Social Psychology

with Study Guide

Eighth Edition

Kassin | Fein | Markus

CENGAGE
Learning

Australia • Brazil • Japan • Korea • Mexico • Singapore • Spain • United Kingdom • United States

CENGAGE
Learning™

Social Psychology: with Study Guide, Eighth Edition

Kassin | Fein | Markus

Executive Editors:
 Maureen Staudt
 Michael Stranz

Senior Project Development Manager:
 Linda DeStefano

Marketing Specialist:
 Sara Mercurio
 Lindsay Shapiro

Senior Production / Manufacturing Manager:
 Donna M. Brown

PreMedia Supervisor:
 Joel Brennecke

Rights & Permissions Specialist:
 Kalina Hintz
 Todd Osborne

Cover Image:
 Getty Images*

* Unless otherwise noted, all cover images used by Custom Solutions, a part of Cengage Learning, have been supplied courtesy of Getty Images with the exception of the Earthview cover image, which has been supplied by the National Aeronautics and Space Administration (NASA).

ISBN-13: 978-1-111-06675-8

ISBN-10: 1-111-06675-2

Cengage Learning
5191 Natorp Boulevard
Mason, Ohio 45040
USA

Cengage Learning is a leading provider of customized learning solutions with office locations around the globe, including Singapore, the United Kingdom, Australia, Mexico, Brazil, and Japan. Locate your local office at:
international.cengage.com/region

Cengage Learning products are represented in Canada by Nelson Education, Ltd.

For your lifelong learning solutions, visit **www.cengage.com/custom**

Visit our corporate website at **www.cengage.com**

Printed in the United States of America

Brief Custom Contents

Social Psychology with Study Guide
Eighth Edition
Kassin | Fein | Markus

Social Psychology
Eighth Edition
Kassin | Fein | Markus

with

Social Psychology Study Guide
Eighth Edition
(located after page I-28)

*We dedicate this book to Bob Zajonc,
an inspiration to us all.*

Brief Contents

Contents

PART II	Social Perception

3   The Social Self   55

4 Perceiving Persons   101

5 Stereotypes, Prejudice, and Discrimination   145

PART III	Social Influence

6 Attitudes   203

Putting Common Sense to the Test   203

7 Conformity   251

Putting Common Sense to the Test   251

8 Group Processes   293

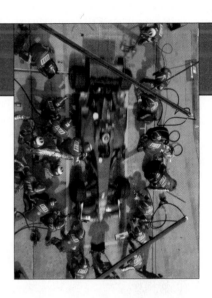

11   Aggression   435

14 Health   569

Preface

The world of the twenty-first century is both an exciting and tumultuous place right now—more so, it seems, than any time in recent memory. On the one hand, it's never been easier to share information, opinions, pictures, music, and footage of live events as they occur with people from all corners of the world. On the other hand, we are surrounded by deep social and political divisions, ethnic conflict, economic turmoil, and an ever present threat of terrorism and other acts of violence. As Charles Dickens (1859) said in *A Tale of Two Cities,* "It was the best of times, it was the worst of times."

Encircled by its place in science and by current world events, social psychology—its theories, research methods, and basic findings—has never been more relevant or more important. We used to think of social psychology as a discipline that is slow to change. As in other sciences, we thought, knowledge accumulates in small increments, one step at a time. Social psychology has no "critical" experiments, no single study can "prove" a theory, and no single theory can fully explain the complexities of human social behavior. While all this remains true, the process of revising this textbook always shows us how complex, dynamic, and responsive our field can be. As the world around us rapidly changes—socially, politically, technologically, and in other disciplines—so too does social psychology.

As always, we had two main goals for this revision. Our first was to present the most important and exciting perspectives in the field as a whole. To communicate the depth of social psychology, we have self-consciously expanded our coverage to include recent developments in social neuroscience and cultural influences, and in other ways that we will soon describe. Second, we want this book to serve as a good teacher outside the classroom. While speaking the student's language, we always want to connect social psychology to current events in politics, sports, business, law, entertainment, uses of the Internet, and other life domains.

What's New in This Edition

As in the past, we have tried to capture some subtle but important shifts within the field so that the reader can feel the pulse of social psychology *today* in each and every page of this textbook.

The Content

Comprehensive, Up-to-Date Scholarship Like its predecessors, the eighth edition offers a broad, balanced, mainstream look at social psychology. Thus, it includes detailed descriptions of classic studies from social psychology's historical warehouse as well as the latest research findings from hundreds of new references. In particular, we draw your attention to the following topics, which are either new to this edition or have received expanded coverage:

- Introduction to social neuroscience and brain-imaging research (Chapter 1)
- Introduction to cultural perspectives in social psychology (Chapter 1)
- The challenges of doing research across cultures (Chapter 2)
- Limitations of self report and its alternatives (Chapter 2)

- Cultural differences in dialecticism (Chapter 3)
- Self-regulation and its aftereffects (Chapter 3)
- Costs and benefits of self-esteem and its pursuit (Chapter 3)
- Mind perception (Chapter 4)
- Recent research on human lie detection (Chapter 4)
- Implicit racism and other forms of implicit prejudice (Chapter 5)
- Evolutionary perspectives on intergroup perception biases (Chapter 5)
- Social neuroscience perspectives on intergroup perception biases (Chapter 5)
- Cultural influences on social identity (Chapter 5)
- Self regulation of prejudice (Chapter 5)
- Stereotype threat effects in nonacademic domains (Chapter 5)
- Political attitudes and the "political brain" (Chapter 6)
- Links between implicit attitudes and behavior (Chapter 6)
- Perceptual consequences of cognitive dissonance (Chapter 6)
- Imitation in nonhumans and infants (Chapter 7)
- Obedience in the twenty-first century (Chapter 7)
- fMRI images of conformity and exclusion (Chapter 7)
- Cultural influences on group cohesiveness (Chapter 8)
- Group dynamics in the economic collapse of 2008–09 (Chapter 8)
- The under use of expertise in groups (Chapter 8)
- Group dynamics challenges posed by "virtual teams" (Chapter 8)
- The associative link between the color red and sexual attraction (Chapter 9)
- The speed dating phenomenon and research paradigm (Chapter 9)
- Cultural influences on romantic love (Chapter 9)
- Longitudinal effects of having children on marital satisfaction (Chapter 9)
- Intergroup biases in helping behavior (Chapter 10)
- Biological and evolutionary approaches to helping (Chapter 10)
- Empathy and helping among animals and human infants (Chapter 10)
- The role of self esteem and narcissism in aggression (Chapter 11)
- Social neuroscience perspectives on aggression and its control (Chapter 11)
- Effects of social rejection and ostracism on aggression (Chapter 11)
- Race effects in jury selection and decision making (Chapter 12)
- New issues and debate over the Stanford Prison Experiment (Chapter 12)
- Cultural perspectives on law and justice (Chapter 12)
- Multicultural vs. colorblind workplace effects on minority employees (Chapter 13)
- The symbolic power of money (Chapter 13)
- The American Psychological Association's recent national survey of stress in America (Chapter 14)
- Cultural differences in social support seeking as a means of coping (Chapter 14)
- Positive emotions as the building blocks of emotion-focused coping (Chapter 14)

As this nonexhaustive list shows, this eighth edition contains a good deal of new material. In particular, you will see that we have zeroed in on developments within four important domains: social neuroscience, implicit processes, evolutionary theory, and cultural perspectives. Across chapters, as always, we have also made it a point to illustrate the relevance of social psychology to current events and to ask students to stop and reflect on their commonsense conceptions.

Social Neuroscience The first domain concerns social neuroscience and the fMRI brain-imaging studies that are poised to enlighten our understanding of the human social experience. Social neuroscience has not fully arrived, and researchers are still raising questions about how to interpret the newly observed links between brain activity and self-referential thoughts, social perceptions, motives, emotions, and behavior. While we acknowledge the current limitations, we also want to provide students with a glimpse of this exciting new fusion of social psychology and neuroscience.

Implicit Processes We have expanded coverage and integrated the increasingly developed distinction between implicit and explicit processes. In matters relating to the unconscious, psychology owes a debt of gratitude to Freud. After some resistance, social psychologists have also come to realize the importance of the conscious-unconscious distinction when it comes to self-esteem, priming, stereotyping, prejudice, attitudes, ambivalence, social influence, and other core topics. Hence, we describe recent work involving the Implicit Association Test, or IAT, and the ongoing debate about what it measures, what it means, and what behaviors it predicts.

Evolutionary Theory We continue in this edition to represent various evolutionary perspectives on human nature, at the heart of which is the notion that we humans, like other species, have an ancestral past that predisposes us, albeit flexibly, to behave in ways that are adapted to promote survival and reproduction. Evolutionary psychologists today seek to explain a wide range of social phenomena—such as snap judgments in social perception, prejudice, helping, aggression, beauty, mate selection, and romantic jealousy. To some extent, this perspective is still controversial. To another extent, it has become part of the mainstream, with respected journals filled with studies and critiques of evolutionary psychology. This edition fully integrates the approach, its findings, and its limitations with the rest of social psychology.

Cultural Perspectives On the heels of our highly expanded coverage of the last edition, we have continued in this edition not only to cover but to fully integrate current research on cultural influences in social behavior. Social psychologists have long been fascinated by similarity and difference—among cultural groups and between racial and ethnic groups within cultures. As the people of the world have come into closer contact, researchers have broadened their scope from the situational snapshot to a fuller account of people in their cultural milieu. Cultural phenomena, once marginalized, are now fully integrated into social psychology. As in our previous edition, every chapter now contains one, two, or three sections on the role of culture. These sections appear within the body of the text and are richly accompanied by photographs, not boxed or set apart.

As social psychology is now a truly international discipline, this book also includes many new citations to research conducted throughout Europe, Asia, Australia, and other parts of the world. We believe that the study of human diversity—from the perspectives of researchers who themselves are a diverse lot—can help students become better informed about social relations as well as about ethics and values.

Connections with Current Events To cover social psychology is one thing; to use its principles to explain events in the real world is quite another. The events of 9/11 changed the world. In different ways not yet fully discernible, so did the more recent and severe economic recession and the U.S. presidential election of Barack Obama. More than ever, we remain convinced that connecting theory to real life is the single best way to heighten student interest and involvement. Over the years, teachers and students alike have told us how much they value the "newsy" features of our book.

The eighth edition, like other editions, is committed to making social psychology *relevant*. Almost every page includes a passage, a quote, a figure, a table, a photo, or a cartoon that refers to people, places, events, social trends, and issues that are prominent in contemporary culture. The reader will find stories about the purported racism, sexism, and ageism in the 2008 presidential election; the torture controversy; Bernie Madoff's elaborate Ponzi scheme; speed dating; Michael Phelps and his historic performance in the Beijing Olympics; the war in Afghanistan; the near economic collapse and its aftermath; the popular TV show *American Idol*; ongoing political debates over health care reform, immigration policy, and gay marriage; the fatal shooting at the Holocaust Museum in Washington, D.C.; the story of a New York City security guard who jumped in front of an oncoming train to save a man lying on the tracks; the controversial police arrest of African American Harvard professor Henry Louis Gates; the 2009 election and massive protests in Iran; and Facebook, Twitter, and other social networking sites.

As in our last edition, you will also find—in the margins—various quotations, song lyrics, public opinion poll results, "factoids," and website addresses. These high-interest items are designed to further illustrate the connectedness of social psychology to a world that extends beyond the borders of a college campus.

Social Psychology and Common Sense   In an earlier edition, we introduced a feature that we remain excited about. Building on a discussion in Chapter 1 about the links (and lack thereof) between social psychology and common sense, each substantive chapter opens with *Putting Common Sense to the Test,* a set of true-false questions designed to assess the student's intuitive beliefs about material later contained in that chapter. Some examples: "Sometimes the harder you try to control a thought, feeling, or behavior, the less likely you are to succeed," "People often come to like what they suffer for," "Opposites attract," and "Groups are less likely than individuals to invest more in a project that is failing." The answers to these questions are revealed in a marginal box after the topic is presented in the text. These answers are then explained at the end of each chapter. We think that students will find this exercise engaging. It will also enable them, as they read, to check their intuitive beliefs against the findings of social psychology and to notice the discrepancies that exist.

The Organization

Of all the challenges faced by teachers and textbooks, perhaps the greatest is to put information together in a way that is accurate and easy to understand. A strong organizational framework helps in meeting this challenge. There is nothing worse for a student than having to wade through a "laundry list" of studies whose interconnections remain a profound mystery. A strong structure thus facilitates the development of conceptual understanding.

But the tail should not wag the dog. Since organizational structure is a means to an end, not an end in itself, we wanted to keep it simple and unobtrusive. Look through the Table of Contents, and you will see that we present social psychology in five major parts—a heuristic structure that instructors and students have found sensible and easy to follow. The book opens with two *Introduction* chapters on the history, subject matter, and research methods of social psychology (Part I). As before, we then move to an intraindividual focus on *Social Perception* (Part II), shift outward to *Social Influence* (Part III) and *Social Relations* (Part IV), and conclude with *Applying Social Psychology* (Part V). We realize that some instructors like to reshuffle the deck to develop a chapter order that better fits their own approach. There is no problem in doing this. Each chapter stands on its own and does not require that others be read first.

The Presentation

Even when the content of a textbook is accurate and up-to-date, and even when its organization is sound, there is still the matter of presentation. As the "teacher outside the classroom," a good textbook should facilitate learning. Thus, every chapter contains the following pedagogical features:

- A narrative preview, chapter outline, and common-sense quiz (beginning with Chapter 3).

- Key terms highlighted in the text, defined in the margin, listed at the end of the chapter, and reprinted in an alphabetized glossary at the end of the book. Both the list and the glossary provide page numbers for easy location of each term.

- Numerous bar graphs, line graphs, tables, sketches, photographs, flowcharts, and cartoons that illustrate, extend, enhance, and enliven material in the text. Some of these depict classic images and studies from social psychology's history; others, new to the eighth edition, are contemporary and often "newsy."

- At the end of each chapter, a comprehensive bulleted review summarizing the major sections and points.

Teaching and Learning Support Package

For the Instructor

Instructor's Resource Manual with Test Bank This manual contains learning objectives, detailed chapter outlines, discussion ideas, classroom activities, handouts, and audiovisual resource suggestions. The classroom exercises feature a unique and popular "What If This Bombs?" section that offers tips for making the most of every activity—even if it does not work. The test bank portion features an extensive set of multiple-choice questions and essay questions with sample answers. Three types of objective questions are provided—factual, conceptual, and applied—and all answers are keyed to learning objectives and text pages.

PowerLecture with JoinIn and ExamView This one-stop lecture and class preparation tool contains ready-to-use PowerPoint slides enabling you to assemble, edit, publish, and present custom lectures for your course. PowerLecture lets you bring together text-specific lecture outlines and art from the eighth edition along with videos or your own materials, culminating in a powerful, personalized, media-enhanced presentation. PowerLecture also includes the JoinIn Student Response System that lets you pose book-specific questions and display students' answers seamlessly within the PowerPoint slides of your own lecture. The ExamView assessment and tutorial system is also available, which guides you step by step through the process of creating tests.

Book Companion Website This dynamic website gives students access to a variety of study tools, practice activities, web quizzes by chapter, and more to encourage review and test preparation. To visit the companion website, go to www.cengage.com/psychology/kassin.

Webtutor Toolbox   WebTutor™ Toolbox for WebCT™ or Blackboard® provides access to all the content of this text's rich Book Companion Website from within your course management system. Robust communication tools—such as a course calendar, asynchronous discussion, real-time chat, a whiteboard, and an integrated e-mail system—make it easy for your students to stay connected to the course.

CengageNOW™   CengageNOW™ is an easy-to-use online resource that helps students study in less time to get the grade they want—NOW. Featuring CengageNOW™ Personalized Study (a diagnostic study tool containing valuable text-specific resources), students focus on just what they don't know and learn more in less time to get a better grade. If the textbook does not include an access code card, students can go to www.CengageBrain.com to get CengageNOW™.

Revealing Psychology   This feature provides a series of social psychology video segments that are informative, engaging, and fun. Hidden cameras reveal people's surprising and amusing reactions when social forces conspire against them. How do you behave when people invade your personal space? Do you help a person who lies sprawled on a busy street? How often do you lie in a ten-minute conversation? These real-world vignettes reveal human foibles and at the same time dramatically illustrate underlying psychological principles. They are available to instructors on DVD for classroom presentation.

Social Psych in Film DVD   This DVD, with closed captioning, contains over 25 clips from popular films and classic experiments that illustrate key concepts in social psychology. Clips from films like *Apollo 13, Schindler's List, Snow Falling on Cedars, In the Name of the Father,* and many others are combined with overviews and discussion questions to help bring psychology alive for students and to demonstrate its relevance to contemporary life and culture.

ABC Video: Social Psychology, Volumes I & II   ABC Videos feature short, high-interest clips from current news events as well as historic raw footage going back 40 years. Perfect for discussion starters or to enrich your lectures and spark interest in the material in the text, these brief videos provide students with a new lens through which to view the past and present, one that will greatly enhance their knowledge and understanding of significant events and open up to them new dimensions in learning. Clips are drawn from such programs as *World News Tonight, Good Morning America, This Week, PrimeTime Live, 20/20,* and *Nightline,* as well as numerous ABC News specials and material from the Associated Press Television News and British Movietone News collections.

Research in Action, Volumes I & II   *Research in Action* features the work of research psychologists to give students an opportunity to learn about cutting-edge research—not just who is doing it, but also how it is done, and how and where the results are being used. By taking students into the laboratories of both established and up-and-coming researchers, and by showing research results being applied outside of the laboratory, these videos offer insight into both the research process and the many ways in which real people's lives are affected by research in the fields of psychology and neuroscience.

For the Student

Readings in Social Psychology: The Art and Science of Research, Fifth Edition   This item contains original articles, each with a brief introduction, and questions to stimulate critical thinking about "doing" social psychology. The articles represent some of the most creative and accessible research, both classic and contemporary, on topics of interest to students.

Study Guide This print *Study Guide* facilitates student learning through the use of a chapter outline, learning objectives, a review of key terms and concepts, multiple-choice questions with explanations for why the correct answer is the best choice, and a practice essay questions with sample answers.

Book Companion Website This outstanding site features chapter outlines, flashcards, tutorial quizzes, and more to help you succeed in your social psychology course. To access the site, go to www.cengage.com/psychology/kassin.

Acknowledgments

Textbooks are the product of a team effort. We are grateful to Cengage Learning for its commitment to quality as the first priority. First, we want to thank Tangelique Williams, our developmental editor. We also want to express our gratitude to Roman Barnes, our photo researcher, who has helped to make this book so photographically interesting. Finally, we want to thank all those whose considerable talents and countless hours of hard work can be seen on every page: Holly Rudelitsch and Pat Waldo, Senior Project Managers; Kate Babbitt, Copyeditor; Jennifer Bonnar, Lachina Publishing Services, Project Manager; Rebecca Rosenberg, Assistant Editor; Lauren Keyes, Media Editor; and Alicia McLaughlin, Editorial Assistant. We also thank Senior Sponsoring Editors Jane Potter and Jon-David Hague, and Marketing Managers Liz Rhoden and Molly Felz.

Several colleagues have guided us through their feedback on this and all prior editions. Every one of these teachers and scholars has helped to make this a better book. For their invaluable insights, comments, and suggestions, we thank reviewers of the eighth edition:

Craig Anderson, *Iowa State University*
Austin Baldwin, *Southern Methodist University*
Nicholas Christenfeld, *University of California, San Diego*
Jack Dovidio, *Yale University*
Donelson Forsyth, *University of Richmond*
Paul A. Franco, *Calumet College of St. Joseph*
MarYam G. Hamedani, *Stanford University*
Alisha Janowsky, *University of Central Florida*
Rusty McIntyre, *Wayne State University*
Margo Monteith, *Purdue University*
Richard Moreland, *University of Pittsburgh*
Todd Shackelford, *Florida Atlantic University*
Nicole M. Stephens, *Northwestern University, Kellogg School of Management*
Kari Terzino, *Iowa State University*

We also thank past edition reviewers:

Shelley N. Aikman, *Syracuse University*
Scott Allison, *University of Richmond*
Thomas William Altermatt, *Hanover College*
Sowmya Anand, *The Ohio State University*
Robin A. Anderson, *St. Ambrose University*
C. Daniel Batson, *University of Kansas*
Arnold James Benjamin, Jr., *Oklahoma Panhandle State University*

Lisa M. Bohon, *California State University*
Bryan Bonner, *The University of Utah*
Jennifer K. Bosson, *The University of Oklahoma*
Martin Bourgeois, *University of Wyoming*
Nyla Branscombe, *University of Kansas*
Brad J. Bushman, *University of Michigan*
Melissa A. Cahoon, *University of Dayton*
Nathaniel Carter, *Lane College*

Serena Chen, *University of California, Berkeley*
James E. Collins, *Carson Newman College*
Eric Cooley, *Western Oregon University*
Keith E. Davis, *University of South Carolina*
Richard Ennis, *University of Waterloo*
Leandre R. Fabrigar, *Queen's University*
Mark A. Ferguson, *University of Kansas*
Joseph R. Ferrari, *DePaul University*
J. H. Forthman, *San Antonio College*
Timothy M. Franz, *St. John Fisher College*
Traci Giuliano, *Southwestern University*
Diana Odom Gunn, *McNeese State University*
Karen L. Harris, *Western Illinois University*
Lora D. Haynes, *University of Louisville*
James Hobbs, *Ulster County Community College*
L. Rowell Huesmann, *University of Michigan*
Karen Huxtable-Jester, *University of Texas at Dallas*
Robert D. Johnson, *Arkansas State University*
Warren H. Jones, *University of Tennessee*
Cheryl Kaiser, *Michigan State University*
Steven J. Karau, *Southern Illinois University*
Suzanne C. Kieffer, *University of Houston*
William M. Klein, *University of Pittsburgh*
LaRue Kobrin, *College of the Redwoods*
Vladimir J. Konecni, *University of California, San Diego*
Doug Krull, *Northern Kentucky University*
Kevin Lanning, *Florida Atlantic University*

Patrick Laughlin, *University of Illinois*
Herbert L. Leff, *University of Vermont*
Margaret A. Lloyd, *Georgia Southern University*
David C. Lundgren, *University of Cincinnati*
Judith McIlwee, *Mira Costa College*
Roque V. Mendez, *Southwest Texas State University*
Daniel Molden, *Northwestern University*
Cynthia R. Nordstrom, *Illinois State University*
Randall E. Osborne, *Indiana University East*
Patricia A. Oswald, *Iona College*
Carol K. Oyster, *University of Wisconsin-La Crosse*
Paul Paulus, *University of Texas at Arlington*
David Pillow, *University of Texas at San Antonio*
Louis H. Porter, *Westchester University of Pennsylvania*
Margaret M. Pulsifer, *Harvard Medical School*
Sally Radmacher, *Missouri Western State University*
Chris Robert, *University of Missouri*
Laura S. Sidorowicz, *Nassau Community College*
Paul Silvia, *University of North Carolina at Greensboro*
Anthony Stahelski, *Central Washington University*
Charles Stangor, *University of Maryland*
Jeffrey Stone, *University of Arizona*
JoNell Strough, *West Virginia University*
Courtney von Hippel, *University of Queensland*
William von Hippel, *University of Queensland*
Kipling D. Williams, *Purdue University*
Ann Zak, *College of St. Rose*

Finally, we are very grateful to Billa Reiss, St. John's University, for helping to create a top-of-the-line *Study Guide*. We are also deeply indebted to Sam Sommers, Tufts University, author of the excellent *Instructor's Resource Manual with Test Bank*; and Tom Finn, Bentley University, author of the PowerPoint lecture outlines. These works have added a whole new dimension to this text.

Saul Kassin
Steven Fein
Hazel Rose Markus

About the Authors

Saul Kassin is Distinguished Professor of Psychology at John Jay College of Criminal Justice, in New York, and Massachusetts Professor of Psychology at Williams College, Williamstown, Massachusetts. Born and raised in Brooklyn, New York, he received his Ph.D. from the University of Connecticut followed by a postdoctoral fellowship at the University of Kansas, a U.S. Supreme Court Judicial Fellowship, and a visiting professorship at Stanford University. In addition to authoring textbooks, he has co-authored and edited *Confessions in the Courtroom, The Psychology of Evidence and Trial Procedure, The American Jury on Trial,* and *Developmental Social Psychology.* Several years ago, Kassin pioneered the scientific study of false confessions, an interest that continues to this day. He has also studied the impact of this and other evidence on the attributions, social perceptions, and verdicts of juries. Kassin is a Fellow of APS, APA, and Divisions 8 and 41. He has testified as an expert witness; lectures frequently to judges, lawyers, and law enforcement groups; and has appeared as a media consultant on national and syndicated news programs.

Steven Fein is Professor of Psychology at Williams College, Williamstown, Massachusetts. Born and raised in Bayonne, New Jersey, he received his A.B. from Princeton University and his Ph.D. in social psychology from the University of Michigan. He has been teaching at Williams College since 1991, with time spent teaching at Stanford University in 1999. His edited books include *Emotion: Interdisciplinary Perspectives, Readings in Social Psychology: The Art and Science of Research,* and *Motivated Social Perception: The Ontario Symposium.* He has served on the executive committee of the Society of Personality and Social Psychology and as the social and personality psychology representative at the American Psychological Association. His research interests concern stereotyping and prejudice, suspicion and attributional processes, social influence, and self-affirmation theory.

Hazel Rose Markus is the Davis-Brack Professor in the Behavioral Sciences at Stanford University. She also co-directs the Research Institute of the Stanford Center for Comparative Studies in Race and Ethnicity. Before moving to Stanford in 1994, she was a professor at the University of Michigan, where she received her Ph.D. Her work focuses on how the self-system, including current conceptions of self and possible selves, structures and lends meaning to experience. Born in England of English parents and raised in San Diego, California, she has been persistently fascinated by how nation of origin, region of the country, gender, ethnicity, race, religion, and social class shape self and identity. With her colleague Shinobu Kitayama at the University of Michigan, she has pioneered the experimental study of how culture and self influence one another. Markus was elected to the American Academy of Arts and Sciences in 1994 and is a Fellow of APS, APA, and Division 8. Some of her recent co-edited books include *Culture and Emotion: Empirical Studies of Mutual Influence, Engaging Cultural Differences: The Multicultural Challenge in Liberal Democracies, Just Schools: Pursuing Equal Education in Societies of Difference,* and *Doing Race: 21 Essays for the 21st Century.*

1

Andreas Pollok/Getty Images

What Is Social Psychology?

This chapter introduces you to the study of social psychology. We begin by defining social psychology and identifying how it is distinct from but related to some other areas of study, both outside and within psychology. Next, we review the history of the field. We conclude by looking forward, with a discussion of the important themes and perspectives that are propelling social psychology into a new century.

A few years from now, you may receive a letter in the mail inviting you to a high school or college reunion. You'll probably feel a bit nostalgic, and you'll begin to think about those old school days. What thoughts will come to mind first? Will you remember the poetry you finally began to appreciate in your junior year? Will you think about the excitement you felt when you completed your first chemistry lab? Will a tear form in your eye as you remember how inspiring your social psychology class was?

Perhaps. But what will probably dominate your thoughts are the people you knew in school and the interactions you had with them—the long and intense discussions about everything imaginable: the loves you had, lost, or wanted so desperately to experience; the time you made a fool of yourself at a party; the effort of trying to be accepted by a fraternity, sorority, or clique of popular people; the day you sat in the pouring rain with your friends while watching a football game.

We focus on these social situations because we are social beings. We forge our individual identities not alone but in the context of other people. We work, play, and live together. We hurt and help each other. We define happiness and success for each other. And we don't fall passively into social interactions; we actively seek them. We visit family, make friends, give parties, build networks, go on dates, pledge an enduring commitment, decide to have children. We watch others, speculate about them, and predict who will wind up with whom, whether in real life or on "reality" TV shows such as *The Real World* or *The Bachelor*. Many of us text or twitter each other about everything we're up to, or we spend lots of time on social networking sites such as Facebook, interacting with countless peers from around the world, adding hundreds or even thousands of "friends" to our social networks.

You've probably seen the movie *It's a Wonderful Life*. When the hero, George Bailey, was about to kill himself, the would-be angel Clarence didn't save him by showing him how much personal happiness he'd miss if he ended his life. Instead, he showed George how much his life had touched the lives of others and how many people would be hurt if he was not a part of their world. It was these social relationships that saved George's life, just as they define our own.

One of the exciting aspects of learning about social psychology is discovering how basic and profoundly important these social relationships are to the human animal.

And research continues to find new evidence for and point to new implications of our social nature. Consider, for example, this set of conclusions from recent research:

■ Having close friends and staying in contact with family members is associated with health benefits such as protecting against heart disease, infection, diabetes, and cancer, and with living longer and more actively (Aggarwal et al., 2008; Kim et al., 2008; Miller et al., 2009; Hawkley et al., 2009).

■ Children who are socially excluded from activities by their peers are more likely than other children to suffer academically as well as socially in school several years later (Bush et al., 2006; Ladd et al., 2008).

■ Experiencing a social rejection or loss is so painful that it produces activity in the same parts of the brain as when we feel physical pain. Experiencing social rewards, on the other hand, such as being treated fairly, activates parts of the brain associated with physical rewards such as desirable food and drink (Lieberman & Eisenberger, 2009; Takahasi et al., 2009).

Man is a social animal.
—Benedict Spinoza, *Ethics*

Adam Larkey/© ABC/Courtesy Everett Collection

Millions of people tune in to watch strangers relate to each other on popular "reality" shows. Pictured here is a group who appeared in a recent season of *The Bachelor*, as viewers wondered which woman might get engaged to the featured bachelor. The enormous popularity of shows like these illustrates part of the appeal of social psychology—people are fascinated with how we relate to one another.

Precisely because we need and care so much about social interactions and relationships, the social contexts in which we find ourselves can influence us profoundly. You can find many examples of this kind of influence in your own life. Have you ever laughed at a joke you didn't get just because those around you were laughing? Do you present yourself in one way with one group of people and in quite a different way with another group? The power of the situation can also be much more subtle, and yet more powerful, than in these examples, as when another's unspoken expectations about you literally seem to cause you to become a different person.

The relevance of social psychology is evident in everyday life, of course, such as when two people become attracted to each other or when a group tries to coordinate its efforts on a project. Dramatic events can heighten its significance all the more, as is evident in people's behavior during and after war, terrorist attacks, or natural disasters. In these traumatic times, a spotlight shines on how people help or exploit each other and we witness some of the worst and best that human relations have to offer. These events invariably call attention to the kinds of questions that social psychologists study—questions about hatred and violence, about intergroup conflict and suspicion, as well as about heroism, cooperation, and the capacity for understanding across cultural, ethnic, racial, religious, and geographic divides. We are reminded of the need for a better understanding of social psychological issues as we see footage of death and destruction in the Middle East or Congo or are confronted with the reality of an all-too-violent world as nearby as our own neighborhoods and campuses. We also appreciate the majesty and power of social connections as we recognize the courage of a firefighter, read about the charity of a donor, or see the glow in the eyes of a new parent. These are all—the bad and the good, the mundane and the extraordinary—part of the fascinating landscape of social psychology.

Think of some of the stories that have been in the news as you read this. No doubt many concern issues about which social psychology can offer some insight. For example, at the time of this writing, a controversy that has been debated in the news for several years concerns the role of torture in interrogation of prisoners of war and captured terrorists. There are a whole host of legal, moral, and political questions inherent in this debate, but it is clear that social psychological research can speak to some of the important issues. In Chapters 8 and 12, for example, we discuss research that

The relevance of social psychology is evident both in everyday situations—such as the fun of socializing with fellow fans at a basketball game, which even the president of the United States occasionally gets to do (left)—and in dramatic, life-changing events, such as the shootings at Virginia Tech University on April 16, 2007 (right). The scope of social psychology is part of what makes it not only so fascinating, but also so applicable to many careers and interests.

can help explain why good men and women may temporarily lose their own sense of right and wrong and engage in horrific abuse of prisoners. Chapter 12 also reports studies that demonstrate how confessions that are extracted under extreme conditions can be false, and what some of the most important factors are that make false confessions more likely.

Not only will you learn interesting and relevant research findings throughout the book, you also will learn *how* social psychologists have discovered this evidence. It is an exciting process and one that we are enthusiastic about sharing with you. The purpose of this first chapter is to provide you with a broad overview of the field of social psychology. By the time you finish it, you should be ready and (we hope) eager for what lies ahead.

What Is Social Psychology?

We begin by previewing the new territory you're about to enter. Then we define social psychology and map out its relationship to sociology and some other disciplines within the field of psychology.

Defining Social Psychology

Social psychology is the scientific study of how individuals think, feel, and behave in a social context. Let's look at each part of this definition.

Scientific Study There are many approaches to understanding how people think, feel, and behave. We can learn about human behavior from novels, films, history, and philosophy, to name just a few possibilities. What makes social psychology different from these artistic and humanistic endeavors is that social psychology is a science. It applies the *scientific method* of systematic observation, description, and measurement to the study of the human condition. How, and why, social psychologists do this is explained in Chapter 2.

social psychology
The scientific study of how individuals think, feel, and behave in a social context.

How Individuals Think, Feel, and Behave   Social psychology concerns an amazingly diverse set of topics. People's private, even nonconscious beliefs and attitudes; their most passionate emotions; their heroic, cowardly, or merely mundane public behaviors—these all fall within the broad scope of social psychology. In this way, social psychology differs from other social sciences such as economics and political science. Research on attitudes (see Chapter 6) offers a good illustration. Whereas economists and political scientists may be interested in people's economic and political attitudes, respectively, social psychologists investigate a wide variety of attitudes and contexts, such as individuals' attitudes toward particular groups of people or how their attitudes are affected by their peers or their mood. In doing so, social psychologists strive to establish general principles of attitude formation and change that apply in a variety of situations rather than exclusively to particular domains.

Note the word *individuals* in our definition of social psychology. This word points to another important way in which social psychology differs from some other social sciences. Sociology, for instance, typically classifies people in terms of their nationality, race, socioeconomic class, and other *group factors*. In contrast, social psychology typically focuses on the psychology of the *individual*. Even when social psychologists study groups of people, they usually emphasize the behavior of the individual in the group context.

Our social relationships and interactions are extremely important to us. Most people seek out and are profoundly affected by other people. This social nature of the human animal is what social psychology is all about.

A Social Context   Here is where the "social" in social psychology comes into play and how social psychology is distinguished from other branches of psychology. As a whole, the discipline of psychology is an immense, sprawling enterprise, the 800-pound gorilla of the social sciences, concerned with everything from the actions of neurotransmitters in the brain to the actions of music fans in a mosh pit. What makes social psychology unique is its emphasis on the social nature of individuals.

However, the "socialness" of social psychology varies. In attempting to establish general principles of human behavior, social psychologists sometimes examine nonsocial factors that affect people's thoughts, emotions, motives, and actions. For example, they may study whether hot weather causes people to behave more aggressively (Anderson, 2001). What is social about this is the behavior: people hurting each other. In addition, social psychologists sometimes study people's thoughts or feelings about nonsocial things, such as people's attitudes toward Nike versus New Balance basketball shoes. How can attitudes toward basketball shoes be of interest to social psychologists? One way is if these attitudes are influenced by something social, such as whether LeBron James's endorsement of Nike makes people like Nike. Both examples—determining whether heat causes an increase in aggression or whether LeBron James causes an increase in sales of Nike shoes—are *social* psychological pursuits because the thoughts, feelings, or behaviors either (a) *concern other people* or (b) *are influenced by other people*.

A well-liked celebrity such as Oprah Winfrey can influence the attitudes and behaviors of millions of people. When Oprah recommends a book, for example, sales of the book are likely to skyrocket.

The "social context" referred to in the definition of social psychology does not have to be real or present. Even the implied or imagined presence of others can have important effects on individuals (Allport, 1985). For example, if people imagine receiving positive or negative reactions from others, their self-esteem can be affected significantly (Smart Richman & Leary, 2009). And if college students imagine living a day in the life of a professor, they are likely to perform better later on an analytic test; if they imagine instead being a cheerleader, however, they perform worse (Galinsky et al., 2008)!

Social Psychological Questions and Applications

For those of us fascinated by social behavior, social psychology is a dream come true. Just look at Table 1.1 and consider a small sample of the questions you'll explore in this textbook. As you can see, the social nature of the human animal is what social psychology is all about. Learning about social psychology is learning about ourselves and our social worlds. And because social psychology is scientific rather than anecdotal, systematic rather than haphazard, it provides insights that would be impossible to gain through intuition or experience alone.

The value of social psychology's perspective on human behavior is widely recognized. Courses in social psychology are often required for undergraduate majors in business, education, and journalism as well as in psychology and sociology. Although many advanced graduates with a Ph.D. in social psychology hold faculty appointments in colleges or universities, others work in medical centers, law firms, government agencies, and a variety of business settings involving investment banking, marketing, advertising, human resources, negotiating, and social networking.

The number and importance of these applications continue to grow. Judges are drawing on social psychological research to render landmark decisions, and lawyers are depending on it to select juries and to support or refute evidence. Businesses are using cross-cultural social psychological research to operate in the global marketplace and group-dynamics research to foster the best conditions for their work forces. Health care professionals are increasingly aware of the role of social psychological factors in the prevention and treatment of disease. Indeed, we can think of no other field of study that offers expertise that is more clearly relevant to so many different career paths.

TABLE 1.1
Examples of Social Psychological Questions
Social Perception: What Affects the Way We Perceive Ourselves and Others?
■ Why do people sometimes sabotage their own performance, making it more likely that they will fail? (Chapter 3)
■ How do people in East Asia often differ from North Americans in the way they explain people's behavior? (Chapter 4)
■ Where do stereotypes come from, and why are they so resistant to change? (Chapter 5)
Social Influence: How Do We Influence Each Other?
■ Why do we often like what we suffer for? (Chapter 6)
■ How do salespeople sometimes trick us into buying things we never really wanted? (Chapter 7)
■ Why do people often perform worse in groups than they would have alone? (Chapter 8)
Social Interaction: What Causes Us to Like, Love, Help, and Hurt Others?
■ How similar or different are the sexes in what they look for in an intimate relationship? (Chapter 9)
■ When is a bystander more or less likely to help you in an emergency? (Chapter 10)
■ Does exposure to TV violence or to pornography trigger aggressive behavior? (Chapter 11)
Applying Social Psychology: How Does Social Psychology Help Us Understand Questions About Law, Business, and Health?
■ Can interrogators really get people to confess to serious crimes they did not commit? (Chapter 12)
■ How can business leaders most effectively motivate their employees? (Chapter 13)
■ How does stress affect one's health, and what are the most effective ways of coping with stressful experiences? (Chapter 14)

The Power of the Social Context: An Example of a Social Psychology Experiment

The social nature of people runs so deep that our perceptions of something can be influenced more by the reactions of others to it than by the thing itself. Consider a controversy concerning a major cable news network's coverage of the 2008 presidential debates between Barack Obama and John McCain. While televising the debates live, CNN continuously showed a graph depicting the second-by-second opinions of a small group of undecided voters from Ohio. Could these reactions of a couple dozen individuals influence the millions of viewers at home (Schechner, 2008)?

Some media stories addressed this issue by citing recent research conducted by one of the authors of this text that relates to this point (Fein, Goethals, & Kugler, 2007). In one experiment, college students watched a tape of a 1984 debate between Ronald Reagan and Walter Mondale, two candidates for the presidency of the United States. During that debate Reagan fired off a pair of one-liners that elicited a great deal of laughter from the audience. Political analysts have wondered whether those one-liners may have won the debate, and possibly the election, for Reagan. The one-liners comprised only seconds of a 90-minute debate concerning the most important issues of the day. Could these few seconds have made such a difference?

To study this issue, we had students watch the debate under one of three conditions. One-third of the students saw the debate as it was, without any editing. One-third of the students saw the debate with the one-liners and the ensuing audience reaction edited out. By comparing these two conditions, we could see whether the presence versus absence of this pair of jokes could make a large difference in people's impressions of Reagan from the debate. However, there was also a third condition. One-third of the students saw the debate with the one-liners intact but with the audience reaction edited out. That is, Reagan told his jokes but there appeared to be no audience response, and the debate continued uninterrupted.

After watching the debate, the students judged the performance of the candidates on a scale ranging from 0 (terrible) to 100 (excellent). As you can see from the first two bars in ▶ Figure 1.1, the students who saw the entire unedited tape did not rate Reagan much more positively than did the students who saw the debate without the one-liners. This suggests that Reagan's jokes did not have much impact on these viewers'

As Hillary Clinton speaks, people watching on TV can see a graph depicting the reactions of other people. During the 2008 presidential election campaign in the United States, some news networks displayed such graphs while broadcasting important debates. Could seeing the reactions of others affect the judgments of the millions of viewers watching at home? According to social psychology research described in this chapter, seeing or hearing other people's reactions can have a strong influence on individuals.

© Ron Sachs/CNP/Corbis

perceptions of him. But look at the third bar in the figure. It illustrates that the students who saw the version of the debate with the one-liners kept in but the audience reaction edited out rated Reagan much less positively than did either of the other groups. What could explain their negativity toward Reagan's debate performance? Perhaps when Reagan's jokes appeared to elicit no reaction, the students unknowingly used the lack of reaction as an indication that Reagan's attempts at wit were inept, and this conclusion caused them to see Reagan in a much less positive light.

What is interesting about these results from a social psychological standpoint is that the students' judgments were influenced more by other people's *reactions* to what Reagan said (that is, whether or not the audience appeared to laugh) than by the *content* of what he said (that is, whether or not the one-liners were edited out of the tape). And it is important to note that these "other people" were not in the room with the students; they were simply sounds on a videotape recorded many years before. Findings such as this demonstrate that the "social context" can be very subtle and yet can have very powerful effects on our thoughts, feelings, and behaviors.

◼ Social Psychology and Related Fields: Distinctions and Intersections

Social psychology is sometimes confused with certain other fields of study. Before we go on, it is important to clarify how social psychology is distinct from these other fields. At the same time, it is important to illustrate some of the ways that interesting and significant questions can be addressed through interactions between social psychology and these other fields (see Table 1.2 on page 10).

Social Psychology and Sociology　Sociologists and social psychologists share an interest in many issues, such as violence, prejudice, cultural differences, and marriage. As noted, however, sociology tends to focus on the group level, whereas social psychology tends to focus on the individual level. For example, sociologists might track the racial attitudes of the middle class in the United States, whereas social psychologists might examine some of the specific factors that make individuals more or less likely to behave in a racist way toward members of some group.

In addition, although there are many exceptions, social psychologists are more likely than sociologists to conduct experiments in which they manipulate some variable and determine the effects of this manipulation using precise, quantifiable measures.

Despite these differences, sociology and social psychology are clearly related. Indeed, many sociologists and social psychologists share the same training and publish in the same journals. When these two fields intersect, the result can be a more complete understanding of important issues. For example, interdisciplinary research on stereotyping and prejudice has examined the dynamic roles of both societal and immediate factors, such as how particular social systems or institutional norms and beliefs affect individuals' attitudes and behaviors (Eagly & Fischer, 2009; Jost et al., 2009; Rabinowitz et al., 2009; Smith & Collins, 2009).

▶ **FIGURE 1.1**

Influence of Others' Reactions

This graph shows the results of research in which participants saw different versions of a tape of a 1984 presidential debate between Ronald Reagan and Walter Mondale. During the debate, Reagan had delivered a pair of witty one-liners that elicited a positive audience reaction. Participants who saw an unedited version of the tape and participants who saw a version with the jokes and the audience reaction edited out judged Reagan's performance similarly. Participants who saw a version with the jokes left in but the audience reaction edited out (suggesting that the audience didn't find the jokes funny) rated Reagan much more negatively.

Adapted from Fein, Goethals, & Kugler, 2007.

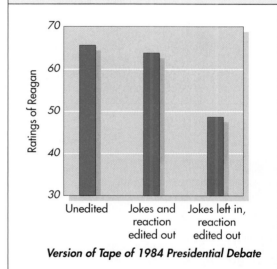

TABLE 1.2

Distinctions Between Social Psychology and Related Fields: The Case of Research on Prejudice

To see the differences between social psychology and related fields, consider an example of how researchers in each field might conduct a study of prejudice.

Field of Study	Example of How a Researcher in the Field Might Study Prejudice
Sociology	Measure how prejudice varies as a function of social or economic class
Clinical psychology	Test various therapies for people with antisocial personalities who exhibit great degrees of prejudice
Personality psychology	Develop a questionnaire to identify men who are very high or low in degree of prejudice toward women
Cognitive psychology	Manipulate exposure to a member of some category of people and measure the thoughts and concepts that are automatically activated (*A study of prejudice in this field would, by definition, be at the intersection of cognitive and social psychology.*)
Social psychology	Manipulate various kinds of contact between individuals of different groups and examine the effect of these manipulations on the degree of prejudice exhibited

Social Psychology and Clinical Psychology Tell people not very familiar with psychology that you are taking a social psychology class, and they are likely to say things like "Oh, great, now you're going to start psychoanalyzing me" or "Finally, maybe you can tell me why everyone in my family is so messed up." The assumption underlying these reactions, of course, is that you are studying clinical, or abnormal, psychology. Clinical psychologists seek to understand and treat people with psychological difficulties or disorders. Social psychologists do not focus on disorders; rather, they focus on the more typical ways in which individuals think, feel, behave, and influence each other.

There are, however, many fascinating ways in which clinical and social psychology intersect. Both, for example, may address how people cope with anxiety or pressure in social situations; how depressed and nondepressed individuals differ in the way they perceive or act toward other people; or how being bullied or stereotyped by others can affect individuals' health and feelings of self-worth (Amodio, 2009; Bosson, Pinel, & Thompson, 2008; Brodish & Devine, 2009; Conklin et al., 2009; Kestilä et al., 2009).

Social Psychology and Personality Psychology Both personality psychology and social psychology are concerned with individuals and their thoughts, feelings, and behaviors. However, personality psychology seeks to understand differences between individuals that remain relatively stable across a variety of situations, whereas social psychology seeks to understand how social factors affect most individuals *regardless of* their different personalities.

In other words, personality psychologists are interested in cross-situational consistency. They may ask, "Is this person outgoing and friendly almost all the time, in just about any setting?" Social psychologists are interested in how different situations cause different behaviors. They may ask, "Are people in general more likely to seek out companionship when they are made anxious by a situation than when they are made to feel relaxed?"

These examples show the contrast between the fields; but in fact, personality psychology and social psychology are very closely linked. The American Psychological Association has more than fifty different divisions, and yet personality psychologists

Do provocative, sexualized images in advertisings, such as on the billboard seen here (near the sign about "student body cards"), make people more sexist or prone to sexual aggression? This is one of the questions that social psychology addresses.

Michael Newman/Photo Edit Inc.

and social psychologists share the same division. Many of these scholars belong to an organization called the Society for Personality and Social Psychology, attend the same conferences, and publish their research in the same journals. So personality and social psychologists see a lot of each other.

The reason for the high degree of connection between social and personality psychology is that the two areas complement each other so well. For example, some social psychologists examine how receiving negative feedback (a situational factor) can have different effects on people as a function of whether their self-esteem is high or low (an individual-difference factor), or whether playing violent video games (a situational factor) is especially likely to trigger aggressiveness in particular types of children (an individual-difference factor) (Nije Bijvank et al., 2009; Park & Maner, 2009; Thomaes et al., 2009).

Social Psychology and Cognitive Psychology Cognitive psychologists study mental processes such as thinking, learning, remembering, and reasoning. Social psychologists are often interested in these same processes. More specifically, though, social psychologists are interested in how people think, learn, remember, and reason with respect to social information and in how these processes are relevant to social behavior.

The last few decades have seen an explosion of interest in the intersection of cognitive and social psychology. The study of *social cognition* is discussed in more detail later in this chapter, and it is a focus throughout this text, especially in Part II on Social Perception.

Social Psychology and Common Sense

After reading about a theory or finding of social psychology, you may sometimes think, "Of course. I knew that all along. Anyone could have told me that." This "knew-it-all-along" phenomenon often causes people to question how social psychology is different from common sense, or traditional folk wisdom. After all, why would any of the following social psychological findings be surprising?

- Beauty and brains don't mix: Physically attractive people tend to be seen as less smart than physically unattractive people.
- People will like an activity more if you offer them a large reward for doing it, causing them to associate the activity with the positive reinforcement.
- People think that they're more unique than they really are: They tend to underestimate the extent to which others share the same opinions or interests.
- Playing contact sports or violent video games releases aggression and makes people less likely to vent their anger in violent ways.

In a minute we will have more to say about each of these statements.

Common sense may seem to explain many social psychological findings after the fact. The problem is distinguishing commonsense fact from commonsense myth. After all, for most commonsense notions, there is an equally sensible-sounding notion that says the opposite. Is it "Birds of a feather flock together" or "Opposites attract"? Is it "Two heads are better than one" or "Too many cooks spoil the broth"? Which are correct? We have no reliable way to answer such questions through common sense or intuition alone.

Social psychology, unlike common sense, uses the scientific method to put its theories to the test. How it does so will be discussed in greater detail in the next chapter. But before we leave this section, one word of caution: Those four "findings" listed above? *They are all false*. Although there may be sensible reasons to believe each of the statements to be true, research indicates otherwise. Therein lies another problem with relying on common sense: despite offering very compelling predictions and explanations, it is sometimes wildly inaccurate. And even when it is not completely wrong, common sense can be misleading in its simplicity. Often there is no simple answer to a question such as "Does absence make the heart grow fonder?" In reality, the answer is more complex than common sense would suggest, and social psychological research reveals how such an answer depends on a variety of factors.

To emphasize these points and to encourage you to think critically about social psychological issues *before* as well as after learning about them, this textbook contains a feature called "Putting Common Sense to the Test." Beginning with Chapter 3, each chapter opens with a few statements about social psychological issues that will be covered in that chapter. Some of the statements are true and some are false. As you read each statement, make a prediction about whether it is true or false and think about why this is your prediction. Marginal notes throughout the chapter will tell you whether the statements are true or false. In reading the chapter, check not only whether your prediction was correct but also whether your reasons for the prediction were appropriate. If your intuition wasn't quite on the mark, think about what the right answer is and how the evidence supports that answer. There are few better ways of learning and remembering than through this kind of critical thinking.

From Past to Present: A Brief History of Social Psychology

People have probably been asking social psychological questions for as long as humans could think about each other. Certainly early philosophers such as Plato offered keen insights into many social psychological issues. But no systematic and scientific study of social psychological issues developed until the end of the nineteenth century. The field of social psychology is therefore a relatively young one. Recent years have marked a tremendous interest in social psychology and an injection of many new scholars into the field. As social psychology is now early in its second century, it is instructive to look back to see how the field today has been shaped by the people and events of its first century.

The Birth and Infancy of Social Psychology: 1880s–1920s

Psychology has a long past, but only a short history.
—Herman Ebbinghaus, *Summary of Psychology*

Like most such honors, the title "founder of social psychology" has many potential recipients, and not everyone agrees on who should prevail. Most point to the American psychologist Norman Triplett, who is credited with having published the first research article in social psychology at the end of the nineteenth century (1897–1898). Triplett's work was noteworthy because after observing that bicyclists tended to race faster when racing in the presence of others than when simply racing against a clock, he designed an experiment to study this phenomenon in a carefully controlled, precise way. This scientific approach to studying the effects of the social context on individuals' behavior can be seen as marking the birth of social psychology.

A case can also be made for the French agricultural engineer Max Ringelmann. Ringelmann's research was conducted in the 1880s but wasn't published until 1913. In an interesting coincidence, Ringelmann also studied the effects of the presence of others on the performance of individuals. In contrast to Triplett, however, Ringelmann noted that individuals often performed worse on simple tasks such as pulling rope when they performed the tasks with other people. The issues addressed by these two early researchers continue to be of vital interest, as will be seen later in Chapter 8, "Group Processes."

Despite their place in the history of social psychology, neither Triplett nor Ringelmann actually established social psychology as a distinct field of study. Credit for this creation goes to the writers of the first three textbooks in social psychology: the English psychologist William McDougall (1908) and two Americans, Edward Ross (1908) and Floyd Allport (1924). Allport's book in particular, with its focus on the interaction of individuals and their social context and its emphasis on the use of experimentation and the scientific method, helped establish social psychology

AP Photo/Christophe Ena

as the discipline it is today. These authors announced the arrival of a new approach to the social aspects of human behavior. Social psychology was born.

Racers from around the world compete in one the stages of the Tour de France in July 2009. Would these cyclists have raced faster or slower if they were racing individually against the clock rather than racing simultaneously with their competitors? More generally, how does the presence of others affect an individual's performance? The earliest social psychology experiments ever done sought to answer questions such as these. Chapter 8 on Group Processes brings you up to date on the latest research in this area.

A Call to Action: 1930s–1950s

What one person would you guess has had the strongest influence on the field of social psychology? Various social psychologists, as well as psychologists outside of social psychology, might be mentioned in response to this question. But someone who was not a psychologist at all may have had the most dramatic impact on the field: Adolf Hitler.

Hitler's rise to power and the ensuing turmoil caused people around the world to become desperate for answers to social psychological questions about what causes violence, prejudice, genocide, conformity and obedience, and a host of other social problems and behaviors. In addition, many social psychologists living in Europe in the 1930s fled to the United States and helped establish a critical mass of social psychologists who would give shape to the rapidly maturing field. The years just before, during, and soon after World War II marked an explosion of interest in social psychology.

In 1936, Gordon Allport (younger brother of Floyd, author of the 1924 textbook) and a number of other social psychologists formed the Society for the Psychological Study of Social Issues. The name of the society illustrates these psychologists' concern for making important, practical contributions to society. Also in 1936, a social psychologist named Muzafer Sherif published groundbreaking experimental research on social influence. As a youth in Turkey, Sherif had witnessed groups of Greek soldiers brutally killing his friends. After immigrating to the United States, Sherif drew on this experience and began to conduct research on the powerful influences groups can exert on their individual members. Sherif's research was crucial for the development of social psychology because it demonstrated that it is possible to study complex social processes such as conformity and social influence in a rigorous, scientific manner.

This innovation laid the foundation for what was to become one of the major topics in social psychology. Research and theory on social influence are discussed throughout this text, particularly in Part III on Social Influence.

Another great contributor to social psychology, Kurt Lewin, fled the Nazi onslaught in Germany and immigrated to the United States in the early 1930s. Lewin was a bold and creative theorist whose concepts have had lasting effects on the field (e.g., Lewin, 1935, 1947). One of the fundamental principles of social psychology that Lewin helped establish was that behavior is a function of the interaction between the person and the environment. This position, which later became known as the **interactionist perspective** (Blass, 1991), emphasized the dynamic interplay of internal and external factors, and it marked a sharp contrast from other major psychological paradigms during his lifetime: psychoanalysis, with its emphasis on internal motives and fantasies; and behaviorism, with its focus on external rewards and punishments.

Lewin also profoundly influenced the field by advocating for social psychological theories to be applied to important, practical issues. Lewin researched a number of practical issues, such as how to persuade Americans at home during the war to conserve materials to help the war effort, how to promote more economical and nutritious eating habits, and what kinds of leaders elicit the best work from group members. Through these studies, Lewin showed how social psychology could enlarge our understanding of social problems and contribute to their solution. Built on Lewin's legacy, applied social psychology flourishes today in areas such as advertising, business, education, environmental protection, health, law, politics, public policy, religion, and sports. Throughout this text, we draw on the findings of applied social psychology to illustrate the implications of social psychological principles for our daily lives. In Part V, three prominent areas of applied social psychology are discussed in detail: law, business, and health. One of Lewin's statements can be seen as a call to action for the entire field: "No research without action, no action without research."

During World War II, many social psychologists answered Lewin's call as they worked for their government to investigate how to protect soldiers from the propaganda of the enemy, how to persuade citizens to support the war effort, how to select officers for various positions, and other practical issues. During and after the war, social psychologists sought to understand the prejudice, aggression, and conformity the war had brought to light. The 1950s saw many major contributions to the

What determines whether people are likely to act to conserve their environment, as these individuals did by volunteering their time to clean up a beach in Hong Kong? Built on the legacy of Kurt Lewin, applied social psychology contributes to the solution of numerous social problems, such as environmental degradation.

interactionist perspective
An emphasis on how both an individual's personality and environmental characteristics influence behavior.

Antony Dickson/AFP/Getty Images

field of social psychology. For example, Gordon Allport (1954) published *The Nature of Prejudice*, a book that continues to inspire research on stereotyping and prejudice more than a half century later. Solomon Asch's (1951) demonstration of how willing people are to conform to an obviously wrong majority amazes students even today. Leon Festinger (1954, 1957) introduced two important theories—one concerning how people try to learn about themselves by comparing themselves to other people, and one about how people's attitudes can be changed by their own behavior—that remain among the most influential theories in the field. These are just a sample of a long list of landmark contributions made during the 1950s. With this remarkable burst of activity and impact, social psychology was clearly, and irrevocably, on the map.

Confidence and Crisis: 1960s–Mid-1970s

In spectacular fashion, Stanley Milgram's research in the early and middle 1960s linked the post–World War II era with the coming era of social revolution. Milgram's research was inspired by the destructive obedience demonstrated by Nazi officers and ordinary citizens in World War II, but it also looked ahead to the civil disobedience that was beginning to challenge institutions in many parts of the world. Milgram's experiments, which demonstrated individuals' vulnerability to the destructive commands of authority, became the most famous research in the history of social psychology. This research is discussed in detail in Chapter 7.

With its foundation firmly in place, social psychology entered a period of expansion and enthusiasm. The sheer range of its investigations was staggering. Social psychologists considered how people thought and felt about themselves and others. They studied interactions in groups and social problems, such as why people fail to help others in distress. They also examined aggression, physical attractiveness, and stress. For the field as a whole, it was a time of great productivity.

Ironically, it was also a time of crisis and heated debate. Many of the strong disagreements during this period can be understood as a reaction to the dominant research method of the day: the laboratory experiment. Critics of this method asserted that certain practices were unethical, that experimenters' expectations influenced their participants' behavior, and that the theories being tested in the laboratory were historically and culturally limited (Gergen, 1973; Kelman, 1967; Rosenthal, 1976). Those who favored laboratory experimentation, on the other hand, contended that their procedures were ethical, their results were valid, and their theoretical principles were widely applicable (McGuire, 1967). For a while, social psychology seemed split in two.

An Era of Pluralism: Mid-1970s–1990s

Fortunately, both sides won. As we will see in the next chapter, more rigorous ethical standards for research were instituted, more stringent procedures to guard against bias were adopted, and more attention was paid to possible cross-cultural differences in behavior. But the baby was not thrown out with the bathwater. Laboratory experiments continued. They did, however, get some company, as a single-minded attachment to one research method evolved into a broader acceptance of many methods. A pluralistic approach recognizes that because no one research method is perfect and

(vertical credit) Courtesy of The National Archives and Records Administration

We Can Do It!

WAR PRODUCTION CO-ORDINATING COMMITTEE

This World War II poster featuring Rosie the Riveter was part of the U.S. government's campaign to encourage women to take jobs in traditionally male-dominated occupations, such as in welding. When the war was over and the men who had served in the military returned to the work force, new advertisements were designed to encourage women to leave these jobs and concentrate on raising families.

Social psychologists are becoming increasingly interested in cross-cultural research, which helps us break out of our culture-bound perspective. Many of our behaviors differ across cultures. In some cultures, for example, people are expected to negotiate about the price of the products they buy, as in this market in Tunisia. In other cultures, such bargaining would be highly unusual and cause confusion and distress.

because different topics require different kinds of investigations, a range of research techniques is needed. The various research methods used by today's social psychologists are described in the next chapter.

Pluralism in social psychology extends far beyond its methods. There are also important variations in what aspects of human behavior are emphasized. Some social psychology research takes what we might call a "hot" perspective, focusing on *emotion* and *motivation* as determinants of our thoughts and actions. Other research in this field takes a "cold" perspective that emphasizes the role of *cognition*, examining the ways that people's thoughts affect how they feel, what they want, and what they do. Of course, some social psychologists examine behavior from both perspectives separately as well as interactively. Integrating such different perspectives is characteristic of the pluralism that the field began to embrace during this period and that continues today.

Another source of pluralism in social psychology is its development of international and multicultural perspectives. Although, as we have seen, individuals from many countries helped establish the field, social psychology achieved its greatest professional recognition in the United States and Canada. At one point, it was estimated that 75 to 90 percent of social psychologists lived in North America (Smith & Bond, 1993; Triandis, 1994). However, this aspect of social psychology began to change rapidly in the 1990s, reflecting not only the different geographic and cultural backgrounds of its researchers and participants but also the recognition that many social psychological phenomena once assumed to be universal may actually vary dramatically as a function of culture. You can find evidence of this new appreciation of the role of culture in every chapter of this book.

Social Psychology in a New Century

As we began the twenty-first century, social psychology began its second hundred years. The field today continues to grow in numbers and diversity of researchers and research topics, areas of the world in which research is conducted, and industries that hire social psychologists and apply their work.

Throughout this text, we emphasize the most current, cutting-edge research in the field, along with the classic findings of the past. In the remainder of the chapter we focus on a few of the exciting themes and perspectives emerging from current research—research that is helping to shape the social psychology of the new century.

Integration of Emotion, Motivation, and Cognition

If any one perspective dominated the final quarter of social psychology's first century, it may have been **social cognition**, the study of how we perceive, remember, and interpret information about ourselves and others. Social psychologists demonstrated that these social-cognitive processes are critically important to virtually every area in the field. Social-cognitive explanations were so powerful that the roles of "hotter" influences, such as emotions and motivations, often took a back seat. Social cognition continues to flourish, but one of the more exciting developments in the field is the reemergence of interest in how individuals' emotions and motivations influence their thoughts and actions. Especially exciting is the fact that the social-cognitive approach is not necessarily seen as being at odds with approaches that emphasize motivations and emotions. Instead, there is a new push to integrate these perspectives, as in research investigating how people's motivations influence nonconscious cognitive processes and vice versa (Bargh & Morsella, 2009; Forgas & Fitness, 2008; Moskowitz & Grant, 2009; Smith & Collins, 2009; Spencer et al., 2003).

One issue illustrating the integration of "hot" and "cold" variables concerns the conflict between wanting to be right and wanting to feel good about oneself. Most of us hold two very different motivations simultaneously. On the one hand, we want to be accurate in our judgments about ourselves and others. On the other hand, we don't want to be accurate if it means we will learn something bad about ourselves or those closest to us. These goals can pull our cognitive processes in very different directions. How we perform the required mental gymnastics is an ongoing concern for social psychologists.

Another theme running through many chapters of this book is the growing interest in distinguishing between automatic and controllable processes and in understanding the dynamic relationship between them (Hassin, Bargh, & Zimerman, 2009; Moons, Mackie, & Garcia-Marques, 2009; Stewart & Payne, 2009). For example, there is a great deal of new evidence showing that stereotypes can be activated in one's mind automatically— that is, quickly and spontaneously, with no awareness, intention, or effort, and possibly even against one's will. Participants in many social psychology experiments are often surprised—to their great dismay—when they learn that their reactions during the study were biased by stereotypes (such as about the person's race or age) that they in fact did not believe in. On the other hand, there also is growing evidence that even such automatic reactions can be controlled under particular conditions. The

> Our desire to be accurate in our judgments can sometimes interfere with our desire to feel good about ourselves.

"On the one hand, eliminating the middleman would result in lower costs, increased sales, and greater consumer satisfaction; on the other hand, we're the middleman."

social cognition The study of how people perceive, remember, and interpret information about themselves and others.

automatic and controlled nature of a variety of processes and behaviors relevant to social psychology will no doubt continue to be an exciting area of research in the coming years.

Biological and Evolutionary Perspectives

As the technology available to researchers evolves, biological perspectives are increasingly being integrated into all branches of psychology, and this integration should continue to grow in social psychology. We are, of course, biological organisms, and it is clear that our brains and bodies influence, and are influenced by, our social experiences. This dynamic can be seen in a great deal of contemporary research, such as in studies demonstrating the cardiovascular effects of being the target of racism, or research illustrating that the manner in which people respond to stress can influence their athletic performance (Salomon & Jagusztyn, 2008; Sherman et al., 2009; Worthy, Markman, & Maddox, 2009).

Social psychologists have been concerned with physiological influences and responses for many years. Examples of this interest can be found throughout the textbook. A particularly exciting recent development is the emergence of the subfield of **social neuroscience**—the study of the relationship between neural and social processes. Social neuroscience is part of a flourishing set of research that explores how the social world affects the brain and biology and vice versa. Recent research has investigated such issues as how individuals' likelihood of acting aggressively may be influenced by their neurological responses to social rejection; gender differences in neuroendocrine reaction to stress; and the relationship between activity in various brain structures, such as the amygdala, and how people respond to members of their own or a different racial group (Eisenberger et al., 2007; Kelly et al., 2008; Lieberman, 2010; Van Bavel, Packer, & Cunningham, 2008).

Recent advances in **behavioral genetics**—a subfield of psychology that examines the effects of genes on behavior—has triggered new research to investigate such matters as the extent to which aggression is an inherited trait and the roles that genes play in individuals' sexual orientation or identity (Buckholtz & Meyer-Lindenberg, 2008; James, 2005).

Evolutionary psychology, which uses the principles of evolution to understand human behavior, is another growing area that is sparking new research in social psychology. According to this perspective, to understand a social psychological issue such as jealousy, we should ask how the psychological mechanisms underlying jealousy today may have evolved from the natural-selection pressures our ancestors faced. Evolutionary psychological theories can then be used to explain and predict gender differences in jealousy, the situational factors most likely to trigger jealousy, and so on (Buss, 2007; Easton & Shackelford, 2009; Edlund & Sagarin, 2009). This perspective is discussed in many places throughout the textbook, especially in Part IV on Social Relations.

Cultural Perspectives

Because of the fantastic advancements in communication technologies in recent years and the globalization of the world's economies, it is faster, easier, and more necessary than ever before for people from vastly different cultures to interact with one another. Thus, our need and desire to understand how we are similar to and different from one another are greater than ever as well. Social psychology is currently experi-

social neuroscience   The study of the relationship between neural and social processes.

behavioral genetics   A subfield of psychology that examines the role of genetic factors in behavior.

evolutionary psychology   A subfield of psychology that uses the principles of evolution to understand human social behavior.

encing tremendous growth in research designed to give us a better understanding and appreciation of the role of culture in all aspects of social psychology.

What is meant by "culture" is not easy to pin down, as many researchers think of culture in very different ways. Broadly speaking, **culture** may be considered to be a system of enduring meanings, beliefs, values, assumptions, institutions, and practices shared by a large group of people and transmitted from one generation to the next. Whatever the specific definition, it is clear that how individuals perceive and derive meaning from their world are influenced profoundly by the beliefs, norms, and practices of the people and institutions around them.

Increasing numbers of social psychologists are evaluating the universal generality or cultural specificity of their theories and findings by conducting **cross-cultural research**, in which they examine similarities and differences across a variety of cultures. More and more social psychologists are also conducting **multicultural research**, in which they examine racial and ethnic groups within cultures.

These developments are already profoundly influencing our view of human behavior. For example, a rapidly growing body of cross-cultural research has revealed important distinctions between the collectivist cultures typically found in Africa, Asia, and Latin America and the individualistic ones more commonly found in North America and Europe. The implications of these differences can be seen throughout the textbook. Consider, for instance, our earlier discussion of the integration of "hot" and "cold" variables in contemporary social psychology, in which we mentioned the conflict people have between wanting to be right and wanting to feel good about themselves. Cross-cultural research has shown that how people try to juggle these two goals can differ dramatically across cultures. Several researchers have found, for example, that people from individualistic cultures are more likely than people from collectivist cultures to seek out or focus on information that makes them feel good about themselves rather than information that points to the need for improvement (Heine, 2007). For example, Carl Falk and others (2009) asked Japanese or European-Canadian individuals to indicate which of a variety of desirable and undesirable traits characterized themselves. ▶ Figure 1.2 illustrates the results of the study, demonstrating that European-Canadian participants were far more likely to choose desirable than undesirable traits as characteristic of themselves, but the Japanese participants were much more balanced between desirable and undesirable traits.

Within a particular society, people are often treated differently as a function of social categories such as gender, race, physical appearance, and so on. Boys and girls, for example, may be raised differently by their parents, confronted with different expectations by teachers, exposed to different types of advertising and marketing, and offered different kinds of jobs. In a sense, then, despite their frequent and intimate contact, women and men may develop and live in distinct subcultures. Social psychologists have studied the role of sociocultural factors in a variety of domains, such as conformity, leadership style, and aggression. Recent research is not only extending this tradition, it is also sometimes turning it on its ear by illustrating that many previous research programs were flawed as a result of taking a male-dominated approach. New research on aggression, for example, illustrates that most of the older research

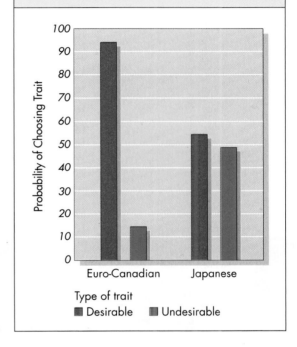

▶FIGURE 1. 2
Self-Descriptions Across Cultures
Japanese or European-Canadian research participants were presented with a list of desirable (e.g., sincere, intelligent) and undesirable (e.g., cruel, indecisive) traits and asked which traits were characteristic of themselves. The European-Canadian participants (the two bars on the left) were much more likely to choose desirable than undesirable traits, but the Japanese participants (the two bars on the right) chose a much more balanced mix of traits.

Based on Falk et al., 2009.

culture A system of enduring meanings, beliefs, values, assumptions, institutions, and practices shared by a large group of people and transmitted from one generation to the next.

cross-cultural research Research designed to compare and contrast people of different cultures.

multicultural research Research designed to examine racial and ethnic groups within cultures.

focused almost exclusively on the forms of aggression typical of boys, thereby failing to recognize important issues relevant to aggression among girls.

These are but a few examples of the cultural research taking place today. In this text, we describe studies conducted in dozens of countries, representing every populated continent on earth. As our knowledge expands, we should be able to see much more clearly both the behavioral differences among cultures and the similarities we all share.

Some social psychology textbooks devote a separate chapter to culture or to culture and gender. We chose not to do so. Because we believe that sociocultural influences are inherent in all aspects of social psychology, we chose instead to integrate discussions of the role of culture and gender in every chapter of the textbook.

New Technologies

Advances in technologies that allow researchers to see images of the brain at work through noninvasive procedures have had a profound effect on several areas of psychology, including social psychology. A growing number of social psychologists are using techniques such as *positron emission tomography (PET)*, *event-related potential (ERP)*, *transcranial magnetic stimulation (TMS)*, and *functional magnetic resonance imaging (fMRI)* to study the interplay of the brain and discrete thoughts, feelings, and behaviors. Social psychology research today benefits from other technological advances as well, such as new and better techniques to measure hormone levels, to code people's everyday dialogue into quantifiable units, and to present visual stimuli to research participants at fractions of a second and then record the number of milliseconds it takes the participants to respond to these stimuli. Some researchers are using virtual reality technology to examine a number of social psychological questions. James Blascovich and others have created the Research Center for Virtual Environments and Behavior at the University of California at Santa Barbara and have been conducting fascinating research on issues such as conformity, group dynamics, aggression and altruism, and eyewitness testimony (e.g., McCall et al., 2009). Because participants in these experiments are immersed in a virtual reality that the experimenters create for them, the researchers can test questions that would be impractical, impossible, or unethical without this technology.

Awesome is an overused word, but it surely describes the revolution that is taking place in how we access information and communicate with each other. The waves of this revolution have carried social psychology research along with it. Social psychologists around the world can now not only communicate and collaborate much more easily but can also gain access to research participants from populations that would otherwise never have been available. These developments have sparked the field's internationalization, perhaps its most exciting course in this new century. World War II triggered an explosion of social psychological research in the United States; the Internet is extending this research to the rest of the world.

Jeff Miller/University of Wisconsin-Madison

Advances in technology enable social psychologists to extend their research in exciting new directions, such as by using functional magnetic resonance imaging (fMRI) to study activity in the brain in response to various thoughts or stimuli.

The Internet itself is also becoming a provocative topic of study. As more people interact with each other through e-mail and social networking sites, there is growing interest in studying how attraction, prejudice, group dynamics, and a host of other social psychological phenomena unfold online versus offline (Toma et al., 2008; Weisbuch et al., 2009; Williams & Mendelsohn, 2008).

We would be presumptuous, and probably naive, to try to predict how new communication and new technologies will influence the ways that people will interact in the coming years, but it probably is safe to predict that their influence will be great. As more and more people fall in love online, or fall into social isolation, or react with anxiety or violence to the loss of individual privacy, social psychology will explore these issues. We expect that some of the students reading this textbook today will be among those explorers in the years to come.

REVIEW

What Is Social Psychology?

Defining Social Psychology

- Social psychology is the scientific study of how individuals think, feel, and behave in a social context.
- Like other sciences, social psychology relies on the systematic approach of the scientific method.
- Distinctive characteristics of social psychology include a focus on the individual as well as a broad perspective on a variety of social contexts and behaviors.
- The "socialness" of social psychology varies, as social psychologists sometimes examine how nonsocial factors affect social thoughts, feelings, and behaviors and sometimes study how social factors influence nonsocial thoughts, feelings, and behaviors.

Social Psychological Questions and Applications

- Social psychologists study a large variety of fascinating questions about people and their social worlds. The scope and relevance of these questions to so many important aspects of our lives make social psychology applicable to many careers and interests.

The Power of the Social Context: An Example of a Social Psychology Experiment

- In one experiment that illustrates the power of the social context, participants' judgments of a political candidate's performance in a debate were influenced more by the reactions of other people to some remarks made by the candidate than by the remarks themselves.

Social Psychology and Related Fields: Distinctions and Intersections

- Social psychology is related to a number of different areas of study, including sociology, clinical psychology, personality psychology, and cognitive psychology. Important work is being done at the intersection of social psychology and each of these fields.

- Social psychology tends to focus on individuals, whereas sociology tends to focus on groups. In addition, social psychology is less likely than sociology to study the relation between broad societal variables and people's behaviors and is more likely to use experimentation.
- In contrast to clinical psychology, social psychology focuses not on disorders but rather on the more typical ways that individuals think, feel, behave, and interact.
- Personality psychology focuses on differences between individuals that remain relatively stable across a variety of situations; social psychology focuses on how social factors affect most individuals, regardless of their different personalities.
- Cognitive and social psychologists share an interest in mental processes such as thinking, learning, remembering, and reasoning, but social psychologists focus on the relevance of these processes to social behavior.

Social Psychology and Common Sense

- Many social psychological theories and findings appear to be like common sense. One problem with common sense, however, is that it may offer conflicting explanations and provide no way to test which is correct. Another problem is that common sense is often oversimplified and therefore misleading.

From Past to Present: A Brief History of Social Psychology

The Birth and Infancy of Social Psychology: 1880s–1920s

■ Early research by Triplett and Ringelmann established an enduring topic in social psychology: how the presence of others affects an individual's performance.

■ The first social psychology textbooks in 1908 and 1924 began to give the emerging field of social psychology its shape.

A Call to Action: 1930s–1950s

■ Social psychology began to flourish because the world needed an explanation for the violence of war and solutions to it.

■ Sherif's work laid the foundation for later studies of social influence, and the legacy of Kurt Lewin is still evident throughout much of social psychology.

■ The 1940s and 1950s saw a burst of activity in social psychology that firmly established it as a major social science.

Confidence and Crisis: 1960s–Mid-1970s

■ Stanley Milgram's experiments demonstrated individuals' vulnerability to the destructive commands of authority.

■ While social psychology was expanding in many new directions, there was also intense debate about the ethics of research procedures, the validity of research results, and the generalizability of conclusions drawn from research.

An Era of Pluralism: Mid-1970s–1990s

■ During the 1970s, social psychology began to take a pluralistic approach to its research methods, views on human behavior, and development of international and multicultural perspectives; this approach continues today.

Social Psychology in a New Century

■ Several exciting themes and perspectives are helping to shape the beginning of social psychology's second century.

Integration of Emotion, Motivation, and Cognition

■ Researchers are becoming more interested in how emotion, motivation, and cognition can operate together in influencing individuals' thoughts, feelings, and behaviors.

■ A great deal of recent social psychological research has explored the automatic versus controllable nature of a number of processes, such as stereotyping.

Biological and Evolutionary Perspectives

■ Biological perspectives, including perspectives based on neuroscience, genetics, and evolutionary principles, are being applied to the study of social psychological issues such as gender differences, relationships, and aggression.

Cultural Perspectives

■ Increasing numbers of social psychologists are evaluating the universal generality or cultural specificity of their theories and findings by examining similarities and differences across cultures as well as between racial and ethnic groups within cultures.

■ For example, in one experiment Canadian participants chose more desirable than undesirable traits as characteristic of themselves, whereas Japanese participants chose a balance of desirable and desirable traits.

New Technologies

■ Advances in technology, such as improved brain-imaging techniques, have given rise to groundbreaking research in social psychology.

■ Virtual reality technology enables researchers to test questions that otherwise would be impractical, impossible, or unethical.

■ The Internet has fostered communication and collaboration among researchers around the world, enabled researchers to study participants from diverse populations, and inspired researchers to investigate whether various social psychological phenomena are similar or different online versus offline.

■ As rapidly advancing technologies change how individuals communicate and access information, the ways that they interact are also likely to change. The social psychology of the next era will explore these issues.

Key Terms

behavioral genetics (18)
cross-cultural research (19)
culture (19)

evolutionary psychology (18)
interactionist perspective (14)
multicultural research (19)

social cognition (17)
social neuroscience (18)
social psychology (5)

Media Resources

Social Psychology 8th Edition Companion Website

Visit your book companion website **www.cengage.com/psychology/kassin** where you will find flash cards, practice quizzes, Internet links, and more to help you study.

CENGAGENOW™ Just what you need to know NOW! Spend time on what you need to master rather than on information you already have learned. Take a pre-test for this chapter and CengageNOW will generate a personalized study plan based on your results. The study plan will identify the topics you need to review and direct you to online resources to help you master those topics. You can then take a post-test to help you determine the concepts you have mastered and what you will need to work on. Try it out! Go to **academic.cengage.com/login** to sign in with an access code or to purchase access to this product.

2

© Matthias Tunger/Corbis

Doing Social Psychology Research

This chapter examines how social psychologists do their research. We begin by asking, "Why should you learn about research methods?" We answer this question by discussing how learning about research methods can benefit you both in this course and beyond. Then we consider how researchers come up with and develop ideas and begin the research process. *Next, we provide an overview of the* research designs *that social psychologists use* to *test their ideas. Finally, we turn to important questions about* ethics and values in social psychology.

It's a familiar situation. You're starting a new semester or quarter at school, and you're just beginning to settle into a new schedule and routine. You're looking forward to your new courses. In general, it's an exciting time. But there's one major catch: As you spend more and more time with your new classmates and new responsibilities, you're leaving someone behind. It could be a boyfriend or girlfriend, a spouse, or a close friend—someone who is not involved in what you are doing now. You may now live far apart from each other or your new commitments in school may be keeping you apart from each other much more than you'd like. The romantic in you says, "Together forever." Or at least, "No problem." But the realist in you worries a bit. Will your love or friendship be the same? Can it survive the long distance, or the new demands on your time, or the new people in your respective environments? Your friends or family may have advice to offer in this situation. Some might smile and reassure you: "Don't worry. Remember what they say, 'Absence makes the heart grow fonder.' This will only strengthen your relationship." Others might call you aside and whisper, "Don't listen to them. Everybody knows, 'Out of sight, out of mind.' You'd better be careful."

Taking your mind off this problem, you begin to work on a class project. You have the option of working alone or as part of a group. Which should you do? You consult the wisdom of common sense. Maybe you should work in a group. After all, everyone knows that "two heads are better than one." As some members of your group begin to miss meetings and shirk responsibilities, though, you remember that "too many cooks spoil the broth." Will you regret having been so quick to decide to join this group? After all, haven't you been taught to "look before you leap"? Then again, if you had waited and missed the chance to join the group, you might have regretted your inaction, recalling that "he who hesitates is lost."

Questions about the course of relationships, the efficiency of working in groups, and the regret from action versus inaction are social psychological questions. And because we all are interested in predicting and explaining people's behaviors and their thoughts and feelings about each other, we all have our own opinions and intuitions about social psychological matters. If the discipline of social psychology were built on the personal experiences, observations, and intuitions of everyone who is interested in social psychological questions, it would be chock-full of interesting theories and ideas, but it would also be a morass of contradictions, ambiguities, and relativism. Instead, social psychology is built on the scientific method.

Scientific? It's easy to see how chemistry is scientific. When you mix two specific compounds in the lab, you can predict exactly what will happen. The compounds will act the same way every time you mix them if the general conditions in the lab are the same. But what happens when you mix together two chemists, or any two people, in a social context? Sometimes you get great chemistry between them; other times you get apathy or even repulsion. How, then, can social behavior, which seems so variable, be studied scientifically?

To many of us in the field, that's the great excitement and challenge of social psychology—the fact that it *is* so dynamic and diverse. Furthermore, in spite of these characteristics, social psychology can, and should, be studied according to scientific principles. Social psychologists develop specific, quantifiable hypotheses that can be tested empirically. If these hypotheses are wrong, they can be proven wrong. In addition, social scientists report the details of how they conduct their tests so that others can try to replicate their findings. They integrate evidence from across time and place. And slowly but steadily they build a consistent and ever more precise understanding of human nature. How social psychologists investigate social psychological questions scientifically is the focus of this chapter. Before we explain the methodology they use, we first explain why it's important and interesting for you to learn about these matters.

The most exciting phrase to hear in science, the one that heralds new discoveries, is not "Eureka!" (I found it!) but "That's funny. . . ."

—Isaac Asimov

Why Should You Learn About Research Methods?

One very practical reason for learning about research methods is that it will help you better understand and learn the material in this book, which will in turn help you on tests and in subsequent courses. Let's look more closely at why this is so. Because social psychology is so relevant to our everyday lives, and because there are so many commonsense notions about social psychological questions, separating myths from truths can be difficult. Most of us don't have an intuition about particular questions concerning quantum mechanics, but we do have intuitions about, say, whether people work better alone or in groups. If you simply read a list of social psychological findings about issues such as this without knowing and understanding the evidence that social psychologists have produced to support the findings, you may discover later that the task of remembering which were the actual findings and which were merely your own intuitions is difficult. This task is sometimes especially challenging in multiple-choice exams. The right answer might seem very plausible, but then again, based only on common sense, so might some of the wrong answers! Learning about the evidence on which the true research findings and theories are based should help you distinguish the correct from the plausible but incorrect answers.

But the benefits of learning about research methods go far beyond the academic. Training in research methods in psychology can improve your reasoning about real-life events and problems (Lehman et al., 1988; Leshowitz et al., 2002; VanderStoep & Shaughnessy 1997). It can make you a better, more sophisticated consumer of information in general. We are constantly bombarded with "facts" from the media, from sales pitches, and from other people. Much of this information turns out to be wrong or, at best, oversimplified and misleading. We are told about the health benefits of eating certain kinds of food, the college entrance exam score benefits of certain preparation courses, or the social status benefits of driving a certain kind of car or wearing a certain kind of shoe. To each of these pronouncements, we should say, "Prove it." What is the evidence? What alternative explanations might there be? For example, a commercial tells us that most doctors prefer a particular (and relatively expensive) brand of aspirin. So should we buy this brand? Think about what it was compared with. Perhaps the doctors didn't prefer that brand of aspirin over other (and cheaper) brands of aspirin but rather were asked to compare that brand of aspirin with several non-aspirin products for a particular problem. In that event, the doctors may have preferred any brand of aspirin over nonaspirin products for that need. Thinking like a scientist while reading this text will foster a healthy sense of doubt about claims such as these. You will be in a better position to critically evaluate the information to which you're exposed and separate fact from fiction.

Mitchell Funk/Getty Images

We are bombarded with information in our everyday lives, such as in the countless advertisements designed to persuade us to buy particular products or adopt particular opinions or attitudes. Learning the methods used in social psychology research can help students become more sophisticated consumers of this information.

Developing Ideas: Beginning the Research Process

The research process involves coming up with ideas, refining them, testing them, and interpreting the meaning of the results obtained. This section describes the first stage of research—coming up with ideas. It also discusses the role of hypotheses and theories and of basic and applied research.

Asking Questions

Every social psychology study begins with a question. And the questions come from everywhere. As discussed in Chapter 1, the first social psychology experiment published was triggered by the question "Why do bicyclists race faster in the presence of other bicyclists?" (Triplett, 1897–1898). Questions can come from a variety of sources, from something tragic, such as a controversial interracial shooting of an unarmed man; to something perplexing, such as the underrepresentation of women in math and science; to something amusing, such as the lyrics of a country song suggesting that female patrons seem prettier to the men in a bar as closing time approaches (Ceci et al., 2009; Payne, 2006; Pennebaker et al., 1979).

Questions also come from reading about research that has already been done. Solomon Asch (1946), for example, read about Muzafer Sherif's (1936) demonstration

Education is not the filling of a pail, but the lighting of a fire.
—William Butler Yeats

Give people facts and you feed their minds for an hour. Awaken curiosity and they feed their own minds for a lifetime.

—Ian Russell

People lay candles by a high school in Kauhajoki, Western Finland, after a young man opened fire on students there in September 2008, killing ten people before shooting himself. Over the years, tragic incidents like this one have inspired social psychologists to conduct research on violence and a wide variety of other important social problems.

of how individuals in a group conform to others in the group when making judgments about a very ambiguous stimulus (mentioned in Chapter 1 and described in Chapter 7 on Conformity). Asch questioned whether people would conform to the opinions of others in a group even when it was quite clear that the group was wrong. He tested this question, and the results surprised him and the rest of the field: People often did conform even though it was clear that the group was wrong. Thus, one of the most famous experiments in the field inspired an even more famous experiment.

Searching the Literature

Once the researcher has an idea, whether it came from personal observation, folk wisdom, a news story, or previous findings, it is important to see what research has already been done on this topic and related topics. Textbooks such as this one offer a starting point. You may find information about many research findings by searching the Internet using a search engine such as Google or on sites such as Wikipedia. While these approaches may be informative, they can also be wildly variable in the relevance, quality, and accuracy of the information presented. One of the best ways to search for published materials on topics of interest is by using an electronic database of published research. Some of these databases, such as PsycINFO, are specific to the psychology literature; others are more general. When you use an electronic database, you can search hundreds of thousands of published articles and books in seconds. You can type in names of authors, key words or phrases, years, or the like and instantly receive summaries of articles that fit your search criteria. Once you have found some relevant articles, there is a good chance that they will refer to other articles that are also relevant. Going from article to article, sometimes called *treeing*, can prove very valuable in tracking down information about the research question.

More often than not, the researcher's original question is changed in one way or another during the course of searching the literature. The question should become more precise, more specific to particular sets of conditions that are likely to have different effects, and more readily testable.

Hypotheses and Theories

An initial idea for research may be so vague that it amounts to little more than a hunch or an educated guess. Some ideas vanish with the break of day. But others can be shaped into a **hypothesis**—an explicit, testable prediction about the conditions under which an event will occur. Based on observation, existing theory, or previous research findings, one might test a hypothesis such as "Teenage boys are more likely to be aggressive toward others if they have just played a violent video game for an hour than if they played a nonviolent video game for an hour." This is a specific prediction, and it can be tested empirically. Formulating a hypothesis is a critical step toward

hypothesis A testable prediction about the conditions under which an event will occur.

planning and conducting research. It allows us to move from the realm of common sense to the rigors of the scientific method.

As hypotheses proliferate and data are collected to test the hypotheses, a more advanced step in the research process may take place: the proposal of a **theory**—an organized set of principles used to explain observed phenomena. Theories are usually evaluated in terms of three criteria: simplicity, comprehensiveness, and generativity. All else being equal, the best theories are elegant and precise; encompass all of the relevant information; and lead to new hypotheses, further research, and better understanding.

In social psychology, there are many theories. Social psychologists do not attempt the all-encompassing grand theory, such as those of Freud or Piaget, which you may have studied in introductory psychology. Instead, they rely on more precise "mini-theories" that address limited and specific aspects of the way people behave, make explicit predictions about behavior, and allow meaningful empirical investigation. Consider, for example, Daryl Bem's (1967, 1972) self-perception theory, which is discussed in Chapter 3 on the Social Self. Bem proposed that when people's internal states, such as a feeling or attitude, are difficult for them to interpret, they infer what this feeling or attitude is by observing their own behavior and taking into account the context in which it takes place. This theory did not apply to all situations; rather, it was specific to situations in which people make inferences about their own actions, and to when their own internal states are somewhat ambiguous. Though more limited in scope than a grand theory of personality or development, self-perception theory did generate numerous specific, empirically testable hypotheses.

Good social psychological theories inspire subsequent research. Specifically, they stimulate systematic studies designed to test various aspects of the theories and the specific hypotheses that are derived from them. A theory may be quite accurate and yet have little worth if it cannot be tested. Conversely, a theory may make an important contribution to the field even if it turns out to be wrong. The research it inspires may prove more valuable than the theory itself, as the results shed light on new truths that might not have been discovered without the directions suggested by the theory.

Indeed, when Bem introduced self-perception theory to the field, it generated a great deal of attention and controversy. Part of its value as a good theory was that it helped organize and make sense of evidence that had been found in previous studies. Furthermore, it generated testable new hypotheses. Many scholars doubted the validity of the theory, however, and conducted research designed to prove it wrong. In short, both supporters and doubters of the theory launched a wave of studies, which ultimately led to a greater understanding of the processes described in Bem's theory.

Beginning students of social psychology are often surprised by the lack of consensus in the field. In part, such disagreement reflects the fact that social psychology is a relatively young science (Kruglanski, 2001). At this stage in its development, premature closure is a worse sin than contradiction or even confusion. But debate is an essential feature of even the most mature science. It is the fate of all scientific theories to be criticized and, eventually, surpassed.

▌ Basic and Applied Research

Is testing a theory the purpose of research in social psychology? For some researchers, yes. **Basic research** seeks to increase our understanding of human behavior and is often designed to test a specific hypothesis from a specific theory. **Applied research**

The currency of science is not truth, but doubt.
—Dennis Overbye

Close cooperation between theoretical and applied psychology can be accomplished . . . if the theorist does not look toward applied problems with highbrow aversion or with a fear of social problems, and if the applied psychologist realizes that there is nothing so practical as a good theory.
—Kurt Lewin

theory An organized set of principles used to explain observed phenomena.

basic research Research whose goal is to increase the understanding of human behavior, often by testing hypotheses based on a theory.

applied research Research whose goals are to enlarge the understanding of naturally occurring events and to find solutions to practical problems.

has a different purpose: to make use of social psychology's theories or methods to enlarge our understanding of naturally occurring events and to contribute to the solution of social problems.

Despite their differences, basic and applied research are closely connected in social psychology. Some researchers switch back and forth between the two—today basic, tomorrow applied. Some studies test a theory and examine a real-world phenomenon simultaneously. As a pioneer in both approaches, Kurt Lewin (1951) set the tone when he encouraged basic researchers to be concerned with complex social problems and urged applied researchers to recognize how important and practical good theories are.

Refining Ideas: Defining and Measuring Social Psychological Variables

To test their hypotheses, researchers always must decide how they will define and measure the variables in which they are interested. This is sometimes a straightforward process. For example, if you are interested in comparing how quickly people run a 100-meter dash when alone and when racing against another person, you can rely on well-established ways to define and measure the variables in question. Many other times, however, the process is less straightforward. For example, imagine you are interested in studying the effects of self-esteem on altruistic behavior. You need to step back and ask yourself, "What do I mean by self-esteem? What do I mean by altruistic behavior?" You will need to define these concepts, and there may be countless ways to do this. Which ones should you pick?

From this picture, we can guess that the boy sitting by himself on the playground is lonely, but how do researchers precisely define and measure conceptual variables such as loneliness? Researchers may use any of a number of approaches, such as asking people how they feel or observing their behavior.

Conceptual Variables and Operational Definitions: From the Abstract to the Specific

When a researcher first develops a hypothesis, the variables typically are in an abstract, general form. These are *conceptual variables*. Examples of conceptual variables include prejudice, conformity, attraction, love, group pressure, and social anxiety. In order to test specific hypotheses, we must then transform these conceptual variables into variables that can be manipulated or measured in a study. The specific way in which a conceptual variable is manipulated or measured is called the **operational definition** of the variable. For example, "conformity" in a particular study may be defined as the number of times a participant indicated agreement with the obviously wrong judgments made by a group of confederates. Part of the challenge and fun of designing research in social psychology is taking an abstract conceptual variable such as love or group pressure and deciding how to operationally define it so as to manipulate or measure it.

Imagine, for example, wanting to conduct a study on the effects of alcohol intoxication on aggression. One of the conceptual variables might be whether or not participants are intoxicated. There are several ways of measuring this variable, most of which are relatively straightforward. For instance, one researcher might operationally define intoxication as when a participant has a blood alcohol level of .10 or more, while another might define it as when a participant says that he or she feels drunk. A second conceptual variable in this study would be aggression. Measuring aggression in experiments is particularly difficult because of ethical and practical issues—researchers can't let participants in their studies attack each other. Researchers interested in measuring aggression are thus often forced to measure relatively unusual behaviors, such as administering shocks or blasts of noise to another person as part of a specific task.

Often there is no single best way to transform a variable from the abstract (conceptual) to the specific (operational). A great deal of trial and error may be involved. However, sometimes there are systematic, statistical ways of checking how valid various manipulations and measures are, and researchers spend a great deal of time fine-tuning their operational definitions to best capture the conceptual variables they wish to study.

Researchers evaluate the manipulation and measurement of variables in terms of their **construct validity**. Construct validity refers to the extent to which (1) the manipulations in an experiment really manipulate the conceptual variables they were designed to manipulate; and (2) the measures used in a study (experimental or otherwise) really measure the conceptual variables they were designed to measure.

"Clemson here, how may I disappoint you?"

This person would probably score low on Rosenberg's Self-Esteem Scale.

Measuring Variables: Using Self-Reports, Observations, and Technology

Social psychologists measure variables in many ways, but most can be placed into one of two categories: self-reports and observations. We discuss each of these methods in the next sections, along with how advances in technology are enabling social psychologists to measure variables in new ways.

Self-Reports   Collecting *self-reports*—in which participants disclose their thoughts, feelings, desires, and actions—is a widely used measurement technique in social psychology. Self-reports can consist of individual questions or sets of questions that together measure a single conceptual variable. One popular self-report measure, the Rosenberg Self-Esteem Scale, consists of a set of questions that measures individuals' overall self-esteem. For example, respondents are asked the extent to which they agree with statements such as "I feel that I have a number of good qualities," and "All in all, I am inclined to feel that I'm a failure." This scale is used in a wide variety of settings, and many researchers from around the world consider it to have good construct validity (Heatherton & Wyland, 2003; Martin-Albo et al., 2007; Vermillion & Dodder, 2007).

Self-reports give the researcher access to an individual's beliefs and perceptions. But self-reports are not always accurate and can be misleading. For example, the

operational definition The specific procedures for manipulating or measuring a conceptual variable.

construct validity   The extent to which the measures used in a study measure the variables they were designed to measure and the manipulations in an experiment manipulate the variables they were designed to manipulate.

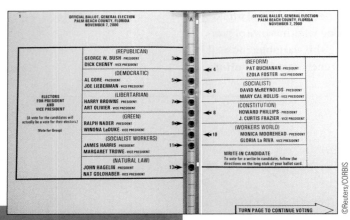

The importance of well-designed questions and response options may never have been more evident than in the aftermath of the U.S. presidential election of November 2000. The positioning of the choices on this "butterfly" ballot design confused countless voters in Palm Beach County, Florida, apparently causing thousands of people to mistakenly vote for Pat Buchanan when they had intended to vote for Al Gore. This confusion may well have caused Gore to lose the presidency to George W. Bush.

desire to look good to ourselves and others can influence how we respond. This is evident in the results of research using the **bogus pipeline technique**—a procedure in which participants are led to believe that their responses will be verified by an infallible lie detector. When participants believe their lies would be detected, they report facts about themselves more accurately and endorse socially unacceptable opinions more frequently. The bogus pipeline is, in fact, bogus; no such infallible device exists. But belief in its powers discourages people from lying (Adams et al., 2008; Gannon et al., 2007; Roese & Jamieson, 1993).

Self-reports are also affected by the way that questions are asked, such as how they are worded or in what order or context they are asked (Schwarz, 1999; Schwarz & Oyserman, 2010). For instance, when UCLA freshmen were asked on a survey, "How much special consideration should black students receive in college admissions?" more than 70 percent said that at least some special consideration should be given. However, when asked, "Should affirmative action be abolished?" 50 percent said yes (Shea, 1996). In another study, a large majority of participants indicated that they thought condoms were effective in stopping AIDS when condoms were said to have a "95 percent success rate" (see Table 2.1). However, when condoms were said to have a "5 percent failure rate" (which is merely another way of saying the same thing as a 95 percent success rate), less than half of the participants indicated that they thought condoms were effective (Linville et al., 1992).

Even the exact same question can elicit very different responses depending on the context in which the question occurs. For example, all individuals contacted in one telephone survey were asked how important the issue of skin cancer was in their lives, but this question was asked either before or after a series of questions about other health concerns. As the bottom of Table 2.1 shows, even though the wording of the question was identical, respondents rated skin cancer as significantly more important if the question was asked first than if it came after the other health questions (Rimal & Real, 2005).

Another reason self-reports can be inaccurate is that they often ask participants to report on thoughts or behaviors from the past, and people's memory of their thoughts or behaviors is very prone to error. To minimize this problem, psychologists have developed ways to reduce the time that elapses between an actual experience and the person's report of it. For example, some use *interval-contingent* self-reports, in which respondents report their experiences at regular intervals, usually once a day. Researchers may also collect *signal-contingent* self-reports. Here, respondents report their experiences as soon as possible after being signaled to do so, usually by means of a beeper or text message. Finally, some researchers collect *event-contingent* self-reports, in which respon-

TABLE 2.1

How Self-Reports Can Be Affected by Context

Are condoms effective in preventing the spread of AIDS? How important is the issue of skin cancer in your life? Responses to these questions can differ significantly depending on context. For the condom question, participants told that condoms had a "95% success rate" were much more likely to say that condoms were effective than were participants told they had a "5% failure rate," even though these two rates are functionally the same thing. For the skin cancer question, respondents rated skin cancer as more important (on a 0–9 scale, with 9 being most important) if it was the first health question asked than if it followed other health questions.

Statement Given to Participants	Percent Who Said Condoms Were Effective
"Condoms have a 95% success rate."	88
"Condoms have a 5% failure rate."	42
Question Order	**Rating of Importance of Skin Cancer**
Skin cancer question asked first	6.10
Skin cancer question asked after others	5.12

Linville et al., 1992; Rimal & Real, 2005.

bogus pipeline technique
A procedure in which research participants are (falsely) led to believe that their responses will be verified by an infallible lie-detector.

dents report on a designated set of events as soon as possible after such events have occurred. For example, the Rochester Interaction Record (RIR) is an event-contingent self-report questionnaire used by respondents to record every social interaction lasting ten minutes or more that occurs during the course of the study, usually a week or two (Downie et al., 2008; Nezlek et al., 2008).

Whatever their differences, most self-report methods require participants to provide specific answers to specific questions. In contrast, *narrative studies* collect lengthy responses on a general topic. Narrative materials can be generated by participants at the researcher's request or taken from other sources (such as diaries, speeches, books, or chatroom discussions). These accounts are then analyzed in terms of a coding scheme developed by the researcher. For example, the researcher might code a series of open-ended self-descriptions for evidence of particular personality traits, diaries for evidence of changes in self-esteem or behavior toward other groups, or interviews for evidence of athletes' explanations for winning or losing (Chung & Pennebaker, 2008; Knee et al., 2008; Page-Gould et al., 2008; Ross et al., 2004).

Observations   Self-reports are but one tool social psychologists use to measure variables. Researchers can also observe people's actions. Sometimes these observations are very simple, as when a researcher notes which of two items a person selects. At other times, however, the observations are more elaborate and (like the coding of narrative accounts) require that interrater reliability be established. **Interrater reliability** refers to the level of agreement among multiple observers of the same behavior. Only when different observers agree can the data be trusted.

The advantage of observational methods is that they avoid our sometimes-faulty recollections and distorted interpretations of our own behavior. Actions can speak louder than words. Of course, if individuals know they are being observed, their behaviors, like their self-reports, may be biased by the desire to present themselves in a favorable light. Therefore, researchers sometimes make observations much more subtly. For example, in experiments concerning interracial interactions, researchers may record participants' eye contact and seating distance to demonstrate biases that would not be revealed using more overt measures (Castelli et al, 2008; Goff, Steele, & Davies, 2008).

Technology   Social psychologists use more than merely their eyes and ears to observe their subjects, of course. Advances in technology offer researchers exciting new tools that enable them to make extremely precise, subtle, and complex observations that were beyond the dreams of social psychologists just a generation or so ago. Various kinds of equipment are used to measure physiological responses such as changes in heart rate, levels of particular hormones, and sexual arousal. Computers are used to record the speed with which participants respond to stimuli, such as how quickly they can identify the race of people in photographs or the presence of a weapon in the hands of a white or black man (Bishara & Payne, 2009; Klauer & Voss, 2008). Eye-tracking technology is used to measure exactly where and for how long participants look at particular parts of a stimulus, such as an advertisement or a video (Crosby et al., 2008; DeWall et al., 2009).

Most recently, social psychologists have begun opening a window into the live human brain—fortunately, without having to lift a scalpel. Brain-imaging technologies take and combine thousands of images of the brain in action. As mentioned in

Joanne Pasila/one[2]

Observational methods provide a useful alternative to self-reports. Here an experimenter behind a one-way mirror observes and records notes from a conversation between two research participants in a psychology lab.

interrater reliability
The degree to which different observers agree on their observations.

Chapter 1, many social psychology studies today use fMRI (functional magnetic resonance imaging) scans to provide researchers with visual images of activity in parts of the brain while the research subject is thinking, making decisions, responding to audio or visual stimuli, and so on. These images can show researchers what parts of the brain seem to "light up"—or show increased activity—in response to a particular stimulus or situation. For example, although participants in a study of racism may show no signs of any racial or sexist biases on their self-reports or through easily observable behavior in the lab, these same participants may show increased activity in parts of their brain associated with feelings of threat or strong emotion when they see pictures of or think about people from a particular racial group or gender (Mitchell et al., 2009; Van Bavel et al., 2008).

Testing Ideas: Research Designs

Social psychologists use several different methods to test their research hypotheses and theories. Although methods vary, the field generally emphasizes objective, systematic, and quantifiable approaches. Social psychologists do not simply seek out evidence that supports their ideas; rather, they test their ideas in ways that could very clearly prove them wrong.

The most popular research method in social psychology is experimentation, in which researchers can test cause-and-effect relationships, such as whether exposure to a violent television program causes viewers to behave more aggressively. We emphasize the experimental approach in this book. In addition, we report the results of many studies that use another popular approach: correlational research, which looks for associations between two variables without establishing cause and effect. We also report the results of studies that use a relatively new technique called meta-analysis, which integrates the research findings of many different studies. Before describing these approaches, though, we turn to an approach with which we all are very familiar: descriptive research. This is the approach used in opinion polls, ratings of the popularity of TV shows, box scores in the sports section, and the like.

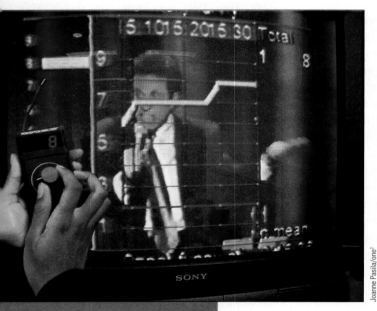

Joanne Pasila/one[2]

Computerized video technology, such as this Perception Analyzer™, allows researchers to track participants' moment-by-moment reactions to events on the screen (in this case, a comedian's performance). It can also simultaneously display the average ratings of groups of participants in a graph superimposed over the video. This technology can help researchers study the dynamics of social influence.

Descriptive Research: Discovering Trends and Tendencies

One obvious way of testing ideas about people is simply to record how frequently or how typically people think, feel, or behave in particular ways. The goal of *descriptive research* in social psychology is, as the term implies, to describe people and their thoughts, feelings, and behaviors. This method can test questions such as: Do most people support capital punishment? What percentage of people who encounter a person lying on the sidewalk would offer to help that person? What do men and women say are the things most likely to make them jealous of their partner? Particular methods of doing descriptive research include observing people, studying records of past events and behaviors, and surveying people. We discuss each of these methods in this section.

Observational Studies   We can learn about other people simply by observing them, of course, and some social psychological questions can be addressed through observational studies. For example, a number of social psychologists interested in the topic of bullying have used observational studies to determine its prevalence among schoolchildren in many places around the world. Although some studies use self-report measures to ask children and teachers about the frequency and severity of bullying, some researchers have gotten a more direct look at the problem by spending time in playgrounds and schoolyards carefully watching and taking notes on the children's interactions, and some have used hidden cameras and microphones (with the schools and parents' consent) to record incidents of bullying (Frey et al., 2009; Hawkins et al., 2001).

Archival Studies   Archival research involves examining existing records of past events and behaviors, such as newspaper articles, medical records, diaries, sports statistics, personal ads, crime statistics, or hits on a web page. A major advantage of archival measures is that because the researchers are observing behavior secondhand, they can be sure that they did not influence the behavior by their presence. A limitation of this approach is that available records are not always complete or sufficiently detailed, and they may have been collected in a nonsystematic manner.

Archival measures are particularly valuable for examining cultural and historical trends. In Chapter 11 on Aggression, for example, we report a number of trends concerning the rate of violent crime in the United States and how it has changed in recent years, and we report differences in homicide rates in countries around the world. These data come from archival records, such as the records of police stations, the Federal Bureau of Investigation (FBI), and the United Nations. Recent examples of archival research include a study that analyzed how black and white defendants in death-penalty cases were described in newspaper articles over a 20-year period and a study that examined the waist-to-hip ratio of *Playboy* centerfolds across two decades (Goff, Eberhardt et al., 2008; Sypeck et al., 2006).

Surveys   It seems that nobody in politics these days sneezes without first conducting an opinion poll. Surveys have become increasingly popular in recent years, and they are conducted on everything from politics to attitudes about social issues to the percentages of people who squeeze rather than fold or roll their toothpaste tubes (OK, we'll tell you: 63 percent say they squeeze, according to a June 2009 poll on Vizu.com). Conducting surveys involves asking people questions about their attitudes, beliefs, and behaviors. Surveys can be conducted in person, over the phone, by mail, or via the Internet. Many social psychological questions can be addressed only with surveys because they involve variables that are impossible or unethical to observe directly or manipulate, such as people's sexual behaviors or their optimism about the future.

Although anyone can conduct a survey (and sometimes it seems that everyone does), there is a science to designing, conducting, and interpreting the results of surveys. Like other self-report measures, surveys can be affected strongly by subtle aspects of the wording and context of questions, and survey researchers are trained

"Just as we suspected—they're beginning to form a boy band."

Observational research can reveal some fascinating—and sometimes disturbing!—insights into social behavior.

Many social psychological questions are addressed using surveys, which can be conducted over the phone, by mail, via the Internet, or face to face in field settings.

In the 1948 U.S. presidential election, pollsters nationwide predicted that Thomas Dewey would defeat Harry Truman by a wide margin. As Truman basked in his victory, pollsters realized that their predictions were based on nonrandom samples of voters. Random sampling would have led to much more accurate predictions.

to consider these issues and to test various kinds of wording and question ordering before conducting their surveys.

One of the most important issues that survey researchers face is how to select the people who will take part in the survey. The researchers first must identify the *population* in which they are interested. Is this survey supposed to tell us about the attitudes of North Americans in general, shoppers at Wal-Mart, or students in an Introduction to Social Psychology course at University X, for example? From this general population, the researchers select a subset, or *sample*, of individuals. For a survey to be accurate, the sample must be similar to, or representative of, the population on important characteristics such as age, sex, race, income, education, and cultural background. The best way to achieve this representativeness is to use **random sampling**, a method of selection in which everyone in a population has an equal chance of being selected for the sample. Survey researchers use randomizing procedures, such as tables of randomly distributed numbers generated by computers, to decide how to select individuals for their samples.

To see the importance of random sampling, consider a pair of U.S. presidential elections (Rosnow & Rosenthal, 1993). Just before the 1936 election, a magazine called the *Literary Digest* predicted that Alfred Landon, the Republican governor of Kansas, would win by 14 percentage points over Franklin Roosevelt. The *Digest* based its prediction on a survey of more than 2 million Americans. In fact, though, Landon *lost* the election by 24 percentage points. The magazine, which had been in financial trouble before the election, declared bankruptcy soon after.

Twenty years later, the Gallup survey's prediction of Dwight Eisenhower's victory was almost perfect—it was off by less than 2 percent. The size of its sample? Only about 8,000. How could the 1936 survey, with its much larger sample, be so wrong and the 1956 survey be so right? The answer is that the 1936 sample was not randomly selected. The *Digest* contacted people through sources such as phone books and club membership lists. In 1936, many people could not afford to have telephones or belong to clubs. The people in the sample, therefore, tended to be wealthier than much of the population, and wealthier people preferred Landon. In 1956, by contrast, Gallup pollsters randomly selected election districts throughout the country and then randomly selected households within those districts. Today, because of improved sampling procedures, surveys conducted on little more than 1,000 Americans can be used to make accurate predictions about the entire U.S. population.

▣ Correlational Research: Looking for Associations

Although there is much to learn from descriptive research, social psychologists typically want to know more. Most research hypotheses in social psychology concern the relationship between variables. For example, is there a relationship between people's gender and their willingness to ask for help from others or between how physically attractive people are and how much money they make?

One way to test such hypotheses is with correlational research. Like descriptive research, **correlational research** can be conducted using observational, archival, or survey methods. Unlike descriptive research, however, correlational approaches measure the *relationship* between different variables. The extent to which variables relate to each other, or correlate, can suggest how similar or distinct two different measures are (for example, how related people's self-esteem and popularity are) and how well one variable can be used to predict another (for example, how well we can predict academic success in college from college entrance exam scores). It is important to note that researchers doing correlational research typically do not manipulate the variables they study; they simply measure them.

Correlation Coefficient When researchers examine the relationship between variables that vary in quantity (such as temperature or degree of self-esteem), they can measure the strength and direction of the relationship between the variables and calculate a statistic called a **correlation coefficient**. Correlation coefficients can range from +1.0 to −1.0. The absolute value of the number (the number itself, without the positive or negative sign) indicates how strongly the two variables are associated. The larger the absolute value of the number, the stronger the association between the two variables, and thus the better either of the variables is as a predictor of the other. Whether the coefficient is positive or negative indicates the direction of the relationship. A positive correlation coefficient indicates that as one variable increases, so does the other. For example, college entrance exam scores correlate positively with grades. The positive direction of this relationship indicates that higher entrance exam scores are associated with higher grades and lower entrance exam scores are associated with lower grades. This correlation is not perfect; some people with high entrance exam scores have poor grades and vice versa. Therefore, the correlation is less than +1.0, but it is greater than 0 because there is some association between the two. A negative coefficient indicates that the two variables go in opposite directions: As one goes up, the other tends to go down. For example, number of classes missed and GPA are likely to be negatively correlated. And a correlation close to 0 indicates that there is no consistent relationship at all. These three types of patterns are illustrated in ▶ Figure 2.1. Because few variables are perfectly related to each other, most correlation coefficients do not approach +1.0 or −1.0 but have more moderate values, such as +.39 or −.57.

Some correlational studies involve a variable that does not vary in quantity, such as race, gender, political affiliation or whether Italian, Mexican, or Thai food is their favorite. In this case, researchers cannot compute a typical correlation coefficient. Nevertheless, such studies can reveal relationships between variables. For example, some research indicates that students who study Latin and take the Latin Achievement Test do more than 100 points better on verbal and math SATs than other students (Costa, 1982). This research indicates a relationship between whether or not a student studies Latin (which is an either/or variable that does not vary in quantity—a student either does or does not study Latin) and students' success on the SAT (which is a variable that does vary in quantity from zero points to a perfect score). Does this correlation mean that studying Latin causes students to do better on the SAT? Think about it; we'll return to this question later.

Advantages and Disadvantages of Correlational Research Correlational research has many advantages. It can study the associations of naturally occurring variables that cannot be manipulated or induced—such as gender, race, ethnicity, and age. It can examine phenomena that would be difficult or unethical to create for research purposes, such as love, hate, and abuse. And it offers researchers a great deal of freedom in where variables are measured. Participants can be brought into a laboratory specially constructed for research purposes or they can be approached in a real-world setting (often called "the field") such as a shopping mall or airport.

© Mike Watson Images/Corbis

Similarity is correlated with attraction—the more similar two people are, the more attractive they are likely to find each other. But a correlation cannot identify the cause of this association. Chapter 9 on Attraction and Close Relationships discusses both correlational and experimental research on the role of similarity in the attraction process.

random sampling A method of selecting participants for a study so that everyone in a population has an equal chance of being in the study.

correlational research Research designed to measure the association between variables that are not manipulated by the researcher.

correlation coefficient A statistical measure of the strength and direction of the association between two variables.

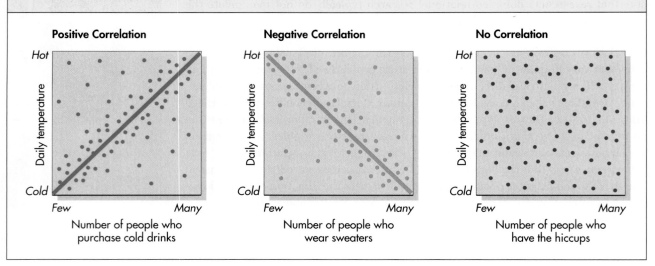

▶**FIGURE 2.1**

Correlations: Positive, Negative, and None

Correlations reveal a systematic association between two variables. Positive correlations indicate that variables are in sync: increases in one variable are associated with increases in the other, decreases with decreases. Negative correlations indicate that variables go in opposite directions: increases in one variable are associated with decreases in the other. When two variables are not systematically associated, there is no correlation.

Despite these advantages, however, correlational research has one very serious disadvantage. And here it is in bold letters: **Correlation is not causation**.

In other words, a correlation cannot demonstrate a cause-and-effect relationship. Instead of revealing a specific causal pathway from one variable, A, to another variable, B, a correlation between variables A and B contains within it three possible causal effects: A could cause B; B could cause A; or a third variable, C, could cause both A and B. For example, imagine learning that the number of hours per night one sleeps is negatively correlated with the number of colds one gets. This means that as the amount of sleep increases, colds decrease in frequency; conversely as sleep decreases, colds become more frequent. One reasonable explanation for this relationship is that lack of sleep (variable A) causes people to become more vulnerable to colds (variable B). Another reasonable explanation, however, is that people who have colds can't sleep well, and so colds (variable B) cause lack of sleep (variable A). A third reasonable explanation is that some other variable (C) causes both lack of sleep and greater frequency of colds. This third variable could be stress. Indeed, stress has many effects on people, as will be discussed in Chapter 14 on Health. ▶ Figure 2.2 describes another correlation that can be explained in many ways—the correlation between playing violent video games and aggression.

As sure as death and taxes, there will be many, many times in your life when you'll encounter reports in the media that suggest cause-and-effect relationships based on correlational research. One of the great benefits of learning and gaining experience with the material in this chapter is that you can see the flaws in media reports such as these and not be taken in by them. Correlation is not causation.

To illustrate how even such respected representatives of the media as the *New York Times* make this mistake, let's return to the Latin and SAT correlation discussed above. This relationship was reported in an op-ed piece in the *Times* entitled "Latin and Greek Are Good for You" (Costa, 1982). The author cited the SAT figures indicating that students who took the Latin Achievement Test did much better on their SATs than other students and concluded that "Latin is good for you." So why is this conclusion wrong? It *is* possible that studying Latin caused an improvement in SAT scores, but other causal explanations are possible as well. In terms of Figure 2.2, A (Latin) might have caused B (elevated SAT scores). Although B could not have caused A, because the students took the SATs only after they had been studying Latin, it is very possible that some other variable (C) caused both A and B. For example, high school students who decide to study Latin may in general be more intelligent than students who show no interest in the subject, or schools that offer study in languages such as Latin and Greek may in general be better academically than schools that do not. So it is possible that studying Latin had no effect on the students' SAT scores, despite the correlation between these two variables (Lehman et al., 1988).

If you Google "why study Latin?" you are likely to find dozens of web pages that claim, quite emphatically, that research shows that studying Latin improves SAT scores. Most, or all, of the data on which they base their claims will be correlational. By now you should know better: correlation is not causation.

Do we learn nothing, then, from correlations? To say that would be to take caution too far. Correlations tell researchers about the strength and direction of relationships between variables, thus helping them understand these variables better and allowing them to use one variable to predict the other. Correlations can be extremely useful in developing new hypotheses to guide future research. And by gathering large sets of correlations and using complicated statistical techniques to crunch the data, we can develop highly accurate predictions of future events.

Experiments: Looking for Cause and Effect

Social psychologists often do want to examine cause-and-effect relationships. Although it is informative to know, for example, that playing a lot of violent video games is correlated with violent behavior in real life, the inevitable next question is whether playing these video games *causes* an increase in violent behavior. If we want to examine cause-and-effect relationships, we need to conduct an **experiment**. Experiments in social psychology range from the very simple to the incredibly elaborate. All of them, however, share two essential characteristics.

1. The researcher has *control* over the experimental procedures, manipulating the variables of interest while ensuring uniformity elsewhere. In other words, all participants in the research are treated in exactly the same manner—except for the specific differences the experimenter wants to create. By exercising control, the researcher attempts to ensure that differences obtained after the experimental manipulation are produced only by that manipulation and are not affected by other events in the experiment.

2. Participants in the study are *randomly* assigned to the different manipulations (called "conditions") included in the experiment. If there are two conditions, who goes where may be determined by simply flipping a coin. If there are many conditions, a computer program may be used. But however it's done, **random assignment** means that participants are not assigned to a condition on the basis of their personal or behavioral characteristics. Through random assignment, the

▶ **FIGURE 2.2**

Explaining Correlations: Three Possibilities

The correlation between one variable (A) and another variable (B) could be explained in three ways. Variable A could cause changes in variable B, or variable B could cause changes in variable A, or a third variable (C) could cause similar changes in both A and B, even if A and B did not influence each other. For example, a correlation between how much children play violent video games and how aggressively they behave could be explained in the following ways:

1. Playing violent video games causes aggressive behavior.
2. Children who behave aggressively like to play a lot of violent video games.
3. Children who have family troubles, such as parents who are not very involved in the children's development, tend both to play a lot of violent video games and to behave aggressively.

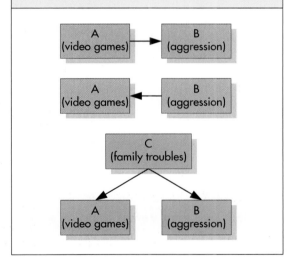

experiment A form of research that can demonstrate causal relationships because (1) the experimenter has control over the events that occur and (2) participants are randomly assigned to conditions.

random assignment A method of assigning participants to the various conditions of an experiment so that each participant in the experiment has an equal chance of being in any of the conditions.

TABLE 2.2

Correlations Versus Experiments

	Correlational Research	Experimental Research
What does it involve?	Measuring variables and the degree of association between them	Random assignment to conditions and control over the events that occur; determining the effects of manipulations of the independent variable(s) on changes in the dependent variable(s)
What is the biggest advantage of using this method?	Enables researchers to study naturally occurring variables, including variables that would be too difficult or unethical to manipulate	Enables researchers to determine cause-and-effect relationships—that is, whether the independent variable can cause a change in the dependent variable

experimenter attempts to ensure a level playing field. *On average, the participants randomly assigned to one condition are no different from those assigned to another condition.* Differences that appear between conditions after an experimental manipulation can therefore be attributed to the impact of that manipulation and not to any preexisting differences between participants.

Because of experimenter control and random assignment of participants, an experiment is a powerful technique for examining cause and effect. Both characteristics serve the same goal: to eliminate the influence of any factors other than the experimental manipulation. By ruling out alternative explanations for research results, we become more confident that we understand just what has, in fact, caused a certain behavior to occur. Table 2.2 summarizes the distinctions between correlational and experimental research.

Random Sampling Versus Random Assignment   You may recall that we mentioned random sampling earlier, in connection with surveys. It's important to remember the differences between random *sampling* and random *assignment*. Table 2.3 summarizes these differences. Random sampling concerns how individuals are selected to be in a study. It is important for generalizing the results obtained from a sample to a broader population, and it is therefore very important for survey research. Random assignment concerns not who is selected to be in the study but rather how participants in the study

TABLE 2.3

Random Sampling Versus Random Assignment

	Random Sampling	Random Assignment
What does it involve?	Selecting participants to be in the study so that everyone from a population has an equal chance of being a participant in the study	Assigning participants (who are already in the study) to the various conditions of the experiment so that each participant has an equal chance of being in any of the conditions
What is the biggest advantage of using this procedure?	Enables researchers to collect data from samples that are representative of the broader population; important for being able to generalize the results to the broader population	Equalizes the conditions of the experiment so that it is very unlikely that the conditions differ in terms of preexisting differences among the participants; essential to determine that the independent variable(s) caused an effect on the dependent variable(s)

are assigned to different conditions, as explained above. Random assignment is essential to experiments because it is necessary for determining cause-and-effect relationships; without it, there is always the possibility that any differences found between the conditions in a study were caused by preexisting differences among participants. Random sampling, in contrast, is not necessary for establishing causality. For that reason, and because random sampling is difficult and expensive, very few experiments use random sampling. We consider the implications of this fact later in the chapter.

Laboratory and Field Experiments   Most experiments in social psychology are conducted in a *laboratory* setting, usually located in a university, so that the environment can be controlled and the participants carefully studied. Social psychology labs do not necessarily look like stereotypical laboratories with liquid bubbling in beakers or expensive equipment everywhere (although many social psychology labs are indeed very high-tech). They can resemble ordinary living rooms or even game rooms. The key point here is that the laboratory setting enables researchers to have control over the setting, measure participants' behaviors precisely, and keep conditions identical for participants.

Field research is conducted in real-world settings outside the laboratory. Researchers interested in studying helping behavior, for example, might conduct an experiment in a public park. The advantage of field experiments is that people are more likely to act naturally in a natural setting than in a laboratory in which they know they are being studied. The disadvantage of field settings is that the experimenter often has less control and cannot ensure that the participants in the various conditions of the experiment will be exposed to the same things.

Because of the important role that experiments play in social psychology, let's take a closer look at the elements of experiments by focusing on two recent experiments.

Experiment 1: Can Song Lyrics Make You More Helpful?   As we will see in Chapter 11 on Aggression, a growing number of studies demonstrate the harmful effects of exposure to violent media, including from television, video games, and music videos. But can positive images and messages from our sources of entertainment produce positive consequences? Tobias Greitemeyer (2009) conducted a set of experiments to address this kind of question. More specifically, he tested the hypothesis that listening to music lyrics that promoted socially positive messages would make people more helpful. In one of his experiments with college students in Germany, he randomly assigned some students to listen to songs with socially positive lyrics (e.g., Bob Sinclair's "Love Generation"—which promotes peace and love) and the other students to listen to songs with neutral lyrics. After listening to the songs and thinking that the study was over, the students were paid for their participation. Before they left, however, the students were asked if they would be interested in donating the money to a nonprofit organization. As ▶ Figure 2.3 shows, students were much more likely to donate their money if they had listened to socially positive than neutral song lyrics.

Experiment 2: Moods and Culture   Imagine that someone shows you a handful of pens. Most of the pens are of one color (e.g., black), and a minority of the pens are of a different color (e.g., blue). You can choose to keep one of the pens. Do you choose a color from the majority or the minority? Believe it or not, there is a consistent cultural difference in how people make this choice. People from Western cultures, such as the United States, tend to choose the uncommon pen color, whereas people from East Asian cultures, such as Korea, tend to choose the majority pen color.

This cultural difference was explored in an interesting way in a recent experiment by Claire Ashton-James and others (2009). The researchers hypothesized that being in a positive mood makes people more likely to explore novel thoughts and behaviors, which can result in their acting in ways that are inconsistent with how people in their culture

© Gideon Mendel/Corbis

In field research, people are observed in real-world settings. Field researchers may observe children in a schoolyard, for example, to study any of a variety of social psychological issues, such as friendship patterns, group dynamics, conformity, helping, aggression, and cultural differences.

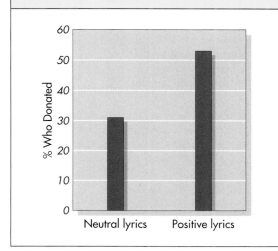

▶ **FIGURE 2.3**

Can Song Lyrics Make You More Helpful?

Participants in Greitemeyer's experiment were asked if they would like to donate the money they had earned from the study to a nonprofit organization. This graph shows that the students who had listened to songs with socially positive lyrics were more likely to donate the money than were the students who had listened to songs with neutral lyrics.

Based on Greitemeyer, 2009.

typically behave. In one of their experiments, research participants were from either Western (European, Euro-Canadian) or East Asian background, and they were presented with the pen choice described above. Before looking at the pens, though, the participants were randomly assigned to be placed into a positive or negative mood. How was mood manipulated? The participants in the positive-mood condition listened to a very pleasant, upbeat piece of classical music (by Mozart), and those in the negative-mood condition listened to a much more serious, rather depressing piece (by Rachmaninov). Table 2.4 summarizes the design of this experiment.

▶ Figure 2.4 depicts the results of this study. The bars in this graph depict what percentage of participants in each condition chose the uncommon pen. Among the Western participants, as can be seen in the left half of the graph, those put in a positive mood were *less* likely to choose the uncommon pen compared to those in the negative-mood condition. The opposite was true for the East Asian participants: those put in a positive mood were *more* likely to choose the uncommon pen compared to those in the negative-mood condition. The results, therefore, supported the researchers' predictions: positive moods did make individuals more likely to act in ways that deviated from the norms of their cultures.

TABLE 2.4

Moods and Culture: The Conditions

In Ashton-James et al.'s experiment, participants from Western or East Asian backgrounds were put in a positive or negative mood. Combining these two variables—culture and the manipulation of mood—creates the four conditions displayed here.

	Western	East Asian
	Condition 1	**Condition 2**
Positive mood	Western/Positive	East Asian/Positive
	Condition 3	**Condition 4**
Negative mood	Western /Negative	East Asian/ Negative

Based on Vandello & Cohen, 2003.

Independent and Dependent Variables   Now that we've looked at a couple experiments, let's focus on some of the specific elements. In an experiment, researchers manipulate one or more **independent variables** and examine the effect of these manipulations on one or more **dependent variables**. In the first experiment above, some participants were randomly assigned to listen to music with socially positive lyrics and the others listened to music with neutral lyrics. This was the independent variable. The dependent variable in that experiment was whether or not the participants agreed to donate their money to a nonprofit organization. It was the dependent variable because the researchers were interested in seeing if it would *depend* on (that is, be influenced by) the manipulation of the independent variable.

Subject Variables   Some experiments include variables that are neither dependent nor truly independent. The gender, ethnicity, and prior political leanings of the participants may vary, for example, and researchers may be interested in examining some of these differences. These variables cannot be manipulated and randomly assigned, so they are not true independent variables, and they are not influenced by the independent variables, so they are not a dependent variable. Variables such as these are called **subject variables**, because they characterize preexisting differences among the subjects, or participants, in the experiment. If a study includes subject variables but no true, randomly assigned independent variable, it is not a true experiment. But experiments often include subject variables along with independent variables so that researchers can test whether the independent variables have the same or different effects on different kinds of participants. The second experiment described above, by Ashton-James and colleagues on mood and culture, is an example of an experiment with one true independent variable and one subject variable. The randomly assigned independent variable was the manipulation of mood—some

independent variable
In an experiment, a factor that experimenters manipulate to see if it affects the dependent variable.

dependent variable
In an experiment, a factor that experimenters measure to see if it is affected by the independent variable.

subject variable   A variable that characterizes pre-existing differences among the participants in a study.

were placed into a good mood, others into a bad mood. The subject variable was the participants' cultural background—some were of Western background, some were of East Asian background. The dependent variable in this study was which pen the participants chose to keep.

Statistical Significance   In the Greitemeyer experiment on song lyrics and helping behavior, 53 percent of the participants who listened to the socially positive song lyrics donated their money, but only 31 percent of those who listened to the neutral song lyrics did so. Is the difference between 53 percent and 31 percent large enough to be meaningful, or could this difference simply be due to chance? After all, if you flip a coin 10 times, you might get six tails and four heads. Is this difference between six and four a meaningful difference? Surely it isn't—one could expect differences like this from random luck alone. Results obtained in an experiment are examined with statistical analyses that allow the researcher to determine how likely it is that the results could have occurred by chance. The standard convention is that if the results could have occurred by chance five or fewer times in 100 possible outcomes, then the result is *statistically significant* and should be taken seriously.

The fact that results are statistically significant does not mean, however, that they are absolutely certain. In essence, statistical significance is an attractive betting proposition. The odds are quite good (at least 95 out of 100) that the effects obtained in the study were due to the experimental manipulation of the independent variable. But there is still the possibility (as high as five out of 100) that the findings occurred by chance. This is one reason why it is important to try to *replicate* the results of an experiment—to repeat the experiment and see if similar results are found. If similar results are found, the probability that these results could have occurred by chance both times is less than one out of 400.

Statistical significance is relevant not only for the results of experiments but also for many other kinds of data as well, such as correlations. A correlation between two variables may be statistically significant or not, depending on the strength of the correlation and the number of participants or observations in the data.

When the results of some research are reported in the media or an advertisement, it's not always clear from the reporting whether the results are statistically significant, so it is important to be very cautious when learning about them. You can be sure, however, that whenever we report in this textbook that there is a difference between conditions of an experiment or that two variables are correlated, these results are statistically significant.

Internal Validity: Did the Independent Variable Cause the Effect?   When an experiment is properly conducted, its results are said to have **internal validity**: there is reasonable certainty that the independent variable did, in fact, cause the effects obtained on the dependent variable (Cook & Campbell, 1979). As noted earlier, both experimenter control and random assignment seek to rule out alternative explanations of the research results, thereby strengthening the internal validity of the research.

▶**FIGURE 2.4**

Mood and Culture

Research participants from Western or East Asian backgrounds were put in a positive or negative mood and then were given a choice to keep one of several pens. Most of the pens were in one color, but one or two were in a different color. Western participants were more likely to choose the uncommon color when in a negative mood than a positive mood, whereas East Asian participants showed the opposite pattern. These results supported the hypothesis that positive moods can make individuals act in ways that are inconsistent with their cultural norms.

Based on Ashton-James et al., 2009.

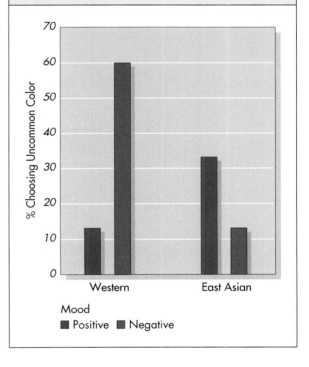

Mood
■ Positive ■ Negative

internal validity   The degree to which there can be reasonable certainty that the independent variables in an experiment caused the effects obtained on the dependent variables.

Experiments also include *control groups* for this purpose. Typically, a control group consists of participants who experience all of the procedures except the experimental treatment. In Greitemeyer's study, for example, the participants in the condition in which the song lyrics were neutral could be considered a control group, which provided a baseline against which to compare the behavior of participants who listened to socially positive lyrics.

Outside the laboratory, creating control groups in natural settings that examine real-life events raises many practical and ethical problems. For example, researchers testing new medical treatments for deadly diseases, such as AIDS, face a terrible dilemma. Individuals randomly assigned to the control group receive the standard treatment, but they are excluded for the duration of the study from what could turn out to be a life-saving new intervention. Yet without such a comparison, it is extremely difficult to determine which new treatments are effective and which are useless. Although some AIDS activists oppose including control groups in treatment research, others have become more supportive of this approach (Gorman, 1994; Rothman & Rothman, 2006).

In assessing internal validity, researchers need to consider their own role as well. Unwittingly, they can sometimes sabotage their own research. For example, imagine you are a researcher and you know which participants are in which conditions of your experiment. You will no doubt have expectations (and possibly even fervent hopes) about how your participants will respond differently between conditions. Because of these expectations, and without realizing it, you may treat the participants a little differently between conditions. It turns out that even very subtle differences in an experimenter's behavior can influence participants' behavior (Rosenthal, 1976). Therefore, because of these **experimenter expectancy effects**, the results you find in your experiment may be produced by *your own* actions rather than by the independent variable!

The best way to protect an experiment from these effects is to keep experimenters uninformed about assignments to conditions. If they do not know the condition to which a participant has been assigned, they cannot treat participants differently as a function of their condition. In the Greitemeyer experiment, for example, if the experimenter knew which participants listened to which songs, this knowledge might have subtly affected how they asked the participants if they wanted to donate their money, such as by being slightly nicer to the participants who listened to the socially positive music. To avoid this problem, Greitemeyer had a second experimenter, who did not know which music each participant had heard, ask about the donation.

Of course, there may be times when keeping experimenters uninformed is impossible or impractical. In such cases, the opportunity for experimenter expectancy effects to occur can at least be reduced somewhat by minimizing the interaction between experimenters and participants. For example, rather than receiving instructions directly from an experimenter, participants can be asked to read the instructions on a computer screen.

External Validity: Do the Results Generalize?   In addition to guarding internal validity, researchers are concerned about **external validity**, the extent to which the results obtained under one set of circumstances would also occur in a different set of circumstances (Berkowitz & Donnerstein, 1982). When an experiment has external validity, its findings can be assumed to generalize to other people and to other situations. Both the participants in the experiment and the setting in which it takes place affect external validity.

Because social psychologists often seek to establish universal principles of human behavior, their ideal sample of participants should be representative of all human

---

experimenter expectancy effects   The effects produced when an experimenter's expectations about the results of an experiment affect his or her behavior toward a participant and thereby influence the participant's responses.

external validity   The degree to which there can be reasonable confidence that the results of a study would be obtained for other people and in other situations.

beings all over the world. Such an all-inclusive representative sample has never been seen and probably never will be. Representative samples of more limited populations do exist and can be achieved by random sampling of a population, which was discussed earlier in the chapter. But, as also mentioned earlier, social psychologists rarely study representative samples. Usually they rely on convenience samples drawn from populations that are readily available to them, which explains why so much of social psychological research is conducted on college students.

There are very practical reasons for the use of convenience samples. Representative samples are fine for surveys that require short answers to a short list of questions. But what about complex, time-consuming experiments? The costs and logistical problems associated with this would be staggering. Fortunately, researchers are using Internet-based data collection more and more frequently, which can allow for far more diverse sets of participants. There are numerous challenges associated with this approach as well, however, such as having less control over what participants are seeing or doing as they participate in the study from afar.

© Fabian Cevallos/CORBIS SYGMA

The settings in which children attend school can vary dramatically across cultures. Here students sit outside in a class in Imbabura, Ecuador. Recognizing cultural variation has become increasingly important in social psychology today, and social psychologists are conducting their research across a wider range of cultures and contexts than ever before.

Advocates of convenience samples contend that there is no contradiction between universal principles and particular participants. Indeed, the more basic the principle, the less it matters who participates in the research. For example, people from different cultures, regions, and ages might differ in the *form* of aggression they typically exhibit when angry, but the situational factors that cause people to be *more likely to* aggress—in whatever way that aggression is expressed—may be similar for most individuals across time and place. Yet in spite of these arguments, the drawbacks to convenience samples are clear—an important consideration given the need for social psychology to become more inclusive (Glick, 2008; Henry, 2008). The growing interest in cross-cultural research in the field is certainly one step in the right direction.

External validity is also affected by the setting in which the research is conducted. Because field research occurs in real-life natural settings rather than in the artificial arrangements of a laboratory, aren't its results more generalizable to actual behavior? The answer depends on where you stand on the issue of mundane versus experimental realism (Aronson & Carlsmith, 1968).

Mundane realism refers to the extent to which the research setting resembles the real-world setting of interest. In order to study interpersonal attraction, Theodore Newcomb (1961) set up an entire college dormitory—a striking example of mundane realism. Advocates of mundane realism contend that if research procedures are more realistic, research findings are more likely to reveal what really goes on.

In contrast, **experimental realism** refers to the degree to which the experimental setting and procedures are real and involving to the participant, regardless of whether they resemble real life or not. According to those who favor experimental realism, if the experimental situation is compelling and real to the participants while they are participating in the study, their behavior in the lab—even if the lab is in the basement

mundane realism The degree to which the experimental situation resembles places and events in the real world.

experimental realism The degree to which experimental procedures are involving to participants and lead them to behave naturally and spontaneously.

of the psychology building—will be as natural and spontaneous as their behavior in the real world. The majority of social psychologists who conduct experiments emphasize experimental realism.

Deception in Experiments   Researchers who strive to create a highly involving experience for participants often rely on **deception**, providing participants with false information about experimental procedures. Toward this end, social psychologists sometimes employ **confederates**, people who act as though they are participants in the experiment but are really working for the experimenter. For example, in Solomon Asch's (1956) classic research on conformity, research participants made judgments about the lengths of lines while in the midst of a number of confederates—who were pretending to be ordinary participants—who at various times all gave wrong answers. The researchers wanted to see if the real participants would conform to the confederates and give the obviously wrong answer that the confederates had given. Although it was a very odd setting, the situation was a very real one to the participants, many of whom clearly struggled with the decision about whether or not to conform.

Deception not only strengthens experimental realism but also confers other benefits: It allows the experimenter to manufacture situations in the laboratory that would be difficult to find in a natural setting, such as a regulated, safe environment in which to study a potentially harmful behavior such as aggression. Studies have shown that participants are rarely bothered by deception and often particularly enjoy studies that use it (Smith & Richardson, 1983). Nevertheless, the use of deception creates some serious ethical concerns, which we examine later in this chapter.

▊ Meta-Analysis: Combining Results Across Studies

We have seen that social psychologists conduct original descriptive, correlational, and experimental studies to test their hypotheses. Another way to test hypotheses in social psychology is to use a set of statistical procedures to examine, in a new way, relevant research that has already been conducted and reported. This technique is called **meta-analysis**. By "meta-analyzing" the results of a number of studies that have been conducted in different places and by different researchers, a social psychologist can measure precisely how strong and reliable particular effects are. For example, studies published concerning the effects of alcohol on aggression may sometimes contradict each other. Sometimes alcohol increases aggression; sometimes it doesn't. By combining the data from all the studies that are relevant to this hypothesis and conducting a meta-analysis, a researcher can determine what effect alcohol typically has, how strong that effect typically is, and perhaps under what specific conditions that effect is most likely to occur. This technique, which was developed relatively recently, is being used with increasing frequency in social psychology today, and we report the results of many meta-analyses in this textbook.

▊ Culture and Research Methods

The study by Ashton-James and others (2009) on the effects of mood on Western and East Asian participants' pen choices is but one example of the growing interest in studying culture in social psychology. One of the advantages of this approach is that it provides better tests of the external validity of research that has been conducted in any one setting. By examining whether the results of an experiment generalize to a very different culture, social psychologists can begin to answer questions about the universality or cultural specificity of their research. It is important to keep in mind that

deception In the context of research, a method that provides false information to participants.

confederate Accomplice of an experimenter who, in dealing with the real participants in an experiment, acts as if he or she is also a participant.

meta-analysis A set of statistical procedures used to review a body of evidence by combining the results of individual studies to measure the overall reliability and strength of particular effects.

when a finding in one culture does not generalize well to another culture, this should be seen not simply as a failure to replicate but also as an opportunity to learn about potentially interesting and important cultural differences and about how and why these differences affect the issue being studied.

As important and exciting as these cultural investigations are, however, they offer special challenges to researchers. For one thing, there are important cultural differences in the assumptions individuals make and the information they tend to give as they respond to questions on a survey (Schwarz et al., 2010). Susanne Haberstroh and others (2002), for example, found that individuals from a culture that promotes interdependent, collectivistic values and self-concepts (such as China) are more likely to take into account question context when completing a questionnaire than are respondents from cultures associated with a more independent, individualistic orientation (such as Germany). Another difference between cultures concerns how willing people are to answer personal questions as part of a research study. North Americans are used to answering personal questions, for example, but people in some cultures feel much more uncomfortable talking about themselves (Fiske, 2002).

Nairán Ramírez-Esparza and others (2009) recently demonstrated an interesting difference in data from self-report and observational measures as a function of culture. Ramírez-Esparza and her colleagues compared Mexican participants and native English-speaking American participants (none of whom were foreign or bicultural) in how sociable they rated themselves on a questionnaire and how sociable their actual behavior was. The behavior was assessed by means of voice-activated digital recorders that all participants wore during their daily activities for two days. As can be seen in ▶ Figure 2.5, although the Mexican participants rated themselves as no more sociable than did the American participants on a questionnaire, the Mexican participants' behavior was observed to be significantly more sociable than Americans' behavior (such as in time spent talking with other people).

When doing cross-cultural or multicultural studies, researchers must be careful also about issues as basic as language. Another study by Ramírez-Esparza and others (2008) illustrates this point. They found that bilingual Mexican-American participants rated themselves as less agreeable on a questionnaire if the questions were in Spanish than English, but their behavior was observed to be higher in agreeableness during an interview if it was conducted in Spanish than if it was conducted in English.

Another issue with language is that it can be difficult for researchers to translate materials from one language into another. Although it is relatively easy to create literal translations, it can be surprisingly challenging to create translations that have the same meaning to people from various cultures. Table 2.5 presents examples—from signs displayed around the world—of what can go wrong when simple sentences are poorly translated.

▶ **FIGURE 2.5**

Culture and Sociability: Self-Reports Versus Observations

Mexican and American participants completed questionnaires that assessed how sociable they were. This self-report measure showed no significant difference between the two groups. However, through the use of voice recorders worn by the participants for two days, the researchers could observe and measure how sociably the participants behaved, such as in how much they socialized or talked with other people. On this observational measure, Mexican participants were judged to be much more sociable than were the American participants.

Based on Ramírez-Esparza et al., 2009.

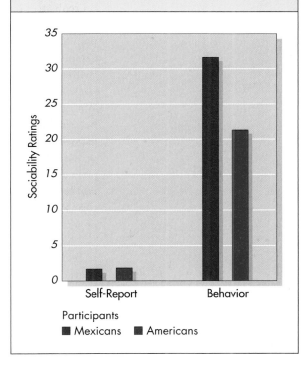

TABLE 2.5

Lost in Translation

- "Drop your trousers here for best results." (a dry cleaner in Thailand)
- "You are invited to take advantage of the chambermaid." (a hotel in Japan)
- "Ladies are requested not to have children in the bar." (a cocktail lounge in Mexico)
- "Take one of our horse-driven city tours—we guarantee no miscarriages." (a tourist agency in the former Czechoslovakia)
- "We take your bags and send them in all directions." (an airline in Denmark)

Triandis (1994).

Ethics and Values in Social Psychology

Regardless of where research is conducted and what method is used, ethical issues must always be considered. Researchers in all fields have a moral and legal responsibility to abide by ethical principles. In social psychology, the use of deception has caused particular concern (Cook & Yamagishi, 2008; Hertwig & Ortmann, 2008), and several studies have provoked fierce debate about whether they went beyond the bounds of ethical acceptability. For example, Stanley Milgram (1963) designed a series of experiments to address the question "Would people obey orders to harm an innocent person?" To test this question, he put volunteers into a situation in which an experimenter commanded them to administer painful electric shocks to someone they thought was another volunteer participant. (In fact, the other person was a confederate who was not actually receiving any shocks.) The experiment had extremely high experimental realism—many of the participants experienced a great deal of anxiety and stress as they debated whether they should disobey the experimenter or continue to inflict pain on another person. The details and results of this experiment will be discussed in Chapter 7 on Conformity, but suffice it to say that the results of the study made people realize how prevalent and powerful obedience can be.

Milgram's research was inspired by the obedience displayed by Nazi officers in World War II. No one disputes the importance of his research question. What has been debated, however, is whether the significance of the research topic justified exposing participants to possibly harmful psychological consequences. Under today's provisions for the protection of human participants, Milgram's classic experiments probably could not be conducted in their original form. (In an interesting twist, while conducting an experiment like Milgram's might be impossible now, in popular culture today individuals endure far greater stress and even humiliation in numerous unscripted TV shows for the entertainment of viewers at home.)

Milgram's research was by no means the only social psychological research to trigger debates about ethics. Several studies in the history of social psychology have sparked a great deal of controversy. And it is not only the controversial studies that receive scrutiny. Today, virtually every social psychology study is evaluated for its ethics by other people before the study can be conducted. In the following sections, we describe current policies and procedures as well as continuing concerns about ethics and values in social psychological research.

Institutional Review Boards and Informed Consent: Protecting Research Participants

In 1974, the agency then called the United States Department of Health, Education, and Welfare established regulations designed to protect human participants in research. These regulations created institutional review boards (IRBs) at all institutions seeking federal funding for research involving human participants. Charged with the responsibility for reviewing research proposals to ensure that the welfare of participants was adequately protected, IRBs were to be the "watchdogs" of research.

Besides submitting their research to IRBs, researchers must also abide by their profession's code of ethics. The statement of ethics of the American Psychological Association (APA), called *Ethical Principles of Psychologists and Code of Conduct* (2002), considers a wide range of ethical issues, including those related to research procedures and practices. The APA code stipulates that researchers are obligated to guard the rights and welfare of all those who participate in their studies.

One such obligation is to obtain **informed consent**. Individuals must be asked whether they wish to participate in the research project and must be given enough information to make an informed decision. Participants must also know that they are free to withdraw from participation in the research at any point. The APA code also recognizes that research "involving only anonymous questionnaires, naturalistic observations, or certain kinds of archival research" may not require informed consent.

Debriefing: Telling All

Have you ever participated in psychological research? If so, what was your reaction to this experience? Have you ever been deceived about the hypothesis or procedures of a study in which you were a participant? If so, how did you feel about it? Most research on participants' reactions indicates that they have positive attitudes about their participation, even when they were deceived about some aspects of a study (Christensen, 1988; Epley & Huff, 1998). Indeed, deceived participants sometimes have expressed more favorable opinions than those who have not been deceived, presumably because studies involving deception are often interesting and creative (Smith & Richardson, 1983).

These findings are reassuring, but they do not remove the obligation of researchers to use deception only when nondeceptive alternatives are not feasible. In addition, whenever deception has been used, there is a special urgency to the requirement that once the data have been collected, researchers fully inform their participants about the nature of the research in which they have participated. This process of disclosure is called **debriefing**. During a debriefing, the researcher goes over all procedures, explaining exactly what happened and why. Deceptions are revealed, the purpose of the research is discussed, and the researcher makes every effort to help the participant feel good about having participated. A skillful debriefing takes time and requires close attention to the individual participant. Indeed, we have known students who became so fascinated by what they learned during a debriefing that it sparked their interest in social psychology, and eventually they became social psychologists themselves!

"What if these guys in white coats who bring us food are, like, studying us and we're part of some kind of big experiment?"

One reason for the use of deception in an experiment is so that the participants will act more naturally when they are not aware of what is being studied. In these cases it is especially important for the researchers to provide a full and thorough debriefing.

informed consent
An individual's deliberate, voluntary decision to participate in research, based on the researcher's description of what will be required during such participation.

debriefing A disclosure, made to participants after research procedures are completed, in which the researcher explains the purpose of the research, attempts to resolve any negative feelings, and emphasizes the scientific contribution made by the participants' involvement.

Values and Science: Points of View

Ethical principles are based on moral values. These values set standards for and impose limits on the conduct of research, just as they influence individuals' personal behavior. Ethical issues are an appropriate focus for moral values in science, but do values affect science in other ways as well? Although many people hold science to a standard of complete objectivity, science can probably never be completely unbiased and objective because it is a human enterprise. Scientists choose what to study and how to study it; their choices are affected by personal values as well as by professional rewards. Indeed, some think that values *should* fuel scientific research and that scientists would be not only naive but also irresponsible to try to keep values out of the picture.

Most—although certainly not all—social psychologists would probably agree with a position offered by Stanley Parkinson (1994): "Scientists are not necessarily more objective than other people; rather, they use methods that have been developed to minimize self-deception" (p. 137). By scrutinizing their own behavior and adopting the rigors of the scientific method, scientists attempt to free themselves of their pre-conceptions and, thereby, to see reality more clearly, even if never perfectly.

As you read about the research reported throughout this book, you might stop every now and then to consider what *you* think about the role of values in science. Do you think values influence the work done by social psychologists? Do you think values *should* affect scientific inquiry?

Your introduction to the field of social psychology is now complete. In these first two chapters, you have gone step by step through a definition of social psychology, a review of its history and discussion of its future, an overview of its research methods, and a consideration of ethics and values. As you study the material presented in the coming chapters, the three of us who wrote this book invite you to share our enthusiasm. You can look forward to information that overturns commonsense assumptions, to lively debate and heated controversy, and to a better understanding of yourself and other people. Welcome to the world according to social psychology. We hope you enjoy it!

[Objectivity in science] is willingness (even the eagerness in truly honorable practitioners) to abandon a favored notion when testable evidence disconfirms key expectations.

—Stephen Jay Gould

REVIEW

Why Should You Learn About Research Methods?

- Because common sense and intuitive ideas about social psychological issues can be misleading and contradictory, it is important to understand the scientific evidence on which social psychological theories and findings are based.

- Studying research methods in psychology improves people's reasoning about real-life events and information presented by the media and other sources.

Developing Ideas: Beginning the Research Process

Asking Questions

- Ideas for research in social psychology come from everywhere—personal experiences and observations, events in the news, and other research.

Searching the Literature

- Before pursuing a research idea, it is important to see what research has already been done on that idea and related topics.

- Electronic databases provide access to a wealth of information, both in the psychology literature and in more general sources.

Hypotheses and Theories

- Formulating a hypothesis is a critical step toward planning and conducting research.

- Theories in social psychology are specific rather than comprehensive and generate research that can support or disconfirm them. They should be revised and improved as a result of the research they inspire.

Basic and Applied Research

- The goal of basic research is to increase understanding of human behavior.

- The goal of applied research is to increase understanding of real-world events and contribute to the solution of social problems.

Refining Ideas: Defining and Measuring Social Psychological Variables

Conceptual Variables and Operational Definitions: From the Abstract to the Specific

- Researchers often must transform abstract, conceptual variables into specific operational definitions that indicate exactly how the variables are to be manipulated or measured.

- Construct validity is the extent to which the operational definitions successfully manipulate or measure the conceptual variables to which they correspond.

Measuring Variables: Using Self-Reports, Observations, and Technology

- In self-reports, participants indicate their thoughts, feelings, desires, and actions.

- Self-reports can be distorted by efforts to make a good impression as well as by the effects of the wording and context of questions.

- In studies using the bogus pipeline technique, participants' self-reports tend to be more accurate and less socially desirable when they are led to believe that a machine can tell whether or not they are telling the truth.

- To increase the accuracy of self-reports, some approaches emphasize the need to collect self-reports as soon as possible after participants experience the relevant thoughts, feelings, or behaviors.

- Narrative studies analyze the content of lengthy responses on a general topic.

- Observations are another way for social psychologists to measure variables.

- Interrater reliability, or the level of agreement among multiple observers of the same behavior, is important when measuring variables using observation.

- New and improved technologies enable researchers to measure physiological responses, reaction times, eye movements, and activity in regions of the brain.

Testing Ideas: Research Designs

- Most social psychologists test their ideas by using objective, systematic, and quantifiable methods.

Descriptive Research: Discovering Trends and Tendencies

- In descriptive research, social psychologists record how frequently or typically people think, feel, or behave in particular ways.

- One form of descriptive research is observational research, in which researchers observe individuals systematically, often in natural settings.

- In archival research, researchers examine existing records and documents such as newspaper articles, diaries, and published crime statistics.

- Surveys involve asking people questions about their attitudes, beliefs, and behaviors.

- Survey researchers identify the population to which they want the results of the survey to generalize, and they select a sample of people from that population to take the survey.

- To best ensure a sample that is representative of the broader population, researchers should randomly select people from the population to be in the survey.

Correlational Research: Looking for Associations

- Correlational research examines the association between variables.

- A correlation coefficient is a measure of the strength and direction of the association between two variables.

- Positive correlations indicate that as scores on one variable increase, scores on the other variable increase, and that as scores on one variable decrease, scores on the other decrease.

- Negative correlations indicate that as scores on one variable increase, scores on the other decrease.

- Correlation does not indicate causation; the fact that two variables are correlated does not necessarily mean that one causes the other.

- Correlations can be used for prediction and for generating hypotheses.

Experiments: Looking for Cause and Effect

- Experiments require (1) control by the experimenter over events in the study; and (2) random assignment of participants to conditions.

- Random sampling concerns how people are selected to be in a study, whereas random assignment concerns how people who are in the study are assigned to the different conditions of the study.

- Experiments are often conducted in a laboratory so that the researchers can have control over the context and can measure variables precisely.

- Field experiments are conducted in real-world settings outside the laboratory.

- Participants in one experiment were more likely to act charitably if they listened to music with socially positive lyrics than with neutral lyrics.

- Participants in another experiment were more likely to act in ways that deviated from cultural norms if they were put in a positive rather than a negative mood.

- Experiments examine the effects of one or more independent variables on one or more dependent variables.
- Subject variables are variables that characterize preexisting differences among the participants.
- Results that are statistically significant could have occurred by chance five or fewer times in 100 possible outcomes.
- Experimental findings have internal validity to the extent that changes in the dependent variable can be attributed to the independent variables.
- Control groups strengthen internal validity; experimenter expectancy effects weaken it.
- Research results have external validity to the extent that they can be generalized to other people and other situations.
- Although using a representative sample would strengthen a study's external validity, most social psychology studies use convenience samples.
- Mundane realism is the extent to which the research setting seems similar to real-world situations.

- Experimental realism is the extent to which the participants experience the experimental setting and procedures as real and involving.
- Deception is sometimes used to increase experimental realism.
- Confederates act as though they are participants in an experiment but actually work for the experimenter.

Meta-Analysis: Combining Results Across Studies

- Meta-analysis uses statistical techniques to integrate the quantitative results of different studies.

Culture and Research Methods

- There is growing interest in studying the role of culture in social psychology.
- As important and exciting as these cultural investigations are, they offer special challenges to researchers.

Ethics and Values in Social Psychology

- Ethical issues are particularly important in social psychology because of the use of deception in some research.

Institutional Review Boards and Informed Consent: Protecting Research Participants

- Established by the federal government, IRBs are responsible for reviewing research proposals to ensure that the welfare of participants is adequately protected.
- The American Psychological Association's code of ethics requires psychologists to secure informed consent from research participants.

Debriefing: Telling All

- Most participants have positive attitudes about their participation in research, even if they were deceived about some aspects of the study.

- Whenever deception has been used in a study, a full debriefing is essential; the researchers must disclose the facts about the study and make sure that the participant does not experience any distress.

Values and Science: Points of View

- Moral values set standards for and impose limits on the conduct of research.
- Various views exist on the relation between values and science. Few believe that there can be a completely value-free science, but some advocate trying to minimize the influence of values on science, whereas others argue that values should be recognized and encouraged as an important factor in science.

Key Terms

applied research (29)
basic research (29)
bogus pipeline technique (32)
confederate (46)
construct validity (31)
correlation coefficient (37)
correlational research (36)
debriefing (49)
deception (46)
dependent variables (42)

experiment (39)
experimental realism (45)
experimenter expectancy effects (44)
external validity (44)
hypothesis (28)
independent variables (42)
informed consent (49)
internal validity (43)
interrater reliability (33)

meta-analysis (46)
mundane realism (45)
operational definition (30)
random assignment (39)
random sampling (36)
subject variables (42)
theory (29)

Media Resources

Social Psychology 8th Edition Companion Website

Visit your book companion website

www.cengage.com/psychology/kassin

where you will find flash cards, practice quizzes, Internet links, and more to help you study.

CENGAGENOW™ Just what you need to know NOW! Spend time on what you need to master rather than on information you already have learned. Take a pre-test for this chapter and CengageNOW will generate a personalized study plan based on your results. The study plan will identify the topics you need to review and direct you to online resources to help you master those topics. You can then take a post-test to help you determine the concepts you have mastered and what you will need to work on. Try it out! Go to **academic.cengage.com/login** to sign in with an access code or to purchase access to this product.

3

Gail Mooney/Corbis

The Social Self

This chapter examines three interrelated aspects of the "social self." First, it considers the self-concept and the question of how people come to understand their own actions, emotions, and motivations. Second, it considers self-esteem, the affective component, and the question of how people evaluate themselves and defend against threats to their self-esteem. Third, it considers self-presentation, a behavioral manifestation of the self, and the question of how people present themselves to others. As we will see, the self is complex and multifaceted.

Can you imagine living a meaningful or coherent life without a clear sense of who you are? In *The Man Who Mistook His Wife for a Hat*, neurologist Oliver Sacks (1985) described such a person—a patient named William Thompson. According to Sacks, Thompson suffered from an organic brain disorder that impairs a person's memory of recent events. Unable to recall anything for more than a few seconds, Thompson was always disoriented and lacked a sense of inner continuity. The effect on his behavior was startling. Trying to grasp a constantly vanishing identity, Thompson would construct one tale after another to account for who he was, where he was, and what he was doing. From one moment to the next, he would improvise new identities—a grocery store clerk, a minister, or a medical patient, to name just a few. In social settings, Thompson's behavior was especially intriguing. As Sacks (1985) observed,

> The presence of others, other people, excite and rattle him, force him into an endless, frenzied, social chatter, a veritable delirium of identity-making and -seeking; the presence of plants, a quiet garden, the nonhuman order, making no social demands upon him, allow this identity-delirium to relax, to subside. (p. 110)

Thompson's plight is unusual, but it highlights two important points—one about the private "inner" self, the other about the "outer" self we show to others. First, the capacity for self-reflection is necessary for people to feel as if they understand their own motives and emotions and the causes of their behavior. Unable to ponder his own actions, Thompson appeared vacant and without feeling—"desouled," as Sacks put it. Second, the self is heavily influenced by social factors. Thompson himself seemed compelled to put on a face for others and to improvise characters for the company he kept. We all do, to some extent. We may not create a kaleidoscope of multiple identities as Thompson did, but the way we manage ourselves is influenced by the people around us.

This chapter examines the ABCs of the self: A for *affect*, B for *behavior*, and C for *cognition*. First, we ask a cognitive question: How do people come to know themselves, develop a self-concept, and maintain a stable sense of identity? Second, we explore an affective, or emotional, question: How do people evaluate themselves, enhance their self-images, and defend against threats to their self-esteem? Third, we confront a behavioral question: How do people regulate their own actions and present themselves to others according to interpersonal demands? As we'll see, the self is a topic that in recent years has attracted unprecedented interest among social psychologists (Leary & Tangney, 2003; Sedikides & Spencer, 2007; Swann & Bosson, 2010; Vohs & Finkel, 2006).

The Self-Concept

Have you ever been at a noisy gathering—holding a drink in one hand and a spring roll in the other, struggling to have a conversation over music and the chatter of voices—and yet managed to hear someone at the other end of the room mention your name? If so, then you have experienced the "cocktail party effect"—the tendency of people to pick a personally relevant stimulus, like a name, out of a complex and noisy environment (Cherry, 1953; Wood & Cowan, 1995). Even infants who are too young to walk or talk exhibit this tendency (Newman, 2005). To the cognitive psychologist, this phenomenon shows that human beings are selective in their attention. To the social psychologist, it also shows that the self is an important object of our own attention.

The term **self-concept** refers to the sum total of beliefs that people have about themselves. But what specifically does the self-concept consist of? According to Hazel Markus (1977), the self-concept is made up of cognitive molecules called **self-schemas**: beliefs about oneself that guide the processing of self-relevant information. Self-schemas are to an individual's total self-concept what hypotheses are to a theory or what books are to a library. You can think of yourself as masculine or feminine, as independent or dependent, as liberal or conservative, as introverted or extroverted. Indeed, any specific attribute may have relevance to the self-concept for some people but not for others. The self-schema for body weight is a good example. Men and women who regard themselves as extremely overweight or underweight, or for whom body image is a conspicuous aspect of the self-concept, are considered *schematic* with respect to weight. For body-weight schematics, a wide range of otherwise mundane events—a trip to the supermarket, new clothing, dinner at a restaurant, a day at the beach, or a friend's eating habits—may trigger thoughts about the self. In contrast, those who do not regard their own weight as extreme or as an important part of their lives are *aschematic* on that attribute (Markus et al., 1987).

Rudiments of the Self-Concept

Clearly the self is a special object of our attention. Whether you are mentally focused on a memory, a conversation, a foul odor, the song in your head, your growling stomach, or this sentence, consciousness is like a "spotlight." It can shine on only one object at a point in time, but it can shift rapidly from one object to another and process information outside of awareness. In this spotlight, the self is front and center. But is the self so special that it is uniquely represented in the neural circuitry of the brain? And is the self a uniquely human concept, or do other animals also distinguish the self from everything else?

self-concept The sum total of an individual's beliefs about his or her own personal attributes.

self-schema A belief people hold about themselves that guides the processing of self-relevant information.

Is the Self Specially Represented in the Brain?   As illustrated by the story of William Thompson that opened this chapter, our sense of identity is biologically rooted. In *The Synaptic Self: How Our Brains Become Who We Are*, neuroscientist Joseph LeDoux (2002) argues that the synaptic connections within the brain provide the biological base for memory, which makes possible the sense of continuity that is needed for a normal identity. In *The Lost Self: Pathologies of the Brain and Identity*, Todd Feinberg and Julian Keenan (2005) describe how the self can be transformed and even completely destroyed by severe head injuries, brain tumors, diseases, and exposure to toxic substances that damage the brain and nervous system.

Social neuroscientists are starting to explore these possibilities. Using PET scans, fMRI, and other imaging techniques that can capture the brain in action, these researchers are finding that certain areas become more active when laboratory participants see a picture of themselves rather than a picture of others (Platek et al., 2008), when they try to judge whether trait words are descriptive of themselves rather than of others (Kelley et al., 2002), and when they take a first-person perspective while playing a video game as opposed to a third-person perspective (David et al., 2006). As we will see throughout this chapter, the self is a frame of reference that powerfully influences our thoughts, feelings, and behaviors. Not all aspects of the self are housed in a single structure of the brain. However, the bulk of research does seem to suggest that various self-based processes can be traced to activities occurring in certain areas of the brain (Northoff et al., 2006; Northoff & Panskepp, 2008).

LWA/Sharie Kennedy/Getty Images

Infants begin to recognize themselves in the mirror at 18 to 24 months of age.

Do Nonhuman Animals Show Self-Recognition?   When you stand in front of a mirror, you recognize the image as a reflection of yourself. But what about dogs, cats, and other animals—how can we possibly know what nonhumans think about mirrors? In a series of studies, Gordon Gallup (1977) placed different species of animals in a room with a large mirror. At first, they greeted their own images by vocalizing, gesturing, and making other social responses. After several days, only great apes (chimpanzees, gorillas, and orangutans)—but not other animals—seemed capable of self-recognition, using the mirror to pick food out of their teeth, groom themselves, blow bubbles, and make faces for their own entertainment. From all appearances, the apes recognized themselves.

In other studies, Gallup anesthetized the animals, then painted an odorless red dye on their brows and returned them to the mirror. Upon seeing the red spot, only the apes spontaneously reached for their own brows—proof that they perceived the image as their own (Povinelli et al., 1997; Keenan et al., 2003). Among apes, this form of self-recognition emerges in young adolescence and is stable across the life span, at least until old age (de Veer et al., 2003). By using a similar red dye test (without anesthetizing the infants), developmental psychologists have found that most human infants begin to recognize themselves in the mirror between the ages of 18 and 24 months (Lewis & Brooks-Gunn, 1979). Today, many researchers believe that self-recognition among great apes and human infants is the first clear expression of the concept "me" (Boysen & Himes, 1999). Recent research suggests that certain intelligent nonprimates can also recognize themselves. In one study, researchers at a New York aquarium found that two bottlenose dolphins marked with black ink often stopped to examine themselves in a mirror (Reiss & Marino, 2001). In a second study, researchers found that three Asian elephants placed in front of a jumbo-sized mirror used the mirror to inspect themselves—as when they moved their trunks to see the insides of their mouths, a part of the body they usually cannot see (Plotnick et al., 2006).

What Makes the Self a Social Concept?   The ability to see yourself as a distinct entity in the world is a necessary first step in the evolution and development of a self-concept. The second step involves social factors. Sociologist Charles Horton Cooley (1902) introduced the term *looking-glass self* to suggest that other people serve as a mirror in which we see ourselves. Expanding on this idea, George Herbert Mead (1934) added that we often come to know ourselves by imagining what significant others think of us and then incorporating these perceptions into our self-concepts.

Picking up where the classic sociologists left off, Susan Andersen and Serena Chen (2002) theorized that the self is "relational"—that we draw our sense of who we are from our past and current relationships with the significant others in our lives. It is interesting that when Gallup tested his apes, those that had been raised in isolation—without exposure to peers—did not recognize themselves in the mirror. Only after such exposure did they begin to show signs of self-recognition. Among human beings, our self-concepts match our *perceptions* of what others think of us. But there's an important hitch: What we think of ourselves often does not match what specific others *actually* think of us (Kenny & DePaulo, 1993; Shrauger & Schoeneman, 1979; Tice & Wallace, 2003).

In recent years, social psychologists have broken new ground in the effort to understand the social self. People are not born thinking of themselves as reckless, likable, shy, or outgoing. So where do their self-concepts come from? In the coming pages, five sources are considered: introspection, perceptions of our own behavior, the influences of other people, autobiographical memories, and the cultures in which we live.

Humans are the only animals who recognize themselves in the mirror. **FALSE.**

▌ Introspection

Let's start at the beginning: How do people achieve insight into their own beliefs, attitudes, emotions, and motivations? Common sense makes this question seem ludicrous. After all, don't you know what you think because *you* think it? And don't you know how you feel because *you* feel it? Look through popular books on how to achieve self-insight, and you'll find the unambiguous answers to these questions to be yes. Whether the prescribed technique is yoga, meditation, psychotherapy, religion, dream analysis, or hypnosis, the advice is basically the same: Self-knowledge is derived from introspection, a looking inward at one's own thoughts and feelings.

If these how-to books are correct, it stands to reason that no one can know you as well as you know yourself. Thus, people tend to assume that for others to know you at all, they would need information about your private thoughts, feelings, and other inner states—not just your behavior. But is this really the case? Most social psychologists are not sure that this faith in introspection is justified. Several years ago, Richard Nisbett and Timothy Wilson (1977) found that research participants often cannot accurately explain the causes or correlates of their own behavior. This observation forced researchers to confront a thorny question: Does introspection provide a direct pipeline to self-knowledge?

In *Strangers to Ourselves*, Wilson (2002) argues that it does not. In fact, he finds that introspection can sometimes impair self-knowledge. In a series of studies, he found that the attitudes people reported having about different objects corresponded closely to their behavior toward those objects. The more participants said they enjoyed a task, the more time they spent on it; the more attractive they found a scenic landscape, the more pleasure they revealed in their facial expressions; the happier they said they were with a current dating partner, the longer the relationship with that partner ultimately lasted. Yet after participants were told to analyze the reasons for how they felt, the attitudes that they reported no longer corresponded to their behavior. There are two problems. The first, as described by Wilson, is that human beings are mentally busy processing information, which is why we so often fail to understand our own thoughts, feelings, and behaviors. Apparently, it is possible to think too much and be too analytical, only to get confused.

In *Self-Insight: Roadblocks and Detours on the Path to Knowing Thyself*, David Dunning (2005) points to a second type of problem in self-assessment: that people overestimate the positives. Most people, most of the time, think they are better than average, even though it is statistically impossible for this to happen. As we will see in our later discussion of self-enhancement, people from all walks of life tend to overrate their own skills, their prospects for success, the accuracy of their opinions, and the impressions they form of others—sometimes with dire consequences for their health and well-being.

"Look, babe. At this point, you've reinvented yourself so many times you're back to who you were at the start."

In some ways, our sense of self is malleable and subject to change.

People also have difficulty projecting forward and predicting how they would feel in response to future emotional events—a process referred to as **affective forecasting**. Imagine that you have a favorite candidate in an upcoming political campaign. Can you anticipate how happy you would be one month after the election if this candidate were to win? How unhappy would you be if he or she were to lose? Closer to home, how happy would you be six months after winning a million-dollar lottery? Or how unhappy would you be if injured in an automobile accident?

In a series of studies, Timothy Wilson and Daniel Gilbert (2003, 2005) asked research participants to predict how they would feel after various positive and negative life events and compared their predictions to how others experiencing those events said they actually felt. Consistently, they found that people overestimate the strength and duration of their emotional reactions, a phenomenon they call the "impact bias." In one study, junior professors predicted that receiving tenure would increase their happiness levels for several years, yet professors who actually received tenure were no happier at that later point than those not granted tenure. In a second study, voters predicted they would be happier a month after an election if their candidate won than if he or she lost. In actuality, supporters of the winning and losing candidates did not differ in their happiness levels one month after the election. In a third study, subway passengers anticipated that they would experience more regret and self-blame if they missed their train by a short minute than by a wider margin. Yet when actual subway riders who missed a train were questioned, they did *not*, as predicted, report feeling intensely regretful in this close situation (Gilbert et al., 2004).

affective forecasting   The process of predicting how one would feel in response to future.

There are two possible reasons for the impact bias in affective forecasting. First, when it comes to negative life events—such as an injury, illness, or big financial loss—people do not fully appreciate the extent to which our psychological coping mechanisms help us to cushion the blow. In the face of adversity, human beings can be remarkably resilient—and not as devastated as we fear we will be (Gilbert et al., 1998). In fact, people are even more likely to overlook the coping mechanisms that *others* use. The result is a self-other difference by which we tend to predict that others will suffer even longer than we will (Igou, 2008). A second reason for these overestimates is that when we introspect about the emotional impact on us of a future event—say, the breakup of a close relationship—we become so focused on that single event that we neglect to take into account the effects of other life experiences. To become more accurate in our predictions, then, we need to force ourselves to think more broadly, about *all* the events that impact us. In one study, college students were asked to predict their emotional reactions to their school football team's winning or losing an important game. As usual, they tended to overestimate how long it would take them to recover from the victory or defeat. This bias disappeared, however, when the students first completed a "prospective diary" in which they estimated the amount of future time they will spend on everyday activities like going to class, talking to friends, studying, and eating meals (Wilson et al., 2000).

◼ Perceptions of Our Own Behavior

Regardless of what we can learn from introspection, Daryl Bem (1972) believes that people can learn about themselves the same way outside observers do—by watching their own behavior. Bem's **self-perception theory** is simple yet profound. To the extent that internal states are weak or difficult to interpret, people infer what they think or how they feel by observing their own behavior and the situation in which that behavior takes place. Have you ever listened to yourself arguing with someone in an e-mail exchange, only to realize with amazement how angry you were? Have you ever devoured a sandwich in record time, only then to conclude that you must have been incredibly hungry? In each case, you made an inference about yourself by watching your own actions.

There are limits to self-perception, of course. According to Bern, people do not infer their own internal states from behavior that occurred in the presence of compelling situational pressures such as reward or punishment. If you argued vehemently or wolfed down a sandwich because you were paid to do so, you probably would not assume that you were angry or hungry. In other words, people learn about themselves through self-perception only when the situation alone seems insufficient to have caused their behavior.

A good deal of research supports self-perception theory. When people are gently coaxed into saying or doing something and when they are not otherwise certain about how they feel, they often come to view themselves in ways that are consistent with their public statements and behavior (Chaiken & Baldwin, 1981; Schlenker & Trudeau, 1990; Kelly & Rodriguez, 2006). Thus, research participants induced to describe themselves in flattering terms scored higher on a later test of self-esteem than did those who were led to describe themselves more modestly (Jones et al., 1981; Rhodewalt & Agustsdottir, 1986). Similarly, those who were maneuvered by leading questions into describing themselves as introverted or extroverted—whether or not they really were—came to define themselves as such later on, unless they were certain of this aspect of their personality (Fazio et al., 1981; Swann & Ely, 1984). British author E. M. Forster long ago anticipated the theory when he asked, "How can I tell what I think 'til I see what I say?"

self-perception theory
The theory that when internal cues are difficult to interpret, people gain self-insight by observing their own behavior.

Self-perception theory may have even more reach than Bem had anticipated. Bem argued that people sometimes learn about themselves by observing their *own* freely chosen behavior. But might you also infer something about yourself by observing the behavior of *someone else* with whom you completely identify? In a series of studies, Noah Goldstein and Robert Cialdini (2007) demonstrated this phenomenon, which they call vicarious self-perception. In one experiment, for example, they asked college students to listen to an interview with a fellow student who had agreed afterward to spend a few extra minutes helping out on a project on homelessness. Before listening to the interview, all the participants were fitted with an EEG recording device on their foreheads that allegedly measured brain activity as they viewed a series of images and words. By random assignment, some participants but not others were then told that their brain-wave patterns closely resembled that of the person whose interview they would soon hear—a level of resemblance, they were told, that signaled genetic similarity and relationship closeness. Would participants in this similarity feedback condition draw inferences about themselves by observing the behavior of a fellow student? Yes. In a post-interview questionnaire, these participants (compared to those in the no-feedback control group) rated themselves as more sensitive and as more self-sacrificing if the student whose helpfulness they observed was said to be similar, biologically. What's more, when the session was over, 93 percent of those in the similarity condition agreed to spend some extra time themselves helping the experimenter—compared to only 61 percent in the no-feedback control group.

"I don't sing because I am happy. I am happy because I sing."

As suggested by self-perception theory, we sometimes infer how we feel by observing our own behavior.

Self-Perceptions of Emotion Draw the corners of your mouth back and up and tense your eye muscles. Okay, relax. Now raise your eyebrows, open your eyes wide, and let your mouth drop open slightly. Relax. Now pull your brows down and together and clench your teeth. Relax. If you followed these directions, you would have appeared to others to be feeling first happy, then fearful, and finally angry. The question is, How would you have appeared to yourself?

Social psychologists who study emotion have asked precisely that question. Viewed within the framework of self-perception theory, the **facial feedback hypothesis** states that changes in facial expression can trigger corresponding changes in the subjective experience of emotion. In the first test of this hypothesis, James Laird (1974) told participants that they were taking part in an experiment on activity of the facial muscles. After attaching electrodes to their faces, he showed them a series of cartoons. Before each one, the participants were instructed to contract certain facial muscles in ways that created either a smile or a frown. As Laird predicted, participants rated what they saw as funnier and reported feeling happier when they were smiling than when they were frowning. In follow-up research, people were similarly induced through posed expressions to experience fear, anger, sadness, and disgust (Duclos et al., 1989)—and even a reduction in racial bias (Ito et al., 2006).

Facial feedback can evoke and magnify certain emotional states. It's important to note, however, that the face is not *necessary* to the subjective experience of emotion. When neuropsychologists recently tested a young woman who suffered from bilateral facial paralysis, they found that despite her inability to outwardly *show* emotion, she

facial feedback hypothesis The hypothesis that changes in facial expression can lead to corresponding changes in emotion.

reported *feeling* various emotions in response to positive and negative visual images (Keillor et al., 2003).

How does facial feedback work? With 80 muscles in the human face that can create over 7,000 expressions, can we actually vary our own emotions by contracting certain muscles and wearing different expressions? Research suggests that we can, though it is not clear what the results mean. Laird argues that facial expressions affect emotion through a process of self-perception: "If I'm smiling, I must be happy." Consistent with this hypothesis, Chris Kleinke and others (1998) asked people to emulate either the happy or angry facial expressions that were depicted in a series of photographs. Half the participants saw themselves in a mirror during the task; the others did not. Did these manipulations affect mood states? Yes. Compared to participants in a no-expression control group, those who put on happy faces felt better, and those who put on angry faces felt worse. As predicted by self-perception theory, the differences were particularly pronounced among participants who saw themselves in a mirror.

Other researchers maintain that facial movements spark emotion by producing physiological changes in the brain (Izard, 1990). For example, Robert Zajonc (1993) argues that smiling causes facial muscles to increase the flow of air-cooled blood to the brain, a process that produces a pleasant state by lowering brain temperature. Conversely, frowning decreases blood flow, producing an unpleasant state by raising temperature. To demonstrate, Zajonc and his colleagues (1989) conducted a study in which they asked participants to repeat certain vowels 20 times each, including the sounds *ah*, *e*, *u*, and the German vowel *ü*. In the meantime, temperature changes in the forehead were measured and participants reported on how they felt. As it turned out, *ah* and e (sounds that cause people to mimic smiling) lowered forehead temperature and elevated mood, whereas *u* and *ü* (sounds that cause us to mimic frowning) increased temperature and dampened mood. In short, people need not infer how they feel. Rather, facial expressions evoke physiological changes that produce an emotional experience.

Other expressive behaviors, such as body posture, can also provide us with sensory feedback and influence the way we feel. When people feel proud, they stand erect with their shoulders raised, chest expanded, and head held high (*expansion*). When dejected, however, people slump over with their shoulders drooping and head bowed (*contraction*). Clearly, your emotional state is revealed in the way you carry yourself. But is it also possible that the way you carry yourself affects your emotional state? Can people lift their spirits by expansion or lower their spirits by contraction? Yes. Sabine Stepper and Fritz Strack (1993) arranged for people to sit in either a slumped or an upright position by varying the height of the table they had to write on. Those forced to sit upright reported feeling more pride after succeeding at a task than did those who were placed in a slumped position. In another study, participants who were instructed to lean forward with their fists clenched during the experiment reported feeling anger, while those who sat slumped with their heads down said they felt sadness (Duclos et al., 1989; Flack et al., 1999).

Smiling can make you feel happier. TRUE.

Self-Perceptions of Motivation   Without quite realizing it, the author Mark Twain was a self-perception theorist. In *The Adventures of Tom Sawyer*, written in the late 1800s, he quipped, "There are wealthy gentlemen in England who drive four-horse passenger coaches 20 or 30 miles on a daily line, in the summer, because the privilege costs them considerable money; but if they were offered wages for the service that would turn it into work then they would resign." Twain's hypothesis—that reward for an enjoyable activity can undermine interest in that activity—seems to contradict both our intuition and the results of psychological research. After all, aren't we all motivated by reward, as B. F. Skinner and other behaviorists have declared? The answer depends on how *motivation* is defined.

As a keen observer of human behavior, Twain anticipated a key distinction between intrinsic and extrinsic motivation. *Intrinsic motivation* originates in factors within a person. People are said to be intrinsically motivated when they engage in an activity for the sake of their own interest, the challenge, or sheer enjoyment. Eating a fine meal, listening to music, spending time with friends, and having a hobby are among the activities that you might find intrinsically motivating. In contrast, *extrinsic motivation* originates in factors outside the person. People are said to be extrinsically motivated when they engage in an activity as a means to an end, for tangible benefits. It might be for money, grades, or recognition; to fulfill obligations; or to avoid punishment. As the behaviorists have always said, people do strive for reward. The question is, What happens to the intrinsic motivation once that reward is no longer available?

From the standpoint of self-perception theory, Twain's hypothesis makes sense. When someone is rewarded for listening to music, playing a game, or eating a tasty food, his or her behavior becomes *over*justified, or *over*rewarded, which means that it can be attributed to extrinsic as well as intrinsic motives. This **overjustification effect** can be dangerous: Observing that their own efforts have paid off, people begin to wonder if the activity was ever worth pursuing in its own right.

Research has shown that when people start getting "paid" for a task they already enjoy, they sometimes lose interest in it. In an early demonstration of this phenomenon, Mark Lepper and his colleagues (1973) gave preschool children an opportunity to play with colorful felt-tipped markers—an opportunity most could not resist. By observing how much time the children spent on the activity, the researchers were able to measure their intrinsic motivation. Two weeks later, the children were divided into three groups, all about equal in terms of initial levels of intrinsic motivation. In one, the children were simply asked to draw some pictures with the markers. In the second, they were told that if they used the markers they would receive a "Good Player Award," a certificate with a gold star and a red ribbon. In a third group, the children were not offered a reward for drawing pictures, but—like those in the second group—they received a reward when they were done.

About a week later, the teachers placed the markers and paper on a table in the classroom while the experimenters observed through a one-way mirror. Since no rewards were offered on this occasion, the amount of free time the children spent playing with the markers reflected their intrinsic motivation. As predicted, those who had expected and received a reward for their efforts were no longer as interested in the markers as they had been. Children who had not received a reward were not adversely affected, nor were those who had received the unexpected reward. Having played with the markers without the promise of tangible benefit, these children remained intrinsically motivated (see ▶ Figure 3.1).

The paradox that reward can undermine rather than enhance intrinsic motivation has been observed in many settings and with both children and adults (Deci & Ryan, 1985; Pittman & Heller, 1987; Tang & Hall, 1995). Accept money for a leisure activity, and before you know it, what used to be "play" comes to feel more like "work." In the long run, this can have negative effects on the quality of your performance. In

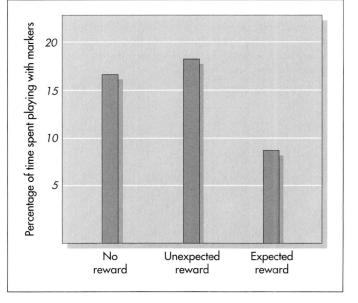

▶ **FIGURE 3.1**

Paradoxical Effects of Reward on Intrinsic Motivation

In this study, an expected reward undermined children's intrinsic motivation to play with felt-tipped markers. Children who received an unexpected reward or no reward did not lose interest.

Lepper et al., 1973.

overjustification effect
The tendency for intrinsic motivation to diminish for activities that have become associated with reward or other extrinsic factors.

a series of studies, Teresa Amabile (1996) and others had participants write poems, draw or paint pictures, make paper collages, and generate creative solutions to business dilemmas. Consistently, they found that people are more creative when they feel interested and challenged by the work itself than when they feel pressured to make money, fulfill obligations, meet deadlines, win competitions, or impress others. When Amabile had art experts rate the works of professional artists, she found that the artists' commissioned work (art they were contracted for) was judged as lower in quality than their noncommissioned work. People are likely to be more creative when they are intrinsically motivated in relation to the task, not compelled by outside forces.

But wait. If extrinsic benefits serve to undermine intrinsic motivation, should teachers and parents *not* offer rewards to their children? Are the employee incentive programs that are so often used to motivate workers in the business world doomed to fail, as some have suggested? (Kohn, 1993) It all depends on how the reward is perceived and by whom. If a reward is presented in the form of verbal praise that is perceived to be sincere or as a special "bonus" for superior performance, then sometimes it can actually *enhance* intrinsic motivation by providing positive feedback about competence—as when people win competitions, scholarships, or a pat on the back from people they respect (Cameron & Pierce, 1994; Cameron et al., 2005; Eisenberger & Cameron, 1996; Henderlong & Lepper, 2002).

The notion that intrinsic motivation is undermined by some types of reward but not others was observed even among 20-month-old babies. In a clever study, Felix Warneken and Michael Tomasello (2008) brought babies into the lab, where the experimenter accidentally dropped a pen or crumpled paper onto the floor and appeared unable to reach it. The child could help by picking up the object and handing it to the experimenter. Most of the babies helped in this situation. In a treatment phase, the researchers responded to the assistance by giving the child a toy cube ("For this you get a cube"), verbal praise ("Thank you, that's really nice!"), or nothing at all. Would these same children continue to help? ▶ Figure 3.2 shows that in a later test phase, when presented with a number of helping opportunities, those in the no-response condition continued to help 89 percent of the time and that this tendency remained high at 81 percent in the verbal praise condition. Yet among children who had earlier received a reward, helping in the test phase dropped to 53 percent when that reward was no longer available.

Individual differences in people's motivational orientation toward work must also be considered. For intrinsically oriented people who say, "What matters most to me is enjoying what I do" and "I seldom think about salary and promotions," reward may be unnecessary and may even be detrimental (Amabile et al., 1994). Yet for people who are highly focused on the achievement of certain goals—whether at school, at work, or in sports—inducements such as grades, scores, bonuses, awards, trophies, and the sheer thrill of competition, as in team sports, tend to boost intrinsic motivation (Durik & Harackiewicz, 2007; Harackiewicz & Elliot, 1993).

▶ **FIGURE 3.2**

In front of 20-month-old babies on the floor of a laboratory, an experimenter accidentally dropped a pen or crumpled paper. Most of the babies helped pick up the fallen object in this situation—a positive act that was met with a tangible reward, verbal praise, or nothing at all. Would the babies help the experimenter again if needed? As shown, babies in the no-response and verbal praise conditions continued to help at high rate. However, those who had received a reward became less likely to help later when that reward was no longer available, suggesting that tangible rewards undermined altruistic tendencies.

Warneken & Tomasello, 2008.

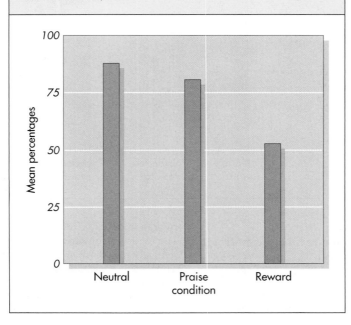

▊ Influences of Other People

As we noted earlier, Cooley's (1902) theory of the looking-glass self emphasized that other people help us define ourselves. In this section, we will see the importance of this proposition to our self-concepts.

Social Comparison Theory   Suppose a stranger were to ask, "Who are you?" If you had only a minute or two to answer, would you mention your religion or your ethnic background? What about your hometown? Would you describe your talents and your interests or your likes and dislikes? When asked this question, people tend to describe themselves in ways that set them apart from others in their immediate vicinity (McGuire & McGuire, 1988). Among children, boys are more likely to cite their gender when they grow up in families that are predominantly female; girls do the same when living in families that are predominantly male (McGuire et al., 1979). Similarly, on the college campus, "nontraditional" older students are more likely to mention age than are traditional younger students (Kite, 1992). Regardless of whether the unique attribute is gender, age, height, or eye color, this pattern is basically the same. The implication is intriguing: Change someone's social surroundings, and you can change that person's spontaneous self-description.

This reliance on distinguishing features in self-description indicates that the self is "relative," a social construct, and that each of us defines ourselves in part by using family members, friends, acquaintances, and others as a benchmark (Mussweiler & Riiter, 2003; Mussweiler & Strack, 2000). Temporarily, our standards of self-comparison can even be influenced by our fleeting, everyday exposures to strangers (Mussweiler et al., 2004). Indeed, that is what Leon Festinger (1954) proposed in his **social comparison theory**. Festinger argued that when people are uncertain of their abilities or opinions—that is, when objective information is not readily available—they evaluate themselves through comparisons with similar others. The theory seems reasonable, but is it valid? Over the years, social psychologists have put social comparison theory to the test, focusing on two key questions: (1) *When* do we turn to others for comparative information? (2) Of all the people who inhabit the earth, *with whom* do we choose to compare ourselves? (Stapel & Blanton, 2006; Suls & Wheeler, 2000)

As Festinger proposed, the answer to the "when" question appears to be that people engage in social comparison in states of uncertainty, when more objective means of self-evaluation are not available. In fact, recent studies suggest that Festinger may have understated the importance of social comparison processes—that people may judge themselves in relation to others even when more objective standards are available. For example, William Klein (1997) asked college students to make a series of judgments of artwork. Giving false feedback, he then told the students that 60 percent or 40 percent of their answers were correct and that this was 20 percent higher or lower than the average among students. When they later rated their own skill at the task, the participants were influenced not by their absolute scores but by where they stood in relation to their peers. For them, it was better to have had a 40 percent score that was above average than a 60 percent score that was below average.

The "with whom" question has also been the subject of many studies. The answer seems to be that when we evaluate our own taste in music, value on the job market, or athletic ability, we look to others who are similar to us in relevant ways (Goethals & Darley, 1977; Wheeler et al., 1982)—a choice that we make automatically, without thinking or necessarily being aware of it (Gilbert et al., 1995). If you are curious about your flair for writing, for example, you're more likely to compare yourself with other

social comparison theory
The theory that people evaluate their own abilities and opinions by comparing themselves to others.

college students than with high schoolers or best-selling authors. There are exceptions to this rule, of course. Later in this chapter, we will see that people often cope with personal inadequacies by focusing on others who are *less* able or *less* fortunate than themselves.

Two-Factor Theory of Emotion   People seek social comparison information to evaluate their abilities and opinions. Do they also turn to others to determine something as personal and subjective as their own emotions? In classic experiments on affiliation, Stanley Schachter (1959) found that when people were frightened into thinking they would receive painful electric shocks, most sought the company of others who were in the same predicament. Nervous and uncertain about how they should be feeling, participants wanted to affiliate with similar others, presumably for the purpose of comparison. Yet when they were not fearful and expected only mild shocks or when the "others" were not taking part in the same experiment, participants preferred to be alone. As Schachter put it, "Misery doesn't just love any kind of company; it loves only miserable company" (p. 24).

Intrigued by the possibilities, Schachter and his research team took the next step. Could it be, they wondered, that when people are uncertain about how they feel, their emotional state is actually determined by the reactions of others around them? In answer to this question, the researchers proposed that two factors are necessary to feel a specific emotion. First, the person must experience the symptoms of physiological arousal—such as a racing heart, perspiration, rapid breathing, and tightening of the stomach. Second, the person must make a *cognitive interpretation* that explains the source of the arousal. And that is where the people around us come in: Their reactions help us interpret our own arousal.

To test this provocative **two-factor theory of emotion**, Schachter and Jerome Singer (1962) injected male volunteers with epinephrine, a drug that heightens physiological arousal. Although one group was forewarned about the drug's effects, a second group was not. Members of a third group were injected with a harmless placebo. Before the drug (which was described as a vitamin supplement) actually took effect, participants were left alone with a male confederate introduced as another participant who had received the same injection. In some sessions, the confederate behaved in a euphoric manner. For 20 minutes, he bounced around happily, doodling on scratch paper, sinking jump shots into the wastebasket, flying paper airplanes across the room, and playing with a Hula-Hoop. In other sessions, the confederate displayed anger, ridiculing a questionnaire they were filling out and, in a fit of rage, ripping it up and hurling it into the wastebasket.

Think for a moment about these various combinations of situations. As the drug takes effect, participants in the *drug-informed* group will begin to feel their hearts pound, their hands shake, and their faces flush. Having been told to expect these symptoms, however, they need not search for an explanation. Participants in the *placebo* group will not become aroused in the first place, so they will have no symptoms to explain. But now consider the plight of those in the *drug-uninformed* group, who suddenly become aroused without knowing why. Trying to identify the sensations, these participants, according to the theory, should take their cues from someone else in the same predicament—namely, the confederate.

In general, the experimental results supported Schachter and Singer's line of reasoning. Drug-uninformed participants reported feeling relatively happy or angry depending on the confederate's performance. In many instances, they even exhibited similar kinds of behavior. One participant, for example, "threw open the window and, laughing, hurled paper basketballs at passersby." In the drug-informed and placebo groups, however, participants were, as expected, less influenced by these social cues.

two-factor theory of emotion
The theory that the experience of emotion is based on two factors: physiological arousal and a cognitive interpretation of that arousal.

Schachter and Singer's two-factor theory has attracted a good deal of controversy, as some studies have corroborated their findings but others have not. In one experiment, for example, participants who were injected with epinephrine and not forewarned about the symptoms later exhibited more fear in response to a scary film, but they were not more angry or amused while seeing films that tend to elicit these other emotions (Mezzacappa et al., 1999). Overall, it now appears that one limited but important conclusion can safely be drawn: When people are unclear about their own emotional states, they sometimes interpret how they feel by watching others (Reisenzein, 1983). The "sometimes" part of the conclusion is important. For other people to influence your emotion, your level of physiological arousal cannot be too intense or else it will be experienced as aversive, regardless of the situation (Maslach, 1979; Zimbardo et al., 1993). Also, research shows that other people must be present as a possible explanation for arousal *before* its onset. Once people are aroused, they turn for an explanation to events that preceded the change in their physiological state (Schachter & Singer, 1979; Sinclair et al., 1994).

In subsequent chapters, we will see that the two-factor theory of emotion has far-reaching implications for passionate love, anger and aggression, and other affective experiences.

▊ Autobiographical Memories

Philosopher James Mill once said, "The phenomenon of the Self and that of Memory are merely two sides of the same fact." If the story of patient William Thompson at the start of this chapter is any indication, Mill was right. Without autobiographical memories—recollections of the sequences of events that have touched your life (Bernsten, 2009; Fivush et al., 2003; Rubin, 1996; Thompson et al., 1998)—you would have no coherent self-concept. After all, who would you be if you could not remember your parents or your childhood playmates, your successes and failures, the places you lived, the schools you attended, the books you read, and the teams you played for? Clearly, memories shape the self-concept. In this section, we'll see that the self-concept shapes our personal memories as well (Conway & Pleydell-Pearce, 2000).

When people are prompted to recall their own experiences, they typically report more events from the recent past than from the distant past. There are, however, two consistent exceptions to this simple recency rule. The first is that older adults tend to retrieve a large number of personal memories from their adolescence and early adulthood years—a "reminiscence bump" found across many cultures that may occur because these are busy and formative years in one's life (Conway et al., 2005; Fitzgerald, 1988; Jansari & Parkin, 1996). A second exception is that people tend to remember transitional "firsts." Reflect for a moment on your own college career. What events pop to mind—and when did they occur? Did you come up with the day you arrived on campus or the first time you met your closest friend? What about notable classes, parties, or sports events? When David Pillemer and his colleagues (1996) asked college juniors and seniors to recount the most memorable experiences of their first year, 32 percent of all recollections were from the transitional month of September. When college graduates were given the same task, they too cited a disproportionate number of events from the opening two months of their first year, followed by the next major transitional period, the last month of their senior year. Among students, these busy transitional periods are important regardless of whether their schools follow a semester calendar or some other academic schedule (Kurbat et al., 1998).

Obviously, not all experiences leave the same impression. Ask people old enough to remember November 22, 1963, and they probably can tell you exactly where they were,

The nice thing about having memories is that you can choose.

—William Trevor

who they were with, and what was happening the moment they heard the news that President John F. Kennedy had been shot. Roger Brown and James Kulik (1977) coined the term *flashbulb memories* to describe these enduring, detailed, high-resolution recollections and speculated that humans are biologically equipped for survival purposes to "print" dramatic events in memory. These flashbulb memories are not necessarily accurate or even consistent over time. When asked, for example, how he heard about the infamous September 11, 2001, terrorist attacks, President George W. Bush gave different accounts on three occasions when asked what he was doing and who told him the news (Greenberg, 2004). Accurate or not, these recollections "feel" special and serve as prominent landmarks in the biographies that we tell about ourselves (Conway, 1995; Talarico & Rubin, 2007).

By linking the present to the past and providing us with an inner sense of continuity, autobiographical memory is a vital part of—and can be shaped by—our identity. In particular, people are often motivated to distort the past in ways that are self-inflated. According to Anthony Greenwald (1980), "The past is remembered as if it were a drama in which the self was the leading player" (p. 604). To illustrate this bias, let's turn the clock back to a momentous event in American history: the Senate Watergate hearings of 1973. The witness was John Dean, former counsel to President Richard Nixon. Dean had submitted a 245-page statement in which he recounted word for word the details of many conversations. Dean's memory seemed so impressive that he was called "the human tape recorder." But then, in an ironic twist of fate, investigators discovered that Nixon had taped the meetings that Dean recalled. Was Dean accurate? A comparison of his testimony with the actual tapes revealed that although he correctly remembered

the gist of his White House meetings, he consistently exaggerated his own role and importance in these events. Cognitive psychologist Ulric Neisser (1981), who analyzed Dean's testimony, wondered, "Are we all like this? Is everyone's memory constructed, staged, self-centered?" The answer is yes—there is a bit of John Dean in all of us (Ross & Sicoly 1979).

In other ways, too, people tend to revise their fading personal histories to reflect favorably on th e self. In one study, George Goethals and Richard Reckman (1973) found that people whose attitudes about school busing were changed by a persuasive speaker later assumed that they had held their new attitude all along. In a second study, Harry Bahrick and others (1996) had 99 college students try to recall all of their high school grades and then checked their reports against the actual transcripts. Overall, the majority of grades were recalled correctly. But most of the errors in memory were grade *inflations*—and most of these were made when the actual grades were *low* (see ▶ Figure 3.3). In a third study, Simone Schlagman and others (2006) talked to young and old volunteers for a period of one week and then analyzed the autobiographical memories that they spontaneously recounted—about births, deaths, holidays, accidents, school events, special occasions, and the like. Both groups recalled plenty of positive events, but older adults recalled fewer negative memories. Together, these findings bring to mind sociologist George Herbert Mead's (1934) contention that our visions of the past are like pure "escape fancies . . . in which we rebuild the world according to our hearts' desires" (pp. 348–349).

Although adults recall more events from the recent than distant past, people are filled with memories from late adolescence and early adulthood. These formative years are nicely captured by high school yearbook photos, such as those of American actresses Angelina Jolie (left) and Jennifer Aniston (right).

Culture and the Self-Concept

The self-concept is also heavily influenced by cultural factors. In America, it is said that "the squeaky wheel gets the grease"; in Japan, it is said that "the nail that stands out gets pounded down." Thus, American parents try to raise their children to be independent, self-reliant, and assertive (a "cut above the rest"), whereas Japanese children are raised to fit into their groups and community.

The preceding example illustrates two contrasting cultural orientations. One values *individualism* and the virtues of independence, autonomy, and self-reliance. The other orientation values *collectivism* and the virtues of interdependence, cooperation, and social harmony. Under the banner of individualism, one's personal goals take priority over group allegiances. In collectivist cultures, by contrast, a person is first and foremost a loyal member of a family, team, company, church, and state, motivated to be part of a group—not different, better, or worse (Triandis, 1994). In what countries are these orientations the most extreme? In a worldwide study of 116,000 employees of IBM, Geert Hofstede (1980) found that the most fiercely individualistic people were from the United States, Australia, Great Britain, Canada, and the Netherlands—in that order. The most collectivist people were from Venezuela, Colombia, Pakistan, Peru, Taiwan, and China.

It's also important to realize that individualism and collectivism are not simple opposites on a continuum and that the similarities and differences between countries do not fit a simple pattern. Daphna Oyserman and others (2002) conducted a meta-analysis of many thousands of respondents in 83 studies. Within the United States, they found that African Americans were the most individualistic subgroup and that Asian Americans and Latino Americans were the most collectivistic. Comparing nations, they found that collectivist orientations varied within Asia, as the Chinese were more collectivistic than Japanese and Korean respondents.

Individualism and collectivism are so deeply ingrained in a culture that they mold our very self-conceptions and identities. According to Hazel Markus and Shinobu Kitayama (1991), most North Americans and Europeans have an *independent* view of the self. In this view, the self is an entity that is distinct, autonomous, self-contained, and endowed with unique dispositions. Yet in much of Asia, Africa, and Latin America, people hold an *interdependent* view of the self. Here, the self is part of a larger social network that includes one's family, co-workers, and others with whom one is socially connected. People with an independent view say that "the only person you can count on is yourself" and "I enjoy being unique and different from others." In contrast, those with an interdependent view are more likely to agree that "I'm partly to blame if one of my family members or co-workers fails" and "my happiness depends on the happiness of those around me" (Rhee et al., 1995; Singelis, 1994; Triandis et al., 1998). These contrasting orientations—one focused on the personal self, the other on a collective self—are depicted in ▶ Figure 3.4.

Research confirms that there is a close link between cultural orientation and conceptions of the self. David Trafimow and others (1991) had North American and Chinese college students complete 20 sentences beginning with "I am. . . ." The Americans were more likely to fill in the blank with trait descriptions ("I am shy"), whereas the Chinese were more likely to identify themselves by group affiliations ("I am a college student"). It's no wonder that in China, one's family name comes *before* one's

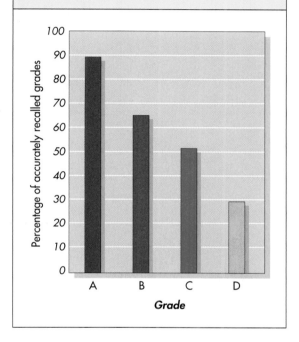

▶ **FIGURE 3.3**

Distortions in Memory of High School Grades

College students were asked to recall their high school grades, which were then checked against their actual transcripts. These comparisons revealed that most errors in memory were grade inflations. Lower grades were recalled with the least accuracy (and the most inflation). It appears that people sometimes revise their own past to suit their current self-image.

Bahrick et al., 1996.

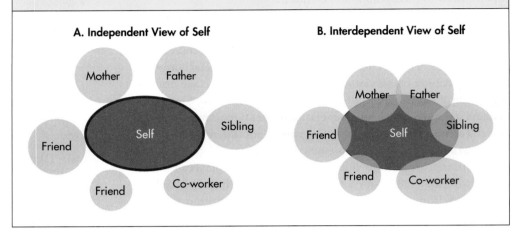

▶ **FIGURE 3.4**

Cultural Conceptions of Self

As depicted here, different cultures foster different conceptions of the self. Many Western-ers have an *independent view* of the self as an entity that is distinct, autonomous, and self-contained. Yet many Asians, Africans, and Latin Americans hold an *interdependent view* of the self that encompasses others in a larger social network.

Markus & Kitayama, 1991.

personal name. Similar differences are found between Australians and Malaysians (Bochner, 1994).

Our cultural orientations can color the way people perceive, evaluate, and present themselves in relation to others. Markus and Kitayama (1991) identified two particu-larly interesting differences between East and West. The first is that people in indi-vidualistic cultures strive for personal achievement, while those living in collectivist cultures derive more satisfaction from the status of a valued group. Thus, whereas North Americans tend to overestimate their own contributions to a team effort, seize the credit for success, and blame others for failure, people from collectivist cultures tend to underestimate their own role and present themselves in more modest, self-effacing terms in relation to other members of the group (Akimoto & Sanbonmatsu, 1999; Heine et al., 2000).

A second consequence of these differing conceptions of the self is that American college students see themselves as less similar to other people than do Asian Indian students. This difference reinforces the idea that individuals with independent con-

Reflecting an interdependent view of the self, children in Japan are taught to fit into the community. Reflect-ing a more independent view of the self, children in the United States are encouraged to express their individuality.

ceptions of the self believe they are unique. In fact, our cultural orientations toward conformity or independence may lead us to favor similarity or uniqueness *in all things*. In a study that illustrates the point, Heejung Kim and Hazel Markus (1999) showed abstract figures to subjects from the United States and Korea. Each figure contained nine parts. Most of the parts were identical in shape, position, and direction. One or more were different. Look at ▶ Figure 3.5. Which of the nine subfigures within each group do you like most? The American subjects liked the subfigures that were unique or in the minority, while Korean subjects preferred those that "fit in" as part of the group. In another study, these same researchers approached pedestrians of American and East Asian heritage at San Francisco's airport and had them fill out a questionnaire. Afterward, as a gift, they offered the participants a choice of one pen from a handful of pens, three or four of which had the same color barrel, green or orange. The result: 74 percent of the Americans chose a uniquely colored pen and 76 percent of the East Asians selected one of the commonly colored pens! It seems that our culturally ingrained orientations to conformity and independence leave a mark on us, leading us to form preferences for things that "fit in" or "stand out."

▶ **FIGURE 3.5**

What's Your Preference: Similarity or Uniqueness?

Which subfigure within each set do you prefer? Kim and Markus (1999) found that Americans tend to like subfigures that "stand out" as unique or in the minority, while Koreans tend to like subfigures that "fit in" with the surrounding group.

Kim & Markus, 1999.

Are people from disparate cultures locked into thinking about the self in either personal or collective terms, or are both aspects of the self present in everyone, to be expressed according to the situation? Reconsider the study noted above, where American students described themselves more in terms of personal traits and Chinese students cited more group affiliations. In a follow-up to that study, Trafimow and others (1997) tested students from Hong Kong, all of whom spoke English as a second language. One half of the students were given the "Who am I?" test in Chinese, and the other half took the test in English. Did this variation influence the results? Yes. Students who took the test in English focused more on personal traits, while those who took the test in Chinese focused more on group affiliations. It appears that each of us have both personal and collective aspects of the self to draw on—and that the part that comes to mind depends on the situation we are in.

The more closely social psychologists examine cultures and their impact on how people think, the more complex is the picture that emerges. Clearly, research documents the extent to which self conceptions are influenced by the individualist and collectivist impulses within a culture. But there are other core differences as well. Kaiping Peng and Richard Nisbett (1999) note that people in East Asian cultures think in dialectical terms about contradictory characteristics—accepting, for example, that apparent opposites (such as black and white, friend and enemy, and strong and weak) can coexist within a single person either at the same time or as a result of changes over time. Grounded in Eastern traditions, **dialecticism** is a system of thought characterized by the acceptance of such contradictions through compromise, as implied by the Chinese proverb "Beware of your friends, not your enemies." This thought style contrasts sharply with the American and European perspective, grounded in Western logic, by which people differentiate seeming opposites on the assumption that if one is right, the other must be wrong.

Wondering if a dialectical style of thought has implications for the self, Tammy English and Serena Chen (2007) conducted a series of studies in which they questioned American college students who were of European or Asian descent about what kind of person they are in such different everyday situations as a classroom, a cafeteria, a party, or the gym. Overall, they found that compared to European Americans who

dialecticism An Eastern system of thought that accepts the coexistence of contradictory characteristics within a single person.

portray their "true selves" as stable across the board, Asian Americans vary their self-concepts more to suit different relationship situations—though they are consistent within these situations. Other research too has shown that East Asians are more willing than Americans to see and accept contradictory aspects of themselves (Spencer-Rodgers et al., 2009)—as seen in their willingness to accept both positive and negative aspects of themselves at the same time (Boucher et al., 2009).

The study of cultural aspects of the self is also expanded by social psychologists interested in Latin American cultures, where social and emotional relationships are a particularly important part of the collectivist orientation. According to Renee Holloway and others (2009), Latino cultures prize the concept of *simpatico*, which emphasizes expressive displays of personable charm, graciousness, and hospitality. Does this cultural value become part of the Latino self concept? Clearly, no two individuals are the same. But when these researchers presented Latino and white Americans with the "Who am I?" task described earlier, they found that the Latino participants on average were more likely to describe themselves using simpatico-related terms such as likable, friendly, sympathetic, amiable, and gracious.

Self-Esteem

How do you feel about yourself? Are you generally satisfied with the way you look, your personality, academic and athletic abilities, your accomplishments, and your friendships? Are you optimistic about your future? When it comes to the self, people are not cool, objective, dispassionate observers. Rather, we are judgmental, motivated, emotional, and highly protective of our **self-esteem**—an affectively charged component of the self.

The word *esteem* comes from the Latin *aestimare*, which means "to estimate or appraise." Self-esteem thus refers to our positive and negative evaluations of ourselves (Coopersmith, 1967). Some individuals have a higher self-esteem than others do—an attribute that can have a profound impact on the way they think about, feel about, and present themselves. It's important to keep in mind, however, that although some of us have higher self-esteem than others, a feeling of self-worth is not a single trait etched permanently in stone. Rather, it is a state of mind that fluctuates in response to success, failure, ups and downs in fortune, social relations, and other life experiences (Heatherton & Polivy, 1991). Also, because the self-concept is made up of many self-schemas, people typically view parts of the self differently: Some parts they judge more favorably or see more clearly or as more important than other parts (Pelham, 1995; Pelham & Swann, 1989). Indeed, just as individuals differ according to how high or low their self-esteem is, they also differ in the extent to which their self-esteem is stable or unstable. As a general rule, self-esteem stays roughly the same from childhood through old age (Trzesniewski et al., 2003). Yet for some people in particular, self-esteem seems to fluctuate in response to daily experiences, which makes them highly responsive to praise and overly sensitive to criticism (Baldwin & Sinclair, 1996; Kernis & Waschull, 1995; Schimel et al., 2001).

■ The Need for Self-Esteem

self-esteem An affective component of the self, consisting of a person's positive and negative self-evaluations.

You, me, and just about everyone else on the planet seem to have a need for self-esteem, wanting to see ourselves in a positive light. As a result of who we are and the culture we live in, each of us may value different attributes and pursue this need in different ways. Some people derive a sense of worth from their appearance; others value physical strength, professional accomplishments, wealth, people skills, or group affiliations. Whatever the source, it is clear that the pursuit of self-worth is an aspect of human motivation that runs deep. But let's step back for a moment and ask, why? Why do we seem to need self-esteem the way we need food, air, sleep, and water?

At present, there are two social psychological answers to this basic question. One theory, proposed by Mark Leary and Roy Baumeister (2000), is that people are inherently social animals and that the desire for self-esteem is driven by this more primitive need to connect with others and gain their approval. In this way, our sense of self-esteem serves as a "sociometer," a rough indicator of how we're doing in the eyes of others. The threat of social rejection thus lowers self-esteem, which activates the need to regain approval and acceptance.

Alternatively, Jeff Greenberg, Sheldon Solomon, and Thomas Pyszczynski (1997) proposed **Terror Management Theory** to help explain our relentless need for self-esteem. According to this provocative and influential theory, we humans are biologically programmed for life and self-preservation. Yet we are conscious of—and terrified by—the inevitability of our own death. To cope with this paralyzing, deeply rooted fear, we construct and accept cultural worldviews about how, why, and by whom the earth was created; religious explanations of the purpose of our existence; and a sense of history filled with heroes, villains, and momentous events. These world views provide meaning and purpose and a buffer against anxiety. In a series of experiments, these investigators found that people react to graphic scenes of death or to the thought of their own death with intense defensiveness and anxiety. When people are given positive feedback on a test, however, which boosts their self-esteem, that reaction is muted. Other research has since confirmed this type of result (Schmeichel et al., 2009). As we'll see in later chapters, this theory has been used to explain how Americans are likely to cope with the trauma of 9/11 and the terror that it triggered (Pyszczynski et al., 2002).

As for the need for self-esteem, Pyszczynski and his colleagues (2004) put it this way:

> Self-esteem is a protective shield designed to control the potential for terror that results from awareness of the horrifying possibility that we humans are merely transient animals groping to survive in a meaningless universe, designed only to die and decay. From this perspective, each individual human's name and identity, family and social identifications, goals and aspirations, occupation and title, and humanly created adornments are draped over an animal that, in the cosmic scheme of things, may be no more significant or enduring than any individual potato, pineapple, or porcupine. (p. 436)

Confirming folk wisdom, a good deal of research suggests that high self-esteem colors our outlook on life. People with positive self-images tend to be happy, healthy, productive, and successful. They also tend to be confident, bringing to new challenges a winning attitude that leads them to persist longer at difficult tasks, sleep better at night, maintain their independence in the face of peer pressure, and suffer from fewer ulcers. In contrast, people with negative self-images tend to be more depressed, pessimistic about the future, and prone to failure. Lacking confidence, they bring to new

Terror Management Theory
The theory that humans cope with the fear of their own death by constructing worldviews that help to preserve their self-esteem.

tasks a losing attitude that traps them in a vicious, self-defeating cycle. Expecting to fail and fearing the worst, they become anxious, exert less effort, and "tune out" on important challenges. People with low self-esteem don't trust their own positive self-appraisals (Josephs et al., 2003). And when they fail, they tend to blame themselves, which makes them feel even less competent (Brockner, 1983; Brown & Dutton, 1995). Low self-esteem may even be hazardous to your health. Indeed, some research suggests that becoming aware of one's own negative attributes adversely affects the activity of certain white blood cells in the immune system, thus compromising the body's capacity to ward off disease (Strauman et al., 1993, 2004).

Does high self-esteem ensure desirable life outcomes? This seemingly simple question is now the subject of debate. On the one hand, based on an extensive review of the research, Roy Baumeister and others (2003) conclude that although high self-esteem leads people to feel good, take on new challenges, and persist through failure, the correlational evidence does not clearly support the strong conclusion that boosting self-esteem *causes* people to perform well in school or at work, to be socially popular, or to behave in ways that foster physical health. What's more, Jennifer Crocker and Lora Park (2004) argue that the process of pursuing self-esteem itself is costly. Specifically, they point to research showing that in trying hard to boost and maintain their self-esteem, people often become anxious, avoid activities that risk failure, neglect the needs of others, and suffer from stress-related health problems. Self-esteem has its benefits, they concede, but striving for it can also be costly. Challenging the conclusion that self-esteem is not worth striving for, William Swann and others (2007) note that although a person's overall, or *global*, sense of self-worth may not be predictive of positive life outcomes, people with specific domains of self-esteem benefit in more circumscribed ways. In other words, research suggests that individuals with high self-esteem specifically for public speaking, mathematics, or social situations will outperform those who have less self-confidence in the domains of public speaking, math, and social situations, respectively.

▌ Are There Gender and Race Differences?

Just as individuals differ in their self-esteem, so too do social and cultural groups. If you were to administer a self-esteem test to thousands of people all over the world, would you find that some segments of the population score higher than others? Would you expect to see differences in the averages of men and women, blacks and whites, or inhabitants of different cultures? Believing that self-esteem promotes health, happiness, and success and concerned that some groups are disadvantaged in this regard, researchers have indeed made these types of comparisons.

Are there gender differences in self-esteem? Over the years, a lot has been written in the popular press about the inflated but fragile "male ego," the low self-regard among adolescent girls and young women, and the resulting gender-related "confidence gap" (Orenstein, 1994). So does the research support this assumption? To find out, Kristin Kling and others (1999) statistically combined the results of 216 studies involving 97,000 respondents and then analyzed the surveys of 48,000 American students conducted by the National Center for Education Statistics. The result: Among adolescents and adults, males outscored females on various general measures of self-esteem. Contrary to popular belief, however, the difference was very small, particularly among older adults.

Researchers have also wondered if low self-esteem is a problem for members of stigmatized minority groups who historically have been victims of prejudice and discrimination. Does membership in a minority group, such as African Americans, deflate one's sense of self-worth? Based on the combined results of studies involving more than half a million respondents, Bernadette Gray-Little and Adam Hafdahl (2000) reported that black American children, adolescents, and adults consistently score higher—not lower—than their white counterparts on measures of self-esteem.

In a meta-analysis of hundreds of studies that compared all age groups and different American minorities, Jean Twenge and Jennifer Crocker (2002) confirmed the African American advantage in self-esteem relative to whites but found that Hispanic, Asian, and Native American minorities have lower self-esteem scores. This self-esteem advantage, as illustrated in ▶ Figure 3.6, is not easy to interpret. Surprised by the high African American scores, some researchers have suggested that perhaps African Americans—more than other minorities—are able to preserve their self-esteem in the face of adversity by attributing negative outcomes to the forces of discrimination and using this adversity to build a sense of group pride. In this regard, Twenge and Crocker found that self-esteem scores of black Americans, relative to those of whites, have risen over time from the pre–civil rights days of the 1950s to the present.

▮ Self-Discrepancy Theory

What determines how people feel about themselves? According to E. Tory Higgins (1989), our self-esteem is defined by the match or mismatch between how we see ourselves and how we want to see ourselves. To demonstrate, try the following exercise. On a blank sheet of paper, write down 10 traits that describe the kind of person you think you *actually* are (smart? easygoing? sexy? excitable?). Next, list 10 traits that describe the kind of person you think you *ought* to be, characteristics that would enable you to meet your sense of duty, obligation, and responsibility. Then make a list of traits that describe the kind of person you *would like* to be, an *ideal* that embodies your hopes, wishes, and dreams. If you follow these instructions, you should have three lists: your actual self, your ought self, and your ideal self.

Research has shown that these lists can be used to predict your self-esteem and your emotional well-being. The first list is your self-concept. The others represent your personal standards, or *self-guides*. To the extent that you fall short of these standards, you will experience lowered self-esteem, negative emotion, and, in extreme cases, a serious affective disorder. The specific consequence depends on which self-guide you fail to achieve. If there's a discrepancy between your actual and ought selves, you will feel guilty, ashamed, and resentful. You might even suffer from excessive fears and anxiety-related disorders. If the mismatch is between your actual and ideal selves, you'll feel disappointed, frustrated, unfulfilled, and sad. In the worst-case scenario you might even become depressed (Boldero & Francis, 2000; Higgins, 1999; Strauman, 1992). Our self-discrepancies may even set into motion a self-perpetuating process. Participating in a study of body images, college women with high rather than low discrepancies between their actual and ideal selves were more likely to compare themselves with thin models in TV commercials, which further increased their body dissatisfaction and depression (Bessenoff, 2006).

Each and every one of us must cope with some degree of self-discrepancy. Nobody's perfect. Yet we do not all suffer from the emotional consequences. The reason, according to Higgins, is that self-esteem depends on a number of factors. One is simply the

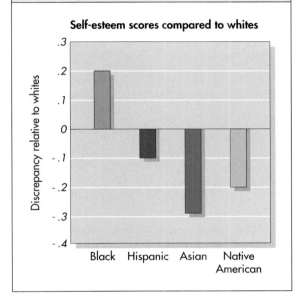

▶ **FIGURE 3.6**

Self-Esteem in U.S. Minorities

Through a meta-analysis, Twenge and Crocker (2002) found that African Americans score higher on self-esteem tests relative to whites, but that Hispanic-American, Asian-American, and Native American minorities score lower.

Twenge & Crocker, 2002.

Self-esteem scores compared to whites

amount of discrepancy. The more of it there is, the worse we feel. Another is the importance of the discrepancy to the self. The more important the domain in which we fall short, again, the worse we feel. A third factor is the degree to which we focus on our self-discrepancies. The more focused we are, the greater the harm. This last observation raises an important question: What causes us to be more or less focused on our personal shortcomings? For an answer, we turn to self-awareness theory.

■ The Self-Awareness "Trap"

If you carefully review your daily routine—classes, work, chores at home, leisure activities, social interactions, and meals—you will probably be surprised at how little time you actually spend thinking about yourself. In a study that illustrates this point, more than a hundred people, ranging in age from 19 to 63, were equipped for a week with electronic beepers that sounded every two hours or so between 7:30 A.M. and 10:30 P.M. Each time the beepers went off, participants interrupted whatever they were doing, wrote down what they were thinking at that moment, and filled out a brief questionnaire. Out of 4,700 recorded thoughts, only 8 percent were about the self. For the most part, attention was focused on work and other activities. In fact, when participants were thinking about themselves, they reported feeling relatively unhappy and wished they were doing something else (Csikszentmihalyi & Figurski, 1982).

I have the true feeling of myself only when I am unbearably unhappy.
—Franz Kafka

Self-Focusing Situations   The finding that people may be unhappy while they think about themselves is interesting, but what does it mean? Does self-reflection bring out our personal shortcomings the way staring into a mirror draws our gaze to every blemish on the face? Is self-awareness an unpleasant mental state from which we need to retreat?

Many years ago, Robert Wicklund and his colleagues theorized that the answer is yes (Duval & Wicklund, 1972; Wicklund, 1975; Silvia & Duval, 2001). According to their **self-awareness theory**, most people are not usually self-focused, but certain situations predictably force us to turn inward and become the objects of our own attention. When we talk about ourselves, glance in a mirror, stand before an audience or camera, watch ourselves on videotape, or behave in a conspicuous manner, we enter into a state of heightened self-awareness that leads us naturally to compare our behavior to some standard. This comparison often results in a negative discrepancy and a temporary reduction in self-esteem as we discover that we fall short. Thus, research participants who are seated in front of a mirror tend to react more negatively to their self-discrepancies, often slipping into a negative mood state (Fejfar & Hoyle, 2000; Hass & Eisenstadt, 1990; Phillips & Silvia, 2005). Interestingly, Japanese people—already highly concerned about their public "face"—are unaffected by the added presence of a mirror (Heine et al., 2009).

The real-life consequences can be substantial. The more self-focused people are in general, the more likely they are to find themselves in a bad mood (Flory et al., 2000) or depressed (Pyszczynski & Greenberg, 1987). People who are self-absorbed are also more likely to suffer from alcoholism, anxiety, and other clinical disorders (Ingram, 1990; Mor & Winquist, 2002).

self-awareness theory
The theory that self-focused attention leads people to notice self-discrepancies, thereby motivating either an escape from self-awareness or a change in behavior.

Is there a solution? Self-awareness theory suggests two basic ways of coping with such discomfort: (1) "shape up" by behaving in ways that reduce our self-discrepancies or (2) "ship out" by withdrawing from self-awareness. According to Charles Carver and Michael Scheier (1981), the solution chosen depends on whether people think they can reduce their self-discrepancy and whether they're pleased with the progress they make once they try (Duval et al., 1992). If so, they tend to match their behavior to personal or societal standards; if not, they tune out, look for distractions, and turn attention away from the self. This process is depicted in ▶ Figure 3.7.

In general, research supports the prediction that when people are self-focused, they are more likely to behave in ways that are consistent either with their own personal values or with socially accepted ideals (Gibbons, 1990). Two interesting field studies illustrate this point. In one, Halloween trick-or-treaters—children with masks, costumes, and painted faces—were greeted at a researcher's door and left alone to help themselves from a bowl of candy. Although the children were asked to take only one piece, 34 percent violated the request. When a full-length mirror was placed behind the candy bowl, however, that number dropped to 12 percent. Apparently, the mirror forced the children to become self-focused, leading them to behave in a way that was consistent with public standards of desirable conduct (Beaman et al., 1979). In a second study, conducted in England, customers at a lunch counter were trusted to pay for their coffee, tea, and milk by depositing money into an unsupervised "honesty box." Hanging on the wall behind the counter was a poster that featured a picture of flowers or a pair of eyes. By calculating the ratio of money deposited to drinks consumed, researchers observed that people paid nearly three times more money in the presence of the eyes (Bateson et al., 2006).

Self-awareness theory states that if a successful reduction of self-discrepancy seems unlikely, individuals will take a second route: escape from self-awareness. Roy Baumeister (1991) speculates that drug abuse, sexual masochism, spiritual ecstasy, binge eating, and suicide all serve this escapist function. Even television may serve as a form of escape. In one study, Sophia Moskalenko and Steven Heine (2003) brought college students into a laboratory and tested their actual-ideal self-discrepancies twice. Half watched a brief TV show on nature before the second test. In a second study, students were sent home with the questionnaire and instructed to fill it out either before or after watching TV. In both cases, those who watched TV had lower self-discrepancies on the second measure. In yet a third study, students who were told they had done poorly on an IQ test spent more time watching TV while waiting in the lab than those who were told they had succeeded. Perhaps TV and other forms of entertainment enable people to "watch their troubles away."

One particularly disturbing health implication concerns the use of alcohol. According to Jay Hull, people often drown their sorrows in a bottle as a way to escape the negative implications of self-awareness. To test this hypothesis, Hull and Richard Young (1983) administered what was supposed to be an IQ test to male participants

▶ FIGURE 3.7

The Causes and Effects of Self-Awareness

Self-awareness pressures people to reduce self-discrepancies either by matching their behavior to personal or societal standards or by withdrawing from self-awareness.

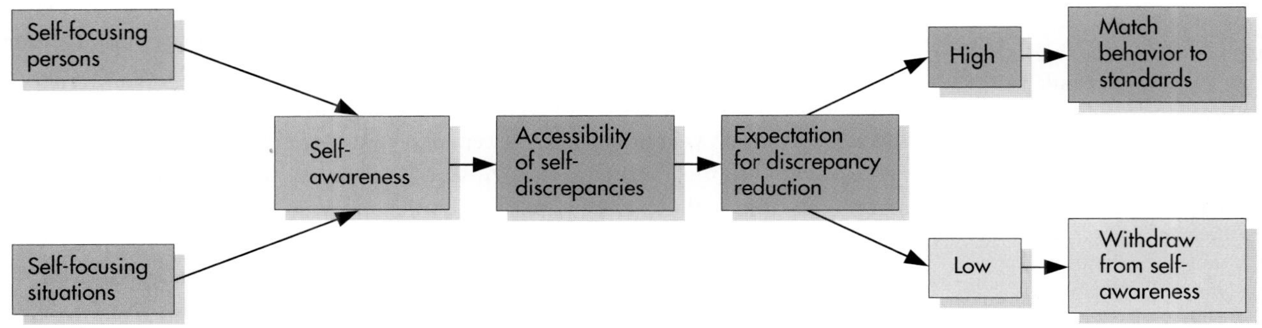

and gave false feedback suggesting that they had either succeeded or failed. Supposedly as part of a separate study, those participants were then asked to taste and rate different wines. As they did so, experimenters kept track of how much they drank during a 15-minute tasting period. As predicted, participants who were prone to self-awareness drank more wine after failure than after success, presumably to dodge the blow to their self-esteem. Among participants not prone to self-awareness, there was no difference in alcohol consumption. These results come as no surprise. Indeed, many of us expect alcohol to grant this form of relief (Leigh & Stacy, 1993) and help us manage our emotional highs and lows (Cooper et al., 1995).

Claude Steele and Robert Josephs (1990) believe that alcoholic intoxication offers more than just a means of tuning out on the self. By causing people to lose touch with reality and shed their inhibitions, it also evokes a state of "drunken self-inflation." In one study, for example, participants rated their actual and ideal selves on various traits—some important to self-esteem, others not important. After drinking either an 80-proof vodka cocktail or a harmless placebo, they re-rated themselves on the same traits. As measured by the perceived discrepancy between actual and ideal selves, participants who were drinking expressed inflated views of themselves on traits they considered important (Banaji & Steele, 1989).

Self-Focusing Persons Just as *situations* evoke a state of self-awareness, some *individuals* are generally more self-focused than others. Research has revealed an important distinction between **private self-consciousness**—the tendency to introspect about our inner thoughts and feelings—and **public self-consciousness**—the tendency to focus on our outer public image (Buss, 1980; Fenigstein et al., 1975). Table 3.1 presents a sample of items used to measure these traits.

Private and public self-consciousness are distinct traits. People who score high on a test of private self-consciousness tend to fill in incomplete sentences with first-person pronouns. They also make self-descriptive statements and recognize self-relevant words more quickly than other words (Mueller, 1982; Eichstaedt & Silvia, 2003). In contrast, those who score high on a measure of public self-consciousness are sensitive to the way they are viewed from an outsider's perspective. Thus, when people were asked to draw a capital letter E on their foreheads, 43 percent of those with high levels of public self-consciousness, compared with only 6 percent of those with low levels, oriented the E so that it was backward from their own standpoint but correct for an outside observer (Hass, 1984). People who are high in public self-consciousness are also particularly sensitive to the extent to which others share their opinions (Fenigstein & Abrams, 1993).

The distinction between private and public self-awareness has implications for the ways in which we reduce self-discrepancies. According to Higgins (1989), people are motivated to meet either their own standards or the standards held for them by significant others. If you're privately self-conscious, you listen to an inner voice and try to reduce discrepancies relative to your own standards; if you're publicly self-conscious, however, you try to match your behavior to socially accepted norms. As illustrated in ▶ Figure 3.8, there may be "two sides of the self: one for you and one for me" (Scheier & Carver, 1983, p. 123).

TABLE 3.1

How Self-Conscious Are You?

These sample items appear in the Self-Consciousness Scale. How many of these statements indicating private or public self-consciousness would you use to describe yourself?

Items That Measure Private Self-Consciousness

- I'm always trying to figure myself out.
- I'm constantly examining my motives.
- I'm often the subject of my fantasies.
- I'm alert to changes in my mood.
- I'm aware of the way my mind works when I work on a problem.

Items That Measure Public Self-Consciousness

- I'm concerned about what other people think of me.
- I'm self-conscious about the way I look.
- I'm concerned about the way I present myself.
- I usually worry about making a good impression.
- One of the last things I do before leaving my house is look in the mirror.

Fenigstein et al., 1975.

---

private self-consciousness
A personality characteristic of individuals who are introspective, often attending to their own inner states.

public self-consciousness
A personality characteristic of individuals who focus on themselves as social objects, as seen by others.

Self-Regulation and Its Limits

To this point, we have seen that self-focused attention can motivate us to control our behavior and strive toward personal or social ideals. Achieving these goals—which enables us to reduce the self-discrepancies that haunt us—means that we must constantly engage in self-regulation, the processes by which we seek to control or alter our thoughts, feelings, behaviors, and urges. From lifting ourselves out of bed in the morning to dieting, running the extra mile, limiting how much we drink at a party, practicing safe sex, smiling politely at people we really don't like, and working when we have more fun things to do, the exercise of self-control is something we do all the time (Carver & Scheier, 1998; Baumeister & Vohs, 2004; Forgas et al., 2009).

Mark Muraven and Roy Baumeister (2000) theorize that self-control is a limited inner resource that can temporarily be depleted by usage. There are two components to their theory. The first is that all self-control efforts draw from a single common reservoir. The second is that exercising self-control is like flexing a muscle: Once used, it becomes fatigued and loses strength, making it more difficult to reexert self-control—at least for a while, until the resource is replenished. Deny yourself the ice cream sundae that tickles your sweet tooth and you'll find it more difficult to hold your temper when angered. Try to conceal your stage fright as you stand before an audience and you'll find it harder to resist the urge to watch TV when you should be studying.

Research has supported this provocative hypothesis. In one study, Muraven and Baumeister (1998) had participants watch a brief clip from an upsetting film that shows scenes of sick and dying animals exposed to radioactive waste. Some of the participants were instructed to stifle their emotional responses to the clip, including their facial expressions; others were told to amplify or exaggerate their facial responses; a third group received no special instructions. Both before and after the movie, self-control was measured by the length of time participants were able to squeeze a handgrip exerciser without letting go. As predicted, those who had to inhibit or amplify their emotions during the film—but not those in the third group—lost their willpower in the handgrip task from the first time they tried it to the second (see ▶ Figure 3.9). Other studies have since confirmed the point: After people exert self-control in one task, their capacity for self-regulation is weakened—causing them to talk too much, disclose too much, or brag too much in a later social situation (Vohs et al., 2005).

It appears that we can control ourselves only so much before self-regulation fatigue sets in, causing us to "lose it." What might this mean, then, for people who are constantly regulating their behavior? To find out, Kathleen Vohs and Todd Heatherton (2000) showed a brief and dull documentary to individual female college students, half of whom were chronic dieters. Placed in the viewing room—either within arm's reach (high temptation) or 10 feet away (low temptation)—was a bowl filled with Skittles, M&Ms, Doritos, and salted peanuts that participants were free to sample. After watching the movie, they were taken to another room for an ice-cream taste test and told they could eat as much as they wanted. How much ice cream did they consume? The researchers predicted that dieters seated within reach of the bowl would have to fight the hardest to avoid snacking—an act of self-control that would cost them later. The prediction was confirmed. As measured by the amount of ice cream consumed in the taste test, dieters in the high-temptation condition ate more ice cream than did all nondieters and dieters in the low-temptation situation. What's more, a second study showed that dieters who had to fight the urge in the high-temptation situation were later less persistent and quicker to give up on a set of impossible cognitive problems they were asked to solve.

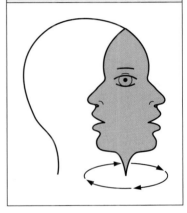

▶ **FIGURE 3.8**
Revolving Images of Self

According to self-awareness theory, people try to meet either their own standards or standards held for them by others—depending, perhaps, on whether they are in a state of private or public self-consciousness (Snyder et al., 1983). As Scheier and Carver (1983, p. 123) put it, there are "two sides of the self: one for you and one for me."

Snyder et al., 1983.

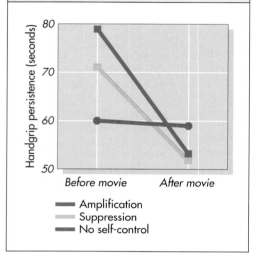

▶FIGURE 3.9

Self-Control as a Limited Inner Resource

Participants were shown an upsetting film and told to amplify or suppress their emotional responses to it (a third group received no self-control instruction). Before and afterward, self-control was measured by persistence at squeezing a handgrip exerciser. As shown, the two groups that had to control their emotions during the film—but not those in the third group—later lost their willpower on the handgrip.

Muraven & Baumeister, 1998.

The highest possible stage in moral culture is when we recognize that we ought to control our thoughts.

—Charles Darwin

New research suggests that self-regulation fatigue sets in because exerting self-control is physically taxing, as measured by the extent to which it consumes glucose, a vital source of bodily energy. Across a range of experiments, Matthew Gailliot and others (2007) had participants engage in an act of self-control—such as suppressing a word, thought, or emotion—before and after which blood samples were taken. Consistently, they found that acts of self-control—relative to similar acts not requiring self-control—were followed by reduced blood glucose levels and a lessened capacity for additional self-control. What's more, these researchers were able to counteract these adverse effects merely by feeding participants sugared lemonade between tasks, which restored glucose to the bloodstream.

Is it possible to counteract self-regulation fatigue through psychological intervention alone, without the calories associated with glucose consumption? Brandon Schmeichel and Kathleen Vohs (2009) reasoned that people may be able to restore their capacity for self-control by stopping to mentally bolster or "affirm" their sense of who they are. To test this hypothesis, they asked participants to write a short story. To vary the exercise of self-control, some but not others were prohibited from using certain letters of the alphabet (try writing even a short paragraph without using the letters *a* or *n* and you will appreciate the discipline that is needed!). Afterward, all participants were administered a classic pain tolerance task that required them to soak one hand in a tub of circulating ice-cold water for as long as they could, until it was too painful to continue. Between the two tasks, "self-affirmation" participants were given a chance to express a core value by writing an essay about the one personal characteristic they find most important (such as family relations, friendships, creativity, or athletics). Others wrote about some less important characteristic. Can a small act of self-affirmation counteract the effects of self-regulation fatigue on cold tolerance? Yes. Among participants in the no-affirmation condition, the prior act of self-control sharply reduced their tolerance to cold pain from an average of 78 seconds to 27 seconds. Among those who were prompted to self-affirm, however, the adverse effect of the first self-control task on pain tolerance was erased.

◼ Ironic Mental Processes

There's another possible downside to self-control that is often seen in sports when athletes become so self-focused under pressure that they stiffen up and "choke." While many athletes rise to the occasion, the pages of sports history are filled with stories of basketball players who lose their touch in the final minute of a championship game, of golfers who cannot sink a routine final putt to win a tournament, and of tennis players who lose their serve, double-faulting when it matters most. "Choking" in these ways seems to be a paradoxical type of failure caused by trying too hard and thinking too much. When you learn a new motor activity like how to throw a curve ball or land a jump, you must think through the mechanics in a slow and cautious manner. As you get better, however, your movements become automatic, so you do not have to think about timing, breathing, the position of your head and limbs, or the distribution of your weight. You relax and just do it. Unless trained to perform while self-focused, athletes under pressure often try their hardest not to fail, become self-conscious, and think too much—all of which disrupts the fluid and natural flow of their performance (Baumeister, 1984; Beilock & Carr, 2001; Gray, 2004; Lewis & Linder, 1997).

The paradoxical effects of attempted self-control are evident in other situations, too. Studying what he calls *ironic processes*, Daniel Wegner (1994) has found that at times, the harder you try to inhibit a thought, feeling, or behavior, the less likely you are to succeed. Try not to think about a white bear for the next 30 seconds, he finds, and that very image intrudes upon consciousness with remarkable frequency. Instruct the members of a jury to disregard inadmissible evidence and the censored material is sure to pop to mind as they deliberate. Try not to worry about how long it's taking to fall asleep and you'll stay awake. Try not to laugh in class, think about the chocolate cake in the fridge, or scratch the itch on your nose—well, you get the idea.

According to Wegner, every conscious effort at maintaining control is met by a concern about failing to do so. This concern automatically triggers an "ironic operating process" as the person, trying hard *not* to fail, searches his or her mind for the unwanted thought. The ironic process will not necessarily prevail, says Wegner. Sometimes we can put the imaginary white bear out of mind. But if the person is cognitively busy, tired, distracted, hurried, or under stress, then the ironic process, because it "just happens," will prevail over the intentional process, which requires conscious attention and effort. As Wegner (1997) put it, "Any attempt at mental control contains the seeds of its own undoing" (p. 148).

Sometimes the harder you try to control a thought, feeling, or behavior, the less likely you are to succeed. **TRUE.**

Ironic processes have been observed in a wide range of behaviors. In an intriguing study of this effect on the control of motor behavior, Wegner and his colleagues (1998) had participants hold a pendulum (a crystalline pendant suspended from a nylon fishing line) over the center of two intersecting axes on a glass grid, which formed a +. Some participants were instructed simply to keep the pendulum steady, while others were pointedly told not to allow it to swing back and forth along the horizontal axis. Try this yourself and you'll see that it's not easy to prevent all movement. In this experiment, however, the pendulum was more likely to swing horizontally when this direction was specifically forbidden. To further examine the role of mental distraction, the researchers instructed some participants to count backward from a thousand by sevens while trying to control the pendulum. In this situation, the ironic effect was even greater. Among those who tried to prevent horizontal movement but could not concentrate fully on the task, the pendulum swayed freely back and forth in the forbidden direction (see ▶ Figure 3.10). Applying this logic to keeping secrets, other researchers have found that instructing word-game players to conceal hidden clues from a fellow player increased rather than decreased their tendency to leak that information (Lane et al., 2006). It may seem both comic and tragic, but at times our efforts at self-control backfire, thwarting even the best of intentions.

▶ **FIGURE 3.10**

Ironic Effects of Mental Control

In this study, participants tried to hold a pendulum motionless over a grid. As illustrated in the tracings shown here, they were better at the task when simply instructed to keep the pendulum steady (a) than when specifically told to prevent horizontal movement (c). Among participants who were mentally distracted during the task, this ironic effect was even greater (b and d).

Wegner et al., 1998.

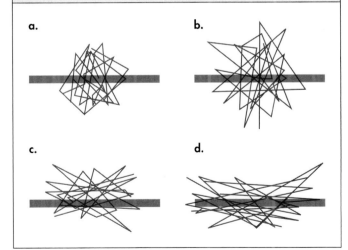

◼ Mechanisms of Self-Enhancement

We have seen that self-awareness can create discomfort and lower self-esteem by focusing attention on discrepancies. We have seen that people often avoid focusing on themselves and turn away from unpleasant truths but that such avoidance is not always possible. And we have seen that efforts at self-regulation often fail and sometimes even

AP/Wide World Photos

© Anatoly Maltsev/epa/Corbis

Why do some athletes choke under pressure and others rise to the occasion? Heading into the 2006 Winter Olympics in Turin, Italy, American downhill racer Bode Miller, a daredevil from New Hampshire, was favored to win several gold medals. Yet after slipping, falling, and missing gates, he failed to win a single medal, gold or otherwise (left). In contrast, Japan's unassuming figure skater Shizuka Arakawa was not favored to win a medal. But then, as if feeling no pressure, she skated a strong and fluid final program, landed her triple jump combinations cleanly, and won the gold (right).

backfire. How, then, does the average person cope with his or her faults, inadequacies, and uncertain future?

At least in Western cultures, most people think highly of themselves most of the time. Consistently, and across a broad range of life domains, research has shown that people see positive traits as more self-descriptive than negative traits, evaluate themselves more highly than they do others, rate themselves more highly than they are rated by others, exaggerate their control over life events, and predict that they have a bright future (Dunning et al., 2004; Sedikides & Gregg, 2008; Taylor, 1989).

Research shows that people overrate their effectiveness as speakers to an audience (Keysar & Henly 2002), overestimate their own contributions to a group and the extent to which they would be missed if absent (Savitsky et al., 2003), and selectively recall positive feedback about themselves while neglecting the negative (Green et al., 2008). People also overestimate their intellectual and social abilities across a wide range of domains. What's particularly interesting about this tendency is that those who are least competent are the most likely to overrate their own performance. In a series of studies, Justin Kruger and David Dunning (1999) found that college students with the lowest scores on tests of logic, grammar, and humor were the ones who most grossly overjudged their own abilities (on average, their scores were in the lowest 12 percent among peers, yet they estimated themselves to be in the 62nd percentile). These investigators found that when the low scorers were trained to be more competent in these areas, they became more realistic in their self-assessments. Ignorance, as they say, is bliss.

Other research, too, shows that people exhibit **implicit egotism**, an unconscious and subtle form of self-enhancement. This is well illustrated in the finding that people rate the letters contained within their name more favorably than the other letters of the alphabet (Hoorens & Nuttin, 1993). In an article entitled "Why Susie Sells Seashells by the Seashore," Brett Pelham and his colleagues (2002) argue that people form positive associations with the sight and sound of their own name and thus are drawn to other people, places, and entities that share this most personal aspect of "self." In a thought-provoking series of studies, these researchers examined several important life choices that we make and found that people exhibit small but statistically detectable preferences for things that contain the letters of their own first or last name. For

implicit egotism
A nonconscious form of self-enhancement.

example, men and women are more likely than would be predicted by chance to live in places (Michelle in Michigan, George in Georgia), attend schools (Kari from the University of Kansas, Preston from Penn State University), and choose careers (Dennis and Denise as dentists) whose names resemble their own. Indeed, marriage records found on various genealogical websites reveal that people are disproportionately likely to marry others with first or last names that resemble their own (Jones et al., 2004). In a subtle but remarkable way, we unconsciously seek out reflections of the self in our surroundings (Pelham et al., 2005).

This recent research on implicit egotism shows that people hold themselves in high regard. It's not that we consciously or openly flatter ourselves. The response is more like a reflex. Indeed, when research participants are busy or distracted as they make self-ratings, their judgments are quicker and even more favorable (Hixon & Swann, 1993; Paulhus et al., 1989). We can't all be perfect, nor can we all be better than average. So what supports this common illusion? In this section, we examine four methods that people use to rationalize or otherwise enhance their self-esteem: self-serving cognitions, self-handicapping, basking in the glory of others, and downward social comparisons.

We don't see things as they are, we see them as we are.

—Anais Nin

Self-Serving Cognitions   How well did you do on the Scholastic Assessment Test (SAT)? When James Shepperd (1993b) asked college students about their performance on this infamous test, he uncovered two interesting patterns. First, the students over-estimated their actual scores by an average of 17 points. This inflationary distortion was most pronounced among those with relatively low scores, and it persisted some-what even when students knew that the experimenter would check their academic files. Second, a majority of students whose SAT scores were low described their scores as inaccurate and the test in general as invalid. In fact, the SATs for the group as a whole were predictive of their grade point averages.

When students receive exam grades, those who do well take credit for the success; those who do poorly complain about the instructor or test questions. When research-ers have articles accepted for publication, they credit the quality of their work; when articles are rejected, they blame the editors and reviewers. When gamblers win a bet, they marvel at their skillfulness; when they lose, they blame fluke events that transformed near-victory into defeat. Whether people have high or low self-esteem, explain their own outcomes publicly or in private, and try to be honest or to make a good impression, there is bias. Across a range of cultures, peo-ple tend to take credit for success and dis-tance themselves from failure (Mezulis et al., 2004; Schlenker et al., 1990)—all while seeing themselves as objective, not biased (Pronin, Gilovich, & Ross, 2004).

Most of us are also unrealistically opti-mistic. College students who were asked to predict their own future compared with that of the average peer believed that they would graduate higher in their class, get a better job, have a happier marriage, and bear a gifted child. They also believed that they were less

In casinos, racetracks, and lotteries, gamblers lose billions of dollars a year. This self-defeating behavior persists in part because people exaggerate their control over random events. For example, many slot-machine addicts mistakenly think that they can find "hot" machines that have not recently surrendered a jackpot.

© Corbis

likely to get fired or divorced, have a car accident, become depressed, be victimized by crime, or suffer a heart attack (Weinstein, 1980). In sports, politics, health, and social issues, people exhibit an optimistic bias—essentially a case of wishful thinking—about their own future, judging desirable events as more likely to occur than undesirable events (Krizan & Windschitl, 2007; Lench, 2009).

Perhaps one reason that people are eternally optimistic is that they harbor illusions of control, overestimating the extent to which they can influence personal outcomes that are not, in fact, within their power to control (Thompson, 1999). In a series of classic experiments on the illusion of control, Ellen Langer (1975) found that college students bet more money in a chance game of high-card when their opponent seemed nervous rather than confident and were more reluctant to sell a lottery ticket if they'd chosen the number themselves than if it was assigned. Emily Pronin and others (2006) tested the related hypothesis that imagining an event before it occurs can lead people to think they had influenced it. In one study, for example, participants watched a trained confederate shoot hoops on a basketball court. Before each shot, they were instructed to visualize his success ("the shooter releases the ball and it swooshes through the net") or an irrelevant event ("the shooter's arm curls to lift a dumbbell"). After the confederate's successful shooting spree, spectators rated the extent of their influence over his performance. As if linking thoughts to outcomes, they exhibited an illusion of mental causation, taking more credit for influence when they had visualized the shooter's success than when they had not.

Self-Handicapping   "My dog ate my homework." "I had a flat tire." "My alarm didn't go off." "My computer crashed." "I had a bad headache." "The referee blew the call." On occasion, people make excuses for their past performance. Sometimes they even come up with excuses in anticipation of future performance. Particularly when people are afraid that they might fail in an important situation, they use illness, shyness, anxiety, pain, trauma, and other complaints as excuses (Kowalski, 1996; Snyder & Higgins, 1988). The reason people do this is simple: By admitting to a limited physical or mental weakness, they can shield themselves from what could be the most shattering implication of failure—a lack of ability.

One form of excuse-making that many of us can relate to is *procrastination*—a purposive delay in starting or completing a task that is due at a particular time (Ferrari et al., 1995). Some people procrastinate chronically, while others do so only in certain situations. There are many reasons why someone might put off what needs to get done—whether it's studying for a test, shopping for Christmas, or preparing for the April 15 tax deadline. According to Joseph Ferrari (1998), one "benefit" of procrastinating is that it helps to provide an excuse for possible failure.

Making verbal excuses is one way to cope with the threatening implications of failure. Under certain conditions, this strategy is taken one step further, as when people actually sabotage their own performance. It seems like the ultimate paradox, but there are times when we purposely set ourselves up for failure in order to preserve our precious self-esteem. As first described by Stephen Berglas and Edward Jones (1978), **self-handicapping** refers to actions people take to handicap their own performance in order to build an excuse for anticipated failure. To demonstrate, Berglas and Jones recruited college students for an experiment supposedly concerning the effects of drugs on intellectual performance. All the participants worked on a 20-item test of analogies and were told that they had done well, after which they expected to work on a second, similar test. For one group, the problems in the first test were relatively easy, leading participants to expect more success in the second test; for a second group, the problems were insoluble, leaving participants confused about their initial success and worried about possible failure. Before seeing or taking the second test, partici-

self-handicapping   Behaviors designed to sabotage one's own performance in order to provide a subsequent excuse for failure.

pants were given a choice of two drugs: Actavil, which was supposed to improve performance, and Pandocrin, which was supposed to impair it.

Although no drugs were actually administered, most participants who were confident about the upcoming test selected the Actavil. In contrast, most males (but not females) who feared the outcome of the second test chose the Pandocrin. By handicapping themselves, these men set up a convenient excuse for failure—an excuse, we should add, that may have been intended more for the experimenter's benefit than for the benefit of the participants themselves. Indeed, a follow-up study showed that although self-handicapping occurs when the experimenter witnesses the participants' drug choice, it is reduced when the experimenter is not present while that choice is being made (Kolditz & Arkin, 1982).

Some people use self-handicapping as a defense more than others do (Rhodewalt, 1990), and there are different ways to use it. For example, some men self-handicap by taking drugs (Higgins & Harris, 1988) or neglecting to practice (Hirt et al., 1991), while women tend to report stress and physical symptoms (Smith et al., 1983). Another tactic is to set one's goals too high, as perfectionists like to do, which sets up failure that would not be interpreted to reflect a lack of ability (Hewitt et al., 2003). Yet another paradoxical tactic used to reduce performance pressure is for people to play down their own ability, lower expectations, and publicly predict that they will fail—a self-presentation strategy known as "sandbagging" (Gibson & Sachau, 2000). People also differ in their reasons for self-handicapping. Dianne Tice (1991) found that people who are low in self-esteem use self-handicapping to set up a defensive, face-saving excuse in case they fail, while those who are high in self-esteem use it as an opportunity to claim extra credit if they succeed.

Whatever the tactics and whatever the goal, self-handicapping appears to be an ingenious strategy: With the odds seemingly stacked against us, the self is insulated from failure and enhanced by success. By easing the pressure to succeed, self-handicapping might even enable us to enjoy what we're doing without worrying so much about how well we do it (Deppe & Harackiewicz, 1996). Of course, this strategy is not without a cost. Sabotaging ourselves—by not practicing or by drinking too much, using drugs, faking illness, or setting goals too high—objectively increases the risk of failure. What's worse, it does not exactly endear us to others. Frederick Rhodewalt and his colleagues (1995) found that participants did not like their partners in an experiment when they thought that these partners had self-handicapped by claiming they did not care, were anxious, or were medically impaired. Women in particular are suspicious and critical of people who self-handicap (Hirt et al., 2003).

People often sabotage their own performance in order to protect their self-esteem. **TRUE.**

Basking in the Glory of Others   To some extent, your self-esteem is influenced by individuals and groups with whom you identify. According to Robert Cialdini and his colleagues (1976), people often **bask in reflected glory (BIRG)** by showing off their connections to successful others. Cialdini's team first observed BIRGing on the university campuses of Arizona State, Louisiana State, Notre Dame, Michigan, Pittsburgh, Ohio State, and Southern California. On the Monday mornings after football games, they counted the number of school sweatshirts worn on campus and found that more of them were worn if the team had won its game on the previous Saturday. In fact, the larger the margin of victory was, the more school shirts they counted.

To evaluate the effects of self-esteem on BIRGing, Cialdini gave students a general-knowledge test and rigged the results so half would succeed and half would fail. The students were then asked to describe in their own words the outcome of a recent football game. In these descriptions, students who thought they had just failed a test were more likely than those who thought they had succeeded to share in their team's victory by exclaiming that "we won" and to distance themselves from defeat by lamenting

bask in reflected glory (BIRG) To increase self-esteem by associating with others who are successful.

how "*they* lost." In another study, participants coming off a recent failure were quick to point out that they had the same birth date as someone known to be successful—thus BIRGing by a merely coincidental association (Cialdini & De Nicholas, 1989).

If self-esteem is influenced by our links to others, how do we cope with friends, family members, teammates, and co-workers of low status? Again, consider sports fans, an interesting breed. They loudly cheer their team in victory, but they often turn and jeer their team in defeat. This behavior seems fickle, but it is consistent with the notion that people derive part of their self-esteem from associations with others. In one study, participants took part in a problem-solving team that then succeeded, failed, or received no feedback about its performance. Participants were later offered a chance to take home a team badge. In the success and no-feedback groups, 68 and 50 percent, respectively, took badges; in the failure group, only 9 percent did (Snyder et al., 1986). It seems that the tendency to bask in reflected glory is matched by an equally powerful tendency to CORF—that is, to cut off reflected failure.

Additional research confirms that the failures of others with whom we identify can influence our own sense of well-being. Edward Hirt and others (1992) found that avid sports fans temporarily lost faith in their own mental and social abilities after a favorite team suffered defeat. Reflected failure may even have physiological effects on the body. Paul Bernhardt and others (1998) took saliva samples from male college students before and after they watched a basketball or soccer game between their favorite team and an archrival. By measuring changes in testosterone levels after the game, these investigators found that men who witnessed their team in defeat had lowered levels of testosterone, the male sex hormone, compare to those who had watched their team win.

© J. L. Atlan/CORBIS SYGMA

When Vietnam veterans returned in defeat more than 25 years ago, they were neglected, even scorned, by the American public. It seems that the tendency to bask in reflected glory is matched by an equally powerful need to cut off reflected failure.

Downward Social Comparisons   Earlier, we discussed Festinger's (1954) theory that people evaluate themselves by social comparison with similar others. But contemplate the implications. If the people around us achieve more than we do, what does that do to our self-esteem? Perhaps adults who shy away from class reunions in order to avoid having to compare themselves with former classmates are acting out an answer to that question.

Festinger fully realized that people don't always seek out objective information and that social comparisons are sometimes made in self-defense. When a person's self-esteem is at stake, he or she often benefits from making **downward social comparisons** with others who are less successful, less happy, or less fortunate (Hakmiller, 1966; Wills, 1981; Wood, 1989). Research shows that people who suffer some form of setback or failure adjust their social comparisons in a downward direction (Gibbons et al., 2002) and that these comparisons have an uplifting effect on their mood and on their outlook for the future (Aspinwall & Taylor, 1993; Gibbons & McCoy, 1991).

Although Festinger never addressed the issue, Anne Wilson and Michael Ross (2000) note that in addition to making social comparisons between ourselves and similar others, we make *temporal* comparisons between our past and present selves.

downward social comparison The defensive tendency to compare ourselves with others who are worse off than we are.

In one study, these investigators had college students describe themselves; in another, they analyzed the autobiographical accounts of celebrities appearing in popular magazines. In both cases, they counted the number of times the self-descriptions contained references to past selves, to future selves, and to others. The result was that people made more comparisons to their own past selves than to others, and most of these temporal comparisons were favorable. Other research has confirmed the basic point. Keenly aware of how "I'm better today than when I was in the past," people use downward temporal comparisons the way they use downward social comparisons as a means of self-enhancement (Zell & Alicke, 2009).

Whether people make upward or downward social comparisons can have striking health implications. When victimized by tragic life events (perhaps a crime, an accident, a disease, or the death of a loved one), people like to *affiliate* with others in the same predicament who have adjusted well, role models who offer hope and guidance. But they tend to *compare* themselves with others who are worse off, a form of downward social comparison (Taylor & Lobel, 1989).

Clearly it helps to know that life could be worse, which is why most cancer patients tend to compare themselves with others in the same predicament but who are adjusting less well than they are. In a study of 312 women who had early-stage breast cancer and were in peer support groups, Laura Bogart and Vicki Helgeson (2000) had the patients report every week for seven weeks on instances in which they talked to, heard about, or thought about another patient. They found that 53 percent of all the social comparisons made were downward, to others who were worse off, while only 12 percent were upward, to others who were better off (the rest were "lateral" comparisons to similar or dissimilar others). Bogart and Helgeson also found that the more often patients made these social comparisons, the better they felt. Downward social comparison is also associated with an ability to cope with the kinds of life regrets that often haunt people as they get older. Adult development researchers have observed that aging adults often experience intense feelings of regret over decisions made, contacts lost, opportunities passed up, and the like—and these regrets can compromise the quality of their lives. Isabelle Bauer and others (2008) asked adults ranging from 18 to 83 years old to disclose their biggest regret and then indicate whether their same-age peers had regrets that were more or less severe. Among the older adults in the sample, those who tended to see others as having more severe regrets than their own felt better than those who saw their others as less regretful.

Unfortunately, it's not always possible to defend the self via downward social comparison. Think about it. When a sibling, spouse, or close friend has more success than you do, what happens to your self-esteem? Abraham Tesser (1988) predicted two possible reactions. On the one hand, you might feel proud of your association with this successful other, as in the process of basking in reflected glory. If you've ever bragged about the achievements of a loved one as if they were your own, you know how "reflection" can bolster self-esteem. On the other hand, you may feel overshadowed by the success of this other person and experience social comparison jealousy—a mixture of emotions that include resentment, envy, and a drop in self-esteem. According to Tesser, the key to whether one feels the pleasure of reflection or the pain of jealousy is whether the other person's success is self-relevant. When close friends surpass us in ways that are vital to our self-concepts, we become jealous and distance ourselves from them in order to keep up our own self-esteem. When intimate others surpass us in ways that are not important, however, we take pride in their triumphs through a process of reflection (Tesser & Collins, 1988; Tesser et al., 1989).

Personal and cultural factors may also influence the way people react to the success of others. For some people—as in those from collectivist cultures, whose concept of self is expanded to include friends, relatives, co-workers, classmates, and others with whom they identify—the success of another may bolster, not threaten, self-esteem. To test this hypothesis, Wendi Gardner and others (2002) brought pairs of friends into the laboratory together for a problem-solving task. They found that when they led the friends to think in collectivist terms, each derived pleasure, not jealousy and threat, from the other's greater success.

▌▌ Are Positive Illusions Adaptive?

Psychologists used to maintain that an accurate perception of reality is vital to mental health. In recent years, however, this view has been challenged by research on the mechanisms of self-defense. Consistently, as we have seen, people preserve their self-esteem by deluding themselves and others with biased cognitions, self-handicapping, BIRGing, and downward comparisons. Are these strategies a sign of health and well-being or are they symptoms of disorder?

When Shelley Taylor and Jonathon Brown (1988) first reviewed the research, they found that individuals who are depressed or low in self-esteem actually have more realistic views of themselves than do most others who are better adjusted. Their self-appraisals are more likely to match appraisals of them made by neutral observers, they make fewer self-serving attributions to account for success and failure, they are less likely to exaggerate their control over uncontrollable events, and they make more balanced predictions about their future. Based on these results, Taylor and Brown reached the provocative conclusion that positive illusions promote happiness, the desire to care for others, and the ability to engage in productive work—hallmark attributes of mental health: "These illusions help make each individual's world a warmer and more active and beneficent place in which to live" (p. 205). People with high self-esteem thus appear to be better adjusted in personality tests and in interviews rated by friends, strangers, and mental health professionals (Taylor et al., 2003).

Not everyone agrees with the notion that it is adaptive in the long run to wear rose-colored glasses. Roy Baumeister and Steven Scher (1988) immediately warned that positive illusions can give rise to chronic patterns of self-defeating behavior, as when people escape from self-awareness through alcohol and other drugs, self-handicap themselves into failure and underachievement, deny health-related problems until it's too late for treatment, and rely on the illusion of control to protect them from the inescapable odds of the gambling casino. Others have similarly noted that people sometimes need to be self-critical in order to improve. In a study on success and failure feedback, Heine and others (2001) found that whereas North American college students persisted less on a task after an initial failure than after success, Japanese students persisted more in this situation. Sometimes we have to face up to our shortcomings in order to correct them.

From an interpersonal standpoint, C. Randall Colvin and others (1995) found that people with inflated rather than realistic views of themselves were rated less favorably on certain dimensions by their own friends. In their studies, self-enhancing men were seen as boastful, condescending, hostile, and less considerate of others; self-enhancing women were seen as more hostile, more defensive and sensitive to criticism, more likely to overreact to minor setbacks, and less well liked. People with inflated self-images may make a good first impression on others, but they are liked less and less as time wears on (Paulhus, 1998).

In a study that illustrates this possible dark side of high self-esteem, Todd Heatherton and Kathleen Vohs (2000) administered a self-esteem test to pairs of unacquainted college students and then brought them together for a brief conversation. Just before meeting, one student within each pair took a "Remote Associates Test," which involved finding one word that connects sets of three seemingly unrelated words (for example, *lick*, *sprinkle*, and *mines* were linked by the word *salt*). For half of these target students, the test was pitched as experimental and the problems given to them were easy to solve. Others were told that the test measured achievement potential and were given very difficult problems, leading them to perform, supposedly, worse than average. Did this ego-threatening feedback affect the students' behavior—and the impressions they made on their interaction partners? In the no-ego-threat group, the high and low self-esteem students were equally well liked. In the ego-threat situation, however, students with high self-esteem became less likable; in fact, they were rated by their partners as rude, unfriendly, and arrogant.

Realism or illusion—which orientation is more adaptive? As social psychologists debate the short-term and long-term effects of positive illusions, it's clear that there is no simple answer. For now, the picture that has emerged is this: People who harbor positive illusions of themselves are likely to enjoy the benefits and achievements of high self-esteem. But these same individuals may pay a price in other ways, as in their relations with others. So what are we to conclude? Do positive illusions motivate personal achievement but alienate us socially from others? Is it adaptive to see oneself in slightly inflated terms but maladaptive to take a view that is too biased? It will be interesting to see how this thorny debate is resolved in the years to come.

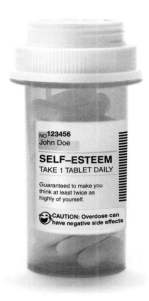

Burazin/Getty Images

Culture and Self-Esteem

Earlier we saw that inhabitants of individualistic cultures tend to view themselves as distinct and autonomous, whereas those in collectivist cultures view the self as part of an interdependent social network. Do these different orientations have implications for self-esteem? This turns out to be a tricky question.

Steven Heine and his colleagues (1999) have argued that cultures have differing effects on the pursuit of self-esteem. Comparing the distribution of self-esteem test scores in Canada and Japan, they found that whereas most Canadians' scores clustered in the high-end range, the majority of Japanese respondents scored in the center of that same range. In other studies, they also observed that Japanese respondents can sometimes be quite self-critical, talking about themselves in negative, self-effacing terms.

Do Japanese people really have a less positive self-esteem compared to North Americans? Or do Japanese respondents have positive self-esteem and simply feel compelled to present themselves modestly *to others* (as a function of the collectivist need to "fit in" rather than "stand out")? To answer this question, some researchers have tried to develop indirect, subtle, "implicit" tests of self esteem—tests that would enable them to measure a person's self-esteem without his or her awareness. In a timed word-association study, researchers found that despite their lower scores on overt self-esteem tests, Asian Americans—just like their European American counterparts—are quicker to associate themselves with positive words like *happy* and *sunshine* than with negative words such as *vomit* and *poison* (Greenwald & Farnham, 2000; Kitayama & Uchida, 2003). In keeping with the Eastern dialectical perspective described earlier, other implicit self-esteem research has shown that while East Asians, like Westerners, are quick to associate the self with positive traits, they are more likely to associate the self with contradictory negative traits as well (Boucher et al., 2009).

Drawing on these results, Constantine Sedikides and his colleagues (2003) maintain that people from individualist and collectivist cultures are similarly motivated to think highly of themselves—that the burning need for positive self-regard is universal, or "pancultural." The observed differences, they argue, stem from the fact that cultures influence *how* we seek to fulfill that need: Individualists present themselves as unique and self-confident, while collectivists present themselves as modest, equal members of a group. From this perspective, people are tactical in their self-enhancements, exhibiting self-praise or humility depending on what is desirable within their cultural surroundings (J. D. Brown, 2003; Lalwani et al., 2006; Sedikides et al., 2005).

Heine and his colleagues agree only in part with this interpretation of the research. They too argue that all people have a need for positive self-regard, wanting to become "good selves" within their own culture. They note, however, that in the effort to achieve this goal, Westerners and other individualists tend to use self-enhancement tactics to stand out, confirm, and express themselves, while East Asians and other collectivists tend to maintain face in order to fit in, improve the self, and adjust to the standards set by their groups. In short, the basic need for positive self-regard is universal but the specific drive toward self-enhancement is culturally ingrained (Heine, 2005; Heine & Hamamura, 2007).

Self-Presentation

Chris Jackson/Getty Images

These days, people self-consciously present a public self to others on Facebook and other online social networking sites.

The human quest for self-knowledge and self-esteem tells us about the inner self. The portrait is not complete, however, until we paint in the outermost layer, the behavioral expression of the social self. Most people are acutely concerned about the image they present to others. The fashion industry, diet centers, cosmetic surgeries designed to reshape everything from eyelids to breasts, and the endless search for miracle drugs that grow hair, remove hair, whiten teeth, freshen breath, and smooth out wrinkles all exploit our preoccupation with physical appearance. Similarly, we are concerned about the impressions we convey through our public behavior, not only in person, but on Facebook, MySpace, and other social networking sites.

Thomas Gilovich and others (2000) found that people are so self-conscious in public settings that they are often subject to the *spotlight effect*, a tendency to believe that the social spotlight shines more brightly on them than it really does. In one set of studies, participants were asked to wear a T-shirt with a flattering or embarrassing image into a room full of strangers, after which they estimated how many of those strangers would be able to identify the image. Demonstrating that people self-consciously feel as if all eyes are upon them, the T-shirted participants overestimated by 23–40 percent the number of observers who had noticed and could recall what they were wearing. Follow-up studies have similarly shown that when people commit a public social blunder, they later overestimate the negative impact of their behavior on those who had observed them (Savitsky et al., 2001).

In *As You Like It*, William Shakespeare wrote, "All the world's a stage, and all the men and women merely players." This insight was first put into social science terms by sociologist Erving Goffman (1959), who argued that life is like a theater and that each of us acts out certain *lines*, as if from a script. Most important, said Goffman, is that each of us assumes a certain *face*, or social identity, that others politely help us maintain. Inspired by Goffman's theory, social psychologists study **self-presentation**: the process by which we try to shape what other people think of us and what we think of ourselves (Schlenker, 2003). An act of self-presentation may take many different forms. It may be conscious or unconscious, accurate or misleading, or intended for an external audience or for ourselves. In this section, we look at the various goals of self-presentation and the ways that people try to achieve these goals.

Strategic Self-Presentation

There are basically two types of self-presentation, each serving a different motive. *Strategic self-presentation* consists of our efforts to shape others' impressions in specific ways in order to gain influence, power, sympathy, or approval. Prominent examples of strategic self-presentation are everywhere: in personal ads, in online message boards, in political campaign promises, in defendants' appeals to the jury. The specific goals vary and include the desire to be seen as likable, competent, moral, dangerous, or helpless. Whatever the goal may be, people find it less effortful to present themselves in ways that are accurate rather than contrived (Vohs et al., 2005).

To illustrate this point, Beth Pontari and Barry Schlenker (2000) instructed research participants who tested as introverted or extroverted to present themselves to a job interviewer in a way that was consistent or inconsistent with their true personality. Without distraction, all participants successfully presented themselves as introverted or extroverted, depending on the task they were given. But could they present themselves as needed if, during the interview, they also had to keep an eight-digit number in mind for a memorization test? In this situation, cognitively busy participants self-presented successfully when asked to convey their true personalities but not when asked to portray themselves in a way that was out of character.

The specific identities that people try to present may vary from one person and situation to another. However, two strategic self-presentation goals are very common. The first is *ingratiation*, a term used to describe acts that are motivated by the

TABLE 3.2
Strategic Self-Presentation in the Employment Interview
In studies of the influence tactics that job applicants report using in employment interviews, the following uses of ingratiation and self-promotion were commonly reported.
Ingratiation
▨ I complimented the interviewer or organization.
▨ I discussed interests I shared in common with the recruiter.
▨ I indicated my interest in the position and the company.
▨ I indicated my enthusiasm for working for this organization.
▨ I smiled a lot or used other friendly nonverbal behaviors.
Self- Promotion
▨ I played up the value of positive events that I took credit for.
▨ I described my skills and abilities in an attractive way.
▨ I took charge during the interview to get my main points across.
▨ I took credit for positive events even if I was not solely responsible.
▨ I made positive events I was responsible for appear better than they actually were.
Higgins & Judge, 2004; Stevens & Kristof, 1995.

desire to "get along" with others and be liked. The other is *self-promotion*, a term used to describe acts that are motivated by a desire to "get ahead" and gain respect for one's competence (Arkin, 1981; Jones & Pittman, 1982). As shown in Table 3.2, observations of employment interviews reveal that ingratiation and self-promotion are the most common self-presentation tactics that job applicants use (Stevens & Kristof, 1995) and that these tactics lead recruiters to form positive impressions (Higgins & Judge, 2004).

On the surface, it seems easy to achieve these goals. When people want to be liked, they put their best foot forward, smile a lot, nod their heads, express agreement, and,

self-presentation Strategies people use to shape what others think of them.

"Great-looking tie!"

Ingratiation is a strategy often used to curry favor.

if necessary, use favors, compliments, and flattery. When people want to be admired for their competence, they try to impress others by talking about themselves and immodestly showing off their status, knowledge, and exploits. In both cases, there are trade-offs. As the term brown-nosing graphically suggests, ingratiation tactics need to be subtle or else they will backfire (Jones, 1964). People also do not like those who relentlessly trumpet and brag about their own achievements (Godfrey et al., 1986) or who exhibit a "slimy" pattern of being friendly to their superiors but not to subordinates (Vonk, 1998).

Self-presentation may give rise to other problems as well. Suggesting that "Self-Presentation Can Be Hazardous to Your Health," Mark Leary and his colleagues (1994) reviewed evidence suggesting that the need to project a favorable public image can lure us into unsafe patterns of behavior. For example, self-presentation concerns can increase the risk of AIDS (as when men are too embarrassed to buy condoms and talk openly with their sex partners), skin cancer (as when people bake under the sun to get an attractive tan), eating disorders (as when women over-diet or use amphetamines, laxatives, and forced vomiting to stay thin), drug abuse (as when teenagers smoke, drink, and use drugs to impress their peers), and accidental injury (as when young men drive recklessly to look fearless to others).

■ Self-Verification

In contrast to strategic self-presentation is a second motive, *self-verification*: the desire to have others perceive us as we truly perceive ourselves. According to William Swann (1987), people are highly motivated in their social encounters to confirm or verify their existing self-concept in the eyes of others. Swann and his colleagues have gathered a great deal of evidence for this hypothesis and have found, for example, that people selectively elicit, recall, and accept personality feedback that confirms their self-conceptions. In fact, people sometimes bend over backward to correct others whose impressions are positive but mistaken. In one study, participants interacted with a confederate who later said that they seemed dominant or submissive. When the comment was consistent with the participant's self-concept, it was accepted at face value. Yet when it was inconsistent, participants went out of their way to prove the confederate wrong: Those who perceived themselves as dominant but were labeled submissive later behaved more assertively than usual; those who viewed themselves as submissive but were labeled dominant subsequently became even more docile (Swann & Hill, 1982).

Self-verification seems desirable, but wait: Do people who harbor a negative self-concept want others to share that impression? Nobody is perfect, and everyone has some faults. But do we really want to verify these faults in the eyes of others? Do those of us who feel painfully shy, socially awkward, or insecure about an ability want others to see these weaknesses? Or would we prefer to present ourselves in public as bold, graceful, or competent? What happens when the desire for self-verification clashes with the need for self-enhancement?

Seeking to answer this question, Swann and his colleagues (1992) asked each student participant in a laboratory study to fill out a self-concept questionnaire and then choose an interaction partner from two other participants—one who supposedly had evaluated them favorably and a second who had supposedly evaluated them unfavorably. The result? Although participants with a positive self-concept chose partners who viewed them in a positive light, a majority of those with a negative self-concept preferred partners who confirmed their admitted shortcomings. In a later study, 64 percent of participants with low self-esteem (compared with only 25 percent of those with high self-esteem) sought clinical feedback about their weaknesses rather than strengths when given a choice (Giesler et al., 1996). Indeed, research suggests that people also prefer to interact with others who verify their group memberships, an aspect of their collective self (Chen et al., 2004).

"I don't want to be defined by who I am."

People often distinguish between their public and private self. However, research on self-verification suggests that this cartoon is wrong—that people do want to be defined by who they are.

If people seek self-verification from laboratory partners, it stands to reason that they would want the same from their close relationships. In a study of married couples, husbands and wives separately answered questions about their self-concepts, their spouse, and their commitment to the marriage. As predicted, people who had a positive self-concept expressed more commitment to partners who appraised them favorably, while those with a negative self-concept felt more committed to partners who appraised them unfavorably (Swann, Hixon, and De La Ronde, 1992).

On important aspects of the self-concept, research shows that people would rather reflect on and learn more about their positive qualities than negative ones (Sedikides, 1993). Still, it appears that the desire for self-verification is powerful and can even, at times, trump the need for self-enhancement. We all want to make a good impression, but we also want others in our lives to have an accurate impression, one that is compatible with our own self-concept (Swann, 1999).

Individual Differences in Self-Monitoring

Although self-presentation is a way of life for all of us, it differs considerably among individuals. Some people are generally more conscious of their public image than others. Also, some people are more likely to engage in strategic self-presentation, while others seem to prefer self-verification. According to Mark Snyder (1987), these differences are related to a personality trait he called **self-monitoring**: the tendency to regulate one's own behavior to meet the demands of social situations.

Individuals who are high in self-monitoring appear to have a repertoire of selves from which to draw. Sensitive to strategic self-presentation concerns, they are poised, ready, and able to modify their behavior as they move from one setting to another. As measured by the Self-Monitoring Scale (Snyder, 1974; Snyder & Gangestad, 1986), they are likely to agree with such statements as "I would probably make a good actor" and "In different situations and with different people, I often act like very different persons." In contrast, low self-monitors are self-verifiers by nature, appearing less concerned about the propriety of their behavior. Like character actors always cast

self-monitoring   The tendency to change behavior in response to the self-presentation concerns of the situation.

TABLE 3.3

Self-Monitoring Scale

Are you a high or low self-monitor? For each statement, answer True or False. When you are done, give yourself one point if you answered T to items 4, 5, 6, 8, 10, 12, 17, and 18. Then give yourself one point if you answered F to items 1, 2, 3, 7, 9, 11, 13, 14, 15, and 16. Count your total number of points. This total represents your Self-Monitoring Score. Among North American college students, the average score is about 10 or 11.

1. I find it hard to imitate the behavior of other people.
2. At parties and social gatherings, I do not attempt to do or say things that others will like.
3. I can only argue for ideas which I already believe.
4. I can make impromptu speeches even on topics about which I have almost no information.
5. I guess I put on a show to impress or entertain others.
6. I would probably make a good actor.
7. In a group of people I am rarely the center of attention.
8. In different situations and with different people, I often act like very different persons.
9. I am not particularly good at making other people like me.
10. I'm not always the person I appear to be.
11. I would not change my opinions (or the way I do things) in order to please someone or win their favor.
12. I have considered being an entertainer.
13. I have never been good at games like charades or improvisational acting.
14. I have trouble changing my behavior to suit different people and different situations.
15. At a party I let others keep the jokes and stories going.
16. I feel a bit awkward in company and do not show up quite as well as I should.
17. I can look anyone in the eye and tell a lie with a straight face (if for a right end).
18. I may deceive people by being friendly when I really dislike them.

Snyder & Gangestad, 1986.

It's more adaptive to alter one's behavior than to stay consistent from one social situation to the next. **FALSE.**

in the same role, they express themselves in a consistent manner from one situation to the next, exhibiting what they regard as their true and honest self. On the Self-Monitoring Scale, low self-monitors say that "I can only argue for ideas which I already believe" and "I have never been good at games like charades or improvisational acting" (see Table 3.3).

Social psychologists disagree on whether the Self-Monitoring Scale measures one global trait or a combination of two or more specific traits. They also disagree about whether high and low self-monitors represent two discrete types of people or just points along a continuum. Either way, the test scores do appear to predict important social behaviors (Gangestad & Snyder, 2000).

Concerned with public image, high self-monitors go out of their way to learn about others with whom they might interact and about the rules for appropriate conduct. Then, once they have the situation sized up, they modify their behavior accordingly. If a situation calls for conformity, high self-monitors conform; if the same situation calls for autonomy, they refuse to conform. Unconsciously adapting to social situations, high self-monitors are likely to mimic the demeanor of others in subtle ways that facilitate smooth social interactions (Cheng & Chartrand, 2003). By contrast, low self-monitors maintain a relatively consistent posture across a range of situations (Snyder & Monson, 1975). As they are highly attuned to their own inner dispositions, low self-monitors may adjust their behavior in response to feedback about their own characteristics (DeMarree et al., 2005). Consistent with the finding that high self-monitors are more concerned than lows about what *other people* think of them, research conducted in work settings shows that high self-monitors receive higher performance ratings and more promotions and that they are more likely to emerge as leaders (Day et al., 2002).

In the coming chapters, we will see that because so much of our behavior is influenced by social norms, self-monitoring is relevant to many aspects of social psychology. There are also interesting developmental implications. A survey of 18- to 73-year-olds revealed that self-monitoring scores tend to drop with age, presumably because people become more settled and secure about their personal identities as they get older (Reifman et al., 1989). For now, however, ponder this question: Is it better to be a high or low self-monitor? Is one orientation inherently more adaptive than the other?

The existing research does not enable us to make this kind of value judgment. Consider high self-monitors. Quite accurately, they regard themselves as *pragmatic*, flexible, and adaptive and as able to cope with the diversity of life's roles. But they could also be described as fickle or phony opportunists, more concerned with appearances than with reality and willing to change colors like a chameleon just to fit in. Now think about low self-monitors. They describe themselves as *principled* and forthright; they are without pretense, always speaking their minds so others know where they stand. Of course, they could also be viewed as stubborn, insensitive to their surroundings, and unwilling to compromise in order to get along. Concerning the relative value of these two orientations, then, it is safe to conclude that neither high nor low self-monitoring is necessarily undesirable—unless carried to the extreme. Goffman (1955) made the same point many years ago, when he wrote:

> Too little perceptiveness, too little savoir faire, too little pride and considerateness, and the person ceases to be someone who can be trusted to take a hint about himself or give a hint that will save others embarrassment. . . . Too much savoir faire or too much considerateness and he becomes someone who is too socialized, who leaves others with the feeling that they do not know how they really stand with him, nor what they should do to make an effective long-term adjustment. (p. 227)

Epilogue: The Multifaceted Self

Throughout human history, writers, poets, philosophers, and personality theorists have portrayed the self as an enduring aspect of personality, as an invisible "inner core" that is stable over time and slow to change. The struggle to find your "true self" is based on this portrait. Indeed, when people over 85 years old were asked to reflect on their lives, almost all said that despite having changed in certain ways, they had remained essentially the same person (Troll & Skaff, 1997). In recent years, however, social psychologists have focused on change. In doing so, they have discovered that at least part of the self is malleable—molded by life experiences and varying from one situation to the next. From this perspective, the self has many different faces.

When you look into the mirror, what do you see, one self or many? Do you see a person whose self-concept is enduring or one whose identity seems to change from time to time? Do you see a person whose strengths and weaknesses are evaluated with an objective eye or one who is insulated from unpleasant truths by mechanisms of self-defense? Do you see a person who has an inner, hidden self that is different from the face shown to others?

Based on the material presented in this chapter, the answer to such questions seems always to be the same: The self has all these characteristics. More than a hundred years ago, William James (1890) said that the self is not simple but complex and multifaceted. Based on current theories and research, we can now appreciate just how right James was. Sure, there's an aspect of the self-concept that we can come to know only through introspection and that is stable over time. But there's also an aspect that changes with the company we keep and the information we get from others. When it comes to self-esteem, there are times when we are self-focused enough to become acutely aware of our short comings. Yet there are also times when we guard ourselves through self-serving cognitions, self-handicapping, BIRGing, and downward social comparisons. Then there is the matter of self-presentation. It's clear that each of us has a private self that consists of our inner thoughts, feelings, and memories. But it is equally clear that we also have an outer self, portrayed by the roles we play and the masks we wear in public. As you read through the pages of this text, you will see that the cognitive, affective, and behavioral components of the self are not separate and distinct but interrelated. They are also of great significance for the rest of social psychology.

REVIEW

The Self-Concept

- The self-concept is the sum total of a person's beliefs about his or her own attributes. It is the cognitive component of the self.

Rudiments of the Self-Concept

- Using brain scans, social neuroscientists find that certain areas become relatively more active when people process self-relevant information.
- Recognizing oneself as a distinct entity is the first step in the development of a self-concept.
- Human beings and apes are the only animals to recognize their mirror-image reflections as their own.
- Cooley's "looking-glass" self suggests that social factors are a necessary second step.

Introspection

- People believe that introspection is a key to knowing the true self.
- But research shows that introspection sometimes diminishes the accuracy of self-reports.
- People also tend to overestimate their emotional reactions to future positive and negative events.

Perceptions of Our Own Behavior

- Bem's self-perception theory holds that when internal states are difficult to interpret, we infer our inner states by observing our own behavior and the surrounding situation.
- Based on self-perception theory, the facial feedback hypothesis states that facial expressions can produce—not just reflect—an emotion state (smiling can cause us to feel happy).
- But it's unclear if the emotion occurs via self-perception or because facial expressions trigger physiological changes that produce the emotional response.
- Also derived from self-perception theory, the overjustification effect shows that people sometimes lose interest in activities for which they were rewarded.

- But if a reward is seen as a "bonus" for superior performance, then it can enhance intrinsic motivation by providing positive feedback.

Influences of Other People

- According to social comparison theory, people often evaluate their own opinions and abilities by comparing themselves to similar others.
- Schachter and Singer proposed that the experience of emotion is based on two factors: physiological arousal and a cognitive label for that arousal.
- Under certain conditions, people interpret their own arousal by watching others in the same situation.

Autobiographical Memories

- Memory of one's life events is critical to the self-concept.
- When people recall life experiences, they typically report more events from the recent past than from the distant past, though some types of memories are generally more vivid and lasting than others.
- Autobiographical memories are shaped by self-serving motives, as people overemphasize their own roles in past events.

Culture and the Self-Concept

- Cultures foster different conceptions of self.
- Many Europeans and North Americans hold an independent view of the self that emphasizes autonomy.
- People in certain Asian, African, and Latin American cultures hold an interdependent view of the self that encompasses social connections.
- These cultural differences influence the way we perceive, feel about, and present ourselves in relation to others.

Self-Esteem

- Self-esteem refers to a person's positive and negative evaluations of the self.

The Need for Self-Esteem

- People have a need for high self-esteem and want to see themselves in a positive light.
- People with low self-esteem often find themselves caught in a vicious cycle of self-defeating behavior.

Are There Gender and Race Differences?

- Among adolescents and young adults, males have higher self-esteem than females do, though the difference is very small, particularly among older adults.
- African Americans outscore white Americans on self-esteem tests, indicating, perhaps, that stigmatized minorities focus on their positive attributes.

Self-Discrepancy Theory

- Self-esteem can be defined by the match between how we see ourselves and how we want to see ourselves. Large self-discrepancies are associated with negative emotional states.
- Discrepancies between the actual and ideal selves are related to feelings of disappointment and depression.
- Discrepancies between the actual and the ought selves are related to shame, guilt, and anxiety.
- These emotional effects depend on the amount of discrepancy and whether we are consciously focused on it.

The Self-Awareness "Trap"

- In general, people spend little time actually thinking about themselves.
- But certain situations (mirrors, cameras, audiences) increase self-awareness, and certain people are generally more self-conscious than others.
- Self-awareness forces us to notice self-discrepancies and can produce a temporary reduction in self-esteem.
- To cope, we either adjust our behavior to meet our standards or withdraw from the self-focusing situation.
- Heavy drinking can be viewed as a means of escaping from self-awareness.

Self-Regulation and Its Limits

- Requiring effort, self-control can temporarily be depleted by usage.
- This depletion effect can be reversed, enabling additional self-control, by the consumption of glucose and by self-affirmation.

Ironic Mental Processes

- Due to the operation of ironic processes, our efforts at self-control may also backfire, causing us to think, feel, and act in ways that are opposite to our intentions.
- Choking under pressure is an ironic phenomenon often seen in sports.

Mechanisms of Self-Enhancement

- Most people think highly of themselves and have unconscious positive associations with things related to the self.
- People protect their self-esteem in four major ways: through self-serving cognitions, such as taking credit for success and denying the blame for failure; self-handicapping, in order to excuse anticipated failure; basking in reflected glory, which boosts their self-esteem through associations with successful others; and downward social comparisons to others who are less well off.
- When others surpass us in ways that are important to us, we become jealous and distance ourselves from them. When surpassed in ways that are not self-relevant, we feel pride and seek closeness.

Are Positive Illusions Adaptive?

- Recent research suggests that certain positive illusions may foster high self-esteem and mental health.
- An alternative view is that such illusions promote self-defeating behavior patterns and that people with inflated views of themselves are liked less by others.

Culture and Self-Esteem

- Cross-cultural comparisons indicate that people from collectivist cultures present themselves as modest in their self-esteem relative to people from individualistic cultures.
- Researchers are seeking to determine whether collectivists have a less inflated self-esteem or simply feel compelled to present themselves modestly to others.
- Everyone has a need for positive self-regard; individualists and collectivists seek to fulfill that need in different ways.

Self-Presentation

- We care deeply about what others think of us and often believe that the social spotlight shines more brightly on us than it really does.
- Self-presentation is the process by which we try to shape what others think of us and even what we think of ourselves. There are two general motives in self-presentation: strategic self-presentation and self-verification.

Strategic Self-Presentation

- Strategic self-presentation is the process by which we try to shape others' impressions of us.
- In social encounters, people often try to get others to see them in a positive light, as likable or competent, for example.

Self-Verification

- Apart from the desire to be seen in a positive light, people seek self-verification, a process by which we try to get others to perceive us "accurately," as we see ourselves.
- Research shows that self-verification motives often trump the desire to be seen in a positive light.

Individual Differences in Self-Monitoring

- Individuals differ in their tendency to regulate their behavior to meet the demands of social situations.
- High self-monitors modify their behavior, as appropriate, from one situation to the next.
- Low self-monitors express themselves in a more consistent manner, exhibiting at all times what they see as their true self.

Epilogue: The Multifaceted Self

- As this chapter has shown, the self is not simple but complex and multifaceted.

Key Terms

affective forecasting (59)
bask in reflected glory (BIRG) (85)
dialecticism (71)
downward social comparisons (86)
facial feedback hypothesis (61)
implicit egotism (82)
overjustification effect (63)

private self-consciousness (78)
public self-consciousness (78)
self-awareness theory (76)
self-concept (56)
self-esteem (72)
self-handicapping (84)
self-monitoring (93)

self-perception theory (60)
self-presentation (91)
self-schemas (56)
social comparison theory (65)
Terror Management Theory (73)
two-factor theory of emotion (66)

Media Resources

Social Psychology 8th Edition Companion Website
Visit your book companion website
www.cengage.com/psychology/kassin
where you will find flash cards, practice quizzes, Internet links, and more to help you study.

CENGAGENOW Just what you need to know NOW! Spend time on what you need to master rather than on information you already have learned. Take a pre-test for this chapter and CengageNOW will generate a personalized study plan based on your results. The study plan will identify the topics you need to review and direct you to online resources to help you master those topics. You can then take a post-test to help you determine the concepts you have mastered and what you will need to work on. Try it out! Go to **academic .cengage.com/login** to sign in with an access code or to purchase access to this product.

Putting **COMMON SENSE** *to the Test*

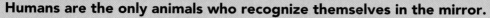

Humans are the only animals who recognize themselves in the mirror.

False. *Studies have shown that the great apes (chimpanzees, gorillas, and orangutans) are also capable of self-recognition.*

Smiling can make you feel happier.

True. *Consistent with the facial feedback hypothesis, facial expressions can trigger or amplify the subjective experience of emotion.*

Sometimes the harder you try to control a thought, feeling, or behavior, the less likely you are to succeed.

True. *Research on ironic processes in mental control have revealed that trying to inhibit a thought, feeling, or behavior often backfires.*

People often sabotage their own performance in order to protect their self-esteem.

True. *Studies have shown that people often handicap their own performance in order to build an excuse for anticipated failure.*

It's more adaptive to alter one's behavior than to stay consistent from one social situation to the next.

False. *High and low self-monitors differ in the extent to which they alter their behavior to suit the situation they are in, but neither style is inherently more adaptive.*

4

Perceiving Persons

This chapter examines how people come to know (or think that they know) other persons. First, we introduce the elements of social perception—those aspects of persons, situations, and behavior that guide initial observations. Next, we examine how people make explanations, or attributions, for the behavior of others and how they form integrated impressions based on initial perceptions and attributions. We then consider confirmation biases, the subtle ways that initial impressions lead people to distort later information, setting in motion a self-fulfilling prophecy.

Putting
COMMON SENSE
to the Test

Circle Your Answer

T	F	The impressions we form of others are influenced by superficial aspects of their appearance.
T	F	Adaptively, people are skilled at knowing when someone is lying rather than telling the truth.
T	F	Like social psychologists, people are sensitive to situational causes when explaining the behavior of others.
T	F	People are slow to change their first impressions on the basis of new information.
T	F	The notion that we can create a "self-fulfilling prophecy" by getting others to behave in ways we expect is a myth.
T	F	People are more accurate at judging the personalities of friends and acquaintances than of strangers.

On July 9, 2006, in front of the 66,000 flag-draped, face-painted fans who filled Olympic Stadium in Berlin, Italy and France squared off for the World Cup soccer final. To get to this point, Italy had most recently defeated Australia, Ukraine, and Germany; France had beaten Spain, Brazil, and Portugal. Tied 1-1 and in overtime, the coveted World Cup championship was still in doubt. Suddenly, France's Zinedine Zidane, voted the most valuable player of the tournament, lowered his head and rammed Italy's Marco Materazzi in the chest, knocking him to the ground. Zidane was ejected from the game, and Italy won on penalty kicks. Why did Zidane head-butt his opponent at this time? Does he have a violent streak he cannot control? Was he overly aroused by the competition and frustrated by Italy's defense? Was he provoked by something Materazzi said? Sports fans wanted to know: What caused this World Cup soccer star to erupt?

Two years later, in the fall of 2008, former NASDAQ chairman Bernie Madoff was arrested for running an elaborate $50 billion Ponzi scheme that fooled and claimed more than 14,000 individual and institutional victims. It was the largest fraud of its kind ever, completely draining individual fortunes and retirement nest eggs, destroying charitable foundations, and even pushing one investor to commit suicide. The 70-year-old Madoff had first started this scheme many years ago. Yet remarkably, despite servicing an elite group of clients who were intelligent and motivated by their high-stakes investments, Madoff demonstrated what research to be described later has shown: that people are notoriously inept at distinguishing truths and lies. Why did Madoff, a respected financial leader and millionaire, perpetrate this fraud? Was he a narcissist, or what clinical psychologists would call a "white-collar psychopath" who harms others with calloused and vicious indifference? Or were his actions triggered by life circumstances? Is it possible that once he started, Madoff was unable to stop, having put himself into a gradually escalating trap from which he could not escape without punishment? Whatever the explanation, Madoff was sentenced for his offenses to 150 years in prison.

In the World Cup soccer final of 2006, France's Zinedine Zidane head-butted Italy's Marco Materazzi. Zidane was ejected from the game and Italy went on to win the championship. What caused Zidane to erupt? Is he a violent person by nature, was he aroused by the intensity of the competition, or was he provoked by his opponent? As social perceivers, this is the type of question we often ask ourselves in trying to understand people.

FIFA/Infront Sports & Media AG

JOHN MACDOUGALL/AFP/Getty Images

Whatever the topic—sports, business, or personal events closer to home—we are all active and interested participants in **social perception**, the processes by which people come to understand one another. This chapter is divided into four sections. First we look at the "raw data" of social perception: persons, situations, and behavior. Second, we examine how people explain and analyze behavior. Third, we consider how people integrate their observations into a coherent impression of other persons. Fourth, we discuss some of the subtle ways that our impressions create a distorted picture of reality, often setting in motion a self-fulfilling prophecy. As you read this chapter, you will notice that the various processes are considered from a perceiver's vantage point. Keep in mind, however, that in the events of life, you are both a *perceiver* and a *target* of others' perceptions.

Observation: The Elements of Social Perception

As our opening examples suggest, understanding others may be difficult, but it's a common and vital part of everyday life. How do we do it? What kinds of evidence do we use? We cannot actually "see" someone's mental or emotional state or his or her motives or intentions any more than a detective can see a crime that has already been committed. So like a detective who tries to reconstruct events by turning up witnesses, fingerprints, blood samples, and other evidence, the social perceiver comes to know others by relying on indirect clues—the elements of social perception. These clues arise from an interplay of three sources: persons, situations, and behavior.

Persons: Judging a Book by Its Cover

Have you ever met someone for the first time and formed a quick impression based only on a quick "snapshot" of information? As children, we were told that we should not judge a book by its cover, that things are not always what they seem, that surface appearances are deceptive, and that all that glitters is not gold. Yet as adults we can't seem to help ourselves.

To illustrate the rapid-fire nature of the process, Janine Willis and Alexander Todorov (2006) showed college students photographs of unfamiliar faces for one-tenth of a second, half a second, or a full second. Whether the students judged the faces for how attractive, likable, competent, trustworthy, or aggressive they were, their ratings—even at the briefest exposure—were quick and were highly correlated with judgments

social perception A general term for the processes by which people come to understand one another.

that other observers made without time-exposure limits (see Table 4.1). Flip quickly through the pages of an illustrated magazine, and you may see for yourself that it takes a mere fraction of a second to form an impression of a stranger from his or her face.

If first impressions are quick to form, on what are they based? In 500 B.C.E., the mathematician Pythagoras looked into the eyes of prospective students to determine if they were gifted. At about the same time, Hippocrates, the founder of modern medicine, used facial features to make diagnoses of life and death. In the nineteenth century, Viennese physician Franz Gall introduced a carnival-like science called phrenology and claimed that he could assess people's character by the shape of their skulls. And in 1954, psychologist William Sheldon concluded from flawed studies of adult men that there is a strong link between physique and personality.

People may not measure each other by bumps on the head, as phrenologists used to do, but first impressions are influenced in subtle ways by a person's height, weight, skin color, hair color, tattoos, piercings, eyeglasses, and other aspects of physical appearance. As social perceivers, we also form impressions of people that are often accurate based on a host of indirect telltale cues. In *Snoop: What Your Stuff Says About You*, Sam Gosling (2008) describes research he has conducted showing that people's personalities can be revealed in the knick-knacks found in their offices and dormitory rooms, the identity claims they make on Facebook pages, the books that line their shelves, and the types of music that inhabit their iPods. In one study, fictional characters with "old-generation" names such as Harry, Walter, Dorothy, and Edith were judged to be less popular and less intelligent than those with younger-generation names such as Kevin, Michael, Lisa, and

TABLE 4.1

First Impressions in a Fraction of a Second

Participants rated unfamiliar faces based on pictures they saw for one-tenth of a second, half a second, or a full second. Would their impressions stay the same or change with unlimited time? As measured by the correlations of these ratings with those made by observers who had no exposure time limits, the results showed that ratings were highly correlated even at the briefest exposure times. Giving participants more time did not increase these correlations.

Traits being judged	.10 sec	.50 sec	1 sec
Trustworthy	.73	.66	.74
Competent	.52	.67	.59
Likable	.59	.57	.63
Aggressive	.52	.56	.59
Attractive	.69	.57	.66

Willis & Todorov, 2006.

Look at these two office cubicles, side by side. Do these images lead you to form any impressions of their inhabitants? If so, do you suppose these impressions would be accurate or misleading?

Monalyn Gracia/PhotoLibrary

Michelle (Young et al., 1993). In another study, both men and women were seen as more feminine when they spoke in high-pitched voices than in lower-pitched voices (Ko et al., 2006).

The human face in particular attracts more than its share of attention. Since the time of ancient Greece, human beings have attended to physiognomy—the art of reading character from faces. Although we may not realize it, this tendency persists today. For example, Ran Hassin and Yaacov Trope (2000) found that people prejudge others in photographs as kind-hearted rather than mean-spirited based on such features as a full, round face, curly hair, long eyelashes, large eyes, a short nose, full lips, and an upturned mouth. Interestingly, these researchers also found that just as people read traits from faces, at times they read traits into faces based on prior information. In one study, for example, participants who were told that a man was kind—compared to those told he was mean—later judged his face to be fuller, rounder, and more attractive.

In social perception studies of the human face, researchers have found that adults who have baby-faced features—large, round eyes; high eyebrows; round cheeks; a large forehead; smooth skin; and a rounded chin—tend to be seen as warm, kind, naive, weak, honest, and submissive. In contrast, adults who have mature features—small eyes, low brows and a small forehead, wrinkled skin, and an angular chin—are seen as stronger, more dominant, and more competent (Berry & Zebrowitz-McArthur, 1986). Thus, in small claims court, judges are more likely to favor baby-faced defendants who are accused of intentional wrongdoing but rule against them when accused of negligence. And in the work setting, baby-faced job applicants are more likely to be recommended for employment as day-care teachers, whereas mature-faced adults are considered to be better suited for work as bankers. Results like these have led Leslie Zebrowitz and Joann Montepare (2005) to conclude that baby-facedness "profoundly affects human behavior in the blink of an eye" (p. 1565).

What accounts for these findings? And why, in general, are people so quick to judge others by appearances? To begin with, human beings are programmed by evolution to respond gently to infantile features so that real babies are treated with tender loving care. Many years ago, Nobel prize–winning ethologist Konrad Lorenz noted that infantile features in many animal species seem to trigger a special nurturing response to cuteness. Recently, this old idea derived new support from a brain-imaging study showing that a frontal brain region associated with love and other positive emotions is activated when people are exposed, even fleetingly, to pictures of babies' faces but not to pictures of the faces of other adults (Kringelbach et al., 2008).

Our reflex-like response to babies is understandable. But do we really respond in the same way to baby-faced adults and, if so, why? Leslie Zebrowitz believes that we do—that we associate infantile features with helplessness traits and then overgeneralize this expectation to baby-faced adults. Consistent with this point, she and her colleagues found in a recent brain-imaging study that the region of the brain that was activated by pictures of babies' faces was also activated by pictures of baby-faced men (Zebrowitz et al., 2009).

Other researchers also believe that people as social perceivers have a tendency to overgeneralize in making snap judgments. Alexander Todorov and others (2008) find that people are quick to perceive unfamiliar faces as more or less trustworthy—an important judgment we must often make—and that we do so by focusing on features that resemble the expressions of happiness and anger (a trustworthy face has a U-shaped mouth and raised eyebrows; in an untrustworthy face, the mouth curls down and the eyebrows form a V). In other words, faces are seen as trustworthy if they look happy, an emotion that signals a person who is safe to approach, and untrustworthy if they look angry, an emotion that signals danger to be avoided.

Our faces, together with our language, are social tools that help us navigate the social encounters that define our "selves" and fashion our lives.
—Alan J. Fridlund

The impressions we form of others are influenced by superficial aspects of their appearance. **TRUE.**

Situations: The Scripts of Life

In addition to the beliefs we hold about persons, each of us has preset notions about certain types of situations—"scripts" that enable us to anticipate the goals, behaviors, and outcomes that are likely to occur in a particular setting (Abelson, 1981; Read, 1987). Based on past experience, people can easily imagine the sequences of events likely to unfold in a typical greeting or at a shopping mall, the dinner table, or a tennis match. The more experience you have in a given situation, the more detail your scripts will contain.

In *Do's and Taboos Around the World*, Roger Axtell (1993) describes many scripts that are culture specific. In Bolivia, dinner guests are expected to fully clean their plates to prove that they enjoyed the meal. Eat in an Indian home, however, and you'll see that many native guests will leave some food on the plate to show the host that they had enough to eat. Social scripts of this nature can influence perceptions and behavior. As we'll see in Chapter 11 on aggression, in places that foster a "culture of honor," men are expected to defend against insult, women are expected to remain modest and loyal, and indications of female infidelity can trigger domestic violence (Vandello & Cohen, 2003).

Behavioral scripts can be quite elaborate. Studying the "first date" script, John Pryor and Thomas Merluzzi (1985) asked U.S. college students to list the sequence of events that take place in this situation. From these lists, a picture of a typical American first date emerged. Sixteen steps were identified, including: (1) male arrives; (2) female greets male at door; (3) female introduces date to parents or roommate; (4) male and female discuss plans and make small talk; (5) they go to a movie; (6) they get something to eat or drink; (7) male takes female home; (8) if interested, he remarks about a future date; (9) they kiss; (10) they say good night. Sound familiar? Pryor and Merluzzi then randomized their list of events and asked participants to arrange them into the appropriate order. They found that those with extensive dating experience were able to organize the statements more quickly than those who had less dating experience. For people who are familiar with a script, the events fall into place like pieces of a puzzle. In fact, more than 20 years later, despite changes in gender and dating norms, research shows that this basic script has remained essentially the same (Morr Serewicz & Gale, 2008).

Knowledge of social settings provides an important context for understanding other people's verbal and nonverbal behavior. For example, this knowledge leads us to expect someone to be polite during a job interview, playful at a picnic, and rowdy at a keg party. Scripts influence social perceptions in two ways. First, we sometimes see what we expect to see in a particular situation. In one study, participants looked at photographs of human faces that had ambiguous expressions. When told that the person in the photo was being threatened by a vicious dog, they saw the facial expression as fearful; when told that the individual had just won money, participants interpreted the same expression as a sign of happiness (Trope, 1986). Second, people use what they know about social situations to explain the causes of human behavior. As described later in this chapter, an action seems to offer more information about a person when it departs from the norm than when it is common. In other words, you would learn more about someone who is rowdy during a job interview or polite at a keg party than if they were polite at the interview and rowdy at the party (Jones & Davis, 1965).

Behavioral Evidence

An essential first step in social perception is recognizing what someone is doing at a given moment. Identifying actions from movement is surprisingly easy. Even when actors dressed in black move about in a dark room with point lights attached only to the joints of their bodies, people quickly and easily recognize such complex acts as walking, running, jumping, exercising, and falling (Johansson et al., 1980). This ability is found in people of all cultures (Barrett et al., 2005) and enables us to recognize themselves and other specific individuals, such as friends, strictly on the basis of their movements (Loula et al., 2005).

More interesting, perhaps, is that people derive *meaning* from their observations by dividing the continuous stream of human behavior into discrete "units." By having participants observe someone on videotape and press a button whenever they detect a meaningful action, Darren Newtson and his colleagues (1987) found that some perceivers break the behavior stream into a large number of fine units, whereas others break it into a small number of gross units. While watching a baseball game, for example, you might press the button after each pitch, after each batter, after every inning, or only after runs are scored. The manner in which people divide a stream of behavior can influence their perceptions in important ways. Research participants who were told to break an event into fine units rather than gross units attended more closely, detected more meaningful actions, and remembered more details about the actor's behavior than did participants who were told to break events into gross units (Lassiter et al., 1988).

In a new and developing area of research, social psychologists are interested in **mind perception**, the process by which people attribute humanlike mental states to various animate and inanimate objects, including other people. Studies show that people who identify someone's actions in high-level terms rather than low-level terms (for example, by describing the act of "painting a house" as "trying to make a house look new," not just "applying brush strokes") are also more likely to attribute humanizing thoughts, feelings, intentions, consciousness, and other states of mind to that actor (Kozak et al., 2006).

Although people do not tend to attribute mental states to inanimate objects, in general the more humanlike a target object is, the more likely we are to attribute to it qualities of "mind." In a series of studies, Carey Morewedge and others (2007) found that whether people are asked to rate different animals in nature (such as a sloth, turtle, housefly, deer, wolf, and hummingbird); cartoon robots or human beings whose motion was presented in slow, medium, and fast speeds; or a purple blob oozing down a city street at the same, slower, or faster pace than the people around it, the result is always the same: People see inner qualities of mind in target objects that superficially resemble humans in their speed of movement.

Asking "What kinds of things have minds?", Heather Gray and her colleagues (2007) conducted an online survey in which they presented more than 2,000 respondents with an array of human and nonhuman characters such as a 7-week-old fetus, a 5-month-old infant, an adult man, a man in a vegetative state, a dead woman, a frog, the family dog, a chimpanzee, God, and a sociable robot. They then asked respondents to rate the extent to which each character possessed various mental capacities such as pleasure, pain, fear, pride, embarrassment, memory, self-control, and morality. Once statistically combined, the results showed that people perceive minds along two dimensions: agency (a target's ability to plan and execute behavior) and experience (the capacity to feel pleasure, pain, and other sensations). Overall, the more "mind" respondents attributed to a character, the more they liked it, valued it, wanted to make it happy, and wanted to rescue it from destruction.

mind perception The process by which people attribute humanlike mental states to various animate and inanimate objects, including other people.

The Silent Language of Nonverbal Behavior   Behavioral cues are used not only to identify someone's physical actions but also to determine his or her inner states. Knowing how another person is feeling can be tricky because people often try to hide their true emotions from others. Have you ever had to suppress your rage at someone, mask your disappointment after failure, feign surprise, make excuses, or pretend to

Guido Alberto Rossi/Tips Images

Alan S. Weiner

© Peter Dazeley/zefa/ Corbis

© Warner Brothers/Courtesy Everett Collection

© M. Thomsen/zefa/Corbis

Carl Durocher/Creative Stock

Can you tell how these individuals are feeling? If you are like most people, regardless of your culture, you will have little trouble recognizing the emotions portrayed.

like something just to be polite? Sometimes people come right out and tell us how they feel. At other times, however, they do not tell us, they are themselves not sure, or they actively try to conceal their true feelings. For these reasons, we often tune in to the silent language of **nonverbal behavior**.

What kinds of nonverbal cues do people use in judging how someone else is feeling? In *The Expression of the Emotions in Man and Animals*, Charles Darwin (1872) proposed that the face expresses emotion in ways that are innate and understood by people all over the world. Contemporary research supports this notion. Numerous studies have shown that when presented with photographs similar to those on page 106, people can reliably identify at least six "primary" emotions: happiness, sadness, anger, fear, surprise, and disgust. In one study, participants from 10 different countries—Estonia, Germany, Greece, Hong Kong, Italy, Japan, Scotland, Sumatra, Turkey, and the United States—exhibited high levels of agreement in their recognition of these emotions (Ekman et al., 1987).

From one end of the world to the other, it is clear that a smile is a smile and a frown is a frown and that just about everyone knows what they mean, even when the expressions are "put on" by actors and are not genuinely felt. But do the results fully support the claim that basic emotions are "universally" recognized from the face, or is the link culturally specific? (Russell, 1994) To answer this question, Hillary Elfenbein and Nalini Ambady (2002) meta-analyzed 97 studies involving a total of 22,148 social perceivers from 42 different countries. As shown in ▶ Figure 4.1, they found support for both points of view. On the one hand, people all over the world are able to recognize the primary emotions from photographs of facial expressions. On the other hand, people are 9 percent more accurate at judging faces from their own national, ethnic, or regional groups than from members of less familiar groups—indicating that we enjoy an "in-group advantage" when it comes to knowing how those who are closest to us are feeling.

In a study that illustrates the point, Elfenbein and Ambady (2003) showed pictures of American faces to groups with varying degrees of exposure to Americans. As predicted, more life exposure was associated with greater accuracy, from a low of 60 percent among Chinese participants living in China up to 83 percent among Chinese living in the United States and 93 percent among non–Chinese Americans. When it

nonverbal behavior Behavior that reveals a person's feelings without words, through facial expressions, body language, and vocal cues.

▶ **FIGURE 4.1**

How Good Are People at Identifying Emotions in the Face?

A meta-analysis of emotion recognition studies involving 22,148 participants from 42 countries confirmed that people all over the world can recognize the six basic emotions from posed facial expressions.

Elfenbein & Ambady, 2002.

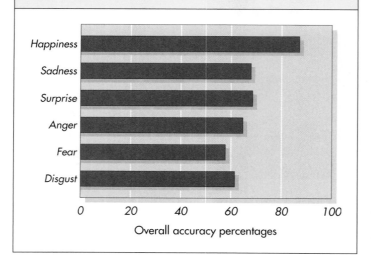

Overall accuracy percentages

comes to recognizing emotions in the face, it appears that familiarity breeds accuracy.

Darwin believed that the ability to recognize emotion in others has survival value for all members of a species. This hypothesis suggests that it is more important to identify some emotions than others. For example, it may be more adaptive to be wary of someone who is angry, and hence prone to lash out in violence, than of someone who is happy, a nonthreatening emotion. Indeed, studies have shown that angry faces arouse us and cause us to frown even when presented subliminally and without our awareness (Dimberg & Ohman, 1996; Dimberg et al., 2000). Illustrating what Christine and Ranald Hansen (1988) called the "anger superiority effect," researchers have found that people are quicker to spot—and slower to look away from—angry faces in a crowd than faces with neutral and less threatening emotions (Fox et al., 2002; Horstmann & Bauland, 2006). Of course, what people search for may be conditioned by a current motivational state. In a visual search task resembling "Where's Waldo?" research participants who were led to fear social rejection and loneliness were quicker to spot faces in diverse crowds that wore welcoming smiles than other expressions (DeWall et al., 2009).

Disgust is another basic emotion that has adaptive significance. When confronted with an offensive stimulus such as a foul odor, spoiled food, feces, rotting flesh, or the sight of mutilation, people react with an aversion that shows in the way they wrinkle the nose, raise the upper lip, and gape. This visceral reaction is often accompanied by nausea; in the case of bad food, this can facilitate expulsion from the mouth (Rozin & Fallon, 1987). In nature, food poisoning is a real threat, so it is adaptive for us to recognize disgust in the face of others. To illustrate, Bruno Wicker and others (2003) had 14 men watch video clips of people smelling pleasant, disgusting, or neutral odors. Afterward, these same men were exposed to the odors themselves. If you've ever inhaled the sweet, floury aroma of a bakery or inserted your nose into a carton of soured milk, you'll appreciate the different reactions that would appear on your face. Using fMRI, researchers monitored activity in the participants' brains throughout the experiment. They found that a structure in the brain known as the *insula* was activated not only when participants sniffed the disgusting odor but also when they watched *others* sniffing it. This result suggests that people more than recognize the face of disgust; they experience it at a neural level.

The social value of the human face is evident to those who communicate online. When e-mail first became popular, the written word was often misinterpreted, especially when the writer tried to be funny, because it lacked the nonverbal cues that normally animate and clarify live interactions. To fill in this gap, e-mailers created smiley faces and other "emoticons" (emotion icons) from standard keyboard characters. A sampling of routinely used emoticons, which are meant to be viewed with one's head tilted 90 degrees to the left, are shown in ▶ Figure 4.2. To simplify the task, Google, Yahoo!, and other e-mail providers now offer a large number of emoticon faces to communicate a wide assortment of emotions and other mental states.

Other nonverbal cues can also influence social perception, enabling us to make quick and sometimes accurate judgments of others based on "thin slices" of expressive behavior (Ambady & Rosenthal, 1993). "Thin slicing is not an exotic gift," notes Malcolm Gladwell (2005), author of the best seller *Blink*. "It is a central part of what it means to be human" (p. 43). In one study, for example, research participants were able to judge the intelligence of strangers accurately, as measured by standardized test scores, based only on hearing them read short sentences (Borkenau et al., 2004). In another study, 100 college students rated the faces of CEOs from the top- and bottom-ranked Fortune 1000 companies on key leadership traits related to power (competent, dominant, mature-faced) and warmth (likable, trustworthy). As it turned out, the CEOs whose faces the students had rated as more powerful—based on nothing more than cropped head shots—were in fact more successful, as measured by their company's most recent profits (Rule & Ambady, 2008).

Eye contact, or *gaze*, is another powerful form of nonverbal communication. As social beings, people are highly attentive to eyes, often following the gaze of others. Look up, down, left, or right, and someone observing you will likely follow the direction of your eyes (Langton et al., 2000). Even one-year-old infants tend to follow gaze, looking toward or pointing at the object of an adult researcher's attention (Brooks & Meltzoff, 2002). Clearly, each of us is drawn like a magnet to another person's direct gaze. Controlled laboratory studies of this "eye contact effect" show that people who look us straight in the eye quickly draw and then hold our attention, increase arousal, and activate key "social" areas of the brain and that this sensitivity is present at birth (Senju & Johnson, 2009).

Eyes have been called the "windows of the soul." In many cultures, people tend to assume that someone who avoids eye contact is evasive, cold, fearful, shy, or indifferent; that frequent gazing signals intimacy, sincerity, self-confidence, and respect; and that the person who stares is tense, angry, and unfriendly. If you've ever conversed with someone who kept looking away, as if uninterested, then you would understand why people might form negative impressions from "gaze disengagement" (Mason et al., 2005). Sometimes eye contact is interpreted in light of a preexisting relationship. If two people are friendly, frequent eye contact elicits a positive impression. If a relationship is not so friendly, that same eye contact is seen in negative terms. Hence, it is said that if two people lock eyes for more than a few seconds, they will either make love or kill each other (Kleinke, 1986).

Another powerful and primitive form of nonverbal signal is *touch*—as in the congratulatory high-five, the chest thump, the sympathetic pat on the back, the joking elbow in the ribs, the painfully strong handshake, and the lingering loving embrace. Physical touching has long been regarded as an expression of friendship, nurturance, and sexual interest. But it may also serve other functions. Many years ago, Nancy Henley (1977) observed that men, older persons, and those of high socioeconomic status

▶ **FIGURE 4.2**

Some Common E-mail "Emoticons"

In order to clarify meaning of their written words, e-mailers often add smiles, winks, and other face-like symbols, or emoticons, to their electronic messages. One set of emoticons is shown here; you may be familiar with others.

Sanderson, 1997.

Wink	Smirk	Said smiling	Said frowning	Sardonic incredulity
'-)	:-,	:-)	:-(	;-)

Disgusted	Kiss, kiss	Clowning around	Said late at night	Said tongue-in-cheek
:-|	:-X	:*)	|-(	:-J

John Stillwell/PA Photos/Landov

Touch is a powerful form of nonverbal behavior and is often subject to strict cultural norms. In April 2009, First Lady Michelle Obama, meeting Queen Elizabeth II for the first time, put her arm around the Queen. Aghast, some commentators noted that this gesture breached protocol; others said it was appropriate because the Queen herself had embraced the First Lady.

were more likely to touch women, younger persons, and individuals of lower status than the other way around. Henley's interpretation: that touching may be an expression not only of intimacy but also of dominance and control. Is social touching reserved for those in power? It appears that the answer is no. After an exhaustive review of past research, Judith Hall and her colleagues (2005) found that although we tend to believe that people touch others more when they are dominant than when they are subordinate, there is no behavioral support for this hypothesis (though dominant people are more facially expressive, encroach more on others' personal space, speak louder, and are more likely to interrupt).

As described by Axtell (1993), nonverbal communication norms vary a great deal from one culture to the next. So watch out! In Bulgaria, nodding your head means "no" and shaking your head sideways means "yes." In Germany and Brazil, the American "okay" sign (forming a circle with your thumb and forefinger) is an obscene gesture. Personal-space habits also vary across cultures. Japanese people like to maintain a comfortable distance while interacting. But in Puerto Rico and much of Latin America, people stand very close and backing off is considered an insult. Also beware of what you do with your eyes. In Latin America, locking eyes is a must, yet in Japan, too much eye contact shows a lack of respect. If you're in the habit of stroking your cheek, you should know that in Italy, Greece, and Spain it means that you find the person you're talking to attractive. And whatever you do, don't ever touch someone's head in predominantly Buddhist countries, especially Thailand. The head is sacred there.

Different cultures also have vastly different rules for the common greeting. In Finland, you should give a firm handshake; in France, you should loosen the grip; in Zambia, you should use your left hand to support the right; and in Bolivia, you should extend your arm if your hand is dirty. In Japan, people bow; in Thailand, they put both hands together in a praying position on the chest; and in Fiji, they smile and raise their eyebrows. In certain parts of Latin America, it is common for people to hug, embrace, and kiss upon meeting. And in most Arab countries, men greet one another by saying *salaam alaykum*, then shaking hands, saying *kaif halak*, and kissing each other on the cheek.

"I knew the suspect was lying because of certain telltale discrepancies between his voice and nonverbal gestures. Also his pants were on fire."

Distinguishing Truth from Deception

Social perception is tricky because people often try to hide or stretch the truth about themselves. Poker players bluff to win money, witnesses lie to protect themselves, public officials make campaign promises they don't really intend to keep, and acquaintances pass compliments to each other to be polite and supportive. On occasion, everyone tells something less than "the truth, the whole truth, and nothing but the truth." Can social perceivers tell the difference? Can *you* tell when someone is lying?

Sigmund Freud, the founder of psychoanalysis, once said that "no mortal can keep a secret. If his lips are silent, he chatters with his fingertips; betrayal oozes out of him at every pore" (1905, p. 94). Paul Ekman and Wallace Friesen (1974) later revised Freud's observation by pointing out that some pores "ooze" more than others. Ekman and Friesen proposed that some channels of communication are difficult for deceivers to control, while others are relatively easy. To test this hypothesis, they showed a series of films—some pleasant, others disgusting—to a group of female nurses. While watching, the nurses were instructed either to report their honest impressions of these films or to conceal their true feelings. Through the use of hidden cameras, these participants were videotaped. Others, acting as observers, then viewed the tapes and judged whether the participants had been truthful or deceptive. The results showed that judgment accuracy rates were influenced by which types of nonverbal cues the observers were exposed to. Observers who watched tapes that focused on the body were better at detecting deception than were those who saw tapes focused on the face. The face can communicate emotion but is relatively easy for deceivers to control,

Research on lying and its detection has shown that there is no one behavioral cue, like Pinocchio's growing wooden nose, that can be used to signal deception.

unlike nervous movements of the hands and feet. Clearly, there is nothing like the wooden Pinocchio's nose to reveal whether someone is lying or telling the truth.

This study was the first of hundreds. In all this research, one group of participants makes truthful or deceptive statements while another group reads the transcripts, listens to audiotapes or watches videotapes, and then tries to judge the statements. Consistently, in laboratories all over the world, results show that people are only about 54 percent accurate in judging truth and deception, too often accepting what others say at face value (Bond & DePaulo, 2006; Vrij, 2008). Although some social perceivers may be better than others at distinguishing truths and lies, individual differences are small (Bond & DePaulo, 2008). In fact, a good deal of research shows that professionals who are specially trained and who regularly make these kinds of judgments for a living—such as police detectives, judges, psychiatrists, customs inspectors, and those who administer lie-detector tests for the CIA, the FBI, and the military—are also highly prone to error (Ekman & O'Sullivan, 1991; Granhag & Strömwall, 2004; Meissner & Kassin, 2002; Vrij, 2008; see Table 4.2).

There are two reasons for this problem. The first is that there is a mismatch between the behavioral cues that actually signal deception and those we use to detect deception (Zuckerman et al., 1981; DePaulo et al., 2003). Think about it. There are four channels of communication that provide potentially relevant information: the spoken word, the face, the body, and the voice. Yet when people have a reason to lie, the words they choose cannot be trusted, and they are generally able to control both their face and body (the voice is the most telling channel; when people lie, they tend to hesitate, then speed up and raise the pitch of their voice). In a survey of some 2,500 adults in 63 countries, Charles Bond found that more than 70 percent believed that liars tend to avert their eyes—a cue that is not supported by any research. Similarly, most of Bond's survey respondents believed that

TABLE 4.2

Can the "Experts" Distinguish Truth and Deception?

Lie-detection experts with experience at making judgments of truth and deception were shown brief videotapes of 10 women telling the truth or lying about their feelings. Considering that there was a 50-50 chance of guessing correctly, the accuracy rates were remarkably low. Only a sample of U.S. Secret Service agents posted a better-than-chance performance.

Observer Groups	Accuracy Rates (%)
College students	52.82
CIA, FBI, and military	55.67
Police investigators	55.79
Trial judges	56.73
Psychiatrists	57.61
U.S. Secret Service agents	64.12

Ekman & O'Sullivan, 1991.

Greg "Fossilman" Raymer was the 2004 World Series of Poker champion, winning $5 million for his first-place finish. So that his eyes would not betray his inner thoughts and feelings, Raymer, like many other poker players, wore reflective sunglasses for the entire tournament.

Adaptively, people are skilled at knowing when someone is lying rather than telling the truth. **FALSE.**

people squirm, stutter, fidget, and touch themselves when they lie—also cues not supported by the research (Henig, 2006).

The second problem is that people tend to assume that the way to spot a liar is to watch for signs of stress in his or her behavior. Yet in important real-life situations—for example, at a high-stakes poker table, the security screening area of an airport, or a police interrogation room—truth tellers are also likely to exhibit signs of stress. For this reason, researchers are seeking a different approach. For example, Aldert Vrij (2008) theorizes that lying is harder to do and requires more thinking than telling the truth. Therefore, he argues, we should focus on behavioral cues that betray cognitive effort. This realization has led Vrij and others to create more challenging types of interviews that could expose deception. In one study, they asked truth tellers and liars to recount their stories in reverse chronological order. This task was a lot harder and more effortful for the deceivers to do, which made the interviewers better able to distinguish between truths and lies (Vrij et al., 2008). In a second study, those interviewing suspects who had committed a mock crime withheld certain details of that crime while questioning some suspects but not others. Using this "strategic disclosure" technique, the interviewers made more accurate judgments of who was lying by catching those who had committed the mock crime in various inconsistencies—such as claiming that they were never present at the crime scene, unaware that they had left fingerprints—which the interviewers did not disclose until later (Hartwig et al., 2005).

In the wake of the September 11 terrorist attacks and heightened worldwide concerns about security, the ability to distinguish truths and lies is essential, potentially a matter of life and death. Yet research shows that social perceivers tune in to the wrong channels. Too easily seduced by the silver tongue, the smiling face, and the restless body, we often fail to notice the quivering voice. Too focused on how stressed a person seems while speaking—an emotional state that afflicts not only guilty liars but innocent truth tellers who stand falsely accused—we fail to notice the amount of effort it takes someone to recite their story or answer a question. With social psychologists in hot pursuit of ways to improve upon human lie detection skills, stay tuned for further developments in years to come.

Attribution: From Elements to Dispositions

To interact effectively with others, we need to know how they feel and when they can be trusted. But to understand people well enough to predict their future behavior, we must also identify their inner *dispositions*—stable characteristics such as personality traits, attitudes, and abilities. Since we cannot actually see dispositions, we infer them indirectly from what a person says and does. In this section, we look at the processes that lead us to make these inferences.

■ Attribution Theories

Do you ever think about the influence you have on other people? What about the roles of heredity, childhood experiences, and social forces? Do you wonder why some people succeed while others fail? Individuals differ in the extent to which they feel a need to explain the uncertain events of human behavior (Weary & Edwards, 1994). Among college students, for example, those who major in psychology are more curious about people than are those who major in one of the natural sciences (Fletcher et al.,

1986). Although there are vast differences among us, people in general tend to ask "why?" when they confront events that are important, negative, or unexpected (Weiner, 1985) and when understanding these events has personal relevance (Malle & Knobe, 1997).

To make sense of our social world, we try to understand the causes of other people's behavior. But what kinds of explanations do we make, and how do we go about making them? In a classic book entitled *The Psychology of Interpersonal Relations*, Fritz Heider (1958) took the first step toward answering these questions. To Heider, we are all scientists of a sort. Motivated to understand others well enough to manage our social lives, we observe, analyze, and explain their behavior. The explanations we come up with are called *attributions*, and the theory that describes the process is called **attribution theory**. The questions posed at the beginning of the chapter regarding the behavior of French soccer star Zinedine Zidane and Wall Street criminal Bernie Madoff are questions of attribution.

"It's not you, Frank, it's me—I don't like you."

People make personal and situational attributions all the time in an effort to make sense of their social world. But what kind of attribution is being made here?

Ask people to explain why their fellow human beings behave as they do—why they succeed or fail, laugh or cry, work or play, or help or hurt others—and you'll see that they come up with complex explanations often focused on whether the behavior is intentional or unintentional (Malle et al., 2000). Interested in how people answer these kinds of *why* questions, Heider found it particularly useful to group the explanations people give into two categories: *personal* and *situational*. In the 2006 World Cup Soccer example, everyone wanted to know what caused Zidane to lash out, forcefully head-butting his Italian opponent to the ground. Immediately, some observers pointed the finger of blame at Zidane, an aggressive player with a short temper (a **personal attribution**). Yet others speculated that his actions were provoked by an accumulation of frustration or something his opponent said (a **situational attribution**). (Materazzi later admitted to making an insulting remark about Zidane's sister; Zidane later apologized for his outburst.) The task for the attribution theorist is not to determine the true *causes* of such an event but rather to understand people's *perceptions* of causality. Heider's insights provided an initial spark for a number of formal models that together came to be known as attribution theory (Weiner, 2008). For now, we describe two of these theories.

Jones's Correspondent Inference Theory   According to Edward Jones and Keith Davis (1965), each of us tries to understand other people by observing and analyzing their behavior. Jones and Davis's *correspondent inference theory* predicts that people try to infer from an action whether the act corresponds to an enduring personal characteristic of the actor. Is the person who commits an act of aggression a beast? Is the person who donates money to charity an altruist? To answer these kinds of questions, people make inferences on the basis of three factors.

The first factor is a person's degree of *choice*. Behavior that is freely chosen is more informative about a person than behavior that is coerced. In one study, participants read a speech, presumably written by a college student, that either favored or opposed Fidel Castro, then the communist leader of Cuba. Some participants were told that the student had freely chosen this position and others were told that the student had been assigned the position by a professor. When asked to judge the student's true attitude, participants were more likely to assume a correspondence

attribution theory   A group of theories that describe how people explain the causes of behavior.

personal attribution   Attribution to internal characteristics of an actor, such as ability, personality, mood, or effort.

situational attribution   Attribution to factors external to an actor, such as the task, other people, or luck.

between the essay (behavior) and the student's attitude (disposition) when the student had had a choice than when he or she had been assigned to the role (Jones & Harris, 1967; see ▶ Figure 4.3). Keep this study in mind. It supports correspondent inference theory, but as we will see later, it also demonstrates one of the most tenacious biases of social perception.

The second factor that leads people to make dispositional inferences is the *expectedness* of behavior. As previously noted, an action tells us more about a person when it departs from the norm than when it is typical, part of a social role, or otherwise expected under the circumstances (Jones et al., 1961). Thus, people think they know more about a student who wears three-piece suits to class or a citizen who openly refuses to pay taxes than about a student who wears blue jeans to class or a citizen who files tax returns on April 15.

Third, social perceivers take into account the intended *effects* or consequences of someone's behavior. Acts that produce many desirable outcomes do not reveal a person's specific motives as clearly as acts that produce only a single desirable outcome (Newtson, 1974). For example, you are likely to be uncertain about exactly why a person stays on a job that is enjoyable, high paying, and in an attractive location—three desirable outcomes, each sufficient to explain the behavior. In contrast, you may feel more certain about why a person stays on a job that is tedious and low paying but is in an attractive location—only one desirable outcome.

Kelley's Covariation Theory   Correspondent inference theory seeks to describe how perceivers try to discern an individual's personal characteristics from a slice of behavioral evidence. However, behavior can be attributed not only to personal factors but to situational factors as well. How is this distinction made? In the opening chapter, we noted that the causes of human behavior can be derived only through experiments. That is, one has to make more than a single observation and compare behavior in two or more settings in which everything stays the same except for the independent variables. Like Heider, Harold Kelley (1967) believes that people are much like scientists in this regard. They may not observe others in a controlled laboratory, but they too search for clues, make comparisons, and think in terms of "experiments."

According to Kelley, people make attributions by using the **covariation principle**: In order for something to be the cause of a behavior, it must be present when the behavior occurs and absent when it does not. Three kinds of covariation information in particular are useful: consensus, distinctiveness, and consistency. To illustrate these concepts, imagine you are standing on a street corner one hot, steamy evening minding your own business, when all of a sudden a stranger comes out of a cool air-conditioned movie theater and blurts out, "Great flick!" Looking up, you don't recognize the movie title, so you wonder what to make of this "recommendation." Was the behavior (the rave review) caused by something about the person (the stranger), the stimulus (the film), or the circumstances (say, the comfortable

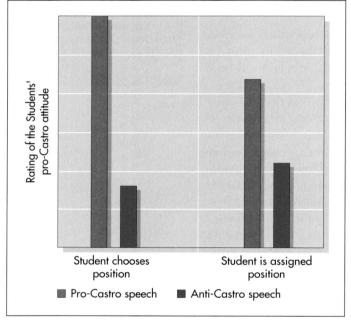

▶ FIGURE 4.3

What Does This Speechwriter Really Believe?

As predicted by correspondent inference theory, participants who read a student's speech (behavior) were more likely to assume that it reflected the student's true attitude (disposition) when the position taken was freely chosen (left) rather than assigned (right). But also note the evidence for the fundamental attribution error. Even participants who thought the student had been assigned a position inferred the student's attitude from the speech.

Jones & Harris, 1967.

Rating of the Students' pro-Castro attitude

Student chooses position   Student is assigned position

■ Pro-Castro speech   ■ Anti-Castro speech

covariation principle
A principle of attribution theory that holds that people attribute behavior to factors that are present when a behavior occurs and are absent when it does not.

theater)? If you are possibly interested in spending a night at the movie, how would you proceed to explain what happened? What kinds of information would you want to obtain?

Thinking like a scientist, you might seek out *consensus information* to see how different persons react to the same stimulus. In other words, what do other moviegoers think about this film? If others also rave about it, then this stranger's behavior is high in consensus and is attributed to the stimulus. If others are critical of this film, however, then the behavior is low in consensus and is attributed to the person.

Still thinking like a scientist, you might also want to have *distinctiveness information* to see how the same person reacts to different stimuli. In other words, what does this moviegoer think of other films? If the stranger is generally critical of other films, then the target behavior is high in distinctiveness and is attributed to the stimulus. If the stranger raves about everything he or she sees, however, then the behavior is low in distinctiveness and is attributed to the person.

Finally, you might seek *consistency information* to see what happens to the behavior at another time when the person and the stimulus both remain the same. How does this moviegoer feel about this film on other occasions? If the stranger raves about the film on video as well as in the theater, regardless of surroundings, then the behavior is high in consistency. If the stranger does not always enjoy the film, the behavior is low in consistency. According to Kelley, behavior that is consistent is attributed to the stimulus when consensus and distinctiveness are also high and to the person when they are low. In contrast, behavior that is low in consistency is attributed to transient circumstances, such as the temperature of the movie theater.

Kelley's theory and the predictions it makes are represented in ▶ Figure 4.4. Does this model describe the kinds of information you seek when you try to determine what causes people to behave as they do? Often it does. Research shows that people who are asked to make attributions for various events do, in general, follow the logic of covariation (Cheng & Novick, 1990; Fosterling, 1992; McArthur, 1972). However, this research

▶**FIGURE 4.4**

Kelley's Covariation Theory

For behaviors that are high in consistency, people make personal attributions when there is low consensus and distinctiveness (top row) and stimulus attributions when there is high consensus and distinctiveness (bottom row). Behaviors that are low in consistency (not shown) are attributed to passing circumstances.

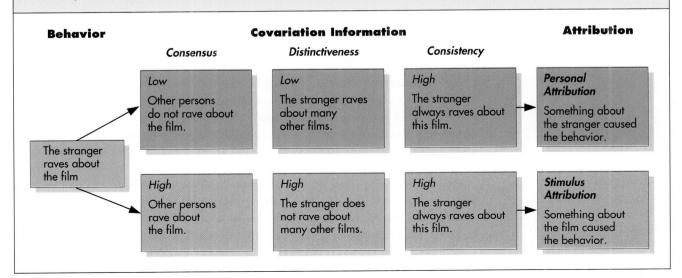

also shows that individuals have their own attributional styles, so people often disagree about what caused a particular behavior (Robins et al., 2004). There are two ways in which social perceivers differ. First, individuals vary in the extent to which they believe that human behaviors are caused by personal characteristics that are fixed ("Everyone is a certain kind of person; there is not much that can be done to really change that") or malleable ("People can change even their most basic qualities") (Dweck et al., 1995). Second, some individuals are more likely than others to process information in ways that are colored by self-serving motivations (von Hippel et al., 2005).

Attribution Biases

When the theories of attribution were first proposed, they were represented by such elaborate flow charts, formulas, and diagrams that many social psychologists began to wonder: Do people really analyze behavior in the way that one might expect of computers? Do people have the time, the motivation, or the cognitive capacity for such elaborate and mindful processes? The answer is sometimes yes, sometimes no. As social perceivers, we are limited in our ability to process all relevant information or we may lack the kinds of training needed to employ fully the principles of attribution theory. More important, we often don't make an effort to think carefully about our attributions. With so much to explain and not enough time in a day, people take mental shortcuts, cross their fingers, hope for the best, and get on with life. The problem is that speed brings bias and perhaps even a loss of accuracy. In this section, we examine some of these shortcuts and their consequences.

Cognitive Heuristics   According to Daniel Kahneman, Amos Tversky, and others, people often make attributions and other types of social judgments by using certain cognitive heuristics: information-processing rules of thumb that enable us to think in ways that are quick and easy but that frequently lead to error (Gilovich et al., 2002; Kahneman et al., 1982; Nisbett & Ross, 1980).

One rule of thumb that has particularly troublesome effects on attribution is the **availability heuristic**, a tendency to estimate the odds that an event will occur by how easily instances of it pop to mind. To demonstrate this phenomenon, Tversky and Kahneman (1973) asked research participants: Which is more common, words that start with the letter *r* or words that contain *r* as the third letter? In actuality, the English language has many more words with *r* as the third letter than as the first. Yet most people guessed that more words begin with *r*. The reason? It's easier to bring to mind words in which *r* appears first. Apparently, our estimates of likelihood are heavily influenced by events that are readily available in memory (MacLeod & Campbell, 1992). The availability heuristic can lead us astray in two ways. First, it gives rise to the **false-consensus effect**, a tendency for people to overestimate the extent to which others share their opinions, attributes, and behaviors. This bias is pervasive. Regardless of whether people are asked to predict how others feel about military spending, abortion, gun control, Campbell's soup, certain types of music, or norms for appropriate behavior, they exaggerate the percentage of others who behave similarly or share their views (Krueger, 1998; Ross, Greene, & House, 1977).

To illustrate the effect, Joachim Krueger (2000) asked participants in a study to indicate whether or not they had certain personality traits. Then they were asked to estimate the percentage of people in general who have these same traits. As shown in Table 4.3, participants' beliefs about other people's personalities were biased by their own self-perceptions. In part, the false-consensus bias is a by-product of the availability heuristic. We tend to associate with others who are like us in important

availability heuristic
The tendency to estimate the likelihood that an event will occur by how easily instances of it come to mind.

false-consensus effect
The tendency for people to overestimate the extent to which others share their opinions, attributes, and behaviors.

ways, so we are more likely to notice and recall instances of similar rather than dissimilar behavior (Deutsch, 1989). Interestingly, people do *not* exhibit this bias when asked to predict the behavior of groups other than their own (Mullen et al., 1992) or when predicting aspects of others that they share but see as particular to themselves rather than typical (Karniol, 2003).

A second consequence of the availability heuristic is that social perceptions are influenced more by one vivid life story than by hard statistical facts. Have you ever wondered why so many people buy lottery tickets despite the astonishingly low odds or why so many travelers are afraid to fly even though they are more likely to perish in a car accident? These behaviors are symptomatic of the **base-rate fallacy**—the fact that people are relatively insensitive to numerical base rates, or probabilities; they are influenced more by graphic, dramatic events such as the sight of a multimillion-dollar lottery winner celebrating on TV or a photograph of bodies being pulled from the wreckage of a plane crash.

TABLE 4.3		
The False-Consensus Effect		
In this study, participants who did and participants who did not rate various personality traits as descriptive of themselves estimated the percentage of other people who had these traits. As shown below, participants' estimates of the population consensus were biased by their own self-perceptions.		
Traits	Self Yes (%)	Self No (%)
Alert	75	65
Discontented	48	33
Loud	46	43
Meticulous	52	41
Sly	36	28
Smug	41	33
Krueger, 2000.		

The base-rate fallacy can thus lead to various misperceptions of risk. Indeed, people overestimate the number of those who die in shootings, fires, floods, and terrorist bombings and underestimate the death toll caused by heart attacks, strokes, diabetes, and other mundane events. Perceptions of risk seem more relevant now than in the past by newly acquired fears of terrorism, and research shows that such perceptions are affected more by fear, anxiety, and other emotions than by cold and objective probabilities (Loewenstein et al., 2001; Slovic, 2000). At times the result can be capricious and downright irrational. Consistent with the fact that people tend to fear things that sound unfamiliar, participants in one study rated fictional food additives as more hazardous to health when the names were difficult to pronounce, such as Hnegripitrom, than when they were easier to pronounce, such as Magnalroxate (Song & Schwarz, 2009).

Every day, we are besieged by both types of information: We read and hear about the unemployment rate and we watch personal interviews with people who were recently laid off; we read the casualty figures of war and we witness the agony of a parent who has lost a child in combat. Logically, statistics that summarize the experiences of large numbers of people are more informative than a single and perhaps atypical case, but perceivers march to a different drummer. As long as the personal anecdote is seen as relevant (Schwarz et al., 1991) and the source as credible (Hinsz et al., 1988), it seems that one good image is worth a thousand numbers.

People can also be influenced by how easy it is to imagine events that did *not* occur. As thoughtful and curious beings, we often are not content to accept what happens to us or to others without wondering, at least in private, "What if. . . ?" According to Daniel Kahneman and Dale Miller (1986), people's emotional reactions to events are often colored by **counterfactual thinking**, the tendency to imagine alternative outcomes that might have occurred but did not. There are different types of counterfactual thoughts. If we imagine a result that is better than the actual result, then we're likely to experience disappointment, regret, and frustration. If the imagined result is worse, then we react with emotions that range from relief and satisfaction to elation. Thus, the psychological impact of positive and negative events depends on the way we think about "what might have been" (Roese, 1997; Roese & Olson, 1995).

What domains of life trigger the most counterfactual thinking—and the regret that often follows? Summarizing past research, Neal Roese and Amy Summerville

A single death is a tragedy; a million is a statistic.

—Joseph Stalin

base-rate fallacy The finding that people are relatively insensitive to consensus information presented in the form of numerical base rates.

counterfactual thinking The tendency to imagine alternative events or outcomes that might have occurred but did not.

(2005) found that people's top three regrets center, in order, on education ("I should have stayed in school"), career ("If only I had applied for that job"), and romance ("If only I had asked her out")—all domains that present us with opportunities that we may or may not realize.

Obviously, people don't immerse themselves in counterfactual thought after every experience. Research shows that we are more likely to think about what might have been—often with feelings of regret—after negative outcomes that result from actions we take rather than from actions we don't take (Byrne & McEleney 2000). Consider an experience that may sound all too familiar: You take a multiple-choice test and after reviewing an item you had struggled over, you want to change the answer. What do you do? Over the years, research has shown that most changes in test answers are from incorrect to correct. Yet most college students harbor the "first instinct fallacy" that it is best to stick with one's original answer. Why? Justin Kruger and his colleagues (2005) found that this myth arises from counterfactual thinking: that students are more likely to react with regret and frustration ("If only I had . . .") after changing a correct answer than after failing to change an incorrect answer.

According to Victoria Medvec and Kenneth Savitsky (1997), certain situations—such as being on the *verge* of a better or worse outcome, just above or below some cutoff point—also make it especially easy to conjure up images of what might have been. The implications are intriguing. Imagine, for example, that you are an Olympic athlete and have just won a silver medal—a remarkable feat. Now imagine that you have just won the bronze medal. Which situation would make you feel better? Rationally speaking, you should feel more pride and satisfaction with a silver medal. But what if your achievement had prompted you to engage in counterfactual thinking? What alternative would haunt your mind if you had finished in second place? Where would your focus be if you had placed third? Is it possible that the athlete who is better off objectively will feel worse?

To examine this question, Medvec and others (1995) videotaped 41 athletes in the 1992 summer Olympic Games at the moment they realized that they had won a silver or a bronze medal and again, later, during the medal ceremony. Then they showed these tapes, without sound, to people who did not know the order of finish. These participants were asked to observe the medalists and rate their emotional states on a scale ranging from "agony" to "ecstasy." The intriguing result, as you might expect, was that the bronze medalists, on average, seemed happier than the silver medalists. Was there any more direct evidence of counterfactual thinking? In a second study, participants who watched interviews with many of these same athletes rated the silver medalists as more negatively focused on finishing second rather than first and the bronze medalists as more positively focused on finishing third rather than fourth. For these world-class athletes, feelings of satisfaction were based more on their thoughts of what might have been than on the reality of what was.

The Fundamental Attribution Error   By the time you finish reading this textbook, you will know the cardinal lesson of social psychology: People are profoundly influenced by the *situational* contexts of behavior. This point is not as obvious as it may seem. For instance, parents are often surprised to hear that their mischievous child, the family monster, is a perfect angel in the classroom. And students are often surprised to observe that their favorite professor, so eloquent in the lecture hall, may stumble over words in less formal gatherings. These reactions are symptomatic of a well-documented aspect of social perception. When people explain the behavior of others, they tend to overestimate the role of personal factors and overlook the impact of situations. Because this bias is so pervasive (and sometimes so misleading) it has been called the **fundamental attribution error** (Ross, 1977).

During the 1996 Olympics, Nike ran a counterfactual (and controversial) ad: "You don't win silver, you lose gold."

fundamental attribution error
The tendency to focus on the role of personal causes and underestimate the impact of situations on other people's behavior.

Evidence of the fundamental attribution error was first reported in the Jones and Harris (1967) study described earlier, in which participants read an essay presumably written by a student. In that study participants were more likely to infer the student's true attitude when the position taken had been freely chosen than when they thought that the student had been assigned to it. But look again at Figure 4.3, and you'll notice that even when participants thought that the student had no choice but to assert a position, they still used the speech to infer his or her attitude. This finding has been repeated many times. Whether the essay topic is nuclear power, abortion, drug laws, or the death penalty, the results are essentially the same (Jones, 1990).

People fall prey to the fundamental attribution error even when they are fully aware of the situation's impact on behavior. In one experiment, the participants were themselves assigned to take a position, whereupon they swapped essays and rated each other. Remarkably, they still jumped to conclusions about each other's attitudes (Miller et al., 1981). In another experiment, participants inferred attitudes from a speech even when they were the ones who had assigned the position to be taken (Gilbert & Jones, 1986).

A fascinating study by Lee Ross and his colleagues (1977) demonstrates the fundamental attribution error in a familiar setting, the TV quiz show. By a flip of the coin, participants in this study were randomly assigned to play the role of either the questioner or the contestant in a quiz game while spectators looked on. In front of the contestant and spectators, the experimenter instructed each questioner to write 10 challenging questions from his or her own store of general knowledge. If you are a trivia buff, you can imagine how esoteric such questions can be: Who was the founder of e-Bay? What team won the NHL Stanley Cup in 1976? It is no wonder that contestants correctly answered only about 40 percent of the questions asked. When the game was over, all participants rated the questioner's and contestant's general knowledge on a scale of 0 to 100.

Picture the events that transpired. The questioners appeared more knowledgeable than the contestants. After all, they knew all the answers. But a moment's reflection should remind us that the situation put the questioner at a distinct advantage (there were no differences between the two groups on an objective test of general knowledge). Did participants take the questioner's advantage into account, or did they assume that the questioners actually had greater knowledge? The results were startling. Spectators rated the questioners as above average in their general knowledge and the contestants as below average. The contestants even rated themselves as inferior to their partners. Like the spectators, they too were fooled by the loaded situation (see ▶ Figure 4.5).

What's going on here? Why do social perceivers consistently make assumptions about persons and fail to appreciate the impact of situations? According to Daniel Gilbert and Patrick Malone (1995), the problem stems in part from *how* we make attributions. Attribution theorists used to assume that people survey all the evidence

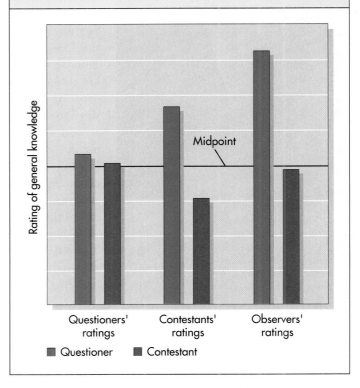

▶ **FIGURE 4.5**

Fundamental Attribution Error and the TV Quiz Show

Even though the simulated quiz show situation placed questioners in an obvious position of advantage over contestants, observers rated the questioners as more knowledgeable (right). Questioners did not overrate their general knowledge (left), but contestants rated themselves as inferior (middle) and observers rated them as inferior as well. These results illustrate the fundamental attribution error.

Ross et al., 1977.

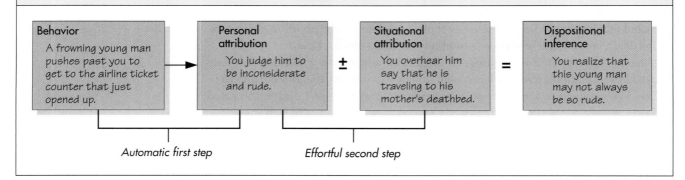

▶**FIGURE 4.6**

Two-Step Model of the Attribution Process

Traditional attribution theories assume that we analyze behavior by searching for a personal or situational cause. The two-step model suggests that people make personal attributions automatically and then must consciously adjust that inference in order to account for situational factors.

Behavior	Personal attribution		Situational attribution		Dispositional inference
A frowning young man pushes past you to get to the airline ticket counter that just opened up.	You judge him to be inconsiderate and rude.	±	You overhear him say that he is traveling to his mother's deathbed.	=	You realize that this young man may not always be so rude.

Automatic first step   Effortful second step

and then decide on whether to make a personal or a situational attribution. Instead, it appears that social perception is a two-step process: First we identify the behavior and make a quick personal attribution, then we correct or adjust that inference to account for situational influences. At least for those raised in a Western culture, the first step is simple and automatic, like a reflex; the second requires attention, thought, and effort (see ▶ Figure 4.6). At present, social neuroscience researchers are beginning to use neuroimaging to probe the brain for evidence of this model (Lieberman et al., 2004).

Several research findings support this hypothesis. First, without realizing it, people often form impressions of others based on a quick glimpse at a face or fleeting sample of behavior (Newman & Uleman, 1989; Todorov & Uleman, 2004). Second, perceivers are *more* likely to commit the fundamental attribution error when they are cognitively busy, or distracted, as they observe the target person than when they pay full attention (Gilbert et al., 1992; Trope & Alfieri, 1997). Since the two-step model predicts that personal attributions are automatic but that the later adjustment for situational factors requires conscious thought, it makes sense to suggest that when attention is divided, when the attribution is made hastily, or when perceivers lack motivation, the second step suffers more than the first. As Gilbert and his colleagues (1988) put it, "The first step is a snap, but the second one's a doozy" (p. 738).

Why is the first step such a snap, and why does it seem so natural for people to assume a link between acts and personal dispositions? One possible explanation is based on Heider's (1958) insight that people see others' dispositions in behavior because of a perceptual bias, something like an optical illusion. When you listen to a speech or watch a quiz show, the actor is the conspicuous *figure* of your attention; the situation fades into the *background* ("out of sight, out of mind," as they say). According to Heider, people attribute events to factors that are perceptually conspicuous, or *salient*. To test this hypothesis, Shelley Taylor and Susan Fiske (1975) varied the seating arrangements of observers who watched as two actors engaged in a carefully staged conversation. In each session, the participants were seated so that they faced actor A, actor B, or both actors. When later questioned about their observations, most participants rated the actor they faced as the more dominant member of the pair, the one who set the tone and direction.

© Roth Stock/Everett Collection

How knowledgeable is this man? Alex Trebek has hosted the TV quiz show *Jeopardy!* since 1984. As host, Trebek reads questions to contestants and then reveals the correct answers. In light of the quiz show study by Ross and others (1977), which illustrates the fundamental attribution error, viewers probably see Trebek as highly knowledgeable, despite knowing that the answers he recites are provided to him as part of his job.

Culture and Attribution

In the fifth century B.C.E., Herodotus, a Greek historian, argued that the Greeks and Egyptians thought differently because the Greeks wrote from left to right and the Egyptians from right to left. Many years later, inspired by anthropologist Edward Sapir, Benjamin Lee Whorf (1956) theorized that the language people speak—the words, the rules, and so on—determines the way they conceptualize the world. To illustrate, he pointed to cultural variations in the use of words to represent reality. He noted that the Hanunoo of the Philippines have 92 different terms for rice, in contrast to the crude distinction North Americans make between "white rice" and "brown rice." Similarly, while English speakers have one word for snow, Eskimos have several words, which, Whorf argued, enables them to make distinctions that others may miss between "falling snow, snow on the ground, snow packed hard like ice, slushy snow, wind-driven flying snow—whatever the situation may be" (p. 216).

Like social psychologists, people are sensitive to situational causes when explaining the behavior of others. **FALSE.**

As a result of many years of research, it is now clear that language and culture can influence the way people think about time, space, objects, and other aspects of the physical world around them (Bloom, 1981; Hardin & Banaji, 1993). Consider our perceptions of color. The rainbow is a continuum of light varying smoothly between the shortest and longest wavelengths of the visible spectrum. Yet when we look at it, we see distinct categories of color that correspond to "red," "orange," "yellow," "green," "blue," and so on. Languages differ in the parts of the color spectrum that are named. In Papua, New Guinea, where Berinmo speakers distinguish between green and brown (they single out a form of "khaki" as the color of dead leaves), an object reflecting light at 450 nanometers would be called green. Yet many English speakers, who distinguish between colors that cross the blue-green part of the spectrum, might see that same object as blue (Özgen, 2004).

Just as culture influences the way people perceive the physical world, so it also influences the way we view social events. Hence, although attribution researchers used to assume that people all over the world explained human behavior in the same ways, it is now clear that cultures shape in subtle but profound ways the kinds of attributions we make about people, their behavior, and social situations (Nisbett, 2003).

Consider the contrasting orientations between Western cultures (whose members tend to believe that persons are autonomous, motivated by internal forces, and responsible for their own actions) and non-Western "collectivist" cultures (whose members take a more holistic view that emphasizes the relationship between persons and their surroundings). Do these differing world views influence the attributions we make? Is it possible that the fundamental attribution error is a uniquely Western phenomenon? To answer these questions, Joan Miller (1984) asked Americans and Asian Indians of varying ages to describe the causes of positive and negative behaviors they had observed in their lives. Among young children, there were no cultural differences. With increasing age, however, the American participants made more personal attributions, while the Indians made more situational attributions (see ▶ Figure 4.7). Testing this hypothesis in different ways, other studies as well have revealed that people form habits of thought, learning to make attributions according to culturally formed beliefs about the causes of human behavior (Lieberman et al., 2005; Masuda & Kitayama, 2004; Miyamoto & Kitayama, 2002).

On this point, Ara Norenzayan and Richard Nisbett (2000) argue that cultural differences in attribution are founded on varying folk theories about human causality. Western cultures, they note, emphasize the individual person and his or her attributes, whereas East Asian cultures focus on the background or field that surrounds that person. To test this hypothesis, they showed American and Japanese college students underwater scenes featuring a cast of small fish, small animals, plants,

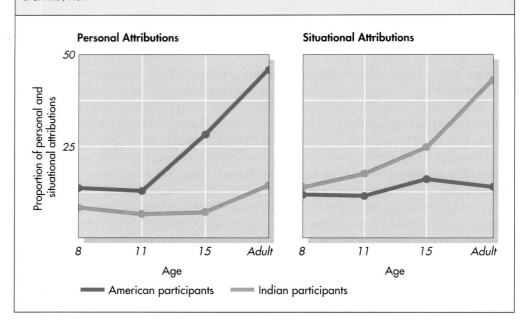

▶ **FIGURE 4.7**

Fundamental Attribution Error: A Western Bias?

American and Asian Indian participants of varying ages described the causes of negative actions they had observed. Among young children, there were no cultural differences. With increasing age, however, Americans made more personal attributions and Indian participants made more situational attributions. Explanations for positive behaviors followed a similar pattern. This finding suggests that the fundamental error is a Western phenomenon.

J. G. Miller, 1984.

Personal Attributions

Situational Attributions

Proportion of personal and situational attributions

50

25

8   11   15   Adic

Age

8   11   15   Adult

Age

━━ American participants   ━━ Indian participants

Look at this tropical underwater scene, then turn away and try to recount as much of it as you can. What did you notice? What did you forget? When researchers showed American and Japanese students underwater scenes, they found that while both groups recalled the focal fish (like the large blue one shown here), the Japanese recalled more about the elements of the background.

James T. Spencer/Photo-Researchers

rocks, and coral and one or more large, fast-moving *focal* fish, the stars of the show. Moments later, when asked to recount what they had seen, both groups recalled details about the focal fish to a nearly equal extent, but the Japanese reported far more details about the supporting cast in the background. Other researchers have also observed cultural differences in the extent to which people notice, think about, and remember the details of focal objects and their contexts (Ishii et al., 2003; Kitayama et al., 2003; Masuda & Nisbett, 2001).

These cultural differences can also be observed in naturally occurring settings outside a psychology laboratory. In an article entitled "Going for the Gold," Hazel Rose Markus and her colleagues (2006) compared the way Olympic performances were described in the United States and Japan. By analyzing the newspaper and TV coverage in these countries, these researchers discovered that although everyone attributed victory and defeat to the athletes, American media were more likely to focus on each athlete's unique personal attributes (such as strength, speed, health, and determination). "I just stayed focused," said Misty Hyman, American gold medalist swimmer. "It was time to show the world what I could do." In addition to reflecting on personal attributes, Japanese media were also more likely to report more wholly on an athlete's background, his or her mental state, and the role of others such as parents, coaches, and competitors. Woman's marathon gold medalist Naoko Takahashi explained her own success this way: "Here is the best coach in the world, the best manager in the world, and all of the people who support me—all of these things were getting together and became a gold medal."

Clearly, the world is becoming a global village characterized by increasing racial and ethnic diversity within countries. Many people who migrate from one country to another become *bicultural* in their identity, retaining some ancestral manners of thought while adopting some of the lifestyles and values of their new homeland. How might these bicultural individuals make attributions for human behavior? Is it possible that they view people through one cultural frame or the other, depending on which one is brought to mind? It's interesting that when shown a picture of one fish swimming ahead of a group, and asked why, Americans see the lone fish as *leading* the others (a personal attribution), while Chinese see the same fish as being *chased* by the others (a situational attribution). But what about bicultural social perceivers? In a study of China-born students attending college in California, researchers presented images symbolizing one of the two cultures (such as the U.S. and Chinese flags), administered the fish test, and found that compared to students exposed to the American images, those who saw the Chinese images made more situational attributions, seeing the lone fish as being chased rather than as leading (see ▶ Figure 4.8). Apparently, it is possible for us to hold differing cultural worldviews at the same time and to perceive others through either lens, depending on which culture is brought to mind (Hong et al., 2000; Oyserman & Lee, 2008).

▦ Motivational Biases

As objective as we try to be, our social perceptions are sometimes colored by personal needs, wishes, and preferences. This tendency shows itself in the officiating controversies of the Olympics every four years, in other competitive sports, and in talent contests such as *American Idol*. To illustrate, look at the object in ▶ Figure 4.9. What do you see? In a series of studies, Emily Balcetis and David Dunning (2006) showed stimuli like this one to college students who thought they were participating in a taste-testing experiment. The students were told that they would be randomly assigned to taste either freshly squeezed orange juice or a vile, greenish, foul-smelling "organic" drink—depending on whether a letter or a number was flashed on a laptop computer. For those told that a letter would assign them to the orange juice condition, 72 percent saw the letter "B." For those told that a number would assign them to the orange juice, 61 percent saw the number "13." In some very basic ways, people have a tendency to see what they want to see.

People have a strong need for self-esteem, a motive that can lead us to make favorable, self-serving, and one-sided attributions for our own behavior. In Chapter 3, we saw that research with students, teachers, parents, workers, athletes, and others shows that people tend to take more credit for success than blame for failure. Similarly, people seek more information about their strengths than about weaknesses, overestimate their contributions to group efforts, exaggerate their control, and predict a rosy future. The false-consensus effect described earlier also has a self-serving side to it. It seems that we overestimate the extent to which others think, feel, and behave as we do, in part to assure ourselves that our ways are correct, normal, and socially appropriate

▶ **FIGURE 4.8**

Attributions Within Cultural Frames

When one fish swims ahead of the others in a group, Americans see that fish as leading the others (a personal attribution), while Chinese see it as being chased by the others (a situational attribution). In a study of bicultural Chinese students attending college in California, Ying-yi Hong and others (2000) displayed visual images that symbolized the United States or China before administering the fish test. As you can see, compared to students who were not shown any images (center), the tendency to make situational attributions was more common among those exposed to Chinese images (right) and less common among those exposed to American images (left). It appears that social perceptions are fluid for people who are familiar with more than one world view and that their perceptions depend on which culture is brought to mind.

Hong et al., 2000.

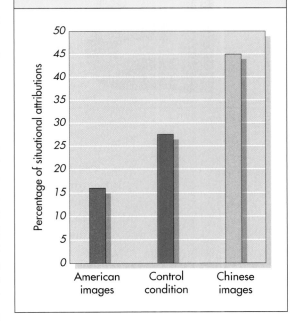

▶**FIGURE 4.9**

Motivated Visual Perception: How People See What They Want to See

Look at the image below. What do you see, the letter B or the number 13? The stimulus itself is ambiguous and can plausibly be seen either way. Research participants who thought they were in a taste-testing experiment were told that they'd be assigned to taste orange juice or a foul-smelling green drink depending on whether a letter or a number was flashed on a laptop computer. For those told that a *letter* would yield orange juice, 72 percent saw the image as "B." For those told that a *number* would yield orange juice, 61 percent saw a "13." This difference shows that sometimes people see what they *want* to see.

Balcetis & Dunning, 2006.

belief in a just world The belief that individuals get what they deserve in life, an orientation that leads people to disparage victims.

(Alicke & Largo, 1995). This positivity bias in attributions is ubiquitous. Through a meta-analysis of 266 studies involving thousands of participants, Amy Mezulis and others (2004) found that except in some Asian cultures, "the self-serving bias is pervasive in the general population" (p. 711).

According to Dunning (2005), the need for self-esteem can bias social perceptions in other subtle ways, too, even when we don't realize that the self is implicated. For example, do you consider yourself to be a "people person," or are you more of a "task-oriented" type? And which of the two styles do you think makes for great leadership? It turns out that students who describe themselves as people-oriented see social skills as necessary for good leadership, while those who are more task-focused see a task orientation as better for leadership. Hence, people tend to judge favorably others who are similar to themselves rather than different on key characteristics (McElwee et al., 2001).

Sometimes ideological motives can color our attributions for the behavior of others. In the United States, it is common for political conservatives to blame poverty, crime, and other social problems on an "underclass" of people who are uneducated, lazy, immoral, or self-indulgent; in contrast, liberals often attribute these same problems to social and economic institutions that favor some groups over others. Do conservatives and liberals think differently about the causes of human behavior, or do the attributions they make depend on whether the particular behavior they're trying to explain fits with their ideology? In a series of studies, Linda Skitka and others (2002) had college students who identified themselves as conservative or liberal make attributions for various events. They found that while participants in general made personal attributions, as Westerners reflexively tend to do, they corrected for situational factors when ideologically motivated to do so. To explain why a prisoner was paroled, conservatives were more likely to believe that the facility was overcrowded (a situational attribution) than that the prisoner had reformed (a personal attribution); to explain why a man lost his job, liberals were more likely to blame the company's finances (a situational attribution) than the worker's poor performance (a personal attribution).

At times, personal defensive motives lead us to blame others for their misfortunes. Consider the following classic experiment. Participants thought they were taking part in an emotion-perception study. One person, actually a confederate, was selected randomly to take a memory test while the others looked on. Each time the confederate made a mistake, she was jolted by a painful electric shock (actually, there was no shock; what participants saw was a staged videotape). Since participants knew that only the luck of the draw had kept them off the "hot seat," you might think they would react with sympathy and compassion. Not so. In fact, they belittled the hapless confederate (Lerner & Simmons, 1966).

Melvin Lerner (1980) argues that the tendency to be critical of victims stems from our deep-seated **belief in a just world**. According to Lerner, people need to view the world as a just place in which we "get what we deserve" and "deserve what we get"—a world where hard work and clean living always pay off and where laziness and a sinful lifestyle are punished. To believe otherwise is to concede that we, too, are vulnerable to the cruel twists and turns of fate. Research suggests that the belief in a just world can help victims cope and serves as a buffer against stress. But how might this belief system influence our perceptions of *others*? If people cannot help or compensate the victims of misfortune, they turn on them. Thus, it is often assumed that poor people are lazy, that crime victims are careless, that battered wives provoke their abusive husbands, and that gay men and women with AIDS are promiscuous. As you might expect, cross-national comparisons reveal that people in poorer countries are less likely than those in more affluent countries to believe in a just world (Furnham, 2003).

The tendency to disparage victims may seem like just another symptom of the fundamental attribution error: too much focus on the person and not enough on the situation. But the conditions that trigger this tendency suggest there is more to it. Over the years, studies have shown that accident victims are held more responsible for their fate when the consequences of the accident are severe rather than mild (Walster, 1966), when the victim's situation is similar to the perceiver's (Shaver, 1970), when the perceiver is generally anxious about threats to the self (Thornton, 1992), and when the perceiver identifies with the victim (Aguiar et al., 2008). Apparently, the more threatened we feel by an apparent injustice, the greater is the need to protect ourselves from the dreadful implication that it could happen to us, an implication we defend by disparaging the victim. Ironically, recent research shows that people may also satisfy their belief in a just world by *enhancing* members of disadvantaged groups—for example, by inferring that poor people are happy and that obese people are sociable, both attributes that restore justice by compensation (Kay & Jost, 2003; Kay et al., 2005).

"And see that you place the blame where it will do the most good."

Attributions of blame are often biased by self-serving motivations.

In a laboratory experiment that reveals part of this process at work, participants watched a TV news story about a boy who was robbed and beaten. Some were told that the boy's assailants were captured, tried, and sent to prison. Others were told that the assailants fled the country, never to be brought to trial—a story that strains one's belief in a just world. Afterward, participants were asked to name as quickly as they could the colors in which various words in a list were typed (for example, the word *chair* may have been written in blue, *floor* in yellow, and *wide* in red). When the words themselves were neutral, all participants—regardless of which story they had seen—were equally fast at naming the colors. But when the words pertained to justice (words such as *fair* and *unequal*), those who had seen the justice-threatened version of the story were more distracted by the words and hence slower to name the colors. In fact, the more distracted they were, the more they derogated the victim. With their cherished belief in a just world threatened, these participants became highly sensitive to the concept of "justice" and quick to disparage the innocent victim (Hafer, 2000).

Integration: From Dispositions to Impressions

When behavior is attributed to situational factors, we do not generally make inferences about the actor. However, personal attributions often lead us to infer that a person has a certain disposition—that the leader of a failing business is incompetent, for example, or that the enemy who extends the olive branch seeks peace. Human beings are not one-dimensional, however, and one trait does not a person make. To have a complete picture of someone, social perceivers must assemble the various bits and pieces into a unified impression.

◫ Information Integration: The Arithmetic

Once personal attributions are made, how are they combined into a single coherent picture of a person? How do we approach the process of **impression formation**? Do we simply add up all of a person's traits and calculate a mental average or do we combine the information in more complicated ways? Anyone who has written or received letters of recommendation will surely appreciate the practical implications. Suppose you're told that an applicant is friendly and intelligent, two highly favorable qualities. Would you be more or less impressed if you then learned that this applicant was also prudent and even-tempered, two moderately favorable qualities? If you are more impressed, then you are intuitively following a *summation* model of impression formation: The more positive traits there are, the better. If you are less impressed, then you are using an *averaging* model: The higher the average value of all the various traits, the better.

To quantify the formation of impressions, Norman Anderson (1968) had research participants rate the desirability of 555 traits on a 7-point scale. By calculating the average ratings, he obtained a *scale value* for each trait (*sincere* had the highest scale value; *liar* had the lowest). In an earlier study, Anderson (1965) used similar values and compared the summation and averaging models. Specifically, he asked a group of participants to rate how much they liked a person described by two traits with extremely high scale values (*H, H*). A second group received a list of four traits that included two that were high and two that were moderately high in their scale values (*H, H, Ml, Ml*). In a third group, participants received two extremely low, negative traits (*L, L*). In a fourth group, they received four traits, including two that were low and two that were moderately low (*L, L, M2, M2*). What effect did the moderate traits have on impressions? As predicted by an averaging model, the moderate traits diluted from rather than added to the impact of the highly positive and negative traits. The practical implication for those who write letters of recommendation is clear. Applicants are better off if their letters include only the most glowing comments and omit favorable remarks that are somewhat more guarded in nature.

After extensive amounts of research, it appears that although people tend to combine traits by averaging, the process is somewhat more complicated. Consistent with Anderson's (1981) **information integration theory**, impressions formed of others are based on a combination, or integration, of (1) personal dispositions of the perceiver and (2) a *weighted* average, not a simple average, of the target person's characteristics (Kashima & Kerekes, 1994). Let's look more closely at these two sets of factors.

◫ Deviations from the Arithmetic

Like other aspects of our social perceptions, impression formation does not follow the rules of cold logic. Weighted averaging may describe the way most people combine different traits, but the whole process begins with a warm-blooded human perceiver, not a computer. Thus, certain deviations from the "arithmetic" are inevitable.

Perceiver Characteristics   To begin with, each of us differs in terms of the kinds of impressions we form of others. Some people seem to measure everyone with an intellectual yardstick; others look for physical beauty, a warm smile, a good sense of humor, or a firm handshake. Whatever the attribute, each of us is more likely to notice and recall certain traits than others (Bargh et al., 1988; Higgins et al., 1982). Thus, when people are asked to describe a group of target individuals, there's typically more overlap between the various descriptions provided by the same perceiver than there is between those provided for the same target (Dornbusch et al., 1965; Park, 1986). Part of

impression formation
The process of integrating information about a person to form a coherent impression.

information integration theory
The theory that impressions are based on (1) perceiver dispositions; and (2) a weighted average of a target person's traits.

the reason for differences among perceivers is that we tend to use ourselves as a standard, or frame of reference, when evaluating others. Compared with the inert couch potato, for example, the serious jock is more likely to see others as less active and athletic (Dunning & Hayes, 1996). As we saw earlier, people also tend to see their own skills and traits as particularly desirable for others to have (McElwee et al., 2001).

A perceiver's current, temporary mood can also influence the impressions formed of others (Forgas, 2000). For example, Joseph Forgas and Gordon Bower (1987) told research participants that they had performed very well or poorly on a test of social adjustment. As expected, this feedback altered their moods, but it also affected their view of others. When presented with behavioral information about various characters, participants spent more time attending to positive facts and formed more favorable impressions when they were happy than when they were sad. Follow-up research shows that people who are induced into a happy mood are also more optimistic, more lenient, and less critical in the attributions they make for others who succeed or fail (Forgas & Locke, 2005). They are also more likely to interpret another person's smile as genuine and heartfelt (Forgas & East, 2008).

Priming Effects   Clearly, the combined effects of stable perceiver differences and fluctuating moods point to an important conclusion: that to some extent, impression formation is in the eye of the beholder. The characteristics we tend to see in other people also change from time to time, depending on recent experiences. Have you ever noticed that once a seldom-used word slips into a conversation or appears on a blog, it is often repeated over and over again? If so, then you have observed **priming**, the tendency for frequently or recently used concepts to come to mind easily and influence the way we interpret new information.

The effect of priming on person impressions was first demonstrated by E. Tory Higgins and others (1977). Research participants were presented with a list of trait words, ostensibly as part of an experiment on memory. In fact, the task was designed as a priming device to plant certain ideas in their minds. Some participants read words that evoked a positive image: *brave, independent, adventurous*. Others read words that evoked a more negative image: *reckless, foolish, careless*. Later, in what they thought to be an unrelated experiment, participants read about a man named Donald who climbed mountains, drove in a demolition derby, and tried to cross the Atlantic Ocean in a sailboat. As predicted, their impressions of Donald were shaped by the trait words they had earlier memorized. Those exposed to positive words later formed more favorable impressions of him than those exposed to negative words. All the participants read exactly the same description, yet they formed different impressions depending on what concept was already on their minds to be used as a basis for comparison (Mussweiler & Damisch, 2008). In fact, priming seems to work best when the prime words are presented so rapidly that people are not even aware of the exposure (Bargh & Pietromonaco, 1982).

Additional research has shown that our motivation and even our social behavior are also subject to the automatic effects of priming without awareness. In one provocative study, John Bargh and Tanya Chartrand (1999) gave participants a "word search" puzzle that contained either neutral words or words associated with achievement motivation (*strive, win, master, compete, succeed*). Afterward, the participants were left alone and given three minutes to write down as many words as they could form from a set of Scrabble letter tiles. When the three-minute limit was up, they were signaled over an intercom to stop. Did these participants, who were driven to obtain a high score, stop on cue or continue to write? Through the use of hidden cameras, the experimenters observed that 57 percent of those primed with achievement-related words continued to write after the stop signal, compared to only 22 percent in the control group.

priming   The tendency for recently used or perceived words or ideas to come to mind easily and influence the interpretation of new information.

Looking at priming effects on social behavior, Bargh, Chen, and Burrows (1996) gave people 30 sets of words presented in scrambled order ("he it hides finds instantly") and told them to use some of the words in each set to form grammatical sentences. After explaining the test, which would take five minutes, the experimenter told participants to locate him down the hall when they were finished so he could administer a second task. So far so good. But when participants found the experimenter, he was in the hallway immersed in conversation, and he stayed in that conversation for 10 full minutes without acknowledging their presence. What's a person to do, wait patiently or interrupt? The participants didn't know it, but some had worked on a scrambled word test that contained many "politeness" words (*yield, respect, considerate, courteous*), while others had been exposed to words related to rudeness (*disturb, intrude, bold, bluntly*). Would these test words secretly prime participants, a few minutes later, to behave in one way or the other? Yes. Compared with those given the neutral words to unscramble, participants primed for rudeness were more likely—and those primed for politeness were less likely—to break in and interrupt the experimenter (see ▶ Figure 4.10).

What accounts for this effect of priming, not only on our social perceptions but also on our behavior? The link between perception and behavior is automatic; it happens like a mindless reflex. Present scrambled words that prime the "elderly" stereotype (*old, bingo*) and research participants walk out of the experiment more slowly as if mimicking an elderly person (Dijksterhuis & Bargh, 2001). But why? Joseph Cesario and others (2006) suggest that the automatic priming of behavior is an adaptive social mechanism that helps us to prepare for upcoming encounters with a primed target—if we are so motivated. After measuring participants' attitudes toward the elderly, these researchers predicted and found that those who liked old people walked more slowly after priming (as if synchronizing with a slow friend), while those who disliked old people walked more quickly (as if fleeing from such an interaction).

Target Characteristics   Just as not all social perceivers are created equal, neither are all traits created equal. In recent years, personality researchers have discovered, across cultures, that individuals can reliably be distinguished from one another along five broad traits, or factors: extroversion, emotional stability, openness to experience, agreeableness, and conscientiousness (De Raad, 2000; McCrae & Costa, 2003; Wiggins, 1996). Some of these factors are easier to judge than others. Based on their review of 32 studies, David Kenny and others (1994) found that social perceivers are most likely to agree in their judgments of a target's extroversion: that is, the extent to which he or she is sociable, friendly, fun-loving, outgoing, and adventurous. It seems that this characteristic is easy to spot, and different perceivers often agree on it even when rating a target person whom they are seeing for the first time.

The valence of a trait—whether it is considered good or bad—also affects its impact on our final impressions. Over the years, research has shown that people exhibit a *trait negativity bias*, the tendency for negative information to weigh more heavily on our impressions than positive information (Rozin & Royzman, 2001; Skowronski & Carlston, 1989). This means that we form more extreme impressions of a person who is said to be dishonest than of one who is said to be honest. It seems that we tend to view others favorably, so we are quick to take notice and pay more careful

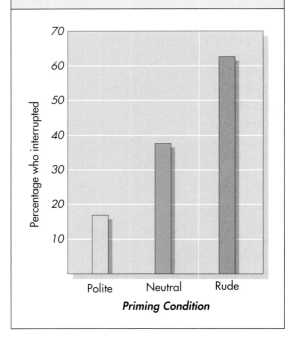

▶ **FIGURE 4.10**

The Priming of Social Behavior Without Awareness

Would waiting participants interrupt the busy experimenter? Compared with those who had previously been given neutral words to unscramble (center), participants given politeness words were less likely to cut in (left) and those given rudeness words were more likely to cut in (right). These results show that priming can influence not only our social judgments but our behavior as well.

Bargh et al., 1996.

attention when this expectation is violated (Pratto & John, 1991). One bad trait may well be enough to destroy a person's reputation, regardless of other qualities. Research on American political campaigns confirms the point: Public opinion is shaped more by a candidate's "negatives" than by positive information (Klein, 1991; Lau, 1985). In light of all this research, Baumeister and others (2001) have concluded that bad is stronger than good in a "disappointingly relentless pattern" (p. 362).

When you think about it, it's probably adaptive for people to stay alert for and pay particularly close attention to negative, potentially threatening information. Recent research suggests that people are quicker to sense their exposure to subliminally pre-sented negative words such as *bomb, thief, shark,* and *cancer* than to positive words such as *baby, sweet, friend,* and *beach* (Dijkster-huis & Aarts, 2003). This sensitivity to nega-tive information is found in infants less than a year old (Vaish et al., 2008). It can also be "seen" in the brain (N. K. Smith et al., 2003). In one study, Tiffany Ito and others (1998) exposed research participants to slides that depicted images that were positive (a red Fer-rari, people enjoying a roller coaster), nega-tive (a mutilated face, a handgun pointed at the camera), or neutral (a plate, a hair dryer). Using electrodes attached to participants' scalps, these researchers recorded electrical activity in different areas of the brain dur-ing the slide presentation. Sure enough, they

Brain research shows that when peo-ple are exposed to negative emotional images—such as the car bomb on the right as opposed to the beach scene on the left—activity in certain parts of the brain is more pronounced.

observed that certain types of activity were more pronounced when participants saw negative images than when they saw stimuli that were positive or neutral. It appears, as these researchers commented, that "negative information weighs more heavily on the brain" (p. 887).

The impact of trait information on our impressions of others depends not only on characteristics of the perceiver and target but on context as well. Two contextual fac-tors are particularly important in this regard: (1) implicit theories of personality; and (2) the order in which we receive information about one trait relative to other traits.

Implicit Personality Theories   Years ago, when O. J. Simpson was charged with brutally murdering his ex-wife Nicole and her friend Ron Goldman, everyone was shocked. Simpson was a national hero: athletic, attractive, charming, intelligent, and successful. Once the premier running back in the National Football League, Simpson went on to become a sports broadcaster, Hollywood actor, and father of four children.

It's easy to understand why people initially reacted to the charges with disbelief. Simpson just didn't seem like *the kind of person* who would commit a cold-blooded murder. The reaction was based on an **implicit personality theory**—a network of assumptions that we hold about relationships among various types of people, traits, and behaviors. Knowing that someone has one trait thus leads us to infer that he or she has other traits as well (Bruner & Tagiuri, 1954; Schneider, 1973; Sedikides & Ander-son, 1994). For example, you might assume that a person who is unpredictable is prob-ably also dangerous or that someone who speaks slowly is also slow-witted. You might also assume that certain traits and behaviors are linked together (Reeder, 1993; Reeder & Brewer, 1979)—that a beloved sports hero like O. J. Simpson, for example, could not possibly stab two people to death.

implicit personality theory
A network of assumptions people make about the relationships among traits and behaviors.

Solomon Asch (1946) was the first to discover that the presence of one trait often implies the presence of other traits. Asch told one group of research participants that an individual was "intelligent, skillful, industrious, warm, determined, practical and cautious." Another group read an identical list of traits, except that the word *warm* was replaced by *cold*. Only the one term was changed, but the two groups formed very different impressions. Participants inferred that the warm person was also happier and more generous, good-natured, and humorous than the cold person. Yet when two other words were varied (*polite* and *blunt*), the differences were less pronounced. Why? Asch concluded that *warm* and *cold* are **central traits**, meaning that they imply the presence of certain other traits and exert a powerful influence on final impressions. Other researchers have observed similar effects (Stapel & Koomen, 2000). In fact, when college students in different classes were told ahead of time that a guest lecturer was a warm or cold person, their impressions after the lecture were consistent with these beliefs, even though he gave the same lecture to everyone (Kelley 1950; Widmeyer & Loy 1988).

Is there something magical about the traits warm and cold? To learn more about the structure of implicit personality theories, Seymour Rosenberg and his colleagues (1968) handed research participants 60 cards, each with a trait word written on it, and asked them to sort the cards into piles that represented specific people, perhaps friends, coworkers, acquaintances, or celebrities. The traits were then statistically correlated to determine how often they appeared together in the same pile. The results were plotted to display the psychological distance between the various characteristics. The "map" shown in ▶ Figure 4.11 shows that the traits—positive and negative alike— were best captured by two dimensions: social and intellectual. More recent research has since confirmed this basic point that people differentiate each other first in terms of warmth ("warm" is seen in such traits as friendly, helpful, and sincere), and second in terms of their competence ("competent" is seen in such traits as smart, skillful, and determined). According to Susan Fiske and her colleagues (2007), warmth and competence are "universal dimensions of social cognition."

The Primacy Effect The order in which a trait is discovered can also influence its impact. It is often said that first impressions are critical, and social psychologists are quick to agree. Studies show that information often has greater impact when presented early in a sequence rather than late, a common phenomenon known as the **primacy effect**.

In another of Asch's (1946) classic experiments, one group of participants learned that a person was "intelligent, industrious, impulsive, critical, stubborn, and envious." A second group received exactly the same list but in reverse order. Rationally speaking, the two groups should have felt the same way about the person. But instead, participants who heard the first list in which the more positive traits came first formed more favorable impressions than did those who heard the second list. Similar findings were obtained among participants who watched a videotape of a woman taking an SAT-like test. In all cases, she correctly answered 15 out of 30 multiple-choice questions. But participants who observed a pattern of initial success followed by failure perceived the woman as more intelligent than did those who observed the opposite pattern of failure followed by success (Jones et al., 1968). There are exceptions, but as a general rule, people tend to be more heavily influenced by the "early returns."

What accounts for this primacy effect? There are two basic explanations. The first is that once perceivers think they have formed an accurate impression of someone, they tend to pay less attention to subsequent information. Thus, when research participants read a series of statements about a person, the amount of time they spent reading each of the items declined steadily with each succeeding statement (Belmore, 1987).

central traits Traits that exert a powerful influence on overall impressions.

primacy effect The tendency for information presented early in a sequence to have more impact on impressions than information presented later.

► **FIGURE 4.11**

Universal Dimensions of Social Cognition

Rosenberg and others (1968) asked people to sort 60 cards, each with a trait word on it, into piles that depicted specific individuals. Through a statistical procedure used to plot how frequently the various traits appeared together, an implicit personality theory "map" emerged. This map shows that both positive and negative traits can be ordered along two dimensions: social (warmth) and intellectual (competent). Since this study, other research has confirmed that warmth and competence are universal dimensions by which people perceive each other.

Rosenberg et al., 1968.

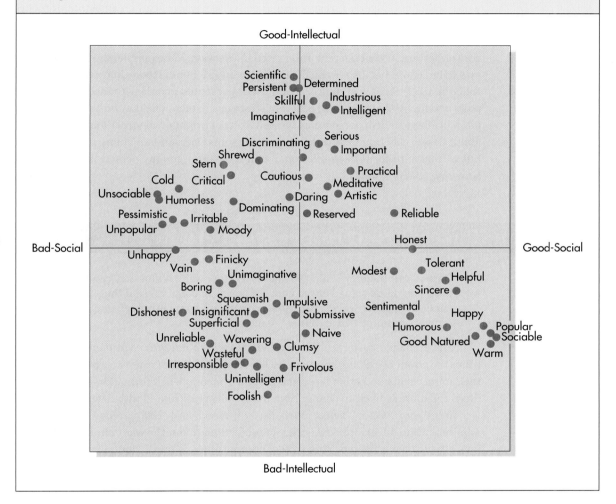

Does this mean we are doomed to a life of primacy? Not at all. If we are unstimulated or mentally tired, our attention may wane. But if perceivers are sufficiently motivated to avoid tuning out and are not pressured to form a quick first impression, then primacy effects are diminished (Anderson & Hubert, 1963; Kruglanski & Freund, 1983). In one study, college students "leaped to conclusions" about a target person on the basis of preliminary information when they were mentally fatigued from having just taken a two-hour exam but not when they were fresh, alert, and motivated to pay attention (Webster et al., 1996). In addition, Arie Kruglanski and Donna Webster (1996) found that some people are more likely than others to "seize" upon and "freeze" their first impressions. Apparently, individuals differ in their **need for closure**, the desire to reduce ambiguity. People who are low in this regard are open-minded, deliberate, and perhaps even reluctant to draw firm conclusions about others. In contrast,

need for closure The desire to reduce cognitive uncertainty, which heightens the importance of first impressions.

those who are high in the need for closure tend to be impulsive and impatient and to form quick and lasting judgments of others.

More unsettling is the second reason for primacy, known as the *change-of-meaning hypothesis*. Once people have formed an impression, they start to interpret inconsistent information in light of that impression. Asch's research shows just how malleable the meaning of a trait can be. When people are told that a kind person is *calm*, they assume that he or she is gentle, peaceful, and serene. When a cruel person is said to be *calm*, however, the same word is interpreted to mean cool, shrewd, and calculating. There are many examples to illustrate the point. Based on your first impression, the word *proud* can mean self-respecting or conceited, *critical* can mean astute or picky, and *impulsive* can mean spontaneous or reckless.

It is remarkable just how creative we are in our efforts to transform a bundle of contradictions into a coherent, integrated impression. For example, the person who is said to be "good" but also "a thief" can be viewed as a Robin Hood character (Burnstein & Schul, 1982). Asch and Henri Zukier (1984) presented people with inconsistent trait pairs and found that they used different strategies to reconcile the conflicts. For example, a brilliant-foolish person may be seen as "very bright on abstract matters, but silly about day-to-day practical tasks," a sociable-lonely person has "many superficial ties but is unable to form deep relations," and a cheerful-gloomy person may simply be someone who is "moody."

Confirmation Biases: From Impressions to Reality

"Please your majesty," said the knave, "I didn't write it and they can't prove I did; there's no name signed at the end." "If you didn't sign it," said the King, "that only makes the matter worse. You must have meant some mischief, or else you'd have signed your name like an honest man."

It is a capital mistake to theorize before you have all the evidence. It biases the judgment.

—Arthur Conan Doyle

This exchange, taken from Lewis Carroll's *Alice's Adventures in Wonderland*, illustrates the power of existing impressions. It is striking but often true: Once people make up their minds about something—even if they have incomplete information—they become more and more unlikely to change their minds when confronted with new evidence.

In his book *State of Denial*, journalist Bob Woodward (2006) argued that the Bush administration never altered its original projections about the war in Iraq despite military intelligence warnings. This type of stubbornness is hardly unique. Political leaders often refuse to withdraw support for government programs that don't work, just as scientists steadfastly defend their pet theories in the face of contradictory research data. All these instances are easy to explain. Presidents, politicians, and scientists have personal stakes in their opinions, as votes, pride, funding, and reputation may be at risk. But what about people who more innocently fail to revise their opinions, often to their own detriment? What about the baseball manager who clings to old strategies that are ineffective or the trial lawyer who consistently selects juries according to false stereotypes? Why are they often slow to face the facts? As we will see, people are subject to various **confirmation biases**—tendencies to interpret, seek, and create information in ways that verify existing beliefs.

confirmation bias The tendency to seek, interpret, and create information that verifies existing beliefs.

■ Perseverance of Beliefs

Imagine you are looking at a slide that is completely out of focus. Gradually, it becomes focused enough so that the image is less blurry. At this point, the experimenter wants to know if you can recognize the picture. The response you're likely to make is interesting. Participants in experiments of this type have more trouble making an identification if they watch the gradual focusing procedure than if they simply view the final, blurry image. In the mechanics of the perceptual process, people apparently form early impressions that interfere with their subsequent ability to "see straight" once presented with improved evidence (Bruner & Potter, 1964). As we will see in this section, social perception is subject to the same kind of interference, which is another reason why first impressions often stick like glue even after we are forced to confront information that discredits them.

Consider what happens when you're led to expect something that does not materialize. In one study, John Darley and Paget Gross (1983) asked participants to evaluate the academic potential of a 9-year-old girl named Hannah. One group was led to believe that Hannah came from an affluent community in which both parents were well-educated professionals (high expectations). A second group thought that she was from a run-down urban neighborhood and that both parents were uneducated blue-collar workers (low expectations). As shown in ▶ Figure 4.12, participants in the first group were slightly more optimistic in their ratings of Hannah's potential than were those in the second group. In each of these groups, however, half the participants then watched a videotape of Hannah taking an achievement test. Her performance on the tape seemed average. She correctly answered some difficult questions but missed others that were relatively easy. Look again at Figure 4.12 and you'll see that even though all participants saw the same tape, Hannah now received much lower ratings of ability from those who thought she was poor and higher ratings from those who thought she was affluent. Apparently, presenting an identical body of mixed evidence did not extinguish the biasing effects of beliefs; it *fueled* these effects.

Events that are ambiguous enough to support contrasting interpretations are like inkblots: We see in them what we want or expect to see. Illustrating the point, researchers had people rate from photographs the extent to which pairs of adults and children resembled each other. Interestingly, the participants did not see more resemblance in parents and offspring than in random pairs of adults and children. Yet when told that certain pairs were related, they did "see" a resemblance, even when the relatedness information was false (Bressan & Martello, 2002).

What about information that plainly disconfirms our beliefs? What then happens to our first impressions? Craig Anderson and his colleagues (1980) addressed this question by supplying participants with false information. After they had time to think

▶ **FIGURE 4.12**

Mixed Evidence: Does It Extinguish or Fuel First Impressions?

Participants evaluated the potential of a schoolgirl. Without seeing her test performance, those with high expectations rated her slightly higher than did those with low expectations. Among the participants who watched a tape of the girl taking a test, the expectations effect was even greater.

Darley & Gross, 1983.

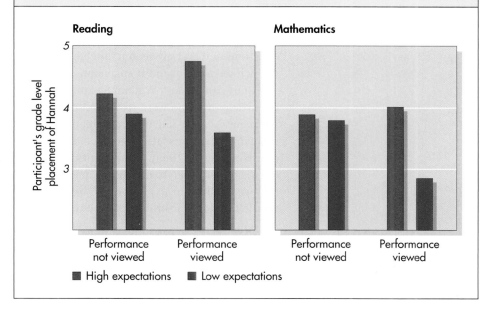

about it, they were told that it was untrue. In one experiment, half the participants read case studies suggesting that people who take risks make better firefighters than do those who are cautious. The others read cases suggesting the opposite conclusion. Next, participants were asked to come up with a theory for the suggested correlation. The possibilities are easy to imagine: "He who hesitates is lost" supports risk-taking, whereas "You have to look before you leap" supports caution. Finally, participants were led to believe that the session was over and were told that the information they had received was false, manufactured for the sake of the experiment. Participants, however, did not abandon their theories about firefighters. Instead they exhibited **belief perseverance**, sticking to initial beliefs even after these had been discredited. Apparently, it's easier to get people to build a theory than to convince them to tear it down. Thus, five full months after the terrorist attack on the World Trade Center, the Gallup Organization interviewed some 10,000 residents of nine Muslim countries and found that 61 percent did *not* believe—despite hard evidence—that the attacks were carried out by Arab men (Gallup Poll Editors, 2002).

Why do beliefs often outlive the evidence on which they are supposed to be based? The reason is that when people conjure up explanations that make sense, those explanations take on a life of their own. In fact, once people form an opinion, that opinion becomes strengthened when they merely *think* about the topic, even if they do not articulate the reasons for it (Tesser, 1978). And therein lies a possible solution. By asking people to consider why an *alternative* theory might be true, we can reduce or eliminate the belief perseverance effects to which they are vulnerable (Anderson & Sechler, 1986).

People are slow to change their first impressions on the basis of new information. **TRUE.**

▮ Confirmatory Hypothesis Testing

Social perceivers are not passive recipients of information. Like detectives, we ask questions and actively search for clues. But do we seek information objectively or are we inclined to confirm the suspicions we already hold?

Mark Snyder and William Swann (1978) addressed this question by having pairs of participants who were strangers to one another take part in a getting-acquainted interview. In each pair, one participant was supposed to interview the other. But first, that participant was falsely led to believe that his or her partner was either introverted or extroverted (actually, participants were assigned to these conditions on a random basis) and was then told to select questions from a prepared list. Those who thought they were talking to an introvert chose mostly introvert-oriented questions ("Have you ever felt left out of some social group?"), while those who thought they were talking to an extrovert asked extrovert-oriented questions ("How do you liven up a party?"). Expecting a certain kind of person, participants unwittingly sought evidence that would confirm their expectations. By asking loaded questions, in fact, the interviewers actually gathered support for their beliefs. Thus, neutral observers who later listened to the tapes were also left with the mistaken impression that the interviewees really were as introverted or extroverted as the interviewers had assumed.

This last part of the study is powerful but in hindsight not all that surprising. Imagine yourself on the receiving end of an interview. Asked about what you do to liven up parties, you would probably talk about organizing group games, playing dance music, and telling jokes. On the other hand, if you were asked about difficult social situations, you might talk about being nervous before oral presentations or about what it feels like to be the new kid on the block. In other words, simply by going along with the questions that are asked, you supply evidence confirming the interviewer's beliefs. Thus, perceivers set in motion a vicious cycle: Thinking someone has a certain trait,

belief perseverance
The tendency to maintain beliefs even after they have been discredited.

they engage in a one-sided search for information and in doing so, they create a reality that ultimately supports their beliefs (Zuckerman et al., 1995).

Are people so blinded by their existing beliefs that they cannot manage an open and objective search for evidence? It depends. In the type of task devised by Snyder and Swann, different circumstances produce less biasing results. Specifically, when people are not certain of their beliefs and are concerned about the accuracy of their impressions (Kruglanski & Mayseless, 1988), when they are allowed to prepare their own interviews (Trope et al., 1984), or when available nonconfirmatory questions are better than the confirmatory questions (Skov & Sherman, 1986), they tend to pursue a more balanced search for information.

Let's stop for a moment and contemplate what this research means for the broader question of why we often seem to resist changing our negative but mistaken impressions of others more than our positive but mistaken impressions. Jerker Denrell (2005) argues that even when we form a negative first impression on the basis of all available evidence and even when we interpret that evidence accurately, our impression may be misleading. The reason: *biased experience sampling*. Meet someone who seems likable and you may interact with that person again. Then if he or she turns out to be twisted, dishonest, or self-centered, you'll be in a position to observe these traits and revise your impression. But if you meet someone you don't like, you will try to avoid that person in the future, cutting yourself off from new information and limiting the opportunity to revise your opinion. Attraction breeds interaction, which is why our negative first impressions in particular tend to persist.

The Self-Fulfilling Prophecy

In 1948, sociologist Robert Merton told a story that is particularly instructive for us today in light of the recent economic downturn. The story was about Cartwright Millingville, president of the Last National Bank during the Great Depression of the 1930s. The bank was solvent, yet a rumor began to spread that it was floundering. Within hours, hundreds of depositors were lined up to withdraw their savings before no money was left to withdraw. The rumor was false, but the bank eventually failed. Using stories such as this, Merton proposed what seemed like an outrageous hypothesis: that a perceiver's expectation can actually lead to its own fulfillment, a **self-fulfilling prophecy**.

Merton's hypothesis lay dormant within psychology until Robert Rosenthal and Lenore Jacobson (1968) published the results of a study in a book entitled *Pygmalion in the Classroom*. Noticing that teachers had higher expectations for better students, they wondered if teacher expectations *influenced* student performance rather than the other way around. To address the question, they told teachers in a San Francisco elementary school that certain pupils were on the verge of an intellectual growth spurt. The results of an IQ test were cited, but in fact, the pupils had been randomly selected. Eight months later, when real tests were administered, the "late bloomers" exhibited an increase in their IQ scores compared with children assigned to a control group. They were also evaluated more favorably by their classroom teachers.

When the Pygmalion study was first published, it was greeted with chagrin. If positive teacher expectations can boost student performance, can negative expectations have the opposite effect? What about the social implications? Could it be that affluent children are destined for success and disadvantaged children are doomed to failure because educators hold different expectations for them? Many researchers were critical of the study and skeptical about the generality of the results. Unfortunately though, these findings cannot be swept under the proverbial rug. In a review of additional studies, Rosenthal (1985) found that teachers' expectations significantly

self-fulfilling prophecy
The process by which one's expectations about a person eventually lead that person to behave in ways that confirm those expectations.

predicted their students' performance 36 percent of the time. Mercifully, the predictive value of teacher expectancies seems to wear off, not accumulate, as children graduate from one grade to the next (A. Smith et al., 1999).

How might teacher expectations be transformed into reality? There are two points of view. According to Rosenthal (2002), the process involves covert communication. The teacher forms an initial impression of students early in the school year based, perhaps, on their background or reputation, physical appearance, initial classroom performance, and standardized test scores. The teacher then alters his or her behavior in ways that are consistent with that impression. If initial expectations are high rather than low, the teacher gives the student more praise, more attention, more challenging homework, and better feedback. In turn, the student adjusts his or her own behavior. If the signals are positive, the student may become energized, work hard, and succeed. If negative, there may be a loss of interest and self-confidence. The cycle is thus complete and the expectations confirmed.

While recognizing that this effect can occur, Lee Jussim and his colleagues (1996; Jussim & Harber, 2005) question whether teachers in real life are so prone in the first place to form erroneous impressions of their students. It's true that in many naturalistic studies, occurring in real classrooms, the expectations teachers have at the start of a school year are ultimately confirmed by their students—a result that is consistent with the notion that the teachers had a hand in producing that outcome. But wait. That same result is also consistent with a more innocent possibility: that perhaps the expectations that teachers form of their students are *accurate*. There are times, Jussim admits, when teachers may stereotype a student and, without realizing it, behave in ways that create a self-fulfilling prophecy. But there are also times when teachers can predict how their students will perform without necessarily influencing that performance (Alvidrez & Weinstein, 1999).

Addressing this question in a longitudinal study of mothers and their children, Stephanie Madon and others (2003) found that underage adolescents are more likely to drink when their mothers had earlier expected them to. Statistical analyses revealed that this prophecy was fulfilled in part because the mothers *influence* their sons and daughters, as Rosenthal's work would suggest, and in part because the mothers are able to *predict* their children's behavior, as Jussim's model would suggest. In fact, a follow-up study suggests that the link between a mother's expectations and her adolescent's later alcohol consumption did not strengthen or weaken over time, remaining stable as the child moved from the seventh grade through the twelfth (Madon et al., 2006).

It's clear that self-fulfilling prophecies are at work in many settings, not only schools but also a wide range of organizations, including the military (Kierein & Gold, 2000; McNatt, 2000). In a study of 1,000 men assigned to 29 platoons in the Israel Defense Forces, Dov Eden (1990) led some platoon leaders but not others to expect that the groups of trainees they were about to receive had great potential (in fact, these groups were of average ability). After 10 weeks, the trainees assigned to the high-expectation platoons scored higher than the others on written exams and on the ability to operate a weapon.

The process may also be found in the criminal justice system when police interrogate suspects. To illustrate, Kassin and others (2003) had some college students but not others commit a mock crime, stealing $100 from a laboratory. All suspects were then questioned by student interrogators who were led to believe that their suspect was probably guilty or probably innocent. Interrogators who presumed guilt asked more incriminating questions, conducted more coercive interrogations, and tried harder to get the suspect to confess. In turn, this more aggressive style made the suspects sound defensive and led observers who later listened to the tapes to judge them guilty, even when they were innocent. Follow-up research has confirmed this self-fulfilling prophecy in the police interrogation room (Hill et al., 2008). Still other studies have shown that judges unwittingly bias juries through their nonverbal behavior (Hart, 1995) and that negotiators settle for lesser outcomes if they believe that their counterparts are highly competitive (Diekmann et al., 2003).

The self-fulfilling prophecy is a powerful phenomenon (Darley & Fazio, 1980; Harris & Rosenthal, 1985). But how does it work? How do social perceivers transform their expectations of others into reality? Research indicates that the phenomenon occurs as a three-step process. First, a perceiver forms an impression of a target person, which may be based on interactions with the target or on other information. Second, the perceiver behaves in a manner that is consistent with that first impression. Third, the target person unwittingly adjusts his or her behavior to the perceiver's actions. The net result: behavioral confirmation of the first impression (see ▶ Figure 4.13).

But now let's straighten out this picture. It would be a sad commentary on human nature if each of us were so easily molded by others' perceptions into appearing brilliant or stupid, introverted or extroverted, competitive or cooperative, warm or cold. The effects are well established, but there are limits.

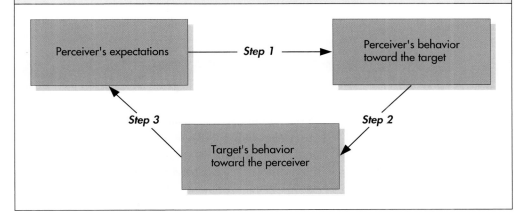

▶ FIGURE 4.13

The Self-Fulfilling Prophecy as a Three-Step Process

How do people transform their expectations into reality? (1) A perceiver has expectations of a target person; (2) the perceiver then behaves in a manner consistent with those expectations; and (3) the target unwittingly adjusts his or her behavior according to the perceiver's actions.

By viewing the self-fulfilling prophecy as a three-step process, social psychologists can identify the links in the chain that can be broken to prevent the vicious cycle.

Consider the first step, the link between one's expectations and one's behavior toward the target person. In the typical study, perceivers try to get to know the target on only a casual basis and are not necessarily driven to form an accurate impression. But when perceivers are highly motivated to seek the truth (as when they are considering the target as a possible teammate or opponent), they become more objective and often do not confirm prior expectations (Harris & Perkins, 1995; Hilton & Darley 1991).

The link between expectations and behavior depends in other ways as well on a perceiver's goals and motivations in the interaction (Snyder & Stukas, 1999). In one study, John Copeland (1994) put either the perceiver or the target into a position of relative power. In all cases, the perceiver interacted with a target who was said to be introverted or extroverted. In half the pairs, the perceiver was given the power to accept or reject the target as a teammate for a money-winning game. In the other half, it was the target who was empowered to choose a teammate. The two participants interacted, the interaction was recorded, and neutral observers listened to the tapes and rated the target person. So did perceivers cause the targets to behave as introverted or extroverted, depending on initial expectations? Yes and no. Illustrating what Copeland called "prophecies of power," the results showed that high-power perceivers triggered the self-fulfilling prophecy, as in past research, but that low-power perceivers did not. In the low-power situation, the perceivers spent less time getting to know the target person and more time trying to be liked.

The notion that we can create a "self-fulfilling prophecy" by getting others to behave in ways we expect is a myth. **FALSE.**

Now consider the second step, the link between a perceiver's behavior and the target's response. In the designs of much of the past research (as in much of life), target persons were not aware of the false impressions held by others. Thus, it is unlikely that Rosenthal and Jacobson's (1968) "late bloomers" knew of their teachers' high expectations or that Snyder and Swann's (1978) "introverts" and "extroverts" knew of their interviewers' misconceptions. But what if they had known? How would *you* react if you found yourself being cast in a particular light? When it happened to participants in one experiment, they managed to overcome the effect by behaving in ways that forced the perceivers to abandon their expectations (Hilton & Darley, 1985).

As you may recall from the discussion of self-verification in Chapter 3, this result is most likely to occur when the expectations of perceivers clash with a target person's own self-concept. When targets who viewed themselves as extroverted were interviewed by perceivers who believed they were introverted (and vice versa), what changed as a result of the interaction were the perceivers' beliefs, not the targets' behavior (Swann & Ely, 1984). Social perception is a two-way street; the persons we judge have their own prophecies to fulfill.

Social Perception: The Bottom Line

Trying to understand people—whether they are professional athletes, world leaders, trial lawyers, or loved ones closer to home—is no easy task. As you reflect on the material in this chapter, you will notice that there are two radically different views of social perception. One suggests that the process is quick and relatively automatic. At the drop of a hat, without much thought, effort, or awareness, people make rapid-fire snap judgments about others based on physical appearance, preconceptions, cognitive heuristics, or just a hint of behavioral evidence. According to a second view, however, the process is far more mindful. People observe others carefully and reserve judgment until their analysis of the target person, behavior, and situation is complete. As suggested by theories of attribution and information integration, the process is eminently logical. In light of recent research, it is now safe to conclude that both accounts of social perception are correct. Sometimes our judgments are made instantly; at other times, they are based on a more painstaking analysis of behavior. Either way, we often steer our interactions with others along a path that is narrowed by first impressions, a process that can set in motion a self-fulfilling prophecy. The various aspects of social perception, as described in this chapter, are summarized in ▶ Figure 4.14.

At this point, we must confront an important question: How *accurate* are people's impressions of each other? For years, this question has proved provocative but hard to answer (Cronbach, 1955; Kenny, 1994). Granted, people often depart from the ideals of logic and exhibit bias in their social perceptions. In this chapter alone, we have seen that perceivers typically focus on the wrong cues to judge if someone is lying, use cognitive heuristics without regard for numerical base rates, overlook the situational influences on behavior, disparage victims whose misfortunes threaten their sense of justice, form premature first impressions, and interpret, seek, and create evidence in ways that support these impressions.

To make matters worse, we often have little awareness of our limitations, leading us to feel *overconfident* in our judgments. In a series of studies, David Dunning and his colleagues (1990) asked college students to predict how a target person would react in various situations. Some made predictions about a fellow student whom they had just met and interviewed and others made predictions about their roommates.

> **FIGURE 4.14**

The Processes of Social Perception

Summarizing Chapter 4, this diagram depicts the processes of social perception. As shown, it begins with the observation of persons, situations, and behavior. Sometimes we make snap judgments from these cues. At other times, we form impressions only after making attributions and integrating these attributions. Either way, our impressions are subject to confirmation biases and the risk of self-fulfilling prophecy.

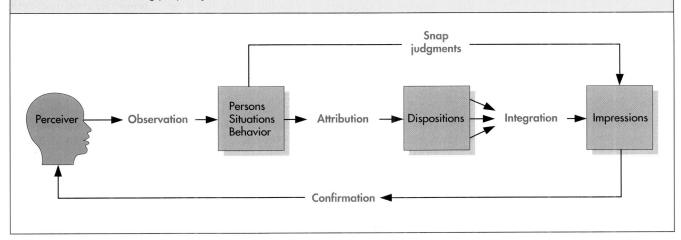

In both cases, participants reported their confidence in each prediction and accuracy was determined by the responses of the target persons themselves. The results were clear: Regardless of whether they judged a stranger or a roommate, the students consistently overestimated the accuracy of their predictions. In fact, Kruger and Dunning (1999) found that people who scored low on tests of spelling, logic, grammar, and humor appreciation were later the most likely to overestimate their own performance. Apparently, poor performers are doubly cursed: They don't know what they don't know (Dunning et al., 2003)—and they don't know they are biased (Ehrlinger et al., 2005).

Standing back from the material presented in this chapter, you may find the list of shortcomings, punctuated by the problem of overconfidence, to be long and depressing. So how can this list be reconciled with the triumphs of civilization? Or to put it another way, "If we're so dumb, how come we made it to the moon?" (Nisbett & Ross, 1980, p. 249)

A number of years ago, Herbert Simon (1956) coined the term *satisficing* (by combining *satisfying* and *sufficing*) to describe the way people make judgments that while not logically perfect are good enough. Today, many psychologists believe that people operate by a principle of "bounded rationality"—that we are rational *within bounds* depending on our abilities, motives, available time, and other factors. In a book entitled *Simple Heuristics That Make Us Smart*, Gerd Gigerenzer and others (1999) noted that people seldom compute intricate probabilities to make decisions; rather, they "reach into an adaptive toolbox filled with fast and frugal heuristics" (p. 5). They also note that these heuristics often serve us well enough. As an example, consider a simple heuristic: that people, objects, or places we recognize have greater value than those we don't recognize. In a study of investment decision making in the stock market, Bernhard Borges and others (1999) asked people to indicate which publicly traded companies they had heard of such as Kodak, Ford Motors, Coca-Cola, Intel, and American Express. These researchers then created two stock portfolios, one containing high-recognition companies and the other, low-recognition companies. After six months, the group of high-recognition stocks actually made more money than did the low-recognition stocks. In general, it even outperformed the market. So can a naive and ignorant investor pick winning stocks based on name recognition? The heuristic in question is not perfect, but it may be good enough.

It is true that people fall prey to the biases identified by social psychologists and probably even to some that have not yet been noticed. It is also true that we often get fooled by con artists such as Bernie Madoff, misjudge our partners in marriage, and hire the wrong job applicants. As Thomas Gilovich (1991) pointed out many years ago, more Americans believe in ESP than in evolution and there are 20 times more astrologers in the world than astronomers. The problem is, our biases can have harmful consequences and give rise, as we'll see in Chapter 5, to stereotypes, prejudice, and discrimination.

Despite our imperfections, there are four reasons to be guardedly optimistic about our competence as social perceivers:

1. The more experience people have with each other, the more accurate they are. For example, although people have a limited ability to assess the personality of strangers they meet in a laboratory, they are generally better at judging their own friends and acquaintances (Kenny & Acitelli, 2001; Levesque, 1997; Malloy & Albright, 1990).

2. Although we are not good at making global judgments of others (that is, at knowing what people are like across a range of settings), we are able to make more precise circumscribed predictions of how others will behave in our own presence. You may well misjudge the personality of a roommate or co-worker, but to the extent that you can predict your roommate's actions at home or your co-worker's actions on the job, the mistakes may not matter (Swann, 1984).

3. Certain social perception skills can be improved in people who are taught the rules of probability and logic (Kosonen & Winne, 1995; Nisbett et al., 1987). For example, graduate students in psychology—because they take courses in statistics—tend to improve in their ability to reason about everyday social events (Lehman et al., 1988).

4. People can form more accurate impressions of others when motivated by concerns for accuracy and open-mindedness (Kruglanski & Webster, 1996). Many of the studies described in this chapter have shown that people exhibit less bias when there is an incentive for accuracy within the experiment, as when participants are asked to judge a prospective teammate's ability to facilitate success in a future task (Fiske & Neuberg, 1990) or a future dating partner's social competence (Goodwin et al., 2002).

To summarize, research on the accuracy of social perceptions offers a valuable lesson: To the extent that we observe others with whom we have had time to interact, make judgments that are reasonably specific, have some knowledge of the rules of logic, and are sufficiently motivated to form an accurate impression, the problems that plague us can be minimized. Indeed, just being aware of the biases described in this chapter may well be a necessary first step toward a better understanding of others.

People are more accurate at judging the personalities of friends and acquaintances than of strangers. **TRUE.**

REVIEW

Observation: The Elements of Social Perception

- To understand others, social perceivers rely on indirect clues—the elements of social perception.

Persons: Judging a Book by Its Cover

- People often make snap judgments of others based on physical appearances (for example, adults with baby-faced features are seen as having childlike qualities).

Situations: The Scripts of Life

- People have preconceptions, or "scripts," about certain types of situations. These scripts guide our interpretations of behavior.

Behavioral Evidence

- People derive meaning from behavior by dividing it into discrete, meaningful units.
- Nonverbal behaviors are often used to determine how others are feeling.
- From facial expressions, people all over the world can identify the emotions of happiness, fear, sadness, surprise, anger, and disgust.
- Body language, gaze, and touch are also important forms of nonverbal communication.
- People use nonverbal cues to detect deception but are often not accurate in making these judgments because they pay too much attention to the face and neglect cues that are more revealing.

Attribution: From Elements to Dispositions

- Attribution is the process by which we explain people's behavior.

Attribution Theories

- People begin to understand others by making personal or situational attributions for their behavior.
- Correspondent inference theory states that people learn about others from behavior that is freely chosen, that is unexpected, and that results in a small number of desirable outcomes.
- From multiple behaviors, we base our attributions on three kinds of covariation information: consensus, distinctiveness, and consistency.

Attribution Biases

- People depart from the logic of attribution theory in two major ways.
- First, we use cognitive heuristics—rules of thumb that enable us to make judgments that are quick but often in error.
- Second, we tend to commit the fundamental attribution error—overestimating the role of personal factors and underestimating the impact of situations.

Culture and Attribution

- Cultures differ in their implicit theories about the causes of human behavior.
- Studies show, for example, that East Asians are more likely than Americans to consider the impact of the social and situational contexts of which they are a part.

Motivational Biases

- Our attributions for the behavior of others are often biased by our own self-esteem motives.
- Needing to believe in a just world, people often criticize victims and blame them for their fate.

Integration: From Dispositions to Impressions

Information Integration: The Arithmetic

- The impressions we form are usually based on an averaging of a person's traits, not on a summation.
- According to information integration theory, impressions are based on perceiver predispositions and a weighted average of individual traits.

Deviations from the Arithmetic

- Perceivers differ in their sensitivity to certain traits and in the impressions they form.
- Differences stem from stable perceiver characteristics, priming from recent experiences, implicit personality theories, and the primacy effect.

Confirmation Biases: From Impressions to Reality

- Once an impression is formed, people become less likely to change their minds when confronted with nonsupportive evidence.
- People tend to interpret, seek, and create information in ways that confirm existing beliefs.

Perseverance of Beliefs

- First impressions may survive in the face of inconsistent information.
- Ambiguous evidence is interpreted in ways that bolster first impressions.
- The effect of evidence that is later discredited perseveres because people formulate theories to support their initial beliefs.

Confirmatory Hypothesis Testing

- Once perceivers have beliefs about someone, they seek further information in ways that confirm those beliefs.

The Self-Fulfilling Prophecy

- As shown by the effects of teacher expectancies on student achievement, first impressions set in motion a self-fulfilling prophecy.

- This is the product of a three-step process: (1) A perceiver forms an expectation of a target person; (2) the perceiver behaves accordingly; and (3) the target adjusts to the perceiver's actions.

- This self-fulfilling prophecy effect is powerful but limited in important ways.

Social Perception: The Bottom Line

- Sometimes people make snap judgments; at other times, they evaluate others by carefully analyzing their behavior.

- Research suggests that our judgments are often biased and that we are overconfident.

- Still, there are conditions under which we are more competent as social perceivers.

Key Terms

attribution theory (113)
availability heuristic (116)
base-rate fallacy (117)
belief in a just world (124)
belief perseverance (134)
central traits (130)
confirmation bias (132)
counterfactual thinking (117)
covariation principle (114)

false-consensus effect (116)
fundamental attribution error (118)
implicit personality theory (129)
impression formation (126)
information integration theory (126)
mind perception (106)
need for closure (131)

nonverbal behavior (107)
personal attribution (113)
primacy effect (130)
priming (127)
self-fulfilling prophecy (135)
situational attribution (113)
social perception (102)

Media Resources

Social Psychology 8th Edition Companion Website
Visit your book companion website
www.cengage.com/psychology/kassin
where you will find flash cards, practice quizzes, Internet links, and more to help you study.

CENGAGENOW™ Just what you need to know NOW! Spend time on what you need to master rather than on information you already have learned. Take a pre-test for this chapter and CengageNOW will generate a personalized study plan based on your results. The study plan will identify the topics you need to review and direct you to online resources to help you master those topics. You can then take a post-test to help you determine the concepts you have mastered and what you will need to work on. Try it out! Go to **academic .cengage.com/login** to sign in with an access code or to purchase access to this product.

Putting COMMON SENSE *to the Test*

The impressions we form of others are influenced by superficial aspects of their appearance.

True. *Research shows that first impressions are influenced by height, weight, clothing, facial characteristics, and other aspects of appearance.*

Adaptively, people are skilled at knowing when someone is lying rather than telling the truth.

False. *People frequently make mistakes in their judgments of truth and deception, too often accepting what others say at face value.*

Like social psychologists, people are sensitive to situational causes when explaining the behavior of others.

False. *In explaining the behavior of others, people overestimate the importance of personal factors and overlook the impact of situations, a bias known as the "fundamental attribution error."*

People are slow to change their first impressions on the basis of new information.

True. *Studies have shown that once people form an impression of someone, they become resistant to change even when faced with contradictory new evidence.*

The notion that we can create a "self-fulfilling prophecy" by getting others to behave in ways we expect is a myth.

False. *In the laboratory and in the classroom, a perceiver's expectation can actually lead to its own fulfillment.*

People are more accurate at judging the personalities of friends and acquaintances than of strangers.

True. *People often form erroneous impressions of strangers but tend to be more accurate in their judgments of friends and acquaintances.*

5

Stereotypes, Prejudice, and Discrimination

This chapter considers how people think, feel, and behave toward members of social groups. We begin by examining the nature of the problem—how aspects of stereotyping, prejudice, and discrimination have changed dramatically in recent years, as well as how persistent they can be. Next, we examine two sets of causes underlying these problems: The first set emphasizes intergroup and motivational factors, and the second set emphasizes cognitive and cultural factors. We then considering some of the effects of being the targets of these biases, and we conclude with some ways to reduce stereotypes, prejudice, and discrimination today and in the future.

It was one of those moments when everyone present knew history was being made. When Barack Obama was sworn in as the 44th president of the United States on January 20, 2009, the ceremonies were like those of so many inaugural days that had come before. But the record number of people braving the chilly winter day at the National Mall in Washington, D.C. and the unprecedented number of people watching from around the world knew that this was different. Although it was not a focus of his inaugural speech, Obama acknowledged the significance of being the first African American to assume the highest office in the land:

> This is the meaning of our liberty and our creed—why men and women and children of every race and every faith can join in celebration across this magnificent Mall, and why a man whose father less than 60 years ago might not have been served at a local restaurant can now stand before you to take a most sacred oath.

The magnitude of change reflected in that simple observation—from a father not being served at a restaurant to a son being elected president of the nation—is staggering. And only a few lifetimes before, African slaves did much of the work to build the U.S. Capitol, from which Obama would take that presidential oath. This stunning evolution in race relations has played out not only on the grand stage of the nation's capital but also in countless ways throughout the land and, indeed, throughout much of the world. We note some of this progress in the pages to come in this chapter. But much of this chapter also reveals ways that stereotypes, prejudice, and discrimination continue to play a profoundly important and destructive—though often more subtle—role in contemporary life.

Some signs of the persistence of the problem were evident during the heated presidential campaign of the previous year. E-mails and online commentaries were

Barack Obama at his historic inauguration on January 20, 2009, when he became the first member of a minority group to become president of the United States.

Along with the signs of progress, signs of the persistent challenges of racism also were evident during Barack Obama's historic presidential campaign. A magazine cover depicts the fears of some people that Barack and his wife Michelle were un-American and on the side of terrorists (left). A bar owner sells T-shirts depicting Obama as the cartoon chimp Curious George (right).

flooded with torrents of racist jokes or dire warnings about what would happen to the country if a black man with a Muslim-sounding name would become president. A supporter at a campaign rally for Republican vice-presidential nominee Sarah Palin carried a Curious George (chimpanzee) doll with an Obama bumper sticker wrapped around its head, while a bar owner in Georgia sold T-shirts depicting Obama as Curious George. White supremacist and other hate groups saw huge growths in number and activity. A video of an angry sermon by the African American former pastor at Obama's church in Chicago saying hateful things about white Americans played repeatedly on the news and over the Internet. Once Obama became president, a number of signs pointed to a huge swelling of hatred and fear: threats against the president's life jumped by about 400 percent compared to those made against his (white) predecessor and activity in hate groups and antigovernment militia groups skyrocketed, as did sales of guns and ammunition. "The face of the federal government today is black," said Mark Potok, the director of the Southern Poverty Law Center, "and that has injected a whole new element into the militia movement" (Meek, 2009).

Examples of prejudice during the campaign were not limited to race. Many supporters and pundits felt that Democratic candidate Hillary Clinton was treated especially harshly and unfairly because she was a woman. Republican presidential nominee John McCain was the target of countless jokes about his age. Defenders of Sarah Palin claimed that she was mocked in the media because of her socioeconomic background or her beauty-pageant looks. Obama was feared and despised by some not only because of racial prejudice but also because of false rumors that he was Muslim.

The frenzy and significance of the presidential campaign shed light on stereotypes, prejudice, and discrimination that remain all too prevalent in our culture but that often go unrecognized because they tend to remain hidden beneath surfaces or in dark corners. And these are problems that are not at all unique to politically charged people or issues or to the United States. The progress reflected in one man's journey from son of a man denied basic human rights to father of two daughters growing up in the most famous house in America is real and significant. But so too are the numerous ways that stereotypes, prejudice, and discrimination continue to reveal that the journey is far from complete.

To address these issues, we begin by taking a close look at the nature of the problem of intergroup bias in contemporary life. Although there is a long list of groups that are the targets of stereotypes, prejudice, and discrimination, in this first section we focus primarily on racism and sexism, as they have been the focus of the large majority of research. Later in the chapter we address some of the key causes and important consequences of intergroup biases, and we close by discussing some of the most promising directions in efforts to reduce these problems.

The Nature of the Problem: Persistence and Change

The election of a member of a historically oppressed minority group to the highest office in the United States, coupled with the prejudices that were revealed during and after the campaign, together reflect the dynamic nature of stereotypes, prejudice, and discrimination today. While examples of blatant, overt prejudice and discrimination remain all too prevalent, it certainly is the case that much progress has been made. How much and how satisfactory that progress is remains open for some debate. White Americans tend to perceive greater racial progress than other Americans, in part because the former see things more from the perspective of how far things have come, whereas the latter see things more from the perspective of how far the country still has to go (Brodish et al., 2008; Eibach & Ehrlinger, 2006). What is harder to debate is the fact that in general, stereotyping, prejudice, and discrimination are seen as less acceptable than ever before, although exceptions to this exist—such as the recent increase in prejudice against immigrants or people perceived to be "foreigners" in many countries around the world (Coenders et al., 2008; Zick et al., 2008) (see ▶ Figure 5.1).

Like germs lurking beneath a seemingly clean countertop, prejudice and discrimination in contemporary life live on under the surface to a much, much greater extent than most people realize. And like germs, their existence can have a profound effect on us, despite how hidden they may be.

In this section, we discuss some of the progress that has been made along with the persistence of more subtle forms of bias. To provide a focus for reviewing the relevant research and to reflect the topics that have most dominated the research literature, we will concentrate in this section on racism and sexism in particular—even though many of the points hold true across a wide variety of targets of stereotypes, prejudice, and discrimination. Before turning to racism and sexism, however, we begin by defining these terms, along with several other relevant concepts.

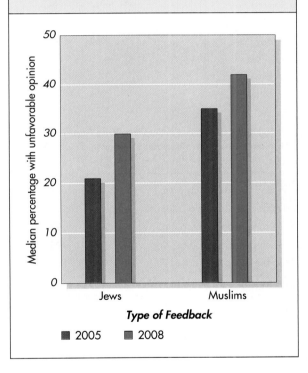

▶ FIGURE 5.1

Unfavorable Views Toward Jews and Muslims in Europe

This graph shows the median percentages of respondents from six countries (Britain, France, Germany, Poland, Russia, and Spain) with unfavorable opinions of Jews and Muslims in 2005 and 2008. Attitudes became more negative during this three-year period.

Kohut & Wike, 2008.

■ Defining Our Terms

Given the complexity of these issues, defining concepts such as prejudice or racism is no simple matter. Debates persist about how best to define the terms—how broad or specific they should be, whether they should focus on individual or institutional levels, and so on. For example, one way to define **racism** is as prejudice and discrimination based on a person's racial background. It is important to realize, however, that racism exists at several different levels. At the individual level, as this definition reflects, any of us can be racist toward anyone else. At the institutional and cultural levels, in contrast, some people are privileged while others are advantaged. For example, institutions that tend to accept or hire individuals connected to the people who already are in the institution, or cultural values that favor the status quo, may unwittingly perpetuate racism. Therefore, another way to define racism is as institutional and cultural practices that promote the domination of one racial group over another (Jones, 1997b). Similarly, **sexism** may be defined as prejudice and discrimination based on a

racism Prejudice and discrimination based on a person's racial background, or institutional and cultural practices that promote the domination of one racial group over another.

sexism Prejudice and discrimination based on a person's gender, or institutional and cultural practices that promote the domination of one gender over another.

person's gender or as institutional and cultural practices that promote the domination of one gender (typically men) over another (typically women).

For the purposes of this chapter, we define **stereotypes** as beliefs or associations that link whole groups of people with certain traits or characteristics. **Prejudice** consists of negative feelings about others because of their connection to a social group. While stereotypes concern associations or beliefs and prejudice concerns feelings, **discrimination** concerns behaviors—specifically, negative behaviors directed against persons because of their membership in a particular group. Stereotypes, prejudice, and discrimination can operate somewhat independently, but they often influence and reinforce each other.

Finally, a **group** is defined as two or more people perceived as having at least one of the following characteristics: (1) direct interactions with each other over a period of time; (2) joint membership in a social category based on sex, race, or other attributes; (3) a shared, common fate, identity, or set of goals. We see people in fundamentally different ways if we consider them to constitute a group rather than simply an aggregate of individuals. We also see people in fundamentally different ways if we consider them to be part of our ingroup or as part of an outgroup. Groups that we identify with—our country, religion, political party, even our hometown sports team—are called **ingroups**, whereas groups other than our own are called **outgroups**.

▌ Racism: Current Forms and Challenges

A close examination of legislation, opinion polls, sociological data, and social psychological research indicates that racial prejudice and discrimination have been decreasing in the United States over the last several decades (Dovidio et al., 2002; Pew Research Center for People & the Press, 2009), although elements of it may once again be on the rise, particularly in Western Europe. In a classic study of ethnic stereotypes published in 1933, Daniel Katz and Kenneth Braly found that white college students viewed the average white American as smart, industrious, and ambitious. Yet they saw the average African American as superstitious, ignorant, lazy, and happy-go-lucky. In multiple follow-up surveys with demographically similar samples of white students conducted from 1951 through 2001, these negative images of blacks largely faded and were replaced by more favorable images (Dovidio et al., 1996; Madon et al., 2001). Similarly, public opinion polls have indicated that racial prejudice in the United States has dropped sharply since World War II. Table 5.1 reports some of the changes in racial prejudice illustrated by these and other studies.

The election of Barack Obama has been seen by many, both within and outside the United States, as a significant sign of racial progress. For example, University of Washington students in a study by Cheryl Kaiser and others (2009) completed questionnaires about their perception of racial progress both just before and soon after the election. In only the span of a few weeks, the students' perception of racial prog-

---

TABLE 5.1

Changes in Overt Racism

The results of many studies and surveys like these demonstrate that overt negative stereotyping and racism have declined dramatically over the years. Although these results are encouraging, research on more subtle modern racism reveals that the picture is much more complex than these self-reports suggest.

Percentage of White Participants Who Selected a Trait to Describe Black Americans

Trait	1933	1967	1993
Superstitious	84%	13%	1%
Lazy	75	26	5
Happy-Go-Lucky	38	27	2
Ignorant	38	11	5
Musical	26	47	12
Very Religious	24	8	17
Stupid	22	4	0

Percentage of White Participants Who Report Being Willing to Admit Blacks into Various Relationships with Them

	1949	1968	1992
Willing to Admit Blacks to:			
Employment in my occupation	78%	98%	99%
My club as personal friends	51	97	96
My street as neighbors	41	95	95
Close kinship by marriage	0	66	74

Percentage of Adult Participants Who Agree with the Statement "It's All Right for Blacks and Whites to Date Each Other."

	1987	2009
Agree	48%	83%

Sources: Dovidio et al., 1996; Peterson, 1997; Pew, 2009.

---

stereotype A belief or association that links a whole group of people with certain traits or characteristics.

prejudice Negative feelings toward persons based on their membership in certain groups.

discrimination Behavior directed against persons because of their membership in a particular group.

ress in the United States increased significantly (see ► Figure 5.2). The flip side of the coin, however, is that support for policies that address racial inequality and perceptions of how much farther the country still needs to go to achieve racial equality decreased significantly. The authors of this research found these latter findings troubling because, as they report, "there are pervasive racial disparities in virtually all aspects of American society" (p. 558). Indeed, racial biases in employment, salaries, housing, bank credit, charges from car dealerships, and a whole host of other measures continue to exist (Pager & Shepherd, 2008). In sum, then, there are legitimate reasons to celebrate racial progress. Racism, however, remains a fact of life and is by no means limited merely to the actions of some fringe individuals or groups. And as we will see in the following section, it exists in ways that escape the recognition of most people.

Modern Racism   Consider two stories from the world of sports:

1. During the 2006 World Cup soccer tournament, which featured the very best players from around the world, racist taunts and even aggression from fans were so prevalent and extreme that the international soccer agency running the World Cup announced it would suspend national associations that did not impose new rules designed to reduce such racist behavior (BBC, July 31, 2006). For example, Oguchi Onyewu, an African American player, said about a game in Europe, "I was going to throw the ball in, and some fans started doing monkey chants and I made a gesture like, 'Whatever.' And a guy reached over and punched me in the mouth" (Whiteside, 2006, p. 12C).

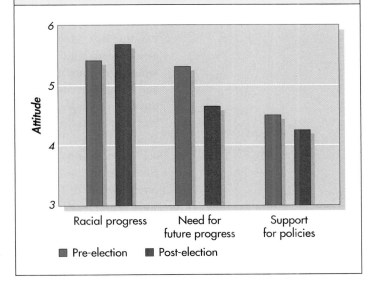

►FIGURE 5.2

Perception of Racial Progress Before and After 2008 Election

University of Washington students completed questionnaires about racial progress both just before and soon after Barack Obama was elected president in November 2008. In the span of a few weeks, students' perceptions of how much racial progress the nation has made increased, whereas their perceptions of how much the country still needed to go to achieve racial equality and how much they supported policies that address racial inequality decreased.

Based on Kaiser et al., 2009.

An opponent tries to prevent Barcelona's Samuel Eto from leaving the game after he was targeted by racist taunts from Spanish League fans.

group   Two or more persons perceived as related because of their interactions, membership in the same social category, or common fate.

ingroups   Groups with which an individual feels a sense of membership, belonging, and identity.

outgroups   Groups with which an individual does not feel a sense of membership, belonging, or identity.

2. Christopher Parsons and others (2009) analyzed every pitch from four Major League Baseball seasons from 2004 through 2008—more than three-and-a-half million pitches in all—and found a fascinating set of results. Umpires were more likely to call strikes for pitchers who were of the same race/ethnicity as they were. Even more interesting is the fact that this bias emerged only under three conditions: (1) if the game was played in the subset of ballparks that did not have a computerized monitoring system the league uses to review umpires' performance in calling balls and strikes; (2) if the number of people attending the game was relatively low; and (3) if the call would not be the final ball or strike of the player at bat. In other words, the racial/ethnic bias was evident only under the conditions when there would be the least accountability or public outcry.

The first of these examples illustrates what some call old-fashioned racism. It is blatant, explicit, and unmistakable. The second is what some call **modern racism**, a subtle form of prejudice that tends to surface when it is safe, socially acceptable, or easy to rationalize. Modern racism is far more subtle and most likely to be present under the cloud of ambiguity. According to theories of modern racism, many people are racially ambivalent. They want to see themselves as fair, but they still harbor feelings of anxiety and discomfort about other racial groups (Hass et al., 1992). There are several specific theories of modern racism, but they all emphasize contradictions and tensions that lead to subtle, often unconscious forms of prejudice and discrimination (Gawronski et al., 2008; Levy et al., 2006; Sears & Henry, 2005; Son Hing et al., 2008). For example, Samuel Gaertner and John Dovidio (1986; Dovidio & Gaertner, 2004) proposed the related concept of *aversive racism*, which concerns the ambivalence between individuals' sincerely fair-minded attitudes and beliefs, on the one hand, and their largely unconscious and unrecognized negative feelings and beliefs about blacks, on the other hand.

In modern forms of racism, prejudice against minorities surfaces primarily under circumstances when the expression of prejudice is safe, socially acceptable, and easy to rationalize as nonracial because of its ambiguity. For example, white British students in a study by Gordon Hodson and others (2005) read about either a white or a black defendant in a robbery case. When the evidence against the defendant was strong and unambiguous, the students were as likely to judge the white defendant guilty as the black defendant. However, when the situation was more ambiguous because some of the most incriminating information against the defendant was ruled inadmissible and therefore technically should be ignored (but often is used by jurors somewhat anyway), the students were significantly more likely to judge the black defendant guilty than the white defendant. This situation was ambiguous because although the students knew that they weren't supposed to use the inadmissible evidence, they also knew that the evidence suggested that the defendant was indeed guilty. So either a guilty or not-guilty verdict could be justified. According to the aversive racism perspective, it is in ambiguous situations such as this that racial biases are more likely to emerge.

Many whites who feel that they are not prejudiced admit that on some occasions they do not react toward blacks (or to other groups, such as gay men) as they should—an insight that causes them to feel embarrassed, guilty, and ashamed (Monteith et al., 2002). Indeed, when they have reason to suspect that racism could bias their judgments, low-prejudice whites may show an *opposite* bias on explicit, consciously controlled tasks, responding more favorably to blacks than to whites (Dovidio et al., 1997; Fein et al., 1997; Norton et al., 2006; Wyer, 2004).

Implicit Racism To contrast it from explicit racism, many scholars call racism that operates unconsciously and unintentionally **implicit racism**. Undetected by individuals who want to be fair and unbiased, implicit racism—along with other forms of implicit prejudice—can skew judgments, feelings, and behaviors—without inducing the guilt that more obvious, explicit forms of racism would trigger.

modern racism A form of prejudice that surfaces in subtle ways when it is safe, socially acceptable, and easy to rationalize.

implicit racism Racism that operates unconsciously and unintentionally.

Implicit racism may be subtle, but its effects can be profound. For example, Jennifer Eberhardt and others (2006) studied predictors of whether a criminal defendant was likely to be sentenced to death. Examining more than 600 death-penalty-eligible cases tried in Philadelphia, Pennsylvania, between 1979 and 1999, these researchers found that in cases involving a white victim, the more the defendant's physical appearance was stereotypically black (see ▶ Figure 5.3), the more likely he would be sentenced to death. It is very unlikely that many of the judges or jurors were consciously aware of this bias, just as it is unlikely that the umpires in Major League Baseball were aware of the bias in how they called strikes, but the evidence in both cases reveals significant discrimination.

The question of how to detect and measure implicit racism is a challenging one. Because of its implicit nature, covert measures that do not require individuals to answer questions about their attitudes typically are used. By far the most well-known measure of this kind is the Implicit Association Test (IAT), first developed and tested by Anthony Greenwald and others (1998). The IAT measures the extent to which two concepts are associated. It measures implicit racism toward African Americans, for example, by comparing how quickly or slowly participants associate African American cues (such as a black face) with negative and positive concepts compared to how quickly or slowly they make the same kinds of associations with European American cues. Other IATs focus on associations concerning older versus younger people, men versus women, and so on. The IAT is discussed in more detail in Chapter 6. It has sparked an explosion of research in the past decade about racism and other forms of prejudice and discrimination, with more than 500 scientific publications already (Smith & Nosek, 2010). The IAT has been so popular that between October 1998 and October 2009 approximately 11 *million* IATs were completed by visitors to the IAT website (Nosek, 2009)!

Implicit racial bias as measured by the IAT has been found between groups around the world and even among children as young as 6 years old (Baron & Banaji, 2006; Dunham et al., 2008). And as can be seen in ▶ Figure 5.4, whereas older children and adults begin to control or change their explicit prejudices and show less bias on explicit measures, the IAT continues to reveal implicit racism throughout development.

Additional measures of implicit biases are being added to researchers' toolboxes (Bluemke & Friese, 2008; Olson & Fazio, 2004; Payne et al., 2005; Sekaquaptewa et al., 2003; Sriram & Greenwald, 2009; von Hippel et al., 2009). Regardless of the specific measure, social psychologists have found that individuals' degree of implicit racism sometimes predicts differences in their perceptions of and reactions to others as a function of race, particularly regarding very subtle, often nonverbal behaviors, such as how far one chooses to sit from a member of a different race or how much eye contact one makes with a member of a different race (Amodio & Devine, 2006; Greenwald et al., 2009). This research is not without some controversy, however. On the one hand, some scholars have raised important questions about implicit measures, particularly the IAT, asking what they really measure, how useful they are for predicting behavior, and how their results should be interpreted (Blanton et al., 2009; Karpinski & Hilton, 2001). On the other hand, a recent meta-analysis of a decade's worth of studies on the IAT found that in socially sensitive domains of interracial and other intergroup behavior, when norms against explicit prejudice are likely to be strong, IAT measures of implicit prejudice predicted biased reactions and behavior

▶ **FIGURE 5.3**

Facial Features and the Death Penalty

In a study by Jennifer Eberhardt and others (2006), the face on the right would be considered more stereotypically black than the face on the left. (Neither of these two individuals have any criminal history and their pictures here are for illustrative purposes only.) Eberhardt's research suggests that if these two people were each found guilty of a crime and were eligible for the death penalty, the man on the right would be more likely to be sentenced to death than the man on the left.

Eberhardt et al., 2006.

Children do not tend to show biases based on race; it is only after they become adolescents that they learn to respond to people differently based on race. **FALSE.**

▶ FIGURE 5.4

Development of Explicit Versus Implicit Racial Preferences

On an explicit attitude measure (left), 6-year-old children showed a strong preference for a white child over a black child. This preference was reduced in 10-year-olds and completely eliminated in adults. However, implicit attitudes, as measured by the Implicit Association Test (right), showed a consistent pro-white bias across all three age groups.

Based on Baron & Banaji, 2006; Dunham et al., 2008.

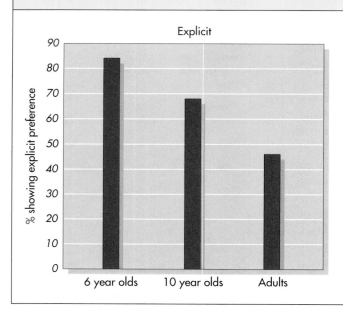

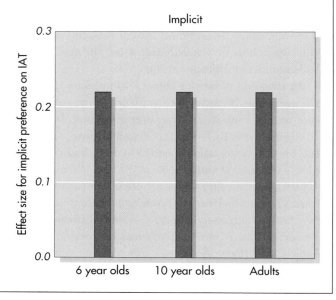

Although Charleston High School in Mississippi has been integrated for decades, it was not until 2008 that the school board allowed a racially integrated senior prom, although some at the school organized a "white prom" as an alternative. Pictured here are two of the students who attended the prom standing in front of a poster for the movie *Prom Night in Mississippi*, an award-winning documentary about this story. Some integrated schools in the United States still hold racially separate proms.

Jason LaVeris/WireImage/Getty Images

significantly better than measures of explicit prejudice did (Greenwald et al., 2009). It is to the sensitive domains of interracial perceptions and interactions that we turn in the following section.

Interracial Perceptions   The divides between racial and ethnic groups tend to be more vast and may promote stronger feelings of hostility, fear, and distrust than the divides based on other social categories, such as those based on gender, appearance, age, and so on. One factor that can keep these negative feelings strong is the relative lack of contact between people of different racial and ethnic groups. In addition, in contemporary society, the stigma of being perceived as racist is especially troubling for most people (Crandall & Eshleman, 2003). This combination of stronger negative emotions, less contact, and greater anxiety about appearing racist makes interracial perception and interaction particularly challenging and fraught with emotion and tension.

A number of studies have demonstrated that whites may be quicker to perceive hostility or anger in black faces than white faces and that this may be especially true for people relatively high in implicit racism. For example, research by Kurt Hugenberg and Galen Bodenhausen (2003, 2004) found that individuals' levels of implicit racism predicted how biased they were in perceiving hostility in black faces. White American participants watched brief movies of facial expressions of white or black targets. In their first study, the facial expression began as displaying hostility and gradually became more neutral. In a second study, the expression began as neutral and gradually became more hostile. The participants' task was to indicate when the face no longer expressed the initial emotion—in other words, when did the emotion change from hostile to neutral in the first study or from neutral to hostile in the second study? The researchers found that participants with relatively high levels of implicit bias, as measured by the IAT, saw the black faces as staying hostile longer in the first study and as becoming hostile quicker in the second study, relative to the white faces. Participants who showed relatively low racism on the IAT did not show this bias. In a later study, these authors found that participants who showed a strong race bias on the IAT were more likely to categorize a racially ambiguous face as African American if the face expressed hostility than if it expressed happiness.

More recently, Paul Hutchings and Geoffrey Haddock (2008) found similar effects with white British students. When students saw pictures of racially ambiguous faces, for example, those students high in implicit racism, as measured by the IAT, were more likely to categorize the faces as black if the faces were angry than if they were happy or neutral (see ▶ Figure 5.5). Students low in implicit racism, in contrast, did not show this bias.

Research using brain-imaging techniques has shown that just perceiving a member of a racial outgroup may trigger different, more emotional reactions than perceiving an ingroup member. This is a conclusion suggested by a study by Allen Hart and others (2000). They monitored the brain activity of European American and African American participants using an fMRI technique while they showed the participants pictures of individuals from their racial ingroup or individuals from an outgroup. The fMRI revealed differential responses in the amygdala, a structure in the brain associated with emotion. Pictures of racial outgroup members tended to elicit stronger amygdala activation than did pictures of ingroup members. Elizabeth Phelps and others (2000) also found that European Americans showed greater amygdala activation in response to black faces than they did in response to white faces. In addition, this greater activation was associated with higher levels of implicit prejudice.

> ### ▶ FIGURE 5.5
>
> #### Seeing Anger in Black Faces
>
> White British students saw pictures of racially ambiguous faces such as these. Students high in implicit racism, as measured by the IAT, were more likely to categorize the faces as black if the faces were angry than if they were happy or neutral. Students low in implicit racism did not show this bias.
>
> Hutchings & Haddock, 2008.

Since these initial studies, several other researchers have found further support for heightened amygdala activity in response to racial outgroup faces (e.g., Amodio, 2008; Cunningham et al., 2004; Ronquillo et al., 2007; Wheeler & Fiske, 2005). Interestingly, the effect of black faces on white participants' amygdala activity may depend on the direction of the eye gaze of the faces depicted. Jennifer Richeson, Sophie Trawalter, and their colleagues (Richeson et al., 2008; Trawalter et al., 2008) found that white participants showed greater amygdala activity and paid greater attention in response to black than white faces, but only if the faces displayed direct eye gaze (as if the person was looking at the participant). The effects were eliminated if the targets' eyes were closed or appeared to be looking elsewhere. The researchers believe these results reflect the fact that direct eye contact from an outgroup member is much more likely to convey threat.

Interracial Interactions   If perceptions of a member of a racial outgroup are associated with various biases and emotional reactions, interracial interactions are even more complex and challenging. One example that illustrates this is from a study by Wendy Mendes and others (2002) in which nonblack participants interacted with either a black or a white confederate on a series of tasks. Participants were more likely to exhibit cardiovascular reactions (such as changes in the amount of blood pumped by the heart per minute) associated with feelings of threat if the confederate was black than if the confederate was white.

When engaging in interracial interactions, whites may be concerned about a number of things, including not wanting to be, or appear to be, racist. They may therefore try to regulate their behaviors, become particularly vigilant for signs of distrust or dislike from their interaction partners, and so on. What should ideally be a smooth-flowing normal interaction can become awkward and even exhausting. This, in turn, can affect their partner's perceptions of them, possibly leading to the ironic outcome of their appearing to be racist because they were trying not to be. A number of researchers have been examining such phenomena (e.g., Amodio et al., 2007; Devine et al., 2005; Dovidio et al., 2002). According to Jacquie Vorauer (2003; Vorauer et al., 2009), for example, individuals engaging in intergroup interactions often activate *metastereotypes*, or thoughts about the outgroup's stereotypes about them, and worry about being seen as consistent with these stereotypes.

Jennifer Richeson, Nicole Shelton, and their colleagues have found across a variety of recent experiments that for white participants, particularly if they score relatively high on a measure of implicit racism, interacting with a black individual can be cognitively and emotionally exhausting because they are so worried about appearing racist (Richeson & Shelton, 2010; Richeson & Trawalter, 2008; Shelton & Richeson, 2007; Shelton et al., 2009). Indeed, participants high in implicit racism are more likely to perform worse on a simple cognitive task after interacting with a black than a white confederate—evidence that the interaction was cognitively draining for them.

In one interesting recent study, Tessa West and others (2009) examined pairs of same-race or cross-race roommates who were randomly assigned to live together. One of the intriguing findings was that in interracial pairs, when one roommate felt anxious on a particular day, his or her roommate became more likely to feel anxious and to desire less interaction with the roommate on the following day. This was not the case for same-race roommates.

It should not be surprising, then, that people sometimes try to avoid interracial interaction for fear of appearing racist or being treated in a racist way, and this avoidant behavior can have the ironic effect of making things all the worse. Ashby Plant and David Butz (2006), for example, found that when nonblack participants with this avoidant concern interacted with a black confederate, they had shorter and less pleasant interactions. Another example of the threat that many whites experience when confronted with issues of race is illustrated in the work of Philip Goff, Claude Steele, and Paul Davies (2008). White male students were led to believe that they would engage in a conversation with either two white partners or two black partners. The students sat farther away from their partners if they thought the conversation was going to be about a racially sensitive topic (racial profiling) than they did if they thought they would be discussing a less racially relevant topic (relationships).

In a clever demonstration of the kind of anxiety whites sometimes feel about race, Michael Norton and others (2006) paired white participants with either a white or black confederate in a game (similar to the children's board game *Guess Who?*) that required the participants to ask the confederate questions so they could guess which of a series of photographs the confederate had been given. As can be seen in ▶ Figure 5.6, participants were significantly less likely to ask about the race of the person in the photograph when playing the game with a black confederate than a white confederate, even though this hurt their ability to win the game. It seemed that the white participants would rather lose the game than run the risk of appearing racist by paying any attention to the race of the people in the photographs.

An interesting follow-up to this study examined the performance of children in this task (Apfelbaum et al., 2008). On a race-neutral version of the game, older children (10- and 11-year-olds), not surprisingly, outperformed younger children (8- and 9-year-olds). However, when race was a relevant category, the older children were much more likely to avoid asking about race, presumably because they are more aware of the sensitivities surrounding race. The result of this was that in the race-relevant version of the game, the younger children significantly outperformed the older children!

Anxieties and challenges associated with intergroup interactions are not limited to those between whites and blacks, of course, despite the fact that the majority of research has focused on this particular intergroup dynamic. Some social psychologists are studying related issues involving other social categories, such as those concerning gays, overweight people, and native peoples of Canada (Blair et al., 2003; Hebl et al., 2009; Vorauer & Turpie, 2004).

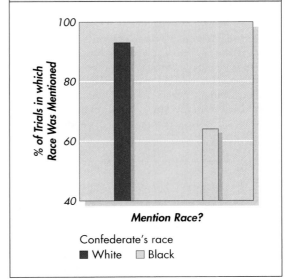

▶ **FIGURE 5.6**

Colorblind?

When white participants played a face-matching game with a confederate in which they had to ask questions of the confederate to guess which of a series of photographs the confederate had, they were much less likely to ask about the race of the people in the photographs if they were interacting with a black confederate than a white confederate, even though this hurt their performance in the game.

Sexism: Ambivalence and Double Standards

As with racism, old-fashioned blatant displays of sexism are less socially accepted than in years past, although they continue to exist at a frequency and with an intensity that would surprise many. As with racism, researchers have been documenting and studying modern and implicit forms of sexism that tend to escape the notice of most people but that can exert powerful discriminatory effects (Swim & Hyers, 2009).

There are some ways that sexism is different, however. Gender stereotypes are distinct from virtually all other stereotypes in that they often are *prescriptive* rather than merely *descriptive*. That is, they indicate what many people in a given culture believe men and women *should* be. Few Americans, for example, think that gays *should* be artistic and sensitive or that old people *should* be forgetful and conservative, but many think that women *should* be nurturing and that men *should* be unemotional. Even though ambition and drive are valued in our society, women who exhibit such traits may be viewed in especially harsh terms, contributing to the double standards that are hallmark of sexism (Cuddy et al., 2004; Prentice & Carranza, 2002; Rudman & Glick, 2001).

Another way that sexism is unique concerns the degree to which the ingroup and outgroup members interact. Men and women are intimately familiar with each other. They come from the same families, and typically (although certainly not always) grow up together, are attracted to one another, live together, and produce and raise children together. Because of this, sexism involves more of an ambivalence between positive and negative feelings and beliefs than is typical of racism and other forms of prejudice and discrimination.

In this section we will focus on this ambivalence and on some of the double standards that exist in sexism in degrees that are not as evident in most other forms of discrimination. Later in the chapter we explore the related issues of gender stereotypes and how they are perpetuated.

Ambivalent Sexism   Overall, stereotypes of women tend to be more positive than stereotypes about men (Eagly et al., 1994). However, the positive traits associated with women are less valued in important domains such as the business world than the positive traits associated with men.

These contradictions are reflected in Peter Glick and Susan Fiske's (2001) concept of **ambivalent sexism**. Ambivalent sexism consists of two elements: *hostile sexism*, characterized by negative, resentful feelings about women's abilities, value, and ability to challenge men's power, and *benevolent sexism*, characterized by affectionate, chivalrous feelings founded on the potentially patronizing belief that women need and deserve protection. Although hostile sexism is clearly more negative and many women feel favorably toward men who exhibit benevolent sexism (Kilianski & Rudman, 1998; Swim et al., 2005), the two forms of sexism are positively correlated. In a study of 15,000 men and women in nineteen nations across six continents, Glick, Fiske, and others (2000) found evidence of prevalent ambivalent sexism around the world. Among their most intriguing findings is the fact that people from countries with the greatest degree of economic and political inequality between the sexes tend to exhibit the most hostile and benevolent sexism. ▶ Figure 5.7 depicts the average hostile sexism scores for each of several countries.

Benevolent sexism, on the surface, does not strike many women or men as terribly troubling, but it certainly fuels sexism and contributes to negative reactions, particularly to women who defy traditional gender roles and stereotypes. Indeed, studies from several countries around the world have found links between benevolent sexism and accepting myths about rape or evaluating women more negatively if they have been acquaintance-raped, particularly if the women are perceived to have acted inappropriately for a woman (such as being "unlady-like") (Chapleau et al., 2007; Viki et al., 2004; Yamawaki, 2007).

▶ **FIGURE 5.7**

Hostile Sexism Across Countries

Respondents from nineteen countries completed measures of hostile and benevolent sexism. The average hostile sexism scores for male respondents from eleven of these countries are depicted here. The countries are listed from left to right in order of how unequal the sexes are in terms of political and economic power as defined by United Nations criteria. It is clear both from this figure and from the data more generally that hostile sexism is positively correlated with gender inequality.

Author's correspondence with Peter Glick.

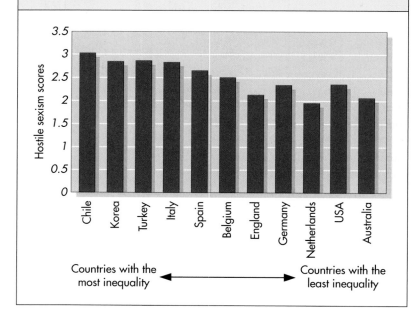

Sex Discrimination: Double Standards and Pervasive Stereotypes   Many years ago, Philip Goldberg (1968) asked students at a small women's college to evaluate the content and writing style of some articles. When the material was supposedly written by John McKay rather than Joan McKay it received higher ratings, a result that led Goldberg to wonder if even women were prejudiced against women. Certain other studies showed that people often devalue the performance of women who take on tasks usually reserved for men (Lott, 1985) and attribute women's achievements to luck rather than ability (Deaux & Emswiller, 1974; Nieva & Gutek, 1981). These studies generated a lot of attention, but it now appears that this kind of devaluation of women is not commonly found in similar studies. More than a hundred studies modeled after Goldberg's indicate that people are not generally biased by gender in the evaluation of performance (Swim & Sanna, 1996; Top, 1991).

ambivalent sexism A form of sexism characterized by attitudes about women that reflect both negative, resentful beliefs and feelings and affectionate and chivalrous but potentially patronizing beliefs and feelings.

This does not mean, however, that sex discrimination no longer exists all these years after the Goldberg study. In many parts of the world, blatant sexism is still quite evident, of course. For example, in Iran, some people supported recent attempts at reforms to benefit women but those in power reacted with hostile resistance. China is notorious for policies such as selective abortion to support a cultural preference for sons over daughters (Saleton, 2009). Other examples are less dramatic but still important. Look at Tables 5.2 and 5.3, for instance, and you'll notice some striking sex differences in occupational choice. How many female airline pilots have you met lately? What about male secretaries? The question is, of course, what explains these differences? Decades of social science research point to sexist attitudes and discrimination as a key part of the equation. Sex discrimination during the early school years may pave the way for diverging career paths in adulthood. Then, when equally qualified men and women compete for a job, gender considerations enter in once again, as some research indicates that business professionals favor men for so-called masculine jobs (such as a manager for a machinery company) and women for so-called feminine jobs (such as a receptionist) (Eagly 2004; Kmec, 2005).

Even when women and men have comparable jobs, the odds are good that the women will be paid less than their male counterparts and will be confronted with a so-called glass ceiling that makes it harder or impossible for women to rise to the highest positions of power in a business or organization (Barreto et al., 2009; Gorman & Kmec, 2009; Leicht, 2008). Women are also frequently confronted with a hostile and unfair work environment. Although American society is becoming less tolerant of sexual harassment, Ida Castro, chair of the U.S. Equal Employment Opportunity Commission, reported that women on Wall Street frequently file complaints of "sexual jokes, derogatory comments, pornographic material, strippers at the office and company-sponsored trips to strip clubs and male-only golf and ski outings" (Knox, 2000, p. IB).

Women vying for jobs and career advancement often face a virtually impossible dilemma: They are seen as more competent if they present themselves with

TABLE 5.2

Gender Differences in Specific Occupations in the United States

Recent labor statistics reveal that men and women occupy very different positions in the U.S. work force.

Occupation	% Women	% Men	Occupation	% Women	% Men
Architect	25.0	75.0	Mechanical engineer	7.0	93.0
Athlete/coach/umpire	32.5	67.5	Physician	30.5	69.5
Bartender	58.0	42.0	Physician's assistant	67.0	33.0
Child-care worker	96.0	4.0	Police detective	19.0	81.0
Computer systems analyst	28.0	72.0	Psychologist	67.0	33.0
Chefs	17.0	83.0	Sales (retail)	52.0	48.0
Construction worker	3.0	97.0	Sales (motorized vehicles and boats)	11.0	89.0
Dental hygienist	98.0	2.0	Secretary	96.0	4.0
Dentist	27.0	73.0	Speech therapist	98.0	2.0
Dietician	90.0	10.0	Teacher (college)	46.0	54.0
Firefighter	5.0	95.0	Teacher (elementary school)	81.0	19.0
Lawyer	34.0	66.0	Truck driver	5.0	95.0
Licensed nurse	92.0	8.0	Waitress/waiter	73.0	27.0

Data from U.S. Bureau of Labor Statistics, 2008.

TABLE 5.3

Women in Work Settings in Selected Countries Around the World (by percent)

These international labor statistics show some of the differences across nations in the distribution of women in the workforce as well as the fairly consistent tendency for women to be especially likely to work in clerical occupations and as service and sales workers rather than in positions as legislators, senior officials, managers, or craft and trade workers. The numbers below indicate the percent of workers in each category who are women.

	Total Workforce	Clerks	Craft and Trade Workers	Legislators, Senior Officials, Managers	Sales and Service Workers
Australia	45%	67%	5%	37%	68%
Canada	47	77	8	37	63
Columbia	39	58	19	46	61
Costa Rica	37	57	14	27	54
Egypt	21	29	3	11	10
Iran	18	24	23	13	11
Israel	46	74	5	30	60
Italy	39	59	14	33	57
Republic of Korea	42	52	15	9	63
Mexico	37	61	24	31	54
Morocco	27	25	19	12	6
Netherlands	45	69	5	28	69
United Kingdom	46	78	8	34	76

Data from International Labor Office, 2008.

Saturday Night Live's popular parodies of Sarah Palin (played by Tina Fey, left) and Hillary Clinton (Amy Poehler, right) raised the question of whether these strong-willed and ambitious political candidates were treated especially harshly by the media because they were women.

Dana Edelson/© NBC/Courtesy: Everett Collection

stereotypically masculine rather than feminine traits, yet when they do this they are also perceived as less socially skilled and attractive—a perception that may ultimately cost them the job or career advancement they were seeking (Eagly, 2004; Fiske et al., 1991; Jackson et al., 2001; Rudman & Glick, 2001). For example, male and female participants in a study by Julie Phelan and others (2008) read about a male or female job candidate for a managerial position. Some candidates emphasized their "agentic" qualities—that is, technical competence, independence, and leadership ability. Others emphasized "communal" qualities—interpersonal and social skills. Phelan and her colleagues found that compared to agentic male candidates, agentic female candidates were perceived as high in competence but low in social skills. In addition, when judging how hirable the candidates were, participants tended to weigh perceptions of the candidates' competence more than their judgments about their social skills—except when judging agentic women! For agentic women, the participants deemphasized these candidates' strong suit—their competence—and instead weighed their (lack of) social skills more heavily.

In a study using people who recently had gone through a real job search, Rebecca

Holloway and Lucy Johnston (2006) found that men who recently had an unsuccessful job interview rated the competence of the interviewer lower if the interviewer was a woman than if the interviewer was a man. Women did not show this bias in the ratings they gave after an unsuccessful job interview.

Causes of the Problem: Intergroup and Motivational Factors

No one is immune from stereotyping, prejudice, and discrimination. Therefore, although there are individual differences—clearly some people are more prejudiced than others, for example—social psychological explanations tend to address factors that make most of us either more or less vulnerable to these intergroup biases. In this section we focus on perspectives that emphasize intergroup and motivational factors. In the section that follows we examine perspectives that emphasize cultural and cognitive factors. It is important to point out here, though, that these different perspectives are not mutually exclusive. They often overlap and work together in accounting for the complexities and pervasiveness of stereotyping, prejudice, and discrimination.

Fundamental Motives Between Groups

A fundamental tenet of social psychology is the social nature of the human animal. Both in our evolutionary history, and in contemporary life, humans live, play, work, and fight in groups. This was true in our evolutionary history and remains true today. A fundamental motive that evolved in our species and in other primates is the need to affiliate with relatively small groups of similar others. These affiliations serve the more basic motive of self-protection. One implication of this is the evolved tendency in people even today to divide the world into ingroups and outgroups—"us" versus "them"—and to favor the former over the latter in numerous ways. Negative stereotypes of outgroups can help justify the desire to exclude outgroups, and the stereotypes in turn can fuel even more prejudice and discrimination.

Mark Schaller and his colleagues (2003; Kenrick et al., 2009; Neuberg et al., 2010) have conducted some fascinating studies that address these points. For example, one set of studies demonstrated that when people's motive to protect themselves was aroused (such as by watching frightening scenes from a movie in which a serial killer stalks a woman through a dark basement), they are more likely to misperceive the emotion of an outgroup member—but not an ingroup member—as anger (Maner et al., 2005). In one particularly creative set of experiments, Schaller and others (2003) hypothesized that being in a completely dark environment would trigger people's self-protective motive more than being in a bright environment and that this would activate stereotypes about the threatening nature of outgroups. Consistent with this hypothesis, Canadian participants in one of their experiments showed greater outgroup bias against Iraqis (relative to ingroup Canadians) when evaluating groups on threat-relevant traits (hostile, untrustworthy) when they were in a dark room than they did when they were in a light room. Darkness did not affect ratings on low-threat traits (ignorant, closed-minded) (see ▶ Figure 5.8).

▶ **FIGURE 5.8**

Fears in the Dark

Canadian participants evaluated Canadians (their ingroup) and Iraqis (an outgroup) on traits that were associated with high threat or low threat. They did this while in a bright or extremely dark room. The higher the bars on this graph, the more favorably they evaluated Canadians than Iraqis on these traits. Participants showed greater ingroup favoritism in ratings of high-threat traits when in a dark environment compared to a bright environment. Darkness did not affect ratings on low-threat traits.

Schaller et al., 2003.

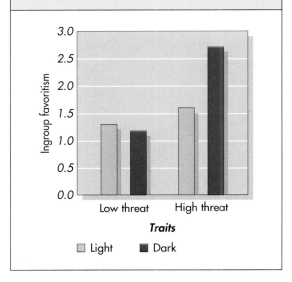

The desire to form ingroups and exclude outsiders from them is reflected in a number of ways. According to *optimal distinctiveness theory*, for example, people try to balance the desire to belong and affiliate with others, on the one hand, and the desire to be distinct and differentiated from others, on the other hand (Abrams, 2009; Brewer, 2007). This may drive people to identify with relatively small ingroups and to distance themselves from outgroups and from individuals whose group status is ambiguous (Castano et al., 2002).

From time to time, our fundamental motivation for self-protection and preservation runs smack into the ultimate obstacle: Thoughts about death and mortality. According to *Terror Management Theory*, which was discussed in Chapter 3, people cope with the fear of their own death by constructing worldviews that help preserve their self-esteem. According to this perspective, favoring ingroups over outgroups is one important way that people preserve their cultural worldviews and, by doing so, try to attain a kind of immortality (Greenberg et al., 2009). Consistent with this theory, a number of studies have demonstrated that making research participants think about mortality—such as with images of cemeteries or with thoughts of decomposing bodies or terrorism—triggers various ingroup biases, including negatively stereotyping and exhibiting prejudice toward a variety of outgroups.

> Being reminded of one's own mortality makes people put things into greater perspective, thereby tending to reduce ingroup-outgroup distinctions and hostilities. **FALSE.**

◼ Robbers Cave: A Field Study in Intergroup Conflict

The 2006–2007 season of the hit reality television show *Survivor* began with great controversy. Each season of *Survivor* features a number of individuals who are placed in very remote locations around the world and compete against each other through often brutal challenges and harsh elements to win a huge cash prize. On this season, however, the producers introduced a new social experiment: They divided the contestants into four rival "tribes" based entirely on race. Many critics attacked this move as exploiting and perpetuating racial stereotypes and prejudices. After only two episodes, the producers dropped the racial division and merged the tribes into two mixed-race groups.

Survivor's experiment probably reminded more than a few social psychologists of a real study conducted more than a half-century before that illustrated how quickly and intensely prejudice can be created between competing groups in the wilderness. The study took place in an unlikely place for a social psychology study: Robbers Cave State Park, Oklahoma. In the summer of 1954, a small group of 11-year-old boys—all white middle-class youngsters, all strangers to one another—arrived at a 200-acre camp located in a densely wooded area of the park. The boys spent the first week or so hiking, swimming, boating, and camping out. After a while, they gave themselves a group name and printed it on their caps and T-shirts. At first, the boys thought they were the only ones at the camp. Soon, however, they discovered that there was a second group and that tournaments had been arranged between the two groups.

What these boys didn't know was that they were participants in an elaborate study conducted by Muzafer Sherif and his colleagues (1961). Parents had given permission for their sons to take part in an experiment for a study of competitiveness and cooperation. The two groups were brought in separately, and only after each had formed its own culture was the other's presence revealed. Now, the "Rattlers" and the "Eagles" were ready to meet. They did so under tense circumstances, competing against each other in football, a treasure hunt, tug of war, and other events. For each event, the winning team was awarded points; the tournament winner was promised a trophy, medals, and other prizes. Almost overnight, the groups turned into hostile antagonists and their rivalry escalated into a full-scale war. Group flags were burned, cabins were ransacked, and a food fight that resembled a riot exploded in the mess hall. Keep in mind that the participants in this study were well-adjusted boys. Yet as Sherif (1966) noted, a naive observer would have thought the boys were "wicked, disturbed, and vicious" (p. 85).

Creating a monster through competition was easy. Restoring the peace, however, was not. First the experimenters tried saying nice things to the Rattlers about the Eagles and vice versa, but the propaganda campaign did not work. Then the two groups were brought together under noncompetitive circumstances, but that didn't help either. What did eventually work was the introduction of **superordinate goals**, mutual goals that could be achieved only through cooperation between the groups. For example, the experimenters arranged for the camp truck to break down, and both groups were needed to pull it up a steep hill. This strategy worked like a charm. By the end of camp, the two groups were so friendly that they insisted on traveling home on the same bus. In just three weeks, the Rattlers and Eagles experienced the kinds of changes that often take generations to unfold: They formed close-knit groups, went to war, and made peace.

The events of Robbers Cave mimicked the kinds of conflict that plague people all over the world. The simplest explanation for this conflict is competition. Assign strangers to groups, throw the groups into contention, stir the pot, and soon there's conflict. Similarly, the intergroup benefits of reducing the focus on competition by activating superordinate goals are also evident around the world. Consider, for example, the remarkable aftermath of the natural disasters that befell Greece and Turkey in 1999, two nations that for many generations had often been in conflict and mistrusted each other. However, Greek-Turkish relations improved dramatically in the wake of earthquakes that rocked both countries. Television images of Turkish rescue workers pulling a Greek child from under a pile of rubble in Athens generated an outpouring of good will. Uniting against a shared threat, as the boys in Robbers Cave did when the camp truck broke down, the two nations began to bridge a deep divide (Kinzer, 1999).

Realistic Conflict Theory

The view that direct competition for valuable but limited resources breeds hostility between groups is called **realistic conflict theory** (Levine & Campbell, 1972). As a simple matter of economics, one group may fare better in the struggle for land, jobs, or power than another group. The losing group becomes frustrated and resentful, the winning group feels threatened and protective—and before long, conflict heats to a rapid boil. It is likely that a good deal of prejudice in the world is driven by the realities of competition (Coenders et al., 2008; Duckitt & Mphuthing, 1998; Stephan et al., 2005; Zárate et al., 2004).

But there is much more to prejudice than real competition. "Realistic" competition for resources may in fact be imagined—a perception in the mind of an individual who is not engaged in any real conflict. In addition, people may become resentful of other groups not because of their conviction that their own security or resources are threatened by these groups but because of their sense of **relative deprivation**, the belief that they fare poorly compared with others. What matters to the proverbial Smiths is not the size of their house per se but whether it is larger than the Jones's house next door (Pettigrew et al., 2008; Walker & Smith, 2002).

superordinate goal A shared goal that can be achieved only through cooperation among individuals or groups.

realistic conflict theory The theory that hostility between groups is caused by direct competition for limited resources.

relative deprivation Feelings of discontent aroused by the belief that one fares poorly compared with others.

Social Identity Theory

Why are people so sensitive about the status and integrity of their ingroups relative to rival outgroups, even when personal interests are not at stake? Could it be that personal interests really *are* at stake but that these interests are more subtle and psychological than a simple competition for valuable resources? If so, could that explain why people all over the world believe that their own nation, culture, language, and religion are better and more deserving than others?

American fans bask in the glory of their team's success at a World Cup soccer game.

These questions were first raised in a study of high school boys in Bristol, England, conducted by Henri Tajfel and his colleagues (1971). The boys were shown a series of dotted slides, and their task was to estimate the number of dots on each. The slides were presented in rapid-fire succession so the dots could not be counted. Later, the experimenter told the participants that some people are chronic "overestimators" and that others are "underestimators." As part of a second, entirely separate task, participants were divided into two groups. They were told that for the sake of convenience one group consisted of overestimators and the other of underestimators, and participants knew which group they were in. (In fact, they were divided randomly.) Participants were then told to allocate points to other participants that could be cashed in for money.

This procedure was designed to create *minimal groups* in which people are categorized on the basis of trivial, minimally important similarities. Tajfel's overestimators and underestimators were not long-term rivals, did not have a history of antagonism, were not frustrated, did not compete for a limited resource, and were not even acquainted with each other. Still, participants consistently allocated more points to members of their own group than to members of the other group. This pattern of discrimination, called **ingroup favoritism**, has been found in studies performed in many countries and using a variety of different measures (Capozza & Brown, 2000; Scheepers et al., 2006).

To explain ingroup favoritism, Tajfel (1982) and John Turner (1987) proposed **social identity theory**. According to this theory, which is illustrated in ▶ Figure 5.9, each of us strives to enhance our self-esteem, which has two components: (1) a *personal* identity; and (2) various collective or *social* identities that are based on the groups to which we belong. In other words, people can boost their self-esteem through their own personal achievements or through affiliation with successful groups. What's nice about the need for social identity is that it leads us to derive pride from our connections with others even if we don't receive any direct benefits from these others (Gagnon & Bourhis, 1996). What's sad, however, is that we often feel the need to belittle "them" in order to feel secure about "us." Religious fervor, racial and ethnic conceit, and aggressive nationalism may all fulfill this more negative side of our social identity. Even gossiping can play this role; Jennifer Bosson and others (2006) found that when people shared negative attitudes about a third party, they felt closer to each other.

Basic Predictions Two basic predictions arose from social identity theory: (1) Threats to one's self-esteem heighten the need for ingroup favoritism, and (2) expressions of ingroup favoritism enhance one's self-esteem. Research generally supports these predictions (Baray et al., 2009; Ellemers et al., 2003; Postmes & Jetten, 2006; Scheepers, 2009; Smurda et al., 2006).

ingroup favoritism
The tendency to discriminate in favor of ingroups over outgroups.

social identity theory
The theory that people favor ingroups over outgroups in order to enhance their self-esteem.

▶**FIGURE 5.9**

Social Identity Theory

According to social identity theory people strive to enhance self-esteem, which has two components: a personal identity and various social identities that derive from the groups to which we belong. Thus, people may boost their self-esteem by viewing their ingroups more favorably than outgroups.

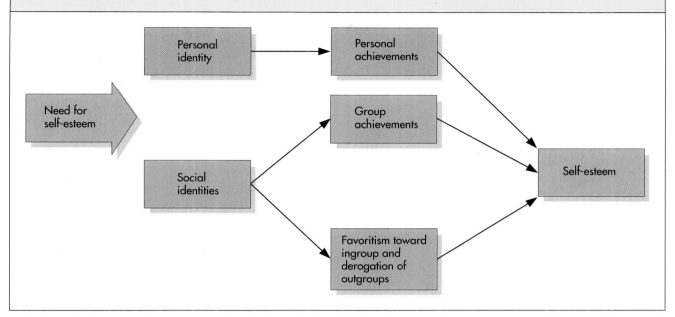

Steven Fein and Steven Spencer (1997) proposed that threats to one's self-esteem can lead individuals to use available negative stereotypes to derogate members of stereotyped groups, and that by derogating others they can feel better about themselves. In one study, for example, Fein and Spencer gave participants positive or negative feedback about their performance on a test of social and verbal skills—feedback that temporarily bolstered or threatened their self-esteem. These participants then took part in what was supposedly a second experiment in which they evaluated a job applicant. All participants received a photograph of a young woman, her résumé, and a videotape of a job interview. Half the participants were given information that suggested that the woman (named Julie Goldberg) was Jewish. The other half was given information that suggested that the woman (named Maria D'Agostino) was not Jewish. On the campus where the study was held, there was a popular negative stereotype of the "Jewish American Princess" that often targeted upper-middle-class Jewish women from the New York area.

As predicted, there were two important results (see ▶ Figure 5.10). First, among participants whose self-esteem had been lowered by negative feedback, they rated the woman more negatively if she seemed to be Jewish than if she did not, even though the pictures and credentials of the two women were the same. Second, participants who had received negative feedback and were given an opportunity to belittle the Jewish woman later exhibited a post-experiment increase in self-esteem—the more negatively they evaluated the Jewish woman, the better these participants felt about themselves. In sum, the results of this experiment suggests that a blow to one's self-image evokes prejudice and the expression of prejudice helps restore self-image.

Situational and Individual Differences   Recent work has extended social identity theory by making more specific distinctions among types of esteem-relevant threats (such as whether the threat is to the group's status or to the individual's role within

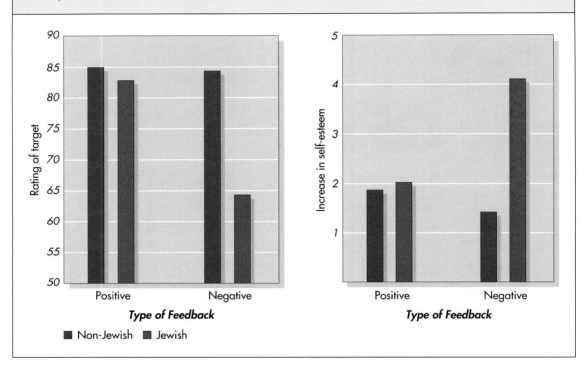

▶ FIGURE 5.10

Self-Esteem and Prejudice

Participants in a 1997 study by Fein and Spencer, participants received positive or negative feedback and then evaluated a female job applicant who was believed to be either Jewish or not Jewish. This study had two key results: (1) Participants whose self-esteem had been lowered by negative feedback evaluated the woman more negatively if they thought she was Jewish than if they thought she was not (left); and (2) negative-feedback participants given the opportunity to belittle the Jewish woman showed a post-experiment increase in self-esteem (right).

Fein and Spencer, 1997.

the group), types of groups (such as whether a group has high or low status in a culture), and types of ingroup members (such as whether the members are strongly or weakly identified with their group) (Platow et al., 2005; Scheepers & Ellemers, 2005; Schmitt et al., 2006; Wann & Grieve, 2005). Greater ingroup identification, for example, has been found across many studies to be associated with stronger social identity effects. In one of the early demonstrations of this point, Nyla Branscombe and Daniel Wann (1994) found that U.S. students who identified strongly with the group "Americans" were especially likely to derogate outgroups in response to a threat to America's status. Manfred Schmitt and Juergen Maes (2002) found that the more East Germans identified with East Germany, the more they showed increased ingroup bias when making comparisons with West Germany during the German unification process—an effect heightened by increased feelings of relative deprivation during unification.

▌ Culture and Social Identity

Individuals' social identities are clearly important to people across cultures. Collectivists are more likely than individualists to value their connectedness and interdependence with the people and groups around them, and their personal identities are tied closely with their social identities. However, according to a number of researchers, people from collectivist cultures are less likely than people from individualist cultures to show biases favoring their ingroups in order to boost their self-esteem (Heine, 2005; Lehman et al., 2004; Snibbe et al., 2003; Yuki, 2003). It isn't the case that collectivists do not favor their ingroup at all. Rather, it's that they are not as compelled to enhance their ingroup as a way of enhancing their own self-esteem. For example, Kenichiro Nakashima and others (2008) showed that when participants' self-esteem was threatened, individuals with independent self-construals showed more ingroup favoritism, whereas individuals with interdependent self-construals did not.

Although they tend not to be driven by self-esteem desires, collectivists do show some biases favoring their ingroups—indeed, being oriented strongly toward one's ingroup may be considered a highly desired and valued way of being (Capozza et al., 2000; Chen et al., 2002; Ruffle & Sosis, 2006). And although collectivists may be less likely to overtly exaggerate the strengths of their ingroups, some research indicates that they draw sharper distinctions between ingroup and outgroup members than individualists do (Gudykunst & Bond, 1997).

Mark Graham/AP/Wide World Photos

Being part of a small, close-knit group can be an important, rewarding part of one's personal identity.

Motives Concerning Intergroup Dominance and Status

Some people are especially motivated to preserve inequities between groups of people in society. Individuals in groups that benefit from advantages that other groups do not have may be motivated to justify and protect those advantages. For example, a growing body of research has examined the **social dominance orientation**: a desire to see one's ingroups as dominant over other groups and a willingness to adopt cultural values that facilitate the oppression of other groups. Such an orientation would be illustrated when individuals endorse sentiments such as "Some groups of people are simply inferior to other groups," and "If certain groups stayed in their place, we would have fewer problems." A person with a social dominance orientation would also likely disagree with statements such as "Group equality should be our ideal." Research in numerous countries throughout the world has found that ingroup identification and outgroup derogation can be especially strong among people with a social dominance orientation (Duckitt & Sibley, 2009; Levin et al., 2009; Sidanius et al., 2007).

Social dominance orientations promote self-interest. But some ideologies support a social structure that may actually oppose one's self-interest, depending on the status of one's groups. John Jost and his colleagues (2009a, 2009b) have focused on what they call *system justification*: processes that endorse and legitimize existing social arrangements. System-justifying beliefs protect the status quo. Groups with power, of course, may promote the status quo to preserve their own advantaged position. But although some disadvantaged groups might be able to improve their circumstances if they were to challenge an economic or political system, members of disadvantaged groups with a system-justification orientation think that the system is fair and just, and they may admire and even show outgroup favoritism to outgroups that thrive in this system.

social dominance orientation
A desire to see one's ingroup as dominant over other groups and a willingness to adopt cultural values that facilitate oppression over other groups.

Causes of the Problem: Cognitive and Cultural Factors

The previous section focused on causes of stereotyping, prejudice, and discrimination that on some level serve individuals' needs or motives, such as the motive to feel good about oneself and one's groups. In this section we turn to perspectives that put greater emphasis on how stereotyping, prejudice, and discrimination result from the basic ways that people learn information available in their culture and process information about people. This is not to say that motivations and intergroup conflicts are not relevant to these cognitive processes. Indeed, we will see in this section a number of ways that people's goals or fears can influence how they process or apply information. The emphasis, however, is on causes that are rooted in cognitive and cultural factors.

Social Categorization

As perceivers, we routinely sort single objects into groups rather than think of each as unique. Biologists classify animals into species; archaeologists divide time into eras; geographers split the earth into regions. Likewise, people sort each other into groups on the basis of gender, race, and other common attributes in a process called **social categorization**. In some ways, social categorization is natural and adaptive. When we group people the way we group foods, animals, and other objects, we can form impressions quickly and use past experience to guide new interactions. With so many things to pay attention to in our social worlds, we can save time and effort by using people's group memberships to make inferences about them (Bodenhausen & Hugenberg, 2009; Fiske & Taylor, 2008; Gaertner et al., 2010). Children learn about social categories quite early and therefore become aware of and use stereotypes when they are very young (Levy & Hughes, 2009; Stangor, 2009).

The time and energy saved through social categorization does come at a cost, however. Categorizing people leads us to overestimate the differences between groups and to underestimate the differences within groups (Ford & Tonander, 1998; Krueger et al., 1989; Spears, 2002; Stangor & Lange, 1994; Wyer et al., 2002). According to Jeffrey Sherman and others (2009), people tend to learn features about majority groups earlier than features about minority groups. When they learn about minority groups, they tend to focus more on features that differentiate them from the majority, thereby magnifying the perceived differences between groups.

The distinctions between social categories may be seen as more rigid, even more biologically rooted, than they actually are. Many people assume, for example, that there is a clear genetic basis for classifying people by race. The fact is, however, that how societies make distinctions between races can change dramatically as a function of historical contexts. For instance, it was fairly common for Americans in the early part of the twentieth century to consider Irish Americans as a racial group distinct from whites, but today such thinking is quite rare. Moreover, biologists, anthropologists, and psychologists have noted that there is more genetic variation within races than between them and emphasize the social, cultural, and historical variables that affect people's conceptions of race (Eberhardt & Goff, 2004; Marks, 1995; Markus, 2008; Ore, 2000). The categories we apply to others often say more about ourselves than they say about them. For example, Melissa Williams and Jennifer Eberhardt (2008) found that people who tend to think of race as a stable, biologically determined entity are less likely to interact with racial outgroup members and are more likely to accept racial inequalities than are people who see race as more socially determined.

social categorization
The classification of persons into groups on the basis of common attributes.

Each of us is a member of multiple social categories, but some categorizations—particularly race, gender, and age—are more likely to quickly dominate our perceptions than others (Ito & Urland, 2003; Yzerbyt & Demoulin, 2010). Other factors can influence how we categorize others. Cognitive factors, such as whether we have been primed to think about a particular category, as well as motivational factors, such as our immediate needs in a situation, can determine whether, for example, we will see a black male firefighter primarily by race, gender, or occupation (Bodenhausen & Macrae, 1998; Castelli et al., 2004).

Ingroups Versus Outgroups   Although grouping humans is much like grouping objects, there is a key difference. When it comes to social categorization, perceivers themselves are members or nonmembers of the categories they use. As we have already discussed in this chapter, the strong tendency to carve the world into "us" (ingroups) and "them" (outgroups) has important consequences.

One cognitive consequence is that we exaggerate the differences between our ingroup and other outgroups. Because perceived similarities are minimized and perceived differences are maximized, stereotypes are formed and reinforced. Another consequence is a phenomenon known as the **outgroup homogeneity effect**, whereby perceivers assume that there is a greater similarity among members of outgroups than among members of one's own group. In other words, there may be fine and subtle differences among "us," but "they" are all alike (Linville & Jones, 1980).

The outgroup homogeneity effect is common and evident around the world (Bartsch et al., 1997; Linville, 1998; Read & Urada, 2003). Indeed, it is easy to think of real-life examples. People from China, Korea, Taiwan, and Vietnam see themselves as different from one another, of course, but to many Western eyes they are all Asian. Business majors like to talk about "engineering types"; engineers talk about "business types"; liberals and conservatives see themselves as individuals but the other side as "one big mass of unthinking extremists"; teenagers lump together all "old people" and older adults talk about "all those rude teenagers"; and while the natives of California proclaim their cultural and ethnic diversity, outsiders talk of the "typical Californian." To people outside the group, outgroup members can even seem to *look* alike: People are less accurate in distinguishing and recognizing the faces of members of racial outgroups, especially if they are unfamiliar with those other groups (Chiroro et al., 2008; Meissner et al., 2005; Pauker et al., 2009; Stahl et al., 2008).

There are several reasons for the tendency to perceive outgroups as homogeneous. First, we often do not notice subtle differences among outgroups because we have little personal contact with them. Think about your family or your favorite sports team, and specific individuals come to mind. Think about an unfamiliar outgroup, however, and you are likely to think in abstract terms about the group as a whole. Indeed, the more familiar people are with an outgroup, the less likely they are to perceive it as homogeneous.

A second problem is that people often do not encounter a representative sample of outgroup members. A student from one school who encounters students from a rival school only when they cruise into town for a Saturday football game, screaming at the top of their lungs, sees only the most avid rival fans—hardly a diverse lot (Linville et al., 1989; Quattrone, 1986). People sometimes perceive their own group to be homogeneous when they first join it, but over time, as they become more familiar

Richard Pasley/Stock Boston

Whether people are likely to immediately categorize this person by his race, gender, or occupation depends on a combination of cognitive, cultural, and motivational factors.

outgroup homogeneity effect
The tendency to assume that there is greater similarity among members of outgroups than among members of ingroups.

with fellow group members, they see their group as more diverse relative to outgroups (Ryan & Bogart, 1997).

Lack of familiarity and lack of diversity of experiences with outgroup members are two reasons why "*they* all look alike," but there's more to the story than that. Research using brain imaging or cognitive methods has found that merely categorizing people as ingroup or outgroup members influences how perceivers process information about them, even if familiarity is held constant. For example, student participants in experiments by Kurt Hugenberg and Olivier Corneille (2009) were exposed to unfamiliar faces of people who were the same race as the participants. These faces were categorized as ingroup members (from the same university as the participants) or outgroup members (from a rival university). The students processed faces more holistically (that is, they integrated the features of the faces into a global representation of the overall face) when they had been categorized as being from their ingroup than they did when they had been categorized as members of the outgroup.

Jay Van Bavel and others (2008) found related results when they exposed participants to unfamiliar white or black faces. The participants showed greater neural activity in particular areas of the brain, such as the orbitofrontal cortex, when the faces were labeled as being from an ingroup than when they were labeled as being from an outgroup (see ▶ Figure 5.11). In addition, this greater activity in the orbitofrontal cortex was correlated significantly with the degree to which the participants reported preferring the ingroup faces over the outgroup faces. It is interesting to note that the categorization of faces as ingroup or outgroup had a much stronger effect on orbitofrontal cortex activity and on preference for the faces than did the variable of whether the faces were white or black.

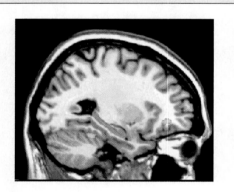

▶ FIGURE 5.11

Neural Activity and Ingroup Bias

Participants saw photographs of unfamiliar white and black faces. When the faces were said to be members of their ingroup, participants showed greater neural activity in particular areas of the brain, including the two areas highlighted here, the fusiform gyrus and the orbitofrontal cortex. Greater activation in the orbitofrontal cortex was also associated with stronger self-reported preference for ingroup faces.

Van Bavel et al., 2008.

Dehumanizing Outgroups Perceivers may not only process outgroup members' faces more superficially—they also sometimes process them more like objects than like fellow human beings. This was a conclusion suggested by Lasana Harris and Susan Fiske (2006). When participants in their research saw pictures of people from a variety of groups, fMRI showed activation in their medial prefrontal cortex, which is thought to be necessary for social cognition. However, this activation was not evident in response to images of either nonhuman objects or people from particularly extreme outgroups, such as addicts or the homeless.

A rapidly growing number of social psychological investigations have illustrated both the subtle and not-so-subtle ways that people see or treat outgroup members as less than fully human (Demoulin et al., 2009; Haslam et al., 2008; Kwan & Fiske, 2008). As but one example, Amy Cuddy and others (2007) conducted a study two weeks after Hurricane Katrina devastated the lives of numerous people in the southeastern United States in 2005. The researchers found that participants were less likely to infer that racial outgroup members were experiencing complex emotions considered uniquely human, such as remorse and mourning, than were racial ingroup members. Those who did infer such humanizing emotions, however, were more likely to report that they intended to take actions to help the victims of the hurricane.

Dehumanization has played a role in atrocities throughout history, such as in the Nazi propaganda that characterized the Jews in Germany as disease-spreading rats and blacks as half-apes. Elements of dehumanization certainly seemed to be evident in the examples discussed in the introduction of this chapter of Barack Obama being portrayed as a chimpanzee during the presidential campaign. The bar owner who was selling T-shirts of Obama as Curious George, for example, defended himself by saying that Obama simply looked so much like the cartoon chimp. This example illustrates several points: the simplistic processing of faces of outgroup members, dehumanization, and a remarkable insensitivity to a persistent and degrading stereotype linking African Americans with monkeys and apes. This insensitivity was evident repeatedly even after Obama became president. For example, an editorial cartoon in the *New York Post* in February 2009 depicted the police killing a chim-

panzee who apparently had written an economic stimulus bill (which President Obama had just signed into law and was the centerpiece of his first months as president). A few months later, a Republican Party activist joked on his Facebook page that a gorilla who escaped from a zoo was probably one of First Lady Michelle Obama's ancestors (Kennedy, 2009).

The persistence of this stereotype was illustrated in the chilling findings from a set of experiments by Phillip Goff, Jennifer Eberhardt, and others (2008). These studies revealed that participants—regardless of their own race—had such well-learned associations between apes and black male faces that even extremely quick exposure to images of one (that is, of either apes or of black male faces) made them quicker to identify or more likely to pay attention to the other. For example, participants were quicker to identify which of a series of animals were apes if they had first been exposed very briefly to photographs of black male faces than if they had been exposed to white male faces or random drawings.

The image in this cartoon from the *New York Post* of February 18, 2009, referred to a chimpanzee that was shot to death by police in Connecticut after it had mauled a friend of its owner. However, the reference in the cartoon's text to the stimulus bill, which President Obama had just signed and championed during his first month in office, caused many to believe that the cartoon was depicting Obama as the chimpanzee.

How Stereotypes Survive and Self-Perpetuate

Social categorization helps give rise to stereotypes, which offer us quick and convenient summaries of social groups. It is clear, however, that they often cause us to overlook the diversity within categories and to form mistaken impressions of specific individuals. Given their shortcomings, why do stereotypes endure? We turn now to some of the mechanisms that help perpetuate stereotypes.

Illusory Correlations   One way that stereotypes endure is through the **illusory correlation**, a tendency for people to overestimate the link between variables that are only slightly or not at all correlated (Meiser & Hewstone, 2006; Risen et al., 2007; Sherman et al., 2009; Stroessner & Plaks, 2001). Illusory correlations result from two different processes. First, people tend to overestimate the association between variables that are *distinctive*: variables that capture attention simply because they are novel or deviant. When two relatively unusual events happen together, that combination may stick in people's minds, and this can lead people to overestimate an association between the two events. For example, if people see a story on the news about a person who was recently released from a mental institution (a rarely encountered category of person) committing a brutal murder (an uncommon behavior), they may remember the link between mental patient and murder better than if a more commonly encountered type of person committed the murder or than if a former mental patient did something more common.

The implications for stereotyping are important. First, unless otherwise motivated, people overestimate the association between distinctive variables such as

illusory correlation   An overestimate of the association between variables that are only slightly or not at all correlated.

Sean Delonas/Splash News

minority groups and deviant acts. Even children in second grade may perceive these false associations (Johnston & Jacobs, 2003).

Second, people tend to overestimate the association between variables they already expect to go together (Hamilton & Rose, 1980; Susskind, 2003). The implications for stereotyping are important here as well: People overestimate the joint occurrence of variables they expect to be associated with each other, such as stereotyped groups and stereotypic behaviors. For example, if perceivers witness 10 men from a group of 100 men get into car accidents, and they also witness 10 women from a group of 100 women get into car accidents, perceivers who believe that women are worse drivers than men are likely to remember more of the women and fewer of the men getting into accidents.

Attributions   People also maintain their stereotypes through how they explain the behaviors of others. Chapter 4 discusses how perceivers make attributions, or explanations, about the causes of other people's behaviors and how these attributions can sometimes be flawed. These flaws can help perpetuate stereotypes. For example, although we know from research that discrimination can impair the performance of stereotyped individuals, perceivers may fail to take this effect into account when explaining this underperformance and instead see it as evidence that supports the negative stereotype. In this way, perceivers may see confirmation of the stereotype instead of recognizing the consequences of discrimination.

On the other hand, when people see others acting in ways that seem to contradict a stereotype, they may be *more* likely to think about situational factors in order to explain the surprising behavior. Rather than accept a stereotype-disconfirming behavior at face value, such as a woman defeating a man in an athletic contest, perceivers imagine the situational factors that might explain away this apparent exception to the rule, such as random luck, ulterior motives, or other special circumstances. In this way, perceivers can more easily maintain their stereotypes of these groups (Karpinski & von Hippel, 1996; Philippot, 2005; Sekaquaptewa et al., 2003; Seta et al., 2003; Sherman et al., 2005).

Subtyping   Have you ever noticed that people often manage to hold negative views about a social group even when they like individual members of that group? Gordon Allport (1954) recognized this phenomenon more than half a century ago. He wrote, "There is a common mental device that permits people to hold prejudgments even in the face of much contradictory evidence. It is the device of admitting exceptions. . . . By excluding a few favored cases, the negative rubric is kept intact for all other cases" (p. 23). Confronted with a woman who does not seem particularly warm and nurturing, for example, people can either develop a more diversified image of females or toss the mismatch into a special subtype—say, "career women." To the extent that people create this subtype, their existing image of women in general will remain relatively intact (Carnaghi & Yzerbyt, 2007; Hewstone & Lord, 1998; Wilder et al., 1996).

Women who play rough contact sports—such as these members of the Canadian women's hockey team—defy gender stereotypes. But rather than change their gender stereotypes, many perceivers subtype these women and dismiss them as exceptions.

© VALDRIN XHEMAJ/epa/Corbis

Confirmation Biases and Self-Fulfilling Prophecies Imagine learning that a mother yelled at a 16-year-old girl, that a lawyer behaved aggressively, and that a Boy Scout grabbed the arm of an elderly woman crossing the street. Now imagine that a construction worker yelled at a 16-year-old girl, that a homeless man behaved aggressively, and that an ex-con grabbed the arm of an elderly woman crossing the street. Do very different images of these actions come to mind? This is a fundamental effect of stereotyping: Stereotypes of groups influence people's perceptions and interpretations of the behaviors of group members. This is especially likely when a target of a stereotype behaves in an ambiguous way; perceivers reduce the ambiguity by interpreting the behavior as consistent with the stereotype (Dunning & Sherman, 1997; Kunda et al., 1997). For example, in one study, black and white sixth-grade boys saw pictures and descriptions of ambiguously aggressive behaviors (such as one child bumping into another). Both the black and the white boys judged the behaviors as more mean and threatening if the behaviors were performed by black boys than if they were done by white boys (Sagar & Schofield, 1980).

The effect of stereotypes on individuals' perceptions is a type of confirmation bias, which, as we saw in Chapter 4, involves people's tendencies to interpret, seek, and create information that seems to confirm their expectations. In a clever demonstration of this bias (specifically in the context of interpreting information), Jeff Stone and his colleagues (1997) had students listen to a college basketball game. Some were led to believe that a particular player was white; others were led to believe he was black. After listening to the game, all of the students were asked to evaluate how the player had performed in the game. Consistent with racial stereotypes, those students who believed the player was black rated him as having played better and more athletically, whereas those who thought he was white rated him as having played with more intelligence and hustle (see ▶ Figure 5.12).

Stereotypes typically are held not just by individuals but by many people within a culture, and they are often perpetuated through repeated communications. In a classic demonstration, Gordon Allport and Leo Postman (1947) showed participants a picture of a subway train filled with passengers. In the picture were a black man dressed in a suit and a white man holding a razor. One participant viewed the scene briefly and then described it to a second participant who had not seen it. The second participant communicated the description to a third participant and so on, through six rounds of communication. The result: In more than half the sessions, the final participant's report indicated that the black man, not the white man, held the razor.

In a more recent demonstration of a similar point, Anthony Lyons and Yoshihisa Kashima (2001) had Australian students read a story about an Australian Rules Football player. The students were put in groups of four. One person read the story, and after a delay of a few minutes transmitted the story to the next student, and so on down the four-person chain. The students were supposed to relay the story as accurately as possible. Some of the information in the story was consistent with stereotypes about Australian Rules Football players (e.g., "On the way, Gary and his mate drank several beers in the car"), and some of it was inconsistent with the stereotype (e.g., "He switched on some classical music"). Although the first student in the chain was likely to communicate both stereotype-consistent and stereotype-inconsistent information, as the story went from person to person the

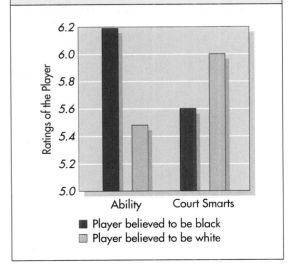

▶ **FIGURE 5.12**

"White Men Can't Jump"?

Students listened to a college basketball game and evaluated one particular player. Half of the students were led to believe the player was black; the other half, that he was white. Consistent with their stereotypes, the students perceived the player as having more physical ability if they thought he was black and as having more "court smarts" if they thought he was white.

Stone et al., 1997.

stereotype-inconsistent information was progressively screened out. By the time the fourth person told the story, the football player seemed much more clearly stereotypical than he had seemed in the original story.

Confirmation biases are bad enough. But even more disturbing are situations in which stereotyped group members are led to actually behave in stereotype-confirming ways. In other words, stereotypes can create self-fulfilling prophecies. As noted in Chapter 4, a self-fulfilling prophecy occurs when a perceiver's false expectations about a person cause the person to behave in ways that confirm those expectations. Stereotypes can trigger such behavioral confirmation (Rosenthal, 2002). Consider a classic experiment by Carl Word and others (1974) involving a situation of great importance in people's lives: the job interview. White participants, without realizing it, sat farther away, made more speech errors, and held shorter interviews when interviewing black applicants than they did when interviewing white applicants. This colder interpersonal style, in turn, caused the black applicants to behave in a nervous and awkward manner. In short, the whites' racial stereotypes and prejudice actually hurt the interview performance of the black candidates. Since the black candidates' interview performance tended to be objectively worse than that of the white candidates, it seemed to confirm the interviewers' negative stereotypes—but this poor performance was caused by the interviewers, not the interviewees.

Are Stereotypes Ever Accurate?   We have been discussing how stereotypes survive despite evidence that should disconfirm them, or how stereotypes distort perceptions and behaviors based on false expectations. But this can raise the question of whether stereotypes are ever accurate. Like people, stereotypes are not all alike. Some are more accurate than others. Although many stereotypes are based on completely illusory information or perceptions, some do stem from a kernel of truth, and still others may be fairly accurate. Lee Jussim and others (2009; Madon et al., 1998) argue that stereotypes tend to be much more accurate than the majority of researchers who study stereotypes acknowledge.

But the question of accuracy is more complicated than it may appear. First, the meaning of "accurate" can be debated. "Accurate" could mean that stereotypes reflect universal, stable, possibly genetic differences or it could mean that stereotypes reflect differences that exist under particular sets of societal and historic conditions (with the qualification that these differences may well change if conditions change). Most social psychologists focus on the latter meaning.

Second, imagine that you believe that members of a particular social category tend to be rude. If you encounter a member of this group and anticipate that she is likely to be rude, you may react to her in a cold, unfriendly way. This in turn may cause her to act rudely toward you in return. Was your expectation of that person accurate? In a sense, it was: She *was* rude to you, just as you expected. But clearly your own behavior may have caused the rudeness. This self-fulfilling prophecy creates a reality that seems to render the stereotype accurate, even if it was false in the first place.

Culture and Socialization

The list of familiar stereotypes is quite long. Athletes are dumb, math majors are geeks, Americans are loud, Italians are emotional, Japanese are sneaky, Californians are laid back, white men can't jump, and used-car salesmen can't be trusted as far as you can throw them. And on and on. Dividing people into social categories, including ingroups and outgroups, certainly is a key factor in the formation of stereotypes and prejudices. But with so many stereotypes and prejudices, many of which are shared around the

Not everyone's life is what they make it. Some people's life is what other people make it.
—Anastasia, a character in Alice Walker's short story "You Can't Keep a Good Woman Down"

world, it is clear that at some level we are somehow taught these stereotypes from our culture. We turn now to examine those processes.

Socialization refers to the processes by which people learn the norms, rules, and information of a culture or group. We learn a tremendous amount of information (often without even realizing it) by absorbing what we see around us in our culture, groups, and families. These lessons include what various stereotypes are, how valued or devalued various groups are, and which prejudices are acceptable to have.

Consider the story of something that happened to one of the authors of this book. When he was about 8 years old, his two best friends one day turned on him and derisively called him a "Jew ball." They had never thought of him as different from them or categorized him as Jewish before, and yet on this day, suddenly Jewishness was relevant—and negative to them. But why *then*, and how did they come up with "Jew ball"?! Only much later did it become clear that they had misheard their father say "Jew boy." Trying to model their father's values, they used an approximation of this expression against their friend, and thereafter they saw him in a different way. The biased lens through which the father saw people was passed down to the next generation.

Although it certainly isn't always the case, the stereotypes and prejudices of a parent can influence the stereotypes and prejudices of a child, often in implicit ways (Castelli et al., 2009). More generally, and more pervasively, the stereotypes and prejudices exhibited by peers, the popular media, and one's culture are part of the air each of us breathes as we develop, and the influences can be obvious or subtle.

To narrow our discussion of these cultural and socialization processes we will focus on gender stereotypes and sexism, but it is important to recognize that these processes are relevant to all kinds and targets of stereotypes, prejudice, and discrimination.

Gender Stereotypes: Blue for Boys, Pink for Girls

We begin with what are often the first words uttered when a baby is born: "It's a boy!" or "It's a girl!" In many hospitals, the newborn boy is immediately given a blue hat and the newborn girl a pink hat. The infant receives a gender-appropriate name and is showered with gender-appropriate gifts. Over the next few years, the typical boy is supplied with toy trucks, baseballs, pretend tools, guns, and chemistry sets; the typical girl is furnished with dolls, stuffed animals, pretend make-up kits, kitchen sets, and tea sets. As they enter school, many expect the boy to earn money by mowing lawns and to enjoy math and video games, while they expect the girl to babysit and to enjoy crafts, music, and social activities.

These distinctions persist in college, as more male students major in economics and the sciences and more female students major in the arts, languages, and humanities. In the work force, more men become doctors, construction workers, auto mechanics, airplane pilots, investment bankers, and engineers. In contrast, more women become secretaries, schoolteachers, nurses, flight attendants, bank tellers, and housewives. Back on the home front, the life cycle begins again when a man and woman have their first baby and discover that "It's a girl!" or "It's a boy!"

The Blues and the Pinks. Even a very quick look at a toy store illustrates dramatic differences in how boys and girls are socialized. For example, boys are encouraged to play active, loud, and violent games (top), while girls are encouraged to engage in quieter, nurturing role play (bottom).

© UrbanZone/Alamy

AP Photo/Nick Ut

The traditional pinks and blues are not as distinct today as they used to be. Many gender barriers of the past have broken down, and the colors have somewhat blended together. Nevertheless, the stereotypes—and, as we discussed earlier, sexism—persists.

What do people say when asked to describe the typical man and woman? Males are said to be more adventurous, assertive, aggressive, independent, and task oriented; females are thought to be more sensitive, gentle, dependent, emotional, and people oriented. These images are so universal that they were reported by 2,800 college students from thirty different countries located in North and South America, Europe, Africa, Asia, and Australia (Williams & Best, 1982). The images are also salient to young children, who distinguish men from women well before their first birthday; identify themselves and others as boys or girls by 3 years of age; form gender-stereotypic beliefs and preferences about stories, toys, and other objects soon after that; and then use their simplified stereotypes in judging others and favoring their own gender over the other in intergroup situations (Golombok & Hines, 2002; Knobloch et al., 2005; Leinbach & Fagot, 1993; Ruble & Martin, 1998).

Children also begin quite early to distinguish between stereotypically masculine and feminine behaviors. One study, for instance, found that by their second birthday toddlers exhibited more surprise when adults performed behaviors inconsistent with gender roles (Serbin et al., 2002). In another study, preschool-age boys and girls liked a new toy less if they were told that it was a toy that opposite-sex children liked (Martin et al., 1995).

Gerianne Alexander (2003), citing data about children exposed prenatally to atypical levels of sex hormones and data about sex differences in toy preferences among nonhuman primates, argues that children's preferences about sex-based toys, while partly due to gender socialization, may also have neurobiological and evolutionary roots. For example, one intriguing study reported that vervet monkeys showed sex differences in toy preferences similar to those seen in human children (Alexander & Hines, 2002).

Although biological and evolutionary factors may play a role in some of these preferences, it is clear that children have ample opportunity to learn gender stereotypes and roles from their parents and other role models. A meta-analysis of more than forty studies showed a significant correlation between parents' gender stereotypes and their children's gender-related thinking (Tenenbaum & Leaper, 2002).

Beliefs about males and females are so deeply ingrained that they influence the behavior of adults literally the moment a baby is born. In one fascinating study, the first-time parents of fifteen girls and fifteen boys were interviewed within twenty-four hours of the babies' births. There were no differences between the male and female newborns in height, weight, or other aspects of physical appearance. Yet the parents of girls rated their babies as softer, smaller, and more finely featured. The fathers of boys saw their sons as stronger, larger, more alert, and better coordinated (Rubin et al., 1974). Could it be there really were differences that only the parents were able to discern? Doubtful. In another study, Emily Mondschein and others (2000) found that mothers of eleven-month-olds underestimated their infants' crawling ability if they were girls but overestimated it if they were boys.

As they develop, boys and girls receive many divergent messages in many different settings. Barbara Morrongiello and Tess Dawber (2000) conducted a study that was relevant to this point. They showed mothers videotapes of children engaging in somewhat risky activities on a playground and asked them to stop the tape and indicate whatever they would ordinarily say to their own child in the situation shown. Mothers of daughters intervened more frequently and more quickly than did mothers of sons. As shown in Table 5.4, mothers of daughters were more likely to caution the child about getting hurt, whereas mothers of sons were more likely to encourage the child's risky playing.

Another study by Morrongiello and others (2000) revealed that although boys typically experience more injuries from risky playing than girls, all children by the age of 6 tend to think that girls are at greater risk of injury than boys.

Social Role Theory As children develop, they begin to look at the larger culture around them and see who occupies what roles in society as well as how these roles are valued. According to Alice Eagly's (1987; Eagly et al., 2004) **social role theory**, although the perception of sex differences may be based on some real differences, it is magnified by the unequal social roles men and women occupy.

The process involves three steps. First, through a combination of biological and social factors, a division of labor between the sexes has emerged over time, both at home and in the work setting. Men are more likely to work in construction or business; women are more likely to care for children and to take lower-status jobs. Second, since people behave in ways that fit the roles they play, men are more likely than women to wield physical, social, and economic power. Third, these behavioral differences provide a continuing basis for social perception, leading us to perceive men as dominant and women as domestic "by nature," when in fact the differences reflect the roles they play. In short, sex stereotypes are shaped by—and often confused with—the unequal distribution of men and women into different social roles. According to this theory, perceived differences between men and women are based on real behavioral differences that are mistakenly assumed to arise from gender rather than from social roles.

Social role theory and socialization processes more generally can of course be extended beyond gender stereotypes and sexism. Seeing that some groups of people occupy particular roles in society more than other people do can fuel numerous stereotypes and prejudices. One extremely important factor in determining what kinds of people we see in what kinds of roles is the popular media. We examine some of the effects associated with media exposure next.

Media Effects More than ever, children, adolescents, and adults seem to be immersed in popular culture transmitted via the mass media. Watching TV shows on our iPods or cell phones while on the stationary bike at the gym, checking out the latest viral video sweeping the Internet while taking a break at the office or coffee shop, seeing advertisements popping up on our computer screens like weeds, glancing at the tabloid cover shots of the latest starlet hounded by relentless paparazzi—there often seems no escape. Through the ever-present media, we are fed a steady diet of images of people. These images have the potential to perpetuate stereotypes and discrimination.

Fortunately, the days when the media portrayed women and people of color in almost exclusively stereotypical, powerless roles are gone. Still, research indicates that some stereotyping persists—for example, in music videos and TV commercials, programs, and cartoons in countries around the world (Bartsch et al., 2000; Klein & Shiffman, 2009; Messineo, 2008; Nassif & Gunter, 2008; Ward et al., 2005).

TABLE 5.4

What Mothers Would Say

Mothers of young boys or girls watched a videotape of another child engaging in somewhat risky behavior on a playground. The mothers were instructed to stop the videotape whenever they would say something to the child if the child were theirs and to indicate what they would say. Mothers of daughters stopped the tape much more often than mothers of sons to express caution ("Be careful!"), worry about injury ("You could fall!"), and directives to stop ("Stop that this instant!"). In contrast, mothers of sons were more likely to indicate encouragement ("Good job! Let me see you go higher!").

Context of Statement	Frequency of Statement by	
	Mothers of Girls	Mothers of Boys
Caution	3.9	0.7
Worry about injury	9.2	0.2
Directive to stop	9.3	0.6
Encouragement	0.5	3.0

Adapted from Morrongiello & Dawber, 2000.

---

social role theory The theory that small gender differences are magnified in perception by the contrasting social roles occupied by men and women.

Although images of attractive people sell magazines and many consumers enjoy looking at them, they do raise the question of whether exposure to so many of these kinds of images also produce negative consequences. For example, does repeated exposure to such images perpetuate stereotypes or cause some people to engage in dangerous behaviors to try to achieve what are often impossible and unhealthy standards of masculinity and femininity?

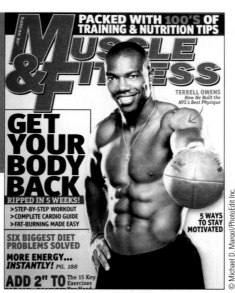

More to the point is the fact that media depictions can influence viewers, often without the viewers realizing it (Ward & Friedman, 2006). Think about TV commercials for beer or men's cologne. There's a good chance that the commercials that come to mind include images of women as sex objects whose primary purpose in the ads is to serve as "the implied 'reward' for product consumption" (Rudman & Borgida, 1995, p. 495). Can these commercials affect not only men's attitudes toward women but their immediate behavior as well? Yes, according to research by Laurie Rudman and Eugene Borgida (1995). They conducted a study in which male undergraduates watched a videotape containing either sexist TV commercials or TV commercials for similar products that contained no sexual imagery.

After watching the commercials, each participant went to a room to meet and interview a woman, who actually was a confederate of the experimenter. Each student's interaction with the woman was secretly videotaped. Later, female judges watched these videotaped interactions and evaluated the male students' behavior toward the female confederate on several dimensions. The results revealed that the men who had seen sexist commercials were rated as behaving in a more sexualized, objectifying manner than the men who had seen the neutral ads. Having been primed with images of women as sex objects on TV, the men treated the woman in objectifying ways.

TV commercials influence not only men's but also women's attitudes and behavior. Studies have shown that female college students who had just watched a set of commercials in which the female characters were portrayed in stereotypical fashion tended to express lower self-confidence, less independence, and fewer career aspirations, and even performed more poorly on a math test, than did those who viewed stereotype-irrelevant or counter-stereotypical ads (Davies et al., 2002; Geis et al., 1984; Jennings et al., 1980).

Immersed in popular culture, people implicitly learn stereotypes about how men and women are supposed to look. Media images of impossibly thin or proportioned female models can have powerful effects on women's body images and esteem and are implicated in the near-epidemic incidence of eating disorders and debilitating anxiety over physical appearance, particularly among young European American women (Henderson-King et al., 2001; Moradi et al., 2005; Ward & Friedman, 2006). The media's impact may be especially negative among individuals who already have concerns

Even brief exposure to sexist television commercials can significantly influence the behaviors of men and women. **TRUE.**

about their appearance or are particularly concerned with other people's opinions (Henderson-King & Henderson-King, 1997; Ricciardelli et al., 2000).

Men's body images may also be affected by the media. A meta-analysis of 25 studies—some correlational and some experimental—found a significant relationship between men's perceptions that the mass media was creating pressure about acceptable male bodies and feeling dissatisfied with their bodies (Barlett et al., 2008). Research points to a growing number of teenage boys and men who are hurting themselves through their obsession with their bodies as they try to gain muscle mass while remaining extremely lean. Here, too, the media appear to play a critical role. Indeed, graphic images of muscular and lean male models have become increasingly prevalent of late. More and more cases come to light every year of boys and young men copying star athletes by taking steroids and other drugs that can make them look more like their role models but that can seriously threaten their health (Gray & Ginsberg, 2007; Hanc, 2006; Hargreaves & Tiggemann, 2009; Hobza & Rochlen, 2009; Taylor, 2006).

It is clear that the portrayals of different groups of people can vary dramatically from one culture to another. This is true also for body image—what is considered the norm or ideal in the mainstream media in Western culture is not the same as the norm or ideal in other cultures or even in subcultures within Western culture. What is considered beautiful in one culture may be considered too thin, too heavy, or too muscular in another culture, and these differences in ideals as represented in the most popular media of a culture lead to different effects on the body-related self-esteem and behaviors of individuals (Bailey, 2008; Jung & Lee, 2006; Schooler, 2008).

The media can also play a role in promoting *positive* norms. This was demonstrated recently in an unusual yearlong field experiment in Rwanda, which has been the site of terrible war, genocide, and intergroup conflict, particularly between the Hutus and Tutsis. Elizabeth Levy Paluck (2009) had Rwandans listen to a radio soap opera (radio being the most important form of mass media there) over the course of a year. She randomly assigned half to listen to a soap opera about conflicts that paralleled real conflicts in the country but that were solved in ways that modeled intergroup cooperation and communication, nonviolence, and opposition to prejudice. The other half of the participants listened to a soap opera about health issues. At the end of the year, those Rwandans who listened to the soap opera promoting positive intergroup norms had significantly more positive feelings about intergroup cooperation, trust, and interactions.

▓ Stereotype Content Model

The relative status and relations between groups in a culture influence the content of the culture's stereotypes about these groups. This is a central point in the **stereotype content model** (Cuddy et al., 2008; Fiske et al., 2009). According to this model, many group stereotypes vary along two dimensions: warmth and competence. Groups may be considered high on both dimensions, low on both, or high on one dimension but low on the other. For example, the elderly may be stereotyped as high on warmth but low on competence.

The stereotype content model proposes that stereotypes about the competence of a group are influenced by the relative *status* of that group in society—higher relative status is associated with higher competence. Stereotypes about the warmth of a group are influenced by perceived *competition* with the group—greater perceived competition is associated with lower warmth. For example, groups that are of low status but that remain compliant and do not try to upset the status quo are likely

stereotype content model
A model proposing that the relative status and competition between groups influence group stereotypes along the dimensions of competence and warmth.

to be stereotyped as low in competence but high in warmth. A wave of immigrants who enter a country with low status but compete for jobs and resources, on the other hand, may be seen as low in both competence and warmth.

To put it into concrete terms, think about stereotypes about two categories of women. Housewives may be seen as having warm traits, such as being caring and nurturing, and having traits associated with lack of competence, such as being passive. Stereotypes of female executives in the corporate world, however, consist of much colder attributes, such as being demanding and cutthroat, along with competent attributes such as being strong. When stereotypes are high on one dimension but low on the other, group members can face a difficult challenge. A female business leader who comes off as very warm may be seen as less competent, for example. Similarly, if she comes off as very competent, she may be seen as less warm.

Researchers have found support for the stereotype content model both with experiments—in which perceived status and intergroup competition are manipulated—and from correlational studies conducted around the world (Caprariello et al., 2009; Cuddy et al., 2009).

Is Stereotyping Inevitable? Automatic Versus Intentional Processes

Part of the power of stereotypes is they can bias our perceptions and responses even if we don't personally agree with them. In other words, we don't have to believe a stereotype for it to trigger illusory correlations and self-fulfilling prophecies or to bias how we think, feel, and behave toward group members. Sometimes just being aware of stereotypes in one's culture is enough to cause these effects. Moreover, stereotypes can be activated without our awareness.

These findings raise a provocative (and potentially depressing) question: Is stereotyping inevitable? When we encounter people from other groups, do our stereotypes of these groups always become activated in our minds? Can we do anything to prevent this from happening? Most people believe that they can resist stereotyping others, but the research paints a far more complex picture.

Stereotypes as (Sometimes) Automatic　Patricia Devine (1989) distinguishes between automatic and controlled processes in stereotyping. She argues that people have become highly aware of the content of many stereotypes through cultural influences, such as lessons learned from parents and images in the media. Because of this high awareness, people automatically activate stereotypes whenever they are exposed to members of groups for which popular stereotypes exist. Thus, just as many of us are automatically primed to think *eggs* after hearing *bacon and*, we are also primed to think of concepts relevant to a stereotype when we think of a stereotyped group. To be sure, we can try to prevent this activated stereotype from influencing our judgments or behaviors. However, we are often unaware that a particular stereotype has been activated or how it can influence our perceptions and behaviors (Bargh, 1997). Thus, the stereotype can affect us in spite of our good intentions.

In her study, Devine exposed white participants to **subliminal presentations** on a computer monitor. For one group, these presentations consisted of words relevant to stereotypes about black people, such as *Africa, ghetto, welfare,* and *basketball*. Subliminally presented information is presented so quickly that perceivers do not even realize that they have been exposed to it. Thus, these students were not consciously aware that they had seen these words. Those who were subliminally primed with many of these words activated the African American stereotype and saw another person's

subliminal presentation
A method of presenting stimuli so faintly or rapidly that people do not have any conscious awareness of having been exposed to them.

behavior in a more negative, hostile light. Especially noteworthy is the fact that these effects occurred *even among participants who did not consciously endorse the stereotypes in question.*

Devine's theory sparked an explosion of interest in these issues. Are we automatically biased by stereotypes, including those we disagree with? And are we inevitably prone to stereotyping after merely being exposed to stereotypes prevalent in our culture? Such questions are very complex, but within the past two decades social psychologists have made great strides in addressing them. It is now clear that stereotype activation can be triggered implicitly and automatically, influencing subsequent thoughts, feelings, and behaviors even among perceivers who are relatively low in prejudice. But it also is clear that several factors can make such activation more or less likely to happen.

For example, some stereotypes are more likely than others to come to mind quickly and easily for any given person. How much exposure individuals have to a stereotype, and therefore how accessible the stereotype is in their mind, varies across time and cultures. People in Western Europe may be quicker to activate the "skinhead" stereotype than people in South America; students from El Paso, Texas, may be more prone to activate Mexican American stereotypes than students in Madison, Wisconsin.

Another factor is how prejudiced the perceiver is. Although stereotypes can be activated automatically even among perceivers very low in prejudice, the threshold for what triggers stereotype activation may be lower for those relatively high in prejudice (Kawakami et al., 1998; Lepore & Brown, 1997, 2002; Wittenbrink et al., 1997).

In the following sections, we explore several other sets of factors that help determine when stereotyping is and isn't inevitable. See Table 5.5 for a summary.

Very brief exposure to a member of a stereotyped group does not lead to biased judgments or responses, but longer exposure typically does. FALSE.

TABLE 5.5

Automatic Stereotype Activation: Important Factors

Based on the relevant research, we can propose the following as some of the factors that are important in determining when people are more or less likely to activate stereotypes automatically.

Factors That Make Automatic Activation More Likely	Factors That Make Automatic Activation Less Likely
Cognitive Factors	
Accessible stereotype (e.g., recently activated or primed)	Exposure to counter-stereotypic group members
Depleted cognitive resources due to prior attempts to suppress stereotypical thinking, fatigue, age, intoxication	Knowledge of personal information about the individual
Cultural Factors	
Popular stereotype in culture	Not common stereotype in culture
Norms and values that accept stereotyping	Norms and values that are opposed to stereotyping
Motivational Factors	
Motivated to make inferences about the person quickly	Motivated to avoid prejudice
Motivated to feel superior to other person	Motivated to be fair, egalitarian
Personal Factors	
Endorses stereotypes, high in prejudice	Disagrees with stereotypes, low in prejudice

Motivation: Fueling Activation

There is a growing recognition of the role that motivational factors can play in stereotype activation (Blair, 2002; Bodenhausen et al., 2003; Gollwitzer & Schaal, 2001; Kunda & Spencer, 2003; Spencer et al., 2003). Whether or not we realize it, we often have particular goals when we encounter others, such as wanting to learn about them, impress them, get to our next task and not be interrupted by them, and so on. Some sets of goals make us more likely to activate stereotypes and others have the opposite effect.

One important goal is the desire to maintain, protect, and perhaps enhance one's self-image and self-esteem. These goals can lead even people low in prejudice to activate negative stereotypes. For example, when their self-esteem is threatened, people may become motivated to stereotype others so that they will feel better about themselves

(Fein & Spencer, 1997). Motivated in this way, they also become more likely to activate stereotypes automatically. To demonstrate these points, Steven Spencer and others (1998) conducted a series of experiments in which they threatened some participants' self-esteem by making them think that they had done poorly on an intelligence test. These participants became more likely to automatically activate negative stereotypes about African Americans or Asians when exposed briefly, even subliminally, to a drawing or videotape of a member of the stereotyped group.

Trying to protect one's self-image can not only promote activation of some stereotypes but can also inhibit activation of others. For example, imagine interacting with a black doctor. Two different stereotypes could come to mind about this person—about doctors and about blacks. Lisa Sinclair and Ziva Kunda found that when white Canadian students in their study received praise from a black doctor, not only did they activate positive stereotypes about doctors but they also simultaneously *inhibited* activation of negative stereotypes about blacks—a pattern presumably driven by the desire to see the person who praised them as especially smart and successful. If this is the effect that praise brings about, will criticism have the opposite effect? Sinclair and Kunda's (1999, 2000) research suggests that it can. They found that when a stereotyped group member criticizes or even simply disagrees with participants, the participants become more likely to activate negative stereotypes about the group (see ▶ Figure 5.13).

Motivation: Putting on the Brakes   Although we may have nonconscious motives to stereotype others, clearly many people today often are motivated to not stereotype or discriminate against others. This motivation may be *externally* driven—not wanting to *appear* to others to be prejudiced. It may also or instead be *internally* driven—not wanting to *be* prejudiced, regardless of whether or not others would find out (Dunton & Fazio, 1997; Plant & Devine, 1998, 2009). Internally motivated individuals are likely to be more successful at controlling stereotyping and prejudice, even on implicit measures, but even they are vulnerable to the strong power of automatic stereotyping and implicit biases.

You may wonder: What if I just try really hard to not think about a stereotype? Research suggests that sometimes the harder you try to suppress an unwanted thought, the less likely you are to succeed. Try not to think about a white bear, and that image may pop into your mind despite your best intentions. Try not to worry about how long it's taking you to fall asleep, and you'll stay awake. Try not to think about an itch, or the chocolate cheesecake in the fridge, or a particular sexist thought—well, you get the idea (Wegner, 1997).

Research on the effectiveness of trying to suppress stereotyping is mixed. On the one hand, it can sometimes cause a post-suppression rebound: After a person spends energy suppressing a stereotype, the stereotype pops up even more, like a volleyball that's been held under water (e.g., Macrae et al., 1994). On the other hand, research suggests that when people are intrinsically motivated to suppress a stereotype that they truly don't believe in, they may be successful at avoiding rebound effects. People who care deeply about not being prejudiced or who are often motivated by egalitar-

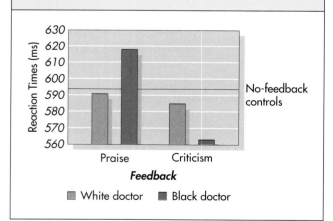

▶ **FIGURE 5.13**

Motivated Stereotype Inhibition and Activation

Participants received either praise or criticism about their performance from either a black man or a white man who they were led to believe was a doctor. A computer task subsequently measured the degree to which participants activated or inhibited stereotypes about blacks. The reaction times of a control group that received neither praise nor criticism are represented in this graph as a horizontal line. Reaction times quicker than this line indicate stereotype *activation*, whereas slower reaction times suggest stereotype *suppression*. Consistent with the idea that people's motivations can influence stereotype activation, participants who had been criticized by the black doctor strongly activated stereotypes about blacks, whereas participants who had been praised by the black doctor inhibited stereotypes about blacks.

Sinclair & Kunda, 1999.

ian goals can become much more efficient and successful in suppressing stereotypes (Gordijn et al., 2004; Monteith et al., 1998; Moskowitz et al., 2004; Wyer, 2007).

For example, according to the *self-regulation of prejudiced responses model* proposed by Margo Monteith and others (2002; Monteith & Mark, 2005, 2009), people who are truly motivated to be fair and unprejudiced are often confronted with the sad reality that they have failed to live up to that goal. These realizations lead to unpleasant emotions such as guilt. As individuals experience such feelings of guilt repeatedly, they begin to develop expertise at recognizing the situations and stimuli that tend to trigger these failures, and therefore they can exert more control over them. In so doing, they begin to interrupt what had been automatic stereotype activation.

Exerting Control: The Need for Cognitive Resources   Trying to suppress stereotyping takes mental effort, and using this effort can drain individuals of cognitive resources for some period of time (Gordijn et al., 2004; Richeson & Trawalter, 2005). Some people are more likely than others to have the cognitive resources available to inhibit stereotyping. One factor is age. Older people have a harder time suppressing stereotypes than younger people, which may explain in part why older people often appear more prejudiced than younger people (Henry et al., 2009; Stewart et al., 2009; von Hippel & Ronay, 2009). Being intoxicated makes even younger people have a difficult time with suppressing thoughts or inhibiting impulses (e.g., consider the dreaded drunk dialing or texting). It may come as little surprise, therefore, that intoxication impairs people's ability to control stereotype activation and application (Bartholow et al., 2006; Schlauch et al., 2009).

Being physically tired or being affected by strong emotion or arousal can sap perceivers of the cognitive resources necessary to avoid stereotyping (Bless et al., 1996; Gilbert & Hixon, 1991; Lambert et al., 2003). In an intriguing demonstration of this, Galen Bodenhausen (1990) classified participants by their circadian arousal patterns, or biological rhythms, into two types: "morning people" (who describe themselves as most alert early in the morning) and "night people" (who say they peak much later, in the evening). By random assignment, participants took part in an experiment in human judgment that was scheduled at either 9 P.M. or 8 P.M. The result? Morning people were more likely to use stereotypes when tested at night; night owls were more likely to do so early in the morning.

As discussed in Chapter 3, exercising self-control is like flexing a muscle, and muscles can become fatigued from use. This fatigue seems to be not just metaphorical—exerting self-control actually seems to consume glucose—a source of energy—in people's blood (Gailliot et al., 2007). In a particularly creative recent experiment, Matthew Gailliot and others (2009) had participants consume a drink sweetened either with sugar or an artificial sweetener (the sugar would raise their blood glucose level, but the artificial sweetener would not). After a brief delay to allow time for the drink manipulation to have its effect on blood glucose, participants were presented a picture of a young man said to be gay and they were asked to write for five minutes about a typical day in his life. The participants' prejudice toward homosexuals was assessed using a questionnaire.

As can be seen in ▶ Figure 5.14, participants who scored low in prejudice toward homosexuals on the questionnaire tended to avoid making derogatory statements about the gay man in their essays—

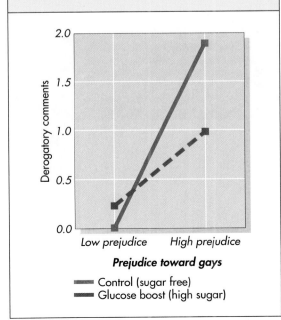

▶FIGURE 5.14

Needing Sugar to Stay Sweet?

Participants wrote a brief essay about a young man who they learned was gay. Participants whose scores on a measure of prejudice toward gays suggested that they were relatively low in prejudice tended to not make derogatory statements about the gay man in their essays, regardless of whether they drank a glucose-boosting high-sugar drink or a glucose-neutral sugarless drink. However, the participants who were relatively high in anti-gay prejudice were much more likely to make derogatory comments if they drank the sugarless drink. By raising their blood glucose, the high-sugar drink presumably gave these participants the energy needed to successfully inhibit expression of their prejudice.

Gaertner et al., 2010.

regardless of which drink they consumed. However, among the participants who were relatively high in anti-gay prejudice, those who consumed the sugarless drink made significantly more derogatory statements than did those who consumed the high-sugar drink. In other words, the energy boost from the sugar drink seemed to give the high-prejudice participants the energy they needed to control their prejudice.

Exerting Control: Additional Factors   Rather than to try not to think about it, one of the best strategies for avoiding the influence of stereotypes is to try instead to activate thoughts about the *individual* who happens to be a member of that group. When we have specific, personal information about an individual, stereotypes and other preconceptions can lose relevance and have less impact on how we respond to that person (Brewer & Feinstein, 1999; Fiske et al., 1999; Hilton & Fein, 1989; Kunda et al., 2003; Yzerbyt et al., 1998). Researchers continue to explore ways to give people control over stereotyping. Techniques include receiving training and practice in resisting stereotype activation when confronted with information about a group; being primed with counter-stereotypic examples (such as female business leaders and scientists, or well-loved members of outgroups); and taking the perspective of a member of the stereotyped group (Dasgupta, 2009; Galinsky & Ku, 2004; Kawakami et al., 2000, 2007; Olson & Fazio, 2006).

▋ "41 Shots": A Focus on the Tragic Shooting of Amadou Diallo

The issue of automatic activation of stereotypes and its effects can be seen in concrete terms by focusing on one particular tragedy that not only sparked controversy but also inspired a wave of social psychological research.

The Tragedy   On February 4, 1999, just after midnight, Amadou Diallo entered his apartment building. He was spotted by members of the Street Crime Unit, an elite unit of officers who patrolled crime-ridden areas of the city. The unit had been extraordinarily successful in reducing crime, but its methods were often criticized for being too aggressive. In particular, critics charged that it singled out African American and His-

Protesters against police violence walk down Broadway in New York City on April 5, 2000. At the center is a photo of Amadou Diallo, an unarmed African immigrant who was killed in a burst of forty-one gunshots by New York City police.

Chris Hondros/Getty Images

panic men. Thousands had been routinely stopped, frisked, and searched. That winter night in 1999, Amadou Diallo would have been one more. Four white police officers from the unit spotted Diallo. He matched the general description of a suspected rapist they were searching for. The police thought that Diallo looked suspicious as he appeared to duck into his building to avoid them. As they approached, he reached into his pocket and began pulling out a black object. Thinking that the object was a gun, the police opened fire. Forty-one shots. Nineteen of them hit Diallo, and he lay dead in the vestibule. The police removed the black object from his hand. It was a wallet. Diallo did not have a weapon.

Protesters held rallies in the days that followed, chanting "forty-one shots" and holding up wallets. "Racial profiling," the controversial use of race as a factor in determining who to stop and search for possible criminal activities, came under renewed attack. The Street Crime Unit was disbanded. Many politicians, columnists, and citizens defended the police officers, noting how difficult it is to make life-or-death decisions in the blink of an eye. In March 2000, all four officers were found not guilty of any criminal charges.

The Song When Bruce Springsteen debuted a song called "American Skin (41 Shots)" about this tragedy during a concert in Atlanta, Georgia, in the summer of 2000, it set off another firestorm of controversy. Heads of two police unions called for a boycott of Springsteen's upcoming concerts in New York. One called him "a dirtbag" and "a floating fag" for singing a song about this issue. Fans and activists called the song "brilliant" and "compassionate." To this day, years later, many police officers and others have never forgiven Springsteen for this song. If you read its lyrics (you can read them by going to brucespringsteen.net and selecting "American Skin (41 Shots)" under Songs), however, you may be struck by how fair and balanced the song actually is, neither condemning nor condoning the police's actions but instead highlighting the tragic consequences of living in a violent, dangerous society.

The controversy about the song was never really about the song itself. Rather, it reflects how difficult it is for people to discuss the issues of race and prejudice. The vast majority of those who protested against the song had never read or listened to its lyrics—they simply were offended by an artist raising questions about a tragic shooting they wanted to put behind them.

The Research A central question, of course, was whether stereotypes associated with the color of Diallo's skin made the officers more likely to misperceive the wallet as a gun. Although none of us can ever know whether this was the case in the Diallo tragedy, it is possible to apply social psychology research to answer related questions, such as whether, in general, a black person is more likely than a white person to be misperceived as holding a gun when they are actually holding a wallet, and whether making such a mistake signals that a perceiver is prejudiced. Indeed, the Diallo shooting inspired a number of social psychology experiments to examine these very questions.

Keith Payne (2001) was the first to publish a study directly inspired by these questions. The participants in his study were undergraduate students, not police officers, but their task was to try to make the kind of decision the police had to make: very quickly identify an object as a weapon or not. Pictures of these objects (such as guns or tools) were presented on a computer screen, immediately preceded by a quick presentation of a black or a white male face. The pictures were presented for fractions of a second. Payne found that the participants were more likely to mistake a harmless object for a weapon if it was preceded by a black face than if the object was preceded by a white face. This difference was less likely to emerge if the participants were given more time to make this judgment.

41 shots . . . cut through the night
You're kneeling over his body in the
*   vestibule*
Praying for his life

Is it a gun, is it a knife
Is it a wallet, this is your life
It ain't no secret, no secret my friend
You can get killed just for living in
*   your American skin*

*   —"American Skin (41 Shots)" by*
*   Bruce Springsteen. Copyright © 2001*
*   Bruce Springsteen (ASCAP). Reprinted*
*   by permission. International copyright*
*   secured. All rights reserved.*

▶ FIGURE 5.15

Shoot or Not?

These are examples of scenes from the video game that Joshua Correll and his colleagues created to investigate whether perceivers, playing the role of police officers, would be biased by the target's race when trying to determine very quickly whether they should shoot him because he is holding a weapon or refrain from shooting because he is holding a harmless object.

Correll et al., 2002.

Police receive training to make them more sensitive to weapons, but they don't get training to undo unconscious race stereotypes or biases.

—Anthony Greenwald

Joshua Correll and his colleagues (2002) also investigated this issue, but they made the situation even more like the one faced by the police. Rather than first present the race of a person and then present an object, these researchers designed a video game to present them together, and the participants had to decide whether or not to shoot the person who appeared on their screen (see ▶ Figure 5.15). Some of these targets were white men and others were black men. Some of them held guns and others held harmless objects (such as a black cell phone or a wallet). If the target held a gun, the participants were supposed to hit a "shoot" button as quickly as possible. If he held a harmless object, they were to hit a "don't shoot" button as quickly as they could.

As in the Payne study, these participants showed a bias consistent with racial stereotypes. If the target held a gun, they were quicker to press the "shoot" button if he was black than if he was white. If the target held a harmless object, they took longer to press the "don't shoot" button if he was black than if he was white. In addition, participants were more likely to mistakenly "shoot" an unarmed target if he was black than they were if he was white.

Since these first publications, a rapidly growing number of others followed to examine the processes involved more closely (e.g., Greenwald et al., 2003; Govorun & Payne, 2006; Klauer & Voss, 2008). For example, in one provocative experiment, Joshua Correll and others (2006) found additional evidence for this racial bias, but they also used physiological measures to determine that when participants exhibited this bias, they also tended to show brain activity that is associated with the perception of being threatened.

Taken together, the results of these studies suggest that when the decision must be made very quickly, a black man in the United States is more likely to be mistakenly perceived as holding a gun than is a white man. It is important to note, though, that the participants in the initial studies were not police officers; they were undergraduate students or individuals from a community sample. Police officers receive extensive training in these kinds of tasks. But as the quote in the margin by social psychologist Anthony Greenwald indicates, the police may not be trained to avoid activating racial stereotypes, and given the prevalence and power of these stereotypes in our society, there is no reason to be confident that they would be impervious to them in split-second decisions.

Researchers have begun to examine police officers' responses in the "shoot" or "don't shoot" simulations that most closely relate to the Diallo tragedy. In one set of experiments using over 200 police officers from fifteen U.S. states, Joshua Correll and others (2007b) found that in contrast to a civilian sample that did show the typical racial bias, trained police officers were not more likely to "shoot" an unarmed black target than an unarmed white target. Like the civilians, however, they did take longer to decide to not shoot an unarmed black target than an unarmed white target, and they decided to shoot an armed black target more quickly than they decided to shoot an armed white target. In other words, the police officers did not show evidence of racial bias in the mistakes they made, but they did have a harder time making decisions that went against the racial stereotype.

In a different experiment with fifty police officers, Michelle Peruche and Ashby Plant (2006) found that in initial trials the officers were more likely to erroneously decide to "shoot" an unarmed target when the target was black rather than when the target was white. With more and more trials, however, this racial bias was eventually reduced. This greater accuracy with practice is consistent with the encouraging results of another line of research by Ashby Plant and her colleagues (2005). In a series of studies using undergraduate students playing the role of police officers, the researchers replicated the finding of a racial bias in the decision to shoot or not, but they also found that training the participants by exposing them to repeated trials in which the race of the target was unrelated to criminality eliminated this bias both immediately after the training and twenty-four hours later.

A second question we posed above was whether exhibiting this racial bias signals that a perceiver has racist attitudes and beliefs. The evidence thus far suggests that this may not be the case. For example, Correll and others (2002) found that the magnitude of the bias was not related to participants' levels of racial prejudice as measured by a series of questionnaires. In addition, these researchers also found that African American participants showed the same bias against black targets as white participants did, again suggesting that racial prejudice is not necessarily reflected in this bias. Consistent with much of the research we've reported in this chapter, *awareness* of the stereotype was a necessary factor, but endorsing it was not. Indeed, Correll and others (2007a) found that by manipulating the accessibility of stereotypes that associate blacks with danger in perceivers' minds (such as by having them first read newspaper articles about black or white criminals), they could strengthen or weaken this bias.

"You look like this sketch of someone who is thinking about committing a crime."

The Diallo shooting was by no means the first incident of its kind to raise controversy about mistaken shootings of African American men by police officers. Nor will it be the last. Indeed, in November 2006, New York City police officers fired fifty shots at a small group of African American men, killing one of them—just hours before he was supposed to get married later that day. Although at least one of the officers thought one of the men had a gun, no evidence that any of them was armed was found. In May 2009, an off-duty African American police officer named Omar Edwards was chasing after a car thief in New York. A white police officer saw Edwards running with a gun drawn and ordered him to freeze. When Edwards turned toward him, the officer opened fire and killed Edwards.

The issue also is not limited to the United States or to black men. Controversies about racism by the police toward immigrants—and by terrorist groups toward the police—have been more common in Europe recently, for example. A recent study in Australia extended the shooter bias studies from the United States by demonstrating that Australian participants were more likely to shoot at targets wearing Muslim headgear than bareheaded targets who did not appear Muslim (Unkelbach et al., 2008).

A Threat in the Air: Effects on the Targets of Stereotypes and Prejudice

We are all targets of other people's stereotypes and prejudices. We are stereotyped and treated differently based on how we look, how we talk, and where we come from. None of us is immune from having our work evaluated in a biased way, our motives questioned, or our attempts at making new friends rejected because of stereotypes and prejudices.

But for the targets of some stereotypes and prejudices, these concerns are relentless and profound. For them, there seem to be few safe havens. Social psychologists often refer to these targets as *stigmatized*—individuals who are targets of negative stereotypes, perceived as deviant, and devalued in society because they are members of a particular social group or because they have a particular characteristic (Major & Crocker, 1993). What are some of the effects of being stigmatized by stereotypes and prejudice? In this section we first examine some of the effects that perceiving that one is being discriminated against can have on individuals. We then focus on the impact that a perceived threat of being stereotyped can have on individuals' performance, particularly regarding the academic achievement of women and minorities.

Perceiving Discrimination

In *Color-Blind*, writer Ellis Cose (1997), who is African American, tells a story about how he was treated in a job interview twenty years earlier. He was an award-winning newspaper reporter at the time and was hoping to land a job with a national magazine. The editor he met with was pleasant and gracious, but he said that the magazine didn't have many black readers. "All the editor saw was a young black guy, and since *Esquire* was not in need of a young black guy, they were not in need of me. . . . He had been so busy focusing on my race that he was incapable of seeing me or my work" (p. 150). Then, a few years later, and in light of affirmative action policies, Cose was asked if he was interested in a position in a firm as corporate director of equal opportunity. "I was stunned, for the question made no sense. I was an expert neither on personnel nor on equal employment law; I was, however, black, which seemed to be the most important qualification" (p. 156).

The targets of stigmatizing stereotypes frequently wonder whether and to what extent others' impressions of them are distorted through the warped lens of social categorization. Over time, such suspicions can be deeply frustrating. In particular situations, though, they can have both positive and negative consequences. In a study by Jennifer Crocker and her colleagues (1991), black participants described themselves on a questionnaire. They were told that the questionnaire would be evaluated by an unknown white student who sat in an adjacent room. Participants were told that they were either liked or disliked by this student on the basis of the student's evaluation of the questionnaire. Then they took a self-esteem test. If the participants thought that the white student could not see them and did not know their race, their self-esteem scores predictably rose after positive feedback and declined after negative feedback.

But when participants thought the evaluating student had seen them through a one-way mirror, negative feedback did not lower their self-esteem. In this situation, participants blamed the unfavorable evaluations on prejudice. However, there was a drawback: Participants who received positive feedback and thought they had been observed through a one-way mirror showed a *decrease* in self-esteem. The reason? Instead of internalizing the credit for success, these participants attributed the praise to patronizing reverse discrimination.

Attributing negative feedback to discrimination can sometimes protect one's self-esteem, but it can have costs as well. First, such an attribution can sometimes be inaccurate, and the recipient of the feedback might miss an opportunity to learn information relevant for self-improvement. Consider the dilemma faced by a white teacher who wants to give negative feedback to a black student regarding an essay the student has written. If the student dismisses this criticism as biased, he or she may fail to learn from the teacher's advice. But if the teacher sugarcoats the feedback in an attempt to avoid the appearance of racism, the student may likewise fail to learn.

Studying this dilemma in a pair of experiments, Geoffrey Cohen and others (1999) came up with a twofold prescription for solving it. They found that black students responded most positively to negative feedback when the teacher both (a) made it clear that he or she had high standards; and (b) assured the students that they had the capacity to achieve those standards. Without such wise mentoring, the students' frequent experience of ambiguity about the sincerity or fairness of feedback can diminish their confidence in and accuracy about what they really do and do not know well (Aronson & Inzlicht, 2004).

Second, although attributing negative feedback to discrimination can protect one's overall self-esteem, it can also make people feel as if they have less personal control over their lives. Individuals from low-status groups may be threatened by this vulnerability to discrimination and thus feel worse about themselves when they perceive that they were discriminated against, especially when they have reason to think that the discrimination against them could persist over time (Schmitt et al., 2002). Such concerns can have tremendous costs: Perceiving persistent discrimination over time is associated with a number of physical and mental health problems and with drug use (Gibbons et al., 2004; Pascoe & Smart Richman, 2009; Williams et al., 2003).

Research on stereotype threat illustrates some of the challenges that can undermine the effectiveness of a white teacher providing feedback and mentorship to a black student as well as strategies for overcoming these challenges.

Whether individuals are more or less likely to perceive discrimination or to be affected negatively by the perception that they have been discriminated against depends on a number of factors, including their beliefs and expectations and the extent to which they identify with their stigmatized group. Several studies have shown, for example, that individuals are more likely to perceive discrimination against them based on their membership in a group if they are highly identified with their group or if they believe that others are often prejudiced against their group (Inzlicht et al., 2008; Major et al., 2003, 2007; Sellers & Shelton, 2003).

◼ Stereotype Threat

Easily one of the most exciting developments in the field has been the tremendous wave of research triggered by a theory introduced by Claude Steele in the mid-1990s. Steele proposed that in situations where a negative stereotype can apply to certain groups, members of these groups can fear being seen "through the lens of diminishing stereotypes and low expectations" (1999, p. 44). Steele (1997) called this predicament **stereotype threat**,

stereotype threat The experience of concern about being evaluated based on negative stereotypes about one's group.

for it hangs like "a threat in the air" when the individual is in the stereotype-relevant situation. The predicament can be particularly threatening for individuals whose identity and self-esteem are invested in domains where the stereotype is relevant. Steele argued that stereotype threat plays a crucial role in influencing the intellectual performance and identity of stereotyped group members. More recently, Steele and his colleagues (2002; Adams et al., 2006) have broadened the scope of their analysis to include *social identity threats* more generally. These threats are not necessarily tied to specific stereotypes but instead reflect a more general devaluing of a person's social group.

According to Steele's theory, stereotype threat can hamper achievement in academic domains in two ways. First, reactions to the "threat in the air" can directly interfere with performance—for example, by increasing anxiety and triggering distracting thoughts. Second, if this stereotype threat is chronic in the academic domain, it can cause individuals to *disidentify* from that domain—to dismiss the domain as no longer relevant to their self-esteem and identity.

To illustrate, imagine a black student and a white student who enter high school equally qualified in academic performance. Imagine that while taking a particularly difficult test at the beginning of the school year, each student struggles on the first few problems. Both students may begin to worry about failing, but the black student may have a whole set of additional worries about appearing to confirm a negative stereotype. Even if the black student doesn't believe the stereotype at all, the threat of being reduced to a stereotype in the eyes of those around her can trigger anxiety and distraction, impairing her performance. And if she experiences this threat in school often—perhaps because she stands out as one of only a few black students in the school or because she is treated by others in a particular way—the situation may become too threatening to her self-esteem. To buffer herself against the threat, she may disidentify with school. If she does this, her academic performance will become less relevant to her identity and self-esteem. In its place, some other domain of life, such as social success or a particular nonacademic talent, will become a more important source of identity and pride.

The Original Experiments Steele and others conducted a series of experiments in which they manipulated factors likely to increase or decrease stereotype threat as students took academic tests. For example, Steele and Joshua Aronson (1995) had black and white students from a highly selective university take a very difficult standardized verbal test. To some participants, it was introduced as a test of intellectual ability; to others, it was introduced as a problem-solving task unrelated to ability. Steele and Aronson reasoned that because of the difficulty of the test, *all* the students would struggle with it. If the test was said to be related to intellectual ability, however, the black students would feel the threat of a negative stereotype in addition to the stress of struggling with the test. In contrast, if the test was simply a research task and not a real test of intelligence, then negative stereotypes would be less applicable and the stereotype threat would be reduced. In that case, black students would be less impaired while taking the test. As shown in ▶ Figure 5.16, the results supported these predictions.

Thus, a seemingly minor change in the setting—a few words about the meaning of a test—had a powerful effect on the black

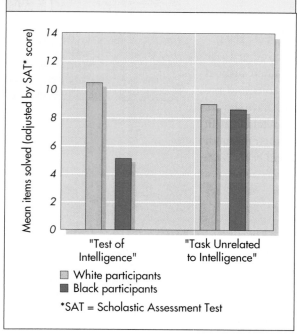

▶ **FIGURE 5.16**

Stereotype Threat and Academic Performance

Black and white students took a very difficult standardized verbal test. Before taking the test, some students were told that it was a test of their intellectual ability, but others were told that it was simply a research task unrelated to intellectual ability. All students' scores on this test were adjusted based on their scores from standardized college entrance verbal examinations. Despite this adjustment, black students did significantly worse than white students on the test if it was introduced as a test of intellectual ability (left). In contrast, among the students who had been told the test was unrelated to ability, black students and white students performed equally well (right).

Steele & Aronson, 1995.

students' performance. In a second study, the researchers used an even more subtle manipulation of stereotype threat: whether or not the students were asked to report their race just before taking the test. (In this study, the researchers described the test as unrelated to ability.) Making them think about race for a few seconds just before taking the test impaired the performance of black students but had no effect on white students. Think about the implications of such findings for important real-world contexts.

Steele's theory predicts that because negative stereotypes concerning women's advanced math skills are prevalent, women may often experience stereotype threat in settings relevant to these skills. Reducing stereotype threat in these settings, therefore, should reduce the underperformance that women tend to exhibit in these areas. To test this idea, Steven Spencer and others (1999) recruited male and female students who were good at math and felt that math was important to their identities. The researchers gave these students a very difficult standardized math test, one on which all of them would perform poorly. Before taking the test, some students were told that the test generally showed no gender differences, thereby implying that the negative stereotype of women's ability in math was *not* relevant to this particular test. Other students were told that the test *did* generally show gender differences. As Steele's theory predicted, women performed worse than men when they were told that the test typically produced gender differences, but they performed as well as men when they were told that the test typically did not produce gender differences.

The Prevalence and Diversity of Threats   Since these original studies, research inspired by the theory of stereotype threat grew at a stunningly fast pace. The evidence for underperformance due to stereotype threat is quite strong and broad. It has been found both in the laboratory and in real-world settings, including schools and businesses. Although much of the research has documented the power of the effects of stereotype threat on African Americans and women (Nguyen & Ryan, 2008), the scope of the research extends much farther. Stereotype threats can affect any group for which strong, well-known negative stereotypes are relevant in particular settings. Social identity threats can be more general than that, affecting groups that may be devalued even in the absence of specific negative stereotypes about a particular domain.

The examples of these threats run far and wide. For instance, many white athletes feel stereotype threat whenever they step onto a court or playing field where they constitute the minority. Will the white athlete feel the added weight of this threat while struggling against the other athletes in a game? To address this question, Jeff Stone and others (1999) had black and white students play miniature golf. When the experimenters characterized the game as diagnostic of "natural athletic ability," the white students did worse. But when they characterized it as diagnostic of "sports intelligence," the black students did worse.

Here is a small sample of groups whose performance in various domains was hurt by stereotype threat, as demonstrated in experiments around the world (Aronson et al., 1999; Ben-Zeev et al., 2005; Chasteen et al., 2005; Croizet & Claire, 1998; Frantz et al., 2004; Gonzales et al., 2002; Kray et al., 2002; Maass et al., 2008; Quinn et al., 2004; Seacat & Mickelson, 2009; Sekaquaptewa & Thompson, 2003; Spencer & Castano, 2007; Yeung & von Hippel, 2008; Yopyk & Prentice, 2005):

Stereotype threat can undermine the performance of individuals from any group for which strong, well-known, negative stereotypes are relevant. White male basketball players, for example, may experience stereotype threat in the presence of an African American majority.

Otto Greule Jr/Getty Images

- Low-socioeconomic-status students in France and the United States on a verbal test when the test was said to be diagnostic of intellectual ability

- European American men on a math test when compared with Asians

- Women on a math test in a co-ed rather than an all-female setting

- Women playing chess on the computer when they were told that their opponent was male

- Women on an engineering test after interacting with sexist men

- White participants taking an IAT when they thought the test was diagnostic of racism

- Individuals with a history of mental illness on a test of reasoning ability when asked about their illness before taking the test

- Women on a negotiation task when success on the task was said to be associated with masculine traits

- Men on a negotiation task when success on the task was said to be associated with feminine traits

- Student athletes primed to think about their identity as athletes before taking a difficult math test

- Overweight individuals primed to think about weight-related stereotypes

- Older adults on a memory test when it was presented as a memory test rather than an impression formation task

- Women driving after being reminded of demeaning stereotypes about female drivers (causing women in a driving simulator to crash into jaywalkers!)

Because individuals are members of multiple groups, they sometimes can feel either threatened or emboldened by a stereotype, depending on which of their social identities has been activated. Consider, for example, a study by Margaret Shih and others (1999) in which Asian American women were examined. In the United States, there is a negative stereotype about women and math but a positive stereotype about Asians and math. The researchers found that these women performed worse on a math test when their gender identity was made salient (by means of questions they had to answer about their gender before taking the test), whereas they performed better on the test when their ethnic identity was made salient. In an interesting follow-up, though, Sapna Cheryan and Galen Bodenhausen (2000) reported that if the high expectations of Asian American women's math abilities are made particularly salient to them as they are about to take a math test, the concern about living up to these expectations can itself be distracting, leading to a "choking" effect and worse performance.

In general, though, members of a group that has the relative advantage of being favorably compared to an outgroup that is targeted by a negative stereotype (for example, that men are better than women at math) may benefit from what Gregory Walton and Geoffrey Cohen (2003) call *stereotype lift*. In a meta-analysis of forty-three relevant studies, members of groups that are not stereotyped tended to perform better on tasks when the stereotype threat against the outgroup was relevant than when it was reduced. Research has shown that reducing the threat, such as by assuring the targeted group that a particular test is not relevant to a negative stereotype, not only improves the performance of the targeted group but also seems to remove some of the boost that the nonstereotyped group members get from being in the allegedly "superior" group.

An African American student is likely to perform worse on an athletic task if the task is described as one reflecting sports intelligence than if it is described as reflecting natural athletic ability. **TRUE.**

Stereotype Threat Effects: Causes and Solutions   How exactly does stereotype threat interfere with performance? And who within a target group is most vulnerable to these effects? These are among the questions currently being investigated. It is clear that one does not need to *believe in* a negative stereotype in order for it to have an effect. Just knowing about the stereotype seems to be enough, particularly if the individual identifies strongly with the targeted group and cares about performing well.

Stereotype threat exerts its effects through multiple processes (Schmader et al., 2008). One of these is by triggering physiological arousal, which may interfere with people's ability to perform well on the task at hand (Ben-Zeev et al., 2005; Blascovich et al., 2001; O'Brien & Crandall, 2003). Another is by causing threatened individuals to try to suppress thoughts about the stereotype, which can have the ironic effect of draining cognitive resources away from the task they are working on (Logel et al., 2009). Stereotype threat also impairs threatened individuals' working memory, which of course impairs task performance (Schmader & Johns, 2003). Stereotype threat also can cause negative thoughts, worry, and feelings of dejection, and can cause individuals to focus more on trying to avoid failure than to achieve success. Each of these effects can undermine performance (Brodish & Devine, 2009; Croizet et al., 2004; Keller & Dauenheimer, 2003).

But although stereotype threat effects are widespread, the growing body of research on this subject also gives us reason to hope. Social psychologists have been uncovering some ways that people can be better protected against these threats. These include being reminded of traits, qualities, or other things that make them feel good about themselves, even about things unrelated to the domain under threat; blurring boundaries between groups; coping with threat by using humor; attributing the arousal triggered by the threat to something nonthreatening; thinking of examples of other group members who have been successful in the domain under threat; and being reminded of other categories to which one belongs that are considered favorably in the domain (such as women taking a math test being reminded of positive stereotypes of "college students") (Ben-Zeev et al., 2005; Ford et al., 2004; McIntyre et al., 2003; Rosenthal & Crisp, 2006; Rydell et al., 2009).

One encouraging example of a successful experiment in a real school setting was a pair of experiments conducted by Geoffrey Cohen and others (2006) with seventh-graders from lower-middle-class and middle-class families in a school in the United States. When they were first measured, the grades of the African American students tended to be significantly lower than those of the European American students. Half of the students were then given a task in which they wrote about values and aspects of their lives they cared deeply about—a process that previous research has shown reaffirms individuals' images of themselves as good, valued people. The other half wrote about values and aspects of life they did not care much about. African American students performed significantly better in the class if they had written about values they cared about, but the writing manipulation had no effect on the European American students. Cohen and his colleagues reported that this subtle, simple manipulation reduced the racial achievement gap among these students by 40 percent.

Perhaps most encouraging for readers of this section of the textbook is the finding that simply learning about stereotype threat may help protect individuals from its effects. Women who were educated about stereotype threat in one study did not show the underperformance that women who had not learned about this research did (Johns et al., 2005).

Part of the reason for the initial excitement when Claude Steele introduced this theory was that it spoke to a profound social problem but offered encouragement rather than pessimism. It illustrated that making even small changes in the situational factors that give rise to stereotype threat can reduce the tremendous weight of negative stereotypes, allowing the targets of stereotypes to perform to their potential. In fact, outside the laboratory, Steele and his colleagues were quick to apply their theory by creating a model program in a real university setting, what Steele called a "wise" environment that fostered interracial contact and cooperation and reduced factors that contribute to stereotype threat. Researchers found that the black students in this program showed almost no underperformance in their grades and were much less likely than other black students to drop out of school (Steele, 1997).

Reducing Stereotypes, Prejudice, and Discrimination

We have discussed some of the issues involved in controlling the activation or expression of stereotypes and prejudice. In this final section, we focus on some of the approaches that have been suggested for combating stereotypes, prejudice, and discrimination more generally, and we point to directions we expect future research to follow on the road toward more progress.

■ Intergroup Contact

"See that man over there?"
"Yes."
"Well, I hate him."
"But you don't know him."
"That's why I hate him."
—Gordon Allport

One of the classic books written on prejudice is Gordon Allport's (1954) *The Nature of Prejudice*. The book was unprecedented in its scope and gave important insights into the social psychology of prejudice. One of the many enduring ideas that Allport advanced was the **contact hypothesis**, which states that under certain conditions, direct contact between members of rival groups will reduce stereotyping, prejudice, and discrimination.

Around the time of the publication of this book, the U.S. Supreme Court ruled in the historic 1954 case of *Brown v. Board of Education of Topeka* that racially separate schools were inherently unequal and violated the U.S. Constitution. In part, the decision was informed by empirical evidence supplied by thirty-two eminent social scientists on the harmful effects of segregation on both race relations and the self-esteem and academic achievement of black students (Allport et al., 1953). The Supreme Court's decision propelled the nation into a large-scale social experiment. What would be the effect?

Despite the Court's ruling, desegregation proceeded slowly. There were stalling tactics, lawsuits, and vocal opposition. Many schools remained untouched until the early 1970s. Then, as the dust began to settle, research brought the grave realization that little had changed—that contact between black and white schoolchildren was not having the intended effect. Walter Stephan (1986) reviewed studies conducted during and after desegregation and found that although 13 percent of the studies reported a decrease in prejudice among whites, 34 percent reported no change, and 53 percent reported an *increase*. These findings forced social psychologists to challenge the wisdom of their testimony to the Supreme Court and to reexamine the contact hypothesis that had guided that advice in the first place.

Is the original contact hypothesis wrong? No. Although desegregation did not immediately produce the desired changes, it's important to realize that the ideal conditions for successful intergroup contact did not exist in the public schools that desegregated. Nobody ever said that deeply rooted prejudices could be erased just by throwing groups together. According to the contact hypothesis, four conditions must exist for contact to succeed. These conditions are summarized in Table 5.6.

contact hypothesis The theory that direct contact between hostile groups will reduce prejudice under certain conditions.

A series of meta-analyses by Thomas Pettigrew and Linda Tropp (2000, 2006, 2008) involving more than 500 studies and a quarter of a million participants in 38 nations has found reliable support for the benefits of intergroup contact in reducing prejudice, particularly when the contact satisfies at least some of the conditions in Table 5.6. Pettigrew and Tropp (2008) propose that contact reduces prejudice by (1) enhancing knowledge about the out-group; (2) reducing anxiety about intergroup contact; and (3) increasing empathy and perspective taking. Although many problems have plagued school desegregation and other desegregation efforts, findings such as Pettigrew and Tropp's are cause for optimism.

TABLE 5.6
The Contact Hypothesis: Conditions
Four conditions are deemed very important for intergroup contact to serve as a treatment for racism. However, many desegregated schools have failed to create a setting that meets these conditions.
1. *Equal status* The contact should occur in circumstances that give the two groups equal status.
2. *Personal interaction* The contact should involve one-on-one interactions among individual members of the two groups.
3. *Cooperative activities* Members of the two groups should join together in an effort to achieve superordinate goals.
4. *Social norms* The social norms, defined in part by relevant authorities, should favor intergroup contact.

One of the most successful demonstrations of desegregation took place on the baseball diamond. On April 15, 1947, Jackie Robinson played for baseball's Brooklyn Dodgers and became the first black man to break the color barrier in a major American sport. Robinson's opportunity came through Dodgers owner Branch Rickey, who felt that integrating baseball was both moral and good for the game (Pratkanis & Turner, 1994). Rickey knew all about the contact hypothesis and was assured by a social scientist friend that a team could furnish the conditions needed for it to work: equal status among teammates, personal interactions, dedication to a common goal, and a positive climate from the owner, managers, and coaches. The rest is history. Rickey signed Robinson and tried to create the situation necessary for success. Although Robinson did face a great deal of racism, he endured, and baseball was integrated. At the end of his first year, Jackie Robinson was named rookie of the year, and in 1962 he was elected to the Baseball Hall of Fame. At his induction ceremony, Robinson asked three people to stand beside him: his mother, his wife, and his friend Branch Rickey.

(Left) Students at Central High School in Little Rock, Arkansas, in September 1957 shout insults at 16-year-old Elizabeth Eckford as she walks toward the school entrance. National Guardsmen blocked the entrance and would not let her enter. (Right) Jackie Robinson and Branch Rickey discuss Robinson's contract with the Brooklyn Dodgers. In 1947, Robinson became the first African American to cross "the color line" and play Major League Baseball, thereby beginning the integration of major American sports.

AP/Wide World Photos

AP/Wide World Photos

Another potential cause for optimism, although coupled perhaps with reasons to feel regret, is the finding by Nicole Shelton and Jennifer Richeson (2005) that both whites and blacks would like to have more contact with each other but believe that the other group does not want to have contact with them! As with stereotype threat, this may be a case in which education about the problem can be an important tool in correcting it.

With more frequent and more meaningful contact across racial and ethnic divides, a variety of the kinds of barriers we've discussed in this chapter can be weakened. For example, a longitudinal study of dating in college by Shana Levin and others (2007) revealed that white, Asian American, and Latino students who dated outside their group more during college showed less ingroup bias and intergroup anxiety at the end of college than students who did not date outside their own racial group. Elizabeth Page-Gould and others (2008) actually created cross-group friendships between Latinos/as and whites in an experiment by having them meet for a few weeks and perform closeness-building tasks together. This experience had a number of positive intergroup effects, one of which was that participants who had initially been relatively high in implicit prejudice began to initiate more intergroup interactions.

The Jigsaw Classroom

As the third condition in Table 5.6 indicates, cooperation and shared goals are necessary for intergroup contact to be successful. Yet the typical classroom is filled with competition—exactly the wrong ingredient. Picture the scene. The teacher stands in front of the class and asks a question. Many children wave their hands, each straining to catch the teacher's eye. Then, as soon as one student is called on, the others groan in frustration. In the competition for the teacher's approval, they are losers—hardly a scenario suited to positive intergroup contact. To combat this problem in the classroom, Elliot Aronson and his colleagues (1978) developed a cooperative learning method called the **jigsaw classroom**. In newly desegregated public schools in Texas and California, they assigned fifth graders to small racially and academically mixed groups. The material to be learned within each group was divided into subtopics, much the way a jigsaw puzzle is broken into pieces. Each student was responsible for learning one piece of the puzzle, after which all members took turns teaching their material to one another. In this system, everyone—regardless of race, ability, or self-confidence—needs everyone else if the group as a whole is to succeed.

The method produced impressive results (Aronson, 2004). Compared with children in traditional classes, those in jigsaw classrooms grew to like each other more, liked school more, were less prejudiced, and had higher self-esteem. What's more, academic test scores improved for minority students and remained the same for white students. Much like an interracial sports team, the jigsaw classroom offers a promising way to create a truly integrated educational experience. It also provides a model of how to use interpersonal contact to promote greater tolerance of diversity.

Shared Identities

jigsaw classroom
A cooperative learning method used to reduce racial prejudice through interaction in group efforts.

One important consequence of the jigsaw classroom technique is that individuals became more likely to classify outgroup members as part of their own ingroup. Instead of seeing racial or ethnic "others" within the classroom, the students now see fellow classmates. Students feel that they are all in the same boat together. A growing body of research has emerged that supports the idea that intergroup contact that emphasizes shared goals and fates and that involves overlapping group memberships (such that individuals who are in different groups in one context also are in the same group in some other context), can be very successful at reducing prejudice and discrimination—specifically by changing how group members categorize each other (Bettencourt & Dorr, 1998; Brewer & Gaertner, 2004; Ray et al., 2008; Van Bavel & Cunningham, 2009).

According to the Common Ingroup Identity Model developed by Samuel Gaertner and John Dovidio (Dovidio et al., 2009; Gaertner & Dovidio 2009; Gaertner et al., 2010), this change comes about through two separate processes: decategorization and recategorization. Decategorization leads people not only to pay less attention to categories and intergroup boundaries but also to perceive outgroup members as individuals. Recategorization, in turn, leads people to change their conception of groups, allowing them to develop a more inclusive sense of the diversity that characterizes their own ingroup. By recognizing members of an outgroup as ingroup members, just as the Rattlers and Eagles did when they changed from competitors to collaborators in Robbers Cave, "they" become "we," and a common ingroup identity can be forged. A recent study that illustrated this point was conducted by Devin Ray and others (2008). American students reported feeling less anger and more respect toward Muslim students if they had been reminded of their membership in the shared ingroup "students" than if they had been reminded of their membership in the ingroup "Americans."

Changing Cultures and Motivations

Earlier in the chapter we reported some of the research that shows the role culture can play in perpetuating stereotypes and prejudice. It is at the cultural level that much potential for positive change can be found as well. Exposure to images that reflect the diversity within social groups, for example, can help weaken stereotypes and combat their automatic activation. These images might also change people's tendency to see

Soccer players from Mexico and Argentina line up with an anti-racism banner before their match in Hanover, Germany, in response to the racist taunts and other actions by fans that had been plaguing the sport during international tournaments.

Andreas Rentz/Bongarts/Getty Images

groups as relatively fixed entities and help them see groups as dynamic entities with less rigid borders.

Motivations, norms, and values can and often do change over time. Here again popular culture is a key player. People—especially younger people—look to images in popular culture as well as to their peers and role models for information about what attitudes and behaviors are cool or out of date. We also look to our peers to get a sense of the local norms around us, including norms about stereotypes and prejudice (e.g., Crandall & Eshleman, 2003; Fein et al., 2003; Paluck, 2009; Stangor et al., 2001). In a particular high school, a senior might feel comfortable calling a friend a "fag" and mean little by it and think nothing of it. Yet several months later in college, this student might realize how wrong that is and feel guilty for ever having done so. If this lesson is learned, it's more likely to have been learned by watching and interacting with one's peers than from having been lectured to about diversity and sensitivity by a campus speaker. Learning these norms can motivate us to adopt them. Legislating against hate speech, unequal treatment, and hostile environments can also be an important weapon, of course. Although they can create resistance and backlashes, laws and policies that require behavior change can—if done right, with no suggestion of compromise and with important leaders clearly behind them—cause hearts and minds to follow (Aronson, 1992).

Social psychologists today recognize that more and more people are motivated to not be prejudiced. The motivation may begin as a concern with not appearing to others to be prejudiced, but for many it becomes internalized—a much more effective antidote (Devine et al., 2005; Monteith et al., 2002).

Much of the hope, therefore, rests with what is at the very core of social psychology: the social nature of the human animal. Some of our baser instincts, such as intergroup competition that breeds intergroup biases, may always be present, but we also can learn from each other the thoughts, values, and goals that make us less vulnerable to perpetuating or being the targets of stereotypes, prejudice, and discrimination.

REVIEW

- The election of an African American to the presidency of the United States and the disturbing signs of racism and other prejudices evident before and after the election illustrate both the progress and the persistent challenges regarding stereotyping, prejudice, and discrimination in contemporary life.

The Nature of the Problem: Persistence and Change

Defining Our Terms

- At the individual level, racism and sexism are forms of prejudice and discrimination based on a person's racial or gender background. At the institutional and cultural level, racism and sexism involve practices that promote the domination of one racial group or gender over another.

- Stereotypes are beliefs or associations that link groups of people with certain characteristics.

- Prejudice refers to negative feelings toward persons based on their membership in certain groups.

- Discrimination is negative behavior directed against persons because of their membership in a particular group.

- Ingroups are groups we identify with; we contrast these with outgroups.

Racism: Current Forms and Challenges

- Over the years, various data show a decline in negative views of black Americans.

- However, modern racism is more subtle and surfaces in less direct ways, particularly in situations where people can rationalize racist behavior.

- People's ambivalence concerning race can lead them to exhibit biases in favor of or against particular groups, depending on the context.

- Racism often works implicitly, as stereotypes and prejudice can fuel discrimination without conscious intent or awareness on the part of perceivers.

- Researchers use covert measures to detect and measure modern and implicit racism and other subtle forms of prejudice and discrimination.

- Individual differences in implicit racism can predict differences in perceptions of and reactions to others based on their race. For example, white perceivers who are relatively high in implicit racism are more likely to perceive hostility in the facial expressions of a black person than in the facial expressions of a white person.

- Seeing a member of a racial outgroup is associated with increased activation in the amygdala, a brain structure associated with emotion.

- Interracial interactions can feel threatening, can provoke anxiety, and can drain cognitive resources, particularly among people relatively high in implicit racism.

- Worried about appearing racist in these interactions, whites in particular may try to avoid interracial interactions or they may go out of their way to avoid any mention of race even when it is relevant.

Sexism: Ambivalence and Double Standards

- Although similar in many other ways, sexism differs from other forms of prejudice and discrimination in part because gender stereotypes are more than just descriptive: They also indicate what the majority of people in a society believe men and women should be. Sexism is also unusual in that ingroup and outgroup members are so intimately familiar with each other.

- Ambivalent sexism reflects both hostile sexism, characterized by negative and resentful feelings toward women, and benevolent sexism, characterized by affectionate, chivalrous, but potentially patronizing feelings toward women.

- Individuals from countries with the greatest degree of economic and political inequality between men and women tend to exhibit high levels of both hostile and benevolent sexism.

- There are some striking sex differences in occupational choices and in the treatment individuals experience in the workplace.

- Women often face a difficult dilemma: If they behave consistently with gender stereotypes, they may be liked more but respected less.

Causes of the Problem: Intergroup and Motivational Factors

Fundamental Motives Between Groups

- The tendency in people to divide the world into ingroups and outgroups—"us" versus "them"—and to favor the former over the latter in numerous ways is likely to be an evolved tendency due to the social nature of our species.

- When people's motives for self-protection are aroused, they show stronger biases against threatening outgroups.

- According to optimal distinctiveness theory, people try to balance the desire to belong with the desire to be distinct and differentiated from others.

- Being reminded about mortality triggers various ingroup biases, including negative stereotypes, and behavior that demonstrates prejudice toward a variety of outgroups.

Robbers Cave: A Field Study in Intergroup Conflict

- In the Robbers Cave study, boys divided into rival groups quickly showed intergroup prejudice. This prejudice was reduced when the boys were brought together through tasks that required intergroup cooperation.

Realistic Conflict Theory

- Realistic conflict theory maintains that direct competition for resources gives rise to prejudice.

Social Identity Theory

- Participants categorized into arbitrary minimal groups discriminate in favor of the ingroup.

- Social identity theory proposes that self-esteem is influenced by the fate of social groups with which we identify.

- Research shows that threats to the self cause individuals to derogate outgroups and that this behavior in turn increases self-esteem.

- Ingroup favoritism is more intense among people whose identity is closely tied to their group.

Culture and Social Identity

- Cultural differences can influence social identity processes. Individualists are more likely than collectivists to try to boost their self-esteem through overt ingroup-enhancing biases.

Motives Concerning Intergroup Dominance and Status

- People with a social dominance orientation exhibit a desire to see their ingroups as dominant over other groups, and they tend to identify more strongly with their ingroup and to be more likely to disparage members of outgroups.

- People who tend to endorse and legitimize existing social arrangements can show signs of outgroup favoritism even when their group holds a relatively disadvantaged position in society.

Causes of the Problem: Cognitive and Cultural Factors

Social Categorization

- The tendency for people to group themselves and others into social categories is a key factor in stereotype formation and prejudice.

- Social categories can be energy-saving devices that allow perceivers to make quick inferences about group members, but these categories can lead to inaccurate judgments.

- People tend to exaggerate the differences between ingroups and outgroups.

- The outgroup homogeneity effect is the tendency to assume that there is more similarity among members of outgroups than there is among members of ingroups.

- Research using brain imaging and cognitive methods has found that merely categorizing people as outgroup members can lead perceivers to process information about outgroup members less deeply.

- Perceivers sometimes dehumanize outgroups in a variety of ways.

How Stereotypes Survive and Self-Perpetuate

- People perceive illusory correlations between groups and traits when the traits are distinctive or when the correlations fit prior notions.

- People tend to make attributions about the causes of group members' behaviors in ways that help maintain their stereotypes.

- Group members who do not fit the mold are often subtyped, leaving the overall stereotype intact.

- The stereotypes that people hold about group members can lead them to behave in biased ways toward those members, sometimes causing the latter to behave consistently with the stereotypes. The stereotypes thus produce a self-fulfilling prophecy.

- Some stereotypes are more accurate than others, but judging the accuracy of stereotypes is challenging, in part because "accuracy" can have different meanings.

Culture and Socialization

- We often learn a tremendous amount of information relevant to stereotypes, prejudice, and discrimination without even realizing it by absorbing what we see around us in our culture, groups, and families.

- Boys and girls tend to show gender-stereotypical preferences for things like toys at very early ages.

- Gender stereotypes are so deeply ingrained that they bias perceptions of males and females from the moment they are born.

- Perceived differences between men and women are magnified by the contrasting social roles they occupy.

- The mass media foster stereotypes of various groups.

- Portrayals of men and women in advertising and other forms of media can influence the behavior and attitudes of men and women.

- A recent field experiment in Rwanda demonstrated the positive effect the media can have in promoting anti-prejudice norms.

Stereotype Content Model

- Many group stereotypes vary along two dimensions: warmth and competence.

- The stereotype content model proposes that stereotypes about the competence of a group are influenced by the relative status of that group in society and that stereotypes about the warmth of a group are influenced by perceived competition with the group.

Is Stereotyping Inevitable? Automatic Versus Intentional Processes

- Stereotypes are often activated without our awareness and operate at an unconscious, or implicit, level.

- Stereotype activation occurs automatically under some conditions. In these cases, stereotypes can influence individuals' perceptions and reactions concerning others even when they don't believe in the stereotypes.

- Stereotype activation can be influenced by a number of factors, including how accessible various stereotypes are in perceivers' minds and how prejudiced the perceivers are.

- Some motivations make stereotype activation more likely to occur and others make it less likely. For example, when perceivers are highly motivated to feel better about themselves, they may become more likely to activate some stereotypes and suppress others.

- Simply trying to suppress stereotypes from being activated can sometimes backfire, although it can work for people who are intrinsically motivated and do not believe the stereotype.

- Some individuals can become relatively expert at regulating prejudiced responses because they recognize the situational factors that have caused them to fail to live up to their egalitarian ideals in the past.

- Trying to suppress stereotyping can be cognitively tiring. When age, fatigue, intoxication, or other cognitive impairment reduces people's cognitive resources, they are less able to control their stereotypes.

- One experiment found that high-prejudice individuals were better able to inhibit their prejudice if their glucose levels were raised by a high-sugar drink.

- Recent research suggests that a variety of strategies—such as training, taking the perspective of others, and thinking of examples that counter stereotypes—can help suppress automatic activation of stereotypes.

"41 Shots": A Focus on the Tragic Shooting of Amadou Diallo

- The shooting of an unarmed African man by New York City police officers triggered a great deal of controversy and inspired social psychology experiments designed to contribute to an understanding of the issues involved.

- Several studies have found that perceivers tend to be more biased toward seeing an unarmed man as holding a weapon and posing a threat if he is black than if he is white.

- Training may be effective in reducing the tendency of civilians or police officers to exhibit this bias.

- This bias is evident even among perceivers who do not endorse negative stereotypes or prejudiced attitudes. Awareness of the stereotype seems to be a key factor.

A Threat in the Air: Effects on the Targets of Stereotypes and Prejudice

- Stigmatized groups are negatively stereotyped and devalued in society.

Perceiving Discrimination

- When members of stigmatized groups perceive others' reactions to them as discrimination, they experience both benefits and drawbacks to their self-esteem and feelings of control.

Stereotype Threat

- Situations that activate stereotype threat cause individuals to worry that others will see them in negative and stereotypical ways.

- Stereotype threat can impair the performance and affect the identity of members of stereotyped or devalued groups. Slight changes in a setting can reduce stereotype threat and its negative effects significantly.

- Stereotype threat can cause African American and female students to fail to perform to their potential in academic settings.

- Research has documented a huge and growing list of groups whose members show underperformance and performance-impairing behaviors when a negative stereotype about their abilities is made relevant.

- Stereotype threat causes its effects through multiple processes. Stereotype threat can lead to increased arousal, trigger attempts to suppress negative stereotypes, impair working memory, and cause individuals to feel dejection-related emotions or to engage in negative thinking.

- Research points to ways that members of stereotyped groups can be protected against these negative effects.

- A study of seventh-graders showed that the simple intervention of asking students to think about values that were important to them dramatically improved the performance of African American students.

- Learning about stereotype threat may protect members of targeted groups against its negative effects.

Reducing Stereotypes, Prejudice, and Discrimination

Intergroup Contact

- Although according to the contact hypothesis, desegregation should reduce prejudice, it did not cure the problem in the absence of key conditions of intergroup contact: equal status, personal interactions, the need to achieve a common goal, and social norms. When these conditions are met, intergroup contact tends to be much more successful in reducing prejudice.

The Jigsaw Classroom

- Schools often fail to meet the conditions for reducing prejudice, in part because competition is too high. One program that is designed to foster intergroup cooperation and interdependence suggests that the right kinds of contact can improve attitudes and behaviors in a school setting.

Shared Identities

- Recent research has demonstrated that changing how group members categorize each other can reduce prejudice and discrimination, for example by recognizing the ways they share a common identity with members of other groups.

Changing Cultures and Motivations

- Changes in the kinds of information perpetuated in one's culture can alter how one perceives social groups.

- As the general culture and local norms change to promote values that are consistent with fairness and diversity and that are not consistent with prejudice and discrimination, individuals' motivations can change accordingly.

Key Terms

ambivalent sexism (156)
contact hypothesis (192)
discrimination (148)
group (148)
illusory correlation (169)
implicit racism (150)
ingroup favoritism (162)
ingroups (148)
jigsaw classroom (194)

modern racism (150)
outgroup homogeneity effect (167)
outgroups (148)
prejudice (148)
racism (147)
realistic conflict theory (161)
relative deprivation (161)
sexism (147)

social categorization (166)
social dominance orientation (165)
social identity theory (162)
social role theory (175)
stereotype (148)
stereotype content model (177)
stereotype threat (187)
subliminal presentation (178)
superordinate goal (161)

Media Resources

Social Psychology 8th Edition Companion Website

Visit your book companion website

www.cengage.com/psychology/kassin

where you will find flash cards, practice quizzes, Internet links, and more to help you study.

CENGAGENOW Just what you need to know NOW! Spend time on what you need to master rather than on information you already have learned. Take a pre-test for this chapter and CengageNOW will generate a personalized study plan based on your results. The study plan will identify the topics you need to review and direct you to online resources to help you master those topics. You can then take a post-test to help you determine the concepts you have mastered and what you will need to work on. Try it out! Go to **academic .cengage.com/login** to sign in with an access code or to purchase access to this product.

Putting COMMON SENSE *to the Test*

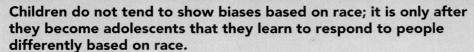

Children do not tend to show biases based on race; it is only after they become adolescents that they learn to respond to people differently based on race.

False. *Children learn about social categories quite early and use stereotypes when they are very young. Children show biases in favor of their racial ingroup on both explicit and implicit measures.*

Being reminded of one's own mortality makes people put things into greater perspective, thereby tending to reduce ingroup-outgroup distinctions and hostilities.

False. *Research has shown that when people feel threatened by thoughts of their own mortality, they tend to seek greater affiliation with their ingroups and exhibit greater prejudice against outgroups, in part to reaffirm their sense of place and purpose in the world.*

Even brief exposure to sexist television commercials can significantly influence the behaviors of men and women.

True. *Exposure to sexist commercials can make men behave in more sexist ways toward women and can make women engage in more stereotypical behaviors.*

Very brief exposure to a member of a stereotyped group does not lead to biased judgments or responses, but longer exposure typically does.

False. *Even very brief exposure to a member of a stereotyped group can activate the stereotype about the group, and this activation can bias subsequent judgments and reactions. Learning more information about the individual, however, sometimes reduces the effects of the stereotype.*

An African American student is likely to perform worse on an athletic task if the task is described as one reflecting sports intelligence than if it is described as reflecting natural athletic ability.

True. *Research suggests that African American students are likely to experience stereotype threat and therefore underperform if the task is described as one that is diagnostic of their sports intelligence. White students tend to show the opposite effect: Their performance is worse if the task is described as reflecting natural athletic ability.*

6

Attitudes

This chapter examines social influences on attitudes. We define attitudes and then discuss how they are measured and when they are related to behavior. Then we consider two methods of changing attitudes. First, we look at source, message, and audience factors that win persuasion through the media of communication. Second, we consider theories and research showing that people often change their attitudes as a consequence of their own actions.

Al Qaeda. Abortion rights. The death penalty. Gay marriage. Rush Limbaugh. Gun control. Barack Obama. Israelis and Palestinians. Anyone who has followed recent events in the United States—or anywhere else in the world, for that matter—knows how passionately people feel about the issues of the day. Attitudes and the mechanisms of attitude change, or persuasion, are a vital part of human social life. This chapter addresses three sets of questions: (1) What is an attitude, how can it be measured, and what is its link to behavior? (2) What kinds of persuasive messages lead people to change their attitudes? (3) Why do we often change our attitudes as a result of our own actions?

The Study of Attitudes

Are you a Democrat, Republican, or Independent? Do you favor or oppose universal health insurance? Should smoking be prohibited in public places? Would you rather listen to alternative rock or hip-hop, drink Coke or Pepsi, work on a PC or Mac, and use an iPhone or a BlackBerry? Should terrorism be contained by war or conciliation? As these questions suggest, each of us has positive and negative reactions to various persons, objects, and ideas. These reactions are called **attitudes**. Skim the chapters in this book, and you'll see just how pervasive attitudes are. You'll see, for example, that self-esteem is an attitude we hold about ourselves, that attraction is a positive attitude toward another person, and that prejudice is a negative attitude often directed against certain groups. Indeed, the study of attitudes—what they are, where they come from, how they can be measured, what causes them to change, and how they interact with behavior—is central to the whole field of social psychology (Albarracín, Johnson, & Zanna, 2005; Crano & Prislin, 2008; Fazio & Petty, 2008).

An attitude is a positive, negative, or mixed evaluation of an object that is expressed at some level of intensity—nothing more, nothing less. *Like, love, dislike, hate, admire,* and *detest* are the kinds of words that people use to describe their attitudes.

attitude A positive, negative, or mixed reaction to a person, object, or idea.

203

It's important to realize that attitudes cannot simply be represented along a single continuum ranging from wholly positive to wholly negative—as you might expect if attitudes were like the balance knob on a stereo that directs sound to the left or right speaker or like the lever on a thermostat that raises or lowers temperature. Rather, as depicted in ▶ Figure 6.1, our attitudes can vary in strength along both positive and negative dimensions. In other words, we can react to something with positive affect, with negative affect, with ambivalence (strong but mixed emotions), or with apathy and indifference (Cacioppo et al., 1997). Some people more than others are troubled by this type of inconsistency (Newby-Clark et al., 2002). In fact, at times people can have both positive and negative reactions to the same attitude object without feeling conflict, as when we are conscious of one reaction but not the other. Someone who is openly positive toward racial minorities but harbors unconscious prejudice is a case in point (Wilson et al., 2000).

> ▶ **FIGURE 6.1**
>
> **Four Possible Reactions to Attitude Objects**
>
> As shown, people evaluate objects along both positive and negative dimensions. As a result, our attitudes can be positive, negative, ambivalent, or indifferent.
>
> Cacioppo et al., 1997.

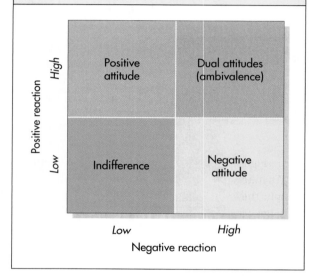

Everyone routinely forms positive and/or negative evaluations of the people, places, objects, and ideas they encounter. This process is often immediate and automatic—much like a reflex action (Bargh et al., 1996; Cunningham et al., 2003; Duckworth et al., 2002; Ferguson, 2007). It now appears, however, that individuals differ in the extent to which they tend to react to stimuli in strong positive and negative terms. What about you—do you form opinions easily? Do you have strong likes and dislikes? Or do you tend to react in more objective, nonevaluative ways? People who describe themselves as high rather than low in the *need for evaluation* are more likely to view their daily experiences in judgmental terms. They are also more opinionated on a whole range of social, moral, and political issues (Bizer et al., 2004; Jarvis & Petty, 1996).

Before we examine the elusive science of attitude measurement, let's stop for a moment and ponder this question: Why do human beings bother to form and have attitudes? Does forming a positive or negative judgment of people, objects, and ideas serve any useful purpose?

Over the years, researchers have found that attitudes serve important functions, such as enabling us to judge, quickly and without much thought, whether something we encounter is good or bad, helpful or hurtful, and to be sought or avoided (Maio & Olson, 2000). The downside is that having preexisting attitudes toward persons, objects, and ideas can lead us to become closed-minded, bias the way we interpret new information, and make us more resistant to change. For example, Russell Fazio and others (2000) found that people who were focused on their positive or negative attitudes toward computerized faces, compared to those who were not, were later slower to notice when the faces were "morphed" and no longer the same.

■ How Attitudes Are Measured

In 1928, Louis Thurstone published an article entitled "Attitudes Can Be Measured." What Thurstone failed to anticipate, however, is that attitude measurement is tricky business. One review of research uncovered more than 500 different methods of determining an individual's attitudes (Fishbein & Ajzen, 1972).

Self-Report Measures   The easiest way to assess a person's attitude about something is to ask. All over the world, public opinions are assessed on a range of issues—

As seen in this Mexican-American rally for immigration rights that was part of a nationwide work boycott, people can be very passionate about the attitudes they hold.

AP/Wide World Photos

in politics, the economy, health care, foreign affairs, science and technology, sports, entertainment, religion, and lifestyles. Simply by asking, recent Harris polls have revealed that Americans prefer football to baseball as a favorite sport; prefer reading to watching TV; rate scientists, firefighters, doctors, and teachers as the most prestigious occupations; like California, Florida, Hawaii, and Colorado as states to live in other than their own; are most eager to vacation in Australia, Italy, Great Britain, and France; and like chocolate more than any other flavor of ice cream (http://www .harrisinteractive.com/).

Self-report measures are direct and straightforward. But attitudes are sometimes too complex to be measured by a single question. As you may recall from Chapter 2, one problem recognized by public opinion pollsters is that responses to attitude questions can be influenced by their wording, the order and context in which they are asked, and other extraneous factors (Schwarz, 1999, 2007; Tourangeau et al., 2000). Recently, for example, the National Opinion Research Center asked several hundred Americans if the U.S. government spent too little money on "assistance to the poor" and 65 percent said yes. Yet when the very same question was asked using the word "welfare" instead, only 20 percent said the government spent too little (Schneiderman, 2008).

Recognizing the shortcomings of single-question measures, researchers who study people's social and political opinions often use multiple-item questionnaires known as **attitude scales** (Robinson, Shaver, & Wrightsman, 1991, 1998). Attitude scales come in different forms, perhaps the most popular being the Likert Scale, named after its inventor, Rensis Likert (1932). In this technique, respondents are presented with a list of statements about an attitude object and are asked to indicate on a multiple-point scale how strongly they agree or disagree with each statement. Each respondent's total attitude score is derived by summing his or her responses to all the items. However, regardless of whether attitudes are measured by one question or by a full-blown scale, the results should be taken with caution. All self-report measures assume that people honestly express their true opinions. Sometimes this assumption is reasonable and correct, but often it is not. Wanting to make a good impression on others, people are often reluctant to admit to their failures, vices, weaknesses, unpopular opinions, and prejudices.

attitude scale A multiple-item questionnaire designed to measure a person's attitude toward some object.

One approach to this problem is to increase the accuracy of self-report measures. To get respondents to answer attitude questions more truthfully, researchers have sometimes used the **bogus pipeline**, an elaborate mechanical device that supposedly records our true feelings physiologically, like a lie-detector test. Not wanting to get caught in a lie, respondents tend to answer attitude questions more honestly, and with less positive spin, when they think that deception would be detected by the bogus pipeline (Jones & Sigall, 1971; Roese & Jamieson, 1993). In one study, for example, people were more likely to admit to drinking too much, using cocaine, having frequent oral sex, and not exercising enough when the bogus pipeline was used than when it was not (Tourangeau et al., 1997). In another study, adolescents were more likely to admit to smoking when the bogus pipeline was used than when it was not (Adams et al., 2008).

Covert Measures   A second general approach to the self-report problem is to collect indirect, covert measures of attitudes that cannot be controlled. One possibility in this regard is to use observable behavior such as facial expressions, tone of voice, and body language. In one study, Gary Wells and Richard Petty (1980) secretly videotaped college students as they listened to a speech and noticed that when the speaker took a position that the students agreed with (that tuition costs should be lowered), most made vertical head movements. But when the speaker took a contrary position (that tuition costs should be raised), head movements were in a horizontal direction. Without realizing it, the students had signaled their attitudes by nodding and shaking their heads.

Although behavior provides clues, it is far from perfect as a measure of attitudes. Sometimes we nod our heads because we agree; at other times, we nod to be polite. The problem is that people monitor their overt behavior just as they monitor self-reports. But what about internal physiological reactions that are difficult if not impossible to control? Does the body betray how we feel? In the past, researchers tried to divine attitudes from involuntary physical reactions such as perspiration, heart rate, and pupil dilation. The result, however, was always the same: Measures of arousal reveal the intensity of one's attitude toward an object but not whether that attitude itself is positive or negative. On the physiological record, love and hate look very much the same (Petty & Cacioppo, 1983).

Although physiological arousal measures cannot distinguish between positive and negative attitudes, some exciting alternatives have been discovered. One is the **facial electromyograph (EMG)**. As shown in ▶ Figure 6.2, certain muscles in the face contract when we are happy and different facial muscles contract when we are sad. Some of the muscular changes cannot be seen with the naked eye, however, so the facial EMG is used. To determine whether the EMG can be used to measure the affect associated with attitudes, John Cacioppo and Richard Petty (1981) recorded facial muscle activity of college students as they listened to a message with which they agreed or disagreed. The agreeable message increased activity in the cheek muscles—the facial pattern that is characteristic of happiness. The disagreeable message sparked activity in the forehead and brow area—the facial patterns that are associated with sadness and distress. Outside observers who later watched the participants were unable to see these subtle changes. Apparently, the muscles in the human face reveal smiles, frowns, feelings of disgust, and other reactions to attitude objects that might otherwise be hid-

"No, I <u>don't</u> want to know what my approval rating is."

These days, it seems, attitude measurement is all around us.

bogus pipeline   A phony lie-detector device that is sometimes used to get respondents to give truthful answers to sensitive questions.

facial electromyograph (EMG) An electronic instrument that records facial muscle activity associated with emotions and attitudes.

den from view (Cacioppo et al., 1986; Larsen et al., 2003; Tassinary & Cacioppo, 1992).

From a social neuroscience perspective, electrical activity in the brain may also assist in the measure of attitudes. In 1929, Hans Burger invented a machine that could detect, amplify, and record "waves" of electrical activity in the brain using electrodes pasted to the surface of the scalp. The instrument is called an *electroencephalograph*, or EEG, and the information it provides takes the form of line tracings called *brain waves*. Based on an earlier discovery that certain patterns of electrical brain activity are triggered by exposure to stimuli that are novel or inconsistent, Cacioppo and others (1993) had participants list 10 items they liked and 10 they did not like within various object categories (fruits, sports, movies, universities, etc.). Later, these participants were brought into the laboratory, wired to an EEG, and presented with a list of category words that depicted objects they liked and disliked. The result: Brainwave patterns that are normally triggered by inconsistency increased more when a disliked stimulus appeared after a string of positive items or when a liked stimulus was shown after a string of negative items than when either stimulus evoked the same attitude as the items that preceded it.

Today, social psychologists are also starting to use new forms of brain imaging in the measurement of attitudes. In one study, researchers used fMRI to record brain activity in participants as they read names of famous—and infamous—figures such as Bill Cosby and Adolf Hitler. When the names were read, they observed greater activity in the amygdala, a structure in the brain associated with emotion, regardless of whether or not participants were asked to evaluate the famous figures (Cunningham et al., 2003). In a study focused on political attitudes, other researchers used fMRI to record brain activity in opinionated men during the 2004 presidential election as they listened to positive and negative statements about the candidate of their choice. They found that although the brain areas associated with cognitive reasoning were unaffected during these presentations, activity increased in areas that are typically associated with emotion (Westen et al., 2006). Together, this new research suggests that people react automatically to positive and negative attitude objects. Although more work is needed, it appears that attitudes may be measurable by electrical activity in the brain.

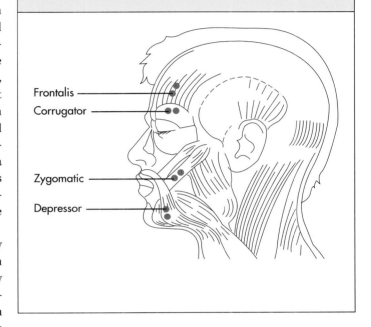

▶ **FIGURE 6.2**

The Facial EMG: A Covert Measure of Attitudes?

The facial EMG makes it possible to detect differences between positive and negative attitudes. Notice the major facial muscles and recording sites for electrodes. When people hear a message with which they agree rather than disagree, there is a relative increase in EMG activity in the depressor and zygomatic muscles but a relative decrease in corrugator and frontalis muscles. These changes cannot be seen with the naked eye.

Cacioppo & Petty, 1981.

Frontalis

Corrugator

Zygomatic

Depressor

Researchers can tell if someone has a positive or negative attitude by measuring physiological arousal. **FALSE.**

The Implicit Association Test (IAT)   When it comes to covert measurement, one particularly interesting development is based on the notion that each of us has all sorts of **implicit attitudes** that we cannot self-report in questionnaires because we are not aware of having them (Fazio & Olson, 2003). To measure these "unconscious" attitudes, Anthony Greenwald, Mahzarin Banaji, Brian Nosek, and others have developed the **Implicit Association Test (IAT)**. As we saw in Chapter 5, the IAT measures the speed with which people associate pairs of concepts (Greenwald et al., 1998). To see how it works, try visiting the IAT website by searching "Implicit Association Test" or typing www.yale.edu/implicit in your browser window.

To take a test that measures your implicit racial attitudes, you go through a series of stages. First, you are asked to categorize black or white faces as quickly as

implicit attitude   An attitude, such as prejudice, that one is not aware of having.

Implicit Association Test (IAT)   A covert measure of unconscious attitudes derived from the speed at which people respond to pairings of concepts—such as black or white with good or bad.

you can, for example, by pressing a left-hand key in response to a black face and a right-hand key for a white face. Next, you are asked to categorize a set of words, for example, by pressing a left-hand key for positive words (*love, laughter, friend*) and a right-hand key for negative words (*war, failure, evil*). Once you have become familiar with the categorization task, the test combines faces and words. You may be asked, for example, to press the left-hand key if you see a black face or positive word and a right-hand key for a white face or negative word. Then, in the fourth stage, the opposite pairings are presented—black or negative, white or positive. Black and white faces are then interspersed in a quick sequence of trials, each time paired with a positive or negative word. In rapid-fire succession, you have to press one key or another in response to stimulus pairs such as *black-wonderful, black-failure, white-love, black-laughter, white-evil, white-awful, black-war,* and *white-joy*. As you work through the list, you may find that some pairings are harder and take longer to respond to than others. In general, people are quicker to respond when liked faces are paired with positive words and disliked faces are paired with negative words than the other way around. Using the IAT, your implicit attitudes about African Americans can thus be detected by the speed it takes you to respond to *black-bad/white-good* pairings relative to *black-good/white-bad* pairings. The test takes only about 10 minutes to complete. When you're done, you receive the results of your test and an explanation of what it means (see ▶ Figure 6.3).

From 1998 to the present, visitors to the IAT website completed more than 5 million tests. In questionnaires, interviews, public opinion polls, and Internet surveys, people don't tend to express stereotypes, prejudices, or other unpopular attitudes. Yet on the IAT, respondents have exhibited a marked implicit preference for self over other, white over black, young over old, straight over gay, able over disabled, thin

▶ FIGURE 6.3

The Implicit Association Test (IAT)

Through a sequence of tasks, the IAT measures implicit racial attitudes toward, for example, African Americans, by measuring how quickly people respond to *black-bad/white-good* word pairings relative to *black-good/white-bad* pairings. Most white Americans are quicker to respond to the first type of pairings than to the second, which suggests that they do not as readily connect black-good and white-bad.

Kassin, 2004.

over obese, and the stereotype that links males with careers and females with family (Greenwald et al., 2003; Nosek et al., 2002). Because more and more researchers are using these kinds of indirect measures, social psychologists who study attitudes find themselves in the midst of a debate over what IAT scores mean, how the implicit attitudes revealed in the IAT are formed and then changed, how these attitudes predict or influence behavior, and how they differ from the more explicit attitudes that we consciously hold and report (Blanton et al., 2009; Gawronski & Bodenhausen, 2006; Petty et al., 2009; Wittenbrink & Schwarz, 2007).

Do implicit attitudes matter? Do millisecond differences in response times on a computerized test really predict behavior in real-world settings of consequence? And what does it mean when one's implicit and explicit attitudes clash? The importance of these questions cannot be overstated. If the IAT reveals unconscious prejudices that people do not self-report, should individuals be scrutinized in the laboratory for hidden motives underlying various potentially unlawful behaviors—as when a police officer shoots a black suspect, fearing that he or she is armed; as when an employer hires a male applicant over a female applicant, citing his credentials as opposed to discrimination; or as when a jury chooses to convict a Latino defendant on the basis of ambiguous evidence?

Kristin Lane and others (2007) have speculated about the relevance of implicit attitudes in law. But is their speculation justified? Some researchers are critical of strong claims concerning the predictive validity of the IAT, citing the need for more behavioral evidence (Blanton et al., 2009). Based on a meta-analysis of 122 IAT studies involving 15,000 participants, Greenwald and others (2009) concede that people's implicit attitudes are generally less predictive of behavior than their explicit attitudes. They also find, however, that IAT measures are better when it comes to socially sensitive topics such as race where people often distort their self-reports.

▉ How Attitudes Are Formed

How did you become liberal or conservative in your political values? Why do you favor or oppose gay marriage? What draws you toward or away from organized religion?

Chances are, these identical twins have more in common than being firefighters. Research suggests that people may be genetically predisposed to hold certain attitudes.

T. K. Wanstal/The Image Works

One hypothesis, first advanced by Abraham Tesser (1993), is that strong likes and dislikes are rooted in our genetic makeup. Research shows that on some issues the attitudes of identical twins are more similar than those of fraternal twins and that twins raised apart are as similar to each other as those who are raised in the same home. This pattern of evidence suggests that people may be predisposed to hold certain attitudes. Indeed, Tesser found that when asked about attitudes for which there seems to be a predisposition (such as attitudes toward sexual promiscuity, religion, and the death penalty), research participants were quicker to respond and less likely to alter their views toward social norms. Tesser speculated that individuals are disposed to hold certain strong attitudes as a result of inborn physical, sensory, and cognitive skills, temperament, and personality traits. Other twin studies, too, have supported the notion that people differ in their attitudes toward a range of issues in part because of genetically rooted differences in their biological makeup (Olson et al., 2001). In a recent study that illustrates the point, researchers brought 40 adults with strong political views into the laboratory for testing and found that those who physiologically were highly reactive to sudden noise and other unpleasant stimuli were more likely to favor capital punishment, the right to bear arms, defense spending, the war in Iraq, and other policies seen as protective against domestic and foreign threats (Oxley et al., 2008).

Whatever dispositions nature provides to us, our most cherished attitudes often form as a result of our exposure to attitude objects; our history of rewards and punishments; the attitudes that our parents, friends, and enemies express; the social and cultural context in which we live; and other types of experiences. In a classic naturalistic study, Theodore Newcomb (1943) surveyed the political attitudes of students at Bennington College in Vermont. At the time, Bennington was a women's college that drew its students from conservative and mostly affluent families. Once there, however, the students encountered professors and older peers who held more liberal views. Newcomb found that as the women moved from their first year to graduation, they became progressively more liberal. (In the 1936 presidential election, 62 percent of first-year Bennington students preferred the Republican Landon to the Democrat Roosevelt, compared to only 43 percent of sophomores and 15 percent of juniors and seniors.) This link between cultural environment and attitudes is particularly evident in the current political landscape of America—a "house divided" by ideology into red states and blue states (Seyle & Newman, 2006).

Clearly, attitudes are formed through basic processes of learning. For example, numerous studies have shown that people can form strong positive and negative attitudes toward neutral objects that somehow are linked to emotionally charged stimuli. In a classic study, college students were presented with a list of adjectives that indicate nationality (*German, Swedish, Dutch, Italian, French,* and *Greek*), each of which was repeatedly presented with words that had very pleasant (*happy, gift, sacred*) or unpleasant (*bitter, ugly, failure*) connotations. When the participants later evaluated the nationalities by name, they were more positive in their ratings of those that had been paired with pleasant words than with unpleasant words (Staats & Staats, 1958).

More recent studies of "evaluative conditioning" have further shown that implicit and explicit attitudes toward neutral objects can form by their association with positive and negative stimuli, even in people who are not conscious of this association (De Houwer et al., 2001; Olson & Fazio, 2001; Walther et al., 2005). That's why political leaders all over the world wrap themselves in national flags to derive the benefit of positive associations, while advertisers strategically pair their products with sexy models, uplifting music, beloved celebrities, nostalgic images, and other positive emotional symbols.

The Link Between Attitudes and Behavior

People take for granted the notion that attitudes influence behavior. We assume that voters' opinions of opposing candidates predict the decisions they make on Election Day, that consumers' attitudes toward competing products influence the purchases they make, and that feelings of prejudice trigger negative acts of discrimination. Yet as sensible as these assumptions seem, the link between attitudes and behavior is far from perfect.

Sociologist Richard LaPiere (1934) was the first to notice that attitudes and behavior don't always go hand in hand. In the 1930s, LaPiere took a young Chinese-American couple on a three-month, 10,000-mile automobile trip, visiting 250 restaurants, campgrounds, and hotels across the United States. Although prejudice against Asians was widespread at the time, the couple was refused service only once. Yet when LaPiere wrote back to the places they had visited and asked if they would accept Chinese patrons, more than 90 percent of those who returned an answer said they would not. Self-reported attitudes did not correspond with behavior.

This study was provocative but seriously flawed. LaPiere measured attitudes several months after his trip, and during that time the attitudes may have changed. He also did not know whether those who responded to his letter were the same people who had greeted the couple in person. It was even possible that the Chinese couple were served wherever they went only because they were accompanied by LaPiere.

Despite these problems, LaPiere's study was the first of many to reveal a lack of correspondence between attitudes and behavior. In 1969, Allan Wicker reviewed the applicable research and concluded that attitudes and behavior are correlated only weakly, if at all. Sobered by this conclusion, researchers were puzzled: Could it be that the votes we cast do *not* follow from our political opinions, that consumers' purchases are *not* based on their attitudes toward a product, or that discrimination is *not* related to underlying prejudice? Is the study of attitudes useless to those interested in human social behavior? Not at all. During subsequent years, researchers went on to identify the conditions under which attitudes and behavior are correlated. Thus, when Stephen Kraus (1995) meta-analyzed all of this research, he concluded that "attitudes significantly and substantially predict future behavior" (p. 58). In fact, he calculated that there would have to be 60,983 new studies reporting a zero correlation before this conclusion would have to be revised. Based on their recent meta-analysis of 41 additional studies, Laura Glasman and Dolores Albarraín (2006) went on to identify some of the conditions under which attitudes most clearly predict future behavior.

Attitudes in Context   One important condition is the level of *correspondence*, or similarity, between attitude measures and behavior. Perhaps the reason that LaPiere (1934) did not find a correlation between self-reported prejudice and discrimination was that he had asked proprietors about Asians in general but then observed their actions toward only one couple. To predict a single act of discrimination, he should have measured people's more specific attitudes toward a young, well-dressed, attractive Chinese couple accompanied by an American professor.

Icek Ajzen and Martin Fishbein (1977) analyzed more than 100 studies and found that attitudes correlate with behavior only when attitude measures closely match the behavior in question. Illustrating the point, Andrew Davidson and James Jaccard (1979) tried to use attitudes to predict whether women would use birth control pills within the next two years. Attitudes were measured in a series of questions ranging from very general ("How do you feel about birth control?") to very specific ("How do you feel about using birth control pills during the next two years?"). The more specific the initial attitude question was, the better it predicted the behavior. Other researchers as well have replicated this finding (Kraus, 1995).

The link between our feelings and our actions should also be placed within a broader context. Attitudes are one determinant of social behavior, but there are other determinants as well. This limitation formed the basis for Fishbein's (1980) theory of reasoned action, which Ajzen (1991) expanded into his **theory of planned behavior**. According to these theories, our attitudes influence our behavior through a process of deliberate decision making, and their impact is limited in four respects (see ▶ Figure 6.4).

First, as just described, behavior is influenced less by general attitudes than by attitudes toward a specific behavior. Second, behavior is influenced not only by attitudes but by *subjective norms*—our beliefs about what others think we should do. As we'll see in Chapter 7, social pressures to conform often lead us to behave in ways that are at odds with our inner convictions. Third, according to Ajzen, attitudes give rise to behavior only when we perceive the behavior to be within our *control*. To the extent that people lack confidence in their ability to engage in some behavior, they are unlikely to form an intention to do so. Fourth, although attitudes (along with subjective norms and perceived control) contribute to an *intention* to behave in a particular manner, people often do not or cannot follow through on their intentions.

A good deal of research supports the theories of reasoned action and planned behavior (Madden et al., 1992; Ajzen & Fishbein, 2005). Indeed, this general approach, which places the link between attitudes and behaviors within a broader context, has successfully been used to predict a wide range of important and practical behaviors, such as using condoms, obeying speed limits, eating healthy foods, and registering to become an organ donor (Albarracín et al., 2001; Conner et al., 2002; Elliott et al., 2003; Hyde & White, 2009).

Strength of the Attitude According to the theories of reasoned action and planned behavior, specific attitudes combine with social factors to produce behavior. Sometimes attitudes have more influence on behavior than do the other factors; sometimes they have less influence. In large part, it depends on the importance, or *strength*, of the

theory of planned behavior
The theory that attitudes toward a specific behavior combine with subjective norms and perceived control to influence a person's actions.

▶**FIGURE 6.4**

Theory of Planned Behavior

According to the theory of planned behavior, attitudes toward a specific behavior combine with subjective norms and perceived behavior control to influence a person's intentions. These intentions, in turn, guide but do not completely determine behavior. This theory places the link between attitudes and behavior within a broader context.

Ajzen, 1991.

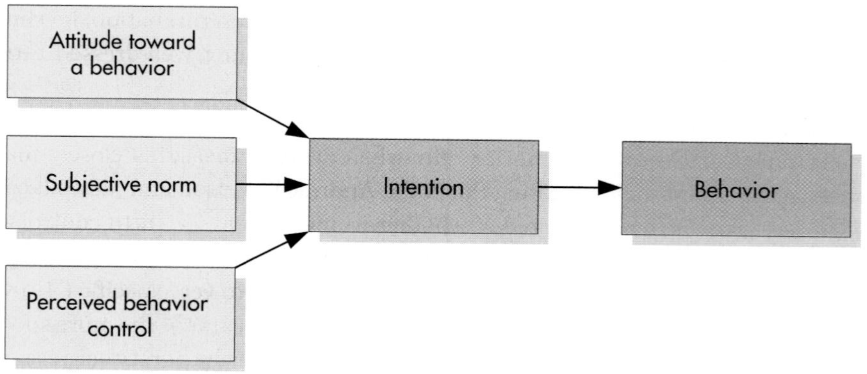

attitude. Each of us has some views that are nearer and dearer to the heart than others. Computer jocks often become attached to PCs or Macs, religious fundamentalists care deeply about issues pertaining to life and death, and political activists have fiery passions for one political party or policy over others. In each case, the attitude is held with great confidence and is difficult to change (Petty & Krosnick, 1995).

Why are some attitudes stronger than others? David Boninger and others (1995) identified three psychological factors that consistently seem to distinguish between our strongest and weakest attitudes. These investigators asked people to reflect on their views toward defense spending, gun control, the legalization of marijuana, abortion rights, and other issues. They found that the attitudes people held most passionately were those that concerned issues that (1) directly affected their own self-interests; (2) related to deeply held philosophical, political, and religious values; and (3) were of concern to their close friends, family, and social ingroups. This last, highly social, point is important. Research shows that when people are surrounded by others who are like-minded, the attitudes they hold are stronger and more resistant to change (Visser & Mirabile, 2004).

Several factors indicate the strength of an attitude and its link to behavior. One is that people tend to behave in ways that are consistent with their attitudes when they are well informed. For example, college students were asked which of two candidates they preferred in an upcoming local election for mayor. Those who knew the factual campaign issues were later the most likely to actually vote for their favored candidate (Davidson et al., 1985). In another study, college students were questioned about their views on various environmental issues and later were asked to take action—to sign petitions, participate in a recycling project, and so on. Again, the more informed the students were, the more consistent their attitudes about the environment were with their behavior (Kallgren & Wood, 1986).

The strength of an attitude is indicated not only by the *amount* of information on which it is based but also by *how* that information was acquired. Research shows that attitudes are more stable and more predictive of behavior when they are born of direct personal experience than when based on indirect, secondhand information. In a series of experiments, for example, Russell Fazio and Mark Zanna (1981) introduced two groups of participants to a set of puzzles. One group worked on sample puzzles; the other group merely watched someone else work on them. All participants were then asked to rate their interest in the puzzles (attitude) and were given an opportunity to spend time on them (behavior). As it turned out, attitudes and behaviors were more consistent among participants who had previously sampled the puzzles.

Third, an attitude can be strengthened, ironically, by an attack against it from a persuasive message. According to Zakary Tormala and Richard Petty (2002), people hold attitudes with varying degrees of certainty and they become more confident in their positions after they successfully resist changing that attitude in response to a persuasive communication. In one study, researchers confronted university students with an unpopular proposal to add senior comprehensive exams as a graduation requirement. Each student read a pro-exam argument that was described as strong or weak, after which they were asked to write down counterarguments and indicate their attitude toward the policy. The result: Students who continued to oppose the policy despite reading what they thought to be a strong argument became even more certain of their opinion.

Additional studies have shown that this effect depends on how satisfied people are with their own resistance. When people resist a strong message and believe that they have done so in a compelling way, they become more certain of their attitude and more likely to form a behavioral intention that is consistent with it. When people resist a persuasive message "by the skin of their teeth," however, and see their own counterarguments as weak, they become less certain of their initial attitude and more vulnerable to subsequent attack (Tormala et al., 2006). Even if a person's belief in their own thoughtful response is incorrect, it can influence the strength of the attitude in question (Barden & Petty, 2008).

A fourth key factor is that strong attitudes are highly accessible to awareness, which means that they are quickly and easily brought to mind (Fazio, 1990). To return to our earlier examples, computer jocks think often about their computer preferences and political activists think often about their allegiances to political parties. It turns out that many attitudes—not just those we feel strongly about—easily pop to mind by the mere sight or even just the mention of an attitude object (Bargh et al., 1992). When this happens, the attitude can trigger behavior in a quick, spontaneous way or by leading us to think carefully about how we feel and how to respond (Fazio & Towles-Schwen, 1999).

To summarize, research on the link between attitudes and behavior leads to an important conclusion. Our evaluations of an object do not always determine our actions because other factors must be taken into account. However, when attitudes are strong and specific to a behavior, the effects are beyond dispute. Under these conditions, voting is influenced by political opinions, consumer purchasing is affected by product attitudes, and racial discrimination is rooted in feelings of prejudice. Attitudes are important determinants of behavior. The question now is How can attitudes be changed?

Persuasion by Communication

On a day-to-day basis, we are all involved in the process of changing attitudes. On TV, on the internet, in magazines, and on billboards, advertisers flood consumers with ad campaigns designed to sell cars, soft drinks, MP3 players, sneakers, and travel destinations. Likewise, politicians make speeches, run TV commercials, pass out bumper stickers, and kiss babies to win votes. Attitude change is sought whenever parents socialize their children, scientists advance theories, religious groups seek converts, financial analysts recommend stocks, or trial lawyers argue cases to a jury. Some appeals work; others do not. Some are soft and subtle; others are hard and blatant. Some serve the public interest, whereas others serve personal interests. The point is, there is nothing inherently evil or virtuous about changing attitudes, a process known as **persuasion**. We do it all the time.

If you wanted to change someone's attitude on an issue, you'd probably try to do it by making a persuasive *communication*. Appeals made in person and through the mass media rely on the spoken word, the written word, and the image that is worth a thousand words. What determines whether an appeal succeeds or fails? To understand why certain approaches are effective while others are not, social psychologists have for many years sought to understand *how* and *why* persuasive communications work. For that, we need a road map of the persuasion process.

■ Two Routes to Persuasion

It's a familiar scene in American politics: Every four years, two or more presidential candidates launch extensive—and expensive—campaigns for office. In a way, if you've seen one election, you've seen them all. The names and dates may change, but over and

persuasion The process by which attitudes are changed.

In U.S. presidential politics, candidates try to win votes by addressing the issues, as in debates and speeches delivered from a podium (the central route) or through the use of banners, balloons, music, and other theatrics (the peripheral route).

over again, opposing candidates accuse each other of ducking the substantive issues and turning the election into a flag-waving popularity contest.

True or not, these accusations show that politicians are keenly aware that they can win votes through two different methods. They can stick to policy and issues or they can base their appeals on other grounds. Interestingly, these "other grounds" can well determine who wins an election. In *The Political Brain*, Drew Westen (2007) presents a wealth of research evidence indicating that in the marketplace of politics, emotions trump reason. Based on a combination of laboratory experiments and public opinion polls, other political psychologists agree (Brader, 2006; Neuman et al., 2007).

To account for the two alternative approaches to persuasion, Richard Petty and John Cacioppo (1986) proposed a dual-process model. This model assumes that we do not always process communications the same way. When people think critically about the contents of a message, they are said to take a **central route to persuasion** and are influenced by the strength and quality of the arguments. When people do not think critically about the contents of a message but focus instead on other cues, they take a **peripheral route to persuasion**. As we'll see, the route taken depends on whether one is willing and able to scrutinize the information contained in the message itself. Over the years, this model has provided an important framework for understanding the factors that elicit persuasion (Petty & Wegener, 1998).

The Central Route   In the first systematic attempt to study persuasion, Carl Hovland and colleagues (1949, 1953) started the Yale Communication and Attitude Change Program. They proposed that for a persuasive message to have influence, the recipients of that message must learn its contents and be motivated to accept it. According to this view, people can be persuaded only by an argument they attend to, comprehend, and retain in memory for later use. Regardless of whether the message takes the form of a live personal appeal, a newspaper editorial, a Sunday sermon, a TV commercial, or a pop-up window on a website, these basic requirements remain the same.

A few years later, William McGuire (1969) reiterated the information-processing steps necessary for persuasion and like the Yale group before him distinguished between the learning, or *reception*, of a message, a necessary first step, and its later *acceptance*. In fact, McGuire (1968) used this distinction to explain the surprising finding that a recipient's self-esteem and intelligence are unrelated to persuasion. In McGuire's analysis, these characteristics have opposite effects on reception and

central route to persuasion
The process by which a person thinks carefully about a communication and is influenced by the strength of its arguments.

peripheral route to persuasion
The process by which a person does not think carefully about a communication and is influenced instead by superficial cues.

acceptance. People who are smart or high in self-esteem are better able to learn a message but are less likely to accept its call for a change in attitude. People who are less smart or low in self-esteem are more willing to accept the message but they may have trouble learning its contents. Overall, then, neither group is generally more vulnerable to persuasion than the other—a prediction that is supported by a good deal of research (Rhodes & Wood, 1992).

Anthony Greenwald (1968) and others then argued that persuasion requires a third, intermediate step: **elaboration.** To illustrate, imagine you are offered a job and your prospective employer tries to convince you over lunch to accept. You listen closely, learn the terms of the offer, and understand what it means. But if it's a really important interview, your head will spin with questions as you weigh all the pros and cons and contemplate the implications: What would it cost to move? Is there potential for advancement? Am I better off staying where I am? When confronted with personally significant messages, we don't listen just for the sake of collecting information, we think about that information. When this happens, the message is effective to the extent that it leads us to focus on favorable rather than unfavorable thoughts.

These theories of attitude change all share the assumption that the recipients of persuasive appeals are attentive, active, critical, and thoughtful of every word spoken. This assumption is correct—some of the time. When it is and when people consider a message carefully, their reaction to it depends on the strength of its contents. In these instances, messages have greater impact when they are easily learned rather than difficult, when they are memorable rather than forgettable, and when they stimulate favorable rather than unfavorable elaboration. Ultimately, strong arguments are persuasive and weak arguments are not.

On the central route to persuasion, the process is eminently rational. It's important to note, however, that thinking carefully about a persuasive message does not guarantee that the process is objective or that it necessarily promotes truth-seeking. At times, each of us prefers to hold a particular attitude and become biased in the way we process information (Petty & Wegener, 1998). Among college students who were politically conservative or liberal, the tendency to agree with a social welfare policy was influenced more by whether it was said to have the support of Democrats or Republicans than by the logical merits of the policy itself (Cohen, 2003). Similarly, college students were less likely to be persuaded by a proposed tuition hike to fund campus improvements when the increase would take effect in one year, thus raising the personal stakes, than by a proposal to raise tuition in eight years (Darke & Chaiken, 2005). To further complicate matters, people who want to hold the right attitudes may fear that they are biased or overly influenced by nonrelevant factors and then try to correct for that bias, sometimes with an ironic result: *overcorrection*. In one study, for example, audience members who were forewarned that people are prone to agree with speakers they like later exhibited more attitude change in response to a speaker who was clearly not likable (Petty et al., 1998).

The Peripheral Route   "The receptive ability of the masses is very limited, their understanding small; on the other hand, they have a great power of forgetting." The author of this statement was Adolf Hitler (1933, p. 77). Believing that human beings are incompetent processors of information, Hitler relied in his propaganda on the use of slogans, uniforms, marching bands, swastika-covered flags, a special salute, and other symbols. For Hitler, "meetings were not just occasions to make speeches; they were carefully planned theatrical productions in which settings, lighting, background music, and the timing of entrances were devised to maximize the emotional fervor of an audience" (Qualter, 1962, p. 112).

elaboration   The process of thinking about and scrutinizing the arguments contained in a persuasive communication.

Do these ploys work? Can the masses be handily manipulated into persuasion? History shows that they can. Audiences are not always thoughtful. Sometimes people do not follow the central route to persuasion but instead take a shortcut through the peripheral route. Rather than try to learn about a message and think through the issues, they respond with little effort on the basis of superficial peripheral cues.

On the peripheral route to persuasion, people will often evaluate a communication by using simple-minded heuristics, or rules of thumb (Chaiken, 1987; Chen & Chaiken, 1999). If a communicator has a good reputation, speaks fluently, or writes well, we tend to assume that his or her message must be correct. And when a speaker has a reputation for being honest, people think less critically about the specific contents of his or her communication (Priester & Petty, 1995). Likewise, we assume that a message must be correct if it contains a long litany of arguments or statistics or an impressive list of supporting experts, if it's familiar, if it elicits cheers from an audience, or if the speaker seems to be arguing against his or her own interests. In some cases, people will change their attitudes simply because they know that an argument has majority support (Giner-Sorolla & Chaiken, 1997).

On the mindless peripheral route, people are also influenced by a host of factors that are not relevant to attitudes, such as cues from their own body movements. In one study, participants were coaxed into nodding their heads up and down (as if saying yes) or shaking them from side to side (as if saying no) while listening via headphones to an editorial, presumably to test whether the headphones could endure the physical activity. Those coaxed into nodding later agreed more with the arguments than those coaxed into shaking their heads from side to side (Wells & Petty, 1980). In other studies, participants viewed and rated graphic symbols or word-like stimuli (*surtel, primet*) while using an exercise bar to either stretch their arms out (which mimics what we do to push something away) or flex their arms in (which we do to bring something closer). The participants later judged these stimuli to be more pleasant when they were associated with the flexing of the arm than when they were associated with the stretching-out motion (Cacioppo et al., 1993; Priester et al., 1996).

Route Selection Thanks to Petty and Cacioppo's (1986) two-track distinction between the central and peripheral routes, it is easy to understand why the persuasion process seems so logical on some occasions yet so illogical on others—why voters may select candidates according to issues or images, why juries may base their verdicts on evidence or a defendant's appearance, and why consumers may base their purchases on marketing reports or product images. The process that is engaged depends on whether the recipients of a persuasive message have the *ability* and the *motivation* to take the central route or whether they rely on peripheral cues instead.

To understand the conditions that lead people to take one route or the other, it's helpful to view persuasive communication as the outcome of three factors: a *source* (who), a *message* (says what and in what context), and an *audience* (to whom). Each of these factors steers a recipient's approach to a persuasive communication. If a source speaks clearly, if the message is important, if there is a bright, captive, and involved audience that cares deeply about the issue and has time to absorb the information, then audience members will be willing and able to take the effortful central route. But if the source speaks at a rate too fast to comprehend, if the message is trivial or too complex to process, or if audience members are distracted, pressed for time, or uninterested, then the less strenuous peripheral route is taken.

▶ Figure 6.5 presents a road map of persuasive communication. In the next three sections, we will follow this map from the input factors (source, message, and audience) through the central or peripheral processing routes to reach the final destination: persuasion.

In reacting to persuasive communications, people are influenced more by superficial images than by logical arguments. **FALSE.**

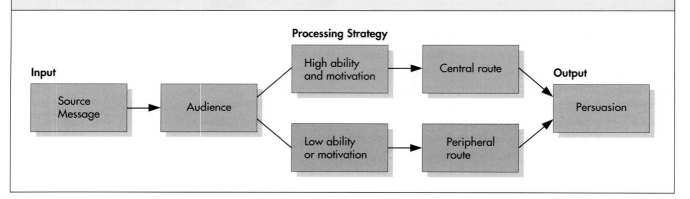

▶**FIGURE 6.5**

Two Routes to Persuasion

Based on characteristics of the source, message, and audience, recipients of a communication take either a central or peripheral route to persuasion. On the central route, people are influenced by strong arguments and evidence. On the peripheral route, persuasion is based more on heuristics and other superficial cues. This two-process model helps explain how persuasion can seem logical on some occasions and illogical on others.

■ The Source

Golfer Tiger Woods is a living legend, one of the most gifted athletes of our time. He has also been paid more millions of dollars per year than just about anyone else—to endorse Nike, American Express, and other products. Why is Woods considered an effective spokesman? What makes some communicators in general more effective than others? As we'll see, there are two key attributes: credibility and likability.

Credibility Imagine you are waiting in line in a supermarket and you catch a glimpse of a swollen headline: "Doctors Discover Cure for AIDS!" As your eye wanders across the front page, you discover that you are reading a supermarket tabloid. What would you think? Next, imagine that you are reading through scientific periodicals in a university library and you come across a similar article, but this time it appears in the *New England Journal of Medicine*. Now what would you think?

Chances are, you'd react with more excitement to the medical journal than to the tabloid, even though both sources report the same news item. In a study conducted during the Cold War era of the 1950s, participants read a speech that advocated for the development of nuclear submarines. The speech elicited more agreement when it was attributed to an eminent American physicist than when the source was said to be the Soviet government–controlled newspaper (Hovland & Weiss, 1951). Likewise, when participants read a lecture favoring more lenient treatment of juvenile offenders, they changed their attitudes more when they thought the speaker was a judge than when they believed the speaker was a convicted drug dealer (Kelman & Hovland, 1953). Now, after more than 50 years of research, it is clear that high-credibility sources are generally more persuasive than low-credibility sources (Pornpitakpan, 2004).

Why are some sources more believable than others? Why were the medical journal, the physicist, and the judge more credible than the tabloid, the Soviet-controlled newspaper, and the drug dealer? For communicators to be seen as credible, they must have two characteristics:

When legendary news anchorman Walter Cronkite died in July of 2009 at the age of 92, he was nicknamed "Uncle Walter." Cronkite delivered the CBS nightly news for 20 years to more viewers than any other anchor in history. Because he reported the news in a manner that was calm, straightforward, and objective, not fiery and opinionated, Cronkite was widely regarded as "the most trusted man in America."

Joe Kohen/Contributor/Getty Images

competence and trustworthiness. *Competence* refers to a speaker's ability. People who are knowledgeable, smart, or well spoken or who have impressive credentials are persuasive by virtue of their expertise (Hass, 1981). Experts can have a disarming effect on us. We assume they know what they're talking about. So when they speak, we listen. And when they take a position, even one that is extreme, we often yield. Unless an expert contradicts us on issues that are personally important, we tend to accept what he or she says without too much scrutiny (Maddux & Rogers, 1980), even when the message is ambiguous (Chaiken & Maheswaran, 1994).

Still, each of us is confronted by plenty of experts in life whose opinions do not sway us. The reason is that expertise alone is not enough. To have credibility, sources must also be *trustworthy*—that is, they must be seen as willing to report what they know truthfully and without compromise. What determines whether we trust a communicator? To some extent, we make these judgments on the basis of stereotypes. For example, the Gallup Organization asked 1,000 Americans to rate how honest people were in various occupational categories. As shown in Table 6.1, nurses topped the list as the most trusted occupational group. Car salesmen were the least trusted.

In judging the credibility of a source, common sense arms us with a simple rule of caution: Beware of those who have something to gain from successful persuasion. If a speaker has been paid off, has an ax to grind, or is simply telling us what we want to hear, we suspect some degree of bias. This rule sheds light on a classic dilemma in advertising concerning the value of celebrity spokespersons: The more products a celebrity endorses, the less trustworthy he or she appears to consumers (Tripp et al., 1994). In the courtroom, the same rule of caution can be used to evaluate witnesses. In one study, research participants served as jurors in a mock trial in which a man claimed that his exposure to an industrial chemical at work had caused him to contract cancer. Testifying in support of this claim was a biochemist who was paid either $4,800 or $75 for his expert testimony. You might think that jurors would be more impressed by the scientist who commanded the higher fee. Yet while he was highly paid, the expert was perceived to be a "hired gun" and was as a result less believable and less persuasive (Cooper & Neuhaus, 2000).

The self-interest rule has other interesting implications. One is that people are impressed by others who take unpopular stands or argue against their own interests. When research participants read a political speech accusing a large corporation of polluting a local river, those who thought that the speechmaker was a pro-environment candidate addressing a staunch environmentalist group perceived him to be biased, while those who thought he was a pro-business candidate talking to company supporters assumed he was sincere (Eagly et al., 1978). Trust is also established by speakers who are not purposely trying to change our views. Thus, people are influenced more when they think that they are accidentally overhearing a communication than when they receive a sales pitch clearly intended for their ears (Walster & Festinger, 1962). That's why advertisers sometimes use the "overheard communicator" trick, in which the source tells a buddy about a new product that really works. As if eavesdropping on a personal conversation, viewers assume that what one friend says to another can be trusted.

TABLE 6.1

Who Do You Trust?

In 2006, a CNN/USA Today/Gallup poll was conducted to determine the level of honesty attributed to people from various occupational groups. Indicated below are the percentages of respondents who rated each group as "high" or "very high" in honesty.

Occupation	Honest? (%)
Nurses	84
Pharmacists	73
Medical doctors	69
College teachers	58
Clergy	58
Police officers	54
Bankers	37
Journalists	26
Business executives	18
Lawyers	18
Stockbrokers	17
Insurance salespersons	13
Car salespersons	7

Likability More than anything else, the celebrity power of Tiger Woods is based on his athletic dominance, his popularity, his youthful charm, and his winning smile. But do these qualities enhance someone's impact as a communicator? Yes. As Dale Carnegie (1936) implied in the title of his classic bestseller, *How to Win Friends and Influence People*, being liked and being persuasive go hand in hand. The question is, What makes a communicator likable? As we'll see in Chapter 9, two factors that spark attraction are *similarity* and *physical attractiveness*.

A study by Diane Mackie and others (1990) illustrates the persuasive power of similarity. Students enrolled at the University of California, Santa Barbara read a strong or a weak speech that argued against continued use of the SATs in college admissions. Half the participants were led to believe that the speech was written by a fellow UCSB student; the other half thought the author was a student from the University of New Hampshire. Very few participants were persuaded by the weak arguments. In contrast, many of those who read the strong message did change their attitudes, but only when they believed it was given by a fellow UCSB student.

Just as source similarity can spark persuasion, dissimilarity can have the opposite inhibiting effect. In a study of people's taste in music, Clayton Hilmert and others (2006) introduced participants to a confederate who seemed to like the same or different kinds of music, such as rock, pop, country, or classical. Others did not meet a confederate. When later asked to rate a particular song, participants were positively influenced by the similar confederate's opinion and negatively influenced by the dissimilar confederate's opinion. In fact, although the effect is more potent when the points of similarity seem relevant to the attitude in question (Berscheid, 1966), the participants in this study were also more or less persuaded by a confederate whose similarities or differences were wholly unrelated to music—for example, when the

Just out of high school, basketball star LeBron James (left) signed a multimillion-dollar contract with Nike. Even more recently, Russian tennis star Maria Sharapova (right) was signed by a number of companies to promote cameras, tennis rackets, cell phones, cars, and watches. Can celebrities sell products? Targeting the peripheral route to persuasion, the advertising industry seems to think so.

Allen Einstein/Getty Images

© David N. Berkwitz/NewSport/Corbis

confederate had similar or different interests in shopping, world politics, museums, trying new foods, or surfing the Internet.

The effect of source similarity on persuasion has obvious implications for those who wish to exert influence. We're all similar to one another in some respects. We might agree in politics, share a common friend, have similar tastes in food, or enjoy spending summers on the same beach. If aware of the social benefits of similarity and the social costs of dissimilarity, the astute communicator can use common bonds to enhance his or her impact on an audience.

Advertising practices presuppose that beauty is also persuasive. After all, billboards, magazine ads, and TV commercials routinely feature young and glamorous "supermodels" who are tall and slender (for women) or muscular (for men) and who have hard bodies, glowing complexions, and radiant smiles. Sure, these models can turn heads, you may think, but can they change minds? In a study that addressed this question, Shelly Chaiken (1979) had male and female college students approach others on campus. They introduced themselves as members of an organization that wanted the university to stop serving meat during breakfast and lunch. In each case, these student assistants gave reasons for the position and then asked respondents to sign a petition. The result: Attractive sources were able to get 41 percent of respondents to sign the petition, whereas those who were less attractive succeeded only 32 percent of the time. Additional research has shown that attractive male and female salespersons elicit more positive attitudes and purchasing intentions from customers then less attractive salespersons, even when they are up front about their desire to make a sale (Reinhard et al., 2006).

Image courtesy of The Advertising Archives

Advertisers are so convinced that beauty sells products that they pay millions of dollars for supermodels to appear in their ads. Here, supermodel Kate Moss appears in an ad for Italian fashion house Versace.

When What You Say Is More Important Than Who You Are To this point, it must seem as if the source of a persuasive communication is more important than the communication itself. Is this true? Certainly there are enough real-life examples—as when books skyrocket to the top of the best seller list once recommended by Oprah Winfrey. The advertising industry has long debated the value of high-priced celebrity endorsements. David Ogilvy (1985), often referred to as "the king of advertising," used to say that celebrities are not effective because viewers know they've been bought and paid for. Ogilvy was not alone in his skepticism. Still, many advertisers scramble furiously to sign up famous entertainers and athletes. From Tiger Woods to Derek Jeter, LeBron James, Peyton Manning, Maria Sharapova, Oprah Winfrey, Jerry Seinfeld, Bono, and Beyonce, TV commercials regularly feature a parade of stars. The bigger the star, they say, the more valuable the testimonial.

Compared with the contents of a message, does the source really make the big difference that advertisers pay for? Are we so impressed by the expert, so enamored of the physical talent, and so drawn to the charming face that we embrace whatever they have to say? And are we so scornful of ordinary or unattractive people that their presentations fall on deaf ears? In light of what is known about the central and peripheral routes to persuasion, the answer to these questions is "it depends."

First, a recipient's level of involvement plays an important role. When a message has personal relevance to your life, you pay attention to the source and think critically about the message, the arguments, and the implications. When a message does not have personal relevance, however, you may take the source at face value and spend little time scrutinizing the information. In a classic study, Richard Petty and others

▶**FIGURE 6.6**

Source Versus Message: The Role of Audience Involvement

People who were high or low in their personal involvement heard a strong or weak message from an expert or non-expert. For high-involvement participants (left), persuasion was based on the strength of arguments, not on source expertise. For low-involvement participants (right), persuasion was based more on the source than on the arguments. Source characteristics have more impact on those who don't care enough to take the central route.

Petty et al., 1981.

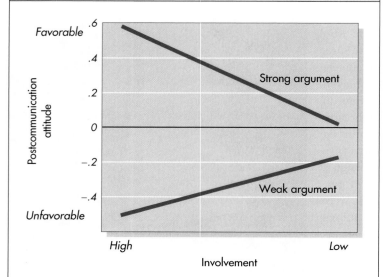

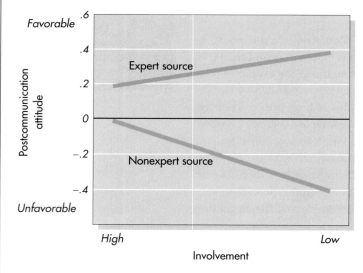

(1981) had students listen to a speaker who proposed that all seniors should be required to take comprehensive exams in order to graduate. Three aspects of the communication situation were varied. First, participants were led to believe that the speaker was either an education professor at Princeton University or a high school student. Second, participants heard either well-reasoned arguments and hard evidence or a weak message based only on anecdotes and personal opinion. Third, participants were told either that the proposed exams might be used the following year (Uh oh, that means me!) or that they would not take effect for another 10 years (Who cares, I'll be long gone by then!).

As predicted, personal involvement determined the relative impact of the expertise of the source and the quality of speech. Among participants who would not be affected by the proposed change, attitudes were based largely on the speaker's credibility: The professor was persuasive; the high school student was not. Among participants who thought that the proposed change would affect them directly, attitudes were based on the quality of the speaker's proposal. Strong arguments were persuasive; weak arguments were not. As depicted in ▶ Figure 6.6, people followed the source rather than the message under low levels of involvement, illustrating the peripheral route to persuasion. But message factors did outweigh source characteristics under high levels of involvement, when participants cared enough to take the central route to persuasion. Likewise, research has shown that the tilt toward likable and attractive communicators is reduced when recipients take the central route (Chaiken, 1980).

There is a second limit to source effects. It is often said that time heals all wounds. Well, time may also heal the effects of a bad reputation. Hovland and Weiss (1951) varied communicator credibility (for example, the physicist versus the Soviet-controlled newspaper) and found that the change had a large and immediate effect on persuasion. But when they measured attitudes again four weeks later, the effect had vanished. Over time, the attitude change produced by the high-credibility source had decreased and the change caused by the low-credibility source had increased. This finding of a delayed persuasive impact of a low-credibility communicator is called the **sleeper effect**.

To explain this unforeseen result, the Hovland research group proposed the *discounting cue hypothesis*. According to this hypothesis, people immediately discount the arguments made by noncredible communicators, but over time, they dissociate what was said from who said it. In other words, we tend to remember the message

sleeper effect A delayed increase in the persuasive impact of a noncredible source.

but forget the source (Pratkanis et al., 1988). To examine the role of memory in this process, Kelman and Hovland (1953) reminded a group of participants of the source's identity before reassessing their attitudes. If the sleeper effect was caused by forgetting, they reasoned, then it could be eliminated through reinstatement of the link between the source and the message. As shown in ▶ Figure 6.7, they were right. When attitudes were measured after three weeks, participants who were not reminded of the source showed the usual sleeper effect. Yet those who did receive a source reminder did not. For these latter participants, the effects of high and low credibility endured. Recent studies by cognitive psychologists have confirmed that over time, people "forget" the connection between information and its source (Underwood & Pezdek, 1998).

The sleeper effect generated a good deal of controversy. There was never a doubt that credible communicators lose some impact over time. But researchers had a harder time finding evidence for delayed persuasion by noncredible sources. Exasperated at one point by their own failures to obtain this result, Paulette Gillig and Anthony Greenwald (1974) wondered, "Is it time to lay the sleeper effect to rest?" As it turned out, the answer was no. More recent research showed that the sleeper effect is reliable provided that participants do not learn who the source is until *after* they have received the original message (Greenwald et al., 1986; Kumkale & Albarracín, 2004).

To appreciate the importance of timing, imagine that you're surfing the Internet and you come across what appears to be a review of a new CD. Before you begin reading, however, you notice in the fine print that this so-called review is really an

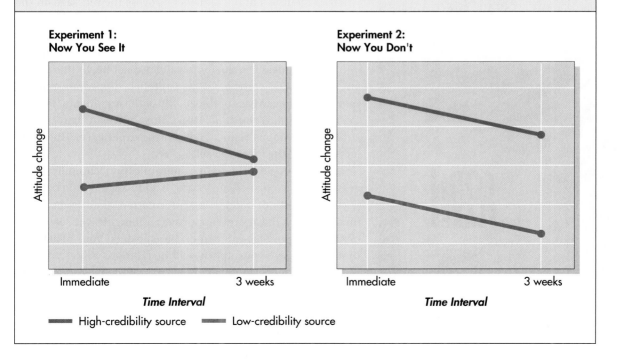

▶ FIGURE 6.7

The Sleeper Effect

In Experiment 1, participants changed their immediate attitudes more in response to a message from a high-credibility source than from a low-credibility source. When attitudes were measured again after three weeks, the high-credibility source had lost impact and the low-credibility source had gained impact—the sleeper effect. In Experiment 2, the sleeper effect disappeared when participants were reminded of the source.

Kelman & Hovland, 1953.

**Experiment 1:
Now You See It**

**Experiment 2:
Now You Don't**

Attitude change

Attitude change

Immediate   3 weeks

Immediate   3 weeks

Time Interval

Time Interval

━━ High-credibility source   ━━ Low-credibility source

advertisement. Aware that you can't always trust what you read, you skim the ad and reject it. Now imagine the same situation, except that you read the entire ad before realizing what it is. Again you reject it. But notice the difference. This time, you have read the message with an open mind. You may still reject it but after a few weeks, the information will have sunk in to influence your evaluation of the music. This scenario illustrates the sleeper effect.

The truth is always the strongest argument.

—Sophocles

When American swimmer Michael Phelps won eight gold medals in the 2008 Beijing Olympics, he was inundated with endorsement offers, including a lucrative deal with Kellogg's Frosted Flakes. After he was suspended for a photo that showed him puffing on a bong, Kellogg's declined to renew the contract.

AP Photo/Rob Carr

■ The Message

Obviously, not all sources are created equal; some are more credible or likable than others. Some are effective when they succeed but lose their luster when they stumble.

On the peripheral route to persuasion, audiences are influenced heavily, maybe too heavily, by these various source characteristics. But when people care about an issue, the strength of a message determines its impact. On the central route to persuasion, what matters most is whether a scientist's theory is supported by the data or whether a company has a sound product. Keep in mind, however, that the target of a persuasive appeal comes to know a message only through the medium of communication—*what* a person has to say and *how* that person says it.

Informational Strategies Communicators often struggle with how to structure and then present an argument to maximize its impact. Should a message be long and crammed with facts or short and to the point? Is it better to present a highly partisan, one-sided message or take a more balanced, two-sided approach? And how should the various arguments be ordered— from strongest to weakest or the other way around? These are the kinds of questions often studied by persuasion researchers (Crano & Prislin, 2008; Petty et al., 1997), including those interested in advertising and consumer behavior (Loken, 2006).

Often the most effective strategy to use will depend on whether members of the audience process the message on the central or the peripheral route. Consider the length of a communication. When people process a message lazily, with their eyes and ears half-closed, they often fall back on a simple heuristic: The longer a message, the more valid it must be. In this case, a large number of words gives the superficial appearance of factual support regardless of the quality of the arguments (Petty & Cacioppo, 1984; Wood et al., 1985). Thus, as David Ogilvy (1985) concluded from his years of advertising experience, "The more facts you tell, the more you sell" (p. 88).

When people process a communication carefully, however, length is a two-edged sword. If a message is long because it contains lots of supporting information, then longer does mean better. The more supportive arguments you can offer or the more sources you can find to speak on your behalf, the more persuasive your appeal will be (Harkins & Petty, 1981). But if the added arguments are weak or if the new sources are redundant, then an alert audience will not be fooled by length alone. When adding to the length of a message dilutes its quality, an appeal might well *lose* impact (Friedrich et al., 1996; Harkins & Petty, 1987).

When two opposing sides try to persuade the same audience, order of presentation becomes a relevant factor as well. During the summer of 2008, before the November presidential election, the Democrats held their national convention a few days before the incumbent Republicans held theirs. These events were watched on television by millions of voters. Do you think the order in which they were scheduled gave one party an advantage? If you believe that information that is presented first has more impact, you'd predict *a primacy effect* (advantage to the Democrats). If you believe that the information presented last has the edge, you'd predict a *recency effect* (advantage to the Republicans).

There are good reasons for both predictions. On the one hand, first impressions are important. On the other hand, memory fades over time, and people often recall only the last argument they hear before making a decision. In light of these contrasting predictions, Norman Miller and Donald Campbell (1959) searched for the "missing link" that would determine the relative effects of primacy and recency. They discovered that the missing link is *time*. In a study of jury simulations, they had people (1) read a summary of the plaintiff's case; (2) read a summary of the defendant's case; and (3) make a decision. The researchers varied how much time separated the two messages and then how much time elapsed between the second message and the decisions. When participants read the second message right after the first and then waited a whole week before reporting their opinion, a primacy effect prevailed and the side that came first was favored. Both messages faded equally from memory, so only the greater impact of first impressions was left. Yet when participants made a decision immediately after the second message but a full week after the first, there was a recency effect. The second argument was fresher in memory, thus favoring the side that went last. Using these results as a guideline, let's return to our original question: What is the impact on Election Day of how the national conventions are scheduled? Think for a moment about the placement and timing of these events. The answer appears in Table 6.2.

"It is a superb vision of America, all right, but I can't remember which candidate projected it."

Research on the sleeper effect shows that people often remember the message but forget the source.

Message Discrepancy Persuasion is a process of changing attitudes. But just how much change should a communicator seek? Before addressing any audience, speakers confront what is perhaps the most critical strategic question: How extreme a position should they take? How *discrepant* should a message be from the audience's existing position in order to have the greatest impact? Common sense suggests two opposite answers. One approach is to take an extreme position in the hope that the more change you advocate, the more you will get. Another approach is to exercise caution and not push for too much change so that the audience will not reject the

TABLE 6.2

Effects of Presentation Order and Timing on Persuasion

A study by Miller and Campbell (1959) demonstrated the effect of presentation order and the timing of opposing arguments on persuasion. As applied to our example, the Democratic and Republican conventions resemble the fourth row of this table. From these results, it seems that the scheduling of such events is fair, promoting neither primacy nor recency.

		Conditions				Results
1. **Message 1**	**Message 2**	One week	Decision			**Primacy**
2. **Message 1**	One week	**Message 2**	Decision			**Recency**
3. **Message 1**	**Message 2**	Decision				None
4. **Message 1**	One week	**Message 2**	One week	Decision		None

message outright. Which approach seems more effective? Imagine trying to convert your politically conservative friends into liberals or the other way around. Would you stake out a radical position in order to move them toward the center or would you preach moderation so as not to be cast aside?

Research shows that communicators should adopt the second, more cautious approach. To be sure, some discrepancy is needed to produce a change in attitude. But the relationship to persuasion can be pictured as an upside-down U with the most change being produced at moderate amounts of discrepancy (Bochner & Insko, 1966). A study by Kari Edwards and Edward Smith (1996) helps explain why taking a more extreme position is counterproductive. These investigators first measured people's attitudes on a number of hot social issues—for example, whether lesbian and gay couples should adopt children, whether employers should give preference in hiring to minorities, and whether the death penalty should be abolished. Several weeks later, they asked the same people to read, think about, and rate arguments that were either consistent or inconsistent with their own prior attitudes. The result: When given arguments to read that preached attitudes that were discrepant from their own, the participants spent more time scrutinizing the material and judged the arguments to be weak. Apparently, people tend to refute and reject persuasive messages they don't agree with. In fact, the more personally important an issue is to us, the more stubborn and resistant to change we become (Zuwerink & Devine, 1996).

Fear Appeals   Many trial lawyers say that to win cases they have to appeal to jurors through the heart rather than through the mind. The evidence is important, they admit, but it also matters whether the jury reacts to their client with anger, disgust, sympathy, or sadness. Of course, very few messages are entirely based on rational argument or on emotion.

Fear is a particularly primitive and powerful emotion, serving as an early warning system that signals danger. Neuroscience research shows that fear is aroused instantly in response to pain, stimulation from noxious substances, or threat, enabling us to respond quickly without having to stop to think about it (LeDoux, 1996). Not surprisingly, the use of fear-based appeals to change attitudes is common. Certain religious cults use scare tactics to indoctrinate new members. So do public health organizations that often graphically portray the damage done to those who smoke cigarettes, use drugs, overeat, and engage in unprotected sex.

Political campaigns are notorious for exploiting fear through negative advertising. The most hard-hitting and controversial ever was a TV commercial that aired just once, on September 7, 1964. In an ad to reelect Democratic president Lyndon Johnson, who was running against Republican Barry Goldwater, a young girl pictured in a field counted to 10 as she picked the petals off a daisy. As she reached 9, an adult voice broke in to count down from 10 to 0, followed by a blinding nuclear explosion and this message: "Vote for President Johnson on November 3. The stakes are too high for you to stay home."

The effects of fear arousal in politics are still evident today. Guided by Terror Management Theory (Greenberg et al., 1997; Pyszczynski et al., 2003; see Chapter 3) and the prediction that a deeply rooted fear of death motivates people to rally around their leaders as a way to ward off anxiety, Mark Landau and his colleagues (2004) found that college students expressed more support for former president George W. Bush and his policies when they were reminded of their own mortality or subliminally exposed to

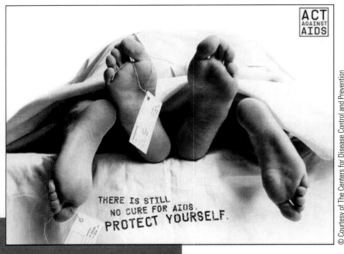

ACT AGAINST AIDS

THERE IS STILL NO CURE FOR AIDS. PROTECT YOURSELF.

© Courtesy of The Centers for Disease Control and Prevention

Public health organizations often use fear, or scare tactics, to change health-related attitudes and behavior.

images of 9/11 than when they were not. This result is not limited to the laboratory. Analyzing patterns of government-issued terror warnings and Gallup polls, Robb Willer (2004) found that increased terror alerts were predictably followed by increases in presidential approval ratings.

Is fear similarly effective for commercial purposes? What about using fear to promote health and safety? If you're interested in public service advertising, visit the website of the Ad Council, the organization that created Smokey the Bear ("Only you can prevent forest fires") and the crash test dummies ("Don't be a dummy—buckle up"). Currently, the Ad Council is running campaigns on a range of issues, including the use of steroids, flu prevention, cyberbullying, and the online sexploitation of youth. To get people to change behavior in domains of this nature, is it better to arouse a little nervousness or

"How often have you asked yourselves 'who would pay the ransom if I were kidnapped by terrorists?' "

a full-blown anxiety attack? To answer these questions, social psychologists over the years have compared communications that vary in the levels of fear they arouse. In the first such study, Irving Janis and Seymour Feshbach (1953) found that high levels of fear did not generate increased agreement with a persuasive communication. Since then, however, research has shown that appeals that arouse high levels of fear can be highly effective (de Hoog et al., 2007).

Fear arousal increases the incentive to change for those who do not actively resist it, but its ultimate impact depends on the strength of the arguments and on whether the message also contains reassuring advice on how to cope with the threatened danger (Keller, 1999; Leventhal, 1970; Rogers, 1983). This last point is important. Without specific instructions on how to cope, people feel helpless and they panic and tune out the message. In one study, for example, participants with a chronic fear of cancer were less likely than others to detect the logical errors in a message that called for regular cancer checkups (Jepson & Chaiken, 1990). When clear instructions are included, however, high dosages of fear can be effective. In the past, research had shown that antismoking films elicit more negative attitudes toward cigarettes when they show gory lung-cancer operations than when they show charts filled with dry statistics (Leventhal et al., 1967) and that films about driving safety are more effective when they show bloody accident victims than when they show plastic crash test dummies (Rogers & Mewborn, 1976). In a recent meta-analysis of 105 studies, however, Natascha de Hoog and others (2007) found that communications that arouse fear need not be gruesome to be effective. Simply put, the more personally vulnerable people feel about a threatened outcome, the more attentive they are to the message and the more likely they are to follow the recommendations contained within it (Das et al., 2003; de Hoog et al., 2005).

Positive Emotions   It's interesting that just as fear helps induce a change in attitude, so does positive emotion. In one study, people were more likely to agree with a series of controversial arguments when they snacked on peanuts and soda than when they did not eat (Janis et al., 1965). In another study, participants liked a television commercial more when it was embedded in a program that was upbeat rather than sad (Mathur & Chattopadhyay, 1991). Research shows that people are "soft touches" when they are in a good mood. Depending on the situation, food, drinks, a soft reclining chair, tender memories, an experience of success, breathtaking scenery, and

Suggesting that a fear of death leads people to rally around their leaders, public opinion polls have shown that as terror threat levels increase, so do presidential approval ratings.

pleasant music can lull us into a positive emotional state that is ripe for persuasion (Schwarz et al., 1991).

According to Alice Isen (1984), people see the world through rose-colored glasses when they are feeling good. Filled with high spirits, we become more sociable, more generous, and generally more positive in our outlook. We also make decisions more quickly and with relatively little thought. The result: Positive feelings activate the peripheral route to persuasion, facilitating change and allowing superficial cues to take on added importance (Petty et al., 1993; Worth & Mackie, 1987).

What is it about feeling good that leads us to take shortcuts to persuasion rather than the more effortful central route? There are three possible explanations. One is that a positive emotional state is cognitively distracting, causing the mind to wander and impairing our ability to think critically about the persuasive arguments (Mackie & Worth, 1989; Mackie et al., 1992). A second explanation is that when people are in a good mood, they assume that all is well, let down their guard, and become somewhat lazy processors of information (Schwarz, 1990). A third explanation is that when people are happy, they become motivated to savor the moment and maintain their happy mood rather than spoiling it by thinking critically about new information (Wegener & Petty, 1994).

This last notion raises an interesting question: What if happy people are presented with a positive and uplifting persuasive message? Would they still appear cognitively distracted, or lazy, or would they pay close attention in order to prolong the rosy glow? To find out, Duane Wegener and others (1995) showed some college students a funny segment from *The Late Show with David Letterman*. Others, less fortunate, watched a somber scene from an HBO movie called *You Don't Have to Die*. The students were then asked to read and evaluate either an uplifting article they agreed with about a new plan to cut tuition or a distressing article they disagreed with about a new plan to raise tuition. In half the cases, the article they read contained strong arguments; in the other cases, the arguments were weak. Did the students read the material carefully enough to distinguish between the strong and weak arguments? Those in the somber condition clearly did. Among those in the happy condition, however, the response depended on whether they expected the message to be one they wanted to hear. When the happy students read about a tuition increase, they tuned out and were equally persuaded by the strong and weak arguments. When they read about the proposal to cut tuition, however, they were persuaded more when the arguments were strong than when they were weak. Because they were in a good mood and were receiving an agreeable message that would not spoil it, these happy students took the effortful central route to persuasion.

Subliminal Messages   In 1957, Vance Packard published *The Hidden Persuaders*, an exposé of Madison Avenue. As the book climbed the best-seller list, it awakened in the public a fear of being manipulated by forces they could not see or hear. What had Packard uncovered? In the 1950s, amid growing fears of communism and the birth of rock 'n' roll, a number of advertisers were said to have used *subliminal advertising*, the presentation of commercial messages outside of conscious awareness. It all started in a drive-in movie theater in New Jersey, where the words "Drink Coke" and "Eat popcorn" were secretly flashed on the screen during intermissions for a third of a millisecond. Although the audience never noticed the message, Coke sales were said to have increased 18 percent and popcorn sales 58 percent over a six-week period (Brean, 1958).

This incident was followed by several others. A Seattle radio station presented subaudible anti-TV messages during its programs ("TV is a bore"), and department stores played music tapes over public address systems that contained subaudible warnings about theft ("If you steal, you'll get caught"). Later, in books entitled *Subliminal Seduction* (1973) and *The Age of Manipulation* (1989), William Bryan Key charged that advertisers routinely sneak faint sexual images in visual ads to heighten the appeal of their products. Several years ago, concerns were also raised about subliminal messages in rock music. In one case, the families of two boys who committed suicide blamed the British rock group Judas Priest for subliminal lyrics ("Do it") that promoted satanism and suicide (*National Law Journal*, 1990). Although the families lost their case, it's clear that many people believe in the power of hidden persuaders.

At the time the story about the New Jersey theater broke, research on the topic was so sketchy and the public so outraged by the sinister implications that the matter was quickly dropped. But today there is renewed interest in subliminal influences as well as new research developments. In one recent field study, for example, researchers played traditional German or French music on alternating days for two weeks at a supermarket display of wines. Keeping track of sales, the researchers found that of the total number of wines bought, 83 percent were German on German-music days and 65 percent were French on French-music days. Yet when asked the reasons for their choices, customers did not cite the music as a factor, suggesting that they were not aware of the effect it had on them (North et al., 1999).

Current uses of subliminal influence are varied. In what is a multimillion-dollar industry, companies today sell self-help videos, tapes, and CDs that play New Age music or nature sounds and also contain fleeting messages that promise to help you relax, lose weight, stop smoking, make friends, raise self-esteem, and even improve your sex life. Can subliminal messages reflexively trigger behavior without our awareness? In 1982, Timothy Moore reviewed the existing research and concluded that "what you see is what you get"—nothing, "complete scams." Moore was right. The original story about the Coke-and-popcorn messages at the New Jersey theater was later exposed as a publicity stunt and hoax (Pratkanis, 1992). To further complicate matters, controlled experiments using subliminal self-help CDs that promise to raise self-esteem, improve memory, or lose weight show that these products offer no therapeutic benefits (Greenwald et al., 1991; Merikle & Skanes, 1992).

If there is no solid evidence of subliminal influence, why, you may wonder, does research demonstrate perception without awareness in studies of priming (described elsewhere in this book) but not in studies of subliminal persuasion? If you think about it, the two sets of claims are different. In the laboratory, subliminal exposures have a short-term effect on simple judgments and actions. But in claims of subliminal persuasion, the exposure is presumed to have long-term effects on eating, drinking, consumer purchases, voter sentiment, or even the most profound of violent acts, suicide. Psychologists agree that people can process information at an unconscious level, but they're quick to caution that this processing is "analytically limited" (Greenwald, 1992).

Perhaps people *perceive* subliminal cues but are not *persuaded* into action unless they are motivated to do so. To test this hypothesis, Erin Strahan and others (2002) brought thirsty college students into the laboratory for a marketing study

PEOPLE HAVE BEEN TRYING TO FIND THE BREASTS IN THESE ICE CUBES SINCE 1957.

The advertising industry is sometimes charged with sneaking seductive little pictures into ads.

Supposedly, these pictures can get you to buy a product without your even seeing them.

Consider the photograph above. According to some people, there's a pair of female breasts hidden in the patterns of light refracted by the ice cubes.

Well, if you really searched you probably *could* see the breasts. For that matter, you could also see Millard Fillmore, a stuffed pork chop and a 1946 Dodge.

The point is that so-called "subliminal advertising" simply doesn't exist. Overactive imaginations, however, most certainly do.

So if anyone claims to see breasts in that drink up there, they aren't in the ice cubes.

They're in the eye of the beholder.

ADVERTISING
ANOTHER WORD FOR FREEDOM OF CHOICE.
American Association of Advertising Agencies

Courtesy of American Association of Advertising Agencies

For years, advertisers have defended against the charge that they embed suggestive and sexual images in print ads. This piece by the American Association of Advertising Agencies addresses the claim.

People are most easily persuaded by commercial messages that are presented without their awareness. **FALSE.**

and provided drinking water to some but not to others. Then, as part of a test administered by computer, they subliminally exposed these students to neutral words (*pirate*, *won*) or to thirst-related words (*thirst*, *dry*). Did the subliminal "thirsty" message later lead the students, like automatons, to drink more in a taste test of Kool-Aid beverages? Yes and no. ▶ Figure 6.8 shows that the subliminal thirst primes had little impact on students whose thirst had just been quenched, but they quite clearly increased consumption among those who were thirsty and had been deprived of water. For a subliminal message to influence behavior, it has to strike "while the iron is hot."

Other researchers have since extended this interesting effect in important ways. In one study, participants who were subliminally presented with the name of a specific soft drink, Lipton Ice, were later more likely to report that they would select that particular brand over others—provided they were thirsty (Karremans et al., 2006). In a second study, participants were subliminally presented with a logo for one brand of dextrose (a sugar pill) or another, after which they worked on a task that required intense concentration. The results showed that when given an opportunity to enhance their concentration, participants were more likely to select and consume the subliminally advertised brand than the other brand—provided they were mentally tired and in need of a boost (Bermeitinger et al., 2009).

◼ The Audience

Although source and message factors are important, the astute communicator must also take his or her audience into account. Presentation strategies that succeed with some people fail with others. Audiences on the central route to persuasion, for example, bear little resemblance to those found strolling along the peripheral route. In this section, we'll see that the impact of a message is influenced by two additional factors: the recipient's personality and his or her expectations.

Right from the start, social psychologists tried to identify types of people who were more or less vulnerable to persuasion. But it turned out that very few individuals are *consistently* easy or difficult to persuade. Based on this insight, the search for individual and group differences is now guided by an interactionist perspective. Assuming that each of us can be persuaded more in some settings than in others, researchers look for an appropriate "match" between characteristics of the message and the audience. So, what kinds of messages turn you on?

The Need for Cognition Earlier, we saw that people tend to process information more carefully when they are highly involved. Involvement can be determined by the importance and self-relevance of a message. According to Cacioppo and Petty (1982), however, there are also individual differences in the extent to which people become involved and take the central route to persuasion. Specifically, they have found that individuals differ in the extent to which they enjoy and participate in effortful cognitive activities, or, as they call it, the **need for cognition (NC)**. People who are high rather than low in their need for cognition like to work on hard problems, search for clues, make fine distinctions, and analyze situations. These differences can be identi-

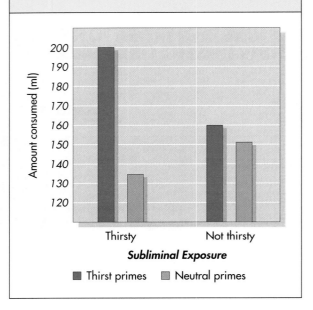

▶FIGURE 6.8

Subliminal Influence

Thirsty and nonthirsty research participants were subliminally exposed to neutral or thirst-related words. Afterward they participated in a beverage taste test in which the amount they drank was measured. You can see that the subliminal thirst cues had little impact on nonthirsty participants but that they did increase consumption among those who were thirsty. Apparently, subliminal cues can influence our behavior when we are otherwise predisposed.

Strahan et al., 2002.

need for cognition (NC)
A personality variable that distinguishes people on the basis of how much they enjoy effortful cognitive activities.

fied by the items contained in the Need for Cognition Scale, some of which appear in Table 6.3.

The need for cognition has interesting implications for changing attitudes. If people are prone to approach or avoid effortful cognitive activities, then the prepared communicator could design messages unique to a particular audience. In theory, the high-NC audience should receive information-oriented appeals and the low-NC audience should be treated to appeals that rely on the use of peripheral cues. The theory is fine, but does it work? Can a message be customized to fit the information-processing style of its recipients? In one test of this hypothesis, participants read an editorial that consisted of either a strong or a weak set of arguments. As predicted, the higher their NC scores were, the more the participants thought about the material, the better they later recalled it, and the more persuaded they were by the strength of its arguments (Cacioppo et al., 1983). In contrast, people who are low in the need for cognition are persuaded by cues found along the peripheral route, such as a speaker's reputation and physical appearance, the overt reactions of others in the audience, and a positive mood state (Cacioppo et al., 1996). At times, they are mindlessly influenced by a reputable source even when his or her arguments are weak (Kaufman et al., 1999).

TABLE 6.3
Need for Cognition Scale: Sample Items
Are you high or low in the need for cognition? These statements are taken from the NC Scale. If you agree with items 1, 3, and 5 and disagree with items 2, 4, and 6, you would probably be regarded as high in NC.
1. I really enjoy a task that involves coming up with new solutions to problems.
2. Thinking is not my idea of fun.
3. The notion of thinking abstractly is appealing to me.
4. I like tasks that require little thought once I've learned them.
5. I usually end up deliberating about issues even when they do not affect me personally.
5. It's enough for me that something gets the job done; I don't care how or why it works.
Cacioppo & Petty, 1982.

Self-Monitoring   Just as people high in the need for cognition crave information, other personality traits are associated with an attraction to other kinds of messages. Consider the trait of *self-monitoring*. As described in Chapter 3, high self-monitors regulate their behavior from one situation to another out of concern for public self-presentation. Low self-monitors are less image conscious and behave instead according to their own beliefs, values, and preferences. In the context of persuasion, high self-monitors may be particularly responsive to messages that promise desirable social images. Whether the product is beer, soda, blue jeans, or cars, this technique is common in advertising, where often the image is the message.

To test the self-monitoring hypothesis, Mark Snyder and Kenneth DeBono (1985) showed image- or information-oriented print ads to high and low self-monitors. In an ad for Irish Mocha Mint coffee, for example, a man and woman were depicted as relaxing in a candlelit room over a steamy cup of coffee. The image-oriented version promised to "Make a chilly night become a cozy evening," while the informational version offered "a delicious blend of three great flavors—coffee, chocolate, and mint." As predicted, high self-monitors were willing to pay more for products after reading imagery ads, while low self-monitors were influenced more by information-oriented appeals. Imagery can even influence the way that high self-monitors evaluate a product, independent of its quality. DeBono and his colleagues (2003) presented people with one of two perfume samples packaged in more or less attractive bottles. Whereas low self-monitors preferred the more pleasant-scented fragrance, high self-monitors preferred whatever scent came from the more attractive bottles.

Regulatory Fit   Setting aside your political views, do you find yourself drawn to some *types* of speeches, arguments, editorials, and television commercials more than others? Joseph Cesario and others (2004) proposed that people are more likely to be influenced by messages that fit their frame of mind and "feel right." In particular, they noted that in an effort to regulate their own emotion state, some individuals are promotion-oriented (drawn to the pursuit of success, achievement, and their ideals), while others are more prevention-oriented (protective of what they have, fearful of failure, and vigilant about avoiding loss). Do these differing outlooks on life make people more responsive to some types of persuasive messages than others? To find out, these researchers presented two versions of an article advocating for a new after-school children's program. They found that promotion-motivated participants were more persuaded by the article when the arguments in it were framed in promotional terms ("because it will *advance* children's education and *support* more children to *succeed*"), while prevention-motivated participants were persuaded more when the very same arguments were framed in more defensive terms ("because it will *secure* children's education and *prevent* more children from *failing*").

In a follow-up study, Cesario and Higgins (2008) found that audience members are also influenced when a speaker's nonverbal style fits their motivational orientations. Watching a high school teacher deliver the same communication concerning a new after-school program, promotion-motivated participants were more receptive when the speaker exhibited an "eager" delivery style (fast, animated, and forward leaning, with hand gestures projecting outward), while prevention-oriented participants were more receptive when he displayed a cautious style (slow, precise, and backward leaning, with hand gestures pushing in).

There are plenty of other ways that you may be more comfortable with some types of messages than others. We saw earlier that some of us are high in the need for cognition, enjoying effortful forms of reasoning and problem solving. Some of us are also high in the need for affect, seeking out and enjoying feelings of strong emotion. In matters of persuasion, these traits lead people to be more receptive to messages that are presented in primarily cognitive or emotional terms (Haddock et al., 2008).

Forewarning and Resistance   When our attitudes or values come under attack, we can succumb to the challenge and change the attitude or we can resist it and maintain the attitude. There are different means of resistance. In a series of studies, Julia Jacks and Kimberly Cameron (2003) asked people to describe and rate the ways that they manage to resist persuasion in their attitudes on abortion or the death penalty. They identified seven strategies, the most common being attitude bolstering ("I think about all the reasons I believe the way I do") and the least common being source derogation ("I look for faults in the person who challenges my belief"). These means of resistance are listed in Table 6.4.

What leads people to invoke these mechanisms of resistance? Does it help to be forewarned that your attitude is about to come under attack? Perhaps the toughest audience to persuade is the one that knows you're coming. When people are aware that someone is trying to change their attitude, they become more likely to resist. All they need is some time to collect their thoughts and come up with a good defense. Jonathan Freedman and David Sears (1965) first discovered this when they told high school seniors to expect a speech on why teenagers should not be allowed to drive (an unpopular position, as you can imagine). The students were warned either two or ten minutes before the talk began or not at all. Those who were the victims of a sneak attack were the most likely to succumb to

TABLE 6.4	
Strategies for Resisting Persuasion	
Strategy	Example
Attitude bolstering	"I reassure myself of facts that support the validity of my belief."
Counterarguing	"I would talk to myself and play devil's advocate."
Social validation	"I also rely on others with the same opinion to be there for me."
Negative affect	"I tend to get angry when someone tries to change my beliefs."
Assertions of confidence	"I doubt anybody could change my viewpoint."
Selective exposure	"Most of the time I just ignore them."
Source derogation	"I look for faults in the person presenting the challenging belief."

the speaker's position. Those who had a full ten minutes' warning were the least likely to agree. To be forewarned is to be forearmed. But why?

At least two processes are at work here. To understand them, let's take a closer look at what forewarning does. Participants in the Freedman and Sears (1965) study were put on notice in two ways: (1) They were informed of the position the speaker would take; and (2) they were told that the speaker intended to change their opinion. Psychologically, these two aspects of forewarning have different effects.

The first effect is purely cognitive. Knowing in advance what position a speaker will take enables us to come up with counterarguments and, as a result, to become more resistant to change. To explain this effect, William McGuire (1964) drew an analogy: Protecting a person's attitudes from persuasion, he said, is like inoculating the human body against disease. In medicine, injecting a small dose of infection into a patient stimulates the body to build up a resistance to it. According to this **inoculation hypothesis**, an attitude can be immunized the same way. As with flu shots and other vaccines, our defenses can be reinforced by exposure to weak doses of the opposing position before we actually encounter the full presentation. Studies of negative political ads show that inoculation can be used to combat the kinds of attack messages that sometimes win elections (Pfau et al., 1990).

Simply knowing that someone is trying to persuade us also elicits a motivational reaction as we brace ourselves to resist the attempt regardless of what position is taken. As a TV viewer, you have no doubt heard the phrase "And now, we pause for a message from our sponsor." What does this warning tell us? Not knowing yet who the sponsor is, even the grouchiest among us is in no position to object. Yet imagine how you would feel if an experimenter said to you, "In just a few minutes, you will hear a message prepared according to well-established principles of persuasion and designed to induce you to change your attitudes." If you are like the participants who actually heard this forewarning, you might be tempted to reply, "Oh yeah? Try me!" Indeed, subjects rejected that message without counterargument and without much advance notice (Hass & Grady, 1975).

When people think that someone is trying to change their attitude or otherwise manipulate them, a red flag goes up. That red flag is called **psychological reactance**. According to Jack Brehm's theory of psychological reactance, all of us want the freedom to think, feel, and act as we (not others) choose. When we sense that a cherished freedom is being threatened, we become motivated to maintain it. And when we sense that a freedom is slipping away, we try to restore it (Brehm & Brehm, 1981). One possible result is that when a communicator comes on too strongly, we may react with *negative attitude change* by moving in the direction that is the opposite of the one being advocated—even, ironically, when the speaker's position agrees with our own (Heller et al., 1973). Sometimes, the motive to protect our freedom to think as we choose trumps our desire to hold a specific opinion. Reactance can trigger resistance to persuasion in two ways. Once aroused, the reactant target of attempted persuasion may simply shut down in a reflex-like response or disagree in a more thoughtful manner by questioning the credibility of the source and counterarguing the message (Silvia, 2006).

It's important to realize that forewarning does not always increase resistance to persuasion because the effects are not that simple. Based on a meta-analysis of 48 experiments, Wendy Wood and Jeffrey Quinn (2003) found that when people are forewarned about an impending persuasive appeal on a topic that is personally not that important, they start to agree before they even receive the message in order to keep from appearing vulnerable to influence. Yet when people are forewarned about a persuasive appeal on a topic of personal importance, they feel threatened and think up counterarguments to bolster their attitude. This cognitive response strengthens their resistance to change once that appeal is delivered.

To do just the opposite is also a form of imitation.

—Lichtenberg

inoculation hypothesis
The idea that exposure to weak versions of a persuasive argument increases later resistance to that argument.

psychological reactance
The theory that people react against threats to their freedom by asserting themselves and perceiving the threatened freedom as more attractive.

In a series of print ads, Apple Computer featured Thomas Edison and other creative geniuses who dared to "think different." In a marketing campaign that paid tribute to individualism, Apple saluted "the crazy ones. The misfits. The rebels. The troublemakers. The round pegs in the square holes. The ones who see things differently."

Culture and Persuasion

A communication is persuasive to the extent that the source is favorable and the message, however it is presented, meets the psychological needs of its audience. In this regard, cultural factors also play a subtle but important role.

In earlier chapters, we saw that cultures differ in the extent to which people are oriented toward individualism or collectivism. In light of these differences, Sang-Pil Han and Sharon Shavitt (1994) compared the contents of magazine advertisements in the United States, an individualistic country, and Korea, a country with a collectivistic orientation. They found that while American advertising campaigns were focused more on personal benefits, individuality, competition, and self-improvement ("She's got a style all her own"; "Make your way through the crowd"), Korean ads appealed more to the integrity, achievement, and well-being of one's ingroups ("An exhilarating way to provide for your family"; "Celebrating a half-century of partnership"). Clearly, there are different ways to appeal to the members of these two cultures. In a second study, Han and Shavitt created two sets of ads for various products. One set portrayed individuals ("Treat yourself to a breath-freshening experience"), and the other set featured groups ("Share this breath-freshening experience"). Both sets were presented to American and Korean participants. The result: Americans were persuaded more by individualistic ads and Koreans preferred collectivistic ads. Similar differences are found in the way celebrity endorsements are used in the two cultures. In the United States, celebrities tend to portray themselves using or talking directly about a product; in Korean commercials that appeal to belongingness, family, and traditional values, celebrities are more likely to play the role of someone else without being singled out (Choi et al., 2005).

As people from all over the world come into contact with each other through travel, satellite television, international trade agreements, and the Internet, cultural values begin to change. Just as humans develop as they get older, cultures sometimes change over time from one generation to the next. Recent and substantial modernization efforts in China—home to 21 out of every 100 people on the planet—illustrate the point. There is so much recent change that Zhang and Shavitt (2003) sought to compare the contents of television commercials, which are primarily directed at the traditional mass market, with advertisements in new magazines that specifically target 18- to 35-year-old, educated, high-income citizens who constitute China's "X-generation." Based on their analysis of 463 ads, they found that while traditional and collectivist values predominated on mainstream TV, magazine ads were characterized by more modern and individualistic impulses. To be persuasive, a message should appeal to the culturally shared values of its audience.

Persuasion by Our Own Actions

Anyone who has ever acted on stage knows how easy it is to become so absorbed in a role that the experience seems real. Feigned laughter can make an actor feel happy, and crocodile tears can turn into sadness. Even in real life, the effect can be dramatic. In 1974, Patty Hearst, a sheltered college student from a wealthy California family, was kidnapped. By the time she was arrested months later, she was a gun-toting revolutionary who called herself Tania. How could someone be so totally converted? In Hearst's own words, "I had thought I was humoring [my captors] by parroting their clichés and buzzwords without believing in them. . . . In trying to convince them I convinced myself" (Hearst, 1982).

▣ Role Playing: All the World's a Stage

The Patty Hearst case illustrates the powerful effects of *role playing*. Of course, you don't have to be kidnapped or terrorized to know how it feels to be coaxed into behavior that is at odds with your inner convictions. People frequently engage in attitude-discrepant behavior as part of a job, for example, or to please others. As commonplace as this seems, it raises a profound question. When we play along, saying and doing things that are privately discrepant from our own attitudes, do we begin to change those attitudes as a result? How we feel can determine the way we act. Is it also possible that the way we act can determine how we feel?

According to Irving Janis (1968), attitude change persists more when it is inspired by our own behavior than when it stems from a passive exposure to a persuasive communication. Janis conducted a study in which one group of participants listened to a speech that challenged their positions on a topic and others were handed an outline and asked to give the speech themselves. As predicted, participants changed their attitudes more after giving the speech than after listening to it (Janis & King, 1954). According to Janis, role playing works to change attitudes because it forces people to learn the message. Hence, people tend to remember arguments they come up with on their own better than they remember arguments provided to them by other people (Slamecka & Graff, 1978). In fact, attitude change is more enduring even when people who read a persuasive message merely *expect* that they will later have to communicate it to others (Boninger et al., 1990).

Posing as a revolutionary named Tania, Patty Hearst was converted by the role her captors forced her to play. "In trying to convince them I convinced myself," she said.

But there's more to role playing than improved memory. The effects of enacting a role can be staggering, in part because it is so easy to confuse what we do or what we say with how we really feel. Think about the times you've dished out compliments you didn't mean or flashed a smile at someone you didn't like or nodded your head in response to a statement you disagreed with. We often shade what we say just to please a particular listener. What's fascinating is not that we make adjustments to suit others but that this role playing has such powerful effects on our own private attitudes. For example, participants in one study read about a man and then described him to someone else, who supposedly liked or disliked him. As you might expect, they described the man in more positive terms when their listener was favorably disposed. In the process, however, they also convinced themselves. At least to some extent, "saying is believing" (Higgins & Rholes, 1978).

Consider the implications. We know that attitudes influence behavior, as when people help those whom they like and hurt those whom they dislike. But research on role playing emphasizes the flip side of the coin—that behavior can change attitudes. Perhaps we come to like people because we have helped them and blame people whom we have hurt. To change people's inner feelings, then, maybe we should begin by focusing on their behavior. Why do people experience changes of attitude in response to changes in their own behavior? One answer to this question is provided by the theory of cognitive dissonance.

Cognitive Dissonance Theory: The Classic Version

Many social psychologists believe that people are strongly motivated by a desire for cognitive consistency—a state of mind in which one's beliefs, attitudes, and behaviors are compatible with each other (Abelson et al., 1968). Cognitive consistency theories seem to presuppose that people are generally logical. However, Leon Festinger (1957) turned this assumption on its head. Struck by the irrationalities of human behavior, Festinger proposed **cognitive dissonance theory**, which states that a powerful motive to maintain cognitive consistency can give rise to irrational, sometimes maladaptive behavior.

According to Festinger, all of us hold many cognitions about ourselves and the world around us. These cognitions include everything we know about our own beliefs, attitudes, and behavior. Although generally our cognitions coexist peacefully, at times they clash. Consider some examples. You say you're on a diet, yet you just dove head-first into a tub of chocolate fudge brownie ice cream. Or you waited in line for hours to get into a concert and then the band proved to be disappointing. Or you baked for hours under the hot summer sun while listening to your iPod even though you knew the health risks. Each of these scenarios harbors inconsistency and conflict. You have already committed yourself to a course of action, yet you realize that the action is inconsistent with your attitude.

Under certain conditions, discrepancies such as these can evoke an unpleasant state of tension known as cognitive dissonance. But discrepancy doesn't always produce dissonance. If you broke a diet for a Thanksgiving dinner with family, your indiscretion would not lead you to experience dissonance. Or if you mistakenly thought the ice cream you ate was low in calories only to find out the truth later, then, again, you would not experience much dissonance. As we'll see, what really hurts is the knowledge that you committed yourself to an attitude-discrepant behavior freely and with some knowledge of the consequences. When that happens, dissonance is aroused and you become motivated to reduce it. As shown in Table 6.5, there are many possible ways to reduce dissonance, such as rationalizing that everyone else is also a hypocrite (McKimmie et al., 2003), denying personal responsibility for the behavior (Gosling et al., 2006), and trivializing the issue in question (Starzyk et al., 2009). Of course, sometimes the easiest way to reduce dissonance is to change your attitude to bring it in line with your behavior.

Right from the start, cognitive dissonance theory captured the imagination. Festinger's basic proposition is simple, yet its implications are far-reaching. In this section, we examine three research areas that demonstrate the breadth of what dissonance theory has to say about attitude change.

Justifying Attitude-Discrepant Behavior: When Doing Is Believing   Imagine for a moment that you are a participant in the classic study by Leon Festinger and J. Merrill Carlsmith (1959). As soon as you arrive, you are greeted by an experimenter who says that he is interested in various measures of performance. Wondering what that means, you all too quickly find out. The experimenter hands you a wooden board con-

---

TABLE 6.5

Ways to Reduce Dissonance

"I need to be on a diet, yet I just dove head first into a tub of chocolate fudge brownie ice cream." If this were you, how would you reduce dissonance aroused by the discrepancy between your attitude and your behavior?

Techniques	Examples
Change your attitude.	"I don't really need to be on a diet."
Change your perception of the behavior.	"I hardly ate any ice cream."
Add consonant cognitions.	"Chocolate ice cream is very nutritious."
Minimize the importance. of the conflict	"I don't care if I'm overweight—life is short!"
Reduce perceived choice.	"I had no choice; the ice cream was served for this special occasion."

Man is the only animal that learns by being hypocritical. He pretends to be polite and then, eventually, he becomes polite.

—Jean Kerr

cognitive dissonance theory The theory that holding inconsistent cognitions arouses psychological tension that people become motivated to reduce.

taining 48 square pegs in square holes and asks you to turn each peg a quarter turn to the left, then a quarter turn back to the right, then back to the left, then back again to the right. The routine seems endless. After 30 minutes, the experimenter comes to your rescue. Or does he? Just when you think things are looking up, he hands you another board, another assignment. For the next half-hour, you are to take 12 spools of thread off the board, put them back, take them off, and put them back again. By now, you're just about ready to tear your hair out. As you think back over better times, even the first task begins to look good.

Finally, you're done. After one of the longest hours of your life, the experimenter lets you in on a secret: There's more to this experiment than meets the eye. You were in the control group. To test the effects of motivation on performance, other participants are being told that the experiment will be fun and exciting. You don't realize it, but you are now being set up for the critical part of the study. Would you be willing to tell the next participant that the experiment is enjoyable? As you hem and haw, the experimenter offers to pay for your services. Some participants are offered one dollar; others are offered 20 dollars. In either case, you agree to help out. Before you know it, you find yourself in the waiting room trying to dupe an unsuspecting fellow student (who is really a confederate).

By means of this elaborate staged presentation, participants were goaded into an attitude-discrepant behavior, an action that was inconsistent with their private attitudes. They knew how dull the experiment really was, yet they raved about it. Did this conflict arouse cognitive dissonance? It depends on how much the participants were paid. Suppose you were one of the lucky ones offered 20 dollars for your assistance. By today's standards, that payment would be worth 80 dollars—surely a sufficient justification for telling a little white lie, right? Feeling well compensated, these participants experienced little if any dissonance. But wait. Suppose you were paid only one dollar. Surely your integrity is worth more than that, don't you think? In this instance, you have **insufficient justification** for going along, so you need a way to cope. According to Festinger (1957), unless you can deny your actions (which is not usually possible), you'll feel pressured to change your attitude about the task. If you can convince yourself that the experiment wasn't that bad, then saying it was interesting is all right.

The results were as Festinger and Carlsmith had predicted. When the experiment was presumably over, participants were asked how they felt about the peg-board tasks. Those in the control group who did not mislead a confederate openly admitted that the tasks were boring. So did those in the 20-dollar condition, who had ample justification for what they did. However, participants who were paid only one dollar rated the experiment as somewhat enjoyable. Having engaged in an attitude-discrepant act without sufficient justification, these participants reduced cognitive dissonance by changing their attitude. The results can be seen in ▶ Figure 6.9.

Two aspects of this classic study are noteworthy. First, it showed the phenomenon of self-persuasion: When people behave in ways that contradict their attitudes, they sometimes go on to change those attitudes without any exposure to a persuasive communication. Demonstrating the power of this phenomenon, Michael Leippe and Donna Eisenstadt (1994) found that white college students who were coaxed into writing essays in favor of new scholarship funds only for black students later reported

"It's a crazy idea, but it just might work."

One way to reduce dissonance is to minimize the importance of the conflict.

insufficient justification
A condition in which people freely perform an attitude-discrepant behavior without receiving a large reward.

▶ **FIGURE 6.9**

The Dissonance Classic

Participants in a boring experiment (attitude) were asked to say that it was enjoyable (behavior) to a fellow student. Those in one group were paid a dollar to lie; those in a second group were offered 20 dollars. Members of a third group, who did not have to lie, admitted that the task was boring. So did the participants paid 20 dollars, which was ample justification for telling a lie. Participants paid only one dollar, however, rated the task as more enjoyable. Behaving in an attitude-discrepant manner without justification, these latter participants reduced dissonance by changing their attitude.

Festinger & Carlsmith, 1959.

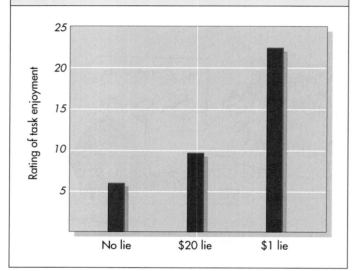

The more money you pay people to tell a lie, the more they will come to believe it. **FALSE.**

insufficient deterrence
A condition in which people refrain from engaging in a desirable activity, even when only mild punishment is threatened.

more favorable attitudes in general toward African Americans. The second major contribution of Festinger and Carlsmith's results is that they contradicted the time-honored belief that big rewards produce greater change. In fact, the more money participants were offered for their inconsistent behavior, the more justified they felt and the less likely they were to change their attitudes.

Just as a small reward provides insufficient justification for attitude-discrepant behavior, mild punishment is **insufficient deterrence** for attitude-discrepant non-behavior. Think about it. What happens when people refrain from doing something they really want to do? Do they devalue the activity and convince themselves that they never really wanted to do it in the first place? In one study, children were prohibited from playing with an attractive toy by being threatened with a mild or a severe punishment. All participants refrained. As cognitive dissonance theory predicts, however, only those faced with the mild punishment—an insufficient deterrent—later showed disdain for the forbidden toy. Those who confronted the threat of severe punishment did not (Aronson & Carlsmith, 1963). Once again, cognitive dissonance theory turned common sense on its head: The less severe the threatened punishment, the greater the attitude change produced.

Justifying Effort: Coming to Like What We Suffer For   Have you ever spent tons of money or tried really hard to achieve something, only to discover later that it wasn't worth all the effort? This kind of inconsistency between effort and outcome can arouse cognitive dissonance and motivate a change of heart toward the unsatisfying outcome. The hypothesis is simple but profound: We alter our attitudes to justify our suffering.

In a classic test of this hypothesis, Elliot Aronson and Judson Mills (1959) invited female students to take part in a series of group discussions about sex. But there was a hitch. Because sex is a sensitive topic, participants were told that they would have to pass an "embarrassment test" before joining the group. The test consisted of reading sexual material aloud in front of a male experimenter. One group of participants experienced what amounted to a *severe* initiation in which they had to recite obscene words and lurid passages taken from paperback novels. A second group underwent a *mild* initiation in which they read a list of more ordinary words pertaining to sex. A third group was admitted to the discussions without an initiation test.

Moments later, all participants were given headphones and permitted to eavesdrop on the group they would soon be joining. Actually, what they heard was a tape-recorded discussion about "secondary sex behavior in the lower animals." It was dreadfully boring. When it was over, participants were asked to rate how much they liked the group members and their discussion. Keep in mind what dissonance theory predicts: The more time or money or effort you choose to invest in something, the more anxious you will feel if the outcome proves disappointing. One way to cope with this inconsistency is to alter your attitudes. That's exactly what happened. Participants who had endured a severe initiation rated the discussion group more favorably than did those who had endured little or no initiation.

Social embarrassment is not the only kind of "effort" we feel we need to justify to ourselves. As a general rule, the more you pay for something—whether you pay in physical exertion, pain, time, or money—the more you will come to like it. This principle has provocative implications for hazing practices in fraternities and sororities, on sports teams, and in the military. Research even suggests that the harder psychotherapy patients have to work at their own treatment, the more likely they are to feel better when that treatment is over (Axsom, 1989; Axsom & Cooper, 1985).

People often come to like what they suffer for. **TRUE.**

Justifying Difficult Decisions: When Good Choices Get Even Better Whenever we make difficult decisions—whether to marry, what school to attend, or what job to accept—we feel dissonance. By definition, a decision is difficult when the alternative courses of action are about equally desirable. Marriage offers comfort and stability; staying single enables us to seek out exciting new relationships. One job might pay more money; the other may offer more interesting work. Once people make tough decisions like these, they are at risk, as negative aspects of the chosen alternatives and positive aspects of the unchosen alternatives are at odds with their decisions. According to dissonance theory, people rationalize whatever they decide by exaggerating the positive features of the chosen alternative and the negative features of the unchosen alternative.

In an early test of this hypothesis, Jack Brehm (1956) asked female participants to evaluate various consumer products, presumably as part of a marketing research project. After rating a toaster, a coffee pot, a radio, a stopwatch, and other products, participants were told that they could take one home as a gift. In the high-dissonance condition, they were offered a difficult choice between two items they found equally attractive. In the low-dissonance group, they were offered an easier choice between a desirable and an undesirable item. After receiving the gift, participants read a few research reports and then reevaluated all the products. The results provided strong support for dissonance theory. In the low-dissonance group, the participants' post-decision ratings were about the same as their pre-decision ratings. But in the high-dissonance condition, ratings increased for the chosen item and decreased for the item that was not chosen. Participants torn between two equivalent alternatives coped by reassuring themselves that they had made the right choice.

This phenomenon appears in a wide range of settings. For example, Robert Knox and James Inskter (1968) took dissonance theory to the racetrack and found that bettors who had already placed two-dollar bets on a horse were more optimistic about winning than were those still standing in line. This type of optimism may even begin to set in once a thoughtful decision is made, even before the bet is placed (Brownstein et al., 2004). Similarly, Dennis Regan and Martin Kilduff (1988) visited several polling stations on Election Day and found that voters were more likely to think that their candidates would win when they were interviewed after submitting their ballots than when they were interviewed before they submitted them. Since bets and votes cannot be taken back, people who had committed to a decision were motivated to reduce post-decision dissonance. So they convinced themselves that the decision they made was right.

© Shannon Stapleton/Reuters/Corbis

Suggesting that people need to justify difficult irrevocable decisions to quell the dissonance they arouse, researchers found that gamblers who had already bet on a horse rated themselves as more certain of winning than those who were still waiting to place a bet.

◼ Cognitive Dissonance Theory: A New Look

Following in Festinger's bold footsteps, generations of social psychologists have studied and refined the basic theory (Cooper, 2007; Harmon-Jones & Mills, 1999). Nobody disputes the fact that when people are gently coaxed into performing an attitude-discrepant behavior, they often go on to change their attitudes. In fact, people will feel discomfort and change their attitudes when they disagree with others in a group (Matz & Wood, 2005) or even when they observe inconsistent behavior from others with whom they identify—a process of vicarious dissonance (Cooper & Hogg, 2007).

Researchers have also examined possible perceptual consequences of cognitive dissonance. In one study, Emily Balcetis and David Dunning (2007) took college students to the crowded center of campus and asked them to put on—and walk around in—a costume consisting of a grass skirt, a coconut bra, a flower lei around the neck, and a plastic fruit basket on the head. Embarrassing as it was to appear this way in public, all the participants walked across campus in this costume. In a high-choice condition, they were led to believe that they could decline in favor of a different task (insufficient justification). In a low-choice condition, they were told that no alternative tasks were available (sufficient justification). How bad was it? Afterward, all the students were asked to estimate the distance they had walked from one point to the other. Needing to justify their embarrassing antics, those in the high-choice condition underestimated how far they had walked relative to those in the low-choice condition. Apparently, the motivation to reduce dissonance can alter our visual representations of the natural environment.

Through systematic research, it became evident early on that Festinger's (1957) original theory was not to be the last word. People do change their attitudes to justify attitude-discrepant behavior, effort, and difficult decisions. But for dissonance to be aroused, certain specific conditions must be present. As first summarized by Joel Cooper and Russell Fazio's (1984) "new look" at dissonance theory, we now have a pretty good idea of what those conditions are.

According to Cooper and Fazio, four steps are necessary for both the arousal and reduction of dissonance. First, the attitude-discrepant behavior must produce unwanted *negative consequences*. Recall the initial Festinger and Carlsmith (1959) study. Not only did participants say something they knew to be false but they also deceived a fellow student into taking part in a painfully boring experiment. Had these participants lied without causing hardship, they would *not* have changed their attitudes to justify the action (Cooper et al., 1974). To borrow an expression from schoolyard basketball, "no harm, no foul." In fact, negative consequences can arouse dissonance even when people's actions are consistent with their attitudes, as when college students who wrote against fee hikes were led to believe that their essays had backfired, prompting a university committee to favor an increase (Scher & Cooper, 1989).

The second necessary step in the process is a feeling of *personal responsibility* for the unpleasant outcomes of behavior. Personal responsibility consists of two factors. The first is the freedom of *choice*. When people believe they had no choice but to act as they did, there is no dissonance and no attitude change (Linder et al., 1967). Had Festinger and Carlsmith coerced participants into raving about the boring experiment, the participants would not have felt the need to further justify what they did by changing their attitudes. But the experimental situation led participants to think that their actions were voluntary and the choice was theirs. Participants were pressured without realizing it and believed that they did not have to comply with the experimenter's request.

For people to feel personally responsible, they must also believe that the potential negative consequences of their actions were *foreseeable* at the time (Goethals et al., 1979). When the outcome could not realistically have been anticipated, then there is no dissonance and no attitude change. Had Festinger and Carlsmith's participants lied in private and found out only later that their statements had been tape-recorded for subsequent use, then, again, they would not have felt the need to further justify their behavior.

The third necessary step in the process is physiological *arousal*. Right from the start, Festinger viewed cognitive dissonance as a state of discomfort and tension that people seek to reduce—much like hunger, thirst, and other basic drives. Research has shown that this emphasis was well placed. In a study by Robert Croyle and Joel Cooper (1983), participants wrote essays that supported or contradicted their own attitudes. Some were ordered to do so, but others were led to believe that the choice was theirs. During the session, electrodes were attached to each participant's fingertips to record levels of physiological arousal. As predicted by cognitive dissonance theory, those who freely wrote attitude-discrepant essays were the most aroused, an observation made by other researchers as well (Elkin & Leippe, 1986). In fact, participants who write attitude-discrepant essays in a "free-choice" situation report feeling high levels of discomfort—which subside once they change their attitudes (Elliot & Devine, 1994).

The fourth step in the dissonance process is closely related to the third. It isn't enough to feel generally aroused. A person must also make an *attribution* for that arousal to his or her own behavior. Suppose you just lied to a friend or studied for an exam that was canceled or made a tough decision that you might soon regret. Suppose further that although you are upset, you believe that your discomfort is caused by some external factor, not by your dissonance-producing behavior. Under these circumstances, will you exhibit attitude change as a symptom of cognitive dissonance? Probably not. When participants were led to attribute their dissonance-related arousal to a drug they had supposedly taken (Zanna & Cooper, 1974), to the anticipation of painful electric shocks (Pittman, 1975), or to a pair of prism goggles that they had to wear (Losch & Cacioppo, 1990), attitude change did not occur. ▶ Figure 6.10 summarizes these four steps in the production and reduction of dissonance.

To this day, social psychologists continue to debate the "classic" and "new look" theories of cognitive dissonance. On the one hand, research has shown that attitude-discrepant actions do not always produce dissonance, in part because not everyone cares about being cognitively consistent (Cialdini et al., 1995) and in part because a change in attitude often seems to require the production of negative consequences (Johnson et al., 1995). On the other hand, some researchers have found that mere

▶**FIGURE 6.10**

Necessary Conditions for the Arousal and Reduction of Dissonance

Research suggests that four steps are necessary for attitude change to result from the production and reduction of dissonance.

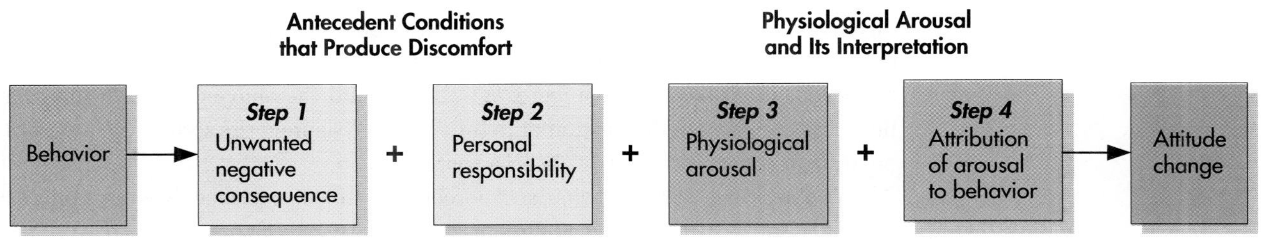

inconsistency can trigger cognitive dissonance, even without negative consequences. For example, Eddie Harmon-Jones and others (1996) had people drink a Kool-Aid beverage that was mixed with sugar or vinegar. They either told the participants (no choice) or asked them (high choice) to state in writing that they liked the beverage and then toss these notes, which were not really needed, into the wastebasket. Afterward, they rated how much they really liked the drink. You may have noticed that this experiment parallels the Festinger and Carlsmith study with one key exception: For participants in the high-choice situation who consumed vinegar and said they liked it, the lie—although it contradicted their true attitudes—did not cause harm to anyone. Did they experience dissonance that they would have to reduce by overrating the vinegar Kool-Aid? Yes. Compared with participants who lied about the vinegar in the no-choice situation, those in the high-choice situation rated its taste as more pleasant. The lie was harmless, but the feeling of inconsistency still forced a change in attitude.

◼ Alternative Routes to Self-Persuasion

It is important to distinguish between the empirical facts uncovered by dissonance researchers and the theory that is used to explain them. The facts themselves are clear: Under certain conditions, people who behave in attitude-discrepant ways go on to change their attitudes. Whether this phenomenon reflects a human need to reduce dissonance, however, is a matter of some controversy. Over the years, three other explanations have been proposed.

Self-Perception Theory   Daryl Bem's (1965) *self-perception theory*, as described in Chapter 3, posed the first serious challenge to dissonance theory. Noting that we don't always have firsthand knowledge of our own attitudes, Bem proposed that we infer how we feel by observing ourselves and the circumstances of our own behavior. This sort of self-persuasion is not fueled by the need to reduce tension or justify our actions. Instead, it is a cool, calm, and rational process in which people interpret ambiguous feelings by observing their own behavior. But can Bem's theory replace dissonance theory as an explanation of self-persuasion?

Bem confronted this question head-on. What if neutral observers who are not motivated by the need to reduce dissonance were to read a step-by-step description of a dissonance study and predict the results? This approach to the problem was ingenious. Bem reasoned that observers can have the same behavioral information as the participants themselves but not experience the same personal conflict. If observers generate the same results as real participants, it shows that dissonance arousal is not necessary for the resulting changes in attitudes.

To test his hypothesis, Bem (1967) described the Festinger and Carlsmith study to observers and had them guess participants' attitudes. Some were told about the one-dollar condition, some were told about the 20-dollar condition, and others read about the control group procedure. The results closely paralleled the original study. As observers saw it, participants who said the task was interesting for 20 dollars didn't mean it; they just went along for the money. But those who made the claim for only one dollar must have been sincere. Why else would they have gone along? As far as Bem was concerned, the participants themselves reasoned the same way. No conflict, no arousal—just inference by observation.

So should we conclude that self-perception, not dissonance, is what's necessary to bring about attitude change? That's a tough question. It's not easy to come up with a critical experiment to distinguish between the two theories. Both predict the same results, but for different reasons. And both offer unique support for their own points of view. On the one hand, Bem's observer studies show that dissonance-like results can be obtained without arousal. On the other hand, the participants of dissonance studies *do* experience arousal, which seems necessary for attitude change to take place. Can we say that one theory is right and the other wrong?

Fazio and others (1977) concluded that both theories are right but in different situations. When people behave in ways that are strikingly at odds with their attitudes, they feel the unnerving effects of dissonance and change their attitudes to rationalize their actions. When people behave in ways that are not terribly discrepant from how they feel, however, they experience relatively little tension and form their attitudes as a matter of inference. In short, highly discrepant behavior produces attitude change through dissonance, whereas slightly discrepant behavior produces change through self-perception.

Impression-Management Theory Another alternative to a dissonance view of self-persuasion is *impression-management theory*, which says that what matters is not a motive to be consistent but a motive to *appear* consistent. Nobody wants to be called fickle or be seen by others as a hypocrite. So we calibrate our attitudes and behaviors publicly in order to present ourselves to others in a particular light (Baumeister, 1982; Tedeschi et al., 1971). Or perhaps we are motivated not by a desire to appear consistent but by a desire to avoid being held responsible for the unpleasant consequences of our actions (Schlenker, 1982). Either way this theory places the emphasis on our concern for self-presentation. According to this view, participants in the Festinger and Carlsmith study mostly did not want the experimenter to think they had sold out for a paltry sum of money.

If the impression-management approach is correct, then cognitive dissonance does not produce attitude change at all—only reported change. In other words, if research participants were to state their attitudes anonymously or if they were to think that the experimenter could determine their true feelings through covert measures, then dissonance-like effects should vanish. Sometimes the effects do vanish, but other times they do not. In general, studies have shown that although self-persuasion can be motivated by impression management, it can also occur in situations that do not clearly arouse self-presentation concerns (Baumeister & Tice, 1984).

Self-Esteem Theories A third competing explanation relates self-persuasion to the self. According to Elliot Aronson, acts that arouse dissonance do so because they threaten the self-concept, making the person feel guilty, dishonest, or hypocritical, and motivating a change in attitude or future behavior (Aronson, 1999; Stone et al., 1997). This being the case, perhaps Festinger and Carlsmith's participants needed to change their attitudes toward the boring task in order to repair damage to the self, not to resolve cognitive inconsistency.

If cognitive dissonance is aroused only by behavior that lowers self-esteem, then people with already low expectations of themselves should not be affected: "If a person conceives of himself as a 'schnook,' he will expect to behave like a schnook" (Aronson, 1969, p. 24). In fact, Jeff Stone (2003) found that when college students were coaxed into writing an essay in favor of a tuition increase (a position that contradicted their attitude) and into thinking about their own standards of behavior, those who had high self-esteem changed their attitude to meet their behavior, as dissonance theory would predict, more than those who had low self-esteem. Claude Steele (1988) takes this notion two steps further. First, he suggests that a dissonance-producing situation—engaging in attitude-discrepant behavior, exerting wasted effort, or making a difficult decision—

▶ **FIGURE 6.11**

When Self-Affirmation Fails

Students gave a dissonant speech advocating a ban on a popular campus tradition. Compared to those in a low-choice situation, students in a high-choice group changed their attitude more to favor the ban. As self-affirmation theory predicts, those given a chance to express their values afterward did not then favor the ban—unless their values were poorly received. Self-affirmation can repair the dissonance-damaged self. When it fails, however, cognitive dissonance returns to pressure the change in attitude.

Galinsky et al., 2000.

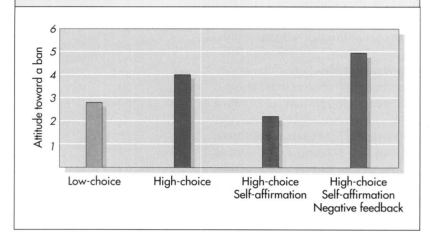

sets in motion a process of *self-affirmation* that serves to revalidate the integrity of the self-concept. Second, this revalidation can be achieved in many ways, not just by resolving dissonance. Self-affirmation theory makes a unique prediction: If the active ingredient in dissonance situations is a threat to the self, then people who have an opportunity to affirm the self in other ways will not suffer from the effects of dissonance. Give Festinger and Carlsmith's one-dollar participants a chance to donate money, help a victim in distress, or solve a problem, and their self-concepts should bounce back without further need to justify their actions.

Research provides support for this hypothesis. For example, Steele and others (1993) gave people positive or negative feedback about a personality test they had taken. Next, they asked them to rate 10 popular music CDs and then offered them a choice of keeping either their fifth- or sixth-ranked CD. Soon after making the decision, the participants were asked to rate the CDs again. As predicted by dissonance theory, most inflated their ratings of the chosen CD relative to the unchosen one. The key word, however, is *most*. The ratings of the participants who had received positive feedback did not change. Why not? According to Steele, it was because they had just enjoyed a self-affirming experience that was enough to overcome the need to reduce dissonance.

▶ **FIGURE 6.12**

Theories of Self-Persuasion: Critical Comparisons

Here we compare the major theories of self-persuasion. Each alternative challenges a different aspect of dissonance theory. Self-perception theory assumes that attitude change is a matter of inference, not motivation. Impression-management theory maintains that the change is more apparent than real, reported for the sake of public self-presentation. Self-affirmation theory contends that the motivating force is a concern for the self and that attitude change will not occur when the self-concept is affirmed in other ways.

	Theories			
	Cognitive Dissonance	Self-Perception	Impression Management	Self-Affirmation
Is the attitude change motivated by a desire to reduce discomfort?	Yes	No	Yes	Yes
Does a person's private attitude really change?	Yes	Yes	No	Yes
Must the change be directly related to the attitude-discrepant behavior?	Yes	Yes	Yes	No

Steele's research suggests that there are many possible ways for people to repair a dissonance-damaged self. But if these efforts at indirect self-affirmation fail, would cognitive dissonance return and create pressure to make a change in attitude? Yes. In one study, college students were asked (high-choice) or told (low-choice) to deliver an attitude-discrepant speech advocating that a popular campus tradition (running nude on the evening of the first snowfall) be banned. For those in the basic high-choice condition, cognitive dissonance was aroused, creating pressure on them to change their attitude favoring the ban. Students in another high-choice group who were subsequently given an opportunity to self-affirm by expressing some cherished values felt less discomfort and exhibited less attitude change. For them, self-affirmation provided the necessary relief. However, among students in a fourth group (also high in choice) who self-affirmed but then received negative feedback about the values they expressed, cognitive dissonance returned, creating pressure to change their attitude toward the ban. In essence, cognitive dissonance and its impact on attitudes reemerged from the failed attempt at self-affirmation (Galinsky et al., 2000; see ▶ Figure 6.11).

To summarize, dissonance theory maintains that people change their attitudes to justify their attitude-discrepant behaviors, efforts, and decisions. Self-perception theory argues that the change occurs because people infer how they feel by observing their own behavior. Impression-management theory claims that the attitude change is spurred by concerns about self-presentation. And self-affirmation theory says that the change is motivated by threats to the self-concept (see ▶ Figure 6.12).

▌ Cultural Influences on Cognitive Dissonance

Over the years, social psychologists have presumed that the cognitive dissonance effects uncovered in 50 years of research and described in this chapter are universal and characteristic of human nature. More and more, however, it appears that cultural context may influence both the arousal and reduction of cognitive dissonance.

In Western cultures, individuals are expected to make decisions that are consistent with their personal attitudes and to make those decisions free from outside influences. In East Asian cultures, however, individuals are also expected to make decisions that benefit their ingroup members and to take the well-being of others into account in making those decisions. In light of these differences, Etsuko Hoshino-Browne and colleagues (2005) compared the reactions of European-Canadian and Japanese research participants in a post-decision dissonance experiment in which they rank-ordered items on a menu by choosing their top 10 dishes. Then they ranked the list again: half made the choices for themselves and the others were asked to imagine a close friend whose tastes they knew and choose on behalf of that friend. Did participants show the classic post-decision justification effect, becoming more positive in their ratings of the chosen items relative to nonchosen items? Yes and no. When they made decisions for themselves, only the Canadian participants exhibited a significant justification effect. When Japanese participants made decisions for a friend, however, they exhibited the stronger effect (see ▶ Figure 6.13). Similar results have been found in other studies (Kitayama et al., 2004).

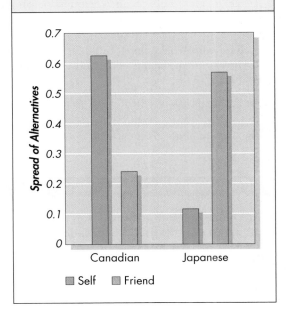

▶ **FIGURE 6.13**

Cognitive Dissonance as Both Universal and Culturally Dependent

Researchers compared Canadian and Japanese research participants in a post-decision dissonance study in which they rank ordered items on a menu, chose their top dishes, then ranked the list again. Half made the choices for themselves; the others were asked to imagine a close friend. When deciding for themselves, only the Canadians exhibited a significant justification effect; when deciding for a friend, however, Japanese participants exhibited the stronger effect.

Hoshino-Browne et al., 2005.

To sum up: Cognitive dissonance is both universal and dependent on culture. At times everyone feels and tries to reduce dissonance, but cultures influence the conditions under which these processes occur.

Changing Attitudes

Attitudes and attitude change are an important part of social life. In this chapter, we have seen that persuasion can be achieved in different ways. The most common approach is through communication from *others*. Faced with newspaper editorials, junk mail, books, TV commercials, blogs, websites, and other messages, we take one of two routes to persuasion. On the central route, attitude change is based on the merits of the source and his or her communication. On the peripheral route, it is based on superficial cues. Either way, the change in attitude often precipitates a change in behavior.

A second, less obvious means of persuasion originates within *ourselves*. When people behave in ways that run afoul of their true convictions, they often go on to change their attitudes. Once again, there are many routes to change, not just one. Cognitive dissonance, self-perception, impression management, and self-esteem concerns are among the possible avenues. From attitudes to behavior and back again, the processes of persuasion are complex and interwoven.

REVIEW

The Study of Attitudes

- An attitude is an affective, evaluative reaction toward a person, place, issue, or object.

How Attitudes Are Measured

- The most common way to measure attitudes is through self-reports, such as attitude scales.
- To get respondents to answer questions honestly, the bogus pipeline may be used.
- Covert measures may also be used. Such measures include nonverbal behavior, the facial electromyograph (EMG), brain-wave patterns, and the Implicit Association Test (IAT).

How Attitudes Are Formed

- Twin studies suggest that people may be genetically predisposed to hold certain attitudes.

- However, research shows that attitudes are formed by experience and learning, as when people develop strong attitudes toward neutral objects because of their association with positive and negative stimuli.

The Link Between Attitudes and Behavior

- Attitudes do not necessarily correlate with behavior, but under certain conditions, there is a high correlation.
- Attitudes predict behavior best when they're specific rather than general and strong rather than weak.
- Attitudes compete with other influences on behavior.

Persuasion by Communication

- The most common approach to changing attitudes is through a persuasive communication.

Two Routes to Persuasion

- When people think critically about a message, they take the central route to persuasion and are influenced by the strength of the arguments.

- When people do not think carefully about a message, they take the peripheral route to persuasion and are influenced by peripheral cues.
- The route taken depends on whether people have the ability and the motivation to fully process the communication.

The Source

- Attitude change is greater for messages delivered by a source that is credible (competent and trustworthy).
- Attitude change is also greater when the source is likable (similar and attractive).
- When an audience has a high level of personal involvement, source factors are less important than the quality of the message.
- The sleeper effect shows that people often forget the source but not the message, so the effects of the credibility of the source dissipate over time.

The Message

- On the peripheral route, lengthy messages are persuasive. On the central route, length works only if the added information does not dilute the message.
- Whether it is best to present an argument first or second depends on how much time elapses—both between the two arguments and between the second argument and the final decision.
- Messages that are moderately discrepant from an audience's attitudes will inspire change, but highly discrepant messages will be scrutinized and rejected.
- High-fear messages motivate attitude change when they contain strong arguments and instructions about how to avoid the threatened danger.
- Positive emotion also facilitates attitude change because people are easier to persuade when they're in a good mood.

- Research shows that subliminal messages do not produce meaningful or lasting changes in attitudes.

The Audience

- People are not consistently difficult or easy to persuade. Rather, different kinds of messages influence different kinds of people.
- People who are high in the need for cognition are persuaded more by the strength of the arguments.
- People who are high in self-monitoring are influenced more by appeals to social images.
- Messages are persuasive to the extent that they are presented in a way that "feels right," fitting the individual orientations of audience members.
- Forewarning increases resistance to persuasive influence. It inoculates the audience by providing the opportunity to generate counterarguments, and it arouses psychological reactance.

Culture and Persuasion

- Communications are successful to the extent that they appeal to the cultural values of an audience.
- Research shows that North Americans are persuaded more by individualistic ads, whereas East Asians prefer collectivistic ads.

Persuasion by Our Own Actions

Role Playing: All the World's a Stage

- The way people act can influence how they feel because behavior can determine attitudes.

Cognitive Dissonance Theory: The Classic Version

- Under certain conditions, inconsistency between attitudes and behavior produces an unpleasant psychological state called cognitive dissonance.
- Motivated to reduce the tension, people often change their attitudes to justify (1) attitude-discrepant behavior; (2) wasted effort; and (3) difficult decisions.

Cognitive Dissonance Theory: A New Look

- According to the "new look" version of cognitive dissonance theory, four conditions must be met for dissonance to be aroused: (1) an act with unwanted consequences; (2) a feeling of personal responsibility; (3) arousal or discomfort; and (4) attribution of the arousal to the attitude-discrepant act.
- Social psychologists continue to debate whether dissonance can be aroused by cognitive inconsistency when no unwanted consequences are produced.

Alternative Routes to Self-Persuasion

- Alternative explanations of dissonance-related attitude change have been proposed.
- Self-perception theory states that people logically infer their attitudes by observing their own behavior.
- Impression-management theory says that people are motivated to change their attitudes only to appear consistent to others.
- Self-esteem theories state that dissonance is triggered by threats to the self-concept and can be reduced indirectly, without a change in attitude, through self-affirming experiences.

Cultural Influences on Cognitive Dissonance

- Recently, social psychologists have wondered whether cognitive dissonance effects are universal or specific to Western cultures.
- Research suggests that people all over the world will try to reduce dissonance when it arises but that the conditions that arouse it are influenced by cultural context.

Changing Attitudes

- Through persuasive communications and the mechanisms of self-persuasion, the processes of changing attitudes and behavior are complex and interwoven.

Key Terms

attitude (203)
attitude scale (205)
bogus pipeline (206)
central route to persuasion (215)
cognitive dissonance theory (236)
elaboration (216)
facial electromyograph (EMG) (206)

Implicit Association Test (IAT) (207)
implicit attitude (207)
inoculation hypothesis (233)
insufficient deterrence (238)
insufficient justification (237)
need for cognition (NC) (230)

peripheral route to persuasion (215)
persuasion (214)
psychological reactance (233)
sleeper effect (222)
theory of planned behavior (212)

Media Resources

Social Psychology 8th Edition Companion Website
Visit your book companion website
www.cengage.com/psychology/kassin
where you will find flash cards, practice quizzes, Internet links, and more to help you study.

CENGAGENOW Just what you need to know NOW! Spend time on what you need to master rather than on information you already have learned. Take a pre-test for this chapter and CengageNOW will generate a personalized study plan based on your results. The study plan will identify the topics you need to review and direct you to online resources to help you master those topics. You can then take a post-test to help you determine the concepts you have mastered and what you will need to work on. Try it out! Go to **academic .cengage.com/login** to sign in with an access code or to purchase access to this product.

Putting COMMON SENSE to the Test

Researchers can tell if someone has a positive or negative attitude by measuring physiological arousal.

False. Measures of arousal can reveal how intensely someone feels, but not whether the person's attitude is positive or negative.

In reacting to persuasive communications, people are influenced more by superficial images than by logical arguments.

False. As indicated by the dual-process model of persuasion, people can be influenced by images or arguments, depending on their ability and motivation to think critically about the information.

People are most easily persuaded by commercial messages that are presented without their awareness.

False. There is no research evidence to support the presumed effects of subliminal ads.

The more money you pay people to tell a lie, the more they will come to believe it.

False. Cognitive dissonance studies show that people believe the lies they are underpaid to tell as a way to justify their own actions.

People often come to like what they suffer for.

True. Studies show that the more people work or suffer for something, the more they come to like it as a way to justify their effort.

7

Conformity

This chapter examines ways in which social influences are "automatic." We then look at three processes. First, we consider the reasons why people exhibit conformity to group norms. Second, we describe the strategies used to elicit compliance with direct requests. Third, we analyze the causes and effects of obedience to the commands of authority. The chapter concludes with a discussion of the continuum of social influence.

On Thursday evening of June 11, 2009, a couple hundred ordinary people who were strangers to one another showed up in San Francisco's Union Square. At precisely 6 P.M., on cue, the impromptu group belted out the Beatles' song "With a Little Help from My Friends." Earlier that week, in York, England, feathers flew outside of the well-known Yorkshire Museum and Gardens when 500 good natured Facebook users appeared, pillows in hand, for a mass pillow fight that lasted five minutes. In both cases, participants had received instructions on the Internet, gathered voluntarily at a set time and place, performed a silly but harmless action, and quickly dispersed. Illustrating the viral power of the Internet to serve as a vehicle for social influence, other "flash mobs" have in recent years formed in New York, Rome, Paris, Amsterdam, Berlin, Oslo, Melbourne, Budapest, Boston, Chicago, Los Angeles, Denver, Houston, and other cities.

Sometimes the social influences that move us are not entertaining and funny but potentially hazardous to our health. Consider the unusual events that occurred in a Tennessee high school. It started when a teacher noticed a gas-like smell in her classroom and then came down with a headache, nausea, shortness of breath, and dizziness. Word spread. Others soon reported the same symptoms and the school was evacuated. Eighty students and several staff members were taken to a local emergency room. Nothing showed up in blood tests, urine tests, or other medical procedures, nor were gases, pesticides, or other toxins detected. What the investigation did turn up was that students who reported feeling ill that day were more likely than others to have seen someone with symptoms, heard about someone with symptoms, or known a classmate who was ill. Reporting these findings in the *New England Journal of Medicine*, researchers concluded that the problems were the product of "mass psychogenic illness"—a profound, almost contagious form of social influence (Jones et al., 2000; Wang, 2006).

Flash mobs and the illness at the Tennessee school reveal the awesome power of social influence. The effects that people have on each other can also be seen in mundane human events. Thus, sports fans spread the "wave" around massive stadiums or chant "de-fense" in a spectacular show of unison. TV producers insert canned

Putting COMMON SENSE to the Test

Circle Your Answer

T	F	When all members of a group give an incorrect response to an easy question, most people most of the time conform to that response.
T	F	An effective way to get someone to do you a favor is to make a first request that is so large the person is sure to reject it.
T	F	In experiments on obedience, most participants who were ordered to administer severe shocks to an innocent person refused to do so.
T	F	As the number of people in a group increases, so does the group's impact on an individual.
T	F	Conformity rates vary across different cultures and from one generation to the next.

We are discreet sheep; we wait to see how the drove is going and then go with the drove.

—Mark Twain

laughter into sitcoms to increase viewer responsiveness. Politicians trumpet the inflated results of their own favorable public opinion polls to attract voters. And bartenders, waiters, and waitresses stuff dollar bills into their tip jars as a way to get customers to follow suit. As they say, "Monkey see, monkey do."

You don't need to be a social psychologist to know that people have an impact on each other's behavior. The trickier question is How and with what effect? The term *social influence* refers to the ways that people are affected by the real and imagined pressures of others (Cialdini & Goldstein, 2004; Kiesler & Kiesler, 1969). The kinds of influences brought to bear on an individual come in different shapes and sizes. In this chapter, we look at social influences that are mindless and automatic, then we consider three forms of influence that vary in the degree of pressure exerted on an individual—*conformity*, *compliance*, and *obedience*. As depicted in ▶ Figure 7.1, conformity, compliance, and obedience are not distinct, qualitatively different "types" of influence. In all three cases, the influence may emanate from a person, a group, or an institution. And in all instances, the behavior in question maybe constructive (helping oneself or others) or destructive (hurting oneself or others) or neutral. It is useful to note, once again, that social influence varies as points along a continuum according to the degree of pressure exerted on the individual. It is also useful to note that we do not always succumb under pressure. People may conform or maintain their independence from others, they may comply with direct requests or react with assertiveness, or they may obey the commands of authority or oppose powerful others in an act of defiance. In this chapter, we examine the factors that lead human beings to yield to or resist social influence.

Social Influence as "Automatic"

Before we consider the explicit forms of social influence depicted in Figure 7.1, whereby individuals choose whether or not to "go along," it's important to note that as social animals humans are vulnerable to a host of subtle, almost reflex-like influences. Without realizing it, we often crack open a yawn when we see others yawning, laugh aloud when we hear others laughing, and grimace when we see others in pain. In an early demonstration, Stanley Milgram and others (1969) had research confederates stop on a busy street in New York City, look up, and gawk at the sixth-floor window of a nearby building. Films shot from behind the window indicated that about 80 percent of passersby stopped and gazed up when they saw the confederates.

Rudimentary forms of imitation have been observed in various animal species, such as pigeons, monkeys, hamsters, and fish (Heyes & Galef, 1996; Zentall, 2003).

▶ **FIGURE 7.1**

Continuum of Social Influence

Social influences vary in the degree of pressure they bring to bear on an individual. People may (1) conform to group norms or maintain their independence; (2) comply with requests or be assertive; and (3) obey or defy the commands of authority.

Yielding to Influence   Resisting Influence

Obedience   Compliance   Conformity   Independence   Assertiveness   Defiance

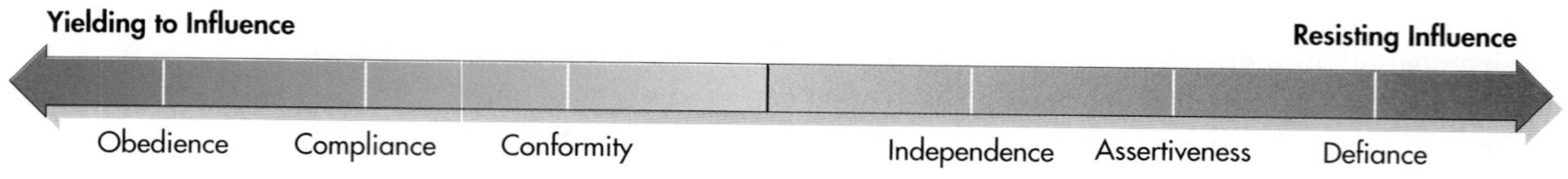

There is even evidence to suggest that "cultures" are transmitted through imitation in groups of whales, as when humpback whales off the coast of Maine use lobtail feeding, a technique in which they slam their tail flukes onto the water, then dive and exhale, forming clouds of bubbles that envelop schools of prey fish. This complex behavior was first observed in 1981. By 1989 it was measurably adopted by 50 percent of the whale population in that area (Rendell & Whitehead, 2001).

Do we really imitate one another automatically, without thought, effort, or conflict? It appears that we do. In recent years, controlled studies of human infants have shown that sometimes shortly after birth, babies not only look at faces but (to the delight of parents all over the world) often mimic simple gestures such as moving the head, pursing the lips, and sticking out the tongue (Bremner, 2002; Gopnik et al., 1999). Studying 162 infants from 6 to 20 months old, Susan Jones (2007) found that imitation developed at different rates for different behaviors. Using parents as models, she found, for example, that infants mimicked opening the mouth wide, tapping their fingers on a table, and waving bye-bye before they mimicked clapping hands, flexing their fingers, or putting their hands on the head.

You may not realize it, but human adults unwittingly mimic each other all the time. To demonstrate, Tanya Chartrand and John Bargh (1999) set up participants to work on a task with a partner, a confederate who exhibited the habit of rubbing his face or shaking his foot. Hidden cameras recording the interaction revealed that without realizing it, participants mimicked these motor behaviors, rubbing their face or shaking a foot to match their partner's behavior. Chartrand and Bargh dubbed this phenomenon the "chameleon effect," after the lizard that changes colors according to its physical environment (see ▶ Figure 7.2).

There are two possible reasons for this nonconscious form of imitation. Chartrand and Bargh speculated that such mimicry serves an important *social* function, that being "in sync" in their pace, posture, mannerisms, facial expressions, tone of voice, accents, speech patterns, and other behaviors enables people to interact more smoothly with one another. Accordingly, Chartrand and Bargh (1999) turned the tables in a second study in which they instructed their confederate to match in subtle ways the mannerisms of some participants but not others. Sure enough, participants who had been mimicked liked the confederate more than those who had not. Further demonstrating the social aspect of mimicry, research shows that people mimic others more when they are highly motivated to affiliate—say, because they are similar to these others or are feeling excluded—than when they are not (Guéguen & Martin, 2009; Huntsinger et al., 2009; Lakin et al., 2008).

Social mimicry is so powerful that it can influence us even when the mimicker is not a real person. In a study entitled "digital chameleons," Jeremy Bailenson and Nick Yee (2005) immersed college students, one at a time, in a virtual reality environment in which they found themselves seated at a table across from a humanlike person that looked something like a three-dimensional cartoon character. This character proceeded to argue that students should be required to carry identification cards at all times for security purposes. In half the sessions, this virtual speaker's back-and-forth head movements perfectly mimicked the participant's head movements at a four-second delay. In the other half, the speaker repeated the head movements of an earlier

Among humpback whales off the coast of Maine, "lobtail feeding" (a complex behavior that traps prey fish) was first observed in 1981. Through imitation, it soon spread across the entire whale population in the region.

▶ **FIGURE 7.2**

The Chameleon Effect

This graph shows the number of times per minute participants rubbed their face or shook their foot when they were with a confederate who was rubbing or shaking his foot.

Kassin, 1997.

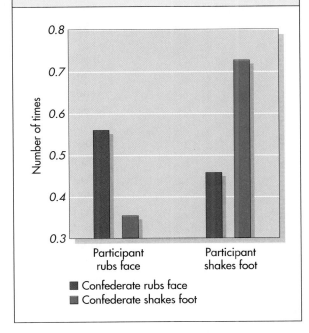

"I don't know why. I just suddenly felt like calling."

Often we are not aware of the influence other people have on our behavior.

recorded participant. Very few of the students who were mimicked were aware of it. Yet when later asked about the experience, they rated the virtual character as more likable and were persuaded by its speech more if it imitated their head movements than if it imitated the movements of the previous participant.

The human impulse to mimic others may have adaptive social value, but these types of effects can also be found in *nonsocial* situations. In one study, Roland Neumann and Fritz Strack (2000) had people listen to an abstract philosophical speech that was recited on tape in a happy, sad, or neutral voice. Afterward, participants rated their own mood as more positive when they heard the happy voice and as more negative when they heard the sad voice. Even though the speakers and participants never interacted, the speaker's emotional state was infectious, an automatic effect that can be described as a form of "mood contagion."

It is also important to realize that mimicry is a dynamic process, as when two people who are walking together or dancing become more and more coordinated over time. To demonstrate, Michael Richardson and others (2005) sat pairs of college students side by side to work on visual problems while swinging a handheld pendulum as "a distraction task." The students did not need to be synchronized in their swinging tempo in order to get along or solve the problems. Yet when each could see the other's pendulum (and even without speaking), their tempos gradually converged over time—like two hearts beating as one.

Conformity

It is hard to find behaviors that are not in some way affected by exposure to the actions of others. When social psychologists talk of **conformity**, they specifically refer to the tendency of people to change their perceptions, opinions, and behavior in ways that are consistent with group norms.

Using this definition, would you call yourself a conformist or a nonconformist? How often do you feel inclined to follow what others are saying or doing? At first, you may deny the tendency to conform and, instead, declare your individuality and uniqueness. But think about it. When was the last time you appeared at a formal wedding dressed in blue jeans or remained seated during the national anthem at a sports event? People find it difficult to breach social norms. In an early demonstration of this point, social psychology research assistants were supposed to ask subway passengers to give up their seats—a conspicuous violation of the norm of acceptable conduct. Many of the assistants could not carry out their assignment. In fact, some of those who tried it became so anxious that they pretended to be ill just to make their request appear justified (Milgram & Sabini, 1978).

Because conformity is so widespread, it is interesting and ironic that research participants (at least in North America) who are coaxed into following a group norm will often not admit to being influenced. Instead, they try to reinterpret the task and rationalize their own behavior as a way to see themselves in more positive terms, as independent (Hornsey & Jetten, 2004). This resistance to the conformity label is partic-

conformity The tendency to change our perceptions, opinions, or behavior in ways that are consistent with group norms.

ularly characteristic of individuals who have high status and seniority within a group (Jetten et al., 2006). But there is a second reason why people tend to not see themselves as conformist. In a series of studies, Emily Pronin and others (2007) found that people perceive others to be more conforming than themselves in all sorts of domains—from why they bought an iPod to why they hold a popular opinion. Part of the reason for this asymmetry is that whereas people judge others by their overt behavior and the degree to which it matches what others are doing, they tend to judge themselves by focusing inward and introspecting about their thought processes, which blinds them to their own conformity.

People understandably have mixed feelings about conformity After all, some degree of it is essential if individuals are to maintain communities and coexist peacefully, as when people assume their rightful place in a waiting line. Yet at other times, conformity can have harmful consequences, as when people drink too heavily at parties or tell offensive ethnic jokes because others are doing the same. For the social psychologist, the goal is to understand the conditions that promote conformity or independence and the reasons for these behaviors.

▌ The Early Classics

In 1936, Muzafer Sherif published a classic laboratory study of how norms develop in small groups. His method was ingenious. Male students, who believed they were participating in a visual perception experiment, sat in a totally darkened room. Fifteen feet in front of them, a small dot of light appeared for two seconds, after which participants were asked to estimate how far it had moved. This procedure was repeated several times. Although participants didn't realize it, the dot of light always remained

motionless. The movement they thought they saw was merely an optical illusion known as the *autokinetic effect*: In darkness, a stationary point of light appears to move, sometimes erratically, in various directions.

At first, participants sat alone and reported their judgments to the experimenter. After several trials, Sherif found that they settled in on their own stable perceptions of movement, with most estimates ranging from one to ten inches (although one participant gave an estimate of 80 feet!). Over the next three days, people returned to participate openly in three-person groups. As before, lights were flashed and the participants, one by one, announced their estimates. As shown in ▶ Figure 7.3, initial estimates varied considerably, but participants later converged on a common perception. Eventually, each group established its own set of norms.

Some 15 years after Sherif's demonstration, Solomon Asch (1951) constructed a very different task for testing how people's beliefs affect the beliefs of others. To appreciate what Asch did, imagine yourself in the following situation. You sign up for a psychology

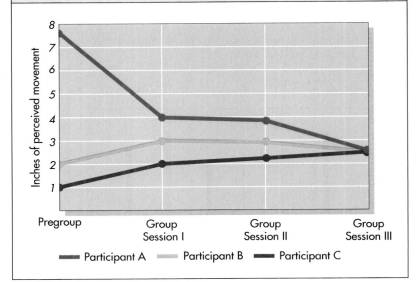

▶ **FIGURE 7.3**

A Classic Case of Suggestibility

This graph, taken from Sherif's study, shows how three participants' estimates of the apparent movement of light gradually converged. Before they came together, their perceptions varied considerably. Once in groups, however, participants conformed to the norm that had developed.

Sherif, 1936.

After two uneventful rounds in Asch's study, the participant (seated second from the right) faces a dilemma. The answer he wants to give in the third test of visual discrimination differs from that of the first five confederates, who are all in agreement. Should he give his own answers or conform to theirs?

William Vandevert

experiment and when you arrive, you find six other students waiting around a table. Soon after you take an empty seat, the experimenter explains that he is interested in the ability to make visual discriminations. As an example, he asks you and the others to indicate which of three comparison lines is identical in length to a standard line.

That seems easy enough. The experimenter then says that after each set of lines is shown, you and the others should take turns announcing your judgments out loud in the order of your seating position. Beginning on his left, the experimenter asks the first person for his judgment. Seeing that you are in the next-to-last position, you patiently await your turn. The opening moments pass uneventfully. The task and discriminations are clear and everyone agrees on the answers. On the third set of lines, however, the first participant selects what is quite clearly the wrong line. Huh? What happened? Did he suddenly lose his mind, his eyesight, or both? Before you have the chance to figure this one out, the next four participants choose the same wrong line. Now what? Feeling as if you have entered the twilight zone, you wonder if you misunderstood the task. And you wonder what the others will think if you have the nerve to disagree. It's your turn now. You rub your eyes and take another look. What do you see? More to the point, what do you do?

▶ Figure 7.4 gives you a sense of the bind in which Asch's participants found themselves—caught between the need to be right and the desire to be liked (Insko et al., 1982; Ross et al., 1976). As you may suspect by now, the other "participants" were actually confederates and had been trained to make incorrect judgments on 12 out of 18 presentations. There seems little doubt that the real participants knew the correct answers. In a control group, where they made judgments in isolation, they made

▶ FIGURE 7.4

Line Judgment Task Used in Asch's Conformity Studies

Which comparison line—A, B, or C—is the same in length as the standard line? What would you say if you found yourself in the presence of a unanimous majority that answered A or C? The participants in Asch's experiments conformed to the majority about a third of the time.

Asch, 1955.

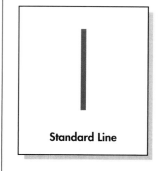

Standard Line

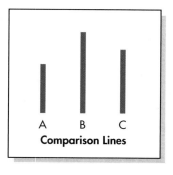

A   B   C
Comparison Lines

almost no errors. Yet Asch's participants went along with the incorrect majority 37 percent of the time—far more often than most of us would ever predict. Not everyone conformed, of course. About 25 percent refused to agree on any of the incorrect group judgments. Yet 50 percent went along on at least half of the critical presentations and the remaining participants conformed on an occasional basis. Similarly high levels of conformity were observed when Asch's study was repeated 30 years later and in recent studies involving other cognitive tasks (Larsen, 1990; Schneider & Watkins, 1996).

Let's compare Sherif's and Asch's classic studies of social influence. Obviously, both demonstrate that our visual perceptions can be heavily influenced by others. But how similar are they really? Did Sherif's and Asch's participants exhibit the same kind of conformity and for the same reasons or was the resemblance in their behavior more apparent than real?

From the start, it was clear that these studies differed in some important ways. In Sherif's research, participants were quite literally "in the dark," so they naturally turned to others for guidance. When physical reality is ambiguous and we are uncertain of our own judgments, as in the autokinetic situation, others can serve as a valuable source of information (Festinger, 1954). Asch's participants found themselves in a much more awkward position. Their task was relatively simple and they could see with their own eyes which answers were correct. Still, they often followed the incorrect majority. In interviews, many of Asch's participants reported afterward that they went along with the group even though they were not convinced that the group was right. Many who did not conform said they felt "conspicuous" and "crazy," like a "misfit" (Asch, 1956, p. 31).

Worldwide, 1.5 billion people, accounting for almost 25 percent of the planet's population, have access to the Internet (Internet World Stats 2009). This being the case, you may wonder: Do the social forces that influence people in the face-to-face encounters studied by Sherif and Asch also operate in virtual groups whose members are nameless, faceless, and anonymous? The answer is yes. McKenna and Bargh (1998) observed behavior in a number of Internet newsgroups, or blogs, in which people with common interests posted and responded to messages on a whole range of topics, from obesity and sexual orientation to money and the stock market. The social nature of the medium in this virtual situation was "remote." Still, these researchers found that in newsgroups that brought together people with "hidden identities" (such as gays and lesbians who had concealed their sexuality), members were highly responsive to social feedback. Those who posted messages that were met with approval rather than disapproval later became more active participants of the newsgroup. When it comes to social support and rejection, even remote virtual groups have the power to shape our behavior (Bargh & McKenna, 2004; Williams et al., 2000).

When all members of a group give an incorrect response to an easy question, most people most of the time conform to that response. **FALSE.**

▊ Why Do People Conform?

The Sherif and Asch studies demonstrate that people conform for two very different reasons: one informational, the other normative (Crutchfield, 1955; Deutsch & Gerard, 1955).

Through **informational influence**, people conform because they want to make correct judgments and they assume that when others agree on something, they must be right. In Sherif's autokinetic task, as in other difficult or ambiguous tasks, it's natural to assume that four eyes are better than two. Hence, research shows that eyewitnesses trying to recall a crime or some other event will alter their recollections and even create false memories in response to what they hear other witnesses report (Gabbert et al., 2003). When people are in a state of uncertainty, following the collective wisdom

informational influence
Influence that produces conformity when a person believes others are correct in their judgments.

Kevin Winter/AMA/Getty Images for AMA

Nonconformists pay a price for dissent. At the start of the controversial U.S.-led war in Iraq, Natalie Maines of the Dixie Chicks, a Texas-based band, told a London audience, "We're ashamed the president of the United States is from Texas." At a time when most Americans supported the war, country music fans greeted this remark with scorn and boycotted the Dixie Chicks. Three years later, the band revealed in a new Grammy award–winning CD that they were still being ostracized for their dissent.

of others may prove to be an effective strategy. In the popular TV game show *Who Wants to Be a Millionaire?* contestants who are stumped on a question can invoke one of two human forms of assistance: (1) calling a friend or relative who serves as a designated "expert"; or (2) polling the studio audience, which casts votes by computer for instant feedback. Overall, the "experts" are useful, offering the correct answer 65 percent of the time. Illustrating the wisdom of crowds, however, the studio audiences pick the right answer 91 percent of the time (Surowiecki, 2005).

In contrast to the informational value of conformity, **normative influence** leads people to conform because they fear the consequences of appearing deviant. It's easy to see why. Early on, research showed that individuals who stray from a group's norm are often disliked, rejected, ridiculed, and dismissed (Schachter, 1951). Although some people are more resilient than others, these forms of interpersonal rejection can be hard to take (Smart Richman & Leary, 2009). In a series of controlled studies, people who were socially *ostracized* by being neglected, ignored, and excluded in a live or Internet chatroom conversation felt hurt, angry, and alone and lacked self-esteem (Williams et al., 2002). Even being left out of a three-way text-messaging conversation on a cell phone can have this effect on us (Smith & Williams, 2004). Kipling Williams (2007a) notes that the research on this point is clear: Some people become so distressed when they are rejected or excluded from a group that they become passive, numb, and lethargic—as though they have been hit with an emotional stun gun.

Why does being ostracized hurt so much? Increasingly, social psychologists are coming to appreciate the extent to which human beings, over the course of evolution, have needed each other in order to survive and flourish. According to Geoff MacDonald and Mark Leary (2005), this need is so primitive that rejection inflicts a social pain that feels just like physical pain. You can sense the connection in the way people describe their emotional reactions to social loss using such words as "hurt," "brokenhearted," and "crushed." Recent research lends provocative support to this linkage. In brain-imaging studies, for example, young people who were left out by other players in a three-person Internet game called "Cyberball" exhibited elevated neural activity in a part of the brain that is normally associated with physical pain (Eisenberger et al., 2003, 2007).

In group settings, both informational and normative influences are typically at work. Consider the Asch experiment. Even though many of his participants said they had conformed just to avoid being different, others said that they came to agree with their group's erroneous judgments. Is that possible? At the time, Asch had to rely on what his participants reported in interviews. Thanks to recent developments in social neuroscience, however, researchers can now peer into the socially active brain. In an ingenious medical school study that illustrates the point, Gregory Berns and others (2005) put 32 adults into a visual-spatial perception experiment in which they were asked to "mentally rotate" two geometric objects to determine if they were the same or different (see ▶ Figure 7.5). As in the original Asch study, the participants were accompanied by four confederates who unanimously made incorrect judgments on certain trials. Unlike in the original study, however, participants were placed in an fMRI scanner while engaged in the task. There were two noteworthy results. First, participants conformed to 41 percent of the group's incorrect judgments. Second, these conform-

normative influence Influence that produces conformity when a person fears the negative social consequences of appearing deviant.

▶ FIGURE 7.5

Conformity Effects on Perception

In this study, participants tried to determine if pairs of geometric objects were the same or different after observing the responses of four unanimous confederates. Participants followed the incorrect group 41 percent of the time. Suggesting that the group had altered perceptions, not just behavior, fMRI results showed that these conforming judgments were accompanied by increased activity in a part of the brain that controls spatial awareness.

Berns et al., 2005.

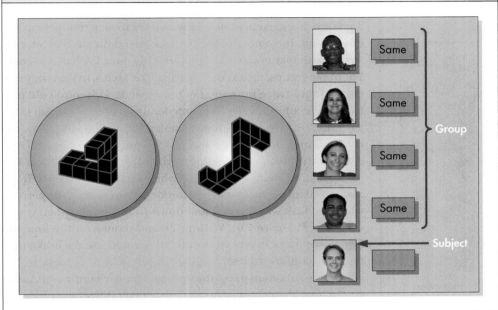

Courtesy Gregory Berns

ing judgments were accompanied by heightened activity in a part of the brain that controls spatial awareness—not in areas associated with conscious decision making. These results suggest that the group altered perceptions, not just behavior.

The distinction between the two types of social influence—informational and normative—is important, not just for understanding why people conform but because the two sources of influence produce different types of conformity: private and public (Allen, 1965; Kelman, 1961). Like beauty, conformity may be skin deep or it may penetrate beneath the surface. **Private conformity**, also called true acceptance or conversion, describes instances in which others cause us to change not only our overt behavior but our minds as well. To conform at this level is to be truly persuaded that others in a group are correct. In contrast, **public conformity** (sometimes called *compliance*, a term used later in this chapter to describe a different form of influence) refers to a more superficial change in behavior. People often respond to normative pressures by pretending to agree even when privately they do not. This often happens when we want to curry favor with others. The politician who tells constituents whatever they want to hear is a case in point.

How, you might be wondering, can social psychologists ever tell the difference between the private and public conformist? After all, both exhibit the same change in their observable behavior. The difference is that compared with someone who merely acquiesces in public, the individual who is truly persuaded maintains that change long after the group is out of the picture. When this distinction is applied to Sherif's and Asch's research, the results come out as expected. At the end of his study, Sherif (1936)

private conformity The change of beliefs that occurs when a person privately accepts the position taken by others.

public conformity A superficial change in overt behavior without a corresponding change of opinion that is produced by real or imagined group pressure.

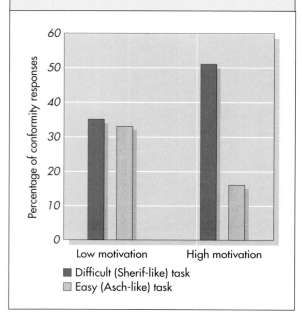

▶FIGURE 7.6

Distinguishing Types of Conformity

People made judgments under conditions in which they had a high or low level of motivation. Regardless of whether the judgment task was difficult or easy, there were moderate levels of conformity when participants had low motivation (left). But when they were highly motivated (right), participants conformed more when the task was difficult (as in Sherif's study) and less when it was easy (as in Asch's study).

Baron et al., 1996.

retested participants alone and found that their estimates continued to reflect the norm previously established in their group—even among those who were retested a full year after the experiment (Rohrer et al., 1954). In contrast, when Asch (1956) had participants write their answers privately, so that others in the group could not see, their level of conformity dropped sharply (Deutsch & Gerard, 1955; Mouton et al., 1956).

In a study that demonstrated both processes, Robert S. Baron and others (1996) had people in groups of three (one participant and two confederates) act as eyewitnesses: First they would see a picture of a person, then they would try to pick that person out of a lineup. In some groups, the task was difficult, like Sherif's, since participants saw each picture only once for half a second. For other groups, the task was easier, like Asch's, in that they saw each picture twice for a total of ten seconds. How often did participants conform when the confederates made the wrong identification? It depended on how motivated they were. When the experimenter downplayed the task as only a "pilot study," the conformity rates were 35 percent when the task was difficult and 33 percent when it was easy. But when participants were offered a financial incentive to do well, conformity went up to 51 percent when the task was difficult and down to 16 percent when it was easy (see ▶ Figure 7.6). With pride and money on the line, the Sherif-like participants conformed more and the Asch-like participants conformed less.

Table 7.1 summarizes the comparison of Sherif's and Asch's studies and the depths of social influence that they demonstrate. Looking at this table, you can see that the difficulty of the task is crucial. When reality cannot easily be validated by physical evidence, as in the autokinetic situation, people turn to others for information and conform because they are truly persuaded by that information. When reality is clear, however, the cost of dissent becomes the major issue. As Asch found, it can be difficult to depart too much from others even when you know that they—not you—are wrong. So you play along. Privately you don't change your mind. But you nod your head in agreement anyway.

TABLE 7.1

Two Types of Conformity

A comparison of Sherif's and Asch's studies suggests different kinds of conformity for different reasons. Sherif used an ambiguous task, so others provided a source of information and influenced the participants' true opinions. Asch used a task that required simple judgments of a clear stimulus, so most participants exhibited occasional public conformity in response to normative pressure but privately did not accept the group's judgments.

Experimental Task	Primary Effect of Group	Depth of Conformity Produced
Sherif's ambiguous autokinetic effect	Informational influence	Private acceptance
Asch's simple line judgments	Normative influence	Public conformity

▮ Majority Influence

Realizing that people often succumb to pressure from peers is only a first step in understanding the process of social influence. The next step is to identify the situational and personal factors that make us more or less likely to conform. We know that people tend to conform when the social pressure is intense and they are insecure about how to behave. But what creates these feelings of pressure and insecurity? Here, we look at four factors: the size of the group, a focus on norms, the presence of an ally, and gender.

Group Size: The Power in Numbers Common sense would suggest that as the number of other people in a majority increases, so should their impact. Actually, it is not that simple. Asch (1956) varied the size of groups, using one, two, three, four, eight, or fifteen confederates, and he found that conformity increased with group size—but only up to a point. Once there were three or four confederates, the amount of *additional* influence exerted by the rest was negligible. Other researchers have obtained similar results (Gerard et al., 1968).

Beyond the presence of three or four others, additions to a group are subject to the law of "diminishing returns" (Knowles, 1983; Mullen, 1983). As we will see later, Bibb Latané (1981) likens the influence of people on an individual to the way light bulbs illuminate a surface. When a second bulb is added to a room, the effect is dramatic. When the tenth bulb is added, however, its impact is barely felt, if at all. Economists say the same about the perception of money. An additional dollar seems greater to the person who has only three dollars than it does to the person who has 300.

Another possible explanation is that as more and more people express the same opinion, an individual is likely to suspect that they are acting either in "collusion" or as "spineless sheep." According to David Wilder (1977), what matters is not the actual number of others in a group but one's perception of how many distinct others who are thinking independently the group includes. Indeed, Wilder found that people were more influenced by two groups of two than by one four-person group and by two groups of three than by one six-person group. Conformity increased even more when people were exposed to three two-person groups. When faced with a majority opinion, we do more than just count the number of warm bodies—we try to assess the number of independent minds.

A Focus on Norms The size of a majority may influence the amount of pressure that is felt, but social norms give rise to conformity only when we know and focus on those norms. This may sound like an obvious point, yet we often misperceive what is normative, particularly when others are too afraid or embarrassed to publicly present their true thoughts, feelings, and behaviors.

One common example of this "pluralistic ignorance" concerns perceptions of alcohol usage. In a number of college-wide surveys, Deborah Prentice and Dale Miller (1996) found that most students overestimated how comfortable their peers were with the level of drinking on campus. Those who most overestimated how others felt about drinking at the start of the school year eventually conformed to this misperception in their own attitudes and behavior. In contrast, students who took part in discussion sessions that were designed to correct these misperceptions actually consumed less alcohol six months later. These findings are important. Additional research has shown that both male and female college students overestimate how frequently their same-sex peers drink and the quantities they consume. The more normative students perceive drinking to be, the more alcohol they consume (Lewis & Neighbors, 2004).

Knowing how others are behaving in a situation is necessary for conformity, but these norms are likely to influence us only when they are brought to our awareness, or "activated." Robert Cialdini (2003) and his colleagues have demonstrated this point in studies on littering. In one study, researchers had confederates pass out handbills to amusement park visitors and varied the amount of litter that appeared in one section of the park (an indication of how others behave in that setting). The result: The more litter there was, the more likely visitors were to toss their handbills to the ground (Cialdini et al., 1990). A second study showed that passersby were most influenced by the prior behavior of others when their attention was drawn to the existing norm. In this instance, people were observed in a parking garage that was either clean or cluttered with cigarette butts, candy wrappers, paper cups, and trash. In half of the cases,

In sports stadiums, restaurants, and other settings, social norms influence us when they are brought to awareness by the current or past behavior of others.

the norm that was already in place—clean or cluttered—was brought to participants' attention by a confederate who threw paper to the ground as he walked by. In the other half, the confederate passed by without incident. As participants reached their cars, they found a "Please Drive Safely" handbill tucked under the windshield wiper. Did they toss the paper to the ground or take it with them? The results showed that people were most likely to conform (by littering more when the garage was cluttered than when it was clean) when the confederate had littered—an act that drew attention to the norm (Cialdini et al., 1991).

An Ally in Dissent: Getting By with a Little Help   In Asch's initial experiment, unwitting participants found themselves pitted against unanimous majorities. But what if they had an ally, a partner in dissent? Asch investigated this issue and found that the presence of a single confederate who agreed with the participant reduced conformity by almost 80 percent. This finding, however, does not tell us why the presence of an ally was so effective. Was it because he or she *agreed with the participant* or because he or she *disagreed with the majority*? In other words, were the views of the participants strengthened because a dissenting confederate offered validating information or because dissent per se reduced normative pressures?

A series of experiments explored these two possibilities. In one, Vernon Allen and John Levine (1969) led participants to believe that they were working together with four confederates. Three of these others consistently agreed on the wrong judgment. The fourth then followed the majority, agreed with the participant, or made a third judgment, which was also incorrect. This last variation was the most interesting: Even when the confederate did not validate their own judgment, participants conformed less often to the majority. In another experiment, Allen and Levine (1971) varied the competence of the ally. Some participants received support from an average person. In contrast, others found themselves supported by someone who wore very thick glasses and complained that he could not see the visual displays. Not a very reassuring ally, right? Wrong. Even though participants derived less comfort from this supporter than from one who seemed more competent at the task, his presence still reduced their level of conformity.

Two important conclusions follow from this research. First, it is substantially more difficult for people to stand alone for their convictions than to be part of even a tiny minority. Second, *any* dissent—whether it validates an individual's opinion or not—can break the spell cast by a unanimous majority and reduce the normative pressures to conform. In an interesting possible illustration of how uncommon it is for individuals to single-handedly oppose a majority, researchers examined voting patterns on the

U.S. Supreme Court from 1953 to 2001. Table 7.2 shows that out of 4,178 decisions in which all nine justices voted, the 8 to 1 split was the least frequent, occurring in only 10 percent of all decisions (Granberg & Barrels, 2005).

Gender Differences Are there gender differences in conformity? Based on Asch's initial studies, social psychologists used to think that women, once considered the "weaker" sex, conform more than men. In light of all the research, however, it appears that two additional factors have to be considered. First, sex differences depend on how comfortable people are with the experimental task. Frank Sistrunk and John McDavid (1971) had male and female participants answer questions on stereotypically mas-culine, feminine, and gender-neutral topics. Along with each question, participants were told the percentage of others who agreed or disagreed. Although females conformed to the contrived majority more on the masculine items, males conformed more on the feminine items (there were no sex differences on the neutral questions). This finding suggests that one's familiarity with the issue at hand, not gender, is what affects conformity. Ask about football or video war games and most women acquiesce more than most men. Ask about family planning and fashion design and the pattern is reversed (Eagly & Carli, 1981).

A second factor is the type of social pressure people face. As a general rule, gender differences are weak and unreliable. But there is an important exception: In face-to-face encoun-ters, where people must disagree with each other openly, small differences do emerge. In fact, when participants think they are being observed, women conform more and men conform less than they do in a more private situation. Why does being "in public" create such a divergence in behavior? Alice Eagly (1987) argues that in front of others, people worry about how they come across and feel pressured to behave in ways that are viewed as acceptable according to traditional gender-role constraints. At least in public, men behave with fierce independence and autonomy, while women play a gentler, more docile role. From an evolutionary perspective, Vladas Griskevicius and others (2006) add that people are most likely to behave in gender-stereotyped ways when motivated to attract someone of the opposite sex. Consistent with research showing that women tend to like men who are independent whereas men prefer women who are agreeable, their research shows that women conform more and that men conform less when primed to think about themselves in a romantic situation.

TABLE 7.2

On Being a Lone Dissenter: Voting Patterns on the U.S. Supreme Court

Out of 4,178 U.S. Supreme Court decisions handed down from 1953 to 2001, the 8 to 1 breakdown involving a lone dissenter was the least common type of vote. This historical observation is consistent with conformity research showing the power of the majority over an individual who lacks an ally

Vote Breakdowns	Frequency
9 to 0	35%
8 to 1	10%
7 to 2	14%
6 to 3	20%
5 to 4	21%

Granberg & Battels, 2005.

Minority Influence

In a book entitled *Dissent in Dangerous Times*, Austin Sarat (2005) notes that while the freedom to dissent is highly valued in the American national psyche, individual dissent-ers are often vilified for their beliefs—especially in today's post-9/11 war on terrorism.

The fact is, it has never been easy for individuals to express unpopular views and enlist support for these views from others. Philosopher Bertrand Russell once said, "Conventional people are roused to frenzy by departure from convention, largely because they regard such departure as criticism of themselves." He may have been right. Although people who assert their beliefs against the majority are generally seen as com-petent and honest, they are also disliked and roundly rejected (Bassili & Provencal, 1988;

Levine, 1989). It's no wonder that most people think twice before expressing unpopular positions. In a series of survey studies of what he called the "minority slowness effect," John Bassili (2003) asked people about their attitudes on social policy issues such as affirmative action or about their likes and dislikes for various celebrities, sports, foods, places, and activities. Consistently, and regardless of the topic, respondents who held minority opinions were slower to answer the questions than those in the majority.

Resisting the pressure to conform and maintaining one's independence may be socially difficult, but it is not impossible. History's famous heroes, villains, and creative minds are living proof: Joan of Arc, Jesus Christ, Charles Darwin, and Mahatma Gandhi, to name just a few, were dissenters of their time who continue to capture the imagination. Then there is human behavior in the laboratory. Social psychologists have been so intrigued by Asch's initial finding that participants conformed 37 percent of the time that textbooks such as this one routinely refer to "Asch's conformity study." Yet the overlooked flip side of the coin is that Asch's participants refused to acquiesce 63 percent of the time—thus also indicating the power of independence, truth telling, and a concern for social harmony (Friend et al., 1990; Hodges & Geyer, 2006).

Twelve Angry Men, a classic film starring Henry Fonda, illustrates how a lone dissenter can resist the pressure to conform and convince others to follow. Almost as soon as the door of the jury room closes, the jury in this film takes a show-of-hands vote. The result is an 11 to 1 majority in favor of conviction with Fonda the lone hold-out. Through 90 minutes of heated deliberation, Fonda works relentlessly to plant a seed of doubt in the minds of his peers. In the end, the jury reaches a unanimous verdict: *not* guilty.

Sometimes art imitates life; sometimes it does not. In this instance, Henry Fonda's heroics are highly atypical. When it comes to jury decision making, as we'll see in Chapter 12, the majority usually wins. Yet in trial juries, as in other small groups, there are occasional exceptions. Thanks to Serge Moscovici, Edwin Hollander, and others, we now know quite a bit about **minority influence** and the strategies that astute nonconformists use to act as agents of social change (De Dreu & De Vries, 2001; Hollander, 1985; Maass & Clark, 1984; Moscovici et al., 1985; Mugny & Perez, 1991).

The Power of Style According to Moscovici, majorities are powerful by virtue of their sheer *numbers*, while nonconformists derive power from the *style* of their behavior. It is not just what nonconformists say that matters but how they say it. To exert influence, says Moscovici, those in the minority must be forceful, persistent, and unwavering in support of their position. Yet at the same time, they must appear flexible and open-minded. Confronted with a consistent but evenhanded dissenter, members of the majority will sit up, take notice, and rethink their own positions.

Why should a consistent behavioral style prove effective? One possible reason is that unwavering repetition draws attention from those in the mainstream, which is a necessary first step to social influence. Another possibility is that consistency signals that the dissenter is unlikely to yield, which leads those in the majority to feel pressured to seek compromise. A third possible reason is that when confronted with someone who has the self-confidence and dedication to take an unpopular stand without backing down, people assume that he or she must have a point. Unless a dissenter is perceived in negative terms—as biased, obstinate, or just plain crazy—this situation stimulates others to reexamine their own views (Moskowitz, 1996). Of course, it helps to be seen as part of "us" rather than "them." Research shows that dissenters have more influence when people identify with them and perceive them to be similar in ways that are relevant and desirable (Turner, 1991; Wood et al., 1996).

Based on a meta-analysis of 97 experiments investigating minority influence, Wendy Wood and her colleagues (1994) concluded that there is strong support for the

minority influence The process by which dissenters produce change within a group.

consistency hypothesis. In one classic study, for example, Moscovici and others (1969) turned Asch's procedure on its head by confronting people with a *minority* of confederates who made incorrect judgments. In groups of six, participants took part in what was supposed to be a study of color perception. They viewed a series of slides that all were blue but varied in intensity. For each slide, the participants took turns naming the color. The task was simple, but two confederates announced that the slides were green. When the confederates were *consistent*—that is, when both made incorrect green judgments for all slides—they had a surprising degree of influence. About a third of all participants incorrectly reported seeing at least one green slide, and 8 percent of all responses were incorrect. Subsequent research confirmed that the perception of consistency increases minority influence (Clark, 2001; Crano, 2000).

Based on the fact that dissent often breeds hostility, Edwin Hollander (1958) recommended a different approach. Hollander warned that people who seek positions of leadership or challenge a group without first becoming accepted full-fledged members of that group run the risk that their opinions will fall on deaf ears. As an alternative to Moscovici's consistency strategy, Hollander suggested that to influence a majority, people should first conform in order to establish their credentials as competent insiders. By becoming members of the mainstream, they accumulate **idiosyncrasy credits**, or "brownie points." Once they have accumulated enough goodwill within the group, a certain amount of their deviance will then be tolerated. Several studies have shown that this "first conform, then dissent" strategy, like the "consistent dissent" approach, can be effective (Bray et al., 1982; Lortie-Lussier, 1987).

A Chip Off the Old Block?   Regardless of which strategy is used, minority influence is a force to be reckoned with. But does it work just like the process of conformity, or is there something different about the way that minorities and majorities effect change? Some theorists believe that a *single process* accounts for both directions of social influence—that minority influence is like a "chip off the old block" (Latané & Wolf, 1981; Tanford & Penrod, 1984). Others have taken a *dual-process* approach (Moscovici, 1980; Nemeth, 1986). In this second view, majorities and minorities exert influence in very different ways and for different reasons. Majorities, because they have power and control, elicit *public* conformity by bringing stressful normative pressures to bear on the individual. But minorities, because they are seen as seriously committed to their views, produce a deeper and more lasting form of *private* conformity, or *conversion*, by leading others to rethink their original positions.

To evaluate these single- and dual-process theories, researchers have compared the effects of majority and minority viewpoints on participants who are otherwise neutral on an issue in dispute. On the basis of this research, two conclusions can be drawn. First, the relative impact of majorities and minorities depends on whether the judgment that is being made is objective or subjective, a matter of fact or opinion. In a study conducted in Italy, Anne Maass and others (1996) found that majorities have greater influence on factual questions, for which only one answer is correct ("What percentage of its raw oil does Italy import from Venezuela?"), but that minorities exert equal impact on opinion questions, for which there is a range of acceptable responses ("What percentage of its raw oil *should* Italy import from Venezuela?"). People feel freer to stray from the mainstream on matters of opinion, when there is no right or wrong answer.

The second conclusion is that the relative effects of majority and minority points of view depend on how conformity is measured. To be sure, majorities have a decisive upper hand on direct or public measures of conformity. After all, people are reluctant to stray conspicuously from the group norm. But on more indirect or private measures of conformity—when participants can respond without a fear of appearing deviant—minorities exert a strong impact (Clark & Maass, 1990; Moscovici & Personnaz, 1991;

idiosyncrasy credits
Interpersonal "credits" that a person earns by following group norms.

Wood et al., 1996). As Moscovici cogently argued, each of us is changed in a meaningful but subtle way by minority opinion. Because of social pressures, we may not openly admit to the influence, but the change is unmistakable (Wood et al., 1994).

According to Charlan Nemeth (1986), dissenters serve another valuable purpose regardless of whether their views are correct. Simply by their willingness to stay firmly independent, minorities can force other group members to think more carefully, more openly, and more creatively about a problem, enhancing the quality of a group's decision making. In one study, participants exposed to a minority viewpoint on how to solve anagram problems later found more novel solutions themselves (Nemeth & Kwan, 1987). In a second study, those exposed to a consistent minority viewpoint on how to recall information later recalled more words from a list they were trying to memorize (Nemeth et al., 1990). In a third study, interacting groups that contained one dissenting confederate produced more original analyses of complex business problems (Van Dyne & Saavedra, 1996). Interestingly, Nemeth and others (2001) have found that in order to have influence on a group, lone individuals must exhibit "authentic dissent," not merely play "devil's advocate," a tactic that actually bolsters a majority's position.

▌ Culture and Conformity

We humans are a heterogeneous and diverse lot. As a matter of *geography*, some of us live in large, heavily populated cities while others live in small towns, affluent suburbs, rural farming or fishing communities, hot and humid jungles, expansive deserts, high-altitude mountains, tropical islands, and vast arctic plains. Excluding dialects, more than 6,800 different *languages* are spoken. There are also hundreds of *religions* that people identify with—the most common being Christianity (33 percent), Islam (21 percent), Hinduism (14 percent), and Buddhism (6 percent), with Judaism (0.22 percent) and others claiming fewer adherents. Roughly 16 percent of the world's population is not affiliated with a religion (Adherents.com 2009).

Linked together by historical time and geographical space, each culture has its own ideology, music, fashions, foods, laws, customs, and manners of expression. As many tourists and exchange students traveling abroad have come to learn, sometimes the hard way, the social norms that influence human conduct can vary in significant ways from one part of the world to another.

Cultures differ in their unique, often colorful norms. In Ecuador, many men wear handwoven Panama hats (top left). In India, brightly colored powders are sold for the Hindu religious festival of Holi, which marks the beginning of spring (bottom left). In Spain, revelers in Pamplona hold up their bandanas before the start of the festival of San Fermin, during which six bulls run through crowded streets in the center of town (right).

© Robert van der Hilst/CORBIS

© RAJ PATIDAR/Reuters/Corbis

© Reuters NewMedia Inc./CORBIS

These photographs were taken of average-income families posing in front of their homes and material possessions. Representing the individualistic orientation common among affluent societies is the Skeen family of Pearland, Texas (left). Representing the collectivist orientation found in more impoverished societies is the Natoma family of Kouakourou, Mali (right).

In *Do's and Taboos Around the World*, R. E. Axtell (1993) warns world travelers about some of these differences. Dine in an Indian home, he notes, and you should leave food on the plate to show the host that the portions were generous and you had enough to eat. Yet as a dinner guest in Bolivia, you would show your appreciation by cleaning your plate. Shop in an outdoor market in Iraq, and you should expect to negotiate the price of everything you buy. Plan an appointment in Brazil, and the person you're scheduled to meet is likely to be late; it's nothing personal. In North America, it is common to sit casually opposite someone with your legs outstretched. Yet in Nepal, as in many Muslim countries, it is an insult to point the bottoms of your feet at someone. Even the way we space ourselves from each other is influenced by culture. Americans, Canadians, British, and northern Europeans keep a polite distance between themselves and others and feel "crowded" by the touchier, nose-to-nose style of the French, Greeks, Arabs, Mexicans, and people of South America. In the affairs of day-to-day living, each culture operates by its own rules of conduct.

Just as cultures differ in their social norms, so too they differ in the extent to which people are expected to adhere to those norms. As we saw in Chapter 3, there are different cultural orientations toward persons and their relationships to groups. Some cultures primarily value **individualism** and the virtues of independence, autonomy, and self-reliance, whereas others value **collectivism** and the virtues of interdependence, cooperation, and social harmony. Under the banner of individualism, personal goals take priority over group allegiances. Yet in collectivistic cultures, the person is first and foremost a loyal member of a family, team, company, church, and state.

What determines whether a culture becomes individualistic or collectivistic? Speculating on the origins of these orientations, Harry Triandis (1995) suggests that there are three key factors. The first is the *complexity* of a society. As people come to live in more complex industrialized societies (compared, for example, with a simpler life of food gathering among desert nomads), there are more groups to identify with, which means less loyalty to any one group and a greater focus on personal rather than collective goals. Second is the *affluence* of a society. As people prosper, they gain financial independence from each other, a condition that promotes social independence as well as mobility and a focus on personal rather than collective goals. The third factor is *heterogeneity*. Societies that are homogeneous or "tight" (where members share the same language, religion, and social customs) tend to be rigid and intolerant of those who veer from the norm. Societies that are culturally diverse or "loose" (where two or more cultures coexist) tend to be more permissive of dissent, thus allowing for more individual expression. According to Edward Sampson (2000), cultural orientations may also be rooted in religious ideologies, as in the link between Christianity and individualism.

individualism A cultural orientation in which independence, autonomy, and self-reliance take priority over group allegiances.

collectivism A cultural orientation in which interdependence, cooperation, and social harmony take priority over personal goals.

Early research across nations showed that autonomy and independence are most highly valued in the United States, Australia, Great Britain, Canada, and the Netherlands, in that order. In contrast, other cultures value social harmony and "fitting in" for the sake of community, the most collectivist people being from Venezuela, Colombia, Pakistan, Peru, Taiwan, and China (Hofstede, 1980). Although it now appears that cultures differ in other more complicated ways and that individuals differ even within cultures (Oyserman et al., 2002), it is clear that nations on average vary in their orientations on the dimension of individualism (Schimmack et al., 2005).

Do cultural orientations influence conformity? Among the Bantu of Zimbabwe, an African people in which deviance is scorned, 51 percent of participants who were placed in an Asch-like study conformed—more than the number typically seen in the United States (Whittaker & Meade, 1967). In fact, when John Berry (1979) compared participants from 17 cultures, he found that conformity rates ranged from a low of 18 percent among Inuit hunters of Baffin Island to a high of 60 percent among village-dwelling Temne farmers of West Africa. Additional analyses have shown that conformity rates are generally higher in cultures that are collectivistic rather than individualistic in orientation (Bond & Smith, 1996). Hence, many anthropologists—interested in culture and its influence over individuals—study the processes of conformity and independence (Spradley & McCurdy 2009).

Compliance

In conformity situations, people follow implicit or explicit group norms. But another common form of social influence occurs when others make *direct requests* of us in the hope that we will comply. Situations calling for **compliance** take many forms. These include a friend's plea for help, sheepishly prefaced by the question "Can you do me a favor?" They also include the pop-up ads on the Internet designed to lure you into a commercial site and the salesperson's pitch for business prefaced by the dangerous words "Have I got a deal for you!" Sometimes, the request is up front and direct; what you see is what you get. At other times, it is part of a subtle and more elaborate manipulation.

How do people get others to comply with self-serving requests? How do police interrogators get crime suspects to confess? How do political parties draw millions of dollars in contributions from voters? How do *you* exert influence over others? Do you use threats, promises, politeness, deceit, or reason? Do you hint, coax, sulk, negotiate, throw tantrums, or pull rank whenever you can? To a large extent, the compliance strategies we use depend on how well we know the person we target, our status within a relationship, our personality, our culture, and the nature of the request.

By observing the masters of influence—advertisers, fund-raisers, politicians, and business leaders—social psychologists have learned a great deal about the subtle but effective strategies that are commonly used. What we see is that people often get others to comply with their requests by setting traps. Once caught in these traps, the unwary victim often finds it difficult to escape.

Mindlessness and Compliance

Sometimes people can be disarmed by the simple phrasing of a request, regardless of its merit. Consider, for example, requests that sound reasonable but offer no real basis for compliance. Ellen Langer and her colleagues (1978) have found that words alone can sometimes trick us into submission. In their research, an experimenter approached

compliance Changes in behavior that are elicited by direct requests.

people who were using a library copying machine and asked to cut in. Three different versions of the request were used. In one, participants were simply asked, "Excuse me. I have five pages. May I use the Xerox machine?" In a second version, the request was justified by the added phrase "because I'm in a rush." As you would expect, more participants stepped aside when the request was justified (94 percent) than when it was not (60 percent). A third version of the request, however, suggests that the reason offered had little to do with the increase in compliance. In this case, participants heard the following: "Excuse me. I have five pages. May I use the Xerox machine because I have to make some copies?" If you read this request closely, you'll see that it really offered no reason at all. Yet 93 percent in this condition complied! It was as if the appearance of a reason, triggered by the word *because*, was all that was necessary. Indeed, Langer (1989) finds that the mind is often on "automatic pilot"—we respond *mindlessly* to words without fully processing the information they are supposed to convey. At least for requests that are small, "sweet little nothings" may be enough to win compliance.

It is interesting that although a state of mindlessness can make us vulnerable to compliance, it can also have the opposite effect. For example, many city dwellers will automatically walk past panhandlers on the street looking for a handout. Perhaps the way to increase compliance in such situations is to disrupt this mindless refusal response by making a request that is so unusual that it piques the target person's interest. To test this hypothesis, researchers had a confederate approach people on the street and make a request that was either typical ("Can you spare a quarter?") or atypical ("Can you spare 17 cents?"). The result: Atypical pleas elicited more comments and questions from those who were targeted—and produced a 60 percent increase in the number of people who gave money (Santos et al., 1994). In another study, researchers who went door to door selling holiday cards gained more compliance when they disrupted the mindless process and reframed the sales pitch. They sold more cards when they said the price was "three hundred pennies—that's three dollars, it's a bargain" than when they simply asked for three dollars (Davis & Knowles, 1999).

Con artists prosper from the tendency for people to respond mindlessly to requests that sound reasonable but offer no real basis for compliance.

The Norm of Reciprocity

A simple, unstated, but powerful rule of social behavior known as the *norm of reciprocity* dictates that we treat others as they have treated us (Gouldner, 1960). On the negative side, this norm can be used to sanction retaliation against those who cause us harm—"an eye for an eye." On the positive side, it leads us to feel obligated to repay others for acts of kindness. Thus, whenever we receive gifts, invitations, and free samples, we usually go out of our way to return the favor.

The norm of reciprocity contributes to the predictability and fairness of social interaction. However, it can also be used to exploit us. Dennis Regan (1971) examined this possibility in the following laboratory study. Individuals were brought together with a confederate who was trained to act in a likable or unlikable manner for an experiment on "aesthetics." In one condition, the confederate did the participant an unsolicited favor. He left during a break and returned with two bottles of Coca-Cola, one for himself and the other for the participant. In a second condition, he returned from the break empty-handed. In a third condition, participants were treated to a Coke, but by the experimenter, not the confederate. The confederate then told participants in all conditions that he was selling raffle tickets at 25 cents apiece and asked if they would be willing to buy any. On average, participants bought more raffle tickets when the confederate had earlier brought them a soft drink than when he had not. The norm of reciprocity was so strong that they returned the favor even when the confederate was not otherwise a likable character. In fact, participants in this condition spent an average of 43 cents on raffle tickets. At a time when soft drinks cost less than a quarter, the confederate made a handsome quick profit on his investment!

It's clear that the norm of reciprocity can be used to trap us, unwittingly, into acts of compliance. For example, research conducted in restaurants shows that waiters and waitresses can increase their tip percentages by writing, "Thank you" on the back of the customer's check, by drawing a happy face on it, or by placing candy on the check tray (Rind & Strohmetz, 2001; Strohmetz et al., 2002). But does receiving a favor make us feel indebted forever or is there a time limit to the social obligation that is so quietly unleashed? In an experiment designed to answer this question, Jerry Burger and others (1997) used Regan's soft drink favor and had the confederate try to "cash in" with a request either immediately or one week later. The result: Compliance levels increased in the immediate condition but not after a full week had passed. People may feel compelled to reciprocate, but that feeling—at least for small acts of kindness—is relatively short-lived.

Some people are more likely than others to trigger and exploit the reciprocity norm. According to Martin Greenberg and David Westcott (1983), individuals who use reciprocity to elicit compliance are called "creditors" because they always try to keep others in their debt so they can cash in when necessary. On a questionnaire that measures *reciprocation ideology*, people are identified as creditors if they endorse such statements as "If someone does you a favor, it's good to repay that person with a greater favor." On the receiving end, some people more than others try not to accept favors that might later set them up to be exploited. On a scale that measures *reciprocation wariness*, people are said to be wary if they express the suspicion, for example, that "asking for another's help gives them power over your life" (Eisenberger et al., 1987).

Setting Traps: Sequential Request Strategies

People who raise money or sell for a living know that it often takes more than a single plea to win over a potential donor or customer. Social psychologists share this knowledge and have studied several compliance techniques that are based on making two or more related requests. *Click!* The first request sets the trap. *Snap!* The second captures the prey. In a fascinating book entitled *Influence: The Psychology of Persuasion*, Robert Cialdini (2007) describes a number of sequential request tactics in vivid detail. These methods are presented in the following pages.

The Foot in the Door Folk wisdom has it that one way to get a person to comply with a sizable request is to start small. First devised by traveling salespeople peddling vacuum cleaners, hairbrushes, cosmetics, magazine subscriptions, and encyclopedias, the trick is to somehow get your "foot in the door." The expression need not be taken literally, of course. The point of the **foot-in-the-door technique** is to break the ice with a small initial request that the customer can't easily refuse. Once that first commitment is elicited, the chances are increased that another, larger request will succeed.

Jonathan Freedman and Scott Fraser (1966) tested the impact of this technique in a series of field experiments. In one, an experimenter pretending to be employed by a consumer organization telephoned a large number of female homemakers in

foot-in-the-door technique
A two-step compliance technique in which an influencer sets the stage for the real request by first getting a person to comply with a much smaller request.

Palo Alto, California, and asked if they would be willing to answer some questions about household products. Those who consented were then asked a few quick and innocuous questions and thanked for their assistance. Three days later, the experimenter called back and made a considerable, almost outrageous, request. He asked the women if they would allow a handful of men into their homes for two hours to rummage through their drawers and cupboards so they could take an inventory of their household products.

The foot-in-the-door technique proved to be very effective. When the participants were confronted with only the very intrusive request, 22 percent consented. Yet the rate of agreement among those who had been surveyed earlier more than doubled, to 53 percent. This basic result has now been repeated over and over again. People are more likely to donate time, money, food, blood, the use of their home, and other resources once they have been induced to go along with a small initial request. Although the effect is not always as dramatic as that obtained by Freedman and Fraser, it does appear in a wide variety of circumstances and it increases compliance rates, on average, by about 13 percent (Burger, 1999).

The practical implications of the foot-in-the-door technique are obvious. But why does it work? Over the years, several explanations have been suggested. One that seems plausible is based on self-perception theory—that people infer their attitudes by observing their own behavior. This explanation suggests that a two-step process is at work. First, by observing your own behavior in the initial situation, you come to see yourself as the kind of person who is generally cooperative when approached with a request. Second, when confronted with the more burdensome request, you seek to respond in ways that maintain this new self-image. By this logic, the foot-in-the-door technique should succeed only when you attribute an initial act of compliance to your own personal characteristics.

Based on a review of dozens of studies, Jerry Burger (1999) concludes that the research generally supports the self-perception account. Thus, if the first request is too trivial or if participants are paid for the first act of compliance, they won't later come to view themselves as inherently cooperative. Under these conditions, the technique *does not* work. Likewise, the effect occurs only when people are motivated to be consistent with their self-images. If participants are unhappy with what the initial behavior implies about them, if they are too young to appreciate the implications, or if they don't care about behaving in ways that are personally consistent, then again the technique does not work. Other processes may be at work, but it appears that the foot opens the door by altering self-perceptions, leading people who agree to the small initial request—without any compensation—to see themselves as helpful (Burger & Caldwell, 2003). In fact, this process can still occur even when a person tries to comply with the initial small request but fails. In a series of studies, Dariusz Dolinski (2000) found that when people were asked if they could find directions to a nonexistent street address or decipher an unreadable message—small favors that they could not satisfy— they, too, become more compliant with the next request.

© Car Culture/Corbis

Lowballing is a common technique used in selling cars. For consumer advice on how to buy a car without falling into this and other compliance traps often set by dealers, visit the Edmunds Automobile Buyer's Guide (www.Edmunds.com).

Knowing that a foot in the door increases compliance rates is both exciting and troubling—exciting for the owner of the foot, troubling for the owner of the door. As Cialdini (2007) put it, "You can use small commitments to manipulate a person's self-image; you can use them to turn citizens into 'public servants,' prospects into 'customers,' prisoners into 'collaborators.' And once you've got a man's self-image where you want it, he should comply *naturally* with a whole range of your requests that are consistent with this view of himself" (p. 74).

Lowballing   Another two-step trap, arguably the most unscrupulous of all compliance techniques, is also based on the "start small" idea. Imagine yourself in the following situation. You're at a local automobile dealership. After some negotiation, the salesperson offers a great price on the car of your choice. You cast aside other considerations and shake hands on the deal and as the salesperson goes off to "write it up," you begin to feel the thrill of owning the car of your dreams. Absorbed in fantasy, you are suddenly interrupted by the return of the salesperson. "I'm sorry," he says. "The manager would not approve the sale. We have to raise the price by another $450. I'm afraid that's the best we can do." As the victim of an all-too-common trick known as **lowballing**, you are now faced with a tough decision. On the one hand, you're wild about the car. You've already enjoyed the pleasure of thinking it's yours; and the more you think about it, the better it looks. On the other hand, you don't want to pay more than you bargained for, and you have an uneasy feeling in the pit of your stomach that you're being duped. What do you do?

Salespeople who use this tactic are betting that you'll go ahead with the purchase despite the added cost. If the way research participants behave is any indication, they are often right. In one study, experimenters phoned introductory psychology students and asked if they would be willing to participate in a study for extra credit. Some were told up front that the session would begin at the uncivilized hour of 7 A.M. Knowing that, only 31 percent volunteered. But other participants were lowballed. Only *after* they agreed to participate did the experimenter inform them of the 7 A.M. starting time. Would that be okay? Whether or not it was, the procedure achieved its objective—the signup rate rose to 56 percent (Cialdini et al., 1978).

Disturbing as it may be, lowballing is an interesting technique. Surely, once the low ball offer has been thrown, many recipients suspect that they were misled. Yet they go along. Why? The reason appears to be based on the psychology of commitment (Kiesler, 1971). Once people make a particular decision, they justify it to themselves by thinking of all its positive aspects. As they get increasingly committed to a course of action, they grow more resistant to changing their mind, even if the initial reasons for the action have been changed or withdrawn entirely. In the automobile dealership scenario, you might very well have decided to purchase the car because of the price. But then you would have thought about its sleek new appearance, the scent of the leather interior, and the brand-new satellite radio. By the time you learned that the price would be more than you'd bargained for, it would be too late—you would already have been hooked.

Lowballing also produces another form of commitment. When people do not suspect duplicity, they feel a nagging sense of unfulfilled obligation to the person with whom they negotiated. Thus, even though the salesperson was unable to complete the original deal, you might feel obligated to buy anyway, having already agreed to make the purchase. This commitment to the other person may account for why lowballing works better when the second request is made by the same person than by someone else (Burger & Petty, 1981). It may also explain why people are most vulnerable to the lowball when they make their commitment in public rather than in private (Burger & Cornelius, 2003).

The Door in the Face   Although shifting from an initial small request to a larger one can be effective, as in the foot-in-the-door and lowball techniques, oddly enough the opposite is also true. Cialdini (2007) describes the time he was approached by a Boy Scout and asked to buy two five-dollar tickets to an upcoming circus. Having better things to do with his time and money, he declined. Then the boy asked if he would be interested in buying chocolate bars at a dollar apiece. Even though he does not particularly like chocolate, Cialdini—an expert on social influence—bought two of them. After a moment's reflection, he realized what had happened. Whether the Boy Scout

lowballing   A two-step compliance technique in which the influencer secures agreement with a request but then increases the size of that request by revealing hidden costs.

planned it that way or not, Cialdini had fallen for what is known as the **door-in-the-face technique**.

The technique is as simple as it sounds. An individual makes an initial request that is so large it is sure to be rejected and then comes back with a second, more reasonable request. Will the second request fare better after the first one has been declined? Plagued by the sight of uneaten chocolate bars, Cialdini and others (1975) tested the effectiveness of the door-in-the-face technique. They stopped college students on campus and asked if they would volunteer to work without pay at a counseling center for juvenile delinquents. The time commitment would be forbidding: roughly two hours a week for the next two years! Not surprisingly, everyone who was approached politely slammed the proverbial door in the experimenter's face. But then the experimenter followed up with a more modest proposal, asking the students if they would be willing to take a group of delinquents on a two-hour trip to the zoo. The strategy worked like a charm. Only 17 percent of the students confronted with only the second request agreed. But of those who initially declined the first request, 50 percent said yes to the zoo trip. You should note that the door-in-the-face technique does not elicit only empty promises. Most research participants who comply subsequently do what they've agreed to do (Cialdini & Ascani, 1976).

Why is the door-in-the-face technique such an effective trap? One possibility involves the principle of *perceptual contrast*: To the person exposed to a very large initial request, the second request "seems smaller." Two dollars' worth of candy bars is not bad compared with ten dollars for circus tickets. Likewise, taking a group of kids to the zoo seems trivial compared with two years of volunteer work. As intuitively sensible as this explanation seems, Cialdini and others (1975) concluded that perceptual contrast is only partly responsible for the effect. When participants heard the large request without actually having to reject it, their rate of compliance with the second request (25 percent) was only slightly larger than the 17 percent rate of compliance exhibited by those who heard only the small request.

A second, more compelling explanation for the effect involves the notion of *reciprocal concessions*. A close cousin of the reciprocity norm, this refers to the pressure to respond to changes in a bargaining position. When an individual backs down from a large request to a smaller one, we view that move as a concession that we should match by our own compliance. Thus, the door-in-the-face technique does not work if the second request is made by a different person (Cialdini et al., 1975). Nor does it work if the first request is so extreme that it comes across as an insincere "first offer" (Schwarzwald et al., 1979). On an emotional level, refusing to help on one request may also trigger feelings of guilt, which we can reduce by complying with the second, smaller request (O'Keefe & Figge, 1997; Millar, 2002).

An effective way to get someone to do you a favor is to make a first request that is so large the person is sure to reject it. **TRUE.**

That's Not All, Folks! If the notion of reciprocal concessions is correct, then a person shouldn't actually have to refuse the initial offer in order for the shift to a smaller request to work. Indeed, another familiar sales strategy manages to use concession without first eliciting refusal. In this strategy, a product is offered at a particular price, but then, before the buyer has a chance to respond, the seller adds, "And that's not all!" At that point, either the original price is reduced or a bonus is offered to sweeten the pot. The seller, of course, intends all along to make the so-called concession.

This ploy, called the **that's-not-all technique**, seems awfully transparent, right? Surely no one falls for it, right? Jerry Burger (1986) was not so sure. He predicted that people are more likely to make a purchase when a deal seems to have improved than when the same deal is offered right from the start. To test this hypothesis, Burger set up a booth at a campus fair and sold cupcakes. Some customers who approached the table were told that the cupcakes cost 75 cents each. Others were told that they cost a

door-in-the-face technique A two-step compliance technique in which an influencer prefaces the real request with one that is so large that it is rejected.

that's-not-all technique A two-step compliance technique in which the influencer begins with an inflated request, then decreases its apparent size by offering a discount or bonus.

TABLE 7.3

Sequential Request Strategies

Various compliance techniques are based on a sequence of two related requests. *Click!* The first request sets the trap. *Snap!* The second captures the prey. Research has shown that the four sequential request strategies summarized in this table are all effective.

Request Shifts	Technique	Description
From small to large	Foot in the door	Begin with a very small request, secure agreement, then make a separate, larger request.
	Lowballing	Secure agreement with a request and then increase the size of that request by revealing hidden costs.
From large to small	Door in the face	Begin with a very large request that will be rejected, then follow that up with a more modest request.
	That's not all	Begin with a somewhat inflated request, then immediately decrease the apparent size of that request by offering a discount or bonus.

dollar, but then, before they could respond, the price was reduced to 75 cents. Rationally speaking, Burger's manipulation did not affect the ultimate price, so it should not have affected sales. But it did. When customers were led to believe that the final price represented a reduction, sales increased from 44 to 73 percent.

At this point, let's step back and look at the various compliance tactics described in this section. All of them are based on a two-step process that involves a shift from a request of one size to another. What differs is whether the small or large request comes first and how the transition between steps is made (see Table 7.3). Moreover, all these strategies work in subtle ways by manipulating the target person's self-image, commitment to the product, feelings of obligation to the seller, or perceptions of the real request. It is even possible to increase compliance by first asking "How are you feeling?" (Howard, 1990) or by claiming some coincidental similarity like having the same first name or birthday (Burger et al., 2004). When you consider these various traps, you have to wonder whether it's ever possible to escape.

■ Assertiveness: When People Say No

Cialdini (2007) opens his book with a confession: "I can admit it freely now. All my life I've been a patsy" (p. xi). As a past victim of compliance traps, he is not alone. Many people find it difficult to assert themselves in interpersonal situations. Faced with an unreasonable request from a friend, spouse, or stranger, they become anxious at the mere thought of putting a foot down and refusing to comply. Indeed, there are times when it is uncomfortable for anyone to say no. However, just as we can maintain our autonomy in the face of conformity pressures, we can also refuse direct requests—even clever ones. The trap may be set, but you don't have to get caught.

According to Cialdini, being able to resist the pressure of compliance rests, first and foremost, on being vigilant. If a stranger hands you a gift and then launches into a sales pitch, you should recognize the tactic for what it is and not feel indebted by the norm of reciprocity. And if you strike a deal with a salesperson who later reneges on the terms, you should be aware that you're being lowballed. Indeed, that is exactly what happened to one of the authors of this book. After a Saturday afternoon of careful

Knowledge is power, and if you know when a clever technique is being used on you, then it becomes easier to ignore.

—Burke Leon

negotiation at a local car dealer, he and his wife finally came to terms on a price. Minutes later, however, the salesman returned with the news that the manager would not approve the deal. The cost of a power moonroof, which was supposed to be included, would have to be added on. Familiar with the research, the author turned to his wife and exclaimed, "It's a trick; they're lowballing us!" Realizing what was happening, she became furious, went straight to the manager, and made such a scene in front of other customers that he backed down and honored the original deal.

What happened in this instance? Why did recognizing the attempted manipulation produce such anger and resistance? As this story illustrates, compliance techniques work smoothly only if they are hidden from view. The problem is, they are not only attempts to influence us, they are also deceptive. Flattery, gifts, and other ploys often elicit compliance, but not if they are perceived as insincere (Jones, 1964) or if the target has a high level of reciprocity wariness (Eisenberger et al., 1987). Likewise, the sequential request traps are powerful only to the extent that they are subtle and cannot be seen for what they are (Schwarzwald et al., 1979). People don't like to be hustled. In fact, feeling manipulated typically leads us to react with anger, psychological reactance, and stubborn noncompliance—unless the request is a command and the requester is a figure of authority.

Obedience

Allen Funt, the creator and producer of the original TV program *Candid Camera* (a forerunner of the show *Punk'd*), spent as much time observing human behavior in the real world as most psychologists do. When asked what he learned from all his people-watching, Funt replied, "The worst thing, and I see it over and over, is how easily people can be led by any kind of authority figure, or even the most minimal signs of authority." He went on to cite the time he put up a road sign that read "Delaware Closed Today." The reaction? "Motorists didn't question it. Instead they asked, 'Is Jersey open?'" (Zimbardo, 1985, p. 47).

Funt was right about the way we react to authority. Taught from birth that it's important to respect legitimate forms of leadership, people think twice before defying parents, teachers, employers, coaches, and government officials. The problem is that mere symbols of authority—titles, uniforms, badges, or the trappings of success, even without the necessary credentials—can sometimes turn ordinary people into docile servants. Leonard Bickman (1974) demonstrated this phenomenon in a series of studies in which a male research assistant stopped passersby on the street and ordered them to do something unusual. Sometimes he pointed to a paper bag on the ground and said, "Pick up this bag for me!" At other times, he pointed to an individual standing beside a parked car and said, "This fellow is overparked at the meter but doesn't have any change. Give him a dime!" Would anyone really take this guy seriously? When he was dressed in

Taken to the extreme, blind obedience can have devastating results. Nazi officials killed millions during World War II, and many said they did it "because I was just following orders."

Syndicated Features Limited/The Image Works, Inc.

street clothes, only a third of the people stopped followed his orders. But when he wore a security guard's uniform, nearly nine out of every ten people obeyed! Even when the uniformed assistant turned the corner and walked away after issuing his command, the vast majority of passersby followed his orders. Clearly, uniforms signify the power of authority (Bushman, 1988).

Blind **obedience** may seem funny, but if people are willing to take orders from a total stranger, how far will they go when it really matters? As the pages of history attest, the implications are sobering. In World War II, Nazi officials participated in the deaths of millions of Jews, as well as Poles, Russians, gypsies, and homosexuals. Yet when tried for these crimes, all of them raised the same defense: "I was following orders."

Surely, you may be thinking, the Holocaust was a historical anomaly that says more about the Nazis as a group of bigoted, hateful, and pathologically frustrated individuals than about the situations that lead people in general to commit acts of destructive obedience. In *Hitler's Willing Executioners*, historian Daniel Goldhagen (1996) argues on the basis of past records that many German officials were willing anti-Semitic participants in the Holocaust—not mere ordinary people forced to follow orders. Citing historical records, others have similarly argued that Nazi killers knew, believed in, and celebrated their mission (Cesarani, 2004; Haslam & Reicher, 2007; Vetlesen, 2005).

Yet two lines of evidence suggest that laying blame on the German people is too simple as an explanation of what happened. First, interviews with Nazi war criminals and doctors who worked in concentration camps suggested, at least to some, the provocative and disturbing conclusion that these people were "utterly ordinary" (Arendt, 1963; Lifton, 1986; Von Lang & Sibyll, 1983). Second, the monstrous events of World War II do not stand alone in modern history. Even today, various crimes of obedience—including both suicide bombings and torture—are being committed in ruthless regimes, militaries, and terrorist organizations throughout the world (Kelman & Hamilton, 1989; Haritos-Fatouros, 2002).

As seen in many recent Wall Street scandals, crimes of obedience are also found in the corporate world, where leaders and their subordinates "morally disengage" from bad actions by denying personal responsibility, minimizing consequences, and dehumanizing victims (Beu & Buckley, 2004). On extraordinary but rare occasions, obedience is carried to its ultimate limit. In 1978, 900 members of the People's Temple cult obeyed a command from Reverend Jim Jones to kill themselves by drinking poison. In 1997, in California, Marshall Applewhite, the leader of the Heaven's Gate cult, killed himself and convinced 37 followers to do the same. Fanatic cult members had committed mass suicide before, and they will likely do so again (Galanter, 1999).

■ Milgram's Research: Forces of Destructive Obedience

During the time that Adolf Eichmann was being tried in Jerusalem for his Nazi war crimes, Stanley Milgram (1963) began a dramatic series of 18 experiments that culminated in his 1974 book *Obedience to Authority*. Milgram did not realize it at the time (and neither did his research participants), but they were about to make history in one of the most famous psychology experiments ever conducted.

For many years, the ethics of this research has been the focus of much debate. Those who say it was not ethical point to the potential psychological harm to which the participants were exposed. In contrast, those who believe that Milgram's research met appropriate ethical standards emphasize the profound contribution it makes to our understanding of an important social problem. They conclude that on balance, the danger that destructive obedience poses for all humankind justified Milgram's unorthodox methods. Consider both sides of the debate, which were summarized in

obedience Behavior change produced by the commands of authority.

From the film *Obedience* by Stanley Milgram copyright 1965 and distributed by The Penn. State University Audio Visual Services

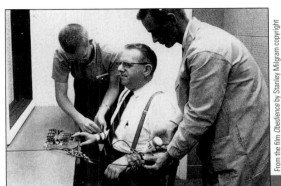

From the film *Obedience* by Stanley Milgram copyright 1965 and distributed by The Penn. State University Audio Visual Services

This is the shock generator Milgram used (left). It still exists and can be seen in the Archives of the History of American Psychology at the University of Akron. Participants in Milgram's studies believed they were shocking Mr. Wallace, the man being strapped into his chair (right).

Chapter 2, and make your own judgment. Now, however, take a more personal look. Imagine yourself as one of the approximately 1,000 participants who found themselves in the following situation.

The experience begins when you arrive at a Yale University laboratory and meet two men. One is the experimenter, a stern young man dressed in a gray lab coat and carrying a clipboard. The other is a middle-aged gentleman named Mr. Wallace, an accountant who is slightly overweight and average in appearance. You exchange quick introductions, and then the experimenter explains that you and your co-participant will take part in a study on the effects of punishment on learning. After lots have been drawn, it is determined that you will serve as the teacher and that Mr. Wallace will be the learner. So far, so good.

Soon, however, the situation takes on a more ominous tone. You find out that your job is to test the learner's memory and administer electric shocks of increasing intensity whenever he makes a mistake. You are then escorted into another room, where the experimenter straps Mr. Wallace into a chair, rolls up his sleeves, attaches electrodes to his arms, and applies "electrode paste" to prevent blisters and burns. As if that isn't bad enough, you may overhear Mr. Wallace telling the experimenter that he has a heart problem. The experimenter responds by conceding that the shocks will be painful but reassures Mr. Wallace that the procedure will not cause "permanent tissue damage." In the meantime, you can personally vouch for how painful the shocks are because the experimenter stings you with one that is supposed to be mild. From there, the experimenter takes you back to the main room, where you are seated in front of a "shock generator," a machine with 30 switches that range from 15 volts, labeled "slight shock," to 450 volts, labeled "XXX."

Your role in this experiment is straightforward. First you read a list of word pairs to Mr. Wallace through a microphone. Then you test his memory with a series of multiple-choice questions. The learner answers each question by pressing one of four switches that light up signals on the shock generator. If his answer is correct, you move on to the next question. If it is incorrect, you announce the correct answer and shock him. When you press the appropriate shock switch, a red light flashes above it, relay switches click inside the machine, and you hear a loud buzzing sound go off in the learner's room. After each wrong answer, you're told, the intensity of the shock should be increased by 15 volts.

You aren't aware, of course, that the experiment is rigged and that Mr. Wallace—who is actually a confederate—is never really shocked. As far as you know, he gets zapped each time you press one of the switches. As the session proceeds, the learner makes more and more errors, leading you to work your way up the shock scale. As you reach 75, 90, and 105 volts, you hear the learner grunt in pain. At 120 volts, he begins to shout. If you're still in it at 150 volts, you can hear the learner cry out, "Experimenter! That's all. Get me out of here. My heart's starting to bother me now. I refuse to go on!" Screams of agony and protest continue. At 300 volts, he says he absolutely refuses to continue. By the time you surpass 330 volts, the learner falls silent and fails to respond—not to be heard from again. Table 7.4 lists his responses in grim detail.

Somewhere along the line, you turn to the experimenter for guidance. "What should I do? Don't you think I should stop? Shouldn't we at least check on him?" You might even confront the experimenter head-on and refuse to continue. Yet in answer to your inquiries, the experimenter—firm in his tone and seemingly unaffected by the learner's distress—prods you along as follows:

- Please continue (or please go on).

- The experiment requires that you continue.

- It is absolutely essential that you continue.

- You have no other choice; you must go on.

TABLE 7.4

The Learner's Protests in the Milgram Experiment

As participants administered progressively more intense shocks, they heard the learner moan, groan, protest, and complain. All participants heard the same programmed set of responses. Eventually, the learner fell silent and ceased to respond.

75 volts	Ugh!
90 volts	Ugh!
105 volts	Ugh! (louder)
120 volts	Ugh! Hey, this really hurts!
135 volts	Ugh!!
150 volts	Ugh!!! Experimenter! That's all. Get me out of here. I told you I had heart trouble. My heart's starting to bother me now. Get me out of here, please. My heart's starting to bother me. I refuse to go on. Let me out.
165 volts	Ugh! Let me out! (shouting)
180 volts	Ugh! I can't stand the pain. Let me out of here! (shouting)
195 volts	Ugh! Let me out of here. Let me out of here. My heart's bothering me. Let me out of here! You have no right to keep me here! Let me out! Let me out of here! Let me out! Let me out of here! My heart's bothering me. Let me out! Let me out!
210 volts	Ugh!! Experimenter! Get me out of here. I've had enough. I won't be in the experiment any more.
225 volts	Ugh!
240 volts	Ugh!
255 volts	Ugh! Get me out of here.
270 volts	(Agonized scream) Let me out of here. Let me out of here. Let me out of here. Let me out. Do you hear? Let me out of here.
285 volts	(Agonized scream)
300 volts	(Agonized scream) I absolutely refuse to answer any more. Get me out of here. You can't hold me here. Get me out. Get me out of here.
315 volts	(Intensely agonized scream) I told you I refuse to answer. I'm no longer part of this experiment.
330 volts	(Intense and prolonged agonized scream) Let me out of here. Let me out of here. My heart's bothering me. Let me out, I tell you. (Hysterically) Let me out of here. Let me out of here. You have no right to hold me here. Let me out! Let me out! Let me out! Let me out of here! Let me out! Let me out!

Milgram, 1974.

What do you do? In a situation that begins to feel more and more like a bad dream, do you follow your own conscience or obey the experimenter?

Milgram described this procedure to psychiatrists, college students, and middle-class adults, and he asked them to predict how they would behave. On average, these groups estimated that they would call it quits at the 135-volt level. Not a single person thought he or she would go all the way to 450 volts. When asked to predict the percentage of *other* people who would deliver the maximum shock, those interviewed gave similar estimates. The psychiatrists estimated that only one out of a thousand people would exhibit that kind of extreme obedience. They were wrong. In Milgram's initial study, involving 40 men from the surrounding New Haven community, participants exhibited an alarming degree of obedience, administering an average of 27 out of 30 possible shocks. In fact, 26 of the 40 participants— that's *65 percent*—delivered the ultimate punishment of 450 volts.

The Obedient Participant At first glance, you may see these results as a lesson in the psychology of cruelty and conclude that Milgram's participants were seriously disturbed. But research does not support such a simple explanation. To begin with, those in a control group who were not prodded along by an experimenter refused to continue early into the shock sequence. What's more, Milgram found that virtually all participants, including those who had administered severe shocks, were tormented by the experience. Many of them pleaded with the experimenter to let them stop. When he refused, they went on. But in the process, they trembled, stuttered, groaned, perspired, bit their lips, and dug their fingernails into their flesh. Some burst into fits of nervous laughter. On one occasion, said Milgram, "we observed a [participant's] seizure so violently convulsive that it was necessary to call a halt to the experiment" (1963, p. 375).

Was Milgram's 65 percent baseline level of obedience attributable to his unique sample of male participants? Not at all. Forty women who participated in a later study exhibited precisely the same level of obedience: 65 percent threw the 450-volt switch. Before you jump to the conclusion that something was amiss in New Haven, consider the fact that Milgram's basic finding has been obtained in several different countries and with children as well as college students and older adults (Shanab & Yahya, 1977, 1978). Obedience in the Milgram situation is so universal that it led one author to ask, "Are we all Nazis?" (Askenasy, 1978).

The answer, of course, is no. An individual's character can make a difference, and some people, depending on the situation, are far more obedient than others. In the aftermath of World War II, a group of social scientists, searching for the root causes of prejudice, sought to identify individuals with an *authoritarian personality* and developed a questionnaire known as the F-Scale to measure it (Adorno et al., 1950; Stone et al., 1993). What they found is that people who get high scores on the F-Scale (F stands for "Fascist") are rigid, dogmatic, sexually repressed, ethnocentric, intolerant of dissent, and punitive. They are submissive toward figures of authority but aggressive toward subordinates. Indeed, people with high F scores are also more willing than low scorers to administer high-intensity shocks in Milgram's obedience situation (Elms & Milgram, 1966).

Although personality characteristics may make someone vulnerable or resistant to destructive obedience, what seems to matter most is the situation in which people find themselves. By carefully altering particular aspects of his basic scenario, Milgram was able to identify factors that increase and decrease the 65 percent baseline rate of obedience in more than 20 variations of the basic experiment (see ▶ Figure 7.7). Three factors in particular are important: the authority figure, the proximity of the victim, and the experimental procedure (Blass, 1992; Miller, 1986).

The Authority   What is perhaps most remarkable about Milgram's findings is that a lab-coated experimenter is *not* a powerful figure of authority. Unlike a military superior, employer, coach, or teacher, the experimenter in Milgram's research could not ultimately enforce his commands. Still, his physical presence and his apparent legitimacy played major roles in drawing obedience. When Milgram diminished the experimenter's status by moving his lab from the distinguished surroundings of Yale University to a run-down urban office building in nearby Bridgeport, Connecticut, the rate of total obedience dropped to 48 percent. When the experimenter was replaced by an ordinary person—supposedly another participant—there was a sharp reduction to 20 percent. Similarly, Milgram found that when the experimenter was in charge but issued his commands by telephone, only 21 percent fully obeyed. (In fact, when the experimenter was not watching, many participants in this condition feigned obedience by pressing the 15-volt switch.) One conclusion, then, is clear. At least in the Milgram setting, destructive obedience requires the physical presence of a prestigious authority figure.

If an experimenter can exert such control over research participants, imagine the control wielded by truly powerful authority figures—whether they are present or not. An intriguing field study examined the extent to which hospital nurses would obey unreasonable orders from a doctor. Using a fictitious name, a male physician called several female nurses on the phone and told them to administer a drug to a specific patient. His order violated hospital regulations: The drug was uncommon, the dosage

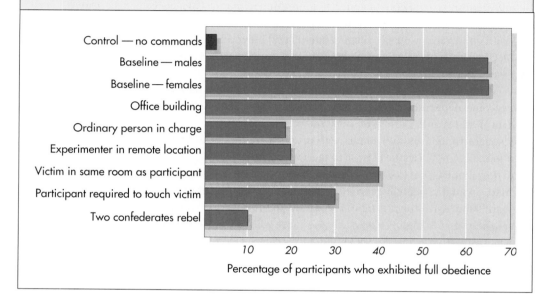

▶**FIGURE 7.7**

Factors That Influence Obedience

Milgram varied many factors in his research program. Without commands from an experimenter, fewer than 3 percent of the participants exhibited full obedience. Yet in the standard baseline condition, 65 percent of male and female participants followed the orders. To identify factors that might reduce this level, Milgram varied the location of the experiment, the status of the authority, the participant's proximity to the victim, and the presence of confederates who rebel. The effects of these variations are illustrated here.

Milgram, 1974.

was too large, and the effects could have been harmful. Yet out of the 22 nurses who were contacted, 21 had to be stopped as they prepared to obey the doctor's orders (Hofling et al., 1966).

The Victim   Situational characteristics of the victim are also important factors in destructive obedience. Milgram noted that Nazi war criminal Adolf Eichmann felt sick when he toured concentration camps but only had to shuffle papers from behind a desk to play his part in the Holocaust. Similarly the B-29 pilot who dropped the atom bomb on Hiroshima in World War II said of his mission, "I had no thoughts, except what I'm supposed to do" (Miller, 1986, p. 228). These events suggest that because Milgram's participants were physically separated from the learner, they were able to distance themselves emotionally from the consequences of their actions.

To test the impact of a victim's proximity on destructive obedience, Milgram seated the learner in one of his studies in the same room as the participant. Under these conditions, only 40 percent fully obeyed. When participants were required to physically grasp the victim's hand and force it onto a metal shock plate, full obedience dropped to 30 percent. These findings represent significant reductions from the 65 percent baseline. Still, three out of ten participants were willing to use brute force in the name of obedience.

The Procedure   Finally, there is the situation created by Milgram. A close look at the dilemma his participants faced reveals two important aspects of the experimental procedure. First, participants were led to feel relieved of any personal sense of *respon-*

sibility for the victim's welfare. The experimenter said up front that he was account-able. When participants were led to believe that they were responsible, their levels of obedience dropped considerably (Tilker, 1970). The ramifications of this finding are immense. In the military and other organizations, individuals often occupy posi-tions in a hierarchical chain of command. Eichmann was a middle-level bureaucrat who received orders from Hitler and transmitted them to others for implementation. Caught between individuals who make policy and those who carry it out, how person-ally responsible do those in the middle feel? Wesley Kilham and Leon Mann (1974) examined this issue in an obedience study that cast participants in one of two roles: the *transmitter* (who took orders from the experimenter and passed them on) and the *executant* (who actually pressed the shock levers). As they predicted, transmitters were more obedient (54 percent) than executants (28 percent).

The second feature of Milgram's scenario that promoted obedience is gradual escalation. Participants began the session by delivering mild shocks and then only gradually escalated to voltage levels of high intensity. After all, what's another 15 volts compared with the current level? By the time participants realized the fright-ening implications of what they were doing, it had become more difficult for them to escape (Gilbert, 1981). This sequence is much like the foot-in-the-door technique. In Milgram's words, people become "integrated into a situation that carries its own momentum. The subject's problem . . . is how to become disengaged from a situation which is moving in an altogether ugly direction" (1974, p. 73). We should point out that obedience by momentum is not unique to Milgram's research paradigm. As reported by Amnesty International, many countries today torture political prisoners, and those who are recruited for the dirty work are trained, in part, through an escalating series of commitments (Haritos-Fatouros, 2002).

In experiments on obedience, most participants who were ordered to administer severe shocks to an innocent person refused to do so. **FALSE.**

Milgram in the Twenty-First Century

When Stanley Milgram published the results of his first experiment in 1963, at the age of 28, a *New York Times* headline read: "Sixty-Five Percent in Test Blindly Obey Order to Inflict Pain." Milgram had pierced the public consciousness and was poised to become an important and controversial figure in psychology—and beyond. In a fascinating biogra-phy, *The Man Who Shocked the World*, Thomas Blass (2004) tells of how Milgram became interested in obedience and the impact his studies have had on social scientists, legal scholars, the U.S. military, and popular culture around the world (Milgram's book has been translated into 11 languages). Now, in an age filled with threats of global conflict, extremism, terrorism, economic desperation, and new forms of lethal weaponry, obedi-ence to authority is an issue of such importance that social psychologists all over the world continue to ponder its ramifications (Benjamin & Simpson, 2009; Blass, 2009).

Today, a grainy black-and-white film that Milgram produced in 1965 in which a number of sessions were recorded from a hidden camera stands as visual proof of this phenomenon. It is clear from looking at this film that this experiment was conducted in another era, an era in which research participants called the young experimenter "sir." Would these results be repeated today? Would *you* obey the commands of Mil-gram's experimenter?

In an effort to answer this question, Dutch researchers Wim Meeus and Quinten Raaijmakers (1995) created a different but analogous situation. They constructed a moral dilemma much like Milgram's. Rather than order participants to inflict physi-cal pain on someone, however, they ordered them to cause psychological harm. When participants arrived at a university laboratory, they met a confederate sup-posedly there to take a test as part of a job interview. If the confederate passed the test, he'd get the job; if he failed, he would not. As part of a study of performance under stress, the experimenter told participants to distract the test-taking applicant by making an escalating series of harassing remarks. On cue, the applicant pleaded with participants to stop, became angry, faltered, and eventually fell into a state of despair and failed. As in Milgram's research, the question was straightforward: How many participants would obey orders through the entire set of 15 stress remarks, despite the apparent harm caused to a real-life job applicant? In a control group that lacked a prodding experimenter, no one persisted. But when the experimenter ordered them to go on, 92 percent exhibited complete obedience despite seeing the task as unfair and distasteful. It appears that obedience is a powerful aspect of human nature brought about by the docile manner in which people relate to figures of authority—even today.

In a more recent—and even more direct—attempt to revisit Milgram, Jerry Burger (2009) conducted a "partial replication" for which he paid $50 to 70 men and women, a diverse group that ranged from 20 to 81 years old, and used the same procedure. In the original experiment, the learner first protested and asked to stop at 150 volts, at which point nearly all participants paused and indicated a reluctance to continue. Some outright refused at this point. Of those participants who did continue, however, most went all the way (Packer, 2008). On the basis of this finding, Burger followed the Milgram protocol up to 150 volts in order to estimate the number of participants who would have pulled the switch at 450 volts. He also added a condition in which a defiant confederate posing as another participant refused to continue.

In light of post-Milgram changes in standards for research ethics, he took additional precautions; he excluded from the study individuals he feared would experience too much stress and then informed and reminded participants three times that they could withdraw from the study at any time without penalty.

Despite all that has changed in 45 years, the obedience rate was not appreciably lower (see ▶ Figure 7.8). In the experiment that Burger modeled, 83 percent of Milgram's participants had continued past 150 volts. In Burger's more recent study, 70 percent did the same (it can be estimated, therefore, that 55 percent would have exhibited full 450-volt obedience in the original experiment). Two additional results proved interesting: (1) Just as Milgram had found, there were no differences between men and women; and (2) the obedience rate declined only slightly, to 63 percent, among participants who saw a defiant confederate refuse to continue.

Already this new replication has drawn a good deal of interest and commentary. Alan Elms (2009), a graduate student and collaborator of Milgram's in the 1960s, is cautious about comparing Burger's "obedience lite" procedure to Milgram's but eager to see it revitalize the research program Milgram had initiated. Arthur Miller (2009), author of *The Obedience Experiments*, voices the

▶ **FIGURE 7.8**

Obedience in the Twenty-First Century

In the version of the experiment that Burger modeled, 83 percent of Milgram's original participants continued past 150 volts. Forty-five years later, Burger saw a slight drop to 70 percent. Note too that the obedience rate dropped only slightly, to 63 percent, among participants who saw a defiant confederate refuse to continue. These results show that obedience to authority may have declined a bit over the years, but it has by no means extinguished.

Burger, 2009.

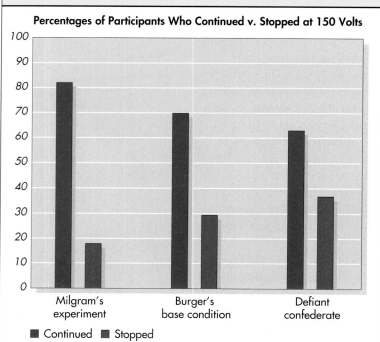

Percentages of Participants Who Continued v. Stopped at 150 Volts

■ Continued ■ Stopped

same cautious excitement. Thomas Blass (2009), author of the Milgram biography, *The Man Who Shocked the World*, sees Burger's experiment as an important milestone and demonstrates the stability and resilience of obedience in human social behavior. In contrast, Jean Twenge (2009), author of *Generation Me*—a 2006 book on how Americans have become more self-centered, narcissistic, and wholly focused on personal rights—is skeptical of that conclusion that nothing has changed. Making precise comparisons, Twenge notes that relative to an obedience rate of 83 percent among Milgram's male participants, only 67 percent of Burger's men exhibited 150-volt obedience, a decline that is statistically comparable to the alarming change in U.S. obesity rates during that same period of time. While impressed with the power of Milgram's situation, Twenge is hopeful that destructive obedience is less prevalent today, in the 21st century, than in the past.

Before leaving the Milgram studies, consider an awkward but important moral question: By providing a situational explanation for the evils of Nazi Germany or of modern-day terrorism, are social psychologists unwittingly excusing the perpetrators? Does blaming what they did on the situation let them off the hook of responsibility? In a series of studies, Miller and others (1999) found that after people were asked to come up with explanations for acts of wrongdoing, they tended to be more forgiving of the individuals who committed those acts and were seen as more forgiving by others. This appearance of forgiveness was certainly not Milgram's intent, nor is it the intent of other researchers today who seek to understand cruelty, even while continuing to condemn it. Miller and his colleagues are thus quick to caution, "To explain is not to forgive" (p. 265).

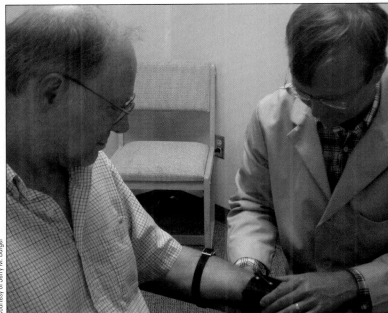

Courtesy of Jerry M. Burger

On January 3, 2007, ABC's *Primetime* news program aired a story titled "Basic Instincts: The Science of Evil." This story reported on Burger's (2009) re-creation of the Milgram obedience experiment. But does this laboratory phenomenon ever play out in the real world?

▌ Defiance: When People Rebel

It is easy to despair in light of the impressive forces that compel people toward blind obedience. But there's also good news. Just as social influence processes can breed subservience to authority, they can also breed rebellion and defiance. Few people realize it, but this phenomenon, too, was seen during World War II. In *Resistance of the Heart*, historian Nathan Stoltzfus (1996) describes a civil protest in Berlin in which the non-Jewish wives of 2,000 newly captured Jews congregated outside the prison. The women were there initially to seek information about their husbands. Soon they were filling the streets, chanting and refusing to leave. After eight straight days of protest, the defiant women prevailed. Fearing the negative impact on public opinion, the Nazis backed down and released the men.

Are the actions of a whole group harder to control than the behavior of a single individual? Consider the following study. Pretending to be part of a marketing research firm, William Gamson and others (1982) recruited people to participate in a supposed discussion of "community standards." Scheduled in groups of nine, participants were told that their discussions would be videotaped for a large oil company that was suing the manager of a local service station who had spoken out against higher gas prices. After receiving a summary of the case, most participants sided with the station manager. But there was a hitch. The oil company wanted evidence to win its case, said the experimenter posing as the discussion coordinator.

A little rebellion now and then is a good thing.

—Thomas Jefferson

He told each of the group members to get in front of the camera and express the company's viewpoint. Then he told them to sign an affidavit giving the company permission to edit the tapes for use in court.

You can see how the obedience script was supposed to unfold. Actually, only one of 33 groups even came close to following the script. In all others, people became incensed by the coordinator's behavior and refused to continue. Some groups were so outraged that they planned to take action. One group even threatened to blow the whistle on the firm by calling the local newspapers. Faced with one emotionally charged mutiny after another, the researchers had to discontinue the experiment.

Why did this study produce such active, often passionate revolt when Milgram's revealed such utterly passive obedience? Could it reflect a change in values from the 1960s, when Milgram's studies were run? Many college students believe that people would conform less today than in the past, but an analysis of obedience studies has revealed that there is no correlation between the year a study was conducted and the level of obedience that it produced (Blass, 1999)—right up through Burger's (2009) recent effort. So what accounts for the contrasting results? One key difference is that people in Milgram's studies took part alone and those in Gamson's were in groups. Perhaps Michael Walzer was right: "Disobedience, when it is not criminally but morally, religiously, or politically motivated, is always a *collective act*" (quoted in Brown, 1986, p. 17).

Obedience to authority seems a timeless phenomenon. Just a few years ago, 18-year-old Louise Ogburn, working at a McDonald's in Kentucky, was accused of stealing money by a prank phone caller and taken into her manager's office. Posing as a police officer, the caller ordered several of the girl's coworkers to have her strip naked. For four hours, she was searched, spanked, and forced into humiliating positions on command. Surveillance footage showed that all but one coworker obeyed the prank caller—and the girl obeyed the coworkers. Remarkably, 70 similar incidents were reported elsewhere. As seen here, Ms. Ogburn sued McDonald's and was awarded $6 million.

AP Photo/Brian Bohannon

Our earlier discussion of conformity indicated that the mere presence of one ally in an otherwise unanimous majority gives individuals the courage to dissent. The same may hold true for obedience. Notably, Milgram never had more than one participant present in the same session. But in one experiment, he did use two confederates who posed as co-teachers along with the real participant. In these sessions, one confederate refused to continue at 150 volts and the second refused at 210 volts. These models of disobedience had a profound influence on participants' willingness to defy the experimenter: In their presence, only 10 percent delivered the maximum level of shock (see Figure 7.7).

We should add that the presence of a group is not a guaranteed safeguard against destructive obedience. Groups can trigger aggression, as we'll see in Chapter 11. For example, the followers of Jim Jones were together when they collectively followed his command to die. And lynch mobs are just that—groups, not individuals. Clearly, there is power in sheer numbers. That power can be destructive, but it can also be used for constructive purposes. Indeed, the presence and support of others often provide the extra ounce of courage that people need to resist orders they find offensive.

The Continuum of Social Influence

As we have seen, social influence on behavior ranges from the implicit pressure of group norms to the traps set by direct requests to the powerful commands of authority. In each case, people choose whether to react with conformity or independence, compliance or assertiveness, obedience or defiance. From all the research, it is tempting to conclude that the more pressure brought to bear on people, the greater the influence. Is it possible, however, that more produces less? In a series of conformity studies, Lucian Conway and Mark Schaller (2005) cast participants into a corporate decision-making task in which they were asked to choose between two business options after watching others make the same decision. Consistently, the participants followed the group more when its members had formed their opinions freely than when they were compelled by a leader. It appears that strong-arm tactics that force people to change their behavior may backfire when it comes to changing opinions.

At this point, let's step back and ask two important questions. First, although different kinds of pressure influence us for different reasons, is it possible to predict all effects with a single overarching principle? Second, what does the theory and research on social influence say about human nature?

Social Impact Theory

In 1981, Bibb Latané proposed that a common bond among the different processes involved in social influence leads people toward or away from such influence. Specifically, Latané proposed **social impact theory**, which states that social influence of any kind—the total impact of others on a target person—is a function of the others' strength, immediacy, and number. According to Latané, social forces act on individuals in the same way that physical forces act on objects. Consider, for example, how overhead lights illuminate a surface. The total amount of light cast on a surface depends on the strength of the bulbs, their distance from the surface, and their number. As illustrated in the left portion of ▶ Figure 7.9, the same factors apply to social impact.

The *strength* of a source is determined by his or her status, ability, or relationship to a target. The stronger the source, the greater the influence. When people view the other members of a group as competent, they are more likely to conform in their judgments. When it comes to compliance, sources enhance their strength by making targets feel obligated to reciprocate a small favor. And to elicit obedience, authority figures gain strength by wearing uniforms or flaunting their prestigious affiliations.

"I invited a few friends over who think you should see a psychiatrist."

Immediacy refers to a source's proximity in time and space to the target. The closer the source, the greater its impact. Milgram's research offers the best example. Obedience rates were higher when the experimenter issued commands in person rather than from a remote location, and when the victim suffered in close proximity to the participant, he acted as a contrary source of influence and obedience levels dropped. Consistent with this hypothesis, Latané and others (1995) asked individuals to name up to seven people in their lives and to indicate how far away those people lived and how many memorable interactions they'd had with them. In three studies,

social impact theory The theory that social influence depends on the strength, immediacy, and number of source persons relative to target persons.

> ▶**FIGURE 7.9**
>
> **Social Impact: Source Factors and Target Factors**
>
> According to social impact theory, the total influence of other people, or "sources," on a target individual depends on three source factors: their strength (size of source circles), immediacy (distance from the target), and number (number of the source circles). Similarly, the total influence is diffused, or reduced, by the strength (size of target circles), immediacy (distance from source circle), and number of target persons.
>
> Latané, 1981.

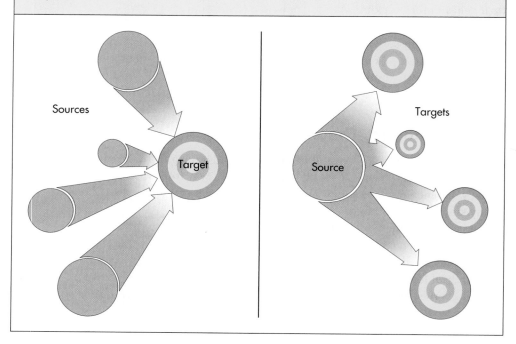

the correlation was the same: The closer others are, geographically, the more impact they have on us.

Finally, the theory predicts that as the *number* of sources increases, so does their influence—at least up to a point. You may recall that when Asch (1956) increased the number of live confederates in his line-judgment studies from one to four, conformity levels rose, yet further increases had only a negligible additional effect.

Social impact theory also predicts that people sometimes resist social pressure. According to Latané, this resistance is most likely to occur when social impact is *divided* among many strong and distant *targets*, as seen in the right part of Figure 7.9. There should be less impact on a target who is strong and far from the source than on one who is weak and close to the source, and there should be less impact on a target who is accompanied by other target persons than on one who stands alone. Thus, we have seen that conformity is reduced by the presence of an ally and that obedience rates drop when people are in the company of rebellious peers.

Over the years, social impact theory has been challenged, defended, and refined on various grounds (Jackson, 1986; Mullen, 1985; Sedikides & Jackson, 1990). On the one hand, critics say that it does not enable us to *explain* the processes that give rise to social influence or answer *why* questions. On the other hand, the theory enables us to predict the emergence of social influence and determine *when* it will occur. Whether the topic is conformity, compliance, or obedience, this theory has set the stage for interesting new research in the years to come.

According to social impact theory, a marine sergeant will exert influence to the extent that he is strong (in a position of power), immediate (physically close), and numerous (backed by others in the institution) relative to his trainees.

A number of social psychologists have recently argued that social impact is a fluid, dynamic, ever-changing process (Vallacher et al., 2002). Latané and L'Herrou (1996) refined the theory in that vein. By having large groups of participants network through e-mail, for example, and by controlling their lines of communication, they found that the individuals within the network formed "clusters." Over time, neighbors (participants who were in direct e-mail contact with each other) became more similar to each other than did those who were more distant (not in direct e-mail contact) within the network. Referring to the geometry of social space, Latané and L'Herrou note that in the real world, immediacy cannot be defined strictly in terms of physical distance. "Walls between houses, rivers through towns, open spaces between cities, these and other spatial discontinuities all tend to prevent the equal flow of influence among all members of a population" (p. 1229). Speculating on the role of computer technology, they also note that social impact theory has to account for the fact that more and more, people interact in cyberspace—perhaps making physical proximity a less relevant factor.

As the number of people in a group increases, so does the group's impact on an individual. **FALSE.**

▊ Perspectives on Human Nature

From the material presented in this chapter, what general conclusions might you draw about human nature? Granted, social influence is more likely to occur in some situations than in others. But are people generally malleable or unyielding? Is there a tilt toward accepting influence or toward putting up resistance?

There is no single universal answer to these questions. As we saw earlier, some cultures value autonomy and independence, while others place more emphasis on conformity to one's group. Even within a given culture, values may change over time. To demonstrate the point, ask yourself: If you were a parent, what traits would you like your child to have? When this question was put to American mothers in 1924, they chose "obedience" and "loyalty," key characteristics of conformity. Yet when mothers were asked the same question in 1978, they cited "independence" and "tolerance of others," key characteristics of autonomy. Similar trends were found in surveys conducted not only in the United States but also in West Germany, Italy, England, and

Conformity rates vary across different cultures and from one generation to the next. **TRUE.**

Japan (Alwin, 1990; Remley 1988) and in laboratory experiments, where conformity rates are somewhat lower today than in the past (Bond & Smith, 1996).

Is it possible that today's children—tomorrow's adults—will exhibit greater resistance to the various forms of social influence? If so, what effects will this trend have on society as a whole? Cast in a positive light, conformity, compliance, and obedience are good and necessary human responses. They promote group solidarity and agreement—qualities that keep groups from being torn apart by dissension. Cast in a negative light, a lack of independence, assertiveness, and defiance are undesirable behaviors that lend themselves to narrow-mindedness, cowardice, and destructive obedience, often with terrible costs. For each of us and for society as a whole, the trick is to strike a balance.

REVIEW

- Conformity, compliance, and obedience are three kinds of social influence, varying in the degree of pressure brought to bear on an individual.

Social Influence as "Automatic"

- Sometimes we are influenced by other people without our awareness.

- Studies show that people mimic each other's behaviors and moods, perhaps as a way of smoothing social interactions.

Conformity

- Conformity is the tendency for people to change their behavior to be consistent with group norms.

The Early Classics

- Two classic experiments illustrate contrasting types of conformity.
- Sherif presented groups of participants with an ambiguous task and found that their judgments gradually converged.
- Using a simpler line-judgment task, Asch had confederates make incorrect responses and found that participants went along about a third of the time.

Why Do People Conform?

- Sherif found that people exhibit private conformity, using others for information in an ambiguous situation.
- Asch's studies indicated that people conform in their public behavior to avoid appearing deviant.

Majority Influence

- As the size of an incorrect unanimous majority increases, so does conformity—up to a point.
- People conform to perceived social norms when these norms are brought to mind.
- The presence of one dissenter reduces conformity, even when he or she disagrees with the participant and lacks competence at the task.
- Women conform more than men on "masculine" tasks and in face-to-face settings but not on "feminine" or gender-neutral tasks or in private settings.

Minority Influence

- Sometimes minorities resist pressures to conform and are able to influence majorities.
- In general, minority influence is greater when the source is an ingroup member.

- According to Moscovici, minorities can exert influence by taking a consistent and unwavering position.

- Hollander claims that to exert influence, a person should first conform, then dissent.

- Majority influence is greater on direct and public measures of conformity, but minorities show their impact in indirect or private measures of conformity.

- By forcing other group members to think more openly about a problem, minorities enhance the quality of a group's decision making.

- People gain courage to resist conformity pressures after watching others do the same.

Culture and Conformity

- Just as cultures differ in their social norms, so too they differ in the extent to which people are expected to adhere to those norms.

- Research shows that people from collectivist cultures conform more than people from individualistic cultures.

Compliance

- A common form of social influence occurs when we respond to direct requests.

Mindlessness and Compliance

- People are more likely to comply when they are taken by surprise and when the request sounds reasonable.

The Norm of Reciprocity

- We often comply when we feel indebted to a requester who has done us a favor.

- People differ in the extent to which they use reciprocity for personal gain and are wary of falling prey to this strategy.

Setting Traps: Sequential Request Strategies

- Four compliance techniques are based on a two-step request: The first step sets a trap, and the second elicits compliance.

- Using the foot-in-the-door technique, a person sets the stage for the "real" request by first getting someone to comply with a smaller request.

- In lowballing, one person gets another to agree to a request but then increases the size of the request by revealing hidden costs. Despite the increase, people often follow through on their agreement.

- With the door-in-the-face technique, the real request is preceded by a large one that is rejected. People then comply with the second request because they see it as a concession to be reciprocated.

- The that's-not-all technique begins with a large request. Then the apparent size of the request is reduced by the offer of a discount or bonus.

Assertiveness: When People Say No

- Many people find it hard to be assertive. Doing so requires that we be vigilant and recognize the traps.

Obedience

- When the request is a command and the requester is a figure of authority, the resulting influence is called obedience.

Milgram's Research: Forces of Destructive Obedience

- In a series of experiments, participants were ordered by an experimenter to administer increasingly painful shocks to a confederate.

- Sixty-five percent obeyed completely but felt tormented by the experience.

- Obedience levels are influenced by various situational factors, including a participant's physical proximity to both the authority figure and the victim.

- Two other aspects of Milgram's procedure contributed to the high levels of obedience: (1) Participants did not feel personally responsible; and (2) the orders escalated gradually.

- In more recent studies, people exhibited high rates of obedience when told to inflict psychological harm on another person.

Milgram in the Twenty-First Century

- Milgram's studies have remained relevant and controversial into the 21st century.

- Researchers note that a situational explanation for acts of destructive obedience does not forgive them.

- A recent "partial replication" of Milgram's shock study suggests that most people are still fully obedient today.

Defiance: When People Rebel

- Just as processes of social influence breed obedience, they can also support acts of defiance, since groups are more difficult to control than individuals

- Provision of a situational explanation for cruel behavior does not excuse that behavior.

The Continuum of Social Influence

Social Impact Theory

■ Social impact theory predicts that social influence depends on the strength, immediacy, and number of sources who exert pressure relative to target persons who absorb that pressure.

Perspectives on Human Nature

■ There is no single answer to the question of whether people are conformists or nonconformists.

■ There are cross-cultural differences in social influence, and values change over time even within specific cultures.

Key Terms

collectivism (267)
compliance (268)
conformity (254)
door-in-the-face technique (273)
foot-in-the-door technique (270)
idiosyncrasy credits (265)

individualism (267)
informational influence (257)
lowballing (272)
minority influence (264)
normative influence (258)
obedience (276)

private conformity (259)
public conformity (259)
social impact theory (285)
that's-not-all technique (273)

Media Resources

Social Psychology 8th Edition Companion Website
Visit your book companion website
www.cengage.com/psychology/kassin
where you will find flash cards, practice quizzes, Internet links, and more to help you study.

CENGAGENOW Just what you need to know NOW! Spend time on what you need to master rather than on information you already have learned. Take a pre-test for this chapter and CengageNOW will generate a personalized study plan based on your results. The study plan will identify the topics you need to review and direct you to online resources to help you master those topics. You can then take a post-test to help you determine the concepts you have mastered and what you will need to work on. Try it out! Go to **academic .cengage.com/login** to sign in with an access code or to purchase access to this product.

Putting COMMON SENSE *to the Test*

When all members of a group give an incorrect response to an easy question, most people most of the time conform to that response.

False. *In Asch's classic conformity experiments, respondents conformed only about a third of the time.*

An effective way to get someone to do you a favor is to make a first request that is so large the person is sure to reject it.

True. *This approach, known as the door-in-the-face technique, increases compliance by making the person feel bound to make a concession.*

In experiments on obedience, most participants who were ordered to administer severe shocks to an innocent person refused to do so.

False. *In Milgram's classic research, 65 percent of all participants obeyed the experimenter and administered the maximum possible shock.*

As the number of people in a group increases, so does the group's impact on an individual.

False. *Increasing group size boosts the impact on an individual only up to a point, beyond which further increases have very little added effect.*

Conformity rates vary across different cultures and from one generation to the next.

True. *Research shows that conformity rates are higher in cultures that are collectivistic rather than individualistic in orientation and that values change over time even within cultures.*

8

Group Processes

This chapter examines social influence in a group context. First, we focus on the fundamentals of groups, *in which we discuss issues such as why people are drawn to groups and how groups develop. We then turn to* how the behavior of individuals is affected by the presence of others. *Then we focus on* group performance *and discuss why the whole (the group decision or performance) so often is different from the sum of its parts (the attitudes and abilities of the group members). In the final section, on* conflict, *we examine how groups intensify or reconcile their differences.*

Toward the end of 2008 much of the world was rocked by an economic crisis that seemed to many to come out of nowhere. Although there were many culprits, much of the blame quickly began to fall on the reckless practices of groups of seemingly very intelligent men and women in the financial markets, particularly in the United States. Numerous columnists, bloggers, and news commentators used the term "the best and the brightest" to describe the individuals who comprised these influential groups, and they all asked versions of the same question: How could such smart people collectively make such incredibly stupid decisions? (e.g., Hedges, 2008; Siris, 2009).

When the U.S. government gave billions of dollars in loans to one of the worst offenders during this crisis—the insurance giant American International Group (AIG)—it did so under the provision that new regulations and oversight must be put in place. Edward Libby, the chief executive officer of AIG at the time, complained that such oversight would hinder AIG's ability to "attract and retain the best and brightest talent" (Seib, 2009).

Most of these commentators (and this CEO) didn't seem to realize that the term "the best and the brightest" was introduced into popular culture not as praise but as irony. The phrase was the title of journalist David Halberstam's 1972 book about U.S. president John F. Kennedy's team of cabinet members and advisors and its foreign policy decision-making, especially regarding the Vietnam War. What was remarkable to Halberstam was how a group of some of the most intelligent, educated, well-intentioned individuals ever to serve a government could make a series of colossal miscalculations and blunders.

Groups, of course, do not always underperform. Indeed, sometimes a group of individuals will develop a kind of chemistry or coordination that enables it to succeed far above what might have been expected of this collection of individuals.

All this reveals a fascinating fact: *Groups can be quite different from the sum of their parts.* When you think about that statement, it suggests something almost mystical or magical about groups, like quantum physics. How can a group be better—or worse—

Putting COMMON SENSE to the Test

Circle Your Answer

T	F	People will cheer louder when they cheer as part of a group than when they cheer alone.
T	F	People brainstorming as a group come up with a greater number of better ideas than the same number of people working individually.
T	F	Group members' attitudes about a course of action usually become more moderate after group discussion.
T	F	Large groups are more likely than small groups to exploit a scarce resource that the members collectively depend on.

You think because you understand "one," you must understand "two," because one and one make two. But you must also understand "and."

—Ancient Sufi saying

293

A trader on Wall Street is stunned and horrified by the financial meltdown he is witnessing in October 2008 (left). Dancers perform at the beautiful opening ceremonies of the 2008 Olympics in Beijing, China (right). The greed-fueled economic collapse and the brilliant teamwork of the opening ceremonies in Beijing together illustrate how people working in groups can make terrible mistakes or achieve great things.

than its individual members? The math may not seem to add up, but the theory and research discussed in this chapter will help answer this question.

People are often at their best—and their worst—in groups. It is through groups that individuals form communities, pool resources, and share successes. But it is also through groups that stereotypes turn into oppression, frustrations turn into mob violence, and conflicts turn into wars.

Clearly, it is important that we understand how groups work and how individuals influence, and are influenced by, groups. The more we learn how to harness the good that groups can bring, and avoid their pitfalls, the better our lives will be. In this chapter we first introduce the fundamentals of what groups are and how they develop, then we examine groups on several levels: At the individual level, we explore how individuals are influenced by groups; at the group level, we explore how groups perform; and at the intergroup level, we explore how groups interact with each other in cooperation and competition.

Fundamentals of Groups

We begin our exploration of groups by asking the basic questions: What is a group? Why do people join groups? We then examine how individuals are socialized into, or out of, groups, and how groups develop over time. We then focus on three important aspects of groups: roles, norms, and cohesiveness.

What Is a Group? Why Join a Group?

What Is a Group?   The question might seem quite simple, but if you step back and think about it, the answer is less obvious. For example, many students are members of a variety of groups on Facebook. Are these really groups? You may be part of a large social psychology class: Is this a group identity that is meaningful to you?

In Chapter 5, we focused on how individuals perceive groups and group members. In that context, we characterized a group as a set of individuals with at least one of the following characteristics: (1) direct interactions with each other over a period of time; (2) joint membership in a social category based on sex, race, or other attributes; (3) a shared fate, identity, or set of goals. The current chapter focuses on groups themselves rather than on others' perceptions of groups and group members. In this context, we emphasize the first and third criteria: *direct interactions among group members over a period of time* and *a shared fate, identity, or set of goals.*

Groups vary in the extent to which they are seen as distinct entities, such as whether they have rigid boundaries that make them distinct from other groups. In other words, some groups seem more "groupy" than others (Meneses et al., 2008; Rutchick et al., 2008). On the very low end of the dimensions of entity or social integration would be people attending a concert or working out near each other in a gym. These often are not considered real groups. Such assemblages are sometimes called *collectives*—people engaging in a common activity but having little direct interaction with each other (Milgram & Toch, 1969). Much more integrated groups include tight-knit clubs, sports teams, or work teams—groups that engage in very purposeful activities with a lot of interaction over time and clear boundaries of who is in and not in the group.

Groups come in all shapes and sizes: large and small, highly organized and quite informal, short term and long lasting. Sometimes group membership is involuntary. You didn't choose your family, for example, or your social class. But membership in many groups is voluntary. You decide to join an existing group or get together with others to create a brand-new one. Why do people join groups? We address this question next.

Why Join a Group? The complexity and ambitions of human life require that we work in groups. Much of what we hope to produce and accomplish can be done only through collective action. Lone individuals cannot play symphonies or football games, build cities or industries, or run governments or universities.

At a more fundamental level, humans may have an innate need to belong to groups, stemming from evolutionary pressures that increased people's chances of survival and reproduction when they lived in groups rather than in isolation. Indeed, according to the *social brain hypothesis*, the unusually large size of primates' brains

The appeal of being a part of groups is evident from the popularity of groups on Facebook. Many people are members of dozens or even hundreds of groups on the social networking site. Whether or not these should be considered *real* groups, and why people may be drawn to join such groups, are among the issues discussed in the text.

People join a group for any of several reasons, such as to affiliate with others, obtain social status, and interact with individual group members.

Sarah Sudhoff/Redux

The individuals which took the greatest pleasure in society would best escape various dangers, whilst those that cared least for their comrades, and lived solitary, would perish in greater numbers.

—Charles Darwin, *The Descent of Man*

evolved because of their unusually complex social worlds (Dunbar, 2008). As Mark Van Vugt and Mark Schaller (2008) state in their review of research on contemporary human group dynamics from an evolutionary perspective: "Humans may well have evolved a range of psychological mechanisms that promote an attraction to and capacity for living in groups" (p. 1).

For humans, attraction to group life serves not only to protect against threat and uncertainty in a physical sense but also to gain a greater sense of personal and social identity. According to social identity theory, which was discussed in Chapter 5, an important part of people's feelings of self-worth comes from their identification with particular groups. This is also at the root of why being rejected by a group is one of life's most painful experiences (Kerr & Levine, 2008; Williams, 2009). As social beings, we come to understand ourselves and our place in the world with reference to the groups that constitute our identities (Bizumic et al., 2009; Haslam et al., 2009; Swann & Bosson, 2010). Certainly the appeal of joining a variety of virtual groups and building a large group of friends on social network sites is fueled by the feelings of social identity and connectedness they foster.

Socialization and Group Development

Once an individual has joined a group, a process of adjustment takes place. The individual assimilates into the group, making whatever changes are necessary to fit in. At the same time, the group may accommodate to the newcomer, making whatever changes are necessary to include that individual. Socialization of a new member into a group often relies heavily on the relationship between newcomers and established members. Newcomers model their behavior on what the old-timers do; old-timers may train newcomers, serve as mentors, or develop personal relationships with them to help them succeed in the group. Effectively socializing new members can produce short-term and long-term benefits for the group as a whole. Conversely, poor socialization can lead to many bad outcomes, including suppressing the potential contributions of newcomers or creating a lot of turnover and instability in the group (Moreland & Levine, 2001; Levine & Choi, 2010).

Just as an individual's relationship with the group changes over time, the dynamics in the group as a whole change across time as well. Group development may proceed through several stages (Wheelan, 2009). Bruce Tuckman (1965; Tuckman & Jensen, 1977) proposed a particularly memorable set of stages through which groups often develop: forming, storming, norming, performing, and adjourning. These stages are described in Table 8.1. According to this model, groups gradually progress from a period of initial orientation through stages of conflict, compromise, and action, followed by a period of withdrawal if the group no longer satisfies members' needs.

Although many groups do seem to pass through these stages, not all groups do. Contemporary theory on group devel-

---

TABLE 8.1

Stages of Group Development

- **Forming:** Members try to orient themselves to the group. They often act in polite, exploratory ways with each other.

- **Storming:** Members try to influence the group so that it best fits their own needs. They become more assertive about the group's direction and what roles they would like to play in the group. A great deal of conflict and hostility may arise as well as feelings of excitement about what might be achieved.

- **Norming:** Members try to reconcile the conflicts that emerge during storming and develop a common sense of purpose and perspective. They establish norms and roles and begin to feel more commitment to the group.

- **Performing:** Members try to perform their tasks and maximize the group's performance. They operate within their roles in the group and try to solve problems in order to achieve their shared goals.

- **Adjourning:** Members disengage from the group, distancing themselves from the other members and reducing their activities within the group. This may occur if members believe that the benefits of staying in the group no longer outweigh the costs.

Based on Tuckman, 1965, and Tuckman & Jensen, 1977.

opment offers more complex models of group development, including the recognition that groups often develop in ways that are not linear and that different groups may develop in different ways (e.g., Chang et al., 2006). For example, Connie Gersick (1988, 1994) observed that groups often do not proceed gradually through a uniform series of stages but instead operate in starts and stops. According to her *punctuated equilibrium* model, groups go through periods of inertia or relative inactivity until triggered by awareness of time and deadlines, which can cause a sudden shift in activity and dynamics. According to Gersick, many groups adopt a problem-solving strategy very quickly—much quicker than Tuckman's theory suggests—but then they procrastinate until they have wasted about half the time they have allotted for the task, after which point they spring into action. Think about the work groups that *you've* been a part of: Do the stages described in Table 8.1 seem to apply, or do the groups described by Gersick seem more familiar to you?

Roles, Norms, and Cohesiveness

Despite their variation in specific characteristics, important features in most groups are an expected set of tasks for members (roles), rules of conduct for members (norms), and forces that push members together (cohesiveness). We consider each of these in the following sections.

Roles   People's *roles* in a group, their set of expected behaviors, can be formal or informal. Formal roles are designated by titles: teacher or student in a class, vice president or account executive in a corporation. Informal roles are less obvious but still powerful. For example, Robert Bales (1958) proposed that regardless of people's titles, enduring groups give rise to two fundamental types of roles: an *instrumental* role to help the group achieve its tasks and an *expressive* role to provide emotional support and maintain morale. The same person can fill both roles but often they are assumed by different individuals, and which of these roles is emphasized in groups may fluctuate over time depending on the needs of the group.

Having a set of clear roles is beneficial to a group (Lu et al., 2008). A meta-analysis of studies involving more than 11,000 individuals found a significant negative correlation between role ambiguity and job performance—the more role ambiguity, the worse one's job performance is (Tubre & Collins, 2000). Teams often strive to organize themselves and distribute task roles based on group members' particular skills and preferences. The better a team does in assigning roles that match the individual's talents, the better the individual will function in the group. However, when a person's role in the group is ambiguous, conflicts with other roles the person has (as when a group member needs to be demanding but also is the person who typically provides emotional support to others) or changes over time, stress, and loss of productivity are likely to result (Bettencourt et al., 2006; Chen et al., 2009; Lu et al., 2008).

Anita Williams Woolley and others (2007) demonstrated the benefits of matching group roles to members' abilities in an experiment that involved the use of tests of brain functioning to

When roles in a group are not distributed properly, group performance suffers.

"I've had to be both hunter and gatherer."

determine role assignment. Participants in the study worked in two-person teams and performed a task that required one member to work on an object identification assignment and the other member to work on a spatial relationship assignment. The researchers used tests of individual differences in object and spatial visualization to assign participants to teams.

The teams in the *homogenous* condition consisted of two individuals who were both strong on the same dimension (object or spatial) and not very strong on the other. The teams in the *congruent* condition consisted of one member strong on object but not spatial visualization and one member with the opposite abilities, and their roles in the group matched their abilities—the spatial person worked on the spatial task and the object person worked on the object task. The teams in the *incongruent* condition also consisted of two members with complementary strengths, but in this condition their roles were incongruent with the skills—an object specialist worked on the spatial task and a spatial specialist worked on the object task. As can be seen in ▶ Figure 8.1, teams in which members' were assigned roles that were congruent with their abilities performed better than the incongruent or homogenous teams.

Norms   In addition to roles for its members, groups also establish *norms*, rules of conduct for members. Like roles, norms may be either formal or informal. Fraternities and sororities, for example, usually have written rules for the behavior expected from their members. Informal norms are more subtle. What do I wear? How hard can I push for what I want? Who pays for this or that? At a more general level, these norms provide individuals with a sense of what it means to be a good group member. Figuring out the unwritten rules of the group can take time and cause anxiety.

Researchers have investigated the development and consequences of a huge array of group norms, involving things as varied as binge drinking, smoking, risky sexual behavior, prejudice, and even the use of language and symbols in Internet groups and gaming (Ahern et al., 2009; Hittner & Kennington, 2008; Martey & Stromer-Galley, 2007; Zitek & Hebl, 2007). Brendan McAuliffe and others (2003) found that even a group norm of individualism can be established, resulting in members who conform to the norm of not conforming!

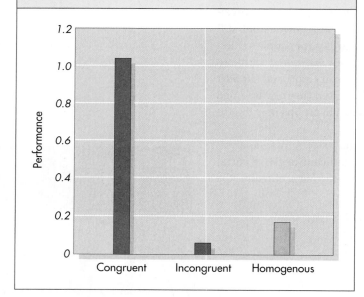

▶ FIGURE 8.1

Matching Abilities to Roles

Two-person teams worked on a project in which one member worked on a task requiring spatial visualization abilities and the other worked on a task requiring object recognition abilities. Teams performed better if the members were assigned to their roles that matched their abilities (*congruent* condition) than if they were assigned to roles that did not match their abilities (*incongruent* condition) or if both members of the team were strong on the same ability (*homogenous* condition).

Based on Woolley et al., 2007.

Blowing the Whistle: Resisting Norms to Reveal Serious Problems   Sometimes breaking a group norm can be very difficult and even traumatic for a group member. Co-workers are especially reluctant to report the unethical behavior of others on their work teams, fearing the social consequences of reporting on a member of the group. Indeed, Benoit Monin and others (2008) demonstrated in a series of experiments how individuals who refused to go along with the norm were strongly disliked by their fellow participants, even when it was clear that the norm was rather immoral. Consultants involved in employee relations frequently observe the dilemma that group members face when they witness unethical conduct. As one consultant noted, "[Team workers] have a fear they'll be seen as divisive. We're social animals, and we so very much want to belong" (Armour, 1998, p. 6B).

Although the 2008–2009 financial collapse that we discussed at the beginning of the chapter caught much of the world by surprise, numerous individuals had tried to warn superiors in their businesses and organizations about the dangerous and sometimes illegal practices they were observing (Goldfarb, 2009; Roig-Franzia, 2009; Sands, 2009). Most of these individuals were ignored; some were threatened. Breaking the "business as usual" norms in the financial sector at the time by warning of impending disaster took great courage, as the pressure to keep silent was enormous. Similarly, a number of individuals working in or with the U.S. government and military received very harsh treatment when they publicly criticized high-ranking officials concerning their actions and decisions in the buildup to and execution of the war in Iraq, or when they revealed secret policies of torture or humiliation of prisoners held by the military (Borger, 2003; Conroy, 2007; Sisk, 2007). Each of the people who came forward did so with the understanding that his or her career and reputation could be threatened and possibly destroyed.

Two officers for the U.S. Army Corps of Engineers, Bunnatine Greenhouse and Christy Watts, testify before a Senate committee in September 2005. These women had reported corruption in the awarding of government contracts and had both lost their jobs after they raised their concerns. Blowing the whistle on corruption in one's group can be a terrifying—and heroic—act.

Cohesiveness   Breaking group norms is especially difficult in groups that are very cohesive. **Group cohesiveness** refers to the forces exerted on a group that push its members closer together (Cartwright & Zander, 1960; Festinger, 1950). Members of cohesive groups tend to feel commitment to the group task, like the other group members, feel group pride, and engage in many—and often intense—interactions in the group (Dion, 2000; Klassen & Krawchuk, 2009).

An interesting question is whether cohesiveness makes groups perform better. It may seem obvious that it should, but in fact the relationship between cohesiveness and performance is not a simple one. The causal relationship works both ways: On the one hand, when a group is cohesive, group performance often improves; on the other hand, when a group performs well, it often becomes more cohesive. Many team athletes recognize that winning creates team chemistry even more than team chemistry creates winning. In their meta-analysis of the research on cohesiveness and group performance, Brian Mullen and Carolyn Copper (1994) found stronger evidence that performance affects cohesiveness than that cohesiveness affects performance. They also found that the positive relationship between cohesiveness and group performance may depend on the size of the group: The relationship tended to be stronger in small groups than in large ones.

An ineffective leader can hurt the cohesiveness of a group, as is evident in the amusingly inept boss (played by Steve Carell) and his disgruntled employees in the TV comedy *The Office*.

Subsequent meta-analyses and longitudinal studies have provided more evidence showing that group cohesion can lead to better performance, but other variables tend to be important in predicting when and to what extent this effect may emerge (Beal et al., 2003; Gully et al., 1995; Tekleab et al., 2009). For example, a meta-analysis of 46 studies of cohesiveness in sports teams found not only a generally positive correlation between cohesiveness and team performance but also that the relationship was particularly strong for female sports teams—possibly because women tend to be more interdependent than men (Carron et al., 2002). And as we will discuss later in the chapter, highly cohesive groups may be especially vulnerable to making terrible decisions because members fear going against a leader or group norm.

group cohesiveness   The extent to which forces push group members closer together, such as through feelings of intimacy, unity, and commitment to group goals.

Culture and Cohesiveness

More than ever before, people work in groups that are diverse culturally. Work teams in the business world may consist of individuals from around the globe. It is becoming all the more important, then, to understand how group dynamics may differ across cultures. For example, Norman Wright and Glyn Drewery (2006) hypothesized that which factors affect a group's cohesiveness will vary as a function of whether the group members are from collectivistic or individualistic cultures. Consistent with this idea, they found that if some group members did not carry their share of the workload or came late to meetings, group cohesiveness was more likely to suffer among Japanese and Pacific Islanders than among Anglos. In a study of 381 work teams in the United States and Hong Kong, Derak Man and Simon Lam (2003) found that increases in task complexity or autonomy, which individualists tend to value more than collectivists, were more likely to increase group cohesiveness among team workers in the United States than in Hong Kong.

How concerned group members are about hurting group cohesiveness by engaging in heated debates—and the effects of such debates on group performance—may also vary across culture. Roger Nibler and Karen Harris (2003) studied five-person groups of strangers and friends in China and the United States. The groups' task was to rank 15 items to be taken aboard a lifeboat from a ship that was about to sink. This task tends to trigger a fair amount of initial disagreement among group members until a consensus can be reached. With the Chinese groups and the groups of American strangers, these kinds of disagreements tended to be perceived as troubling and interfered with group performance. To the groups of American friends, in contrast, these disagreements were more likely to be seen as simply part of a freewheeling debate, and the sense of freedom to exchange opinions and disagree with one another tended to improve performance on this task.

Individuals in Groups: The Presence of Others

When we engage in activities in groups, we are in the presence (either physically or virtually) of others. It's an obvious point, but some of its consequences are profound and surprising. In this section we focus on three important effects that the presence of others can have on individuals: social facilitation, social loafing, and deindividuation.

Social Facilitation: When Others Arouse Us

Social psychologists have long been fascinated by how the presence of others affects behavior. In Chapter 1, we reported that one of the founders of social psychology was Norman Triplett, whose article "The Dynamogenic Factors in Pacemaking and Competition" (1897–1898) is often cited as the earliest publication in the field. Triplett began his research by studying the official bicycle records from the Racing Board of the League of American Wheelmen for the 1897 season. He noticed that cyclists who competed against others performed better than those who cycled alone against the clock. After dismissing various theories of the day (our favorite is "brain worry"), he proposed his own hypothesis: The presence of another rider releases the competitive instinct, which increases nervous energy and enhances performance. To test this proposition, Triplett got 40 children to wind up fishing reels, alternating between performing alone and working in parallel. On average, winding time was faster when the children worked side by side than when they worked alone. (In an interesting contemporary twist on this classic, in 2005 Michael Strube used modern statistical techniques to reanalyze Triplett's original data and found that the results were not as straightforward as Triplett's report suggested.)

Later research following Triplett's studies proved disappointing. Sometimes the presence of others (side by side or with an audience out front) enhanced performance; at other times, performance declined. It seemed that Triplett's promising lead had turned into a blind alley, and social psychologists had largely abandoned this research by World War II. But years later, Robert Zajonc (1965, 1980) saw a way to reconcile the contradictory results by integrating research from experimental psychology with social psychological research. Zajonc offered an elegant solution: The presence of others increases arousal, which can affect performance in different ways, depending on the task at hand. Let's see how this works.

The Zajonc Solution According to Zajonc, the road from presence to performance requires three steps.

1. The presence of others creates general physiological *arousal*, which energizes behavior. Based on experimental psychology research and principles of evolution, Zajonc argued that all animals, including humans, tend to become aroused when in the presence of *conspecifics*—that is, members of their own species.

2. Increased arousal enhances an individual's tendency to perform the *dominant response*. The dominant response is the reaction elicited most quickly and easily by a given stimulus. Here again, Zajonc drew from experimental psychology research, particularly research concerning learning.

3. The quality of an individual's performance varies according to the type of *task*. On an easy task (one that is simple or well learned), the dominant response is usually correct or successful. But on a difficult task (one that is complex or unfamiliar), the dominant response is often incorrect or unsuccessful.

Putting these three steps together (see ▶ Figure 8.2) yields the following scenarios. Suppose you are playing the violin. If you're an excellent player and are performing a well-learned, familiar arrangement, having other people around should enhance your performance; the presence of others will increase your arousal, which will enhance your dominant response. Because this arrangement is so well learned, your dominant response will be to perform it well. However, if you are just learning to play the violin and you are unfamiliar with this arrangement, the presence of others is the last thing you'll want. The increase in arousal should enhance the dominant response, which in this case would be *unsuccessful* violin playing.

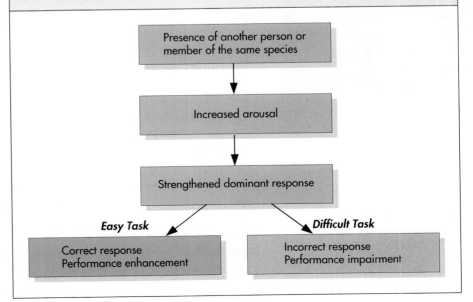

▶**FIGURE 8.2**

Social Facilitation: The Zajonc Solution

According to Zajonc, the presence of others increases arousal, which strengthens the dominant response to a stimulus. On an easy task, the dominant response is usually correct and thus the presence of others enhances performance. On a difficult task, the dominant response is often incorrect and thus the presence of others impairs performance.

When you think about it, this makes intuitive sense. If you are just learning how to perform some complicated task, such as playing the violin or riding a bike, it helps if you are not aroused. In contrast, if you are already good at the task, you may need the extra "juice" that comes from performing in front of others to help you rise to new heights and perform even better than you would if performing alone. Sports fans may be able to think of many instances when the best athletes seem to rise to the occasion when the pressure is on, while lesser athletes "choke" under the same kind of pressure. And physical performances are not the only ones influenced; the effects also hold for social judgment or cognitive tasks, such as forming impressions of others or solving math problems (Lambert et al., 2003; Park & Catrambone, 2007).

Taken as a package, these two effects of the presence of others—helping performance on easy tasks but hurting performance on difficult tasks—are known as **social facilitation**. Unfortunately this term has been a prime source of confusion for countless students. The trick is to remember that the presence of others facilitates the dominant response, not necessarily the task itself. This facilitation of the dominant response does, in effect, facilitate easy tasks, but it makes difficult tasks even more difficult.

Zajonc says that social facilitation is universal, occurring not only in human activities but also among other animals, even insects. Have you ever wondered, for instance, how well a cockroach performs in front of other cockroaches? Neither did we—that is, we wouldn't have if not for the ever-creative Bob Zajonc. Zajonc and his colleagues (1969) had cockroaches placed in a brightly lit start box connected to a darkened goal box. When the track was a simple one, with a straight runway between the start box and the goal box, cockroaches running in pairs ran more quickly toward the goal box than did those running alone. But in a more complex maze that required a right turn to reach the goal box, solitary cockroaches outraced pairs.

In a particularly creative follow-up experiment, Zajonc and his colleagues found that cockroaches completed the easy maze faster, and the difficult maze slower, if they raced in front of a crowd of spectator cockroaches than if they raced with no audience. How did the researchers get cockroaches to participate as spectators? The researchers placed cockroaches in plexiglass "audience boxes" along either side of the maze, and this "audience" produced social facilitation.

Social Facilitation Research Today   Zajonc's formulation revived interest in the issues raised by Triplett's early research, and suddenly the inconsistent findings that had been reported began to make sense. The results of a meta-analysis of 241 studies were consistent with much of Zajonc's account (Bond & Titus, 1983). And despite its long history, research today continues to demonstrate new examples of social facilitation and to test its scope and limitations. Social facilitation effects have been demonstrated recently in settings such as driving tests (a word of advice: Don't take your road test with another test-taker present in the car!), electronic gambling, and neuropsychological testing (Rockloff & Dyer, 2007; Rosenbloom et al., 2007; Yantz & McCaffrey, 2007). Researchers are also beginning to find neurological and physiological evidence consistent with predictions based on the theory, such as evidence concerning patterns of brain activation and cardiovascular responses (Blascovich et al., 1999; Wagstaff et al., 2008).

United States swimmer Michael Phelps takes the lead on the way to one of his record-setting eight gold medals at the 2008 Olympics in Beijing. Through social facilitation, some of the best athletes benefit from the presence of an audience and high pressure when performing well-learned routines.

social facilitation   A process whereby the presence of others enhances performance on easy tasks but impairs performance on difficult tasks.

It is because of the effects of social facilitation that firefighters, police officers, military personnel, and others must train so much to be ready to make split-second decisions under highly arousing situations. They may seem to practice scenarios to the point of overtraining, but it is only through such repetition that their dominant response can be assured to typically be the correct one. When they are in the midst of a raging fire or military firefight, it is often impossible for them to deliberate carefully, and arousal will tend to elicit their dominant responses (e.g., Gladwell, 2005).

Social facilitation effects are triggered by the presence of others, but recent research has pushed the boundaries of what "the presence of others" can mean. For example, many people relate to favorite television characters almost as if they were real people, such as by feeling joy or sadness along with a beloved character. Could the "presence" of such a TV character trigger social facilitation effects? Wendi Gardner and Megan Knowles (2008) found that it could, as participants in their study performed simple tasks better and complex tasks worse in the presence of a picture of a favorite TV character. A picture of a nonfavorite character did not elicit these effects. Even nonhuman characters may be human-like enough to cause arousal and social facilitation effects. Students in Sung Park and Richard Catrambone's (2007) experiment completed tasks either alone, in the company of another person, or next to a computer that showed a "virtual" person—a computer-generated three-dimensional display that seemed to breathe, blink, and display subtle facial movements—that appeared to watch them (see ▶ Figure 8.3). Social facilitation effects were just as strong in the presence of a virtual other as with a real other person.

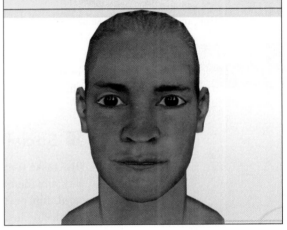

▶ **FIGURE 8.3**
Virtual Human and Social Facilitation
This is an image of what the virtual person looked like in the study by Sung Park and Richard Catrambone (2007). The presence of this virtual human watching participants triggered social facilitation effects.

Alternative Explanations for Social Facilitation   Social facilitation effects have been replicated across many domains, but not all of Zajonc's theory has received universal support. Zajonc proposed that the **mere presence** of others is sufficient to produce social facilitation. Some have argued, however, that the presence of others will produce social facilitation only under certain conditions. These issues have produced various alternative explanations of social facilitation.

The first and most thoroughly researched alternative, **evaluation apprehension theory**, proposes that performance will be enhanced or impaired only in the presence of others who are in a position to evaluate that performance (Geen, 1991; Henchy & Glass, 1968). In other words, it's not simply because others are around that I'm so aroused and therefore inept as I try to learn to snowboard on a crowded mountain. Rather, it's because I worry that the others are watching and probably laughing at me, possibly uploading a video of my performance to YouTube. These concerns increase my dominant response, which, unfortunately, is falling.

Another approach to social facilitation, **distraction-conflict theory**, points out that being distracted while we're working on a task creates attentional conflict (Baron, 1986; Sanders, 1981). We're torn between focusing on the task and inspecting the distracting stimulus. When we are conflicted about where to pay attention, our arousal increases.

Trying to isolate these different causes in an experiment can be challenging. For example, one study tried to manipulate evaluation apprehension while keeping mere presence constant by having confederates in one condition be present but blindfolded (supposedly in preparation for a perception study) while participants

mere presence theory
The proposition that the mere presence of others is sufficient to produce social facilitation effects.

evaluation apprehension theory   A theory that the presence of others will produce social facilitation effects only when those others are seen as potential evaluators.

distraction-conflict theory
A theory that the presence of others will produce social facilitation effects only when those others distract from the task and create attentional conflict.

"God, this is going to be all over YouTube."

Fear of being evaluated by others can sometimes hurt performance.

worked on a task. The presence of confederates who were not blindfolded led to increased dominant responses for participants, but blindfolded confederates did not trigger this effect, presumably because participants would not be concerned about being evaluated by these others (Cottrell et al., 1968).

So is one of these theories right and the others wrong? Probably not. It seems likely that all three of the basic elements described by these theories (mere presence, evaluation, and attention) can contribute to the impact others have on our own performance (Uziel, 2007). For example, the mere presence account can explain social facilitation among cockroaches better than the evaluation apprehension account can, but evaluation apprehension is better than mere presence at explaining why blindfolded others have less impact than others who are not blindfolded. An integration of these different explanations may offer the best account of all. But as we are about to see in the next section, there is even more to the story of how individuals are affected by the presence of others.

Social Loafing: When Others Relax Us

The tasks that participants complete in research on social facilitation produce individually identifiable results. That is, individual behavior can be identified and evaluated. But on some tasks, efforts are pooled so that the specific performance of any one individual cannot be determined. That other founder of social psychology, French agricultural engineer Max Ringelmann, investigated group performance on these kinds of collective endeavors. In research conducted during the 1880s, Ringelmann discovered that compared with what individuals produced when they worked on their own, people's output declined when they worked together on simple tasks like pulling a rope or pushing a cart (Kravitz & Martin, 1986; Ringelmann, 1913).

Why did individual output decline? One explanation is that the individuals exerted less effort when they acted collectively, but another explanation is that the individuals simply demonstrated poor coordination when working together—some pulled while others relaxed and vice versa. How can you distinguish lack of effort from poor coordination in a task like this? Nearly a hundred years after Ringelmann's research, Alan Ingham and his colleagues (1974) answered this question by using a rope-pulling machine and blindfolding participants. In one condition participants were led to *think* that they were pulling with a bunch of other participants, and in another condition the participants were informed that they were pulling alone (which, in fact, they were). The researchers told the participants to pull as hard as they could. Ingham and colleagues were able to measure exactly how hard each individual participant pulled, and they observed that the participants pulled almost 20 percent harder when they thought they were pulling alone than when they thought they were pulling with others. Naoki Kugihara (1999) found a similar decline in rope-pulling among Japanese men (but not women) in a collective setting.

Bibb Latané and his colleagues (1979) found that group-produced reductions in individual output, which they called **social loafing**, are common in other types of tasks as well. For example, imagine being asked as part of a psychology experiment to cheer or clap as loudly as you can. Common sense might lead you to think that you would cheer and clap louder when doing this together with others in a group

social loafing A group-produced reduction in individual output on tasks where contributions are pooled.

than when performing alone because you would be less embarrassed and inhibited if others were doing the same thing as you. But Latané and his colleagues found that when performing collectively, individual students loafed—they exerted less effort. The noise generated by each individual decreased as the size of the group increased (see ▶ Figure 8.4). This social loafing occurred even among cheerleaders, who are supposed to be experts at cheering and clapping with others!

Social loafing is not restricted to simple motor tasks. Sharing responsibility with others reduces the amount of effort that people put into more complex motor tasks, such as swimming in a relay race or playing soccer; cognitive tasks, such as completing memory, math, or verbal tests; and important, enduring real-world behaviors, such as working collaboratively on collective farms or team projects (Hoigaard & Ommundsen, 2007; Liden et al., 2004; Miles & Greenberg, 1993; Plaks & Higgins, 2000; Tan & Tan, 2008; Weldon et al., 2000). When others are there to pick up the slack, people slack off.

But social loafing is not inevitable; a number of factors can reduce it. Social loafing is less likely to occur when one of the following conditions is present:

- People believe that their own performance can be identified and thus evaluated—by themselves or others.

- The task is important or meaningful to those performing it.

- People believe that their own efforts are necessary for a successful outcome.

- The group expects to be punished for poor performance.

- The group is small.

- The group is cohesive—that is, membership in the group is valuable and important to the members and the individuals like each other.

Most college students are quite familiar with having to work on group projects and many have seen the pitfalls of social loafing in these settings. Praveen Aggarwal and Connie O'Brien (2008) recently studied several hundred university students to assess what factors can reduce the incidence of social loafing. They identify three factors that are key to reducing social loafing: (1) limiting the scope of the project—projects that are very large and complex should be broken into smaller components; (2) keeping the groups small; and (3) using peer evaluations—the researchers found that as the number of times when peers evaluated each other's work increased, the incidence of social loafing decreased.

Businesses have taken note of social loafing and have applied these research findings in an effort to reduce it in the workplace. For example, one form of social loafing at the workplace has come to be known as *cyberloafing*, which involves personal use of e-mail and the Internet at work; cyberloafing can be a huge drain on workers' productivity (Blanchard & Henle, 2008; Henle et al., 2009). One result is that workers' actions on the job are coming under increasing surveillance as the number of computer keystrokes they make per hour or the content of their calls, e-mails, or Internet browsing can be recorded electronically.

Although everyone is vulnerable to social loafing, some people may be more or less prone to it than others. Hwee Tan and Min-Li Tan (2008), for example, found that people high in conscientiousness were less likely to engage in social loafing. Other

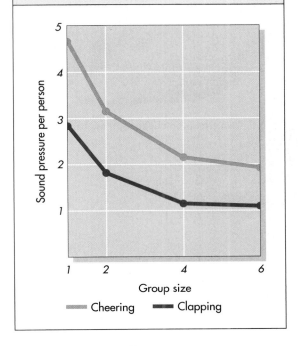

▶ **FIGURE 8.4**

Social Loafing: When Many Produce Less

Social loafing is a group-produced reduction in individual output on simple tasks. In this study, college students were told to cheer or clap as loudly as they could. The noise produced by each of them decreased as the size of the group increased.

Based on Latané et al., 1979.

People will cheer louder when they cheer as part of a group than when they cheer alone. **FALSE.**

"We just haven't been flapping them hard enough."

Individuals often don't try as hard in groups as they do alone. If they can be convinced that their efforts will pay off, however, their output can soar.

factors associated with reduced social loafing include being very task oriented, having "a winning orientation," and being relatively high in achievement motivation (Hart et al., 2004; Hoiggard & Ommundsen, 2007; Stark et al., 2007).

Collective Effort Model   Several researchers have constructed theoretical accounts to explain the findings about when social loafing is more or less likely to occur (e.g., Guerin, 2003; Shepperd & Taylor, 1999). The most influential analysis is by Karau and Williams (2001), who proposed the **collective effort model**. This model asserts that individuals will try hard on a collective task when they think their efforts will help them achieve outcomes they personally value. If the outcome is important to individual members of the group and if they believe they can help achieve the desired outcome, then they are likely to engage in *social compensation* by increasing their efforts on collective tasks to try to compensate for the anticipated social loafing or poor performance of other group members.

Conversely, if the outcome is not personally important to individual members, if they believe that their contribution won't affect the outcome very much, or if they feel they are unable to compensate for the anticipated social loafing of other members, then they are likely to exert less effort. This is sometimes called the *sucker effect*: Nobody wants to be the "sucker" who does all the work while everyone else goofs off, so everyone withholds effort and the result is very poor group performance (Houldsworth & Mathews, 2000; Kerr, 1983; Shepperd, 1993a). The next time you work on a group project, such as a paper that you and several other students are supposed to write together, consider the factors that increase and decrease social loafing. You might want to try to change aspects of the situation so that all group members are motivated to do their share of the work.

Culture and Social Loafing

Steven Karau and Kipling Williams (1993) conducted a meta-analysis of 78 studies and found social loafing to be a reliable phenomenon that is evident across numerous tasks and in countries around the world. Recent research has even demonstrated social loafing among children as young as five years old (Arterberry et al., 2007). Despite its prevalence around the world, some group and cultural differences in tendencies to socially loaf have been found.

Karau and Williams's meta-analysis found that social loafing was less prevalent among women than among men and less prevalent among people from East Asian, collectivist cultures (such as those in China, Japan, and Taiwan) than among people from Western, individualist cultures (such as those in Canada and the United States). Women in general, and people in primarily collectivistic cultural contexts, tend to be relatively more interdependent and connected to others than are men in general, and people in individualistic contexts. Individuals with a more interdependent self concept tend to be more aware of their connections and mutual reliance on others and therefore may be more concerned about the possible negative impact on others of their social loafing.

In an interesting twist, Ying-yi Hong and others (2008) hypothesized that there are times when people from collectivistic cultures may be especially likely to socially loaf. Because people from these cultures tend to be concerned with behaving consis-

collective effort model The theory that individuals will exert effort on a collective task to the degree that they think their individual efforts will be important, relevant, and meaningful for achieving outcomes that they value.

tently with group norms, they may be tempted to socially loaf if they are working in a group that has established a norm of low productivity and effort. The researchers found support for this idea in a set of studies with Chinese students. When these students engaged in a task with co-workers who were not being productive, the participants reduced their own efforts if they thought their effort would be evident to their co-workers. Not wanting to publicly deviate from the group norm, these students conformed to the norm of working less hard.

Deindividuation

Although we spend much of our lives in the presence of others, there are times when behavior in collectives can be quite extraordinary. Nineteenth-century French scholars Gabriel Tarde (1890) and Gustave Le Bon (1895) maintained that under the sway of the crowd, people can turn into copycat automatons or, worse still, uncontrollable mobs. More than a century later, their warnings of what are often known as "the group mind" or "mob behavior" still resonate when the latest example of a group gone wild with rioting or looting makes the news. The destructive capacity of collectives has left and continues to leave a bloody trail through human history.

What turns an unruly crowd into a violent mob? No doubt many of the factors described in Chapter 11 on aggression contribute to group violence as well as violence done by individuals. These include imitation of aggressive models, intense frustration, alcohol consumption, and the presence of weapons that trigger aggressive thoughts and actions. But there's also **deindividuation**, the loss of a person's sense of individuality and the reduction of normal constraints against deviant behavior. Most investigators believe that deindividuation is a collective phenomenon that occurs only in the presence of others (Diener et al., 1976; Festinger et al., 1952).

Philip Zimbardo (1969) observed that *arousal, anonymity,* and reduced feelings of individual *responsibility* together contribute to deindividuation. Consider, for example, the behavior of a group of "knuckleheads" (as the Los Angeles Police Chief called them) who celebrated the Los Angeles Lakers winning the National Basketball Association championship on June 14, 2009 (Knoll et al., 2009). On the way out of the arena, some set fire to Orlando Magic shirts (the Lakers beat the Magic for the title) and then set fire to trash cans and trees. The mayhem quickly spread to stomping car windshields, ripping down signs, and breaking into and looting some stores. All three elements that Zimbardo specified were present here: The fans were very *aroused* by their team's victory, the thousands of fans pouring out of the arena provided the individuals with relative *anonymity,* and these factors, quite possibly along with alcohol consumed during the game, contributed to reduced feelings of individual *responsibility.*

According to Steven Prentice-Dunn and Ronald Rogers (1982, 1983), two types of environmental cues—accountability cues and attentional cues—make deviant behaviors such as this rioting more likely to occur. *Accountability cues* affect the individual's cost-reward calculations. When accountability is low, those who commit deviant acts are less likely to be caught and punished, and people may deliberately choose to engage in gratifying but usually inhibited behaviors. Being in a large crowd or wearing

Here, Chinese farmers cooperate on a task in which individual contributions cannot be identified. Social loafing on such tasks occurs less often in Eastern cultures than in Western ones.

The sentiments and ideas of all the persons in the gathering take one and the same direction, and their conscious personality vanishes.

—Gustave Le Bon (1895)

deindividuation The loss of a person's sense of individuality and the reduction of normal constraints against deviant behavior.

It has become fairly commonplace in recent years for celebrations by groups of fans after their team's victory in a championship to escalate from joy to mayhem and destruction. In this photo soccer fans roll over a car in Sydney, Australia, while celebrating Italy's victory over France in the World Cup. In the midst of a crowd like this, people may feel deindividuated, which can lead to deviant behavior.

Chris McGrath/Getty Images

a mask are two examples of instances when accountability may be low, and these factors are associated with more extreme and destructive behaviors.

Attentional cues focus a person's attention away from the self. In this state the individual attends less to internal standards of conduct, reacts more to the immediate situation, and is less sensitive to long-term consequences of behavior (Diener, 1980). Behavior slips out from the bonds of cognitive control and people act on impulse. When you are at a party with very loud music and flashing lights, you may be swept up with the pulsating crowd and feel your individual identity slipping away. In laboratory research, groups of participants placed in a highly stimulating environment (loud music, colorful video games) were more uninhibited, extreme, and aggressive in their actions (Diener, 1979; Spivey & Prentice-Dunn, 1990).

One context where many people spend a lot of time and where both accountability and attentional cues are likely to be low is online. If you've ever been part of an online community where people can post comments anonymously, there is a good chance that you've witnessed some of the nasty effects of deindividuation. Many well-intentioned sites or discussions or even the comments sections linked to online newspaper stories, videos, or celebrity gossip blogs soon devolve into a torrent of crude, hostile, and prejudiced venting and taunting that would never happen without the cloak of anonymity.

Trick or Treat: Field Experiments on Halloween   One particularly creative set of field experiments by Edward Diener and Arthur Beaman and their colleagues (Beaman et al., 1979; Diener et al., 1976) demonstrated how accountability cues and attentional cues can affect behavior on a night when many otherwise well-behaved individuals act in antisocial ways: Halloween. When you think about it, Halloween is a perfect time to study deindividuation: Children often wear costumes with masks, travel in large groups at night, and are highly aroused. In one study, the researchers unobtrusively observed more than 1,300 children who came trick-or-treating to 27 homes spread around Seattle. At each of these homes, a researcher met and greeted the children, who were either alone or in groups. In one condition, the researcher asked the children their names and where they lived; in another condition, the researcher did not ask them any questions about their identities. When asked to identify themselves, the children should have become more self-aware and more accountable for their actions.

Children who were not asked to reveal their identities should have felt relatively deindividuated, safe and anonymous in their costumes.

The children were then invited to take *one* item from a bowl full of candy and were left alone with the bowl. Hidden observers watched to see how many pieces of candy each child took. What did the observers see? As ▶ Figure 8.5 illustrates, children who were in a group were more likely to break the rule and take extra candy than were children who were alone. Add anonymity to the presence of a group, and children became even more likely to do so. In other words, the children were most likely to take extra candy when they were the most deindividuated: when they were in a group and had not been asked to identify themselves. In another experiment, the researchers placed a mirror behind the candy bowl in some conditions. As noted in Chapter 3, the presence of a mirror tends to increase people's self-awareness. Children who had been asked their names, especially older children, were much less likely to steal candy if there was a mirror present than if there wasn't. Older children are more likely to have internal standards against stealing, and making these children self-aware made them more likely to act according to those standards.

Moving from Personal to Social Identity   The loss of personal identity does not always produce antisocial behavior. In a study conducted by Robert Johnson and Leslie Downing (1979), female undergraduates donned garments resembling either robes worn by Ku Klux Klan members or nurses' uniforms. Half of the participants were individually identified throughout the study; the others were not. All of the participants were then given the opportunity to increase or decrease the intensity of electric shocks delivered to a supposed other participant (actually, a confederate in the experiment) who had previously behaved in an obnoxious manner. Participants wearing Ku Klux Klan costumes increased shock levels in both the identified and anonymous conditions. However, among those in nurse's apparel, anonymous participants *decreased* shock intensity four times more frequently than did identified participants!

These findings make a telling point: Sometimes becoming less accountable or less self-aware allows us to be more responsive to the needs of others. According to the **social identity model of deindividuation effects (SIDE)**, whether deindividuation affects people for better or for worse seems to reflect the characteristics and norms of the group immediately surrounding the individual as well as the group's power to act according to these norms (Cronin & Reicher, 2009; Klein et al., 2007; Lee, 2008). As personal identity and internal controls are submerged, social identity emerges and conformity to the group increases. If a group defines itself in terms of prejudice and hatred against another group, deindividuation can ignite an explosion of violence. The occasional stories of horrendous violation of the human rights of prisoners of war may illustrate this, as the intergroup hostilities the fighting has fueled along with the numerous ways that the military depersonalizes its members create a social identity that can overwhelm personal values of right and wrong. In contrast, if a group defines itself in terms of concern for the welfare of others, deindividuation can spark an expansion of goodness. The consequences of losing your personal identity depend on what you lose it to.

▶ **FIGURE 8.5**

Trick-or-Treat(s)

Children trick-or-treating on Halloween arrived at one of 27 houses around Seattle that were part of a field experiment. Some were alone and some were in groups with other trick-or-treaters. The experimenter who greeted them allowed a random half of the children to remain anonymous but asked the other half to indicate their names and where they lived. The experimenter instructed each child to take only one piece of candy, after which she left the children alone. The bars in this graph represent the percentage of children who took more than the one piece of candy. Consistent with predictions based on deindividuation, the children who were in a group and were anonymous were most likely to cheat by taking extra candy.

Based on Diener et al., 1976.

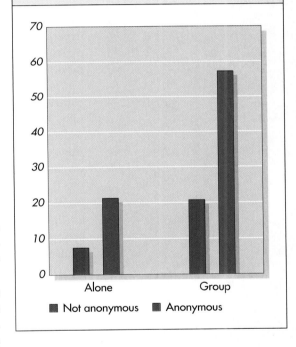

social identity model of deindividuation effects (SIDE) A model of group behavior that explains deindividuation effects as the result of a shift from personal identity to social identity.

Group Performance: Problems and Solutions

Social facilitation, social loafing, and deindividuation can all affect individuals whether they are working in real groups or are merely part of a collective or crowd. In this section, we examine processes that are specific to groups, where interaction among members is more direct and meaningful. We focus on how well groups perform, and in doing so, we address a fundamental question: Aren't two or more heads generally better than one? Although eight people typically can outproduce a lone individual, do eight people working together in a group typically outperform the sum of eight people working individually? Although this often is true, you may be surprised to learn how often and in what ways groups perform worse than their potential would suggest. We also discuss when and how groups are more likely to perform well.

A committee should consist of three men, two of whom are absent.

—Herbert Beerbohm Tree

■ Process Loss and Types of Group Tasks

According to Ivan Steiner (1972), when a group performs worse than its potential, it experiences **process loss**. Process loss refers to the reduction of group productivity due to problems in the dynamics of a group. According to Steiner, some types of group tasks are more vulnerable to process loss than others.

For instance, on an *additive* task, the group product is the *sum* of all the members' contributions. Donating to a charity is an additive task, as is making noise at a pep rally. As we have seen, people often indulge in social loafing during additive tasks, which creates process loss. Of course, groups usually outperform a single individual. However, each member's contribution may be less than it would be if that person worked alone.

On a *conjunctive* task, the group product is determined by the individual with the *poorest* performance. Mountain-climbing teams are engaged in such a task; the "weakest link" will determine their success or failure. Because of this vulnerability to the poor performance of a single group member, group performance on conjunctive tasks tends to be worse than the performance of a single average individual.

On a *disjunctive* task, the group product is (or can be) determined by the performance of the individual with the *best* performance. Trying to solve a problem or develop a strategy may be a disjunctive task: What the group needs is a single successful idea or answer, regardless of the number of failures. In principle, groups have an edge on individuals in the performance of disjunctive tasks. The more people are involved, the more likely it is that someone will make a breakthrough. In practice, however, group processes can interfere with coming up with ideas and getting them accepted, resulting in process loss.

For example, groups may not realize which group members have the best ideas or are most expert. Unless the best solution for a particular problem is easily identifiable once it has been suggested, the group may fail to implement it; as a result, the group will perform worse than its best members (Soll & Larrick, 2009; Stasser et al., 1995; Straus et al., 2009). Have you ever had the experience of *knowing* you had the right idea but being unable to convince others in your group until it was too late? If so, then you have experienced first-hand the problem of process loss on a disjunctive task. Fortunately, as groups gain experience with each other, they can become better at recognizing and utilizing the expertise of their members, especially if the group is not very large (Bonner et al., 2006; Bonner & Baumann, 2008). We will discuss strategies that can help groups recognize and utilize expertise a bit later.

Gordon Wiltsie/Getty Images

Just as the strength of a chain depends on its weakest link, the group product of a conjunctive task is determined by the individual with the poorest performance. In mountain climbing for example, if one person slips or falls, the whole team is endangered.

process loss The reduction in group performance due to obstacles created by group processes, such as problems of coordination and motivation.

On some kinds of tasks, groups can even show *process gain*, in which they outperform even the best members. Patrick Laughlin and his colleagues (2006, 2008) have found that groups performed better than the best individuals on tasks in which the correct answer was clearly evident to everyone in the group once it was presented and the work could be divided up so that various subgroups worked on different aspects of the task.

Brainstorming

During the 1950s, advertising executive Alex Osborn developed a technique called **brainstorming** that was designed to enhance the creativity and productivity of problem-solving groups. The ground rules for brainstorming call for a freewheeling, creative approach:

- Express all ideas that come to mind even if they sound crazy.

- The more ideas, the better.

- Don't worry whether the ideas are good or bad and don't criticize anyone's ideas; they can be evaluated later.

- All ideas belong to the group, so members should feel free to build on each other's work.

Osborn (1953) claimed that by using these procedures, groups could generate more and better ideas than could individuals working alone. The idea caught on. Brainstorming was soon a popular exercise in business, government, and education, and it remains so today. But when the research caught up with the hype, it turned out that Osborn's faith in the group process was unfounded. In fact, "nominal groups" (several individuals working alone) produce a greater number of better ideas than do real groups in which members interact with each other. Brainstorming can indeed be effective, but people brainstorming individually produce more and higher-quality ideas than the same number of people brainstorming together. One meta-analysis concluded that brainstorming groups are only about half as productive as an equal number of individuals working alone (Mullen et al., 1991). Rather than being inspired by each other and building on each other's ideas, people brainstorming in a group underperform (Diehl & Stroebe, 1987; Nijstad & Stroebe, 2006; Paulus & Brown, 2007).

The top half of Table 8.2 presents several explanations that have been proposed for why brainstorming is ineffective. Recall our discussion of social loafing from earlier in the chapter, for example. As you can see in Table 8.2, social loafing is one factor that contributes to process loss in group brainstorming. Despite the research evidence, brainstorming is still a popular device in many organizations. People who participate in interactive brainstorming groups typically think that it works wonderfully and evaluate their performance more favorably than do individuals in nominal groups. They also enjoy themselves more. And those who have not participated in an interactive brainstorming group believe that such groups are highly productive. Both the experienced and the inexperienced cling to the illusion that group brainstorming is much better than individual brainstorming (Nijstad & Stroebe, 2006).

There are strategies to improve productivity while also promoting the enjoyment that group brainstorming can produce. For example, training people in effective brainstorming, alternating types of brainstorming sessions (such as by having members brainstorm alone and then together), or using a trained facilitator during brainstorming sessions are each strategies than have been shown to improve group performance (Oxley et al., 1996; Paulus et al., 2006; Paulus & Brown, 2007).

People brainstorming as a group come up with a greater number of better ideas than the same number of people working individually. **FALSE.**

brainstorming A technique that attempts to increase the production of creative ideas by encouraging group members to speak freely without criticizing their own or others' contributions.

TABLE 8.2

Brainstorming in Groups: Problems and Solutions

Factors That Reduce the Effectiveness of Group Brainstorming

- **Production blocking**: When people have to wait for their turn to speak, they may forget their ideas, may be so busy trying to remember their ideas that they don't listen to others or generate additional ideas, or may simply lose interest.
- **Free riding**: As others contribute ideas, individuals may feel less motivated to work hard themselves. They see their own contributions as less necessary or less likely to have much impact. They therefore engage in social loafing.
- **Evaluation apprehension**: In the presence of others, people may be hesitant to suggest wild, off-the-wall ideas for fear of looking foolish and being criticized. Even if they are willing to suggest such ideas, they may spend time preparing to justify them that they otherwise could have spent coming up with more ideas.
- **Performance matching**: Group members work only as hard as they see others work. Once the other three factors have reduced the performance of a brainstorming group, performance matching can help maintain this relatively inferior performance.

Why Electronic Brainstorming Is Effective

- Production blocking is reduced because members can type in ideas whenever they come to mind.
- Free riding can be reduced by having the computer keep track of each member's amount of input.
- Evaluation apprehension is reduced because group members contribute their ideas anonymously.
- Performance matching is reduced because group members spend less time focusing on the performance of others as they type in their own ideas. In addition, performance matching is less of a problem because the initial performance of groups that brainstorm electronically is likely to be high.
- Group members can benefit by seeing the ideas of others, which can inspire new ideas that they might not otherwise have considered.

A committee is a cul-de-sac down which ideas are lured and then quietly strangled.
—Barnett Cocks

Computers offer a relatively new and promising way to improve group brainstorming. Electronic brainstorming combines the freedom of working alone at a computer with the stimulation of receiving the ideas of others on a screen. The bottom half of Table 8.2 presents some of the factors that make this type of brainstorming effective. The results of a meta-analysis on the existing research on electronic brainstorming is encouraging (DeRosa et al., 2007). Groups using electronic brainstorming tend to perform much better than other brainstorming groups and almost as well as nominal groups. When the group is relatively large (more than eight people), electronic brainstorming groups may even perform better than nominal groups. Brainstorming may have found its true home in a technology that Osborn could have only dreamed of all those years ago.

Group Polarization

People typically are attracted to groups that share their attitudes, and those who disagree with the group usually leave by their own choice or are ejected by the others. But similar does not mean identical. Although the range of opinion is relatively restricted, there are still differences. What do you think should be the result of a group discussion of these differing points of view? For example, imagine that a group is discussing whether someone should behave in a risky or a cautious manner, such as whether an entrepreneur should risk trying to expand his or her business or whether an employee in a stable but boring job should quit and take a more creative job in a new but unproven Internet company. Are groups more likely to advocate risky or cautious decisions about issues like these?

Common sense suggests two alternative predictions. Perhaps the most reasonable prediction is that there will be a compromise as group members move toward the average of all the individuals' attitudes. But common sense also suggests another prediction. Many people familiar with committees agree that forming a committee is a good way *not* to get something done. We think that as lone individuals we are willing to take risks and implement new ideas, but we recognize that groups tend to be cautious and slow moving. Wary of leading the group toward a risky decision, people often become more cautious in their views as they discuss them with other group members.

So which prediction is the correct one: movement toward the average attitude or movement toward caution? James Stoner (1961) tested this question by comparing decisions made by individuals with decisions made by groups, and he found that *neither* prediction was correct: Group decisions tended to be riskier than individuals' decisions. Was this a fluke? Several subsequent studies found similar results, and the tendency for groups to become riskier than the average of the individuals became known as the *risky shift* (Cartwright, 1971).

But the story doesn't end there. Later studies seemed to contradict the idea of the risky shift, finding that for some choices, groups tended to become more *cautious* after group discussion (Knox & Safford, 1976). How can we make sense of these contradictory findings?

Researchers concluded that group discussion tends to enhance or exaggerate the initial leanings of the group. Thus, if most group members initially lean toward a risky position on a particular issue, the group's position becomes even riskier after the discussion. But if group members in general initially lean toward a cautious position, the group discussion leads to greater caution. This effect is called **group polarization**: the exaggeration through group discussion of initial tendencies in the thinking of group members (Moscovici & Zavalloni, 1969; Myers & Lamm, 1976).

Group members' attitudes about a course of action usually become more moderate after group discussion. **FALSE.**

Group polarization is not restricted to decisions involving risk versus caution. Any group decision can be influenced by group polarization, from serious decisions such as how to allocate scarce medical resources to more mundane decisions such as what theme a sorority should use at its next party (Chandrashekaran et al., 1996; Furnham et al., 2000).

Group polarization was demonstrated recently in an experiment by Pi-Yueh Cheng and Wen-Bin Chou (2008) involving students in Taiwan. The students were given sets of choices to make about how to invest some money. Some students were given choices that were framed in terms of how much money they could gain. For example, one choice was between a guaranteed gain of $25,000 versus a 25 percent chance to gain $100,000 (along with a 75 percent chance of gaining nothing). A good deal of previous research has shown that individuals tend to prefer caution in such choices, tending to take the guaranteed money. The other students were given choices framed as losses. For example, would you choose a sure loss of $25,000 of your original $100,000 investment or a 75 percent chance of losing the $100,000 (along with a 25 percent chance of losing nothing)? In this kind of loss framing, most individuals prefer risk, hoping to luck out and not have to lose any money.

The students first made these choices individually, and the results were as expected: Students tended to be cautious when the choices were framed in terms of gains and take more chances when the choices were framed as losses. A week later the students were put into three-person groups to make these decisions. As can be seen in ▶ Figure 8.6, the groups' decisions polarized. Compared to the individuals' preferences, groups became even more cautious in the gain scenarios and they became even more willing to take risks in the loss scenarios.

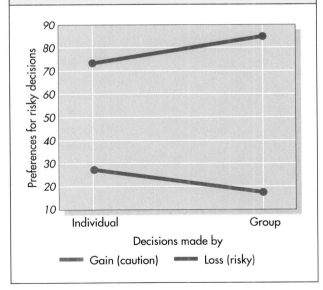

▶ **FIGURE 8.6**

Group Polarization in Investment Decisions

When making choices by themselves about how to invest money, the Taiwanese students in this experiment tended to be cautious when the investment scenarios were framed as potential gains and take more risks when the investment scenarios were framed as potential losses (the higher the bars in this graph, the more risky the decisions were). When the students returned a week later and made these choices in groups, the groups' decisions were polarized. That is, compared to the choices individuals had made alone, the groups became even more cautious in gain scenarios and took even more risks in loss scenarios.

Based on Cheng & Chiou, 2008.

What causes group polarization? According to *persuasive arguments theory*, the greater the number and persuasiveness of the arguments to which group members are exposed, the more extreme their attitudes become. If most group members favor a cautious decision, for example, most of the arguments discussed will favor caution, giving the members more and more reasons to think caution is the correct approach (Pavitt, 1994; Vinokur & Burnstein, 1974).

A second explanation is based on *social comparison theory*. As described in Chapter 3, individuals develop their view of social reality by comparing themselves with

group polarization The exaggeration of initial tendencies in the thinking of group members through group discussion.

others. In the case of group discussions, as individuals learn that most of the other group members lean in one direction on some issue, they may adopt a more extreme attitude in this same direction. In other words, people who are members of a group that believes that X is good may be willing to state to the group that twice X is even better. By advocating for twice X, individuals can distinguish themselves in the group in a manner that is approved by the group (Lamm & Myers, 1978).

There are additional explanations for group polarization. For example, groups may polarize as a way to differentiate themselves from other groups (McGarty et al., 1992). Each of these accounts spotlights particular processes, but taken together they all seem to contribute to the emergence of group polarization. Now that you know about group polarization, you should be able to see evidence of it often as you observe the groups around you. The increasingly risky, reckless behavior of groups in the investment banking, mortgage, and insurance industries that fueled the global economic crisis at the end of 2008 no doubt reflected group polarization run amok. At a broad level, it seems that political groups today have become more and more polarized, moving to extremes rather than toward moderation and compromise. On a smaller level, observe how the culture of a team may evolve over the course of a season or follow the attitudes of a group as it prepares for a debate and you're likely to see group polarization develop through the processes we've just described.

▊ Groupthink

The processes involved in group polarization may set the stage for an even greater and perhaps more dangerous bias in group decision making. For example, several days before the U.S. space shuttle *Columbia* disintegrated on February 1, 2003, as it reentered the earth's atmosphere on its way home, a team of engineers at the National Aeronautics and Space Administration (NASA) reviewed a video of foam breaking off the shuttle during launch and hitting the area near the left wing. The group speculated about whether the impact could have damaged the heat-shielding tiles located there. One engineer, Rodney Rocha, made more than half a dozen requests of NASA managers to go outside the agency and seek images from spy satellite photos or powerful telescopes that could provide a better look at the possible damage to the *Columbia* while it was in space. These requests were ignored or rejected. One manager said that he refused to be a "Chicken Little." The flight director e-mailed his rejection of the engineer's request with these chilling words: "I consider it to be a dead issue" (Glanz & Schwartz, 2003). All seven crew members on *Columbia* died in the ensuing tragedy.

There have been several particularly notable cases where high-level groups associated with the U.S. government made decisions that in hindsight seem remarkably ill conceived. For instance, toward the end of 1941, U.S. intelligence leaders dismissed numerous signs of an imminent attack by the Japanese on Pearl Harbor, leaving the base unprepared and vulnerable. The attack proved disastrous for the United States, costing almost 4,000 lives and a significant portion of the nation's arsenal of ships and planes. Sixty years later, American intelligence leaders again missed and dismissed signs of an imminent attack—the September 11, 2001, terrorist attacks in New York and Washington—such as when they rejected Federal Bureau of Investigations (FBI) attorney Coleen Rowley's pleas to investigate a suspected terrorist who subsequently played a critical role in the attacks.

Or consider one of the greatest fiascoes in U.S. history: the decision to invade Cuba in 1961. When John Kennedy became president of the United States in 1961, he assembled one of the most impressive groups of advisers in the history of American government. As we mentioned in the beginning of this chapter, these individuals—highly intelligent, educated at the best universities, led by a new president brimming with ambition, charisma, and optimism—were called "the best and the brightest" (Halberstam, 1972). But the Kennedy administration had inherited a plan from the previous administration to invade Cuba at the Bay of Pigs in order to spark a people's revolt that would overthrow Fidel Castro's government. After much deliberation, Kennedy and his advisers eventually approved an invasion plan that in hindsight was hopelessly flawed. For example, once the invaders landed at the Bay of Pigs, they were to be supported by anti-Castro guerrillas camped in the mountains nearby. But had Kennedy and his advisers consulted a map, they might have noticed that the invaders were to land eighty miles away from these mountains and were separated from them by a huge swamp. Ultimately the invasion failed miserably. The invaders were quickly killed or captured, the world was outraged at the United States, and Cuba allied itself more closely with the Soviet Union—exactly the opposite of what Kennedy had intended. The United States was humiliated. After the fiasco, Kennedy himself wondered, "How could we have been so stupid?" (Janis, 1982).

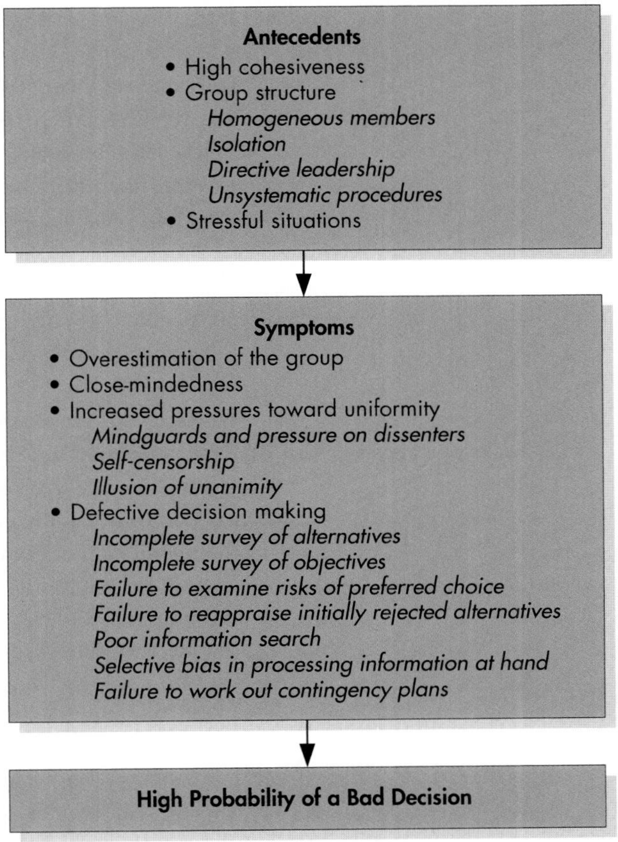

According to Irving Janis (1982), the answer to this question and similar questions that could be posed of any of the other fiascoes we've described lies in a particular kind of flawed group dynamic that he called **groupthink**, an excessive tendency to seek concurrence among group members. Groupthink emerges when the need for agreement takes priority over the motivation to obtain accurate information and make appropriate decisions. ▶ Figure 8.7 outlines the factors that contribute to groupthink, along with its symptoms and consequences.

Janis believed that three characteristics contribute to the development of groupthink:

▶ FIGURE 8.7

Charting the Course of Groupthink

Irving Janis depicted groupthink as a kind of social disease, complete with antecedents and symptoms, that increased the chance of making a bad decision.

Based on Janis, 1982.

Antecedents
- High cohesiveness
- Group structure
  Homogeneous members
  Isolation
  Directive leadership
  Unsystematic procedures
- Stressful situations

Symptoms
- Overestimation of the group
- Close-mindedness
- Increased pressures toward uniformity
  Mindguards and pressure on dissenters
  Self-censorship
  Illusion of unanimity
- Defective decision making
  Incomplete survey of alternatives
  Incomplete survey of objectives
  Failure to examine risks of preferred choice
  Failure to reappraise initially rejected alternatives
  Poor information search
  Selective bias in processing information at hand
  Failure to work out contingency plans

High Probability of a Bad Decision

1. Since *highly cohesive groups* are more likely to reject members with deviant opinions, Janis thought they would be more susceptible to groupthink.

2. *Group structure* is also important. Groups that are composed of people from similar backgrounds, isolated from other people, directed by a strong leader, and lacking in systematic procedures for making and reviewing decisions should be particularly likely to fall prey to groupthink.

3. Finally, Janis emphasized that *stressful situations* can provoke groupthink. Under stress, urgency can overrule accuracy and the reassuring support of other group members becomes highly desirable.

In Janis's formulation, groupthink is a kind of social disease, and infected groups display the behavioral symptoms indicated in the middle of Figure 8.7. For example, NASA's refusal to ask for outside help in obtaining images of the *Columbia* shuttle in space clearly illustrated the symptom of *closed-mindedness*. Another symptom, *pressures toward uniformity*, was evident in all these examples. During the planning of the Bay of Pigs invasion, the president's brother, Robert Kennedy, served as a mindguard

groupthink A group decision-making style characterized by an excessive tendency among group members to seek concurrence.

and warned dissenting members to keep quiet. A chilling example of this occurred during the debate about whether to go ahead with the launch of the space shuttle *Challenger* in 1986 on an unusually cold day in Florida, 17 years before the *Columbia* disaster. When a vice-president for engineering voiced his objection to the *Challenger* being launched on schedule because of fear that the cold weather could cause the O-ring seals in the rocket boosters to fail, a manager pressured him to change his vote by telling him to "take off your engineer hat and put on your management hat." Pressured to abandon one role and adopt the other, he changed his vote, and the tragic fate of the *Challenger* and its crew may have been sealed at that moment. In the end, this vice-president's decision helped foster an *illusion of unanimity* because top-level managers at NASA were unaware of all the dissent voiced by the engineers that morning.

More recently, some scholars have proposed that the group dynamics behind the decision to invade Iraq in 2003 by primarily American and British forces reflected groupthink, particularly in the decision makers' serious failures in information gathering and analysis and in the underestimation of risks (Houghton, 2008; Rodrigues et al., 2005).

When alternatives are not considered, the behavioral symptoms of groupthink can result in the defective decision making outlined in Figure 8.7. In turn, a defective decision-making process increases the likelihood that a group will make bad decisions.

Research on Groupthink: Myth or Reality? Groupthink is a rather distinctive theory in social psychology. On the one hand, its impact has been unusually broad: It is discussed in a variety of disciplines outside psychology including business, political science, and communication, and it has spawned numerous workshops as well as a best-selling management training video. Yet on the other hand, there is not a great deal of empirical support for the model, certainly not in proportion to its fame. This may be partly due to the difficulty of experimentally testing such a broad set of variables in high-pressure group settings. In addition, many researchers disagree with Janis about the specific conditions that make groups vulnerable to groupthink (Baron, 2005; Choi & Kim, 1999; Henningsen et al., 2006; Kramer, 1998; t'Hart et al., 1995; Tetlock, 1998; Whyte, 1998). Some researchers do believe, however, that when multiple antecedents of groupthink are evident simultaneously, such as high cohesiveness, a strong and controlling leader, and a great deal of stress, groups are particularly vulnerable to the kinds of faulty decision making that Janis described (Esser, 1998; Mullen et al., 1994). For now, the bottom line may be that even if one is skeptical about the details of Janis's theory of groupthink, as many scholars are, it does seem clear that many of the factors that Janis specified as antecedents and symptoms of groupthink can contribute to very faulty group decision making, and groups would be wise to be on the lookout for these traps. Whatever the merits or problems with the theory, the steps that Janis advocated to avoid these traps should help most groups. We turn to this advice next.

"On second thought, don't correct me if I'm wrong."

A controlling leader who discourages disagreement can promote groupthink, leading to bad decisions.

Preventing Groupthink To guard against groupthink, Janis urged groups to make an active effort to process information more carefully and accurately. He recommended that decision-making groups use the following strategies:

- To avoid isolation, groups should consult widely with outsiders.

- To reduce group pressures to conform, leaders should explicitly encourage criticism and not take a strong stand early in the group discussion.

■ To establish a strong norm of critical review, subgroups should separately discuss the same issue, a member should be assigned to play devil's advocate and question all decisions and ideas, and a "second chance" meeting should be held to reconsider the group decision before taking action.

President Kennedy appeared to arrive at similar conclusions after the Bay of Pigs disaster. In the following year, 1962, the United States and the Soviet Union appeared to be at the brink of war after U.S. military intelligence discovered that Soviet missiles in Cuba were aimed at the United States. During this crisis, Kennedy stayed away from initial meetings about how to respond to the situation, he consulted with experts outside his inner circle of advisers, and he told his brother Robert to play the devil's advocate and challenge all ideas—in sharp contrast to Robert's role of "mindguard" during the Bay of Pigs planning sessions. Unlike the Bay of Pigs invasion, the Cuban missile crisis ended exactly as Kennedy had hoped: The Soviet Union withdrew its missiles from Cuba and a war was avoided.

Research has shown empirical support for the effectiveness of some strategies in curtailing groupthink tendencies. These include inserting someone in the group to play the role of a "reminder" who is responsible for informing the group about the dangers of biased decision making, making individual group members believe that they will be held personally responsible for the outcome of their group's decisions, increasing the diversity of group members, and creating a group norm that encourages critical thinking and discourages the search for concurrence (Kroon et al., 1991; Postmes et al., 2001; Schultz et al., 1995; t'Hart, 1998). And as we will see a bit later in the chapter, computer-based technology can be used during meetings to help avoid groupthink.

The magnitude of the Boston construction project known as the "Big Dig" is evident in this photo. Construction took more than a decade longer and cost billions of dollars more than planned, and even after the final ramp opened in 2006, significant problems remained. Groups that have spent a great deal of time, effort, or money on a project such as this one often feel trapped, and rather than considering changing their decision they escalate their commitment to try to justify what they have already invested.

Escalation Effects

A specific kind of trap that can be very costly to organizations and businesses is known as the **escalation effect** (sometimes referred to as *entrapment*). Escalation effects occur when commitment to a failing course of action is increased to justify investments already made (Haslam et al., 2006; Keil et al., 2007; Staw, 1997). Laboratory experiments show that groups are more likely to escalate commitment to a failing project and are likely to do so in more extreme ways than are individuals (Dietz-Uhler, 1996; Seibert & Goltz, 2001). In numerous instances, groups, businesses, and governments have incurred huge costs because they continued to throw more money, time, and other resources into a project that should have been terminated long before (Ross & Staw, 1986). We will revisit this concept again in Chapter 13, when we discuss how businesses and individuals can fall into a "sunk cost" trap as they spend more and more money trying to justify an already bad investment of time and money.

A memorable example is the construction project in Boston known as the "Big Dig," which was designed to convert a congested stretch of highway into a high-speed underground tunnel. It was originally budgeted in 1983 for about $2.6 billion and was expected to be completed by 1995. Years of delays and increasing costs led to escalating commitments to try to salvage the troubled project. These 7.5 miles of road were costing millions of dollars a day, but with so much money already spent, commitments

escalation effect The condition in which commitments to a failing course of action are increased to justify investments already made.

Nor is the people's judgment always true: The most may err as grossly as the few.

—John Dryden

to completing the project only increased. As U.S. representative Barney Frank wryly suggested, it would have been cheaper to raise the city than to dig the tunnel (Roane, 2000). The project took more than a decade longer than planned to complete, and in 2008 its total cost was estimated to be a staggering $22 billion (Murphy, 2008).

■ Communicating Information and Utilizing Expertise

One of the biggest flaws in how groups perform is that they often fail to use all the information or skills that group members have (Hackman & Katz, 2010). In this section we will explore some of the dynamics that cause this problem as well as some factors that can help groups better communicate and use important information.

Biased Sampling   Imagine that you are part of a group that is discussing which of several candidates should be supported for an election. You have read some potentially damaging personal information about one of the candidates, and you assume that the others are also aware of it. If you observe during group discussion that nobody else mentions this information, you may further assume that the others don't think the information is relevant or credible, so you may not mention it yourself. Other group members may also have unique bits of information known only to them. For similar reasons, these pieces of information fail to enter the discussion. In the end, the discussion is dominated by information everyone in the group already knew, while the unshared information never makes it to the table.

This illustrates what Garold Stasser (1992; Stasser & Titus, 2003) termed **biased sampling**. Because of biased sampling, a group may fail to consider important information that is not common knowledge in the group. Inadequately informed, the group may make a bad decision. A recent meta-analysis by Jessica Mesmer-Magnus and Leslie DeChurch (2009) of 72 studies involving almost 5,000 groups found that biased sampling is a frequent and significant problem in groups. Groups that do a better job of sharing information tend to perform much better and are more cohesive.

Recent research has discovered several conditions under which biased sampling is less likely to occur. For example, leaders who encourage a lot of group participation are more likely to elicit unshared (as well as shared) information during group discussions than are leaders who are more directive (Larson et al., 1998). As groups gain more experience, they often become better at sharing information (Greitemeyer et al., 2006).

Sometimes biased sampling can have tragic consequences. The commission formed to investigate the explosion of the space shuttle *Challenger* concluded that inadequate sharing of information contributed to the disaster. For example, some engineers had information indicating that it would be unsafe to launch the shuttle that morning because of the low temperature, but this information was not shared with everyone. The people who ultimately made the decision to launch therefore were not aware of all the information that was relevant for their decision. The commission concluded, "If the decision-makers had known all the facts, it is highly unlikely that they would have decided to launch" (Presidential Commission on the Space Shuttle Challenger Accident, 1986, p. 82). Lessons learned after that tragedy appeared to have

The U.S. space shuttle *Challenger* explodes shortly after its launch on January 28, 1986, killing all seven crew members. Inadequate sharing of information and a flawed communication network were among the group dynamics problems that contributed to NASA's flawed, and ultimately fatal, decision to launch the shuttle that cold morning.

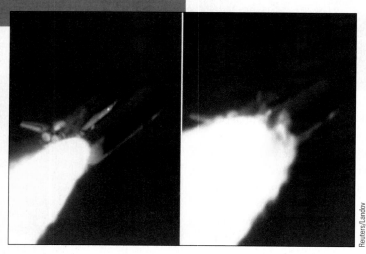

Reuters/Landov

biased sampling   The tendency for groups to spend more time discussing shared information (information already known by all or most group members) than unshared information (information known by only one or a few group members).

been forgotten 17 years later: Inadequate sharing of vital information also appeared to have contributed to the *Columbia* disaster in 2003.

Part of the problem in the NASA disasters was that the *communication network*, which defines who can speak with whom based on a group's structure, made it difficult for information to be distributed to all of the decision makers. In many organizations, information is passed up a chain of command through layers of middle management and only some of this information makes it all the way up to the executives who make the final decisions. This was the case at NASA. The engineers who were most familiar with the physical details of the shuttle could not communicate directly with the NASA officials at the top of the chain of command. According to Rodney Rocha, who was one of the engineers who most emphatically warned about the possible damage to the *Columbia*, "Engineers were often told not to send messages much higher than their own rung in the ladder" (Glanz & Schwartz, 2003). Because warnings were suppressed as the flow of information moved up the chain of command, the people at the top did not know the extent of the concerns of those lower in the chain.

Information Processing and Transactive Memory   Even if a group has all the available information, group members must process that information and use it to make judgments or perform tasks. How well do groups process information compared with individuals? In general, groups are susceptible to the same information-processing biases as individuals, only more so. In reviewing the research on group information processing, Verlin Hinsz and others (1997) concluded, "If some bias, error, or tendency predisposes individuals to process information in a particular way, then groups exaggerate this tendency. However, if this bias, error, or tendency is unlikely among individuals processing the information (e.g., less than half the sample), then groups are even less likely to process information in this fashion" (pp. 49–50).

One key advantage of groups is that they can divide a large body of information into smaller portions and delegate different members to remember these more manageable portions, ideally by matching information to individuals based on their expertise and interest. This shared process is known as **transactive memory**, which helps groups remember more information more efficiently than individuals (Peltokorpi, 2008; Wegner et al., 1991). But process loss can occur in this domain as well. Social loafing may occur, for example, when group members don't do their share of the work while expecting others to pick up the slack. A particularly important problem is that groups may not distribute the tasks and roles among group members in a rational or efficient manner, for example by matching individuals to tasks based on their skills, expertise, and preferences. Groups that develop good transactive memory systems are able to do this well, for example by recognizing who knows what in the group, and this improves group performance significantly (Littlepage et al., 2008; Palazzolo et al., 2006).

Strategies for Improvement

Groups researchers have found a variety of factors that promote better group dynamics, such as through better sharing of information and utilization of expertise. We turn to some of these next.

Norms and Goals   As with so many aspects of group dynamics, group norms play an important role. Tom Postmes and others (2001) conducted an experiment in which groups were induced to develop a norm emphasizing either group consensus or independent critical analysis. Groups with the critical-thinking norm were much more likely to discuss unshared information (thereby avoiding biased sampling) and come

transactive memory   A shared system for remembering information that enables multiple people to remember information together more efficiently than they could do so alone.

to significantly more accurate decisions after group discussion than were groups with the consensus norm.

Groups, like individuals, tend to perform better on a task when they have specific, challenging, and reachable goals, particularly if the group members are committed to the goals and believe they have the ability to achieve them. Such goals are generally more effective than "do your best" goals or no goals at all (Latham & Locke, 2007; Wegge et al., 2007). You've probably worked in many groups for which the goal was simply to "do your best." Despite the popularity of such goals, the research clearly shows that they are not as effective as specific goals. As Edwin Locke and Gary Latham (2002) concluded from their review of 35 years' worth of studies, "When people are asked to do their best, they do not do so" (p. 706). People are indeed capable of better than their vaguely defined "best." In addition to having challenging and specific goals, groups are most likely to benefit when there are incentives in place for achieving these goals.

Training and Interventions Researchers have discovered several other strategies and factors that can enhance group processes. Table 8.3 presents a set of the conditions that Ruth Wageman and her colleagues (2009) suggest are best for team effectiveness. These suggestions are consistent with the principles that we have addressed throughout this chapter, and they help illustrate the tremendous value that understanding the social psychology of groups can have in the business world or wherever group performance is essential. For example, Jane Prichard and Melanie Ashleigh (2007) found that the transactive memory and performance of groups improved with training programs in team skills, which taught skills such as problem solving, goal setting, role allocation, and relationships. A meta-analysis of the literature on group training found reliable evidence supporting the value of training in improving group performance (Salas et al., 2007).

Another approach that research has shown to be effective is adopting interventions that stop the natural flow of behaviors in groups and compel the group members to explicitly think about how they should proceed. For example, Andrea Gurtner and others (2007) found that group performance was improved significantly after an intervention was performed that induced the group to reflect on its performance and make explicit plans to implement strategies for improvement.

An experiment by Anita Williams Woolley and others (2008) demonstrated how important it is for groups to be induced to explicitly plan how to proceed so that they can properly utilize the expertise of its members. Four-person teams were given the task of solving a terrorist plot based on a set of information about suspects, potential locations, and planned activities. To solve the case, the teams would have to share and correctly use different sets of evidence. For some of the evidence, participants with strong verbal memory would be most likely to offer correct analyses. For some other evidence, participants with strong face-recognition ability would be most helpful.

Based on pre-testing of the participants' abilities, the teams were constructed so that some had experts and some did not. Specifically, half the teams had one verbal memory expert, one face-recognition expert, and two nonexperts. The other half of the teams consisted of four nonexperts. The researchers also manipulated whether or not the teams would receive a collaborative planning intervention. The teams that received this were required to discuss explicitly who would be responsible for which type of evidence and plan how they would integrate the various types of evidence they

---

TABLE 8.3

Conditions for Team Effectiveness

Ruth Wageman and her colleagues (2009) reviewed the research on what makes teams most effective. Below is a list of some of the conditions they emphasize.

- Teams should be interdependent for some common purpose and have some stability of membership.
- The team's overall purpose should be challenging, clear, and consequential.
- Teams should be as small as possible and have clear norms that specify what behaviors are valued or are unacceptable.
- A reward system should provide positive consequences for excellent team performance.
- Technical assistance and training should be available to the team.

---

group support systems
Specialized interactive computer programs that are used to guide group meetings, collaborative work, and decision-making processes.

were given. The other teams did not receive this requirement and instead were able to launch immediately into their work.

As ▶ Figure 8.8 shows, groups with experts but no planning did no better (indeed, they even did somewhat worse) than groups without experts. Similarly, groups that engaged in planning but had no experts did no better than groups with no planning. Only the groups that had experts as well as the planning intervention did relatively well on the task. Requiring the groups to think about how they would use the available information and each other's skills enabled them to reap the benefits of the expertise of group members.

Computer Technology and Group Support Systems Some of the obstacles that get in the way of good group discussion and decision making can be reduced through the use of interactive computer programs. Recently there has been an explosion of research on the use of such programs. Often referred to as **group support systems** (or *group decision support systems*), these programs help remove communication barriers and provide structure and incentives for group discussions and decisions. Compared to groups that use more conventional face-to-face modes of discussion, groups that use these systems often do a better job of sampling information, communicating, and arriving at good decisions (Lim & Guo, 2008; Rains, 2005; Vathanophas & Liang, 2007). Table 8.4 lists some of the ways that computerized group support systems can help groups avoid groupthink.

Virtual Teams

Teams consisting of people who may be dispersed widely across the globe are a relatively recent (and rapidly growing) part of the business world. Recent estimates indicate that a majority of professional workers today spend time working in virtual teams (Cordery & Soo, 2008; Mathieu et al., 2008). Virtual teams, sometimes also called dispersed teams, are "groups of people who work interdependently with shared purpose across space, time, and organization boundaries using technology to communicate and collaborate" (Kirkman et al., 2002, p. 67). Due to globalization and a variety of related factors, virtual teams will be increasingly important in businesses and organizations.

Most of the factors that contribute to process loss in groups apply as well to virtual groups, but virtual groups may be especially vulnerable to some of these. Given the physical distances between members and how little interaction they may have with each other, virtual groups may have a harder time building cohesiveness, keeping membership stable, socializing new members, keeping roles clear, sharing information, and developing transactive memory systems that enable the members to recognize or recall who has what knowledge or expertise in the group. Special attention must be paid to virtual groups, therefore, to offset these problems. For example, directories should be available and updated to allow members to access information about who knows

▶ **FIGURE 8.8**

Benefitting from Experts: The Role of Collaborative Planning

Four-person teams sifted through different sets of evidence to try to solve a case. Some teams had two participants who had expert-level abilities relevant to some of the evidence, whereas other teams had no experts. In addition, half the teams were made to engage in collaborative planning before doing their task and the other half did not. The bars on this graph reflect how well the groups performed on the task, with higher scores reflecting better performance. The only condition in which groups tended to perform well was when the group both had experts and engaged in collaborative planning.

Based on Woolley et al., 2008.

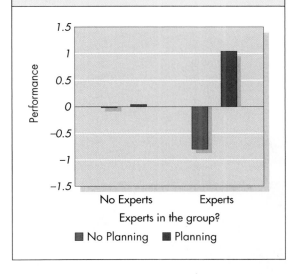

TABLE 8.4

How Computerized Group Support Systems Help Groups Avoid Groupthink

1. Allow group members to raise their concerns anonymously through the computer interface, enabling them to risk challenging group consensus without fear of direct attacks

2. Reduce the directive role of the leader

3. Enable group members to provide input simultaneously, so they don't have to wait for a chance to raise their ideas

4. Allow the least assertive group members to state their ideas as easily as the most dominating

5. Provide a systematic agenda of information gathering and decision making

6. Keep the focus in the group meetings on the ideas themselves rather than on the people and relationships within the group

Based on Miranda, 1994.

what across the virtual team. Frequent teleconferencing sessions and occasional short visits to allow dispersed group members to spend some time together can also help (Cordery & Soo, 2008; Hackman, 2010; Oshri et al., 2008).

Diversity

Along with becoming more dispersed, groups around the world, whether in schools, organizations, businesses, sports, arts, or governments, are becoming increasingly diverse, most obviously in terms of sex, race, ethnicity, and cultural background. How does diversity affect group performance? How can a group best use diversity to its advantage? The answers to such questions—and even the meaning of diversity—are likely to change as society changes in terms of its demographics and attitudes. In addition, diversity is not restricted to demographic differences among group members but can also mean differences in attitudes, personalities, skill levels, and so on. Thus, the issues surrounding diversity are particularly complex.

The evidence from empirical research concerning the effects of diversity on group performance is decidedly mixed (Hackman, 2010; Mannix & Neale, 2005; van Knippenberg & Schippers, 2007). On the one hand, diversity often is associated with negative group dynamics (Levine & Moreland, 1998; Maznevski, 1994). Miscommunications and misunderstandings are more likely to arise among heterogeneous group members, causing frustration and resentment and damaging group performance by weakening coordination, morale, and commitment to the group. Cliques often form in diverse groups, causing some group members to feel alienated. And even if diversity doesn't appear to hurt a group in any objective way, group members may *think* that it does. For example, S. Gayle Baugh and George Graen (1997) compared how diverse and homogeneous project teams rated their own effectiveness. Project teams that were diverse in terms of gender and race rated themselves as less effective, even though external evaluators judged the diverse teams to be no less effective than the homogeneous teams.

On the other hand, research has also demonstrated positive effects of diversity, such as on patterns of socialization, classroom dynamics, and complexity of group discussion (Antonio et al., 2004; Juvonen et al., 2006). Samuel Sommers (2006) found that racially diverse juries exchanged a wider range of information, cited more facts about the case being decided, and made fewer errors in their deliberations than racially homogenous juries, at least when the defendant was black. Sommers and others (2008) also found that merely *anticipating* being in a racially mixed group made white individuals process information relevant to race more thoroughly.

Because groups have become increasingly diverse in many settings today, it is more important than ever that groups learn how to utilize the great benefits and minimize the costs of diversity in group processes.

© Jon Feingersh/zefa/Corbis

As more and more organizations try to attract customers and investors from diverse cultures, diversity in personnel should offer more and more advantages. Cedric Herring (2009) analyzed data from over 1,000 work establishments in the United States from 1996 to 1997 and found that racial diversity was associated with greater profits and market share. (Keep in mind, however, that this is a correlational finding and that the causality is ambiguous. For example, it could be the case that diversity contributed to success or that success made greater diversity possible.) Given trends in populations, business, and attitudes, we can predict that the relationship between diversity and group success is likely to become more positive and consistent in the future. It remains for future research to investigate this hypothesis.

Conflict: Cooperation and Competition Within and Between Groups

Many of the most crucial issues confronting our world today involve conflicts between individuals and their groups or between groups. The desire of some individuals to consume valuable resources conflicts with the need of others to protect the environment for the greater good. A nation's claim to important territory or the right to nuclear arms conflicts with another nation's national security. In this section, we describe some of the dilemmas groups often must confront and what factors influence whether individuals and groups act cooperatively or competitively in dealing with them. We also look at some of the factors that cause conflicts between groups to escalate or be reduced, and we focus on an important mechanism for resolving group conflicts: negotiation.

Mixed Motives and Social Dilemmas

Imagine that you have to choose between cooperating with others in your group and pursuing your own self-interests, which can hurt the others. Examples of these mixed-motive situations are everywhere. An actor in a play may be motivated to try to "steal" a scene, a basketball player may be inclined to hog the ball, an executive may want to keep more of the company's profits, a family member may want to eat more than his fair share of the leftover birthday cake, and a citizen of the earth may want to use more than her fair share of finite valuable resources. Many of the executives and investors whose greedy and reckless actions contributed to the economic crisis discussed in the introduction to the chapter wanted to make huge profits very quickly, despite the risks to the economy as a whole.

In each case, the individual can gain something by pursuing his or her self-interests, but if everyone in the group pursues self-interests, all of the group members will ultimately be worse off than if they had cooperated with each other. Each option, therefore, has possible benefits as well as potential costs. When you are in a situation like this, you may feel torn between wanting to cooperate and wanting to compete, and these mixed motives create a difficult dilemma. What do you do? The notion that the pursuit of self-interest can sometimes be self-destructive forms the basis for what is called a **social dilemma**. In a social dilemma, what is good for one is bad for all. If everyone makes the most self-rewarding choice, everyone suffers the greatest loss. This section examines how people resolve the tension between their cooperative and competitive inclinations in social dilemmas.

The Prisoner's Dilemma   We begin with a crime story. Two partners in crime are picked up by the police for questioning. Although the police believe they have committed a major offense, there is only enough evidence to convict them on a minor charge. In order to sustain a conviction for the more serious crime, the police will have to convince one of them to testify against the other. Separated during questioning, the criminals weigh their alternatives (see ▶ Figure 8.9). If neither confesses, they will both get light sentences on the minor charge. If both confess and plead guilty, they will both receive moderate sentences. But if one confesses and the other stays silent, the confessing criminal will secure immunity from prosecution while the silent criminal will pay the maximum penalty.

This situation forms the basis for the research paradigm known as the **prisoner's dilemma**. In the two-person prisoner's dilemma, participants are given a series of

social dilemma   A situation in which a self-interested choice by everyone will create the worst outcome for everyone.

prisoner's dilemma   A type of dilemma in which one party must make either cooperative or competitive moves in relation to another party. The dilemma is typically designed so that the competitive move appears to be in one's self-interest, but if both sides make this move, they both suffer more than if they had both cooperated.

▶FIGURE 8.9

The Prisoner's Dilemma

In the original prisoner's dilemma, from which the game took its name, each of two criminals is offered immunity from prosecution in exchange for a confession. If both stay silent, both get off with a light sentence on a minor charge (upper left). If both confess, both receive a moderate sentence (lower right). But if one confesses while the other stays mum, the confessing criminal goes free and the silent one spends a long time in jail.

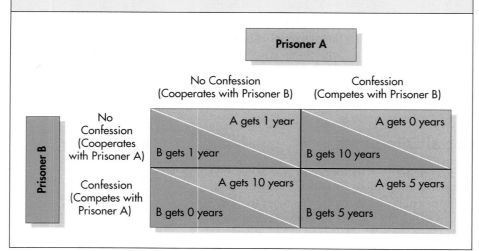

Would you like to try participating in a prisoner's dilemma game online? Some websites offer a chance for you to do this. To find them, search for "Prisoner's Dilemma" in a search engine.

choices that give them the option of cooperating or competing with each other, but either option has potential costs. Consider an example: Imagine that you're Prisoner A in Figure 8.9. It appears that no matter what Prisoner B does, you're better off if you compete with B and confess. If B doesn't confess to the police (in other words, if he cooperates with you by not ratting you out), you will get a lighter penalty if you do confess than if you don't—no jail time versus one year in jail. If B confesses, you still get a lighter sentence if you confess than if you don't—five versus ten years. So clearly, you should confess, right? But here's the dilemma: If you *both* confess, each of you gets five years. If *neither* of you confesses, each of you gets only one year. In other words, each individual is better off selling out his or her partner, but if both individuals do this, they are worse off than if neither did. It's really a perplexing situation. What do you think you would do?

This kind of social dilemma is not limited to situations involving only two individuals at a time. Imagine, for example, being in a burning building or a sinking ship. Each individual might want to race for the exit or the lifeboats as quickly as possible and push others out of the way, but if everyone does that, more people will die in the panic. More lives will be saved if people leave in an orderly fashion. Soldiers engaged in combat may be better off individually if they take no chances and duck for cover, but if their comrades do the same thing, they all will be slaughtered by the enemy. Nations face such dilemmas as well. Two countries locked in an arms race would be better off if they stopped spending money and resources on weapons of mass destruction, but neither country wants to risk falling behind the other (Dawes, 1980).

Resource Dilemmas   The prisoner's dilemma sets up a trap for those who play it: Attempts to gain an advantage will backfire if the other party also makes the competitive choice. This conflict of motives also forms the basis for another category of social dilemmas: **resource dilemmas**, which concern how two or more people share a limited resource. Resource dilemmas come in two basic types: (1) commons dilemmas and (2) public goods dilemmas.

In the *commons dilemma*, if people take as much as they want of a limited resource that does not replenish itself, nothing will be left for anyone. Robyn Dawes (1980) called this situation the *take-some dilemma*. One popular example of this dilemma is known as the "tragedy of the commons" (Hardin, 1968). In earlier times, people would let their animals graze on the town's lush grassy commons. But if all the animals grazed to their hearts' content (and to their owners' benefit), the commons would be stripped, the animals' food supply would be diminished, and the owners' welfare would be threatened. Today, the tragedy of the commons is a clear danger on a global scale. Deforestation, air pollution, carbon emission, ocean dumping, massive irrigation,

If a free society cannot help the many who are poor, it cannot save the few who are rich.

—John F. Kennedy

resource dilemmas Social dilemmas involving how two or more people will share a limited resource.

overfishing, commercial development of wilderness areas, a rapidly increasing population in some developing countries, and an overconsuming population in the richest nations all pit individual self-interest against the common good.

In *public goods dilemmas*, all of the individuals are supposed to contribute resources to a common pool. Examples of these public goods include the blood supply, public broadcasting, schools, libraries, roads, and parks. If no one gives, the service can't continue. If club members don't pay their dues or contribute their time, the club will fail. Again, private gain conflicts with the public good.

Pollution from an oil refinery in Edmonton, Canada, glows in the dusk. A clean environment is a public resource that is vital for all of us, but protecting it often runs into conflict with the economic self-interest of individuals or groups.

Solving Social Dilemmas: Groups and Individuals   When does individual desire prevail in social dilemmas? When, in contrast, do people see beyond their own immediate potential for gain and consider the long-term benefits of cooperation? Social dilemmas pose a serious threat to the quality of life and even to life itself. How do people try to solve them? What factors make them more or less cooperative when faced with these dilemmas?

Fear and greed are two critically important factors in determining reactions to these dilemmas—the fear of being exploited by others and the greedy desire to maximize one's own outcomes. Trust, therefore, is essential in promoting cooperation because it reduces the fear of being exploited. Similarly, a sense of belongingness and identity with the greater group also promotes cooperation, because this perspective can reduce fear and greed (De Cremer et al., 2008; Ishii & Kurzban, 2008; Klapwijk & Van Lange, 2008). Another important factor is threat of punishment (Mulder, 2008). Groups that punish members who exploit the rest of the group are more likely to thrive. Indeed, evolutionary psychologists point to how punishing those who do not cooperate with the group is an evolved psychological mechanism because cooperation was crucial for survival (O'Gormon et al., 2008).

These are just a few of the variables that help determine competition or cooperation in social dilemmas. Table 8.5 summarizes some of the factors that extensive research has identified as facilitating the best solutions to social dilemmas.

Groups tend to be more competitive in mixed-motive situations than individuals (McGlynn et al., 2009). One reason for this is that it can be harder to establish trust between groups than between individuals (Naquin & Kurtzberg, 2009). Because we are prone to perceive groups in less personalized or humanized ways than we perceive individuals, we are more likely to fear groups and to feel less inhibited about behaving in a greedy way toward them. We feel less shame or guilt in hurting an abstract *Other* than we do in hurting a specific person. Another reason why groups are more competitive than individuals is that members of a group feel that they are less identifiable by members of other groups. The greater anonymity that a group offers frees individual group members to act in a self-interested or aggressive manner. This is one reason why large groups are more likely to exploit

TABLE 8.5
Solving Social Dilemmas

Behavior in a social dilemma is influenced by both psychological factors and structural arrangements. The characteristics listed here contribute to the successful solution of social dilemmas.

Psychological Factors

- **Individual and cultural differences**
  Having a prosocial, cooperative orientation
  Trusting others
  Being a member of a collectivistic culture
- **Situational factors**
  Being in a good mood
  Having had successful experience managing resources and working cooperatively
  Being exposed to unselfish models
  Having reason to expec others to cooperate
- **Group dynamics**
  Acting as an individual rather than in a group
  Being in a small group rather than in a large group
  Sharing a social identity or superordinate goals

Structural Arrangements

- Creating a payoff structure that rewards cooperative behavior and/or punishes selfish behavior
- Removing resources from the public domain and handing them over to private ownership
- Establishing an authority to control the resources

scarce resources than small ones are (Pruitt, 1998; Seijts & Latham, 2000; Wildschut et al., 2003).

The fact remains that social dilemmas often do involve very large groups—a city, a state, a nation, the whole world. In these circumstances, the structural arrangements listed in Table 8.5 may be most appropriate. Resolving social dilemmas well is crucial for maintaining the quality of our lives, both immediately and (even more so) for the future. Understanding the psychological and structural factors that affect the behaviors of groups when they confront these dilemmas is therefore one of the most vital contributions that social psychological research can make.

> **Large groups are more likely than small groups to exploit a scarce resource that the members collectively depend on. TRUE.**

Individual and Gender Differences Although all of us struggle with social dilemmas, people differ in their own tendencies toward cooperation and competition. One relevant dimension on which people differ is in their *social value orientation*. Researchers classify individuals into one of three social value orientations: Individuals with a *prosocial, cooperative* orientation seek to maximize joint gains or achieve equal outcomes. Those with an *individualist* orientation seek to maximize their own gain. And people with a *competitive* orientation seek to maximize their own gain relative to that of others. Recent studies have found that individuals with a cooperative orientation are less likely to behave in a competitive, resource-consuming fashion than are people with individualistic or competitive orientations (Bogaert et al., 2008; De Cremer et al., 2008; van Dijk et al., 2009).

Although women often are thought to be more cooperative and less individualistic than men, the evidence that women behave more cooperatively than men in social dilemmas is not very reliable. Some studies have found this difference, but others have not (Simpson, 2003). As with the relationship between gender and many other variables, whether or not a gender difference is likely to emerge may depend on other factors. For example, Ko Kuwabara's (2005) research suggests that that men are more likely to respond competitively in response to motives involving greed, whereas women are more likely to respond competitively in response to motives involving fear of being exploited by others.

"I'm running late—some people were waiting for my table so I had to take my sweet time."

> People with a competitive social value orientation may go out of their way to prevent others from using a resource, even if in doing so, they hurt themselves in the long run as well.

■ Culture and Social Dilemmas

Just as with gender differences, the expectation that there should be reliable cultural differences in responses to social dilemmas is stronger than the evidence found in the research thus far. Some studies have suggested that people and groups from collectivist cultures are more likely to cooperate in social dilemmas than people and groups from individualist cultures, but others have found similarities across cultures (Ishii & Kurzban, 2008; Kopelman, 2009; Takemura & Yuki, 2007; Yamagishi et al., 2005).

More specifically, however, it may be that collectivists tend to cooperate more when dealing with friends or ingroup members but compete more aggressively when dealing with strangers or outgroup members; this difference tends not to be as strong among individualists (De Dreu et al., 2007; Oyserman et al., 2002). This point was supported recently in an interesting experiment by Rosana Yin-mei Wong and Ying-yi Hong (2005). Participants in this experiment were Hong Kong Chinese college students who could be considered bicultural; that is, they were exposed extensively throughout their lives to both Chinese and American cultures. These students played a prisoner's dilemma game with either friends or strangers. Before playing, some of the students were exposed to pictures associated with Chinese culture (such as a Chinese dragon or a person performing kung fu). Others were exposed to pictures associated with American culture (such as the American flag or an American football game). Would seeing the Chinese or American images prime one or the other culture and cause the students to respond in the prisoner's dilemma game differently?

The results revealed that the pictures did make a difference (see ▶ Figure 8.10). When playing the prisoner's dilemma game with a friend, students exposed to the Chinese symbols cooperated much more than students exposed to the American symbols did. When they played with a stranger, in contrast, they demonstrated no significant difference in cooperativeness as a function of which culture was primed. These results suggest that exposure to the Chinese prime led the students to respond in ways that were consistent with collectivistic norms: a lot of cooperation with friends and less cooperation with strangers. Exposure to the American prime led to less cooperation in general, but not a bias for friends and against strangers.

Conflict Escalation and Reduction

Social dilemmas can create important conflicts between groups, and how groups resolve these dilemmas can make the difference between war and peace. There are, of course, many other sources of conflict between groups. The very fact that groups differ from each other on any of a number of dimensions—religious, ethnic, racial, cultural, political—can spark conflict. Again and again, throughout human history, differences between groups explode in hatred and bloodshed. What fans the flames of an escalating conflict? And what can extinguish these flames? We address these questions in the remaining sections of the chapter.

Conflicts between groups are caused by many factors, including competition for scarce resources, stereotypes and prejudice, and competing ideologies. But once a conflict is in place, it can feed on itself. Indeed, *conflict spirals* are frequent, as one party annoys the other party, who retaliates, prompting a more extreme reaction from the first party, and so on (Brett et al., 1998; Rubin et al., 1994). Table 8.6 lists several factors that contribute to conflict escalation. The first three concern group processes discussed earlier in the chapter. The fourth one, concerning the capacity to use threat, may seem more surprising. We discuss this and a fifth factor (perceptions of the other) in the next sections.

Threat Capacity It seems obvious that the ability to punish someone who engages in a prohibited behavior can act as a deterrent to conflict escalation. You're less likely to mess with someone who can mess right back with you. If both parties hold their

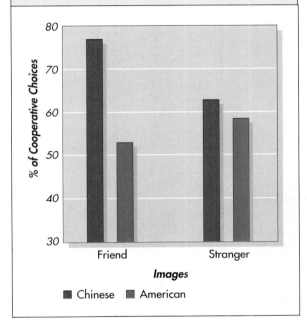

▶ **FIGURE 8.10**
Culture and the Prisoner's Dilemma
Students from Hong Kong who were very familiar with both Chinese and American cultures played the prisoner's dilemma game with a friend or a stranger. Before playing, some participants were exposed to Chinese images and some were exposed to American images. When playing with a friend, students primed with Chinese images cooperated more than did students primed with American pictures. When playing with a stranger, there was no significant difference in cooperativeness as a function of which culture was primed.

Adapted from Wong & Hong, 2005.

TABLE 8.6
Factors That Promote and Sustain the Escalation of Between-Group Conflict

- The group polarization process, which increases the extremity of group members' attitudes and opinions
- Pressures to conform, such as group cohesiveness and groupthink, that make it difficult for individuals to oppose the group's increasingly aggressive position
- Escalation of commitment, which seeks to justify past investments through the commitment of additional resources
- Premature use of threat capacity, which triggers aggressive retaliation
- Negative perceptions of "the other," which promote acceptance of aggressive behavior and enhance cohesiveness of the ingroup "us" against the outgroup "them"

fire, a balance of terror can work. But having the capacity to attack can present an irresistible temptation to do so.

A classic study conducted by Morton Deutsch and Robert Krauss (1960) makes the point. These investigators had pairs of female participants engage in a simulated work environment in which each was in charge of a trucking company that was carrying merchandise over a road to a specific destination. Because they had to share parts of the road, they had to coordinate their efforts. However, in one condition of the study, one of the women in each pair had the capacity to take control of the road and block the other's progress, which would increase her own profit and reduce the other participant's profit. In another condition, both participants in each pair had this capacity. What was the result?

In general, when a participant had the ability to block the other, she did—and both participants suffered. Overall, participants earned more money if neither could block the other than if one of them could, and when *both* members of the pair could block the other, the participants earned least of all. These results suggest that once coercive means are available, people tend to use them, even when doing so damages their own outcomes.

Perceptions of the Other The fifth factor listed in Table 8.6 calls to mind our earlier discussion of stereotypes and prejudice, including the favoring of ingroups over outgroups (see Chapter 5). Seeing the other side in a conflict as an outgroup can exaggerate one's perception of the differences between the groups and lead to less cooperation (Garcia et al., 2005; Yamagishi et al., 2008). During conflict, the opposing group and its members are often perceived as "the other"—strange, foreign, alien. They are characterized in simplistic, exaggerated ways. Held at a psychological distance, the other becomes a screen on which it is possible to project one's worst fears. Indeed, groups often see each other as *mirror images:* They see in their enemies what their enemies see in them. As Urie Bronfenbrenner (1961) discovered when he visited the former Soviet Union during the Cold War, the Soviets saw Americans as aggressive, exploitative, and untrustworthy, just as the Americans saw them. The same is true of Israelis and Palestinians today.

Taken to extremes, negative views of the other can result in *dehumanization,* the perception that people lack human qualities or are "subhuman," and this can play a powerful role in escalating conflict and promoting prejudice or violence (Demoulin et al., 2009; Esses et al., 2008; Maoz & McCauley, 2008). As the Nazis began the Holocaust, they released propaganda that characterized Jews as less than human—as rats that spread disease and needed to be exterminated. During World War II, the United States portrayed the Japanese people as cold, identical robots. At the same time, the Japanese media portrayed Americans as bloodthirsty animals, as in cartoons depicting eagles flying off with bloodied Japanese citizens in their talons.

Dehumanization is the ultimate version of "us" versus "them," removing all religious and ethical constraints against the taking of human life. As George Orwell (1942) discovered during the Spanish Civil War, the cure for dehumanization is to restore the human connection. Sighting an enemy soldier holding up his trousers with both hands while running beside a nearby trench, Orwell was unable to take the easy shot: "I had come here to shoot at 'Fascists'; but a man who is holding up his trousers isn't a 'Fascist,' he is visibly a fellow creature, similar to yourself, and you don't feel like shooting at him" (p. 254).

Group conflict is tragically hard to stop, as in the ongoing struggles between groups in the Middle East. In this photo, Palestinians hurl stones at Egyptian forces at the Egyptian border with the Gaza Strip in February 2008 during a clash in which a civilian was killed.

Ibraheem Abu Mustafa/Reuters/Landov

Reducing Conflict Through GRIT A peacemaking strategy developed by Charles Osgood (1962) offers some hope for breaking a conflict between groups. In this strategy, called **graduated and reciprocated initiatives in tension-reduction (GRIT)**, one group takes the first move toward cooperation by making an initial concession. It then waits for the response from the other side and reciprocates that move: It responds to aggressiveness with aggressiveness and to cooperativeness with even more cooperativeness. Research on GRIT is encouraging; even people with a competitive orientation tend to respond cooperatively to this strategy, and the positive effects of GRIT can be enduring (Lindskold & Han, 1988; Yamagishi et al., 2005).

▌ Negotiation

Unilateral concessions are useful for beginning the peace process, but extended negotiations are usually required to reach a final agreement. Negotiations on complex issues such as nuclear arms control, international environmental protection, and efforts to make peace in volatile regions such as the Middle East often go on for years or even decades.

Negotiations are not restricted to the international scene. Unions and management engage in collective bargaining to establish employee contracts. Divorcing couples negotiate the terms of their divorce, by themselves or through their lawyers. Dating couples negotiate about which movie to attend. Families negotiate about who does which annoying household chores. Indeed, negotiations occur whenever there is a conflict that the parties wish to resolve without getting into an open fight or relying on an imposed legal settlement. There is an immense amount of research on negotiation and bargaining (De Dreu 2010; Malhotra & Bazerman, 2008; Thompson et al., 2010). Here, we focus on those findings most relevant to conflict reduction.

Keys to Successful Negotiating Conflicts can be reduced through successful negotiation. But what constitutes success in this context? Perhaps the most common successful outcome is a 50-50 compromise. Here, the negotiators start at extreme positions and gradually work toward a mutually acceptable midpoint. Some negotiators, however, achieve an even higher level of success. Most negotiations are not simply fixed-sum situations in which each side must give up something until a middle point is reached. Instead, it is often the case that both sides can benefit (Bazerman & Neale, 1992). When an **integrative agreement** is reached, both parties obtain outcomes that are superior to a 50-50 split.

Take, for instance, the tale of the two sisters and the orange (Follett, 1942). One sister wanted the juice to drink; the other wanted the peel for a cake. So they sliced the orange in half and each one took her portion. These sisters suffered from an advanced case of what is known as the "*fixed-pie syndrome*," the belief that whatever one of them won, the other one lost. In fact, however, each of them could have had the whole thing: all of the juice for one, all of the peel for the other. An integrative agreement was well within their grasp, but they failed to see it. Unfortunately, research indicates that this happens all too often. Leigh Thompson and Dennis Hrebec (1996) conducted a meta-analysis of 32 experiments and found that in over 20 percent of negotiations that could have resulted in integrative agreements, the participants agreed to settlements that were worse for both sides. The ability to achieve integrative agreements is an acquired skill: experienced negotiators obtain them more often than inexperienced ones do (Druckman, 1994; Thompson, 1990).

It is always difficult for participants in a dispute to listen carefully to each other and reach some reasonable understanding of each other's perspective. But communication

graduated and reciprocated initiatives in tension-reduction (GRIT) A strategy for unilateral persistent efforts to establish trust and cooperation between opposing parties.

integrative agreement A negotiated resolution to a conflict in which all parties obtain outcomes that are superior to what they would have obtained from an equal division of the contested resources.

in which both sides disclose their goals and needs is critically important in allowing each side to see opportunities for joint benefits (De Dreu et al., 2006). This may seem obvious and yet people in negotiations, just like the two sisters with the orange, very often fail to communicate their goals and needs. For one thing, negotiators tend to think that their goals and objectives are more clear to the other party than they actually are (Vorauer & Claude, 1998). Furthermore, in conflict negotiations each party is likely to distrust and fear the other. Neither wants to reveal too much for fear of losing power at the bargaining table. Again, this is part of the fixed-pie syndrome. But if one party does disclose information, the disclosure can have dramatic effects. If one side discloses, the other party becomes much more likely to do so, enhancing the likelihood of integrative agreement (Thompson, 1991).

In addition to disclosure of information, several other factors can improve negotiations and increase the chances that both sides will benefit. These factors include training negotiators in conflict-resolution techniques and using computerized negotiation support systems (Davis & Hall, 2003; Kersten & Lai, 2007; Taylor et al., 2008). Even simply taking a break can be very effective—as long as during the break everyone can be distracted from thinking about the negotiation (Harinck & De Dreu, 2008).

During particularly difficult or significant negotiations, outside assistance may be sought. Some negotiations rely on an *arbitrator*, a person who has the power to impose a settlement. But it is more common for conflicting parties to request the participation of a *mediator*, a person who works with them to try to reach a voluntary agreement. Traditionally, mediators have been employed in labor-management negotiations and international conflicts. But increasingly, mediators help resolve a wide range of other disputes, such as those involving tenants and landlords, divorcing couples, and feuding neighbors. Trained in negotiation and conflict management, mediators can often increase the likelihood of reaching a cooperative solution (Alexander, 2008; Carnevale, 2002).

Gender Differences As with gender differences concerning social dilemmas, the evidence for gender differences in negotiation is not as clear as many expect them to be. Some studies have shown that compared to men, women tend to negotiate lower outcomes, communicate less assertively, and behave less competitively, but some studies do not support these findings (Katz et al., 2008; Stuhlmacher et al., 2007). The lesson is that there is a great deal of overlap between the sexes and that the emergence of predictable differences is likely to depend on the presence of other factors. For example, Roderick Swaab and Dick Swaab (2009) recently found in a meta-analysis and in their own laboratory experiment that men achieved higher-quality agreements when negotiating under conditions in which there was no visual contact between the parties (such as via the phone or e-mail). If there was visual contact, the men did better when there was no eye contact. Women showed the opposite pattern: Visual contact and eye contact were associated with higher-quality agreements. The authors speculate that the results may reflect differences in what makes men and women most comfortable. Whatever the exact cause, the results support the idea that gender differences in negotiation likely depend on a host of other variables.

Negotiating with car dealers is a form of negotiation that many of us engage in from time to time. Want some tips? Try the Tips & Advice section on the Edmunds website at www.edmunds.com.

▌ Culture and Negotiation

As the world becomes smaller because of advances in technology, the globalization of business and the economy, and global threats concerning the environment and terrorism, the ability to negotiate effectively across cultures becomes increasingly important. Understanding cultural differences relevant to negotiation is therefore vital. Table 8.7

lists some common assumptions made by negotiators from Western, individualistic cultures that are not always shared by representatives from other cultures.

Consider, for example, our statement that good communication is a key ingredient in successful negotiation. Communication across cultures can present special challenges. Whereas an individualistic perspective emphasizes direct communication and confrontation, a collectivistic perspective emphasizes information sharing that is more indirect and a desire to avoid direct conflict. Individualistic negotiators may emphasize rationality, whereas a greater tolerance of contradiction and emotionality is characteristic of a collectivistic style—although collectivists prefer emotionality that is not confrontational. Negotiators from individualistic cultures are more likely to respond with a direct "no" to a proposal; negotiators from collectivistic cultures are more likely to refer to social roles and relationships.

According to Yunxia Zhu and others (2007), for example, relationship building is an important part of the negotiation process among Chinese. Negotiators from

TABLE 8.7

Cultural Assumptions About Negotiating

People from different cultures make different assumptions about the negotiation process. This table summarizes some assumptions commonly made by U.S. and other Western negotiators. It also presents some alternative assumptions that may be held by negotiators from other cultures. As you can see, such different assumptions could make it very difficult to reach a successful agreement.

Assumptions of Negotiators from the United States and Other Western Countries	Assumptions of Negotiators from Non-Western Cultures
Negotiation is a business, not a social activity.	The first step in negotiating is to develop a trusting relationship between the individual negotiators.
Points should be made with rational, analytical arguments without contradiction	Arguments may be more holistic, and emotionality and contradiction may be tolerated.
Communication is direct and verbal.	Some of the most important communication is nonverbal or indirect.
Written contracts are binding; oral commitments are not.	Written contracts are less meaningful than oral communications because the nonverbal context clarifies people's intentions.
Current information and ideas are more valid than historical or traditional opinions and information.	History and tradition are more valid than current information and ideas. Information must be understood in its greater context.
Time is very important; punctuality is expected; deadlines should be set and adhered to.	Building a relationship takes time and is more important than punctuality; setting deadlines is an effort to humiliate the other party.

Based on Brett & Gelfand, 2006, De Dreu et al., 2007, Gelfand et al., 2007, Giebels & Taylor, 2009, and Kimmel, 1994, 2000.

individualistic cultures may need to be uncharacteristically patient with processes that may seem irrelevant to the task at hand because they are important in creating *guanxi*, a Chinese term for relationship. The initial sessions in negotiations with Chinese take on particular importance because they can set the tone for establishing *guanxi*.

Another difference concerns the timing of concessions. Individualists tend to prefer to make compromises and concessions toward the end of a negotiation, whereas

Prakas Singh/AFP/Getty Images

Chief negotiators from the United States and several Central American countries meet in Nicaragua in September 2003 to negotiate a free trade agreement. Such negotiations are both important and complex and involve nations with different resources, needs, relationships, and cultures. They highlight the usefulness of social psychological research, which has specified a number of factors that can make negotiations more or less likely to succeed.

collectivists may prefer to begin with generous concessions and gradually reduce their concessions later. Yet another factor concerns "saving face"—feeling that others continue to respect you and that you have maintained honor. Although saving face in a negotiation is important across cultures, it may be of more central importance in collectivistic cultures (Oetzel et al., 2008; Rodriguez Mosquera et al., 2008; Tjosvold et al., 2004).

Emotional responses may hurt negotiations between members of different cultures if they are deemed inappropriate in one of the cultures. Expressions of pride are more likely to be received positively in individualistic cultures, whereas expressions of shame are more likely to be received positively in collectivistic cultures (Rodriguez Mosquera et al., 2004). A recent experiment that illustrates cultural differences in sensitivity to particular emotions was conducted by Shirli Kopelman and Ashleigh Shelby Rosette (2008) with business students from Hong Kong and Israel. The students participated in a negotiation exercise in which an American female business manager offered them a take-it-or-leave-it proposal by video. For half the students, the manager made the offer displaying positive emotion—she spoke in a friendly tone, smiled and nodded often, and appeared cordial. For the other half, the manager displayed negative emotion—she spoke in a more angry tone and appeared intimidating and irritated.

As the researchers had predicted, the students from Hong Kong responded very differently as a function of the emotion displayed. As can be seen in ▶ Figure 8.11, they were much more likely to accept the offer from the American negotiator if it was made with a display of positive than with negative emotions. Students from Israel, where direct and confrontational negotiations are more commonplace (and perhaps where an American woman would be seen less as an outgroup), were relatively unaffected by the emotional display of the American negotiator when deciding whether or not to accept the offer.

If negotiators are not aware of these kinds of cross-cultural differences or if they cannot respond effectively to them, inevitable misunderstandings may prevent them from achieving a successful outcome. Wendi Adair and Jeanne Brett (2005) describe negotiation as a kind of dance. The partners move with each other according to various rhythms, and the dance will work only if they can synchronize their movements and work together. Negotiations across cultures can be challenging because the participants have different ways of performing these dances. As Adair and Brett put it, "Just as it will take time for a Cuban, who is accustomed to the rapid, staircase movements of Latin social dancing, and an American—accustomed to smooth walking dances like the waltz—to get in sync, it will take time for cross-cultural negotiators to synchronize their movements" (p. 46). It is in the best interest of negotiators, therefore, to learn each other's perspectives so they can work together more effectively and fluently without stepping on each other's toes.

▶ FIGURE 8.11

Emotions During Negotiation: Cross-Cultural Differences

Business students from Hong Kong and Israel participated in a negotiation exercise in which they received a take-it-or-leave-it proposal from an American business manager. The manager displayed either warm, positive emotion or angry, negative emotion while making the offer. Students from Hong Kong were much less likely to accept the offer if it was made with negative emotion rather than with positive emotion. The Israeli students' decisions were not strongly affected by the emotions displayed.

Based on Kopelman & Rosette, 2008.

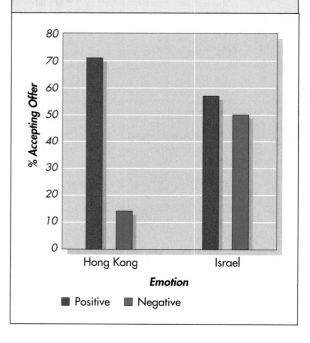

■ Finding Common Ground

Every conflict is unique, as is every attempt at conflict resolution. Still, all efforts to find a constructive solution to conflict require some common ground to build upon. Recognition of a *superordinate identity* is one way to establish common ground between groups in conflict. When group members perceive that they have a shared identity—a sense of belonging to something that is larger than and encompasses their own groups—the attractiveness of outgroup members increases and interactions between the groups often become more peaceful.

Superordinate goals have another valuable characteristic: They can produce a superordinate identity. The experience of intergroup cooperation increases the sense of belonging to a single superordinate group. Even the mere expectation of a cooperative interaction increases empathy, which, in turn, enhances helpfulness and reduces aggression. Indeed, empathic connections between various members of each group can lay the foundation for an inclusive rather than an exclusive social identity (Dovidio & Gaertner, 2010).

On the road to peace, both kinds of common ground are needed. Cooperation to meet shared goals makes similarities more visible, and a sense of a shared identity makes cooperation more likely. Those who would make peace, not war, realize that it is in their own self-interest to do so and understand that the cloak of humanity is large enough to cover a multitude of lesser differences.

REVIEW

Fundamentals of Groups

What Is a Group? Why Join a Group?

- Groups involve direct interactions among group members over a period of time and a shared common fate, identity, or set of goals.
- Groups vary in the extent to which they are seen as distinct entities.
- People join a group for a variety of reasons, including to perform tasks that can't be accomplished alone and to enhance self-esteem and social identity.
- Evolutionary scholars propose that attraction to groups is an evolved psychological mechanism.

Socialization and Group Development

- The socialization of newcomers into a group relies on the relationships they form with old-timers, who act as models, trainers, and mentors.
- Groups often proceed through several stages of development, from initial orientation through periods of conflict, compromise, and action.
- Some groups pass through periods of inactivity followed by sudden action in response to time pressures.

Roles, Norms, and Cohesiveness

- Establishing clear roles can help a group; but when members' roles are assigned poorly, are ambiguous, come in conflict with other roles, or undergo change, stress and poor performance can result.
- Teams in one experiment where group roles were matched to individuals' areas of expertise on the basis of tests of each individual's brain functioning performed especially well.
- Groups often develop norms that group members are expected to conform to. Group members who go against the norm may be disliked, threatened, or rejected.
- The relationship between cohesiveness and group performance is complex and depends on factors such as the size of the group, the kind of task the group is performing, and the kinds of norms that have been established.

Culture and Cohesiveness

- What behaviors affect group cohesiveness can vary significantly across cultures.
- When working in a group, people from collectivistic cultures may distinguish more between working with friends and strangers than people from individualistic cultures do.

Individuals in Groups: The Presence of Others

Social Facilitation: When Others Arouse Us

- In an early experiment, Triplett found that children performed faster when they worked side by side rather than alone.

- Social facilitation refers to two effects that occur when individual contributions are identifiable: The presence of others enhances performance on easy tasks but impairs performance on difficult tasks.

- Social facilitation effects have been found in a variety of domains. Even the "presence" of fictional TV characters or computerized images of people can trigger these effects.

- The theories of mere presence, evaluation apprehension, and distraction conflict give different explanations of the cause of social facilitation effects; all three explanations probably account for some of the social facilitation effects.

Social Loafing: When Others Relax Us

- In early research on easy tasks involving pooled contributions, Ringelmann found that individual output declined when people worked with others. This social loafing effect has been replicated in numerous studies over the years.

- But social loafing is reduced or eliminated when people think that their individual efforts will be important, relevant, and meaningful. In such cases, individuals may engage in social compensation in an effort to offset the anticipated social loafing of others.

Culture and Social Loafing

- Groups in collectivistic cultures may be more likely to have group norms that promote productive teamwork and discourage social loafing.

- People from collectivistic cultures may be likely to socially loaf if they are working in a group that has established a norm of low productivity and effort.

Deindividuation

- Deindividuation diminishes a person's sense of individuality and reduces constraints against deviant behavior.

- Two types of environmental cues can increase deviant behavior: (1) Accountability cues, such as anonymity, signal to individuals that they will not be held responsible for their actions; and (2) attentional cues, such as intense environmental stimulation, produce a deindividuated state in which the individual acts impulsively.

- Large crowds can both increase anonymity and decrease self-awareness; together these two effects can increase violent or other deviant behavior.

- A field experiment of Halloween trick-or-treaters showed that when factors associated with deindividuation were highest—when children were anonymous and in a group—they were most likely to take more candy than permitted.

- The effects of deindividuation depend on the characteristics of the immediate group. In the context of an antagonistic social identity, antisocial behavior increases; in the context of a benevolent social identity, prosocial behavior increases.

Group Performance: Problems and Solutions

Process Loss and Types of Group Tasks

- Because of process loss, a group may perform worse than it would if every individual performed up to his or her potential.

- Group performance is influenced by the type of task (additive, conjunctive, or disjunctive).

- Among the factors that create process loss are social loafing, poor coordination, and failure to recognize the expertise of particular group members.

- Groups can do better than even the best members of the group on tasks that can be divided among subgroups and when the correct approach is clearly demonstrable to the rest of the group members.

Brainstorming

- Contrary to illusions about the effectiveness of interactive brainstorming, groups in which members interact face to face produce fewer creative ideas than the same number of people working alone.

- Computer-based technology can improve group brainstorming.

Group Polarization

- When individuals who have similar though not identical opinions participate in a group discussion, their opinions become more extreme.

- Explanations for group polarization emphasize the number and persuasiveness of arguments heard and social comparison with other group members.

Groupthink

- Groupthink refers to an excessive tendency to seek concurrence among group members.

- The symptoms of groupthink produce defective decision making, which can lead to a bad decision.

- Research to test the theory of groupthink has not produced as much evidence to support the theory as its fame might suggest.

- Groups may be more likely to experience groupthink if multiple contributing factors are present simultaneously, such as high cohesiveness, a strong and controlling leader, and a great deal of stress.

- Strategies that have been successful in helping groups avoid groupthink include consulting with outsiders, having the leader play a less controlling role, encouraging criticism and a thorough search for information, and having a group member play devil's advocate to challenge the consensus.

Escalation Effects

- Groups are susceptible to an escalation effect, which occurs when commitment to a failing course of action is increased to justify investments that have already been made. Instead of cutting its losses, groups essentially throw good money and time after bad.

Communicating Information and Utilizing Expertise

- Biased sampling refers to the tendency for groups to pay more attention to information that is already known by all or most group members than to important information that is known by only one or a few group members.

- Information may not be communicated adequately in a group because of problems in the group's communication network, such as suppression of relevant information at some point in the decision-making chain.

- Groups can remember more information than individuals through transactive memory, a shared process by which the information can be divided among the group members.

Strategies for Improvement

- Group norms that foster critical thinking can prevent biased sampling.

- Setting specific ambitious goals can improve group performance.

- Training groups in better group dynamics, such as how best to develop transactive memory, can be effective.

- Interventions that compel groups to stop and explicitly think about the best way to proceed can also improve group performance.

- One recent experiment demonstrated that having experts in a group was not good enough to improve group performance; the presence of experts helped the group only if their presence was coupled with an intervention that required the group to engage in collaborative planning.

- Computer technology can be used to guide group discussions and decision-making processes, which can help group avoid problems such as groupthink.

Virtual Teams

- There is a growing trend in the business world toward teams that are dispersed across space and work interactively via technology, but such teams may be especially vulnerable to some of the factors that cause process loss. Therefore, special attention needs to be paid to virtual teams to offset these problems.

Diversity

- Research on the effects of diversity on group performance is rather mixed; both positive and negative effects have been found thus far.

Conflict: Cooperation and Competition Within and Between Groups

Mixed Motives and Social Dilemmas

- In mixed-motive situations, such as the prisoner's dilemma, there are incentives to compete as well as incentives to cooperate.

- In a social dilemma, personal benefit conflicts with the overall good.

- Resource dilemmas involve sharing limited resources. In the commons dilemma a group of people can take resources from a common pool, whereas in the public goods dilemma a group of people must make contributions to a shared resource.

- Behavior in a social dilemma is influenced by a number of psychological factors, including situational factors, group dynamics, and structural arrangements.

- Groups tend to be more competitive than individuals in mixed-motive situations.

- Individuals with a prosocial, cooperative orientation are less likely to behave in a competitive, resource-consuming fashion than people with individualistic or competitive orientations are.

Culture and Social Dilemmas

- Some studies have suggested that collectivists are more likely to cooperate in social dilemmas than are individualists, but the evidence is somewhat mixed.

- Collectivists may cooperate more when dealing with friends or ingroup members but compete more aggressively when dealing with strangers or outgroup members.

- In one experiment Chinese participants who were familiar with both American and Chinese cultures were primed with either Chinese or American symbols. Participants cooperated more when playing a prisoner's dilemma with a friend if they were primed with Chinese symbols than if they were primed with American symbols.

Conflict Escalation and Reduction

- Conflicts can escalate for many reasons, including conflict spirals and escalation of commitment.

- The premature use of the capacity to punish can elicit retaliation and escalate conflict.

- Perceptions of the other that contribute to conflict escalation include unfavorable mirror images and dehumanization.
- GRIT—an explicit strategy for the unilateral persistent pursuit of trust and cooperation between opposing parties—is a useful strategy for beginning the peace process.

Negotiation

- Many negotiations have the potential to result in integrative agreements in which outcomes exceed a 50-50 split, but negotiators often fail to achieve such outcomes.
- Communication and an understanding of the other party's perspective are key ingredients of successful negotiation.
- Mediators can often be helpful in achieving success in negotiations.

- Differences between men and women in negotiation most likely emerge only in combination with other variables. For example, one line of research suggests that for women, negotiations go better when there is eye contact between the negotiators; for men, negotiations are more productive when there is no visual contact.

Culture and Negotiation

- People from different cultures may have very different assumptions and styles concerning negotiations, such as whether direct or indirect communication is preferred, how important context and relationship-building is, and whether direct conflict should be avoided.
- One experiment found that business students from Hong Kong were much more affected by the emotion an American negotiator displayed than students from Israel were when deciding whether or not to accept the American's proposal.

Finding Common Ground

- Superordinate goals and a superordinate identity increase the likelihood of a peaceful resolution of differences.

Key Terms

biased sampling (318)

brainstorming (311)

collective effort model (306)

deindividuation (307)

distraction-conflict theory (303)

escalation effect (317)

evaluation apprehension theory (303)

graduated and reciprocated initiatives in tension-reduction (GRIT) (329)

group cohesiveness (299)

group polarization (313)

group support systems (321)

groupthink (315)

integrative agreement (329)

mere presence theory (303)

prisoner's dilemma (323)

process loss (310)

resource dilemmas (324)

social dilemma (323)

social facilitation (302)

social identity model of deindividuation effects (SIDE) (309)

social loafing (304)

transactive memory (319)

Media Resources

Social Psychology 8th Edition Companion Website

Visit your book companion website

www.cengage.com/psychology/kassin

where you will find flash cards, practice quizzes, Internet links, and more to help you study.

CENGAGENOW Just what you need to know NOW! Spend time on what you need to master rather than on information

you already have learned. Take a pre-test for this chapter and CengageNOW will generate a personalized study plan based on your results. The study plan will identify the topics you need to review and direct you to online resources to help you master those topics. You can then take a post-test to help you determine the concepts you have mastered and what you will need to work on. Try it out! Go to **academic .cengage.com/login** to sign in with an access code or to purchase access to this product.

Putting COMMON SENSE *to the Test*

People will cheer louder when they cheer as part of a group than when they cheer alone.

False. *People tend to put less effort into collective tasks, such as group cheering, than into tasks where their individual performance can be identified and evaluated.*

People brainstorming as a group come up with a greater number of better ideas than the same number of people working individually.

False. *Groups in which members interact face to face produce fewer creative ideas when brainstorming than the same number of people brainstorming alone.*

Group members' attitudes about a course of action usually become more moderate after group discussion.

False. *Group discussion often causes attitudes to become more extreme as the initial tendencies of the group are exaggerated.*

Large groups are more likely than small groups to exploit a scarce resource that the members collectively depend on.

True. *Large groups are more likely to behave selfishly when faced with resource dilemmas, in part because people in large groups feel less identifiable and more anonymous.*

9

© Martin Meyer/Corbis

Attraction and Close Relationships

This chapter examines how people form relationships with each other. First, we describe the fundamental human need for being with others, why people affiliate, and the problem of loneliness. Then we consider various personal and situational factors that influence our initial attraction to specific others. Third, we examine different types of close relationships—what makes them rewarding, how they differ, the types of love they arouse, and the factors that keep them together or break them apart.

No topic fascinates the people of this planet more than inter-personal attraction. Needing to belong, we humans are obsessed about friendships, romantic relationships, dating, love, sex, reproduction, sexual orientation, marriage, and divorce. Playwrights, poets, and musicians write with eloquence and emotion about loves desired, won, and lost. In recent years, television has been filled with relationship-centered reality TV shows such as *The Bachelor*, *The Bachelorette*, *The Pickup Artist*, *Wife Swap*, *Blind Date*, *elimiDATE*, *Here Come the Newlyweds*, and *Cheaters*. More and more, people are meeting romantic partners online rather than in bars—on Facebook, in chat rooms, on craigslist, and at dating service websites such as Match.com, eHarmony, and Compatible Partners. Both in our hearts and in our minds, the relationships we seek and enjoy with other people are more important than anything else.

At one time or another, each of us has been startled by our reaction to someone we have met. In general, why are human beings drawn to each other? Why are we so attracted to some people and yet indifferent to or repelled by others? What determines how our intimate relationships evolve? What does it mean to love someone, and what problems are likely to arise along the way? As these questions reveal, the processes of attraction among people—from the first spark through the flames of an intimate connection—often seem like a wild card in the deck of human behavior. This chapter unravels some of the mysteries.

Putting COMMON SENSE to the Test

Circle Your Answer

T	F	People seek out the company of others, even strangers, in times of stress.
T	F	Infants do not discriminate between faces considered attractive and unattractive in their culture.
T	F	People who are physically attractive are happier and have higher self-esteem than those who are unattractive.
T	F	When it comes to romantic relationships, opposites attract.
T	F	Men are more likely than women to interpret friendly gestures by the opposite sex in sexual terms.
T	F	After the honeymoon period, there is an overall decline in levels of marital satisfaction.

Being with Others: A Fundamental Human Motive

Although born helpless, human infants are equipped with reflexes that orient them toward people. They are uniquely responsive to human faces, they turn their head toward voices, and they are able to mimic certain facial gestures on cue. Then, a few weeks later comes a baby's first smile, surely the warmest sign of all. Much to the delight of parents all over the world, the newborn seems an inherently social animal.

But wait. If you reflect on the amount of time that you spend talking to, being with, flirting with, confiding in, pining for, or worrying about other people, you'll realize that we are all social animals. It seems that people need people.

According to Roy Baumeister and Mark Leary (1995), the need to belong is a basic human motive, "a pervasive drive to form and maintain at least a minimum quantity of lasting, positive, and significant interpersonal relationships" (p. 497). This general proposition is supported by everyday observation and a great deal of research. All over the world, people feel joy when they form new social attachments and react with anxiety and grief when these bonds are broken—as when separated from a loved one by distance, divorce, or death. The need to belong runs deep, which is why people get very distressed when they are neglected by others, rejected, excluded, stigmatized, or ostracized, all forms of "social death" (Leary, 2001; Smart Richman & Leary, 2009; Williams, 2007a).

We care deeply about what others think of us, which is why we spend so much time and money to make ourselves presentable and attractive. In fact, some people are so worried about how they appear to others that they suffer from *social anxiety disorders* characterized by intense feelings of discomfort in situations that invite public scrutiny (Leary & Kowalski, 1995). One very familiar example is public-speaking anxiety, or "stage fright"—a performer's worst nightmare. If you've ever had to make a presentation only to feel weak in the knees and hear your voice quiver, you have endured a hint of this disorder. When sufferers are asked what there is to fear, the most common responses are shaking and showing other signs of anxiety, going blank, saying something foolish, and being unable to continue (Stein et al., 1996). For people with high levels of social anxiety, the problem is also evoked by other social situations, such as eating at a public lunch counter, signing a check in front of a store clerk, and, for males, urinating in a crowded men's room. In extreme cases, the reaction can become so debilitating that the person just stays at home (Beidel & Turner, 1998; Crozier & Alden, 2005).

Our need to belong is a fundamental human motive. People who have a network of close social ties—in the form of lovers, friends, family members, and co-workers—have higher self-esteem than those who live more isolated lives (Dennisen et al., 2008; Leary & Baumeister, 2000). They also tend to be happier and more satisfied with life (Diener et al., 1999). In fact, as we'll see in Chapter 14 on health, people who are socially connected are also physically healthier and less likely to die a premature death (Cacioppo & Patrick, 2008; House et al., 1988; Uchino, 2006).

"At this point, my privacy needs are interfering with my intimacy goals."

People are motivated to establish and maintain an optimum level of social contact.

The Thrill of Affiliation

As social beings, humans are drawn to each other like magnets to metal. We work together, play together, live together, and often make lifetime commitments to grow old together. This social motivation begins with the **need for affiliation**, defined as a desire to establish social contact with others (McAdams, 1989). Individuals differ in the strength of their need for affiliation, but it seems that people are highly motivated to establish and maintain an *optimum* balance of social contact—sometimes craving the company of others, sometimes wanting to be alone—the way the body maintains a certain temperature level. In an interesting study, Bibb Latané and Carol Werner (1978) found that laboratory rats were more likely to approach others of their species

need for affiliation The desire to establish and maintain many rewarding interpersonal relationships.

after a period of isolation and were less likely to approach others after prolonged contact. These researchers suggested that rats, like many other animals, have a built-in "sociostat" (social thermostat) to regulate their affiliative tendencies.

Is there evidence of a similar mechanism in humans? Shawn O'Connor and Lorne Rosenblood (1996) recruited college students to carry portable beepers for four days. Whenever the beepers went off (on average, every hour), the students wrote down whether at the time they were *actually* alone or in the company of other people and whether they *wanted* to be alone or with others. The results showed that students were in the state they desired two-thirds of the time. In fact, the situation they desired on one occasion (saying they wanted to be alone at 4 P.M.) predicted their actual situation the next time they were signaled (they would be alone at 5 P.M.). Whether it was solitude or social contact that the students sought, they successfully managed to regulate their own personal needs for affiliation.

When Italy won the World Cup soccer championship in the summer of 2006, the people of Rome and other cities across the country spilled into the streets, piazzas, and fountains in order to be with one another for the occasion.

People may well differ in the strength of their affiliative needs, but there are times when we all want to be with other people. Recall the scenes in Chicago, St. Louis, Dallas, Pittsburgh, Philadelphia, Boston, Los Angeles, and other recent championship sports cities whenever the home team won the final championship game. From one city to the next, jubilant fans stayed long after the game had ended, milling about and exchanging high-fives, slaps on the back, and hugs and kisses. In each of these cities, it's clear that people wanted to celebrate together rather than alone.

Affiliating can satisfy us for other reasons as well, as others provide energy, attention, stimulation, information, and emotional support (Hill, 1987). One condition that strongly arouses our need for affiliation is stress. Have you ever noticed the way neighbors who never stop to say hello come together in snowstorms, hurricanes, power failures, and other major crises? Many years ago, Stanley Schachter (1959) theorized that an external threat triggers fear and motivates us to affiliate, particularly with others who face a similar threat. In a laboratory experiment that demonstrated the point, Schachter found that people who were expecting to receive painful electric shocks chose to wait with other nervous participants rather than alone. So far, so good. But when Irving Sarnoff and Philip Zimbardo (1961) led college students to expect that they would be engaging in an embarrassing behavior—sucking on large bottle nipples and pacifiers—their desire to be with others fell off. It seemed puzzling. Why do people in fearful misery love company while those in embarrassed misery seek solitude?

Yacov Rofé (1984) proposed a simple answer: utility. Rofé argued that stress increases the desire to affiliate only when being with others is seen as useful in reducing the negative impact of the stressful situation. Schachter's participants had good reason to believe that affiliation would be useful. They would have the opportunity to compare their emotional reactions with those of others to determine whether they really needed to be fearful. For those in the Sarnoff and Zimbardo study, however, affiliation had little to offer. When we face embarrassment, being with others is more likely to increase the stress than reduce it.

Let's return to Schachter's initial study. What specific benefit do people get from being in the presence of others in times of stress? Research suggests that people facing an imminent threat seek each other out in order to gain *cognitive clarity* about the danger they are in. In one study, James Kulik and Heike Mahler (1989) found that hospital patients waiting for open-heart surgery preferred to have as roommates other

People seek out the company of others, even strangers, in times of stress. TRUE.

patients who were post-operative rather than pre-operative, presumably because they were in a position to provide information about the experience. Patients in a second study who had been assigned post-operative rather than pre-operative roommates became less anxious about the experience and were later quicker to recover from the surgery (Kulik et al., 1996).

Even within a laboratory setting, Kulik and others (1994) found that study participants anticipating the painful task of soaking a hand in ice-cold water preferred to wait with someone who had already completed the task rather than with someone who had not. They also asked more questions of these experienced peers than participants who did not know that the water would be painful. Under stress, we adaptively become motivated to affiliate with others who can help us cope with an impending threat. Summarizing his own work, Schachter (1959) noted that misery loves miserable company. Based on their more recent studies, Gump and Kulik (1997) further amended this assertion: "Misery loves the company of those in the same miserable situation" (p. 317).

◼ The Agony of Loneliness

Loneliness and the feeling of being unwanted is the most terrible poverty.

—Mother Teresa

People need other people—to celebrate with, share news with, commiserate with, talk to, and learn from. But some people are painfully shy, socially awkward, inhibited, and reluctant to approach others (Bruch et al., 1989; Lane, 2007). Shyness is a pervasive problem. Roughly 49 percent of all Americans describe themselves as shy, as do 31 percent in Israel, 40 percent in Germany, 55 percent in Taiwan, and 57 percent in Japan (Henderson & Zimbardo, 1998). People who are shy find it difficult to approach strangers, make small talk, telephone someone for a date, participate in small groups, or mingle at parties. What's worse, they often reject others, perhaps because they fear being rejected themselves. The sad result is a pattern of risk avoidance that sets them up for unpleasant and unrewarding interactions (Crozier, 2001).

Shyness can arise from different sources. In some cases, it maybe an inborn personality trait. Jerome Kagan (1994) and others have found that some infants are highly sensitive to stimulation, inhibited, and cautious shortly after birth. In other cases, shyness develops as a learned reaction to failed interactions with others. Thus, interpersonal problems of the past can ignite social anxieties about the future (Leary & Kowalski, 1995). Not all shy infants grow up to become inhibited adults. But longitudinal research indicates that there is some continuity, that this aspect of our personalities may be predictable from our temperament and behavior as young children. Thus, toddlers observed to be inhibited, shy, and fearful at age 3 were more likely than toddlers who were more outgoing to be socially isolated and depressed at age 21 (Caspi, 2000). The difference can be seen in the adult brain. Using fMRI, researchers have recently observed that people who are shy, compared to those who are bold, exhibit greater activity in the amygdala—a region of the brain responsible for fear processing—when exposed to pictures of strangers (Beaton et al., 2008; Schwartz et al., 2003).

Whatever the source, shyness is a real problem, and it has painful consequences. Studies show that shy people evaluate themselves negatively, expect to fail in their social encounters, and blame themselves when they do. As a result, many shy people go into self-imposed isolation, which makes them feel lonely (Cheek & Melchior, 1990; Jackson et al., 2002). In part, the problem stems from a paralyzing fear of rejection, which inhibits people from making friendly or romantic overtures to those they are interested in. If you ever wanted to approach someone you liked but stopped yourself, you know that this situation often triggers an approach-avoidance conflict, pulling you between the desire for contact and a fear of being rejected. What's worse, research shows that people who fear rejection think that their friendly or romantic interest is transparent to others, which leads them to back off (Vorauer et al., 2003).

Loneliness is a sad and heart-wrenching emotional state. To be lonely is to feel deprived of human social connections (Cacioppo & Patrick, 2008). Some researchers maintain that loneliness is triggered by a discrepancy between the level of social contact a person has and the level he or she wants (Peplau & Perlman, 1982). Others find, more simply, that the less social contact people have, the lonelier they feel (Archibald et al., 1995). Unfortunately, people in some parts of the world are lonelier today than ever before. In *Bowling Alone*, Harvard professor of public policy Robert Putnam (2001) argued that Americans are more disconnected from their families, neighbors, co-workers, and communities than in the past. Not too long ago, he wrote, thousands of people belonged to bowling leagues. Today they are more likely to bowl alone. Lamenting the adverse effects, Putnam (2006) preaches: "You gotta have friends."

Who is lonely, and when? Loneliness is most likely to occur during times of transition or disruption—as in the first year at college, after a romantic breakup, or when a loved one moves far away. Surveys show that people who are unattached are lonelier than those who have romantic partners, but that those who are widowed, divorced, and separated are lonelier than people who have never been married. Despite the stereotypic image of the lonely old man passing time on a park bench, the loneliest groups in American society are adolescents and young adults 18 to 30 years old. In fact, loneliness seems to decline over the course of adulthood—at least until health problems in old age limit social activities (Peplau & Perlman, 1982).

How do people cope with this distressing state? When college students were asked what behavioral strategies they use to combat loneliness, 96 percent said they often or sometimes try harder to be friendly to other people, 94 percent take their mind off the problem by reading or watching TV, and 93 percent try extra hard to succeed at another aspect of life. Others said that they distract themselves by running, shopping, washing the car, or staying busy at other activities. Still others seek new ways to meet people, try to improve their appearance, or talk to a friend, relative, or therapist about the problem. Though fewer in number, some are so desperate that they use alcohol or drugs to wash away feelings of loneliness (Rook & Peplau, 1982). In Chapter 14 we will see that as people age, loneliness becomes a risk factor—as toxic as smoking and obesity—for a broad range of physical and mental health problems, including physical inactivity and depression (Cacioppo et al., 2006; Hawkley et al., 2009).

The Initial Attraction

Affiliation is a necessary first step in the formation of a social relationship. But each of us is more drawn to some people than to others. If you've ever had a crush on someone, felt the tingly excitement of a first encounter, or enjoyed the first moments of a new friendship, then you know the meaning of the term *attraction*. When you meet someone for the first time, what do *you* look for? Does familiarity breed fondness or contempt? Do birds of a feather flock together or do opposites attract? Is beauty the object of your desire or do you believe that outward appearances are deceiving? And what is it about a situation or the circumstances of an initial meeting that draws you in for more?

According to one classic perspective, people are attracted to those with whom they can have a relationship that is rewarding (Byrne & Clore, 1970; Lott & Lott, 1974). The rewards may be direct, as when people provide us with attention, support, money, status, information, and other valuable commodities. Or the rewards may be

loneliness A feeling of deprivation about existing social relations.

indirect, as when it feels good to be with someone who is beautiful, smart, or funny, or who happens to be in our presence when times are good. A second perspective on attraction has also emerged in recent years—that of evolutionary psychology, the subdiscipline that uses principles of evolution to understand human social behavior. According to this view, human beings all over the world exhibit patterns of attraction and mate selection that favor the conception, birth, and survival of their offspring. This approach has a great deal to say about differences in this regard between men and women (Buss, 2004; Schaller et al., 2006; Simpson & Kenrick, 1997).

Recognizing the role of rewards and the call of our evolutionary past provides broad perspectives for understanding human attraction. But there's more to the story—much more. Over the years, social psychologists have identified many determinants of attraction and the development of intimate relationships (Berscheid & Regan, 2004; Miller & Perlman, 2009; Regan, 2008). It's important to note that most of the research has focused on heterosexuals, so we often do not know how well specific findings apply to the homosexual population. At the same time, it is important to realize that many of the basic processes described in this chapter affect the development of all close relationships, regardless of whether the individuals involved are gay, lesbian, or straight (Herek, 2006; Kurdek, 2005; Peplau & Fingerhut, 2007).

▋ Familiarity: Being There

It seems so obvious that people tend to overlook it: We are most likely to become attracted to someone we have seen and become familiar with. So let's begin with two basic and necessary factors in the attraction process: proximity and exposure.

The Proximity Effect It hardly sounds romantic, but the single best predictor of whether two people will get together is physical proximity or nearness. To be sure, we often interact at remote distances by telephone, e-mail, Twitter, blogs, and message boards. These days it's common for people to find friends, lovers, and sexual partners from a distance. Yet some of our most important social interactions still occur among people who find themselves in the same place at the same time (Latané et al., 1995).

To begin with, where we live influences the friends we make. Many years ago, Leon Festinger and his colleagues (1950) studied friendship patterns in married-student college housing and found that people were more likely to become friends with residents of nearby apartments than with those who lived farther away. More recent research has also shown that college students—who live in off-campus apartments, dormitories, or fraternity and sorority houses—tend to date those who live either nearby (Hays, 1985) or in the same type of housing as they do (Whitbeck & Hoyt, 1994).

"Sometimes I think you only married me because I lived next door!"

The Mere Exposure Effect Proximity does not necessarily spark attraction, but to the extent that it increases frequency of contact, it's a good first step. Folk wisdom often suggests a dim view of familiarity, which is said to "breed contempt." But in a series of experiments, Robert Zajonc (1968) found that the more often people saw a novel stimulus—whether it was a foreign word, a geometric form, or a human face—the more they came to like it. This phenomenon, which Zajonc called the **mere exposure effect**, has since been observed in more than 200 experiments (Bornstein, 1989).

People do not even have to be aware of their prior exposures for this effect to occur. In a typical study, participants are shown pictures of several stimuli, each for one to five milliseconds, which is too quick to register in awareness and too quick for anyone to realize that some stimuli are presented more often than others. After the presentation, participants are shown each of the stimuli and asked two questions: Do you like it, and have you ever seen it before? Perhaps you can predict the result. The more frequently the stimulus is presented, the more people like it. Yet when asked if they've ever seen the liked stimulus before, they say no. These results demonstrate that the mere exposure effect can influence us without our awareness (Kuntz-Wilson & Zajonc, 1980). In fact, the effect is stronger under these conditions (Bornstein & D'Agostino, 1992; Zajonc, 2001).

To appreciate the implications in a naturalistic situation, imagine yourself in a psychology class that is held in a large lecture hall. Three times a week, you trudge over to class, shake the cobwebs out of your head, and try your best to be alert. The room holds several hundred students. You come in and look down the tiered seats to the front where your instructor stands. During the semester, you're vaguely aware of another student who sits up front, but you never talk to her and you probably would not recognize her if you saw her somewhere else. Then, at the end of the semester, you attend a special session where you are shown photographs of four women and asked some questions about them. Only then do you learn that you have participated in a study of the mere exposure effect.

Now view the same events from the perspective of Richard Moreland and Scott Beach (1992). These researchers selected four women who looked like typical students to be confederates in this study. One had a very easy job: She had her picture taken. But the other three also attended the class—five, ten, or fifteen times. Did the frequency of exposure spark attraction among the real students in this situation? Yes. In questionnaires they completed after viewing pictures of all four women, students rated each woman on various traits (such as popularity, honesty, intelligence, and physical attractiveness) and recorded their beliefs about how much they would like her, enjoy spending time with her, and want to work with her on a mutual project. The results lined up like ducks in a row: The more classes a woman attended, the more attracted the students were to her.

Familiarity can even influence our self-evaluations. Imagine that you had a portrait photograph of yourself developed into two pictures: one that depicted your actual appearance and the other a mirror-image copy. Which image would you prefer? Which would a friend prefer? Theodore Mita and others (1977) tried this interesting experiment with female college students and found that most preferred their mirror images, while their friends liked the actual photos. In both cases, the preference was for the view of the face that was most familiar.

■ Physical Attractiveness: Getting Drawn In

What do you look for in a friend or romantic partner? Intelligence? Kindness? A sense of humor? How important, really, are a person's looks? As children, we were told that "beauty is only skin deep" and that we should not "judge a book by its cover." Yet as adults, we react more favorably to others who are physically attractive

mere exposure effect The phenomenon whereby the more often people are exposed to a stimulus, the more positively they evaluate that stimulus.

Beauty is a greater recommendation than any letter of introduction.

—Aristotle

than to those who are not. Over the years, studies have shown that in the affairs of our social world, beauty is a force to be reckoned with (Langlois et al., 2000; Patzer, 2006; Swami & Furnham, 2008).

The human bias for beauty is pervasive. In one study, fifth-grade teachers were given background information about a boy or girl, accompanied by a photograph. All teachers received identical information, yet those who saw an attractive child saw that child as being smarter and more likely to do well in school (Clifford & Walster, 1973). In a second study, male and female experimenters approached students on a college campus and tried to get them to sign a petition. The more attractive the experimenters were, the more signatures they were able to get (Chaiken, 1979). In a third study, Texas judges set lower bail and imposed smaller fines on suspects who were rated as attractive rather than unattractive on the basis of photographs (Downs & Lyons, 1991). Fourth, in a number of other studies conducted in the United States, Canada, and England, economists have discovered that within many occupational groups, physically attractive men and women earn more money than peers who are comparable except for being less attractive (Hamermesh & Biddle, 1994; Judge et al., 2009; Mobius & Rosenblat, 2006). There is no doubt about it: Across a range of settings, people fare better if they are attractive than if they are not (Hosoda et al., 2003).

It all seems so shallow, so superficial. But before we go on to accept the notion that people prefer others who are physically attractive, let's stop for a moment and consider a fundamental question: What constitutes physical beauty? Is it an objective and measurable human characteristic like height, weight, or hair color? Or is beauty a subjective quality, existing in the eye of the beholder? There are advocates on both sides.

What Is Beauty?   No one would argue that there is a "gold standard" for beauty. However, some researchers do believe that certain faces are inherently more attractive than others. There are three sources of evidence for this proposition.

First, when people are asked to rate faces on a 10-point scale, there is typically a high level of agreement among children and adults, men and women, and people from the same or different cultures (Langlois et al., 2000). For example, Michael Cunningham and others (1995) asked Asian and Latino students and black and white American students to rate the appearance of women from all these groups. Overall, some faces were rated more attractive than others, leading these investigators to argue that people everywhere share an image of what is beautiful. It is interesting that people also tend to rate others similarly regardless of their own level of attractiveness. By analyzing the 10-point ratings of pictures that people post of themselves on a rating-and-dating website called HOTorNOT.com, Leonard Lee and others (2008) found that members tend to evaluate specific others similarly regardless of how high or low their own ratings were on the site.

People also tend to agree about what constitutes an attractive body. For example, men tend to be drawn to the "hourglass" figure often seen in women of average weight whose waists are a third narrower than their hips, a shape that is thought to be associated with reproductive fertility. In general, women with a 0.7 WHR (a waist-to-hip ratio where the waist circumference is 70 percent of the hip circumference) are rated as more attractive by men from European cultures. In fact, when shown photographs of women before and after they had microfat grafting surgery (where fat tissue is taken from the waist and implanted on the buttocks, which lowers the WHR), people rated the post-operative photographs as more attractive—independent of any changes in body weight (Singh & Randall, 2007). In contrast, women like men with a waist-to-hip ratio that forms a tapering V-shaped physique, signaling more muscle than fat (Singh, 1993, 1995). If marriage statistics are any indication, women also seem to prefer men

Perceptions of facial beauty are largely consistent across cultures. Those regarded as good-looking in one culture also tend to be judged as attractive by people from other cultures. From left to right, the individuals pictured here are from Venezuela, Kenya, Japan, and the United States (the American is the actress Marilyn Monroe).

with height. Comparisons made in Europe indicate that married men are a full inch taller, on average, than unmarried men (Pawlowski et al., 2000).

Second, a number of researchers have identified physical features of the human face that are reliably associated with ratings of attractiveness, such as smooth skin, a pleasant expression, and youthfulness (Rhodes, 2006). Particularly intriguing are studies showing that people like faces in which the eyes, nose, lips, and other features are not too different from the average. Judith Langlois and Lori Roggman (1990) showed college students both actual yearbook photos and computerized facial composites that "averaged" features from four, eight, sixteen, or thirty-two of the photos. Time and again, they found that the students preferred the averaged composites to the individual faces and that the more faces used to form the composite, the more highly it was rated. Other studies have since confirmed this result (Jones et al., 2007; Langlois et al., 1994; Rhodes et al., 1999).

It seems odd that "averaged" faces are judged attractive when after all, the faces we find the most beautiful are anything but average. What accounts for these findings? Langlois and others (1994) believe that people like averaged faces because they are more prototypically face-like and have features that are less distinctive, so they seem more familiar to us. Consistent with this notion, research shows that just as people are more attracted to averaged human faces than to individual faces, they also prefer averaged dogs, birds, fish, wristwatches, and cars (Halberstadt & Rhodes, 2000, 2003).

Computerized averaging studies also show that people are drawn to faces that are symmetrical, where the paired features of the right and left sides line up and mirror each other (Grammer & Thornhill, 1994; Mealey et al., 1999). Why do people prefer symmetrical faces? Although support is mixed, evolutionary psychologists have speculated that our pursuit of symmetry is adaptive because symmetry is naturally associated with biological health, fitness, and fertility, qualities that are highly desirable in a mate (Rhodes et al., 2001; Shackelford & Larsen, 1999; Thornhill & Gangestad, 1993). Perhaps for that reason, people throughout the world try to enhance their appeal by wearing or painting symmetrical designs on their faces and bodies—designs that others find attractive (Cárdenas & Harris, 2006).

A third source of evidence for the view that beauty is an objective quality is that babies who are far too young to have learned the culture's standards of beauty exhibit a nonverbal preference for faces considered attractive by adults. Picture the scene in an infant laboratory: A baby, lying on its back in a crib, is shown a series of faces previously rated by college students. The first face appears and a clock starts ticking as the baby looks at it. As soon as the baby looks away, the clock stops and the next face is presented. The result: Young infants spend more time tracking and looking at attractive

Infants do not discriminate between faces considered attractive and unattractive in their culture. **FALSE.**

faces than at unattractive ones, regardless of whether the faces are young or old, male or female, or black or white (Game et al., 2003; Langlois et al., 1991). "These kids don't read *Vogue* or watch TV," notes Langlois, "yet they make the same judgments as adults" (Cowley, 1996, p. 66).

In contrast to this objective perspective, other researchers argue that physical attractiveness is subjective, and they point for evidence to the influences of culture, time, and the circumstances of our perception. When Johannes Hönekopp (2006) had large numbers of people rate the same faces, he found that although some faces were seen as more attractive than others, individuals differed a great deal in their private preferences. To some extent, beauty really is in the eye of the beholder.

One source of evidence for our variability in taste, first noted by Charles Darwin (1872), is that people from different cultures enhance their beauty in very different ways through face painting, makeup, plastic surgery, scarring, tattoos, hairstyling, the molding of bones, the filing of teeth, braces, and the piercing of ears and other body parts—all contributing to the "enigma of beauty" (Newman, 2000). In dramatic ways, what people find attractive in one part of the world may be seen as repulsive in another part of the world (Landau, 1989).

Ideals also vary when it comes to bodies. Looking at preferences for female body size in fifty-four cultures, Judith Anderson and others (1992) found that heavy women are judged more attractive than slender women in places where food is frequently in short supply. In one study, for example, Douglas Yu and Glenn Shepard (1998) found that Matsigenka men living in the Andes Mountains of southeastern Peru see female forms with "tubular" shapes—as opposed to hourglass shapes—as healthier, more attractive, and more desirable in a mate.

Differences in preference have also been found among racial groups within a given culture. Michelle Hebl and Todd Heatherton (1998) asked black and white female college students from the United States to rate thin, average, and overweight women from a set of magazine photographs. The result: The white students saw the heavy women as the least attractive, but the black students did not similarly discriminate. A follow-up study showed the same difference in perceptions of black and white men (Hebl & Turchin, 2005). Why the difference? Based on the fact that white Americans are, on average, thinner than black Americans, one possible explanation is that they simply prefer a body type that is more typical of their group. Another possibility is that white Americans identify more with the "mainstream" weight-obsessed culture as portrayed in TV shows, magazine ads, and other media.

Standards of beauty also change over time, from one generation to the next. Many years ago, Brett Silverstein and others (1986) examined the measurements of female models appearing in women's magazines from the years 1901 to 1981, and they found that "curvaceousness" (as measured by the bust-to-waist ratio) varied over time, with a boyish, slender look becoming particularly desirable in recent years. More recently, researchers took body measurements from all *Playboy* centerfolds, beginning with the first issue, in 1953, which featured Marilyn Monroe, through the last issue of 2001, with Eva Herzigova. The result: Over time, models became thinner and had lower bust-to-waist ratios—away from the ample "hourglass" to a more slender, athletic, stick-like shape (Voracek & Fisher, 2002).

Computer-generated images that average the features of different faces are seen as more attractive than the individual faces on which they were based. In fact, up to a point, the more faces are represented in a composite, the more attractive it is. Shown here are sets of male and female composites that combine 2, 4, and 32 faces. Which do you prefer? (Langlois & Roggman, 1990.)

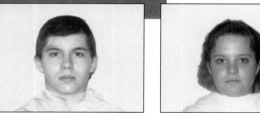

2-Face Composite 2-Face Composite

4-Face Composite 4-Face Composite

32-Face Composite 32-Face Composite

Courtesy of Dr. Judith Langlois; University of Texas, Austin

Still other evidence for the subjective nature of beauty comes from many research laboratories. Time and again, social psychologists have found that our perceptions of someone's beauty can be inflated or deflated by various circumstances. Research shows, for example, that people often see others as more physically attractive if they have nonphysical qualities that make them likable (Kniffin & Wilson, 2004). This link is illustrated in the student evaluations posted on www.RateMyProfessors.com, a popular website. An analysis of actual ratings on this site revealed that both male and female professors who were rated highly for their teaching were also more likely to be described as "hot" (Riniolo et al., 2006). Particularly interesting in this regard is that the more in love people are with their partners, the less attracted they are to others of the opposite sex (Johnson & Rusbult, 1989; Simpson et al., 1990).

When it comes to men's attraction to women, one particularly interesting context factor concerns color. The color red is routinely associated with sex. In many species of primates, females display red swelling on their genitals, chest, or face as they near ovulation. In human rituals that date back thousands of years, girls painted red ochre on their face and body at the emergence of puberty and fertility. Today, women use red lipstick and rouge to enhance their appeal, red hearts symbolize Valentine's Day, red lingerie is worn to entice, and red-light districts signal the availability of sex through prostitution. Are men so conditioned by the color red that its presence boosts their perceptions of attractiveness? In a study of the "red-sex link," Andrew Elliot and Daniela Niesta (2008) had male and female research participants rate female photos that were set against a solid red or white background. Everyone saw the same photos, yet the attractiveness ratings were highest among the men in the red background condition (see ▶ Figure 9.1). In a series of follow-up studies, men continued to rate women as more attractive—and as more sexually desirable (but not generally more likable)—in the presence of red compared to women who were in the presence of gray, blue, or green.

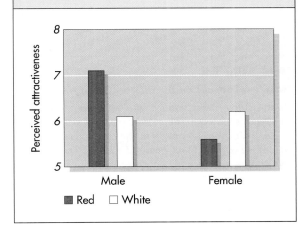

▶ FIGURE 9.1

Romantic Red: The Color of Attraction?

In this experiment, college students rated pictures of women that were set against a solid red or white background. Perhaps illustrating a learned association between the color red and romance, male students—but not their female counterparts—rated the pictured women as more attractive in the red background condition.

Elliot & Niesta, 2008.

Why Are We Blinded by Beauty?   Regardless of how beauty is defined, it's clear that people seen as physically attractive are at a social advantage. Perhaps that's why billions of dollars a year are spent on shaving, waxing, makeup, hair gels, tattoos, body piercings, and cosmetic surgery designed to plump up sunken skin, peel and scrape wrinkles from the face, vacuum out fat deposits, lift faces, reshape noses, tuck in tummies, and enlarge or reduce breasts.

What creates the bias for beauty, and why are we drawn like magnets to people who are physically attractive? One possibility is that it is inherently rewarding to be in the company of people who are aesthetically appealing—that we derive pleasure from beautiful men and women the same way that we enjoy a breathtaking landscape or a magnificent work of art. In an fMRI study of men, for example, researchers found that areas of the brain known to respond to rewards such as food, money, and drugs such as cocaine are also activated by facial beauty (Aharon et al., 2001). Or perhaps the rewards are more extrinsic. Perhaps, for example, we expect the glitter of another's beauty to rub off on us. When average-looking men and women are seen alongside someone else of the same sex, they are rated as more attractive when the other person is good-looking and as less attractive when he or she is plain-looking (Geiselman et al., 1984).

A second possible reason for the bias toward beauty is that people tend to associate physical attractiveness with other desirable qualities, an assumption known as the

There is no known culture in which people do not paint, pierce, tattoo, reshape or simply adorn their bodies.
—Enid Schildkrout, anthropologist

Love looks not with the eyes, but with the mind; And therefore is wing'd Cupid painted blind.

—William Shakespeare, *A Midsummer Night's Dream*

what-is-beautiful-is-good stereotype (Dion et al., 1972). Think about children's fairy tales, where Snow White and Cinderella are portrayed as beautiful *and* kind, while the witch and stepsisters are said to be both ugly *and* cruel. This link between beauty and goodness can even be seen in Hollywood movies. Stephen Smith and others (1999) asked people to watch and rate the main characters who appeared in the 100 top-grossing movies between 1940 and 1990. They found that the more attractive the characters were, the more frequently they were portrayed as virtuous, romantically active, and successful. In a second study, these investigators showed college students a film that depicted either a strong or a weak link between the beauty and goodness of the characters. Then, in a supposedly unrelated experiment, these students were asked to evaluate two graduate school applicants whose credentials were equivalent but whose photographs differed in terms of physical attractiveness. The result was both interesting and disturbing: Students who had watched a film depicting the beautiful-is-good stereotype were more likely than those who had watched a nonstereotypic film to favor the physically attractive applicant in their evaluations (see ▶ Figure 9.2). It appears that the entertainment industry unwittingly helps foster and perpetuate our tendency to judge people by their physical appearance.

Studies have shown that good-looking people are judged to be smart, successful, happy, well-adjusted, socially skilled, confident, and assertive—but also vain (Eagly et al., 1991). So is this physical attractiveness stereotype accurate? Only to a limited extent. Research shows that good-looking people do have more friends, better social skills, and a more active sex life—and they are more successful at attracting a mate (Rhodes et al., 2005). Yet beauty is *not* related to objective measures of intelligence, personality, adjustment, or self-esteem. In these domains, our popular perceptions appear to exaggerate the reality (Feingold, 1992b). It also seems that the specific nature of the stereotype depends on cultural conceptions of what is "good." When Ladd Wheeler and Youngmee Kim (1997) asked people in Korea to rate photos of various men and women, they found that people seen as physically attractive were also assumed to have "integrity" and "a concern for others"—traits that are highly valued in this collectivist culture. In contrast to what is considered desirable in more individualistic cultures, attractive people in Korea were not assumed to be dominant or assertive. What is beautiful is good, but what is good is (in part) culturally defined.

If the physical attractiveness stereotype is true only in part, why does it endure? One possibility is that each of us creates support for the bias via the type of *self-fulfilling prophecy* model described in Chapter 4. In a classic study of interpersonal attraction, Mark Snyder and others (1977) brought together unacquainted pairs of male and female college students. All the students were given biographical sketches of their partners. Each man also received a photograph of a physically attractive or unattractive woman, supposedly his partner. At that point, the students rated each other on several dimensions and had a phone-like conversation over headphones, conversations that were taped and later heard by uninvolved participants. The results were provocative. Men who thought they were interacting with a woman who was attractive (1) formed more positive impressions of her personality and (2) were friendlier in their conversational behavior. And now for the clincher: (3) the female students whose partners had seen the attractive picture were later rated by listeners to the conversation as warmer, more confident, and more animated. Fulfilling the prophecies of

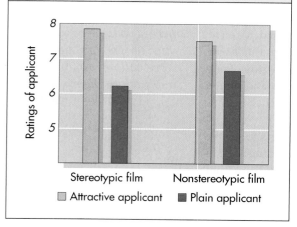

▶ **FIGURE 9.2**

Media Influences on the Bias for Beauty

In this study, participants evaluated graduate school applicants who differed in their physical attractiveness. Indicating the power of the media to influence us, those who had first watched a stereotypic film in which beauty was associated with goodness were more likely to favor the attractive applicant than those who had first seen a nonstereotypic film.

Smith et al., 1999.

what-is-beautiful-is-good stereotype The belief that physically attractive individuals also possess desirable personality characteristics.

their own expectations, men who expected an attractive partner actually created one. These findings call to mind the Greek myth of Pygmalion, who fell in love with a statue he had carved and thus brought it to life.

The Benefits and Costs of Beauty   There's no doubt about it, good-looking people have a significant edge. As a result, they are more popular, more sexually experienced, more socially skilled, and more likely to attract a mate. In light of these advantages, it's interesting that physical attractiveness is not a sure ticket to health, happiness, or high self-esteem (Diener et al., 1995; Feingold, 1992b; Langlois et al., 2000). The life of Marilyn Monroe is a case in point. A celebrity of the 1950s and 1960s, Monroe was considered one of the most ravishing women of her time and one of the hottest actresses in Hollywood. Yet she was terribly vulnerable and insecure. Why?

One possible problem is that highly attractive people can't always tell if the attention and praise they receive from others is due to their talent or just their good looks. A study by Brenda Major and others (1984) illustrates the point. Male and female participants who saw themselves as attractive or unattractive wrote essays that were later positively evaluated by an unknown member of the opposite sex. Half the participants were told that their evaluator would be watching them through a one-way mirror as they wrote the essay; the other half were led to believe that they could not be seen. In actuality, there was no evaluator, and all participants received identical, very positive evaluations of their work. Participants were then asked why their essay was so favorably reviewed. The result: Those who saw themselves as unattractive felt better about the quality of their work after getting a glowing evaluation from someone who had seen them. Yet those who saw themselves as attractive and thought they had been seen attributed the glowing feedback to their looks, not to the quality of their work. For people who are highly attractive, positive feedback is sometimes hard to interpret (see ▶ Figure 9.3). This distrust may be well founded. In one study, many men and women openly admitted that if a prospective date was highly attractive, they would lie to present themselves well (Rowatt et al., 1999).

Another cost of having physical attractiveness as a social asset is the pressure to maintain one's appearance. In today's American society, such pressure is particularly strong when it comes to the body. This focus on the human form can produce a healthy emphasis on nutrition and exercise. But it can also have unhealthy consequences, as when men pop steroids to build muscle and women overdiet to lose weight and inches. Particularly among young women, an obsession with thinness can give rise to serious eating disorders such as *bulimia nervosa* (food binges followed by purging) and *anorexia nervosa* (self-imposed starvation, which can prove fatal). Although estimates vary, recent studies indicate that less than 1 percent of women suffer from anorexia, that 2 to 3 percent have bulimia, and that these rates are higher among female college students than among nonstudents (Fairburn & Brownell, 2002; Smolak & Thompson, 2009; Thompson, 2003).

This painting depicts a Greek myth in which Pygmalion, the king of Cyprus, sculpted his ideal woman in an ivory statue he called Galatea, illustrating the power of a self-fulfilling prophecy. Pygmalion fell in love with his creation, caressed it, adorned it with jewelry, and eventually brought it to life.

▶ **FIGURE 9.3**

When Being Seen Leads to Disbelief

People who believed they were physically unattractive were more likely to cite the quality of their work as the reason for receiving a positive evaluation when they thought they were seen by the evaluator. However, people who believed they were attractive were less likely to credit the quality of their work when they thought they were seen.

Major & Konar, 1984.

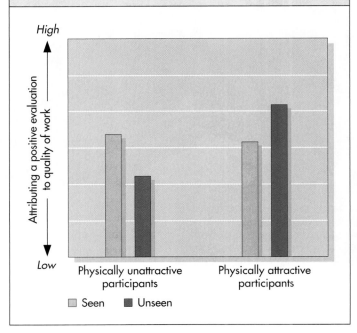

Women are more likely than men to suffer from what Janet Polivy and others (1986) once called the "modern mania for slenderness." This slender ideal is regularly projected in the mass media. Studies have shown that young women who see magazine ads or TV commercials that feature ultra-thin models become more dissatisfied with their own bodies than those who view neutral materials (Posavac et al., 1998). Trying to measure up to the multimillion-dollar supermodels can only prove frustrating to most. What's worse, the cultural ideal for thinness may be set early in childhood. Several years ago, Kevin Norton and his colleagues (1996) projected the life-size dimensions of the original Ken and Barbie dolls that are popular all over the world. They found that both were unnaturally thin compared with the average young adult. In fact, the estimated odds that any young woman would have Barbie's shape are approximately 1 in 100,000.

In sum, being beautiful may be a mixed blessing. There are some real benefits that cannot be denied, but there may be some costs as well. This tradeoff makes you wonder about the long-term effects. Some years ago, Ellen Berscheid and others (1972) compared the physical attractiveness levels of college students (based on yearbook pictures) to their adjustment when they reached middle age. There was little relationship between their appearance in youth and their later happiness. Those who were especially good-looking in college were more likely to be married, but they were not more satisfied with marriage or more content with life. Beauty may confer advantage, but it is not destiny.

> People who are physically attractive are happier and have higher self-esteem than those who are unattractive. **FALSE.**

First Encounters: Getting Acquainted

Speed dating is a fascinating new platform for men and women who are looking for a romantic relationship. In speed-dating events, individuals pay to have between ten and twenty-five very brief "dates" lasting no more than four minutes. After rotating like clockwork from one partner to another, participants—who wear nametags—let the event hosts know which partners, if any, they'd be interested in seeing again. If two participants double-match, the host provides each with the other's contact information so they can schedule a real date (Finkel & Eastwick, 2008).

For a first encounter, does speed dating provide people with enough information? Is four minutes enough time for you to determine if you are romantically attracted to someone? To be sure, you get an up-close-and-personal look at a person's physical appearance. But then what other information would you want? Proximity boosts the odds that we will meet someone, familiarity puts us at ease, and beauty draws us in like magnets to a first encounter. But what determines whether sparks will fly in the early getting-acquainted stages of a relationship? In this section, we consider three characteristics of others that can influence our attraction: similarity, reciprocity, and being hard to get.

Speed dating is a recent phenomenon that can be found all over the world. In London, pictured here, men and women gather for quick pairings in a round robin series of "dates."

© Caroline Cortizo/Alamy

Liking Others Who Are Similar   The problem with proverbial wisdom is that it often contradicts itself. Common sense tells us that "birds of a feather flock together." Yet we also hear that "opposites attract." So which is it? Before answering this question, imagine sitting at a computer, meeting someone in an online chat room, and striking up a conversation about school, sports, restaurants, movies, where you live, where you've traveled, or your favorite band—and you realize that the two of you have a lot in common. Now imagine the opposite experience of chatting with someone who is very different in his or her background, interests, values, and outlook on life. Which of the two strangers would you want to meet, the one who is similar or the one who is different?

Over the years, research has consistently shown that people tend to associate with others who are similar to themselves (Montoya et al., 2008). The vast array of online dating sites illustrates the point. In addition to generic services such as Match.com, eHarmony, Compatible Partners, and HookUp.com, all sorts of specialty services are specifically designed to bring together people of like minds—hence, Conservative Match.com, LiberalHearts.com, Jdate.com, Christian Cafe.com, and HappyBuddhist.com.

Four types of similarity are most relevant. The first is demographic. On a whole range of demographic variables—such as age, education, race, religion, height, level of intelligence, and socioeconomic status—people who go together as friends, dates, lovers, or partners in marriage tend to resemble each other more than randomly paired couples (Warren, 1966). These correlations cannot be used to prove that similarity causes attraction. A more compelling case could be made, however, by first measuring people's demographic characteristics and then determining whether these people, when they met others, liked those who were similar to them more than those who were dissimilar. This is what Theodore Newcomb (1961) did. In an elaborate study, Newcomb set up an experimental college dormitory and found that students who had similar backgrounds grew to like each other more than those who were dissimilar did. Is demographic similarity still a factor even today, with all the choices we have in our diverse and multicultural society? Yes. Commenting on the persistently magnetic appeal of similarity, sociologist John Macionis (2003) notes that "Cupid's arrow is aimed by society more than we like to think." One unfortunate result, as we saw in Chapter 5, is that by associating only with similar others, people form social niches that are homogeneous and divided along the lines of race, ethnic background, age, religion, level of education, and occupation (McPherson et al., 2001).

People can also be similar in other ways, as when they share the same opinions, interests, and values. For example, what about the role of *attitude* similarity in attraction? Here, the time course is slower because people have to get to know each other first. In Newcomb's study, the link between actual similarity and liking increased gradually over the school year. Laboratory experiments have confirmed the point. For example, Donn Byrne (1971) had people give their opinions on a whole range of issues and then presented them with an attitude survey that had supposedly been filled out by another person (the responses were rigged). In study after study, he found that participants liked this other person better when they perceived his or her attitudes as being more similar to theirs (Byrne, 1997).

The link between attitudes and attraction is evident among newly married couples. In a comprehensive study, Shanhong Luo and Eva Klohnen (2005) tested 291 newlywed couples and found that people tended to marry others who shared

Cyberdating works because the courting process is reversed; people get to know each other from the inside out.
—Trish McDermott, Match.com

"I can't wait to see what you're like online."

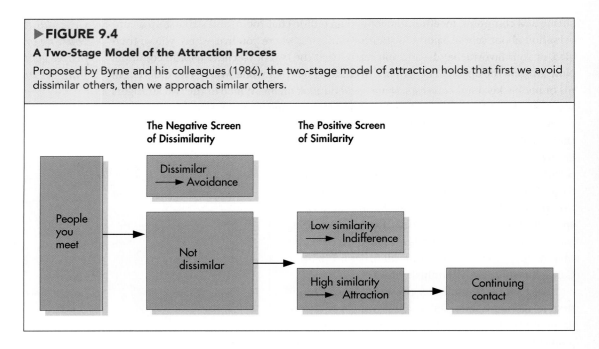

▶ **FIGURE 9.4**

A Two-Stage Model of the Attraction Process

Proposed by Byrne and his colleagues (1986), the two-stage model of attraction holds that first we avoid dissimilar others, then we approach similar others.

their political attitudes, religiosity, and values but who did not necessarily start out having similar personalities (for example, both being introverted or extroverted). Yet once in the relationship, similarities in personality became relevant: The more similar they were, the happier was the marriage. Clearly, birds of a feather both flock together and stay together. But wait. Does this necessarily mean that similarity breeds attraction, or might attraction breed similarity? In all likelihood, both mechanisms are at work. Luo and Klohnen compared couples who had been together for varying lengths of time before marriage and found that similarity was unrelated to the length of the relationship. Yet another study of dating couples showed that when partners who are close discover that they disagree on important moral issues, they bring their views on these issues into alignment and become more similar from that point on (Davis & Rusbult, 2001).

According to Milton Rosenbaum (1986), attraction researchers have overplayed the role of attitudinal similarity. Similarity does not spark attraction, he says. Rather, dissimilarity triggers repulsion: the desire to avoid someone. Rosenbaum maintains that people expect most others to be similar, which is why others who are different grab our attention. Taking this hypothesis one step further, David Lykken and Auke Tellegen (1993) argue that in mate selection, *all* forms of interpersonal similarity are irrelevant. After a person discards the 50 percent of the population who are least similar, they claim, a random selection process takes over.

So which is it: Are we turned on by others who are similar in their attitudes or are we turned off by those who are different? As depicted in ▶ Figure 9.4, Donn Byrne and his colleagues proposed a two-step model that takes both reactions into account. First, they claim, we avoid associating with others who are dissimilar; then, among those who remain, we are drawn to those who are most similar (Byrne et al., 1986; Smeaton et al., 1989). Our reactions may also be influenced by expectations. People expect similarity from ingroup members, like fellow Democrats or Republicans or fellow straights or gays. In a series of studies, Fang Chen and Douglas Kenrick (2002) found that research participants were particularly attracted to outgroup members who expressed similar attitudes and they were most repulsed by ingroup members who expressed dissimilar attitudes.

In addition to demographics and attitudes, a third source of similarity and difference is also at work, at least in romantic relationships. Have you ever noticed the way people react to couples in which one partner is a knockout and the other is not? Typically, we are startled by "mismatches" of this sort, as if expecting people to pair off with others who are similarly attractive—not more, not less. This reaction has a basis in reality. Early on, laboratory studies showed that both men and women yearn for partners who are highly attractive. Thus, when incoming first-year students at the University of Minnesota were randomly coupled for a dance, their desire for a second date was influenced more by their partner's physical attractiveness than by any other variable (Walster et al., 1966). In real-life situations, however, where one can be accepted or rejected by a prospective partner, people tend to shy away from making romantic overtures with others who seem "out of reach" (Berscheid et al., 1971; van Straaten et al., 2009). Correlational studies of couples who are dating, engaged, living together, or married support this "**matching hypothesis**": the idea that people tend to become involved romantically with others who are equivalent in their physical attractiveness (Feingold, 1988).

A fourth type of similarity can trigger attraction among strangers: a similarity in subjective experience. Imagine that a professor says something in class that strikes you as funny. You glance at the student next to you, who glances back, and the two of you burst out laughing, as if bonded by a private joke. Whenever two people who are at a common event laugh, cry, jump to their feet, cheer, shake their heads, or roll their eyes at the same time, they feel as if they have shared a subjective experience. Elizabeth Pinel and others (2006) called this experience "I-sharing" and theorized that people who I-share, even if they are otherwise dissimilar, feel a profound sense of connection to one another—like "kindred spirits." In a series of experiments, participants were asked to imagine themselves with a similar or dissimilar stranger with whom they did or did not react in the same way to an external event. Consistently, the participants liked the I-sharers more than everyone else, even when they had different backgrounds. The implications are intriguing. As Pinel and her colleagues (2006) put it, "A fundamentalist Christian and an atheist can find themselves enjoying the same sunset; a staunch Republican and an equally staunch Democrat can share a laugh. When two objectively different people I-share in these and other ways, their disliking for one another might lessen, if only for a moment" (p. 245).

Before concluding that similarity is the key to attraction, what about the old adage that opposites attract? Many years ago, sociologists proposed the *complementarity hypothesis*, which holds that people seek others whose needs "oppose" their own—that people who need to dominate, for example, are naturally drawn to those who are submissive (Winch et al., 1954). Is there any support for this view? Surprisingly, the answer is no. Of course, most human beings are romantically attracted to others of the opposite sex. But when it comes to fitting mutual needs and personality traits the way keys fit locks, research shows that complementarity does not make for compatible attraction (Gonzaga et al., 2007; Luo & Klohnen, 2005; O'Leary & Smith, 1991). In an interview with the *Washington Post*, Gian Gonzaga—a researcher for eHarmony, the online dating service that matches people according to similarities—debunked the complementarity hypothesis, noting that while opposites may seem exotic at first glance, over time the differences become difficult to negotiate (McCarthy, 2009).

Liking Others Who Like Us
Many years ago, Fritz Heider (1958) theorized that people prefer relationships that are psychologically "balanced" and that a state of imbalance causes distress. In groups of three or more individuals, a balanced social constellation

An estimated 44,000 couples a year get married after meeting on eHarmony.com—including Tanyalee and Joshua, pictured here. "I just remember hearing that number the first time and thinking that can't possibly be right," said Gian Gonzaga, a researcher for eHarmony. "We checked the numbers again and again and again. The idea that about 2 percent of all the marriages in the United States come out of our system? Really cool" (McCarthy, 2009).

When it comes to romantic relationships, opposites attract. **FALSE.**

matching hypothesis The proposition that people are attracted to others who are similar in physical attractiveness.

exists when we like someone whose relationships with others parallel our own. Thus, we want to like the friends of our friends and the enemies of our enemies (Aronson & Cope, 1968). If you've ever had a good friend who dated someone you detested, then you know how awkward and unpleasant an unbalanced relationship can be. The fact is, we don't expect our friends and enemies to get along (Chapdelaine et al., 1994).

Between two people, a state of balance exists when a relationship is character- ized by **reciprocity**: a mutual exchange between what we give and what we receive. Liking is mutual, which is why we tend to like others who indicate that they like us. In one experiment, Rebecca Curtis and Kim Miller (1986) brought pairs of students into the laboratory, arranged for them to talk, and then "revealed" to one member in each pair that he or she was liked by the partner or disliked. When the students were later reunited for conversation, those who thought that they were liked were, in turn, warmer, more agreeable, and more self-disclosing. Feeling liked is important. When groups of men and women were asked to reflect on how they fell in love or developed friendships with specific people, many spontaneously said they had been turned on initially by the realization that they were liked (Aron et al., 1989).

But does reciprocity mean simply that the more people like us, the more we will like them back? Many years ago, Elliot Aronson and Darwyn Linder (1965) conducted an interesting study in which female college students met in pairs several times to discuss various topics. In each pair, one student was a research participant and her partner was a confederate. After each meeting, the participant overheard a follow-up conversation between the experimenter and the confederate in which she was dis- cussed and evaluated. Over time, the confederate's evaluation of the participant either was consistently positive or negative or underwent a change, either from negative to positive (gain) or from positive to negative (loss). Put yourself in the participant's shoes. All else being equal, in which condition would you like your partner most? In this study, participants liked the partner more when her evaluation changed from negative to positive than when it was positive all along. As long as the "conversion" is gradual and believable, people like others more when their affection takes time to earn than when it comes easily.

Pursuing Those Who Are Hard to Get   The Aronson and Linder (1965) finding suggests that we like others who are socially selective. This seems to support the popu- lar notion that you can spark romantic interest by playing hard to get. A few years ago, Ellen Fein and Sherri Schneider (1996) wrote a paperback book for women seductively titled *The Rules: Time-Tested Secrets for Capturing the Heart of Mr. Right*. What were the rules? Here's one: "Don't call him and rarely return his calls." Here's another: "Let him take the lead." In all cases, the theme was that men are charmed by women who are hard to get. It's an interesting hypothesis.

Despite intuition, researchers found that the **hard-to-get effect** is harder to get than originally anticipated (Walster et al., 1973). One problem is that we are turned *off* by those who reject us because they are committed to someone else or have no interest in us (Wright & Contrada, 1986). Another problem is that we tend to prefer people who are moderately selective compared with those who are nonselective (they have poor taste or low standards) or too selective (they are snobs). In a study that illustrates the point, researchers arranged for male and female college students to have four-minute speed dates with ten or so other students of the opposite sex, after which they all rated each other and indicated on a website if they were interested in meeting again. Analyses of the ratings showed that participants liked dates who selectively desired them more than others, but they did not like nondiscriminating dates who had indicated a desire for several of the men they encountered (Eastwick & Finkel, 2008).

reciprocity   A mutual exchange between what we give and receive—for example, liking those who like us.

hard-to-get effect   The tendency to prefer people who are highly selective in their social choices over those who are more readily available.

Now suppose that someone you are interested in is hard to get for external reasons. What if a desired relationship is opposed or forbidden by parents, as in the story of Romeo and Juliet? What about a relationship threatened by catastrophe, as in the love story portrayed in the 1997 movie *Titanic*? What about distance, a lack of time, or renewed interest from a partner's old flame? As you may recall from Chapter 6, the theory of psychological reactance states that people are highly motivated to protect their freedom to choose and behave as they please. When a valued freedom is threatened (not getting the object of one's affection), people reassert themselves, often by wanting that which is unavailable too much—like the proverbial forbidden fruit (Brehm & Brehm, 1981).

Consider what happens when you think that your chance to get a date for the evening is slipping away. Is it true, to quote country-western musician Mickey Gilley, that "the girls all get prettier at closing time"? To find out, researchers entered some bars in Texas and asked patrons three times during the night to rate the physical attractiveness of other patrons of the same and opposite sex. As Gilley's lyrics suggested, people of the opposite sex were seen as more attractive as the night wore on (Pennebaker et al., 1979). The study is cute, but the correlation between time and attraction can be interpreted in other ways (perhaps attractiveness ratings rise with blood-alcohol levels!). In a follow-up study, Scott Madey and his colleagues (1996) also had patrons in a bar make attractiveness ratings throughout the night. They found that these ratings increased as the night wore on only among patrons who were not committed to a relationship. As reactance theory would predict, closing time posed a threat—which sparked desire—only to those on the lookout for a late-night date.

Consistent with reactance theory, studies conducted in bars like this have shown that men and women who are not in committed relationships see each other as more attractive as the night wears on.

Another possible instance of passion fueled by reactance can be seen in "the allure of secret relationships." In a clever experiment, Daniel Wegner and others (1994) paired up male and female college students to play bridge. Within each foursome, one couple was instructed in writing to play footsie under the table, either secretly or in the open. Got the picture? After a few minutes, the game was stopped and the players were asked to indicate privately how attracted they were to their own partner and to the opposite-sex member of the other team. The result: Students who played footsie in secret were more attracted to each other than those who played in the open or not at all. This finding is certainly consistent with reactance theory. But there may be more to it. First, as we'll see later, the thrill of engaging in a forbidden act, or the sheer excitement of having to keep a secret, may help fan the flames of attraction. Second, it is important to realize that over time keeping a secret romance from others can become so much of a burden that the relationship itself will suffer (Foster & Campbell, 2005).

Finally, it's important to realize that sometimes reactance reduces interpersonal attraction. Have you ever tried to play the matchmaker by insisting that two of your unattached single friends get together? Be forewarned: Setting people up can backfire. Determined to preserve the freedom to make their own romantic choices, your friends may become *less* attracted to each other than they would have been without your encouragement (Wright et al., 1992).

■ Mate Selection: The Evolution of Desire

Before moving on to the topic of close relationships, let's stop and consider this question: When it comes to the search for a short-term or long-term mate, are men and women similarly motivated? If not, what are the differences? Later in this chapter,

"Gee, but I miss the heightened eroticism of those five and a half years of conjugal visits."

we'll see that most men appear to be more sex-driven than most women, desiring more frequent and more casual sex, more partners, and more variety, all of which leads researchers in the area to conclude that "men desire sex more than women" (Baumeister et al., 2001, p. 270).

The Evolutionary Perspective   Why do these sex differences exist, and what do they mean? In *The Evolution of Desire*, David Buss (2003) argues that the answer can be derived from evolutionary psychology. According to this perspective, human beings all over the world exhibit mate-selection patterns that favor the conception, birth, and survival of their offspring—and women and men, by necessity, employ different strategies to achieve that common goal (Buss & Schmitt, 1993; Gangestad & Simpson, 2000; Trivers, 1972).

According to Buss, women must be highly selective because they are biologically limited in the number of children they can bear and raise in a lifetime. A woman must, therefore, protect her children and so searches for a mate who possesses (or has the potential to possess) economic resources and is willing to commit those resources to support her offspring. The result is that women should be attracted to men who are older and financially secure or who have ambition, intelligence, stability, and other traits predictive of future success.

In contrast, men can father an unlimited number of children and can ensure their reproductive success by inseminating many women. Men are restricted, however, by their ability to attract fertile partners and by their lack of certainty as to whether the babies born are actually their own. With these motives springing from their evolutionary past, men seek out women who are young and physically attractive (having smooth skin, full lips, lustrous hair, good muscle tone, and other youthful features)—attributes that signal health and reproductive fertility. To minimize their paternal uncertainty, men should also favor chastity, pursuing women they think will be sexually faithful rather than promiscuous.

In an initial test of this theory, Buss (1989) and a team of researchers surveyed 10,047 men and women in thirty-seven cultures in North and South America, Asia, Africa, Eastern and Western Europe, and the Pacific. All respondents were asked to rank-order and rate the importance of various attributes in choosing a mate. The results were consistent with predictions. Both men and women gave equally high ratings to certain attributes, such as "having a pleasant disposition." In the vast majority of countries, however, "good looks" and "no previous experience in sexual intercourse" were valued more by men, whereas "good financial prospect" and "ambitious and industrious" were more important to women. Analyses of personal ads appearing in magazines and newspapers have similarly revealed that in the dating marketplace the "deal" is that women offer beauty, while men offer wealth (Feingold, 1992a; Rajecki et al., 1991; Sprecher et al., 1994). In the words of one investigator, the search for a heterosexual mate seems to feature "men as success objects and women as sex objects" (Davis, 1990).

Some researchers have suggested that these gendered preferences are not mere luxuries but are actually necessities in the mating marketplace. In Buss's (1989) study, men were more likely to prefer good looks and women were more likely to prefer good financial prospects, but both sexes saw other characteristics—such as being funny, dependable, and kind—as more important. But what happens in real life, where mate seekers who can't have it all must prioritize their desires? Studying "the necessities and luxuries in mate preferences," Norman Li and others (2002) asked participants to design their ideal marriage partner by purchasing different characteristics using "mate dollars." In some cases, they were granted a large budget to work with; in other cases, the budget was limited. In the large-budget condition, men spent somewhat more play money on physical attractiveness and women spent somewhat more on social status, but both were just as interested in a partner who was kind, lively, and creative. In the low-budget condition, however, men spent even more of their play money on physical attractiveness and women spent even more on social status. When mate seekers can't have it all and must therefore focus on what's most important, they prioritize their choices in the ways predicted by evolutionary theory (see ▶ Figure 9.5).

Also consistent with the evolutionary perspective is a universal tendency for men to seek younger women (who are most likely to be fertile) and for women to desire older men (who are most likely to have financial resources). Buss (1989) found this age-preference discrepancy in all the cultures he studied, with men on average wanting to marry women who were 2.7 years younger and women wanting men who were 3.4 years older. Based on their analysis of personal ads, Douglas Kenrick and Richard Keefe (1992) found that men in their twenties are equally interested in younger women and slightly older women still of fertile age. But men in their thirties seek out women who are five years younger, while men in their fifties prefer women ten to twenty years younger. In contrast, girls and women of all ages are attracted to men who are older than they are. These patterns can also be seen in marriage statistics taken from different cultures and generations. There is one interesting exception: Teenage boys say they are most attracted to women who are slightly *older* than they are, women in their fertile twenties (Kenrick et al., 1996).

One might think that the mate preferences predicted by evolutionary theory would be limited to fertile men and women of youth. Not so. Recently, 600 Yahoo!

Men seek to propagate widely, whereas women seek to propagate wisely.

—Robert Hinde

▶ FIGURE 9.5

Sex Differences in Mate Preference: Evolutionary Necessities?

In this study, participants built an ideal mate by "purchasing" characteristics. When they were given a large budget, men spent a somewhat higher percentage of money on physical attractiveness and women spent somewhat more on social status than on other characteristics. On a low budget, however, men spent even more on physical attractiveness and women spent even more on social status.

Li et al., 2002.

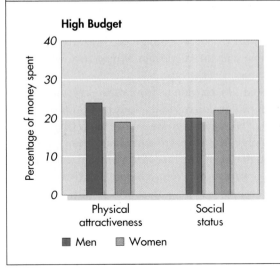
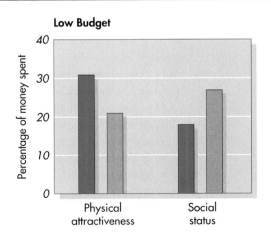

High Budget

Low Budget

Percentage of money spent

■ Men ■ Women

Joel Sartore/National Geographic Image Collection

This young man spies through his sunglasses at women on the beach. From an evolutionary perspective, his attraction is biologically (though not consciously) driven by the search for a fertile reproductive partner.

personal ads were analyzed from four age groups: 20 to 34, 40 to 54, 60-74, and 75+ years. At all ages, men were more likely than women to offer information about their own educational, employment, and income status. They were also more likely to seek indications of physical attractiveness. The older they were, the more the men wanted increasingly younger women. In contrast, women of all ages were more likely to seek out status information and men who were older (at least until the women were 75, at which point they sought men younger than themselves). Apparently, in the United States, the mate preferences predicted by evolutionary theory persist throughout the life span (Alterovitz & Mendelsohn, 2009).

Also supportive of evolutionary theory is research on *jealousy*, "the dangerous passion"—a negative emotional state that arises from a perceived threat to one's relationship. Although jealousy is a common and normal human reaction, men and women may be aroused by different triggering events. According to the theory, a man should be most upset by *sexual* infidelity because a wife's extramarital affair increases the risk that the children he supports are not his own. In contrast, a woman should feel threatened more by *emotional* infidelity because a husband who falls in love with another woman might leave and withdraw his financial support (Buss, 2000).

A number of studies support this hypothesis. In one, male and female college students were asked whether they would be more upset if their romantic partner were to form a deep emotional attachment or have sex with another person. Think for a moment about this choice. Which situation would *you* find more distressing? The results revealed a striking gender difference: 60 percent of the men said they would be more upset by a partner's sexual infidelity, but 83 percent of the women felt that emotional infidelity was worse (Buss et al., 1992). This difference seems to reveal itself whenever men and women are asked which type of infidelity is more upsetting (Schützwohl, 2004; Shackelford et al., 2004).

In a second study, newly married husbands and wives were interviewed about how they would react if they suspected their partner of cheating. Interestingly, the men said they would use more "mate-retention" tactics (concealing or threatening the wife or taking action against the male rival) when their wives were young and attractive. In contrast, women said they would use more mate-retention tactics (being watchful or enhancing their appearance) when married to men who strove for status and made more money (Buss & Shackelford, 1997).

In a third study, male and female students were asked to imagine their girlfriend or boyfriend flirting at a party with a person of the opposite sex—someone depicted as attractive or unattractive and as socially dominant or submissive. The result: Men said they would be most jealous and upset when their imagined rival was dominant and had status, while women were most jealous when their female rival was young and physically attractive (Dijkstra & Buunk, 1998).

In a fourth study, researchers studied 398 individuals from various countries who had been clinically diagnosed with "morbid jealousy." Using information provided in published case histories, they found that whereas men were more likely than women to accuse their partners of sexual infidelity, women were more likely than men to be upset over emotional infidelity. Although only a few case histories contained details concerning the feared rival, jealous men were more likely to report that their rival had greater status and/or resources, while jealous women were more likely to report that their rival was younger and/or more attractive (Easton et al., 2007).

Sociocultural Perspectives   Although the gender differences are intriguing, critics of the evolutionary approach are quick to argue that some of the results can be interpreted in terms that are "psychological" rather than "evolutionary." One common argument is that women trade youth and beauty for money not for reproductive purposes but rather because they often lack *direct* access to economic power. With this hypothesis in mind, Steven Gangestad (1993) examined women's access to wealth in each of the countries in Buss's cross-cultural study. He found that the more economic power women had, the more important male physical attractiveness was to them. This result suggests that it may be the generally low social and economic status of women relative to men that leads them to care less about the physical attributes of a potential mate.

Another argument concerns the finding that men are more fearful of a mate's sexual infidelity (which threatens paternal certainty) while women worry more about emotional infidelity (which threatens future support). The difference is consistent, but what does it mean? There are two criticisms. First, in contrast to the explanation evolutionary theory provides, some researchers have found that men become more upset over sexual infidelity not because of uncertain paternity but because they reasonably assume that a married woman who has a sexual affair is also likely to have intimate feelings for her extramarital partner. In other words, the man's concern, like the woman's, may be over threats to the relationship, not about fatherhood issues (DeSteno & Salovey 1996; Harris & Christenfeld, 1996). Second, although men and women react differently when asked to imagine a partner's sexual or emotional infidelity, they are equally more upset by emotional infidelity when asked to recall actual experiences from a past relationship (Harris, 2002). At present, then, researchers continue to debate what the observed gender differences in romantic jealousy mean and the evolutionary model that is used to explain them (Harris, 2005; Sagarin, 2005).

A third argument is that the self-report differences typically found between the sexes are small compared to the similarities. This is an important point. In Buss's original cross-cultural study, both men and women gave their highest ratings to such attributes as kindness, dependability, a good sense of humor, and a pleasant disposition (physical attractiveness and financial prospects did not top the lists). In fact, research shows that women desire physical attractiveness as much as men do when asked about what they want in a short-term casual sex partner (Li & Kenrick, 2006; Regan & Berscheid, 1997).

Even more limiting is the question of whether the *stated* preferences reported in the Buss (1989) surveys match the *actual* preferences when people find themselves face to face with real flesh-and-blood partners. In a recent study, Paul Eastwick and Eli Finkel (2008) recruited men and women for a speed-dating event. Beforehand, they asked participants about their preferences for an ideal partner. Replicating the usual effect, men were more likely to cite "physically attractive" and women were more likely to cite "earning prospects." Yet the romantic attraction ratings of partners during and after the speed dating revealed that the differences among male and female participants about what characteristics were important had disappeared. In theory, men and women enacted the different roles cast by evolution; yet in practice, their attraction to others was based on similar characteristics. These results can be seen in ▶ Figure 9.6.

Finally, the sex differences often observed are neither predictable nor universal. Human societies are remarkably flexible in terms of the ways people adapt to their environments, and there are revealing exceptions to the rules that are supposed to govern human play on the evolutionary field. For example, David Geary (2000) points out that while human fathers spend less time doing child care than mothers do, they are unique among mammals—including baboons and chimpanzees, our evolutionary cousins—in the amount of care they give to their offspring. Geary speculates that

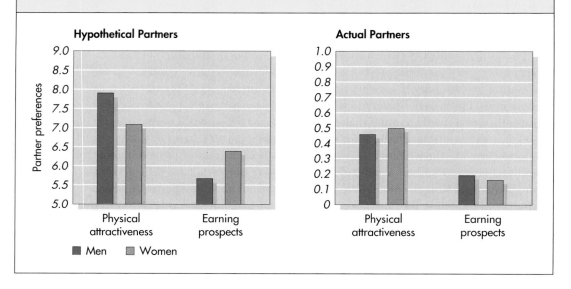

▶ **FIGURE 9.6**

Evolutionary Mate Preferences: In Theory and in Practice

Before they engaged in speed-dating, male and female participants stated their preferences for an ideal partner. Consistent with the evolutionary perspective, males were more likely to cite "physically attractive" and females were more likely to cite "earning prospects" (left). In ratings of actual speed-dating partners, however, male and female participants did not differ in their preferences for these characteristics (right).

Finkel & Eastwick, 2008.

human men care for their children in part because they enjoy more paternal certainty than do other male primates.

Consider, too, the puzzling observation that most women of the Bari tribe in Venezuela are highly promiscuous. From an evolutionary standpoint, this behavior does not seem adaptive since women who "sleep around" may scare off potential mates fearful of wasting their resources on children who are not their own. So why is female promiscuity the norm in this culture? In *Cultures of Multiple Fathers*, anthropologists Stephen Beckerman, Paul Valentine, and others note that the Bari and other aboriginal people in lowland South America believe that a baby can have multiple fathers and that all men who have sex with a pregnant woman make a biological contribution to the unborn child (some groups assume that more than one father, or at least more than one insemination, are *required* to form a fetus). Thus, by taking many lovers a woman increases the number of men who will provide for her child. It appears that this strategy works. A multi-fathered Bari child is 16 percent more likely than a single-fathered child to survive to the age of 15 (Beckerman & Valentine, 2002).

Summing Up   The evolutionary perspective offers social psychologists an interesting but controversial perspective on relationships. The approach continues to draw criticism that the results are weak, limited, or explainable by nonevolutionary means (Harris, 2003; Hazan & Diamond, 2000; Pedersen et al., 2002). However, it also continues to generate new ideas. Currently, scientists in this area are studying a range of issues, such as the possible links between facial appearance and health and fertility (Geary, 2005; Grammer et al., 2005; Weeden & Sabini, 2005); the flexibility or "plasticity" of sexual orientation in men and women (Baumeister, 2000; Lippa, 2006); the potentially deadly link between sexual jealousy and violence (Buss, 2000); the reason that some men refuse to make child support payments (Shackelford et al.,

2005); women's ability to detect and prefer men who are intelligent (Prokosch et al., 2009); and the various sexual motives that can pull our attention toward physically attractive members of the opposite or same sex (Maner et al., 2007).

Close Relationships

Being attracted to people can be exhilarating or frustrating, depending on how the initial encounters develop. How important is a good relationship to you? Researchers asked 300 students to weigh the importance of having a satisfying romantic relationship against the importance of other life goals (such as getting a good education, having a successful career, or contributing to a better society) and found that 73 percent said they would sacrifice most other goals before giving up a good relationship (Hammersla & Frease-McMahan, 1990).

Intimate relationships often involve three basic components: (1) feelings of attachment, affection, and love; (2) fulfillment of psychological needs; and (3) interdependence between partners, each of whom has a meaningful influence on the other. Although people have many significant relationships in their lives that contain one or more of these components, social psychologists have concentrated their research on friends, dating partners, lovers, and married couples (Berscheid & Regan, 2004; Hendrick & Hendrick, 2000; Miller & Perlman, 2009; Sprecher et al., 2008).

Not all intimate relationships contain all three ingredients. A summer romance is emotionally intense, but in the fall, both partners resume their separate lives. An "empty shell" marriage revolves around coordinated daily activities; but emotional attachment is weak and psychological needs go unmet. Clearly, relationships come in different shapes and sizes. Some are sexual; others are not. Some involve partners of the same sex; others, partners of the opposite sex. Some partners commit to a future together; others drop by for a brief stay. Feelings run the gamut from joyful to painful and from loving to hateful, with emotional intensity ranging all the way from mild to megawatt.

How do we advance from our first encounters to the intimate relationships that warm our lives? Do we proceed gradually over time, in stages, step by step, or by leaps and bounds? According to one perspective, relationships progress in order through a series of stages. For example, Bernard Murstein's (1986) *stimulus-value-role (SVR) theory* says there are three: (1) the stimulus stage, in which attraction is sparked by external attributes such as physical appearance; (2) the value stage, in which attachment is based on similarity of values and beliefs; and (3) the role stage, in which commitment is based on the performance of such roles as husband and wife. All three factors are important throughout a relationship, but each one is said to be first and foremost during only one stage.

In evaluating any stage theory, the critical issue is *sequence.* Does the value stage always precede the role stage or might a couple work out roles before exploring whether their values are compatible? Most researchers do not believe that intimate relationships progress through a fixed sequence of stages. What, then, accounts for how they change? Every relationship has a developmental history with ups and downs, stalls and accelerations. What pushes a relationship up, pulls it down, or keeps it steady? One common answer is *rewards.* Love, like attraction, depends on the experience of

The Bari tribeswomen of Venezuela are sexually promiscuous. The Bari believe that a baby can have multiple fathers, so being promiscuous enables a woman to secure child support from many men. This exception to the evolutionary norm illustrates that human behavior is flexible and that people can develop mating strategies to suit their cultural environment.

intimate relationship A close relationship between two adults involving emotional attachment, fulfillment of psychological needs, or interdependence.

positive emotions in the presence of a partner. Step by step, as the rewards pile up, love develops. Or, as rewards diminish, love erodes. In reward theories of love, quantity counts. But some would disagree. Think about your own relationships. Are your feelings toward someone you love simply a more intense version of your feelings toward someone you like? Is the love of a close friend the same as the love of a romantic partner? If not, then you can appreciate that there are qualitative differences among relationships. Both views have something to offer. Progress on the road from attraction to love depends on the quantity of fuel in the tank *and* on the kind of engine providing the power. The next section examines the reward-based approach to building a relationship. Then we consider differences among the various types of relationships.

▌▌ The Intimate Marketplace: Tracking the Gains and Losses

Earlier, we saw that people are initially attracted to others who provide them with direct or indirect rewards. But is "What's in it for me?" still important in a relationship that has blossomed and grown? Can an economic approach be used to predict the future of a close relationship?

Social Exchange Theory **Social exchange theory** is an economic model of human behavior according to which people are motivated by a desire to maximize profit and minimize loss in their social relationships just as they are in business (Homans, 1961; Thibaut & Kelley, 1959). The basic premise is simple: Relationships that provide more rewards and fewer costs will be more satisfying and endure longer. Between intimates, the rewards include love, companionship, consolation in times of distress, and sexual gratification if the relationship is of this nature. The costs include the work it takes to maintain a relationship, work though conflict, compromise, and sacrifice opportunities elsewhere.

The development of an intimate relationship is very clearly associated with the overall level of rewards and costs. Research has shown that dating couples who experience greater increases in rewards as their relationship progresses are more likely to stay together than are those who experience small increases or declines (Berg & McQuinn, 1986). People do not worry about costs during the honeymoon phase of a relationship (Hays, 1985). After a few months, however, both rewards and costs start to contribute to levels of satisfaction, both in married couples (Margolin & Wampold, 1981) and in gay and lesbian couples who are living together (Kurdek, 1991a).

Rewards and costs do not arise in a psychological vacuum. People bring to their relationships certain expectations about the balance sheet to which they are entitled. John Thibaut and Harold Kelley (1959) coined the term *comparison level (CL)* to refer to this average expected outcome in relationships. A person with a high CL expects his or her relationships to be rewarding; someone with a low CL does not. Situations that meet or exceed a person's expectations are more satisfying than those that fall short. Even a bad relationship can look pretty good to someone who has a low CL.

According to Thibaut and Kelley, a second kind of expectation is also important. They coined the term *comparison level for alternatives (CLalt)* to refer to people's expectations about what they would receive in an alternative situation. If the rewards available elsewhere are believed to be high, a person will be less committed to staying in the

"I've done the numbers, and I will marry you."

social exchange theory A perspective that views people as motivated to maximize benefits and minimize costs in their relationships with others.

present relationship (Drigotas & Rusbult, 1992). If people perceive that they have few acceptable alternatives (a low CLalt), they will tend to remain, even in an unsatisfying relationship that fails to meet expectations (CL).

Of course, just as these alternatives can influence our commitment, a sense of commitment can influence our perceptions of the alternatives. If you have ever been in love, you probably were not cold, calculating, and altogether objective in your perceptions of the alternatives. In close and intimate relationships, we tend to act like lovers, not scientists, and harbor positive illusions. Research shows that people who are in love tend to see other prospective partners as less appealing (Johnson & Rusbult, 1989; Simpson et al., 1990). They also tend to see their own partners and relationships through rose-colored glasses (Collins & Feeney 2000; Gagne & Lydon, 2001; Sanderson & Evans, 2001). Fully aware of the bias that love brings, people expect to be judged in this way by their partners (Boyes & Fletcher, 2007). Having a generally positive perspective on one's partner is thus conducive to a happy and stable relationship (Murray et al., 1996; Murray & Holmes, 1999), except when people are in denial about their partners and incorrect in their perceptions of their partners' specific characteristics (Neff & Karney, 2005).

A third element in the social exchange is investment. An *investment* is something a person puts into a relationship that he or she cannot recover if the relationship ends. If you don't like the way an intimate relationship is working out, you can pack your clothes, grab your laptop or DVD player, and drive away. But what about all the time you put into trying to make the relationship last? What about all the romantic and career opportunities you sacrificed along the way? As you might expect, investments increase commitment. Because of those things we can't take with us, we're more likely to stay (Rusbult & Buunk, 1993).

Over the years, research has shown that the building blocks of the social exchange framework—as depicted in ▶ Figure 9.7 and as incorporated into Caryl Rusbult et al.'s (1998) investment model—can be used to determine the level of commitment

▶ **FIGURE 9.7**

Relational Building Blocks

The building blocks of social exchange are rewards, costs, comparison level for alternatives, and investments. These factors are strongly associated with the satisfaction and commitment partners experience in their relationship.

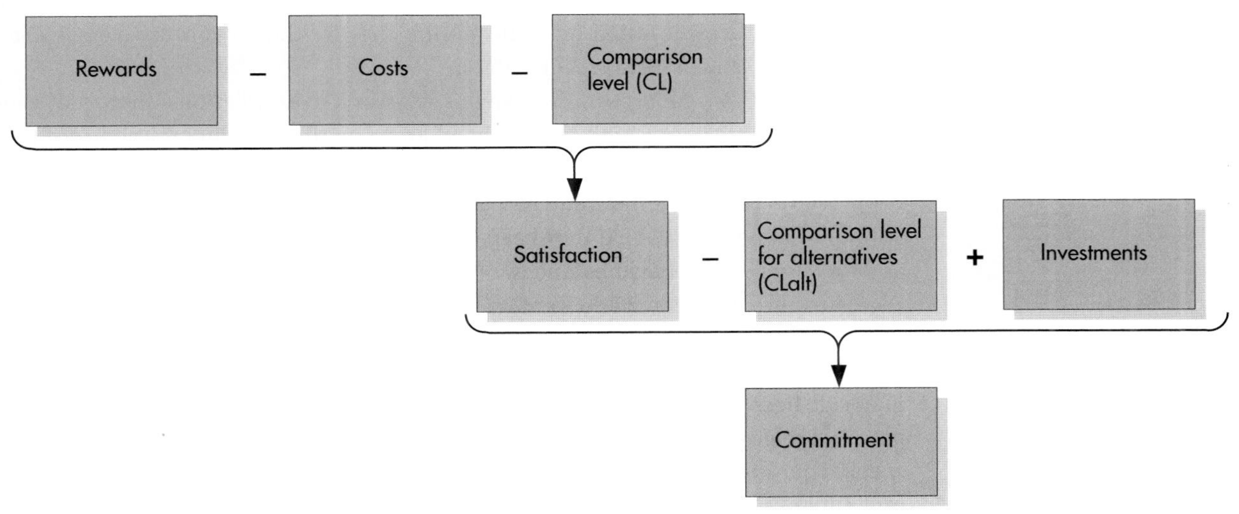

partners bring to a relationship (Le & Agnew, 2003). This model is important because commitment levels predict how long relationships will last. In studies of dating and married couples, research shows that the best-adjusted ones are those in which each partner is committed and sees the other as mutually committed (Drigotas et al., 1999). Particularly important for the durability of a relationship, people who are committed are more likely to forgive and forget when their partners betray a spoken or unspoken relationship norm by flirting, lying, forgetting an anniversary, revealing a private and embarrassing story in public, or having an affair (Finkel et al., 2002). Unfortunately, there are times when commitment can be a trap. A study of battered women showed that the investment model can be used to predict whether battered women will remain in an abusive relationship (Rhatigan & Axsom, 2006).

Equity Theory   **Equity theory** provides a special version of how social exchange operates in interpersonal interactions (Adams, 1965; Messick & Cook, 1983; Walster et al., 1978). According to this theory, an equitable relationship is a matter of social justice (Hatfield et al., 2008). All over the world, people are most content when the ratio between what they get out of a relationship (benefits) and what they put into it (contributions) is similar for both partners. Thus, the basic equity formula is:

$$\frac{\text{Your Benefits}}{\text{Your Contributions}} = \frac{\text{Your Partner's Benefits}}{\text{Your Partner's Contributions}}$$

Equity is different from equality. According to equity theory, the balance is what counts. So if one partner benefits more from a relationship but also makes a greater contribution, then the situation is equitable. In an inequitable relationship, the balance is disturbed: One partner (called the *overbenefited*) receives more benefits than he or she deserves on the basis of contributions made, while the other partner (aptly called the *underbenefited*) receives fewer benefits than deserved.

Both overbenefit and underbenefit are unstable and often unhappy states. As you might expect, underbenefited partners feel angry and resentful because they are giving more than their partner for the benefits they receive, while overbenefited partners feel guilty because they are profiting unfairly. Both kinds of inequity are associated with negative emotions in dating couples (Walster et al., 1978), married couples (Schafer & Keith, 1981; Guerrero et al., 2008), and friendships among elderly widows (Rook, 1987). When it comes to satisfaction with a relationship, as you might expect, it is more unpleasant to feel underbenefited than overbenefited. People prefer to receive too much in life rather than too little, even if they feel bad about it (Grote & Clark, 2001; Hatfield et al., 1982; Sprecher, 2001).

If equity is so important, then any partner in a close relationship may at times feel a need to restore the balance sheet when he or she is feeling inferior as if he or she is falling short, or insecure. According to Sandra Murray and John Holmes (2008), people in relationships naturally and unconsciously maintain something of a "trust-insurance system" by which they keep a tally of costs and benefits in order to detect and then repair possible imbalances.

Murray and others (2009) went on to demonstrate the process in a series of studies of newlyweds. In one of these studies, more than 200 married couples, averaging 27 years of age, were recruited from local city clerk's offices when they applied for their marriage license. Each couple had been married for less than six months. All participants were given a personal digital assistant for keeping a daily diary by answering specific questions—about their feelings, behaviors, and doubts about the marriage— each night before going to bed. By tracking and statistically correlating each partner's answers over time, the researchers observed three steps of the trust-insurance sys-

equity theory   The theory that people are most satisfied with a relationship when the ratio between benefits and contributions is similar for both partners.

tem in action: (1) On days after participants anxiously felt that they were not good enough for their partner, they were more likely to make sacrifices—for example, by doing the dishes, making lunch, or picking up after the partner; (2) these restorative actions were accompanied by lowered feelings of inferiority that same day; and (3) on the next day, the partners who benefited from these actions expressed fewer doubts about their marriage.

Types of Relationships

Social exchange models focus on quantity: The more (rewards, equity), the better (satisfaction, endurance). But is reward always necessary? And what about qualitative differences in our relationships? Does more reward turn casual acquaintances into friends, and friends into lovers, or are these types of relationships different from each other?

Exchange and Communal Relationships According to Margaret Clark and her colleagues, people operate by a reward-based model when they are in **exchange relationships**, which are characterized by an immediate tit-for-tat repayment of benefits. In these situations, people want costs to be quickly offset by compensation, leaving the balance at zero. But not all relationships fit this mold. Clark maintains that in **communal relationships**, partners respond to each other's needs and well-being over time and in different ways, without regard for whether they have given or received a benefit (Clark, 1984; Clark & Mills, 1979).

Exchange relationships typically exist between strangers and casual acquaintances and in certain long-term arrangements such as business partnerships. In contrast, strong communal relationships are usually limited to close friends, romantic partners, and family members (Clark & Mills, 1993). Based on fieldwork in West Africa, Alan Fiske (1992) is convinced that this distinction applies to human interactions all over the world. But the cynics among us wonder: Are communal relationships truly free of social exchange considerations? Can people really give without any desire to receive, or do partners in a communal relationship follow a more subtle version of social exchange, assuming that the benefits will balance out in the long run? Clark and Judson Mills (1993) believe that true communal relationships do exist—that once a communal norm has been adopted in a relationship, regardless of how it started, the motivation to respond to the other's needs becomes automatic.

Secure and Insecure Attachment Styles Another interesting approach to understanding relationships is provided by Phillip Shaver, Cindy Hazan, and their colleagues, who have theorized that just as infants display different kinds of attachment toward their parents, adults also exhibit specific **attachment styles** in their romantic relationships (Cassidy & Shaver, 1999; Mikulincer & Shaver, 2007; Rholes & Simpson, 2004).

For many years, child development psychologists had noticed that infants form intense, exclusive bonds with their primary caretakers. This first relationship is highly charged with emotion, and it emerges with regularity from one culture to the next. By observing the way babies react to both separations from and reunions with the primary caretaker, usually the mother, researchers also noticed that babies have different attachment styles. Those with *secure* attachments cry in distress when the mother leaves and then beam with sheer delight when she returns. Those with *insecure* attachments show one of two patterns. Some babies, described as anxious, cling and cry when the mother leaves but then greet her with anger or apathy upon her return. Others are generally more detached and *avoidant*, not reacting much on either occasion (Ainsworth et al., 1978).

exchange relationship
A relationship in which the participants expect and desire strict reciprocity in their interactions.

communal relationship
A relationship in which the participants expect and desire mutual responsiveness to each other's needs.

attachment style The way a person typically interacts with significant others.

How important is this first attachment? Does a secure and trusting bond in the first year of life set a foundation for close relationships later in life? John Bowlby (1988), a psychiatrist and influential theorist, has argued that there is a link—that infants form "internal working models" of attachment figures and that these models guide their relationships later in life. Research shows that infants classified as securely attached are later more positive in their outlook toward others (Cassidy et al., 1996). Looking back, adults with a secure attachment style described having positive family relationships, while avoidant and anxious adults recalled having problems with one or both parents (Feeney & Noller, 1990; Hazan & Shaver, 1987).

Whether or not adult attachment styles are rooted in the first year of life, the distinction among adults has proved to be a useful one. Read the descriptions of three attachment types in Table 9.1. Which fits you best? Hazan and Shaver (1987) presented this task initially in a "love quiz" that appeared in a Denver newspaper and then in a study of college students. As shown in Table 9.1, the distribution of responses was similar in the two samples, and it proved similar again in a later nationwide sample of 8,000 adults (Mickelson et al., 1997). In addition, the researchers found that people who have a secure attachment style report having satisfying relationships that are happy, friendly, based on mutual trust, and enduring. Cognitively they see people as good-hearted and they believe in romantic love. In contrast, avoidant lovers fear intimacy and believe that romantic love is doomed to fade; and anxious lovers report a love life full of emotional highs and lows, obsessive preoccupation, a greater willingness than others to make long-term commitments, and extreme sexual attraction and jealousy.

To some extent, our attachment styles can be seen in our everyday behavior. For example, Jeffrey Simpson and others (1996) videotaped dating couples as they tried to resolve various conflicts and then showed the tapes to outside observers. They found that men classified from a questionnaire as having an insecure-avoidant attachment style were the least warm and supportive and that women with an insecure-anxious style were the most upset and negative in their behavior. There is also reason to believe that people's attachment styles influence their physiological reactions to relationship conflict. In one study Sally Powers and her colleagues (2006) brought 124 college-age dating couples into the laboratory to discuss a heated conflict they'd been having. Before and after this "conflict negotiation task," the researchers took saliva samples from all participants to measure levels of cortisol, a stress hormone. The results showed that boyfriends and girlfriends who were insecurely attached exhibited more physiological stress in response to the conflict task than did those who were securely attached.

TABLE 9.1

Attachment Styles

Question: Which of the following best describes your feelings?

Answers and Percentages	Newspaper Sample	University Sample
Secure	56	56
I find it relatively easy to get close to others and am comfortable depending on them and having them depend on me. I don't often worry about being abandoned or about someone getting too close to me.		
Avoidant	25	23
I am somewhat uncomfortable being close to others; I find it difficult to trust them completely, and difficult to allow myself to depend on them. I am nervous when anyone gets too close and often love partners want me to be more intimate than I feel comfortable being.		
Anxious	19	21
I find that others are reluctant to get as close as I would like. I often worry that my partner doesn't really love me or won't want to stay with me. I want to merge completely with another person, and this desire sometimes scares people away.		

Hazan & Shaver, 1987.

What about the future? Does the attachment style you endorse today foretell relational outcomes tomorrow? On this question, the evidence is mixed. People who are secure do tend to have more lasting relationships. But the prognosis for those classified as insecure is harder to predict, with the results less consistent. What's important to realize is that although styles of attachment are modestly stable over time—perhaps as holdovers from infancy and childhood—they are not fixed, or set in stone. To illustrate this point, Lee Kirkpatrick and Cindy Hazan (1994) tracked down participants from a study that had taken place four years earlier and found that 30 percent had different attachment styles. In keeping with the central theme of social psychology—that we are profoundly shaped by the situations we are in—research suggests that people may continuously revise their own attachment styles in response to new relationship experiences (Baldwin & Fehr, 1995; Keelan et al., 1994; Scharfe & Bartholomew, 1994).

How Do I Love Thee? Counting the Ways

The poet Elizabeth Barrett Browning asked, "How do I love thee?" and then went on to "count the ways"—of which there are many. When college students were asked to list all kinds of love that came to mind, they produced 216 items, such as friendship, parental, brotherly, sisterly, romantic, sexual, spiritual, obsessive, possessive, and puppy love (Fehr & Russell, 1991).

Over the years, various schemes for classifying different types of love have been proposed (Sternberg & Weis, 2006). On the basis of ancient writings, sociologist John Alan Lee (1988) identified three primary love styles: *eros* (erotic love), *ludus* (game-playing, uncommitted love), and *storge* (friendship love). As with primary colors, Lee theorized, these three styles can be blended together to form new secondary types of love, such as *mania* (demanding and possessive love), *pragma* (pragmatic love), and *agape* (other-oriented, altruistic love). On a scale designed to measure these "colors of love," men tend to score higher than women on *ludus*, while women score higher on *storge*, *mania*, and *pragma* (Hendrick & Hendrick, 1995).

Another popular taxonomy is derived from Robert Sternberg's (1986) **triangular theory of love**. According to Sternberg, there are eight basic subtypes of love (seven different forms of love and an eighth combination that results in the absence of love)—and all can be derived from the presence or absence of three components. The combination can thus be viewed as the vertices of a triangle (see ▶ Figure 9.8). The components—and sample items used to measure each one—are described below:

Intimacy: The emotional component, which involves liking and feelings of closeness. ("I have a comfortable relationship with ___ .")

Passion: The motivational component, which contains drives that trigger attraction, romance, and sexual desire. ("Just seeing ___ is exciting for me.")

Commitment: The cognitive component, which reflects the decision to make a long-term commitment to a loved partner. ("I will always feel a strong responsibility for ___ .")

Research provides fairly good support for this tri-component model of love (Sternberg, 1999). In one study, Arthur Aron and Lori Westbay (1996) asked people to rate 68 prototypical features of love and found that all the various features fell into three categories: passion (*gazing at the other, euphoria, butterflies in the stomach*), intimacy (*feeling free to talk about anything, supportive, understanding*), and commitment (*devotion, putting the other first, long-lasting*). In a second study, Sternberg (1997) asked people to state what they see as important in different kinds of relationships and found that the results were consistent with the theory. For example, "ideal lover" scored high on all

I have studied love because it is my life's difficult problem. Although I have made much progress, the "impossible dream" of a truly fulfilling mutual love remains a goal I have yet to achieve.
—John Alan Lee

triangular theory of love
A theory proposing that love has three basic components—intimacy, passion, and commitment—that can be combined to produce eight subtypes.

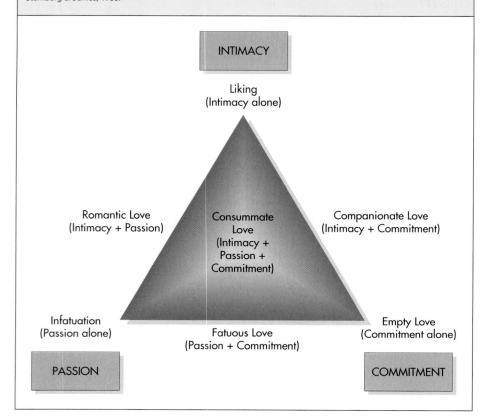

▶ **FIGURE 9.8**

Sternberg's Triangular Theory of Love

According to Sternberg, various combinations of passion, intimacy, and commitment give rise to seven different types of love. (Although it is not shown, the absence of all three components produces an eighth result, nonlove.)

Sternberg & Barnes, 1986.

three components, "friend" scored high on intimacy and commitment but low on passion, and "sibling" scored high on commitment but low on intimacy and passion.

In light of theories involving infant attachment styles, colors, triangles, and other love classification schemes that have been proposed over the years, one wonders: How many types of love are there, really? It's hard to tell. But there are two basic types that are built into all models: *liking*, the type of feeling you would have for a platonic friend, and *loving*, the kind of feeling you would have for a romantic partner. According to Zick Rubin (1973), liking and loving are two distinct reactions to an intimate relationship. There is some question, however, about how sharp the difference is. Kenneth and Karen Dion (1976) questioned casual daters, exclusive daters, engaged couples, and married couples. Although casual daters reported more liking than loving, liking and loving did not differ among those in the more committed dating relationships. The two-pronged distinction Elaine Hatfield (1988) and her colleagues (Hatfield & Rapson, 1993) make between passionate and companionate love is even sharper. According to Hatfield, **passionate love** is an emotionally intense and *often erotic state* of absorption in another person, whereas **companionate love** is a secure, trusting, and stable partnership, similar to what Rubin called liking.

Passionate Love: The Thrill of It   Passionate love is an intense emotional, heart-thumping state of absorption in another person. From ecstatic highs to agonizing lows, it is the bittersweet stuff of romance paperbacks, popular music, poems, and soap operas. What is passionate love, and where does it come from? According to Ellen Berscheid and Elaine Walster (later Hatfield) (1974), the key to understanding passionate love is to recognize that it is an emotion that can be analyzed like any other emotion. Drawing on Schachter's (1964) two-factor theory of emotion (see Chapter 3), they theorized that passionate love is fueled by two ingredients: (1) a heightened state of physiological arousal; and (2) the belief that this arousal was triggered by the beloved person.

Sometimes, the arousal-love connection is obvious, as when a person feels a surge of sexual desire at the sight of a romantic partner. At other times, however, the symptoms of arousal—such as a pounding heart, sweaty palms, and weak knees—can be hard to interpret. When we are in the company of an attractive person, these symptoms may be attributed or "misattributed" to passionate love. Dolf Zillmann (1984)

passionate love   Romantic love characterized by high arousal, intense attraction, and fear of rejection.

companionate love   A secure, trusting, stable partnership.

calls the process **excitation transfer**. According to Zillmann, arousal triggered by one stimulus can be transferred or added to the arousal from a second stimulus. The combined arousal is then perceived as having been caused only by the second stimulus.

Donald Dutton and Arthur Aron (1974) first tested this provocative hypothesis in a field study that took place on two bridges above British Columbia's Capilano River. One was a narrow, wobbly suspension bridge (450 feet long and 5 feet wide, with a low handrail) that sways 230 feet above rocky rapids—a nightmare for anyone the least bit afraid of heights. The other bridge was wide, sturdy, and only 10 feet from the ground. Whenever an unaccompanied young man walked across one of these bridges, he was met by an attractive young woman who introduced herself as a research assistant, asked him to fill out a brief questionnaire, and gave her phone number in case he wanted more information about the project. As predicted, men who crossed the scary bridge were later more likely to call her than those who crossed the stable bridge. In a study of "love at first fright" that took place in two amusement parks, Cindy Meston and Penny Frohlich (2003) similarly found that men and women who were not with a romantic partner rated a photographed person of the opposite sex as more attractive right after they rode on a roller coaster than they did before they began the ride. Perhaps terror can fan the hot flames of romance.

Or maybe not. Maybe it's just a relief to be with someone when we're in distress. To rule out the possibility that relief rather than arousal is what fuels attraction, Gregory White and his colleagues (1981) had to create arousal without distress. How? A little exercise can do it. Male participants ran in place for either two minutes or fifteen seconds and then saw a videotape of a woman they expected to meet. The woman had been made up to look physically attractive or unattractive. After watching the video, participants rated her appearance. The result: Those who exercised for two minutes as opposed to only fifteen seconds saw the physically attractive woman as even more attractive and the unattractive woman as less attractive. This study and others like it (Allen et al., 1989) showed that arousal—even without distress—intensifies emotional reactions, positive or negative.

According to excitation transfer theory, bodily arousal triggered by one stimulus can be misattributed to another stimulus. This theory suggests that the energy that springs from dancing may intensify a person's feelings for his or her partner, fanning the flames of passion.

The implication of this research—that our passions are at the mercy of bridges, roller coasters, exercise, and anything else that causes the heart to race—is intriguing. It is certainly consistent with the common observation that people are vulnerable to falling in love when their lives are turbulent. But does the effect occur, as theorized, because people *mis*attribute their arousal to a person they have just met? Yes and no. Based on their review of 33 experiments, Craig Foster and others (1998) confirmed that the arousal-attraction effect does exist. They also found, however, that the effect occurs even when people know the actual source of their arousal—in other words, even without misattribution. According to these investigators, just being aroused, even if we know why, facilitates whatever is the most natural response. If the person we meet is good-looking and of the right sex, we become more attracted. If the person is not good-looking or is of the wrong sex, we become less attracted. No thought is required. The response is automatic.

It is now clear that passionate love is highly sexualized. In a book entitled *Lust: What We Know About Human Sexual Desire*, Pamela Regan and Ellen Berscheid (1999) present compelling evidence for the proposition that intense sexual desire and excitement are a vital part of passionate love. In this regard, they are quick to note that "loving" is different from "being in love." To illustrate, Berscheid and Meyers (1996) asked college men and women to make three lists: people they loved, people they were in love with, and people they were sexually attracted to. As it turned out, only 2 percent

excitation transfer The process whereby arousal caused by one stimulus is added to arousal from a second stimulus and the combined arousal is attributed to the second stimulus.

of those in the "love" category also appeared in the sex list. Yet among those in the "in love" category, the overlap with sex was 85 percent. And when Regan and her colleagues (1998) asked people to list the characteristics of romantic love, two-thirds cited sexual desire—more than the number who put happiness, loyalty, communication, sharing, or commitment on the list.

Romantic ideals notwithstanding, it is also clear that people have doubts about the staying power of passionate love. Does the fire within a relationship burn hot and bright over time or is it just a passing fancy? Comparisons of couples at different stages of their relationships and longitudinal studies that measure changes in the same couples over time have suggested that intense, sexual, passionate love does tend to diminish somewhat over time (Acker & Davis, 1992). Yet this decline may not be clearly defined or inevitable. In a recent study, Bianca Acevedo and Arthur Aron (2009) meta-analyzed past survey research and asked couples who had been together for varying lengths of time questions about passionate love. They found that although the initial "obsessional" aspect of passionate love clearly does diminish in long-term relationships ("I sometimes find it difficult to concentrate on work because thoughts of my partner occupy my mind"), there is a "romantic" aspect that often endures ("I would rather be with my partner than anyone else," "I want my partner—physically, emotionally, mentally").

Companionate Love: The Self-Disclosure in It   In contrast to the intense, emotional, erotic, and sometimes obsessional nature of passionate love, companionate love is a form of affection that binds close friends as well as lovers. Companionate relationships rest on a foundation of mutual trust, caring, respect, friendship, and long-term commitment—characteristics that John Harvey and Julie Omarzu (2000) see as necessary for "minding the close relationship."

Compared with the passionate form of love, companionate love is less intense but is in some respects deeper and more enduring. Susan Sprecher and Pamela Regan (1998) administered passionate and companionate love scales to heterosexual couples who had been together for varying amounts of time and found that the passionate love scores of both men and women initially rose over time but then peaked and declined somewhat during marriage. Companionate love scores, however, did not similarly decline. In fact, in couples that stay together, partners are likely to report that "I love you more today than yesterday" (Sprecher, 1999). Like the sturdy, steady tortoise in Aesop's fable, companionate love may seem to be outpaced by the flashier start of passionate love, but it can still cross the finish line well ahead.

Companionate love is characterized by high levels of **self-disclosure**, a willingness to open up and share intimate facts and feelings. In a way, self-disclosure is to companionate love what arousal is to passionate love. Think for a moment about your most embarrassing moment, your most cherished ambitions, or your sex life. Would you bare your soul on these private matters to a complete stranger? What about a casual acquaintance, date, friend, or lover? Whether or not to self-disclose—what, when, how much, and to whom—is a decision that each of us makes based on a consideration of what we stand to gain and lose in a relationship (Omarzu, 2000).

The willingness to disclose intimate facts and feelings lies at the heart of our closest and most intimate relationships (Derlega et al., 1993). Research shows that the more emotionally involved people are in a close relationship, the more they self-disclose to each other. Nancy Collins and Lynn Miller (1994) note three possible reasons for this correlation: (1) We disclose to people we like; (2) we like people who disclose to us; and (3) we like people to whom we have disclosed. Thus, among pairs of college students brought together in a laboratory for brief getting-acquainted conversations, the more they self-disclosed, the better they felt about each other afterward (Vittengl & Holt,

True love never grows old.
—Proverb

As soon as you cannot keep anything from a woman, you love her.
—Paul Geraldy

self-disclosure Revelations about the self that a person makes to others.

2000). In a longitudinal study of adult dating couples, partners who reported higher levels of self-disclosure also expressed more satisfaction, commitment, and love (Sprecher & Hendrick, 2004). When it comes to sex, too, partners who self-disclose their likes and dislikes to each other are more satisfied sexually than those who are less open (MacNeil & Byers, 2009).

Over the years, researchers have observed three patterns of self-disclosure in relationships. One is that partners reveal more to each other as their relationship grows over time. According to Irving Altman and Dalmas Taylor (1973), self-disclosure is a basic form of social exchange that unfolds as relationships develop. Their *social penetration theory* holds that relationships progress from superficial exchanges to more intimate ones. At first, people give relatively little of themselves to each other and receive little in return. If the initial encounters prove rewarding, however, the exchanges become both *broader* (covering more areas of their lives) and *deeper* (involving more sensitive areas). As shown in ▶ Figure 9.9, social interaction grows from a narrow, shallow sliver to a wider, more penetrating wedge.

A second observation is that patterns of self-disclosure change according to the state of a relationship. During a first encounter and in the budding stages of a new relationship, people tend to reciprocate another's self-disclosure with their own—at a comparable level of intimacy. If a new acquaintance opens up, it is polite to match that self-disclosure by revealing more of ourselves. Once a relationship is well established, however, strict reciprocity occurs less frequently (Altman, 1973; Derlega et al., 1976). Among couples in distress, two different self-disclosure patterns have been observed. For some, both breadth and depth decrease as partners withdraw from each other and cease to communicate (Baxter, 1987). For others, the breadth of self-disclosure declines but depth increases as the partners hurl cruel and angry statements at each other (Tolstedt & Stokes, 1984). In this case, the social depenetration process resembles neither the sliver of a superficial affiliation nor the wedge of a close relationship but rather a long, thin dagger of discontent.

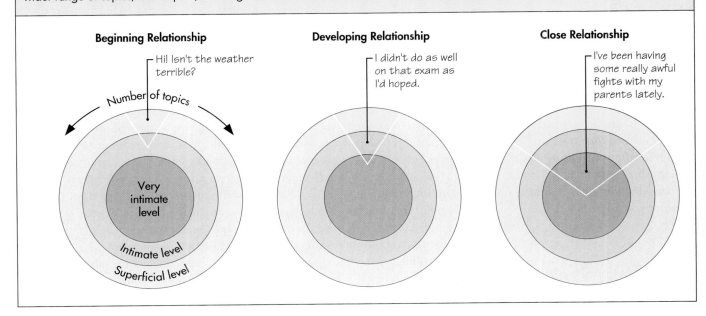

▶FIGURE 9.9

From a Sliver to a Wedge

According to the theory of social penetration, as a relationship becomes closer, partners increase both the breadth (covering a wider range of topics) and depth (revealing more intimate information) of their exchanges.

Beginning Relationship

Hi! Isn't the weather terrible?

Number of topics

Very intimate level

Intimate level

Superficial level

Developing Relationship

I didn't do as well on that exam as I'd hoped.

Close Relationship

I've been having some really awful fights with my parents lately.

A third common observation is that individuals differ in the tendency to share private, intimate thoughts with others. For example, Kathryn Dindia and Mike Allen (1992) conducted a meta-analysis of 205 studies involving 23,702 white North Americans and found, on average, that women are more open than men—and that people in general are more self-disclosing to women than to men. This being the case, it comes as no surprise that women rate their same-sex friendships more highly than men rate theirs. At least in North America, male friends seem to bond more by taking part in common activities, while female friends engage more in a sharing of feelings (Duck & Wright, 1993). As Paul Wright (1982) put it, women tend to interact "face-to-face" but men go "side-by-side."

Culture, Attraction, and Close Relationships

In looking at attraction, desire, relationships, and love, one wonders: Are people all over the world similar or different? To what extent are these processes universal or different from one culture to another? In recent years, several social psychologists have raised these kinds of questions (Hatfield et al., 2007).

In his original cross-cultural study of mate selection, for example, Buss (1989) found that physical attractiveness is more important to men all over the world and that financial resources are more important to women—gender differences that appeared to be universal. Yet even Buss was struck by the powerful impact that culture had on mate preferences. In China, India, Indonesia, Iran, Taiwan, and the Palestinian territories of Israel, for example, people valued chastity in a mate. Yet in Finland, France, Norway, Sweden, the Netherlands, and West Germany, chastity was either unimportant or negatively valued.

When it comes to close relationships, research has shown that passionate love is a widespread and universal emotion. In surveys conducted throughout the world, William Jankowiak and Edward Fischer (1992) detected indications of passionate love in 147 out of 166 cultures as varied as Indonesia, China, Turkey, Nigeria, Trinidad, Morocco, Australia, and Micronesia. Drawing on this universality, some researchers have begun to explore the underlying neuroscience. For example, anthropologist Helen Fisher (2004) believes that romantic love is hard-wired in the neurochemistry of the brain. In particular, Fisher argues that the neurotransmitter dopamine, which drives animals to seek rewards such as food and sex, is essential to the pleasure that is felt when these drives are satisfied. Hence, she argues, dopamine levels are associated with both the highs of romantic passion and the lows of rejection. Citing evidence from studies of humans and other animals, she also points to neurochemical parallels between romantic love and substance addiction.

To an American in love, his/her emotions tend to overshadow everything else . . . to a Chinese in love, his/her love occupies a place among other considerations.

—Hsu

Although most people in the world agree that sexual desire is what injects the passion into passionate love, not everyone sees it as necessary for marriage. Think about this question: If a man or woman had all other qualities you desired, would you marry this person if you were *not* in love? When American students were surveyed in 1967, 35 percent of men and 76 percent of women said yes. Twenty years later, only 14 percent of men and 20 percent of women said they would marry someone with whom they were not in love (Simpson et al., 1986). The shift among women may reflect the pragmatic point that marrying for love is an economic luxury that few women of the past could afford. As seen in the current popularity of prenuptial agreements, pragmatic considerations continue to influence marriage practices, even today.

The willingness to marry without love is also highly subject to cultural variation. In light of the different values that pervade individualist and collectivist cultures, the differences are not surprising. In many cultures, marriage is seen as a transaction between families that is influenced by social, economic, and religious considerations. Indeed, arranged marriages are still common in India, China, many Muslim countries, and sub-Saharan Africa. So, when Robert Levine and others (1995) asked college students from eleven countries about marrying without love, they found that the percentage who said they would do so ranged from 4 percent in the United States, 5 percent in Australia, and 8 percent in England up to 49 percent in India and 51 percent in Pakistan.

In cultures in which love is not a sufficient basis for marriage, other factors play a role. In India, a historically entrenched caste system divides its citizens and holds sway over love and marriage (Singh, 2009). Indeed, while the government legalized intercaste marriage more than 50 years ago and is now offering incentives for intercaste couples to marry, an invisible separation remains between the upper and lower castes that lasts from birth to death—and "honor killings" of couples who dare to cross these traditional lines are not uncommon (Wax, 2008). In China, where a cultural premium is placed on devotion, respect, and obedience of children to parents and other family elders, there is far less emphasis on the Western "fairytale ideals" of love and romance (Higgins et al., 2002; Jackson et al., 2006). In recent surveys, young adults in China, more than in the United States, said they would be influenced in their mate selection decisions by parents and close friends—for example, that they would try to persuade their parents to accept a dating partner and stop dating that partner if their parents did not approve (Zhang & Kline, 2009).

The influence of culture on love is interesting. On the one hand, it could be argued that the rugged individualism found in many Western cultures would inhibit the tendency to become intimate and interdependent with others. On the other hand, individualism leads people to give priority in making marital decisions to their own feelings rather than to family concerns, social obligations, religious constraints, income, and the like (Dion & Dion, 1996). In an illustration of this point, Fred Rothbaum and Bill Yuk-Piu Tsang (1998) compared popular love songs in the United States and China. They found that the American lyrics focused more on the two lovers as isolated entities, independent of social context ("There is nobody here, it's just you and me, the way I want it to be").

DPA/The Image Works

Tushar Agarwal and his bride Richa are married in a wedding ceremony in Bombay. Fulfilling a tradition that seems strange to most Americans, for whom being in love is essential, this Indian marriage was arranged.

■ Relationship Issues: The Male-Female Connection

Browse the offerings of any real or online bookstore and you'll see one paperback title after another on the general topic of gender. There are books for men and books for women, books that preach the masculine ideal and books that tell us how to be more feminine, books that portray men and women as similar and books that accentuate the differences. Is it true, to borrow John Gray's (1997) provocative book title, that *Men Are from Mars, Women Are from Venus*? And if so, what are the implications when it comes to male-female relationships?

Sexuality   More than a hundred years ago, Sigmund Freud shocked the scientific community by proposing psychoanalytic theory, which placed great emphasis on sex as a driving force in human behavior. At the time, Freud's closest associates rejected this focus on sexual motivation. But was he wrong? Sexual images and themes pop up,

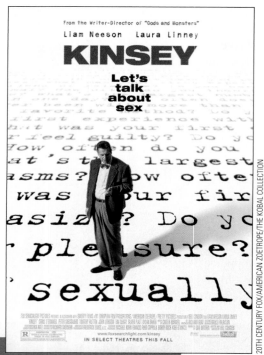

In the movie *Kinsey*, Liam Neeson plays biologist Alfred Kinsey, the first scientist to study sexual practices in the United States.

Men are more likely than women to interpret friendly gestures by the opposite sex in sexual terms. TRUE.

quite literally, in our dreams, in the jokes we tell, in the TV shows we watch, in the novels we read, in the music we hear, and in the sex scandals that swirl around public figures in the news. It's no wonder that advertisers use sex to sell everything from blue jeans to perfume, soft drinks, and cars.

Sex, a most private aspect of human relations, is difficult to study systematically. If you saw the 2004 movie *Kinsey*, starring Liam Neeson, you'd know that during the 1940s biologist Alfred Kinsey and his colleagues (1948, 1953) conducted the first large-scale survey of sexual practices in the United States. Based on confidential interviews of more than 17,000 men and women, these researchers sought for the first time to describe what nobody would openly talk about: sexual activity. Many of his results were shocking; reported sexual activity was more frequent and more varied than anyone had expected. Kinsey's books were instant bestsellers. Certain aspects of his methodology were flawed, however. For example, participants were mostly young, white, urban, and middle class—hardly a representative sample. He also asked leading questions to enable respondents to report on sexual activities—or make up stories (Jones, 1997a). Kinsey died in 1954, but his Institute for Sex Research at Indiana University remains to this day a major center for the study of human sexuality.

Since Kinsey's groundbreaking study, many sex surveys have been conducted, and they form part of the research history that has been chronicled, both seriously and with humor, in books with such titles as *Kiss and Tell: Surveying Sex in the Twentieth Century* (Ericksen & Steffen, 1999), and *Bonk: The Curious Coupling of Science and Sex* (Roach, 2008). The limits of self-reports—regardless of whether they are taken in face-to-face interviews, telephone surveys, or the Internet—is that we can never know for sure how accurate the results are. Part of the problem is that respondents may not be honest in their disclosures. Another limiting factor is that people differ in their interpretations of survey questions.

Consider this deceptively simple question: What does it mean to say you had sex? In an article published in the *Journal of the American Medical Association*, Stephanie Sanders and June Reinisch (1999) asked college students from 29 states, "Would you say you *had sex* with someone if the most intimate behavior you engaged in was . . . ?" The results showed that most students agreed that vaginal and anal intercourse constitute having sex and that deep kissing, oral contact with breasts, and manual contact with genitals do not. Yet there was little consensus about oral-genital contact. At the time this study was published, former President Clinton, mired in a sex scandal, claimed he did not have "sexual relations" with intern Monica Lewinsky despite oral-genital contact. Sanders and Reinisch's findings suggest that there is some ambiguity about what "having sex" actually means (see Table 9.2).

TABLE 9.2

What Constitutes "Having Sex"?

In this study, male and female college students were asked, "Would you say you had sex with someone if the most intimate behavior you engaged in was ___ ?" As you can see, there was consensus for some behaviors but disagreement for others.

Contact	Percent Who Said Yes	Contact	Percent Who Said Yes
Deep kissing	2	Oral contact with genitals	40
Oral contact with breasts	3	Anal intercourse	81
Touching genitals	14	Vaginal intercourse	99

Sanders & Reinisch, 1999.

Researchers have used an array of methods to measure sexual attitudes and behavior. Studies of everyday interactions reveal that men view the world in more sexualized terms than women do. In 1982, Antonia Abbey arranged for pairs of male and female college students to talk for five minutes while other students observed the sessions. When she later questioned the actors and observers, Abbey found that the males were more sexually attracted to the females than vice versa. The males also rated the female actors as being more seductive and more flirtatious than the women had rated themselves as being. Among men more than women, eye contact, a compliment, a friendly remark, a brush against the arm, and an innocent smile are often interpreted as sexual come-ons (Kowalski, 1993). Despite all that has changed in recent years, these gender differences in perceptions of sexual interest still exist (Levesque et al., 2006).

"Sex brought us together, but gender drove us apart."

Gender differences are particularly common in self-report surveys, where in comparison to women, men report being more promiscuous, more likely to think about sex, more permissive, more likely to enjoy casual sex without emotional commitment, and more likely to fantasize about sex with multiple partners (Oliver & Hyde, 1993). When asked to select ten private wishes from a list, for example, most men and women similarly wanted love, health, peace on earth, unlimited ability, and wealth. But more men than women also wanted "to have sex with anyone I choose" (Ehrlichman & Eichenstein, 1992). In a large-scale study of 16,000 respondents from 52 countries all over the world, David Schmitt (2003) found that most men desire more sex partners and more sexual variety than most women do, regardless of their relationship status or sexual orientation. Based on this study and others, Roy Baumeister and others (2001) concluded that "men desire sex more than women" (p. 270).

Sexual Orientation   At a time when policy makers, judges, religious leaders, scholars, and laypeople openly debate the topic of gay marriage, no discussion of human sexuality is complete without a consideration of differences in **sexual orientation**—defined as one's sexual preference for members of the same sex (homosexuality), the opposite sex (heterosexuality), or both sexes (bisexuality).

How common is homosexuality, and where does it come from? Throughout history and in all cultures, a vast majority of people have been heterosexual in their orientation. But how vast a majority is a subject of some debate. A 1970 survey funded by the Kinsey Institute revealed that 3.3 percent of American men sampled said that they had frequent or occasional homosexual sex (Fay et al., 1989). Between 1989 and 1992, the National Opinion Research Center reported that 2.8 percent of American men and 2.5 percent of women had exclusive homosexual activity. Together, large-scale surveys in the United States, Europe, Asia, and the Pacific suggest that the exclusively homosexual population in the world is 3 or 4 percent among men and about half that number among women (Diamond, 1993).

Although an exclusive homosexual orientation is relatively rare among humans and other animals, homosexual *behaviors* are more common. In *Biological Exuberance*, Bruce Bagemihl (1999) reports that sexual encounters among male-male and female-female pairs have been observed in more than 450 species, including giraffes, goats, birds, chimpanzees, and lizards. Among humans, the incidence of homosexual behavior varies from one generation and culture to the next, depending on prevailing attitudes. In *Same Sex, Different Cultures*, Gilbert Herdt (1998) notes that in parts of the world, stretching from Sumatra to Melanesia, it's common for adolescent males

In an ABC Primetime survey of 1,501 American adults, a number of gender differences were found (Longer et al., 2004):

	Men	Women
Think about sex every day	*70%*	*34%*
Have visited a sex website	*34%*	*10%*
Have fantasized about a threesome	*33%*	*9%*

sexual orientation A person's preference for members of the same sex (homosexuality), opposite sex (heterosexuality), or both sexes (bisexuality).

to engage in homosexual activities before being of age for marriage, even though homosexuality as a permanent trait is rare. It's important, then, to realize that sexual orientation cannot be viewed in black-or-white terms but should be seen along a continuum. In the center of that continuum, 1 percent of people describe themselves as actively bisexual.

To explain the roots of homosexuality, various theories have been proposed. The Greek philosopher Aristotle believed that it was inborn but strengthened by habit; post-Freud psychoanalysts argue that it stems from family dynamics, specifically a child's over-attachment to a parent of the same or opposite sex; social learning theorists point to rewarding sexual experiences with same-sex peers in childhood. Yet there is little hard evidence to support these claims. In a particularly comprehensive study, Alan Bell and others (1981) interviewed 1,500 homosexual and heterosexual adults about their lives. There were no differences in past family backgrounds, absence of a male or female parent, relationship with parents, sexual abuse, age of onset of puberty, or high school dating patterns. Except for the fact that homosexual adults described themselves as less conforming as children, the two groups could not be distinguished by past experiences. Both groups felt strongly that their sexual orientation was set long before it was "official."

Increasingly, there is scientific evidence of a biological disposition. In a highly publicized study, neurobiologist Simon LeVay (1991) autopsied the brains of nineteen homosexual men who had died of AIDS, sixteen heterosexual men (some of whom had died of AIDS), and six heterosexual women. LeVay examined a tiny nucleus in the hypothalamus that is involved in regulating sexual behavior and is known to be larger in heterosexual men than in women. The specimens were numerically coded, so LeVay did not know whether a particular donor he was examining was male or female, straight or gay. The result: In the male homosexual brains he studied, the nucleus was half the size as in male heterosexual brains and comparable in size to those found in female heterosexual brains. This research is described in Levy's (1993) book *The Sexual Brain*.

It's important to recognize that this study revealed only a correlation between sexual orientation and the brain and cannot be used to draw conclusions about cause and effect. More convincing support for the biological roots of sexual orientation comes from twin studies suggesting that there is a genetic predisposition. Michael Bailey and Richard Pillard (1991) surveyed 167 gay men and their twins and adopted brothers. Overall, 52 percent of the identical twins were gay, compared to only 22 percent of fraternal twins and 11 percent of adoptive brothers. Two years later, Bailey and others (1993) conducted a companion study of lesbians with similar results.

The origins of sexual orientation are complex for two reasons. First, it's not clear that sexual orientation for men and women is similarly rooted. In Australia, Bailey and others (2000) had hundreds of pairs of twins rate their own sexuality on a seven-point continuum that ranged from "exclusively heterosexual" to "exclusively homosexual." Overall, 92 percent of both men and women saw themselves as exclusively heterosexual. Among the others, however, more women than men said that they had bisexual tendencies and more men than women said they were exclusively homosexual. In another study, a longitudinal investigation of 18- to 25-year-old women, Lisa Diamond (2003) found that more than a quarter of those who had initially identified themselves as lesbian or bisexual changed their orientation over the next five years—far more change than is ever reported among men.

Recent experiments in laboratory settings reinforce the point. In one study, Meredith Chivers and others (2004) recruited men and women who had identified themselves as heterosexual or homosexual in their orientation. In a private, dimly lit room, these participants watched a series of brief sex clips—some involving male couples, others involving female couples. While watching, the participants rated their subjective feelings of sexual attraction on a scale. At the same time, genital arousal was measured using devices that recorded penile erection (for males) and vaginal pulse (for females). Results showed that the women were genitally aroused by both male *and* female sex clips, regardless of whether they identified themselves as straight or lesbian in their orientation. Yet males exhibited more genital arousal in response to men *or* women, depending on their sexual orientation. In fact, although self-identified bisexual men reported an attraction to both sexes, most were genitally aroused by men or by women—but not both (Rieger et al., 2005). These findings and others (Lippa, 2006), compel the conclusion that women are sexually more flexible than men, having more *erotic plasticity*. Simply put, women are more open and more likely to change sexual preferences over the course of a lifetime (Baumeister, 2000; Diamond, 2007; Peplau, 2003).

A second complicating factor is that although there is evidence for a biological disposition, this does not necessarily mean that there's a "gay gene" (Hamer et al., 1999). Daryl Bem (1996, 2000) sees the development of sexual orientation as a *psycho*biological process. According to Bem, genes influence a person's temperament at birth, leading some infants and young children to be naturally more active, energetic, and aggressive than others. These differences in temperament draw some children to male playmates and "masculine" activities and others to female playmates and "feminine" activities. Bem refers to children who prefer same-sex playmates as gender conformists and to those who prefer opposite-sex playmates as gender nonconformists ("sissies" and "tomboys").

Activity preferences in childhood may be biologically rooted, but what happens next is the psychological part. According to Bem, gender-conforming children come to see members of the opposite sex as different, unfamiliar, arousing, and even "exotic." Gender-nonconforming children, in contrast, come to see same-sex peers as different, unfamiliar, arousing, and exotic. Later, at puberty, as children become physically and sexually mature, they find that they are attracted to members of the same or opposite sex—depending on which is the more exotic. Bem describes his proposed chain of events as the "exotic becomes erotic" theory of sexual orientation.

At present, there is only sketchy support for this theory. It is true that genetic makeup can influence temperament and predispose a child to favor certain kinds of activities over others (Kagan, 1994). It is also true that gay men are more likely to have been "sissies" and lesbians to have been "tomboys" as children—differences seen not only in people's self-reported accounts from childhood (Bailey & Zucker, 1995) but also in their behavior, as memorialized in home videos (Rieger et al., 2008). It may even be true that people are genetically hardwired to become sissies and tomboys as children (Bailey et al., 2000). But do peer preferences in childhood alter adult sexual orientation, as Bem suggests, because the exotic becomes erotic? Or is there a "gay gene" that fosters gender nonconformity in childhood as well as homosexuality in adolescence and adulthood? And can a single theory explain homosexuality in both men and women or are separate theories needed, as some have suggested (Peplau et al., 1998)? At present, more research is needed to answer these questions and tease apart the biological and psychological influences. Either way, one point looms large: People, especially men, do not seem to willfully choose their sexual orientation, nor can they easily change it.

Is there any reason to believe that the attraction process and the formation of intimate relationships are any different for same-sex couples? Not really. According to the U.S. census, an estimated 600,000 same-sex couples were living together in the United States in 2000. Recent research shows that gays and lesbians meet people in the same ways as straights, by seeking out others who are attractive and similar in

In 2001, the Netherlands became the first modern nation to grant same-sex marriages full legal status. Same-sex marriage has since become legal in Belgium (2003), Spain (2005), Canada (2005), South Africa (2006), Norway (2009), and Sweden (2009).

On June 17, 2008, Sharon Papo and Amber Weiss exchanged wedding vows on the first full day of same-sex marriages in San Francisco. They remain legally married even though the law itself came to an end five months later when California voters passed Proposition 8, an amendment to the state constitution that limits marriage to heterosexual couples.

their attitudes; that their satisfaction and commitment levels are affected by social exchange and equity concerns just as they are in heterosexual relationships; and that they report levels of liking and loving in their intimate relationships that are comparable to those in heterosexual couples. Same-sex couples differ from straight couples in two ways: They are more likely to retain friendships with former sex partners after breaking up, and they tend to divide chores more equally within a household (Kurdek, 2005; Peplau & Fingerhut, 2007). In light of these striking similarities, and with same-sex marriage now legal in a handful of states, more research on gay and lesbian couples is sure to be conducted in the coming years.

The Marital Trajectory Because we are social beings, having close relationships is important to us all—for our happiness and emotional well-being and even for our physical health and longevity. As noted at the start of this chapter, 73 percent of American college students surveyed said they would sacrifice most other life goals rather than give up a satisfying relationship (Hammersla & Frease-McMahan, 1990). Yet sadly, if they live in the United States or Canada, these students live in a society in which roughly 40 percent of first marriages are likely to end in divorce. With just one previously divorced partner, the odds of divorce are even greater. This discrepancy between the stability most people want and the disruption they may have to confront is dramatic. Couples argue, break up, separate, and divorce. How do marriages evolve over time and why do some last while others dissolve?

Ellen Berscheid and Harry Reis (1998) say that for social psychologists who study intimate relationships, this is the most frequently asked and vexing question. Is there a typical developmental pattern? No and yes. No, it's clear that all marriages are different and cannot be squeezed into a single mold. But yes, certain patterns do emerge when survey results are combined from large numbers of married couples that have been studied over long periods of time. Lawrence Kurdek (1999) reported on a longitudinal study of married couples in which he measured each spouse's satisfaction every year for ten years (of the 522 couples he started with, 93 completed the study). ▶ Figure 9.10 shows that there was an overall decline in ratings of marital quality and that the ratings given by husbands and wives were very similar. There are two marked periods of decline. The first occurs during the first year of marriage. Newlyweds tend to idealize each other and to enjoy an initial state of marital bliss (Murray et al., 1996). However, this "honeymoon" is soon followed by a decline in satisfaction (Bradbury, 1998). After some stabilization, a second decline is observed at about the eighth year of marriage—a finding that is consistent with the popular belief in a "seven-year itch" (Kovacs, 1983).

This marital trajectory is interesting but it represents a crude average of different types of marriages. There is no single mold, however, and one size does not fit all relationships. Realizing this limitation, researchers are actively seeking to plot more precise trend lines for specific marital situations. Thus far, these studies have shown that in heterosexual couples that have a first child, the transition to parenthood hastens the sense of decline in both partners (Lawrence et al., 2008); that cohabiting gay and lesbian couples do not self-report the lowered satisfaction often seen in heterosexual couples (Kurdek, 2008); and that, despite the initial dip, marital satisfaction increases again in middle age for parents whose children grow up, leave home, and empty the nest (Gorchoff et al., 2008).

Do specific factors predict future outcomes? To address this question, Benjamin Karney and Thomas Bradbury (1995) reviewed 115 longitudinal studies of more than 45,000 married couples and found only that certain positively valued variables (education, employment, constructive behaviors, similarity in attitudes) are somewhat predictive of positive outcomes. They did find, however, that the steeper the initial decline in satisfaction, the more likely couples are to break up later. This decline is, in part, related to the stress of having and raising children, a stress that is common among newly married couples. Boredom is also predictive of a loss in satisfaction. In a longitudinal study of 123 married couples, husbands and wives who felt like they were in a rut at one point in time were significantly less satisfied nine years later (Tsapelas et al., 2009).

Is there anything a couple can do to avoid a rut and keep the honeymoon alive? Perhaps there is. Arthur Aron and his colleagues (2000) have theorized that after the exhilaration of a new relationship wears off, partners can combat boredom by engaging together in new and arousing activities. By means of questionnaires and a door-to-door survey, these researchers found that the more new experiences spouses said they'd had together, the more satisfied they were with their marriages. To test this hypothesis in a controlled experiment, they brought randomly selected couples into the laboratory, spread gymnasium mats across the floor, tied the partners together at a wrist and ankle, and had them crawl on their hands and knees, over a barrier, from one end of the room to the other—all while carrying a pillow between their bodies. Other couples were given the more mundane task of rolling a ball across the mat, one partner at a time. A third group received

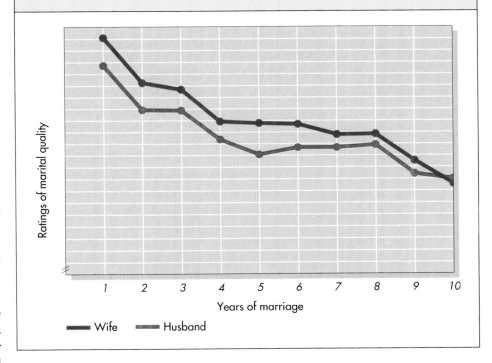

▶ FIGURE 9.10

Marital Satisfaction over Time

In a longitudinal study that spanned ten years, married couples rated the quality of their marriages. On average, these ratings were high, but they declined among both husbands and wives. As you can see, there were two steep drops, occurring during the first and eighth years of marriage.

Kurdek, 1999.

no assignment. Afterward, all participants were surveyed about their relationships. As predicted, the couples that had struggled and laughed their way through the novel and arousing activity reported more satisfaction with the quality of their relationships than did those in the mundane and no-task groups. It's possible that the benefit of shared participation in this study was short-lived. But maybe, just maybe, a steady and changing diet of exciting new experiences can help keep the flames of love burning.

Communication and Conflict Disagreements about sex, children, in-laws, and other matters can stir conflict in close relationships. Of particular relevance during turbulent economic times, research shows that financial pressures can put enormous

After the honeymoon period, there is an overall decline in levels of marital satisfaction. **TRUE.**

amounts of strain on marital relations (Conger et al., 1999). Whatever the cause, all couples experience some degree of friction. The issue is not whether it occurs but how we respond to it. One source of conflict is the difficulty some people have talking about their disagreements. When relationships break up, communication problems are among the most common causes cited by straight and gay couples alike (Kurdek, 1991b; Sprecher, 1994). But what constitutes "bad communication"? Comparisons between happy and distressed couples have revealed a number of communication patterns that often occur in troubled relationships (Fincham, 2003).

One common pattern is called *negative affect reciprocity*—a tit-for-tat exchange of expressions of negative feelings. Generally speaking, expressions of negative affect within a couple trigger more in-kind responses than do expressions of positive affect. But negative affect reciprocity, especially in nonverbal behavior, is greater in couples that are unhappy, distressed, and locked into a duel. For couples in distress, smiles pass by unnoticed, but every glare, every disgusted look, provokes a sharp reflex-like response. The result, as observed in unhappy couples around the world, is an inability to break the vicious cycle and terminate unpleasant interactions (Gottman, 1998).

Men and women react differently to conflict. Most women report more intense emotions and are more expressive than most men (Grossman & Wood, 1993). She tells him to "warm up"; he urges her to "calm down." Thus, many unhappy marriages are also characterized by a *demand/withdraw interaction pattern*, in which the wife demands that the couple discuss the relationship problems, only to become frustrated when her husband withdraws from such discussions (Christensen & Heavey, 1993). This pattern is not unique to married couples. When dating partners were asked about how they typically deal with problems, the same demand/withdraw pattern was found (Vogel et al., 1999). Married or not, then, it's clear that couples caught in this bind often find themselves echoing the title of Deborah Tannen's (1990) once popular book on gender and communication, *You Just Don't Understand*. According to John Gottman (1994), there is nothing wrong with either approach to dealing with conflict. The problem, he says, lies in the discrepancy—that healthy relationships are most likely when both partners have similar styles of dealing with conflict.

Whatever one's style, there are two basic approaches to reducing the negative effects of conflict. The first is so obvious that it is often overlooked: Increase rewarding behavior in other aspects of the relationship. According to Gottman and Levenson (1992), marital stability rests on a "fairly high balance of positive to negative behaviors" (p. 230). If there's conflict over one issue, partners can and should search for other ways to reward each other. As the balance of positives to negatives improves, so should overall levels of satisfaction, which can reduce conflict (Huston & Vangelisti, 1991). A second approach is to try to understand the other's point of view. Being sensitive to what the partner thinks and how he or she feels enhances the quality of the relationship (Honeycutt et al., 1993; Long & Andrews, 1990). What motivates individuals in the heat of battle to make that effort to understand? For starters, it helps if they agree that there is a communication problem.

The attributions that partners make for each other's behaviors and the willingness to forgive are correlated with the quality of their relationship (Bradbury & Fincham, 1992; Fincham et al., 2007; Harvey & Manusov, 2001). As you might expect, happy couples make *relationship-enhancing attributions*: They see the partner's undesirable behaviors as caused by factors that are situational ("a bad day"), temporary ("It'll pass"), and limited in scope ("That's just a sore spot"). Yet they perceive desirable behaviors as caused by factors that are inherent in the partner, permanent, and generalizable to other aspects of the relationship. In contrast, unhappy couples flip the attributional coin on its tail by making the opposite *distress-maintaining attributions*. Thus, while happy couples minimize the bad and maximize the good, distressed couples don't give an inch. In light of these differing attributional patterns, it would seem that over time happy couples would get happier and miserable couples more miserable. Do they? Yes. By tracking married couples longitudinally, researchers have found that husbands and wives who made distress-maintaining attributions early in marriage reported less satisfaction at a later point in time (Fincham et al., 2000; Karney & Bradbury, 2000). The link between causal attributions and levels of marital bliss or distress may be reciprocal, with each influencing the other; causal attributions may influence levels of marital satisfaction and vice versa.

Breaking Up When an intimate relationship ends, as in divorce, the effect can be traumatic (Fine & Harvey, 2006). As part of a longitudinal study of adults in Germany, Richard Lucas (2005) zeroed in on 817 men and women who at some point were divorced. Every year for eighteen years, these participants were interviewed and asked to rate how satisfied they were with life on a scale of 0 to 10. On average, the divorcees were more than a half point less satisfied than their married counterparts. But did time heal the wound? ▶ Figure 9.11 shows three interesting patterns: (1) Participants had become less and less satisfied even before divorce; (2) satisfaction levels rebounded somewhat immediately after divorce; and (3) satisfaction levels never returned to original baseline levels. In short, people adapt but do not fully recover from the experience.

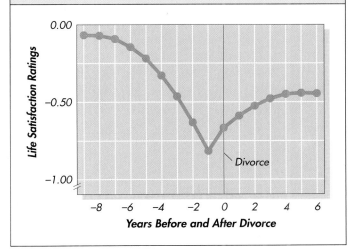

▶ FIGURE 9.11

Changes in Life Satisfaction Before and After Divorce

In this study, 817 men and women who were divorced at some point rated how satisfied they were with life on a scale of 0 to 10 every year for 18 years. Overall, divorcees were less satisfied than their married counterparts—a common result. On the question of whether time heals the wound, you can see that satisfaction levels dipped before divorce and rebounded afterward, but did not return to original levels. It appears that people adapt but do not fully recover from this experience.

Lucas, 2005.

How do people cope with divorce? The answer is, it depends on the nature of the loss. One vital factor is the closeness of a relationship, or the extent to which the line between self and other becomes so blurred that mine and yours are one and the same. Indeed, Aron and others (1992) found that the longevity of a romantic relationship can be predicted by which of the diagrams in ▶ Figure 9.12 people choose to describe their relationship. The more one incorporates a partner into the self, the more lasting the relationship is likely to be—but the more distress one anticipates if there is a breakup.

Another important factor in this regard is interdependence, the social glue that binds us together. Research shows that the more interdependent couples are (as measured by the amount of time they spend together, the variety of activities they share, and the degree of influence each partner has over the other) and the more invested they are in the relationship, the longer it will likely last (Berscheid et al., 1989; Rusbult & Buunk, 1993)—and the more devastated they will become when it ends (Fine & Sacher, 1997; Simpson, 1987). In trying to explain how people regulate the risks of forming close romantic relationships, Sandra Murray and others (2006) note that an ironic theme runs through much of the research: "The relationships that have the most potential to satisfy adult needs for interpersonal connection are the very relationships that activate the most anxiety about rejection" (p. 661). We are, to put it mildly, darned if we do and darned if we don't. The factors that contribute to the endurance of a relationship (closeness and interdependence) turn out to be the same factors that intensify the fear of rejection and make coping more difficult after a relationship ends. So, how do you balance making the psychological investment necessary for a lasting relationship against holding back enough for self-protection?

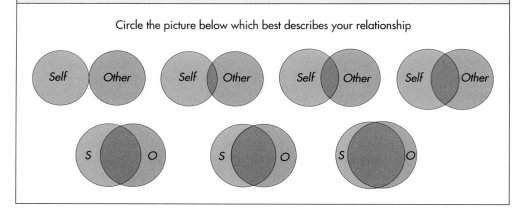

▶ FIGURE 9.12

How Close Is Your Relationship?

The Inclusion of Other in the Self (IOS) Scale is a one-item, pictorial measure of relationship closeness. Choosing a picture with less overlap between the circles indicates less closeness; choosing one with more overlap indicates more closeness.

Aron et al., 1992.

In the United States and other Western countries, various demographic markers indicate how problematic traditional forms of commitment have become: A high divorce rate, more single-parent families, more unmarried couples living together, and more never-married individuals. Yet the desire for long-term intimate relationships has never wavered or disappeared. On the contrary, people spend millions of dollars on online dating sites, gays and lesbians actively seek legal recognition of same-sex marriages, the vast majority of divorced individuals remarry, and stepfamilies forge a new sense of what it means to be a "family." It seems that we are in the midst of a great and compelling search as millions of men and women try to find ways to affiliate with, attract, get closer to, love, and commit themselves with permanence to others.

REVIEW

Being with Others: A Fundamental Human Motive

- The need to belong is a basic human motive, a pervasive drive to form and maintain lasting relationships.

The Thrill of Affiliation

- This social motivation begins with the need for affiliation, a desire to establish social contact with others.
- People differ in the strength of their affiliative needs.
- Stressful situations in particular motivate us to affiliate with others who face a similar threat.

The Agony of Loneliness

- Shyness is a pervasive problem that sets people up to have unrewarding interactions with others.
- People who are painfully shy are at risk for loneliness, a feeling of isolation and social deprivation.

The Initial Attraction

- According to one perspective, people are attracted to others with whom the relationship is rewarding; rewards can be direct or indirect.

- Evolutionary psychologists argue that human beings exhibit patterns of attraction and mate selection that favor the passing on of their own genes.

Familiarity: Being There

- Proximity sets the stage for social interaction, which is why friendships are most likely to form between people who live near each other.

- Supporting the mere exposure effect, studies show that the more often people see a stimulus, the more they come to like it.

- We do not have to be aware of our prior exposures for the increase in liking to occur.

Physical Attractiveness: Getting Drawn In

- In a wide range of social settings, people respond more favorably to men and women who are physically attractive.

- Some researchers believe that certain faces (averaged and symmetrical) are inherently attractive—across cultures and to infants as well as adults.

- Others argue that beauty is in the eye of the beholder and point to the influences of culture, time, and context.

- One reason for the bias for beauty is that it's rewarding to be in the company of others who are attractive.

- A second reason is that people associate beauty with other positive qualities, a belief known as the what-is-beautiful-is-good stereotype.

- People seen as physically attractive are more popular, more sexually experienced, and more socially skilled. However, they are not happier or higher in self-esteem.

- One reason physically attractive people are not happier is that they often discount the praise they get for nonsocial endeavors.

- Another problem with having beauty as a social asset is that people, especially women, feel pressured to keep up their appearance and are often dissatisfied with how they look.

First Encounters: Getting Acquainted

- People tend to associate with, befriend, and marry others whose demographic backgrounds, attitudes, and interests are similar to their own.

- People first avoid others who are dissimilar and then are drawn to those in the remaining group who are most similar to themselves.

- Supporting the matching hypothesis, people tend to become romantically involved with others who are equivalent in physical attractiveness.

- Contrary to popular belief, complementarity in needs or personality does not spark attraction.

- Illustrating the effects of reciprocity, we tend to like others who indicate that they like us.

- But people who are indiscriminate about who they like can be taken for granted and not be liked as much by others.

- Research on the hard-to-get effect shows that people like others best who are moderately selective in their social choices.

Mate Selection: The Evolution of Desire

- Evolutionary psychologists say that women seek men with financial security or traits predictive of future success in order to ensure the survival of their offspring.

- In contrast, men seek women who are young and attractive (physical attributes that signal health and fertility) and are not promiscuous (an attribute that diminishes certainty of paternity).

- Cross-cultural studies tend to support these predicted sex differences, but critics note that many results are not that strong and can be viewed in terms that are more psychological than evolutionary.

Close Relationships

- Intimate relationships include at least one of three components: feelings of attachment, fulfillment of psychological needs, and interdependence.

- Stage theories propose that close relationships go through specific stages, but evidence for a fixed sequence is weak.

- Two other views emphasize either a gradual accumulation of rewards or a sharp distinction between types of relationships.

The Intimate Marketplace: Tracking the Gains and Losses

- According to social exchange theory, people seek to maximize gains and minimize costs in their relationships.

- Higher rewards, lower costs, and an outcome that meets or exceeds a partner's comparison level (CL) predict high levels of satisfaction.

- Lower expectations about alternatives (CLalt) and more investment in the relationship are associated with higher levels of commitment.

- Equity theory holds that satisfaction is greatest when the ratio between benefits and contributions is similar for both partners.

- Both overbenefit and underbenefit elicit negative emotions, but the underbenefited are usually less satisfied.

Types of Relationships

- In exchange relationships, people are oriented toward reward and immediate reciprocity; in communal relationships, partners are responsive to each other's needs.

- People with secure attachment styles have more satisfying romantic relationships than do those with insecure (anxious or avoidant) styles.

How Do I Love Thee? Counting the Ways

- According to the triangular theory of love, there are eight subtypes of love produced by the combinations of intimacy, passion, and commitment.
- Inherent in all classifications of love are two types: passionate and companionate.
- Passionate love is an intense, emotional, often erotic state of positive absorption in another person.
- In one theory, passionate love is sparked by physiological arousal and the belief that the arousal was caused by the loved person.
- Consistent with excitation transfer, arousal can increase or decrease attraction, depending on the initial attractiveness of the person whom one is with.
- Compared with passionate love, companionate love is less intense but in some respects deeper and more enduring.
- Companionate love rests on mutual trust, caring, friendship, commitment, and willingness to share intimate facts and feelings.
- Self-disclosure between partners often becomes broader and deeper over time, though self-disclosure varies with the state of the relationship.

Culture, Attraction, and Relationships

- Although Buss identified universal gender differences in mate preference, he also found some striking cultural differences, for example in differing preferences for chastity.
- The universality of passionate love has led some researchers to explore the neuroscientific bases for this experience.
- Cultures differ in the extent to which romantic love is seen as necessary for marriage.

Relationship Issues: The Male-Female Connection

- People vary in how they define what it means to "have sex."
- On average, men report being sexually more active than women and see opposite-sex interactions in more sexualized terms.
- An estimated 3 or 4 percent of men and 2 percent of women are exclusively homosexual in orientation.
- Both biological and environmental theories are used to explain the origins of homosexuality.
- When relationships break up, communication problems are among the most common causes.
- Unhappy couples often engage in negative affect reciprocity and exhibit a demand/withdraw interaction pattern.
- During conflict, women are more likely to be demanding and men are more likely to withdraw.
- Partners can reduce conflict by behaving in rewarding ways in other areas and by trying to understand each other's point of view.
- Happy couples make relationship-enhancing attributions, while unhappy couples make distress-maintaining attributions.
- On average, marital satisfaction starts high, declines during the first year, stabilizes, and then declines again at about the eighth year.
- Partners who are close and interdependent and for whom relationships are important to the self-concept (characteristics that normally promote stability) suffer more after breaking up.

Key Terms

attachment style (367)

communal relationship (367)

companionate love (370)

equity theory (366)

exchange relationship (367)

excitation transfer (371)

hard-to-get effect (356)

intimate relationship (363)

loneliness (343)

matching hypothesis (355)

mere exposure effect (345)

need for affiliation (340)

passionate love (370)

reciprocity (356)

self-disclosure (372)

sexual orientation (377)

social exchange theory (364)

triangular theory of love (369)

what-is-beautiful-is-good stereotype (350)

Media Resources

Social Psychology 8th Edition Companion Website
Visit your book companion website
www.cengage.com/psychology/kassin
where you will find flash cards, practice quizzes,
Internet links, and more to help you study.

CENGAGENOW™ Just what you need to know NOW! Spend time
on what you need to master rather than on information

you already have learned. Take a pre-test for this chapter
and CengageNOW will generate a personalized study plan
based on your results. The study plan will identify the topics you need to review and direct you to online resources to
help you master those topics. You can then take a post-test
to help you determine the concepts you have mastered and
what you will need to work on. Try it out! Go to **academic
.cengage.com/login** to sign in with an access code or to
purchase access to this product.

Putting COMMON SENSE *to the Test*

People seek out the company of others, even strangers, in times of stress.

True. *Research has shown that external threat causes stress and leads people to affiliate with others who are facing or have faced a similar threat.*

Infants do not discriminate between faces considered attractive and unattractive in their culture.

False. *Two-month-old infants spend more time gazing at attractive than unattractive faces, indicating that they do make the distinction.*

People who are physically attractive are happier and have higher self-esteem than those who are unattractive.

False. *Attractive people are at an advantage in their social lives, but they are not happier, better adjusted, or higher in self-esteem.*

When it comes to romantic relationships, opposites attract.

False. *Consistently, people are attracted to others who are similar—not opposite or complementary—on a whole range of dimensions.*

Men are more likely than women to interpret friendly gestures by the opposite sex in sexual terms.

True. *Experiments have shown that men are more likely than women to interpret friendly interactions with members of the opposite sex as sexual come-ons.*

After the honeymoon period, there is an overall decline in levels of marital satisfaction.

True. *High marital satisfaction levels among newlyweds are often followed by a measurable decline during the first year and then, after a period of stabilization, by another decline at the eighth year—a pattern found among parents and nonparents alike.*

10

© Jon Feingersh/PhotoLibrary

Helping Others

This chapter describes the social psychology of giving and receiving help. We examine the evolutionary, motivational, situational, personal, and interpersonal factors that predict whether a potential helper will provide assistance to a person in need. In the concluding section, we discuss the helping connection, the role of social ties in promoting helpfulness to others.

It was their bravery that compelled them to risk their lives, but it was their compassion that ultimately saved them. Six firefighters from New York City's Ladder Company 6 were among the many firefighters, police officers, and other rescue workers who courageously climbed up the stairs of the World Trade Center on September 11, 2001. The jets that had flown into each of the Twin Towers of the skyscraper were hemorrhaging fuel, causing an inferno of unprecedented proportion. A massive stream of people trying to flee raced down the narrow stairs, passing the firefighters who were going up. Awed by their courage and resolve, people yelled encouragement and blessings to the firefighters as they passed them. Under the burden of more than 100 pounds of equipment, the men of Ladder Company 6 had reached the 27th floor of the North Tower when they heard the horrifying sound of the South Tower collapsing. Their captain ordered them to turn back, realizing that if the other tower could collapse, so could theirs.

On their way down, around the fourteenth or fifteenth floor, they encountered a frail woman named Josephine Harris. She had walked down almost 60 flights already, and she was exhausted. The firefighters helped her walk, but she was slowing them down dangerously. Their captain, John Jonas, was growing more anxious: "I could hear the clock ticking in the back of my head. I'm thinking, 'C'mon, c'mon. We've got to keep moving.'" But none of the six men considered leaving her behind, so they slowly walked down together. Josephine didn't think she could go on, but one of the firefighters asked her about her family and told her that her children and grandchildren wanted to see her again. She continued but finally collapsed as they got near the fourth floor. On the fourth floor they tried to find a chair to carry her in. And then, the 110-story skyscraper collapsed.

Other rescue workers who had passed this slow-moving group on the stairs were killed on the floors below them. Virtually everyone who was still above them was killed. And yet somehow this group survived, trapped in an inexplicable pocket of safety amid the unimaginable wreckage, along with two other firefighters, a fire department chief, and a Port Authority police officer. After a harrowing search for a way out, they eventually found a small ray of light—a literal ray of hope—and followed it to safety.

Putting COMMON SENSE to the Test

Circle Your Answer

T	F	People are more likely to help someone in an emergency if the potential rewards seem high and the potential costs seem low.
T	F	In an emergency, a person who needs help has a much better chance of getting it if three other people are present than if only one other person is present.
T	F	People are much more likely to help someone when they're in a good mood.
T	F	People are much less likely to help someone when they're in a bad mood.
T	F	Attractive people have a better chance than unattractive people of getting help when they need it.
T	F	Women seek help more often than men do.

Displaying bravery that seems to defy instinct, firefighter Mike Kehoe climbs the stairs of one of the towers of the World Trade Center to help with the rescue efforts during the terrorist attacks on the morning of September 11, 2001. This photograph became a famous symbol of the heroism exhibited by so many people on that horrific day. Kehoe was one of the fortunate ones who survived.

A 78-year-old man named Angel Arce Torres lies in the street in Hartford, Connecticut, in May 2008 after being hit by a speeding car. The car sped off, numerous other cars drove past him, and several witnesses on the sidewalk walked on by. As discussed in this chapter, this kind of inaction by bystanders is all too common.

The firefighters later called Josephine Harris their guardian angel and thanked *her* for saving *their* lives. They realized that had they not encountered her, they would have gone down the stairs faster, and had she not kept walking despite exhaustion, they would have been a few floors above. Either way, they would have been killed. But Josephine Harris knew that she owed her life to these brave men who risked not seeing their own children again so that she could see hers.

There were many other heroes that day, including ordinary citizens whose acts of self-sacrifice to help others were not part of their job descriptions. Some of the help was dramatically heroic, like that of the passengers aboard hijacked United Airlines Flight 93. They decided to fight the terrorists on their flight and sacrifice their own lives in order to try to prevent the terrorists from killing many more people on the ground. And much of the help was behind the scenes, as in the cases of people who volunteered endless hours to do the grueling work of cleaning up the disaster area, helping the injured and the grieving, and donating money, clothes, and other resources.

When people read stories such as these, it is natural for them to wonder what they would have done: Would they have risked their lives to help others? What makes some people, at some times, act to help others? The wonderful acts of helping during the chaos of 9/11 are inspiring, to be sure. But there were also many stories that day of people who turned their backs on others, even on people who had just helped them.

Every day there are numerous unheralded acts of helping others and of failing to help others. A volunteer works tirelessly in an AIDS clinic, a college student tutors a child, a congregation raises money for a religious cause, an older sister lets her little brother win at checkers. And yet every day someone ignores the screams outside his or her window, drives past motorists stranded on the side of a road, or tries to avoid making eye contact with a homeless person on the street.

Every few months we see a story like that of Terrence Kelsor, who had been a security guard for only three weeks when he saw a drunken man stumble onto the train tracks in New York City as a train approached in March 2009. Kelsor jumped onto the track, grabbed the man—who outweighed him by 80 pounds—and pulled him off the tracks, just as the speeding train approached. "I had to react quick," he reported. "I knew if I didn't do something, this man was going to die" (Samuels & Goldsmith, 2009, p. 6).

And all too often we also learn stories like that of Angel Arce Torres, a 78-year-old man crossing the street in Hartford, Connecticut, in May 2008. From a video of the incident posted on the Internet, one can see a speeding car driving on the wrong side of the street hit Torres violently, sending him twisting in the air and crashing to the pavement. He lies there motionless. One car after another drives by, pausing only briefly before moving past the injured man. Numerous witnesses look on from the sidewalk. Several appear to consider checking on the man, but then something seems to hold them back. Eventually, finally, one man walks into the street to check on the victim, and only then do several others act as well. The victim, left paralyzed and unable to talk, died a year later. The police chief said, "It's incredible how people could be so inhumane. We no longer have a moral compass" (Cohen & De La Torre, 2009, p. A1).

There is no simple answer to the question of why some people help and others don't or why some situations lead to quick assistance and others to shocking displays of inaction. The determinants of helping behavior are complex and multifaceted. But social psychologists have learned a great deal about these determinants—and therefore about human nature. As you will see in the pages to come, some of their findings are quite surprising.

In this chapter, we examine several questions about helping: *Why* do people help? *When* do they help? *Who* is likely to help? *Whom* do they help? The concluding section concentrates on a major recurring theme—social connection—that underlies much of the theory and research on helping.

Evolutionary and Motivational Factors: Why Do People Help?

Although few individuals reach the heights of heroic helping, virtually everyone helps somebody sometime. People give their friends a ride to the airport; donate money, food, and clothing for disaster relief; babysit for a relative; work as a volunteer for charitable activities; pick up the mail for a neighbor who's out of town. The list of **prosocial behaviors**—actions intended to benefit others—is endless. But *why* do people help? Several factors have an impact.

Evolutionary Factors in Helping

We begin with evolution. Evolutionary scientists use principles of evolution to understand human social behavior. Can evolutionary principles help explain why people help? At first glance, some may think it unlikely. From an evolutionary perspective, what possible function can there be in helping others, especially at the risk of one's own life? Doesn't risking one's life for others fly in the face of evolutionary principles such as "survival of the fittest"?

The "Selfish Gene" In fact, evolutionary perspectives emphasize not the survival of the fittest individuals but the survival of the individuals' genes (Dawkins, 1989; Hamilton, 1964). From the perspective of evolution, human social behavior should be analyzed in terms of its contribution to reproductive success in ancestral environments: the conception, birth, and survival of offspring over the course of many generations. If a specific social behavior enhances reproductive success, then the genetic underpinnings of that behavior are more likely to be passed on to subsequent generations. In this way, the behavior can eventually become part of the common inheritance of the species.

According to a report by the Giving USA Foundation, Americans gave more than $300 billion to charitable causes in 2008, despite a terrible economic recession. Almost 90 percent of households gave. The results of the Canadian Survey of Giving, Volunteering, and Participating show that Canadians donated about $10 billion in 2007; 85 percent of adults gave at least one donation.

prosocial behaviors Actions intended to benefit others.

Of course, in order to reproduce, the individual must survive long enough to do so. Being helped *by* others should increase the chances of survival. But what about being helpful *to* others? Since helping others can be costly in terms of time and effort and it is sometimes dangerous to the helper, being helpful would seem to decrease one's chances of survival. Shouldn't any genetically based propensities for helping have dropped out of the gene pool long ago?

Not necessarily. There is an alternative to individual survival. You can also preserve your genes by promoting the survival of those who share your genetic makeup, even if you perish in the effort to help them. By means of this indirect route to genetic survival, the tendency to help genetic relatives, called **kin selection**, could become an innate characteristic—that is, a characteristic that is not contingent on learning for its development, although it can be influenced by learning, culture, and other factors. Kin selection is evident in the behavior of many organisms. Just as humans often risk their lives to save close relatives, ground squirrels, capuchin monkeys, and many other mammals and birds emit an alarm to warn nearby relatives of a predator. The alarm helps their relatives but makes the individual who sounds the alarm more vulnerable to attack (McCowan & Hooper, 2002; Schel et al., 2009; Wheeler, 2008). Similarly, lemurs sometimes rush to the aid of a fellow lemur held by a snake, putting themselves at risk as they mob the snake to save the lemur (Eberle & Kappeler, 2008).

Because kin selection serves the function of genetic survival, preferential helping of genetic relatives should be strongest when the biological stakes are particularly high. This appears to be the case (Burnstein et al., 1994; Korchmaros et al., 2006; Stewart-Williams, 2007). For example, participants in a study by Carey Fitzgerald (2009) were asked how willing they would be to offer different kinds of help to a friend, a half-sibling, or a sibling. There were three levels of helping behavior: the lowest risk involved picking up items from a store for the person; the medium risk involved loaning the person $10,000; and the highest risk involved trying to rescue the person from a burning house.

As can be seen in ▶ Figure 10.1, for the lowest-risk helping scenario, participants rated themselves as likely to help a friend as a sibling. For the higher-risk scenarios, however, they were significantly more willing to help a sibling than a friend. Their willingness to help a half-sibling fell in between their willingness to help a friend and their willingness to help a sibling.

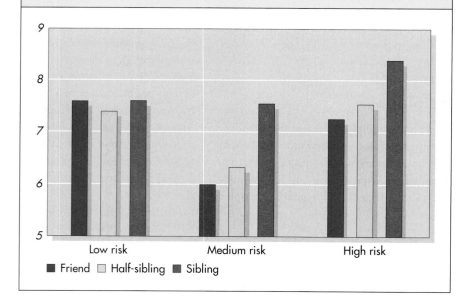

▶ **FIGURE 10.1**

Helping Kin When Risks Are High

Participants indicated how willing they would be to offer different types of help to a friend, a half-sibling, or a sibling. The help was either low risk, medium risk, or high risk. For the lowest-risk help, participants were as willing to help a friend as they were to help a sibling. For higher-risk helping, in contrast, participants were more willing to help a sibling than a friend, with willingness to help a half-sibling coming in the middle.

Based on Fitzgerald, 2009.

■ Friend ☐ Half-sibling ■ Sibling

kin selection Preferential helping of genetic relatives, which results in the greater likelihood that genes held in common will survive.

Participants in a series of studies by Elaine Madsen and others (2007) did more than speculate about what they thought they would do in different hypothetical scenarios— these participants actually suffered in order to help others. Participants in these studies were asked to hold a difficult position with their legs (from an isometric ski-training exercise). The longer they could hold the position, the more money would be earned for another person. However, the position became more and more painful to hold over time.

Consistent with predictions based on kin selection, participants withstood the pain and held the position longer if they were doing so for a genetically close relative than for a more distant relative, a friend, or a charity. This effect was found among British students as well as among participants from Zulu populations in South Africa.

Reciprocal Altruism   Kin selection provides only a partial explanation for helping. Relatives are not always helpful to each other. And even though relatives may get preferential treatment, most people help out nonkin as well. What's the reproductive advantage of helping someone who isn't related to you? The most common answer is reciprocity. Through *reciprocal altruism*, helping someone else can be in your best interests because it increases the likelihood that you will be helped in return (Krebs, 1987; Trivers, 1985). If A helps B and B helps A, both A and B increase their chances of survival and reproductive success. Over the course of evolution, therefore, individuals who engage in reciprocal altruism should survive and reproduce more than individuals who do not, thus enabling this kind of altruism to flourish.

Robert Trivers (1971) cites several examples of reciprocal altruism in animals. Many animals groom each other; for instance, monkeys groom other monkeys and cats groom other cats. Large fish (such as groupers) allow small fish (such as wrasses) to swim in their mouths without eating them; the small fish get food for themselves and at the same time remove parasites from the larger fish. And chimps who share with other chimps at one feeding are repaid by the other chimps at another feeding; those who are selfish are rebuffed, sometimes violently, at a later feeding (de Waal, 1996, 2006b).

An additional illustration is provided by Robert Seyfarth and Dorothy Cheney (1984). In a creative field experiment, these researchers audiotaped female vervet monkeys calling out for help and then played the recorded vocalizations near other female monkeys. Half of these other monkeys heard a female who had recently groomed them; the other half heard a female who had not recently done so. Consistent with the idea of reciprocal altruism, monkeys were significantly more likely to respond attentively to the request for help if the solicitor had just groomed them than if she had not. Interestingly, if the solicitor was genetically related to the monkeys who heard the tape, the monkeys' response was equally strong, whether or not she had groomed them.

Frans de Waal (2003) observed a group of chimpanzees engaged in nearly 7,000 interactions and recorded their grooming and food-sharing behaviors. He noted striking evidence of reciprocal altruism among these chimps. If Chimp A groomed Chimp B, for instance, B became much more likely to then share his or her food with A. Moreover, if Chimp A groomed B but was not reciprocated in some way by B, A became unlikely to then share his or her food with B.

Scratch my back and I'll scratch yours.

—Proverb

Many animals groom each other, whether they are chimpanzees in Tanzania or young girls in the United States. According to evolutionary psychologists, such behavior often reflects reciprocal altruism.

It's interesting that these chimps were able to negotiate this kind of reciprocity across acts: in grooming and food sharing. It was as if they were operating under a norm of "You scratch my back, I'll scratch yours—or maybe I'll give you some of my apples." This more complicated reciprocation is not uncommon. For example, in a meta-analysis of studies involving 14 different primate species, Gabriele Schino (2006) found evidence that grooming is reciprocated with support in fights (against some other individual). You scratch my back and I'll have your back in a fight!

Learning to cooperate, therefore, can be rewarding for both parties. One clever study that illustrates this was conducted by Frans de Waal and Michelle Berger (2000). They observed same-sex pairs of capuchin monkeys working cooperatively in a test chamber to obtain a tray of food. The two monkeys were separated from each other by a mesh partition. One monkey by itself could not pull the tray, but the two monkeys could accomplish the task if they cooperated. When successful, the monkey that wound up with the food consistently shared it with its helper. When they were rewarded in this way, the monkeys became even more likely to help each other on subsequent occasions.

In some human environments, reciprocal altruism is essential for survival even today. Consider, for example, the Northern Ache, who are indigenous peoples of northeastern Paraguay. Wesley Allen-Arave and others (2008) studied a group of Northern Ache who lived in households on a reservation and shared virtually all their food across households. The researchers found that households shared more food with other households that reciprocated in kind. Even among kin, sharing food was contingent on being reciprocated. In other words, households shared more food with kin who were most likely to reciprocate.

Reciprocal altruism is not restricted to basic needs such as food acquisition. Think of file sharing instead of food sharing. Swapping music and videos online through file-sharing services may be considered a form of reciprocal altruism, since an individual makes his or her own files available to others so that he or she can have access to theirs. (Of course, record companies and movie studios have other terms for these activities, such as *criminal* and *unethical*.) Strong norms often develop in these peer-to-peer networks. An individual who downloads songs or videos from others' computers but doesn't make his or her own files available is likely to be chastised quickly and emphatically.

Indeed, the development of norms and the punishment of individuals who deviate from the norm are key factors in maintaining reciprocal altruism, especially in groups of nonkin. Indrikis Krams and others (2008) observed in a field experiment that pied flycatchers (a type of bird) would come to the aid of a captured neighbor and mob the predator—but not if the neighbor had not cooperated by providing assistance earlier! In addition to withholding support, individuals may actively punish violators of the norm of reciprocity, despite the potential cost to themselves in doing so (Nelissen, 2008; Rilling et al., 2008; Singer, 2006).

Group-Level Altruism   Kin selection and reciprocal altruism emphasize helping specific others based on genetic relatedness or the probability of being helped in return. But much helping goes beyond these limits. For example, injured or sick animals are sometimes aided by others in their group, even if they are unrelated and there is little chance that the recipients will return the favor (de Waal, 1996, 2008). Can altruism operate at a broader level than specific genes or specific reciprocal relationships between individuals?

One such example is *indirect reciprocity*, which can be described as "I help you and somebody else helps me" (Nowak & Sigmund, 2005; Stanca, 2009). This kind of more complex system of altruism may play a role in *group selection*. The idea behind group selection is that groups with altruistic members may be more likely to thrive and avoid extinction than groups with only selfish individuals (O'Gorman et al., 2008; Wilson et al., 2008). According to this perspective, cooperation and helpfulness among mem-

Charity begins at home but shouldn't end there.

—Scottish proverb

bers of a social group—especially when the group faces an external threat—could be an evolved tendency. Frans de Waal (1996) reports remarkable instances of within-group helping among animals—for example, a Japanese monkey born without hands and feet who was fully accepted and helped by the other monkeys in its group and a retarded rhesus monkey given special care by the other monkeys in its group. Barry Sinervo and others (2006) recently reported cooperative partnerships among nonrelated lizards to protect their territories. Some evolutionary scientists are skeptical of the concept of group selection, however, and it remains to be seen how this idea itself will evolve in the years to come (Brewer & Caporael, 2006; Price, 2008).

The Evolution of Morality, Parental Caregiving, and Empathy   The research and examples just discussed are among the reasons that some scholars have become more interested in studying seemingly higher-order, very "human" attributes such as morality, gratitude, and empathy from an evolutionary perspective. Although these concepts may seem incompatible with "the selfish gene" perspective, contemporary evolutionary approaches point to their adaptive functions. From this view, morality is not merely a human construction made to constrain us from exhibiting our selfish, aggressive, "animal" true nature but instead evolved due to the social nature of primates, including (but not exclusive to) the human animal (de Waal, 2006a; McCullough et al., 2008; Narvaez & Lapsley, 2009; Sinnott-Armstrong, 2008).

Consider the story of Binti Jua. At the end of 1996, *People* magazine honored her as one of the twenty-five "most intriguing people" of the year and *Newsweek* named her "hero of the year." On August 16, while caring for her own seventeen-month-old daughter, Binti came across a three-year-old boy who had fallen about twenty feet onto a cement floor and been knocked unconscious. She picked up the boy and gently held him, rocking him softly, and then turned him over to paramedics. What was most "intriguing" about Binti? The fact that she was a gorilla.

When the boy climbed over a fence and fell into the primate exhibit at the Brookfield Zoo, near Chicago, witnesses feared the worst. One paramedic said, "I didn't know if she was going to treat him like a doll or a toy." With her own daughter clinging to her back the entire time, Binti "protected the toddler as if he were her own," keeping other gorillas at bay and eventually placing him gently at the entrance where zookeepers and paramedics could get to him. "I could not believe how gentle she was," observed a zoo director (O'Neill et al., 1996, p. 72).

© 1996 Robert Allison/Contact Press Images

Binti Jua, a gorilla at the Brookfield Zoo, near Chicago, gently rocks a three-year-old boy who had fallen eighteen feet into the primate exhibit. The gorilla was acclaimed as a hero for her role in saving the boy. Did Binti Jua act out of kindness and empathy? Or did she simply do what she was taught—fetch objects that fall into her cage? This episode brings the altruism debate to life, even in the animal world.

Was this an act of kindness and compassion, or did the gorilla just do what she had been trained to do—pick up and fetch things dropped into her cage? There is no way to know in this case, but this story is consistent with research on the evolution of parental caregiving (Bell, 2001). Many mammals, and especially humans, display impulses to care for offspring. Parental caregiving, of course, tends to help kin survive, but these behaviors can sometimes generalize to helping offspring who are not kin (Batson et al., 2005).

Empathy is another concept that may not be as uniquely human as some might think. Although the definition of **empathy** has been much debated, most researchers regard empathy as having both cognitive and emotional components (Davis et al., 2004; de Waal, 2009; Eisenberg et al., 2006). The major cognitive component of empathy is *perspective taking*: using the power of imagination to try to see the world through someone else's eyes. A key emotional component of empathy is *empathic concern*, which involves other-oriented feelings, such as sympathy, compassion, and tenderness. In contrast to empathic concern is *personal distress*, which involves self-oriented reactions to a person

empathy Understanding or vicariously experiencing another individual's perspective and feeling sympathy and compassion for that individual.

in need, such as feeling alarmed, troubled, or upset. Researchers today cite numerous examples of animals behaving in ways that seem to show empathy.

For example, a fascinating study suggests that human infants and possibly even young chimpanzees are capable of at least a rudimentary degree of perspective taking and the helping behavior that results. Felix Warneken and Michael Tomasello (2006) placed eighteen-month-old human infants with an adult experimenter. At various points in time, the experimenter appeared to have trouble reaching a goal. For example, he accidentally dropped a marker on the floor and tried unsuccessfully to reach it, or he couldn't put some magazines into a cabinet because the doors were closed. Twenty-two of the twenty-four infants tested in the study helped the experimenter in at least one of the tasks, and many infants helped on several tasks. In doing so, the infants apparently understood that the experimenter needed help—that is, that he was having trouble completing a task by himself.

Two additional details are worth noting about the study. First, the experimenter never requested help from the infants, nor did he praise or reward the infants when they did help. Second, for every task he needed help with, the experimenter created a similar situation in which he did not seem to have a problem. For example, rather than accidentally drop the marker on the floor and try to reach it, the experimenter sometimes intentionally threw the marker on the floor and did not try to retrieve it. In these situations, the infants were not likely to take action such as picking up the marker. This suggested that when they did help the experimenter, the infants did so because they understood he was trying to achieve some goal.

The researchers also tested three young chimpanzees using a similar procedure. The chimpanzees also helped the human experimenter when they saw that he appeared to need help reaching his goal, although not across as many tasks or as reliably as the human infants did. The authors reported that this was the first experimental evidence of helping of this kind (helping others who are struggling to achieve some goal without any benefit to the self) by nonhuman primates.

Frans de Waal (2008, 2009), among others, has cited numerous and startling examples of primates such as chimpanzees and bonobos seeming to show empathy under more natural conditions. For example, ▶ Figure 10.2 depicts a juvenile chimpanzee putting an arm around an adult male who had just been defeated in a fight. This kind of consoling behavior is not uncommon in chimpanzees. De Waal also reports examples of chimpanzees who risked their lives trying to save companions from drowning, even though they themselves were unable to swim. Less dramatically, young chimps have been seen helping to push an old and arthritic group member up onto a climbing frame for a grooming session. The examples de Waal has collected suggest at least some degree of perspective taking

▶ FIGURE 10.2

Consolation in Chimps

A juvenile chimpanzee puts an arm around an adult male who has just lost a fight. Frans de Waal has observed many such acts of consoling behavior among apes.

De Waal, 2008.

and sympathy among nonhuman primates. De Waal (2008) concludes, "There is now increasing evidence that the brain is hardwired for social connection, and that the same empathy mechanism proposed to underlie human altruism may underlie the directed altruism of other animals" (p. 292).

Rewards of Helping: Helping Others to Help Oneself

Whether or not it can be traced to evolutionary factors, one important reason why people help others is because it often is rewarding, even if the rewards are psychological rather than material. We all like the idea of being the hero, lifted onto the shoulders of our peers for coming to the rescue of someone in distress. Helping helps the helper.

The empirical evidence on this point is clear: People are much more likely to help when the potential rewards of helping seem high relative to the potential costs. This effect does not appear to be limited to the very individualistic cultures of the United States, Canada, and Western Europe (Hedge & Yousif, 1992; Imai, 1991). Potential helpers around the world often seem to conduct a cost-benefit analysis not only when making deliberate decisions to behave prosocially, as when donating blood, but also in more impulsive, sudden decisions to intervene in an emergency.

Indeed, the **arousal: cost-reward model** of helping stipulates that both emotional and cognitive factors determine whether bystanders to an emergency will intervene (Dovidio et al., 2006). Emotionally, bystanders experience the shock and alarm of personal distress; this unpleasant state of arousal motivates them to do something to reduce it. What they do, however, depends on the "bystander calculus," their computation of the costs and rewards associated with helping. When potential rewards (to self and victim) outweigh potential costs (to self and victim), bystanders will help. But raise those costs and lower those rewards and it is likely that the victims will not be helped (Fritzsche et al., 2000; Piliavin et al., 1981).

Feeling Good   Helping often simply feels good. A growing body of research reveals a strong relationship between giving help and feeling better, including improvements in mental *and* physical health (Dillard et al., 2008; Omoto et al., 2009; Piliavin, 2003; Post, 2005). Heidi Wayment (2004), for example, found that women who engaged in helping behaviors in the aftermath of the September 11, 2001, terrorist attacks in the United States showed greater reduction in their distress over time than women who did not do so. More recently, a longitudinal study by Jane Piliavin and Erica Siegl (2008) found that doing volunteer work was associated with improvements in psychological well-being and that volunteering for multiple organizations was associated with greater improvement.

In a provocative set of studies using brain-imaging techniques, James Rilling and others (2002) examined the brain activity of women playing a Prisoner's Dilemma game, which, as was discussed in Chapter 8, is a game in which individuals compete or cooperate with each other for individual and joint payoffs. The researchers found that when the women were engaged in mutual cooperation during the game, activation was observed in areas of the brain that are linked to the processing of rewards. Despite the fact that these individuals could have earned more money by competing with their partner after their partner had cooperated, their brain activity suggested that cooperation was intrinsically rewarding. This feeling could reinforce altruism and inhibit selfishness.

Even when helping doesn't feel good immediately, it can pay off in the long run. When parents reluctantly sacrifice relaxing with a good book or DVD at the end of a hard day in order to help their child finish some homework, they might not feel immediate

When you give to someone else, you get so much more.
—Former U.S. Secretary of State Colin Powell

People are more likely to help someone in an emergency if the potential rewards seem high and the potential costs seem low. TRUE.

arousal: cost-reward model The proposition that people react to emergency situations by acting in the most cost-effective way to reduce the arousal of shock and alarm.

A Peace Corps worker teaches English in Honduras. Volunteering one's time, energy, and skills to help others can make one feel good about oneself. Even if they are not financial, the rewards can be tremendous.

Bob Daemmrich/The Image Works

joy from giving help, but in the long run, they can expect to reap the benefits of their behavior (Salovey et al., 1991).

Children learn that helping others can be rewarding. Younger children focus on the rewards they get from parents and others, but as they develop into adolescents, they begin to reward themselves for helping, taking pride in their actions. Their helpful behavior can then be internally motivated, leading them to help even without the promise of immediate material or social rewards (Cialdini et al., 1981; Piliavin & Callero, 1991).

The process of helping others in order to feel good about oneself is often not conscious, but it can be. For example, participants in one study rated the relative importance of a number of considerations in deciding whether to help someone else. Two of the three considerations that the participants rated as most important concerned the rewards ("It would make me feel good about myself") and costs ("I might get hurt") of helping. The other consideration was "It's the right thing to do" (Smitherman, 1992). People's awareness that helping feels good is evident in the words offered by no less an authority than "Dear Abby," the world's most famous syndicated advice columnist. She offered this advice to her readers: "The surest way to forget your own troubles is to do something nice for those less fortunate. The adrenaline rush you'll get is more powerful than speed, and the 'high' is perfectly legal" ("Dear Abby," 2003).

In their **negative state relief model**, Robert Cialdini and his colleagues (1987) propose that because of this positive effect of helping, people who are feeling bad may be inclined to help others in order to improve their mood. Indeed, after experiencing a traumatic event, some individuals seek out opportunities to help others in order to feel better about themselves instead of becoming bitter and antisocial (Staub & Vollhardt, 2008; Vollhardt, 2009). Helping others may help one heal oneself.

Being Good   In addition to wanting to *feel* good, many of us also are motivated to *be* good—that is, to help because we recognize that "it's the right thing to do." Some situations are especially likely to call to mind norms that compel helpful behaviors. These may be everyday situations, as when encountering an elderly person in a parking lot who needs help getting grocery bags in her car. Sometimes norms can compel much more dramatic and risky action, particularly for individuals whose roles in a group or society give them responsibility in a situation. When the firefighters in Ladder Company 6 (described in the introduction of this chapter) risked their lives to stay with Josephine Harris, their actions were consistent with the idea of not leaving anyone behind who could be saved. Another example is that of Chesley "Sully" Sullenberger, pilot of US Airways Flight 1549 on the afternoon of January 15, 2009. When the jet hit a large flock of geese just after takeoff from LaGuardia Airport in New York City, it lost all power in its engines and was heading for catastrophe. Sullenberger somehow guided the jet to a safe landing in the Hudson River. As the plane began to fill up with water, the crew managed to get all 150 passengers out of the plane and onto the wings and rafts and eventually into various rescue crafts. Sullenberger refused to leave the sinking plane until he had walked up and down the cabin two final times to make sure no one was left behind. No matter what, he would be the last person off the plane

negative state relief model
The proposition that people help others in order to counteract their own feelings of sadness.

as well as the last person off the rafts in the frigid river (McClam, 2009).

Acts of helping and courage like these may be triggered by norms and moral principles, but of course they can also serve to make the helpers feel good about themselves. Being good can feel good, and the heroic helper may be rewarded in multiple ways.

The Cost of Helping or of Not Helping Clearly helping has its rewards, but it has its costs as well. The firefighters in Ladder Company 6 who somehow survived the collapse of the North Tower of the World Trade Center while saving Josephine Harris were among the lucky ones. Many people were killed while helping others that day, such as Abraham Zelmanowitz, a computer programmer who refused to leave his quadriplegic friend who could not descend the stairs. And beyond 9/11, we often are moved by stories of the costs paid by those who offer help, such as Charles Bybee, a 62-year-old man who went into a busy street in Fullerton, California, to rescue a suicidal woman who seemed to be trying to get hit by a car in the summer of 2009. While trying to help, he was the one struck and killed by a car (Associated Press, 2009).

AP Photo/Bebeto Matthews

Survivors of a flight that landed in the cold Hudson River on January 15, 2009, stand on the wings and begin to board boats to take them to safety. After his miraculous safe landing in the river after losing all power to his jet's engines, pilot Chesley Sullenberger made sure that he was the last one out of the plane and onto the boats, fulfilling his responsibility to his crew and passengers.

Other helpers have done more sustained and deliberate helping, such as the people who helped hide runaway slaves in the nineteenth-century United States or the people who helped hide Jews during the Holocaust. Sharon Shepela and others (1999) call this type of thoughtful helping in the face of potentially enormous costs *courageous resistance*. And although giving help is often associated with positive affect and health, when the help involves constant and exhausting demands, which is often the case when taking long-term care of a very ill person, the effects on the helper's physical and mental health can be quite negative (Fujino & Okamura, 2009; Mioshi et al., 2009).

To lower some of the costs of helping, some legislatures have created "Good Samaritan" laws that encourage bystanders to intervene in emergencies by offering them legal protection, particularly doctors who volunteer medical care when they happen upon emergencies (Cunningham, 2009; Oleson, 2009). Other kinds of Good Samaritan laws increase the costs of failing to help. Sometimes called "duty to rescue" laws, these laws require people to provide or summon aid in an emergency, so long as they do not endanger themselves in the process. Such laws are not uncommon in Europe and Canada. In fact, several photographers were initially accused by French authorities of breaking France's Good Samaritan laws following the automobile crash that killed Princess Diana, her companion, and their driver in Paris in 1997. Reportedly, these photographers arrived early at the crash scene and took pictures rather than attempting to help the victims. (In the United States, this kind of "duty to rescue" law is relatively rare, but it did play an important role in the final episode of the popular TV series *Seinfeld*, as the four main characters were arrested and sentenced to a year in prison for callously failing to help someone in need.)

> *The charity that hastens to proclaim its good deeds, ceases to be a charity, and is only pride and ostentation.*
> —William Hutton

■ Altruism or Egoism: The Great Debate

We have documented some of the ways that helping others can help the helper. This raises a classic question, however: Are our helpful behaviors always **egoistic**—motivated by selfish concerns or simple conformity to socialized norms? Or are humans

egoistic Motivated by the desire to increase one's own welfare.

ever truly **altruistic**—motivated by the desire to increase another's welfare? Many psychological theories assume an egoistic, self-interested bottom line. It is not difficult to imagine egoistic interpretations for almost any acts of helping, even the most seemingly altruistic ones. Tutoring the disadvantaged? It will look good on your résumé or college application. Anonymously helping the homeless? It reduces your guilt. Donating blood to people you'll never know? It makes you feel a bit more noble. Risking your life for a stranger? Such heroism may benefit your reputation and status. So is all helping at some level egoistic?

Daniel Batson (2009) thinks not. As we will see in the following section, he believes that the motivation behind some helpful actions is truly altruistic and that empathy plays a critically important role in it.

AP Photo/Blake Wolf

Liz Wallace and Mallory Holtman carry their opponent, Sara Tucholosky, around the bases in their college softball tournament game. After hitting the first home run of her career, Tucholosky injured her knee and could not run around the bases to complete the run, and her teammates and coaches were not allowed to help her and preserve the home run. Despite costing their own team a run, Wallace and Holtman volunteered to help her around the bases in an inspiring act of altruism.

altruistic Motivated by the desire to improve another's welfare.

The Empathy-Altruism Hypothesis Batson's model of altruism is based on his view of the consequences of empathy. As we discussed earlier, *empathy* is understood by many researchers to have the cognitive component of taking another's perspective and the emotional component of feeling concerned for that other. According to Batson, both components are the key to altruism. If you perceive someone in need and imagine how *that person* feels, you are likely to experience other-oriented feelings of empathic concern, which in turn produce the altruistic motive to reduce the other person's distress.

There are, however, instances in which people perceive someone in need and focus on their *own* feelings about this person or on how *they* would feel in that person's situation. Although many people may think of this as "empathy," Batson contrasts this with instances in which people's concern is with how the *other person* is feeling. It's when your focus is on the other person that true altruism is possible. This focus on the other person is illustrated in the story described in the beginning of the chapter about Terrence Kelsor rescuing a drunken man from the path of an oncoming train. Kelsor was quoted explaining his motivation, "At the time, I was just concerned about the man's life. I wasn't thinking about being a hero" (Samuels & Goldsmith, 2009, p. 6).

Another story that may illustrate empathy occurred during a college softball tournament game between Central Washington and Western Oregon in April 2008. In the second inning, a short, "really tiny" senior named Sara Tucholsky shocked everyone by hitting the first home run of her career. In her excitement she missed touching first base, and when she turned to go back and touch it, she tore a ligament in her knee and crumpled to the ground in agony. There was no way she could run around the bases, and therefore her home run would not be official. Her coach talked with officials about what to do. They said that no one from her team could help her around the bases and that she would have to be replaced and the home run would not count. Then someone stepped in and asked, "Excuse me, would it be OK if we carried her around and she touched each bag?"

It was the star hitter from the opposing team, Mallory Holtman. She and another player carried Tucholsky around the diamond, lowering her enough at each base to allow her to touch it so that she could preserve the one and only home run of her softball career. They did this despite the fact that it would cost their own team a run in a close and important game—a game they would ultimately lose by just two runs, thereby ending their season. According to Holtman, she didn't do it for any glory. Indeed, she couldn't understand why people made a fuss about it afterward. "Everyone

▶**FIGURE 10.3**

The Empathy-Altruism Hypothesis

According to the empathy-altruism hypothesis, taking the perspective of a person in need creates feelings of empathic concern, which produce the altruistic motive to reduce the other person's distress. When people do not take the other's perspective, they experience feelings of personal distress, which produce the egoistic motive to reduce their own discomfort.

Based on Batson, 1991.

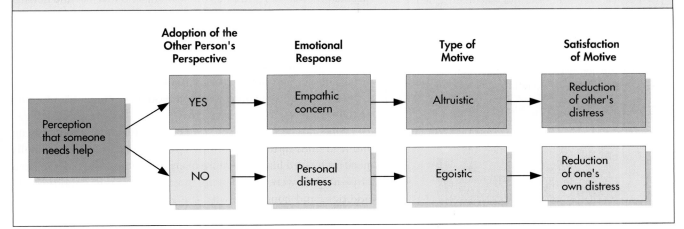

else would have done it," she said (Hays, 2008). It is impossible to know from a story like this exactly what factors could have motivated the helping behavior, but clearly some degree of taking the other person's perspective and feeling sympathy for her were crucial elements behind Mallory Holtman's decision to help her fallen opponent.

The basic features of Batson's **empathy-altruism hypothesis** are outlined in ▶ Figure 10.3. The hard part, though, is this: How can we tell the difference between egoistic and altruistic motives? In both cases people help someone else, but the helpers' reasons are different. Confronted with this puzzle, Batson came up with an elegant solution. It depends, he says, on whether one can obtain the relevant self-benefits without relieving the other's need. For example, when a person's motive is egoistic, helping should decline if it's easy for the individual to escape from the situation and therefore escape from his or her own feelings of distress. When a person's motive is altruistic, however, help will be given regardless of the ease of escape.

Based on this reasoning, Batson and others have conducted more than 30 experiments that have found support for the empathy-altruism hypothesis. For example, participants in one set of studies were given an opportunity to use an excuse that would allow them to both escape from helping someone and avoid feeling guilty about it. Participants who were primed with nothing or primed to think about their own feelings tended to take advantage of the excuse and escape the situation. Participants primed to take the other person's perspective, however, were much more likely to help the other person despite the chance to get out of it and despite the cost associated with giving the help. For these participants, the altruistic motives triggered by empathic concern could be satisfied only through actually helping the other person (Batson et al., 2003).

In a recent study, Batson and his colleagues (2007) demonstrated the role of both perspective taking and having warm emotional reactions to the other person in predicting helping. Students in this study read about a fictitious student named Bryan Banks who was hit by a car while running late to class and was seriously injured. The researchers manipulated perspective taking by varying the instructions given to the students. Those in the objective condition were asked to "try to take an objective perspective toward what is described. Try not to get caught up in how the student facing

The great gift of human beings is that we have the power of empathy.

—Meryl Streep

empathy-altruism hypothesis
The proposition that empathic concern for a person in need produces an altruistic motive for helping.

▶ FIGURE 10.4

Perspective Taking and Positive Emotions Underlying Helping

Students read about a fictitious student named Bryan who was injured. They were instructed either to take an objective perspective or to imagine Bryan's perspective. They also read information designed to make them feel either positive or negative emotions toward him. The bars in this graph reflect the percentage of students in each condition who agreed to help get class notes copied for Bryan. The combination of imagining Bryan's perspective and feeling positive emotions toward him led to the most helping.

Based on Batson et al., 2007.

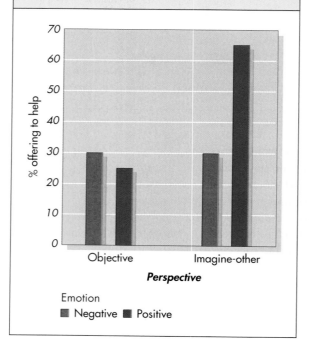

this difficulty feels; just remain objective and detached." The students in the imagine-perspective condition were asked to "try to imagine how the student facing this difficulty feels and how it is affecting his or her life."

The researchers also manipulated emotional reactions to Bryan. Students read that Bryan had been running late to class because he was stopped by an old woman who was lost and needed help finding her house. The students in one condition read that Bryan was very nice to the woman, whereas students in the other condition read that Bryan was rather nasty to her. Later, after they were led to think the study was completed, the students read a letter asking for volunteers to help Bryan by helping get class notes copied for him, a commitment that would take a couple of hours of their time.

As can be seen in ▶ Figure 10.4, participants who had been induced both to take Bryan's perspective and to feel emotionally positive toward him were more likely to sign up to help the injured student than were participants in any of the other conditions. In addition, and consistent with the empathy-altruism hypothesis, the more these students felt empathic concern for Bryan (as measured on a questionnaire), the more likely they were to step up and actually offer to help him.

Despite the evidence that supports the empathy-altruism hypothesis, it has its limits. For example, Batson has never claimed that *all* helping is altruistically motivated. There are multiple motives for helping, and many (and probably most) helpful acts are best explained in terms of the processes we consider elsewhere in this chapter. And any single helpful action can be the result of a mixture of egoistic and altruistic motives. Mark Snyder (1993) suggests, for example, that the most effective way to increase helping is to encourage people to recognize and feel comfortable with the convergence of self-oriented and other-oriented concerns. Another limit is created by the fact that motives do not guarantee behavior. Empathy leads to altruistic motivations but not necessarily to helpful behaviors. For example, someone with empathic concern for another might not help this person if he or she fears that the potential cost of offering the help will be very high (Batson et al., 1983).

It is also the case that some individuals may tend to be more or less altruistic than others. For example, in a set of studies Brent Simpson and Robb Willer (2008) found that individuals they classified as egoists tended to act prosocially when their reputations were at stake, but individuals they classified as altruists tended to act prosocially regardless of whether or not their reputations could be affected.

Convergence of Motivations: Volunteering The debate between egoistic and altruistic motivations may become less relevant when considering more long-term helping behavior, such as volunteerism. People tend to volunteer not because of one single specific motive but due to multiple motives. Some of these motives are associated with empathy, such as perspective taking and empathic concern, whereas other motives are more egoistic, such as wanting to enhance one's résumé, relieve negative emotions, or conform to prosocial norms (Hur, 2006; Penner et al., 2005; Piferi et al., 2006; Reeder et al., 2001). Allen Omoto and others (2009) have found that both other-focused motivation and self-focused motivation predicted volunteerism.

More than 26 percent of the U.S. population did at least some volunteer work between September 2007 and September 2008, according to the U.S. Bureau of Labor Statistics.

Table 10.1 lists five categories of motives that Allen Omoto and Mark Snyder (1995) determined were behind volunteers' decisions to help people with AIDS. One interesting finding was that volunteers who had initially endorsed self-oriented motives, such as gaining understanding and developing personal skills, remained active volunteers longer than did those who had initially emphasized other-oriented motives, such as humanitarian values and community concern. Why were the more egoistic goals associated with longer service? Snyder and Omoto (2008) have observed that purely altruistic motives may not keep individuals motivated long enough to withstand the personal costs associated with some kinds of prolonged helping. As Mark Snyder noted, "The good, and perhaps romanticized, intentions related to humanitarian concern simply may not be strong enough to sustain volunteers faced with the tough realities and personal costs of working with [persons with AIDS]" (Snyder, 1993, p. 258). When helping demands more of us, self-interest may keep us going.

Egoistic motives, therefore, can be put to good use. This was evident in a set of studies by Eamonn Ferguson and others (2008). The researchers first conducted a longitudinal study in which they assessed the beliefs of British students about blood donation and then checked the United Kingdom's National Blood Service database six months later to see which of the students had donated blood during the six months.

According to the empathy-altruism hypothesis, taking the perspective of someone in need is the first step toward altruism. When Sarah DeCristoforo returned to school after receiving chemotherapy for leukemia, her teacher and two friends actually put themselves in her place in one highly visible respect—they shaved their heads. Here, Sarah, wearing a scarf, is surrounded by her supporters.

The Newport News Daily Press

TABLE 10.1

Motivations to Volunteer to Help People with AIDS

Allen Omoto and Mark Snyder identified five categories of motivations underlying people's initial decisions to become volunteers to help people with AIDS. Within each category, three examples of specific statements representative of the general motive are presented.

Values	Community Concern
Because of my humanitarian obligation to help others	Because of my sense of obligation to the gay community
Because I enjoy helping other people	Because I consider myself an advocate for gay-related issues
Because I consider myself a loving and caring person	Because of my concern and worry about the gay community
Understanding	**Esteem Enhancement**
To learn more about how to prevent AIDS	To feel better about myself
To learn how to help people with AIDS	To escape other pressures and stress in my life
To deal with my personal fears and anxiety about AIDS	To feel less lonely
Personal Development	
To get to know people who are similar to myself	
To meet new people and make new friends	
To gain experience dealing with emotionally difficult topics	

Omoto & Snyder, 1995.

The researchers found that having other-oriented beliefs about blood donation (such as that society benefits from blood donation) and having self-oriented beliefs (such as that they would benefit by donating blood) each predicted actual blood donation during the ensuing six-month period. Although both types of motives correlated with actual donations, having the self-oriented beliefs was the stronger predictor.

Based on these results Ferguson and his colleagues reasoned that it might be wise to focus on egoistic rewards when designing a campaign to try to encourage more people to donate blood. They designed an experiment to test this hypothesis. Some students in this study read a leaflet that promoted donation from an altruistic perspective. These students read messages such as that if they donated blood, "You are helping treat patients recovering from diseases such as leukemia, cancer, sickle cell disease, and thalassemia" or that if they did not donate blood, "Accident victims will be unable to use the blood." Other students read a leaflet that promoted donation from an egoistic perspective. Among the messages read by these students was that if they donated blood, "You may be pleased, fulfilled, contented, and proud of yourself," or that if they decided not to donate, "You will miss a personally rewarding experience that will boost your morale." The students then later indicated the extent to which they would be willing to donate blood.

The researchers found that if the students had not previously committed to donating blood, they remained relatively unwilling to donate blood after reading the leaflets. The students who had shown a previous commitment to blood donation, however, became more willing to do so after reading the messages. As can be seen in ▶ Figure 10.5, for these students, the egoistic messages were more effective than the altruistic ones. That is, students indicated greater willingness to donate blood if they had read messages that focused on how personally rewarding blood donation is than if they read messages that focused on the benefits to others of blood donation.

Self-interest as a motive for helping, therefore, is not necessarily a bad thing. Indeed, the fact that many people find helping others to be so personally rewarding is a positive aspect of human nature. One's feelings of empathic concern for others are usually limited to a few other people at a time and perhaps to relatively brief periods. Those people who derive a great deal of personal satisfaction from helping others, however, may be motivated much more frequently and consistently to engage in helping behaviors. Indeed, commitment to prosocial actions can become an important part of one's identity (Piliavin et al., 2002; Snyder & Omoto, 2008).

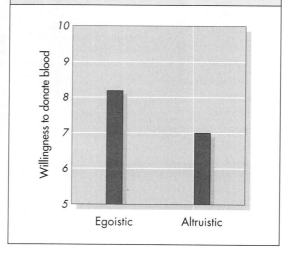

▶ **FIGURE 10.5**

Appealing to Egoistic Motives to Promote Blood Donation

Among students who had previously committed to donating blood, students who read persuasive messages that appealed to egoistic motives (for example, that donating blood makes people feel better about themselves) indicated a greater willingness to donate blood than did students who read messages that appealed to more altruistic motives (for example, that by donating blood people with various diseases would be helped).

Based on Ferguson et al., 2008.

Interested in volunteering? One place to find information is Volunteermatch.org.

Situational Influences: When Do People Help?

Thus far, we have focused on *why* people help others. We now turn to the question of *when* people help. We begin by discussing a remarkably creative and provocative set of research findings that make a surprising point: If you need help in an emergency, you may be better off if there is only one witness to your plight than if there are several. We then focus on a wide range of other situational factors related to helping, including where we live, whether we are experiencing time pressure, what kind of mood we're in, and whether we've been exposed to particular role models or social norms.

The Unhelpful Crowd

On January 15, 2008, a man named Rage Ibrahim was convicted for sexually assaulting a woman in the hallway of an apartment building in St. Paul, Minnesota, the previous summer. Surveillance video from the hallway showed several residents, as many as ten, opening their apartment doors, looking at the man beating and raping the screaming woman, and closing their doors as they went back into their apartments. At one point three men approached them, but they left after Ibrahim got off the woman and shoved one of them in the back. Despite the woman's cries for someone to call the police, no one called 911 for more than an hour. A police commander who saw the video said, "It was horrifying. I can't describe how it sent chills up my back, watching this woman getting assaulted and people turning their backs and doing nothing" (Gottfried, 2007, 2008).

The sad truth is that this kind of story of bystanders failing to act, while chilling, is not as uncommon as most people imagine. The most famous of these stories occurred more than four decades ago. It has remained famous in large part because of the fascinating social psychology research it inspired.

The story begins at about 3:20 in the morning on March 13, 1964, in the New York City borough of Queens. Twenty-eight-year-old Kitty Genovese was returning home from her job as a bar manager. Suddenly, a man attacked her with a knife. She was stalked, stabbed, and sexually assaulted just 35 yards from her own apartment building. Lights went on and windows went up as she screamed, "Oh my God! He stabbed me! Please help me!" She broke free from her attacker twice, but only briefly. Newspaper reports indicated that 38 of her neighbors witnessed her ordeal but not one intervened. Finally, after nearly 45 minutes of terror, one man called the police. But before they got her to the hospital, Genovese was dead.

The murder of Kitty Genovese shocked the nation. Were her neighbors to blame? It seemed unlikely that all 38 of them could have been moral monsters. Most of the media attention focused on the decline of morals and values in contemporary society and on the anonymity and apathy seen in large American cities such as New York. A few days after the incident, John Darley and Bibb Latané discussed over dinner the events and the explanations being offered for it. They were not convinced that these explanations were sufficient to account for why Kitty Genovese didn't get the help she needed; and they wondered if other, more social psychological processes might have been at work. They speculated that because each witness to the attack could see that many other witnesses had turned on their lights and were looking out their windows, each witness may have assumed that others would, or should, take responsibility and call the police. To test their ideas, Darley and Latané (1968) set out to see if they could produce unresponsive bystanders under laboratory conditions. Let's take a look at one of their studies.

The murder of Kitty Genovese, pictured here, shocked the nation in 1964. How could 38 witnesses stand by and do nothing? Research conducted in the aftermath of this tragedy suggests that if there had been only one witness rather than almost 40, Kitty Genovese might have had a better chance of receiving help, and she might be alive today.

NY Times/Redux Stock

When a participant arrived, he or she was taken to one of a series of small rooms located along a corridor. Speaking over an intercom, the experimenter explained that he wanted participants to discuss personal problems college students often face. Participants were told that to protect confidentiality, the group discussion would take place over the intercom system and that the experimenter would not be listening. They were required to speak one at a time, taking turns. Some participants were assigned to talk with one other person, whereas other participants joined larger groups of three or six people.

Although one participant did mention in passing that he suffered from a seizure disorder that was sometimes triggered by study pressures, the opening moments of the conversation were uneventful. But soon, an unexpected problem developed. When the time came for this person to speak again, he stuttered badly, had a hard time speaking clearly, and sounded as if he were in very serious trouble:

> I could really-er-use some help so if somebody would-er-give me a little h-help-uh-er-er-er-er c-could somebody-er-er-help-er-uh-uh-uh [choking sounds] . . . . I'm gonna die-er-er-I'm . . . gonna die-er-help-er-er-seizure-er [chokes, then quiet].

Confronted with this situation, what would *you* do? Would you interrupt the experiment, dash out of your cubicle, and try to find the experimenter? Or would you sit there—concerned, but unsure how to react?

As it turns out, participants' responses to this emergency were strongly influenced by the size of their group. Actually all participants were participating alone, but tape-recorded material led them to believe that others were present. All the participants who thought that only they knew about the emergency quickly left the room to try to get help. In the larger groups, however, participants were less likely and slower to intervene. Indeed, 38 percent of the participants in the six-person groups never left the room at all! This research led Latané and Darley to a chilling conclusion: The more bystanders there are, the *less* likely the victim will be helped. This is the **bystander effect**, whereby the presence of others inhibits helping.

Before the pioneering work of Latané and Darley, most people would have assumed just the opposite. Isn't there safety in numbers? Don't we feel more secure rushing in to help when others are around to lend their support? Latané and Darley overturned this commonsense assumption and provided a careful, step-by-step analysis of the decision-making process involved in emergency interventions. In the following sections, we examine each of five steps in this process: noticing something unusual, interpreting it as an emergency, taking responsibility for getting help, deciding how to help, and providing assistance. We also consider the reasons why people sometimes fail to take one of these steps and therefore do not help. These steps, and the obstacles along the way, are summarized in ▶ Figure 10.6.

Noticing The first step toward being a helpful bystander is to notice that someone needs help or at least that something out of the ordinary is happening. Participants in the seizure study could not help but notice the emergency. In many situations, however, the problem isn't necessarily perceived. The presence of others can be distracting and can divert attention away from indications of a victim's plight. In addition, people may fail to notice that someone needs help because they are caught up in their own concerns. People who live in big cities and noisy environments may become so used to seeing people lying on sidewalks or hearing screams that they begin to tune them out, becoming susceptible to what Stanley Milgram (1970) called *stimulus overload*.

Interpreting Noticing the victim is a necessary first step toward helping, but it is not enough. People must interpret the meaning of what they notice. Cries of pain can be mistaken for shrieks of laughter; heart-attack victims can appear to be drunk. So observers wonder: does that person really need help? In general, the more ambiguous the situation is, the less likely it is that bystanders will intervene (Clark & Word, 1972).

Interpretations of the relationship between a victim and an attacker also affect whether help will be provided. Consider, for example, how people react when they see a woman attacked by a man. Research by Lance Shotland and Margaret Straw (1976) indicates that many observers of such an incident believe that the attacker and the victim have a close relationship as dates, lovers, or spouses—even when no information about the relationship is actually available. This inference can have very serious implications, since, as Shotland and Straw documented, intervening in domestic violence is perceived to be more dangerous to the helper and less desired by the victim

---

In an emergency, a person who needs help has a much better chance of getting it if three other people are present than if only one other person is present. **FALSE.**

bystander effect The effect whereby the presence of others inhibits helping.

▶**FIGURE 10.6**

The Five Steps to Helping in an Emergency

On the basis of their analysis of the decision-making process in emergency interventions, Latané and Darley (1970) outlined five steps that lead to providing assistance. But obstacles can interfere, and if a step is missed, the victim won't be helped.

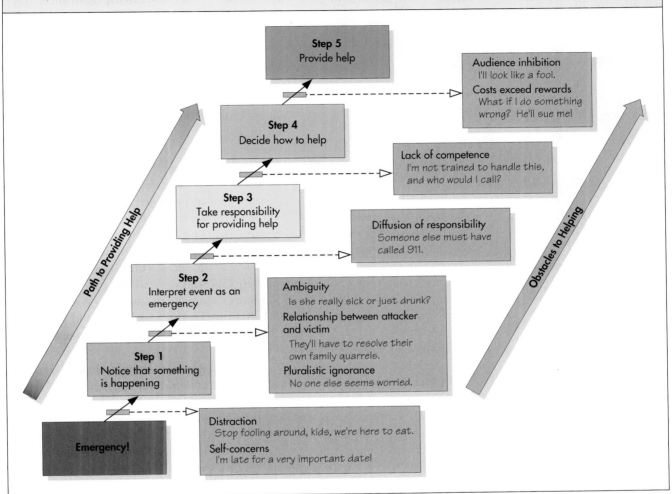

than is intervening in an attack by a stranger. Given such beliefs, the response to a scene staged by Shotland and Straw was predictable: In the scene, a woman was supposedly being assaulted by either a stranger or her husband. More than three times as many observers tried to stop the assault by the stranger.

It's not only women who are in danger if they are perceived as having a close relationship with their attacker: Children also suffer. The 1993 murder of two-year-old James Bulger by two ten-year-old boys was the British equivalent of the Kitty Genovese slaying. James was dragged, kicking and screaming, for two and a half miles from a shopping mall to a railroad track, where he was battered to death. Sixty-one people admitted that they had seen the boys. Most did nothing. One asked a few questions but didn't intervene. The reason? As one witness put it, he thought the boys were "older brothers taking a little one home." When people think "family," they think "It's OK, it's safe." But sometimes it isn't.

Perhaps the most powerful information available during an emergency is the behavior of other people. Startled by a sudden, unexpected, possibly dangerous event,

The first step toward providing help is to notice that someone needs assistance. Distracted by their own concerns or by the overwhelming stimuli of a big, bustling city, these people walking in midtown Manhattan may not even notice the homeless couple begging for spare change.

each person looks quickly to see what others are doing. As everyone looks at everyone else for clues about how to behave, the entire group is paralyzed by indecision. When this happens, the person needing help is a victim of **pluralistic ignorance**. In this state of ignorance, each individual believes that his or her own thoughts and feelings are different from those of other people, when in fact, many of the other people are thinking or feeling the same way. Each bystander thinks that other people aren't acting because somehow they know there isn't an emergency. Actually, everyone is confused and hesitant, but taking cues from each other's inaction, each observer concludes that help is not required.

Latané and Darley (1968) put this phenomenon to the test in an experiment in which participants completed a questionnaire in a room in which they were either (a) alone; (b) with two confederates who remained passive and took no action; or (c) with two other naive participants just like them. A few minutes after participants had started to fill out the questionnaire, smoke began to seep into the room through a vent. Was this an emergency? How do you think you would respond? Within four minutes, half of the participants who were working alone took some action, such as leaving the room to report the smoke to someone. Within six minutes—the maximum time allotted before the researchers terminated the experiment—three-quarters of these participants took action. Clearly, they interpreted the smoke as a potential emergency.

But what about the participants working in groups of three? Common sense suggests that the chances that *somebody* will take action should be greater when more people are present. But only one of the twenty-four participants in this condition took action within four minutes, and only three did so before the end of the study—even though, at that point, the smoke was so thick they had to fan it away from their faces to see the questionnaire! The rate of action was even lower when participants were in a room with two passive confederates; in this condition, only one in ten participants reported the smoke. If the participants in either of the two group conditions had interpreted the smoke as a potential emergency, they would have acted, because their own lives would have been at stake. But instead, they quickly, coolly looked at the reactions of the others in the room, saw that nobody else seemed too concerned, and became convinced that nothing could be wrong.

Pluralistic ignorance is not restricted to emergency situations (Chia & Lee, 2008; Halbesleben et al., 2007; Park et al. 2007; Prentice & Miller, 2003). Have you ever sat through a class feeling totally lost? You want to ask a question, but you're too embarrassed. No one else is saying anything, so you assume they all find the material a snap. Finally, you dare to ask a question. And suddenly, hands shoot up in the air all over the classroom. No one understood the material, yet everyone assumed that everyone else was breezing along. Pluralistic ignorance in the classroom interferes with learning. In an emergency situation, it can lead to disaster unless someone breaks out of the pack and dares to help. Then others are likely to follow.

Taking Responsibility Noticing a victim and recognizing an emergency are crucial steps, but by themselves, they don't ensure that a bystander will come to the rescue. The issue of responsibility remains. When help is needed, who is responsible for providing it? If a person knows that others are around, it's all too easy to place the respon-

pluralistic ignorance The state in which people in a group mistakenly think that their own individual thoughts, feelings, or behaviors are different from those of the others in the group.

sibility on *them*. People often fail to help because of the **diffusion of responsibility**: the belief that others will or should intervene. Presumably, each of those people who watched or listened to Kitty Genovese's murder thought that someone else would do something to stop the attack. The witnesses to the hit-and-run in Hartford, Connecticut, in 2008 (described earlier in the chapter) also looked around and did nothing at first, presumably hoping that someone else would get involved. But remember those helpful participants in the seizure study who thought that they alone heard the other person's cry for help? Diffusion of responsibility cannot occur if an individual believes that only he or she is aware of the victim's need.

An interesting set of experiments by Stephen Garcia and others (2002) found that the presence of others can promote diffusion of responsibility even when those others are present only in one's mind! Garcia and his colleagues (including John Darley) had participants simply *imagine* being in a crowd or being alone. Soon after, these participants were given an opportunity to help someone. The results indicated that participants who had just thought of being with many other people were less likely to help than were the participants who had imagined themselves alone.

Diffusion of responsibility usually takes place under conditions of anonymity. Bystanders who do not know the victim personally are more likely to see others as responsible for providing help. Accordingly, if the psychological distance between a bystander and the victim is reduced, there will be less diffusion of responsibility and more help. Reducing the psychological distance among bystanders can also counteract the diffusion of responsibility. Established groups in which the members know each other are usually more helpful than groups of strangers (Rutkowski et al., 1983). For example, in recent experiments Mark Levine and Simon Crowther (2008) replicated the inhibiting effect of bystanders on helping when the bystanders were strangers, but they found that the effect did not occur when the bystanders were all friends.

In addition, the diffusion of responsibility can be defeated by a person's role. A group leader, even if he or she has only recently been assigned to that position, is more likely than other group members to act in an emergency (Baumeister et al., 1988). And some occupational roles increase the likelihood of intervention. Registered nurses, for example, do not diffuse responsibility when confronted by a possible physical injury (Cramer et al., 1988). Recall Terrence Kelsor, whose daring rescue of a man on the subway tracks in New York City in March 2009 was described in the beginning of the chapter. Kelsor had been a security guard for only three weeks, but he immediately assumed responsibility for saving the man.

Deciding How to Help   Having assumed the responsibility to help, the person must now decide how to help. Bystanders are more likely to offer direct help when they feel competent to perform the actions required. For instance, individuals who have received Red Cross training in first-aid techniques are more likely to provide direct assistance to a bleeding victim than are those without training (Shotland & Heinold, 1985).

But people who do not possess the skills that would make them feel competent to intervene directly often do have an option available. They can decide to help indirectly by calling for assistance from others. In many situations, indirect helping is by far the wiser course of action. Physical injuries are best treated by medical personnel; dangerous situations such as domestic violence are best handled by police officers; and that friendly-looking individual standing by the side of a stalled car on a lonely road is best picked up by the highway patrol. Even people trained in CPR are now advised to call 911 before starting CPR on an adult victim. Calling others in to help is safe, simple, and effective. A prompt phone call can be a lifeline. Such a call might have saved Kitty Genovese's life.

diffusion of responsibility
The belief that others will or should take the responsibility for providing assistance to a person in need.

Providing Help The final step in the intervention process is taking action. Here, too, the presence of others can have an impact. Latané and Darley point out that people sometimes feel too socially awkward and embarrassed to act helpfully in a public setting. When observers do not act in an emergency because they fear making a bad impression on other observers, they are under the influence of **audience inhibition**.

This is a very common obstacle to helping, but sometimes it can be especially tragic. Melanie Carlson (2008) reports about a gang rape of an unconscious 15-year-old girl by four perpetrators in the presence of six bystanders at a party in 2002. The district attorney said that the bystanders did not intervene for fear of being considered "wusses" or being "made fun of" (p. 3). When Carlson interviewed young men from a university in California about how they would respond in situations like the gang rape, many of them raised similar concerns, indicating that their masculinity would be threatened if they intervened.

Worrying about how others will view us does not, however, always reduce helping. When people think they will be scorned by others for failing to help, the presence of an audience *increases* their helpful actions (Schwartz & Gottlieb, 1980).

The Bystander Effect Online One new application of the research on the bystander effect is in the world of electronic-based communication. Daniel Stalder (2008) reviewed recent studies on individuals' responses to e-mail or Internet-based requests for help. Even here, the bystander effect emerged, indicating that the virtual presence of others reduced the likelihood that any one individual would intervene.

A sad example of the bystander effect in cyberspace occurred in February 2003. Brandon Vedas overdosed on drugs and lay dying in front of a crowded room full of people, many of whom egged him on to take even more drugs. The modern-day twist was that this room was virtual; it was a chatroom, and the bystanders watched Vedas, who used the name "Ripper" online, poison himself to death in front of the webcam in his Phoenix, Arizona, bedroom. "That's not much," said a teenager from rural Oklahoma whose alias was "Smoke2K." "Eat more. I wanna see if you survive or if you just black out." Another wrote in, "Ripper—you should try to pass out in front of the cam." Not everyone was so callous. Some wrote in warning Ripper to be careful; one wrote, "Don't OD on us, Ripper." One person did begin to call the police, but—astonishingly—others talked her out of it. Vedas posted his cell number with the instructions "Call if I look dead." The last coherent words Vedas wrote before he died were "I told u I was hardcore" (Kennedy, 2003, p. 5).

This incident was different from the Kitty Genovese one in several ways, including the fact that it was not clear if the onlookers could have done anything about this. Without knowing Ripper's real name or address, the police probably would not have been able to find him in time even if someone had called promptly. But several processes central to Darley and Latané's research clearly were evident. Multiple witnesses suggested that "somebody" call poison control or the police but did not do so themselves. Some questioned whether Ripper was really dying or had just passed out. One person told another *not* to call the police because that could get Ripper arrested. Together, these Internet bystanders were struggling on the decision tree, spreading doubt and diffusion of responsibility.

The Legacy of the Bystander Effect Research As you can see in Figure 10.6, providing help in an emergency is a challenging process. At each step along the way, barriers and diversions can prevent a potential helper from becoming an actual one. In 1981, Bibb Latané and Steve Nida conducted a meta-analysis of more than 50 studies on the bystander effect and concluded, "The original phenomenon discovered by

audience inhibition Reluctance to help for fear of making a bad impression on observers.

Latané and Darley has a firm empirical foundation and has withstood the tests of time and replication" (p. 322).

In his more recent review and analysis of the literature, Daniel Stalder (2008) found that the evidence continues to support the finding that the presence of others inhibits individual bystanders from helping, but he raised one point of clarification: Despite the fact that crowds inhibit individuals from helping, the individual in need may still be more likely to receive help from a large group of witnesses than from a lone witness. In fact, as group size increases, the chances that at least someone will help may increase as well. In other words, if the group size gets sufficiently large, the mathematical odds become better that at least *someone* will defy the forces against action and decide to help, even if the probability that any particular witness would help is reduced by the bystander effect.

The power and relevance of Latané and Darley's analysis are evident in the fact that newspapers around the world typically cite their work when reporting the latest shocking incident of bystander nonintervention. In 1995, for example, Deletha Word

AP/Wide World Photos

was involved in a traffic accident with Martell Welch, Jr., on a traffic-clogged bridge over the Detroit River. Welch, who was over six feet tall and about 270 pounds, dragged Word, who was less than five feet tall and weighed about 115 pounds, out of her car, ripped off some of her clothes, and hit her repeatedly while yelling threats at her in an outburst that lasted at least ten minutes.

The attack itself was shocking, but perhaps more shocking was that about 40 people witnessed it, and not one of them attempted to come to the woman's aid. Finally, as Welch approached Word, allegedly while holding his car jack, she climbed over the bridge rail and jumped into the river. Within moments, she disappeared into the water, and her body was found

Dortha Word, second from the left, and friends pray on the bridge from which Dortha's daughter, Deletha, jumped to her death three days earlier, trying to escape a man who had been attacking her. About 40 people witnessed the attack but did not intervene. Their failure to help her daughter stunned Dortha: "I can't believe all those people stood around and watched."

hours later (*The Detroit News*, 1997). Soon after this incident, *Dateline NBC* interviewed John Darley about this case and his research on the bystander effect, and Darley simulated some of the experiments he had done with Latané.

Earlier in this chapter we discussed the stories of unhelpful witnesses to the hit-and-run in Hartford, Connecticut in 2009 and to the sexual assault in 2007 of a woman in an apartment building hallway in St. Paul, Minnesota. In these and many other similar incidents, reporters and commentators continue to cite the name "Kitty Genovese" and the research we have described here.

Given its enduring legacy, it is interesting to note that some of the original details reported about the witnesses to the Kitty Genovese murder—accounts that have been repeated countless times over the years since then—may, in fact, be inaccurate. Rachel Manning and others (2008) recently published an article suggesting that some of the witnesses may have called the police well before the police finally arrived. These were in the days before "911" calls, and it is impossible to know whether or not these calls were made or what may have been said in them. Manning and her colleagues also question whether thirty-eight was the correct number of witnesses and suggest that far fewer were likely to have actually seen the incident, although possibly even more than thirty-eight heard it.

To us, these questions are interesting but beside the main point. Whether fully accurate or not, these original reports were what inspired John Darley and Bibb Latané to pursue the line of research we have reported in this section, and that research has yielded valuable insight concerning the social psychology of bystander intervention. In addition, we have cited several other more recent stories from the news of tragic inaction of bystanders, and for every one we cite, there are dozens more. Latané and Darley's theorizing continues to help people understand how these incidents can occur.

Many of us who teach social psychology have stories of former students who witnessed an emergency and jumped in to help while consciously thinking of the lessons they'd learned in their social psychology classes about Darley and Latané's bystander intervention research. Indeed, one of the authors of this book remembers being at a lecture in a room filled with social psychologists when a loud crash suddenly emanated from an adjacent room. After a few seconds of delay, dozens of social psychologists burst out of their chairs, almost trampling each other as they rushed to see if there was an emergency. And the only ones who were not explicitly thinking "Darley and Latané" while doing so were the ones thinking "Latané and Darley."

Getting Help in a Crowd: What Should You Do?   But what do all these stories and experiments teach you about what to do if you need help in the presence of many people? Is there anything you can do to enhance the chances that someone will come to your aid? We can offer this advice: Try to counteract the ambiguity of the situation by making it very clear that you do need help and try to reduce diffusion of responsibility by singling out particular individuals for help, such as with eye contact, pointing, or direct requests (Moriarty, 1975; Shotland & Stebbins, 1980).

A study by P. M. Markey (2000) involving people in Internet chat rooms found results consistent with this advice. As the number of people present in each chat room group grew larger, individuals took increasingly more time to respond to someone's plea for help. However, this effect was eliminated when the person asking for help specified a particular individual's name (see ▶ Figure 10.7).

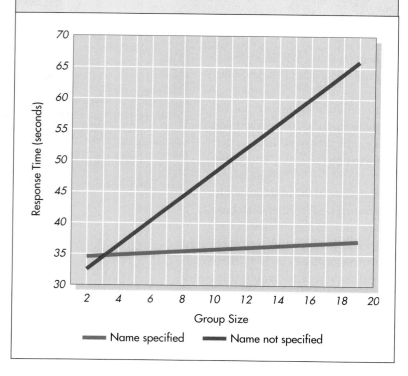

▶ FIGURE 10.7

Cyberhelping

In a study that extends Latané and Darley's research on the bystander effect by bringing it into cyberspace, individuals participating in an online chat room saw a plea for help from another person in the chat room. Consistent with Latané and Darley's findings, individuals responded more slowly if they thought that many other people were in the chat room than if they thought that few others were present. However, if the person seeking help asked an individual by name, that person responded quickly regardless of how many other people were in the chat room.

Markey, 2000.

(Graph: x-axis "Group Size" from 2 to 20; y-axis "Response Time (seconds)" from 30 to 70. Legend: "Name specified" and "Name not specified")

■ Time Pressure

The presence of others can create obstacles at each step on the way toward helping in an emergency. Other factors, too, can affect multiple steps in this process. Our good intentions of helping those in need can sometimes conflict with other motivations. One such source of conflict is time pressure. When we are in a hurry or have a lot on our minds, we may be so preoccupied that we fail to notice others who need help, become less likely to accept responsibility for helping someone, or decide that the costs of helping are too high because of the precious time that will be lost. When we have other demands on us that seem very important, getting involved in someone else's problems may seem like a luxury we can't afford (Batson et al., 1978; Moore, 2005). John Darley and Daniel Batson (1973) examined the role of time pressure in an experiment that produced what may be the most ironic finding in the history of social psychology.

Their study was based on the parable of the Good Samaritan, from the Gospel of Luke. This parable tells the story of three different people—a priest, a Levite, and a Samaritan—each traveling on the road from Jerusalem to Jericho. Each encounters a man lying half-dead by the roadside. The priest and the Levite—both considered busy, important, and relatively holy people—pass by the man without stopping. The only one who helps is the Samaritan, a social and religious outcast of that time. A moral of the tale is that people with low status are sometimes more virtuous than those who enjoy high status and prestige. Why? Perhaps in part because high-status individuals tend to be busy people, preoccupied with their own concerns and rushing around to various engagements. Such characteristics may prevent them from noticing or deciding to help a victim in need of assistance.

Darley and Batson brought this ancient story to life. They asked seminary students to think about what they wanted to say in an upcoming talk. Half of them were told that the talk was to be based on the parable of the Good Samaritan; the other half expected to discuss the jobs that seminary students like best. All participants were then instructed to walk over to a nearby building where the speech would be recorded. At this point, participants were told either that they were running ahead of schedule, that they were right on time, or that they were already a few minutes behind schedule. On the way to the other building, all participants passed a research confederate slumped in a doorway, coughing and groaning. Which of these future ministers stopped to lend a helping hand?

Perhaps surprisingly, the topic of the upcoming speech had little effect on helping. The pressure of time, however, made a real difference. Of those who thought they were ahead of schedule, 63 percent offered help—compared with 45 percent of those who believed they were on time and only 10 percent of those who had been told they were late. In describing the events that took place in their study, Darley and Batson noted that "on several occasions a seminary student going to give his talk on the parable of the Good Samaritan literally stepped over the victim as he hurried on his way!" These seminary students unwittingly demonstrated the very point that the parable they would be discussing warns against.

▌▌ Location and Helping

If the presence of others often inhibits helping, do individuals have a worse chance of being helped in an emergency in a big city than in a small town? In the midst of the hectic pace and large crowds of a big city, are pleas for help more likely to go unanswered?

Although place of residence does not seem to affect how much those in close relationships help each other (Franck, 1980; Korte, 1980), a large city does have a number of characteristics that might reduce help to strangers. For example, as we discussed earlier in the context of noticing an emergency, Stanley Milgram (1970) proposed that cities produce stimulus overload among their inhabitants. Bombarded by sights and sounds, city residents may wear a coat of unresponsive armor to protect themselves from being overwhelmed by stimulation (Korte et al., 1975). Claude Fischer (1976) noted that the residents of large urban areas are a heterogeneous group that is composed of diverse nationalities, races, and ethnic backgrounds. Such diversity could diminish the sense of similarity with others, reduce empathic concern, and result in less helping. Also, residents of large cities may feel more anonymous and less accountable for their actions than residents of smaller communities, where people are more likely to know their neighbors.

Whatever the exact causes, people are less likely to help in urban areas than in rural ones. This relationship has been found in several countries, including Canada, Israel, Great Britain, and the Sudan (Hedge & Yousif, 1992; Steblay, 1987). For example, when Paul Amato (1983) studied fifty-five Australian communities, he found that spontaneous, informal help to strangers was greater where the population was smaller.

In a similar vein, Robert Levine and his colleagues (2008) examined three kinds of spontaneous help offered to strangers in 24 U.S. cities. These measures of helping—all assessed in a downtown area during normal business hours on clear summer days—included picking up a pen that a stranger had apparently dropped accidentally; helping a stranger with a heavy limp pick up a pile of magazines that the stranger had dropped; and responding to a stranger's request for change for a quarter by at least checking to see if they had change.

As you can see in Table 10.2, Knoxville, Tennessee, wins the title of "Most Helpful City" among the 24 studied. You should also be able to see that the biggest cities tended to have the worst scores for helping. Overall, greater population size and population density (population per square mile) were associated with less helping. Levine and his colleagues also found that greater economic well-being of a city was associated with more helping. As we will see a bit later in this section, however, the picture of helping in the United States is different if one focuses specifically on charitable giving or volunteering.

TABLE 10.2

Helping in the U.S.A.

Three types of help offered to strangers, including helping them retrieve things they dropped or trying to make change for them, were studied in 24 U.S. cities. The top six and bottom six cities are listed in this table. Cities with the largest populations tended to have the least amount of helping. The economic well-being of a city was positively correlated with helping.

Top Six Cities for Helping		Bottom Six Cities for Helping	
Overall Rank	Region	Overall Rank	Region
1. Knoxville, TN	South	19. Youngstown, OH	North Central
2. Kansas City, MO	North Central	20. Atlanta, GA	South
3. Louisville, KY	South	21. Chicago, IL	North Central
4. Indianapolis, IN	North Central	22. Los Angeles, CA	West
5. Dallas, TX	South	23. San Francisco, CA	West
6. Nashville, TN	South	24. New York, NY	Northeast

Based on data from Levine et al., 2008.

▋ Culture and Helping

Around the world as well, some cities seem to have more helpful citizens than others. Robert Levine and others (2001) conducted similar field studies in a major city in each of 23 large countries around the world. Table 10.3 reports how the cities ranked in their propensity to help; pedestrians in Rio de Janeiro, Brazil, exhibited the highest rates of helping and pedestrians in Kuala Lampur, Malaysia, exhibited the lowest rates. Levine and his colleagues examined a number of measures of each city to try to determine what factors predicted these differences in helping, such as how hectic the pace of life seemed to be (as determined by pedestrians' walking speed) or how individualistic or collectivistic the culture was. Only two measures correlated with helping rates. One was a measure of economic well-being—cities from countries with the greatest levels of economic well-being tended to exhibit the least helping, although this relationship was not very strong (and is inconsistent with the findings from the research of Levine and his colleagues in the United States).

The other variable that predicted helping concerned the notion of what is called *simpatía* in Spanish or *simpático* in Portuguese. Some researchers report that this is an important element of Spanish and Latin American cultures and involves a concern with the social well-being of others (Markus & Lin, 1999; Sanchez-Burks et al., 2000). The five cultures in the study conducted by Levine and colleagues that value *simpatía* did tend to show higher rates of helping than the *non-simpatía* cultures.

You may find it surprising that collectivism was not a predictor of helping, but the research on the relationship between individualism or collectivism and prosocial behavior is quite mixed at this time. This inconsistency may stem in part from differences in the kinds of helping studied. Compared to individualists, collectivists may be more likely to help ingroup members, but they are less likely to help outgroup members (Conway et al., 2001; Schwartz, 1990).

Lucian Conway and others (2001) studied differences in people's levels of individualism and collectivism within the United States. They found that collectivism was positively associated with the kind of direct, spontaneous, nonserious help

---

TABLE 10.3

Helping Around the World

Three types of spontaneous helping of a stranger were examined in field experiments in a major city in each of 23 different countries around the world. The top six and bottom six cities are listed below, as are their respective ranks on a measure of economic prosperity. Cities with asterisks are considered to have *simpatía* cultural values, which are characterized by a concern with the social well-being of others.

Top Six Cities for Helping

City	Helping Rank	Economic Rank
*Rio de Janeiro, Brazil	1	16
*San Jose, Costa Rica	2	15
Lilongwe, Malawi	3	22
Calcutta, India	4	21
Vienna, Austria	5	4
*Madrid, Spain	6	9

Bottom Six Cities for Helping

City	Helping Rank	Economic Rank
Taipei, Taiwan	18	(data unavailable)
Sofia, Bulgaria	19	17
Amsterdam, Netherlands	20	6
Singapore, Singapore	21	2
New York, United States	22	1
Kuala Lampur, Malaysia	23	10

Based on Levine et al., 2001.

---

assessed in the Levine et al. (2001) cross-cultural study described above, such as picking up a dropped pen for a stranger. However, for helping that is less spontaneous and more deliberate, such as mailing a sealed and stamped letter that someone (unseen) had apparently dropped or making contributions to a particular charity, collectivism was associated with *less* helping. Conway et al. speculated that a possible explanation for these results is that collectivists are more responsive to the immediate needs of a person near them but less responsive in the more abstract situations, as in the found letter situation or making charitable contributions.

Conway et al.'s speculation received support in an investigation of charitable giving and volunteerism in the United States. Using data from random samples drawn from 40 of the 50 states in the United States, Markus Kemmelmeier and others (2006) examined the relationship between the degree of individualism associated with each state and the amount of helping the individuals from within those states offered to strangers in the form of donations and volunteering. The states' degree of individualism had been determined in a previous study by Vandello and Cohen (1999) using a number of variables, such as the percentage of people living alone, the percentage of people with no religious affiliation, and the percentage of self-employed people. In general, states in the Mountain West and the Great Plains were the most individualistic, followed by the Northeast and the Midwest. The least individualistic states tended to be in the South and Southwest.

Kemmelmeier and colleagues found that people from the more individualistic states tended to exhibit greater charitable giving and volunteering than people from the more collectivistic states, particularly donations and volunteering that were not specific to one's ingroup affiliations. The authors propose that when helping involves this more abstract kind of giving—as opposed to, for example, helping someone from within one's ingroup—individualism may be associated with greater helping.

■ Moods and Helping

Helping someone can put people in a better mood, but can being in a good mood increase people's likelihood of helping someone? Are we less likely to help if we're in a bad mood? What's your prediction?

Good Moods and Doing Good   Sunshine in Minneapolis, pleasant odors in Albany, and compliments in Sydney give us some clues about the relationship between good mood and helping. Over the course of a year, pedestrians in Minneapolis, Minnesota, were stopped and asked to participate in a survey of social opinions. When Michael Cunningham (1979) tabulated their responses according to the weather conditions, he discovered that people answered more questions on sunny days than on cloudy ones. Moving his investigation indoors, Cunningham found that sunshine is truly golden: The more the sun was shining, the more generous the tips left by restaurant customers were. Sunshine and helping seem to go together, but what's the connection? Probably it's the mood we're in, as a sunny day cheers us up and a cloudy day damps us down.

When the sun is not shining, many people head for the mall. One of the more powerful sensations you can count on experiencing while strolling through the mall comes when you pass a bakery or coffee shop, as the pleasant aroma of freshly baked chocolate chip cookies or freshly brewed French roast stops you in your tracks. Robert Baron (1997) believed that these pleasant scents put people in a good mood, and he wondered if this good mood would make them more likely to help someone in need. He tested this with passersby in a large shopping mall in Albany, New York. Each selected passerby was approached by a member of the research team and asked for change for a dollar. This interaction took place in a location containing either strong pleasant odors (such as near a bakery or a coffee-roasting café) or no discernible odor (such as near a clothing store).

As can be seen in ▶ Figure 10.8, people approached in a pleasant-smelling location were much more likely to help than people approached in a neutral-smelling location. Baron also found that people were in a better mood when they were in the pleasant-smelling environments. This effect on their mood appears to have caused their greater tendency to help.

▶ **FIGURE 10.8**

Scents and Sensibilities

People walking in a mall were approached by someone who asked them for change. This encounter took place in areas of the mall with either pleasant ambient odors or no clear odors. The stranger also gave the individuals a questionnaire that measured their mood on a 5-point scale, ranging from 1 (very bad) to 5 (very good). As shown on the left, the people approached in a pleasant-smelling area were in a better mood than those approached in neutral-smelling locations. In addition (right), people were more likely to help the stranger by giving him change if they were in a pleasant-smelling area than if they were in a neutral-smelling area.

Data from Baron, 1997.

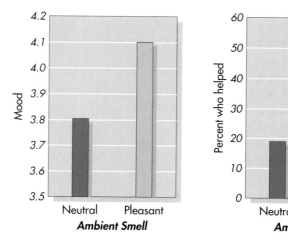
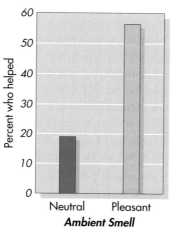

Shoppers are not the only people at the mall affected by mood—the sales staff is affected too. Joseph Forgas and others (2008) conducted a field experiment at four department stores in Sydney, Australia. The moods of salespersons were manipulated by having a confederate approach them and say either very complimentary things (e.g., "I am so impressed with the service at this store"), negative things (e.g., "I am so disappointed with the service at this store"), or neutral things. A few seconds later, a second confederate approached the salesperson and asked for help finding an item that did not really exist. How much did the salesperson attempt to help this confederate?

The researchers predicted that the mood manipulation would not have much effect on the most experienced salespersons, as they would have a well-rehearsed set of responses to customer questions and would therefore respond accordingly. For the less experienced staff, however, Forgas and his colleagues expected that they would exert greater effort to help the customer if they had been put in a good mood. As ▶ Figure 10.9 illustrates, this is exactly what the results indicated.

Of course, sunshine, sweet scents, and sweet sentiments are not the only enhancers of mood and helping. In fact, helping is increased by all kinds of pleasant, mood-lifting experiences, such as being successful on a task, reading pleasant positive statements, being offered a cookie, imagining a Hawaiian vacation, and listening to uplifting music (Aderman, 1972; Isen & Levin, 1972; North et al., 2004). On the job, being in a good mood seems to be the major determinant of a wide range of behaviors (such as helping co-workers, making constructive suggestions, and spreading goodwill) that improve workplace quality and increase organizational effectiveness (Isen, 2008; Tsai et al., 2007). When we're happy, we're helpful—a state of affairs known as the **good mood effect**.

Why do good moods increase helping? There seem to be several factors at work. Table 10.4 summarizes some of the reasons why feeling good often leads to doing good, and it also describes some of the forks in this road that can lead away from helping. Whatever its exact cause, the good mood effect kicks in quite early in life. It occurs among people of all ages, and even young children help more when they feel happy and cheerful (Moore et al., 1973).

Bad Moods and Doing Good   Since a good mood increases helping, does a bad mood decrease it? Not necessarily. Under many circumstances, negative feelings can elicit positive behavior toward others (Carlson & Miller, 1987; Estrada-Hollenbeck & Heatherton, 1998; Staub & Vollhardt, 2008; Zemack-Rugar et al., 2007). One such circumstance is when people feel guilt. Imagine yourself in the following situation. A stranger approaches you on the street and asks you to use his camera to take his picture for a school project. You get ready, aim, and . . . nothing. The camera doesn't work. Looking concerned, the stranger says the camera is rather delicate, asks you if you touched any of the dials, and informs you that it will have to be fixed. You continue on your way down the street. As you pass a young woman, she drops a file folder containing some papers. Now here's the question: Are you more likely to help the woman pick up her papers because you think you broke the other person's camera?

Probably. In an experiment that used this setup, 80 percent of participants who had been led to believe that they had broken the man's camera helped the woman pick up her papers; only 40 percent of participants who had not had a broken-camera

People are much more likely to help someone when they're in a good mood. **TRUE.**

▶ **FIGURE 10.9**

May I Help You?

Salespersons at department stores in Sydney, Australia, were approached by a confederate who put them in a positive, negative, or neutral mood by saying either very positive, negative, or neutral things to them. A few seconds later a different confederate asked the salepersons for help in finding an item that didn't exist. How hard did the staff try to help the confederate? Among the less-experienced staff, those who had been put in a positive mood were much more helpful than were the other salespersons.

Data from Forgas et al., 2008.

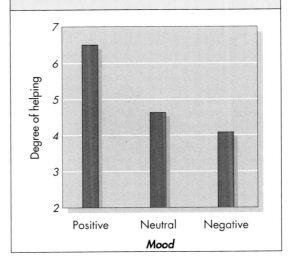

good mood effect   The effect whereby a good mood increases helping behavior.

TABLE 10.4

Good Moods Lead to Helping: Reasons and Limitations

Research shows that people in positive moods are more likely to help someone in need than are people in neutral moods. There are several explanations for this effect as well as some limiting conditions that can weaken or reverse the help-promoting effects of good moods.

Why Feeling Good Leads to Doing Good

- *Desire to maintain one's good mood.* When we are in a good mood, we are motivated to maintain that mood. Helping others makes us feel good, so it can help maintain a positive mood.
- *Positive expectations about helping.* If we have positive expectations about the rewards of helping, we are more likely to help.
- *Positive thoughts.* Positive moods trigger positive thoughts, and if we have positive thoughts about others, we should like them more, which makes us more likely to help them.
- *Positive thoughts and expectations about social activities.* Positive moods trigger positive thoughts and expectations about interacting with others and engaging in social activities. These positive thoughts and expectations can promote interacting with others in prosocial ways, including helping them.

When Feeling Good Might Not Lead to Doing Good

- *Costs of helping are high.* If the anticipated costs of helping in a particular situation seem high, helping would put our good mood at risk. In this case, if we can avoid getting involved and thus maintain our good mood (for example, if we can justify our failure to help), we are less likely to help.
- *Positive thoughts about other social activities that conflict with helping.* If our good mood makes us want to go out and party with our friends, our motivation to engage in this social activity may prevent us from taking the time to notice or take responsibility for helping someone in need.

---

experience stopped to help (Cunningham et al., 1980). Thus, participants who unintentionally harmed one individual were more helpful to the next person. According to Roy Baumeister and others (1994), such spillover effects provide an especially vivid demonstration of the interpersonal nature of guilt and its function of enhancing, maintaining, and repairing relationships. Feeling guilty, they contend, motivates us to strengthen whatever social relations are at hand.

More generally, negative moods often promote helping. Why might this be? As noted earlier, people know that helping makes them feel good. This point underlies the negative state relief model, which we described earlier as proposing that people who are feeling bad are motivated to repair their mood and they realize that one way to do it is by helping others.

Although negative moods can boost helping, it is not as strong and consistent a relationship as that between good moods and helping. As Table 10.5 indicates, there are several limits to this effect. One important variable is whether people accept responsibility for their bad feelings (Rogers et al., 1982). Negative moods are less likely to promote helping if we blame others for them (such as when we're angry at another person) than if we take personal responsibility (such as when we regret a poor decision we have just made). In addition, negative moods are less likely to increase helping if they cause us to become very self-focused (such as when we experience intense grief or depression or when we dwell on our own problems and concerns) than if they direct our focus outward (such as when we feel sad after watching a public service advertisement about child abuse) (Bagozzi & Moore, 1994; Fisher et al., 2008; Tangney et al., 1996).

Some kinds of helping are more difficult and unpleasant than others, of course. When the helping involves particularly unpleasant tasks, the positive effect of sadness on helping is reduced. Guilt, on the other hand, can promote helping even when the helping is relatively unpleasant (Zemack-Rugar et al., 2007).

People are much less likely to help someone when they're in a bad mood. **FALSE.**

Charity sees the need, not the cause.

—German proverb

TABLE 10.5

Bad Moods and Helping: When Does Feeling Bad Lead to Doing Good, and When Doesn't It?

Research shows that people in negative moods are often more likely to help someone in need than are people in neutral moods. However, there are several limitations to this effect. This table summarizes some of the factors that make it more or less likely for people to do good when they feel bad.

When Negative Moods Make Us More Likely to Help Others

- If we take responsibility for what caused our bad mood ("I feel guilty for what I did.")
- If we focus on other people ("Wow, those people have suffered so much.")
- If we think about our personal values that promote helping ("I really shouldn't act like such a jerk next time; I have to be nicer.")

When Negative Moods Make Us Less Likely to Help Others

- If we blame others for our bad mood ("I feel so angry at that jerk who put me in this situation.")
- If we become very self-focused ("I am so depressed.")
- If we think about our personal values that do not promote helping ("I have to wise up and start thinking about my own needs more.")

■ Role Models and Social Norms: A Helpful Standard

We mentioned earlier that children become more aware as they get older of the potential benefits of helping. How, in general, do children learn about helping? One important way is through role models. Seeing important people in their lives behave prosocially or antisocially encourages children to follow suit. Role models can be real people in children's lives or characters they see on television (Moriarty & McCabe, 1977; Rushton, 1981a; Sprafkin et al., 1975). Indeed, although politicians, educators, researchers, and parents pay a great deal of attention to the negative effects of TV on children (discussed in Chapter 11 on Aggression), TV can also have positive effects on children through the modeling of prosocial behavior.

After reviewing extensive research literature, Susan Hearold (1986) concluded that the effect of prosocial TV on prosocial behavior was about twice as large as the effect of TV violence on aggressive behavior. She argued that rather than primarily advocating the elimination of the negative by removing shows with sex and violence, the public should focus more on accentuating the positive by encouraging the creation of more shows with prosocial themes and positive role models. More recently, a meta-analysis of 34 studies involving more than 5,000 children found a reliable positive effect of prosocial television on children's prosocial behavior, especially when specific acts of altruism were modeled on TV (Mares & Woodard, 2005).

Helpful models are important not only for children but for all of us. Observing helpful models increases helping in a variety of situations (Bryan & Test, 1967; Ng & van Dyne, 2005; Sarason et al., 1991; Siu et al., 2006). Even song lyrics can promote a helpful standard: As discussed in Chapter 2, Tobias Greitemeyer (2009) found that exposure to music with prosocial lyrics fostered helpful behavior.

Why do people who exemplify helping inspire us to help? Three reasons stand out. First, they provide an example of behavior for us to imitate directly. Second, when they are rewarded for their helpful behavior, people who model helping behavior teach us that helping is valued and rewarding, which strengthens our own inclination to be helpful. Third, the behavior of these models makes us think about and become more aware of the standards of conduct in our society.

General rules of conduct established by society are called **social norms**. These norms embody standards of socially approved and disapproved behavior. Two sets of

social norm A general rule of conduct reflecting standards of social approval and disapproval.

social norms bear directly on when people are likely to help. The first consists of norms based on fairness. As we mentioned in Chapter 7, the *norm of reciprocity* establishes quid-pro-quo transactions as a socially approved standard: People who give to you should be paid back. We discussed reciprocal altruism earlier in this chapter; many animals, including humans, help those who have helped them.

The norm of reciprocity can be so powerful that many people reciprocate help even when that reciprocation will be unacknowledged. This was demonstrated in an experiment by Jerry Burger and others (2009). While waiting for the experimenter to return during a break in an experiment, participants in one condition of the study were unexpectedly given a bottle of water by a confederate, whereas participants in another condition were not. Later, the confederate asked them if they would help them out for a project by taking a survey home to complete and returning it at a specified time and place. Some participants were told that the confederate would be there to receive the survey (and, therefore, to see if the participant returned it), whereas others were told they would simply drop the survey into a box. Participants who had been given the bottle of water were more likely to return the survey than were participants who had not received the favor, and this held true even if the participants believed that the confederate would not know whether they returned the survey. These participants seemed to think that returning the favor was just something they ought to do.

Equity is the basis of another norm that calls for fairness in our treatment of others. The *norm of equity* prescribes that when people are in a situation in which they feel overbenefited (receiving more benefits than earned), they should help those who are underbenefited (receiving fewer benefits than earned). Such help restores an equitable balance (Walster, Walster, & Berscheid, 1978).

Other social norms related to help go beyond an immediate sense of fairness to a larger sense of what is right. The **norm of social responsibility** dictates that people should help those who need assistance. This norm creates a sense of duty and obligation, to which people respond by giving more help to those in greater need of it (Berkowitz, 1972; Bornstein, 1994). When people are more motivated by concerns about *justice or fairness*, however, their intentions to help someone will be driven more by their belief that this person *deserves* their assistance than by their belief that he or she simply needs it (Lerner, 1998).

Concerns with reciprocity, equity, social responsibility, and justice can have powerful effects. Yet sometimes they fail to produce the helpful behavior they prescribe. Why? One problem with social norms is their generality. They are so general, so abstract, that it is not clear when they apply. When you encounter two people fighting, should you follow the norm prescribing "Help those in need" or the one instructing you to "Mind your own business"? (Darley & Latané, 1970).

Culture and Social Norms for Helping

Social norms can vary dramatically across cultures. For instance, Joan Miller and her colleagues (1990) found that children and adults in the United States were less likely than children and adults in India to believe that people have an obligation to provide assistance to friends or strangers whose need for help is not extreme. It appears that the Hindu Indians who participated in this study regarded social responsibilities as an absolute moral obligation, whereas Americans applied the norm of social responsibility more selectively. Jonathan Baron and Joan Miller (2000) also found that Indian students were more likely than U.S. students to view donating bone marrow to save someone's life as morally required. U.S. students were much more likely than Indian students to say that whether or not to donate was a personal choice for the potential donor to make.

In our increasingly interdependent world, we have seen the terrifying power of individuals to do great harm. Yet there is a more hopeful side of this interconnected age: private citizens have never had more power to advance the common good and secure a brighter future.
—Former U.S. President Bill Clinton

norm of social responsibility A moral standard emphasizing that people should help those who need assistance.

Paul Yablo and Nigel Field (2007) compared attitudes and self-reported altruistic behaviors of American and Thai college students. On both types of measures Thai students appeared more altruistic and helpful than American students. Based in part on interviews they conducted with some of the participants, Yablo and Field believe that an important reason for this difference is the role of religion. Unlike the American students, the Thai students were very likely to cite norms and values based on religion to explain why they would help in various situations.

Personal Influences: Who Is Likely to Help?

As we have just seen, social psychological research addressing the question "When do people help?" has been quite productive. What about the question "Who is likely to help?" In this section, we consider some of the individual differences between people that address this question.

Are Some People More Helpful Than Others?

Although situational factors clearly can overwhelm individual differences in influencing helping behaviors in many contexts (Latané & Darley, 1970), researchers have found some evidence that people who are more helpful than others in one situation are likely to be more helpful in other situations as well (Hampson, 1984; Hay & Cook, 2007; Rushton, 1981b). In addition, longitudinal research suggests that this individual difference may be relatively stable over time (Dovidio et al., 2006). For example, Nancy Eisenberg and others (2002) found that the degree to which preschool children exhibited spontaneous helping behavior predicted how helpful they would be in later childhood and early adulthood.

This individual difference in helpfulness appears to be partly based on genetics. Genetically identical (monozygotic) twins are more similar to each other in their helpful behavioral tendencies and their helping-related emotions and reactions, such as empathy, than are fraternal (dizygotic) twins, who share only a portion of their genetic makeup. These findings suggest that there may be a heritable component to helpfulness (Gregory et al., 2009; Knafo & Plomin, 2006; Knafo et al., 2008).

Movie star Angelina Jolie has used her celebrity as well as her own time and energy to raise awareness and resources for impoverished and malnourished children around the world. In this photo she is at a refugee camp on the Kenya-Somalia border in September 2009.

What Is the Altruistic Personality?

Even if we identify some people who help others a lot and other people who don't, we have not addressed the question of what distinguishes people who help from those who don't—other than their helpfulness, of course. What are the various components of *the altruistic personality*? Can we predict who is likely to be altruistic by looking at people's overall personalities?

Consider some examples of people who have acted very altruistically. Do they seem to have very similar personality traits and characteristics? Take, for example, Oskar Schindler, the wealthy German businessman during the Nazi regime who became the hero of the book and movie *Schindler's List*. Schindler was a shady operator, cheating in business and marriage, partying with sadistic German military officers. From his

The purpose of human life is to serve and to show compassion and the will to help others.

—Albert Schweitzer

Michael J. Okoniewski

AP Photo/Noah Berger

Rock star Bruce Springsteen may not seem to have a lot in common with the Dalai Lama (seen here serving lunch at a soup kitchen in 2009) and many of the other people mentioned on this page as models of altruism, but like them, he donates a tremendous amount of time and money to helping others. At every stop on his concert tours in recent years, Springsteen has raised money for local causes, such as food banks, youth centers, and shelters.

overall personality, could anyone have predicted his altruistic actions of risking his own life to save over 4,000 Jews during the Holocaust? It is doubtful.

What about more contemporary models of altruism? Consider these people: Bill Gates, a computer geek who cofounded Microsoft and became the richest man in the world; Bono, the extraverted Irish rock star; Ted Turner, an eccentric American from the South who started the first 24-hour news cable station (CNN); Dikembe Mutombo, a 7-foot, 2-inch former professional basketball player originally from the Congo; Mother Teresa, a Roman Catholic nun from Macedonia. These well-known figures seem *quite* different from each other in overall personality—except for their concern with helping others. Gates and his wife Melinda have pledged *billions* of dollars to charity, much of it to target health issues around the world. Bono has worked tirelessly to raise money and awareness about the plight of poor African nations. Turner pledged a personal donation of $1 billion to the United Nations. Mutombo has raised millions of dollars for and overseen the construction of hospitals in the Congo. Mother Teresa devoted her life to the poor in India.

The quest to discover the altruistic personality has not been an easy one. Much of the research conducted over the years has failed to find consistent, reliable personality characteristics that predict helping behavior across situations. Some researchers have changed the nature of the quest, however, focusing on personality variables that predict helping in some specific situations rather than across all situations; and their studies have been more successful in identifying traits that predict such behavior (Carlo et al., 2005; Finkelstein, 2009; Penner, 2004).

Research suggests that two of the qualities that are most essential for an altruistic personality are empathy and advanced moral reasoning (e.g., Eisenberg & Eggum, 2008; Hoffman, 2000). We have already discussed empathy in this chapter, such as in the context of Batson's empathy-altruism hypothesis. Being able to take the perspective of others and experience empathy is associated positively with helping and other prosocial behaviors in children and adults (Albiero et al., 2009; Batson, 2009; Nakao & Itakura, 2009; Vaish et al., 2009).

The second characteristic associated with helping is moral reasoning. Children and adults who exhibit internalized and advanced levels of moral reasoning behave more altruistically than others. Such reasoning involves adhering to moral standards independent of external social controls and taking into account the needs of others when making decisions about courses of action. In contrast, people whose reasoning is focused on their own needs or on the concrete personal consequences that their actions are likely to have tend not to engage in many helping behaviors (Carlo et al., 1996; Krebs & Rosenwald, 1994; Malti et al., 2009; Midlarsky et al., 1999; Schonert-Reichl, 1999).

The combination of empathy and advanced moral reasoning may be an especially strong predictor of helping tendencies. Paul Miller and his colleagues (1996) proposed that "cold" cognitive moral principles may not be enough to trigger self-sacrificing prosocial action. When these principles are activated together with the experience of "hot" empathic or sympathetic emotional responses to another's suffering, however, helping is much more likely.

Elizabeth Midlarsky, Stephanie Fagin-Jones, and their colleagues (Fagin-Jones & Midlarsky, 2007; Midlarsky et al., 2005) have conducted one fascinating line of research that suggests the importance of both empathy and moral reasoning. They contrasted the personalities of "non-Jewish heroes of the Holocaust"—people who risked their lives to help Jews despite having no expectation of any extrinsic rewards—with bystanders who did not help during the Holocaust. The researchers found that rescuers did indeed tend to differ from bystanders on a combination of several variables associated with prosocial behavior, particularly empathic concern and moral reasoning. Both of these qualities are reflected in the quote of one woman who sheltered 30 Jews in her home in Poland: "Helping to give shelter was the natural thing to do, the human thing. When I looked into those eyes, how could I not care? Of course I was afraid—always afraid—but there was no choice but to do the only decent thing" (Midlarsky et al., 2005, p. 908).

"It's always poor you, isn't it, Albert?"

Someone relatively low in empathic concern for another.

True kindness presupposes the faculty of imagining as one's own the suffering and joy of others.

—André Gide

Interpersonal Influences: Whom Do People Help?

However influential they might be, personal factors alone do not a helper make. The characteristics of the person in need are important as well. Are some people more likely than others to receive help? Are some helpers particularly responsive to certain kinds of individuals who need assistance? Here, we explore some of the interpersonal aspects of helping.

Perceived Characteristics of the Person in Need

Although many characteristics of a person in need might affect whether that individual is helped, researchers have paid special attention to two: the personal attractiveness of the person in need and whether or not the person seems responsible for being in the position of needing assistance.

Attractiveness   In Chapter 9, we described the social advantages physically attractive individuals enjoy. The bias toward beauty also affects helping. Attractive people are more likely to be offered help and cooperation across a number of different settings, whether it be asking for directions on campus, playing a game that could be either competitive or cooperative, or requesting money in a health emergency (Farrelly et al., 2007; West & Brown, 1975; Wilson, 1978). In addition to physical attractiveness, interpersonal attractiveness is also related to receiving more help (Stürmer et al., 2005).

Certainly one explanation for some of these findings is that people help attractive others in the hope of establishing some kind of relationship with an attractive person. Not many people would be shocked to learn, for example, that male motorists in France were more likely to stop their cars and offer a ride to female hitchhikers whose bust size was enhanced (by a bra worn by a confederate) or who were smiling (Guéguen, 2007; Guéguen & Fischer-Lokou, 2004). What may be surprising, however, is that attractive people receive more help even when the helper does it anonymously, with no chance for any reward. One demonstration of this was a study by Peter Benson and his colleagues (1976) in a large metropolitan airport. Darting into a phone booth to make a call (these were the days long before cell phones), each of 604 travelers discovered some materials supposedly left behind accidentally by the previous caller (but actually planted by the experimenters): a packet containing a completed graduate school application form, a photograph of the applicant, and a stamped, addressed envelope. In some packets, the photo depicted a physically attractive individual; in others, the person was relatively unattractive. What was a busy traveler to do? When the researchers checked their mail, they found that people were more likely to send in the materials of the good-looking applicants than those of the less attractive applicants.

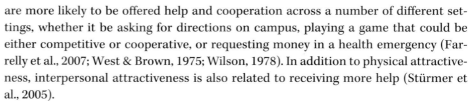

Attractive people have a better chance than unattractive people of getting help when they need it. **TRUE.**

Attributions of Responsibility   At some time or another, most students have had the experience of being asked to lend their class notes to a classmate. Has this ever happened to you? If so, you can compare your reactions with those of the students in a study conducted by Richard Barnes and his colleagues (1979). In this research, students received a call from an experimental confederate posing as another student, who asked to borrow their class notes to prepare for an upcoming exam. The reason for this request varied. To some students, the caller said, "I just don't seem to have the ability to take good notes. I really try to take good notes, but sometimes I just can't do it." Other students were told that "I just don't seem to have the motivation to take good notes. I really can take good notes, but sometimes I just don't try." You probably won't be surprised to learn that the caller received much more help from those who were informed that he had tried and failed than from those who were told he hadn't tried at all.

Bluntly stating that you didn't even try to help yourself may seem like an obvious way to ensure that others won't help you out. But even when the circumstances are more complex and the causes more subtle, people's beliefs about the needy individual's responsibility influence helping. For example, participants in an experiment by Pamela Dooley (1995) read scenarios about someone who had just been diagnosed with AIDS. If the participants read that the person had contracted the disease through a blood transfusion rather than through sexual activity or drug use, they considered the situation less controllable, felt more pity for the person, and indicated a greater desire to engage in helping behaviors. Similarly, Nadine Mackay and Christine Barrowclough (2005) report that the medical and nursing staff at an emergency room felt more negative about and were less helpful to patients whose injuries they felt were more controllable and avoidable. Michelle Lobchuck and others (2008) found that caregivers of people with lung cancer had more negative emotions and gave less supportive help if they believed the patient was largely responsible for their disease.

▌▌ The Fit Between Giver and Receiver

Some potential helpers are particularly responsive to certain kinds of potential recipients. In this section, we look at a variety of ways in which helping depends on the fit between a giver and a receiver.

Similarity and Ingroups: Helping Those Just Like Us   We are more likely to help others who are similar to us. All kinds of similarity—from dress to attitudes to nationality—increase our willingness to help, and signs of dissimilarity decrease it (Dovidio, 1984). There are probably several reasons underlying this effect. For one thing, as seen in Chapter 9, we are more likely to be attracted to and develop relationships with people who are similar to ourselves. In addition, people tend to empathize more with similar others or with people in their ingroups (Xu et al., 2009). The influence of similarity could even be a form of kin selection, as people may use similarity in appearance as a signal of potential kinship.

People are much more likely to help fellow ingroup members than they are to help members of an outgroup (Bernhard et al., 2006; Kogut & Ritov, 2007; Levine et al., 2005; Stürmer et al., 2006). Mark Levine and others (2005) demonstrated this point in a clever field experiment based on the bystander intervention research discussed earlier in the chapter. Participants were British university students who were supporters of a particular popular football (soccer) team. After completing some questions about their support of the team (which served to highlight their identification with it), the participants had to walk to another building on campus, allegedly to watch a video for the next part of the study. On the way they encountered a jogger (actually, a confederate) who fell and seemed to be in pain with an injured ankle. For some of the participants, this jogger happened to be wearing the shirt of the participants' favorite team. For others, the jogger was wearing either a shirt of a rival team or a neutral shirt with no team logo. Would the shirt affect how likely the jogger was to be offered help?

As you can see in ▶ Figure 10.10, the shirt did make a big difference. Participants were much more likely to offer help to a person wearing their favorite team's shirt—a fellow ingroup member—than they were to help a person wearing either a neutral or a rival shirt. In this study, wearing a rival team's shirt did not reduce the jogger's chances of getting help compared to wearing a neutral shirt; it was just that wearing a shirt that signified similar team affiliation led to increased helping.

The effects of similarity and ingroup status on helping suggest that members of the same race should help each other more than they help members of different races. However, in a meta-analysis of more than 30 studies, Donald Saucier and others (2005) found no consistent overall relationship between racial similarity and helping. What accounts for these inconsistencies? First, although helping can be a compassionate response to another, it can also be seen as a sign of superiority over the person who needs help, and this can greatly complicate the decision about helping someone (Ames et al., 2004; Vorauer & Sasaki, 2009). Second, public displays of racial prejudice risk social disapproval, and prejudiced individuals may bend over backward (in public, at least) to avoid revealing their attitudes. As discussed in Chapter 5, however, modern racism relies on more subtle forms of discrimination. Consistent with predictions from

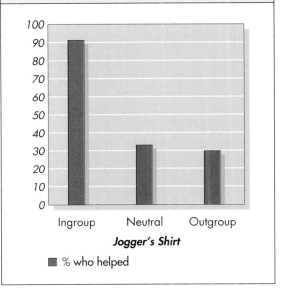

▶ **FIGURE 10.10**

Helping Ingroup Members

Participants who were fans of a particular British football (soccer) team came across a fallen jogger who seemed to be in pain. When the jogger was wearing a shirt of the participants' favorite team, they were much more likely to offer help than if he was wearing either a rival team's shirt or a neutral shirt.

Based on Levine et al., 2005.

theories of modern racism, Saucier et al.'s meta-analysis found that when the situation provides people with excuses or justifications for not helping, racial discrimination in helping is more likely.

Intergroup biases in helping can be reduced significantly, however, if the members of the different groups can perceive themselves as members of a common group. Through fostering perceptions of shared identities and highlighting similarities between individuals across groups, an ingroup and an outgroup can begin to see each other as more similar than different, thereby promoting helping and other positive behaviors (Dovidio et al., 2009; Levine et al., 2005).

Closeness: A Little Help for Our Friends   As we would expect, people are usually more helpful to those they know and care about than they are to strangers or superficial acquaintances (Bell et al., 1995; Clark & Mills, 1993; Stewart-Williams, 2008). People in a *communal* relationship, such as close friends or romantic partners, feel mutual responsibility for each other's needs. People in an *exchange* relationship, such as acquaintances or business associates, give help with the expectation of receiving comparable benefits in return—"If I help you move your furniture, you'd better give me a ride to the airport." When people are, or desire to be, in a communal relationship with each other, they attend more to each other's needs, are more likely to help, and are less likely to be concerned with keeping track of rewards and costs than people in an exchange relationship are. People in a communal relationship also feel better about having helped the other, and they feel worse if they are unable to help (Williamson et al., 1996).

So common sense seems correct here: People help their friends more than they help strangers or acquaintances. But there may be an exception to this general rule, and it has to do with the helper's ego. If we can help a friend succeed in a task that is not very important to our identity or relevant to our ego, we are likely to do so and to delight in their success. But what if they succeed in doing something that we wish we could do at least as well? Would we help a friend shine in this case? According to the *self-evaluation maintenance model* (Erber & Tesser, 1994), people sometimes offer more help to a stranger than to a friend if the help is for something that can be threatening to the helper's ego. We may prefer that a stranger steal the spotlight than a friend whose success we'll be reminded of all too often.

▌ Gender and Helping

Here's a quick, one-question quiz: Who helps more, men or women? Before you answer, consider the following situations:

A. Two strangers pass on the street. Suddenly, one of them needs help that might be dangerous to give. Other people are watching. The person in need is female.

B. Two individuals have a close relationship. Every so often, one of them needs assistance that takes time and energy to provide but is not physically dangerous. No one else is around to notice whether help is given. The person who needs help is either male or female.

Is your answer different for these two situations? It's likely to be. Situation A is a classic male-helper scenario. Here, the helper is a "knight in shining armor"—physically brave and chivalrous—rescuing a lady in distress. Because much of the research on helping used to focus on emergency situations, such as in the bystander intervention studies, older reviews tended to find that on average, men are more helpful than women and women receive more help than men (Eagly & Crowley, 1986).

Situation B is the classic female-helper scenario. Every day, millions of people provide support for their friends and loved ones, and some reviews indicate that women are more likely to provide this kind of help than are men (Becker & Eagly, 2004; George et al., 1998; McGuire, 1994). Though it lacks the high drama of an emergency intervention, this type of helping, called "social support," plays a crucial role in the quality of our lives. Chapter 14 reports evidence indicating that social support is associated with better physical and psychological health.

Many of the stories from September 11, 2001, fit these two classic senses of helping. Most of the dramatic rescue stories were of men engaged in dangerous acts of helping, such as the account of the firefighters featured in the opening to this chapter. And many women worked behind the scenes in the more unheralded acts of helping, such as tending to the wounded, raising money for the families of the victims, and helping with the cleanup of the disaster sites at the World Trade Center and the Pentagon. But as is the case with most gender differences, there were many exceptions. Many men worked along with women to lend support in the aftermath, and several women risked, and lost, their lives while trying to help others in the World Trade Center that morning. Indeed, Susan Hagen and Mary Carouba, outraged at the lack of coverage of women's sacrifices on 9/11, wrote a book in 2002 to address this oversight, *Women at Ground Zero: Stories of Courage and Compassion.*

For types of helping that do not easily fit into either of these categories, the evidence for gender differences is not strong. In a field experiment conducted in six cities that examined whether people help a man or woman who dropped a pen, for example, there were no gender differences in who tended to help or in who was helped (Reysen & Ganz, 2006).

Research has examined not only whether gender is related to differences in helping behavior but also to differences in the willingness to *seek* help. Have you ever had the experience of getting lost while driving with a member of the opposite sex? Who wanted to stop early on and ask for directions? Who kept insisting that help wasn't necessary? In this case, the stereotype is true: Men ask for help less frequently than do women—a difference replicated in several countries around the world (Chang, 2007; Mackenzie et al., 2006; Murray et al., 2008; Sherer, 2007). Help-seeking is less socially acceptable for men and is more threatening to their self-esteem (Wills & DePaulo, 1991).

"Are you telling me you won't even ask the computerized navigational system for directions?"

Men are less likely to seek help than women, possibly because it is more threatening to their self-esteem.

Women seek help more often than men do. **TRUE.**

Reactions to Receiving Help

As the point about men feeling threatened when seeking help suggests, receiving help from someone is not always simply a positive experience. Think about some times when someone helped you. How did you feel? Grateful, relieved, comforted—anything else? Embarrassed, obligated, inferior? Receiving help is often a positive experience, but sometimes it has drawbacks for the recipient. There are costs in providing help, and there can be costs in receiving it. Jeffrey Fisher, Arie Nadler, Daniel Ames, and their collaborators have extensively examined people's reactions to receiving help (Ames et al., 2004; Fisher et al., 1982; Nadler & Fisher, 1986). According to their **threat-to-self-esteem model**, receiving help is experienced as *self-supportive* when

threat-to-self-esteem model
The theory that reactions to receiving assistance depend on whether help is perceived as supportive or threatening.

the recipient feels appreciated and cared for, but it is experienced as *self-threatening* when the recipient feels inferior and overly dependent.

People who are stigmatized by being the targets of negative stereotypes and feeling devalued in the larger society often face a difficult attributional dilemma when they receive help from members of nonstigmatized groups: Is the helping sincere and unassuming, is it well intentioned but patronizing, or is it controlling and designed to keep the recipient dependent? These are questions that members of nonstigmatized groups aren't as likely to consider when they receive help from another. Members of stigmatized groups may feel worse about themselves after receiving help from an outgroup member, particularly if the help was unsolicited (Blaine et al., 1995; Nadler et al., 2009; Schneider et al., 1996).

▊ Culture and Who Receives Help

As we said earlier in the chapter, compared to individualists, collectivists may be more likely to help ingroup members but less likely to help outgroup members (Conway et al., 2001; Schwartz, 1990). Even within a culture, the extent to which individuals are individualistic or collectivistic can matter. For example, Lucian Conway and others (2001) found that Americans with a more collectivistic orientation were less likely to help strangers than were those with an individualistic orientation, particularly when the helping involved planning (as opposed to spontaneous helping).

We al so discussed earlier that people are less likely to help if they think the person is responsible for his or her plight. Elizabeth Mullen and Linda Skitka (2009) recently proposed that this may be a stronger influence on helping in an individualist culture—where individuals may be expected to have more control over their own fates—than in a collectivist one. On the other hand, perceptions of how much the person in need contributes to society might affect the helping decisions of collectivists—who have stronger norms of interdependence—more than of individualists.

To test these ideas, Mullen and Skitka had participants from the United States and the Ukraine (a more collectivistic society) read about 16 individuals who needed an organ transplant. Information about each individual suggested that some were more responsible for their illness than others (e.g., a person continued to eat unhealthy foods and resist exercise despite warnings versus a person had a genetically defective organ). The researchers also varied information about how much contribution the individuals seemed to make to society (e.g., a person who volunteers for multiple organizations versus a person who does not volunteer). After reading about all 16 people, participants were asked to indicate which of up to six of them should receive a transplant.

In both cultures, people were less likely to help patients who were more responsible for their organ failure or who made less contribution to society. However, as can be seen in ▶ Figure 10.11, the issue of personal responsibility played a bigger role in the decisions made by the Americans, whereas the issue of contribution to society played a bigger role in the decisions by the Ukrainians.

There also may be cultural differences in how threatened people are when seeking or receiving help. For example, Shelley Taylor and others (2007) have found that seeking and receiving social support from close others may be more stressful—both psychologically and physiologically—to Asian and Asian American students than it is to European American students. Asian students benefited more from what the researchers called *implicit social support*—support that comes from just thinking about close others but that does not involve actually seeking or receiving their help in coping with stressful events.

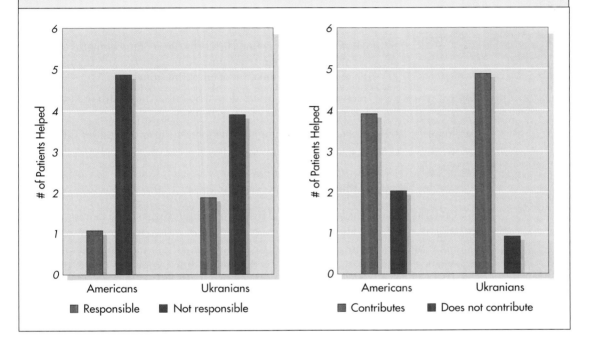

▶**FIGURE 10.11**

Who Should Receive Help? A Cross-Cultural Difference

Americans and Ukrainians were asked to decide which six of up to sixteen individuals should receive an organ transplant. Participants were given information about the individuals that varied in terms of how personally responsible they seemed to be for their illnesses and how much they seemed to contribute to their society. Although participants in both countries preferred helping individuals who were not responsible for their illness and who made contributions to society, Americans' decisions were affected more by how responsible the person seemed, whereas Ukrainians' decisions were affected more by whether the person made contributions to society.

Based on Mullen & Skitka, 2009.

The Helping Connection

Although whether or not people help others can be quite variable, a consistent theme appears repeatedly in this chapter: a sense of connection. Throughout the chapter, this connection has taken various forms—genetic relatedness, empathic concern, sense of responsibility for someone, perceived similarity, shared group membership, and so on.

In the United States, one of the richest countries on earth, thousands of men, women, and children are without a home. Many sleep on the street, carry their belongings in grocery carts, and rummage through piles of garbage to find food. In contrast, among some of the poorest people on earth, no one goes without shelter or remains thirsty as long as anyone has water to drink. How can we account for this difference? Homelessness is, of course, a complex phenomenon affected by many specific economic and political factors. But it may also be a symptom of a profound loss of social connection in American society.

Consider, however, the outpouring of help by Americans after large-scale tragedies. After Hurricane Katrina in August 2005, for example, families throughout the country took in those who lost their homes, schools and colleges offered displaced

Company 6 firefighters are reunited with Josephine Harris, the woman they risked their lives to save in the World Trade Center on September, 11, 2001. The men presented Josephine with a jacket honoring her as their "Guardian Angel"—a reminder of how their selfless act of helping her may have in turn saved their own lives as the 110-story skyscraper collapsed around them.

students the chance to continue their education, countless college students resisted the hedonistic temptations of spring break to volunteer their time to help rebuild New Orleans, young children helped raise money and food, and on and on. A tragedy such as Katrina can remind people of their common humanity, highlighting their social connection while, temporarily at least, rendering their differences insignificant.

The relationship between helping and interpersonal connection runs like a bright red thread through much of the research on helping. For example:

- Evolutionary perspectives emphasize the genetic connection of reciprocal, kin, and within-group helping.

- Two kinds of connections lie at the heart of the empathy-altruism hypothesis: the cognitive connection of perspective taking and the emotional connection of empathic concern.

- In an emergency, bystanders who know the victim or know each other are more likely to intervene.

- People who respond empathically to another's suffering and consider the plight of others in their own moral reasoning are more likely to help than are others.

- Perceived similarity increases helping.

- In a close relationship, it's easier to give and more comfortable to receive.

Taken as a whole, these theories and research findings suggest that helping requires the recognition of individual human beings with whom we can have a meaningful connection. Which brings us back to Ladder Company 6 and the so many others who risked and even lost their lives that day. Most of the people didn't know the others they were helping. But suddenly, horribly, fate had thrown them together, and suddenly their lives deeply mattered to each other. They felt responsible for each other. Many of those who helped in the face of grave danger may never have read the words that English poet John Donne wrote almost 400 years ago. But they would have understood them:

> No man is an island, entire of itself. Every man is a piece of the continent, a part of the main. If a clod be washed away by the sea, Europe is the less, as well as if a promontory were, as well as if a manor of thy friends or of thine own were. Any man's death diminishes me, because I am involved in mankind. And therefore never send to know for whom the bell tolls; it tolls for thee.

REVIEW

Evolutionary and Motivational Factors: Why Do People Help?

Evolutionary Factors in Helping

- Evolutionary perspectives emphasize two ways that helping could become an innate, universal behavioral tendency: kin selection, in which individuals protect their own genes by helping close relatives; and reciprocal altruism, in which those who give also receive.

- Other evolutionary approaches include the idea of group selection, in which members of a social group help each other survive.

- Recent work examines how seemingly higher-order, uniquely human constructs such as morality and empathy are evolved characteristics that can also be seen in some other animals.

- Many primates seem to exhibit empathy both in laboratory and natural settings.

Rewards of Helping: Helping Others to Help Oneself

- People are much more likely to help when the potential rewards of helping seem high relative to the potential costs.

- Helping others often makes the helper feel good, it can relieve negative feelings such as guilt, and it is associated with better health.

- People who are feeling bad may be inclined to help others in order to feel relief from their negative mood.

Altruism or Egoism: The Great Debate

- Scholars have debated whether egoistic motives are always behind helpful behaviors or whether helping is ever truly altruistic.

- According to the empathy-altruism hypothesis, taking the perspective of a person perceived to be in need creates the other-oriented emotion of empathic concern, which in turn produces the altruistic motive to reduce the other's distress.

- A number of studies have supported the empathy-altruism hypothesis, for example by demonstrating that when people are altruistically motivated, they will help even when escaping from the helping situation is easy. However, there are limits to the role of altruism in helping behavior.

- Longer-term acts of helping, such as volunteerism, reflect both altruistic and egoistic motivations. Self-interested goals in this context can be a good thing because they promote a commitment to helping behavior to the extent that such goals are met.

Situational Influences: When Do People Help?

The Unhelpful Crowd

- Research on the bystander effect, in which the presence of others inhibits helping in an emergency, indicates why the five steps necessary for helping—noticing, interpreting, taking responsibility, deciding how to help, and providing help—may not be taken.

- The distractions caused by the presence of other people and by our own self-concerns may impair our ability to notice that someone needs help.

- Under ambiguous circumstances, some interpretations—such as the belief that an attacker and a victim have a close relationship or mistaken inferences drawn from pluralistic ignorance—reduce intervention from bystanders.

- People may fail to take responsibility because they assume that others will do so—a phenomenon called *diffusion of responsibility*.

- Bystanders are less likely to offer direct aid when they do not feel competent to do so. They can, however, call for assistance from others.

- Even if people want to help, they may not do so if they fear that behaving in a helpful fashion will make them look foolish.

- Some recent research has demonstrated the bystander effect even in online contexts, when the bystanders are not physically present.

- The legacy of the bystander effect research and of the Kitty Genovese tragedy that inspired it endures, even as revisions are suggested to some of the research conclusions or to some of the details of the Genovese case.

Time Pressure

- When people are in a hurry, they are less likely to notice or choose to help others in need.

Location and Helping

- Residents of heavily populated areas are less likely to provide spontaneous, informal help to strangers than are residents of smaller or less densely populated communities.

Culture and Helping

- Cross-cultural research has found variation in the helping rates of people in cities around the world. According to one study, people in cities with relatively low levels of economic well-being were somewhat more likely to help strangers, and people from *simpatía* cultures were more likely to help strangers than people from *non-simpatía* cultures.

- Research concerning the relationship between individualism-collectivism and helping has yielded rather mixed results. According to some analyses, collectivists may be more responsive than individualists to the immediate needs of a particular person but less helpful in more abstract situations.

Moods and Helping

- A good mood increases helpfulness.

- People in a good mood may help in order to maintain their positive mood or because they have more positive thoughts and expectations about helpful behavior, about the person in need, or about social activities in general.

- A bad mood can often increase helpfulness, for example when people feel guilty about something.

- People in a bad mood may be motivated to help others in order to improve their mood.

- A bad mood is less likely to increase helpfulness if the bad mood is attributed to the fault of others or if it causes the person to become very self-focused.

Role Models and Social Norms: A Helpful Standard

- Observing a person modeling helpful behavior increases helping.

- Social norms that promote helping are based on a sense of fairness or on standards about what is right.

Culture and Social Norms for Helping

- Cultural differences exist in how people interpret and apply social norms.

- The results of one study suggest that Hindu Indians regard social responsibilities as an absolute moral obligation, whereas Americans apply the norm of social responsibility more selectively.

- Another study found that Thai students reported that religion plays a greater role in their decisions to help someone than did American students.

Personal Influences: Who Is Likely to Help?

Are Some People More Helpful Than Others?

- There is some evidence of relatively stable individual differences in helping tendencies.
- Recent findings suggest that there may be a genetic, heritable component to helpfulness.

What Is the Altruistic Personality?

- Some personality traits are associated with helpful behavioral tendencies in some situations, but no one set of traits appears to define the altruistic personality.
- Two qualities that do predict helping behaviors are empathy and advanced moral reasoning.

Interpersonal Influences: Whom Do People Help?

Perceived Characteristics of the Person in Need

- Attractive individuals are more likely to receive help than are those who are less attractive.
- People are more willing to help when they attribute a person's need for assistance to uncontrollable causes rather than to events under the person's control.

The Fit Between Giver and Receiver

- In general, perceived similarity to a person in need increases willingness to help.
- People are more likely to help members of their ingroups.
- Research on the role of race in helping has yielded inconsistent results.
- People usually help friends more than strangers, except when helping threatens their own egos.

Gender and Helping

- Men help female strangers in potentially dangerous situations more than women do; women help friends and relations with social support more than men do. The evidence for gender differences is not strong for acts of helping that do not easily fit either of these categories.
- Compared to women, men are more hesitant to seek help, especially for relatively minor problems.

Reactions to Receiving Help

- The threat-to-self-esteem model distinguishes between help perceived as supportive, which produces positive reactions, and help perceived as threatening, which creates negative reactions.

- Members of stigmatized groups sometimes feel worse after receiving unsolicited help from members of non-stigmatized groups.

Culture and Who Receives Help

- Some research has shown that people with a collectivistic orientation may be less likely to help outgroup members or strangers than are those with an individualistic orientation.
- A recent study found that attributions of how responsible a person in need was for their situation played a stronger role in individualists' decisions to help the person than it did in collectivists' decisions to help. In contrast, perceptions of how much the person in need contributes to society affected collectivists' decisions to help more than it affected individualists' decisions.
- According to the results of one study, seeking and receiving social support from close others may be more stressful—both psychologically and physiologically—to Asian and Asian American students than to European American students. Asian and Asian American students may prefer social support that is more implicit than explicit, whereas the opposite may be true for American students.

The Helping Connection

- Theory and research seem to indicate that helping requires the recognition of meaningful connections among individuals.

Key Terms

altruistic (400)
arousal: cost-reward model (397)
audience inhibition (410)
bystander effect (406)
diffusion of responsibility (409)
egoistic (399)

empathy (395)
empathy-altruism hypothesis (401)
good mood effect (417)
kin selection (392)
negative state relief model (398)
norm of social responsibility (420)

pluralistic ignorance (408)
prosocial behaviors (391)
social norm (419)
threat-to-self-esteem model (427)

Media Resources

Social Psychology 8th Edition Companion Website
Visit your book companion website
www.cengage.com/psychology/kassin
where you will find flash cards, practice quizzes,
Internet links, and more to help you study.

CENGAGENOW™ Just what you need to know NOW! Spend time on what you need to master rather than on information

you already have learned. Take a pre-test for this chapter and CengageNOW will generate a personalized study plan based on your results. The study plan will identify the topics you need to review and direct you to online resources to help you master those topics. You can then take a post-test to help you determine the concepts you have mastered and what you will need to work on. Try it out! Go to **academic .cengage.com/login** to sign in with an access code or to purchase access to this product.

Putting COMMON SENSE *to the Test*

People are more likely to help someone in an emergency if the potential rewards seem high and the potential costs seem low.

True. *For both emergency situations and more long-term, well-planned helping, people's helping behaviors are determined in part by a cost-benefit analysis.*

In an emergency, a person who needs help has a much better chance of getting it if three other people are present than if only one other person is present.

False. *In several ways, the presence of others inhibits helping.*

People are much more likely to help someone when they're in a good mood.

True. *Compared to neutral moods, good moods tend to elicit more helping and other prosocial behaviors.*

People are much less likely to help someone when they're in a bad mood.

False. *Compared to neutral moods, negative moods often elicit more helping and prosocial behaviors. This effect depends on a number of factors, including whether people take responsibility for their bad mood or blame it on others; but in many circumstances, feeling bad leads to doing good.*

Attractive people have a better chance than unattractive people of getting help when they need it.

True. *People are more likely to help those who are attractive.*

Women seek help more often than men do.

True. *At least for relatively minor problems, men ask for help less frequently than women do.*

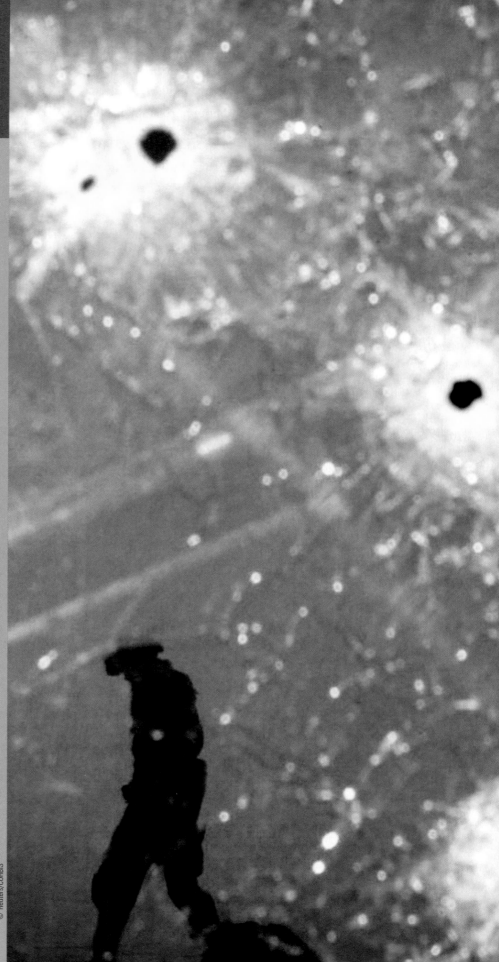

11

Aggression

In this chapter, we examine a disturbing aspect of human behavior: aggression. First, we ask, "What is aggression?" and consider its definition. After describing how aggression may vary across culture, gender, and individual differences, we examine various theories concerning the origins of aggression. We then explore a variety of situational factors that influence when people are likely to behave aggressively. Next, we focus on two critically important issues in our society. One issue concerns the media effects on aggression, including the consequences of exposure to media violence and pornography. The other issue is the intimate violence that can occur in close relationships. We conclude by discussing ways of reducing violence.

Putting COMMON SENSE to the Test

Circle Your Answer

T	F	In virtually every culture, males are more violent than females.
T	F	For virtually any category of aggression, males are more aggressive than females.
T	F	Children who are spanked or otherwise physically disciplined (but not abused) for behaving aggressively tend to become less aggressive.
T	F	Blowing off steam by engaging in safe but aggressive activities (such as sports) makes people less likely to aggress later.
T	F	Exposure to TV violence in childhood is related to aggression later in life.
T	F	Men are much more likely than women to aggress against their spouses or partners.

A church. A museum. A school. These are places in which people should feel safe. But within three months across the spring of 2009 the sense of safety in each of these places was shattered by deadly violence.

On May 31, 2009, Dr. George Tiller was serving as an usher at his church's Sunday morning service in Wichita, Kansas, when he was shot in the head at point blank range. Scott Roeder was arrested and charged with the murder. Tiller was a controversial figure because he was the director of one of the few clinics in the United States that provided what are known as late-term abortions (abortions after the twenty-first week of pregnancy) and had been the target of a great deal of criticism and some threats.

Less than two weeks later, on June 10, an 88-year-old man named James von Brunn reportedly walked up to the entrance of the United States Holocaust Memorial Museum in Washington, D.C. Security guard Stephen Tyrone Johns "was kind enough to open the door" for von Brunn, who then raised the rifle he had been carrying at his side and fired it near the guard's heart, killing him. Other security guards shot and wounded von Brunn as he fired two more shots. A notebook left in von Brunn's car outside the museum read, "You want my weapons—this is how you'll get them. The Holocaust is a lie. Obama was created by Jews" (Meyer, 2009, p. 22).

Less than three months before these two incidents, 17-year-old Tim Kretschmer walked into his former high school in Winnenden, Germany, at about 9:30 in the morning. Armed with his father's gun and hundreds of rounds of ammunition, he went on a shooting spree, killing nine students and three teachers. He shot many of his victims in the head as he moved from room to room. After police arrived he fled and led them on a wild chase, during which he killed three more people before killing himself with a shot to

Alex Grimm/Getty Images

AP Photo/Alex Brandon

© Reuters New Media Inc./Corbis

Snapshots of terror. On the top left is a man holding a sign reading, "God where were you?" in front of the school in Winnenden, Germany, the day after a teenager shot and killed nine students, three teachers, and three others in March 2009. On the top right are bullet-scarred glass doors at the U.S. Holocaust Memorial Museum in Washington, D.C., after an 88-year-old man opened fire on security guards inside the museum in June 2009. Eric Harris and Dylan Klebold are seen in the photo on the bottom as they walk through Columbine High School on the day of their murderous rampage in April 1999.

the head. In the end, he had fired more than 100 rounds and killed 16 people and himself, and had injured several more.

Do you recall reading much about the bloodbath in this high school in southwestern Germany? Unless you are from that area, chances are that you never even heard of it. The sad reality is that there have been so many school shootings in recent years that few of these stories capture very much international attention anymore. Indeed, a month after this incident, many people gathered in Littleton, Colorado, to mark the tenth anniversary of what has come to serve as a chilling icon of this sickening and all-too-frequent kind of aggression: the massacre at Columbine High School. On April 20, 1999, teenagers Dylan Klebold and Eric Harris, armed with a semiautomatic rifle, a semiautomatic handgun, two sawed-off shotguns, and more than 30 homemade bombs, terrorized the school. These boys first shot and killed two students in the school parking lot. Then they entered the cafeteria, where they threw pipe bombs and opened fire, filling the room with bullets. From there, the boys went upstairs, shot a school police officer, and then shot and killed a teacher, ten other students, and themselves.

In many respects, the stories about the killings at the church and at the museum were quite different from those about the school shootings. But together they all raise profound questions about the causes of aggression and violence. Each of these incidents reflects some of the factors associated with aggression that will be discussed in the pages that follow.

This chapter examines the origins and immediate triggers of aggression. It focuses primarily on aggression by individuals; aggression by groups, such as rampaging mobs and warring nations, was discussed in Chapter 8. This chapter also discusses factors that reduce aggression.

What Is Aggression?

aggression   Behavior intended to harm another individual.

Although there are numerous ways one can define **aggression**, the definition that best represents the research today is that aggression is behavior that is intended to harm another individual. Aggressive behaviors come in many forms. Words as well as deeds can be aggressive. Quarreling couples who intend their spiteful remarks to hurt are behaving aggressively. Spreading a vicious rumor about someone is another form of aggression. Even failure to act can be aggressive, if that failure is intended to hurt someone, such as by not helping someone avoid what you know will be a humiliating outcome.

To distinguish them from less harmful behaviors, extreme acts of aggression are called *violence*. Some other terms in the language of aggression refer to emotions and attitudes. *Anger* consists of strong feelings of displeasure in response to a perceived injury; the exact nature of these feelings (for example, outrage, hate, or irritation) depends on the specific situation. *Hostility* is a negative, antagonistic attitude toward another person or group. Anger and hostility are often closely connected to aggression, but not always. People can be angry at others and regard them with great hostility without ever trying to harm them. And aggression can occur without a trace of anger or hostility, as when a contract killer murders a perfect stranger in order to "make a killing" financially.

The aggression of a hired gun is an example of **instrumental aggression**, in which harm is inflicted as a means to a desired end. Aggression aimed at harming someone for personal gain, attention, or even self-defense fits this definition. If the aggressor believes that there is an easier way to obtain the goal, aggression will not occur. Some researchers call this type of aggression *proactive aggression*.

In **emotional aggression**, the means and the end coincide. Harm is inflicted for its own sake. Some researchers call this type of aggression *reactive aggression*. Emotional aggression is often impulsive, carried out in the heat of the moment. The jealous lover strikes out in rage; fans of rival soccer teams go at each other with fists and clubs. Emotional aggression, however, can also be calm, cool, and calculating. Revenge, so the saying goes, is a dish best served cold.

Of course, sometimes it is hard to distinguish between instrumental and emotional aggression. Why does a frustrated fighter illegally head butt his opponent—is it a deliberate, sneaky attempt to gain an advantage over a frustrating opponent, or does it simply reflect someone losing control and lashing out unthinkingly in frustration? It can be difficult to know where to draw the line between the two types of aggression and motives. Indeed, some scholars believe that all aggression is fundamentally instrumental, serving some need, and still others suggest that instrumental and emotional aggression are not distinct categories but endpoints on a continuum (Anderson & Huesmann, 2007; Tedeschi & Bond, 2001).

During their heavyweight boxing championship fight in June 1997, former champion Mike Tyson viciously bites champion Evander Holyfield's ear. After chewing off pieces of both of Holyfield's ears, Tyson was disqualified and a near-riot ensued in the ring. Was Tyson's attack an instance of instrumental aggression, in which he bit Holyfield's ears in order to stop a fight he felt he could not win, or was it an example of emotional aggression, in which he lost his composure and snapped because of the frustration and pain he was experiencing?

Photo by Clint Karlsen/Courtesy Las Vegas Review-Journal

Culture, Gender, and Individual Differences

Just as not all types of aggression are alike, not all groups of people are alike in their attitudes and propensities toward aggression. Before we discuss the causes of aggression and what can be done about it, we need to consider how aggression is similar and how it differs across cultures, gender, and individuals.

■ Culture and Aggression

Cultures vary dramatically in how—and how much—their members aggress against each other. We can see this variation across societies and across specific groups, or subcultures, within a society.

instrumental aggression
Inflicting harm in order to obtain something of value.

emotional aggression
Inflicting harm for its own sake.

Comparisons Across Societies   The United States has enjoyed recent dramatic decreases in its rates of violent crimes, but it continues to be an exceptionally violent country (see Table 11.1). Its murder rate is one of the highest among politically stable, industrialized nations, far worse than the rates for Canada, Australia, New Zealand, and much of Western Europe. However, several countries in Eastern Europe, Africa, Asia, and the Americas have worse rates than the United States. ▶ Figure 11.1 illustrates some of the variation in homicide rates around the world.

Based on data from INTERPOL, the world's largest police organization, Nigel Barber (2006) reports that rates of violent crimes are higher in the Americas than in many other regions in the world. According to these data, the rates of murder, rape, and assault among eleven countries in the Americas (including Argentina, the Bahamas, Chile, Costa Rica, and the United States) were about double the world averages. Barber proposes that a key factor that may explain this difference is the relatively high rate of single parenthood in the Americas, which correlates with violent crime.

TABLE 11.1

The Violent Crime Clock

Although the rates of violent crimes in the United States have declined in recent years, they are still distressingly high, as these averaged statistics illustrate, and are much higher than they were several decades ago.

In the United States in 2007, there was, on average:

One MURDER	every 31 minutes
One FORCIBLE RAPE	every 6 minutes
One AGGRAVATED ASSAULT	every 37 seconds
One VIOLENT CRIME	every 22 seconds

Based on Federal Bureau of Investigation statistics.

Another difference across countries concerns how individualistic or collectivistic cultures tend to be. As discussed throughout the book, individualistic cultures place more emphasis on the values of independence, autonomy, and self-reliance, whereas collectivistic cultures place greater emphasis on the values of interdependence, cooperation, and social harmony. Gordon Forbes and others (2009) hypothesized that individualistic cultures, which are less concerned with social harmony and the avoidance of open conflict, are most likely to have a relatively high rate of aggression. To examine this idea, they asked students in China (a highly collectivistic culture), the United States (a highly individualistic culture), and Poland (a culture with intermediate levels of collectivism and individualism) to complete questionnaires about different types of aggression. The researchers found that aggression levels were highest in the United States and lowest in China, with Poland falling in the middle. Although there may be multiple reasons for these differences, Forbes and his colleagues believe that the results support their hypothesis that individualism is associated with aggression.

The forms violence typically takes, and people's attitudes toward various kinds of aggression, also differ internationally. Relative to most of the world, the United States has a tremendous amount of gun-related violence. The prevalence of handguns in the United States is exceptionally high, and even when compared to countries with which it shares much culturally, such as England and Australia, attitudes about guns tend to be much more permissive and positive in the United States, especially among males (Cooke, 2004). Indeed, although the rate of violent crime is actually lower in the United States than in England and Wales, the murder rate is much higher in the United States than in the U.K. (Barclay & Tavares, 2003). Researchers believe that the higher murder rate in the United States is due to the prevalence of guns. Almost 70 percent of the murders in the United States in 2007 were committed with guns.

The violence in the United States also tends to involve individuals rather than groups of people. Group attacks against other groups in political, ethnic, tribal, or other institutionalized conflict are seen throughout the world but are particularly associated with the Middle East, Africa, Eastern Europe, and parts of South America. And violent mobs of European football (what Americans call soccer) fans are not uncommon in England and other parts of Europe—behavior rarely seen at American sports events.

Cultures also differ in their attitudes about aggression. In a study involving students at 36 universities in 19 different countries around the world, there was considerable variation in how acceptable the students found different actions, such as a husband slapping a wife or vice versa (Douglas & Straus, 2006). For example, almost 80 percent of the respondents from a university in India did not strongly disapprove of a husband slapping a wife, compared to only about 24 percent at a university in the United States. In general, respondents from Europe were more approving of a husband slapping a wife than were respondents from Australia and New Zealand, who in turn tended to be somewhat more approving than respondents from North America. In contrast, these trends were reversed for the question of whether respondents had ever injured a dating partner—on this issue, North American rates tended to be highest. The issue of the acceptability of a husband slapping a wife made the news briefly in May 2009 when a Saudi judge said during a seminar on domestic violence that it is acceptable for a husband to slap his wife if she spends a lot of money because "she deserves the punishment" (Jamjoom, 2009).

Even within the same region, cultural differences can lead to very different attitudes and behaviors regarding aggression between men and women. A study of Israeli youths revealed that rates of dating violence were much higher among Israeli Arabs than Israeli Jews, apparently reflecting the very different norms between the two cultures (Sherer, 2009).

What is considered to be aggression and unacceptable in relation to children also can differ across cultures. For example, in Japan, it is not uncommon for Japanese adult businessmen to grope schoolgirls on public transportation, a practice that would be considered aggressive

▶ **FIGURE 11.1**

Violence Around the World

These figures indicate the number of recorded intentional homicides per 100,000 people in each of several countries in 2004, according to United Nations statistics published in 2006 (the U.S. data come from the U.S. Department of Justice data). Interpret the numbers with caution because there are wide differences in reporting and recording practices in the various countries, but the basic point is clear: There is wide variation in the frequency of murder around the world.

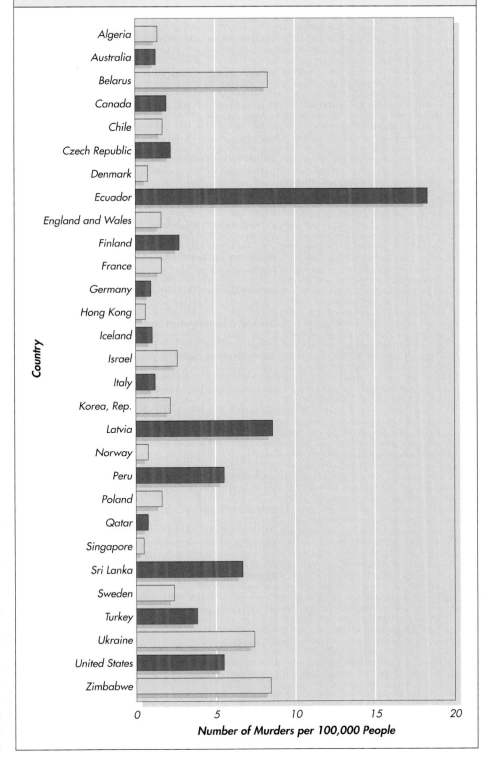

and unacceptable in many other cultures, including the far more violent United States. A 2004 survey conducted in Tokyo found that 64 percent of women in their twenties and thirties said that they had been groped in subways or subway stations (Ronzone, 2009). Indeed, the problem has become so bad that some train companies in Tokyo have introduced female-only cars to protect women and girls against this practice, such as on one train line that was formerly considered "a gropers' paradise" because of long gaps between stops and t he large number of schoolgirl passengers (Joyce, 2005, p. A6). Exploiting this behavior to more extreme ends, a Japanese 3D video game called "Rape-lay" has players simulate raping a woman and her two "virgin schoolgirl" daughters in a subway. This game caused an international uproar in February 2009 when it was discovered to be on sale (temporarily) at Amazon.com (Fennelly, 2009).

Another example concerns female genital mutilation—any of several procedures in which, according to some estimates, the genitals of approximately 6,000 girls a day are cut in several countries around the world, particularly in parts of Africa and Asia. It is estimated that well over 100 million females worldwide have undergone this procedure, mostly in childhood and often without anesthesia or sterile techniques. The cultures that practice this consider it an important, sacred ritual, but the cultures that condemn it consider it an inhumane and dangerous act of violence and have vigorously called for a worldwide ban (Leye et al., 2006; Rosenthal, 2006). In 2009, a man was the first to be arrested in Egypt for performing the operation since a new law had been put in place that criminalized the procedure. The law had been passed after a high-profile case in which a 12-year-old died during the procedure (Méras, 2009).

Bullying Around the World   Children around the world are physically, sexually, or emotionally bullied by other students (Eslea et al., 2003; Kanetsuna et al., 2006; Nesdale & Naito, 2005). The reported prevalence of bullying varies widely across research studies, with estimates on the low end suggesting that 5 or 10 percent of schoolchildren are involved in bullying, and estimates on the high end suggesting numbers as high as 70 to 90 percent (Borntrager et al., 2009; Due & Holstein, 2008; Santalahti et al., 2008; Olweus, 2004). When Wendy Craig and her colleagues (2000; Pepler et al., 2004) set up hidden video cameras and microphones to get an unfiltered peek into aggression in schoolyards in Canada, they saw bullying in midsized schools at a rate of 4.5 episodes per hour. This team of researchers found in a later study that almost half of boys in eighth grade and half the girls in ninth grade reported having recently bullied others (Pepler et al., 2006).

These seemingly ordinary rites of childhood can lead to extraordinary suffering, including feelings of panic, nervousness, and distraction in school; recurring memories of abuse; depression and anxiety that can endure through adulthood; and even suicide (Birkett et al., 2009; Cassidy, 2009; Gladstone et al., 2006; Lund et al., 2009). It is worth noting that the shooters in most of the instances of school shootings during the past decade reportedly felt that they had been bullied or picked on by peers.

Nonviolent Cultures   Although violence seems to be just about everywhere, a handful of societies stand out as nonviolent exceptions. Bruce Bonta (1997) described 25 societies around the world that are almost completely without violence. For example, the Chewong, who live in the mountains of the Malay Peninsula, do not even have words in their language for quarreling, fighting, aggression, or warfare. The most serious act of aggression noted during a year among the Ifaluk, who live on a small atoll in the Federated States of Micronesia, involved a man who "touched another on the shoulder in anger, an offense which resulted in a stiff fine." The Amish, the Hutterites, and the Mennonites are all societies that reside in the relatively violent United States (as well as in Canada) but remain remarkably nonviolent. Table 11.2 lists some of the other societies that Bonta identified as nonviolent. What makes all of these societies so peaceful? According to Bonta, all but two of these 25 societies strongly oppose competition and endorse cooperation in all aspects of their lives. This raises the possibility that cooperation and lack of competition may promote nonviolence.

The peace of one of these nonviolent communities was shattered, however, on the morning of October 2, 2006. A 32-year-old milk truck driver named Charles Roberts, a father of three, burst into a one-room Amish schoolhouse in Pennsylvania, carrying three firearms, two knives, and up to 600 rounds of ammunition, along with other materials to carry out a horrific attack. He let the boys and a few adults leave, and then lined up the girls—ages 6 to 13—against the blackboard, tied them up, and shot them one by one. After police burst in, Roberts shot and killed himself. Five of the girls were killed, and five more were critically injured.

The details of the massacre were truly nightmarish. At least two of the girls who were shot had asked the killer to shoot them first, in the hope of sparing some of the younger girls. And yet, in a

TABLE 11.2

Nonviolent Societies

In addition to those discussed in the text, this table lists a few of the other societies that Bruce Bonta identified as nonviolent.

Society	Comments
Balinese (Indonesian island of Bali)	A researcher who was there for four years never even witnessed two boys fighting.
Glwi (Central Kalahari Desert of southern Africa)	They abhor violence and take pleasure from fortunate events only if they are in the company of group members.
Inuit (Arctic regions, including those in Siberia, Alaska, Canada, and Greenland)	They use strategies to control anger and prevent violence; they have a strong fear of aggression.
Ladakhis (Tibetan Buddhist society in northern India)	Villagers indicate that they have no memory of any fighting in the village.
Zapotec (Native American society in southern Mexico)	"Several researchers have been fascinated that one community is particularly peaceful, with very strong values that oppose violence, in contrast to other communities nearby where fighting and machismo are comparable with the rest of Mexico" (p. 320).

Bonta, 1997.

remarkable display of this community's commitment to its principles of peace and forgiveness, families of the slain and injured children offered prayers for the killer and his family. According to some reports, the very night of the killings some Amish "stood in the kitchen of the murderer's family, their arms around his sobbing father, and said, 'We will forgive Charlie.'" One member of the community suggested that the forgiveness displayed by the Amish in this incident could be "a gift to the world. . . . Maybe there's something to learn about how nations might treat other nations" (Dueck, 2006, p. A25).

Subcultures Within a Country   There are important variations in aggression within particular societies as a function of age, class, race, and region. For example, teenagers and young adults have a much greater rate of involvement in violent crime—as both offenders and victims—than any other age group. The fact that the American population has been aging in recent years is one of the reasons cited for the sharp drop in violent crime rates over the past 15 or so years. (Other factors that are noted frequently include longer jail sentences for criminals, more visible and community-oriented policing, a decline in the market for crack cocaine, and tougher gun-control laws.)

What about race? Despite the stories that get the most attention on the news, the large majority of murders are intraracial rather than interracial. Among incidents when the killer's race was identified in the United States in 2007, 92 percent of black murder victims were killed by black offenders, and 83 percent of white murder victims were slain by white offenders. Nevertheless, African Americans live in a much more violent America than do whites. The proportion of African Americans—particularly African American males—who are the perpetrators or victims of homicide is consistently much higher than that of other racial groups. For example, although African Americans represented about 13 percent of the U.S. population in 2005, they were victims of 49 percent of all murders, and 93 percent of those killed were killed by other black people (U.S. Department of Justice, 2007). Reliable data about homicide rates among other racial or ethnic groups are much more limited.

Regional differences are also striking. In the United States, the murder rate is consistently highest in the South, followed by the West. Some scholars have attributed the greater violence in the South and West to a *culture of honor* that is prevalent among white males in these regions. The culture of honor encourages violent responses to perceived threats against one's status as an honorable, powerful man (Cohen et al., 1998; Hayes & Lee, 2005; Vandello & Cohen, 2004). Other scholars believe that the consistently high rates of murder and violent crime in the South are due to hot weather (Anderson & Anderson, 1996). We will focus more on both the culture of honor and the relationship between heat and aggression later in the chapter.

Gender and Aggression

Despite all the variation across cultures, one thing is universal: Men are more violent than women. This has been found in virtually all cultures studied around the world. According to U.S. Department of Justice data, 90 percent of murderers in 2007 were male and 79 percent of murder victims were male. Despite the significant variation in total violence from one country to another, the gender difference remains remarkably stable over time and place: Men commit the very large majority of homicides, and men constitute the very large majority of murder victims (Buss, 2004; Daly & Wilson, 1989). In the spate of school shootings discussed throughout this chapter, all of the perpetrators were males.

What about aggression in general, as opposed to violence? In meta-analyses involving hundreds of samples from numerous countries, John Archer (2004) and Noel Card and his colleagues (2008) have found that males are consistently more physically aggressive than females. This was true across all ages and cultures sampled. Females were as likely to feel anger as males, but they were much less likely to act on their anger in aggressive ways. Even among children between 1 and 6 years old, boys show higher rates of physical aggression than girls.

So does all this mean that the stereotype that males are more aggressive than females is correct? Not necessarily. Most of the research has focused on the form of aggression that is typical of males: physical aggression. But think back to our definition of aggression: It concerns intent to harm. There are many ways to harm someone other than through physical means. Recent research has recognized this, and the results challenge the notion that males are more aggressive than females. The findings that are emerging can be summarized by a child's remark noted by Britt Galen and Marion Underwood (1997) in their research on aggression among adolescent girls and boys: "Boys may use their fists to fight, but at least it's over with quickly; girls use their tongues, and it goes on forever" (p. 589).

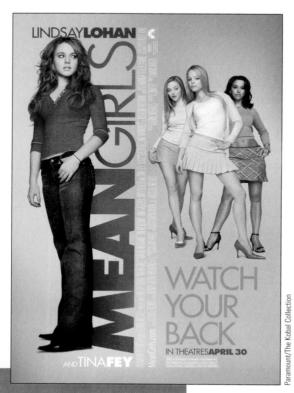

The movie *Mean Girls*, starring Lindsay Lohan and Rachel McAdams, depicted high school girls engaged in an escalating battle of indirect, relational aggression.

Paramount/The Kobal Collection

This research reveals that although boys tend to be more *overtly* aggressive than girls, boys do not tend to be more aggressive than girls when it comes to *indirect* or *relational* aggression. Indeed, for these types of aggression, girls sometimes are more aggressive than boys. Indirect forms of aggression include acts such as telling lies to get someone in trouble or shutting a person out of desired activities. Relational aggression is one kind of indirect aggression that particularly targets a person's relationships and social status, such as by threatening to end a friendship, engaging in gossip and backbiting, and trying to get others to dislike the target. Why are girls at least as aggressive as boys on relational (but not physical) forms of aggression? Researchers believe that one reason is because females typically care more about relationships and intimacy than males do and so may see injuring someone socially as particularly effective. Another reason may be that strong norms encourage boys to aggress physically, but these same norms discourage girls from doing so.

Numerous studies conducted in a variety of countries around the world have found that females tend to engage in indirect aggression more often than males, although many others have found only small or no significant gender differences. The results of meta-analyses (Archer, 2004; Card et al., 2008) that have reviewed the very large research literature on the topic have found a very small but statistically significant gender difference, with girls exhibiting somewhat more indirect aggression than boys (see ▶ Figure 11.2).

In addition to gender differences, there may be differences in the types of aggression people exhibit as a function of sexual orientation. Mark Sergeant and others (2006), for example, found that gay men reported significantly lower levels of physical aggression than straight men did, but there was no difference between the two groups on self-reported rates of indirect aggression.

In virtually every culture, males are more violent than females. **TRUE.**

For virtually any category of aggression, males are more aggressive than females. **FALSE.**

Individual Differences

Although it is clear that aggression can vary across cultures and gender, a different question is whether there is consistency in aggression within specific individuals. In other words, do some people simply tend to be more aggressive than others, across ages and situations? The evidence on this point is fairly clear: Although situational variables (as we will see later in this chapter) certainly do influence whether and how someone will aggress, there are some stable individual differences in aggressiveness. Aggression in childhood does predict aggression in adolescence and adulthood, along with adult criminality, alcohol abuse, and other antisocial behaviors. Similarly, low aggression in childhood predicts low aggression well into adulthood (Huesmann et al., 2009; Kokko et al., 2009; Vierikko et al., 2006).

What types of personalities tend to be associated with aggressiveness? Ann Bettencourt and others (2006) conducted a meta-analysis of 63 studies to answer this question. People who tend to hold hostile cognitions, express anger, and exhibit irritability tend to behave more aggressively. Other traits associated with aggression, however, tend to predict aggression reliably only under conditions of provocation—that is, situations that are perceived to be aversive or stressful. Among these traits are *emotional susceptibility* (the tendency to feel distressed, inadequate, and vulnerable to perceived threats), *narcissism* (the tendency to have an inflated sense of self-worth and self-love but without a strong set of beliefs to support these feelings, thereby leaving the person's self-esteem unstable and sensitive to criticism), *Type A personality* (the tendency to be driven by feelings of inadequacy to try to prove oneself through personal accomplishments), and *impulsivity* (being

▶ **FIGURE 11.2**

Gender and Types of Aggression

A meta-analysis was conducted of 148 studies of direct and indirect aggression involving children and adolescents across several countries. The results indicate that the magnitude and direction of gender differences in aggression depend on the type of aggression. The height of the bars in this graph indicate the degree to which boys show more aggression than girls; the higher the bar, the more aggression than girls boys exhibit. Across these various studies, the boys tend to be much more physically aggressive than girls. Boys also exhibit more direct verbal aggression than girls, but this difference is smaller. Regarding indirect aggression, however, girls tend to be more aggressive than boys. This difference is very small but is statistically reliable across the set of studies.

Based on Card et al., 2008.

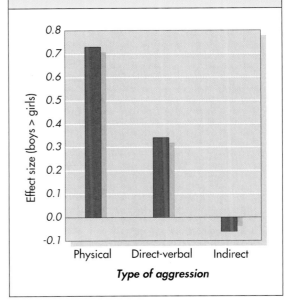

relatively unable to control one's thoughts and behaviors). When not provoked, individuals with these traits are not much more likely than others to behave aggressively. Provocation, however, can light the relatively short fuses of these individuals, leading to the potential explosion of aggression.

Many people have assume that individuals—particularly adolescents—with low self-esteem are more likely to aggress than people with average or high self-esteem. The evidence on this is mixed at best (Bushman et al., 2009; Donnellan et al., 2005; Locke, 2009). In fact, some research suggests not only that low self-esteem does not predict aggression but that people with *high* self-esteem are particularly likely to aggress if (1) they also are high in narcissism; and (2) they have received a threat to their ego, such as from a humiliation or insult (Bushman et al., 2009; Thomaes et al., 2008). Although self-esteem is not a great predictor of aggression, narcissism clearly is: Narcissism is consistently and positively correlated with aggression in response to provocation.

Origins of Aggression

Regardless of these various cultural, gender, and individual differences, aggression has been a prevalent part of human interaction throughout human history and around the world. It is not surprising that many have speculated about the origins of aggression. Where does it come from? Are we *born* aggressive, or are we *taught* to be aggressive? Many have argued for one side or the other of the "nature-nurture" debate—the "nature" side holding that aggression is an innate characteristic of human beings and the "nurture" side holding that aggression is learned through experience. In this section, we look at the theory and research most relevant to tracing the origins of human aggression. In reviewing each perspective, we examine how well it can account for the overall prevalence of aggression as well as for the cultural and gender differences that we have discussed.

■ Is Aggression Innate?

Innate characteristics are not dependent on learning for their development, although they can be influenced by learning, culture, and other factors. Here, we examine two approaches to the issue of whether aggression is innate: (1) evolutionary psychological accounts; and (2) biological factors, including genes, hormones, neurotransmitters, and brain and executive functioning.

Evolutionary Psychology   Evolutionary psychological accounts of aggression use principles of evolution to understand both the roots and the contemporary patterns of human aggression. For example, in his provocative book *The Most Dangerous Animal: Human Nature and the Origins of War*, David Livingstone Smith (2007) takes an evolutionary psychological perspective in his analysis of the origins of human warfare. This account emphasizes that human warfare originated not only to obtain valuable resources but also to attract mates and forge intragroup bonds. While it might seem that in our evolutionary history it would have been the pacifists who would have been more likely to survive than the warriors, Smith argues that it was the warriors who would have been more likely to attract mates and be accepted as part of a group. Therefore, the individuals who could and would fight had greater chances for reproductive success, and they would pass down these tendencies to their offspring, and

The most persistent sound which reverberates through men's history is the beating of war drums.

—Arthur Koestler

so on. The greater reproductive success of warriors over pacifists would result in the tendencies toward aggression and war to evolve to become part of human nature.

Evolutionary social psychology is geared not only to describe the origins of human social behavior but also to generate testable, falsifiable predictions. For example, evolutionary theories emphasize genetic survival rather than the survival of the individual. Because at least some of a person's genes can be transmitted through the reproductive success of genetic relatives, evolution should have favored the inhibition of aggression against those who are genetically related to us. Consistent with that hypothesis, Martin Daly and Margo Wilson (1988, 1996, 2005) report that birth parents are much less likely to abuse or murder their own offspring than stepparents are to harm stepchildren. In two samples studied, preschool children living with a stepparent or foster parent were 70 to 100 times more likely to be fatally abused than were children living with both biological parents.

What can account for the gender differences in aggression? According to an evolutionary perspective, males are competitive with each other because females select high-status males for mating, and aggression is a means by which males traditionally have been able to achieve and maintain status. In addition, because human men, unlike women, cannot be sure that they are the genetic parents of their children, men are predisposed to sexual jealousy. Behaviors triggered by sexual jealousy, including aggression and the threat of aggression, may be designed to enhance the male's confidence in his paternity of offspring. Consistent with evolutionary reasoning, crime statistics indicate that male-to-male violence is most likely to occur when one male is perceived as challenging the other's status or social power, such as by attempting to humiliate him or to challenge his sexual relationships. Male-to-female violence is predominantly triggered by sexual jealousy (Duntley & Buss, 2008; Goetz et al., 2008; Wilson & Daly, 1996).

Of course, as noted earlier, women also aggress. From an evolutionary perspective, reproductive success is dependent on the survival of one's offspring. Because women are much more limited than men in terms of the number of children they can have, evolution presumably favored those women who were committed to protecting their children. Indeed, much research on aggression by females has focused on maternal aggression, whereby females aggress to defend their offspring against threats by others. For example, females in a variety of species attack male strangers who come too close to their offspring (Ferreira et al., 2000; Gammie et al., 2000). In a similar vein, Anne Campbell (1999) proposes that females tend to place a higher value on protecting their own lives— again, in order to protect their offspring. This hypothesis may explain not only why human males engage more often in risky, potentially self-destructive behaviors but also why human females, when they do aggress, are more likely to use less obvious, and thus less dangerous, means—such as indirect or relational aggression rather than overt physical aggression. Relational aggression also may be particularly effective for women because it can harm the reputations of rival females—which can make men less interested in them (Vaillancourt, 2005).

Vladas Griskevicius and others (2009) propose that men are more likely than women to boost their status (and successfully compete for women) through direct, face-to-face aggression against other men, whereas women are more likely to boost their status (and successfully compete for men) through indirect aggression against

"It's a guy thing."

other women. In a series of experiments, Griskevicius and others activated either a status motive for some of the male and female participants (such as by having them think about competing with same-sex others for a high-status job promotion) or an unrelated motive for other participants. All participants then read about a scenario in which a same-sex person is publicly rude to them, and they were asked to indicate how they would respond. Activating a status motive increased direct aggression responses in men, whereas it increased indirect aggressive responses in women.

Behavior Genetics Evolutionary psychology involves tying together evolution, genetic transmission, and behavior. Behavior genetics focuses on the latter two. As we said earlier, aggressiveness is a relatively stable personality characteristic; children relatively high in aggressiveness are more likely to be aggressive later in life. Can this aggressive personality type be due to genes? To answer this question, two types of studies are typically employed in research on humans. In twin studies, monozygotic twins (who are identical in their genetic makeup) are compared with dizygotic twins (who share only part of their genes). On any heritable trait, monozygotic twins will be more similar than dizygotic twins. Adoptee studies are also used in behavior genetics research. On any inherited trait, adopted children will resemble their biological parents more than they resemble their adoptive parents.

The results of twin and adoptee studies have produced somewhat inconsistent results, but the trend in the research supports the heritability of human aggressive behavior to at least some degree (Hines & Saudino, 2002; Miles & Carey, 1997; Rowe et al., 2008; Vierikko et al., 2006). One interesting finding from a study of twins in the Montreal area was that there was much stronger evidence for the role of genes in physical aggression than in indirect, relational aggression (Brendgen et al., 2005).

The Role of Testosterone In addition to the question of heritability, researchers have long been interested in determining what specific biological factors influence aggression (Renfrew, 1997). Because of the persistent sex differences in physical aggression among humans and other animals, many researchers have wondered if testosterone plays a role. Although men and women both have this "male sex hormone," men usually have higher levels than women. Research conducted on a variety of animals has found a strong correlation between testosterone levels and aggression. The relationship is far weaker among humans. Even so, a number of studies have documented an association between testosterone and aggression. Using diverse samples of people, such as young boys, prison inmates, college students, and elderly men, these studies tend to show a positive correlation between testosterone levels and physical aggression or violence (Archer, 2006; Book et al., 2001; Dabbs & Dabbs, 2000; van Bokhoven et al., 2006). For example, one study found that college fraternities whose members tended to have higher testosterone levels were more rambunctious and exhibited more crude behavior than other fraternities; fraternities whose members had lower testosterone levels tended to be more academically successful and socially responsible, and their members smiled more (Dabbs et al., 1996). The relationship between testosterone and aggression is not limited to males. Studies have also shown a positive relationship between testosterone and aggression and related behaviors (such as competitiveness) in women (Cashdan, 2003; Dabbs & Dabbs, 2000; von der Pahlen et al., 2002).

Look at your index and ring fingers. Which is longer? Believe it or not, your answer may be a clue to how aggressive you are likely to be! Well, that may be overstating it a bit, but research has shown some intriguing correlations among finger-length ratio, testosterone, and aggression. Men tend to have relatively longer ring fingers than index fingers; larger ratios (especially on the right hand) are considered more "masculine." Larger ratios are thought to be associated with exposure to higher prenatal testosterone levels. Several studies have found that this finger-length ratio is associated with higher aggression. For example, Alita Cousins and others (2009) found that men with larger, more masculine finger-length ratios reported being more threatening and physically aggressive toward their female dating partners compared to men with less masculine finger-length ratios. Allison Bailey and Peter Hurd (2005) found in a sample of Canadian college students that men with more masculine finger-length ratios had higher scores for the trait of physical aggression. This correlation did not emerge among women (see ▶ Figure 11.3). Sarah Coyne and others (2007) also found that for women this finger-length ratio was not associated with a measure of direct aggression, but it was positively correlated with their indirect aggression.

Intriguing as they are, correlational findings cannot prove that testosterone causes aggression. There are alternative explanations. For example, aggression itself can cause temporary increases in testosterone—if the aggression is successful (Gladue et al., 1989; Mazur et al., 1992). Stress may also be involved in the correlation between testosterone and aggression: Higher levels of stress are associated with higher levels of testosterone (Thompson et al., 1990). Stress may simultaneously elevate both testosterone and aggression, resulting in a correlation that may reflect the effects of stress rather than the effects of testosterone.

For ethical reasons, researchers do not manipulate people's levels of testosterone to measure its effects on aggression and other behaviors. But Stephanie Van Goozen and others (1995; Cohen-Ketteinis & Van Goozen, 1997) have studied individuals who were voluntarily manipulating their sex hormones—transsexuals undergoing sex reassignment treatments. The researchers administered tests of aggression to 35 female-to-male transsexuals and 15 male-to-female transsexuals shortly before and three months after the start of cross-sex hormone treatment in a Dutch hospital. As their levels of male hormones increased, the female-to-male transsexuals exhibited increased aggression-proneness. In contrast, the deprivation of these hormones in the male-to-female group was associated with a decrease in aggression-proneness. It is important to note, however, that these changes in aggressiveness may have been caused not by the hormone treatment per se but rather by indirect factors such as the transsexuals' expectations or other people's reactions to them.

The Role of Serotonin Testosterone is not the only biological factor linked to human aggression. There has been an explosion of interest in the past decade concerning the role of the neurotransmitter serotonin (Beitchman et al., 2006; Carrillo et al., 2009; Crockett et al., 2008; Suarez & Krishnan, 2006). Neurotransmitters such as serotonin act as chemical messengers in the nervous system, transmitting information. Serotonin appears to work like a braking mechanism to restrain impulsive acts of aggression. Low levels of serotonin in the nervous systems of humans and many animals are associated with high levels of aggression. Drugs that boost serotonin's activity can dampen aggressiveness, along with a range of other impulsive and socially deviant behaviors. Such drugs have even been used to treat "road rage"—people's impulsive acts of aggression and violence while driving.

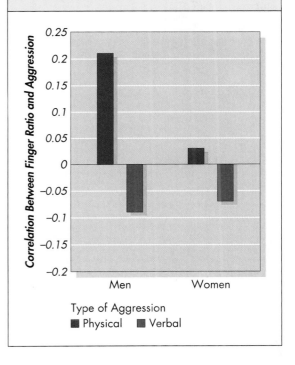

▶**FIGURE 11.3**

Fingers, Testosterone, and Aggression

According to some research, the longer one's right ring finger is relative to one's right index finger, the more "masculine" one's finger ratio is said to be, as these ratios are thought to be associated with exposure to higher prenatal testosterone levels. This figure presents the partial correlations (with some other factors statistically controlled for) found in one study between students' finger ratios and how much physical and verbal aggression they exhibited. Among men, more masculine finger ratios were associated with more physical, but not more verbal, aggression. This correlation did not emerge among women.

Based on Bailey & Hurd, 2005.

▶**FIGURE 11.4**

Brain Functioning and Aggression

This figure shows three slices of the brain. Within each slice, the areas highlighted in color have been found in recent research to be impaired in antisocial, violent, and psychopathic populations.

Raine, 2008.

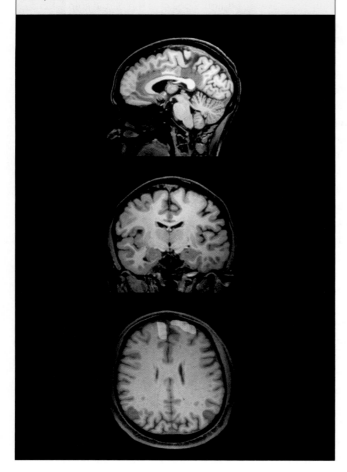

Brain and Executive Functioning In addition to hormones and neurotransmitters, the frontal lobe of the brain is another hot topic in research on the biological underpinnings of human aggression. Researchers using a variety of techniques have found evidence linking abnormalities in frontal lobe structures with tendencies toward aggressive and violent behavior (Miczek et al., 2007; Miura, 2009; Raine, 2008). The prefrontal cortex in particular has been implicated. Impaired prefrontal processing can disrupt what is called *executive functioning*, the cognitive abilities and processes that allow humans to plan or inhibit their actions. Executive functioning enables people to respond to situations in a reasoned, flexible manner, as opposed to being driven purely by external stimuli (Hoaken et al., 2007). A growing body of research finds a link between poor executive functioning and high aggression (Giancola et al., 2006; Raaijmakers et al., 2008; Seguin & Zelazo, 2005; Siever, 2008).

One noteworthy recent finding is that very aggressive teenagers showed different patterns of brain activity in response to witnessing someone else in pain than did less aggressive youth (Decety et al., 2009). In particular, when watching situations in which someone intentionally inflicted pain on another person, healthy teenagers showed brain activity associated with empathy. The highly aggressive teens, however, exhibited a pattern of brain activity associated with experiencing rewards, suggesting that they enjoyed watching others experience pain that someone intentionally inflicted on them. In addition, the aggressive teenagers showed less activation in areas associated with self-regulation and moral reasoning when seeing someone inflict pain on another than did the nonaggressive teenagers.

These are among the lines of research that demonstrate associations between brain functioning and aggression and other antisocial behaviors. ▶ Figure 11.4 illustrates some of the brain regions implicated in these studies.

▊ Is Aggression Learned?

Regardless of the precise contribution of genetic and biological factors, it is clear that aggressive behavior is strongly affected by learning (Bandura, 1973). Rewards obtained by aggression today will increase its use tomorrow. Such rewards come in two flavors: *positive reinforcement*, when aggression produces desired outcomes; and *negative reinforcement*, when aggression prevents or stops undesirable outcomes. The child who gets a toy by hitting the toy's owner is likely to hit again. So, too, the child who can stop other children from teasing by shoving them away has learned the fateful lesson that aggression pays. Children who see aggression producing more good outcomes, and fewer bad outcomes, are more aggressive than other children (Boldizar et al., 1989).

Rewards are one part of the learning equation, but what about punishment? Punishment is often promoted as a way to reduce aggressive behavior. Can people learn not to act aggressively through punishment? Some politicians and police officials in New York City believe that the dramatic reduction in crime in the city in recent years (from 2,245 murders in 1990 to only 516 in 2008—less than a quarter of the 1990 tally!) is due in large part to swift, more effective punishment of all kinds of crimes, even relatively minor crimes such as vandalism, which sends the message that crime will lead to punishment. Research suggests that punishment is most likely to decrease aggression when it (1) immediately follows the aggressive behavior; (2) is strong enough to deter the aggressor; and (3) is consistently applied and perceived as fair and legitimate by the aggressor. However, such stringent conditions are seldom met, and when they are not met, punishment can backfire. When courts are overburdened and prisons are overcrowded, which is often the case, the relationship between crime and punishment can seem more like a lottery than a rational system in which the punishment fits the crime. In short, the *certainty* of punishment is more important than its *severity* (Berkowitz, 1998).

There are other problems with punishment as well. Punishment perceived as unfair or arbitrary can provoke retaliation, creating an escalating cycle of aggression. Perhaps most troubling is that punishment, especially when delivered in an angry or hostile manner, offers a model to imitate. Murray Straus and his colleagues (Donnelly & Straus, 2005; Douglas & Straus, 2007; Straus, 2000; Straus & Douglas, 2008) have been outspoken critics of the use of *corporal punishment*: physical force (such as spanking, hitting, and pinching) intended to cause a child pain, but not injury, for the purpose of controlling or correcting the child's behavior. The large majority of children in the United States experience spanking and other forms of corporal punishment. Numerous studies, however, report a positive relationship between corporal punishment and the likelihood of aggression: More corporal punishment now is associated with more aggression later. Elizabeth Gershoff (2002) investigated this issue with a meta-analysis of 88 studies conducted over six decades and involving more than 36,000 participants. Her analysis revealed strong evidence for a positive correlation between corporal punishment and several categories of subsequent antisocial behaviors, such as aggression later as a child, aggression as an adult, and adult criminal behavior.

The relationship between parental corporal punishment and children's subsequent aggression is influenced by a number of factors, including the overall family environment, the emotions displayed by the parents during the punishment, and cultural and ethnic differences (Benjet & Kazdin, 2003; Pagani et al., 2009; Pinderhughes et al., 2000). For example, corporal punishment is less likely to increase aggressiveness when it is administered in the context of an overall warm and supportive parent-child relationship (Baumrind, 1997; Deater-Deckard et al., 1998).

Children who are spanked or otherwise physically disciplined (but not abused) for behaving aggressively tend to become less aggressive. **FALSE.**

Social Learning Theory One of the authors of this book remembers many a late, cold afternoon during his middle school and high school years playing informal but competitive games of football and hockey with friends. The way he and his friends played them, both games were played without protective equipment and were quite rough, but football was the more physically brutal of the two. Yet despite the fact that virtually every play culminated in a pile of boys jumping on the flattened body of an opponent, it was very rare that an actual fight would break out. When this same group of friends played hockey, on the other hand, virtually every single game they played featured at least one fight. Why? Although he was years away from his first social psychology class, this future social psychologist was quite sure that he and his friends were basing their behavior on role models. Rarely had they seen professional football players stop and fight on the field. But rarely had they seen a professional hockey game in which that *didn't* happen.

The power of models to modify behavior is a crucial tenet of Albert Bandura's (1977) **social learning theory**. Social learning theory emphasizes that we learn from the example of others as well as from direct experience with rewards and punishments.

social learning theory The theory that behavior is learned through the observation of others as well as through the direct experience of rewards and punishments.

"I blame all the violent cave paintings."

The idea that aggression may be learned by observing others behaving aggressively may go back a long, long time.

Models influence the prosocial, helpful behavior described in Chapter 10. They also affect antisocial, aggressive behavior. In a classic study, Bandura and his associates (1961) observed the behavior of mildly frustrated children. Those who had previously watched an adult throw around, punch, and kick an inflatable doll were more aggressive when they later played with the doll than were those who had watched a quiet, subdued adult. These children followed the adult model's lead not only in degree of aggression but also in the kinds of aggression they exhibited. Subsequent research has amply demonstrated that a wide range of aggressive models can elicit a wide range of aggressive imitations. Furthermore, these models do not have to be present; people on TV—even cartoon characters—can serve as powerful models of aggression (Bandura, 1983; Baron & Richardson, 1994; Berkowitz, 1993).

People learn more than specific aggressive behaviors from aggressive models. They also develop more positive attitudes and beliefs about aggression in general, and they construct aggressive "scripts" that serve as guides for how to behave and solve social problems. These scripts can be activated automatically in various situations, leading to quick, often unthinking aggressive responses that follow the scripts they have learned (Bennett et al., 2005; Huesmann, 1998). Learning these scripts from their parents is one of the reasons that there are positive correlations between witnessing parents behaving aggressively or violently with each other during conflicts and individuals' subsequent aggressiveness with peers and others as adolescents or even later as adults themselves (Hill & Nathan, 2008; Underwood et al., 2008).

Boys in Baghdad play with toy guns, imitating the adult behavior they have observed in their war-torn country. When U.S. troops patrolled the area regularly, they traded the toy guns for pens to get them off the streets.

Consider the boys described just above who fought during hockey but not football games. Could their fighting during hockey be due to something about the sport of hockey itself, or did these boys learn aggressive scripts from watching how professional hockey players used their fists to deal with frustrations and provocations? An interesting study by Chris Gee and Larry Leith (2007) supports the social learning hypothesis. Gee and Leith analyzed the penalty records from 200 games of the National Hockey League (NHL). The NHL is the major professional hockey league in North America, and in recent years it has come to include top players from numerous countries around the world. When they were young and developing into hockey players, players born in North America were much more likely to have been exposed to models of aggression and fighting, and to have been rewarded (and not punished severely) for fighting and aggressive play, than were players born in Europe. Subsequently, even though these athletes all were playing the same sport on the same teams in the NHL, Gee and Leith found that the players born in North America were much more likely to be called for aggressive penalties than were players born in Europe (see ▶ Figure 11.5). Also, of all the infractions that the North Americans committed, more than 32 percent were for fighting or "roughing," whereas only 16 percent of the penalties for European players were for these particularly aggressive infractions.

Aggression or violence scripts play important roles in the lives of many young men and women who have committed violent crimes. In a thorough analysis of 416 young violent offenders from two New York City neighborhoods, Deanna Wilkinson and Patrick Carr (2008) found that 93 percent had seen someone get beaten badly, 75 percent had seen someone get knifed, 92 percent had seen someone get shot, and 77 percent had seen someone get killed. More than three-quarters of these violent offenders reported that a close friend had been killed through violence. Wilkinson and Carr collected chilling interviews with these individuals, many of which illustrated how so much early exposure to violence taught these individuals the unfortunate lesson that violence is the appropriate way to deal with conflicts and to attain a degree of high status in the neighborhood.

Just as aggressive models can increase aggressive behavior, nonaggressive models can decrease it. Observing a nonaggressive response to a provoking situation teaches a peaceful alternative and strengthens existing restraints against aggression. In addition, observing someone who is calm and reasonable may help an angry person settle down rather than strike out. Aggression can spread like wildfire. But nonviolence and prosocial behavior can also be contagious (Donnerstein & Donnerstein, 1976; Gibbons & Ebbeck, 1997).

Bandura's social learning theory has been one of the most important social psychological approaches to the study of human aggression since his classic early experiments in the early 1960s. Its simplicity should not obscure the fact that it can help explain a great amount of human behavior. Daniel Batson and Adam Powell (2003) wrote that social learning theory "has probably come closer to [the goal of accounting for the most facts with the fewest principles] than has any other theory in the history of social psychology" (p. 466).

▶ **FIGURE 11.5**

Social Learning of Aggression in Hockey: North America Versus Europe

Researchers examined all the penalties called against National Hockey League players born in North America or Europe during 200 games. North American players were likely to have been exposed to more aggressive role models and positive reinforcement for fighting and aggression in hockey than their European counterparts. Consistent with this cultural difference in norms and role models, the results depicted here show that the North Americans were much more likely to be called for aggressive (but not for nonaggressive) penalties than the Europeans were.

Based on Gee & Leith, 2007.

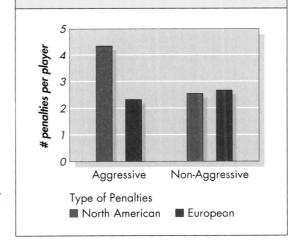

Gender Differences and Socialization: "Boys Will Be Boys"

To account for gender differences in aggression, social learning approaches emphasize that males and females are taught different lessons about aggression: They are rewarded and punished differently for aggression and are presented with different models. Whether or not gender differences in aggressive behavior originated from innate biological factors, today they are maintained and perpetuated through lessons that are passed on from one generation to the next about the acceptability of various kinds and degrees of aggression.

Most researchers agree that social roles have a strong influence on gender differences in physical aggression. As described in Chapter 5, males and females are socialized to fill different roles in society. Overt aggression tends to be more socially acceptable in stereotypically male roles than in female roles. Indeed, highly aggressive boys are sometimes among the most popular and socially connected children in elementary school (Rodkin et al., 2000; Vaillancourt & Hymel, 2006). Boys who use their fists to deal with conflict are much more likely to be rewarded with increased social status than are girls, who might suffer scorn and ridicule for fighting. On the other hand, a girl who successfully uses relational aggression, such as through social manipulation, can reap social benefits more easily than a boy (Crick & Rose, 2000). One recent study reported that girls' (but not boys') beliefs about the acceptability of relational aggression correlated significantly with their mothers' attitudes about relational aggression (Werner & Grant, 2009).

▌ Culture and Socialization: Cultures of Honor

Socialization of aggression also varies from culture to culture. For example, in a study of students at a high school near Detroit, Michigan, Violet Souweidane and Rowell Huesmann (1999) found that those born in the United States were more accepting of aggression than those who had emigrated from the Middle East, especially if they emigrated after the age of 11. Likewise, in a sample of Hispanic schoolchildren in Chicago, those who had been in the United States longer showed greater approval of aggression (Guerra et al., 1993). Giovanna Tomada and Barry Schneider (1997) report that adolescent boys in traditional villages in Italy are encouraged to aggress as an indication of their sexual prowess and in preparation for their dominant role in the household. These authors believe that this is why schoolyard bullying among elementary school boys is significantly higher in central and southern Italy than it is in Norway, England, Spain, or Japan. Similarly, some researchers believe that *machismo*—which in its most stereotyped characterization prescribes that challenges, abuse, and even differences of opinion "must be met with fists or other weapons" (Ingoldsby. 1991, p. 57)—contributes to the fact that rates of violence are higher among Latin American men than among European American men (Harris, 1995).

Machismo may represent one form of what anthropologists call a *culture of honor*, which emphasizes honor and social status, particularly for males, and the role of aggression in protecting that honor. Even minor conflicts or disputes are often seen as challenges to social status and reputation and can therefore trigger aggressive responses. Several such subcultures exist around the world (and *Star Trek* fans might recognize the Klingon empire as an intergalactic example of a culture of honor). In an extensive series of studies, Dov Cohen, Richard Nisbett, Joseph Vandello, and their colleagues have examined various cultures of honor. Their original focus was on white men in the American South (Nisbett & Cohen, 1996). Rates of violence are consistently higher in the South than in all other regions of the country. Southerners are more likely than Northerners to agree that "a man has the right to kill" in order to defend his family and house, and they are more accepting of using violence to protect one's honor than are people from other parts of the country. (Note, however, that Southerners are *not* more likely than other Americans to accept violence unrelated to the protection of honor.)

Data from surveys, field experiments, and laboratory experiments suggest that this culture of honor promotes violent behavior. In one series of experiments, Cohen and others (1996) investigated how white male students who had grown up either in the North or in the South responded to insults. The experiments, conducted on a large Midwestern campus, involved an encounter that took place as the participant and the confederate were passing each other in a narrow hallway. The confederate did not give way to the participant, bumped into him, and hurled an insult. Compared with Northerners, Southerners were more likely to think that their masculine reputations had been threatened, exhibited greater physiological signs of being upset, appeared more physiologically primed for aggression (their testosterone levels rose), and engaged in more aggressive and dominant subsequent behavior, such as giving firmer hand-

▶FIGURE 11.6

Insult, Aggression, and the Southern Culture of Honor

White male participants from either the North or South regions of the United States either were bumped and insulted by a male confederate or they passed the confederate without incident (control condition). As you can see, the incident had a greater effect on Southern participants. Specifically, they thought that they would be seen as less masculine (left); their testosterone levels increased more (center); and they were slower to yield to a confederate who later approached them in a narrow corridor (right).

Cohen et al., 1996.

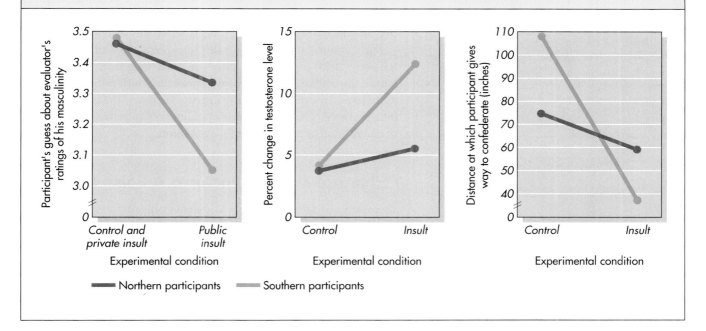

shakes and being more unwilling to yield to a subsequent confederate as they walked toward each other in a very narrow hallway (see ▶ Figure 11.6).

Institutions support norms about the acceptability of honor-based violence. Cohen and Nisbett (1997) illustrated this in a clever experiment in which they sent letters to employers all over the United States from a fictitious job applicant who admitted that he had been convicted of a felony. To half the employers, the applicant reported that he had impulsively killed a man who had been having an affair with his fiancée and then taunted him about it in a crowded bar. To the other half, the applicant reported that he had stolen a car because he needed the money to pay off debts. Employers from the South and the West (which has a culture of honor similar to that of the South) were more likely than their Northern counterparts to respond in an understanding and cooperative way to the letter from the convicted killer—but not to the letter from the auto thief.

Joseph Vandello and Dov Cohen (2003) examined the culture of honor in Brazil in other research. Vandello and Cohen found that a wife's infidelity harmed a man's reputation more in the eyes of Brazilian students than in the eyes of students from the northern United States. In a related study, Vandello, Cohen, and others (2009) had participants from Chile (a culture that emphasizes honor) or Canada (a culture that is neutral concerning honor) listen to a tape of a man describing how he behaved violently toward his wife during a conflict. In one condition, the conflict was triggered when the husband thought she was flirting with another man at a party. In a different condition, the conflict was triggered by something having nothing to do with jealousy or threats to the man's honor. The Chilean participants rated the violence as more

► **FIGURE 11.7**

Culture of Honor and Attitudes About Domestic Violence

Participants from Chile (a culture that emphasizes honor) or Canada (a neutral culture regarding honor) listened to a tape of a man describing his violent behavior toward his wife during a conflict. When the conflict was not triggered by an honor-related issue, Chileans and Canadians did not differ in how acceptable they thought the violence was. When the conflict was triggered by the husband perceiving his wife flirting with another man at a party, however, the Chileans were significantly more accepting of the violence than the Canadians were.

Based on Vandello et al., 2009.

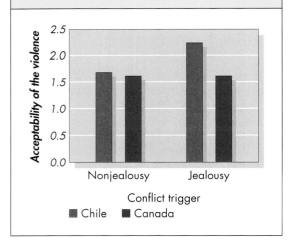

acceptable and rated the husband more positively across several dimensions than the Canadian participants did when the conflict was related to jealousy, but there was no cultural difference when the conflict was not related to jealousy or honor (see ► Figure 11.7).

A key to the aggression associated with cultures of honor is the fact that individuals in these cultures perceive aggressive responses to honor-based threats as the norm among their peers. That is, cultures of honor persist because the individuals believe that most people in their peer group have positive attitudes toward aggression (and negative attitudes toward not acting aggressively) in response to threats to one's honor. Consistent with this idea, Vandello, Cohen, and Sean Ransom (2008) found that relative to white men from the northern part of the United States, white men from the South were significantly more likely to overestimate the aggressiveness of their peers and to interpret others' ambiguous advice about how to respond in an interpersonal conflict as encouraging aggression.

■ Nature Versus Nurture: A False Debate?

The origins of aggression are a source not only of scientific disagreement but also of political controversy. Politicians frequently engage in heated debates about whether to fund research and treatment programs, and they disagree with each other strongly about whether aggression is, to any significant extent, attributable to stable biological characteristics present at birth. However important it may be, this contentious issue should not obscure the considerable agreement that exists on other points. The effects of learning are not disputed; aggression is, at least to some extent, "made" by experience. Nor is there any doubt that in aggression, as in all human behavior, biology and environment interact. The debate between nature and nurture may rage on among politicians, but to scientists it is clear that the origins of human aggression represent a profound interaction of evolved mechanisms and environmental and social factors.

Situational Influences on Aggression

Whatever the ultimate causes of aggression, it is clear that specific, immediate situational factors can promote or inhibit aggressive thoughts and actions. In this section, we take a close look at several of these factors: frustration, negative affect, arousal, and factors that influence people's thoughts and information processing.

■ Frustration: Aggression as a Drive

frustration-aggression hypothesis The idea that (1) frustration always elicits the motive to aggress; and (2) all aggression is caused by frustration.

In 1939, the year that World War II began, John Dollard and his colleagues published *Frustration and Aggression*, one of the most influential books on aggression ever written. This book set forth two major propositions that taken together were called the **frustration-aggression hypothesis**: (1) Frustration—which is produced by interrupting a person's progress toward an expected goal—will always elicit the motive to aggress; and (2) All aggression is caused by frustration.

Dollard and his colleagues claimed that the motive to aggress is a psychological drive that resembles physiological drives like hunger. According to this theory, just as food deprivation elicits a hunger drive, so frustration elicits an aggressive drive. Just as the hunger drive prompts the search for food, so the aggressive drive prompts the attempt to inflict injury. But what if we're unable to aggress against the source of our frustration? After all, we can't hit the boss, nor can we strike out against abstractions such as health problems or financial setbacks. Dollard and his colleagues believed that in such instances the aggressive drive can seep out in the form of **displacement**. Here, the inclination to aggress is deflected from the real target to a substitute. After a bad day at work or at school, do you sometimes come home and yell at the first available target—be it friend, lover, or pet? If so, what is the effect on you? Does yelling at an innocent bystander reduce your inclination to take revenge on the person who gave you a hard time?

Drawing from the ancient idea of **catharsis**, Dollard and his colleagues believed that displacing aggression in these safer ways can be effective. Just as hunger can be satisfied by fast food as well as by an expensive steak, so any aggressive act should reduce the motive to engage in any other aggressive behavior. Since the Dollard group defined aggression quite broadly—to include making hostile jokes, telling violent stories, cursing, and observing the aggression of others, real or fictional—they held out the hope that engaging in some relatively harmless pursuit could drain away energy from more violent tendencies.

The Frustration-Aggression Hypothesis: Does the Evidence Support It?   Obviously, there is a connection between frustration and aggression. Break into a line of shoppers at the supermarket or interrupt a student cramming for an exam, and you can see it for yourself. On a more extreme level, it was clear that Dylan Klebold and Eric Harris of the Columbine massacre had been feeling extremely frustrated by their exclusion from popular cliques. Tim Kretschmer, the perpetrator in the Winnenden, Germany, shootings, reportedly was frustrated about being bullied and having difficulty making friends (Hall, 2009). Indeed, in 13 of the 15 school shootings between 1995 and 2001 that Mark Leary and others (2003) examined, the shooters had apparently been frustrated by social rejection. Social rejection has been cited as the most significant risk factor for adolescent violence (Leary et al., 2006). Similarly, James von Brunn, who shot and killed the security guard at the Holocaust Museum in June 2009, was reportedly filled with frustration before he took his rifle to the museum. An acquaintance said that von Brunn "complained that his Social Security benefits had been reduced, and he suspected that his white supremacist views were the reason" (Zongker & Nuckols, 2009). The ex-wife of the man who assassinated Dr. George Tiller in a Kansas church in May 2009 said that her former husband started gravitating to extreme, hostile viewpoints when he became frustrated with financial troubles ("Anderson Cooper 360 Degrees," 2009).

Soon after the frustration-aggression theory was proposed, however, critics pointed out that the Dollard group had overstated their case. Early on, Neal Miller (1941), one of the originators of the hypothesis, acknowledged that frustration does not always produce aggressive inclinations. The other absolute, that all aggression is caused by frustration, was soon overturned as well. In the following pages, we will consider many other causes of aggression.

The concept of displacement was also subjected to close scrutiny. Some evidence suggested that societal frustrations arising from economic and social difficulties may fuel genocide and other forms of violence (such as lynchings) against outgroups (Hovland & Sears, 1940; Staub, 1996, 2004)—a reaction sometimes called *scapegoating*, which involves blaming a particular minority group or groups for the problems

displacement Aggressing against a substitute target because aggressive acts against the source of the frustration are inhibited by fear or lack of access.

catharsis A reduction of the motive to aggress that is said to result from any imagined, observed, or actual act of aggression.

the overall society is facing. However, acceptance of the role of displacement in channeling aggressive behavior soon diminished within the field after scholars pointed to weaknesses in the theory and inconclusive empirical evidence (Green et al., 1998; Marcus-Newhall et al., 2000; Zillmann, 1979). The tide may be turning yet again, though, as the concept of displacement seems to be making a comeback in recent years, sparked in part by a meta-analysis of 49 published articles that found reliable evidence for displaced aggression in response to provocation (Marcus-Newhall et al., 2000). In a more recent study of workers from a variety of industries, Jenny Hoobler and Daniel Brass (2006) found support for the old idea that when workers feel abused by their supervisors at work, their families at home—rather than their bosses at work—are likely to feel the brunt of their frustration-driven aggression. Although family members can serve as targets of displaced aggression, research by William Pedersen and others (2008) suggests that provoked individuals are especially likely to displace aggression toward others they dislike or others who are outgroup members.

The concept of catharsis also received a great deal of attention, perhaps because it seemed to offer a way to control aggression. Dollard and his colleagues described catharsis as a two-step sequence. First, aggression reduces the level of physiological arousal. Second, because arousal is reduced, people are less angry and less likely to aggress further. It sounds logical, and many people believe it. For example, Gordon Russell and his colleagues (1995) reported that more than two-thirds of Canadian respondents in their research agreed with statements reflecting a belief in the effectiveness of catharsis (such as the statement that participating in aggressive sports is a good way to get rid of aggressive urges). Catharsis has also been used by school administrators and others to justify aggressive sports (Bennett, 1991).

But when put to the test, catharsis has not lived up to its advertisement. Most researchers have concluded that the catharsis idea is a myth. It is more counterproductive than effective in reducing subsequent aggression (Bushman, 2002; Geen & Quanty, 1977). Here's why:

- Imagined aggression or observing aggressive models is more likely to increase arousal and aggression than it is to reduce them. Indeed, this is a central point of social learning theory.

- Actual aggression can lower arousal levels. However, if aggressive intent remains, "cold-blooded" aggression can still occur. Furthermore, if aggression-produced reduction of arousal feels good to the aggressor, this reward makes it more likely that aggression will occur again—another important point from social learning theory.

- Blowing off steam by hitting a punching bag or screaming may feel good to people who intuitively believe in catharsis. Yet their feelings of hostility and anger may persist—and possibly even increase.

- Even relatively low levels of aggression can chip away at restraints against more violent behavior.

Blowing off steam by engaging in safe but aggressive activities (such as sports) makes people less likely to aggress later. **FALSE.**

Aggressive behavior may sometimes reduce the likelihood of further immediate aggression, but so can just letting the frustration simply dissipate over time. For that matter, a response incompatible with aggression, such as distracting oneself with laughter, can be more effective. In the long run, successful aggression sets the stage for more aggression later. In sum, relying on catharsis is dangerous medicine—more likely to inflame aggression than to put it out.

Frustration-Aggression Theory Revised   After bearing so much criticism, the frustration-aggression hypothesis seemed torn and tattered. But Leonard Berkowitz's (1989) reformulation put the hypothesis in a new perspective. According to Berkowitz, frustration is but one of many unpleasant experiences that can lead to aggression by creating negative, uncomfortable feelings. It is these negative feelings, and not the frustration itself, that can trigger aggression. And as we'll see, negative feelings play a major role in influencing aggression.

◼ Negative Affect

In addition to frustrating experiences, a wide variety of noxious stimuli and bad feelings can create negative feelings and increase aggression: noise, crowding, physical pain, threatened self-esteem, feelings of jealousy, social rejection, bad odors, and having your home team lose a professional football playoff game (Baumeister et al., 2000; Berkowitz, 1998; De Steno et al., 2006; Leary et al., 2006; Panee & Ballard, 2002; Verona et al., 2002; Warburton et al., 2006). Most aggressive incidents can be directly linked to some type of provocation, and the negative affect caused by the provocation plays a critically important role in triggering aggression. Reactions to a very common unpleasant condition, hot weather, are especially intriguing. Many people assume that temperature and tempers rise together, while others think it's just a myth. Who is right?

By far, the worst thing about the firehouse was the heat. It got really, really hot inside there the last few weeks of shooting. We had no air conditioning and the hotter it got, the angrier we got.

—Jason, one of the people living in the firehouse on MTV's *The Real World: Boston*

Heat and Aggression: Losing Your Cool   Craig Anderson and others have conducted extensive research on the question of whether heat leads to aggression, and data across time, cultures, and methodologies strongly support the notion that people lose their cool in hot temperatures and behave more aggressively (Anderson et al., 2000; Bushman et al., 2005a, 2005b). More violent crimes occur in the summer than in the winter, in hot years than in cooler years, and in hot cities than in cooler cities at any given time of year. The numbers of political uprisings, riots, homicides, assaults, rapes, and reports of violence peak in the summer months (see ▶ Figure 11.8). Indirect acts of aggression also increase in excessive heat. As temperatures rise to uncomfortable levels, laboratory participants become more likely to interpret ambiguous events in hostile terms (Rule et al., 1987), and drivers in cars without air conditioning honk their horns longer at motorists whose cars are stalled in front of them (Kenrick & MacFarlane, 1986). Alan Reifman and others (1991) found that as the temperature rises, Major League Baseball pitchers are more likely to hit batters with a pitch. The pitchers aren't wilder in general (such as in the number of walks they give up or wild pitches they throw)—they are just more likely to hit batters (see ▶ Figure 11.9).

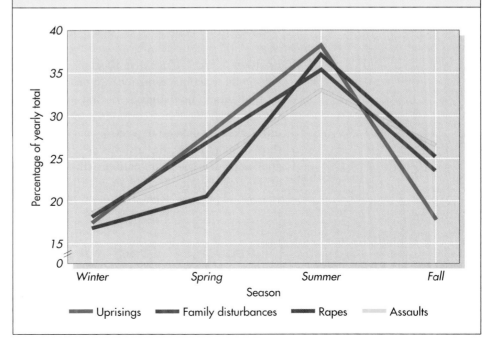

▶**FIGURE 11.8**

The Link Between Heat and Violence

Worldwide weather records and crime statistics reveal that more violent crimes are committed during the summer than in the other seasons.

Anderson, 1989.

Percentage of yearly total

Season

— Uprisings   — Family disturbances   — Rapes   — Assaults

▶**FIGURE 11.9**

Temper and Temperature in Baseball

This figure shows the average number of players hit by pitches (HBPs) per game during the 1986 through 1988 Major League Baseball seasons. As the temperature increased, so did the likelihood that pitchers would hit batters (with balls often thrown around 90 miles per hour and often thrown at a batter's head). Players' general wildness or fatigue, as measured by walks, wild pitches, passed balls, and errors, did not increase with temperature, suggesting that the heat-HBP correlation perhaps was due to hotter temperatures that led to hotter tempers.

Reifman et al., 1991.

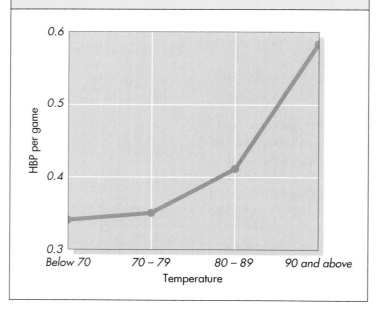

Given the earlier discussion of the culture of honor and the high incidence of violence in the American South, you may wonder whether it is culture or heat that contributes to the violence. At this point, evidence points to both influences as important. Each probably has independent effects on aggression. In addition, they may interact with each other. For example, the relatively high temperatures of the region may support aggressive norms (Anderson et al., 2000; Nisbett & Cohen, 1996).

Social Rejection   One of the most unpleasant feelings that people experience is being rejected or ostracized by others. As we have already indicated, most of the perpetrators of the school shootings we discussed earlier in the chapter had very negative emotional reactions associated with feelings of social rejection and isolation. Of course, stories like these are intriguing but are not scientific evidence for the effects of social rejection. More valid evidence comes from a number of experiments that have manipulated social rejection to examine its causal effect on a number of outcomes including aggression. For example, a participant in an experiment might find himself or herself suddenly ignored by the two other participants in the study, who engage in pleasant interactions only with each other. These studies have shown that social rejection increases the likelihood of aggressive responses (Crescioni & Baumeister, 2009; Williams, 2007b)—especially if the socially rejected individual is particularly sensitive to rejection (Ayduk et al., 2008). Lowell Gaertner and others (2008) found that participants who were socially rejected by someone from an apparently tight-knit group became likely to retaliate aggressively against all the members of the rejector's group.

Positive Affect   If negative affect increases the likelihood of aggressing, can positive emotional reactions reduce it? Some evidence suggests that they can. For example, participants in one study were first angered by an experimental confederate. They were then shown funny cartoons or neutral pictures. Presented with an opportunity to retaliate by delivering electric shocks as part of a supposed learning experiment, those who had seen the cartoons delivered fewer shocks (Baron & Ball, 1974). Feeling good appears to be incompatible with anger and aggression. Feeling concerned about others has similar effects. An empathic response to another person reduces aggression against that individual (Miller & Eisenberg, 1988; Sergeant et al., 2006).

▌ Arousal: "Wired" for Action

Research on affect clearly indicates that the type of emotion (positive or negative) influences aggression. The intensity of arousal is important as well. In Chapter 9, we described the process of *excitation transfer*, in which the arousal created by one stimulus can intensify an individual's emotional response to another stimulus. For example, men who engaged in vigorous exercise were later more attracted to an attractive female than were those who had barely moved (White et al., 1981). Physical exercise is a highly arousing but emotionally neutral experience. Can it increase aggression as well as attraction? The research of Dolf Zillmann (1983, 2003) suggests that it can. The scope of excitation transfer is not limited to physical exercise. Noise, violent movies, arousing music—all have been shown to increase aggression. Heat has an interesting effect on arousal: Although people believe that heat lowers arousal, it actually increases it. This misperception makes heat a prime candidate for excitation transfer, as people are likely to misattribute arousal caused by heat to something else, such as anger, which can then lead to aggression (Anderson et al., 1996). Later in this chapter, we describe the effects of another arousing stimulus—pornography—on the inclination to aggress.

▌▐ Thought: Automatic and Deliberate

Step by step, we have been making our way toward a comprehensive theory of social and situational influences on aggression, particularly emotional aggression. We've examined several kinds of unpleasant experiences (frustration, noxious stimuli, and provocation) that create negative affect. We've considered how arousal can contribute to aggression. The next step is to add cognition. People don't just feel; they also think. These thoughts may be as primitive as automatic, unconscious associations, or they may be higher-order, conscious deliberations. Both automatic and deliberate thoughts play a critically important role in aggressive behavior.

Automatic Cognition: Situational Cues   No other stable, industrialized country in the world comes even close to the United States in terms of the prevalence of guns used in violent crime. Guns of course are only an instrument—it's the people who are pulling the trigger. But social psychologist Leonard Berkowitz wondered whether guns were in fact entirely neutral. He hypothesized that the presence of a weapon can act as a situational cue that automatically triggers aggressive thoughts and feelings, thereby increasing the likelihood of aggression. In a classic study designed to test this idea, he and Anthony LePage (1967) had a confederate provoke male participants who could later respond by giving the confederate electric shocks (although in reality the confederate was not shocked). On a table near the shock apparatus just happened to be some objects scattered about, allegedly left there from a previous experiment.

For half of the participants, these objects were a revolver and rifle, and for the other half, they were badminton racquets and shuttlecocks. Berkowitz and LePage found that participants delivered more shocks to the confederate when a revolver and rifle were present than when badminton racquets and shuttlecocks were. In other words, although they didn't use these weapons, their mere presence seemed to make the participants more aggressive. This tendency for the presence of guns to increase aggression came to be known as the **weapons effect**. As Berkowitz put it: "The finger pulls the trigger, but the trigger may also be pulling the finger" (1968, p. 22).

Individuals may differ in what associations they have with various weapons. Bruce Bartholow and others (2005) found that hunters were less likely than nonhunters to associate hunting guns with aggression. Hunters had more positive associations with hunting guns; for example, they linked guns with sport and the pleasurable experiences they had had hunting with friends and family. Nonhunters not only had more negative, aggressive thoughts after exposure to hunting guns than did hunters but they also behaved more aggressively while doing a subsequent task. However, exposure to assault guns had a very different effect: Hunters had more negative, aggressive associations with assault guns than did nonhunters, and they behaved more aggressively than nonhunters after exposure to them. In other words, hunters cognitively

weapons effect   The tendency that the likelihood of aggression will increase by the mere presence of weapons.

differentiated hunting guns from assault guns more than nonhunters did, and so these two types of weapons triggered very different effects for them.

Jennifer Klinesmith and others (2006) found that weapons had an effect on men's testosterone levels as well as on their aggression. Male college students in this experiment handled either a handgun or a children's game for 15 minutes. Relative to the students who interacted with the game, the students who interacted with the gun showed increased testosterone levels and exhibited greater aggression against another person (by adding a lot of "Frank's Red Hot Sauce" to a cup of water they thought another subject would have to drink!) (▶ Figure 11.10). The greater the increase in testosterone in response to the gun, the more hot sauce the students added to the other person's drink.

In general, any object or external characteristic that is associated with (1) successful aggression; or (2) the negative affect of pain or unpleasantness can serve as an aggression-enhancing situational cue (Berkowitz, 1993, 1998, 2008). Even brief exposure to words associated with hot temperatures can trigger aggressive thoughts (DeWall & Bushman, 2009). Even when they are subtle, aggressive cues can have very strong effects, increasing people's hostility and likelihood of aggressing. In addition, stimuli that would not serve as aggression-enhancing cues for some people can be aggression cues for others. People who tend to be aggressive associate significantly more cues with aggression and hostility than do people who are not as chronically aggressive; thus, they are particularly prone to automatically activating aggression-related thoughts (Bushman, 1996, 1998).

▶ **FIGURE 11.10**

Guns, Testosterone, and Hot Sauce: Evidence for the Weapons Effect

Male college students handled either a gun (actually just a pellet gun, but identical in size, shape, and feel to a real automatic handgun) or a children's game for 15 minutes. The bars on the left show the increase in testosterone measured in the students after interacting with the gun (purple) or the game (teal). The bars on the right illustrate a measure of aggressive behavior: how much hot sauce the students secretly put in a drink they thought the confederate would have to swallow. Consistent with research on the weapons effect, students who handled the gun showed a much greater increase in testosterone as well as significantly more aggressive behavior than did students who handled the game.

Based on Klinesmith et al., 2006.

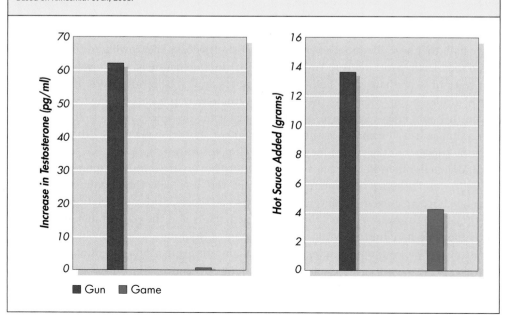

Higher-Order Cognition: Cognitive Control   Situational cues can trigger automatic associations. More complex information about one's situation, however, influences the deliberate, thoughtful consideration that we call higher-order cognitive processing. For example, an angry person might refrain from acting aggressively if the potential costs of fighting seem too high. In this case, the person might choose to flee rather than fight. In addition, people who believe that aggression is inappropriate in a particular situation or whose moral values and principles mandate nonviolent behavior may realize that better alternatives to aggression exist (Huesmann & Guerra, 1997). The behavior of other people in the immediate situation can also influence an individual's considerations. If one or more others in a group are reacting aggressively to the situation, aggression can be contagious (Levy & Nail, 1993).

People's thoughts about the intentions of other people can determine whether they are likely to respond aggressively. Some individuals exhibit a **hostile attribution bias** in that they tend to perceive hostile intent in others. For example, socially maladjusted children who are chronically aggressive and have been rejected by their peers see hostile intent where others don't (Crick & Dodge, 1994). Such perceptions then increase their aggression, and their peers respond by rejecting them further, locking these children into an ever-escalating vicious cycle. Chronically aggressive adults, too, tend to expect and perceive hostility in others' motives and behaviors (Dill et al., 1997). Research has found hostile attribution bias to be associated with both physical and relational aggression (Bailey & Ostrov, 2008). A meta-analysis of more than 40 studies found strong support for the relationship between aggressive behavior and hostile attributions of the intentions of peers (Orobio de Castro et al., 2002).

The effect of social rejection on hostile thinking and aggressive behaviors was demonstrated recently in a set of experiments by Nathan DeWall and others (2009). Some participants in these studies were made to experience social rejection (or thoughts about being socially excluded in the future), and others did not go through this experience. The participants who experienced or thought about social rejection were significantly more likely than the other participants to interpret the ambiguous actions of another person as hostile and to act aggressively against another person, such as by blasting them with painful white noise during a competitive reaction-time task. The more these socially rejected participants made hostile attributions, the more aggressive was their subsequent behavior.

Alcohol   Some conditions make it more difficult to engage in the higher-order cognition that can inhibit aggressive impulses. High arousal, for example, impairs the cognitive control of aggression (Zillmann et al., 1975). So does alcohol. Alcohol is implicated in the majority of violent crimes, suicides, and automobile fatalities. The evidence is quite clear about this point: Alcohol consumption often increases aggressive behavior (Bushman & Cooper, 1990; Exum, 2006; Graham et al., 2006; Leonard et al., 2003). Even among individuals who are usually not aggressive, those who drink more, aggress more (Bailey & Taylor, 1991; Pihl et al., 1997).

But *how* does alcohol increase aggression? A meta-analysis of 49 studies indicates that alcohol reduces anxiety, which in turn lowers people's inhibitions against aggressing (Ito et al., 1996). In addition, drinking disrupts the way we process information (Leonard, 1989). For example, alcohol impairs people's executive functioning, which as we discussed earlier involves cognitive processes that enable people to plan or inhibit actions (Weiss & Marksteiner, 2007). This in turn increases aggression. Another way that alcohol can lead to aggression is through what Claude Steele and Robert Josephs (1990) call *alcohol myopia*. That is, alcohol narrows people's focus of attention. Intoxicated people respond to initial, salient information about the situation but often miss later, more subtle indicators. Alcohol myopia is related to other

hostile attribution bias The tendency to perceive hostile intent in others.

potentially destructive behaviors as well, such as intentions to engage in risky sexual behavior (MacDonald et al., 2000). In combination with the reduced inhibitions that alcohol can produce, this behavior can be lethal.

In addition to its pharmacological effects, alcohol can also affect aggressiveness because of people's *expectations* about alcohol's effects. The more people expect alcohol to affect them and make them more aggressive, the more likely it is that it will have that effect (Bégue et al., 2009; Quigley & Leonard, 2006). And alcohol, even if not consumed, can serve as an aggression cue for some people, priming aggressive thoughts and hostile perceptions through their associations of alcohol with aggression (Bartholow & Heinz, 2006).

Situational Influences: Putting It All Together

We have seen that negative affect, arousal, and aggression-related thoughts can lead to aggression. And a number of factors influence whether one is likely to experience negative affect, arousal, and aggressive thoughts, such as aversive experiences (frustration, crowding, heat, provocation), situational cues (guns, violent movies), and individual and cultural differences (chronic hostility, cultures of honor). ▶ Figure 11.11 diagrams how these various factors interact to lead to emotional aggression. As this figure illustrates, various aversive experiences (such as frustration or heat), situational cues (such as weapons), and individual differences (such as a hostile attribution bias) can create negative affect, high arousal, and/or aggressive thoughts, each of which can lead to aggressive behavior. Whether the affect, arousal, and thoughts translate into aggressive behavior, however, may depend in part on the outcome of higher-order thinking, which can either inhibit aggression (such as by recognizing the danger of the situation or recognizing that what seemed like a provocation was really just an accident) or facilitate it (such as by perceiving that aggression is encouraged by one's peers in this situation or that a provocation was intentional).

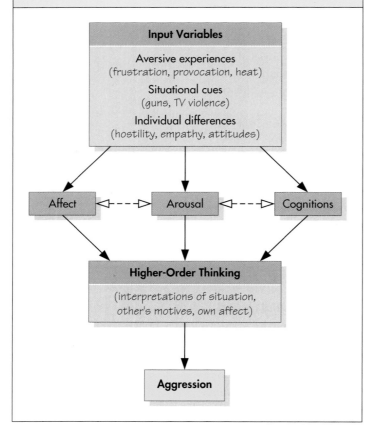

▶ **FIGURE 11.11**

A Model of Situational Influences on Emotional Aggression

Unpleasant experiences and situational cues can trigger negative affect, high arousal, and aggression-related thoughts. Due to individual differences, some people are more likely than others to experience these feelings and thoughts. Higher-order thinking then shapes these feelings and thoughts into more well-defined emotions and behavioral intentions. Depending on the outcome of this thinking (which can occur beneath the individual's conscious awareness and can be affected by factors such as alcohol or stress), the individual may choose to aggress.

Based on Anderson et al., 1996.

Media Effects

Having looked at origins and specific factors that contribute to aggression, we now focus on a special topic that has been a major concern of politicians, families, and social scientists alike for many years: violence in television, film, video games, and other media. We explore two types of mass media presentations—nonsexual violence and pornography—in which the display of aggression may elicit more aggression.

Violence in TV, Movies, Music Lyrics, and Video Games

On September 13, 2006, Kimveer Gill, a 25-year-old man, drove up to Dawson College in Montreal, pulled three guns from his car, and started shooting students. In total, Gill shot 20 people. Gill had no apparent connection or dispute with Dawson College or its students. Rather, it seemed, he had a tremendous amount of hostility toward the world in general. He had written numerous postings on the Internet about his loathing for humanity and about his fascination with guns, death, and violent video games. On a website popular with Goth culture, he had posted entries about his fantasies of killing people, many of which foreshadowed the events of September 13. "Life is a video game. You've got to die sometime," he wrote in one blog (Struck, 2006, p. A12). These are the same words another young killer had used after killing police officers in Alabama in 2003, in a scene similar to one depicted in the killer's favorite violent video game (Kampis, 2005).

According to one report, when Danny Ledonne heard about the shootings at Dawson College in Montreal, he threw up. Ledonne, living in Colorado, had no connection to Kimveer Gill or his victims, but Ledonne had heard that the killer was a big fan of the extremely violent video game he had posted on the Internet, called *Super Columbine Massacre*. The game was based on the massacre at Columbine High School, and Gill was fascinated by the shootings, both the real event and the video game version. "When I heard about the Dawson shootings," Ledonne said, "people asked me, 'Gosh. How do you feel to have blood on your hands?'" (Gerson, 2006, p. A12).

Despite what Ledonne's physical reaction to the Dawson College news might suggest, Ledonne asserts that he doesn't believe his game promotes real violence. But Gill, like the killers in Columbine and in many other school shootings, was an avid fan of several extremely violent, vicious video games. The question is, then: Do these games—and violence depicted in other popular media—cause real-world aggression and violence?

Violence depicted in the media has been a target of attack and counterattack for decades. But the amount, intensity, and graphic nature of the violence have continued to escalate. Testifying before a U.S. Senate subcommittee, social psychologist Leonard Eron estimated that by the end of elementary school a typical American child would have seen 8,000 murders and more than 100,000 other acts of violence (DeAngelis, 1993). And the numbers seem to only rise. A 2003 study by the Parents Television Council, for example, counted 534 separate episodes of prime-time violence on the six major American television networks during the first two weeks of November 2002, compared to 292 from the year before.

The most violent TV shows, ironically enough, are targeted to children directly—namely, cartoons and other children's programming (*National Television Violence Study*, 1998). At the same time, children and adolescents are heavily exposed to depictions of violence in movies and video games. Particularly popular among young males is "professional" wrestling and mixed martial arts, which in recent years have become increasingly violent and graphic. Young men and women are also

People asked me, "Gosh. How do you feel to have blood on your hands?"

—Danny Ledonne, after learning that the school shooter at Dawson College in 2006 was a fan of the video game he had posted on the Internet

Can playing violent video games cause children and young adults to become more aggressive and violent? A growing body of research suggests that it can.

© David Pearson/Alamy

According to a national survey of 12- to 17-year-olds in the United States, 99% of boys and 94% of girls play video games.
—Lenhart et al., 2008

heavy consumers of music that includes violent imagery in its lyrics and accompanying videos. A more recent phenomenon is the abundance of videos that individuals upload to various websites that depict very aggressive, extreme behavior, including fist fights, beatings, and violent pranks. The people seen in these videos are usually of the same age and backgrounds as the people watching them, so their influence may be especially strong in inducing copycat behavior.

If consumers didn't enjoy violence in TV, film, music, videos, and video games, these media would not be featuring it. So can it really be harmful? We explore this question in the sections that follow.

Linking Media Violence to Real-World Violence Does life imitate art? It often seems that way. Brad Bushman, whose work is cited in several places in this chapter, first became interested in research on media violence when a store owner he knew was the victim of a heinous crime: Two armed men came into the store and forced the owner and customers into the basement, forced them to drink Drano (a highly corrosive, toxic fluid used to clean plumbing pipes), and put duct tape over their mouths—the day after these men had allegedly watched (three times) the Clint Eastwood movie *Magnum Force*, which features a scene depicting this very act of brutality (Leland, 1995). People who have lost family members to violence that seemed to be copied directly from violent video games such as *Manhunt* and *Grand Theft Auto* have sued the makers and distributors of these violent games.

Dylan Klebold and Eric Harris were big fans of the violent video game *Doom* when they went on their 1999 shooting spree at Columbine High School, and reports indicate that they based their plans for their massacre on the game. Tim Kretschmer, whose March 2009 rampage at a high school in Winnenden, Germany, was described in the introduction to this chapter, had numerous brutally violent video games and videos. This led one of Germany's largest retail chains to stop selling films or games with very violent material (Roxborough, 2009). Indeed, many of the boys involved in these waves of school shootings had consumed a steady diet of violent video games. Each shooting, moreover, was soon followed by additional threats and violent acts. According to one analysis, there were 400 copycat incidents in the United States and Canada in the month after the Columbine shooting, most of which were not fatal (Tobin, 2006). Table 11.3 lists just a few of the many violent incidents that may have been inspired by exposure to violence depicted in popular media. Yet no one can ever prove that a specific fictional depiction was the primary cause of a specific act of violence. There are always other possibilities.

If you ask people whether exposure to media violence causes real aggression, most would probably say that they doubt that it does or that there has never been clear evidence one way or another on this question. When this issue is discussed on the news or in the media in general, the reports tend to conclude that the relevant scientific evidence is weak and mixed, at best. Defenders of the entertainment industry consistently argue that there is no evidence that viewing media violence causes real-world aggression. Social psychologists and others who study this issue are often confronted by people who assert, "I've played lots of violent video games and I never killed anyone."

The movie *Fight Club*, starring Brad Pitt and Edward Norton, has been linked to numerous copycat acts of aggression and violence, including the 2009 bombing at a Starbucks in New York City by a teenager obsessed with the movie and one of its lead characters, Tyler Durden.

I see television's violent content as therapeutic for the population.
—Jib Fowles, author of *The Case for Television Violence*

TABLE 11.3

Copycat Violence?

Although it's impossible to prove that any specific media depiction caused a specific violent action, there have been some close connections.

Violent Fiction	Subsequent Violent Fact
The Matrix (a trilogy of films starring Keanu Reeves)	Numerous killers have cited the influence of these movies in their violent outbursts. Many of them believed they were in a real-life version of the matrix.
The Sopranos (TV series about a mob family)	Two brothers strangled their mother and chopped off her head and hands to hide her identity. They later told investigators that they had seen this done on *The Sopranos*.
Money Train (movie starring Wesley Snipes and Woody Harrelson)	In several incidents in New York City, people doused subway token collectors with flammable liquids and burned them, just as had been depicted in the movie.
Natural Born Killers (movie starring Woody Harrelson and Juliette Lewis)	At least eight murders have been cited as having been inspired by this violent film, including the case of a student who decapitated a classmate because he "wanted to be famous, like the natural born killers" (Brooks, 2002, p. 10).
"F*** tha Police" (song by gangsta rap group N.W.A.)	Rifles used in the shooting of a police officer in North Carolina were emblazoned with the letters N.W.A.
Scream (movie starring Neve Campbell, Courteney Cox, and Drew Barrymore)	Several brutal attacks apparently copied elements of the movie, including the costume worn and the scare tactics used by the fictional killer. For example, a Belgian man put on a *Scream* costume before killing a 15-year-old girl with two kitchen knives.
Fight Club (movie starring Brad Pitt)	A teen obsessed with *Fight Club* set off a bomb at a Manhattan Starbucks in an act that was similar to an event in the movie. A friend said, "He thought he was Tyler Durden," the lead character from the movie (Gendar et al., 2009, p. 7).
Professional wrestling	Mimicking a dangerous wrestling move he had seen on TV, a 7-year-old boy accidentally killed his 3-year-old brother in Dallas.
The Life and Death of Lord Erroll (a controversial book)	The author's son was killed in an act very similar to the murder that had been described in her book. The author later said, "In some terrible way, I think I pressed the trigger" (Alderson, 2001, p. 6).
Grand Theft Auto (video game)	Two teenagers in Tennessee fired shotgun blasts at passing cars on a highway, leaving one dead and another wounded. They claimed they didn't mean to kill anyone but simply wanted to emulate *Grand Theft Auto*, their favorite video game.

But what does the social psychological research *really* say on this matter? Here, we do not need to qualify the answer with "It depends." Although media violence is neither a necessary nor a sufficient cause of real-world aggression and violence (that is, exposure to media violence does not necessarily cause one to aggress, nor is it ever the only cause of an act of aggression or violence), the evidence is impressive and clear: Media violence contributes to real aggression and violence. In one review, Brad Bushman and Rowell Huesmann (2001) asked and answered this question emphatically: "Does TV violence have any effect on aggressive and violent behavior of children? The answer is yes! The scientific evidence . . . is overwhelming on this point. The relation between TV violence and aggression is about as strong as the relation between smoking and cancer" (p. 223). Not everyone who smokes gets lung cancer, and not everyone who gets lung cancer smoked. But it is clear that smoking is an important cause of lung cancer, and research suggests that the same is true of media violence and real-world aggression. ▶ Figure 11.12 illustrates the relative magnitude of the correlation between TV violence and aggression.

What is the evidence behind these numbers and conclusions? The best way to investigate the issue of media violence is to use multiple methods, each of which has different sets of strengths and weaknesses. This is exactly what researchers in this area

There's an audience of people who love this genre who are not violent. In fact, they sort of use it to vent their violent nature so they don't have to act it out in real life.
—Actress Jamie Lee Curtis, star of *Halloween* and some of its sequels, defending horror movie blood and gore

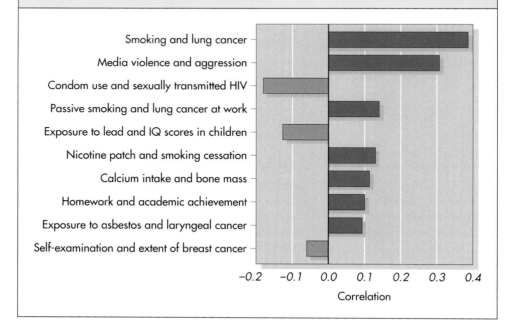

►FIGURE 11.12

How Strong Is the Relationship Between Media Violence and Real-World Aggression?
The correlation between exposure to violence in the media and aggressive behavior is compared here to the correlations of several other well-established relationships. This comparison illustrates the relative magnitude of the link between media violence and aggressive behavior.

Singer & Singer, 2001.

have done. What is particularly impressive about this research is that the results have been strikingly consistent across methods. Longitudinal research, which examines individuals' exposure to violent media early in life and then examines their real-world aggression years later, has found, for example, that the extent to which 8-year-olds watched violent TV predicts their aggressiveness and criminality as adults, even when statistically controlling for other factors such as socioeconomic status and parenting practices (Huesmann et al., 2003) (► Figure 11.13). More recently, in a study of 820 youth, including 390 juvenile delinquents, Paul Boxer and others (2009) found that childhood and adolescent preferences for violent media significantly predicted later violence and aggression.

In experimental research, individuals are randomly assigned to watch or play with violent or nonviolent media, and their aggressive thoughts, feelings, and behaviors are measured immediately after the exposure. In one experiment, for example, adolescent Dutch boys were randomly assigned to play either a violent or a nonviolent video game for 20 minutes. Compared to the boys who played the nonviolent video game, the boys who played the violent game behaved more aggressively after the game by delivering very loud, aversive blasts of noise against an opponent in a reaction-time task. This aggressive effect was especially strong among the boys who reported identifying most strongly with the main character in the video game. Some of these boys chose to blast their opponent with noise so loud that it could—according to the experimenter's instructions—cause permanent hearing loss to the other boy (although, in fact, no one actually received these noise blasts) (Konijn et al., 2007). Another experiment was conducted by a team of researchers in Madrid, who found that 8- to 12-year-old children, particularly boys, were more aggressive after viewing televised bullfights (Graña et al., 2004).

In one extensive review, researchers examined the relationship between exposure to media violence and real aggression in 46 longitudinal studies, 86 cross-sectional surveys (which look, at one point in time, at the relation between individuals' exposure to violent media and their aggressive behavior), 28 field experiments, and 124 laboratory experiments—totaling more than 50,000 participants. The magnitude of the positive relationship between exposure to media violence and real aggressive behavior was consistent across all four types of studies. The laboratory experiments tended to show the strongest effects and the other three types of studies showed only slightly weaker—but still strong—relationships (Anderson & Bushman, 2002a; Anderson et al., 2004).

Violent video games have not been around as long as violent television, but there has been enough research on these games within the past decade that researchers have found reliable effects. A meta-analysis of video-game studies of both experimental and correlational methods reports that exposure to violent video games is significantly linked to increases in aggressive behavior, aggressive cognitions, aggressive affect, and physiological arousal, as well as to decreases in helping behavior (Anderson et al., 2004). One recent experiment found that playing a violent video game had stronger effects on subsequent aggression than merely watching violence (Polman et al., 2008). A large study of German adolescents found that playing violent video games frequently was associated with hostile attribution bias, aggressive norms, and physical aggression. Furthermore, the degree to which the adolescents played violent video games predicted their level of physical aggressiveness 30 months later (Möller & Krahé, 2009).

Based on the accumulated research, six major professional societies in the United States—the American Psychological Association, the American Academy of Pediatrics, the American Academy of Child and Adolescent Psychiatry, the American Medical Association, the American Academy of Family Physicians, and the American Psychiatric Association—together concluded that the research "reveals unequivocal evidence that media violence increases the likelihood of aggressive and violent behavior in both immediate and long-term contexts" (Anderson, Berkowitz, et al., 2003, p. 81). The general public may not be aware of this, but the scientific community is more convinced than ever.

Of course, the media do not operate in a vacuum. People are influenced by their families, peers, social values, and opportunities for education and employment. Nor are all individuals the same; differences in personality can heat up or tone down the impact of exposure to aggressive displays. Media effects tend to be especially strong among people who are high in trait aggressiveness, irritability, or hostility as well as among those who lack empathy (Anderson & Bushman, 2002b; Arriaga et al., 2006; Bushman & Huesmann, 2001).

Physical violence is not the only kind of aggression portrayed in the media. Sarah Coyne and John Archer (2004) found examples of indirect aggression in 92 percent of programs on British television shows that are popular with adolescents, a rate much

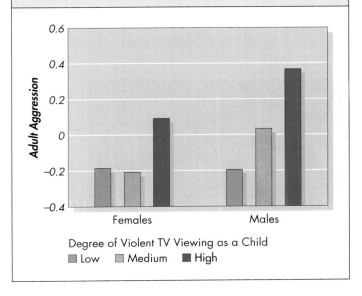

▶ **FIGURE 11.13**

Violent TV Viewing and Aggression 15 Years Later

A longitudinal study tracked individuals over a 15-year period. Based on how much TV violence they viewed as 8-year-olds, individuals were categorized as having viewed low (lower 20 percent), medium (middle 60 percent), or high (upper 20 percent) levels of TV violence. Their aggressiveness as adults was measured 15 years later. For both females and males, those who tended to watch the greatest amount of violent TV as children tended to be the most aggressive as adults.

Based on Huesmann et al., 2003.

higher than physical aggression. Compared to physical aggressors, the indirect aggressors portrayed tended to be more rewarded for their aggression, and they were more likely to be female and attractive. In a later experiment, Coyne and her colleagues (2004) found that television exposure to indirect aggression had immediate effects on adolescents' own behavior, such as leading to less helping behavior, more negative evaluations of others, and greater endorsement of using indirect aggression in response to an ambiguous situation.

More recently, Coyne and others (2008) randomly assigned female college students to watch film clips involving physical aggression (from the movie *Kill Bill*), relational aggression (from the movie *Mean Girls*), or no aggression (from the movie *What Lies Beneath*). Although the different clips produced equal degrees of excitement and arousal, the clips showing either physical or relational aggression led the students to become more aggressive (blasting a confederate with painful noise) than did the non-aggressive clip.

Exposure to TV violence in childhood is related to aggression later in life. **TRUE.**

How Does Media Violence Cause These Effects? The evidence from hundreds of studies makes it clear that media violence—whether from TV, movies, music lyrics or videos, video games, and so on—can have both immediate and long-term effects. Another question, though, is *how* it can have these effects.

Social psychologists have found several paths through which media violence produces real-world aggression. Media violence can trigger aggressive and hostile thoughts, which in turn can lead individuals to interpret others' actions in hostile ways and promote aggression. Playing violent video games, for example, has been found to cause increases in aggressive cognitions and affect, in addition to aggressive behavior (Anderson, 2004).

In one series of experiments, Peter Fischer and Tobias Greitemeyer (2006) found that male participants who had just listened to misogynous song lyrics recalled more negative attributes about women, reported more feelings of vengeance, and behaved more aggressively toward a female confederate than did male participants who had listened to neutral music. Listening to men-hating lyrics had a similar effect on female participants' aggressive-related responses toward men. Because of the sexual and sexist overtones of many video games, they may promote not only aggression but sexist attitudes and behaviors (Dietz, 1998). Steven Fein and Emily Eustis (2001) found that male college students with higher-than-average levels of hostility expressed more sexist attitudes after they participated in a video game that featured sexist behavior.

Rap star 50 Cent has achieved a great deal of popularity and acclaim over the past several years, while at the same time sparking controversy because of the violent nature of many of his songs, which his critics claim promote violence and sexism.

Another effect of media violence is that it desensitizes individuals to violence. **Desensitization** to violence refers to a reduction in emotion-related physiological reactivity to real violence. Desensitization is one form of *habituation*. A novel stimulus gets our attention, and if it's sufficiently interesting or exciting, it elicits physiological arousal. But when we get used to something, our reactions diminish. Familiarity with violence reduces physiological arousal to new incidents of violence (Geen, 1981). Desensitized to violence, we may become more accepting of it.

Desensitization to violence from media exposure can have both immediate and long-term effects. Nicholas Carnagey and others (2007) demonstrated some immediate effects in a pair of experiments in which they had college students play either a violent video game (such as *Duke Nukem* or *Mortal Kombat*) or a nonviolent video game (such as *Glider Pro* or *3D Pinball*) for 20 minutes. In one experiment, the participants then watched a 10-minute videotape depicting several scenes of real violence, such as

desensitization Reduction in emotion-related physiological reactivity in response to a stimulus.

Kevin Winter/Getty Images

shootings and prison fights. Consistent with the idea that violent video games desensitize players to real violence, participants had lower heart rates and lower galvanic skin responses (which is one measure of emotional arousal) while watching the real violence if they had earlier played a violent rather than a nonviolent video game. In a second experiment, after playing the video game, participants overheard a (staged) fight between two people that ended with one of the fighters leaving and the other groaning on the floor, apparently injured. Participants who had played a violent video game were less likely to come to the aid of the injured person than participants who had played a nonviolent game. Those who had played the violent game also rated the fight as sounding less severe than did the participants who had played the nonviolent video game.

These researchers also found in the second experiment that participants who had a history of playing a lot of violent video games were less helpful than were participants who had not been habitual players of violent video games. This finding suggests that playing these violent games can lead to more long-term desensitization to violence. Several other experiments conducted in a variety of countries have since demonstrated the desensitizing effects of violent media (Fanti et al., 2009; Staude-Miller et al., 2008). In one experiment, male and female college students who were randomly assigned to play a violent video game for 20 minutes subsequently took more than 450 percent longer to help an injured stranger than did participants who played a nonviolent video game (see ▶ Figure 11.14). Those who played the violent game also perceived the fight to be less serious than did those who played the nonviolent game (Bushman & Anderson, 2009).

In an interesting field study, these researchers also had a young woman on crutches "accidentally" drop her crutches and struggle to retrieve them outside a movie theater either just before or just after a movie was shown. The movie shown was either violent or nonviolent. Would people going to the violent movie be slower to offer help than people going to the nonviolent one? There was no difference in how quickly people offered to help her *before* the movies began, suggesting that the people going to these movies did not differ in general helpfulness. However, *after* seeing the movie, those who had seen the violent movie were slower to respond to the woman in need than were those who had seen the nonviolent movie.

Media violence can also produce long-term effects by influencing people's values and attitudes toward aggression, making it seem more legitimate and even necessary for social interaction and the resolution of social conflicts. Through the processes of social learning, children may learn that aggression and violence are common, normal ways of dealing with threats or problems and may even be rewarding. Frequent exposure to such imagery fuels the aggression scripts that children and adolescents develop, which they subsequently use to guide their behavior (Anderson & Huesmann, 2007).

Media violence can affect people also through what George Gerbner and his colleagues (1986) call **cultivation**. Cultivation refers to the capacity of the mass media to construct a social reality that people perceive as true, even if it isn't. The media tend to depict the world as much more violent than it actually is. This can make people become more fearful, more distrustful, more likely to arm themselves, and more likely to behave aggressively in what they perceive as a threatening situation (Nabi & Sullivan, 2001).

▶ **FIGURE 11.14**

Desensitizing Effects of Violent Media

Students were randomly assigned to play either a violent or a nonviolent video game for 20 minutes. A few minutes after playing the game, while filling out a questionnaire, they heard what sounded like a fight outside the lab room. They could hear one person get injured and be left alone while clearly needing help. The students were led to believe that the experimenter was not around at this time. Consistent with the idea that violent media can desensitize people, the students who had played the violent game took more than 450 percent longer to come to the aid of this injured stranger than did the students who had played the nonviolent game.

Bushman & Anderson, 2009.

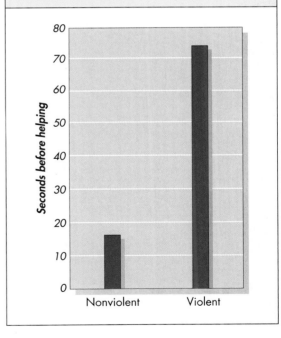

cultivation The process by which the mass media (particularly television) construct a version of social reality for the public.

Can Media Cause Positive, Prosocial Effects? The vast amount of attention and research has focused on the negative effects of media, but can positive media images and messages produce prosocial rather than antisocial effects? Although there is not a great deal of research on this yet, there are some encouraging results. As discussed in Chapter 2 (see Figure 2.3, p. 41), Tobias Greitemeyer (2009) found that listening to music lyrics that promoted socially positive messages caused participants to behave more helpfully. Chapter 10 reported that a meta-analysis of 34 studies found a reliable positive effect of prosocial television on children's prosocial behavior, especially when specific acts of altruism were modeled on TV (Mares & Woodard, 2005).

Although video games have a particularly bad reputation because of how brutally violent so many of them are, some games feature helpful, cooperative behaviors. A recent ambitious international investigation by Douglas Gentile and others (2009) examined the effects of such games in three different countries using three different methods. A correlational study in Singapore revealed that middle-school children who played more prosocial games tended to behave more prosocially. A longitudinal study of two samples of Japanese children and adolescents found that the more the children played prosocial video games when they were initially assessed by the researchers, the more the children engaged in prosocial behavior a few months later. Finally, college students in the United States were randomly assigned to play prosocial (such as *Super Mario Sunshine*) or neutral (such as *Pure Pinball*) video games for 20 minutes, after which they were given the chance to help or harm another participant on some task. Those who played the prosocial games were significantly more helpful than were those who played the neutral games.

The question of whether exposure to erotic or pornographic images can influence aggression toward women has triggered a good deal of social psychological research over the years. The importance of understanding the impact of such material is underscored by the prevalence of such images in our society, as is evident in this picture: The huge billboard of porn star Jenna Jameson is hard to miss for the endless stream of adults and children on one of the busiest streets in the world, in New York's Times Square.

AP/Wide World Photos

Pornography

Just as citizens, scientists, and politicians have been concerned about the consequences of mass media presentations of violence, they have also been troubled by mass media displays of sexual material. Such displays are highly visible and widely available. Magazines, videos, and Internet sites cater to a wide range of sexual interests. Heavy metal, hip-hop, and rap groups often rely on obscenities to get their fans' attention. Pornographic websites and phone services rake in millions of dollars. Opposition to pornography is equally prominent. Parents, religious leaders, consumer groups, and feminist activists lobby legislators and go to court to obtain greater restraints on the availability of sexually explicit materials.

In a meta-analysis of 46 published studies, Elizabeth Oddone-Paolucci and others (2000) found that men were significantly more likely to report sexually aggressive behaviors and attitudes if they also reported exposure to pornography. Of course, this correlational evidence does not prove that pornography caused these behaviors and attitudes. Indeed, such evidence must be supported by experimental research, which we review below. But it is important to recognize the challenges of conducting research on such a controversial and sensitive issue. Even defining the variables is rarely straightforward. Past attempts to ban specific works, such as James Joyce's novel *Ulysses* and Robert Mapplethorpe's photos, illustrate that the definitions of such terms as *obscenity*, *erotica*, and *pornography* are often a matter of personal opinion: One person's smut is another person's master-piece. Because of the subjectivity involved in such definitions, the term **pornography** is used here to refer to explicit sexual material, regardless of its moral or aesthetic qualities. It is crucial, however, to distinguish between nonviolent and violent pornography in discussing the relationship between pornographic displays and aggression.

Nonviolent Pornography   Earlier in this chapter, we described how both arousal and affect can influence aggression. The results of research on nonviolent pornography confirm the importance of these factors (Donnerstein et al., 1987). For many people, viewing attractive nudes elicits a pleasant emotional response and low levels of sexual arousal. This combination of positive affect and only moderate arousal is unlikely to trigger much aggression. Indeed, according to Michael Seto and colleagues (2001), there is little support for a direct causal link between the use of nonviolent pornography and sexual aggression. These researchers do note, however, that men who are already predisposed to sexually offend are the most likely to be affected by pornography exposure. This latter point is also consistent with a conclusion reached by other researchers (Kingston et al., 2009; Vega & Malamuth, 2007). They propose that relatively aggressive men may interpret and react to the same images differently than less aggressive men, making them more likely to be affected by them in negative ways. It may be of interest to note that authorities found child pornography on the computer of James von Brunn, the man who shot and killed the security guard at the Holocaust Museum (Syeed, 2009).

Violent Pornography   Adding violence to pornography greatly increases the possibility of harmful effects. Violent pornography is a triple threat: It brings together high arousal; negative emotional reactions such as shock, alarm, and disgust; and aggressive thoughts. Numerous Internet sites—including many that are free and can be viewed easily by minors—focus specifically on images of sexual violence against women and use depictions of women's pain as a selling point (Gossett & Byrne, 2002).

According to a meta-analysis of 217 studies on the relationship between TV violence and aggression, programs that include violent pornography have a stronger effect than any other type of program (Paik & Comstock, 1994). And there is substantial evidence that this effect is gender-specific. Male-to-male aggression is no greater

The combination of violence, arousal, and sexual imagery is part of the appeal to many fans of professional wrestling (as in this WWE event in 2009). Research on aggression suggests that this combination can also be particularly potent in contributing to real-world aggression among viewers.

© Chris Ryan/Corbis

pornography   Explicit sexual material.

after exposure to violent pornography than it is after exposure to highly arousing but nonviolent pornography, but male-to-female aggression is markedly increased (Donnerstein & Malamuth, 1997; Linz et al., 1987; Malamuth & Donnerstein, 1982). Furthermore, violent pornography is one of the few situational factors (along with guns and alcohol) that has been shown to increase aggression even in the absence of provocation—particularly if the women are portrayed as somehow enjoying (such as becoming sexually aroused by) their own victimization (Donnerstein & Berkowitz, 1981).

Not everyone is affected by violent pornography in the same way. Neil Malamuth has developed what he calls the "rapist's profile." Men fit the profile if they have relatively high levels of sexual arousal in response to violent pornography and also express attitudes and opinions indicating acceptance of violence toward women (see Table 11.4). These individuals report more sexually coercive behavior in the past and more sexually aggressive intentions for the future. Among male college students given an opportunity to retaliate against a female confederate who had angered them, those who fit the rapist's profile were more aggressive (Malamuth, 1983, 1986). In another study illustrating the volatile mix of negative attitudes and violent pornography, Dano Demaré and his colleagues (1993) found that male college students' negative attitudes toward women and their frequent consumption of violent pornography each predicted the students' self-reported sexually aggressive intentions. The strongest prediction, however, was obtained when both pornography *and* attitudes were included in the equation.

The potential dangers of mixing violence and sexual arousal are not limited to the pornography industry. Popular movies, video games, and music videos frequently mix the two. This has been true in the movie industry since the time of silent movies, in which the hero saves the damsel in distress, who is perhaps tied to the train tracks, and it continues a century later as action movies try to top each other with increasingly arousing and graphic scenes that combine fighting and sex.

Numerous violent video games mix intense violence with gratuitously erotic images of women. These games offer what seems to be an especially dangerous combination of ingredients: a tremendous amount of violence; rewards for degrading women and treating them violently; and very arousing action and music. In at least one popular video game, players not only get to have their character kill numerous people and animals in numerous inventive ways, but they also can urinate on a woman before killing her. We earlier described the Japanese video game in which the player can simulate raping a woman and her daughters in a subway. Meanwhile, professional wrestling organizations have become notorious for their frequent use of violence and sexual imagery targeted to young males. Defenders claim that viewing such material is harmless and offers a cathartic release for viewers, thereby reducing real-world violence. Opponents cite evidence pointing strongly against catharsis (Bushman, 2002; Forbes et al., 2006).

TABLE 11.4

Attitudes About Sex and Aggression

Widely used in research on pornography, these two scales assess attitudes about violence toward women and beliefs about the nature of rape. A few items from each scale are shown here.

Acceptance of Interpersonal Violence (Toward Women): AIV Scale

1. Being roughed up is sexually stimulating to many women.
2. Many times a woman will pretend she doesn't want to have intercourse because she doesn't want to seem loose, but she's really hoping the man will force her.
3. A man is never justified in hitting his wife.

Scoring: Persons scoring high in acceptance of violence toward women agree with items 1 and 2 but disagree with item 3.

Rape Myth Acceptance: RMA Scale

1. If a woman engages in necking or petting and she lets things get out of hand, it is her own fault if her partner forces sex on her.
2. Any female can get raped.
3. Many women have an unconscious wish to be raped, and may then unconsciously set up a situation in which they are likely to be attacked.
4. In the majority of rapes, the victim is promiscuous or has a bad reputation.

Scoring: Persons scoring high in acceptance of rape myths agree with items 1, 3, and 4 but disagree with item 2.

Based on Burt, 1980.

Intimate Violence: Trust Betrayed

All violence is troubling, but aggression between intimates is especially disturbing. We want to feel safe with those we know and love, and yet far too often that sense of security is destroyed by violence. Among the homicides committed in the United States in 2007, almost half of the victims knew their murderer. According to a U.S. Department of Justice report released in 2000, nearly 25 percent of surveyed women and 7.6 percent of surveyed men reported that they had been raped and/or physically assaulted by their spouse, date, or other intimate partner. The victims of intimate violence are children as well as adults, and the assault that takes place is often sexual as well as physical. In this section, we examine two major types of intimate violence: sexual aggression among college students and physical aggression between partners or targeted at children.

Sexual Aggression Among College Students

Acquaintance rape (often called "date rape") is a serious problem among college students. According to one recent report (Cole, 2006), the incidence of rape among female college students in the United States is estimated to be 35 per 1,000 female students. This study also estimates that 90 percent of college women who are raped know their assailants and reports that most rapes occur in social situations, such as at a party. These statistics vary across different studies, and some research estimates that the incidence is even higher, such as 15 to 20 percent of female college students (Carr & VanDeusen, 2004). When all types of unwanted sexual interactions are included, a majority of college women and about a third of college men say they have experienced coercive sexual contact (Cate & Lloyd, 1992; Struckman-Johnson & Struckman-Johnson, 1994). Rates of sexual coercion among Canadian college students appear to be similar (DeKeseredy et al., 1993).

A number of factors are associated with sexual aggression among college students. Two of the most important are gender and alcohol. First, both men and women report that men are more likely to engage in coercive behavior—psychological as well as physical—in order to obtain sex (Poppen & Segal, 1988). Second, alcohol consumption is involved in a majority of sexually aggressive incidents between college students (Carr & VanDeusen, 2004; Cate & Lloyd, 1992; Cole, 2006). Not only does actual consumption increase aggressive behavior, but the mere *belief* that one has consumed alcohol (even if one hasn't) heightens sexual arousal and sexual interest (Baron & Richardson, 1994). The cognitive effects of intoxication, in which salient cues are noticed but subtle ones are missed, may disrupt interpersonal communication, and the anxiety-reducing effects of intoxication may weaken inhibitions against aggressive behavior (Farris et al., 2008). These conclusions are consistent with the results of an experiment by Brian Marx and others (1999) in which male college students listened to an audiotape of a simulated date rape. As illustrated in ▶ Figure 11.15, participants who had consumed alcohol took significantly longer to determine that the man should refrain from attempting further sexual contact with the woman.

▶ **FIGURE 11.15**

Alcohol and Perception of Sexual Aggression

Male college students listened to an audiotape of what was designed to sound like a date rape. Before listening to the tape, some of the men consumed alcohol and others did not. The experimenter recorded how long it took each participant to determine that the man on the tape should stop attempting further sexual contact with the woman. Students who had consumed alcohol took significantly longer to determine that the man should refrain from attempting further sexual contact.

Marx et al., 1999.

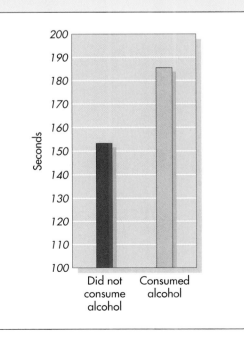

Women's perceptions and behaviors are also affected by alcohol. Several studies have found evidence suggesting that alcohol use (especially binge drinking) can make women more likely not only to take greater risks but also to fail to recognize danger and to feel less able to resist an assault effectively (Howard et al., 2008; Loiselle & Fuqua, 2007; McCauley & Calhoun, 2008; Pumphrey-Gordon & Gross, 2007; Testa et al., 2006).

A recent particularly disturbing development has been the growing use of so-called date-rape drugs, such as Rohypnol (sometimes called "roofies") or Gamma Hydroxy Butyrate (GHB, sometimes called "liquid ecstasy"), to render a person, often a date, helpless. Numerous stories around the world have documented their use in acquaintance rape by methods such as secretly putting the drug in a target's drink at a club or party.

A third important factor concerns attitudes toward rape and toward women. As we indicated earlier, men who fit Malamuth's concept of the rapist's profile—relatively high sexual arousal in response to violent pornography and attitudes indicating acceptance of violence toward women (again, see Table 11.4)—report using more sexually coercive behavior (Malamuth, 1996). In light of these findings, it is encouraging that rape-awareness workshops appear to reduce acceptance of rape myths and increase sympathy for female rape victims (Hong, 2000; Proto-Campise et al., 1998). Education has a crucial role to play in reducing sexual aggression.

Domestic Violence: Partner and Child Abuse

Partner Abuse In the United States, approximately one-third to one-half of female homicide victims are murdered by a husband or a boyfriend. Of course, partner abuse is not limited to the United States; it is a worldwide phenomenon. Nor is it a new development; it has occurred throughout history. Indeed, evolutionary psychologists point to a number of factors that predict such behavior, including males' concerns about paternity (in particular, uncertainty over whether they are the biological fathers of their children). These concerns are known to fuel intense sexual jealousy and distrust, both of which have been implicated in a large percentage of spousal homicides and acts of physical aggression (Buss & Duntley 2005; Shackelford, 2001; Shackelford & Goetz, 2005).

One of the most surprising results of national surveys in 1975 and 1985 was the high level of wife-to-husband violence, which in terms of severe violence (such as kicking, hitting, beating, threatening with a weapon, and using a weapon) was consistently higher than the level of husband-to-wife abuse. Research on aggression during the early years of marriage has also found somewhat higher rates of wife-to-husband aggression than husband-to-wife aggression (Frye & Karney 2006; O'Leary et al., 1989). These statistics were initially met with doubt, but they have since received support from the results of research by Murray Straus and his colleagues (Douglas & Straus, 2006; Straus, 1999; Straus, 2006) and from a series of meta-analyses conducted by John Archer (2000, 2002), involving more than 80 published articles, books, and other sources of data concerning aggression between heterosexual partners in several countries. Across these many studies, the rates of female-to-male aggression in intimate relationships are either higher than or similar to the rates of male-to-female aggression.

These statistics tell only part of the story. Although women aggress against men in intimate relationships as much or somewhat more than men do against women, the consequences of aggression between partners tend to be much more damaging to women, who are more often killed, seriously injured, or sexually assaulted during domestic disputes than are men (Archer, 2000, 2002; Straus & Ramirez, 2005). As Barbara Morse (1995) put it, "Women were more often the victims of severe partner assault and injury not because men strike more often, but because men strike harder" (p. 251).

Like most aggressive actions, violence between partners is caused by multiple factors. Among the factors associated with increased partner aggression are personal characteristics (such as age, attitudes toward violence, drug and alcohol abuse, and personality), socioeconomic status (which includes income and education), interpersonal conflict, stress, social isolation, and the experience of growing up in a violent family (Herzberger, 1996; Tjaden & Thoennes, 2000).

Men are much more likely than women to aggress against their spouses or partners. **FALSE.**

Child Abuse   Children who grow up in a violent family not only witness aggression, they often bear the brunt of it. More than 3 million American children between the ages of 3 and 17 years witness domestic violence every year (U.S. Department of Justice, 1998). Hundreds of thousands of children are themselves abused each year by a parent or close relative. And many other children each year are abused by a caregiver or other trusted person.

Like partner aggression, child abuse is multiply determined. Among the factors associated with increased child abuse are personal characteristics of the abusing parent (such as personality and substance abuse and whether the individual is biologically related to the child) and of the child (younger children are more often abused by family members); the family's socioeconomic status; stressful experiences; social isolation; marital conflict; and the abusing parent's having been abused as a child (Belsky 1993; Davies & Cummings, 1994; Herzberger, 1996).

The Cycle of Violence   At this point, you should begin to see a pattern emerging: the connection between violence in childhood and violence as an adult. This connection is called the **cycle of violence**. Children who witness parental violence or who are themselves abused are more likely as adults to inflict abuse on intimate partners or their children, or, perhaps, to be victims of intimate violence (Fagan, 2005; Frey et al., 2009; Holt & Gillespie, 2008; Ireland & Smith, 2009). This intergenerational transmission of domestic violence is by no means inevitable, however. Most people who witness or experience abuse in their families of origin are not abusive or abused in their families of procreation. The cycle of violence refers to a greater tendency, not an absolute certainty.

Reducing Violence

Multiple Causes, Multiple Cures

A variety of factors contribute to aggression—and, as we have seen, the impact of any one factor often involves other factors simultaneously. Hot temperatures, for instance, influence arousal and aggressive thoughts as well as affect. The effects of watching violence in the media may depend on the chronic level of hostility that a viewer has. Thus we cannot hope for a single, simple cure. The most effective strategies for reducing aggression recognize this complexity and work on multiple levels. Indeed, one of the most successful treatment programs for violent juvenile delinquents is called *multisystemic therapy*. This approach addresses individuals' problems at several different levels, including the needs of the adolescents and the many contexts in which they are embedded, such as family, peer group, school, and neighborhood (Borduin et al., 2009;

cycle of violence   The transmission of domestic violence across generations.

Curtis et al., 2009; Henggeler et al., 2009; Letourneau et al., 2009; Timmons-Mitchell & Bender, 2006).

One group of researchers has been studying an intervention that targets and tries to alter some of the kinds of destructive thinking we have discussed in this chapter, such as aggressive scripts, hostile attributions, and normative beliefs about aggression (such as believing that one's peers and one's culture promote aggression). The intervention is conducted in elementary schools and is led by children's teachers in the classroom setting for an hour a week for 20 weeks per year. Among other things, the curriculum teaches children how to generate prosocial solutions to responding to conflict, has the teachers model and reinforce prosocial rather than aggressive behavior, and helps the children see things from others' perspectives. Thus far, the results of this program have been encouraging in communities with moderate financial resources, but it is less clear if it will prove successful in the poorest communities (Metropolitan Area Child Study Research Group, 2007). Further adjustments and analyses of this approach will no doubt continue.

Situational and Sociocultural Factors   What about steps to reduce aggression more generally? Given that negative affect and thinking contribute to aggression, reducing stressors such as frustration, discomfort, and provocation should reduce aggression. Toward this end, an improved economy, healthier living conditions, and social support are extremely important. The prevalence of weapons has also been associated with aggressive thoughts and emotions. Reducing the number of guns may reduce not only access to the weapons but also the incidence of such thoughts and emotions. At the same time, teaching and modeling nonviolent responses to frustrations and social problems—and encouraging thoughtful responses that are incompatible with anger, such as humor and relaxation—are among the most effective things we can do for our society's children, and for each other.

Having observed the relative nonviolence of cultures that emphasize cooperation over competitiveness, social psychologists have concluded that cooperation and shared goals across groups are effective methods for reducing intergroup hostilities and aggression. In addition, because communities beset by broken windows and petty crime reveal a loss of control and support—thus possibly signaling to those who live there that aggression and antisocial behavior are left unpunished—police departments in numerous cities have begun to crack down on relatively minor acts of vandalism and aggression in the hope that doing so will prevent more serious acts of violence (Taylor, 2000). Finally, changing the cost-reward payoffs associated with aggression can have profound effects on the aggressive tendencies exhibited within a culture. Socialization practices that reward prosocial rather than antisocial behavior therefore have the potential to greatly reduce the tendency to engage in bullying, fighting, and other aggressive behaviors. Conversely, when overt or even indirect aggression is legitimized, we are all at risk.

Media Effects   The media, of course, play an important role in legitimizing—even glorifying—violence. What, then, can we do about it? Government censorship is one answer, but it is not a very popular one, for a number of reasons. Another alternative is to use public pressure to increase media self-censorship. Of course, the most powerful kind of public pressure would be a commercial boycott. If violence did not sell, the media would not produce it. Unfortunately, however, violence continues to be a moneymaker.

Research on the effects of prosocial song lyrics, television, and video games are quite encouraging in this regard. Indeed, as discussed in Chapter 10, an analysis by Susan Hearold (1986) concluded that prosocial TV programs can produce stronger effects on behavior than do antisocial TV programs. If parents can help children select shows and games that provide compelling, vivid prosocial models for their children, the effects may be strong. Parents have also been advised to watch television with their children and to teach them how TV differs from real life, how imitating TV characters can produce undesirable outcomes, and how children might be harmed by watching TV. This kind of ongoing parental tutorial takes significant time and effort. But given the extent of media depictions of violence in our society, strengthening children's critical viewing skills is a wise investment.

At this point, education may well be the most effective approach. In addition to the role of parents in educating and supporting their children concerning consumption of media, school-based interventions may also help curb children's undesirable reactions to TV. For example, Lawrence Rosenkoetter and others (2009) implemented a classroom-based intervention with almost 500 children in more than 30 classrooms (grades 1 to 4) over the course of seven months. The intervention is based on the concepts and research we have reviewed in this chapter, such as social learning theory and the development of aggressive scripts. Some of the techniques used in this program are designed to help children distinguish between what is pretend and what is real, to encourage them to choose good people to admire and imitate (as opposed to fictional superheroes), and even to get them to talk to the TV in response to bad behaviors that are depicted (to encourage critical thinking). The results thus far from this program have been impressive and include reducing not only the amount of violent TV these children watch but also how much they identify with violent superheroes. In addition, Sahara Byrne (2009) recently conducted an experiment that demonstrated that exposing children to a media literacy intervention can reduce their willingness to use aggression after exposure to violent media.

Scott Gries/Getty Images

Singers Rihanna and Chris Brown are seen here performing together in a concert in December 2008. Less than two months later, the image of this happy couple shattered when Brown was charged with assault for brutally beating her. In August 2009, Brown was sentenced to probation and community service. Violence targeting dating partners, spouses, and children occurs at alarming rates, and researchers point to several factors as contributing to this tragic problem.

Daniel Linz and others (1992) similarly advise educational efforts to increase viewers' critical skills in evaluating media depictions that link violence and sex. A model for such efforts can be found in the debriefing provided to research participants exposed to violent pornography in experiments (Donnerstein et al., 1987). This debriefing emphasizes that rape myths are inaccurate and that violent pornography is unrealistic. Among individuals presented with this information, there are long-term reductions in acceptance of rape myths.

Intimate Violence In addition to rape-awareness programs that debunk various rape myths and increase sensitivity, sex education programs that emphasize the desirability of being respectful and considerate toward one's sexual partner are important tools in reducing sexual aggression. Many college campuses experience persistent problems with alcohol abuse, which can be a key factor in many rapes and other forms of sexual aggression. Preventing and treating alcohol abuse, therefore, can make for healthier, safer campuses.

Family violence, too, is a matter of grave societal concern, and, because it is caused by multiple factors, it must be addressed by a variety of approaches. Laws and programs that protect victims of abuse and reduce the likelihood of continued violence by abusers are vitally important. But family violence takes place in a larger context. As Peter Sidebotham and Jon Heron (2006) have observed, "The association between poverty and child maltreatment is one of the most consistent observations in the published research" (p. 499). Thus, protecting families from violence also means providing family members with educational and employment opportunities. Furthermore, because abuse of alcohol and other drugs so often leads to family violence, better education about the effects of such substances, as well as support for individuals who need help dealing with them, would be a worthy investment not only for these individuals but also for the people around them.

Ultimately, effective communication is the key to reducing intimate violence. Jealousy and distrust contribute to much of the violence that occurs between intimate partners. Insensitivities to others' needs and fears as well as acceptance of myths about rape play important roles in sexual aggression. And children who grow up in abusive homes may learn aggressive scripts that teach them that the best way to respond to social problems is through aggression. Better communication can help address all of these problems.

▊ Conclusions

Since war begins in the minds of men, it is in the minds of men that the defenses of peace must be constructed.

—Constitution of UNESCO

We began this chapter with several stories of violence. A review of this chapter will reveal social psychological research in each section that is relevant to various aspects of the lives of the perpetrators involved in these shootings and in the wave of school shootings that we have referenced in the chapter. Some of the people behind these acts of violence grew up in a "culture of honor" that may have glorified violence in response to perceived threats to their status and manhood. Many experienced great frustrations in their lives, felt isolated and lonely, had easy access to weapons and hate-filled propaganda, and were consumers of brutal violence in TV shows, movies, and especially video games. Some were exposed to abuse within their families.

TABLE 11.5

Some Steps to Reduce Aggression and Violence

Although there may be other reasons to endorse or reject the ideas below, social psychological research on aggression suggests that each has the potential to reduce aggression.

- Enlarge opportunities to achieve the goals valued by society (such as social approval, status, financial success) through nonviolent means.
- Reward nonaggressive behavior.
- Provide attractive models of peaceful behavior.
- Reduce all forms of aggression in our society, including physical punishment of children, capital punishment of criminals, and war.
- Reduce frustration by improving the quality of life in housing, health care, employment, and child care.
- Provide fans and air-conditioned shelters when it's hot.
- Reduce access to and display of weapons.
- Apologize when you've angered someone, and regard apologies as a sign of strength—not weakness. Encourage others to do likewise.
- Stop and think when you feel your temper rising. Control it instead of letting it control you.
- Discourage excessive drinking of alcohol and support efforts to provide treatment for alcohol abuse.
- Develop good communication skills in families and relationships, thereby helping to avoid misperceptions, jealousy, and distrust.
- Pay attention and respond to warning signs of trouble in adolescents, including social isolation, talk of violence, and consumption of violence-filled literature and other media.

The problem of school shootings in particular grew to such proportions that the U.S. Secret Service, whose mission is to protect the president, became involved, launching an intensive study. The initial findings indicated that the best way to predict those most likely to aggress was to listen to what the individuals themselves had to say, because many of them revealed, in one way or another, their aggressive thoughts and hostile attitudes before they committed their terrible actions. This conclusion parallels the crucial point we have already stated: Communication and social support are critically important factors in reducing violence.

Table 11.5 lists some of the possible steps suggested by the research we've reviewed. You may not agree that all of these actions are desirable, and you may prefer others that are not mentioned. What's important is to realize that each of us can do something to reduce aggression. There are many paths to take toward this common goal. And because aggression is caused by multiple factors, it is only through multiple paths that we can reach this goal.

REVIEW

What Is Aggression?

- Aggression is behavior intended to harm another individual.
- Anger is an emotional response to perceived injury; hostility is an antagonistic attitude.
- Instrumental aggression is a means to obtain a desired outcome.
- In emotional aggression, harm is inflicted for its own sake.

Culture, Gender, and Individual Differences

Culture and Aggression

- The rates of violence and the forms violence takes vary dramatically from one society to another.
- Some research suggests that individualistic cultures tend to have higher rates of aggression than collectivistic cultures.
- The forms that aggression may take and attitudes about whether various practices should be considered aggression vary across cultures.
- Bullying is a persistent and widespread problem that affects a large number of young people in the world.
- Within a society, different subcultures exhibit different norms concerning aggression.
- Teenagers and young adults, African Americans, and people in the South are the groups most prone to violence in the United States.

Gender and Aggression

- Men are more violent than women in virtually every culture and time period that has been studied.
- Males tend to be more overtly, physically aggressive than females.
- Females are somewhat more indirectly or relationally aggressive than males.

Individual Differences

- There is some stability in aggression: Aggression in childhood predicts aggression in adulthood.
- People who tend to hold hostile cognitions, express anger, and exhibit irritability tend to behave more aggressively.
- Some other personality traits are associated with aggression only after provocation. These include emotional susceptibility, narcissism, Type A personality, and impulsivity.

Origins of Aggression

Is Aggression Innate?

- Evolutionary psychology views aggression as a universal, innate characteristic that has evolved from natural and sexual selection pressures.
- Evolutionary accounts propose that gender differences in aggression can be traced to competition for status (and the most desirable mates) and sexual jealousy.

- Some research suggests that individual differences in aggression are produced by genetic inheritance.
- The sex hormone testosterone and the neurotransmitter serotonin appear to play roles in human aggression.
- Impairments in several areas of the brain, especially to executive functioning, are associated with aggressiveness.
- Biological factors interact with social factors in producing or regulating aggression.

Is Aggression Learned?

- Aggression is increased when it is rewarded.
- Aggression is decreased by punishment only under specific conditions that are often not met in the real world.
- Physical punishment of children is associated with increases in their subsequent aggressive behavior.
- Social learning theory emphasizes the influence of models on the behavior of observers.
- Models who obtain desired goals through the use of aggression and are not punished for their behavior are the most likely to be imitated. But even punished models may encourage aggression in observers.
- Aggressive models teach not only specific behaviors but also more general attitudes and ideas about aggression and aggressive "scripts" that guide behavior.

- Growing up in a household or community with a lot of aggression and violence increases the likelihood that one will become an aggressive person.
- Peaceful models can decrease aggressive responses in observers.

Gender Differences and Socialization: "Boys Will Be Boys"

- Gender and cultural differences in human aggression may be due in part to differences in socialization practices—lessons taught, reinforcements and punishments given, models offered, and roles and norms emphasized.

Culture and Socialization: Cultures of Honor

- A culture of honor promotes status-protecting aggression among white males in the American South and West as well as among men in other parts of the world, such as in Brazil and Chile.

Nature Versus Nurture: A False Debate?

- Human aggression clearly is affected by learning and experience.
- In aggression, as in all human behavior, biological and environmental influences interact.

Situational Influences on Aggression

Frustration: Aggression as a Drive

- The frustration-aggression hypothesis proposes that frustration produces the motive to aggress and that aggression is caused by frustration.
- But in fact, frustration produces many motives, and aggression is caused by many factors.
- According to the frustration-aggression hypothesis, displacement occurs if aggression against the source of frustration is inhibited.
- The frustration-aggression hypothesis holds that engaging in any aggressive action reduces the motive to engage in further aggression, a process called catharsis.
- In the long run, however, aggression now is likely to increase aggression later.
- Frustration is only one of a number of unpleasant experiences that produce negative affect and increase aggression.
- Some studies support the idea of displacement of aggression. However, most research does not support the idea of catharsis as an effective means to reduce aggression.

Negative Affect

- A wide variety of noxious stimuli can create negative feelings and increase aggression.
- The negative affect due to provocation is a key factor behind much aggression.
- Hot temperatures are associated with increased aggression and violence.

- Experiencing social rejection is particularly aversive and can increase aggressive responses.
- Positive emotional responses are incompatible with negative affect and reduce retaliatory aggression.

Arousal: "Wired" for Action

- Highly arousing stimuli increase retaliatory aggression.

Thought: Automatic and Deliberate

- Situational cues associated with aggression, such as the presence of a gun, can automatically activate aggression-related thoughts and increase aggressive behavior.
- Individuals differ in what associations they have with different kinds of weapons.
- Deliberate thoughts that affect aggression include the perception of the cost or appropriateness of aggression.
- The extent to which individuals perceive hostile intent in others is an important factor in predicting aggression.
- Social rejection can cause people to make hostile attributions about the motives of others, which in turn increases aggressive responses.
- High arousal impairs the cognitive control of aggression, as does alcohol.

Situational Influences: Putting It All Together

- Aggression is influenced by separate and interactive effects of affect, arousal, and cognitions.

Media Effects

Violence in TV, Movies, Music Lyrics, and Video Games

- There is a tremendous amount of violence depicted in the media, and much of it is targeted to children and adolescents.
- A large number of studies, using a variety of different methods, have shown a significant positive relationship between exposure to media violence and real-world aggressive cognitions and behaviors.
- Exposure to TV violence in childhood is related to aggression later in life.
- In laboratory and field experiments, exposure to aggressive models increases aggressive behavior among adults and children.
- Exposure to indirect aggression on TV can promote subsequent real-world indirect aggression.
- Observing violence in the media can trigger aggressive cognitions and hostility.
- Because we habituate to familiar stimuli, repeated observation of violence desensitizes people to violence, reducing physiological arousal to new incidents. This desensitization can increase aggressive behavior and decrease helping behavior.
- Habitual viewing of media violence can suggest that aggression is rewarded, encourage imitation, and promote aggressive scripts, which can guide subsequent behavior.
- Through cultivation of a social reality, the mass media can intensify fear of aggression and encourage aggressive behavior.
- Prosocial song lyrics, TV programs, and video games can increase prosocial behavior.

Pornography

- In general, the evidence pointing to a causal link between viewing nonviolent pornography and aggressive behavior is weak, but the effect is stronger among individuals who are already predisposed to sexual aggression.
- Violent pornography increases aggression, particularly male-to-female aggression.
- When a female is portrayed as enjoying violent sex, even unprovoked men become more aggressive and more accepting of violence against women.
- The combination of interest in violent pornography and negative attitudes toward women is a strong predictor of self-reported sexual aggression in the past and sexually aggressive intentions for the future.

Intimate Violence: Trust Betrayed

Sexual Aggression Among College Students

- Men are more likely than women to engage in sexually coercive behavior.
- Alcohol consumption is involved in a majority of sexually aggressive incidents. Alcohol has several effects that increase the risk of sexual aggression.
- The combination of positive attitudes toward rape and negative attitudes toward women is associated with coercive sexual behavior.

Domestic Violence: Partner and Child Abuse

- Sexual jealousy and distrust fuel a great deal of violence between intimate partners.
- National surveys reveal that women engage in as much or more aggressive behavior against a partner as men do, but women are more likely to be killed, seriously injured, or sexually abused by a partner.
- A shockingly high number of children are victimized, often by parents and caretakers.
- Children who witness parental violence or are themselves abused are more likely as adults to abuse their partners and their own children. But most people escape from this cycle of violence.

Reducing Violence

Multiple Causes, Multiple Cures

- Recognizing that aggression has multiple levels of causes, multisystemic therapy has been effective in reducing aggressive behaviors among violent adolescents.
- Situational and sociocultural factors that can help reduce violence include the avoidance of negative affect, aggressive thinking, the presence of weapons, competitiveness, minor acts of aggression and vandalism, and social rewards for aggressive behavior.
- Models of nonviolent responses to social problems are also useful in reducing violent behavior.
- Educational efforts emphasizing the unrealistic nature of violent pornography have proved effective in reducing acceptance of rape myths.
- Sex education and rape-awareness programs can be effective in helping prevent sexual aggression.

- Because of the role of alcohol consumption in rape and other forms of sexual aggression, it is all the more important for college campuses to develop more effective prevention and treatments of alcohol abuse.

- Protecting the victims of family violence and preventing its recurrence require a wide range of interventions.

Conclusions

- Communication and social support are critically important factors in reducing violence.

Key Terms

aggression (436)
catharsis (455)
cultivation (469)
cycle of violence (475)
desensitization (468)

displacement (455)
emotional aggression (437)
frustration-aggression hypothesis (454)
hostile attribution bias (461)

instrumental aggression (437)
pornography (471)
social learning theory (449)
weapons effect (459)

Media Resources

Social Psychology 8th Edition Companion Website
Visit your book companion website
www.cengage.com/psychology/kassin
where you will find flash cards, practice quizzes, Internet links, and more to help you study.

CENGAGENOW Just what you need to know NOW! Spend time on what you need to master rather than on information you already have learned. Take a pre-test for this chapter and CengageNOW will generate a personalized study plan based on your results. The study plan will identify the topics you need to review and direct you to online resources to help you master those topics. You can then take a post-test to help you determine the concepts you have mastered and what you will need to work on. Try it out! Go to **academic .cengage.com/login** to sign in with an access code or to purchase access to this product.

Putting COMMON SENSE *to the Test*

In virtually every culture, males are more violent than females.

True. *In almost all cultures and time periods that have been studied, men commit the large majority of violent crimes.*

For virtually any category of aggression, males are more aggressive than females.

False. *Girls tend to be somewhat more indirectly, or relationally, aggressive than boys.*

Children who are spanked or otherwise physically disciplined (but not abused) for behaving aggressively tend to become less aggressive.

False. *Evidence indicates that the use of even a little physical punishment to discipline children is associated with increases in subsequent aggressive and antisocial behavior by the children, even years later, although this relationship may depend on a variety of other factors.*

Blowing off steam by engaging in safe but aggressive activities (such as sports) makes people less likely to aggress later.

False. *Although people may be less likely to aggress immediately after such activities, initial aggression makes future aggression more—not less—likely.*

Exposure to TV violence in childhood is related to aggression later in life.

True. *Laboratory experiments, field experiments, and correlational research all suggest a link between exposure to violence on TV and subsequent aggressive behavior.*

Men are much more likely than women to aggress against their spouses or partners.

False. *Evidence suggests that women engage in as many or more acts of serious aggression against their partners as men, but men are much more likely to injure, sexually abuse, or kill their partners.*

12

IN GOD WE TRUST

Law

This chapter examines applications of social psychology to the law. First, we consider three stages in the life of a jury trial: jury selection, an often controversial process; the courtroom drama in which confessions, eyewitness identifications, and other types of evidence are presented; and jury deliberation, where the jury reaches a group decision. Next, we consider posttrial factors such as sentencing and prison, the possible result of a guilty verdict. Finally, we discuss perceptions of justice both inside and outside the courtroom.

It seems that there is always a high-profile case in the news that spotlights a crime of sex, violence, money, passion, or celebrity and that captures our interest. The twenty-first century is still young, and yet we have already witnessed the public trials of various corrupt executives, celebrities, and terrorists. We even saw a world leader brought to trial—when former Iraqi president Saddam Hussein was captured in 2003 by American forces, then tried in Baghdad, convicted, and hung for crimes committed against the people of Iraq. There will be more high-profile trials to come, of course; examples include the corruption case against former Illinois governor Rod Blagojevich and the federal trials of Guantánamo Bay detainees.

Then there is Philip Markoff, a 22-year-old medical student who was arrested in the spring of 2009 by Boston police for the hotel room murder of a masseuse and for other crimes of violence against strippers and other women who had advertised for erotic services on Craigslist. Is this man the Craigslist killer? At first, his friends insisted that he is not capable of such violence—and they started a Facebook page in his support. Yet police report that he was seen on a hotel surveillance camera at the time in question and that items belonging to at least two victims were found in his apartment.

Not all spectacular crimes involve violence. In the fall of 2008, former NAS-DAQ chair Bernie Madoff was arrested for running an elaborate $50 billion Ponzi scheme that claimed more than 14,000 individual and institutional victims (Bandler & Varchaver, 2009). Clinical forensic psychologists who study the criminal mind see the narcissistic Madoff as a "white collar psychopath" who harms others with callous and vicious indifference. But this case also raises intriguing questions for social psychologists interested in law. For example, it appears that the 70-year-old Madoff had first started his Ponzi scheme many years ago, putting himself into a gradually escalating trap from which he could not escape without punishment, even if he were inclined to do so. Also troubling is the extent to which Madoff was able to deceive all those whose money he "managed." Remarkably, despite servicing an elite group of clients motivated by high-stakes investments, Madoff demonstrated what social

Philip Markoff, a young medical student, was arrested by Boston police for the murder of a masseuse and for other crimes of violence against women who had offered erotic services on Craigslist (left). Illustrating that not all crimes involve youth and violence, former NASDAQ Chair Bernie Madoff was arrested—and is now in prison for life—for running a $50 billion Ponzi scheme that victimized thousands (right).

perception research has long shown: that people are notoriously inept at telling the difference between truths and lies.

Regardless of how you feel about these cases, they clearly illustrate the profound relevance of social psychology at work in the legal system, raising many questions: What kinds of people do lawyers select as jurors, and why? Can partisans set aside their biases in decision making? How reliable are confessions, eyewitnesses, and other types of evidence presented in court? Are the decision makers contaminated by pretrial publicity and other information not in evidence? How do trial juries reach unanimous verdicts after days, weeks, or months of presentations that are often followed by exhausting deliberation? In this chapter, we take social psychology into the courtroom to answer these questions. But first, let's place the trial process in a broader context.

In the U.S. criminal justice system, the trial is just the tip of an iceberg. Once a crime is committed, it must be detected and then reported if it is to receive further attention. Through investigation, the police must then find a suspect and decide whether to make an arrest. If they do, the suspect is jailed or bail is set and a judge or grand jury decides if there is sufficient evidence for a formal accusation. If there is, the prosecuting and defense lawyers begin a lengthy process known as "discovery," during which they gather evidence. At this point, many defendants plead guilty as part of a deal negotiated by the lawyers. In cases that do go to trial, the ordeal does not then end with a verdict. After conviction, the trial judge imposes a sentence and the defendant decides whether to appeal to a higher court. For those in prison, decisions concerning their release are made by parole boards.

As ▶ Figure 12.1 illustrates, the criminal justice apparatus is complex and the actors behind the scenes are numerous. Yet through it all, the trial—a relatively infrequent event—is the heart and soul of the system. The threat of trial motivates parties to gather evidence and, later, to negotiate a deal. And when it is over, the trial by judge or jury forms the basis for sentencing and appeals decisions. Social psychologists have a lot to say about trials and other aspects of the legal system as well (Brewer & Williams, 2005; Greene et al., 2007; Wrightsman & Fulero, 2008).

The issues that social psychologists are now studying are broad and varied. At present, for example, researchers are looking at whether police can tell when someone is lying and how they can make these judgments more accurately (Granhag & Strömwall, 2004; Vrij, 2008); at how juries make decisions in civil lawsuits involving large sums of

▶ FIGURE 12.1

Overview of the American Criminal Justice System

This flow chart presents the movement of cases through different branches of the criminal justice system. As illustrated here, the trial is just one aspect of the criminal justice system.

Adapted from the President's Commission on Law Enforcement and Administration of Justice, 1967.

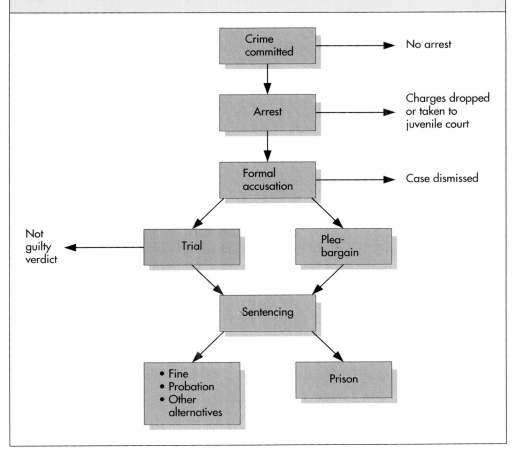

money (Greene & Bornstein, 2003; Bornstein et al., 2008); at how juries react to a battle of opposing experts in the courtroom (Levett & Kovera, 2008); at how people evaluate claims of sexual harassment within different legal frameworks (Wiener et al., 2002); and at how the U.S. Supreme Court receives oral arguments and makes decisions (Wrightsman, 2006, 2008). Importantly, much of what social psychologists have discovered in the legal arena is not known to judges, lawyers, and laypeople as a matter of common sense (Borgida & Fiske, 2007). In the coming pages, we divide the trial process into three basic stages: jury selection, the presentation of evidence, and the jury's deliberations.

Jury Selection

If you're ever accused of a crime in the United States or involved in a lawsuit, you have a constitutional right to a trial by an impartial jury from your community. This right is considered essential to doing justice within a democracy. Yet whenever a controversial verdict is reached in a high-profile case, people, right or wrong, blame the twelve individuals who constituted the jury. That's why it is important to know how juries are selected.

Jury selection is a three-stage process. First, the court uses voter registration lists, telephone directories, and other sources to compile a master list of eligible citizens who live in the community. Second, so that a representative sample can be obtained, a certain number of people from the list are randomly drawn and summoned for duty. If you've ever been called, you know what happens next. Before people who appear in court are placed on a jury, they are subject to what is known as **voir dire**, a pretrial interview in which the judge and lawyers question the prospective jurors for signs of bias. If someone knows one of the parties, has an interest in the outcome of the case, or has already formed an opinion, the judge will excuse that person "for cause." In fact, if it can be proven that an entire community is biased, perhaps because of pretrial publicity, then the trial might be postponed or moved to another location.

Although the procedure seems straightforward, there is more to the story. In addition to de-selecting individuals who are clearly biased, the lawyers are permitted to exercise **peremptory challenges**. That is, they can reject a certain limited number of prospective jurors even if they seem fair and open-minded, and they can do so without having to state reasons or win the judge's approval. Why would a lawyer challenge someone who appears to be impartial? What guides lawyers' decisions to accept some jurors and reject others? These questions make the process of voir dire particularly interesting to social psychologists (Vidmar & Hans, 2007).

"I see jury selection has begun."

Trial Lawyers as Intuitive Psychologists

Rumor has it that trial lawyers have used some unconventional methods to select juries. Under pressure to make choices quickly and without much information, lawyers rely on implicit personality theories and stereotypes. As described in Chapter 4, an implicit personality theory is a set of assumptions that people make about how certain attributes are related to each other and to behavior. When we believe that all members of a group share the same attributes, these implicit theories are called stereotypes.

As far as trial practice is concerned, how-to books claim that the astute lawyer can predict a juror's verdict by his or her gender, race, age, ethnic background, and other simple demographics. It has been suggested, for example, that athletes lack sympathy for fragile and injured victims, that engineers are unemotional, that men with beards resist authority, and that cabinetmakers are so meticulous in their work that they will never be completely satisfied with the evidence. Clarence Darrow, one of the most prominent trial attorneys of the twentieth century, suggested that jurors of southern European descent favored the defense whereas those from Scandinavia favored the prosecution. Other lawyers have theorized that women are more skeptical as jurors than men, particularly in response to attractive female witnesses. Still others offer selection advice based on faces, facial expressions, body language, and clothing. Perhaps the most interesting rule of thumb is also the simplest: "If you don't like a juror's face, chances are he doesn't like yours either!" (Wishman, 1986, pp. 72–73).

voir dire   The pretrial examination of prospective jurors by the judge or opposing lawyers to uncover signs of bias.

peremptory challenge   A means by which lawyers can exclude a limited number of prospective jurors without the judge's approval.

The intuitive approach to jury selection by which lawyers use peremptory challenges may provide for colorful stories from inside the courtroom, but the consequences of this kind of stereotyping for justice can be troubling. For example, what if a prosecutor were to use peremptory challenges to exclude from the jury all whites, blacks, Latinos, or Asians; or all men or all women, possibly stripping the jury of the defendant's peers? In recent years, the U.S. Supreme Court has for the first time limited the use of peremptory challenges to prevent lawyers from systematically excluding prospective jurors on the basis of race. According to the Court, judges can now require lawyers suspected of discriminating in this way to explain the basis of their challenges (*Batson v. Kentucky*, 1986; *Miller-El v. Dretke*, 2005).

Citing social psychological research on stereotyping and prejudice, Sommers and Norton (2008) point to two problems: (1) The influence of conscious and unconscious racial stereotypes on social perceptions is prevalent and likely to influence lawyers in the courtroom; and (2) these racial biases are difficult to identify in specific instances because lawyers, like everyone else, typically do not acknowledge having been influenced by their stereotypes. In a study that illustrated both points, Sommers and Norton (2007) presented college students, law students, and attorneys with a summary of a criminal trial involving a black defendant and asked them to choose between two prospective jurors with various characteristics—one white, the other black. As predicted, all groups were far more likely to challenge the juror who was black rather than the one who was white, yet very few subjects cited race as a factor in their decisions.

The intuitive approach to jury selection sometimes leads to discrimination on the basis of race and other characteristics. This approach is also not very effective. Thus, although some experienced trial attorneys take pride in their jury-selection skills, researchers have found that most lawyers cannot effectively predict how jurors will vote, either on the basis of their intuitive rules of thumb (Olczak et al., 1991) or by relying on how prospective jurors answer questions during the voir dire (Kerr et al., 1991; Zeisel & Diamond, 1978). Apparently, whether a juror characteristic predicts verdicts depends on the specifics of each and every case. Hence a new service industry was born: scientific jury selection.

Contrary to popular opinion, women are harsher as trial jurors than men are. **FALSE.**

Scientific Jury Selection

In a movie based on John Grisham's *The Runaway Jury*, a ruthless jury consultant named Rankin Fitch, played by Gene Hackman, helps lawyers select jurors through the use of intrusive high-tech surveillance work. Burrowing deep into the lives of prospective jurors, Fitch trails them, investigates them, and even resorts at times to bribery, blackmail, and intimidation. Determined to stack the jury in order to defend gun company defendants against a multimillion-dollar wrongful death lawsuit, Fitch declares, "A trial is too important to be left up to juries."

Grisham's depiction of jury consulting is a work of fiction, not fact. But it is based on a kernel of truth. Instead of relying on hunches, successful stock market investors, baseball managers, and poker players play the odds whenever they can. Now many trial lawyers do too. In recent years, the "art" of jury selection has been transformed into a "science" (Lieberman & Sales, 2007).

This use of jury consultants began during the Vietnam War era, when the federal government prosecuted a group of antiwar activists known as the Harrisburg Seven. The case against the defendants was strong, and the trial was to be held in the conservative city of Harrisburg, Pennsylvania. To help the defense select a jury, sociologist Jay Schulman and his colleagues (1973) surveyed the local community by interviewing 840 residents. Two kinds of information were taken from each resident: demographic

In *Runaway Jury*, a film based on John Grisham's novel, actor Gene Hackman played feared jury consultant Rankin Fitch. In a film that blurred fact and fiction, Fitch not only researched prospective jurors for jury selection purposes but also engaged in jury tampering, blackmail, and other illegal tactics in a desperate but failed effort to win the verdict.

(for example, sex, race, age, and education) and attitudes relevant to the trial (for example, attitudes toward the government, the war, and political dissent). By correlating these variables, Schulman's team came up with a profile of the ideal defense juror: "a female Democrat with no religious preference and a white-collar job or a skilled blue-collar job" (p. 40). Guided by this result, the defense selected its jury. The rest is history: Against all odds, the trial ended in a hung jury, split 10 to 2 in favor of acquittal.

Twenty-five years later, in the criminal trial against O. J. Simpson, the defense team hired a jury consultant to help in the selection process. Based on pretrial surveys, this consultant predicted that African American women would prove to be Simpson's strongest defenders. Public opinion polls and other research later confirmed the more general point that race may have played a role in this particular case (Murray et al., 1997). Prosecutor Marcia Clark also had the help of a jury consultant who found exactly the same result. However, Clark rejected his advice in favor of her intuitive belief that black women would be enraged by Simpson's history of domestic violence. Again, the rest is history. After four hours of deliberation, the criminal jury found Simpson not guilty of all charges (Toobin, 1996).

Today, the technique known as **scientific jury selection** is used often, especially in high-profile criminal trials and civil trials in which large sums of money are at stake. Research shows, for example, that jurors are differently predisposed when confronted with cases that pit lone individuals against large corporations, with some people favoring big business and others harboring an anti-business prejudice (Hans, 2000). How is scientific jury selection carried out? What are the methods used? The procedure is simple. Because lawyers are often not allowed to ask jurors intrusive and personal questions, they try to determine jurors' attitudes and verdict tendencies from information that is known about their backgrounds. The relevance of this information can be determined through focus groups, mock juries, or community-wide surveys, in which statistical relationships are sought between general demographic factors and attitudes relevant to a particular case. Then, during the voir dire, lawyers ask prospective jurors about their backgrounds and use peremptory challenges to exclude those whose profiles are associated with unfavorable attitudes.

As you might expect, scientific jury selection is a controversial enterprise. By law, consultants are not permitted to communicate with or approach the prospective jurors themselves, despite the tactics portrayed in *Runaway Jury*. But how effective are the techniques that are employed? It's hard to say. On the one hand, trial lawyers who have used scientific jury selection boast an impressive winning percentage. On the other hand, it is impossible to know the extent to which these victories are attributable to the jury-selection surveys (Strier, 1999). So does scientific jury selection work? Although extensive data are lacking, it appears that attitudes can influence verdicts in some cases and that pretrial research can help lawyers identify these attitudes (Seltzer, 2006). As we'll soon see, the linkage between attitudes and verdicts is particularly strong in cases that involve capital punishment.

Before concluding our review of scientific jury selection, let's stop to consider an ethical question: Is justice enhanced or impaired by the intervention of professional jury consultants? Is the real goal for lawyers to eliminate jurors who are biased or to create juries slanted in their favor? Those who practice scientific jury selection argue

scientific jury selection
A method of selecting juries through surveys that yield correlations between demographics and trial-relevant attitudes.

that picking juries according to survey results is simply a more refined version of what lawyers are permitted to do by intuition. If there's a problem, they say, it is not in the *science* but in the *law* that permits trial attorneys to use peremptory challenges to exclude jurors who are not obviously biased. In response, critics argue that scientific jury selection tips the scales of justice in favor of wealthy clients who can afford the service, an outcome that further widens the socioeconomic gap that exists within the courts. Hence, Neil and Dorit Kressel (2002), authors of *Stack and Sway: The New Science of Jury Consulting*, argue that peremptory challenges, which enable lawyers and their consultants to strike jurors who are not overtly biased, should be abolished.

Juries in Black and White: Does Race Matter?

The year was 1995; the scene was a Los Angeles courthouse. All eyes were focused on the so-called trial of the century. O. J. Simpson was charged with the murders of his ex-wife Nicole Brown and her friend Ronald Goldman. The trial was packed with drama: Simpson was a Hall of Fame football hero, sportscaster, and actor; the crime was violent; and the defense lawyers claimed that Simpson was framed by racist police. To many Americans who followed the case, the evidence against Simpson seemed overwhelming. So when he was found not guilty by a twelve-person jury that included eight African Americans, the verdict was seen as a symptom of the racial divide in America. More recently, when Duke University lacrosse students, who were white, stood accused of raping a local prostitute, who was black, speculation about the biasing effects of race was once again rampant.

To what extent does a juror's race color his or her decision making? Research suggests that there is no simple answer. In one study, Norbert Kerr and others (1995) tested the most intuitive hypothesis of all, that jurors favor defendants who are similar to themselves. They presented mixed-race groups with a strong or weak case involving a black or white defendant. They found that when the evidence was weak, the participants were more lenient in their verdicts toward the defendant of the same race. Yet when the evidence was strong, they were harsher against that similar defendant, as if distancing themselves from his or her wrongdoing.

In a second study, Sommers and Ellsworth (2001) tested the popular notion that jurors will show preference for others of their racial group when a crime involves race, as when it is a motivated hate crime or when attorneys "play the race card" in arguments to the jury. Yet they found the opposite pattern. When race was not an issue that is "on the radar," white jurors predictably treated the defendant more favorably when he was white than when he was black. Yet when race was made a prominent issue at trial, white jurors bent over backward *not* to appear prejudiced and did not discriminate. Other research has shown that jurors may at times be motivated to watch for racist tendencies in themselves, leading them to process trial information even more carefully when a defendant is black than when he or she is white (Sargent & Bradfield, 2004).

The potential for individual jurors to exhibit racial bias may also depend on the composition of the jury with whom they expect to deliberate. In a courthouse located in Ann Arbor, Michigan, Sommers (2006) showed a *Court TV* summary of a sexual assault trial in which the defendant was African American. A total of 200 locals participated in 29 six-person mock juries after a voir dire that either did or did not make race an issue. Ultimately, the juries that were formed were either all white or heterogeneous, consisting of four whites and two blacks. After the videotaped trial summary but before the groups deliberated, each juror was asked to indicate his or her verdict preference. Look at ▶ Figure 12.2, and you'll see that jurors were influenced by the

▶ **FIGURE 12.2**

Effects of Racial Diversity on the Jury

Six-person mock juries watched the trial of an African American defendant in groups that were homogeneous (all white) or diverse (four white, two black). In some cases, the issue of race was raised during the voir dire; in others, it was not. Either way, the white jurors in homogeneous groups were more likely to vote guilty than white jurors in diverse groups who, in turn, were more likely to vote guilty than black jurors in diverse groups. It seems that individual jurors are influenced in their decisions by the racial composition of their groups.

Sommers, 2006.

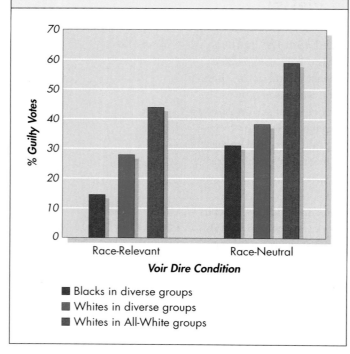

- Blacks in diverse groups
- Whites in diverse groups
- Whites in All-White groups

racial composition of their groups as a whole. In diverse groups, 34 percent of white jurors voted guilty compared to 23 percent of black jurors—a small difference. In the all-white groups, however, 51 percent of jurors voted guilty, which represented a significant jump compared to both blacks and whites in the more diverse groups.

Death Qualification

On February 3, 1998, a 38-year-old convicted ax murderer named Karla Faye Tucker died by lethal injection in Huntsville, Texas. At 6:45 P.M., eight minutes after lethal chemicals were pumped into her arms, Tucker moaned, then moved her lips as in prayer, gasped twice, and died with her eyes open. Outside the prison walls, one group of protesters lit candles and sang, while another crowd cheered and waved signs that read "God bless the death penalty." Because Tucker was a woman and a born-again Christian, her execution drew worldwide attention. Pope John Paul II wrote a letter on her behalf, as did the European Parliament and the United Nations. On the question of her punishment, people were divided.

Over the years, the death penalty has stimulated a heated public debate in America (Bedau & Cassell, 2004). Think about it: If you had to sentence someone to die, could you do it? Not everyone answers this question in the same way. Yet your answer could mean the difference between life and death for a defendant convicted of murder. Today, a majority of American states permit capital punishment. Among those that do, the jury decides not only the verdict but the sentence as well. In these cases, it is not surprising that sentencing decisions are influenced not only by the facts of a specific case but also by jurors' general attitudes toward the death penalty. Kevin O'Neil and his colleagues (2004) found that these attitudes are composed of various beliefs, such as beliefs in the legitimacy of retribution and revenge ("There are some murderers whose death would give me a sense of personal satisfaction"), deterrence ("The death penalty makes criminals think twice before committing murder"), and cost ("Executing a murderer is less expensive than keeping him in jail for the rest of his life"). Monica Miller and David Hayward (2008) found that people who favor the death penalty are more likely to hold fundamentalist religious views and a belief in the literal interpretation of the Bible. Brooke Butler and Gary Moran (2007) found that people who favor the death penalty also tend to harbor authoritarian beliefs and the belief that the world is a just place in which people get what they deserve and deserve what they get.

In cases involving crimes punishable by death and in which the jury makes both decisions, a special jury-selection practice known as **death qualification** is typically used. Through death qualification, judges may exclude all prospective jurors who say that they would refuse to vote for the death penalty. These jurors are excluded for the entire trial. To ensure that *sentencing* decisions are unbiased, it makes sense to exclude those who admit they are close-minded. But does this same selection prac-

death qualification A jury-selection procedure used in capital cases that permits judges to exclude prospective jurors who say they would not vote for the death penalty.

tice tip the balance toward the prosecution when it comes to the *verdict*? In other words, are death-qualified juries prone to convict?

Through a series of studies, Phoebe Ellsworth, Craig Haney, and others have examined this question. Their results have shown that compared to people who oppose the death penalty, those who support it are more prosecution-minded on a host of issues. For example, they are more concerned about crime, more trustful of police, more cynical about defense lawyers, and less tolerant of procedures that are designed to protect the accused (Fitzgerald & Ellsworth, 1984; Haney et al., 1994). When it comes to trial verdicts, the difference can be substantial. In one study, 288 people watched a videotaped murder trial and then participated in mock juries. The results showed that jurors who said they were willing to impose the death penalty were more likely to vote guilty both before and after deliberating than were those who would have been excluded for their refusal to impose a death sentence (Cowan et al., 1984).

Similar results have been found in studies of real jurors (Moran & Comfort, 1986). In fact, Haney (1984) found that hearing death-qualification voir dire questions themselves is biasing because these questions presume the defendant's guilt and communicate to prospective jurors that the courts consider death a desirable form of punishment. In his studies, even randomly selected mock jurors were more likely to vote for conviction—and for the death penalty—when exposed to such questions during the voir dire than when they were not.

As the research evidence mounted, American courts had to face a sobering prospect. Were hundreds of prisoners on death row tried by juries that were biased against them? In the case of *Lockhart v. McCree* (1986), the U.S. Supreme Court considered the issue. To inform the Court of recent research, the American Psychological Association submitted an exhaustive review of the literature (Bersoff & Ogden, 1987)—but to no avail. In an opinion that disappointed many social psychologists, the Court rejected the research and ruled that death qualification does not violate a defendant's right to a fair trial.

Should the Supreme Court have been persuaded by the research findings of social psychologists? Some say yes (Ellsworth, 1991); others say no (Elliott, 1991). Either way, it is now important to devise alternative, non-prejudicial methods that can be used to select capital juries. For example, research shows that many people who would be excluded because of a *general* opposition to capital punishment also admit that they would consider the death penalty for *specific* defendants found guilty of committing atrocious acts of violence—suggesting that perhaps these individuals should not be removed from the jury (Cox & Tanford, 1989). This issue continues to spark interest and concern among social psychologists (Costanzo, 1997). It is especially relevant these days, in light of sobering revelations brought about by DNA tests showing that many prisoners, including many on death row, did not commit the crimes for which they were convicted (Baumgartner et al., 2008).

Worldwide, the most common methods of execution are by hanging, shooting, and beheading. In the United States, the most commonly used methods are electrocution, lethal injection, and poisonous gas—as delivered in this gas chamber. For more information on the death penalty, such as up-to-date lists of death-row inmates, visit http://www.deathpenaltyinfo.org/home.

"Ask the judge whether we can find the defendant not guilty and still execute him."

The Courtroom Drama

Once a jury is selected, the trial officially begins and the evidence previously gathered comes to life. The evidence produced in the courtroom can range far and wide, from confessions to autopsy results, medical tests, bloodstains, hair samples, handwriting samples, diaries, fingerprints, photographs, and business documents. The trial is a well-orchestrated event. Lawyers for both sides make opening statements. Witnesses then answer questions under oath. Lawyers make closing arguments. The judge instructs the jury. Yet there are many problems in this all-too-human enterprise: The evidence may not be accurate or reliable, jurors may be biased by extraneous factors, and judges' instructions may fall on deaf ears. In this section, we identify some of the problems and possible solutions.

▌ Confession Evidence

Every now and then, an extraordinary event comes along that shakes the way you think. The Central Park jogger case was one of these events. In 1989, five boys who were 14 to 16 years old were found guilty of a monstrous assault and rape of a female jogger in New York's Central Park after they confessed (four of them on videotape) in vivid detail. Thirteen years later, a serial rapist named Matias Reyes stepped forward from prison to say that he alone, not the boys, had committed the crime. As part of a thorough investigation of Reyes's claim, the district attorney DNA-tested the semen from the crime scene and found that it was a match: Reyes was the rapist. The five boys, now men, were innocent. Their confessions were false and the convictions were vacated (Kassin, 2002; Saulny, 2002).

Police Interrogations: Social Influence Under Pressure   As these events unfolded, questions mounted: Why would five boys—or anyone else, for that matter—confess to a crime they did not commit? In general, what social influences are brought to bear on suspects interrogated by police? Many years ago, police detectives would use bright lights, brute force, rubber hose, and physical intimidation to get confessions. Today, however, the police are required to warn suspects of their Miranda rights to silence and an attorney, and the "third degree" tactics they use are more psychological in nature. In *Criminal Interrogation and Confessions*, the most popular how-to manual written for police, Fred Inbau and others (2001) have advised interrogators to put suspects alone

In 1989, 16-year-old Kharey Wise (left) and four other teenagers confessed to raping a jogger in New York's Central Park. Based solely on his confession, Wise was convicted and sent to prison. Thirteen years later, Matias Reyes (right) admitted that he alone, not the boys, had committed the crime. DNA tests confirmed that Reyes was the rapist. The boys, despite their confessions, were innocent.

Courtesy ABCNEWS.com

Courtesy of ABCNEWS.com

into a small, bare, soundproof room, a physical environment designed to arouse feelings of social isolation, helplessness, and discomfort. Next, they present a vivid nine-step procedure designed to get suspects to confess (see Table 12.1).

Once a suspect is isolated, this method of interrogation offers two approaches. One approach is to pressure the suspect into submission by expressing certainty in his or her guilt and even, at times, claiming to have damaging evidence such as fingerprints or an eyewitness. In this way, the accused is led to believe that it is futile to mount a defense. A second approach is to befriend the suspect, offer sympathy and friendly advice, and "minimize" the offense by offering face-saving excuses or blaming the victim. Lulled into a false sense of security and led to expect leniency, the suspect caves in. These tactics may sound as if they spring from a *Law & Order* TV script, but in real life they are routinely used (Gudjonsson, 2003; Kassin, 2005, 2008; Kassin & Gudjonsson, 2004; Leo, 2008; Zimbardo, 1967).

TABLE 12.1
The Nine Steps of Interrogation
1. Confront the suspect with assertions of his or her guilt.
2. Develop "themes" that appear to justify or excuse the crime.
3. Interrupt all statements of innocence and denial.
4. Overcome all of the suspect's objections to the charges.
5. Keep the increasingly passive suspect from tuning out.
6. Show sympathy and understanding and urge the suspect to tell all.
7. Offer the suspect a face-saving explanation for his or her guilty action.
8. Get the suspect to recount the details of the crime.
9. Convert that statement into a full written confession.
Inbau et al., 2001.

In an observational study of 182 live and videotaped interrogations, Richard Leo (1996) found that detectives used an average of five to six tactics per suspect. In a survey of 631 police investigators, Kassin and others (2007) found that the most common reported tactics were to physically isolate suspects, identify contradictions in their accounts, establish rapport, confront suspects with evidence of their guilt, appeals to self-interests, and offer sympathy and moral justification. In the years following 9/11, it is now clear that harsher, physically aversive methods of persuasion were also used to interrogate suspected terrorists (Mayer, 2007; McKelvey, 2007).

The Risk of False Confessions   It could be argued that the use of trickery and deception does not pose a serious problem because innocent people never confess to crimes they did not commit. This assumption, however, is incorrect. As hard as it is to believe, a number of chilling cases of false confessions are on record. In fact, research shows that among prisoners who were convicted and later proved innocent by DNA evidence, more than 20 percent had given false confessions to police (Garrett, 2008; Scheck et al., 2000). Importantly, too, this sample represents the mere tip of an iceberg. Although most case studies are based in the United States and England, proven false confessions have been documented in countries all over the world, including Canada, Norway, Finland, Germany, Iceland, Ireland, the Netherlands, Australia, New Zealand, China, and Japan (Kassin et al., 2010).

Sometimes innocent suspects confess as an act of *compliance*, to escape a bad situation. In the Central Park jogger case, the five boys had been in custody and interrogated by several detectives for some 14 to 30 hours before giving their videotaped confessions (most interrogations last an hour or two). Very long periods of time bring fatigue, despair, and a deprivation of sleep and other need states. The jogger, detectives, and suspects disagree about what transpired during these unrecorded hours, so it is impossible to know for sure. The defendants claimed that they were threatened, that promises were made in exchange for cooperation, and that the crime details that appeared in their confessions were suggested to them. Put simply, they said they cooperated thinking they would go home.

There are other instances in which interrogation causes innocent suspects to believe that they might be guilty of the crime, illustrating an even stronger form of social influence known as *internalization*. This process was evident in the recent story of three men and three women in Beatrice, Nebraska. In 1989, they were convicted of

If you're interested in learning more about false confessions, the Innocence Project would be a good place to start (Innocence Project, 2009).

the murder of a 68-year-old woman. Five of them pled guilty; four gave vividly detailed confessions during intense interrogations. Twenty years later, all six were pardoned after a full reinvestigation followed DNA testing that excluded them and identified the actual culprit. Immediately, the Nebraska Attorney General's Office announced that despite their confessions, these individuals were innocent "beyond all doubt." Yet remarkably, all of them had come to internalize the erroneous belief in their own guilt. In fact, one woman stood by her statement until just before she was pardoned, when she concluded, "I guess I was brainwashed" (Hammel, 2008).

Is it really possible to get people to confess to an act they did not commit? Based on the events of actual cases, Kassin and Kiechel (1996) theorized that two factors can increase this risk: (1) a suspect who lacks a clear memory of the event in question; and (2) the presentation of false evidence. To test this hypothesis, they recruited pairs of college students to work on a fast- or slow-paced computer task. At one point, the computer crashed and students were accused of having caused the damage by pressing a key they had been specifically instructed to avoid. All students were truly innocent and denied the charge. In half the sessions, however, the second student (who was really a confederate) said that she had seen the student hit the forbidden key. Demonstrating the process of compliance, many students confronted by this false witness agreed to sign a confession handwritten by the experimenter. Further demonstrating the process of internalization, some students later "admitted" guilt to a stranger (also a confederate) after the study was supposedly over and the two were alone. In short, innocent people who are vulnerable to suggestion can be induced to confess and to internalize guilt by the presentation of false evidence, an interrogation tactic the police sometimes use (see Table 12.2).

TABLE 12.2

Factors That Promote False Confessions

As participants worked on a fast- or slow-paced task, the computer crashed and they were accused of causing the damage. A confederate then said that she had or had not seen the participants hit the forbidden key. As shown, many participants signed a confession (compliance), and some even "admitted" their guilt in private to another confederate (internalization). Despite their innocence, many participants in the fast-false witness condition confessed on both measures.

| | Control | | False Witness | |
	Slow	Fast	Slow	Fast
Compliance	35%	65%	89%	100%
Internalization	0%	12%	44%	65%

Kassin & Kiechel, 1996.

This finding has been replicated on numerous occasions. In a study involving a completely different form of deception, Nash and Wade (2009) used digital editing software to fabricate visual evidence of participants in a computerized gambling experiment "stealing" money from the "bank" during a losing round. Presented with this false proof, all participants confessed—and most internalized the belief in their own guilt.

In another laboratory study, innocent students were led to confess to cheating, a possible violation of their university honor code. In this situation, Melissa Russano and others (2005) asked participants to solve a series of problems, sometimes alone and sometimes with a fellow participant (who was actually a confederate). In the trials, participants were instructed not to seek or provide assistance. In a guilty condition, the confederate asked for help, inducing most participants to break the rule. In an innocent condition, no such request was made. Moments later, the experimenter returned and interrogated everyone as to whether they had cheated. As part of this interrogation, the experimenter offered leniency for cooperation to some participants, minimized the seriousness of the violation to others, used both tactics, or used no tactics at all. Would students sign a confession to cheating? Yes. Table 12.3 shows that both promises and minimization increased the number of true confessions among students who broke the rule. But these same tactics also increased the rate of false confessions among students who did nothing wrong.

Confessions and the Jury: An Attributional Dilemma   How does the legal system treat confessions brought out by various methods of interrogation? The procedure is straightforward. Whenever a suspect confesses but then withdraws the statement, pleads not guilty, and goes to trial, the judge must determine whether the statement was voluntary or coerced. If the confession was clearly coerced—as when a suspect is isolated for long periods of time, deprived of food or sleep, threatened, or abused—it is excluded. If the confession is not coerced, it is admitted into evidence for the jury to evaluate.

In these cases, juries are confronted with a classic attribution dilemma: A suspect's statement may indicate guilt (personal attribution) or it may simply provide the suspect with a way to avoid the unpleasant consequences of silence (situational attribution). According to attribution theory, jurors should reject all confessions made in response to external pressure. But wait. Remember the fundamental attribution error? In Chapter 4, we saw that people tend to overattribute behavior to persons and overlook the influence of situational forces. Is it similarly possible, as in the Central Park jogger case, that jurors view suspects who confess as guilty even if they were highly pressured to confess during interrogation?

To examine this question, Kassin and Holly Sukel (1997) had mock jurors read one of three versions of a double murder trial. In a control version that did not contain a confession, only 19 percent voted guilty. In a low-pressure version in which the defendant was said to have confessed immediately upon questioning, the conviction rate rose considerably, to 62 percent. But there was a third, high-pressure condition in which participants were told that the defendant had confessed out of fear while his hands were cuffed behind his back, causing him pain. How did jurors in this situation react? Reasonably, they judged the confession to be coerced and said it did not influence their verdicts. Yet the conviction rate in this situation increased sharply, this time from 19 to 50 percent. Apparently, people are powerfully influenced by evidence of a confession, even when they concede that it was coerced—and even when it was relayed secondhand by an informant who was motivated to lie (Neuschatz et al., 2008).

The jury's reaction to confession evidence may also depend on how that evidence is presented. Today, many police departments videotape confessions for presentation in court. But could you tell the difference between a true confession and a false confession? Maybe not. Inside prison walls, Kassin, Meissner, and Norwick (2005) videotaped male inmates giving full confessions to the crimes for which they were incarcerated and concocting false confessions to offenses suggested by the researchers that they did not commit. College students and police investigators then watched and judged ten different inmates, each of whom gave a true or false confession to one of five crimes: aggravated assault, armed robbery, burglary, breaking and entering, and car theft. The results showed that although the police were generally confident in their performance, neither group exhibited high levels of accuracy.

In light of recently discovered false confessions, a number of states and cities are beginning to require that

TABLE 12.3

More Factors That Promote False Confessions

Participants were asked to solve a series of problems, sometimes alone and sometimes with a confederate. In a guilty condition, the confederate asked for help during a trial where participants were supposed to work alone, inducing participants to break the rule. In an innocent condition, no such request was made. The experimenter later interrogated everyone by promising leniency, minimizing the seriousness of the violation, using both tactics, or using no tactics at all. As shown by confession rates, both promises of leniency and minimization increased the number of true confessions to cheating by students who broke the rule. But they also increased the number of false confessions in students who did nothing wrong.

Condition	Guilty	Innocent
Control	46%	6%
Promise	72%	14%
Minimization	81%	18%
Both	87%	43%

Russano et al., 2005.

"I'm neither a good cop nor a bad cop, Jerome. Like yourself, I'm a complex amalgam of positive and negative personality traits that emerge or not, depending on circumstances."

the full interrogations be videotaped. This is an important means of reform to current practice, in part because it enables judges and juries to see for themselves how a confession came about and the extent to which the suspect was coerced (Kassin et al., 2010). But how should these events be staged for the camera? In a series of important experiments, Daniel Lassiter and his colleagues (2001) taped mock confessions from three different camera angles so that either the suspect or the interrogator or both were visible. All participants heard the same exchanges of words, but those who watched the suspects saw the situations as less coercive overall than did those who focused on the interrogators. Follow-up research has shown that even the perceptions of experienced trial judges are influenced by these variations in camera perspective (Lassiter et al., 2007). The practical policy implications are clear: When the camera directs all eyes at the accused, jurors are likely to underestimate the amount of pressure exerted by the "hidden" interrogator.

Without being beaten or threatened, innocent people sometimes confess to crimes they did not commit. **TRUE.**

The Lie-Detector Test

Often people confess after being told that they have failed the **polygraph**, or lie-detector, test. A polygraph is an electronic instrument that simultaneously records multiple channels of physiological arousal. The signals are picked up by sensors attached to different parts of the body. For example, rubber tubes are strapped around a suspect's torso to measure breathing, blood-pressure cuffs are wrapped around the upper arm to measure pulse rate, and electrodes are placed on the fingertips to record sweat-gland activity, or perspiration. These signals are then boosted by amplifiers and converted into a visual display.

The polygraph is used to detect deception on the assumption that when people lie, they become anxious and aroused in ways that can be measured. Here's how the test is conducted. After convincing a suspect that the polygraph works and establishing his or her baseline level of arousal, the examiner asks a series of yes-no questions and compares how the suspect reacts to emotionally arousing *crime-relevant questions* ("Did you steal the money?") and *control questions* that are arousing but not relevant to the crime ("Did you take anything that did not belong to you when you were younger?"). In theory, suspects who are innocent—whose denials are truthful—should be more aroused by the control questions, while guilty suspects—whose denials are false—should be more aroused by the crime-relevant questions.

Does the lie-detector test really work? Many laypeople think it is foolproof, but scientific opinion is split (Iacono & Lykken, 1997). Some researchers report accuracy rates of up to 80 to 90 percent (Honts, 1996; Raskin, 1986). Others believe that such claims are exaggerated (Lykken, 1998). One well-documented problem is that truthful persons too often fail the test. A second problem is that people who understand the test can fake the results. Studies show that you can beat the polygraph by tensing your muscles, squeezing your toes, or using other physical countermeasures while answering the *control* questions. By artificially inflating the responses to "innocent" questions, one can mask the stress that is aroused by lying on the crime-relevant questions (Honts et al., 1994).

What, then, are we to conclude? Careful reviews of the research suggest that there is no simple answer (Honts et al., 2002; National Research Council, 2003). Under certain conditions—for example, when the suspect is naive and the examiner is competent—it is possible for the polygraph to detect truth and deception at fairly high levels of accuracy. Still, the problems are hard to overcome, which is why the U.S. Supreme Court recently ruled, in the context of a military court martial, that judges may refuse

polygraph A mechanical instrument that records physiological arousal from multiple channels; it is often used as a lie-detector test.

to admit polygraph test results into evidence (*United States v. Scheffer*, 1998). Seeking an alternative, researchers are now trying to develop tests that distinguish between truth and deception through the measurement of involuntary electrical activity in the brain (Bashore & Rapp, 1993); pupil dilation when the person being tested is asked to lie, which requires more cognitive effort than telling the truth (Dionisio et al., 2001); and the use of fMRI to measure blood oxygen levels in areas of the brain associated with deception (Kozel et al., 2005; Bhatt et al., 2009).

A person can fool a lie-detector test by suppressing arousal when questions about the crime are asked. **FALSE.**

Eyewitness Testimony

"I'll never forget that face!" When these words are uttered, police officers, judges, and juries all take notice. Too often, however, eyewitnesses make mistakes. On March 8, 2009, the CBS show *60 Minutes* aired the story of Jennifer Thompson and Ronald Cotton. One night in 1984, in North Carolina, a young man broke into Thompson's apartment, cut the phone wires, and raped her. She described him to the police, helped construct a composite sketch, and then positively identified Ronald Cotton as her assailant. Cotton had alibis for his whereabouts that night, but based on Thompson's eyewitness identification, he was found guilty and sentenced to life in prison. Ten years later, DNA tests of semen stains revealed that Cotton was innocent and that Bobby Poole, a known offender, was the real assailant. In 1995, after ten years in prison, Cotton was released and offered $5,000 in compensation. He has since put the pieces of his life back together. Thompson, upon realizing that she had identified an innocent man, said, "I remember feeling sick, but also I remember feeling just an overwhelming sense of just guilt. . . . I cried and cried and I wept and I was angry at me and I beat myself up for it for a long time."

Every year, thousands of people are charged with crimes solely on the basis of eyewitness evidence. Many of these eyewitness accounts are accurate, but many are not—which is why psychologists have been interested in the topic for 100 years (Doyle, 2005). Several years ago, the National Institute of Justice reported on 28 wrongful convictions in which convicted felons were proved innocent by DNA evidence after varying numbers of years in prison. Remarkably, as in Ronald Cotton's case, every one of these convictions involved a mistaken identification (Connors et al., 1996). Now, more than 200 DNA exonerations later, it is clear: Eyewitness error is the most common cause of wrongful convictions (Wells, Memon, & Penrod, 2007).

In 1999, the U.S. Department of Justice took a bold step in response to this problem, assembling a group of police, prosecutors, defense attorneys, and research

Jennifer Thompson was traumatized twice: the first time when she was raped, the second when she learned that she had identified a man proved to be innocent by DNA tests ten years later. Here you can see Thompson talking to Ronald Cotton, the man she picked from a lineup. Notice the resemblance between Cotton and Bobby Poole, her actual assailant.

Poole

Cotton

psychologists to devise a set of "how-to" guidelines. Led by social psychologist Gary Wells, this Technical Working Group went on to publish *Eyewitness Evidence: A Guide for Law Enforcement* (U.S. Department of Justice, 1999; Wells et al., 2000).

As eyewitnesses, people can be called upon to remember just about anything—perhaps a face, a weapon, an accident, or a conversation. To date, hundreds of tightly controlled studies of eyewitness testimony have been conducted. Based on this research, three conclusions can be drawn: (1) eyewitnesses are imperfect; (2) certain personal and situational factors can systematically influence their performance, and (3) judges, juries, and lawyers are not adequately informed about these factors (Cutler & Penrod, 1995; Lindsay et al., 2007). Even the U.S. Supreme Court harbors outdated misconceptions about the nature of eyewitness memory (Wells & Quinlivan, 2009).

People tend to think that human memory works like a videotape camera—that if you turn on the power and focus the lens, all events will be recorded for subsequent playback. Unfortunately, it's not that simple. Over the years, researchers have found it useful to view memory as a three-stage process involving the *acquisition, storage,* and *retrieval* of information. The first of these stages, acquisition, refers to a witness's perceptions at the time of the event in question. Second, the witness rehearses and stores that information in memory to avoid forgetting. Third, the witness retrieves the information from storage when needed. This model suggests that errors can occur at three different points.

Acquisition   Some kinds of persons and events are more difficult to perceive than others. Common sense tells us that brief exposure time, poor lighting, long distance, physical disguise, and distraction can all limit a witness's perceptions. Research has uncovered other, less obvious factors as well.

After the tragic assassination of President John F. Kennedy, dozens of eyewitnesses came forward to describe what they saw. Some reported one gunman in the sixth-floor window of a nearby building, others reported two or three gunmen in the building, and still others thought the shots were fired from the ground. Such are the pitfalls of eyewitness testimony.

Consider the effects of a witness's emotional state. Often people are asked to recall a bloody shooting, a car wreck, or an assault—emotional events that trigger high levels of stress. In a study that illustrates the debilitating effects of stress, Charles Morgan and others (2004) randomly assigned trainees in a military survival school to undergo a realistic high-stress or low-stress mock interrogation. Twenty-four hours later, he found that those in the high-stress condition had difficulty identifying their interrogators in a lineup. Other research has shown that arousal has a complex effect on memory. Realizing the importance of what they are observing, highly aroused witnesses zoom in on the central features of an event such as the culprit, the victim, or a weapon. As a direct result of this narrowed field of attention, however, arousal impairs a witness's memory for other less central details (Brown, 2003; Christianson, 1992). Alcohol, a drug often involved in crimes, can also cause problems. When participants in one study witnessed a live staged crime, those who had earlier consumed fruit juice were more accurate in their recollections than were those who had been served an alcoholic beverage (Yuille & Tollestrup, 1990). Under the influence of alcohol, people can recognize the perpetrator in a lineup, but they too often make false identifications when the actual perpetrator is absent (Dysart et al., 2002).

The **weapon-focus effect** is also an important factor. Across a wide range of settings, research shows that when a criminal pulls out a gun, a razor blade, or a knife, witnesses are less able to identify that culprit than if no weapon is present (Pickel,

1999; Steblay 1992). There are two reasons for this effect. First, people are agitated by the sight of a menacing stimulus, as when participants in one study were approached by an experimenter who was holding a syringe or threatening to administer an injection (Maass & Kohnken, 1989). Second, even in a harmless situation, a witness's eyes lock in on a weapon like magnets, drawing attention away from the face (Hope & Wright, 2007). To demonstrate, Elizabeth Loftus and others (1987) showed people slides of a customer who walked up to a bank teller and pulled out either a pistol or a checkbook. By tracking eye movements, these researchers found that people spent more time looking at the gun than at the checkbook. The net result was an impairment in the ability of the research participants to identify the criminal in a lineup.

There is still another important consideration. By varying the racial makeup of participants and target persons in laboratory and real-life interactions, researchers discovered that people find it relatively difficult to recognize members of a race other than their own—an effect known as the **cross-race identification bias** (Malpass & Kravitz, 1969). In one field study, for example, 86 convenience store clerks in El Paso, Texas, were asked to identify three customers—one white, one black, and one Mexican American—all experimental confederates who had stopped in and made a purchase earlier that day. It turned out that the white, black, and Mexican American clerks were all most likely to accurately identify customers belonging to their own racial or ethnic group (Platz & Hosch, 1988).

The finding that "they all look alike" (referring to members of other groups) is found reliably and in many different racial and ethnic groups. Indeed, Christian Meissner and John Brigham (2001) statistically combined the results of 39 studies involving a total of 5,000 mock witnesses. They found that the witnesses were consistently less accurate and more prone to making false identifications when they tried to recognize target persons from racial and ethnic groups other than their own.

Eyewitnesses find it relatively difficult to recognize members of a race other than their own. **TRUE.**

Storage Can remembrances of the remote past be trusted? As you might expect, memory for faces and events tends to decline with the passage of time. Longer intervals between an event and its retrieval are generally associated with increased forgetting (Shapiro & Penrod, 1986). But not all recollections fade, and time alone does not cause memory slippage. Consider the plight of bystanders who witness firsthand such incidents as terrorist bombings, shootings, plane crashes, or fatal car accidents. Afterward, they may talk about what they saw, read about it, hear what other bystanders have to say, and answer questions from investigators and reporters. By the time witnesses to these events are officially questioned, they are likely to have been exposed to so much postevent information that one wonders if their original memory is still "pure."

According to Loftus (1996), it probably is not. Many years ago, based on her own studies of eyewitness testimony, Loftus proposed a now classic theory of reconstructive memory. After people observe an event, she said, later information about that event—whether the information is true or not—becomes integrated into the fabric of their memory. A classic experiment by Loftus and John Palmer (1974) illustrates the point. Participants viewed a film of a traffic accident and then answered questions, including: "About how fast were the cars going when they *hit* each other?" Other participants answered the same question, except that the verb *hit* was replaced by *smashed, collided, bumped,* or *contacted.* All participants saw the same accident, yet the wording of the question affected their reports. ▶ Figure 12.3 shows that participants given the "smashed" question estimated the highest average speed and those responding to the "contacted" question estimated the lowest. But there's more. One week later, participants were called back for more probing. Had the wording of the questions caused them to reconstruct their memories of the accident? Yes. When

weapon-focus effect The tendency for the presence of a weapon to draw attention and impair a witness's ability to identify the culprit.

cross-race identification bias The tendency for people to have difficulty identifying members of a race other than their own.

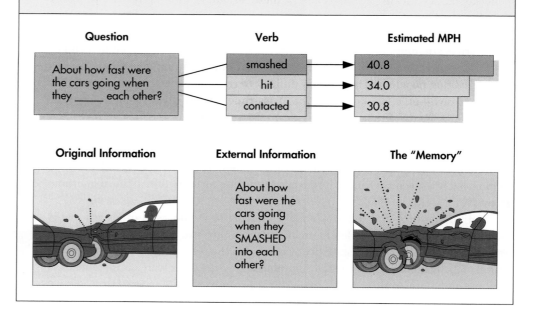

▶ **FIGURE 12.3**

Biasing Eyewitness Reports with Loaded Questions

Participants viewed a film of a traffic accident and then answered this question: "About how fast were these cars going when they (hit, smashed, or contacted) each other?" As shown, the wording of the question influenced speed estimates (top). One week later, it also caused participants to reconstruct their memory of other aspects of the accident (bottom).

Loftus & Loftus, 1976.

asked whether they had seen broken glass at the accident (none was actually present), 32 percent of the "smashed" participants said they had. As Loftus had predicted, what these participants remembered of the accident was based on two sources: the event itself and postevent information.

This **misinformation effect** has aroused a great deal of controversy. It's clear that eyewitnesses can be compromised when exposed to postevent information—as when they are told, for example, that either the person they identified or someone else had confessed during an interrogation (Hasel & Kassin, 2009). But does this information actually alter a witness's real memory so that it can never be retrieved again? Or do participants merely follow the experimenter's suggestion, leaving their true memory intact for retrieval under other conditions? Either way, whether memory is truly altered or not, it is clear that eyewitness *reports* are hopelessly biased by postevent information and that this effect can be hard to erase (Johnson & Seifert, 1998). The effects can also be dramatic. In one laboratory study, people were led through a process of imagination to create false memories of having performed some bizarre behaviors two weeks earlier, such as balancing a spoon on the nose, sitting on dice, and rubbing lotion on a chair (Thomas & Loftus, 2002).

This phenomenon raises an additional, potentially troubling question. If adults can be misled by postevent information, what about young children? On August 2, 1988, Margaret Kelly Michaels, a 26-year-old preschool teacher, was found guilty of 115 counts of sex abuse committed at the Wee Care Nursery School in New Jersey. The charges against her were shocking. For a period of over seven months, the jury was told, she danced nude in the classroom, stripped the children, licked peanut butter off their genitals, and raped them with knives, forks, spoons, and Lego blocks.

misinformation effect The tendency for false post-event misinformation to become integrated into people's memory of an event.

Were the children's stories accurate? On the one hand, there were some striking consistencies in the testimonies of 19 child witnesses. On the other hand, the social workers and investigators who conducted the interviews often prompted the children with suggestive leading questions, told them that Michaels was a bad person, urged them to describe acts they had initially denied, offered bribes for disclosures, and pressured those who claimed ignorance. Except for this testimony, there was no physical evidence of abuse and no other witnesses even though the acts were supposed to have occurred during school hours in an open classroom. Michaels was found guilty and sentenced to 47 years in prison. After serving five of those years, she was released when the state appeals court overturned the conviction on the ground that the children's testimony could not be trusted. "One day you're getting ready for work and making coffee, minding your business," said Michaels, "and the next minute you are an accused child molester."

Can suggestive interview procedures cause young children to confuse appearance and reality? Over the years, thousands of sex abuse charges have been filed against babysitters, preschool teachers, and family members. Rekindling images of the Salem witch trials of the seventeenth century, some of these suspects were falsely accused of participating in satanic cults (Bottoms & Davis, 1997). In light of these events, judges struggled to decide: Are preschoolers competent to take the witness stand, or are they too suggestible, too prone to confuse reality and fantasy? To provide guidance to the courts, researchers have studied the factors that influence children's eyewitness memory (Bruck & Ceci, 1999).

This research has evolved through several stages. At first, simple laboratory experiments showed that preschoolers were more likely than older children and adults to incorporate misleading "trick" questions into their memories for simple stories (Ceci et al., 1987). Other studies showed that interviewers could get young children to change their memories (or at least their answers) simply by repeating a question over and over—a behavior that implies that the answer given is not good enough (Poole & White, 1991). But are young children similarly suggestible about stressful real-life experiences?

In one study, Michelle Leichtman and Stephen Ceci (1995) told nursery school children about a clumsy man named Sam Stone who always broke things. A month later, a man visited the school, spent time in the classroom, and left. The next day, the children were shown a ripped book and a soiled teddy bear and asked what had happened. Reasonably, no one said that they saw Stone cause the damage. But then, over the next ten weeks, they were asked suggestive questions ("I wonder if Sam Stone was wearing long pants or short pants when he ripped the book?"). The result: When a new interviewer asked the children in the class to tell what happened, 72 percent of the 3- and 4-year-olds blamed Stone for the damage and 45 percent said they saw him do it. One child "recalled" that Stone took a paintbrush and painted melted chocolate on the bear. Others "saw" him spill coffee, throw toys in the air, rip the book in anger, and soak the book in warm water until it fell apart. It's important to realize that false memories in children are not necessarily a byproduct of bad questioning procedures. Even when interviews are fair and neutral, false reports can stem from young children's exposure to misinformation from such outside sources as television (Principe et al., 2000), parents (Poole & Lindsay, 2001), and classmates (Principe & Ceci, 2002).

To summarize, research shows that repetition, misinformation, and leading questions can bias a child's memory report and that preschoolers are particularly vulnerable in this regard. The effects can be dramatic. In dozens of studies, these kinds of procedures have led children to falsely report that they were touched, hit, kissed, and hugged; that a thief came

"Do you swear to tell your version of the truth as you perceive it, clouded perhaps by the passage of time and preconceived notions?"

into their classroom; that something "yucky" was put into their mouth; and even that a doctor had cut a bone from their nose to stop it from bleeding. Somehow, the courts must distinguish between true and false claims—and do so on a case-by-case basis. To assist in this endeavor, researchers have proposed that clear interviewing guidelines be set so that future child witnesses will be questioned in an objective, nonbiasing manner (Lamb et al., 2008).

Retrieval For eyewitnesses, testifying is only the last in a series of efforts to retrieve what they saw from memory. Before witnesses reach the courtroom, they are questioned by police and lawyers, view a lineup or mug shots, and even assist in the construction of a facial composite or an artist's sketch of the perpetrator. Yet each of these experiences increases the risk of error and distortion.

Imagine trying to reconstruct a culprit's face by selecting a set of eyes, a nose, a mouth, a hairstyle, and so on, from vast collections of features and then combining them into a composite of the face. Research shows that this process seldom produces a face that resembles the actual culprit (Kovera et al., 1997). To further complicate matters, the face construction process itself may confuse witnesses, making it more difficult for them later to identify the culprit. In one study, for example, participants were asked to select from six pictures a person's face they had seen two days earlier. Sixty percent accurately identified the target. When they first tried to reconstruct the face using a computerized facial composite program, however, their identification accuracy dropped to 18 percent (Wells et al., 2005).

▶**FIGURE 12.4**

Morphing Composite Faces to Catch a Thief

Students from Iowa State University volunteered to use morphing software to answer this question: If there are multiple eyewitnesses to a crime, would it help to average their sketches of the perpetrator's face? In this study, participants constructed sketches of target faces of student volunteers they had viewed. Using the morphing software, a single image that combined four sketches was created for each target. Other participants then rated the similarity of each set of sketches and the morphed image to the original target. Overall, the morphs were more similar to targets than were the individual sketches on which they were based.

Hasel & Wells, 2007.

Sketch 1

Sketch 2

Sketch 3

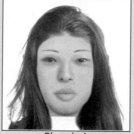
Sketch 4

Sketch 5

Target Face

When there are multiple eyewitnesses to a crime, it is common for descriptions of the culprit to vary from one witness to the next. But what if the various descriptions could somehow be averaged into a single face? Is a collection of witnesses better than one witness? To answer this question, Lisa Hasel and Gary Wells (2007) had participants view a series of target faces and construct a sketch for each one, resulting in four sketches per face. Then for each target they used morphing software to create one composite image that combined the four sketches. To see if these morphs resembled the actual faces better than the average of the individual sketches, a new sample of participants rated the similarity of each set of sketches and morphed composite image to the original target. The results were encouraging: On average, the morphs were rated as more similar to the targets than were the individual sketches on which they were based (see ▶ Figure 12.4).

Nothing an eyewitness does has greater impact than making an identification from a photographic or live lineup. Once police have made an arrest, they often call on their witnesses to view a lineup that includes the suspect and five to seven other individuals. This procedure may take place within days of a crime or months later. Either way, the lineup often results in tragic cases of mistaken identity. Through the application of eyewitness research findings, this risk can be reduced, as we will see (Wells et al., 1998; Wells et al., 2007).

Basically, four factors can affect identification performance at this stage. The first is the lineup *construction*. To be fair, a lineup should contain four to eight innocent persons, or "foils," who match the witness's general description of the culprit. If the witness describes seeing a white male in his 20s with curly hair, for example, foils should not be included that are old, nonwhite, and bald. Also, anything that makes a suspect distinctive compared to the others in the lineup increases his or her chance of being selected (Buckhout, 1974). This is what happened to Steve Titus, who was mistakenly accused of rape when the police showed the victim his photograph alongside those of five other men. Although the foils resembled Titus in appearance, his picture stood out like a sore thumb. It was smaller than the others and was the only one without a border. Titus was also the only man in the group with a smile on his face (Loftus & Ketcham, 1991).

Second, lineup *instructions* to the witness are very important. In a study by Roy Malpass and Patricia Devine (1981), students saw a staged act of vandalism, after which they attended a lineup. Half of the students received "biased" instructions: They were led to believe that the culprit was in the lineup. The others were told that he might or might not be present. Lineups were then presented either with or without the culprit. When the students received biased instructions, they felt compelled to identify *someone* and often picked an innocent person (see Table 12.4). Additional studies have both confirmed and qualified this basic result: When the criminal is present in the lineup, biased instructions are not problematic. When the criminal is not in the lineup, however—which occurs whenever the police suspect is innocent—biased instructions substantially increase the rate of mistaken identifications (Clark, 2005; Steblay, 1997). Again, the story of Steve Titus is a case in point. The police told the victim to pick her assailant from a group of six. After studying the pictures for several minutes and shaking her head in confusion, she was urged to concentrate and make a choice. "This one is the closest," she said. "It has to be this one" (Loftus & Ketcham, 1991, p. 38).

TABLE 12.4

Effects of Lineup and Instructions on False Identifications

After witnessing a crime, participants were told either that the culprit was in the lineup (biased instruction) or that he might or might not be present (unbiased instruction). Participants then viewed a lineup in which the real culprit was present or absent. Notice the percentage of participants in each group who identified an innocent person. Those who received the biased instruction were more likely to make a false identification, picking an innocent person rather than no one at all, especially when the real culprit was not in the lineup.

	Percentage of False Identifications	
	Unbiased Instructions	Biased Instructions
Culprit present	0	25
Culprit absent	33	78

Malpass & Devine, 1981.

Third, the *format* of a lineup also influences whether a witness feels compelled to make a selection. When witnesses are presented with a spread of photographs, they tend to make relative, multiple-choice-like judgments, comparing the different alternatives and picking the one who looks most like the criminal. This strategy increases the tendency to make a false identification. The solution: When the same photos are shown sequentially, one at a time, witnesses tend to make absolute judgments by comparing each target person with their memory of the criminal. This situation diminishes the risk of a forced and often false identification of an innocent suspect (Lindsay & Bellinger, 1999; Lindsay et al., 1991; Lindsay & Wells, 1985). Currently, some researchers are concerned that the benefit of the sequential format will depend on how it is implemented and the extent to which it reduces the rate of correct identifications when the actual perpetrator is in the lineup (McQuiston-Surrett et al., 2006).

The fourth factor is perhaps the most subtle, as it pertains to *familiarity-induced* biases. Research shows that people often remember a face but not the circumstances in which they saw that face. In one study, for example, participants witnessed a staged crime and then looked through mug shots. A few days later, they were asked to view a lineup. The result was startling: Participants were just as likely to identify an innocent person whose picture was in the mug shots as they were to pick the actual criminal (Brown et al., 1977)! Many different studies have shown that witnesses will often identify from a lineup someone they had seen in another context, including innocent bystanders who also happened to be at the crime scene (Deffenbacher et al., 2006).

Courtroom Testimony   Eyewitnesses can be inaccurate, but that's only part of the problem. The other part is that their testimony in court is persuasive and not easy to evaluate. To examine how juries view eyewitness testimony, Gary Wells, Rod Lindsay, and others conducted a series of experiments in which they staged the theft of a calculator in the presence of unsuspecting research participants, who were later cross-examined after trying to pick the culprit from a photo spread. Other participants, who served as mock jurors, observed the questioning and judged the witnesses. The results were sobering: Jurors overestimated how accurate the eyewitnesses were and could not distinguish between witnesses whose identifications were correct and those whose identifications were incorrect (Lindsay et al., 1981; Wells et al., 1979).

There appear to be two problems. First, people generally do not know about these aspects of human perception and memory through common sense. Brian Cutler and others (1988) found that mock jurors were not sensitive enough to the effects of lineup instructions, weapon focus, and other aspects of an eyewitnessing situation, such as the cross-race bias, in evaluating the testimony of an eyewitness (Abshire & Bernstein, 2003). This lack of knowledge is not limited to trial juries. Survey research shows that relative to experts, judges, prosecutors, and defense attorneys also lack awareness of many of the factors described above that influence eyewitness memory (Benton et al., 2006; Wise & Safer, 2004; Magnussen et al., 2008).

The second problem is that people tend to base their judgments of an eyewitness largely on how *confident* that witness is, a factor that only is modestly predictive of accuracy. This statement may seem surprising, but studies have shown that the witness who declares "I am absolutely certain" is often not more likely to be right than the one who appears unsure (Penrod & Cutler, 1995; Sporer et al., 1995; Wells & Murray, 1984). Why are eyewitness confidence and accuracy not highly related? The reason is that confidence levels can be raised and lowered by factors that do not have an impact on identification accuracy.

To demonstrate, Elizabeth Luus and Wells (1994) staged a theft in front of pairs of participants and then had each separately identify the culprit from a photographic lineup. After the participants made their identifications, the experimenters led them to believe that their partner, a co-witness, either had picked the same person, a similar-looking different person, or a dissimilar-looking different person or had said that the thief was not in the lineup. Participants were then questioned by a police officer who asked, "On a scale from 1 to 10, how confident are you in your identification?" The result: Participants became more confident when told that a co-witness picked the same person or a dissimilar alternative and less confident when told that the co-witness picked a similar alternative or none at all. Other research confirms how important such postidentification feedback can be. John Shaw (1996) found that witnesses who are repeatedly questioned about their observations become more and more confident over time but not more accurate.

Wells and Amy Bradfield (1998) then found that eyewitnesses who received positive feedback about their false identifications went on to reconstruct other aspects of their eyewitnessing experience. In a series of studies, they showed participants a security camera videotape of a man who shot a guard followed by a set of photographs that did not contain the actual gunman (in other words, all identifications made were false). The experimenter then said to some witnesses, but not to others, "Oh good. You identified the actual murder suspect." When witnesses were later asked about the whole experience, those given the confirming feedback "recalled" that they had paid more attention to the event, had a better view of the culprit, and found it easier to make the identification (see ▶ Figure 12.5). Apparently, an eyewitness's confidence about the entire experience can be raised or lowered by social feedback—and this makes confidence even less predictive of accuracy (Bradfield et al., 2002; Douglass & Steblay, 2006).

The more confident an eyewitness is about an identification, the more accurate he or she is likely to be. **FALSE.**

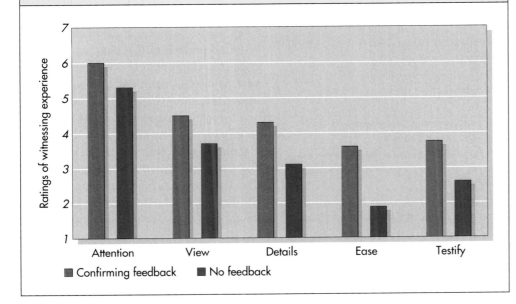

▶ FIGURE 12.5

The Biasing Effects of Post-identification Feedback

Participants saw a gunman on videotape and then tried to make an identification from a set of photographs in which he was absent. Afterward, the experimenter gave some witnesses but not others confirming feedback about their selection. As shown, those given the confirming feedback later recalled that they had paid more attention to the event, had a better view of it, could make out details of the culprit's face, and found it easier to make the identification. They were also more willing to testify in court.

Wells & Bradfield, 1998.

If the police officer who administers the lineup can boost a witness's confidence about the whole witnessing experience, can he or she also influence the witness's identification decision? In a study that specifically addressed this question, Sarah Greathouse and Margaret Bull Kovera (2009) paired student "witnesses" to a staged theft with student "police" who were trained how to administer a simultaneous or sequential photo lineup using either biased or unbiased instructions. In these lineups, a picture of the actual culprit was either present or absent. Half the administrators were *informed* of who the police suspect was in the lineup; the other half was *blind* as to the suspect's identity. The results showed that under relatively biasing conditions (simultaneous photo spreads and biased instructions), witnesses made more suspect identifications—even when the suspect was truly innocent—when the administrator was informed rather than blind. Videotapes of the sessions showed that the informed administrators unwittingly increased identification rates by telling witnesses to look carefully, by asking them to look again when they failed to make a selection, and in some cases by letting on that they knew who the suspect was. This study strongly supports a point of reform that eyewitness researchers have long advocated: the use of a "double-blind" procedure in which not only the suspect but the police administrator does not know who the suspect is within the lineup.

TABLE 12.5

What Eyewitness Experts Say in Court

Presented with a list of eyewitness factors, 64 experts were asked what research findings were strong enough to present in court. In order of how much support they elicited, the following are among the most highly regarded topics of expert testimony.

Eyewitness Factor	Statement
Wording of questions	An eyewitness's testimony about an event can be affected by how the questions put to the witness are worded.
Lineup instructions	Police instructions can affect an eyewitness's willingness to make an identification.
Mug shot-induced bias	Exposure to mug shots of a suspect increases the likelihood that the witness will later choose that suspect in a lineup.
Confidence malleability	An eyewitness's confidence can be influenced by factors that are unrelated to the accuracy of an identification.
Postevent information	Eyewitness testimony about an event often reflects not only what the witness actually saw but also information they obtained later on.
Child suggestibility	Young children are more vulnerable than adults to interviewer suggestion, peer pressures, and other social influences.
Alcoholic intoxication	Alcoholic intoxication impairs an eyewitness's later ability to recall persons and events.
Cross-race bias	Eyewitnesses are more accurate at identifying members of their own race than they are at identifying members of other races.
Weapon focus	The presence of a weapon impairs an eyewitness's ability to accurately identify the perpetrator's face.
Accuracy confidence	An eyewitness's confidence is not a good predictor of the accuracy of his or her identification.

Kassin et al., 2001.

The Eyewitness Expert Having described the problems with information obtained from eyewitnesses, social psychologists are in a position to put their knowledge to use by educating juries so they can better evaluate the evidence. But can this goal be achieved? Just like medical doctors who testify about a patient's physical condition, economists who testify on monopolies and other antitrust matters, and architectural engineers who testify on the structural integrity of buildings, psychologists are often called by one party or the other to tell the jury about relevant aspects of human perception, memory, and behavior (Cutler, 2009).

What, specifically, do these experts say to the jury? What findings do they present in court? A few years ago, researchers surveyed 64 eyewitness experts, many of whose studies are described in this chapter. The principles listed in Table 12.5 were seen by the vast majority as highly reliable and worthy of expert testimony (Kassin et al., 2001).

Does the jury need to be informed? In some cases, yes. As noted earlier, researchers have found that there's a great deal about eyewitnesses that the average person does not know as a matter of common sense (Devenport et al., 1997). Even judges and lawyers are not aware of many of the factors that influence eyewitnesses. Veronica Stinson and others (1996, 1997) presented large groups of Florida judges and defense lawyers with hypothetical cases that included a lineup identification that varied in important ways. In general, the judges and lawyers were able to reasonably distinguish between lineups and instructions that were fair as opposed to suggestive. But they did not understand that witnesses are more likely to pick someone from photographs—even someone innocent—when the pictures are shown all at once (which leads people to make relative judgments) than when they are shown sequentially, one at a time (which leads people to make absolute judgments). Getting it backward, the judges and lawyers criticized the sequential format for not allowing witnesses to compare photographs, which is precisely what should not be done.

Nonevidentiary Influences

A trial is a well-orchestrated event that follows strict rules of evidence and procedure. The goal is to ensure that juries base their verdicts solely on the evidence and testimony presented in court—not on rumors, newspaper stories, a defendant's attire, and other information. The question is: To what extent is this goal achieved, and to what extent are jury verdicts tainted by non-evidentiary influences?

Pretrial Publicity   Many high-profile cases find their way into newspapers and other mass media long before they appear in court. In these instances, the legal system struggles with this dilemma: Does exposure to pretrial news stories corrupt the pool of prospective jurors? Public opinion surveys consistently show that the more people know about a case, the more likely they are to presume the defendant guilty, even when they claim to be impartial (Kovera, 2002; Moran & Cutler, 1991). There is nothing mysterious about this result. The information in news reports usually comes from the police or district attorney's office, so it often reveals facts unfavorable to the defense. The question is whether these reports have an impact on juries that go on to hear evidence in court and deliberate to a verdict.

To examine the effects of pretrial publicity, Geoffrey Kramer and his colleagues (1990) played a videotaped reenactment of an armed robbery trial to hundreds of people participating in 108 mock juries. Before watching the tape, participants were exposed to news clippings about the case. Some read news material that was neutral. Others read information that was incriminating—for example, revealing that the defendant had a prior record or implicating the defendant in a hit-and-run accident in which a child was killed. Even though participants were instructed to base their decisions solely on the evidence, pretrial publicity had a marked effect. Among those exposed to neutral material, 33 percent voted guilty after deliberating in a jury. Among those exposed to the prejudicial material, that figure increased to 48 percent. What's worse, neither judges nor defense lawyers could identify in a simulated voir dire which jurors had been biased by the publicity. As shown in ▶ Figure 12.6, 48 percent of jurors who were questioned and perceived to be impartial—those who said

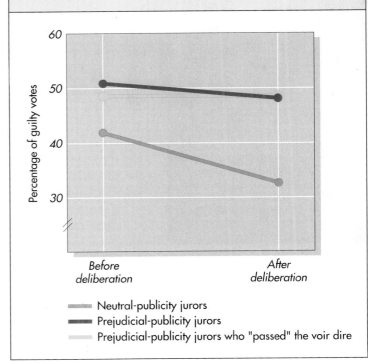

▶ **FIGURE 12.6**

Contaminating Effects of Pretrial Publicity

In this study, participants were exposed to prejudicial or neutral news reports about a defendant, watched a videotaped trial, and voted before and after participating in a mock jury deliberation. As shown, pretrial publicity increased the conviction rate both before and after deliberation, even among participants perceived to be impartial by judges and lawyers.

Kerr et al., 1982.

Percentage of guilty votes

60

50

40

30

Before deliberation

After deliberation

Neutral-publicity jurors
Prejudicial-publicity jurors
Prejudicial-publicity jurors who "passed" the voir dire

they were unaffected—went on to vote guilty (Kerr et al., 1991). The impact of pretrial publicity is even more powerful when the news is seen on television rather than in print (Ogloff & Vidmar, 1994).

Pretrial publicity is potentially dangerous in two respects. First, it often divulges information that is not later allowed into the trial record. Second is the matter of timing. Because many news stories precede the actual trial, jurors learn certain facts even before they enter the courtroom. From what is known about the power of first impressions, the implications are clear. If jurors receive prejudicial news information about a defendant before trial, that information will distort the way they interpret the facts of the case—an effect that has been found in recent research (Hope et al., 2004). So is there a solution? Since the biasing effects persist despite the practices of jury selection, the presentation of hard evidence, cautionary words from the judge, and open jury deliberations, justice may demand that highly publicized cases be postponed or moved to other, less informed communities (Steblay et al., 1999; Studebaker & Penrod, 1997).

Is it possible that juries are influenced by pretrial publicity of a more general nature that is unrelated to their specific case? Perhaps you have watched the popular television drama *CSI* (which stands for "crime scene investigation"), and focuses on the process by which police investigators collect and analyze fingerprints, bodily fluids, and other types of forensic evidence (the original is set in Las Vegas; spinoffs now include *CSI: Miami* and *CSI: New York*). Many legal commentators are speculating that the public's exposure to this show is influencing jury verdicts; they call it the "CSI effect." The fear is that the television programs lead jurors to have unrealistically high expectations that cause them to vote cautiously for acquittal because they find the actual evidence insufficient to support a guilty verdict. If true, then the CSI effect would represent a special type of pretrial publicity potentially influencing an entire population of juries. Tom Tyler (2006a) is quick to note, however, that although the hypothesis is plausible, there is at present no hard evidence to support it.

CSI: Miami is a popular TV show about police investigators who use science to analyze evidence. Does this show lead jurors to set unrealistically high expectations for evidence, causing them to acquit criminals? At least for now, there is no evidence to support this "CSI effect" hypothesis.

Andrew MacPherson/© CBS/Courtesy: Everett Collection

Inadmissible Testimony　Just as jurors are biased by news stories, so they occasionally receive extralegal information within the trial itself. In the 1995 trial of O. J. Simpson, who was acquitted of murder, Simpson's lawyers repeatedly referred to witnesses who would not later testify. With each passing reference, the prosecutor objected. Eventually, the judge issued a warning to Simpson's lawyers and ordered the jury to disregard the information. A few weeks later, the judge then had to warn prosecutors who had leaked biasing facts, again instructing the jury to disregard that information.

If something seems wrong with this series of events, you should know that it is a scene often replayed in the courtroom. Can people really strike information from their minds the way court reporters can strike it from the record? Can people on a jury resist the forbidden fruit of inadmissible testimony? Although common sense suggests they cannot, the research is mixed. In one study, a group of mock jurors read about a murder case based on evidence so weak that not a single juror voted guilty. A second group read the same case, except that the prosecution introduced an illegally obtained tape recording of a phone call made by the defendant: "I finally got the money to pay you off. . . . When you read the papers tomorrow, you'll know what I mean." The defense argued that the illegal tape should not be admissible but the judge disagreed. At this point, the conviction rate increased to 26 percent. In a third group, as in the second, the tape was brought in and the defense objected. Yet this time, the judge sustained the objection and told jurors to disregard the tape. The result: 35 percent voted for conviction (Sue et al., 1973). Other studies as well have revealed that jurors are often not deterred by "limiting instructions" (Steblay et al., 2006).

Why do people not follow a judge's order to disregard inadmissible evidence? There are a number of possible explanations (Lieberman & Arndt, 2000). Imagine yourself in the jury box, and three reasons will become apparent. First, the added instruction draws attention to the information in controversy. It's like being told not to think about white bears. As we saw in Chapter 3, trying to suppress a specific thought increases its tendency to intrude upon our consciousness (Wegner, 1994). A second reason is that a judge's instruction to disregard, much like censorship, restricts a juror's decision-making freedom. Accordingly, it can backfire by arousing reactance. Thus, when a judge emphasizes the ruling by *forbidding* jurors from using the information ("You have no choice but to disregard it"), they become even *more* likely to use it (Wolf & Montgomery, 1977). The third reason is the easiest to understand. Jurors want to reach the right decision. If they stumble onto relevant information, they want to use it whether it satisfies the law's technical rules or not. In other words, jurors find it hard to ignore information that seems relevant to a case (Wissler & Saks, 1985).

To test this third hypothesis, Kassin and Sommers (1997) had mock jurors read a transcript of a double murder trial that was based on weak evidence, leading only 24 percent to vote guilty. Three other groups read the same case except that the state's evidence included a wiretapped phone conversation in which the defendant confessed to a friend. In all cases, the defense lawyer objected to the disclosure. When the judge ruled to admit the tape into evidence, the conviction rate increased considerably, to 79 percent. But when the judge excluded the tape and instructed jurors to disregard it, their reaction depended on the reason that the tape was excluded. When told to disregard the tape because it was barely audible and could not be trusted, participants mentally erased the information, as they should, and delivered the same 24 percent conviction rate as in the no-tape control group. But when told to disregard the item because it had been illegally obtained, 55 percent voted guilty. Despite the judge's warning, these latter participants were unwilling to ignore testimony they saw as highly relevant merely because of a legal technicality.

Additional studies indicate that jurors in this situation may comply with a judge's instruction to disregard when the technicality involves a *serious* violation of the defendant's rights (Fleming et al., 1999) and that the process of deliberation increases compliance, which minimizes the bias (London & Nunez, 2000).

The Judge's Instructions

One of the most important rituals in any trial is the judge's instructions to the jury. It is through these instructions that juries are educated about relevant legal concepts, informed of the verdict options, admonished to disregard extralegal factors, and advised on how to conduct their deliberations. To make verdicts adhere to the law, juries are supposed to comply with these instructions. The task seems simple enough, but there are problems.

To begin with, the jury's intellectual competence has been called into question. For years, the courts have doubted whether jurors understood their instructions. One skeptical judge put it bluntly when he said that "these words may as well be spoken in a foreign language" (Frank, 1949, p. 181). He may well have been right. When actual instructions are tested with community mock jurors, the results reveal high levels of misunderstanding—a serious problem in light of the fact that jurors seem to have many preconceptions about crimes and the requirements of the law.

Comprehensibility is even problematic when it comes to the death penalty instructions that are required in capital cases (Wiener et al., 1995) and for college students as well as ordinary jurors from the community (Rose & Ogloff, 2001). There is, however, reason for hope. Research has shown that when conventional instructions—which are poorly structured, esoteric, and filled with complex legal terms—are rewritten in plain English, comprehension rates increase markedly (Elwork et al., 1982; English & Sales, 1997). Supplementing a judge's instructions with flow charts, computer animations, and other audiovisual aids is also effective (Brewer et al., 2004).

A lack of comprehension is one reason that a judge's instruction may have little impact. But there's a second reason: Sometimes juries disagree with the law, thus raising the controversial issue of **jury nullification**. Because juries deliberate in private, they can choose to disregard, or "nullify," the judge's instructions. The pages of history are filled with poignant examples. Consider the case of someone tried for euthanasia, or "mercy killing." By law, it is murder. But to the defendant, it might be a noble act on behalf of a loved one. Faced with this kind of conflict—an explosive moral issue on which public opinion is sharply divided—juries often evaluate the issue in human terms, use their own notions of commonsense justice, and vote despite the law for acquittal (Finkel, 1995; Horowitz & Willging, 1991; Niedermeier et al., 1999). This nullification tendency is particularly likely to occur when jurors who disagree with the law are informed of their right to nullify it (Meissner et al., 2003).

Jury nullification is what happened in cases pertaining to physician-assisted suicide, as was practiced by Jack Kevorkian, a retired pathologist. During the 1990s, Kevorkian presided over 130 deaths. For three of these incidents, he was tried for murder and the juries, sympathetic to his plight, practiced nullification and acquitted him. Then he injected a terminally ill man with a lethal dose of drugs, videotaped the death,

In this Detroit courtroom, Dr. Jack Kevorkian was tried for an assisted suicide. Although physician-assisted suicide is illegal in Michigan, the jury in this case "nullified" the law in favor of its own conceptions of justice and voted not guilty. However, Kevorkian was eventually convicted and sent to prison.

jury nullification The jury's power to disregard, or "nullify," the law when it conflicts with personal conceptions of justice.

gave the tape to CBS News, and again challenged authorities to take him to court. They did, and in 1999, after having defied the law in the boldest of ways, Kevorkian was found guilty. He was Prisoner #284797 in a Michigan state prison until he was released on parole in June 2007.

Jury Deliberation

Anyone who has seen the original movie *Twelve Angry Men* can appreciate how colorful and passionate a jury's deliberation can be. This film classic opens with a jury eager to convict a young man of murder—no ifs, ands, or buts. The group selects a foreperson and takes a show-of-hands vote. The result is an 11-to-1 majority, with actor Henry Fonda the lone dissenter. After many tense moments, Fonda manages to convert his peers, and the jury votes unanimously for acquittal.

It is often said that the unique power of the jury stems from the wisdom that emerges when individuals come together privately as one *group*. Is this assumption justified? *Twelve Angry Men* is a work of fiction, but does it realistically portray what transpires in the jury room? And in what ways does the legal system influence the group dynamics? By interviewing jurors after trials and by recruiting people to participate on mock juries and then recording their deliberations, researchers have learned a great deal about how juries make their decisions.

Leadership in the Jury Room

In theory, all jurors are created equal. In practice, however, dominance hierarchies tend to develop. As in other decision-making groups, a handful of individuals lead the discussion while others join in at a lower rate or watch from the sidelines, speaking

In the classic movie *Twelve Angry Men*, Henry Fonda plays a lone juror who single-handedly converts his eleven guilty-voting peers to vote for acquittal. Sometimes life imitates art; in this case, it does not. Research shows that majorities on the first jury vote usually prevail in the final verdict.

The Everett Collection

only to cast their votes (Hastie et al., 1983). It's almost as if there is a jury within the jury. The question is, what kinds of people emerge as leaders?

It is often assumed that the foreperson is the leader. The foreperson, after all, calls for votes, acts as a liaison between the judge and jury, and announces the verdict in court. It seems like a position of importance, yet the selection process is very quick and casual. It's interesting that foreperson selection outcomes do follow a predictable pattern (Stasser et al., 1982). People of higher occupational status or with prior experience on a jury are frequently chosen. Interestingly too, the first person who speaks is often chosen to be the foreperson (Strodtbeck et al., 1957). And when jurors deliberate around a rectangular table, those who sit at the heads of the table are more likely to be chosen than are those seated in the middle (Bray et al., 1978; Strodtbeck & Hook, 1961).

If you find such inequalities bothersome, fear not: Forepersons may act as nominal leaders, but they do not exert more than their fair share of influence over the group. In fact, although they spend more time than other jurors talking about procedural matters, they spend less time expressing opinions about the verdict (Hastie et al., 1983). Thus, it may be most accurate to think of the foreperson not as the jury's leader but as its moderator. In *Twelve Angry Men*, actor Martin Balsam—not Henry Fonda—was the foreperson. He was also among the least influential members of the jury.

The Dynamics of Deliberation

If the walls of the jury room could talk, they would tell us that the decision-making process typically passes through three stages (Hastie et al., 1983; Stasser et al., 1982). Like other problem-solving groups, juries begin in a relaxed *orientation* period during which they set an agenda, talk in open-ended terms, raise questions, and explore the facts. Then, once differences of opinion are revealed (usually after the first vote is taken), factions develop and the group shifts abruptly into a period of *open conflict*. With the battle lines sharply drawn, discussion takes on a more focused, argumentative tone. Together, jurors scrutinize the evidence, construct stories to account for that evidence, and discuss the judge's instructions (Pennington & Hastie, 1992). If all jurors agree, they return a verdict. If not, the majority tries to achieve a consensus by converting the holdouts through information and social pressure. If unanimity is achieved, the group enters a period of *reconciliation*, during which it smoothes over the conflicts and affirms its satisfaction with the outcome. If the holdouts continue to disagree, the jury declares itself hung. This process is diagrammed in ▶ Figure 12.7.

When it comes to decision-making *outcomes*, deliberations follow a predictable course first discovered by Harry Kalven and Hans Zeisel (1966). By interviewing the members of 225 juries, they were able to reconstruct how these juries split on their very first vote. Out of 215 juries that opened with an initial majority, 209 reached a final verdict consistent with that first vote. This finding— which was later bolstered by the results of mock jury stud-

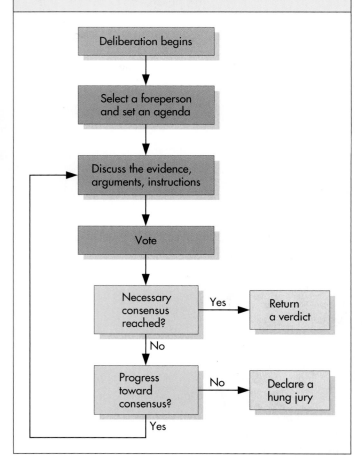

▶ **FIGURE 12.7**

Jury Deliberations: The Process

Juries move through various tasks en route to a verdict. They begin by setting and reviewing the case. If all jurors agree, they return a verdict. If not, they continue to discuss the case until they reach a consensus. If the holdouts refuse to vote with the majority, the jury becomes deadlocked.

ies (Kerr, 1981; Stasser & Davis, 1981; see Table 12.6)—led Kalven and Zeisel (1966) to conclude that "the deliberation process might well be likened to what the developer does for an exposed film; it brings out the picture, but the outcome is predetermined" (p. 489). Setting aside Henry Fonda's *Twelve Angry Men* heroics, one can usually predict the final verdict by knowing where the individual jurors stand the first time they vote. Juries are not generally more or less subject to bias than the individuals who constitute the groups (Kerr et al., 1999). Hence, "majority rules" seems to describe what happens not only in juries but in most other small decision-making groups (Hastie & Kameda, 2005).

There is one exception to this majority-wins rule in the jury room. In criminal trials, deliberation tends to produce a **leniency bias** that favors the defendant. All other factors being equal, individual jurors are more likely to vote guilty on their own than they are in a group; they are also more prone to convict before deliberations than they are afterward (Mac-Coun & Kerr, 1988). Look again at Table 12.6, and you'll see that juries that are equally divided in their initial vote are ultimately likely to return not-guilty verdicts. Perhaps it is easier to raise a "reasonable doubt" in other people's minds than it is to erase all doubt. In this regard, it is interesting to note that in their classic study entitled *The American Jury* (1966), Kalven and Zeisel surveyed 555 judges who reported how they would have voted in some 3,500 jury trials. Judges agreed with their juries 78 percent of the time. When they disagreed, it was usually because the jury acquitted a defendant thought guilty by the judge. Perhaps these disagreements are due, in part, to the fact that juries decide as groups and judges decide as individuals.

Knowing that the majority tends to prevail doesn't tell us how juries manage to resolve disagreements en route to a verdict. From the conformity studies discussed in Chapter 7, we know that there are two possibilities. Sometimes people conform because through a process of *informational influence* they are genuinely persuaded by what others say. At other times, people yield to the pressures of *normative influence* by changing their overt behavior in the majority's direction even though they disagree in private. Justice demands that juries reach a consensus through a vigorous exchange of views and information, not as the result of heavy-handed social pressure. But is that how it works? Research shows that juries achieve unanimity not by one process or the other but by a combination of both (Kaplan & Schersching, 1981). Research also shows that certain factors can upset the delicate balance between informational and normative influences. Social pressure is increased, for example, in juries that vote by a public roll call or show of hands (Davis et al., 1989) and in deadlocked juries that are called back into the courtroom and urged by the judge to resolve their differences (Smith & Kassin, 1993).

Over the years, the U.S. Supreme Court has addressed the decision-making dynamics of the jury in two ways. In the following pages, we look at these important issues and what they mean.

TABLE 12.6

The Road to Agreement: From Individual Votes to a Group Verdict

Research has shown how verdicts are reached by mock juries that begin with different combinations of initial votes. You can see that the results support the majority-wins rule. But also note the evidence for a leniency bias: When the initial vote is split, juries gravitate toward acquittal (Kerr, 1981, as cited in Stasser et al., 1982).

Initial Votes (Guilty-Not Guilty)	Final Jury Verdicts (Percent)		
	Conviction	Acquittal	Hung
6-0	100	0	0
5-1	78	7	16
4-2	44	26	30
3-3	9	51	40
2-4	4	79	17
1-5	0	93	7
0-6	0	100	0

One can usually predict a jury's final verdict by knowing where the individual jurors stand the first time they vote. **TRUE.**

Jury Size: How Small Is Too Small?

How many people does it take to form a jury? In keeping with British tradition, twelve has been the magic number. Then, in the case of *Williams v. Florida* (1970), the defendant was convicted of armed robbery by a six-person jury. He appealed the verdict to the

leniency bias The tendency for jury deliberation to produce a tilt toward acquittal.

U.S. Supreme Court but lost. As a result of this precedent, American courts are now permitted to cut trial costs by using six-person juries in cases that do not involve the death penalty. Juries consisting of fewer than six are not permitted (*Ballew v. Georgia*, 1978).

What is the impact of moving from twelve to six? The Supreme Court approached this question as a social psychologist would. It sought to determine whether the change would affect the decision-making process. Unfortunately, the Court misinterpreted the available research so badly that Michael Saks (1974) concluded that it "would not win a passing grade in a high school psychology class" (p. 18). Consider whether a reduction in size affects the ability of those in the voting minority to resist normative pressures. The Supreme Court did not think it would. Citing Asch's (1956) conformity studies, the Court argued that an individual juror's resistance depends on the *proportional* size of the majority. But is that true? Is the lone dissenter caught in a 5-to-1 bind as well insulated from the group norm as the minority in a 10-to-2 split? The Court argued that these 83-to-17 percent divisions are psychologically identical. But wait. Asch's research showed exactly the opposite—that the mere presence of a single ally enables dissenters to keep their independence better than anything else. Research has shown that the size of a jury has other effects too. Michael Saks and Molli Marti (1997) conducted a meta-analysis of studies involving 15,000 mock jurors who deliberated in over 2,000 six-person or twelve-person juries. Overall, they found that the smaller juries were less likely to represent minority segments of the population. They were also more likely to reach a unanimous verdict and to do so even when they deliberated for shorter periods of time. Even in civil trials, in which juries have to make complex decisions on how much money to award the plaintiff, six-person groups spend less time discussing the case (Davis et al., 1997).

Less-Than-Unanimous Verdicts

The jury's size is not all that has changed. In 1972, the Supreme Court considered whether states may accept jury verdicts that are not unanimous. In one opinion, two defendants had been convicted by jury verdicts that were not unanimous—one by a vote of 11 to 1, the other by 10 to 2 (*Apodaca v. Oregon*, 1972). In a second opinion, a guilty verdict was determined by a 9-to-3 margin (*Johnson v. Louisiana*, 1972). In both decisions, the Supreme Court upheld the convictions.

The Court was divided in its view of these cases. Five justices argued that a rule allowing verdicts that are not unanimous would not adversely affect the jury; four justices believed that it would reduce the intensity of deliberations and undermine the potential for minority influence. Table 12.7 presents these dueling points of view. Which do you find more convincing? Imagine yourself on a jury that needs only a 9-to-3 majority to return a verdict. You begin by polling the group and find that you already have the nine votes needed. What next? According to one script, the group continues to argue vigorously and with open minds. According to the alternative scenario, the group begins to deliberate but the dissenters are quickly cast aside because their votes are not needed. Again, which scenario seems more realistic?

To answer that question, Reid Hastie and others (1983) recruited more than 800 people from the Boston area to take part in 69 mock juries. After watching a reenactment of a murder trial, the groups were instructed to reach a verdict by a 12-to-0, a 10-to-2, or an 8-to-4 margin. The differences were striking. Compared with juries that needed unanimous decisions, the others spent less time discussing the case and more time voting. After reaching the required number of votes, they often rejected the holdouts, terminated discussion, and returned a verdict. Afterward, participants in the non-unanimous juries rated their peers as more close-minded and themselves as less informed and less confident about the verdict. What's worse, Hastie's team saw in tapes of the delibera-

> ## TABLE 12.7
>
> ### *Johnson v. Louisiana* (1972): Contrasting Views
>
> Notice the contrasting views in the U.S. Supreme Court's decision to permit jury verdicts that are not unanimous. Justice White wrote the majority opinion and Justice Douglas wrote the dissent. The decision was reached by a vote of 5 to 4.
>
> ##### *Mr. Justice White, for the Majority*:
>
> We have no grounds for believing that majority jurors, aware of their responsibility and power over the liberty of the defendant, would simply refuse to listen to arguments presented to them in favor of acquittal, terminate discussion, and render a verdict. On the contrary, it is far more likely that a juror presenting reasoned argument in favor of acquittal could either have his arguments answered or would carry enough other jurors with him to prevent conviction. A majority will cease discussion and outvote a minority only after reasoned discussion has ceased to have persuasive effect or to serve any other purpose—when a minority, that is, continues to insist upon acquittal without having persuasive reasons in support of its position.
>
> ##### *Mr. Justice Douglas, for the Minority*:
>
> Non-unanimous juries need not debate and deliberate as fully as most unanimous juries. As soon as the requisite majority is attained, further consideration is not required either by Oregon or by Louisiana even though the dissident jurors might, if given the chance, be able to convince the majority. . . . The collective effort to piece together the puzzle of historical truth . . . is cut short as soon as the requisite majority is reached in Oregon and Louisiana. . . . It is said that there is no evidence that majority jurors will refuse to listen to dissenters whose votes are unneeded for conviction. Yet human experience teaches us that polite and academic conversation is no substitute for the earnest and robust argument necessary to reach unanimity.

tions that majority-rule juries often adopted "a more forceful, bullying, persuasive style" (1983, p. 112). After being permitted to videotape 50 non-unanimous civil juries in Arizona, Shari Diamond and colleagues (2006) similarly observed that thoughtful minorities were sometimes "marginalized" by majorities that had the power to ignore them.

Today, only two states permit less-than-unanimous verdicts in criminal trials. A substantial number do so for civil cases. Yet research has shown that this procedure weakens jurors who are in the voting minority, breeds close-mindedness, short-circuits the discussion, and leaves many jurors uncertain about the decision. Henry Fonda, step aside. The jury has reached its verdict.

Posttrial: To Prison and Beyond

After conspiring in a series of cold-blooded killings, most committed at gas stations and convenience stores, Washington, D.C. snipers John Allen Muhammad, 42, and Lee Boyd Malvo, 18, were caught, tried, and convicted by Virginia juries. Their crimes were identical. In November 2003, Muhammad's jury sentenced him to death, but Malvo's jury sentenced him to life in prison one month later. Both supporters and opponents of the death penalty complained of the disparity. But did the different sentences reflect on the capricious nature of jury decision making (some had suggested that Malvo benefited from a jury's charitable spirit the week of Christmas), or were the differences rationally and morally based on the fact that Muhammad was older and more in control—the "mastermind," not the "puppet"?

■ The Sentencing Process

For defendants convicted of crimes, the jury's verdict is followed by a sentence. Sentencing decisions are usually made by judges, not juries, and they are often controversial. One reason for the controversy is that many people see judges as being too lenient (Stalans & Diamond, 1990). Another is that people disagree on the goals served by imprisonment. For many judges, the goal of a prison sentence is practical: to incapacitate offenders and deter them from committing future crimes. For many citizens, however, there is a more powerful motive at work: to exact retribution, or revenge, against the offender for his or her misdeeds. Research shows that people are driven by this "just deserts" motive, recommending sentences of increasing harshness for crimes of increasing severity, regardless of whether the offender is seen as likely to strike again and regardless of whether such sentences deter crime or serve other useful purposes (Carlsmith et al., 2002; Carlsmith, 2006; Darley et al., 2000; Darley & Pittman, 2003). Interestingly, research also shows that although people think that "sweet revenge" against someone who exploited them will make them feel better, sometimes it has the opposite effect (Carlsmith et al., 2008).

Based on current rates, an estimated 5 percent of all Americans (9 percent of men, 1 percent of women) will serve prison time in the course of their lives.

Judges also disagree about issues related to sentencing. Thus, a recurring public complaint is that there is too much **sentencing disparity**—that punishments for crime are inconsistent from one judge to the next. To document the problem, Anthony Partridge and William Eldridge (1974) compiled identical sets of files from 20 actual cases and sent them to 50 federal judges for sentencing recommendations. They found major disparities in the sentences the judges said they would impose. In one case, for example, judges had read about a man who was convicted of extortion and tax evasion. One judge recommended a three-year prison sentence, while another recommended 20 years in prison and a fine of $65,000. It's hard to believe these two judges read the same case. But other studies have uncovered similar differences.

Some judges are unusually creative in their sentencing of convicted felons. For example, a judge in Houston ordered a piano teacher who molested two students to donate his piano to a local school, a South Dakota judge sentenced cattle rustlers to shovel manure for a week, and a Florida judge ordered drunk drivers to display a bumper sticker on their cars that said "Convicted DUI" (Greene et al., 2006). In recent years, the federal government and many state governments have created sentencing guidelines to minimize the disparities and bring greater consistency to the process (Ruback & Wroblewski, 2001).

Still, sentencing decisions can be influenced by irrelevant factors. For example, Birte Englich and others (2006) theorized that judges would be influenced by the well-known "anchoring effect"—the tendency to use one stimulus as an "anchor," or reference point, in judging a second stimulus (Tversky & Kahneman, 1974). In a series of studies conducted in Germany, these researchers presented legal professionals—mostly judges—with materials about a criminal case. All participants received the same file except that some files suggested a low sentencing number (one year) and others suggested a high number (three years). Regardless of whether the number was presented as a prosecutor's recommendation, a question from a journalist, or a random roll of the dice, those first exposed to the high anchor point assigned harsher sentences than those exposed to the lower anchor point.

Some influences on this very human decision-making process are even more disturbing. By combing through U.S. death penalty statistics, researchers long ago discovered that sentencing decisions are consistently biased by race: All else being equal, convicted murderers are more likely to be sentenced to death if they are black or if the victim is white (Baldus et al., 1990). Informed by the racial stereotyping studies we saw in Chapter 5, Jennifer Eberhardt and her colleagues (2006) revisited a number of capital cases involving black defendants, this time looking for an even more subtle effect. For each case, they obtained a photograph of the defendant and had college students rate the degree to which he had a stereotypically black appearance—for example, a broad nose, thick lips, and dark skin. Using these ratings, they found that when the

sentencing disparity
Inconsistency of sentences for the same offense from one judge to another.

victim was black, the defendant's appearance was unrelated to sentencing. When the victim was white, however, the death penalty odds were predictable by the blackness of the defendant's appearance (24 percent among the least stereotypical; 58 percent among the most stereotypical). It seems that there are shades of black that influence whether judges and juries perceive defendants to be "deathworthy."

The Prison Experience

It is no secret that many prisons are overcrowded and that the situation has worsened as a result of recently toughened sentencing guidelines. It is also no secret that prison life can be cruel, violent, and degrading. The setting is highly oppressive and regimented, many prison guards are abusive, and many inmates fall into a state of despair (Paulus, 1988). Indeed, many are psychologically disturbed and in need of treatment they do not receive (Kupers, 1999). Thus, it is natural for social psychologists to wonder: Is there something in the situation that leads guards and prisoners to behave as they do? Would the rest of us react in the same way?

For ethical reasons, one obviously cannot place research participants inside a real prison. So, many years ago, a team of researchers from Stanford University did the next best thing. They constructed their own prison in the basement of the psychology department building (Haney et al., 1973; Haney & Zimbardo, 1998; Zimbardo et al., 1973). Complete with iron-barred cells, a solitary-confinement closet, and a recreation area for guards, the facility housed 21 participants—all healthy and stable men between the ages of 17 and 30 who had answered a newspaper ad promising 15 dollars a day for a two-week study of prison life. By the flip of a coin, half the participants were designated as guards and the other half became prisoners. Neither group was told specifically how to fulfill its role.

On the first day, each of the participant prisoners was unexpectedly "arrested" at his home, booked, fingerprinted, and driven to the simulated prison by officers of the local police department. These prisoners were then stripped, searched, and dressed in loose-fitting smocks with an identification number, a nylon stocking to cover their hair, and rubber sandals. A chain was bolted to the ankle of each prisoner. The guards were dressed in khaki uniforms and supplied with nightsticks, handcuffs, reflector sunglasses, keys, and whistles. The rules specified that prisoners were to be called by number, routinely lined up to be counted, fed three bland meals, and permitted three supervised toilet visits per day. The stage was set. It remained to be seen just how seriously the participants would take their roles and react to one another in this novel setting.

The events of the next few days were startling. Filled with a sense of power and authority, a few guards became progressively more abusive. They harassed the inmates, forced them into crowded cells, woke them during the night, and subjected them to hard labor and solitary confinement. These guards were particularly cruel when they thought they were alone with a prisoner. The prisoners themselves were rebellious at first, but their efforts were met with retaliation. Soon they all became passive and demoralized. After 36 hours, the experimenters had to release their first prisoner, who was suffering from acute depression. On subsequent days, other prisoners had to be released. By the sixth day, those who remained were so shaken by the experience that the study was terminated. It is reassuring, if not remarkable, that after a series of debriefing sessions, participants seemed to show no signs of lasting distress.

This study has been criticized on methodological and ethical grounds (Banuazizi & Movahedi, 1975; Savin, 1973). Still, the results are fascinating. Within a brief

In this simulation study of prison behavior, subjects were arbitrarily assigned to be prisoners or guards. Local police officers arrested the prisoners, who were brought to a jail constructed at Stanford University. After several days, the guards took on cruel, authoritarian roles that demoralized the prisoners to such an extent that the experiment was terminated.

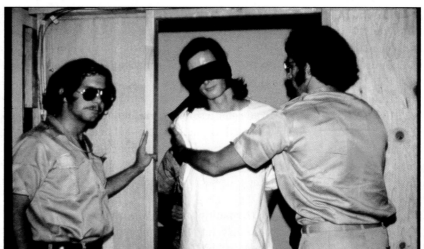

period of time, under relatively mild conditions, and with a group of men not prone to violence, the Stanford study recreated some of the prisoner and guard behaviors actually found behind prison walls. But would this occur today, in the twenty-first century? To find out, social psychologists Steve Reicher and Alex Haslam (2006) worked in the spring of 2002 with the British Broadcasting Corporation, or BBC, to create a survivor-like reality TV special called *The Experiment*, modeled after Zimbardo's study. Shown in four episodes, the television special brought together 15 men, all of whom were carefully screened, were warned that they would be exposed to hardships, and were randomly assigned to prisoner and guard roles. Determined to set limits, monitor events closely, and adhere to ethical guidelines for research with human subjects, Haslam and Reicher did not fully recreate the conditions of the original study and did not observe the same kinds of brutality from the guards. In their view, these findings challenge the conclusion that normal people can be dehumanized by the mere assignment to institutional roles.

One other profound question has arisen concerning the Stanford prison study, the same question that is often raised about Milgram's obedience experiments: Did the behavior of guards reflect on the power of the situation they were in or were the men who took part in the study uniquely prone to violence? Recently, Thomas Carnahan and Sam McFarland (2007) posted two newspaper ads—one, like Zimbardo's, for a study on prison life; the other, identical in every way except that it omitted the words "prison life." Those who volunteered for the prison study scored higher on tests that measure aggressiveness, authoritarianism, and narcissism and lower on tests that measure empathy and altruism. Reflecting on the differences, these researchers suggested that perhaps the Stanford prison study had attracted individuals who were prone to antisocial behavior. In response, Haney and Zimbardo (2009) note that volunteers in the original study were also tested and that no personality differences were found between them and the general population. More importantly, they note, no differences were found between those assigned to prisoner and guard roles within the experiment.

Reiterating his belief in the power of the situation, Zimbardo (2007) points to the striking parallels between the behaviors observed in his simulated prison and the sadistic abuses of real prisoners in 2004, more than 30 years later, by military guards at the Abu Ghraib Prison in Iraq. Noting that various social psychological factors create a "perfect storm" that leads good people to behave in evil ways, Zimbardo refers to this unfortunate transformation as the "Lucifer Effect," named after God's favorite angel, Lucifer, who fell from grace and ultimately became Satan.

Perceptions of Justice

People tend to measure the success of a legal system by its ability to produce fair and accurate results. But is that all there is to justice? Let's step back for a moment from the specifics and ask if it is possible to define justice in a way that is unrelated to outcomes.

Justice as a Matter of Procedure

In a book entitled *Procedural Justice* (1975), John Thibaut and Laurens Walker proposed that our satisfaction with the way legal and other disputes are resolved depends not only on outcomes but also on the procedures used to achieve those outcomes. Two aspects of procedure are important in this regard: One is *decision control*—whether a procedure affords the involved parties the power to accept, reject, or otherwise influence the final decision. The other is *process control*—whether it offers the parties an opportunity to present their case to a third-party decision maker. In the courtroom, of course, the disputants are limited in their decision control. Thus, their satisfaction must depend on whether they feel that they had a chance to express their views.

There are two ways to look at the effects of process control on perceptions of justice. Originally, it was thought that people want an opportunity to express their opinions only because having a voice in the process improves the odds of achieving a favorable ruling. In this view, process control is satisfying only because it increases decision control (Thibaut & Walker, 1978). Recent research, however, suggests that people value the chance to present their side of a story to an impartial decision maker even when they do not prevail in the ultimate outcome. In other words, process control is more than just an instrumental means to an end. When people believe that they have a voice in the proceedings, are treated with respect, and are judged by an impartial decision maker, process control can be an end in itself (Lind et al., 1990).

This aspect of the legal system is very important. It means, for example, that regardless of whether people agree or disagree with how a case turns out, they can find solace in the fact that both sides had their "day in court," at least when the decision

Dario Pignatelli/Reuters/Landov

In the summer of 2009, thousands of Iranian men and women took to the streets of Tehran and other major cities to protest the re-election of Mahmoud Ahmadinejad as president. With evidence suggesting that the vote was rigged, these protests illustrate how frustrated people get when they don't trust that their voices are being heard in a fair manner—an essential aspect of procedural justice.

maker is seen as impartial. Yet certain members of the legal community are openly critical of that so-called day in court. As law professor Alan Dershowitz once put it, "Nobody really wants justice. Winning is the only thing to most participants in the criminal justice system, just as it is to professional athletes" (1982, p. xvi).

Dershowitz's skepticism is centered on something that many of us take for granted: the **adversarial model** of justice. In the adversarial system (as practiced in North America, Great Britain, and a handful of other countries), the prosecution and defense oppose each other, each presenting one side of the story in an effort to win a favorable verdict. In contrast, most other countries use an **inquisitorial model**, in which a neutral investigator gathers the evidence from both sides and presents the findings in court. With two such different methods of doing justice, social psychologists could not resist the temptation to make comparisons (van Koppen & Penrod, 2003).

Interested in which approach people prefer, Laurens Walker and others (1974) constructed a business simulation in which two companies competed for a cash prize. Participants who were assigned to the role of president of a company learned that someone on their staff was accused of spying on the competition. To resolve the dispute, a "trial" was held. In some cases, the trial followed an adversarial procedure in which the two sides were presented by law students who were chosen by participants and whose payment was contingent on winning. Other cases followed an inquisitorial model in which a single law student who was appointed by the experimenter and paid regardless of the outcome presented both sides. Regardless of whether they had won or lost the verdict, participants who took part in an adversarial trial were more satisfied than those involved in an inquisitorial trial. Even impartial observers preferred the adversarial proceedings.

Other researchers found similar results, not only in the United States and Great Britain, where citizens are accustomed to the adversarial system, but in France and West Germany as well (Lind et al., 1978). This perception of procedural justice is not limited to adversarial methods of resolving legal disputes. Rather, it seems that any method that offers participants a *voice* in the proceedings, including methods that are nonadversarial, is seen as most fair and just—not only in law, but also in business, politics, school settings, and intimate relationships (Folger & Greenberg, 1985; Sheppard, 1985). It is also important in this regard for people to perceive that they were granted as much "voice" as others were (Van Prooijen et al., 2006) and that the decision maker was open-minded and not acting out of self-interest (De Cremer, 2004). In matters of justice, people all over the world are motivated not only by the desire for personal gain but by their need to be recognized, respected, and treated fairly by others who are impartial. Research thus shows that for people to accept the rule of law and comply with outcomes they do not like, they must see the decision-making procedures as fair (Tyler, 2006b).

adversarial model A dispute-resolution system in which the prosecution and defense present opposing sides of the story.

inquisitorial model A dispute-resolution system in which a neutral investigator gathers evidence from both sides and presents the findings in court.

▌ Culture, Law, and Justice

When it comes to the basics of human behavior, much of the research in this chapter can be universally applied. In police interrogations, suspects all over the world, including some who are innocent, are more likely to confess when they are isolated and intensely pressured than when they are not. In eyewitness testimony, the problems and limitations of human memory—as seen in our ability to accurately perceive, store, and retrieve certain types of information—are universal. In courtrooms wherever juries are used, their decision making will invariably reflect the joint influences of their personal dispositions, the information they receive in court, and the conformity dynamics that seize hold of small groups. Finally, recurring stories of prison abuses have shown that prison is a social setting that tends to bring out the worst in guards and their prisoners—wherever they are.

Although the similarities are clear, they should not mask important cross-cultural differences. Because cultures have different norms, customs, and values, they also create different laws to regulate their citizens' behavior. To be sure, certain universal values have evolved among humans and are passed from one generation to the next, such as the prohibitions against physical violence, the taking of someone's property without consent, and deception in important transactions. In other ways, however, the world's cultural and religious groups differ markedly in the behaviors they scorn and seek to regulate. In some countries but not in others, it is against the law to have sex outside of marriage, take more than one husband or wife, assist in a suicide, gamble, eat meat, or drink alcohol. Based on the belief in an afterlife, some religions prohibit autopsies. Others impose strict dress codes, particularly for women.

In diverse populations such as the United States, these cultural practices can put governments and cultures into conflict with one another. In one highly publicized case, a Japanese woman living in California was prosecuted for drowning her two children in the Pacific Ocean before being rescued while she was trying to drown herself. At trial, she testified that she had tried to commit *oyaku-shinju*, a Japanese custom of parent-child suicide, after learning that her husband was having an affair. Her motive, she said, was to save her children from the shame that their father had brought to the family. In a second case, a Navajo defendant was prosecuted for using the hallucinogen peyote, an illegal substance in the United States. He argued that the substance is used to achieve spiritual exaltation and should be protected by the freedom of religion. (Immigrants from Yemen, Kenya, and Somalia have similarly been arrested for chewing khat leaves in social gatherings, the way Americans chew tobacco, even though the effect is comparable to drinking three espressos.) In a third case, two Cambodian immigrants were prosecuted for trying to eat a 4-month-old puppy, an acceptable practice in their homeland but not in the United States. As these examples illustrate, judges and juries are sometimes asked to consider *cultural defenses* in their decision making (Renteln, 2004).

Just as nations differ in the crime laws that are set, the study of *comparative law* shows that they also differ in the processes used to enforce these laws. In Great Britain, the United States, Canada, and Australia, the accused has a right to be tried by a jury composed of fellow citizens. In France, Russia, and Brazil, that right is reserved for only the most serious crimes. In India and throughout Asia, all defendants are tried by professional judges, not juries. Yet China recently introduced mixed panels consisting of one judge and two lay jurors. Beginning in 2009, Japan also started to use a quasi-jury system, called *saiban-in*, in which three law-trained judges and six lay citizens chosen by lottery come together to render verdicts and sentencing decisions by a majority vote. Ever since juries were abolished in Japan during World War II, all Japanese defendants have been tried by three-judge panels; almost all have been convicted, typically after confessing to save face and minimize embarrassment to the family.

For people judged guilty of serious crimes, the consequences may also vary from one country to another. As noted earlier, "doing justice" often means punishing those who violate rules as a means of seeking retribution. But whether people are offended enough to seek revenge depends in part on the power of individualist and collectivist norms within the culture. For example, research shows that American college students are offended more when their personal rights are violated—for example, when a co-worker steals the credit for their idea, while Korean students are offended more when their sense of duty and obligation is violated—for example, when a co-worker fails to contribute his or her promised share in a cooperative effort (Shteynberg et al., 2009).

When it comes to punishment, the most notable cultural difference concerns the death penalty. When Iraq's former president Saddam Hussein was executed by hanging in December of 2006, many world leaders, including many of Hussein's enemies, took the opportunity to condemn the execution and, more generally, capital punishment. According to Amnesty International, there are substantial differences of opinion and practice across the world regarding the death penalty (Amnesty International, 2009). Currently, 86 countries prohibit the death penalty for all crimes (Australia, Austria, Belgium, Canada, Colombia, Denmark, England, France, Germany, Greece, Ireland, Italy, Mexico, the Netherlands, Norway, Portugal, Spain, Sweden, Switzerland, Turkey, and Venezuela are prominent examples); 11 ban the death penalty as a general rule but permit it for exceptional crimes, such as espionage, or crimes committed in exceptional circumstances (Brazil, Chile, Israel, and Peru are some examples); 26 countries allow for the death penalty in law but do not execute people as a matter of practice (Algeria, Kenya, Morocco, and Russia are some examples); and 73 countries permit and use the death penalty (in addition to the United States, the others include China, Cuba, Egypt, Iran, Iraq, India, Japan, Pakistan, Saudi Arabia, and Thailand). On matters of crime and punishment, it is clear that cultural influences are substantial.

Closing Statement

This chapter focuses on the trial process, the events that precede it, and the events that follow from it. Yet we've only scratched the surface. In recent years, more and more judges, lawyers, and policy makers have come to recognize that social psychology can make important contributions to the legal system. Thus, with increasing frequency, social psychologists are called on for expert advice in and out of court and are cited in the opinions written by judges. Clearly, the collection, presentation, and evaluation of evidence are imperfect human enterprises and subject to bias. Through an understanding of social psychology, however, we can now identify some of the problems—and perhaps even the solutions.

REVIEW

- Embedded in a large criminal justice system, relatively few cases come to trial.

- Yet the trial is the heart and soul of the system.

Jury Selection

- Once called for service, prospective jurors are questioned by the judge or lawyers in a process known as voir dire.
- Those who exhibit a clear bias are excluded. Lawyers may also strike a limited number through the use of peremptory challenges.

Trial Lawyers as Intuitive Psychologists
- Pressured to make juror selections quickly, lawyers rely on implicit personality theories and stereotypes.
- But general demographic factors do not reliably predict how jurors will vote.

Scientific Jury Selection

- Lawyers sometimes hire psychologists to conduct surveys that identify correlations between demographics and trial-relevant attitudes.
- Scientific jury selection raises ethical issues concerning its effects on justice.

Juries in Black and White: Does Race Matter?

- On the question of whether race influences a juror's decision making, research suggests that there is no simple answer.

- Whether or not jurors are biased by race may depend on the strength of the evidence, the extent to which attention is drawn to race, and the diversity of the jury as a whole.

Death Qualification

- In capital cases, prospective jurors who say they would not vote for the death penalty are excluded in a process known as death qualification.
- Jurors who favor the death penalty are more likely to find defendants guilty than are jurors who oppose the death penalty.

The Courtroom Drama

- Once the jury is selected, evidence previously gathered is presented in court.

Confession Evidence

- The police employ various methods of interrogation.
- One method is to befriend the suspect and "minimize" the offense; a second is to scare the suspect into believing that it is futile to deny the charges.
- Under pressure, people sometimes confess to crimes they did not commit.
- Although juries are supposed to reject coerced confessions, their verdicts are still influenced by such evidence.

The Lie-Detector Test

- By recording physiological arousal, the polygraph can be used as a lie detector.
- Polygraphers report high rates of accuracy; but truthful persons are too often judged guilty, and the test can be fooled.

Eyewitness Testimony

- Eyewitness memory is a three-stage process involving acquisition, storage, and retrieval.
- During acquisition, witnesses who are highly aroused zoom in on the central features of an event but lose memory for peripheral details.
- The presence of a weapon hinders a witness's ability to identify the perpetrator.
- Witnesses have trouble recognizing members of a race other than their own.
- During storage, misleading postevent information biases eyewitness memory.
- Young children are particularly suggestible in this regard.

- Lineups are biased when a suspect is distinctive, when the police imply that the criminal is in the lineup, when witnesses make relative judgments, and when the suspect is familiar for other reasons.
- In court, jurors overestimate eyewitnesses' accuracy and cannot distinguish between accurate and inaccurate witnesses.
- People are too readily persuaded by a witness's confidence—a factor that does not reliably predict identification accuracy.
- Psychologists are sometimes called to testify as experts on eyewitness evidence.

Nonevidentiary Influences

- The more pretrial knowledge people have about a case, the more likely they are to presume the defendant guilty.
- Research shows that pretrial publicity can bias jury verdicts.
- Once inadmissible testimony leaks out in court, the jury is contaminated by it.
- A judge's cautionary instruction may worsen the situation by drawing attention to the forbidden testimony, arousing reactance, or leading jurors to see the information as relevant.

The Judge's Instructions

- The judge's instructions often have little impact, in part because they are often incomprehensible.
- The instructions are usually delivered after the evidence, after many jurors have formed an opinion.
- Jurors may not follow instructions that conflict with their own conceptions of justice, a phenomenon known as jury nullification.

Jury Deliberation

Leadership in the Jury Room

- Dominance hierarchies develop in the jury room.
- Certain people are more likely than others to be elected foreperson, but the foreperson tends to play the role of moderator rather than group leader.

The Dynamics of Deliberation

- Jury deliberations pass through three stages: orientation, open conflict, and reconciliation.
- The period of open conflict is filled with informational and normative pressures.

- When it comes to outcomes, the initial majority typically wins, although deliberation tends to produce a leniency bias.

Jury Size: How Small Is Too Small?

- The U.S. Supreme Court has ruled that the use of six-person juries is acceptable.
- But these smaller groups do not deliberate for as long as twelve-person juries do and contain less minority representation.

Less-Than-Unanimous Verdicts

- In some states, juries are permitted to reach verdicts by a less-than-unanimous majority.
- But research shows that once a required majority is reached, these juries reject the holdouts, terminate discussion, and return a verdict.

Posttrial: To Prison and Beyond

The Sentencing Process

- Many people believe that judges are too lenient and that punishments for the same offense are often inconsistent from one case to another.
- Part of the problem is that people have different views of the goals of sentencing and punishment.

The Prison Experience

- Stanford researchers built a simulated prison and recruited male adults to act as guards and prisoners.
- Some guards were abusive, the prisoners became passive, and the study had to be terminated.
- To this day, the Stanford prison study continues to draw debate concerning the power of the situation and the similarity between these findings and more recent events.

Perceptions of Justice

Justice as a Matter of Procedure

- Satisfaction with justice depends not only on winning and losing but also on the procedures used to achieve the outcome.
- People of all cultures prefer models of justice that offer participants a voice in the proceedings and the opportunity to be judged by an impartial decision maker.

Culture, Law, and Justice

- Reflecting cultural and religious values, countries set different laws in an effort to regulate behavior.
- In diverse populations, differing cultural practices sometimes put governments into conflict with segments of their population.
- Cultures also differ in the processes used to enforce laws and the consequences for those who are convicted.

Closing Statement

- Increasingly social psychologists have become involved in studying the legal system—identifying the problems and seeking solutions.

Key Terms

adversarial model (522)
cross-race identification bias (501)
death qualification (492)
inquisitorial model (522)
jury nullification (512)

leniency bias (515)
misinformation effect (502)
peremptory challenge (488)
polygraph (498)
scientific jury selection (490)

sentencing disparity (518)
voir dire (488)
weapon-focus effect (500)

Media Resources

Social Psychology 8th Edition Companion Website

Visit your book companion website **www.cengage.com/psychology/kassin** where you will find flash cards, practice quizzes, Internet links, and more to help you study.

CENGAGENOW Just what you need to know NOW! Spend time on what you need to master rather than on information you already have learned. Take a pre-test for this chapter and CengageNOW will generate a personalized study plan based on your results. The study plan will identify the topics you need to review and direct you to online resources to help you master those topics. You can then take a post-test to help you determine the concepts you have mastered and what you will need to work on. Try it out! Go to **academic.cengage.com/login** to sign in with an access code or to purchase access to this product.

Putting COMMON SENSE *to the Test*

Contrary to popular opinion, women are harsher as trial jurors than men are.

False. *Demographic factors such as gender do not consistently predict juror verdicts; men may be harsher in some cases, women in others.*

Without being beaten or threatened, innocent people sometimes confess to crimes they did not commit.

True. *Innocent suspects sometimes confess, either to escape an unpleasant situation or because they are led to believe they committed a crime they cannot recall.*

A person can fool a lie-detector test by suppressing arousal when questions about the crime are asked.

False. *It is possible to beat a lie-detector test by elevating arousal when "innocent" questions are asked but not by trying to suppress arousal in response to "guilty" questions.*

Eyewitnesses find it relatively difficult to recognize members of a race other than their own.

True. *Researchers have observed this cross-race identification bias in both laboratory and field settings.*

The more confident an eyewitness is about an identification, the more accurate he or she is likely to be.

False. *Studies have shown that the confidence of an eyewitness does not reliably predict accuracy, in part because confidence is influenced by postidentification factors.*

One can usually predict a jury's final verdict by knowing where the individual jurors stand the first time they vote.

True. *As a result of both informational and normative group influences, the preference of the initial voting majority usually prevails.*

13

Business

This chapter examines the social side of business—specifically, the role of social factors in the workplace and their influence on economic decisions. First, we look at social influences on personnel selection and performance appraisals made within organizations. Then, we examine the roles of leadership and worker motivation. Finally, we explore economic decision making, the stock market, and other business settings.

Every year, around Labor Day, the Harris poll asks Americans to estimate how much time they spend working. Since 1973, there has been a steady increase—from 41 hours per week up to about 50 hours per week. The International Labor Organization reports that Americans in a year work 137 hours more than the Japanese, 260 hours more than the British, and 499 hours more than the French (Greenhause, 2001).

Whenever two adults meet for the first time, the opening line of their conversation is predictable: "So, what do you do?" "Oh, I'm a (social psychologist). And you?" For many people, work is an integral part of their personal identity. Of course, most of us would rather spend next Monday morning lying on a warm and breezy beach, reading a paperback novel, and sipping a tropical fruit drink, but most people spend more time working than playing. In large part, we work to make money. Yet jobs also provide us with activity, a sense of purpose, and a social community. Imagine that you had just won $10 million in a lottery. Would you continue to work? In a 2005 Gallup poll, 59 percent of Americans said they would still continue, either at their current jobs or elsewhere. Thus, it is important to identify the social influences on this significant human experience.

There is a flip side to the importance of work: unemployment. Worldwide, in the summer of 2009, the number of people in a population who were unemployed ranged from a low of nearly 0 (in Andorra) up to 90 percent (in Zimbabwe). As a result of the recent and dramatic economic downturn, unemployment rates have driven up all over the world. According to the U.S. Bureau of Labor Statistics, the unemployment rate in the United States has risen in the past few years from 4 percent to nearly 10 percent—with young adults being hit the hardest (U.S. Bureau of Labor Statistics, 2009). Sadly, behind these numbers are real people—men and women who have lost jobs and are unable to find new jobs, often plunging them into a situation, through no fault of their own, that is financially and psychologically devastating. If you have a job, it is an important part of your life; if you don't have a job, that fact too is an important part of your life.

This chapter considers applications of social psychology to business. First, we'll look at **industrial/organizational (I/O) psychology**, the study of human behavior in the workplace. This subdiscipline of psychology is broad and includes in its ranks both social and nonsocial psychologists who conduct research, teach in business schools or universities, and work in government and private industry. Whatever the setting, I/O psychology raises important practical questions about job interviewing, evaluations

industrial/organizational (I/O) psychology The study of human behavior in business and other organizational settings.

and promotions, leadership, motivation, and other aspects of life on the job. Next, we'll examine some social influences on economic decision making in the stock market and elsewhere in the business world.

The impact of social psychological factors in the workplace was first recognized many years ago—thanks, oddly enough, to a study of industrial lighting. The year was 1927. Calvin Coolidge was president, baseball legend Babe Ruth hit 60 home runs, Charles Lindbergh flew across the Atlantic for the first time, and the U.S. economy seemed sound, though the stock market would soon crash, triggering the Great Depression. Just outside of Chicago, the Hawthorne plant of the Western Electric Company employed 30,000 men and women who manufactured telephones and central office equipment. As in other companies, management wanted to boost productivity. The bottom line was important.

At first, managers thought that they could make workers at the plant more productive by altering the illumination levels in the factory. Proceeding logically, they increased the lighting for one group of workers in a special test room, kept the same lighting in a control room, and compared the effects. Much to their surprise, productivity rates increased in both rooms. At that point, a team of psychologists was brought in to vary other conditions in the factory. Over the next five years, groups of employees from various departments were selected to do their work in a test room where, at different times, they were given more rest periods, coffee breaks, a free mid-morning lunch, shorter work days, shorter weeks, a new location, overtime, financial incentives, dimmer lights, or just a different method of payment. At one point, the researchers even went back and reinstated the original pre-study conditions inside the test room. Yet no matter what changes were made, productivity levels always increased.

The Hawthorne project, described in a classic book entitled *Management and the Worker* (Roethlisberger & Dickson, 1939), has had a great impact on the study of behavior in the workplace. At first, the researchers were puzzled and discouraged. With positive effects observed among all test-room workers (even when the original pretest conditions were in place), it seemed that the project had failed. Ponder the results, however, and you'll see why these studies are so important. With striking consistency, workers became more productive—not because of any of the specific changes made but because they had been singled out for special assignment. Many researchers have criticized the methods used in this study and the ways the results have been interpreted (Adair, 1984; Chiesa & Hobbs, 2008; Parsons, 1974). Still, the phenomenon that has become known as the **Hawthorne effect** laid a foundation for I/O psychology.

The Hawthorne plant no longer exists, but the study conducted there helped psychologists understand the profound impact of social influences in the workplace. Interested in the conditions that affect satisfaction, motivation, and performance, today's researchers study all aspects of life in the workplace, including the effects of monitoring workers' activity on the computer (Alge, 2001); what motivates some people to spend extra hours at work (Brett & Stroh, 2003); perceptions and realities of sexual harassment (O'Leary-Kelly et al., 2009); the relationship between daylight saving time, sleep,

These women were among the assembly plant workers who took part in the classic Hawthorne studies of productivity in the workplace.

Courtesy of AT&T Archives

Hawthorne effect The finding that workers who were given special attention increased their productivity regardless of what actual changes were made in the work setting.

and workplace injuries (Barnes & Wagner, 2009); and the perpetrators and targets of bullying in the workplace (Glasø et al., 2009).

The three of us who wrote this textbook all work on college campuses amid students, professors, and administrators. We spend most of our time in classrooms, offices, and research laboratories. For women and men in other occupations—store clerks, taxicab drivers, carpenters, doctors, Internet companies, farmers, teachers, accountants, firefighters, and airline pilots—the workplace is very different. Yet despite the diversity of roles and settings, certain common concerns arise: How are applicants selected for jobs? How is performance then evaluated? What makes for an effective leader who can influence others and mobilize their support? What motivates people to work hard and feel satisfied with this aspect of their lives? And what factors influence the kinds of economic decisions that people make? Let's enter the workplace and address these important questions.

"And the dim fluorescent lighting is meant to emphasize the general absence of hope."

Personnel Selection

For all kinds of organizations, especially in a tight economy, the secret to success begins with the recruitment and development of a competent work staff. For that reason, personnel selection is the first important step (Sackett & Lievens, 2008).

The Typical Job Interview

Anyone who has ever applied for a desirable job knows that sometimes you have to climb hurdles and jump through hoops to land a position that matches your desires. The routine is a familiar one: You submit a résumé or post one online, fill out an application, and perhaps bring in samples of your work or take a standardized test of your abilities, personality traits, or honesty. You may even be placed on the "hot seat" in a face-to-face interview. In a typical interview, a representative of the organization and an applicant meet in person to discuss the job. Interviews thus provide a two-way opportunity for the applicant and employer to evaluate each other. What a social perception dilemma these opportunities present! As an applicant, you have only a half-hour or so to make a favorable impression. As an interviewer, you have the same brief period of time to penetrate the applicant's self-presentation while at the same time presenting the company in a favorable light.

Even the most elaborate hiring methodologies eventually boil down to one of the dreaded rituals of business life: the job interview.

—Hotjobs.com

Monster.com founder Jeff Taylor (left) talks to employees about the company. Today, many job seekers and companies meet online through websites like Monster.com.

Very few employers would consider hiring a complete stranger for a responsible position without an interview. Would *you*? Like most of us, you probably trust your own ability to size people up. But should you? Do interviews promote sound hiring, or do they produce decisions that are biased by job-irrelevant personal characteristics? Civil rights laws explicitly forbid employers to discriminate on the basis of sex, race, age, religion, national origin, or disability. Does the interview process itself intensify or diminish these possible sources of bias? And are interviews valid and predictive of performance?

Focusing on the possibility of race and ethnic background biases in an interview setting, some

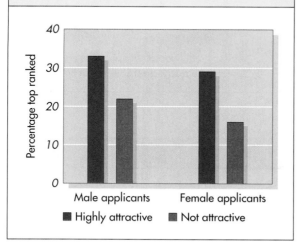

▶**FIGURE 13.1**

The Bias for Beauty in Hiring

In this study, managers rank-ordered four job applicants, two men and two women. One of each gender was attractive, the other plain. As shown, a majority selected an attractive male or female applicant as their top choice.

Marlowe et al., 1996.

researchers have reported good news. By statistically combining the results of 31 studies involving more than 11,000 job applicants, Allen Huffcutt and Philip Roth (1998) found that black and Hispanic applicants receive interview ratings only slightly lower on average than those obtained by their white counterparts. Perhaps the face-to-face interactions provided by interviews humanize applicants, bringing to life their interest in the job, their social skills, and other relevant attributes that do not show up on paper. This relative lack of bias also seems to characterize subjective evaluations of job performance—where supervisor (and peer) ratings of black, white, and Hispanic workers are more similar to one another, not less so, than "objective" measures of performance (Roth et al., 2003).

Although most employers have learned to guard against discriminatory hiring practices, there is one possible source of bias that is difficult to regulate: physical attractiveness. Except for certain types of work (such as modeling), beauty is not relevant to performance on the job. Yet as we saw in Chapter 9, people tend to favor others who are good-looking. Does this bias operate in hiring situations? To answer this question, Cynthia Marlowe and others (1996) presented a set of job application folders—including résumés, data sheets, and photographs—to 112 male and female managers of a financial institution. Believing they were evaluating actual prospective employees, each manager rank-ordered four equivalent and qualified applicants: two men and two women, one of each of whom was highly attractive. Who was selected? Look at ▶ Figure 13.1, and you'll see that there was a slight tendency to favor male applicants but that physical appearance had a greater impact, as 62 percent of all managers selected an attractive applicant as their top choice. Other research has since confirmed that human resource professionals exhibit a hiring preference for male and female applicants who are attractive (Jawahar & Mattsson, 2005). On a positive note, the results of Marlowe and colleagues showed that managers who had the most experience did not exhibit the bias for beauty.

Although interviews often result in the right selection of new employees, they sometimes lack predictive validity (Eder & Harris, 1999). Part of the problem may be that job applicants present themselves in a positive light, as you'd expect, and that those who engage in the most self-promotion—and these are not necessarily the best-qualified—are the most likely to get hired (Stevens & Kristof, 1995). Some college seniors who enter the job market are also more confident in their interviewing skills than others, and confidence predicts success months later (Tay et al., 2006). Researchers have found that even the quality of an applicant's handshake (as determined by its strength and vigor, firmness of grip, duration, and whether it is accompanied by eye contact) predicts how highly he or she will be rated by a real interviewer after an hour-long mock interview (Stewart et al., 2008).

"Faking" in an employment interview—which occurs whenever a job applicant consciously presents himself or herself in distorted ways in order to create a favorable impression—may well compromise the predictive validity of the process. For that reason, researchers have recently sought to develop a questionnaire that measures faking. In a series of studies, Julia Levashina and Michael Campion (2007) asked several hundreds of college seniors who were active on the job market to anonymously rate the degree to which they engaged in various faking behaviors during their most recent interviews. Some of the behaviors involved outright lying ("I claimed that I have skills I do not have"); others involved forms of exaggeration ("I exaggerated my responsibilities on previous jobs"), ingratiation ("I laughed at the interviewer's jokes even when they were not funny"), and image protection ("When asked directly, I did not mention some problems that I had in past jobs"). It will be interesting in future research to see whether applicants' responses on this questionnaire can be used to predict their success or failure—not only during the interview process but also later on the job.

Even if applicants are completely honest in their self-presentations, another potential problem with interviews is that employers often have preconceptions that can distort the process. When participants in an interview experiment were led to believe that the applicant they would meet was not suitable for a particular job, they prepared questions that sought negative rather than positive information (Binning et al., 1988). In a field study that illustrated the problem, Amanda Phillips and Robert Dipboye (1989) surveyed 34 managers from different branch offices of a large corporation and 164 job applicants these managers had interviewed. They found that the managers' pre-interview expectations, which were based on written application materials, influenced the kinds of interviews they conducted as well as the outcomes: The higher their expectations, the more time they spent "recruiting" rather than "evaluating" and the more likely they were to make a favorable hiring decision. Similarly, Thomas Dougherty and others (1994) found that interviewers with positive rather than negative expectations sounded warmer, more outgoing, and more cheerful. They also gave more information and spent more time promoting the company. It seems that job interviews can become part of a vicious cycle, or self-fulfilling prophecy. Without realizing it, employers use the opportunity to create realities that bolster their preexisting beliefs (see ▶ Figure 13.2).

Although flawed, job interviews consistently make for better hiring decisions. **FALSE.**

■ "Scientific" Alternatives to Traditional Interviews

Face-to-face interviews bring to life both job-relevant and not-so-relevant personal characteristics. Given that the process is so variable, should interviews be eliminated? Should they, perhaps, be computerized, leaving applicants to interact with companies via a programmed sequence of questions and answers administered by computer? Online interviews may offer a forum for an initial screening of applicants. Chances are, however, not too many people would feel comfortable making important life decisions in such an impersonal manner. Is it possible, then, to preserve the human touch of an interview while eliminating the bias and error?

Some organizations use the *polygraph*, or lie-detector test, as a screening device. As described in Chapter 12, the polygraph is an instrument that records physiological arousal in different parts of the body. Based on the assumption that lying creates stress, a polygraph examiner conducts an interview and compares the interviewee's level of arousal in response to various questions. Those who administer lie-detector tests argue that it enhances their ability to identify prospective employees who are honest. But opponents argue that the test invades an individual's privacy, that it is too easily misused, and that its results are not sufficiently accurate. For these reasons, the U.S. government in 1988 passed a law that prohibits the use of lie-detector tests except in

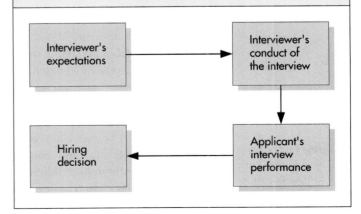

▶ **FIGURE 13.2**

Job Interviews: A Self-Fulfilling Prophecy?

One study indicates that interviewers' expectations influence the kinds of interviews conducted and applicants' performance. The higher the expectations, the more the interviewer tries to impress rather than evaluate the applicant and make a favorable hiring decision. Without realizing it, employers may use job interviews to create a reality that supports their prior beliefs.

Phillips & Dipboye, 1989.

matters involving large sums of money, public safety, and national security, such as for screening FBI agents and scientists who work at nuclear testing facilities (Beardsley, 1999).

Standardized Tests   Today, many companies use standardized written tests in the selection process. Three general types are used for this purpose. Tests of intelligence are designed to measure intellectual and cognitive abilities, job-specific knowledge and skills, or "street smarts" and common sense, which all may contribute to success on the job.

When it comes to measures of general intelligence, the use of cognitive ability tests in the workplace is a matter of serious debate. On the basis of extensive research, some psychologists believe that cognitive ability tests are useful because they are predictive of job success in high-stakes work settings (Gottfredson, 2002; Schmidt, 2002)—importantly, without discriminating against minorities and others who lack the resources to pay for test preparation courses (Sackett et al., 2008). The benefits of cognitive ability testing in the workplace have been amply demonstrated. Still, some researchers caution that general intelligence is only one relevant factor and that this focus discriminates against individuals with other abilities who don't happen to score well on these tests (Sternberg & Hedlund, 2002). For this reason, I/O psychologists as a group are somewhat ambivalent about the use of intelligence testing in personnel selection. When Kevin Murphy and others (2003) surveyed more than 700 professionals in the field, they found that most agreed that intelligence is not fully captured by standardized tests, that different jobs require different cognitive abilities, and that both cognitive and noncognitive selection measures should be used.

Currently, an estimated 2,500 U.S. companies also use personality testing to measure traits that are predictive of such work-related outcomes as leadership potential, helpfulness, lateness, absenteeism, and theft (Cha, 2005). For example, research shows that people who score high rather than low in the trait of conscientiousness—which tends to make them more achievement oriented, dependable, orderly, and cautious—are more likely in general to perform well on the job (Dudley et al., 2006). Another example: People who score as extroverted rather than introverted are especially likely to succeed as business managers and salespersons (Hurtz & Donovan, 2000; Salgado, 1997). Research shows that children and young adults who have high self-esteem, self-confidence, and a sense of control tend to seek out more challenging lines of work and, as a result, are more satisfied with their jobs later in life (Judge et al., 2000). Research also shows that high self-monitors—people who closely regulate their behavior to be socially appropriate—are more likely to get promoted and become leaders within an organization (Day et al., 2002).

These research findings are clear. But does that mean that companies should test all job applicants and hire those with favorable personalities? Reflecting this trend, one *U.S. News & World Report* writer explains "why a psychologist might be at your next interview" (Wolgemuth, 2009). But is this a sound development in the practical world of personnel selection? Not according to five editors of research journals that have published much of this personality research. In an article they collectively wrote, these editors concluded that although certain personality factors may well relate to job performance, researchers would need to devise tests that are more predictive—tests that do not rely on the motivated applicant's self-report and therefore cannot easily be faked (Morgeson et al., 2007).

Third, many companies have recently begun to administer **integrity tests**—questionnaires designed specifically to assess an applicant's honesty and character by asking direct questions concerning illicit drug use, shoplifting, petty theft, and other transgressions. The responses are scored by computer. Narrative profiles are provided,

integrity tests   Questionnaires designed to test a job applicant's honesty and character.

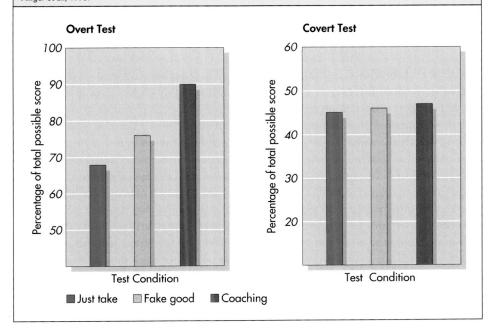

▶ **FIGURE 13.3**

Can Integrity Tests Be Faked?

Alliger and others (1996) gave college students overt and covert integrity tests. Some just took the test; others were told to "fake good"; others were coached. On the overt test, scores increased for subjects who faked good or were coached (left). On the covert test, scores were unaffected by these interventions (right).

Alliger et al., 1996.

and arbitrary cutoff scores are often used to determine if an applicant has passed or failed (Camara & Schneider, 1994).

A major concern about integrity tests and personality tests too, for that matter, is that applicants may be able to fake the tests on their own or with the help of coaching. Specifically, the concern is that applicants will use the tests to present themselves in overly positive ways—for example, as highly stable, conscientious, agreeable, or extroverted (Schmitt & Oswald, 2006). But is this the case with integrity tests? Can they be faked?

Let's consider the two different types of integrity tests that are used: (1) *overt tests*, in which the purpose is obvious to the test-taker; and (2) *covert tests*, in which items measure broad personality characteristics that are not clearly related to the workplace. To examine the susceptibility of these tests to faking, George Alliger and others (1996) gave both overt and covert tests to college students. Some were told to just take the tests, others were instructed to "fake good," and still others were coached and given specific strategies for how to beat the tests. ▶ Figure 13.3 shows how well the students did. On the overt test, the scores increased for those instructed to fake good and then increased again among those who were specifically coached. Yet on the covert personality test, scores were unaffected by these interventions. Other studies, too, demonstrate the point: When it comes to faking, the covert tests, quite literally, pass the test (Alliger & Dwight, 2000).

But are such instruments sufficiently valid to be used for personnel selection? Although there is reason for skepticism, the research suggests that both types of tests do predict various work-related behaviors (Berry et al., 2007; Goldberg et al., 1991; Sackett et al., 1989). In a study using overt integrity tests, Michael Cunningham and others

(1994) found that actual job applicants scored higher on these tests than did non-motivated research participants and that their scores matched those obtained from participants specifically instructed to fake good. So, does this self-presentation bias compromise a test's validity? Not necessarily. In a second experiment, these same investigators overpaid participants by $5 and found that those with high rather than low test scores were also more likely to return the extra cash. Other researchers have arrived at similar findings (Barrick & Mount, 1996). Indeed, when Deniz Ones and others (1993) conducted a meta-analysis of tests taken by thousands of workers, they found that test scores were highly predictive of job performance as well as of such counterproductive behaviors as theft, absenteeism, lateness, and other disciplinary problems.

Structured Interviews   Another way to improve selection judgments is through the use of **structured interviews**. A structured interview is much like a standardized test in that the same information is obtained in the same situation from all applicants, who are then compared on a common, relevant set of dimensions (Campion et al., 1988). By asking exactly the same set of questions or using the same set of tasks, employers can prevent themselves from unwittingly conducting biased interviews that merely confirm their preexisting conceptions. Over the years, studies have shown that structured interviews are better than conventional interviews in the selection of insurance agents, sales clerks, and other workers (Wiesner & Cronshaw, 1988) and that they are more predictive than paper-and-pencil personality tests (Huffcutt et al., 2001), perhaps because they are more difficult to fake (Van Iddekinge et al., 2005). In fact, structured interviews can be conducted over the telephone and later scored from a taped transcript of what was said. Even in this way, the information received can be used to predict a future worker's attendance rate, productivity, and tenure on the job (Schmidt & Rader, 1999).

To create a more structured, multidimensional setting for selection and evaluation purposes, many organizations use **assessment centers**, in which several applicants take part in a group of activities such as written tests, situational tests, and role-playing exercises that are monitored by a group of evaluators. Instead of one method (an interview) and one evaluator (an interviewer), multiple methods and evaluators are used. Assessment centers are widely assumed to be more effective than traditional interviews at identifying applicants who will succeed in a particular position (Thornton & Rupp, 2006). When companies struggle to cut hiring costs, assessments are sometimes streamlined to involve fewer evaluators, fewer exercises, briefer exercises, and other types of shortcuts (Borman et al., 1997). Still, research shows that an assessment center's multidimensional approach is a good way to make hiring decisions that are ultimately quite predictive of job performance (Arthur et al., 2003; Bowler & Woehr, 2006; Meriac et al., 2008).

Personnel Selection as a Two-Way Street   For many years, researchers focused on the ways in which different personnel selection procedures serve employers. As we noted earlier, however, the hiring process is an interpersonal two-way street in which organizations and applicants size each other up. So how do job seekers feel about the methods just described? What is *your* reaction to these methods? Research shows that people generally see concrete, job-specific tests and interview situations as the most fair and they dislike being evaluated by general, standardized tests of intelligence, personality, and honesty (Rosse et al., 1994; Rynes & Connerly, 1993). For employers on the lookout for strong recruits, the perceived fairness of the selection process that is used may well influence whether top applicants accept the offers that are made (Bauer et al., 1998).

Even the format of an interview can leave a lasting impression. Flawed as it may be, how does the face-to-face interview compare with computer-mediated interviews? In today's global economy, interviewers and job applicants are often geographi-

structured interview   An interview in which each job applicant is asked a standard set of questions and evaluated on the same criteria.

assessment center   A structured setting in which job applicants are exhaustively tested and judged by multiple evaluators.

cally separated, which necessitates either costly travel or the use of technology for computer-mediated interviews, telephone interviews, and videoconferencing. If you've ever communicated in these ways, you know how different the interaction can be from a face-to-face interview. But how effective are these media for job interviews for employers and applicants? At the campus recruitment center of a large Canadian university, 970 students who submitted résumés to jobs that were posted on the Internet interviewed with 346 organizations. These were actual interviews. Most were held in person, but some were conducted by telephone or videoconferencing. When questioned about the experience afterward, the students in the in-person interviews saw the process as more fair, saw the outcome as more favorable, and were more likely to accept the job if offered. It may be difficult to replace the connection and caring that are signaled by in-person contact (Chapman et al., 2003).

Affirmative Action

Affirmative action is a policy that gives special consideration to women and members of underrepresented minority groups in recruitment, hiring, admissions, and promotion decisions. This policy is among the most emotional and explosive social issues of our time. On one side of the debate is the argument that preferential treatment is necessary as a way to overcome historical inequities and to bring the benefits of diversity to the workplace. On the other side is the claim that the policy results in unfair reverse discrimination. Surveys show that Americans are sharply divided on the issue: women are more supportive than men and African Americans are more supportive than whites (Crosby et al., 2006; Kravitz & Platania, 1993; Parker et al., 1997).

Differences of opinion were apparent during the summer of 2003, just after the U.S. Supreme Court ruled on a pair of historic affirmative action lawsuits filed by students who had been rejected from the University of Michigan. Upholding the law school's policy but not the undergraduate policy, the Court ruled by a 5-to-4 margin that it is proper for a university to take race into account as a way to bring diversity to the campus as long as a specific quota or point system is not used. That day in a Gallup poll of 1,385 Americans, 59 percent favored affirmative action for women and 49 percent favored affirmative action for racial minorities. In both cases, women and minorities were more favorable toward the policy (see ▶ Figure 13.4).

Representing both sides of the debate about affirmative action, Americans demonstrated their passionate opinions outside the U.S Supreme Court. On June 23, 2003, the Court—by a 5 to 4 margin—upheld a university's right to consider race in admissions in order to create a diverse student body.

Proponents of affirmative action often accuse opponents of harboring conscious or unconscious prejudice. In contrast, the opponents argue that they support a simple meritocracy, a form of justice in which everyone receives an equal opportunity and then rewards are matched to contributions. In support of this reasoning, Ramona Bobocel and others (1998) studied affirmative action attitudes and found that opposition to it was associated with a strong belief in the principle of merit, not with measures of racial prejudice. So, would these opponents favor preferential selection procedures to rectify the injustice of a workplace contaminated by discrimination? It appears that many would. When affirmative action opponents were led to see women and minorities as

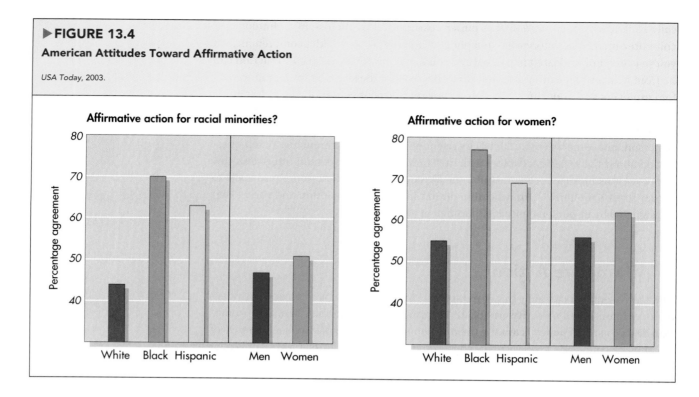

▶ **FIGURE 13.4**

American Attitudes Toward Affirmative Action

USA Today, 2003.

the targets of discrimination in a particular workplace, which itself undermines the principle of merit, they became more favorable toward a system of preferential treatment (Son Hing et al., 2002).

As political debate rages, many questions are being raised. According to Rupert Nacoste (1996), affirmative action affects those the policy is designed to help, those who feel excluded by it, the organizations that implement it, and the interactions among these three interested groups. In addition, Nacoste argues that people react not to the abstract concept of affirmative action but to the procedures that are used to implement the concept and that these reactions can set off "procedural reverberations" within the system. For example, people will be dissatisfied and the system will reverberate to the extent that the policy is set secretly rather than in the open, to the extent that interested parties have no opportunity to express their personal views, and to the extent that group membership considerations are seen as more important than the individual contributions of each applicant. Nacoste's notion of procedural interdependence is diagrammed in ▶ Figure 13.5.

After years of research on attitudes toward affirmative action, it is now clear that although there are sharp differences of opinion, people's reactions depend—and can be changed by—how the policy is implemented. There is no single approach. Faye Crosby and her colleagues (2006) note that policies range from "soft" forms of affirmative action, such as outreach programs designed to identify, recruit, or specially train applicants from underrepresented groups, to "hard" forms of affirmative action that give preference in hiring to applicants from targeted groups who are equally or less qualified than others. Based on a meta-analysis of 126 studies involving 29,000 respondents, David Harrison and others (2006) found that people are most favorable toward softer forms of affirmative action and least favorable toward quotas and other hard policies that favor some applicants over others regardless of their qualifications. By describing different affirmative action programs to business school students, Ariel Levi and Yitzhak Fried (2008) found not only that participants preferred a soft affirmative action policy but that they were most supportive of a policy that influenced the hiring and training of new employees and least supportive of a policy that affected promotions and layoffs for existing employees.

As you might expect, people who do not personally benefit from affirmative action react negatively to both the policy and those who benefit from it (Heilman et al., 1996). But what about the recipients of this policy? Does affirmative action psychologically undermine those it is intended to help? In an early series of studies, Madeline Heilman and others (1987) selected male and female college students to serve as leaders of a two-person task. These students were then led to think that they had been chosen for the leadership role either by a preferential selection process that was based on gender or by a merit selection process based solely on qualifications. The result: The women (but not the men) who believed they were chosen because of their gender later devalued their own performance, even after receiving positive feedback.

There are three explanations as to why preferential selection policies may have a

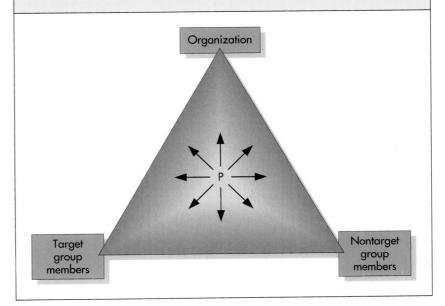

▶ FIGURE 13.5

Affirmative Action: Effects on Individuals, Groups, and Organizations

Affirmative action affects target group members the policy is designed to help, non–target group members who feel excluded by it, organizations that implement it, and the interactions among these groups. According to Nacoste, people's reactions to affirmative action procedures can set off procedural reverberations (P) within the system.

Nacoste, 1996.

range of negative effects. First, people perceive a procedure as unjust to the extent that it excludes those who are qualified simply because of their non-membership in a group (Barnes Nacoste, 1994; Heilman et al., 1996). Second, the recipients become less able to attribute success on the job to their own abilities and efforts, leading them and their co-workers to harbor doubts about their competence (Heilman et al., 1992; Major et al., 1994). Third, preferential selection is seen as a form of assistance, a situation that can lead recipients to feel stigmatized by what they assume to be the negative perceptions of others (Heilman & Alcott, 2001).

Are the recipients of affirmative action doomed to feel stigmatized, like second-class citizens? Not necessarily. We saw earlier that the way people tend to react to a preferential selection procedure depends on how it is structured and for what purpose it is implemented. A good deal of research shows that people draw negative inferences about themselves and others when employment selections are made *solely* on the basis of sex, skin color, or ethnic background. But would they react more favorably to a preferential selection process if it is clear that merit-based factors also play a role and that the person chosen is competent and qualified for the position?

To find out, Heilman and her colleagues (1998) again brought together male and female participants to take part in a joint two-person task that required a leader and a follower. As in prior experiments, the researchers administered a bogus qualifications test and then assigned each female to the leadership role. Some participants were told that the appointment was based strictly on *merit* (that the person with the higher test score had been selected as the leader). Others were told that the process favored the woman in a way that was *preferential equivalent* (that she was chosen only when her score was similar to that of her male counterpart), *preferential minimum*

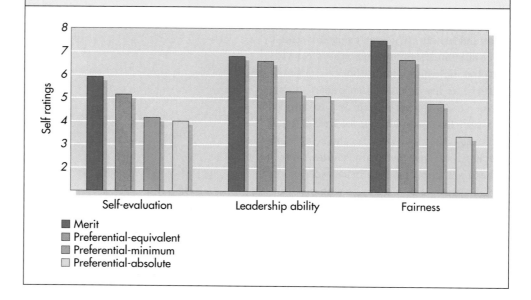

▶FIGURE 13.6

Varying Effects of Affirmative Action on Women

College women appointed as task leaders were told that they were selected by merit or by gender. Those in the gender condition were further told that preference was given: (1) only if they were *equivalent* to their male partner; (2) only if they met a *minimum standard*; or (3) *absolutely* regardless of merit. These participants later rated their performance and leadership highest and saw the process as most fair when their appointment was based on merit rather than on preference. But the score was not much lower in the equivalent condition where merit was taken into account.

Heilman et al., 1998.

standard (that she was chosen only if she was minimally qualified), or *preferential absolute* (that she was chosen regardless of merit). The result: The appointed female leaders later rated their own performance and leadership abilities most favorably and saw the process as most fair when their appointment was based on merit, not gender (see ▶ Figure 13.6). Importantly, they also did not devalue their performance or see the selection process as unfair in the preferential equivalent condition, where merit was clearly taken into account. Similarly, neither male co-participants nor observers were troubled by this type of preferential selection process. In light of these findings, Table 13.1 offers guidelines for managing affirmative action programs in a way that minimizes criticism from all concerned.

■ Culture and Organizational Diversity

For many years, the study of organizational behavior was "culture blind and culture bound" (Gelfand et al., 2007; Triandis, 1994). As a result of two dramatic historical changes, researchers now look at the workplace through a broader lens. The first change has resulted from affirmative action programs, which forced an increase in the number of women and minorities who populate most organizations. The second is the worldwide trend toward globalization, which has brought more and more people from disparate cultures into daily contact with each other as colleagues and co-workers. Georgia Chao and Henry Moon (2005) note that every individual worker has a multidimensional identity that can be characterized within a *cultural mosaic* consisting of the

TABLE 13.1

Managing Affirmative Action

Preferential selection practices are often seen as unjust, and they often lead recipients to doubt their own competence. Pratkanis and Turner (1996) recommend that the steps listed here be taken to minimize these negative effects.

1. Set and communicate clear and explicit qualifications criteria (background, knowledge, skills, etc.) to be used in selection decisions.

2. Be certain that selection procedures are perceived as fair by targeted applicants and their co-workers.

3. Provide the target applicant and co-workers with specific feedback about the target's job qualifications.

4. Develop socialization strategies that keep target applicants from making negative self-attributions.

5. Emphasize the target applicant's unique contributions to the organization.

6. Point out that affirmative action does not imply hiring by quotas, since other job-relevant attributes are considered as well.

7. Recognize that affirmative action is not a panacea and that it cannot be expected to solve all the problems faced by the targeted groups.

various "tiles" of his or her demographic groups (such as age, gender, race, and ethnic heritage), geographical background (such as country of origin, region, climate, and population density), and personal associations (such as with religion, profession, and political affiliation). In some ways, everyone is similar; in other ways, no two people are alike. For researchers who study organizational behavior, the challenge is to represent the full complexity that comes with a diverse workplace.

As diversity has become a fact of life, researchers have sought to understand what effect this change is having on motivation, morale, and performance in the workplace. On the one hand, a pessimist would predict that diversity would breed division and conflict, making worker teams less effective. In Chapter 5, "Stereotypes, Prejudice, and Discrimination," we saw that people categorize one another into ingroups and outgroups based on gender, age, race, and other visible characteristics and show a marked preference for "us" over "them." We also saw in Chapter 9, "Attraction and Close Relationships," that people prefer the company of others who have similar rather than dissimilar attitudes and values. To the extent that people dislike each other, they will not work well together. On the other hand, an optimist would predict that diversity increases the range of perspectives and skills that are brought to bear on a problem, enhancing productivity and creative problem solving by providing a group with a larger pool of resources to draw from.

What is the net impact of diversity on a group's performance? There is a hint of evidence for both effects. At present, researchers agree that there is no single or simple answer because the effect is likely to depend on the nature of the diversity, whether similarities or differences are accentuated, the proportion of majority to minority members, whether there is a culture of smooth integration within the organization, the type of work to be completed, the group's ability and motivation, and other factors (Mannix & Neale, 2005; van Knippenberg & Schippers, 2007; Williams & O'Reilly, 1998).

A workplace may strive for diversity, but its success may well depend on its philosophy and approach. Reflecting a society-wide debate, many companies struggle with this question: Is it better to acknowledge group differences in the workplace by celebrating multiculturalism, or ignore these differences in an effort to encourage a uniform, colorblind environment? To see if there is a relationship between the beliefs

The globalization of business is a fact of life. More than 63,000 multinational corporations and 821,000 foreign subsidiaries now employ 90 million people around the world.
—Gabel & Brunner, 2003

held within a company and how engaged its minority workers feel, Victoria Plaut and others (2009) conducted an online "diversity climate survey" of 5,000 white and minority employees from 18 departments of a large health care organization. By comparing departments, they found that the more multicultural the dominant white employees were in their diversity beliefs (endorsing "employees should recognize and celebrate racial and ethnic differences" rather than "employees should downplay their racial and ethnic differences"), the more engaged their minority workers felt (for example, "I am proud to tell others that I work at this organization").

The real-world correlation is intriguing, but it does not prove that the multicultural beliefs within the organization *caused* minority employees to feel more engaged. To test that hypothesis directly, Valerie Purdie-Vaughns and others (2008) presented African-American corporate professionals with a brochure for a fictitious management consulting firm. For participants assigned to a value-diversity condition, the brochure stated: "While other consulting firms mistakenly try to shape their staff into a single mold, we believe that embracing our diversity enriches our culture." For others in a colorblind condition, the brochure stated: "While other firms mistakenly focus on their staff's diversity, we train our diverse workforce to embrace their similarities." Did the African-American participants, experienced in the corporate world, feel comfortable with this company? If the brochure photographs depicted a high level of minority representation, they were fine. If the photos depicted a low level of minority representation, however, their comfort level depended on the company's diversity beliefs. In this case, they trusted the multicultural firm that celebrated diversity and difference more than the colorblind firm that sought to minimize it.

Performance Appraisals

Even after a person is hired, the evaluation process continues. Nobody enjoys being scrutinized by a boss or anyone else, for that matter. Still, **performance appraisal**—the process of evaluating an employee's work and communicating the results to that person—is an inevitable fact of life in the workplace. Performance appraisals provide a basis for placement decisions, transfers, promotions, raises and salary cuts, bonuses, and layoffs. They also give feedback to employees about the quality of their work and status within the organization. It's no wonder that I/O psychologists have studied this process in great detail.

It would be easy if a worker's performance could be measured by purely *objective* and quantifiable criteria, as when typists are judged by the number of words they type in a minute, automobile dealers by the number of cars they sell, and sales agents by the number of customers they service. These kinds of quantitative measures are often not available, however, and they do not take into account the quality of work. By necessity, then, performance appraisals are usually based on more *subjective* measures such as the perceptions of employees by supervisors, co-workers, and sometimes even the employees themselves (Landy & Farr, 1983).

Supervisor Ratings

performance appraisal
The process of evaluating an employee's work within the organization.

Based on the assumption that supervisors keep themselves informed about the performance of their subordinates, they are most often called on to make evaluations. But are these ratings accurate? And is the process fair? The process has both benefits and drawbacks. On the one hand, research shows that supervisors are influenced more by a worker's job knowledge, ability, technical proficiency, and dependability than by less relevant factors such as friendliness (Borman et al., 1995). On the other hand, as we'll see, evaluators predictably fall prey to many of the social perception biases described elsewhere in this book.

Over the years, a number of appraisal-related problems have been identified. One is the *halo effect*, a failure to discriminate among different and distinct aspects of a worker's performance (Cooper, 1981). In Chapter 4, we saw that people's impressions of one another are guided by implicit personality theories—by the preconceptions they have about the relationships among different traits. Believing that someone is warm, we assume that he or she is also generous and good-natured. In a similar manner, supervisors who believe that a worker is unproductive may also rate that worker negatively on teamwork, independence, creativity, and other distinct dimensions. Halo effects are most pronounced when evaluators rate someone they do not know well or when a time delay has caused their memory of performance to fade (Koslowski et al., 1986; Murphy & Balzer, 1986). Lacking concrete details in these situations, they fall back on their past impressions and implicit theories and assume that one aspect of performance implies other aspects as well.

Second, it's difficult for supervisors to make repeated evaluations of the same worker, each time through fresh eyes. In a series of experiments, participants were asked to watch a teacher present three videotaped lectures and then evaluate his or her speaking ability, clarity, preparation, rapport, and so on (Murphy et al., 1985; Smither et al., 1988). For some, the first two lectures were low in quality; for others, they were high in quality. On the third tape, all participants watched the same average performance. The result: Even though participants rated each lecture independently, their final evaluations showed signs of a *contrast effect*: Those who had first observed negative performances judged the average-quality lecture more favorably than did those who had seen the positive performances. Practically speaking, this finding suggests that supervisors who do multiple performance appraisals may judge an employee's work in light of all previous observations. One performance sets a standard for another. It's no wonder that entertainers worry about taking the stage right after a "tough act to follow."

A third problem is that evaluators differ in the average numerical ratings they give to others. Because of what is known as the *restriction of range problem*, some people provide uniformly high, lenient ratings; others are inclined to give stingy, low ratings; and still others gravitate toward the center of the numerical scale. In all cases, people who use a restricted range fail to make adequate distinctions. Sometimes the differences among raters are considerable, as was seen in a study of managers employed in numerous organizations (Scullen et al., 2000). Other researchers have observed that performance evaluations are influenced by the rater's personality. Individuals who have agreeable personalities, for example, tend to be lenient in their ratings of others, while those who are highly conscientious tend to be more harsh (Bernardin et al., 2000). In a meta-analysis of 25 studies—some conducted in the workplace, others in a laboratory—John Georgesen and Monica Harris (1998) found that people who are in power, compared to those who are not in power, consistently give lower performance ratings to others who are in subordinate positions.

▮ Self-Evaluations

Although performance appraisals are typically made by supervisors, input is often sought from co-workers, subordinates, clients, customers, and others whose opinions are relevant. You may not realize it, but by filling out course-evaluation surveys in college, you may have had an influence on tenure and promotion decisions involving your own professors. As when workers are asked to evaluate their managers, these evaluations provide valuable "upward feedback."

One particularly interesting source of information comes from self-evaluations. If you've ever had to describe yourself in a job application, you know that a self-evaluation is not exactly a lesson in modesty. As discussed in Chapter 3, most people see themselves in overly flattering terms, taking credit for success, denying the blame for failure, having an inflated sense of control, and exhibiting unrealistic optimism about the future. Add the fact that people like to present themselves favorably to others, and it comes as no surprise that self-evaluations in the workplace are consistently more positive than the ratings made by supervisors (Campbell & Lee, 1988) and less predictive of job success (Shore et al., 1992). To illustrate, studies have shown that workers tend to underestimate the number of times they had been absent compared with co-workers (Harrison & Shaffer, 1994; Johns, 1994).

Another reason why self-evaluations should be taken with a grain of salt is that individuals differ in the extent to which they tend to present themselves in a positive light. Research shows that the more power people have in an organization, the higher their self-evaluations are (Georgesen & Harris, 1998). Similarly, men in general are more boastful than women and more likely to overestimate their own performance (Beyer, 1990). Insofar as work appraisals are based on self-evaluations, then, these differences put both subordinates and female employees at a disadvantage.

> A problem with having workers evaluate their own job performance is that self-ratings are overly positive. TRUE.

New and Improved Methods of Appraisal

Performance appraisals cannot always be trusted. When more objective measures of work output are not available, however, organizations have no choice but to rely on the imperfect and sometimes prejudiced human judge. For researchers, the challenge is to find ways to boost the accuracy of the evaluations that are made.

One solution concerns the timing of evaluations in relation to the observation of performance. Evaluations are less prone to error when made right after performance than when there's a delay of days, weeks, or months. Alternatively, evaluators should take notes and keep clear records of their observations, perhaps using behavioral checklists. Part of the problem is that once memory for details begins to fade, evaluators fall back on stereotypes and other biases (Murphy & Balzer, 1986; Sanchez & De La Torre, 1996).

A second possible solution is to teach raters some of the skills necessary for making accurate appraisals. Over the years, various training programs have been developed, and research suggests that accuracy can be boosted by alerting evaluators to the biases of social perception, focusing their attention on job-relevant behaviors, sharpening their memory skills, informing them of performance norms that serve as a frame of reference within the organization, and providing them with practice and feedback in the use of rating scales (Day & Sulsky 1995; Hedge & Kavanagh, 1988). No system will ever be perfect, but much improvement is possible, particularly when people are motivated to be accurate (Salvemini et al., 1993).

Third, it is now common in most organizations to collect and combine a full circle of ratings from multiple evaluators in a process that is referred to as a 360-degree performance appraisal. As in assessment centers, a multiple-rater system in which a final evaluation represents the average of ratings made by independent sources with different perspectives is more complete than the conventional single-rater approach (Conway & Huffcutt, 1997; Lepsinger & Lucia, 2009). In a typical 360-degree assessment, an employee's performance is rated by superiors, peers, subordinates, the employees themselves, and even outside stakeholders such as customers, clients, students, and patients. In this way, whatever idiosyncratic bias a single individual might bring to his or her ratings can be offset by others. Although there is debate over how to combine, compare, and contrast different sources, research shows that this approach is generally an improvement over single-rater methods (Craig & Hannum, 2006; Morgeson et al., 2005).

Due-Process Considerations

In the all-too-human enterprise of performance appraisal, especially in an economy that sees numerous workers laid off, accuracy is not the only concern. There's also another problem: perceptions of fairness. Is it fair that one professor is tenured while another is not or that one worker is laid off while another is retained? Precisely because the stakes are high in decisions that are made about personnel, performance ratings may be biased and sometimes even deliberately distorted by those motivated by political and self-serving agendas within the workplace. Particularly at the executive level, office politics are an organizational fact of life (Gioia & Longnecker, 1994).

To enhance perceptions of fairness, Robert Folger and his colleagues (1992) proposed a "due process" model of performance appraisal. In general, this model is designed to guard the rights of employees in the same way that the criminal justice system seeks to protect the accused. The model consists of three principles. The first is that there should be *adequate notice*—that is, clear performance standards that employees can understand and ask questions about. The second is that employees should receive a *fair hearing* in which they are evaluated by a supervisor who knows their work and in which they receive timely feedback as well as an opportunity to present their own case. The third principle is that appraisals should be based on *evidence* of job performance, not on prejudice, corruption, or external considerations. As indicated by research on how people react to pay raises, pay cuts, promotions, layoffs, and the implementation of affirmative action policies, procedural fairness (*how* decisions are made) can be just as important to people as a favorable outcome (*what* decisions are made). Thus, workers who are dissatisfied with their pay are more likely to retaliate (for example, by calling in sick, stealing or wasting the company's supplies, or damaging equipment) when they see the procedures used to determine pay as unfair and were not consulted about the decision (Skarlicki & Folger, 1997).

Recent research has shown that people judge organizational justice according to a large number of criteria—such as the transparency and fairness of the procedures that are used; the extent to which the procedures and the outcomes they produce are explained; the extent to which affected workers are treated with dignity, politeness, and respect; and the decision-making outcomes by which salaries, promotions, and other resources are allocated. Together, the combination of these specific types of justice influences people's satisfaction, commitment, and on-the-job performance within the workplace (Ambrose & Schminke, 2009).

Leadership

Regardless of where you're employed, the work experience depends in large part on the quality of the leadership in the organization. A leader is someone who can move a group of people toward a common goal. He or she may be a head of state, the president of a college or university, the principal investigator of a research team, the executive

TABLE 13.2

Quotable Conceptions of Leadership

The purpose of all rulers is the well-being of those they rule.

—Saint Augustine

The most important quality in a leader is that of being acknowledged as such.

—Andre Maurois

I am a leader by default, only because nature does not allow a vacuum.

—Bishop Desmond Tutu

If one is lucky, a solitary fantasy can totally transform one million realities.

—Maya Angelou

When the effective leader is finished with his work, the people say it happened naturally.

—Lao Tse

Never tell people how to do things. Tell them what to do and they will surprise you with their ingenuity.

—General George Patton

We must become the change we want to see.

—Mahatma Gandhi

The final test of a leader is that he leaves behind him in other men the conviction and will to carry on.

—Walter J. Lippmann

Leadership should be born out of the understanding of the needs of those who would be affected by it.

—Marian Anderson

No man will make a great leader who wants to do it all himself, or to get all the credit for doing it.

—Andrew Carnegie

The task of the leader is to get his people from where they are to where they have not been.

—Henry Kissinger

officer of a corporation, or the manager or head coach of a sports team. Across a wide range of settings, researchers have long wondered: What personal and situational factors make for effective leadership? There is no single formula. Some leaders succeed by winning supporters; others lead by mending fences, uniting rivals, negotiating deals, building coalitions, solving problems, or stirring emotions (see Table 13.2). Whatever the strategy, there is one common denominator: Good leadership is about social influence (Avolio et al., 2009; Goethals et al., 2004).

■ The Classic Trait Approach

One approach to the study of leadership is to identify the traits that characterize "natural-born" leaders, those who have the "right stuff." According to the Great Person Theory of history, exceptional individuals rise up to determine the course of human events. This approach has had some support over the years, since certain traits—such as ambition, intelligence, a need for power, self-confidence, a high energy level, and an ability to be flexible and adapt to change—are characteristic of people who go on to become leaders (Hogan et al., 1994; Kenny & Zaccaro, 1983). Even physical height may play a role. In this regard, it is striking that across the entire twentieth century, the tallest candidate for United States president won an astonishing 23 out of 25 elections—that's 92 percent of the time (1972 and 1976 were the only exceptions).

On the basis of past research, Shelley Kirkpatrick and Edwin Locke (1991) argued that certain stable characteristics are associated with successful leadership among business executives. In particular, they pointed to the importance of *cognitive ability* (intelligence and an ability to quickly process large amounts of information), *inner drive* (a need for achievement, ambition, and a high energy level), *leadership motivation* (a desire to influence others in order to reach a common goal), *expertise* (specific knowledge of technical issues relevant to the organization), *creativity* (an ability to generate original ideas), *self-confidence* (faith in one's own abilities and ideas), *integrity* (reliability, honesty, and an open communication style), and *flexibility* (an ability to adapt to the needs of followers and to changes in the situation). "Regardless of whether leaders are born or made," they say, "it is unequivocally clear that leaders are not like other people" (p. 58). Locke (2000) picked up on this theme in *The Prime Movers*, a book in which he describes the traits that "great wealth creators"—self-made multimillionaires and billionaires—seem to have in common. Zaccaro (2007) adds that various aspects of leadership can best be predicted by unique combinations of attributes rather than by single traits.

In contrast to this approach, more situationally oriented theories were introduced based on the notion that the emergence of a given leader depends on time, place, and circumstances—that different situations call for different types of leaders (Vroom & Jago, 2007). Thus, as the needs, expectations, and resources of a group change, so too will the person best suited to lead it. This need for a match was evident in New

York City on the day of the terrorist attacks on the World Trade Center, when Mayor Rudolph Giuliani stepped up to address the crisis, offer a visible presence, calm the city, and mobilize rescue, recovery, cleanup, and rebuilding efforts. The same can be said of Barack Obama, who ran for president in 2008 on a platform of change at a time when the economy was in a state of crisis.

Studies of presidential leadership in particular can be used to illustrate the point about situations and leadership (Goethals, 2005). For example, David Winter (1987) found that presidential candidates are more likely to be elected and reelected when their primary motive in life—whether it is for achievement, power, or affiliation—matches what Americans want most at that time. An alternative to the classic trait perspective, then, is a view that leadership is the product of a unique interaction between the person and the surrounding situation.

Situations may well dictate the success of a particular leadership style. During the emergence of the dot-com era, for example, the traditional image of a leader who presides from the top down over a hierarchical command structure gave way to a corporate culture in which a leader should be accessible, fluid, lateral, and relationship oriented. But is this situational doctrine necessarily incompatible with the classic trait approach? Maybe not. In *Primal Leadership*, Daniel Goleman, Richard Boyatzis, and Annie McKee (2002) argue that the primary job of leadership is emotional and that great leaders are endowed with *emotional intelligence*, an ability to know how people are feeling and how to use that information to guide their own actions. Great leaders are men and women who exude interest, enthusiasm, and other positive emotions and whose energy is contagious. Precisely because demands change from one time, situation, and organization to the next, however, leaders with emotional intelligence are by nature flexible in their style, serving as visionaries, coaches, pacesetters, and so on as needed.

▊ Contingency Models of Leadership

Illustrative of this interactional perspective is Fred Fiedler's (1967) **contingency model of leadership**. Fiedler argues that a key difference among leaders is whether they are *primarily task oriented* (single-mindedly focused on the job) or *relations oriented* (concerned about the feelings of employees). The amount of control that a leader has determines which type of leadership is more effective. Leaders enjoy *high situational control* when they have good relations with their staff, a position of power, and a clearly structured task. In contrast, leaders exhibit *low situational control* when they have poor relations with their staff, limited power, and a task that is not clearly defined.

Combining these personal and situational components, studies of various work groups suggest that task-oriented leaders are the most effective in clear-cut situations that are either low or high in control and that relations-oriented leaders perform better in situations that afford a moderate degree of control. In low-control situations, groups need guidance, which task-oriented leaders provide by staying focused on the job. In high-control situations, where conditions are already favorable, these same leaders maintain a relaxed, low profile. Relations-oriented leaders are different. They offer too little guidance in low-control situations and they meddle too much in high-control situations. In ambiguous situations, however, relations-oriented leaders—precisely because of their open, participative, social style—motivate workers to solve problems in creative ways.

Studies of military units, sports teams, schools, hospitals, and other organizations generally support Fiedler's model. While this support is far from unanimous, the main point is well taken: Good leadership requires a match between an individual's personal style and the demands of a specific situation (Fiedler & Chemers, 1984). A mismatch—

contingency model of leadership The theory that leadership effectiveness is determined both by the personal characteristics of leaders and by the control afforded by the situation.

Shown at his famous "I have a dream" speech in Washington, D.C., in August 1963, Martin Luther King Jr. was a transformational leader who inspired massive change by making supporters believe that anything was possible.

that is, the wrong type of person for the situation—can have negative consequences for both the leader and his or her organization. For example, Martin Chemers and others (1985) surveyed college administrators to determine both their leadership style and their situational control. They found that mismatches were associated with increased job stress, stress-related illness, and absence from work, symptoms that diminish a leader's productivity and competence (Fiedler & Garcia, 1987; Fiedler et al., 1992).

Making decisions is one of the most important tasks for any leader. In the two-way street between leaders and followers, however, it is often important to solicit the opinions of others. How much participation should leaders invite? According to the **normative model of leadership** proposed by Victor Vroom and Philip Yetton (1973), leaders vary widely in this regard. Some are highly autocratic and directive (they invite no feedback from workers) while others are highly participative (they frequently seek and use suggestions from workers). For effective long-term leadership, the key is to invite just the right amount of worker participation—not too much (which is often not efficient) and not too little (which can lower morale). As to what constitutes the right amount, Vroom and Yetton argued that it depends on various factors such as the clarity of the problem, the information available to the leader and followers, and whether it's more important that the decision be right or that one have support.

Although the ideal leader is one who adjusts his or her style to meet the situation, people generally prefer leaders who involve them in important decisions. Research shows that participative decision making boosts worker morale, motivation, and productivity and reduces turnover and absenteeism rates. Benefits such as these have been found especially in situations where employees want to have input (Vroom & Jago, 1988) and when they are involved in decision making directly rather than through elected representatives (Rubenowitz et al., 1983).

normative model of leadership The theory that leadership effectiveness is determined by the amount of feedback and participation that leaders invite from workers.

∎ Transactional Leadership

Although contingency models take both the person and the situation into account, Edwin Hollander (1985) criticizes these "top-down" views of leadership in which workers are portrayed as inert, passive, faceless creatures to be soothed or aroused

at the management's discretion. Instead, he sees leadership as a two-way social exchange in which there is mutual and reciprocal influence between a leader and his or her followers. According to Hollander, a good **transactional leader** is one who gains compliance and support from followers by setting clear goals for them, by offering tangible rewards, by providing assistance, and by fulfilling psychological needs in exchange for an expected level of job performance. Transactional leadership thus rests on the leader's willingness and ability to reward subordinates who keep up their end of the bargain and to correct those who do not.

Pioneers of the technology revolution Bill Gates, co-founder of Microsoft (left), and Steve Jobs, co-founder of Apple (right), have been two of the most forward-looking, transformational business leaders of our time.

▥ Transformational Leadership

Think about some of the greatest leaders of the past century, those who were able to transform the status quo by making supporters believe that anything is possible. Martin Luther King Jr. was that kind of leader. So were Franklin D. Roosevelt, Mahatma Gandhi, John F. Kennedy, Ronald Reagan, and Nelson Mandela. In their classic book *In Search of Excellence*, Thomas Peters and Robert Waterman (1982) studied 62 of America's best businesses and found that their success was due largely to the ability of the leaders to elicit extraordinary efforts from ordinary human beings.

Today, two prominent models of such leadership are Bill Gates and Steven Jobs, both of whom are co-founders of two of the most important technology companies in the world. In 1975, Gates dropped out of Harvard and co-founded what was then a small company by the name of Microsoft. Long before it seemed possible, he envisioned a day when there would be a PC in every home and office. Then as it was becoming clear that the future resided in cyberspace, he shocked the business world by refocusing Microsoft around the Internet. He is now one of the richest and most philanthropic people in the world. In 1973, Steven Jobs, like Gates, also dropped out of college. He soon co-founded Apple and helped popularize and innovate the "Mac," bringing to it the mouse, a sleek design, and other creative elements. His most recent innovations are the iPod portable music player and the iPhone, an all-in-one gadget. In an industry that demands an ability to anticipate the future, adapt quickly to change, take great risks, and enlist support from others, both Gates and Jobs have been leaders.

What's special about Gates, Jobs, and other successful leaders? Based on the work of political scientist James MacGregor Burns (1978, 2003), Bernard Bass (1998; Bass & Riggio, 2006) calls them **transformational leaders**. Transformational leaders motivate

transactional leader   A leader who gains compliance and support from followers primarily through goal setting and the use of rewards.

transformational leader   A leader who inspires followers to transcend their own needs in the interest of a common cause.

others to transcend their personal needs in the interest of a common cause, particularly in times of growth, change, and crisis. Through consciousness raising and raw emotional inspiration, they articulate a clear vision for the future and then mobilize others to join in that vision. Over the years, Bass and his colleagues have asked people who work for various business managers and executives, military officers, school principals, government bureaucrats, fire chiefs, and store owners to describe the most outstanding leaders they know (Bass & Avolio, 1990; Hater & Bass, 1988). As shown in Table 13.3, the descriptions they gave revealed four attributes: charisma, inspirational motivation, intellectual stimulation, and an individualized consideration of others. Other studies have shown that transformational leaders are also more extroverted than the average person (Bono & Judge, 2004).

To measure the extent to which individuals possess the attributes of transactional and transformational leadership styles, Bass (1985) devised the Multifactor Leader Questionnaire, or MLQ. Using this instrument, researchers have studied leadership in different cultures and in different types of organizations, including auto manufacturers, express-mail companies, multinational corporations, banks, government agencies, and military groups. Others have varied the use of the different leadership styles in controlled laboratory settings. Indicating that inspiration is universally a more powerful motivator than reward, the results have shown that transformational leaders are more effective than transactional leaders (Bass, 1998; Lowe et al., 1996) and exert influence by getting others to identify personally with them and the social group they represent (Kark et al., 2003). In light of their ability to exert influence, it is not surprising that in a study of 39 managers and 130 employees in six companies, those who emerged as transformational leaders on the MLQ were also more socially networked within their organizations (Bono & Anderson, 2005).

People are drawn like magnets to transformational leaders who have what it takes. But wait. Does this mean that Adolf Hitler, Saddam Hussein, and other authoritarian heads of state were leaders of the same stripe as Mahatma Gandhi, Franklin D. Roosevelt, and Nelson Mandela? One would hope not. To separate human evil

The most effective type of leader is one who knows how to win support through the use of reward. **FALSE.**

TABLE 13.3

Characteristics of Transformational Leaders

When people are asked to describe the best leaders they know, four characteristics are most often cited: charisma, an ability to inspire others, intellectual stimulation, and individualized consideration. These attributes are evident in the self-descriptions given here.

Characteristic	Description	Sample Items
Charisma	Has a vision; gains respect, trust, and confidence; promotes a strong identification of followers.	I have a sense of mission that I communicate to them. They are proud to be associated with me.
Inspiration	Gives pep talks, increases optimism and enthusiasm, and arouses emotion in communications.	I present a vision to spur them on. I use symbols and images to focus their efforts.
Intellectual Stimulation	Actively encourages a reexamination of existing values and assumptions; fosters creativity and the use of intelligence.	I enable them to think about old problems in new ways. I place strong emphasis on careful problem solving before taking action.
Individualized Consideration	Gives personal attention to all members, acts as adviser and gives feedback in ways that are easy to accept, understand, and use for personal development.	I coach individuals who need it. I express my appreciation when they do a good job.

Based on Bass & Avolio, 1990.

from virtue, Bass and Steidlmeier (1999) sought to distinguish between what they call pseudo-transformational leaders, who appeal to emotions rather than to reason and manipulate ignorant followers to further their own personal interests, and *authentic* transformational leaders, who morally uplift followers and help them transform their collective visions into realities.

Leadership Among Women and Minorities

The fact that Americans elected Barack Obama the first African American president of the United States is remarkable in both historical and current contexts. Look at the leaders of America's Fortune 500 companies at the start of 2009, and you'll find that a mere 3 percent of the CEOs are women—a percentage that is only somewhat higher in the health care industry, government, or educational institutions. Look at the percentage of African Americans, Hispanics, and Asians in the top ranks of the same organizations, and you'll see that they don't fare any better. Even today, in the twenty-first century, there are proportionally few U.S. senators who are female or Major League Baseball managers who are black.

Despite progress that has been made in entry- and middle-level positions, working women and minorities who seek positions of leadership have still not fully broken through the "glass ceiling"—a barrier so subtle that it is transparent, yet so strong that it keeps them from reaching the top of the hierarchy (Morrison & Von Glinow, 1990). Indeed, women may also encounter "glass walls" that keep them from moving laterally within an organization—for example, from positions in public relations to those in core areas such as production, marketing, and sales (Lopez, 1992).

Many women are highly qualified for positions of power. Research shows that male and female managers have very similar aspirations, abilities, values, and job-related skills. Reviewing what is now a massive amount of research literature on sex differences in leadership, Alice Eagly and Linda Carli (2007) found that female leaders in the workplace are as task oriented as their male counterparts and that male and female leaders in general are equally effective. The only difference seems to be that men are more controlling and women more democratic in their approaches. As a result, men may be more effective as leaders in positions that require a more directive style (for example, in the military), whereas women may be more effective in managerial settings that require openness and cooperation. Indeed, when college students in one study were assigned to participate in long-term work groups, centralized leadership structures emerged over time in all-male groups, while more balanced decentralized leadership structures emerged in all-female groups (Berdahl & Anderson, 2005).

This portrayal of women leaders is consistent with Judy Rosener's (1995) observation that today's leading women draw effectively on qualities traditionally seen as feminine. It is also consistent with Sally Helgesen's (1995) observation that female managers interact more with subordinates, invite them to participate in the decision-making process, share information and power, and spin more extensive networks, or "webs of inclusion"—a leadership style she sees as a feminine advantage. Research shows that men and women differ in their style, not in the capacity for leadership. A meta-analysis of 45 comparative studies suggests that female leaders may even be slightly more transactional and transformational than men (Eagly et al., 2003). Other researchers are quick to caution that all claims of a gender advantage in favor of men or women are based on stereotypes and are overstated (Vecchio, 2002).

If women are competent to serve as leaders, why have so relatively few managed to reach the top in executive positions? For women, the path to power—from their entry into the labor market, to recruitment in an organization, and up the promotion

"If you were taking a new job and had your choice of boss, would you prefer to work for a man or woman?" According to a 2006 Gallup poll that asked this question, 34 percent of men preferred a male boss and 10 percent preferred a female boss, and 56 percent had no preference. Among women, 40 percent preferred a male boss, 26 percent preferred a female boss, and 32 percent had no preference (Carroll, 2006).

ladder—is something of an obstacle course (Ragins & Sundstrom, 1989)—or, as Eagly & Carli (2007) put it, a labyrinth.

Three sets of impediments have been identified. One is that many women are deeply conflicted about having to juggle a career and family responsibilities and feel as though they have to pick one or the other (Halpern & Cheung, 2008). A second impediment is that some women shy away from competitive, hierarchical positions that offer the potential for leadership in favor of professions that involve helping people (Pratto et al., 1997). Yet a third impediment is societal. Lingering stereotypes portray women as followers, not as leaders, so some people are uneasy about women in leadership roles—particularly women who have a task-oriented and directive style or who occupy "masculine" positions, as in business (Eagly & Karau, 2002).

In a survey of 100 male and female corporate executives, Karen Lyness and Donna Thompson (2000) found that although the men and women were equally successful, the women had overcome more barriers to get where they were going—such as being excluded from informal social networks, being passed over for jobs that required relocating, and not fitting into the corporate culture. To further complicate matters, research shows that people in general exhibit a bias against motherhood when it comes to recommending women with children for promotion (Heilman & Okimoto, 2008).

Statistics show that minorities also fight an uphill battle for leadership positions. President Barack Obama is the most obvious and extraordinary exception. In the world of business, in 2009, only six U.S. companies in the Fortune 500 group had an African American CEO, the most notable being Ursula Burns, who became the first black woman to head a Fortune 500 company when she became CEO of the Xerox Corporation. What seems to be the problem?

Research is mixed on the question of whether employee evaluations are biased by race (Roth et al., 2003; Sackett & DuBois, 1991; Stauffer & Buckley, 2005; Waldman & Avolio, 1991). Still, in light of what social psychologists have discovered about the subtleties of modern racism, as described in Chapter 5, business leaders should beware of the indirect ways in which minorities are handicapped in the pursuit of leadership. Many years ago, in a study of African Americans in the banking industry, many said that they had felt excluded socially from informal work groups, were not "networked," and lacked the sponsors, role models, and mentors needed for advancing within an organization (Irons & Moore, 1985). Similarly, a study of business school graduates revealed that African-American and Hispanic men were less likely than others to have mentoring relationships with the influential white men in their respective companies (Dreher & Cox, 1996).

Overcoming the obstacles, some minorities do manage to break through the racial divide into positions of leadership. How did these individuals, and others who have risen to executive ranks, do it? In *Breaking Through*, David Thomas and John Gabarro (1999) studied the career trajectories and experiences of 54 managers and executives in three large companies. Referring to the corporate career ladder as a tournament, they discovered that the successful African-, Asian-, and Hispanic-American executives they studied climbed slowly at first to positions of middle management but were then fast-tracked relative to their white peers into the executive suite. Minority managers have to build a solid foundation early, they suggested, "because they are promoted only after proving themselves again and again." At every step of this developmental process, they found that mentors played a vital role—by opening doors, offering challenging assignments, and sponsoring them for recruitment into important, high-profile positions. In *Leading in Black and White*, Ancella Livers and Keith Caver (2003) further suggested, based on surveys and interviews of black professionals, that success involved some common ingredients such as having a distinct identity

When Ursula Burns was named chief executive officer of Xerox Corporation in July of 2009, she became the first African American woman ever to serve as CEO of a Fortune 500 company. Forbes lists Burns as one of the most powerful women in business.

Courtesy of Xerox Corporation

and a heightened focus on race, office politics, networking, and again, the need for mentors. People need other people, and the corporate world is no exception.

Motivation at Work

What motivates individuals to work hard, and to work well? What determines your on-the-job satisfaction, or performance? Are you driven strictly by economics, or do you have other personal needs to fulfill? There is no single answer. At work, as in the rest of life, our behavior often stems from the convergence of many different motives. Hence, I/O psychologists over the years have found that people's satisfaction at work depends on a host of factors, economic and otherwise—such as leadership quality, a sense of justice, social relationships and comparisons, and the opportunity for advancement. Even the mere newness of a job can prove invigorating. In a longitudinal one-year study of new workers, Wendy Boswell and others (2009) found that satisfaction peaks during an initial honeymoon period before trending downward and settling in.

Economic Reward Models

Out of necessity, people work to make a living. Yet in strictly economic terms, the issue of payment is more complicated than it may appear. To begin with, someone's overall satisfaction with his or her compensation depends not only on salary (gross income, take-home pay) but also on raises (upward changes in pay, how these changes are determined), how income is distributed (the number of checks received or salary differences within the company), and what benefits an employer offers (stock options, tuition credits, on-site gym facilities, vacation time, sick leave, health insurance, pensions, and other services). Each of these factors constitutes part of a formula for satisfaction (Heneman & Schwab, 1985; Judge & Welbourne, 1994). In fact, many rewards are not monetary but symbolic—such as titles, office size, location, carpeting, furnishings, windows, and the ability to regulate access by others (Becker, 1981; Sundstrom, 1986).

Perhaps the most basic theory of worker motivation is Victor Vroom's (1964) **expectancy theory**. According to Vroom, people are rational decision makers who analyze the benefits and costs of the possible courses of action. Accordingly, he said, workers become motivated and exert effort when they believe that: (1) their effort will result in an improved performance, (2) their performance will be recognized and rewarded, and (3) the monetary and symbolic rewards that are offered are valuable and desirable. Over the years, this theory has been used with some success to predict worker attendance, productivity, and other job-related behaviors (Mitchell, 1974; Van Eerde & Thierry, 1996).

Goal setting is particularly important for motivation. Research shows that people perform better at work and are more productive when they are given specific goals and clear standards for success and failure than when they're simply told to "do your

In January 2007, based on surveys of 105,000 employees from 446 companies, *Fortune* named Google the best company to work for in America. Located in Mountain View, California, Google provides its staff with free gourmet meals, onsite doctors, daycare, a spa, laundry service, and time to spend on independent projects. It's no wonder that Google's employees are so motivated—and that the company gets hundreds of résumés a day.

Scott Barbour/Getty Images

expectancy theory The theory that workers become motivated when they believe that their efforts will produce valued outcomes.

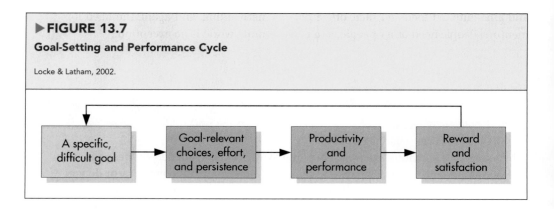

▶ **FIGURE 13.7**
Goal-Setting and Performance Cycle

Locke & Latham, 2002.

best" (Locke & Latham, 1990). Financial incentives, in particular, can effectively boost worker productivity without compromising the quality of the work (Jenkins et al., 1998). Based on past research, Edwin Locke and Gary Latham (2002) offer a practically useful theory of goal setting. The key, they maintain, is for people to set specific and difficult goals for themselves or others. This practice increases goal-related choice, effort, and persistence, increases productivity and other aspects of performance, brings reward and satisfaction, and triggers a willingness to take on new challenges and set new goals, thus setting into motion a self-perpetuating cycle of high performance (see ▶ Figure 13.7).

▮ Bonuses, Bribes, and Intrinsic Motivation

People may strive for reward, but there's more to money than just economics and more to motivation than the size of a paycheck. Social psychological factors must also be considered. Under certain conditions, reward systems that increase *extrinsic motivation* may undermine *intrinsic motivation*. As we saw in Chapter 3, people are thought to be extrinsically motivated when they engage in an activity for money, recognition, or other tangible rewards. In contrast, people are said to be intrinsically motivated when they perform for the sake of interest, challenge, or sheer enjoyment. Business leaders want employees to feel intrinsically motivated and committed to their work. So where do expectancy theory and incentive programs fit in? Is tangible reward the bottom line or not?

Research shows that when people start getting paid for a task they already enjoy, they sometimes lose interest in it. In the first demonstration of this effect, Edward Deci (1971) recruited college students to work for three one-hour sessions on block-building puzzles they found interesting. During the first and third sessions, all participants were treated in the same manner. In the second session, however, half were paid one dollar for each puzzle they completed. To measure intrinsic motivation, Deci left participants alone during a break in the first and third sessions and recorded the amount of time they spent on the puzzles rather than on other available activities. Compared with participants in the unrewarded group, those who had been paid in the second session later showed less interest in the puzzles when the money was no longer available (see ▶ Figure 13.8).

This paradoxical finding that rewards undermine intrinsic motivation has been observed in many laboratory and field studies (Deci & Ryan, 1985; Lepper & Greene, 1978; Tang & Hall, 1995). By making people feel controlled rather than autonomous, various extrinsic factors commonly found in the workplace—deadlines, punishment, close supervision, evaluation, and competition—also have adverse effects on motivation and performance. Thus, Teresa Amabile (1996) found that people who were paid for artistic activities, compared with others who were not paid, produced work that was later judged to be less creative by independent raters. To be maximally productive, people should feel internally driven, not compelled by outside forces.

But wait. If money undermines intrinsic motivation, should employers *not* use monetary incentives? Are the pay-for-performance programs often used in the workplace doomed to fail, as some have suggested (Kohn, 1993)? Not at all. To answer these questions, it's important to realize that any given reward can be interpreted in two ways, depending on how it is presented. On the one hand, being offered payment can make a person feel bribed, bought off, and controlled, which can result in the detrimental effects just described. On the other hand, rewards often provide people with positive feedback about the quality of their performance, as when people earn bonuses, scholarships, and verbal praise from others they respect. Research shows that although controlling rewards tend to lower intrinsic motivation, informational rewards have the opposite positive effect on motivation (Eisenberger & Cameron, 1996) and on creativity (Eisenberger & Rhoades, 2001). In fact, for people who are highly focused on the achievement of certain goals at work, or elsewhere, tangible inducements tend to boost intrinsic motivation (Durik & Harackiewicz, 2007; Harackiewicz & Elliot, 1993).

▶ **FIGURE 13.8**

The Effect of Payment on Intrinsic Motivation: Turning Play into Work

In this study, participants worked three times on puzzles they found interesting. After each session, the amount of free time participants spent on the puzzles served as a record of their intrinsic motivation. During the second session, half of the participants were paid for puzzles they completed and half were not. Those paid in the second session later showed less interest in the puzzles when the money was no longer available.

Deci, 1971.

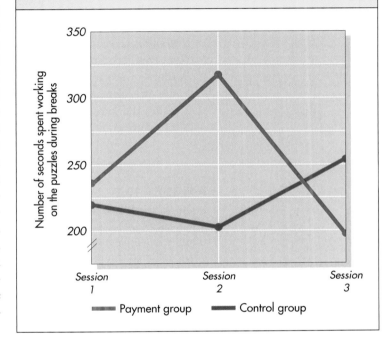

▌ Equity Considerations

A second aspect of payment that influences motivation is the perception that it is fair. According to *equity theory*, presented in Chapter 9, people want rewards to be equitable. In other words, the ratio between inputs and outcomes should be the same for the self as it is for others. Relative to co-workers, then, the more effort you exert and the more you contribute, the more money you should earn. If you feel overpaid or underpaid, however, you will experience distress and try to relieve it by (1) restoring actual equity, say, by working less or getting a raise, or (2) convincing yourself that equity already exists (Cropanzano, 1993).

Equity theory has some fascinating implications for behavior in the workplace. Consider Jerald Greenberg's (1988) study of employees in a large insurance firm. To allow for refurbishing, nearly 200 workers had to be moved temporarily from one office to another. The workers were randomly assigned to offices that usually belonged to others who were higher, lower, or equal in rank. Predictably, the usual occupants with the higher rank had a more spacious office, fewer occupants, and a larger desk. Would the random assignments influence job performance? By keeping track of the number of insurance cases processed and by rating the complexity of the cases and the quality of the decisions made, Greenberg was able to derive a measure of job performance for each worker before, during, and after the office switch. To restore equity, he reasoned, workers assigned to higher-status offices would feel overcompensated and improve their job performance and those sent to lower-status offices would feel undercompensated and slow their performance down. That is exactly what happened. ▶ Figure 13.9 shows that the results offered sound support for equity theory.

Satisfaction depends not only on equity outcomes but also on the belief that the means used to determine those outcomes were fair and clearly communicated (Brockner & Wiesenfeld, 1996; Folger, 1986). For example, Greenberg (1990) studied workers in three manufacturing plants owned by the same parent company. Business was slow, so the company reduced its payroll through temporary pay cuts. Would the cuts make workers feel underpaid? If so, how would the workers restore equity? Concerned that the policy might trigger employee theft, Greenberg randomly varied the conditions in the three plants. In one, the employees were told, without an explanation, that they would receive a 15 percent pay cut for ten weeks. In the second plant, the same pay cut was accompanied by an explanation and expressions of regret. In the third plant, salaries were not cut. By keeping track of inventories for the ten weeks before, during, and after the pay cuts, Greenberg was able to estimate the employee theft rate. The result: Workers whose pay had been cut stole more from the company—presumably to restore equity—but only when they were not provided with an adequate explana-

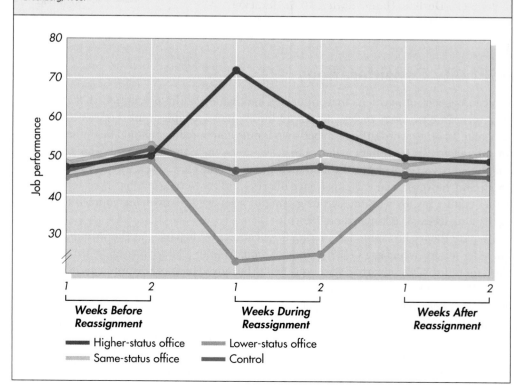

▶FIGURE 13.9

Equity in the Workplace

Insurance company workers were moved temporarily to offices that were the workplaces of those who were higher, lower, or equal in status to their own rank. Supporting equity theory, those assigned to the offices of higher-status individuals increased their job performance, and those sent to offices of lower-status individuals showed a decrease. When workers were reassigned to their original offices, productivity levels returned to normal.

Greenberg, 1988.

tion for their loss. When it comes to getting paid, praised, and treated with respect, people are most dedicated to their jobs when they believe they are being treated fairly (Folger & Cropanzano, 1998).

People are so sensitive to unfairness, underpayment, and maltreatment that these feelings can cause stress and compromise their health. In a survey of more than 3,500 workers, Bennett Tepper (2001) discovered that those who felt victimized by injustice in the workplace also reported the most fatigue, anxiety, and depression. Particularly stressful is the combination of feeling underpaid and unfairly treated. Theorizing that people will lose sleep over these concerns, Greenberg (2006) studied 467 nurses at four private hospitals, two of which cut nurses' salaries by 10 percent and two of which did not. In one hospital from each group, he taught nursing supervisors how to help promote feelings of organizational justice. Across a six-month period, participants periodically reported on their nighttime sleep patterns. The results showed two interesting patterns: (1) Underpaid nurses reported more symptoms of insomnia than those whose salaries were unchanged; and (2) this problem was reduced among underpaid nurses whose supervisors had been trained to treat them fairly (see ▶ Figure 13.10).

Equity in the workplace is important, perhaps more so for men than for women. In studies of reward allocation, people are led to believe that they and a partner are working at a task for which they will be paid. They work separately, receive false feedback on their performance, and then are told that they must decide how to divide a joint reward. In this situation, women typically pay themselves less than men do and react less strongly when they are underpaid by others (Major & Deaux, 1982). Studies of outcomes outside the laboratory reinforce the point. A study of male and female graduates of an Ivy League business school showed that the men were more likely than the women to negotiate starting salaries that were higher than the salaries that companies initially offered (Gerhart & Rynes, 1991). Other studies have confirmed this result: Men negotiate more aggressively than women do (Babcock & Laschever, 2003; Stuhlmacher & Walters, 1999).

The gender wage gap has been narrowing in recent years, but it has not been fully closed. According to the U.S. Bureau of Labor Statistics, American women in 1980 earned only 60 cents for every dollar that men were paid. By 1990, the figure was up slightly, to 72 cents. By 2006, it had climbed to 81 cents. There are many possible explanations for this gender wage gap. One is that women expect less pay than men do, even when they are equally qualified—an expectation that may stem from a long history of discrimination (Major & Konar, 1984). Second, women sometimes care

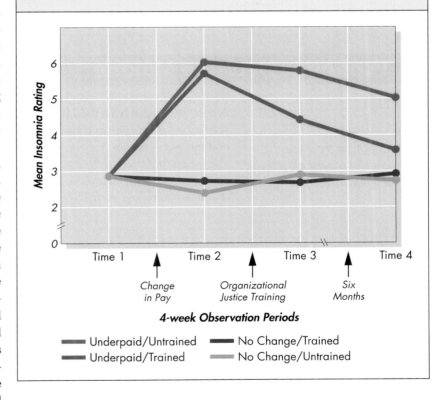

▶ FIGURE 13.10

Losing Sleep over Underpayment and Organizational Injustice

Nurses were studied at four hospitals—two that cut their salaries, two that did not. In one hospital of each group, supervisors were trained to promote feelings of organizational justice. For six months, participating nurses reported on their nighttime sleep patterns. As shown, those whose salaries had been cut reported more sleep loss than the others, but the problem was reduced among nurses whose supervisors had been trained to treat them fairly.

Greenberg, 2006.

People who feel overpaid work harder on the job than those who see their pay as appropriate. **TRUE.**

"Productivity is up nine percent since I made everyone a vice-president."

less about money and more about interpersonal relationships (Crosby, 1982). Third, women may be satisfied with less money because they compare themselves with other women instead of with their more highly paid male counterparts (Bylsma et al., 1995; Chesler & Goodman, 1976). Fourth, women on average tend to rate themselves less favorably than do men, so even when they work harder and perform better, they feel less entitled (Major et al., 1984). Whatever the explanation, it is clear that the gender gap in wages is deeply rooted in history (Goldin, 1990). However, it appears equally clear that today's working women are not content to remain underpaid relative to men. The gender wage gap should thus vanish as successive generations of women become more established in high-paying careers. Supporting this prediction, labor statistics show that compared to their male counterparts, women in the 25-to-34 age group earned 89 cents on the male dollar in 2008 (U.S. Bureau of Labor Statistics, 2008).

Economic Decision Making

*Money is power, freedom,
a cushion, the root of all evil,
the sum of blessings.*
—Carl Sandburg

People are intensely focused on money—anxious to have more of it and afraid to be without it. In powerful and symbolic ways, money arouses emotion, activates thought, and motivates action. We ran a Google search on the word *money* in the fall of 2009 and found that there were 133 million entries, exceeding the 73.3 million entries generated by the word *happiness*. (Being social psychologists, we were interested to find that *love* conquered all at 1.5 billion entries.)

"I wish they'd quit sending my financial statements."

Living alone on a deserted island, money would not be necessary to bolster self-sufficiency or protect against social rejection.

The Symbolic Power of Money

Although actor and comedian W. C. Fields once said that a rich man is nothing but a poor man with money, common sense and recent research suggest that money can change people in interesting ways.

Think about it. If you had a fortune, you would be financially independent. How would that make you feel? In a series of laboratory experiments, Kathleen Vohs and her colleagues (2006) found that when college students were merely primed to think about money, they became more self-sufficient, more autonomous, and less social in relation to others. In each study, the researchers primed money in some participants but not others in subtle ways—for example, by having them read an essay that mentioned money, by presenting them with scrambled sentences that relate to money, by having them count a large stack of Monopoly money, or by seating them at a computer with a screensaver that featured floating bills. Across the board, those who were exposed to money cues later became more independent. Put into a social situation, they preferred working alone rather than on a team, they put more distance between themselves and a fellow participant, they sought less help on a puzzle they could not solve, and they gave less help to someone who needed it. Reflecting on these findings, Vohs speculates that "money changes people at a core, basic level," that "having money makes people feel less connected and more independent, whereas having little money makes you feel more interdependent with others" (Carpenter, 2005, p. 27).

Let's take this speculation one step further. If money leads us to feel more self-sufficient, does it lessen our need for approval and blunt the pain of social rejection? And following rejection, do we attach greater value to money? Through research conducted in China, Xinyue Zhou and others (2009) sought to answer these questions. In one study, they brought a handful of university students together for a getting-acquainted conversation. The students were then separated and asked to pick someone from the group they'd like to work with. At that point, by random assignment, all students were told that they had to be dismissed—either because everyone selected them (social acceptance) or because no one selected them (social rejection). Afterward, they completed a set of money-related tasks. Here's the interesting part: When asked to draw a Chinese coin from memory, students in the rejection condition drew larger coins. They also said they were more willing to permanently give up such pleasures as chocolate, sunshine, and the beach in exchange for the equivalent of $1.4 million. Rejection had increased the subjective value of money. In a second study, students engaged in what they were told was a "finger dexterity" task: They counted out either 80 pieces of paper or 80 $100 bills. Next they played a computerized online ball-tossing game, presumably with three live students. In the normal condition, the game proceeded uneventfully. In a rejection condition, however, the others soon started to exclude the participant from the ball toss. When later asked how they felt about the game, those who had counted paper were more distressed than those who had counted money. Somehow, the money served to buffer students from the distress normally caused by social rejection (see ▶ Figure 13.11).

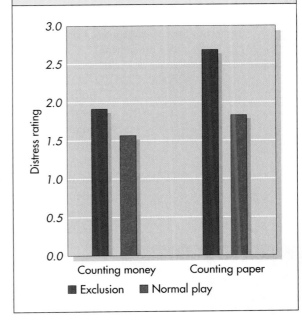

▶ **FIGURE 13.11**

Links Between Money and Social Rejection

After counting blank pieces of either paper or money, some research participants but not others told they had been excluded from an online ball-tossing game by other players. As seen in terms of how they felt about the game, excluded participants who had counted paper were more distressed than before (right) yet those who had counted money were not (left). It appears that money and the self-sufficiency that it symbolizes can mute the adverse effects of social rejection.

Zhou et al., 2009.

■ Social Influences in the Stock Market

For all its tangible and symbolic benefits, money is a prominent source of human motivation. In recent years, therefore, social psychologists have become interested in how people make economic decisions, for example when they invest in the stock market. The stock market can be remarkably volatile, as it has been over the past decade—surging up, plummeting down, and inching its way back up in ways that resemble a roller coaster ride. Why does the market fluctuate so much? Are the companies we invest in unpredictable from day to day or are social psychological factors at work? To what extent are day-to-day price movements determined by rational economic indicators such as the gross domestic product, interest rates, budget surpluses and deficits, inflation, employment statistics, company earnings, political uncertainty, consumer confidence, and stock prices that are too high or too low and need correction? To what extent, for that matter, is the stock market influenced by fear, greed, false beliefs, financial experts like CNBC's Jim Cramer who appear on business shows, rumors that spread over the Internet, conformity pressures, and other social influences, all compounded by the speed with which people can now trade stocks online?

"I don't buy stocks simply because others are buying them. I buy them because many, many others are buying them."

The odds of making money are far better in the stock market than in the slot machines found in gambling casinos. Most of the time, most investors come out ahead. In many ways, however, choosing stocks is like gambling. In *A Random Walk Down Wall Street*, first published in 1981, economist Burton Malkiel (2007) reported that over the long haul, mutual fund portfolios compiled by experts perform no better than randomly selected groups of stocks. Thus, when *Consumer Reports* evaluated the advice given by professional brokers, it concluded that "a monkey throwing darts at the stock pages . . . could probably do as well in overall investment performance, perhaps even better" (Shefrin & Statman, 1986, p. 52).

But don't some professionals turn a greater profit than others? And if stock prices rise and fall in reaction to market conditions and the success of a company in relation to that of its competitors, can't the astute investor or short-term day trader take advantage of these relationships? The answer to both questions is "not necessarily." It is certainly true that some brokers perform better than others do for a period of time, perhaps even for a few years. But individuals are no more likely to succeed after a string of wins than after a string of losses. Since many investors and traders have access to the same information and since stock prices can change at a moment's notice, short-term price movements in the market cannot be predicted with precision or reliability. The only way to guarantee profit is to use confidential inside information, which is illegal. Yet studies show that the average person has a measure of faith in professional investors, overestimating their rate of success relative to their actual performance (Törngren & Montgomery, 2004).

If stock market decisions are not made on strictly economic grounds, then on what are they based? As described in *Greed and Fear*, Hersh Shefrin's (2006) book on the behavioral finance and the psychology of investing, predictions of the future on Wall Street are heavily influenced by social psychological factors. In October 1987, for example, the U.S. stock market crashed, resulting in an estimated loss of $500 billion.

The floor of a stock exchange is a setting fraught with social influence (left). In fact, today's investors are also bombarded by social influences when they watch business shows such as CNBC's hit show *Mad Money*, starring Jim Cramer (right).

Shortly afterward, economist Robert Shiller sent questionnaires to a large group of active traders to try to determine what caused the crisis. For the 1,000 or so investors who responded, the key event was news about the market itself, including a sharp decline that occurred on the morning of the crash. In other words, price movements in the stock market were triggered not by objective economic information but by other price movements in the market. Does this phenomenon ring a bell? Studies on the processes of social comparison and conformity have shown that when people feel they cannot clearly and concretely measure their own opinion, they turn to others for guidance. Perhaps that is why investors are more influenced by news and stock market tips during periods of rising or falling prices than they are during periods of relative stability (Schachter et al., 1985).

With respect to coin flips and other chance events, gamblers too often assume that hot streaks are due to turn cold and vice versa. Yet when it comes to games of skill, such as basketball, people often make the opposite assumptions that a hot streak forecasts continued success and a cold spell predicts failure. Both assumptions are incorrect. One event does not imply another. But what about the ups and downs of a stock market? Do either of these beliefs color the decisions investors make?

To explore this question, Stanley Schachter and his colleagues (1987) presented college students with recent price histories of stocks that had increased, decreased, or remained stable over a three-week period. The conventional wisdom on Wall Street, of course, is that investors should buy low and sell high. Yet most participants indicated they would buy stocks that had risen and sell stocks that had fallen. In a follow-up study, very similar decisions were made by more sophisticated students attending the business school at Columbia University.

Do people always go with the flow of the marketplace, or do they sometimes buck the trend to buy low and sell high? Paul Andreasson (1987) argued that the answer depends on attributions. According to Andreasson, investors may follow conventional wisdom. But, he asked, what about price changes for which they have a ready explanation? What if a rise in a stock's price is attributed to certain company or world events? As far as the stock market is concerned, attributions such as these can produce self-fulfilling prophecies by leading investors to believe that the changes will persist—that rising prices will continue to climb or that declining prices will continue to fall. To test his hypothesis, Andreasson simulated a stock market on the computer and found that without news stories to explain the fluctuations, research participants assumed that prices would gravitate to previous levels. The result: They bought stocks when the price was low and sold when the price was high. However, those who also received *Wall Street Journal* explanations for the changes pursued the less profitable strategy, buying stocks that were climbing (based on the assumption that they would continue to do so) and selling those that were on the decline (based on the same assumption of continuity).

Even unpublished rumors can have this effect. Nicholas DiFonzo and Prashant Bordia (1997) conducted a stock market simulation in which unconfirmed company rumors were leaked to some participants but not others. Interestingly, the participants said that they felt that the rumors were not credible and thus did not sway their decisions. Yet they traded on these rumors as if they were hard facts. It doesn't stretch the imagination to see how all these findings might relate to actual behavior in the stock market. Faced with upward and downward movements, the financial news media often seize upon current events for a quick explanation. In some cases, the rumors spread like wildfire through the business community. Whether the news is true or false is irrelevant. Either way, it can turn an initial rise into a bull rally and an initial dip into a steep dive. At present, researchers are using laboratory simulations to mimic the decision making that causes stock market bubbles, crashes, and other phenomena (Porter & Smith, 2003).

Sometimes emotional factors can lead us astray. Contradicting rational theories of economic decision making, research shows that people often fall prey to the **endowment effect**, a tendency to inflate the value of objects they already own (Thaler, 1980). In a study that demonstrates this point, people demanded a higher price for a coffee mug that had been given to them than they did for a comparable mug they did not yet own (Kahneman et al., 1990). In a second study, researchers observed the orders placed by Australian stock market investors and found that sellers valued their own shares higher than buyers did, regardless of the current market price (Furche & Johnstone, 2006).

▌ Commitment, Entrapment, and Escalation

Stock market behavior, like other business decisions that individuals, groups, and organizations make, is complicated by another social factor. Shefrin and Meir Statman (1985) argued that many investors lack the self-control necessary for sound investment decisions. When people own shares of a stock that is climbing, they sometimes sell too early so they can enjoy the quick pleasure of making a profit. This tendency is easy to understand. But when people own stock that is falling, they often wait too long before selling in the hope that they might avoid a financial loss. Why do people often continue to hang on in a failing situation—a decision-making disease that Shefrin (2006) calls "Get-Evenitis"? When the handwriting is on the wall, why compound the problem by throwing good money after bad?

In *Too Much Invested to Quit*, Alan Teger (1980) described a dollar-auction game that illustrates part of the dilemma. Imagine yourself in this situation: The auctioneer tells you and other participants that a one-dollar bill is about to be sold. As in a typical auction, the highest bidder will receive the dollar in exchange for the amount bid. Yet contrary to convention, the second highest bidder must also pay the amount bid and will receive nothing in return. You and the other participants are asked not to communicate, and the minimum opening bid is set at five cents. Then, before you know it, the bidding begins. In laboratory experiments, two participants compete in the auction. They are supplied with a small amount of money that is theirs to keep, and they are free to quit the experiment at any time. What happens next might seem startling. Some pairs reasonably choose to take the money and run without making a single bid. Other pairs, however, get involved in escalating bidding wars. According to Teger, bidding for the dollar frequently climbs into the five-dollar range—more than the amount allocated for play by the experimenter. On one occasion, the auctioneer had to terminate the game after the two participants had bid $24.95 and $25!

The dollar auction helps us understand how we can become financially overcommitted in real life. In Chapter 8, we saw that individuals and groups can become *entrapped* by their own initial commitments as they try to justify or salvage investments they have already made. In business, the economic conditions in which an investment is made sometimes justify continued commitment. When there is a reasonable likelihood of success and when potential earnings are high relative to the additional necessary costs, it may pay to persist. With certain long-term investments, sizable up-front costs have to be endured before the delayed benefits are likely to materialize. As in the dollar auction, however, entrapment may occur when economic conditions do not provide a basis for optimism.

Why do investors, business executives, and others losing money on a failing investment so often "hang tough," only to sink deeper and deeper? Why do supervisors who recommend that a worker be hired later overrate that worker's job performance compared with others in the company who were not involved in the hiring

endowment effect The tendency for people to inflate the value of objects, goods, or services they already own.

(Schoorman, 1988)? Why do NBA teams continue to start players who were selected as top draft picks but have not performed well (Staw & Hoang, 1995)? One explanation for these *escalation effects* is that while people ordinarily avoid taking large financial risks to gain money, they are often willing to take risks to keep from losing money. When offered a hypothetical choice between a certain gain of $1,000 and a 50-50 shot at a gain of $2,500, most people choose the smaller guaranteed alternative. Yet when offered a choice between a certain loss of $1,000 and a 50-50 shot at a loss of $2,500, most people roll the dice (Kahneman & Tversky, 1979).

Our aversion to loss accounts for part of the problem, but it's clear that social psychological factors also contribute heavily to the escalation effect. Research has shown that individuals who make the decisions that lead to loss are more likely than others to persist or even to invest further when they feel personally responsible. Why? There are two reasons, both of which are valid (Moon, 2001). One is that people are trained to finish what they have started—a desire for completion that can lead people to throw good money or time after bad (Garland & Conlon, 1998). The second, according to Barry Staw, Joel Brockner, and others, is that people often remain committed to a failing course of action in order to justify their prior decisions, protect their self-esteem, or save face in front of others. Thus, Staw and his colleagues (1997) found that banks were less likely to cut their losses on bad business and real estate loans when the executives who had funded those loans were still with the bank than when they were not. Zhang and Baumeister (2006) found that participants whose self-esteem was threatened were more likely to become entrapped in a failing laboratory game, losing more money as a result.

In organizations, escalation effects can be minimized by removing the individuals who made the initial losing investment from the decision making later on. Fortunately, individual investors can also learn to use various de-escalation strategies designed to make them more responsive to available evidence and keep them from throwing good money after bad (Simonson & Staw, 1992). In one study, for example, Richard Larrick and others (1990) found that people often violate the **sunk cost principle** of economics, which states that only future costs and benefits, not past commitments, or "sunk costs," should be considered in making a decision. To appreciate the practical implications, imagine that you've bought a $40 ticket to a basketball game weeks in advance. Now, on the day of the game, you don't feel well, it's snowing, and your favorite player is injured. Do you still go to the game to make sure you use the ticket? Not wanting to "waste" the money, many of us would go even though the money is already sunk, and even though we would have to bear the added costs of getting sick, driving in bad weather, and sitting through a boring game. To see if there is a more rational economic choice, ask yourself this question: Would you go to the game if someone called on game day and offered you a free ticket? If you said that you would go if you'd paid for the ticket but not if it were free, then—like investors who don't know when to cut their losses—you fell into the sunk cost trap and should have stayed home.

Over and over again, studies have shown that human adults fall prey to the sunk cost effect, allowing their economic decisions to be biased by past investments of time, money, and effort, a maladaptive tendency that, curiously, is *not* exhibited by children or laboratory animals (Arkes & Ayton, 1999). Thankfully, we are trainable. In a study of University of Michigan professors, Larrick and others (1990) found that the economists among them were more likely than their counterparts in other disciplines to use the sunk cost principle—not only in hypothetical problems but also in personal decisions. More important, they found that others can be taught to apply the rule as well. Indeed, a full month after exposure to a brief training session, college students were more likely to report that they were using the rule in their own lives. Sometimes a little knowledge can go a long way.

 People losing money on an investment tend to cut their losses rather than hang tough. **FALSE.**

sunk cost principle The economic rule of thumb that only future costs and benefits, not past commitments, should be considered in making a decision.

REVIEW

- The classic Hawthorne studies showed that attention paid to workers increased their productivity.

- In the workplace and other business settings, behavior is heavily influenced by social psychological factors.

Personnel Selection

- Recruiting a competent staff is the first important step in developing a successful organization.

The Typical Job Interview

- Employment interviews may actually diminish the tendency of employers to make simple stereotyped judgments.

- But interviews often give rise to poor selection decisions, in part because of the self-presentations of applicants and by expectations of the interviewer that bias the interview.

"Scientific" Alternatives to Traditional Interviews

- Many companies use standardized tests of cognitive ability, personality, and integrity as part of the selection process.

- Although overt integrity tests are easy to fake, covert tests are not and the results of covert tests are somewhat predictive of job performance.

- A more effective selection method is the structured interview, in which all applicants are evaluated in a standardized manner.

- Many organizations use assessment centers, in which multiple applicants take part in multiple activities monitored by a group of evaluators.

Affirmative Action

- Affirmative action affects those it is designed to help, those who feel excluded by it, organizations that implement it, and interactions among these three groups.

- Research shows that women devalue their own performance when they think they have been preferentially selected.

- But reactions are more favorable when procedures are seen as fair, for example when merit-based factors are thought to play a role.

Culture and Organizational Diversity

- Affirmative action and the globalization of business have combined to increase diversity in the workplace.

- One prediction is that diversity will breed division and conflict, making work teams less effective.

- A more optimistic prediction is that diversity will increase the range of perspectives brought to bear on a problem, enhancing group performance.

- At present, research provides a hint of support for both predictions, suggesting that there is no single or simple effect.

Performance Appraisals

- Performance appraisals involve the evaluation of an employee and communication of the results to that person.

- Sometimes objective measures of performance are available, but usually evaluations are based on subjective judgments.

Supervisor Ratings

- Research shows that supervisor ratings are based largely on job-relevant characteristics.

- These ratings may be biased by halo effects, contrast effects, and individual differences in the tendency to give high, low, or neutral ratings on a numeric scale.

Self-Evaluations

- Self-evaluations also figure into performance appraisals, but they tend to be self-serving and inflated.

- Self-evaluations are higher among those who have power in an organization. They are also higher among men than among women.

New and Improved Methods of Appraisal

- Performance appraisals can be improved when ratings are made shortly after observation, careful notes are taken, multiple raters are used, and raters are trained in the necessary skills.

Due-Process Considerations

- Procedural fairness (not just outcomes) is an important factor in the way people react to evaluations of their performance.

Leadership

- Everyone agrees that leadership requires social influence.

The Classic Trait Approach

- One approach is to identify the traits that characterize people who appear to have leadership qualities.
- Situational theories are based on the notion that different situations call for different types of leaders.

Contingency Models of Leadership

- In Fiedler's contingency model, task-oriented leaders excel in high- and low-control situations, whereas relations-oriented leaders are effective in moderate-control situations.
- According to the normative model, although leaders range from autocratic to participative, the key to good leadership is to invite the right amount of worker participation.

Transactional Leadership

- Transactional leaders reward followers who keep up their end of the bargain and correct those who do not.

Transformational Leadership

- Transformational leaders motivate followers through their charisma, inspiration, intellectual stimulation, and personal concern for others.
- Studies show that transformational leaders are more effective than transactional leaders.

Leadership Among Women and Minorities

- Despite recent gains, working women and minorities are underrepresented in positions of leadership.
- Many women who are qualified encounter obstacles at home and at work, where people hold stereotypes about women in leadership roles.
- Part of the problem for minorities is that they are excluded from social networks and influential mentors in the workplace.

Motivation at Work

- Both economic and social factors influence motivation in the workplace.

Economic Reward Models

- On the economic side, Vroom's expectancy theory states that workers behave in ways designed to produce the most desirable outcome.
- Various incentive programs are thus used to motivate by reward.

Bonuses, Bribes, and Intrinsic Motivation

- When people perceive a reward as a bribe and a means of controlling their behavior, they lose interest in the work itself.

- But when a reward is presented as a bonus, giving positive information about the quality of work, it can enhance intrinsic motivation.

Equity Considerations

- Equity theory says that the ratio between inputs and outcomes should be the same for all workers.
- Research shows that workers adjust their productivity levels upward when they feel overpaid and downward when they feel underpaid.
- For various reasons, women accept as equitable a lower level of pay than men do.

Economic Decision Making

The Symbolic Power of Money

- Research shows that money makes people feel more independent, more self-sufficient, and less in need of others.
- As a result, exposure to money can mute the distressing effects of social rejection.

Social Influences in the Stock Market

- Economic decisions are often influenced by social psychological factors.

- Sharp changes in the stock market can be triggered by news of what other investors are doing.
- The goal in the stock market is to buy low and sell high, yet various factors can lead investors to follow less-profitable strategies.
- Stock market simulations have shown that investors can be influenced by news stories and unconfirmed rumors, which can set in motion a self-fulfilling prophecy.

Commitment, Entrapment, and Escalation

- People often become entrapped by their initial commitments and so stick to failing courses of action and throw good money after bad.

- At an organizational level, escalation can be minimized by removing those who made the initial losing investment from later decision making.

- Individually, people can be taught de-escalation strategies, such as the rule that only future costs and benefits, not sunk costs, are relevant to economic decisions.

Key Terms

assessment center (536)

contingency model of leadership (547)

endowment effect (562)

expectancy theory (553)

Hawthorne effect (530)

industrial/organizational (I/O) psychology (529)

integrity tests (534)

normative model of leadership (548)

performance appraisal (542)

structured interview (536)

sunk cost principle (563)

transactional leader (549)

transformational leader (549)

Media Resources

Social Psychology 8th Edition Companion Website
Visit your book companion website
www.cengage.com/psychology/kassin
where you will find flash cards, practice quizzes, Internet links, and more to help you study.

CENGAGENOW Just what you need to know NOW! Spend time on what you need to master rather than on information you already have learned. Take a pre-test for this chapter and CengageNOW will generate a personalized study plan based on your results. The study plan will identify the topics you need to review and direct you to online resources to help you master those topics. You can then take a post-test to help you determine the concepts you have mastered and what you will need to work on. Try it out! Go to **academic.cengage.com/login** to sign in with an access code or to purchase access to this product.

Putting COMMON SENSE *to the Test*

Although flawed, job interviews consistently make for better hiring decisions.

False. *Although interviews may lessen the tendency among employers to make simple stereotyped judgments, they often lack predictive validity.*

A problem with having workers evaluate their own job performance is that self-ratings are overly positive.

True. *Self-evaluations of job performance are not only more positive than ratings made by others but also less predictive of success.*

The most effective type of leader is one who knows how to win support through the use of reward.

False. *Great leaders articulate a vision and then inspire others to join in that vision and work for a common cause.*

People who feel overpaid work harder on the job than those who see their pay as appropriate.

True. *People who feel overpaid work harder to restore their sense of equity.*

People losing money on an investment tend to cut their losses rather than hang tough.

False. *People often remain committed to a failing course of action in order to justify the initial decision to themselves and others.*

14

Health

This chapter explores the social psychology of physical and mental health. We focus first on the links between stress and health. Four questions are asked in this regard: What causes stress, how does it affect the body, how do we appraise potentially stressful situations, and what are some ways of coping with stress? Next we discuss some of the social influences on treatment and prevention. We then conclude on a positive note, looking at the roots of happiness.

When Laurence Sterne, an eighteenth-century English novelist, weighed the value of good health, he concluded that it was "above all gold and treasure." Most would agree, which is why health care is so important to people and why the subject of reform is such a contentious political topic. The long and complex debate about health care in the United States and elsewhere clearly illustrates the intensity of feelings on this issue. In matters of life and death, everyone cares intensely, including social psychologists.

The reasons that social psychologists study *mental health* and such disorders as anxiety and depression are obvious. We humans are inherently social creatures, and our psychological well-being can be both damaged and repaired by our relationships with other people. But social psychologists are also interested in *physical health*, a domain normally associated with medicine. Working in universities, medical schools, hospitals, and government agencies, many social psychologists are deeply involved in the emerging area of **health psychology**—the application of psychology to the promotion of physical health and the prevention and treatment of illness (Friedman & Silver, 2007; Leventhal et al., 2008; Straub, 2007; Taylor, 2009).

You may wonder: What does social psychology have to do with catching a cold, having a heart attack, or being afflicted by cancer? If you could turn the clock back a few years and ask your family doctor, his or her reply would be "nothing." In the past, physical illness was considered a purely biological event. But this strict medical perspective has given way to a broader model, which holds that health is a joint product of biological, psychological, and social factors.

Part of the reason for this expanded view is that illness patterns over the years have changed in significant ways. In the year 1900, the principal causes of death in the United States were contagious diseases such as polio, smallpox, tuberculosis, typhoid fever, malaria, influenza, and pneumonia. Today, none of these infectious illnesses are leading killers. Instead, Americans are most likely to die (in order of risk) from heart disease, cancers, strokes, respiratory diseases, and accidents (AIDS is twentieth on the list in the United States but fourth worldwide). These diseases are

Putting COMMON SENSE to the Test

Circle Your Answer

T	F	The accumulation of daily hassles does more to make people sick than catastrophes or major life changes.
T	F	Like humans, zebras get ulcers.
T	F	Stress can weaken the heart, but it cannot affect the immune system.
T	F	When it comes to physical health, research does not support popular beliefs about the power of positive thinking.
T	F	People who have lots of friends are healthier and live longer than those who live more isolated lives.
T	F	As role models, celebrities have great influence over public health care decisions.

health psychology The study of physical health and illness by psychologists from various areas of specialization.

sometimes preventable through changes in lifestyle, outlook, and behavior. In light of useful research that has been conducted in recent years, this chapter focuses first on stress: what causes it, what it does to the body, and how we appraise stressful situations in order to cope with them. Next, we look at some social influences on the treatment and prevention of illness. Finally, we consider the pursuit of happiness and life satisfaction.

Stress and Health

According to the World Health Organization, the average life expectancy ranges from a low of 33 years in Swaziland to a high of 83 in Andorra. (The average life expectancy is 78 in the United States and 80 in Canada.) For up-to-date health statistics, you can visit online the World Health Organization (www.who.org) and the National Center for Health Statistics (www.cdc.gov/nchs).

Stress is an unpleasant state of arousal that arises when we perceive that the demands of a situation threaten our ability to cope effectively. Nobody knows the precise extent of the problem, but stress is a potent killer. Regardless of who you are, when you were born, or where you live, you have no doubt experienced stress. Sitting in rush-hour traffic, packing your belongings to move, losing your job and looking for work, getting married or divorced, getting into an argument with a close friend, worrying about an unwanted pregnancy or the health of your child, living in a high-crime neighborhood, struggling to make financial ends meet, and caring for a loved one who is sick are examples of stresses and strains we all must live with.

Clearly, what stresses a generation or entire population can be influenced by world events. In a nationwide survey of thousands of men and women commissioned by the American Psychological Association (2008), respondents were asked to indicate the sources of stress in their lives. Four out of five cited money and the economy. In fact, five of the top 10 stressors related to money, the others being work, housing costs, and job stability (see Table 14.1). The effects on a person's health and well-being are clear. Among the symptoms most commonly reported were irritability and anger, fatigue, nervousness, lack of energy and motivation, sadness, depression, headaches, wanting to cry, stomach upset, and muscular tension. Whether the stress is short term or long term, serious or mild, no one is immune and there is no escape. But there are ways to cope.

According to Richard Lazarus and Susan Folkman (1984), the stress-and-coping process is an ongoing transaction between a person and his or her environment. Faced with an event that may prove threatening, our subjective **appraisal** of the situation determines how we will experience the stress and what **coping** strategies we will use—in other words, what thoughts, feelings, and behaviors we will employ to try to reduce the stress. At times, people also take proactive steps to keep a potentially stressful event from occurring in the first place. As we'll see, effective coping helps to maintain good health; ineffective coping can cause harm (Monat et al., 2007).

In the next two sections, we examine two questions that are relevant to health and well-being: (1) What causes stress, and (2) how does stress "get into" the body? Then we look at appraisal and coping, processes that account for why an event that flattens one person can prove harmless to another. As all the pieces come together, we'll see that the answers to these questions provide a broad and useful model of the stress-and-coping process (see ▶ Figure 14.1).

TABLE 14.1

What Americans Cite as Top Stressors

Stressors	Percent of Americans
Money	81
The economy	80
Work	67
Family health problems	67
Family responsibilities	64
Housing costs	62
Relationships	62
Personal health concerns	61
Job stability	56
Personal safety	48

American Psychological Association, 2008.

Anthony Robbins offers a simple two-step formula for handling stress: (1) Don't sweat the small stuff; and (2) remember that it's all small stuff.

What Causes Stress?

There are many different sources of stress, or **stressors**, and these can be defined and measured in different ways (Cohen et al., 1995). What events do *you* find stressful? Try jotting down some of the stressors in your own life, and you'll probably find that the items on your list can be sorted into three major categories: catastrophes, major life events, and daily hassles.

Crises and Catastrophes

> We are running from the wave, and we can see the water right behind us. We run toward the other side of the island. When we get about halfway across, we meet people running and screaming from the other direction. Then we see the water in front of us too. The waves meet, and we are under water. (Dittmann, 2005, p. 36)

On December 26, 2004, one of the worst natural disasters in history spread over Southeast Asia, India, Indonesia, and Africa. It started when a powerful earthquake struck deep under the Indian Ocean, triggering massive tsunamis that obliterated cities, seaside communities, and holiday resorts. Approximately 320,000 people in a dozen countries were killed; thousands of survivors were injured and traumatized in the process.

Eight months later, in August 2005, Hurricane Katrina stampeded through the Gulf Coast of the United States with winds of up to 175 miles per hour, devastating areas in Florida, Mississippi, Alabama, and Louisiana and killing nearly 2,000 people. In New Orleans, the surge breached the levees, ultimately flooding 80 percent of the city and many neighboring parishes. Causing an estimated $81 billion in damage, Hurricane Katrina quickly became the costliest natural disaster in U.S. history.

The intense stress that natural catastrophes impose on a population can also be caused by human beings. The terrorist assault on the World Trade Center and the Pentagon on September 11, 2001, was a different kind of tragedy that no one who was old enough to witness it will ever forget. Americans all over the world took the attack personally and were touched by it, whether they were present or not. In a nationwide telephone survey of 560 adults conducted later that week, 90 percent said they were experiencing some symptoms of stress and 44 percent reported "substantial" symptoms such as recurring thoughts, dreams, and memories; difficulty falling or staying asleep; difficulty concentrating on work; and unprovoked outbursts of anger (Schuster et al., 2001). These problems were far more common among New Yorkers than in people living in other areas (Schlenger et al., 2002). Even within Manhattan, researchers found that the closer residents lived to Ground Zero, the more traumatized and depressed they were by the experience (Galea et al., 2002). The most profoundly affected were those who worked in the towers or nearby, those who had friends and family in the vicinity, and rescue workers who were called to the scene.

Other events that can have similarly traumatic effects include war, motor vehicle accidents, plane crashes, violent crimes, physical or sexual abuse, the death of a loved one, and natural disasters such as fires, tornadoes, earthquakes, and floods (Kubany et

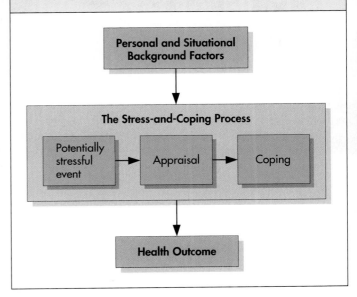

▶ **FIGURE 14.1**

The Stress-and-Coping Process

This process involves a potentially stressful event, the appraisal of that event, and attempts to cope. Played out against a variety of background factors unique to each individual, the stress-and-coping process influences health outcomes.

stress An unpleasant state of arousal in which people perceive the demands of an event as taxing or exceeding their ability to satisfy or alter those demands.

appraisal The process by which people make judgments about the demands of potentially stressful events and their ability to meet those demands.

coping Efforts to reduce stress.

stressor Anything that causes stress.

Natural disasters can devastate entire populations. In December 2004, the tsunami that destroyed parts of South Asia traumatized survivors on Phi Phi Island, a beautiful vacation resort in Thailand (left). Months later, in August 2005, Hurricane Katrina stormed through the U.S. Gulf Coast. In New Orleans, where 80 percent of the city was flooded, residents waiting for help hugged the rooftops of flooded buildings (right).

al., 2000). The harmful effects of catastrophic stressors on health are well documented. Paul and Gerald Adams (1984) examined the public records in Othello, Washington, before and after the 1980 eruption of the Mount St. Helens volcano, which spewed thick layers of ash all over the area. After the eruption, they observed increases in calls made to a mental health crisis line, police reports of domestic violence, referrals to a local alcohol treatment center, and visits to the emergency room. Then there was an earthquake that shook San Francisco in 1989. Houses collapsed, highways buckled, overpasses fell apart, water mains burst, and fires raged out of control, leaving thousands of people homeless. By coincidence, Susan Nolen-Hoeksema and Jannay Morrow (1991) had administered some trauma-relevant measures to a group of Stanford University students two weeks before the earthquake. Follow-up assessments ten days later and again after six weeks provided these investigators with a before-and-after examination of coping. They found that people who had initially been more distressed and those who had encountered more danger during the quake experienced the most psychological distress afterward.

The scarring effects of large-scale disasters are without dispute. Based on their review of 52 studies, Anthony Rubonis and Leonard Bickman (1991) found that high rates of psychological disorders—such as anxiety, phobias, depression, alcohol abuse, and somatic complaints—are common among residents of areas that have been hit by these catastrophic events. In a more recent study of disasters involving 377 counties, a team of researchers found that compared with the years preceding each disaster, the suicide rate increased by 14 percent after floods, by 31 percent after hurricanes, and by 63 percent after earthquakes (Krug et al., 1998).

War in particular leaves deep, permanent psychological scars. Soldiers in combat believe that they have to kill or be killed. They suffer intense anxiety and see horrifying injuries, death, and destruction, all of which leaves them with images and emotions that do not fade. Given this level of stress, it's not surprising that when a war is over, some veterans suffer greatly. In World War I, the problem was called "shell shock." In World War II, it was called "combat fatigue." Now the problem is considered a specific form of **posttraumatic stress disorder (PTSD)** and is identified by such enduring symptoms as recurring anxiety, sleeplessness, nightmares, intrusive bad thoughts, flashbacks, attention problems, and social withdrawal. What's worse, families are often shattered when a loved one returns from war and seems different, as if still trapped in combat (McCarty-Gould, 2000). Apparently, time alone does not heal the wounds of war-induced PTSD. In a longitudinal study of 88,000 American soldiers who had returned from the war in Iraq, researchers found that soldiers had more mental health problems three to six months after their return than immediately afterward, with the number of reported PTSD cases rising from 49 percent to 59 percent (Milliken et al., 2007).

War can traumatize civilian populations as well. In Israel, 16 percent of adults had personally been exposed to a terrorist attack and 37 percent had a close friend or family member who had been exposed (Bleich et al., 2003). As for the mental health con-

sequences of such exposure, a study of 905 Jewish and Palestinian citizens revealed that exposure to terrorism was associated with PTSD symptoms in both groups—more so among the Palestinian citizens, members of an ethnic minority who have fewer coping resources to turn to when in distress (Hobfoll et al., 2006).

Over the years, clinical psychologists have studied PTSD and the life experiences that precipitate its onset (Friedman et al., 2007). Based on a nationwide survey of 6,000 Americans aged 15 to 54 years, Ronald Kessler and others (1995) estimated that 8 percent of the population (5 percent of men, 10 percent of women) suffer posttraumatic stress disorder in the course of a lifetime and that the symptoms often persist for many years. Among the experiences that produced these traumas were witnessing a murder or injury, the death of a loved one, life-threatening accidents, serious illness, war, fires and natural disasters, physical and sexual assaults, and prison. From a meta-analysis of 290 studies involving

These soldiers, like thousands of other troops and civilians, have experienced the recent wars in Iraq and Afganistan first-hand. It has long been recognized that combat leaves psychological scars and increases the risk of posttraumatic stress disorder.

thousands of participants, it is clear that PTSD is more prevalent among women than among men, even though men are more likely to experience potentially traumatic events (Tolin & Foa, 2006).

▮▮ Major Life Events

Some people are lucky enough to avoid major catastrophes. But nobody can completely avoid stress. Indeed, change itself may cause stress by forcing us to adapt to new circumstances. This hypothesis was first proposed by Thomas Holmes and Richard Rahe (1967), who interviewed hospital patients and found that their illnesses had often been preceded by major changes in some aspect of their lives. Some of the changes were negative (getting hurt, divorced, or fired), but others were positive (getting married or promoted or having a baby). To measure life stress, Holmes and Rahe then devised the Social Readjustment Rating Scale (SRRS), a checklist of 43 major life events each assigned a numerical value based on the amount of readjustment it requires. Among the events sampled (and the numerical values they were assigned) were the death of a spouse (100), divorce (73), imprisonment (63), marriage (50), job loss (47), pregnancy (40), school transfer (20), and even vacations (13).

posttraumatic stress disorder (PTSD) A condition in which a person experiences enduring physical and psychological symptoms after an extremely stressful event.

Tyler Hicks/The New York Times/Redux

The simple notion that change is inherently stressful has an intuitive ring about it. But is change per se, positive or negative, necessarily harmful? There are two problems with this notion. First, although there is a statistical link between negative events and illness, research does not similarly support the claim that positive "stressors" such as taking a vacation, graduating, winning a lottery, starting a new career, or getting married are similarly harmful (Stewart et al., 1986). Happiness is not the absence of distress, nor is distress the absence of happiness. A person can simultaneously experience both emotions (Carver & Scheier, 1990), and the health consequences are different (Taylor, 1991). The second complicating factor is that the impact of any change depends on who the person is and how the change is interpreted. Moving to a new country, for example, is less stressful to immigrants who can speak the new language (Berry et al., 1992); a diagnosis of infertility is less devastating to married couples who want children when they confront the issue, emotionally, than when they avoid it (Berghuis & Stanton, 2002). Victims of physical assault who engage in counterfactual "what if?" thinking take longer to recover emotionally than those who do not (El Leithy et al., 2006). The amount of change in a person's life may provide crude estimates of stress and future health, but the predictive equation is not that simple.

■ Microstressors: The Hassles of Everyday Life

Think again about the sources of stress in your life, and catastrophes and other exceptional events will spring to mind. Yet the most common source of stress arises from the hassles that irritate us every day. Environmental factors such as population density, loud noise, extreme heat or cold, and cigarette smoke are all sources of stress. Car

problems, gas prices, waiting in lines, losing keys, bad work days, money troubles, and other "microstressors" also place a constant strain on us. Unfortunately, there is nothing "micro" about the impact of these stressors on health and well-being. Studies suggest that the accumulation of daily hassles contributes more to illness than do major life events (Kohn et al., 1991). Interpersonal conflicts are the most upsetting of our daily stressors and have a longer-lasting impact than most others (Bolger et al., 1989).

One problem that plagues many people in the workplace is occupational stress (Barling et al., 2005). One type of reaction is *burnout*—a prolonged response to job stress that is characterized by emotional exhaustion, cynicism, disengagement, and a lack of personal accomplishment. Teachers, doctors, nurses, police officers, social workers, and others in human-service professions are especially at risk. Under relentless job pressures, those who are burned out describe themselves as feeling drained, frustrated, hardened, apathetic, and lacking in energy and motivation (Maslach, 1982; Maslach et al., 2001). People are most likely to have this experience when they do not have enough resources at work—such as support from supervisors and friendly relations with co-workers—to meet the demands of the job (Lee & Ashforth, 1996; Viswesvaran et al., 1999). To make matters worse, research shows that people who experience burnout at work are more at risk for cardiovascular disease (Melamed et al., 2006).

Waiting in line at Chicago's O'Hare Airport, a common occurrence in these days of heightened security, is the kind of microstressor that plagues air travelers on a daily basis.

Tim Boyle/Getty Images

Another form of daily stress comes from commuting. At present, an estimated 100 million Americans commute to work each weekday—and for longer periods of time than ever before. Research has shown that driving to work can increase stress (Koslowsky et al., 1995). It now appears that commuting long distances by train can have the same effect. In a study of railroad commuters who traveled regularly from their homes in suburban New Jersey to work in Manhattan, Gary Evans and Richard Wener (2006) found that the longer their commute was, the more stress they reported feeling, the sloppier they were at a simple proofreading task, and the higher was their level of cortisol—a stress hormone that was measured by taking saliva samples after the morning trips.

On the home front, financial pressure is a particularly common source of stress (American Psychological Association, 2008). Even before the recent economic crisis in the United States, a three-year study of over 400 married American couples showed that those who are strained by a tight budget and have difficulty paying the bills experience more distress and conflict in their marriages (Conger et al., 1999). A follow-up study of African American families later showed that economic hardship spells emotional distress for parents and adjustment problems for their children (Conger et al., 2002).

The accumulation of daily hassles does more to make people sick than catastrophes or major life changes. **TRUE.**

How Does Stress Affect the Body?

The term *stress* was first popularized by Hans Selye (1936), an endocrinologist. As a young medical student, Selye noticed that patients who were hospitalized for many different illnesses often had similar symptoms, such as muscle weakness, a loss of weight and appetite, and a lack of ambition. Maybe these symptoms were part of a generalized response to an attack on the body, he thought. In the 1930s, Selye tested this hypothesis by exposing laboratory rats to various stressors, including heat, cold, heavy exercise, toxic substances, food deprivation, and electric shock. As anticipated, the different stressors all produced a similar physiological response: enlarged adrenal glands, shrunken lymph nodes, and bleeding stomach ulcers. Borrowing a term from engineering, Selye called the reaction *stress*—a word that quickly became part of everyday language.

The General Adaptation Syndrome

According to Selye, the body naturally responds to stress in a three-stage process that he called the **general adaptation syndrome** (see ▶ Figure 14.2). Sparked by the recognition of a threat—such as a predator, an enemy soldier, a speeding car, or a virus—the body has an initial *alarm* reaction. To meet the challenge, adrenaline and other hormones are poured into the bloodstream, creating physiological arousal. Heart rate, blood pressure, and breathing rates increase, while slower, long-term functions such as growth, digestion, and the operation of the immune system are inhibited. At this stage, the body mobilizes all of its resources to ward off the threat. Next comes a *resistance* stage, during which the body remains aroused and on the alert. There is continued release of stress hormones, and local defenses are activated. But if the stress persists for a prolonged period of time, the body will fall into an *exhaustion* stage. According to Selye, our anti-stress resources are limited. In fact, however, research has shown that exhaustion occurs not because our stress-fighting resources are limited but because their overuse causes other systems in the body to break down, which puts us at risk for illness and even death. Selye's basic model thus makes an important point:

general adaptation syndrome
A three-stage process (alarm, resistance, and exhaustion) by which the body responds to stress.

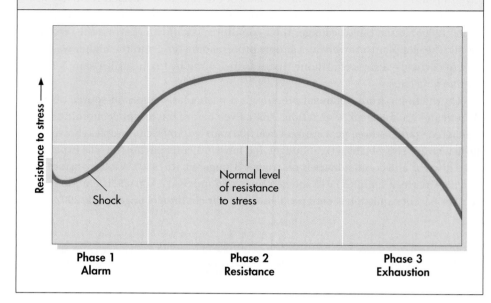

► **FIGURE 14.2**

The General Adaptation Syndrome

According to Selye (1936), the human body responds to threat in three phases: alarm, resistance, and exhaustion.

Stress may be an adaptive short-term reaction to threat, but over time it compromises our health and well-being.

A stress response is found in all mammals. So why, asks neuroscientist Robert Sapolsky (2004), don't zebras get ulcers? Sapolsky notes that the physiological stress response is superbly designed through evolution to help animals mobilize to fight or escape in acute emergencies. For the zebra, this occurs when a hungry lion leaps out from a bush and sprints at top speed across the savanna. For humans, it occurs during combat or competitive sports and perhaps even on first dates and in job interviews. But think about the list of situations you find stressful, and you'll see that people become anxious over things that would make no sense to a zebra. "We humans live well enough and long enough, and are smart enough, to generate all sorts of stressful events purely in our heads," says Sapolsky. From the perspective of the evolution of the animal kingdom, he notes, psychological stress is a "recent invention" (p. 5). The reason stress causes ulcers and other illnesses, then, is that the response is designed for acute physical emergencies, yet we turn it on often and for prolonged periods of time as we worry about taxes, mortgages, oral presentations, the job market, marital problems, and the inevitability of death.

All humans respond bodily to stress, which is what enables us to mount a defense. Physiologically, the sympathetic nervous system is activated and more adrenaline is secreted, which increases the heart rate and heightens arousal. Then all at once the liver pours extra sugar into the bloodstream for energy, the pupils dilate to let in more light, breathing speeds up for more oxygen, perspiration increases to cool down the body, blood clots faster to heal wounds, saliva flow is inhibited, and digestion slows down to divert blood to the brain and skeletal muscles. Faced with threat, the body readies itself for action. But what, behaviorally, is the nature of the defense?

Many years ago, Walter Cannon (1932) described the body as prepared for "fight or flight." To be sure, men often lash out aggressively when under siege. But do women respond similarly? In her book *The Tending Instinct*, Shelley Taylor (2002) argues that while men frequently exhibit the classic fight-or-flight reaction to stress, women are more likely to exhibit a "tend-and-befriend" response. Prepared by evolution, in order to enhance the survival of their offspring, she argues, women adapt to hardship by caring for their children and seeking out others who might help. Consistent with this argument, studies have shown that, under stress, women become more nurturing than men—and more affiliative. Interestingly, animal and human studies show that when females are isolated, unsupported, and in social distress, they exhibit elevated levels of the hormone oxytocin, which, in turn, increases their tendency to seek out social contact (Taylor, 2006).

Like humans, zebras get ulcers. **FALSE.**

What Stress Does to the Heart

Coronary heart disease (CHD) is a narrowing of the blood vessels that carry oxygen and nutrients to the heart muscle. It is by far the leading cause of death in the United States among both men and women. According to the American Heart Association, an estimated 80 million American adults (one in three) suffer from CHD. For many, the result is a heart attack, which occurs when the precious blood supply to the heart is blocked. This causes an uncomfortable feeling of pressure, fullness, squeezing, or pain in the center of the chest—and sometimes sweating, dizziness, nausea, fainting, and shortness of breath. Every year, 1.5 million Americans have heart attacks. One-third do not survive. (For more information, you can visit www.americanheart.org.)

Several factors are known to increase the risk of CHD. The three most important are hypertension, or high blood pressure; cigarette smoking; and high cholesterol. (Others include a family history of CHD, a high-fat diet, obesity, and a lack of exercise.) People with one of the three major risk factors are twice as likely to develop CHD, those with two risk factors are three and a half times as likely, and those with all three are six times as likely. These statistics are compelling and should not be taken lightly. Combined, however, these variables account for fewer than half the known cases of CHD. What's missing from the equation is the fourth major risk factor: psychological stress—from work, from marital troubles, and from the negative life events that plague people who lack resources because of low socioeconomic status (Gallo & Matthews, 2003; Matthews, 2005).

In 1956, cardiologists Meyer Friedman and Ray Rosenman were studying the relationship between cholesterol and coronary heart disease. After noticing that husbands were more likely than their wives to have CHD, they speculated that work-related stress might be the reason (at the time, most women did not work outside the home). To test this hypothesis, Friedman and Rosenman interviewed 3,000 healthy middle-aged men. Those who seemed the most hard-driving, competitive, impatient, time-conscious, and quick to anger were classified as having a **Type A personality** (also called coronary-prone behavior pattern—a more optimistic label since it is easier to change a behavior pattern than a personality). Roughly an equal number of men who were easygoing, relaxed, and laid back were classified as having a Type B personality. Interestingly, out of 258 men who went on to have heart attacks over the following nine years, 69 percent had been classified as Type A and only 31 percent as Type B (Rosenman et al., 1975).

The Type A, or coronary-prone, behavior pattern is made up of a cluster of traits, including competitive drive, a sense of time urgency, and a dangerous mix of anger, cynicism, and hostility (Friedman & Booth-Kewley 1987; Matthews, 1988). In interviews and written questionnaires, Type As report that they walk fast, talk fast, work late, interrupt speakers in mid-sentence, detest waiting in lines, race through yellow lights when they drive, lash out at others in frustration, strive to win at all costs, and save time by

Type A personality A pattern of behavior characterized by extremes of competitive striving for achievement, a sense of time urgency, hostility, and aggression.

multitasking. In contrast, "there are those who breeze through the day as pleased as park rangers—despite having deadlines and kids and a broken down car and charity work and scowling Aunt Agnes living in the spare bedroom" (Carey, 1997, p. 75).

By the early 1980s, the influence of the Type A behavior pattern on CHD was widely accepted. A panel of distinguished scientists convened by the National Heart, Lung and Blood Institute concluded that the Type A pattern was a risk factor for CHD, comparable to more traditional risks such as high blood pressure, smoking, high blood cholesterol, and obesity. But science, like time, moves on. Later studies of Type A and CHD obtained weaker results that varied depending on how Type A was measured and the kind of population that was studied (Matthews, 1988). Certainty about the bad effects of "hurry sickness" and "workaholism" began to crumble.

One issue that arose concerned measurement. Specifically, it turns out that the strength of the link between Type A behavior and coronary heart disease depends on how people are diagnosed. In the original study, Friedman and Rosenman classified men by means of a structured interview in which they could observe the men's verbal and nonverbal behavior. Afterward, however, many psychologists—in their haste to pursue this vital line of research—tried to identify Type A people using quick, easy-to-take questionnaires instead of time-consuming interviews. The questionnaires were not nearly as predictive. Apparently, the Type A pattern is more evident from a person's interview *behavior* (whether he or she constantly checks the time, speaks quickly, interrupts the interviewer, and makes restless fidgety movements) than from *self-reports*. When interviews are used to make the diagnosis, 70 percent of men who have CHD also have a Type A behavior pattern—compared with only 46 percent of those who are healthy (Miller et al., 1991).

The Type A behavior pattern was also refined conceptually, and a new line of inquiry sprang up. This research showed the primary toxic ingredient in CHD is *hostility*—as seen in people who are constantly angry, resentful, cynical, suspicious, and mistrustful of others (see Table 14.2). Apparently, people who are always in a negative emotional state and are quick to explode are besieged by stress. Because the heart is just a dumb pump and the blood vessels mere hoses, the health result is predictable: "The cardiovascular stress-response basically consists of making them work harder for a while, and if you do that on a regular basis, they will wear out, just like any pump or hoses you could buy at Sears" (Sapolsky, 1994, p. 42). In the long run, chronic hostility and anger can be lethal (Miller et al., 1996; Siegman & Smith, 1994). In fact, people who have lots of anger and suppress it are as likely to develop high blood pressure as those with anger who express it. It's the emotion that is toxic, not whether you hold it in or let it out (Everson et al., 1998; Everson-Rose & Lewis, 2005).

What else explains the connection between hostility and coronary heart disease? One possibility is that hostile people are less health-conscious—that they tend to smoke more, consume more caffeine and alcohol, exercise less, sleep less, and eat less healthy foods. They are also less likely to comply with advice from doctors (Leiker & Hailey, 1988; Siegler, 1994). A second explanation is that hostile people are physiologically reactive, so in tense social situations they exhibit greater increases in blood

TABLE 14.2

How "Hostile" Is Your Pattern of Behavior?

- When in the express checkout line at the supermarket, do you often count the items in the baskets of the people ahead of you to be sure they aren't over the limit?
- When an elevator doesn't come as quickly as it should, do your thoughts quickly focus on the inconsiderate behavior of the person on another floor who's holding it up?
- When someone criticizes you, do you quickly begin to feel annoyed?
- Do you frequently find yourself muttering at the television during a news broadcast?
- When you are held up in a slow line in traffic, do you quickly sense your heart pounding and your breath quickening?

Williams, 1993.

pressure, pulse rate, and adrenaline, a hormone that accelerates the buildup of fatty plaques on the artery walls, causing hardening of the arteries (Krantz & McCeney, 2002). In fact, research shows that people who are hostile exhibit more intense cardiovascular reactions not only during the event that makes them angry—say, being involved in a heated argument (Davis et al., 2000)—but long afterward as well, when asked to relive the event (Frederickson et al., 2000).

As a result of all this research and its many offshoots, a whole new subfield has developed that is sure to produce more valuable and practical insights in the years to come. Appropriately enough, this new subfield, which brings together the heart and the mind, has been called *psychocardiology* (Jordan et al., 2007).

What Stress Does to the Immune System

Increasingly, it has become clear that psychological stress produces a wide range of effects on the body, including increases in the risk of chronic back pain, diabetes, appendicitis, upper respiratory infections, arthritis, herpes, gum disease, common colds, and some forms of cancer. How can stress have so broad a range of disabling effects? Answer: By compromising the body's immune system, the first line of defense against illness (Ader, 2007).

The **immune system** is a complex surveillance system that fights bacteria, viruses, parasites, fungi, and other "nonself" substances that invade the body. The system contains more than a trillion specialized white blood cells called *lymphocytes* that circulate throughout the bloodstream and secrete chemical antibodies. These shark-like search-and-destroy cells protect us 24 hours a day by patrolling the body and attacking trespassers. The immune system is also equipped with large scavenger cells that zero in on viruses and cancerous tumors. Serving as a "sixth sense" for foreign invaders, the immune system continually renews itself. For example, during the few seconds it took to read this sentence, your body produced 10 million new lymphocytes.

Today, many health psychologists specializing in **psychoneuroimmunology**, or **PNI** (*psycho* for the mind, *neuro* for the nervous system, and *immunology* for the immune system) study the connections among the brain, behavior, the immune system, health, and illness. Before we get into some of the fascinating results, let's pause

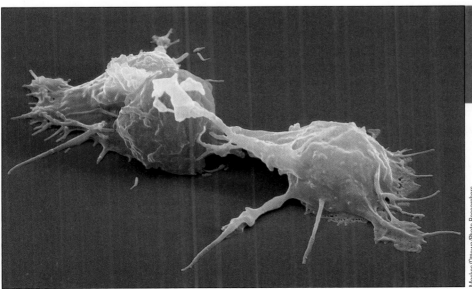

This color-enhanced microscopic image shows two "natural killer" immune cells (in yellow) engulfing and destroying a leukemia cell (in red). The human immune system contains more than a trillion specialized white blood cells.

Meckes/Ottowa/Photo Researchers

immune system   A biological surveillance system that detects and destroys "nonself" substances that invade the body.

psychoneuroimmunology (PNI)   A subfield of psychology that examines the links among psychological factors, the brain and nervous system, and the immune system.

for a moment and consider three of the methods these researchers use to spy on the operations of the immune system. One method is to take blood samples from animal or human participants exposed to varying degrees of stress and count the number of lymphocytes and other white blood cells circulating in the bloodstream. A second is to extract blood, add cancerous tumor cells to the mix, and measure the extent to which the natural killer cells destroy the tumors. A third method is to "challenge" the living organism by injecting a foreign agent into the skin and measuring the amount of swelling that arises at the site of the injection. The more swelling there is, the more potent the immune reaction is assumed to be (Ader, 2007).

It is now clear that stress can affect the immune system, at least temporarily. The medical community used to reject the idea outright, but no longer. What changed? First, animal experiments showed that rats exposed to noise, overcrowding, or inescapable shocks, and primates separated from their social companions, exhibit a drop in immune cell activity compared with non-exposed animals (Coe, 1993; Moynihan & Ader, 1996). A link was also observed in humans. Intrigued by the fact that people often become sick and die shortly after they are widowed, R. W. Barthrop and others (1977) took blood samples from 26 men and women whose spouses had recently died. Compared with non-widowed controls, these grief-stricken spouses exhibited a weakened immune response. This demonstration was the first of its kind.

Additional studies soon revealed weakened immune responses in NASA astronauts after their reentry into the atmosphere and splashdown, in people deprived of sleep for a prolonged period of time, in students in the midst of final exams, in men and women recently divorced or separated, in people caring for a family member with Alzheimer's disease, in snake-phobic people who are exposed to a live snake, and in workers who have just lost their jobs. Even in the laboratory, people who are given complex arithmetic problems to solve or painful stimuli to tolerate exhibit changes in immune cell activity that last for one or more hours after the stress has subsided (Cohen & Herbert, 1996).

In an intriguing study, Arthur Stone and others (1994) paid 48 adult volunteers to take a harmless but novel protein pill every day for twelve weeks—a substance that would lead the immune system to respond by producing an antibody. Every day, the participants completed a diary in which they reported about their moods and experiences at work, at home, in financial matters, in leisure activities, and in social relationships with their friends, spouses, and children. The participants also gave daily saliva samples that were later used to measure the amount of antibody produced. The results were striking, as are their implications: The more positive events participants experienced in a given day, the more antibody was produced. The more negative events they experienced, the less antibody was produced.

In many ways, it is now clear that negative experiences and the emotions they elicit can weaken our immune system's ability to protect us from injuries, infections, and a wide range of illnesses (Kiecolt-Glaser et al., 2002). In an experiment that well illustrates this point in action, researchers brought healthy male and female volunteers into a clinical research laboratory, administered a battery of questionnaires, injected them with a needle in the arm, and then used a vacuum pump to raise a blister. In follow-up visits during the next eight days, the researchers measured the speed with which the wounds were healing. They found that participants whose questionnaires indicated that they had anger control problems—for example, losing their temper or boiling inside—secreted more of the stress hormone cortisol in response to the blistering procedure and the wound was slower to heal over time (Gouin et al., 2008).

Clearly, psychological states can "get into" the immune system. As illustrated in ▶ Figure 14.3, there are two possible ways this can happen. First, people who are under intense stress tend to smoke more, ingest more alcohol and drugs, sleep less, exercise

> **FIGURE 14.3**
>
> **Pathways from Stress to Illness**
>
> Hostility, stress, and other negative emotional states may cause illness in two ways: (1) by promoting unhealthful behaviors (more alcohol, less sleep, and so on); and (2) by triggering the release of hormones that weaken the immune system.

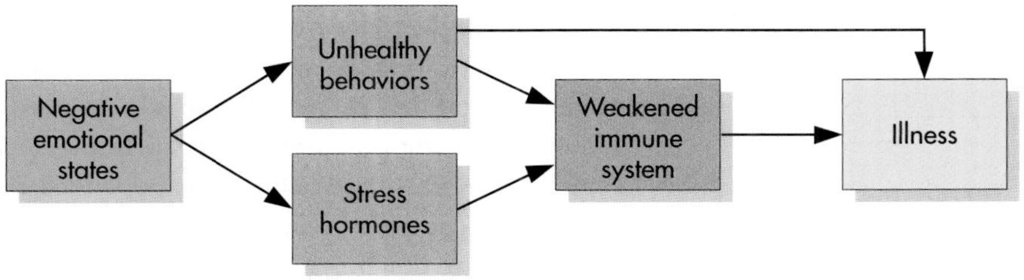

less, and have poorer diets, behaviors that tend to compromise the immune system. For example, one study showed that when healthy male adults were kept awake between 3:00 and 7:00 A.M., immune cell activity diminished and returned to normal only after a full night of uninterrupted sleep (Irwin et al., 1994). Second, stress triggers the release of adrenaline and other stress hormones into the bloodstream, and these hormones tend to suppress immune cell activity. The result is a temporary lowering of the body's resistance (Cohen & Williamson, 1991). Either way, hundreds of studies now show that the effects of stress on the immune system are complex. Brief stressors (such as a shark attack, a difficult exam, or an injury) can enhance the immune response in ways that are adaptive in the short term, but chronic life stressors (such as a high-pressure job, a distressed marriage, or a family illness) can suppress the immune response over time, putting the organism at risk (Segerstrom & Miller, 2004).

The Links Between Stress and Illness

If chronic stress can weaken the immune system, are people who are stressed in life more likely to become sick? Might some people, for example, be psychologically more susceptible than others to catching the H1N1 (swine) flu? Sheldon Cohen and his colleagues (1993) conducted a fascinating and elaborate study to help answer this question. They paid 420 volunteers to spend nine days in a medical experiment and risk exposure to a common cold virus. In the first two days, participants filled out several questionnaires, including one that measured recent stressful experiences in their lives. They also received a physical examination, including a blood test. Then, to simulate the person-to-person transmission of a virus, the researchers dropped a clear liquid solution into each participant's nose. Those randomly assigned to the control group received a placebo saline solution. Others, less fortunate, received a cold virus in doses that tend to produce illness rates of 20 to 60 percent.

For the next week, participants were quarantined in large apartments, where they were examined daily by a nurse who took their temperature, extracted mucus samples, and looked for signs of colds, such as sneezing, watery eyes, stuffy nose, and sore throat. (The participants did not realize it, but the nurse also kept track of the number of tissues they used.) All participants were healthy at the start of the project, and not a single one in the saline control group developed a cold. Yet among those exposed to a virus, 82 percent became infected and 46 percent of those who were infected caught a cold, symptoms and all. A virus is a virus, so often there is no escape. Most interesting, however, is

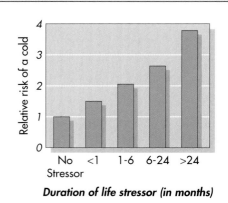

> **FIGURE 14.4**
>
> **Stress Duration and Illness**
>
> Two hundred seventy-six volunteers were inter-
> viewed about recent life stress, then infected with
> a cold virus. As shown above, the more months a
> stressor had lasted, the more likely a person was
> to catch the cold. Over time, stress breaks down
> the body's immune system.
>
> Cohen et al., 1998.

Duration of life stressor (in months)

that life stress made a difference. Among those who became infected, high-stress participants were more likely to catch a cold than were the low-stress participants—53 percent compared with 40 percent. In short, people whose lives are filled with stress are particularly vulnerable to contagious illness.

In a follow-up of this experiment, Cohen and others (1998) interviewed 276 volunteers about recent life stressors, infected them with a cold virus, and then measured whether or not they developed a cold. They found that some types of stress were more toxic than others. Specifically, people who had endured *chronic* stressors that lasted for more than a month (like ongoing marital problems or unemployment) were more likely to catch a cold than those who had experienced *acute* short-term stress (such as a fight with a spouse or a reprimand at work). ▶ Figure 14.4 shows that the longer a stressor had lasted, the more likely a person was to catch a cold. Over time, stress breaks down the body's immune system.

The effects of stress are clear. But it appears that certain personal characteristics can buffer people against the adverse health effects. In yet another follow-up study, Cohen and his colleagues (2006) found that the more sociable people were in life, the more resistant they were to developing the lab-induced cold. They also found that the more positively people *see themselves* on the socioeconomic status (SES) ladder relative to others in the population—regardless of their *actual* levels of education, occupation, and income—the less likely they were to catch the lab-induced cold (Cohen et al., 2008).

These common-cold studies are important because they demonstrate not only that stress can weaken the immune system but also that it can leave us vulnerable to illness as a result. Does stress have similar effects on more serious illnesses? Can it, for example, hasten the spread of HIV/AIDS or cancer? In an early test of this hypothesis, Madeline Visintainer and others (1982) implanted tumorous cancer cells into laboratory rats, some of which were then exposed repeatedly to shocks they could not escape. After one month, 50 percent of the animals not shocked died of cancer. Yet relative to that baseline, the death rate climbed to 73 percent among those subjected to the inescapable shock. This study was among the first to show that psychological states such as a feeling of helplessness can influence the spread of cancer.

The growth of tumors in helpless white laboratory rats is interesting, but does the same principle apply to people? For obvious ethical reasons, researchers cannot fill humans with despair or inject lethal tumors into their bodies to test the cause-and-effect chain directly. But they can examine the medical records of people whose lives have been struck by tragedy. Investigations of this sort have revealed that cancer appears more often than normal in people who are prone to being in a negative emotional state (Sklar & Anisman, 1981). In one large-scale study, investigators looked up 2,000 male employees of the Western Electric Company in Chicago whose personalities had been assessed in 1958. At that time, test scores had shown that some of the men were low in self-esteem, unhappy, and depressed. The outcome: Some 20 years later, these men were more likely than their coworkers to have died of cancer (Persky et al., 1987).

Let's be clear about what these results mean. Nobody disputes that cancer is caused by exposure to toxic substances and other biological factors. But individuals who are clinically depressed or under great stress have weakened immune systems and a heightened susceptibility to infectious agents, which, in some cases, may result in a higher death rate from cancer and other diseases as well (Cohen et al., 2007; Kiecolt-Glaser, 2009; Miller et al., 2009).

Stress can weaken the heart, but it cannot affect the immune system. **FALSE.**

Processes of Appraisal

Some 2,500 years ago, an anonymous author wrote an extraordinary poem about human suffering: the Book of Job. A pious and prosperous man when the poem opens, Job is soon beset by great calamities. He loses his property, his children, and his health. Job and his friends try to understand how these terrible things could happen. His friends argue that Job's plight must be a punishment sent by God and tell Job to repent. Because he believes that his sufferings far exceed any wrongdoing on his part, Job cannot accept this explanation. In despair, he doubts his capacity to withstand continued hardship and longs for death. But eventually Job finds strength and peace through trusting in God's will. From the perspective of the stress-and-coping model shown in Figure 14.1, Job and his friends were engaged in the process of appraisal. They considered possible explanations for Job's suffering and formed expectations about his ability to cope with his situation. These same themes are found in research on stress and coping.

Attributions and Explanatory Styles

Depression is a mood disorder characterized by feelings of sadness, pessimism, and apathy and slowed thought processes. Other symptoms include disturbances in sleeping and eating patterns and a reduced interest in sex. Every year, between 6 and 7 percent of the U.S. population experiences a major depression. Many more suffer from briefer, milder bouts with the blues. Sometimes called the "common cold" of psychological disorders, depression is universal and widespread (Gotlib & Hammen, 2009).

About twice as many women as men seek treatment for being depressed. During the course of a lifetime, an estimated 12 percent of American men and 21 percent of women will suffer from a major depression (Kessler et al., 1994). This sex difference first begins to appear in adolescence, although the disparity is a bit smaller in less developed nations (Culbertson, 1997). While depression has many causes, some researchers have focused on the attributions people make for the positive and negative events of their lives.

In 1975, Martin Seligman argued that depression results from a feeling of **learned helplessness,** the acquired expectation that one cannot control important outcomes. In a classic series of experiments, Seligman found that dogs strapped into a harness and exposed to painful electric shocks soon became passive and gave up trying to escape, even in new situations where escape was possible. In contrast, dogs that had not received uncontrollable shocks quickly learned the escape routine. As applied to humans, this finding suggested that prolonged exposure to uncontrollable events might similarly cause apathy, inactivity, a loss of motivation, and pessimism. In human research participants, those exposed to inescapable bursts of noise thus failed to protect themselves in a later situation where the noise could be easily avoided. Seligman was quick to note that people who are exposed to uncontrollable events become, in many ways, like depressed individuals: discouraged, pessimistic about the future, and lacking initiative. Thus, he saw depression as a form of learned helplessness.

Lynn Abramson and her colleagues (1989) later proposed that depression is a state of *hopelessness* brought on by the negative self-attributions people make for failure. In fact, some people have a **depressive explanatory style**—a tendency to attribute bad events to factors that are internal rather than external ("It's my fault"), stable rather than unstable ("It will not change"), and global rather than specific ("It spreads to all parts of my life"). Research supports this proposition. Whether people are trying to explain social rejection, a sports defeat, low grades, or their inability to solve an

learned helplessness A phenomenon in which experience with an uncontrollable event creates passive behavior in the face of subsequent threats to well-being.

depressive explanatory style A habitual tendency to attribute negative events to causes that are stable, global, and internal.

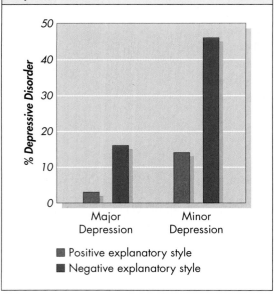

▶**FIGURE 14.5**

Using Attributional Styles to Predict Depression

In this study, researchers measured the explanatory styles of first-year college students. As juniors two years later, those with a negative rather than positive style in their first year were more likely to suffer from a major or minor depressive disorder.

Alloy et al., 2006.

experimenter's puzzle, those who are depressed are more likely than others to blame factors that are within the self, unlikely to change, and broad enough to impair other aspects of life. The result: hopelessness and despair (Abramson et al., 1989; Metalsky et al., 1993). This way of thinking may signal a vulnerability to future depression. Indeed, when Lauren Alloy and her colleagues (2006) measured the explanatory styles of nondepressed newly entered college students and then followed up on these students in their junior year, they found that those with a negative explanatory style in their first year—compared to classmates with a more positive style—were far more likely to have suffered from a major or minor depressive disorder (see ▶ Figure 14.5).

■ The Human Capacity for Resilience

Stress affects people differently, an observation that led Suzanne Kobasa and her colleagues (1982) to wonder why some of us are more resilient than others in the face of stress. Kobasa studied some 200 business executives who were under stress. Many said they were frequently sick, affirming the link between stress and illness; others had managed to stay healthy. The two groups were similar in terms of age, education, job status, income, and ethnic and religious background. But it was clear from various tests that they differed in their attitudes toward themselves, their jobs, and the people in their lives. Based on these differences, Kobasa identified a personality style that she called *hardiness* and concluded that hardy people have three characteristics: (1) commitment—a sense of purpose with regard to one's work, family, and other domains; (2) challenge—an openness to new experiences and a desire to embrace change; and (3) control—the belief that one has the power to influence important future outcomes.

Research supports the general point that resilience, or hardiness, serves as a buffer against stress (Funk, 1992). As you might expect, most people are exposed to at least one highly traumatic event during the course of a lifetime. Yet while many react with PTSD, others maintain their equilibrium and mental health: "Roughly 50 percent to 60 percent of the U.S. population is exposed to traumatic stress but only 5 percent to 10 percent develop PTSD" (Ozer et al., 2003, p. 54). Thus, Ann Masten (2001) and George Bonanno (2004) both argue that most human beings are highly resilient and exhibit a remarkable capacity to thrive in the wake of highly aversive events. In fact, Vicki Helgeson and her colleagues (2006) note that many people who confront heart attacks, cancer, divorce, war, family illness, and other traumas will often find ways to accept, benefit, and grow from the experience.

What are the characteristics of hardiness, resilience, and the ability to find benefit in loss? In two-part longitudinal interviews of Israeli Jews and Arabs during a period of intense terrorist and rocket attacks, Steven Hobfoll and others (2009) found that 64 percent of those interviewed experienced chronic or delayed distress, while 36 percent were mostly resistant to symptoms or completely resilient. Comparisons of the two groups showed that resilience in this population was more common among men than women; among Jews, who are in the majority of the population, than Arabs, an ethnic minority; and among people in general with more education, more money, and more social support from friends. These findings may be specific to the populations and events of Israel. More likely, however, they tell us something more generally about the characteristics of resilience. Let's see.

Self-Efficacy When Kobasa and others (1982) first identified hardiness as an adaptive trait, they—and other researchers—were quick to notice that the perception of control is an important ingredient (Florian et al., 1995). Early on, research showed that the harmful effects of crowding, noise, heat, and other stressors are reduced when people think they can exert control over these aspects of their environment (Glass & Singer, 1972). The perception of control is especially meaningful for people whose lives are regulated to a large extent by others. For example, elderly residents of nursing homes who were given more control over daily routines became happier and more active (Langer & Rodin, 1976; Schulz, 1976). Other studies showed that patients with heart disease, cancer, and AIDS were better adjusted emotionally when they felt that they could influence the course of their illness (Helgeson, 1992; Rodin, 1986; Thompson et al., 1993).

MANKOFF

"Amazing, three failed marriages, scores of disastrous relationships, many financial reversals, and countless physical ailments, but through it all I've always had good luck parking."

People often have feelings of self-efficacy in some life domains but not others.

The perception of control refers to the expectation that our behaviors can produce satisfying outcomes. But people also differ in the extent to which they believe that they can perform these behaviors in the first place. These concepts seem related, but in fact they refer to different beliefs, both of which are necessary for us to feel that we control important outcomes in our lives (Skinner, 1996). According to Albert Bandura (1997), these latter expectations are based on feelings of competence, or **self-efficacy**. Some individuals may be generally more confident than others, says Bandura, but self-efficacy is a state of mind that varies from one specific task and situation to another. In other words, you may have high self-efficacy about meeting new people but not about raising your grades. Or you may have high self-efficacy about solving a math problem but not about writing a paper.

Research on self-efficacy has shown that the more of it you have at a particular task, the more likely you are to take on that task, try hard, persist in the face of failure, and succeed. The implications for mental and physical health are particularly striking. For example, individuals with high self-efficacy on health-related matters are more likely, if they want, to stay physically fit, abstain from alcohol, and tolerate the pain of arthritis, childbirth, and migraine headaches (Maddux, 1995)—and even to stop smoking (Baldwin et al., 2006) or lose weight (Linde et al., 2006).

At times, having a strong sense of self-efficacy may literally mean the difference between life and death. In one recent study, Urmimala Sarkar and colleagues (2009) recruited 1,024 heart disease patients and tracked their health over time. At the start of the study, all participants completed a Cardiac Self-Efficacy Scale in which they indicated how confident they were in their ability to maintain their usual activities, engage in sexual activity, and get aerobic exercise. Over the ensuing years, 124 of the patients were hospitalized and 235 died. When the patients were sorted into four categories of self-efficacy—from the highest scores to the lowest—the results showed that the higher their self-efficacy at the start of the study, the more likely they were to survive hospitalization years later (see ▶ Figure 14.6).

self-efficacy A person's belief that he or she is capable of the specific behavior required to produce a desired outcome in a given situation.

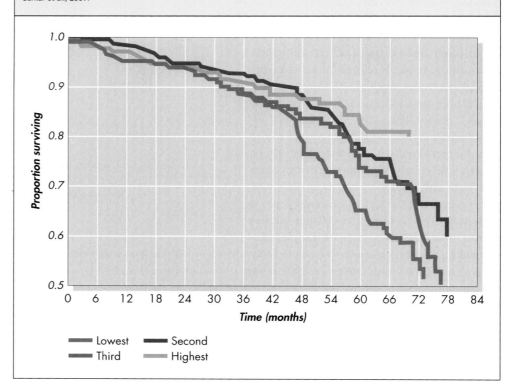

▶**FIGURE 14.6**

Self-Efficacy: A Matter of Life and Death?

One thousand and twenty-four heart disease patients varying in "cardiac self-efficacy" were tracked over time. As shown, the higher their cardiac self-efficacy scores were at the start of the study, the more likely they were to survive hospitalization up to 78 months later.

Sarkar et al., 2009.

Dispositional Optimism The reason it's important to understand our attributions for past outcomes and our perceptions of control in present situations is that both have implications for our outlook on the future. In *Learned Optimism*, Seligman (1991) argues that a generalized tendency to expect positive outcomes is characterized by a nondepressive explanatory style. According to Seligman, optimists tend to blame failure on factors that are external, temporary, and specific, and to credit success to factors that are internal, permanent, and global. Thankfully, in light of the advantages that optimism brings, Suzanne Segerstrom (2006a), like Seligman, notes that even pessimists can retrain themselves to think in optimistic ways.

Consider your own view of the future. Are you the eternal optimist who looks on the bright side and generally expects good things to happen, or do you tend to believe in Murphy's Law, that if something can go wrong it will? By asking questions such as these, Michael Scheier and Charles Carver (1985) categorized college students along this dimension and found that dispositional optimists reported fewer illness symptoms during the semester than did pessimists. Correlations between optimism and health are common. Studies have shown that optimists are more likely to take an active problem-focused approach in coping with stress (Nes & Segerstrom, 2006). As a result, they are more likely to complete a rehabilitation program for alcoholics; make a quicker, fuller recovery from coronary artery bypass surgery; and, among gay men concerned about AIDS, take a more active approach to the threat (Scheier & Carver, 1992). In a study of 1,306 healthy adult men from the Boston area, those reporting high levels of optimism rather than pessimism were half as likely to have coronary heart disease ten years later (Kubzansky et al., 2001). In a study of 5,000 municipal workers in Finland, those who were high rather than low in optimism were healthier and missed fewer days from work if they were struck by a death or serious illness in the family over the next five years (Kivimäki et al., 2005).

In the course of a lifetime, everyone has setbacks. But an optimistic disposition may help us weather the storms better. There may even be long-term health implications. In one study, researchers collected personal essays written in the 1940s by 99 men who had just graduated from Harvard and then analyzed these materials to determine what each man's explanatory style had been in his youth. Thirty-five years later, those who in their youth had an optimistic outlook were healthier than their more pessimistic peers (Peterson et al., 1988).

How can these results be explained? There are two possibilities: one biological, the other behavioral. In research that supports a biological explanation, investigators analyzing blood samples have found that optimists exhibit a stronger immune response to stress than pessimists do (Kamen-Siegel et al., 1991; Segerstrom et al., 1998). In research that supports a behavioral explanation, Christopher Peterson and others (1988) scored the explanatory styles of 1,528 healthy young adults from questionnaires they had filled out between 1936 and 1940. Astonishingly, after 50 years, the optimists (specifically, those who had made global rather than specific attributions for good events) were less likely to have died an accidental, reckless, or violent death.

There's an old saying: "Where there's life, there's hope." Perhaps the opposite is also true: "Where there's hope, there's life." In a stunning illustration of this possibility, Susan Everson and others (1996) studied 2,428 middle-aged men in Finland. Based on the extent to which they agreed with two simple statements ("I feel that it is impossible to reach the goals I would like to strive for" and "The future seems hopeless, and I can't believe that things are changing for the better"), the men were initially classified as having a high, medium, or low sense of hopelessness. When the investigators checked the death records roughly six years later, they

The optimist proclaims we live in the best of all possible worlds; and the pessimist fears this is true.

—James Cabell

The most important thing in illness is never to lose heart.

—Nikolai Lenin

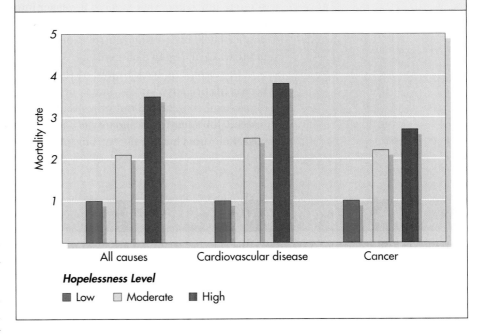

▶ **FIGURE 14.7**

Hopelessness and the Risk of Death

Among middle-aged men in Finland, those who were initially high rather than low in hopelessness were more likely to die within six years—overall, from cancer, and from cardiovascular disease. Those who were moderate in hopelessness fell between the two extremes.

Everson et al., 1996.

Hopelessness Level
■ Low   ☐ Moderate   ■ High

found that the more hopeless the men were at the start, the more likely they were to have died of various causes—even when the men were otherwise equated for their age and prior health status. Compared with those who were low in hopelessness, the highs were more than twice as likely to die from cancer and four times more likely to die of cardiovascular disease (see ▶ Figure 14.7). These results bring to life what Norman Cousins (1989) described as "the biology of hope," reminding us that "positive expectations can be self-fulfilling" (Peterson, 2000).

When it comes to physical health, research does not support popular beliefs about the power of positive thinking. **FALSE.**

▍ Pollyanna's Health

Pollyanna is the upbeat heroine created by American writer Eleanor Porter. Although she used to get bad press for her boundless belief that even the most ominous cloud has a bright silver lining, the research in this section suggests that Pollyanna should be an extraordinarily healthy person.

Let's be clear about what the research means. The mind is a powerful tool that can be used to hurt, heal, and protect the body (Ray, 2004). Still, no credible scientist believes that our attributions, perceptions of control, optimism, or other sources of resilience are the sole determinants of a long life. A positive outlook cannot guarantee future good health. So although we should appreciate the powers of the mind to influence the body, it would be a cruel mistake to blame victims of illness for having a bad outlook on life. As Howard Friedman (1991) put it in *The Self-Healing Personality*, "We must walk a fine line between blaming patients on the one hand and absolving them of any role in their health on the other" (p. 96).

It's also important to recognize that there may be drawbacks to positive thinking, especially if it leads us to see ourselves and the events around us in ways that are grossly unrealistic. As we saw in Chapter 3, people with overly positive views of themselves are sometimes disliked by their friends and seen as boastful, inconsiderate, and oversensitive to criticism (Colvin et al., 1995; Heatherton & Vohs, 2000). It may also be detrimental for people to believe that they have control over events when they do not. In a study of patients suffering from a loss of kidney function, those who felt that they had control over their health became more depressed, not less, after having a transplant that failed (Christensen et al., 1991). In a study of first-year law students, optimists exhibited a stronger immune response than did pessimists when their transition to law school was easy but a weaker immune response when the transition was difficult (Segerstrom, 2006b). Faced with some setbacks, a sense of control can help us bounce back. But setting control expectations too high can do more harm than good in the wake of negative outcomes.

This brings us back to Job. At the end of this biblical account, Job recovers his health, his property, and his family prosperity. He does not, however, regain the sense of personal control and optimism that he enjoyed prior to being struck by calamity. Instead, Job's hard-won serenity is based on his belief that life has meaning and purpose. Pollyanna has her charm, but Job is a hero of the human condition.

Ways of Coping with Stress

Leaving home. Studying for final exams. Breaking up with a boyfriend or girlfriend. Working long nights—or not at all. Waiting on long security lines at the airport. Feeling squeezed in a tight job market. Having children. Raising children. Struggling to meet the deadline to complete a textbook. Stress is inevitable. No one can prevent it. The best we can do is to minimize its harmful effects on our health. Depending on the person and stressor, people can cope by trying to solve the problem, talking to friends, inviting distractions, sleeping or drinking too much to escape, praying, brooding, venting, lashing out, laughing it off, getting outside help, pretending that all is well—or freaking out. Combining all psychological theories and research, it appears that there are about 400 specific ways to cope with stress (Skinner et al., 2003). In a recent nationwide survey, men and women were asked about how they manage the

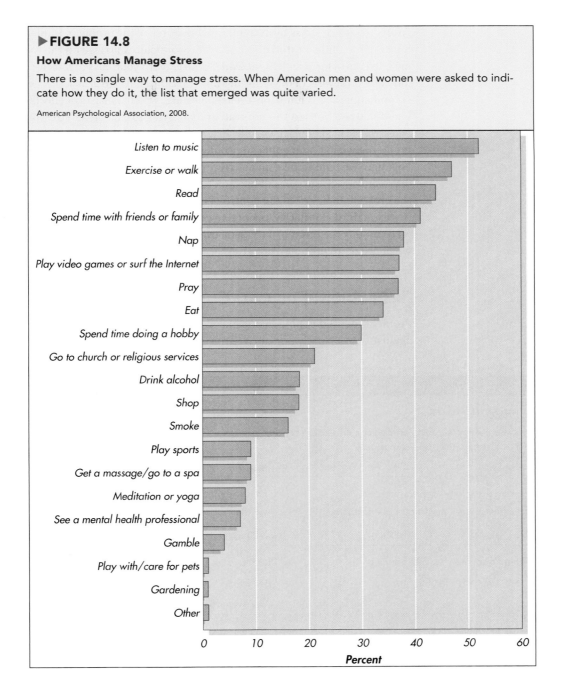

▶ **FIGURE 14.8**

How Americans Manage Stress

There is no single way to manage stress. When American men and women were asked to indicate how they do it, the list that emerged was quite varied.

American Psychological Association, 2008.

stress in their lives. As you can see in ▶ Figure 14.8, people cope in a wide variety of ways—some healthy, others not (American Psychological Association, 2008).

By grouping specific strategies that are similar, researchers study different general types of coping. Based on the self-reports of large numbers of people, Charles Carver and others (1989) constructed a multidimensional questionnaire they called COPE that measures twelve distinct methods of coping (see Table 14.3). While noting that people can use different coping strategies, Richard Lazarus and Susan Folkman (1984) distinguished two general types. The first is **problem-focused coping**, cognitive and behavioral

problem-focused coping
Cognitive and behavioral efforts to alter a stressful situation.

efforts to reduce stress by overcoming the source of the problem. Difficulties in school? Study harder, hire a tutor, or reduce your workload. Marriage on the rocks? Talk it out or see a counselor. Problems at work? Consult with your boss or look for another job. As indicated in several of the items in Table 14.3, the goal is to attack the source of stress. A second approach is **emotion-focused coping**, which consists of efforts to manage our emotional reactions to stressors rather than trying to change the stressors themselves. If you struggle at school, at work, or in a romantic relationship, you can keep a stiff upper lip, accept what is happening, tune out, or vent your emotions. According to Lazarus and Folkman, we tend to take an active, problem-focused approach when we think we can overcome a stressor but fall back on an emotion-focused approach when we perceive the problem to be out of our control. Lisa Aspinwall and Shelley Taylor (1997) note that there is a third alternative: **proactive coping**, which consists of up-front efforts to ward off or modify the onset of a stressful event. As we'll see, coping is an ongoing process by which we try to prevent—not just react to—life's bumps and bruises.

▌▌ Problem-Focused Coping

Problem-focused coping seems like the prime candidate for a starring role in the war against stress. Surely our most active and assertive efforts are associated with better

---

TABLE 14.3

Ways of Coping with Stress

These statements describe some coping strategies that people say they use. The strategies are listed in order from those that are relatively common to those that are less common.

Planning/Active Coping	Suppression of Competing Activities
▪ I try to come up with a strategy about what to do.	▪ I put aside other activities to concentrate on this.
▪ I take additional action to try to get rid of the problem.	▪ If necessary I let other things slide a little.
Positive Reinterpretation	**Mental Disengagement**
▪ I look for something good in what is happening.	▪ I turn to work . . . to take my mind off things.
▪ I try to make it seem more positive.	▪ I go to the movies or watch TV, to think about it less.
Acceptance	**Turning to Religion**
▪ I learn to live with it.	▪ I seek God's help.
▪ I accept that this has happened and can't be changed.	▪ I try to find comfort in my religion.
Seeking Social Support	**Behavioral Disengagement**
▪ I talk to someone about how I feel.	▪ I give up the attempt to get what I want.
▪ I ask people who had similar experiences what they did.	▪ I admit to myself that I can't deal with it.
Restraint Coping	**Denial**
▪ I force myself to wait for the right time to do something.	▪ I refuse to believe that it has happened.
▪ I make sure not to make matters worse by acting too soon.	▪ I pretend that it hasn't really happened.
Focusing on/Venting Emotions	**Alcohol and Drugs**
▪ I get upset and let my emotions out.	▪ I drink alcohol or take drugs to think about it less.
▪ I let my feelings out.	

Carver et al., 1989.

health (Aspinwall & Taylor, 1992). And clearly we often benefit from confronting a stressor head on rather than avoiding it. Consider something we all are guilty of on occasion: procrastination, a purposive delay in beginning or completing a task, often accompanied by feelings of discomfort (Ferrari et al., 1995). In a longitudinal study of college students enrolled in a health psychology class, Dianne Tice and Roy Baumeister (1997) administered a questionnaire at the start of the semester that assesses the extent to which people tend to procrastinate. True to their word, those students who were classified from their test scores as procrastinators turned in their term papers later than did their classmates and received lower grades. More interesting was the relationship to daily reports of stress and physical health. Early on, while procrastinators were in the "putting it off" stage of their projects, they were relatively stress-free compared with others. Later in the semester, however, as the deadline neared and passed, procrastinators were under greater stress and reported having more symptoms of illness. In the end, the short-term benefits of avoidance were outweighed by the long-term costs.

In dealing with essential tasks, it is better to confront and control than to avoid. But is this always the more beneficial approach? There are two reasons why sometimes it is not. First, to exert control a person must stay vigilant, alert, and actively engaged, which is physiologically taxing (Light & Obrist, 1980). Second, a controlling orientation can cause problems if it leads us to develop an overcontrolling, stress-inducing, Type A pattern of behavior—whether that means always having the last word in an argument, "driving" from the back seat of a car, or planning every last detail of a leisurely vacation. Not all events are within our control or important enough to worry about. There are times when it's better to just let go (Friedland et al., 1992; Wright et al., 1990).

When we use the word *control*, we usually have in mind active efforts to manage something: win an argument, work out a marital problem, or solve a problem at work. But control comes in many guises. Knowledge, for instance, is a form of control. Knowing why something happens increases your chance of making sure it goes your way—if not now, then the next time. Sometimes we can cope effectively with tragedies such as technological disasters, terrorist acts, and spousal abuse by blaming the perpetrators for their actions. In these situations, holding others responsible can force a helpful response, such as financial compensation or police protection.

But what about self-blame? Is it ever adaptive to cope with a bad situation by blaming oneself? According to Ronnie Janoff-Bulman (1979), it depends on whether you blame your behavior or yourself as a person. People can change their own behavior, she notes, so behavioral self-blame paves the way for control in an effort to reduce current stresses or avoid future ones. But it is not similarly adaptive, she warns, to blame your own enduring personal characteristics, which are harder to change. Janoff-Bulman (1992) later amended this hypothesis, noting that it may take time to realize the mental health benefits of behavioral self-blame. This prediction was tested in studies of how female rape victims adjust to the trauma. Consistently, both behavioral and characterological self-blame were associated with an increase in distress. Contrary to prediction, rape victims who blame their own behavior for what happened do *not* cope better than those who blame their character (Frazier & Schauben, 1994; Hall et al., 2003).

In light of past research, Patricia Frazier (2003) offers a somewhat more complex perspective on blame, control, and coping. Clearly, she notes, it can be adaptive for the victims of rape and other traumas to own a sense of future control (Carver et al., 2000; Frazier et al., 2004). But noting that behavioral self-blame for a past trauma does not guarantee the prevention of future trauma, she distinguishes past, present, and future control—and what each implies about the dreaded possibility of a future recurrence. In a longitudinal study of female rape victims appearing in an emergency room, she

emotion-focused coping Cognitive and behavioral efforts to reduce the distress produced by a stressful situation.

proactive coping Up-front efforts to ward off or modify the onset of a stressful event.

assessed attributions of blame and responsibility, perceptions of control, and feelings of distress periodically from two weeks up to a year later. Overall, women blamed the rapist more than they blamed themselves, a tendency that strengthened over time. As in other studies, however, those who assigned more blame either to the rapist or to themselves were more distressed. Apparently, the problem with behavioral self-blame, once thought to be adaptive, is that it did not engender feelings of future safety. In this regard, the most useful sense of control was over the *present*: women who believed that they could help themselves get better and facilitate their own recovery were more optimistic about the future and the least distressed.

▌ Emotion-Focused Coping

Stress is by definition an unpleasant and arousing experience that fills people with negative and unhealthy emotions. Do some coping mechanisms focus on this emotional aspect of adversity?

Positive Emotions: Building Blocks of Emotion-Focused Coping   Following the terrorist attacks of 9/11, many Americans reported in public opinion polls that they cried and felt sad, angry, fearful, anxious, and disgusted. Under conditions so tragic, one would not also expect people to experience positive emotions. Yet it is possible for positive and negative feelings to coexist—as when we find consolation in loss or a silver lining in the dense gray clouds (Folkman & Moskowitz, 2000).

People who cope well and are resilient tend to experience positive emotions in the face of stress—a common capacity that Ann Masten (2001) termed "ordinary magic." How is it that positive emotions work like magic? On the basis of numerous studies, Barbara Frederickson (2009) offers a two-step theory of why our fleeting but pleasant positive emotions are so effective. First, she notes that positive emotions help people to *broaden* their outlook in times of stress so they can cope with adversity—in part by providing a welcome distraction from the anger, fear, and other negative states that increase blood pressure and arousal and narrow the focusing of attention.

To test the hypothesis that positive emotion is adaptive in this way, Frederickson and colleagues (2003) contacted 46 college students days after September 11, 2001, who had previously taken part in a study on stress and coping. Across the board, the students felt angry, sad and fearful; they also felt scorn toward the attackers. But many also expressed positive feelings of gratitude (to be alive), love (a renewed appreciation for loved ones), and interest (in unfolding world events). In fact, those who scored as most resilient before the crisis were later the most likely to have these positive emotions and least likely to suffer depression after the crisis. By coping with positive emotions in one specific situation after another, Frederickson (2009) suggests, people over time *build* personal resources—learning, for example, how to stay calm, focused, in control, and capable of giving and receiving emotional support.

Research on positive emotions reminds us not to overintellectualize the coping process and underestimate the value of emotion-focused coping. Look back at Table 14.3, and you will see many instances of emotion-focused coping, such as acceptance, denial, focusing on or venting of emotions, disengaging mentally and behaviorally, or turning to religion. By and large, we will see that there are two other general ways to cope with the emotional aspects of stress: shutting down and opening up. Let's examine the health effects of each of these strategies.

Shutting Down: Suppressing Unwanted Thoughts   Often we react to stress by shutting down and trying to deny or suppress the unpleasant thoughts and feelings.

One specific form of avoidance coping is distraction. Consider what happens when criminals take innocent victims hostage. Police surround the vehicle or building site and negotiations begin. Are certain ways of coping with this frightening situation particularly effective? To help answer this question, 57 airline employees voluntarily participated in a remarkable training exercise conducted by the Special Operations and Research Staff of the FBI Academy (Auerbach et al., 1994; Strentz & Auerbach, 1988). Some volunteers were trained in problem-focused coping techniques such as helping each other, interacting with their captors, and gathering intelligence. Others were trained in emotion-focused techniques designed to decrease anxiety—such as distraction, deep breathing, and muscle relaxation. Volunteers in a control condition did not receive any specific instruction.

After the training session, the volunteers were "abducted" by FBI agents acting as terrorists. Automatic weapons were fired (with blanks), and bloody injuries were simulated. The volunteers were then "held captive" in one room and isolated by having pillowcases placed over their heads. A few cooperative "hostages" were released. Four days later, other FBI agents "stormed" the building and "rescued" the remaining hostages. The exercise was conducted in a realistic manner, and the volunteers found it exceedingly stressful. Those who had been instructed in anxiety-management techniques coped better than those given problem-solving training or no training at all. In this kind of situation, where individuals have little actual control over events, distraction and other emotion-focused techniques were more effective in reducing distress than were problem-focused efforts to exert control.

In a daring rescue, French commandos stormed an Air France jetliner, killed four Algerian terrorists who had hijacked the plane and murdered two passengers, and freed 173 passengers and crew. Simulation research conducted by the FBI has examined what techniques will help people cope effectively if they are held hostage.

Although potentially effective, suppression of unwanted thoughts from awareness can also have a peculiar, paradoxical effect. As described in Chapter 3, Daniel Wegner (1994, 1997) conducted a series of studies in which he told people not to think of a white bear and found that they could not then keep the image from popping to mind. What's more, he found that among participants who were permitted later to think about the bear, those who had earlier tried to suppress the image were unusually preoccupied with it, providing evidence of a rebound effect. Sometimes, the harder you try not to think about something, the less likely you are to succeed (Wegner et al., 1998). The solution: focused distraction. When participants were told to imagine a tiny red Volkswagen every time the forbidden bear intruded into consciousness, the rebound effect vanished (Wenzlaff & Wegner, 2000).

What do white bears and red cars have to do with coping? A lot. When people try to block stressful thoughts from awareness, the problem may worsen. That's where focused distraction comes in. In a study of pain tolerance, Delia Cioffi and James Holloway (1993) had people put a hand into a bucket of ice-cold water and keep it there until they could no longer bear the pain. One group was instructed to avoid thinking about the sensation. A second group was told to form a mental picture of their home. Afterward, those who had coped through suppression were slower to recover from the pain than were those who had used focused self-distraction. To manage stress—whether it's caused by physical pain, a strained romance, final exams, or problems at work—distraction ("think about lying on the beach") is a better coping strategy than mere suppression ("don't think about the pain").

Keeping secrets and holding in strong emotions may also be physically taxing. In the laboratory, James Gross and Robert Levenson (1997) showed female students funny, sad, and neutral films. Half the time, they told the students to not let their feelings show. From a hidden camera, videotapes confirmed that when they were asked to conceal their feelings, the students were less expressive. But physiological recordings revealed that as they watched the funny and sad films, the students exhibited a greater cardiovascular response when they tried to inhibit their feelings than when they did not. Physiologically, the effort to suppress the display of emotion backfired.

A study by Steve Cole and his colleagues (1996) may push this point a profound step further. These investigators identified 80 gay men in the Los Angeles area who were newly infected with the HIV virus but had no symptoms, administered various psychological tests, and monitored their progress every six months for nine years. They found that in men who were partly "in the closet"—compared with those who were open about their homosexuality—the infection spread more rapidly, causing them to die sooner. This provocative correlation does not prove that "coming out" is healthier than "staying in." In a controlled laboratory experiment, however, participants who were instructed to suppress rather than express turbulent emotional thoughts exhibited a temporary decrease in the activity of certain immune cells (Petrie et al., 1998). At least in Western cultures that encourage self-expression, actively concealing your innermost thoughts and feelings can be hazardous to your health.

Opening Up: Confronting One's Demons   The research just described suggests that just as shutting down can sometimes have benefits, so too can the opposite form of coping: opening up. There are two aspects to this emotional means of coping with stress. The first is acknowledging and understanding our emotional reactions to important events; the second is expressing these inner feelings to ourselves and others (Stanton et al., 2000).

According to James Pennebaker (1997), psychotherapy, self-help groups, and various religious rituals have something in common: All offer a chance for people to confide in someone, spill their guts, confess, and talk freely about their troubles—maybe for the first time. To test for the healing power of opening up, Pennebaker conducted a series of controlled studies in which he brought college students into a laboratory and asked them to talk into a tape recorder or write for 20 minutes either about past traumas or about trivial daily events. While speaking or writing, the students were upset and physiologically aroused. Many tearfully recounted accidents, failures, instances of physical or sexual abuse, loneliness, the death or divorce of their parents, shattered relationships, and their fears about the future. Soon these students felt better than ever. Pennebaker found that when they opened up, their systolic blood pressure levels rose during the disclosures but then later dipped below their pre-experiment levels. The students even exhibited a decline in the number of times they visited the campus health center over the next six months. Other studies, too, have shown that keeping personal secrets can be stressful and that "letting it out" and "getting it off your chest" can have true therapeutic effects on mental and physical health. These effects are especially strong when participants are comfortable with disclosure, when the disclosures are made across multiple sessions, and when the events being described are recent and traumatic (Frattaroli, 2006; Lepore & Smyth, 2002).

It appears that confession may be good for the body as well as the soul. But why does it help to open up? Why do *you* sometimes feel the need to talk out your problems? One possibility, recognized a full century ago by Sigmund Freud, is that the experience provides a much-needed *catharsis*, a discharge of tension—like taking the lid off a boiling pot of water to slow the boiling. People who experience trauma—whether it's a bout with cancer, death, an accident, a natural disaster, or exposure to violence—are often haunted by intrusive images of their stressor that pop to mind and cannot be stopped. In these cases, disclosure may bring closure. Research shows, for example, that women who had an abortion and who talked about it to an experimenter were later less distressed by intrusive thoughts about the traumatic experience than women who had also had an abortion but were not asked to open up about it (Major & Gramzow, 1999).

Another explanation for the benefits of opening up, one favored by Pennebaker, is that talking about a problem can help you to sort out your thoughts, understand the problem better, and gain *insight*, in cognitive terms. Whatever the reason, it's clear that opening up, perhaps to someone else, can be therapeutic—provided that the listener can be trusted. This last point is critical: Despite the potential for gain, opening up can also cause great distress when the people we confide in react with rejection or unwanted advice or, worse, betray what was said to others (Kelly & McKillop, 1996).

Indicating the importance of the "to whom" part of opening up, Stephen Lepore and colleagues (2000) exposed college students to disturbing Nazi Holocaust images. Afterward, the students were randomly divided into groups and asked to talk about their reactions to themselves while alone in a room, to a validating confederate who smiled and agreed, or to an invalidating confederate who avoided eye contact and disagreed. An additional group was given no opportunity to talk. As reported two days later, students who talked alone or to a validating confederate—compared to those who did not talk—said they had fewer intrusive Holocaust thoughts in the intervening period and were less stressed when re-exposed to the original images. However, for students who talked to an invalidating confederate the benefits of opening up were muted. This finding supports our earlier conclusion: It is better to discuss one's demons than to conceal them—but the extent of the benefit depends on whether the people we talk to are supportive. It's no wonder, then, that people are more likely to join mutual support groups, both live and online, when they suffer from stigmatizing disorders such as AIDS, alcoholism, breast cancer, and prostate cancer than when they have less embarrassing but equally toxic illnesses such as heart disease and diabetes (Davison et al., 2000).

Self-Focus: Getting Trapped Versus Getting Out In Chapter 3, we saw that people spend little time actually thinking about the self—and when they do, they wish they were doing something else (Csikszentmihalyi & Figurski, 1982). According to self-awareness theory, self-focus brings out our personal shortcomings the way staring in a mirror draws our attention to every blemish on the face. It comes as no surprise, then, that self-focus seems to intensify some of the most undesirable consequences of emotion-focused coping. Here's the script.

The state of self-awareness can be induced in us by external stimuli such as mirrors, cameras, and audiences. Mood, too, plays a role. Peter Salovey (1992) found that, compared with a neutral mood state, both positive and negative moods increase awareness of the self. Thus, when a stressful event occurs, the negative feelings that arise magnify self-focus. What happens next depends on a person's self-esteem, as people with a negative self-concept experience more negative moods when self-focused than do those with a positive self-concept (Sedikides, 1992). The end result is a self-perpetuating feedback loop: Being in a bad mood triggers self-focus, which in people with low self-esteem further worsens the mood. This vicious circle forms the basis for a self-focusing model of depression according to which coping with stress by attending to your own feelings only makes things worse (Mor & Winquist, 2002; Pyszczynski & Greenberg, 1992).

A great deal of research has shown that individuals who respond to distress by rumination and repetitive thought—by constantly fixating on themselves, their feelings, their symptoms, and the source of their distress—are more likely to become

Healthy distractions such as exercise are a good way to break out of the trap of self-focused depression. Unhealthy distractions, such as an alcohol binge, reduce self-focus at a self-destructive cost.

anxious and depressed than those who allow themselves to be distracted (Nolen-Hoeksema, 1991; Nolen-Hoeksema et al., 2008). Although some types of self-focus may be useful, as when people react to a stressful event by focusing on the positives or worrying in ways that lead them to plan, problem solve, and alter their expectations in adaptive ways, the adverse effects are clear (Watkins, 2008). Over the years, and across a range of different cultures, research has also shown that girls and women in particular have a tendency to ruminate, confront their negative feelings, and seek treatment for being depressed, while boys and men resort to alcohol and other drugs, physical activity, antisocial behavior, and other means of distraction. As a general rule, it appears that women who are upset tend to brood, while men who are upset are more likely to act out (Culbertson, 1997; Nolen-Hoeksema & Girgus, 1994).

Thankfully, there are healthier alternatives. To redirect attention away from the self, it helps to become absorbed in an activity such as aerobic exercise, gardening, writing, or reading a book. Whatever the activity, it should be difficult, demanding, and fully engaging. Ralph Erber and Abraham Tesser (1992) found that people who were in a bad mood felt better after performing a difficult task than a simple task or none at all. Difficult tasks, it appears, can "absorb" a bad mood. Meditation—which calls on participants to focus their attention on a chosen nonself object—can have positive effects for the same reason (Lutz et al., 2008). Referring to techniques of focused relaxation that he had developed, Cardiologist Herbert Benson recommended that people sit comfortably, close their eyes, relax the muscles, breathe deeply, and silently utter some word over and over again. Says Benson (1993), "By practicing two basic steps—the repetition of a sound, word, phrase, prayer, or muscular activity; and a passive return to the repetition whenever distracting thoughts recur—you can trigger a series of physiological changes that offer protection against stress" (p. 256).

■ Proactive Coping

According to Lisa Aspinwall and Shelley Taylor (1997), people often benefit from *proactive coping*, which consists of up-front efforts to ward off or modify the onset of a stressful event. As illustrated in ▶ Figure 14.9, coping can be seen as an ongoing process by which we try to prevent as well as react to the bumps and bruises of daily life. Also as shown, the first line of defense involves the accumulation of resources—

personal, financial, social, and otherwise—that can later, if needed, serve as a buffer against stress. In this section, we look at two possible resources: social support and religion.

Social Support If the world is crashing down around you, what do you do? Do you try to stop it? Do you try to manage your emotions? Or do you try to get help from others? Throughout this book, we have seen that no man or woman is an island, that human beings are social animals, that people need people, and that to get by you need a little help from friends. But do our social nature and our connections to others have anything to do with health? Do close family ties, lovers, buddies, online support groups, and relationships at work serve as a buffer against stress? The answer is yes. The evidence is now overwhelming that **social support** has therapeutic effects on our physical and psychological well-being (Cohen, 2004; Uchino, 2009).

David Spiegel, of Stanford University's School of Medicine, came to appreciate the value of social connections many years ago when he organized support groups for women with advanced breast cancer. The groups met weekly in 90-minute sessions to laugh, cry, share stories, and discuss ways of coping. Spiegel had fully expected the women to benefit emotionally from the experience. But he found something else he did not expect: These women lived an average of 18 months longer than did similar others who did not attend the groups. According to Spiegel (1993), "The added survival time was longer than any medication or other known medical treatment could be expected to provide for women with breast cancer so far advanced" (pp. 331–332).

Similar discoveries were then made by other researchers. In one study, Lisa Berkman and Leonard Syme (1979) surveyed 7,000 residents of Alameda County, California and conducted a nine-year follow-up of mortality rates. They found that the more social contacts people had, the longer they lived. This was true of men and women, young and old, rich and poor, and people from all racial and ethnic backgrounds. James House and others (1988) studied 2,754 adults interviewed during visits to their doctors. He found that the most socially active men were two to three times less likely to die within nine to twelve years than others of similar age who were more isolated. According to House, social isolation was statistically just as predictive of an early death as smoking or high cholesterol.

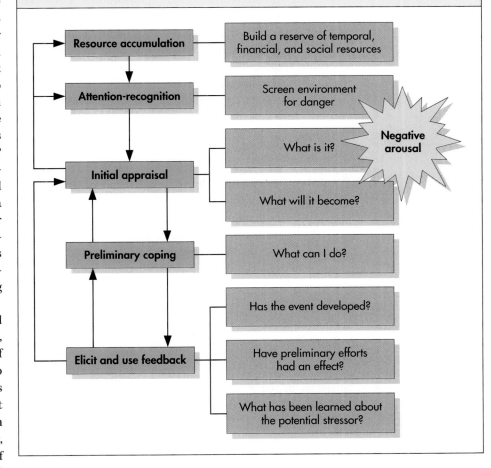

▶ **FIGURE 14.9**

Aspinwall and Taylor's Model of Proactive Coping

Coping can be seen as an ongoing, multi-step process by which people try to prevent, not just react to, life's daily stressors.

Aspinwall & Taylor, 1997.

social support The helpful coping resources provided by friends and other people.

Research findings like these are common. For example, married people are more likely than those who are single, divorced, or widowed to survive cancer for five years (Taylor, 1990), gay men infected with HIV are less likely to contemplate suicide if they have close ties than if they do not (Schneider et al., 1991), people who have a heart attack are less likely to have a second one if they live with someone than if they live alone (Case et al., 1992), and people, once married, who are then separated or divorced for long periods of time, are at an increased risk of early death (Sbarra & Nietert, 2009). Based on this type of research, Bert Uchino and his colleagues (1996) concluded that in times of stress, having social support lowers blood pressure, lessens the secretion of stress hormones, and strengthens immune responses.

On the flip side of the coin, people who are lonely suffer greater age-related increases in blood pressure and have more difficulty sleeping at night (Cacioppo et al., 2002; Hawkley et al., 2003). In fact, a study of first-year college students showed that feelings of loneliness during the semester were associated with elevated levels of the stress hormone cortisol and a weakened immune response to a flu shot they had received at the university health clinic (Pressman et al., 2005). There's no doubt about it: Being isolated from other people can be hazardous to your health.

There is, however, a vital exception to this rule. Of all the social networks that support us, romantic partnerships, as in marriage, are the most powerful. But while men and women who are happily married live longer than those who are single or divorced, marital conflict breeds stress, elevated blood pressure, ulcers, depression, alcohol and drug abuse, changes in immune function, and other unhealthy effects, especially for women (Kiecolt-Glaser & Newton, 2001).

Our social connections are therapeutic for many reasons. Friends may encourage us to get out, eat well, exercise, and take care of ourselves. They also give sympathy, reassurance, someone to talk to, advice, and a second opinion. The value of social support is so basic that people who support us don't need to be physically present. In one study, for example, the physiological responses of research participants were measured as they played a competitive fire-fighting simulation on computer. Via closed-circuit monitor, some participants thought they were being watched, spoken to, and comforted by a friendly person of the same sex, while others were left alone. The result: Social support delivered over a monitor, even from a confederate who was not physically present, had a calming influence on participants. It lowered their heart rate, reduced the level of cortisol in their saliva, and led them to see the task as easier (Thorsteinsson et al., 1998).

The health benefits of social support show just how important it is to connect with others. Are there any drawbacks to an active social life? Is it possible, for example, that the more people we see in a day—such as family, friends, classmates, teammates, co-workers, and neighbors—the more exposed we are to colds or the flu? Natalie Hamrick and others (2002) asked 18- to 30-year-old adults about recent stressful events and about their social lives, then had them keep a health diary for three months. Based on past research, they expected that participants who were under high stress would get sick more than those under low stress. But what about people with high versus low levels of social contact? What do you think? Would their social connections make them vulnerable to illness or protect them? It depends. Look at ▶ Figure 14.10 and you'll see that for people under low stress, social connections did not matter. For people under high stress, however, those with high

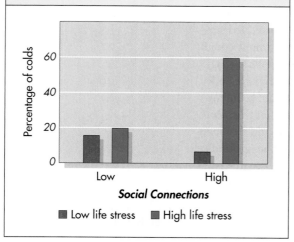

▶ **FIGURE 14.10**

Does Being Popular Always Promote Health?

Young adults were asked about recent stressful events and about their social lives—and then kept a health diary for three months. As you can see, social contact made no difference for people under low stress. For people under high stress, however, those with active social lives were more likely to get sick. Social contact increases exposure to infectious agents—and can bring illness for those whose resistance is compromised by stress.

Hamrick et al., 2002.

levels of social contact were *more* likely to catch a cold or flu. It's healthy to be popular except, perhaps, during flu season.

Precisely because researchers agree that social support is vital to health, they have struggled mightily to come up with ways to measure it (Cohen et al., 2000). In some studies, social support is defined by the sheer *number of social contacts* a person has. This measure can be useful, but a simple social contact model has some limitations. One is that it glosses over the fact that people who are stuck in bad relationships are sometimes more distressed, not less (Rook, 1984). Another problem is that having too many contacts can actually reduce levels of support. Consider the plight of the urban poor in India who are packed into overcrowded residences of up to 11 people per room. They are more stressed than people in less crowded conditions and have *less* social support, in part because they tend to withdraw (Evans & Lepore, 1993).

A second model of social support focuses on the *diversity* of a person's social network, one that consists, for example, of a spouse, close family members, friends, co-workers, and neighbors. Over the years, research has shown that people who are socially "integrated," who have connections to different types of people in different types of relationships, are healthier and live longer lives (Cohen & Janicki-Deverts, 2009).

A third model focuses on the quality of a person's relationships rather than their quantity. This *intimacy model* predicts that the key is to have a close relationship with a significant other who is emotionally on call for late-night conversations. Having one special relationship may be all a person needs. Thus, while many women with breast cancer benefit physically and emotionally from peer discussion groups, these groups are not needed by—and do not help—women who have supportive partners at home (Helgeson et al., 2000).

A fourth approach defines social support by *its perceived availability* (Sarason et al., 1983). Compared with people who are uncertain of what social resources they have, those who believe that ample support is available when needed cope more effectively. In almost any demanding situation you can imagine, perceived support is associated with better adjustment—even when these perceptions are not entirely accurate (Lakey & Cassady, 1990).

The Religious Connection   Finally, it is clear that religion provides a deeply important source of social and emotional support for many people. There are more than 6 billion people on earth who belong to hundreds of religions—the most populated, in order, being Christianity, Islam, Hinduism, and Buddhism (Judaism and others have many fewer adherents). Only about 15 to 20 percent of the world's population is unaffiliated with a religious group. In the United States, two-thirds of all adults describe religion as a very important part of their lives. Is there a link between religiosity and health?

This is an interesting but controversial question. On the one hand, population surveys suggest that people who regularly attend religious services live longer than those who do not (McCullough et al., 2000). When you think about it, this correlation makes some intuitive sense. Religious faith may fill people with hope and optimism rather than with despair, offer the physiological benefits of relaxation in prayer, provide a community lifeline of social support to prevent isolation, and promote a safe and healthy way of life by discouraging such toxic habits as drinking and smoking. After analyzing 30 years of health data from 2,600 California adults, for example, William Strawbridge and others (2001) found that men and women who regularly

People who have lots of friends are healthier and live longer than those who live more isolated lives. **TRUE.**

Religion provides an important source of support for many people. Here, people meditate in New York's Central Park during "Change Your Mind Day," which consists of yoga, meditation, music, and various spiritual practices from Buddhist traditions.

AP/Wide World Photos

attend religious services drink less, smoke less, and exercise more. On the other hand, some researchers caution that the correlations between religiosity and longevity are modest and can be interpreted in other ways. It's possible, for example, that non-smokers, teetotalers, and others who regularly abstain from unhealthful behaviors are more likely to adopt religion as part of their lives than smokers, drinkers, and risk-takers, and that their survival comes from who they are, not from their attendance at religious services (Sloan et al., 1999).

At this point, the research is suggestive but not conclusive: A religious way of life is associated with physiological benefits, health, and longevity, but the basis for these correlations—and the ultimate causal question of whether becoming religious will increase one's health—is a compelling question that remains to be determined (Miller & Thoresen, 2003; Plante & Thoresen, 2007; Powell et al., 2003; Seeman et al., 2003).

TABLE 14.4

Collectivist Coping Styles

The following sample statements describe five common types of coping styles, in order of frequency of usage, that have emerged from studies in Taiwan.

Acceptance, Reframing, and Striving	91%

- Tried to accept the trauma for what it offered me
- Believed I would grow from surviving the traumatic event
- Realized that the trauma served an important purpose in my life

Avoidance and Detachment	71%

- Saved face by not telling anyone
- Pretended to be okay
- Kept my feelings within myself in order not to worry my parents

Family Support	66%

- Shared my feelings with my family
- Knew that I could ask assistance from my family
- Followed the guidance of my elders

Religion and Spirituality	40%

- Found comfort in my religion or spirituality
- Found guidance from my religion
- Found comfort through prayer or other religious rituals

Private Emotional Outlets	30%

- Saved face by seeking advice from a professional I did not know
- Chatted with people about the trauma on the Internet
- Ate in excess

Heppner et al., 2006.

Culture and Coping

Everyone in the world feels stress during the course of a lifetime. Whether the result of a natural disaster, the death of a loved one, the breakup of a relationship, war, serious illness, an accident, or the chronic microstressors of studying, working, and trying to make ends meet, stress is universal to the human experience. But do people in all cultures solve problems and cope in the same ways?

Most of the research on coping is conducted with people from Western cultures, in which individualism and independence are highly valued. Do people from collectivist cultures that value interdependence use the same coping mechanisms that are listed in Table 14.3? The answer may not be as obvious as it seems. In view of the differences between Eastern and Western cultures, for example, one might predict that Asians are more likely than European Americans to cope with stress by turning to others for support. Yet Shelley Taylor and her colleagues (2004) found that when they asked college students to describe what they do to relieve stress, only 39 percent of South Koreans (compared to 57 percent of Americans) said they sought social support. Additional research has confirmed this surprising cultural difference. Regardless of whether the source of stress is social, academic, financial, or health related; across age groups; and in diverse Asian samples that included Chinese, Japanese, Korean, and Vietnamese participants, the result is always the same: People from Asian cultures are less likely to seek out social support in times of stress.

Additional probing has shed light on this difference. In individualistic cultures, people often use others to service their personal goals. Yet in collectivist cultures, where social groups take precedence over the self, people are reluctant to strain their relationships by calling on others for support. This being the case, Heejung Kim and her colleagues (2008) distinguished between *explicit social support* (disclosing one's distress to others and seeking their advice, aid, or comfort) and *implicit social support* (merely thinking about or being with close others without openly asking for help). In a study that asked participants to imagine themselves in one of these two situations, Asian Americans reacted with more stress to the explicit social support situation, while European Americans found the more contained implicit situation more stressful (Taylor et al., 2007).

To better understand the "collectivist coping style," Paul Heppner and others (2006) administered extensive questionnaires to more than 3,000 Asian college students in Taiwan, many of whom had endured the kinds of traumatic events described in this chapter (the three most frequent were breakups, academic pressure, and the death or illness of a loved one). Table 14.4 shows five ways of coping that were identified. In order of how often they are used, the strategies are (1) acceptance, reframing, and striving; (2) avoidance and detachment; (3) family support; (4) religion and spirituality; and (5) private emotional outlets. Of the five strategies, participants rated acceptance as the most helpful. Do these results describe how Taiwanese adults cope with stress? What about Asians from Korea, Japan, China, and elsewhere? Stay tuned. Interest is growing in these questions and, more generally, in the intersections of social psychology, culture, and health (Gurung, 2010).

Treatment and Prevention

Understanding what social support is and how it operates is important in the study of health because so many of life's problems and prospects occur in a social context and so many of our efforts to cope with stress involve other people. Indeed, as we'll see in this section, health psychologists are actively trying to find ways in which social influences can be used to improve the development of treatment and prevention programs.

■ Treatment: The "Social" Ingredients

Often, what ails us can be treated through medical intervention. The treatments vary widely—from a simple change in diet to vitamin supplements, aspirin, antibiotics, surgery, and the like. There's no doubt about it: Medicine is vital to health. In addition, however, treatment has a social component, what the family doctor used to call "bedside manner." What are the active social ingredients?

To begin to answer this question, let's consider research on the benefits of psychotherapy. Over the years, studies have shown that although there are vastly different schools of thought and techniques for doing psychotherapy, all approaches are somewhat effective and, surprisingly, all are generally equivalent (Smith et al., 1980; Wampold et al., 1997). Apparently, despite the surface differences, all psychotherapies have a great deal in common at a deeper level and these common factors—more than the specific techniques used—provide the active ingredients necessary for change. What are some of these factors?

First, all healers—regardless of whether they are medical doctors, psychologists, or others—provide *social support*, a close human relationship characterized by warmth, expressions of concern, a shoulder to cry on, and someone to talk to. Earlier, we discussed the benefits to health and longevity of having social contacts. In psychological therapy, studies have shown that the better the "working alliance" is between a therapist and client, the more favorable the outcome is likely to be (Horvath & Luborsky, 1993). As psychotherapist Hans Strupp (1996) put it, "The simple and incontrovertible truth is that if you are anxious or depressed, or if you are experiencing difficulties with significant people in your life, chances are that you feel better if you talk to someone you can trust" (p. 1017).

Second, all therapies offer a ray of *hope* to people who are sick, demoralized, unhappy, or in pain. In all aspects of life, people are motivated by upbeat, positive expectations. Although some of us are more optimistic than others, optimism is a specific expectation that can be increased or decreased in certain situations (Armor & Taylor, 1998). Indeed, a common aspect of all treatments is that they communicate and instill positive expectations. It has been suggested that high expectations can spark change even when they are not justified (Prioleau et al., 1983). This suggestion is consistent with the well-known placebo effect in medicine, whereby patients improve after being given an inactive drug or treatment. Believing can help make it so, which is how faith healers, shamans, and witch doctors all over the world have managed to perform "miracle cures" with elaborate rituals. Even modern medicine exploits the power of hope. As Walter Brown (1998) puts it, "The symbols and rituals of healing—the doctor's office, the stethoscope, the physical examination—offer reassurance" (p. 91).

A third important ingredient is *choice*. Allowing patients to make meaningful choices, such as deciding on a type of treatment, increases the effectiveness of treatments for alcoholism (Miller, 1985) and obesity (Mendonca & Brehm, 1983). Choosing to undergo an effortful or costly treatment is particularly beneficial in this regard. The person who voluntarily pays in time, money, or discomfort needs to self-justify that investment—a predicament sure to arouse cognitive dissonance (see Chapter 6). One way to reduce dissonance is to become ultra-motivated to succeed: "Why have I chosen to do this? Because I really want to get better." Perhaps because highly motivated individuals are more careful and conscientious about carrying out the prescribed treatment, they tend to improve more.

Danny Axsom (1989) tested this specific proposition in a study of snake phobias. Participants, all of whom were highly snake-phobic, were or were not given an explicit choice about undertaking a treatment that was described as either requiring "extreme exertion" or being "easy." Among the four experimental conditions, participants who were given an explicit choice about continuing an effortful treatment reported the greatest motivation to change their phobic behavior and came closest to the five-foot-long New Jersey corn snake used to measure approach behavior.

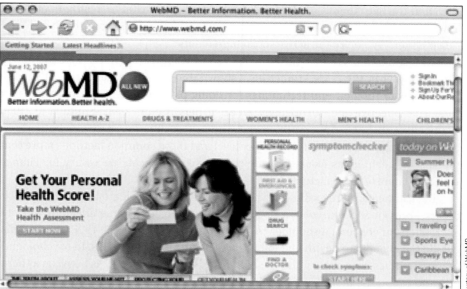

Today, people can find all sorts of information and advice on health-related issues on WebMD and other Internet sites.

Prevention: Getting the Message Across

We live in what could aptly be described as the era of prevention in that many serious health threats are preventable. Just watch TV, leaf through a magazine, or surf the Internet: There are programs for AIDS prevention, campaigns to persuade smokers to break the habit, sunscreens that protect the skin from harmful rays, and laws that mandate the use of seat belts. To a large extent, we know what to do and what not to do to promote good health and avoid disease and injury. But just how do we convince ourselves and others to translate that knowledge into action?

Nowhere is this problem more acute than among people who suffer from AIDS. Earlier in the chapter, we noted that heart attacks, cancer, strokes, and accidents are now more common causes of death than infectious diseases. But AIDS, the first truly global epidemic, has spread at an alarming rate. Years ago, AIDS was described as a microbiological time bomb. In 1981, five homosexual men in North America were diagnosed with AIDS and were among only 189 cases reported that year. By 1996, the number of cases in North America had skyrocketed to three-quarters of a million and included heterosexual men, women, and children (Mann, 1992). In 2009, the World Health Organization estimated that 34 million people worldwide were infected with HIV; an estimated 2 million died in that year alone. Worldwide, both numbers are down from previous years. However, the number of new infections continues to climb in parts of Latin America, sub-Saharan Africa, North Africa, the Middle East, Eastern Europe, and parts of Asia.

The AIDS virus is transmitted from one person to another in infected blood, semen, and vaginal secretions. People who are HIV-positive may have no symptoms for several years and may not even realize they are infected. Eventually, however, the virus will ravage the immune system by destroying lymphocytes that help ward off disease. What's frightening about AIDS is that it appears fatal, that it is increasing at a rate of one new case every few seconds, and that there is no vaccine that can prevent its occurrence (Stine, 2007). At present, the most effective way to control the spread of AIDS is to alter people's beliefs, motivations, and risk-taking behaviors (Fisher & Fisher, 1992; Fisher et al., 1994; Gerrard et al., 1996; Kalichman, 2006)—and that's where social psychology comes in. Across a range of perspectives, several basic steps emerge (see ▶ Figure 14.11).

▶ **FIGURE 14.11**

Aiming for Good Health

Several major factors help convince people to engage in healthy practices. Recognition that a threat to health exists is a necessary first step. Positive models and healthy subjective norms encourage people to adopt health-protective behaviors. A sense of self-efficacy about being able to carry out healthy behaviors and the belief that such behaviors will be effective increase the likelihood of active efforts.

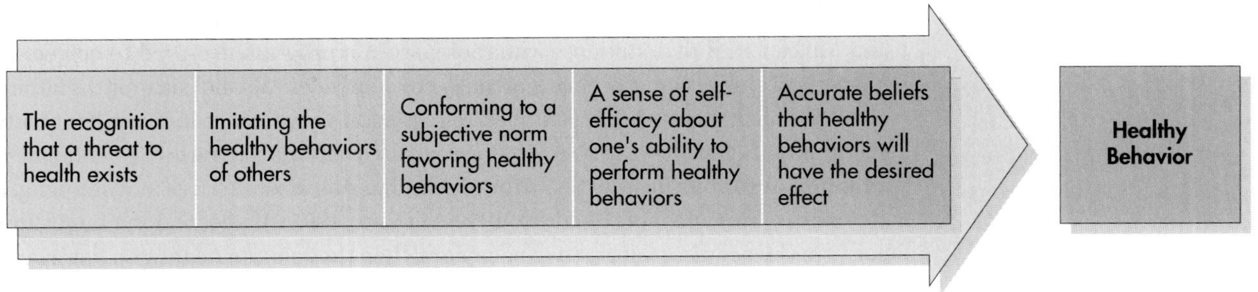

The first step toward good health depends on the relative pleasure to be derived from healthy versus unhealthy behaviors. If a healthy behavior is more enjoyable than an unhealthy one, then presumably all we need to do is try it out and we'll be convinced. Usually, however, it's not this easy. Many unhealthy habits are sinfully enjoyable, and many healthy behaviors require self-control. If they are to be convinced to switch, people have to recognize that their health is at risk. As described in Chapter 6, graphic fear appeals are a popular method of persuasion in commercial and public service advertisements: the gruesome lung-cancer operation to scare smokers into quitting, the bloody accident victim to get people to use seat belts. Fear appeals can be incredibly effective at changing attitudes and behavior (de Hoog et al., 2007).

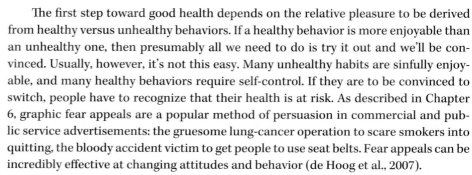

As role models, celebrities have great influence over public health care decisions. TRUE.

The next two steps toward good health involve other people. When those around us behave in healthful ways, they serve as role models that help set healthy norms. Direct modeling can be especially useful. Celebrities in particular have a great deal of influence over public health issues. In a poignant moment of the 1996 Olympics, heavyweight boxing legend Muhammad Ali—who, like actor Michael J. Fox, suffers from Parkinson's disease, a motor disorder—stood upright with his arm trembling and his face frozen as he lit the ceremonial flame. The National Parkinson's Foundation, which went on to adopt a torch as its symbol, was flooded with donations (Nattinger et al., 1998). Unfortunately, the sword of influence cuts both ways, which is why it is so troubling to see role models of *un*healthy behavior among high-profile athletes, entertainers, and other celebrities who occupy center stage.

Besides eliciting direct imitation, spokespersons contribute to the development of subjective norms, beliefs we hold about how people expect us to behave. According to the theories of reasoned action (Fishbein, 1980) and planned behavior (Ajzen, 1991) presented in Chapter 6, both attitudes and subjective norms affect our intentions to take action. Indeed, both positive attitudes toward safe sex and felt pressure from significant others increase intentions to practice safe sex (Chan & Fishbein, 1993; Cochran et al., 1992). As to who the most effective spokespersons might be, a recent meta-analysis of 354 HIV intervention programs spanning 17 years revealed that health professionals promote greater behavioral change than peers and other community sources (Durantini et al., 2006).

Intervention strategies that make use of social pressure can be very effective. In a series of studies, Jeffrey Kelly and others (1991) found that self-reports by gay men of high-risk sexual behavior diminished after opinion leaders in the gay community had been trained to advocate safe-sex practices to their peers. Unfortunately, subjective norms often sustain unhealthy behaviors. There are two reasons why this occurs. First, people who smoke or drink excessively overestimate the prevalence of such practices among their peers. Second, these inflated estimates serve to support and increase unhealthy practices at a later time. For example, Deborah Prentice and Dale Miller (1996) found that college students who overestimate the level of alcohol use on campus at the start of a school year are eventually more likely to conform to this misperception in their own attitudes and behavior. For those trapped within this closed circle, the best way to cut through it is to provide accurate information about *who* does *what*. Prentice and Miller found that students who took part in a program designed to correct their misperceptions of campus norms actually consumed less alcohol six months later.

The fourth step to health emphasizes a person's confidence in his or her ability to succeed. Self-efficacy—the belief that we can do what needs to be done—enhances the adoption of various healthy behaviors, including safe-sex practices, not smoking, and abstinence from alcohol (Bandura, 1999; Maddux, 1995). If people don't know how to perform the necessary corrective behaviors, then they should be taught. For example, smoking-prevention programs often teach children techniques for resisting peer pressures and refusing the offer of a cigarette (Baum, 1984; Evans et al., 1984).

Finally, people need reliable and accurate information about the effectiveness of the healthy behaviors they are urged to adopt (Weinstein, 1989). If people believe that something works, they will be more likely to try it out. Beware, however, of someone who is too easily convinced. In one study, participants who had been reassured that a proposed prevention program would be successful were positive in their evaluation of the program regardless of the quality of the arguments that supported it. Those given a lower expectation of success were more discerning and based their evaluations on the quality of the arguments presented (Gleicher & Petty, 1992). In the short run, people can be tricked by false promises. In the long run, accurate information will prevail.

For social psychologists, the challenge in addressing the HIV crisis is to convert the science into a practice that works. In an excellent illustration, Jeffrey Fisher and his colleagues (2002) theorized that HIV prevention in city schools, which is essential for controlling the number of newly infected teens, requires a three-pronged attack. In their model, students must be provided with accurate *information* about HIV transmission and how to prevent it, with a personal and social *motivation* to engage in HIV-preventative behaviors, and with the *behavioral skills* necessary to follow through—notably, by using condoms. Armed with this model, these investigators set up HIV prevention programs in four urban high schools, devised a control group that lacked these "active ingredients," and found that the program, when administered by the classroom teachers, changed HIV-prevention behavior, increasing condom use up to a year later—all for an estimated cost of $2.22 per student. Other similarly oriented efforts have been developed as well, also with good success (Albarracín et al., 2005).

Armed with a theory and various effective techniques, social psychologists are looking to make important strides in the fight against AIDS. There are two caveats, however. First, it is necessary (and not that easy) for prevention programs to attract the kinds of high-risk participants for whom they are designed. Yet this is exactly the group, ironically, that is least likely to attend. In a study of 350 inhabitants of a high-risk community, Allison Earl and her colleagues (2009) found that people who were the most informed, most motivated, and most skilled at using condoms to prevent the spread of HIV were also the most likely to accept an offer to participate in the program. Those who were less informed, less motivated, and less skilled were less receptive. Clearly, for any HIV prevention program to work, it must bring in those members of the community who need it most.

The second caveat is that a focus on educating "healthy" people in the use of condoms addresses the spread of HIV prevention from one perspective. A second approach is to focus prevention efforts on HIV positive individuals who can transmit the virus. To achieve this objective, it is necessary to increase the number of HIV positive individuals who are aware of their infections. It is also necessary to educate the few who know they are infected and yet still engage in behaviors that put sex partners at risk. With an eye on this objective, Ann O'Leary and Richard Wolitski (2009) describe a number of possible ways to encourage those who are knowingly infected to take responsibility, reject rationalization and excuse making, humanize and empathize with their sex partners, and bring their behavior in line with their own moral standards.

The Pursuit of Happiness

Long before the emergence of social psychology, philosophers regarded happiness as the ultimate state of being. In the U.S. Declaration of Independence, Thomas Jefferson thus cited life, liberty, and "the pursuit of happiness" as the most cherished of human rights. But what is happiness, and how is it achieved? Aristotle said it was the reward of an active life. Freud linked it with both work and love. Others have variously suggested that happiness requires money and power, health and fitness, religion, beauty, the satisfaction of basic needs, and an ability to derive pleasure from the events of everyday life. In recent years, social psychologists have applied their theories and methods to the study of this most basic human motive: the pursuit of happiness (Diener & Biswas-Diener, 2008; Gilbert, 2006; Haidt, 2006; Lyubomirsky, 2007).

To study happiness—or **subjective well-being**, as social psychologists like to call it—one must be able to measure it. How do researchers know whether someone is happy? Simple: They ask. Better yet, they use questionnaires such as the Satisfaction with Life Scale, in which people respond to statements such as "If I could live my life over, I would change almost nothing" (Diener et al., 1984; Pavot & Diener, 1993). As Marcus Aurelius said, "No man is happy who does not think himself so."

Using self-reports, surveys show that 75 percent of American adults describe themselves as happy and that in 86 percent of all nations sampled, the ratings are, on average, more often positive than neutral (Diener, 2000). In general, people who are happy also have cheerful moods, high self-esteem, physical health, a sense of personal control, more memories of positive as opposed to negative events, and optimism about the future (Myers & Diener, 1995). It's no secret that our outlook on life becomes rosy right after we win a big game, fall in love, land a great job, or make money and that the world seems gloomy right after we lose, fall out of love, or suffer a personal tragedy or financial setback. Predictably, the events of everyday life trigger fluctuations in mood. For example, people are most happy on Fridays and Saturdays and least happy on Mondays and Tuesdays (Larsen & Kasimatis, 1990). Even during the day, happiness levels fluctuate like clockwork. For example, David Watson and others (1999) asked college students to rate their mood states once a day for 45 days, always at a different hour. They found, on average, that the students felt best during the middle of the day (noon to 6 P.M.) and worst in the early morning and late evening hours.

But what determines our long-term satisfaction, and why are some of us happier in general than others? Seeking the roots of happiness, Ed Diener and his colleagues (1999) reviewed many years of research and found that subjective well-being is not meaningfully related to demographic factors such as age, sex, racial and ethnic background, IQ, education level, or physical attractiveness. Contrary to popular belief, people are not less happy during the so-called crisis years of midlife or in old age than during their youth and "peak" young-adult years. Men and women do not differ on this measure, and, in the United States, African and Hispanic Americans are as happy as white Americans.

Overall, there are three key predictors of happiness: *social relationships* (people with an active social life, close friends, and a happy marriage are more satisfied than those who lack these intimate connections), *employment status* (regardless of income, employed people are happier than those who are out of work), and *physical and mental health* (people who are healthy are happier than those who are not). Reflecting the impact of these factors, worldwide surveys of more than 100,000 respondents in 55 countries have shown that happiness levels vary from one culture to the next (Diener & Suh, 2000). Although rankings fluctuate a bit from one survey to the next, national happiness ratings are consistently high in Denmark, Sweden, Switzerland, and Australia. Canada ranks fifth in the world, and the United States ranks seventh (Veenhoven, 1993).

Perhaps the most interesting statistical relationship is between income and subjective well-being. We all know the saying that "money can't buy happiness"—though some people (particularly those who are financially strapped) do not believe it. But is

subjective well-being One's happiness, or life satisfaction, as measured by self-report.

wealth truly a key to happiness? To some extent, yes, but the evidence is complex. Ed Diener and Martin Seligman (2004) note that multimillionaires from the Forbes list of the 400 richest Americans report high levels of life satisfaction (5.8 on a 7-point scale), but so do the Masai, a herding people in East Africa with no electricity or running water who live in huts made with dung (5.7 on the same 7-point scale).

Cross-national studies reveal a strong positive association between a nation's wealth and the subjective well-being of its people. There are some exceptions. But as a general rule, the more money a country has, the happier its citizens are, at least up to a point. Within any given country, however, the differences between wealthy and middle-income people are modest. In one survey, for example, a group of the wealthiest Americans said they were happy 77 percent of the time, which was only moderately higher than the 62 percent figure reported by those of average income. And when comparisons within a single culture are made over time, there is no relationship between affluence and happiness. Americans on average are two to three times richer now than 50 years ago—before we had computers, flat-screen TVs, BlackBerrys, iPhones, and digital cameras that fit into the palm of your hand. Yet the number of respondents who said they were "very happy" was 35 percent in 1957 and only 32 percent in 1998 (see ▶ Figure 14.12).

So what are we to conclude? At this point, it appears that having shelter, food, safety, and security is essential for subjective well-being. But once these basic needs

© Alan Schein Photography/Corbis

This image probably arouses positive feelings. But can money buy happiness? Recent research shows that there is no simple answer.

▶**FIGURE 14.12**

Wealth and Subjective Well-Being

Over a period of more than 40 years, Americans became twice as wealthy, as measured by adjusted per person income—but they were no happier, as measured in public opinion polls.

Kassin, 1997.

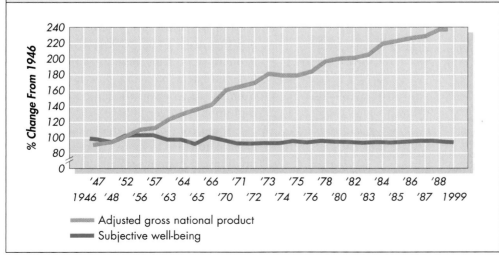

are met, particularly in an already prosperous society, additional increases in wealth do not appreciably raise levels of happiness. Why doesn't money contribute more to subjective well-being? One reason is that our perceptions of wealth are not absolute but, instead, are relative to certain personally set standards (Parducci, 1995). These standards are derived from two sources: other people and our own past.

According to *social comparison theory*, as described in Chapter 3, people tend to naturally compare themselves to others and feel contented or deprived depending on how they fare in this comparison. To demonstrate, Ladd Wheeler and Kunitate Miyake (1992) had college students for two weeks keep a written record of every time they mentally compared their own grades, appearance, abilities, possessions, or personality traits to someone else's. Consistently, these diaries revealed that making "upward comparisons" (to others who were better off) sparked negative feelings, while making "downward comparisons" (to others who were worse off) triggered positive feelings. That is why the middle-class worker whose neighbors can't pay their bills feels fortunate but the upper-class social climber who rubs elbows with the rich and famous feels deprived. This relativity may also help explain why there are only modest relationships between happiness and actual income and perceptions of financial status (Johnson & Krueger, 2006).

It is also natural for people to use their own recent past as a basis of comparison. According to *adaptation-level theory*, our satisfaction with the present depends on the level of success to which we are accustomed. Get married, buy a new house, or make a killing in the stock market and you will surely enjoy a wave of euphoria. Before long, however, the glitter will wear off, and you'll adapt to your better situation and raise your standard of comparison. Indeed, when Philip Brickman and others (1978) interviewed 22 people who had won between $50,000 and $1 million in a lottery, they found that these people did not rate themselves as happier than in the past. Compared to others from similar backgrounds, the winners said that they now derived less pleasure from routine activities such as shopping, reading, and talking to a friend. Perhaps the more money you have, the more you need to stay happy. The results of a Chicago public opinion poll suggest that this is the case: Whereas people who earned less than $30,000 a year said that $50,000 would fulfill their dreams, those who earned more than $100,000 said it would take $250,000 to make them happy (Csikszentmihalyi, 1999). Highlighting a dark side of the "American dream," research shows that the more materialistic people are, the less satisfied they seem to be (Nickerson et al., 2003). Economists are thus coming to appreciate that to some extent, our sense of well-being stems from the gap between income and material aspirations (Stutzer, 2004).

There's one other possible and intriguing explanation for why money, per se, is not more predictive of happiness: Perhaps each of us, as a result of both biological and environmental factors, has a set baseline level of happiness, a "set point" toward which we gravitate. This notion is supported by three recent findings. One is that ratings of happiness are higher among pairs of identical twins than among fraternal twins—leading David

"Remember how I said I was happiest when we had nothing?"

Lykken (2000) to suggest that there may be a genetic basis for having a certain set level of contentment. A second finding is that the fluctuations in mood that accompany positive and negative life events tend to wear off over time. For example, in a study spanning two years, Eunkook Suh and others (1996) studied participants for two years and found that only experiences occurring in the last three months correlated with reports of subjective well-being. Getting engaged or married, breaking up, starting a new job, and being hospitalized are the kinds of high-impact experiences that people assume have lasting if not permanent effects on happiness levels (Gilbert et al., 1998)—but in fact, the impacts are temporary. A third finding is that happiness levels, like personality traits, are relatively stable over time and place, which leads to the conclusion that some people are, in general, happier than others (DeNeve & Cooper, 1998).

The pursuit of happiness is a powerful human motive that is not fully understood. Although it appears that people are predisposed toward a particular set point, it is clear that happiness is not completely set in stone. In a 17-year study of individuals in Germany, researchers found that 24 percent of the respondents had significantly higher or lower levels of life satisfaction in the last five years of the study than they did in the first five years (Fujita & Diener, 2005). In a study of national surveys that spanned from 1981 to 2007, other researchers found that average happiness ratings increased in 45 out of 52 countries in which multiple surveys were administered over time—an increase that was linked to increasing democratization in these countries (Inglehart et al., 2008). Realizing that happiness is malleable, both for individuals and for large populations, researchers are now seeking ways to produce sustainable increases in subjective well-being (Lyubomirsky et al., 2005).

REVIEW

Stress and Health

- Stress is an unpleasant state that arises when we perceive that the demands of an event strain our ability to cope effectively.
- A person's appraisal of a situation determines how stress is experienced and how he or she copes.

- Coping responses consist of the thoughts, feelings, and behaviors by which people attempt to reduce stress.

What Causes Stress?

- There are many different causes of stress, or stressors.

Crises and Catastrophes

- Natural disasters and other catastrophic events can have harmful and long-term effects on mental and physical health.
- People with posttraumatic stress disorder suffer from psychological and physical symptoms long after the event is over.
- Soldiers exposed to combat often suffer from posttraumatic stress.

Major Life Events

- Early research suggested that all change is stressful.
- However, more recent studies suggest that only negative events are harmful.

Microstressors: The Hassles of Everyday Life

- The most common sources of stress are minor everyday hassles.
- Constant noise, job pressures, and living in shared space are all stressful in this regard.

How Does Stress Affect the Body?

- Selye coined the term *stress* upon observing that different stressors produce similar physiological effects on the body.

The General Adaptation Syndrome

- The body responds to stress in three stages: alarm, resistance, and exhaustion.
- The stress response is designed for acute emergencies, not for the constant long-term stress that humans often experience.

What Stress Does to the Heart

- Stress is a major risk factor in coronary heart disease (CHD).
- Early research suggested that the hard-driving Type A personality, also called coronary behavior pattern, is associated with CHD.
- This link was found when the Type A pattern was assessed in structured interviews but not when it was measured by questionnaire.
- Hostility is now known to be the "toxic" element in the Type A behavior pattern.

What Stress Does to the Immune System

- The immune system contains specialized white blood cells called lymphocytes that detect and destroy foreign substances in the body.
- Laboratory and field research shows that stress affects the activity of these cells, sometimes resulting in a weakened immune response.
- Stress can "get into" the immune system by causing people to behave in unhealthy ways or by triggering the release of stress hormones that suppress immune cell activity.

The Links Between Stress and Illness

- Stress weakens the immune system, so people under stress are more likely to catch a cold when exposed to a virus.
- There may also be a link between negative emotional states and serious diseases such as cancer, but the evidence is less strong.

Processes of Appraisal

Attributions and Explanatory Styles

- According to the learned helplessness model of depression, exposure to an uncontrollable event sparks passive, apathetic, depression-like symptoms.
- Research shows that the attributions people make for their lack of control are of central importance.
- The depressive explanatory style is a tendency to make stable, global, internal attributions for bad events; it is associated with depression and perhaps with physical illness.

The Human Capacity for Resilience

- Some individuals are more resilient than others in the face of stress, a trait called hardiness.

- The key ingredient of hardiness is the belief that one has the power to control future outcomes through one's own behavior.
- Depending on the situation, people may have a high or low self-efficacy—the belief that they can perform the behaviors needed to produce positive outcomes.
- Some individuals are characteristically more optimistic than others, and optimism at one point in time is predictive of later positive health outcomes.

Pollyanna's Health

- Positive thinking is associated with good health, but the causal relationship is unclear.
- Unrealistic positive illusions may have undesirable interpersonal and health consequences.

Ways of Coping with Stress

Problem-Focused Coping

- In problem-focused coping, people try to reduce stress by overcoming the source of the problem.
- Problem-focused coping is often effective, but at times there are drawbacks.
- For example, exerting control is physiologically taxing and can increase stress rather than reduce it.

- Also, both behavioral and characterological self-blame are associated with increased distress.

Emotion-Focused Coping

- In emotion-focused coping, people try to manage the emotional turmoil produced by a stressful situation.
- The best starting point is the experience of positive emotions.

- In situations that one cannot control, mental distraction and avoidance can reduce stress.

- But the suppression from awareness of unwanted thoughts and feelings can backfire, causing us to become preoccupied with them.

- Research shows that opening up and confronting one's feelings about upsetting events improves mental and physical health.

- Among people with low self-esteem, self-focus worsens their mood and heightens their distress.

- In contrast, it is helpful to become absorbed in demanding external activities such as reading, exercise, and gardening.

Proactive Coping

- As a first line of defense, people can ward off stress through proactive coping efforts such as the accumulation of resources.

- Having many different roles and identities serves as a buffer against stressors in any one domain of life.

- Friendships and other sources of social support have strong beneficial effects on physical health and psychological well-being.

- All researchers agree that social support is healthy, but they measure it in different ways, focusing on such factors as the number of social contacts a person has, the presence of special close relationships, or perceptions that social support is available.

- Social psychologists are also studying the role of religion in reducing stress.

Culture and Coping

- Stress is universal, but people from collectivist cultures appear to rely less often on social support as a means of coping than do people from individualist cultures.

- Recent research has identified that acceptance, avoidance, family support, religion, and private emotional outlets are the coping styles members of collectivist cultures use.

Treatment and Prevention

Treatment: The "Social" Ingredients

- Medical treatment includes an important social component.

- Doctors, therapists, and other health care workers provide patients with social support and a ray of hope.

- Choice of treatment is also an important factor, particularly when patients choose an effortful treatment, which increases commitment.

Prevention: Getting the Message Across

- Many causes of death are preventable through changes in lifestyle and behavior, which is where social psychology comes in.

- First, people have to recognize that a threat to their health exists.

- Others serve as important role models and spokespersons for healthy or unhealthy behavior.

- Subjective norms can also encourage healthy or unhealthy behaviors.

- A sense of self-efficacy enhances a person's adoption and maintenance of healthy behaviors.

- Accurate information is needed to sustain people's commitment to healthy behaviors.

The Pursuit of Happiness

- Most people report being relatively happy, but there are individual differences.

- Three important factors are social relationships, employment, and health.

- Evidence that money can buy happiness is mixed. More affluent nations tend to have happier citizens than less affluent nations, but correlations with groups of citizens within nations are modest.

- One reason for the limited association between wealth and happiness is that our perceptions of wealth are relative, not only to what others have but also to what we have become accustomed to.

- Research suggests that each of us has a baseline level of happiness toward which we gravitate over time.

- Still, research shows that happiness levels are somewhat malleable in individuals and in nations.

Key Terms

appraisal (570)

coping (570)

depressive explanatory
    style (583)

emotion-focused coping (590)

general adaptation
    syndrome (575)

health psychology (569)

immune system (579)

learned helplessness (583)

posttraumatic stress disorder
    (PTSD) (573)

proactive coping (590)

problem-focused coping (589)

psychoneuroimmunology
    (PNI) (579)

self-efficacy (585)

social support (597)

stress (570)

stressor (571)

subjective well-being (606)

Type A personality (577)

Media Resources

Social Psychology 8th Edition Companion Website

Visit your book companion website

www.cengage.com/psychology/kassin

where you will find flash cards, practice quizzes, Internet links, and more to help you study.

CENGAGENOW™ Just what you need to know NOW! Spend time on what you need to master rather than on information you already have learned. Take a pre-test for this chapter and CengageNOW will generate a personalized study plan based on your results. The study plan will identify the topics you need to review and direct you to online resources to help you master those topics. You can then take a post-test to help you determine the concepts you have mastered and what you will need to work on. Try it out! Go to **academic .cengage.com/login** to sign in with an access code or to purchase access to this product.

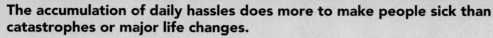

Putting COMMON SENSE *to the Test*

The accumulation of daily hassles does more to make people sick than catastrophes or major life changes.

True. *Car problems, arguments with friends, and other "microstressors" contribute more to our levels of stress than larger but less frequent stressors.*

Like humans, zebras get ulcers.

False. *Stress causes ulcers in humans, not zebras. That's because the stress response is designed for acute emergencies; but in people, it is activated often and for long periods of time.*

Stress can weaken the heart, but it cannot affect the immune system.

False. *Recent research has shown that stress and other psychological states can alter the activity of white blood cells in the immune system and affect our resistance to illness.*

When it comes to physical health, research does not support popular beliefs about the power of positive thinking.

False. *Consistently, people who are optimistic—and situations that promote optimism—are associated with better health outcomes.*

People who have lots of friends are healthier and live longer than those who live more isolated lives.

True. *Across a range of studies, researchers have found that social support is strongly associated with positive health outcomes.*

As role models, celebrities have great influence over public health care decisions.

True. *As a result of all the media attention given to celebrities, the health care decisions they make exert a great deal of influence on others.*

Glossary

adversarial model   A dispute-resolution system in which the prosecution and defense present opposing sides of the story. *(p. 522)*

affective forecasting   The process of predicting how one would feel in response to future events. *(p. 59)*

aggression   Behavior intended to harm another individual. *(p. 436)*

altruistic   Motivated by the desire to improve another's welfare. *(p. 400)*

ambivalent sexism   A form of sexism characterized by attitudes about women that reflect both negative, resentful beliefs and feelings and affectionate and chivalrous but potentially patronizing beliefs and feelings. *(p. 156)*

applied research   Research whose goals are to enlarge the understanding of naturally occurring events and to find solutions to practical problems. *(p. 29)*

appraisal   The process by which people make judgments about the demands of potentially stressful events and their ability to meet those demands. *(p. 570)*

arousal: cost-reward model   The proposition that people react to emergency situations by acting in the most cost-effective way to reduce the arousal of shock and alarm. *(p. 397)*

assessment center   A structured setting in which job applicants are exhaustively tested and judged by multiple evaluators. *(p. 536)*

attachment style   The way a person typically interacts with significant others. *(p. 367)*

attitude   A positive, negative, or mixed reaction to a person, object, or idea. *(p. 203)*

attitude scale   A multiple-item questionnaire designed to measure a person's attitude toward some object. *(p. 205)*

attribution theory   A group of theories that describe how people explain the causes of behavior. *(p. 113)*

audience inhibition   Reluctance to help for fear of making a bad impression on observers. *(p. 410)*

availability heuristic   The tendency to estimate the likelihood that an event will occur by how easily instances of it come to mind. *(p. 116)*

base-rate fallacy   The finding that people are relatively insensitive to consensus information presented in the form of numerical base rates. *(p. 117)*

basic research   Research whose goal is to increase the understanding of human behavior, often by testing hypotheses based on a theory. *(p. 29)*

bask in reflected glory (BIRG)   To increase self-esteem by associating with others who are successful. *(p. 85)*

behavioral genetics   A subfield of psychology that examines the role of genetic factors in behavior. *(p. 18)*

belief in a just world   The belief that individuals get what they deserve in life, an orientation that leads people to disparage victims. *(p. 124)*

belief perseverance   The tendency to maintain beliefs even after they have been discredited. *(p. 134)*

biased sampling   The tendency for groups to spend more time discussing shared information (information already known by all or most group members) than unshared information (information known by only one or a few group members). *(p. 318)*

bogus pipeline   A phony lie-detector device that is sometimes used to get respondents to give truthful answers to sensitive questions. *(p. 206)*

bogus pipeline technique   A procedure in which research participants are (falsely) led to believe that their responses will be verified by an infallible lie-detector. *(p. 32)*

brainstorming   A technique that attempts to increase the production of creative ideas by encouraging group members to speak freely without criticizing their own or others' contributions. *(p. 311)*

bystander effect   The effect whereby the presence of others inhibits helping. *(p. 406)*

catharsis   A reduction of the motive to aggress that is said to result from any imagined, observed, or actual act of aggression. *(p. 455)*

central route to persuasion   The process by which a person thinks carefully about a communication and is influenced by the strength of its arguments. *(p. 215)*

central traits   Traits that exert a powerful influence on overall impressions. *(p. 130)*

cognitive dissonance theory   The theory that holding inconsistent cognitions arouses psychological tension that people become motivated to reduce. *(p. 236)*

collective effort model   The theory that individuals will exert effort on a collective task to the degree that they think their individual efforts will be important, relevant, and meaningful for achieving outcomes that they value. *(p. 306)*

collectivism   A cultural orientation in which interdependence, cooperation, and social harmony take priority over personal goals. *(p. 267)*

communal relationship   A relationship in which the participants expect and desire mutual responsiveness to each other's needs. *(p. 367)*

companionate love   A secure, trusting, stable partnership. *(p. 370)*

compliance   Changes in behavior that are elicited by direct requests. *(p. 268)*

confederate   Accomplice of an experimenter who, in dealing with the real participants in an experiment, acts as if he or she is also a participant. *(p. 46)*

confirmation bias   The tendency to seek, interpret, and create information that verifies existing beliefs. *(p. 132)*

conformity   The tendency to change our perceptions, opinions, or behavior in ways that are consistent with group norms. *(p. 254)*

construct validity   The extent to which the measures used in a study measure the variables they were designed to measure and the manipulations in an experiment manipulate the variables they were designed to manipulate. *(p. 31)*

contact hypothesis   The theory that direct contact between hostile groups will reduce prejudice under certain conditions. *(p. 192)*

contingency model of leadership   The theory that leadership effectiveness is determined both by the personal characteristics of leaders and by the control afforded by the situation. *(p. 547)*

coping   Efforts to reduce stress. *(p. 570)*

correlational research   Research designed to measure the association between variables that are not manipulated by the researcher. *(p. 36)*

correlation coefficient   A statistical measure of the strength and direction of the association between two variables. *(p. 37)*

counterfactual thinking   The tendency to imagine alternative events or outcomes that might have occurred but did not. *(p. 117)*

covariation principle   A principle of attribution theory that holds that people attribute behavior to factors that are present when a behavior occurs and are absent when it does not. *(p. 114)*

cross-cultural research   Research designed to compare and contrast people of different cultures. *(p. 19)*

cross-race identification bias   The tendency for people to have difficulty identifying members of a race other than their own. *(p. 501)*

cultivation   The process by which the mass media (particularly television) construct a version of social reality for the public. *(p. 469)*

culture   A system of enduring meanings, beliefs, values, assumptions, institutions, and practices shared by a large group of people and transmitted from one generation to the next. *(p. 19)*

cycle of violence   The transmission of domestic violence across generations. *(p. 475)*

death qualification   A jury-selection procedure used in capital cases that permits judges to exclude prospective jurors who say they would not vote for the death penalty. *(p. 492)*

debriefing   A disclosure, made to participants after research procedures are completed, in which the researcher explains the purpose of the research, attempts to resolve any negative feelings, and emphasizes the scientific contribution made by the participants' involvement. *(p. 49)*

deception   In the context of research, a method that provides false information to participants. *(p. 46)*

deindividuation   The loss of a person's sense of individuality and the reduction of normal constraints against deviant behavior. *(p. 307)*

dependent variable   In an experiment, a factor that experimenters measure to see if it is affected by the independent variable. *(p. 42)*

depressive explanatory style   A habitual tendency to attribute negative events to causes that are stable, global, and internal. *(p. 583)*

desensitization   Reduction in emotion-related physiological reactivity in response to a stimulus. *(p. 468)*

dialecticism   An Eastern system of thought that accepts the coexistence of contradictory characteristics within a single person. *(p. 71)*

diffusion of responsibility   The belief that others will or should take the responsibility for providing assistance to a person in need. *(p. 409)*

discrimination   Behavior directed against persons because of their membership in a particular group. *(p. 148)*

displacement   Aggressing against a substitute target because aggressive acts against the source of the frustration are inhibited by fear or lack of access. *(p. 455)*

distraction-conflict theory   A theory that the presence of others will produce social facilitation effects only when those others distract from the task and create attentional conflict. *(p. 303)*

door-in-the-face technique   A two-step compliance technique in which an influencer prefaces the real request with one that is so large that it is rejected. *(p. 273)*

downward social comparison   The defensive tendency to compare ourselves with others who are worse off than we are. *(p. 86)*

egoistic   Motivated by the desire to increase one's own welfare. *(p. 399)*

elaboration   The process of thinking about and scrutinizing the arguments contained in a persuasive communication. *(p. 216)*

emotional aggression   Inflicting harm for its own sake. *(p. 437)*

emotion-focused coping   Cognitive and behavioral efforts to reduce the distress produced by a stressful situation. *(p. 590)*

empathy   Understanding or vicariously experiencing another individual's perspective and feeling sympathy and compassion for that individual. *(p. 395)*

empathy-altruism hypothesis   The proposition that empathic concern for a person in need produces an altruistic motive for helping. *(p. 401)*

endowment effect   The tendency for people to inflate the value of objects, goods, or services they already own. *(p. 562)*

equity theory   The theory that people are most satisfied with a relationship when the ratio between benefits and contributions is similar for both partners. *(p. 366)*

escalation effect   The condition in which commitments to a failing course of action are increased to justify investments already made. *(p. 317)*

evaluation apprehension theory   A theory that the presence of others will produce social facilitation effects only when those others are seen as potential evaluators. *(p. 303)*

evolutionary psychology   A subfield of psychology that uses the principles of evolution to understand human social behavior. *(p. 18)*

exchange relationship   A relationship in which the participants expect and desire strict reciprocity in their interactions. *(p. 367)*

excitation transfer   The process whereby arousal caused by one stimulus is added to arousal from a second stimulus and the combined arousal is attributed to the second stimulus. *(p. 371)*

expectancy theory   The theory that workers become motivated when they believe that their efforts will produce valued outcomes. *(p. 553)*

experiment   A form of research that can demonstrate causal relationships because (1) the experimenter has control over the events that occur and (2) participants are randomly assigned to conditions. *(p. 39)*

experimental realism The degree to which experimental procedures are involving to participants and lead them to behave naturally and spontaneously. *(p. 45)*

experimenter expectancy effects The effects produced when an experimenter's expectations about the results of an experiment affect his or her behavior toward a participant and thereby influence the participant's responses. *(p. 44)*

external validity The degree to which there can be reasonable confidence that the results of a study would be obtained for other people and in other situations. *(p. 44)*

facial electromyograph (EMG) An electronic instrument that records facial muscle activity associated with emotions and attitudes. *(p. 206)*

facial feedback hypothesis The hypothesis that changes in facial expression can lead to corresponding changes in emotion. *(p. 61)*

false-consensus effect The tendency for people to overestimate the extent to which others share their opinions, attributes, and behaviors. *(p. 116)*

foot-in-the-door technique A two-step compliance technique in which an influencer sets the stage for the real request by first getting a person to comply with a much smaller request. *(p. 270)*

frustration-aggression hypothesis The idea that (1) frustration always elicits the motive to aggress; and (2) all aggression is caused by frustration. *(p. 454)*

fundamental attribution error The tendency to focus on the role of personal causes and underestimate the impact of situations on other people's behavior. *(p. 118)*

general adaptation syndrome A three-stage process (alarm, resistance, and exhaustion) by which the body responds to stress. *(p. 575)*

good mood effect The effect whereby a good mood increases helping behavior. *(p. 417)*

graduated and reciprocated initiatives in tension-reduction (GRIT) A strategy for unilateral persistent efforts to establish trust and cooperation between opposing parties. *(p. 329)*

group Two or more persons perceived as related because of their interactions, membership in the same social category, or common fate. *(p. 148)*

group cohesiveness The extent to which forces push group members closer together, such as through feelings of intimacy, unity, and commitment to group goals. *(p. 299)*

group polarization The exaggeration of initial tendencies in the thinking of group members through group discussion. *(p. 313)*

group support systems Specialized interactive computer programs that are used to guide group meetings, collaborative work, and decision-making processes. *(p. 321)*

groupthink A group decision-making style characterized by an excessive tendency among group members to seek concurrence. *(p. 315)*

hard-to-get effect The tendency to prefer people who are highly selective in their social choices over those who are more readily available. *(p. 356)*

Hawthorne effect The finding that workers who were given special attention increased their productivity regardless of what actual changes were made in the work setting. *(p. 530)*

health psychology The study of physical health and illness by psychologists from various areas of specialization. *(p. 569)*

hostile attribution bias The tendency to perceive hostile intent in others. *(p. 461)*

hypothesis A testable prediction about the conditions under which an event will occur. *(p. 28)*

idiosyncrasy credits Interpersonal "credits" that a person earns by following group norms. *(p. 265)*

illusory correlation An overestimate of the association between variables that are only slightly or not at all correlated. *(p. 169)*

immune system A biological surveillance system that detects and destroys "nonself" substances that invade the body. *(p. 579)*

Implicit Association Test (IAT) A covert measure of unconscious attitudes derived from the speed at which people respond to pairings of concepts—such as black or white with good or bad. *(p. 207)*

implicit attitude An attitude, such as prejudice, that one is not aware of having. *(p. 207)*

implicit egotism A nonconscious form of self-enhancement. *(p. 82)*

implicit personality theory A network of assumptions people make about the relationships among traits and behaviors. *(p. 129)*

implicit racism Racism that operates unconsciously and unintentionally. *(p. 150)*

impression formation The process of integrating information about a person to form a coherent impression. *(p. 126)*

independent variable In an experiment, a factor that experimenters manipulate to see if it affects the dependent variable. *(p. 42)*

individualism A cultural orientation in which independence, autonomy, and self-reliance take priority over group allegiances. *(p. 267)*

industrial/organizational (I/O) psychology The study of human behavior in business and other organizational settings. *(p. 529)*

informational influence Influence that produces conformity when a person believes others are correct in their judgments. *(p. 257)*

information integration theory The theory that impressions are based on (1) perceiver dispositions; and (2) a weighted average of a target person's traits. *(p. 126)*

informed consent An individual's deliberate, voluntary decision to participate in research, based on the researcher's description of what will be required during such participation. *(p. 49)*

ingroup favoritism The tendency to discriminate in favor of ingroups over outgroups. *(p. 162)*

ingroups Groups with which an individual feels a sense of membership, belonging, and identity. *(p. 148)*

inoculation hypothesis The idea that exposure to weak versions of a persuasive argument increases later resistance to that argument. *(p. 233)*

inquisitorial model A dispute-resolution system in which a neutral investigator gathers evidence from both sides and presents the findings in court. *(p. 522)*

instrumental aggression Inflicting harm in order to obtain something of value. *(p. 437)*

insufficient deterrence A condition in which people refrain from engaging in a desirable activity, even when only mild punishment is threatened. *(p. 238)*

insufficient justification A condition in which people freely perform an attitude-discrepant behavior without receiving a large reward. *(p. 237)*

integrative agreement A negotiated resolution to a conflict in which all parties obtain outcomes that are superior to what they would have obtained from an equal division of the contested resources. *(p. 329)*

integrity tests Questionnaires designed to test a job applicant's honesty and character. *(p. 534)*

interactionist perspective An emphasis on how both an individual's personality and environmental characteristics influence behavior. *(p. 14)*

internal validity The degree to which there can be reasonable certainty that the independent variables in an experiment caused the effects obtained on the dependent variables. *(p. 43)*

interrater reliability The degree to which different observers agree on their observations. *(p. 33)*

intimate relationship A close relationship between two adults involving emotional attachment, fulfillment of psychological needs, or interdependence. *(p. 363)*

jigsaw classroom A cooperative learning method used to reduce racial prejudice through interaction in group efforts. *(p. 194)*

jury nullification The jury's power to disregard, or "nullify," the law when it conflicts with personal conceptions of justice. *(p. 512)*

kin selection Preferential helping of genetic relatives, which results in the greater likelihood that genes held in common will survive. *(p. 392)*

learned helplessness A phenomenon in which experience with an uncontrollable event creates passive behavior in the face of subsequent threats to well-being. *(p. 583)*

leniency bias The tendency for jury deliberation to produce a tilt toward acquittal. *(p. 515)*

loneliness A feeling of deprivation about existing social relations. *(p. 343)*

lowballing A two-step compliance technique in which the influencer secures agreement with a request but then increases the size of that request by revealing hidden costs. *(p. 272)*

matching hypothesis The proposition that people are attracted to others who are similar in physical attractiveness. *(p. 355)*

mere exposure effect The phenomenon whereby the more often people are exposed to a stimulus, the more positively they evaluate that stimulus. *(p. 345)*

mere presence theory The proposition that the mere presence of others is sufficient to produce social facilitation effects. *(p. 303)*

meta-analysis A set of statistical procedures used to review a body of evidence by combining the results of individual studies to measure the overall reliability and strength of particular effects. *(p. 46)*

mind perception The process by which people attribute humanlike mental states to various animate and inanimate objects, including other people. *(p. 106)*

minority influence The process by which dissenters produce change within a group. *(p. 264)*

misinformation effect The tendency for false post-event misinformation to become integrated into people's memory of an event. *(p. 502)*

modern racism A form of prejudice that surfaces in subtle ways when it is safe, socially acceptable, and easy to rationalize. *(p. 150)*

multicultural research Research designed to examine racial and ethnic groups within cultures. *(p. 19)*

mundane realism The degree to which the experimental situation resembles places and events in the real world. *(p. 45)*

need for affiliation The desire to establish and maintain many rewarding interpersonal relationships. *(p. 340)*

need for closure The desire to reduce cognitive uncertainty, which heightens the importance of first impressions. *(p. 131)*

need for cognition (NC) A personality variable that distinguishes people on the basis of how much they enjoy effortful cognitive activities. *(p. 230)*

negative state relief model The proposition that people help others in order to counteract their own feelings of sadness. *(p. 398)*

nonverbal behavior Behavior that reveals a person's feelings without words, through facial expressions, body language, and vocal cues. *(p. 107)*

normative influence Influence that produces conformity when a person fears the negative social consequences of appearing deviant. *(p. 258)*

normative model of leadership The theory that leadership effectiveness is determined by the amount of feedback and participation that leaders invite from workers. *(p. 548)*

norm of social responsibility A moral standard emphasizing that people should help those who need assistance. *(p. 420)*

obedience Behavior change produced by the commands of authority. *(p. 276)*

operational definition The specific procedures for manipulating or measuring a conceptual variable. *(p. 30)*

outgroup homogeneity effect The tendency to assume that there is greater similarity among members of outgroups than among members of ingroups. *(p. 167)*

outgroups Groups with which an individual does not feel a sense of membership, belonging, or identity. *(p. 148)*

overjustification effect The tendency for intrinsic motivation to diminish for activities that have become associated with reward or other extrinsic factors. *(p. 63)*

passionate love Romantic love characterized by high arousal, intense attraction, and fear of rejection. *(p. 370)*

peremptory challenge A means by which lawyers can exclude a limited number of prospective jurors without the judge's approval. *(p. 488)*

performance appraisal The process of evaluating an employee's work within the organization. *(p. 542)*

peripheral route to persuasion The process by which a person does not think carefully about a communication and is influenced instead by superficial cues. *(p. 215)*

personal attribution Attribution to internal characteristics of an actor, such as ability, personality, mood, or effort. *(p. 113)*

persuasion The process by which attitudes are changed. *(p. 214)*

pluralistic ignorance The state in which people in a group mistakenly think that their own individual thoughts, feelings, or behaviors are different from those of the others in the group. *(p. 408)*

polygraph A mechanical instrument that records physiological arousal from multiple channels; it is often used as a lie-detector test. *(p. 498)*

pornography Explicit sexual material. *(p. 471)*

posttraumatic stress disorder (PTSD) A condition in which a person experiences enduring physical and psychological symptoms after an extremely stressful event. *(p. 573)*

prejudice Negative feelings toward persons based on their membership in certain groups. *(p. 148)*

primacy effect The tendency for information presented early in a sequence to have more impact on impressions than information presented later. *(p. 130)*

priming The tendency for recently used or perceived words or ideas to come to mind easily and influence the interpretation of new information. *(p. 127)*

prisoner's dilemma A type of dilemma in which one party must make either cooperative or competitive moves in relation to another party. The dilemma is typically designed so that the competitive move appears to be in one's self-interest, but if both sides make this move, they both suffer more than if they had both cooperated. *(p. 323)*

private conformity The change of beliefs that occurs when a person privately accepts the position taken by others. *(p. 259)*

private self-consciousness A personality characteristic of individuals who are introspective, often attending to their own inner states. *(p. 78)*

proactive coping Up-front efforts to ward off or modify the onset of a stressful event. *(p. 590)*

problem-focused coping Cognitive and behavioral efforts to alter a stressful situation. *(p. 589)*

process loss The reduction in group performance due to obstacles created by group processes, such as problems of coordination and motivation. *(p. 310)*

prosocial behaviors Actions intended to benefit others. *(p. 391)*

psychological reactance The theory that people react against threats to their freedom by asserting themselves and perceiving the threatened freedom as more attractive. *(p. 233)*

psychoneuroimmunology (PNI) A subfield of psychology that examines the links among psychological factors, the brain and nervous system, and the immune system. *(p. 579)*

public conformity A superficial change in overt behavior without a corresponding change of opinion that is produced by real or imagined group pressure. *(p. 259)*

public self-consciousness A personality characteristic of individuals who focus on themselves as social objects, as seen by others. *(p. 78)*

racism Prejudice and discrimination based on a person's racial background, or institutional and cultural practices that promote the domination of one racial group over another. *(p. 147)*

random assignment A method of assigning participants to the various conditions of an experiment so that each participant in the experiment has an equal chance of being in any of the conditions. *(p. 39)*

random sampling A method of selecting participants for a study so that everyone in a population has an equal chance of being in the study. *(p. 36)*

realistic conflict theory The theory that hostility between groups is caused by direct competition for limited resources. *(p. 161)*

reciprocity A mutual exchange between what we give and receive—for example, liking those who like us. *(p. 356)*

relative deprivation Feelings of discontent aroused by the belief that one fares poorly compared with others. *(p. 161)*

resource dilemmas Social dilemmas involving how two or more people will share a limited resource. *(p. 324)*

scientific jury selection A method of selecting juries through surveys that yield correlations between demographics and trial-relevant attitudes. *(p. 490)*

self-awareness theory The theory that self-focused attention leads people to notice self-discrepancies, thereby motivating either an escape from self-awareness or a change in behavior. *(p. 76)*

self-concept The sum total of an individual's beliefs about his or her own personal attributes. *(p. 56)*

self-disclosure Revelations about the self that a person makes to others. *(p. 372)*

self-efficacy A person's belief that he or she is capable of the specific behavior required to produce a desired outcome in a given situation. *(p. 585)*

self-esteem An affective component of the self, consisting of a person's positive and negative self-evaluations. *(p. 72)*

self-fulfilling prophecy The process by which one's expectations about a person eventually lead that person to behave in ways that confirm those expectations. *(p. 135)*

self-handicapping Behaviors designed to sabotage one's own performance in order to provide a subsequent excuse for failure. *(p. 84)*

self-monitoring The tendency to change behavior in response to the self-presentation concerns of the situation. *(p. 93)*

self-perception theory The theory that when internal cues are difficult to interpret, people gain self-insight by observing their own behavior. *(p. 60)*

self-presentation Strategies people use to shape what others think of them. *(p. 91)*

self-schema A belief people hold about themselves that guides the processing of self-relevant information. *(p. 56)*

sentencing disparity Inconsistency of sentences for the same offense from one judge to another. *(p. 518)*

sexism Prejudice and discrimination based on a person's gender, or institutional and cultural practices that promote the domination of one gender over another. *(p. 147)*

sexual orientation A person's preference for members of the same sex (homosexuality), opposite sex (heterosexuality), or both sexes (bisexuality). *(p. 377)*

situational attribution Attribution to factors external to an actor, such as the task, other people, or luck. *(p. 113)*

sleeper effect A delayed increase in the persuasive impact of a noncredible source. *(p. 222)*

social categorization The classification of persons into groups on the basis of common attributes. *(p. 166)*

social cognition The study of how people perceive, remember, and interpret information about themselves and others. *(p. 17)*

social comparison theory The theory that people evaluate their own abilities and opinions by comparing themselves to others. *(p. 65)*

social dilemma A situation in which a self-interested choice by everyone will create the worst outcome for everyone. *(p. 323)*

social dominance orientation A desire to see one's ingroup as dominant over other groups and a willingness to adopt cultural values that facilitate oppression over other groups. *(p. 165)*

social exchange theory A perspective that views people as motivated to maximize benefits and minimize costs in their relationships with others. *(p. 364)*

social facilitation A process whereby the presence of others enhances performance on easy tasks but impairs performance on difficult tasks. *(p. 302)*

social identity model of deindividuation effects (SIDE) A model of group behavior that explains deindividuation effects as the result of a shift from personal identity to social identity. *(p. 309)*

social identity theory The theory that people favor ingroups over outgroups in order to enhance their self-esteem. *(p. 162)*

social impact theory The theory that social influence depends on the strength, immediacy, and number of source persons relative to target persons. *(p. 285)*

social learning theory The theory that behavior is learned through the observation of others as well as through the direct experience of rewards and punishments. *(p. 449)*

social loafing A group-produced reduction in individual output on tasks where contributions are pooled. *(p. 304)*

social neuroscience The study of the relationship between neural and social processes. *(p. 18)*

social norm A general rule of conduct reflecting standards of social approval and disapproval. *(p. 419)*

social perception A general term for the processes by which people come to understand one another. *(p. 102)*

social psychology The scientific study of how individuals think, feel, and behave in a social context. *(p. 5)*

social role theory The theory that small gender differences are magnified in perception by the contrasting social roles occupied by men and women. *(p. 175)*

social support The helpful coping resources provided by friends and other people. *(p. 597)*

stereotype A belief or association that links a whole group of people with certain traits or characteristics. *(p. 148)*

stereotype content model A model proposing that the relative status and competition between groups influence group stereotypes along the dimensions of competence and warmth. *(p. 177)*

stereotype threat The experience of concern about being evaluated based on negative stereotypes about one's group. *(p. 187)*

stress An unpleasant state of arousal in which people perceive the demands of an event as taxing or exceeding their ability to satisfy or alter those demands. *(p. 570)*

stressor Anything that causes stress. *(p. 571)*

structured interview An interview in which each job applicant is asked a standard set of questions and evaluated on the same criteria. *(p. 536)*

subjective well-being One's happiness, or life satisfaction, as measured by self-report. *(p. 606)*

subject variable A variable that characterizes pre-existing differences among the participants in a study. *(p. 42)*

subliminal presentation A method of presenting stimuli so faintly or rapidly that people do not have any conscious awareness of having been exposed to them. *(p. 178)*

sunk cost principle The economic rule of thumb that only future costs and benefits, not past commitments, should be considered in making a decision. *(p. 563)*

superordinate goal A shared goal that can be achieved only through cooperation among individuals or groups. *(p. 161)*

Terror Management Theory The theory that humans cope with the fear of their own death by constructing worldviews that help to preserve their self-esteem. *(p. 73)*

that's-not-all technique A two-step compliance technique in which the influencer begins with an inflated request, then decreases its apparent size by offering a discount or bonus. *(p. 273)*

theory An organized set of principles used to explain observed phenomena. *(p. 29)*

theory of planned behavior The theory that attitudes toward a specific behavior combine with subjective norms and perceived control to influence a person's actions. *(p. 212)*

threat-to-self-esteem model The theory that reactions to receiving assistance depend on whether help is perceived as supportive or threatening. *(p. 427)*

transactional leader A leader who gains compliance and support from followers primarily through goal setting and the use of rewards. *(p. 549)*

transactive memory A shared system for remembering information that enables multiple people to remember information together more efficiently than they could do so alone. *(p. 319)*

transformational leader A leader who inspires followers to transcend their own needs in the interest of a common cause. *(p. 549)*

triangular theory of love A theory proposing that love has three basic components—intimacy, passion, and commitment—that can be combined to produce eight subtypes. *(p. 369)*

two-factor theory of emotion The theory that the experience of emotion is based on two factors: physiological arousal and a cognitive interpretation of that arousal. *(p. 66)*

Type A personality A pattern of behavior characterized by extremes of competitive striving for achievement, a sense of time urgency, hostility, and aggression. *(p. 577)*

voir dire The pretrial examination of prospective jurors by the judge or opposing lawyers to uncover signs of bias. *(p. 488)*

weapon-focus effect The tendency for the presence of a weapon to draw attention and impair a witness's ability to identify the culprit. *(p. 500)*

weapons effect The tendency that the likelihood of aggression will increase by the mere presence of weapons. *(p. 459)*

what-is-beautiful-is-good stereotype The belief that physically attractive individuals also possess desirable personality characteristics. *(p. 350)*

References

Abelson, R. P. (1981). Psychological status of the script concept. *American Psychologist, 36,* 715–729.

Abrams, D. (2009). Social identity on a national scale: Optimal distinctiveness and young people's self-expression through musical preference. *Group Processes & Intergroup Relations, 12,* 303–317.

Abramson, L. Y., Metalsky, G. I., & Alloy, L. B. (1989). Hopelessness depression: A theory-based subtype of depression. *Psychological Review, 96,* 358–372.

Abshire, J., & Bernstein, B. H. (2003). Juror sensitivity to the cross-race effect. *Law and Human Behavior, 27,* 471–480.

Acevedo, B. P., & Aron, A. (2009). Does a long-term relationship kill romantic love? *Review of General Psychology, 13,* 59–65.

Acker, M., & Davis, M. H. (1992). Intimacy, passion, and commitment in adult romantic relationships: A test of the triangular theory of love. *Journal of Social and Personal Relationships, 9,* 21–50.

Adair, J. G. (1984). The Hawthorne effect: A reconsideration of the methodological artifact. *Journal of Applied Psychology, 69,* 334–345.

Adair, W. L., & Brett, J. M. (2005). The negotiation dance: Time, culture, and behavioral sequences in negotiation. *Organization Science, 16,* 33–51.

Adams, G., Garcia, D. M., Purdie-Vaughns, V., & Steele, C. M. (2006). The detrimental effects of a suggestion of sexism in an instruction situation. *Journal of Experimental Social Psychology, 42,* 602–615.

Adams, J., Parkinson, L., Sanson-Fisher, R. W., & Walsh, R. A. (2008). Enhancing self-report of adolescent smoking: The effects of bogus pipeline and anonymity. *Addictive Behaviors, 33,* 1291–1296.

Adams, J. S. (1965). Equity in social exchange. *Advances in Experimental Social Psychology, 2,* 267–299.

Adams, P. R., & Adams, G. R. (1984). Mount Saint Helens's ash-fall: Evidence for a disaster stress reaction. *American Psychologist, 39,* 252–260.

Ader, R. (Ed.). (2007). *Psychoneuroimmunology* (4th ed.). Burlington, MA: Elsevier.

Aderman, D. (1972). Elation, depression, and helping behavior. *Journal of Personality and Social Psychology, 24,* 91–101.

Adherents.com. (2009). Major religions of the world ranked by number of adherents. Retrieved September 20, 2009, from http://www.adherents.com/Religions_By_Adherents.html.

Adorno, T., Frenkel-Brunswik, E., Levinson, D., & Sanford, R. N. (1950). *The authoritarian personality.* New York: Harper.

Aggarwal, B. A. F., Liao, M., & Mosca, L. (2008). Physical activity as a potential mechanism through which social support may reduce cardiovascular disease risk. *Journal of Cardiovascular Nursing, 23,* 90–96.

Aggarwal, P., & O'Brien, C. L. (2008). Social loafing on group projects: Structural antecedents and effect on student satisfaction. *Journal of Marketing Education, 30,* 255–264.

Aguiar, P., Vala, J., Correia, I., & Pereira, C. (2008). Justice in our world and in that of others: Belief in a just world and reactions to victims. *Social Justice Research, 21,* 50–68.

Aharon, I., Etcoff, N., Ariely, D., Chabris, C. F., O'Connor, E., & Breiter, H. C. (2001). Beautiful faces have variable reward value: fMRI and behavioral evidence. *Neuron, 32,* 537–551.

Ahern, J., Galea, S., Hubbarde, A., & Syme, S. L. (2009). Neighborhood smoking norms modify the relation between collective efficacy and smoking behavior. *Drug and Alcohol Dependence, 100,* 138–145.

Ainsworth, M., Blehar, M. C., Waters, E., & Wall, S. (1978). *Patterns of attachment: A psychological study of the strange situation.* Hillsdale, NJ: Erlbaum.

Ajzen, I. (1991). The theory of planned behavior. *Organizational Behavior and Human Decision Processes, 50,* 179–211.

Ajzen, I., & Fishbein, M. (1977). Attitude-behavior relations: A theoretical analysis and review of empirical research. *Psychological Bulletin, 84,* 888–918.

Ajzen, I., & Fishbein, M. (2005). The influence of attitudes on behavior. In D. Albarracín, B. T. Johnson, & M. P. Zanna (Eds.), *The handbook of attitudes* (pp. 173–221). Hillsdale, NJ: Erlbaum.

Akimoto, S. A., & Sanbonmatsu, D. M. (1999). Differences in self-effacing behavior between European and Japanese Americans: Effect on competence evaluations. *Journal of Cross-Cultural Psychology, 30,* 159–177.

Albarracín, D., Gillette, J. C., Earl, A. N., Glasman, L. R., Durantini, M. R., & Ho, M.-H. (2005). A test of major assumptions about behavior change: A comprehensive look at the effects of passive and active HIV-prevention interventions since the beginning of the epidemic. *Psychological Bulletin, 131,* 856–897.

Albarracín, D., Johnson, B. T., & Zanna, M. P. (Eds.). (2005). *The handbook of attitudes.* Hillsdale, NJ: Erlbaum.

Albarracín, D., Johnson, B. T., Fishbein, M., & Muellerleile, P. A. (2001). Theories of reasoned action and planned behavior as models of condom use: A meta-analysis. *Psychological Bulletin, 127,* 142–161.

Albiero, P., Matricardi, G., Speltri, D., & Toso, D. (2009). The assessment of empathy in adolescence: A contribution to the Italian validation of the 'Basic Empathy Scale.' *Journal of Adolescence, 32,* 393–408.

Alexander, G. M. (2003). An evolutionary perspective of sex-typed toy preferences: Pink, blue, and the brain. *Archives of Sexual Behavior, 32,* 7–14.

Alexander, G. M., & Hines, M. (2002). Sex differences in response to children's toys in nonhuman primates *(Cercopithecus aethiops sabaeus). Evolution and Human Behavior, 23,* 467–479.

Alexander, N. (2008). The mediation metamodel: Understanding practice. *Conflict Resolution Quarterly, 26,* 97–122.

Alicke, M. D., & Largo, E. (1995). The role of the self in the false consensus effect. *Journal of Experimental Social Psychology, 31,* 28–47.

Allen, J. B., Kenrick, D. T., Linder, D. E., & McCall, M. A. (1989). Arousal and attribution: A response-facilitation alternative to misattribution and negative-reinforcement models. *Journal of Personality and Social Psychology, 57,* 261–270.

Allen, V. L. (1965). Situational factors in conformity. In L. Berkowitz (Ed.), *Advances in Experimental Social Psychology, 2,* 133–175.

Allen, V. L., & Levine, J. M. (1969). Consensus and conformity. *Journal of Experimental Social Psychology, 5,* 389–399.

Allen-Arave, W., Gurven, M., & Hill, K. (2008). Reciprocal altruism, rather than kin selection, maintains nepotistic food transfers on an Ache reservation. *Evolution and Human Behavior, 29,* 305–318.

Alliger, G. M., & Dwight, S. A. (2000). A meta-analytic investigation of the susceptibility of integrity tests to faking and coaching. *Educational and Psychological Measurement, 60,* 59–72.

Alliger, G. M., Lilienfeld, S. O., & Mitchell, K. E. (1996). The susceptibility of overt and covert integrity tests to coaching and faking. *Psychological Science, 7,* 32–39.

Alloy, L. B., Abramson, L. Y., Whitehouse, W. G., Hogan, M. E., Panzarella, C., & Rose, D. T. (2006). Prospective incidence of first onsets and recurrences of depression in individuals at high and low cognitive risk for depression. *Journal of Abnormal Psychology, 115,* 145–156.

Allport, F. H. (1924). *Social psychology.* Boston: Houghton Mifflin.

Allport, F. H., et al. (1953). The effects of segregation and the consequences of desegregation: A social science statement. *Minneapolis Law Review, 37,* 429–440.

Allport, G. W. (1954). *The nature of prejudice.* Reading, MA: Addison-Wesley.

Allport, G. W. (1985). The historical background of social psychology. In G. Lindzey & E. Aronson (Eds.), *Handbook of social psychology* (3rd ed., Vol. I, pp. 1–46). New York: Random House.

Allport, G. W., & Postman, L. J. (1947). *The psychology of rumor.* New York: Holt.

Alterovitz, S. S.-R., & Mendelsohn, G. A. (2009). Partner preferences across the life span: Online dating by older adults. *Psychology and Aging, 24,* 513–517.

Altman, I. (1973). Reciprocity of interpersonal exchange. *Journal for Theory of Social Behavior, 3,* 249–261.

Altman, I., & Taylor, D. A. (1973). *Social penetration: The development of interpersonal relationships.* New York: Holt, Rinehart and Winston.

Alvidrez, A., & Weinstein, R. S. (1999). Early teacher perceptions and later student academic achievement. *Journal of Educational Psychology, 91,* 731–746.

Alwin, D. F. (1990). Cohort replacement and changes in parental socialization values. *Journal of Marriage and the Family 52,* 347–360.

Amabile, T. M. (1996). *Creativity in context.* New York: Westview.

Amabile, T. M., Hill, K. G., Hennessey, B. A., & Tighe, E. M. (1994). The work preference inventory: Assessing intrinsic and extrinsic motivation orientations. *Journal of Personality and Social Psychology, 66,* 950–967.

Amato, P. R. (1983). Helping behavior in urban and rural environments: Field studies based on a taxonomic organization of helping episodes. *Journal of Personality and Social Psychology, 45,* 571–586.

Ambady, N., & Rosenthal, R. (1993). Half a minute: Predicting teacher evaluations from thin slices of nonverbal behavior and physical attractiveness. *Journal of Personality and Social Psychology, 64,* 431–441.

Ambrose, M. L., & Schminke, M. (2009). The role of overall justice judgments in organizational justice research: A test of mediation. *Journal of Applied Psychology, 94,* 491–500.

American Psychological Association. (2002). Ethical principles of psychologists and code of conduct. *American Psychologist, 57,* 1060–1073.

American Psychological Association. (2008, October 7). *Stress in America 2008 Survey: Executive summary.* Washington, DC: American Psychological Association. Retrieved August 15, 2009, from http://apahelpcenter.mediaroom.com/index.php?s=pageC.

Ames, D. R., Flynn, F. J., & Weber, E. U. (2004). It's the thought that counts: On perceiving how helpers decide to lend a hand. *Personality and Social Psychology Bulletin, 30,* 461–474.

Amnesty International. (2009). http://www.amnesty.org.

Amodio, D. (2008). The social neuroscience of intergroup relations. *European Review of Social Psychology, 19,* 1–54.

Amodio, D. (2009). Intergroup anxiety effects on the control of racial stereotypes: A psychoneuroendocrine analysis. *Journal of Experimental Social Psychology, 45,* 60–67.

Amodio, D. M., & Devine, P. G. (2006). Stereotyping and evaluation in implicit race bias: Evidence for independent constructs and unique effects on behavior. *Journal of Personality and Social Psychology, 91,* 652–661.

Amodio, D. M., Kubota, J. T., Harmon-Jones, E., & Devine, P. G. (2007). Alternative mechanisms for regulating racial responses according to internal vs. external cues. *Social Cognitive and Affective Neuroscience, 1, 1–26.*

Andersen, S. M., & Chen, S. (2002). The relational self: An interpersonal social-cognitive theory. *Psychological Review, 109,* 619–645.

Anderson, C. A. (1989). Temperature and aggression: Ubiquitous effects of heat on occurrence of human violence. *Psychological Bulletin, 106,* 74–96.

Anderson, C. A. (2001). Heat and violence. *Current Directions in Psychological Science, 10,* 33–38.

Anderson, C. A. (2004). An update on the effects of playing violent video games. *Journal of Adolescence, 27,* 113–122.

Anderson, C. A., & Anderson, K. B. (1996). Violent crime rate statistics in philosophical context: A destructive testing approach to heat and southern culture of violence effects. *Journal of Personality and Social Psychology, 70,* 740–756.

Anderson, C. A., Anderson, K. B., & Deuser, W. E. (1996). Examining an affective framework: Weapon and temperature effects on aggressive thoughts, affect, and attitudes. *Personality and Social Psychology Bulletin, 22,* 366–376.

Anderson, C. A., Anderson, K. B., Dorr, N., DeNeve, K. M., & Flanagan, M. (2000). Temperature and aggression. In M. P. Zanna (Ed.), *Advances in experimental social psychology* (Vol. 32, pp. 63–133). San Diego, CA: Academic Press.

Anderson, C. A., Berkowitz, L., Donnerstein, E., Huesmann, L. R., Johnson, J. D., Linz, D., Malamuth, N. M., & Wartella, E. (2003). The influence of media violence on youth. *Psychological Science in the Public Interest, 4,* 81–110.

Anderson, C. A., & Bushman, B. J. (2002a). The effects of media violence on society. *Science, 295,* 2377–2379.

Anderson, C. A., & Bushman, B. J. (2002b). The general aggression model: An integrated social-cognitive model of human aggression. *Annual Review of Psychology, 53,* 27–51.

Anderson, C. A., Carnagey, N. L., Flanagan, M., Benjamin, A. J., Eubanks, J., & Valentine, J. C. (2004). Violent video games: Specific effects of violent content on aggressive thoughts and behavior. *Advances in Experimental Social Psychology, 36,* 199–249.

Anderson, C. A., & Huesmann, L. R. (2007). Human aggression: A social-cognitive review. In M. A. Hogg & J. Cooper (Eds.), *The Sage handbook of social psychology* (pp. 259–287). London: Sage.

Anderson, C. A., Lepper, M. R., & Ross, L. (1980). Perseverance of social theories: The role of explanation in the persistence of discredited information. *Journal of Personality and Social Psychology, 39,* 1037–1049.

Anderson, C. A., & Sechler, E. S. (1986). Effects of explanation and counterexplanation on the development and use of social theories. *Journal of Personality and Social Psychology, 50,* 24–34.

Anderson Cooper 360 Degrees. (2009, June 2). Air France jet wreckage found; abortion doctor's murder suspect in court; shooting suggests homegrown terror. Retrieved August 10, 2009, from http://transcripts.cnn.com/TRANSCRIPTS/0906/02/acd.02.html.

Anderson, J. L., Crawford, C. B., Nadeau, J., & Lindberg, T. (1992). Was the Duchess of Windsor right? A cross-cultural review of the socioecology of ideals of female body shape. *Ethology and Sociobiology, 13,* 197–227.

Anderson, N. H. (1965). Averaging versus adding as a stimulus combination rule in impression formation. *Journal of Experimental Social Psychology, 70,* 394–400.

Anderson, N. H. (1968). Likableness ratings of 555 personality-trait words. *Journal of Personality and Social Psychology, 9,* 272–279.

Anderson, N. H., & Hubert, S. (1963). Effects of concomitant verbal recall on order effects in personality impression formation. *Journal of Verbal Learning and Verbal Behavior, 2,* 379–391.

Andreasson, P. B. (1987). On the social psychology of the stock market: Aggregate attributional effects and the regressiveness of prediction. *Journal of Personality and Social Psychology, 53,* 490–496.

Antonio, A. L., Chang, M. J., Hakuta, K., Kenny, D. A., Levin, S., & Milem, J. F. (2004). Effects of racial diversity on complex thinking in college students. *Psychological Science, 15,* 507–510.

Apfelbaum, E. P., Pauker, K., Ambady, N., Sommers, S. R., & Norton, M. I. (2008). Learning (not) to talk about race: When older children underperform in social categorization. *Developmental Psychology, 44,* 1513–1518.

Apodaca v. Oregon, 406 U.S. 404 (1972).

Archer, J. (2000). Sex differences in aggression between heterosexual partners: A meta-analytic review. *Psychological Bulletin, 126,* 651–680.

Archer, J. (2002). Sex differences in physically aggressive acts between heterosexual partners: A meta-analytic review. *Aggression and Violent Behavior: A Review Journal, 7,* 313–351.

Archer, J. (2004). Sex differences in aggression in real-world settings: A meta-analytic review. *Review of General Psychology, 8,* 291–322.

Archer, J. (2006). Testosterone and human aggression: An evaluation of the challenge hypothesis. *Neuroscience and Biobehavioral Reviews, 30,* 319–345.

Arendt, H. (1963). *Eichmann in Jerusalem: A report on the banality of evil.* New York: Viking.

Arkes, H. R., & Ayton, P. (1999). The sunk cost and Concorde effects: Are humans less rational than lower animals? *Psychological Bulletin, 125,* 591–600.

Arkin, R. M. (1981). Self-presentation styles. In J. T. Tedeschi (Ed.), *Impression management theory and social psychological research* (pp. 311–333). New York: Academic Press.

Armor, D. A., & Taylor, S. E. (1998). Situated optimism: Specific outcome expectancies and self-regulation. *Advances in Experimental Social Psychology, 30,* 309–379.

Armour, S. (1998, February 17). Office ethics: Teams make it hard to tattle. *USA Today,* p. 6B.

Aron, A., Aron, E. N., & Smollan, D. (1992). Inclusion of Other in the Self Scale and the structure of interpersonal closeness. *Journal of Personality and Social Psychology, 63,* 596–612.

Aron, A., Dutton, D. G., Aron, E. N., & Iverson, A. (1989). Experiences of falling in love. *Journal of Social and Personal Relationships, 6,* 243–257.

Aron, A., Norman, C. C., Aron, E. N., McKenna, C., & Heyman, R. E. (2000). Couples' shared participation in novel and arousing activities and experienced relationship quality. *Journal of Personality and Social Psychology, 78,* 273–284.

Aron, A., & Westbay L. (1996). Dimensions of the prototype of love. *Journal of Personality and Social Psychology, 70,* 535–551.

Aronson, E. (1969). The theory of cognitive dissonance: A current perspective. *Advances in Experimental Social Psychology, 4,* 1–34.

Aronson, E. (1992). Stateways can change folkways. In R. M. Baird & S. E. Rosenbaum (Eds.), *Bigotry, prejudice, and hatred: Definitions, causes, and solutions* (pp. 185–201). Buffalo, NY: Prometheus.

Aronson, E. (1999). Dissonance, hypocrisy, and the self-concept. In E. Harmon-Jones & J. Mills (Eds.), *Cognitive dissonance: Progress on a pivotal theory in social psychology* (pp. 103–126). Washington, DC: American Psychological Association.

Aronson, E. (2004). Reducing hostility and building compassion: Lessons from the jigsaw classroom. In A. G. Miller (Ed.), *The social psychology of good and evil* (pp. 469–488). New York: Guilford.

Aronson, E., & Carlsmith, J. M. (1963). Effect of severity of threat on the devaluation of forbidden behavior. *Journal of Abnormal and Social Psychology, 66,* 584–588.

Aronson, E., & Carlsmith, J. M. (1968). Experimentation in social psychology. In G. Lindzey & E. Aronson (Eds.), *Handbook of social psychology* (2nd ed., Vol. 2, pp. 1–79). Reading, MA: Addison-Wesley.

Aronson, E., & Cope, V. (1968). My enemy's enemy is my friend. *Journal of Personality and Social Psychology, 8,* 8–12.

Aronson, E., & Linder, D. (1965). Gain and loss of esteem as determinants of interpersonal attractiveness. *Journal of Experimental Social Psychology, 1,* 156–172.

Aronson, E., Blaney, N., Stephan, C., Sikes, J., & Snapp, M. (1978). *The jigsaw classroom.* Beverly Hills, CA: Sage.

Aronson, J., & Inzlicht, M. (2004). The ups and downs of attributional ambiguity: Stereotype vulnerability and the academic self-knowledge of African American college students. *Psychological Science, 15,* 829–836.

Aronson, J., Lustina, M. J., Good, C., Keough, K., Steele, C. M., & Brown, J. (1999). When white men can't do math: Necessary and sufficient factors in stereotype threat. *Journal of Experimental Social Psychology, 35,* 29–46.

Arriaga, P., Esteves, F., Carneiro, P., & Monteiro, M. B. (2006). Violent computer games and their effects on state hostility and physiological arousal. *Aggressive Behavior, 32,* 358–371.

Arterberry, M. E., Cain, K. M., & Chopko, S. A. (2007). Collaborative problem solving in five-year-old children: Evidence of social facilitation and social loafing. *Educational Psychology, 27,* 577–596.

Arthur, W., Day, E. D., McNelly, T. L., & Edens, P. S. (2003). A meta-analysis of the criterion-related validity of assessment center dimensions. *Personnel Psychology, 56,* 125–154.

Asch, S. E. (1946). Forming impressions of personality. *Journal of Abnormal and Social Psychology, 41,* 258–290.

Asch, S. E. (1951). Effects of group pressure upon the modification and distortion of judgments. In H. Guetzkow (Ed.), *Groups, leadership, and men.* Pittsburgh, PA: Carnegie Press.

Asch, S. E. (1955, November). Opinions and social pressure. *Scientific American,* pp. 31–35.

Asch, S. E. (1956). Studies of independence and conformity: A minority of one against a unanimous majority. *Psychological Monographs, 70,* 416.

Asch, S. E., & Zukier, H. (1984). Thinking about persons. *Journal of Personality and Social Psychology, 46,* 1230–1240.

Ashton-James, C. E., Maddux, W. W., Galinsky, A. D., & Chartrand, T. L. (2009). Who I am depends on how I feel: The role of affect in the expression of culture. *Psychological Science, 20,* 340–346.

Askenasy, H. (1978). *Are we all Nazis?* Secaucus, NJ: Lyle Stuart.

Aspinwall, L. G., & Taylor, S. E. (1992). Modeling cognitive adaptation: A longitudinal investigation of the impact of individual differences and coping on college adjustment and performance. *Journal of Personality and Social Psychology, 63,* 989–1003.

Aspinwall, L. G., & Taylor, S. E. (1993). The effects of social comparison direction, threat, and self-esteem on affect, self-evaluation, and expected success. *Journal of Personality and Social Psychology, 64,* 708–722.

Aspinwall, L. G., & Taylor, S. E. (1997). A stitch in time: Self-regulation and proactive coping. *Psychological Bulletin, 121,* 417–436.

Associated Press. (2009, July 4). Man who tried to rescue suicidal OC woman dies. The Associated Press State and Local Wire.

Auerbach, S. M., Kiesler, D. J., Strentz, T., Schmidt, J. A., & Serio, C. D. (1994). Interpersonal impacts and adjunctment to the stress of simulated captivity: An empirical test of the Stockholm Syndrome. *Journal of Social and Clinical Psychology, 13,* 207–221.

Avolio, B. J., Walumbwa, F. O., & Weber, T. J. (2009). Leadership: Current theories, research, and future directions. *Annual Review of Psychology, 60,* 421–444.

Axsom, D. (1989). Cognitive dissonance and behavior change in psychotherapy. *Journal of Experimental Social Psychology, 25,* 234–252.

Axsom, D., & Cooper, J. (1985). Cognitive dissonance and psychotherapy: The role of effort justification in inducing weight loss. *Journal of Experimental Social Psychology, 21,* 149–160.

Axtell, R. E. (1993). *Do's and taboos around the world* (3rd ed.). New York: John Wiley.

Ayduk, Ö., Gyurak, A., & Luerssen, A. (2008, May). Individual differences in the rejection-aggression link in the hot sauce paradigm: The case of rejection sensitivity. *Journal of Experimental Social Psychology, 44,* 775–782.

Babcock, L., & Laschever, S. (2003). *Women don't ask: Negotiation and the gender divide.* Princeton, NJ: Princeton University Press.

Bagemihl, B. (1999). *Biological exuberance: Animal homosexuality and natural diversity.* New York: St. Martin's Press.

Bagozzi, R. P., & Moore, D. J. (1994). Public service advertisements: Emotions and empathy guide prosocial behavior. *Journal of Marketing, 58,* 56–70.

Bahrick, H. P., Hall, L. K., & Berger, S. A. (1996). Accuracy and distortion in memory for high school grades. *Psychological Science, 7,* 265–271.

Bailenson, J. N., & Yee, N. (2005). Digital chameleons: Automatic assimilation of nonverbal gestures in immersive virtual environments. *Psychological Science, 16,* 814–819.

Bailey, A. A., & Hurd, P. L. (2005). Finger length ratio (2D:4D) correlates with physical aggression in men but not in women. *Biological Psychology, 68,* 215–222.

Bailey, C. A., & Ostrov, J. M. (2008). Differentiating forms and functions of aggression in emerging adults: Associations with hostile attribution biases and normative beliefs. *Journal of Youth and Adolescence, 37,* 713–722.

Bailey, D. S., & Taylor, S. P. (1991). Effects of alcohol and aggressive disposition on human physical aggression. *Journal of Research in Personality, 25,* 334–342.

Bailey, E. J. (2008). *Black America, body beautiful: How the African American image is changing fashion, fitness, and other industries.* Westport, CT: Praeger.

Bailey, J. M., Dunne, M. P., & Martin, N. G. (2000). Genetic and environmental influences on sexual orientation and its correlates in an Australian twin sample. *Journal of Personality and Social Psychology 78,* 524–536.

Bailey, J. M., & Pillard, R. C. (1991). A genetic study of male sexual orientation. *Archives of General Psychiatry, 48,* 1089–1096.

Bailey, J. M., Pillard, R. C., Neale, M. C., & Agyei, Y. (1993). Heritable factors influence sexual orientation in women. *Archives of General Psychiatry, 50,* 217–223.

Bailey, J. M., & Zucker, K. J. (1995). Childhood sex-typed behavior and sexual orientation: A conceptual analysis and quantitative review. *Developmental Psychology, 31,* 43–55.

Balcetis, E., & Dunning, D. (2006). See what you want to see: Motivational influences on visual perception. *Journal of Personality and Social Psychology, 91,* 612–625.

Balcetis, E., & Dunning, D. (2007). Cognitive dissonance and the perception of natural environments. *Psychological Science, 18,* 917–921.

Baldus, D. C., Woodworth, G., & Pulaski, C. A. (1990). *Equal justice and the death penalty: A legal and empirical analysis.* Boston: Northeastern University Press.

Baldwin, A. S., Rothman, A. J., Hertel, A. W., Linde, J. A., Jeffery, R. W., Finch, E. A., & Lando, H. A. (2006). Specifying the determinants of the initiation and maintenance of behavior change: An examination of self-efficacy, satisfaction, and smoking cessation. *Health Psychology, 25,* 626–634.

Baldwin, M., & Fehr, B. (1995). On the instability of attachment style ratings. *Personal Relationships, 2,* 247–261.

Baldwin, M. W., & Sinclair, L. (1996). Self-esteem and "if . . . then" contingencies of interpersonal acceptance. *Journal of Personality and Social Psychology, 71,* 1130–1141.

Bales, R. F. (1958). Task roles and social roles in problem-solving groups. In E. E. Maccoby, T. M. Newcomb, & E. L. Hartley (Eds.), *Readings in social psychology* (3rd ed., pp. 437–447). New York: Holt.

Ballew v. Georgia, 435 U.S. 223 (1978).

Banaji, M. R., & Steele, C. M. (1989). Alcohol and self-evaluation: Is a social cognition approach beneficial? *Social Cognition, 7,* 137–151.

Bandler, J., & Varchaver, N. (2009, May 11). How Bernie did it. *Fortune, 159*(10).

Bandura, A. (1973). *Aggression: A social learning analysis.* Englewood Cliffs, NJ: Prentice-Hall.

Bandura, A. (1977). *Social learning theory.* Englewood Cliffs, NJ: Prentice-Hall.

Bandura, A. (1983). Psychological mechanisms of aggression. In R. G. Geen & E. I. Donnerstein (Eds.), *Aggression: Theoretical and empirical reviews: Vol. l. Theoretical and methodological issues* (pp. 1–40). New York: Academic Press.

Bandura, A. (1997). *Self-efficacy: The exercise of control.* New York: W. H. Freeman.

Bandura, A. (1999). A sociocognitive analysis of substance abuse: An agentic perspective. *Psychological Science, 10,* 214–218.

Bandura, A., Ross, R., & Ross, S. (1961). Transmission of aggression through imitation of aggressive models. *Journal of Abnormal and Social Psychology, 63,* 575–582.

Banuazizi, A., & Movahedi, S. (1975). Interpersonal dynamics in a simulated prison: A methodological analysis. *American Psychologist, 30,* 152–160.

Baray, G., Postmes, T., & Jetten, J. (2009). When "I" equals "We": Exploring the relation between social and personal identity of extreme right-wing political party members. *British Journal of Social Psychology, 48,* 625–647.

Barber, N. (2006). Why is violent crime so common in the Americas? *Aggressive Behavior, 32,* 442–450.

Barclay, G., & Tavares, C. (2003). *International comparisons of criminal justice statistics 2001.* London: Home Office Statistical Bulletin.

Barden, J., & Petty, R. E. (2008). The mere perception of elaboration creates attitude certainty: Exploring the thoughtfulness heuristic. *Journal of Personality and Social Psychology, 95,* 489–509.

Bargh, J. A. (1997). The automaticity of everyday life. In R. S. Wyer (Ed.), *The automaticity of everyday life: Advances in social cognition* (Vol. 10, pp. 1–61). Mahwah, NJ: Erlbaum.

Bargh, J. A., & Chartrand, T. L. (2000). The mind in the middle: A practical guide for priming and automaticity research. In H. T. Reis and C. M. Judd (Eds.), *Handbook of research methods in social and personality psychology* (pp. 253–285). New York: Cambridge University Press.

Bargh, J. A., & McKenna, K. Y. A. (2004). The internet and social life. *Annual Review of Psychology, 55,* 1–20.

Bargh, J. A., & Morsella, E. (2009). Unconscious behavioral guidance systems. In C. Agnew, D. Carlston, W. Graziano, & J. Kelly (Eds.), *Then a miracle occurs: Focusing on behavior in social psychological theory and research.* New York: Oxford University Press.

Bargh, J. A., & Pietromonaco, P. (1982). Automatic information processing and social perception: The influence of trait information presented outside of conscious awareness on impression formation. *Journal of Personality and Social Psychology, 43,* 437–449.

Bargh, J. A., Chaiken, S., Govender, R., & Pratto, F. (1992). The generality of the automatic attitude activation effect. *Journal of Personality and Social Psychology, 62,* 893–912.

Bargh, J. A., Chaiken, S., Raymond, P., & Hymes, C. (1996). The automatic evaluation effect: Unconditional automatic attitude activation with a pronunciation task. *Journal of Experimental Social Psychology, 31,* 104–128.

Bargh, J. A., Chen, M., & Burrows, L. (1996). Automaticity of social behavior: Direct effects of trait construct and stereotype activation on action. *Journal of Personality and Social Psychology, 71,* 230–244.

Bargh, J. A., Lombardi, W. J., & Higgins, E. T. (1988). Automaticity of chronically accessible constructs in person x situation effects on person perception: It's just a matter of time. *Journal of Personality and Social Psychology, 55,* 599–605.

Barlett, C. P., Vowels, C. L., & Saucier, D. A. (2008). Meta-analyses of the effects of media images on men's body-image concerns. *Journal of Social and Clinical Psychology, 27,* 279–310.

Barling, J., Kelloway, K., & Frone, M. (2005). *Handbook of occupational stress.* Los Angeles: Sage.

Barnes, C. M., & Wagner, D. T. (2009). Changing to daylight saving time cuts into sleep and increases workplace injuries. *Journal of Applied Psychology, 94,* 1305–1317.

Barnes Nacoste, R. (1994). If empowerment is the goal . . . : Affirmative action and social interaction. *Basic and Applied Social Psychology, 15,* 87–112.

Barnes, R. D., Ickes, W., & Kidd, R. F. (1979). Effects of the perceived intentionality and stability of another's dependency on helping behavior. *Personality and Social Psychology Bulletin, 5,* 367–372.

Baron, A. S., & Banaji, M. R. (2006). The development of implicit attitudes: Evidence of race evaluations from ages 6 and 10 and adulthood. *Psychological Science, 17,* 53–58.

Baron, J., & Miller, J. G. (2000). Limiting the scope of moral obligations to help: A cross-cultural investigation. *Journal of Cross Cultural Psychology, 31,* 703–725.

Baron, R. A. (1997). The sweet smell of helping: Effects of pleasant ambient fragrance on prosocial behavior in shopping malls. *Journal of Personality and Social Psychology, 23*(5), 498–503.

Baron, R. A., & Ball, R. L. (1974). The aggression-inhibiting influence of nonhostile behavior. *Journal of Experimental Social Psychology, 10,* 23–33.

Baron, R. A., & Richardson, D. R. (1994). *Human aggression* (2nd ed.). New York: Plenum.

Baron, R. S. (1986). Distraction-conflict theory: Progress and problems. In L. Berkowitz (Ed.), *Advances in experimental social psychology* (Vol. 19, pp. 1–40). Orlando, FL: Academic Press.

Baron, R. S. (2005). So right it's wrong: Groupthink and the ubiquitous nature of polarized group decision making. In M. P. Zanna (Ed.), *Advances in experimental social psychology* (pp. 219–253). San Diego: Elsevier Academic Press.

Baron, R. S., Hoppe, S. I., Kao, C. F., Brunsman, B., Linneweh, B., & Rogers, D. (1996). Social corroboration and opinion extremity. *Journal of Experimental Social Psychology, 32,* 537–560.

Barreto, M., Ryan, M. K., & Schmitt, M. T. (2009). *The glass ceiling in the 21st century: Understanding barriers to gender equality.* Washington, DC: American Psychological Association.

Barrett, H. C., Todd, P. M., Miller, G. F., & Blythe, P. W. (2005). Accurate judgments of intention from motion cues alone: A cross-cultural study. *Evolution and Human Behavior, 26,* 313–331.

Barrick, M. R., & Mount, M. K. (1996). Effects of impression management and self-deception on the predictive validity of personality constructs. *Journal of Applied Psychology, 81,* 261–272.

Bartholow, B. D., & Heinz, A. (2006). Alcohol and aggression without consumption: Alcohol cues, aggressive thoughts, and hostile perception bias. *Psychological Science, 17,* 30–37.

Bartholow, B. D., Anderson, C. A., Carnagey, N. L., & Benjamin, A. J., Jr. (2005). Interactive effects of life experience and situational cues on aggression: The weapons priming effect in hunters and nonhunters. *Journal of Experimental Social Psychology, 41,* 48–60.

Bartholow, B. D., Dickter, C. L., & Sestir, M. A. (2006). Stereotype activation and control of race bias: Cognitive control of inhibition and its impairment by alcohol. *Journal of Personality and Social Psychology, 90,* 272–287.

Barthrop, R. W., Lazarus, L., Luckhurst, E., Kiloh, L. G., & Penny, R. (1977). Depressed lymphocyte function after bereavement. *Lancet, 1,* 834–839.

Bartsch, R. A., Burnett, T., Diller, T. R., & Rankin-Williams, E. E. (2000). Gender representation in television commercials: Updating an update. *Sex Roles, 43,* 735–743.

Bartsch, R. A., Judd, C. M., Louw, D. A., Park, B., & Ryan, C. S. (1997). Cross-national outgroup homogeneity: United States and South African stereotypes. *South African Journal of Psychology, 27,* 166–170.

Bashore, T. R., & Rapp, P. E. (1993). Are there alternatives to traditional polygraph procedures? *Psychological Bulletin, 113,* 3–22.

Bass, B. M. (1985). *Leadership and performance beyond expectations.* New York: Free Press.

Bass, B. M. (1998). *Transformational leadership: Industry, military, and educational impact.* Mahwah, NJ: Erlbaum.

Bass, B. M., & Avolio, B. J. (1990). *Manual: The multifactor leadership questionnaire.* Palo Alto, CA: Consulting Psychologists Press.

Bass, B. M., & Riggio, R. E. (2006). *Transformational leadership* (2nd ed.). Mahwah, NJ: Erlbaum.

Bass, B. M., & Steidlmeier, P. (1999). Ethics, character, and the authentic transformational leadership behavior. *Leadership Quarterly, 10,* 181–217.

Bassili, J. N. (2003). The minority slowness effect: Subtle inhibitions in the expression of views not shared by others. *Journal of Personality and Social Psychology, 84,* 261–276.

Bassili, J. N., & Provencal, A. (1988). Perceiving minorities: A factor-analytic approach. *Personality and Social Psychology Bulletin, 14,* 5–15.

Batson, C. D. (1991). *The altruism question.* Hillsdale, NJ: Erlbaum.

Batson, C. D. (2009). Empathy and altruism. In C. R. Snyder & S. J. Lopez (Eds.), *Oxford handbook of positive psychology* (2nd ed., pp. 417–426). New York: Oxford University Press.

Batson, C. D., Cochran, P. J., Biederman, M. F., Blosser, J. L., Ryan, M. J., & Vogt, B. (1978). Failure to help when in a hurry: Callousness or conflict? *Personality and Social Psychology Bulletin, 4,* 97–101.

Batson, C. D., Eklund, J. H., Chermok, V. L., Hoyt, J. L., & Ortiz, B. G. (2007). An additional antecedent of empathic concern: Valuing the welfare of the person in need. *Journal of Personality and Social Psychology, 93,* 65–74.

Batson, C. D., Lishner, D. A., Cook, J., & Sawyer, S. (2005). Similarity and nurturance: Two possible sources of empathy for strangers. *Basic and Applied Social Psychology, 27,* 15–25.

Batson, C. D., O'Quin, K., Fultz, J., Vanderplas, M., & Isen, A. M. (1983). Influence of self-reported distress and empathy on egoistic versus altruistic motivation to help. *Journal of Personality and Social Psychology, 45,* 706–718.

Batson, C. D., & Powell, A. A. (2003). Altruism and prosocial behavior. In T. Millon & M. J. Lerner (Eds.), *Handbook of psychology: Personality and social psychology* (Vol. 5, pp. 463–484). New York: Wiley.

Batson v. Kentucky, 476 U.S. 79 (1986).

Bauer, I., Wrosch, C., & Jobin, J. (2008). I'm better off than most other people: The role of social comparisons for coping with regret in young adulthood and old age. *Psychology and Aging, 23,* 800–811.

Bauer, T. N., Maertz, C. P., Dolen, M. R., & Campion, M. A. (1998). Longitudinal assessment of applicant reactions to employment testing and test outcome feedback. *Journal of Applied Psychology, 83,* 892–903.

Baugh, S. G., & Graen, G. B. (1997). Effects of team gender and racial composition on perceptions of team performance in cross-functional teams. *Group and Organization Management, 22,* 366–383.

Baum, A. (Ed.). (1984). Social psychology and cigarette smoking [Special issue]. *Journal of Applied Social Psychology, 14*(3).

Baumeister, R. F. (1982). A self-presentational view of social phenomena. *Psychological Bulletin, 91,* 3–26.

Baumeister, R. F. (1984). Choking under pressure: Self-consciousness and paradoxical effects of incentives on skillful performance. *Journal of Personality and Social Psychology, 46,* 610–620.

Baumeister, R. F. (1991). *Escaping the self.* New York: Basic Books.

Baumeister, R. F. (2000). Gender differences in erotic plasticity: The female sex drive as socially flexible and responsive. *Psychological Bulletin, 126,* 347–374.

Baumeister, R. F., & Leary, M. R. (1995). The need to belong: Desire for interpersonal attachments as a fundamental human motivation. *Psychological Bulletin, 117,* 497–529.

Baumeister, R. F., & Scher, S. J. (1988). Self-defeating behavior patterns among normal individuals: Review and analysis of common self-destructive tendencies. *Psychological Bulletin, 104,* 3–22.

Baumeister, R. F., & Tice, D. M. (1984). Role of self-presentation and choice in cognitive dissonance under forced compliance: Necessary or sufficient causes? *Journal of Personality and Social Psychology, 46,* 5–13.

Baumeister, R. F., & Vohs, K. D. (Eds.). (2004). *Handbook of self-regulation: Research, theory, and applications.* New York: Guilford.

Baumeister, R. F., Bratslavsky, E., Finkenauer, C., & Vohs, K. D. (2001). Bad is stronger than good. *Review of General Psychology, 5,* 323–370.

Baumeister, R. F., Bushman, B. J., & Campbell, W. K. (2000). Self-esteem, narcissism, and aggression: Does violence result from low self-esteem or from threatened egotism? *Current Directions in Psychological Science, 9,* 26–29.

Baumeister, R. F., Campbell, J. D., Krueger, J. I., & Vohs, K. D. (2003). Does high self-esteem cause better performance, interpersonal success, happiness, or healthier lifestyles? *Psychological Science in the Public Interest, 4,* 1–44.

Baumeister, R. F., Chesner, S. P., Sanders, P. S., & Tice, D. M. (1988). Who's in charge here? Group leaders do lend help in emergencies. *Personality and Social Psychology Bulletin, 14,* 17–22.

Baumeister, R., Stillwell, A. M., & Hetherington, T. F. (1994). Guilt: An interpersonal approach. *Psychological Bulletin, 115,* 243–267.

Baumgartner, F. R., De Bouf, S. L., & Boydstun, A. E. (2008). *The decline of the death penalty and the discovery of innocence.* New York: Cambridge University Press.

Baumrind, D. (1997). Necessary distinctions. *Psychological Inquiry, 8,* 176–229.

Baxter, L. A. (1987). Self-disclosure and disengagement. In V. J. Derleg & J. H. Berg (Eds.), *Self-disclosure: Theory, research, and therapy* (pp. 155–174). New York: Plenum.

Bazerman, M. H., & Neale, M. A. (1992). *Negotiating rationally.* New York: Free Press.

BBC. (2006, July 31). UEFA issues new anti-racism rules. Retrieved June 9, 2006, from http://news.bbc.co.uk/sport2/hi/football/europe/5232208.stm.

Beaman, A. L., Klentz, B., Diener, E., & Svanum, S. (1979). Objective self-awareness and transgression in children: A field study. *Journal of Personality and Social Psychology, 37,* 1835–1846.

Beal, D. J., Cohen, R. R., Burke, M. J., & McLendon, C. L. (2003, December). Cohesion and performance in groups: A meta-analytic clarification of construct relations. *Journal of Applied Psychology, 88,* 989–1004.

Beardsley, T. (1999, October). Truth or consequences. *Scientific American,* pp. 21, 24.

Beaton, E. A., Schmidt, L. A., Schulkin, J., Antony, M. M., Swinson, R. P., & Hall, G. B. (2008). Different neural responses to stranger and personally familiar faces in shy and bold adults. *Behavioral Neuroscience, 122,* 704–709.

Becker, F. D. (1981). *Workspace.* New York: Praeger.

Beckerman, S., & Valentine, P. (Eds.). (2002). *Cultures of multiple fathers: The theory and practice of partible paternity in lowland South America.* Gainesville: University Press of Florida.

Becker, S. W., & Eagly, A. H. (2004). The heroism of women and men. *American Psychologist, 59,* 163–178.

Bedau, H., & Cassell, P. (Eds.). (2004). *Debating the death penalty: Should America have capital punishment?* New York: Oxford University Press.

Bègue, L., Subra, B., Arvers, P., Muller, D., Bricout, V., & Zorman, M. (2009). A message in a bottle: Extrapharmacological effects of alcohol on aggression. *Journal of Experimental Social Psychology, 45,* 137–142.

Beidel, D. C., & Turner, S. M. (1998). *Shy children, phobic adults: Nature and treatment of social phobia.* Washington, DC: American Psychological Association.

Beilock, S. L., & Carr, T. H. (2001). On the fragility of skilled performance: What governs choking under pressure? *Journal of Experimental Psychology: General, 130,* 701–725.

Beitchman, J. H., Baldassarra, L., Mik, H., De Luca, V., King, N., Bender, D., Ehtesham, S., & Kennedy, J. L. (2006). Serotonin transporter polymorphisms and persistent, persuasive childhood aggression. *American Journal of Psychiatry, 163,* 1103–1105.

Bell, A. P., Weinberg, M. S., & Hammersmith, S. K. (1981). *Sexual preference: Its development in men and women.* Bloomington: Indiana University Press.

Bell, D. C. (2001). Evolution of parental caregiving. *Personality and Social Psychology Review, 5,* 216–229.

Bell, J., Grekul, J., Lamba, N., Minas, C., & Harrell, W. A. (1995). The impact of cost on student helping behavior. *Journal of Social Psychology, 135,* 49–56.

Belmore, S. M. (1987). Determinants of attention during impression formation. *Journal of Experimental Psychology: Learning, Memory, and Cognition, 13,* 480–489.

Belsky J. (1993). Etiology of child maltreatment: A developmental-ecological analysis. *Psychological Bulletin, 114,* 413–434.

Bem, D. J. (1965). An experimental analysis of self-persuasion. *Journal of Experimental Social Psychology, 1,* 199–218.

Bem, D. J. (1967). Self-perception: An alternative interpretation of cognitive dissonance phenomena. *Psychological Review, 74,* 183–200.

Bem, D. J. (1972). Self-perception theory. In L. Berkowitz (Ed.), *Advances in experimental social psychology* (Vol. 6, pp. 1–62). New York: Academic Press.

Bem, D. J. (1996). Exotic becomes erotic: A developmental theory of sexual orientation. *Psychological Review, 103,* 320–335.

Bem, D. J. (2000). Exotic becomes erotic: Interpreting the biological correlates of sexual orientation. *Archives of Sexual Behavior, 29,* 531–548.

Benjamin, L. T., & Simpson, J. A. (2009). The power of the situation: The impact of Milgram's obedience studies on personality and social psychology. *American Psychologist, 64,* 12–19.

Benjet, C., & Kazdin, A. E. (2003). Spanking children: The controversies, findings and new directions. *Clinical Psychology Review, 23,* 197–224.

Bennett, J. C. (1991). The irrationality of the catharsis theory of aggression as justification for educators' support of interscholastic football. *Perceptual and Motor Skills, 72,* 415–418.

Bennett, S., Farrington, D. P., & Huesmann, L. R. (2005). Explaining gender differences in crime and violence: The importance of social cognitive skills. *Aggression and Violent Behavior, 10,* 263–288.

Benson, H. (1993). The relaxation response. In D. Goleman & J. Gurin (Eds.), *Mind body medicine: How to use your mind for better health* (pp. 233–257). Yonkers, NY: Consumer Reports Books.

Benson, P. L., Karabenick, S. A., & Lerner, R. M. (1976). Pretty pleases: The effects of physical attractiveness, race, and sex on receiving help. *Journal of Experimental Social Psychology, 12,* 409–415.

Benton, R. B., Ross, D. F., Bradshaw, E., Thomas, W. N., & Bradshaw, G. S. (2005). Eyewitness memory is still not common sense: Comparing jurors, judges, and law enforcement to eyewitness experts. *Applied Cognitive Psychology, 20,* 115–129.

Ben-Zeev, T., Fein, S., & Inzlicht, M. (2005). Arousal and stereotype threat. *Journal of Experimental Social Psychology, 41,* 174–181.

Berdahl, J. L., & Anderson, C. (2005). Men, women, and leadership centralization in groups over time. *Group Dynamics: Theory, Research, and Practice, 9,* 45–57.

Berg, J. H., & McQuinn, R. D. (1986). Attraction and exchange in continuing and noncontinuing dating relationships. *Journal of Personality and Social Psychology, 50,* 942–952.

Berghuis, J. P., & Stanton, A. L. (2002). Adjustment to a dyadic stressor: A longitudinal study of coping and depressive symptoms in infertile couples over an insemination attempt. *Journal of Consulting and Clinical Psychology, 70,* 433–438.

Berglas, S., & Jones, E. E. (1978). Drug choice as a self-handicapping strategy in response to noncontingent success. *Journal of Personality and Social Psychology, 36,* 405–417.

Berkman, L., & Syme, S. L. (1979). Social networks, host resistance, and mortality: A nine-year follow-up study of Alameda County residents. *American Journal of Epidemiology, 109,* 186–204.

Berkowitz, L. (1968). Impulse, aggression, and the gun. *Psychology Today, 2*(4), 18–22.

Berkowitz, L. (1972). Social norms, feelings, and other factors affecting helping and altruism. In L. Berkowitz (Ed.), *Advances in experimental social psychology* (Vol. 6, pp. 63–108). New York: Academic Press.

Berkowitz, L. (1993). *Aggression: Its causes, consequences, and control.* New York: McGraw-Hill.

Berkowitz, L. (1998). Affective aggression: The role of stress, pain, and negative affect. In R. G. Geen & E. Donnerstein (Eds.), *Human aggression: Theories, research, and implications for social policy* (pp. 49–72). San Diego: Academic Press.

Berkowitz, L. (2008). On the consideration of automatic as well as controlled psychological processes in aggression. *Aggressive Behavior, 34,* 117–129.

Berkowitz, L., & Donnerstein, E. (1982). External validity is more than skin deep: Some answers to criticisms of laboratory experiments. *American Psychologist, 37,* 245–257.

Berkowitz, L., & LePage, A. (1967). Weapons as aggression-eliciting stimuli. *Journal of Personality and Social Psychology, 7,* 202–207.

Bermeitinger, C., Goelz, R., Johr, N., Neumann, M., Ecker, U., & Doerr, R. (2009). The hidden persuaders break into the tired brain. *Journal of Experimental Social Psychology, 45,* 320–326.

Bernardin, H. J., Cooke, D. K., & Villanova, P. (2000). Conscientiousness and agreeableness as predictors of rating leniency. *Journal of Applied Psychology, 85,* 232–236.

Bernhard, H., Fischbacher, U., & Fehr, E. (2006). Parochial altruism in humans. *Nature, 442,* 912–915.

Bernhardt, P. C., Dabbs, J. M., Fielden, J. A., & Lutter, C. D. (1998). Testosterone changes during vicarious experiences of winning and losing among fans at sporting events. *Physiology and Behavior, 65,* 59–62.

Berns, G. S., Chappelow, J., Zink, C. F., Pagnoni, G., Martin-Skurski, M. E., & Richards, J. (2005). Neurobiological correlates of social conformity and independence during mental rotation. *Biological Psychiatry, 58,* 245–253.

Bernsten, D. (2009). *Involuntary autobiographical memories: An introduction to the unbidden past.* New York: Cambridge University Press.

Berry, C. M., Sackett, P. R., & Wiemann, S. (2007). A review of recent developments in integrity test research. *Personnel Psychology, 60,* 271–301.

Berry, D. S., & Zebrowitz-McArthur, L. (1986). Perceiving character in faces: The impact of age-related craniofacial changes in social perception. *Psychological Bulletin, 100,* 3–18.

Berry, J. W. (1979). A cultural ecology of social behavior. *Advances in Experimental Social Psychology, 12,* 177–206.

Berry, J. W., Poortinga, Y. H., Segall, M. H., & Dasen, P. R. (1992). *Cross-cultural psychology: Research and application.* Cambridge, UK: Cambridge University Press.

Berscheid, E. (1966). Opinion change and communicator-communicatee similarity and dissimilarity. *Journal of Personality and Social Psychology, 4,* 670–680.

Berscheid, E., Dion, K., Walster, E., & Walster, G. W. (1971). Physical attractiveness and dating choice: A test of the matching hypothesis. *Journal of Experimental Social Psychology, 7,* 173–189.

Berscheid, E., & Meyers, S. A. (1996). A social categorical approach to a question about love. *Personal Relationships, 3,* 19–43.

Berscheid, E., & Reis, H. T. (1998). Attraction and close relationships. In D. Gilbert, S. Fiske, & G. Lindzey (Eds.), *Handbook of social psychology* (4th ed.). New York: McGraw-Hill.

Berscheid, E., & Regan, P. (2004). *The psychology of interpersonal relationships.* Upper Saddle River, NJ: Prentice-Hall.

Berscheid, E., Snyder, M., & Omoto, A. M. (1989). The relationship closeness inventory: Assessing the closeness of interpersonal relationships. *Journal of Personality and Social Psychology, 57,* 792–807.

Berscheid, E., & Walster, E. (1974). A little bit about love. In T. Huston (Ed.), *Foundations of interpersonal attraction* (pp. 355–381). New York: Academic Press.

Berscheid, E., Walster, E., & Campbell, R. (1972). *Grow old along with me.* Unpublished manuscript, Department of Psychology, University of Minnesota.

Bersoff, D. N., & Ogden, D. W. (1987). In the Supreme Court of the United States: *Lockhart v. McCree. American Psychologist, 42,* 59–68.

Bessenoff, G. R. (2006). Can the media affect us? Social comparison, self-discrepancy, and the thin ideal. *Psychology of Women Quarterly, 30,* 239–251.

Bettencourt, B. A., & Dorr, N. (1998). Cooperative interaction and intergroup bias: Effects of numerical representation and cross-cut role assignment. *Personality and Social Psychology Bulletin, 24,* 1276–1293.

Bettencourt, B. A., Molix, L., Talley, A. E., Sheldon, K. M. (2006). Psychological need satisfaction through social roles. In T. Postmes & J. Jetten (Eds.), *Individuality and the group: Advances in social identity* (pp. 196–214). Thousand Oaks, CA: Sage.

Bettencourt, B. A., Talley, A., Benjamin, A. J., & Valentine, J. (2006). Personality and aggressive behavior under provoking and neutral conditions: A meta-analytic review. *Psychological Bulletin, 132,* 751–777.

Beu, D. S., & Buckley, M. R. (2004). This is war: How the politically astute achieve crimes of obedience through the use of moral disengagement. *Leadership Quarterly, 15,* 551–568.

Beyer, S. (1990). Gender differences in the accuracy of self-evaluations of performance. *Journal of Personality and Social Psychology, 59,* 960–970.

Bhatt, S., Mbwana, J., Adeyemo, A., Sawyer, A., Hailu, A., & VanMeter, J. (2009). Lying about facial recognition: An fMRI study. *Brain and Cognition, 69,* 382–390.

Bickman, L. (1974). The social power of a uniform. *Journal of Applied Social Psychology, 4,* 47–61.

Binning, J. F., Goldstein, M. A., Garcia, M. F., & Scatteregia, J. H. (1988). Effects of preinterview impressions on questioning strategies in same- and opposite-sex employment interviews. *Journal of Applied Psychology, 73,* 30–37.

Birkett, M., Espelage, D. L., & Koenig, B. (2009). LGB and questioning students in schools: The moderating effects of homophobic bullying and school climate on negative outcomes. *Journal of Youth and Adolescence, 38,* 989–1000.

Bishara, A. J., & Payne, B. K. (2009). Multinomial process tree models of control and automaticity in weapon misidentification. *Journal of Experimental Social Psychology, 45,* 524–534.

Bizer, G., Krosnick, J., Holbrook, A., Wheeler, S., Rucker, D., & Petty, R. E. (2004). The impact of personality on cognitive, behavioral, and affective political processes: The effects of need to evaluate. *Journal of Personality, 72,* 995–1027.

Bizumic, B., Reynolds, K. J., Turner, J. C., Bromhead, D., & Subasic, E. (2009). The role of the group in individual functioning: School identification and the psychological well-being of staff and students. *Applied Psychology: An International Review, 58,* 171–192.

Blaine, B., Crocker, J., & Major, B. (1995). The unintended negative consequences of sympathy for the stigmatized. *Journal of Applied Social Psychology, 25,* 889–905.

Blair, I. V. (2002). The malleability of automatic stereotypes and prejudice. *Personality and Social Psychology Review, 6,* 242–261.

Blair, I. V., Park, B., & Bachelor, J. (2003). Understanding intergroup anxiety: Are some people more anxious than others? *Group Processes and Intergroup Relations, 6,* 151–169.

Blanchard, A. L., & Henle, C. A. (2008). Correlates of different forms of cyberloafing: The role of norms and external locus of control. *Computers in Human Behavior, 24,* 1067–1084.

Blanton, H., & Jaccard, J. (2006). Arbitrary metrics in psychology. *American Psychologist, 61,* 27–41.

Blanton, H., & Jaccard, J. (2008). Unconscious racism: A concept in pursuit of a measure. *Annual Review of Sociology, 34,* 277–297.

Blanton, H., Jaccard, J., Gonzales, P. M., & Christie, C. (2006). Decoding the implicit association test: Implications for criterion prediction. *Journal of Experimental Social Psychology, 42,* 192–212.

Blanton, H., Jaccard, J., Klick, J., Mellers, B., Mitchell, G., & Tetlock, P. E. (2009). Strong claims and weak evidence: Reassessing the predictive validity of the IAT. *Journal of Applied Psychology, 94,* 567–582.

Blascovich, J., Mendes, W. B., Hunter, S. B., & Salomon, K. (1999). Social "facilitation" as challenge and threat. *Journal of Personality and Social Psychology, 77,* 68–77.

Blascovich, J., Spencer, S. J., Quinn, D., & Steele, C. (2001). African Americans and high blood pressure: The role of stereotype threat. *Psychological Science, 12,* 225–229.

Blass, T. (1991). Understanding behavior in the Milgram obedience experiment: The role of personality, situations, and their interactions. *Journal of Personality and Social Psychology, 60,* 398–413.

Blass, T. (1992). The social psychology of Stanley Milgram. *Advances in Experimental Social Psychology, 25,* 227–329.

Blass, T. (1999). The Milgram paradigm after 35 years: Some things we now know about obedience to authority. *Journal of Applied Social Psychology, 25,* 955–978.

Blass, T. (2004). *The man who shocked the world.* New York: Basic Books.

Blass, T. (2009). From New Haven to Santa Clara: A historical perspective on the Milgram obedience experiments. *American Psychologist, 64,* 37–45.

Bleich, A., Gelkopf, M., & Solomon, Z. (2003). Exposure to terrorism, stress-related mental health symptoms, and coping behaviors among a nationally representative sample in Israel. *Journal of the American Medical Association, 290,* 612–620.

Bless, H., Schwarz, N., & Wieland, R. (1996). Mood and stereotyping: The impact of category membership and individuating information. *European Journal of Social Psychology, 26,* 935–959.

Bloom, A. (1981). *The linguistic shaping of thought.* Hillsdale, NJ: Erlbaum.

Bluemke, M., & Friese, M. (2008). Reliability and validity of the Single-Target IAT (ST-IAT): Assessing automatic affect towards multiple attitude objects. *European Journal of Social Psychology, 38,* 977–997.

Bobocel, D. R., Son Hing, L. S., Davey, L. M., Stanley, D. J., & Zanna, M. P. (1998). Justice-based opposition to social policies: Is it genuine? *Journal of Personality and Social Psychology, 75,* 653–669.

Bochner, S. (1994). Cross-cultural differences in the self-concept: A test of Hofstede's individualism/collectivism distinction. *Journal of Cross Cultural Psychology, 25,* 273–283.

Bochner, S., & Insko, C. A. (1966). Communicator discrepancy, source credibility, and opinion change. *Journal of Personality and Social Psychology, 4,* 614–621.

Bodenhausen, G. V. (1990). Stereotypes as judgmental heuristics: Evidence of circadian variations in discrimination. *Psychological Science, 1,* 319–322.

Bodenhausen, G. V., & Hugenberg, K. (2009). Attention, perception, and social cognition. In F. Strack & J. Förster (Eds.), *Social cognition: The basis of human interaction* (pp. 1–22). Philadelphia: Psychology Press.

Bodenhausen, G. V., & Macrae, C. N. (1998). Stereotype activation and inhibition. In R. S. Wyer, Jr. (Ed.), *Stereotype activation and inhibition: Advances in social cognition* (Vol. 11, pp. 1–52). Mahwah, NJ: Erlbaum.

Bodenhausen, G. V., Macrae, C. N., & Hugenberg, K. (2003). Social cognition. In T. Millon & M. J. Lerner (Eds.), *Handbook of psychology: Personality and social psychology* (Vol. 5., pp. 257–282). New York: Wiley.

Bogaert, S., Boone, C., & Declerck, C. (2008). Social value orientation and cooperation in social dilemmas: A review and conceptual model. *British Journal of Social Psychology, 47,* 453–480.

Bogart, L. M., & Helgeson, V. S. (2000). Social comparisons among women with breast cancer: A longitudinal investigation. *Journal of Applied Social Psychology, 30,* 547–575.

Boldero, J., & Francis, J. (2000). The relation between self-discrepancies and emotion: The moderating roles of self-guide importance, location relevance, and social self-domain centrality. *Journal of Personality and Social Psychology, 78,* 38–52.

Boldizar, J. P., Perry, D. G., & Perry, L. (1989). Outcome values and aggression. *Child Development, 60,* 571–579.

Bolger, N., DeLongis, A., Kessler, R. C., & Schilling, E. A. (1989). Effects of daily stress and negative mood. *Journal of Personality and Social Psychology, 57,* 808–818.

Bonanno, G. A. (2004). Loss, trauma, and human resilience: Have we underestimated the human capacity to thrive after extremely aversive events? *American Psychologist, 59,* 20–28.

Bond, C. F., & DePaulo, B. M. (2008). Individual differences in judging deception: Accuracy and bias. *Psychological Bulletin, 134,* 477–492.

Bond, C. F., Jr., & Titus, L. T. (1983). Social facilitation: A metaanalysis of 241 studies. *Psychological Bulletin, 94,* 265–292.

Bond, C., & DePaulo, B. (2006). Accuracy of deception judgments. *Personality and Social Psychology Review, 10,* 214–234.

Bond, R., & Smith, P. B. (1996). Culture and conformity: A metaanalysis of studies using Asch's (1952b, 1956) line judgment task. *Psychological Bulletin, 119,* 111–137.

Boninger, D. S., Brock, T. C., Cook, T. D., Gruder, C. L., & Romer, D. (1990). Discovery of reliable attitude change persistence resulting from a transmitter tuning set. *Psychological Science, 1,* 268–271.

Boninger, D. S., Krosnick, J. A., & Berent, M. K. (1995). Origins of attitude importance: Self-interest, social identification, and value relevance. *Journal of Personality and Social Psychology, 68,* 61–80.

Bonner, B. L., & Baumann, M. R. (2008). Informational intra-group influence: The effects of time pressure and group size. *European Journal of Social Psychology, 38,* 46–66.

Bonner, B. L., Baumann, M. R., Lehn, A. K., Pierce, D. M., & Wheeler, E. C. (2006). Modeling collective choice: Decision-making on complex intellective tasks. *European Journal of Social Psychology, 36,* 617–633.

Bono, J. E., & Anderson, M. H. (2005). The advice and influence networks of transformational leaders. *Journal of Applied Psychology, 90,* 1306–1314.

Bono, J. E., & Judge, T. A. (2004). Personality and transformational and transactional leadership: A meta-analysis. *Journal of Applied Psychology, 89,* 901–910.

Bonta, B. D. (1997). Cooperation and competition in peaceful societies. *Psychological Bulletin, 121,* 299–320.

Book, A. S., Starzyk, K. B., & Qunisey, V. L. (2001). The relationship between testosterone and aggression: A meta-analysis. *Aggression and Violent Behavior, 6,* 579–599.

Borduin, C. M., Schaeffer, C. M., & Heiblum, N. (2009). A randomized clinical trial of multisystemic therapy with juvenile sexual offenders: Effects on youth social ecology and criminal activity. *Journal of Consulting and Clinical Psychology, 77,* 26–37.

Borger, J. (2003, July 10). White House "lied about Saddam threat." *Guardian* (London), p. 11.

Borges, B., Gigerenzer, G., & Goldstein, D. (1999). Can ignorance beat the stock market? In G. Gigerenzer, P. Todd & the ABC Research Group (Eds.), *Simple heuristics that make us smart.* New York: Oxford University Press.

Borgida, E., & Fiske, S. T. (Eds.). (2007). *Psychological science in court: Beyond common knowledge.* Oxford, UK: Blackwell.

Borkenau, P., Mauer, N., Riemann, R., Spinath, F. M., & Angleitner, A. (2004). Thin slices of behavior as cues of personality and intelligence. *Journal of Personality and Social Psychology, 86,* 599–614.

Borman, W. C., Hanson, M. A., & Hedge, J. W. (1997). Personnel selection. *Annual Review of Psychology, 48,* 299–337.

Borman, W. C., White, L. A., & Dorsey, D. W. (1995). Effects of ratee task performance and interpersonal factors on supervisor and peer performance ratings. *Journal of Applied Psychology, 80,* 168–177.

Bornstein, R. F. (1989). Exposure and affect: Overview and metaanalysis of research, 1968–1987. *Psychological Bulletin, 106,* 265–289.

Bornstein, R. F. (1994). Dependency as a social cue: A meta-analytic review of research on the dependency–helping relationship. *Journal of Research in Personality, 28,* 182–213.

Bornstein, R. F., & D'Agostino, P. R. (1992). Stimulus recognition and the mere exposure effect. *Journal of Personality and Social Psychology, 63,* 545–552.

Bornstein, B. H., Wiener, R. L., Schopp, R., & Willborn, S. L. (Eds.). (2008). *Civil juries and civil justice: Psychological and legal perspectives.* New York: Springer.

Borntrager, C., Davis, J. L., Bernstein, A., & Gorman, H. (2009). A cross-national perspective on bullying. *Child and Youth Care Forum, 38,* 121–134.

Bosson, J. K., Johnson, A. B., Niederhoffer, K., & Swann, W. B., Jr. (2006). Interpersonal chemistry through negativity: Bonding by sharing negative attitudes about others. *Personal Relationships, 13,* 135–150.

Bosson, J. K., Pinel, E. C., & Thompson, J. K. (2008). The affective consequences of minimizing women's body image concerns. *Psychology of Women Quarterly, 32,* 257–266.

Boswell, W. R., Shipp, A. J., Payne, S. C., & Culbertson, S. S. (2009). Changes in newcomer job satisfaction over time: Examining the pattern of honeymoons and hangovers. *Journal of Applied Psychology, 94,* 844–858.

Bottoms, B. L., & Davis, S. L. (1997). The creation of satanic ritual abuse. *Journal of Social and Clinical Psychology, 16,* 112–132.

Boucher, H. C., Peng, K., Shi, J., & Wang, L. (2009). Culture and implicit self-esteem: Chinese are 'good' and 'bad' at the same time. *Journal of Cross-Cultural Psychology, 40,* 24–45.

Bowlby, J. (1988). *A secure base.* New York: Basic Books.

Bowler, M. C., & Woehr, D. J. (2006). A meta-analytic evaluation of the impact of dimension and exercise factors on assessment center ratings. *Journal of Applied Psychology, 91,* 1114–1124.

Boxer, P., Huesmann, L., Bushman, B. J., O'Brien, M., & Moceri, D. (2009). The role of violent media preference in cumulative developmental risk for violence and general aggression. *Journal of Youth and Adolescence, 38,* 417–428.

Boyes, A. D., & Fletcher, G. J. O. (2007). Meta-awareness of bias in intimate relationships. *Journal of Personality and Social Psychology, 92,* 286–306.

Boysen, S. T., & Himes, G. T. (1999). Current issues and emerging theories in animal cognition. *Annual Review of Psychology, 50,* 683–705.

Bradbury, T. N. (Ed.). (1998). *The developmental course of marital dysfunction.* New York: Cambridge University Press.

Bradbury, T. N., & Fincham, F. D. (1992). Attributions and behavior in marital interaction. *Journal of Personality and Social Psychology, 63,* 613–628.

Brader, T. (2006). *Campaigning for hearts and minds: How emotional appeals in political ads work.* Chicago: University of Chicago Press.

Bradfield, A. L., Wells, G. L., & Olson, E. A. (2002). The damaging effect of confirming feedback on the relation between eyewitness certainty and identification accuracy. *Journal of Applied Psychology, 87,* 112–120.

Branscombe, N. R., & Wann, D. L. (1994). Collective self-esteem consequences of outgroup derogation when a valued social identity is on trial. *European Journal of Social Psychology, 24,* 641–657.

Bray, R. M., Johnson, D., & Chilstrom, J. T., Jr. (1982). Social influence by group members with minority opinions: A comparison of Hollander & Moscovici. *Journal of Personality and Social Psychology, 43,* 78–88.

Bray, R. M., Struckman-Johnson, C., Osborne, M., McFarlane, J., & Scott, J. (1978). The effects of defendant status on decisions of student and community juries. *Social Psychology, 41,* 256–260.

Brean, H. (1958, March 31). What hidden sell is all about. *Life,* pp. 104–114.

Brehm, J. W. (1956). Post-decision changes in desirability of alternatives. *Journal of Abnormal and Social Psychology, 52,* 384–389.

Brehm, S. S., & Brehm, J. W. (1981). *Psychological reactance: A theory of freedom and control.* New York: Academic Press.

Bremner, J. G. (2002). The nature of imitation by infants. *Infant Behavior and Development, 25,* 65–67.

Brendgen, M., Dionne, G., Girard, A., Boivin, M., Vitaro, F., & Pérusse, D. (2005). Examining genetic and environmental effects on social aggression: A study of 6-year-old twins. *Child Development, 76,* 930–946.

Bressan, P., & Martello, M. F. D. (2002). Talis Pater, Talis Filius: Perceived resemblance and the belief in genetic relatedness. *Psychological Science, 13,* 213–218.

Brett, J. M., & Gelfand, M. (2006). A cultural analysis of the underlying assumptions of negotiation theory. In L. L. Thompson (Ed.), *Negotiation theory and research* (pp. 173–201). Madison, CT: Psychological Press.

Brett, J. M., & Stroh, L. K. (2003). Working 61 plus hours a week: Why do managers do it? *Journal of Applied Psychology, 88,* 67–78.

Brett, J. M., Shapiro, D. L., & Lytle, A. L. (1998). Breaking the bonds of reciprocity in negotiations. *Academy of Management Journal, 41,* 410–424.

Brewer, M. B. (2007). The importance of being we: Human nature and intergroup relations. *American Psychologist, 62,* 728–738.

Brewer, M. B., & Caporael, L. R. (2006). An evolutionary perspective on social identity: Revisiting groups. In M. Schaller (Ed.), *Evolution and social psychology* (pp. 143–161). Madison, CT: Psychosocial Press.

Brewer, M. B., & Feinstein, A. S. H. (1999). Dual processes in the cognitive representation of persons and social categories. In S. Chaiken & Y. Trope (Eds.), *Dual-process theories in social psychology* (pp. 255–270). New York: Guilford.

Brewer, M. B., & Gaertner, S. L. (2004). Toward reduction of prejudice: Intergroup contact and social categorization. In M. B. Brewer & M. Hewstone (Eds.), *Self and social identity* (pp. 298–318). Malden, MA: Blackwell.

Brewer, N., & Williams, K. D. (Eds.). (2005). *Psychology and law: An empirical perspective.* New York: Guilford.

Brewer, N., Harvey, S., & Semmler, C. (2004). Improving comprehension of jury instructions with audio-visual presentation. *Applied Cognitive Psychology, 18,* 765–776.

Brickman, P., Coates, D., & Janoff-Bulman, R. J. (1978). Lottery winners and accident victims: Is happiness relative? *Journal of Personality and Social Psychology, 36,* 917–927.

Brockner, J. (1983). Low self-esteem and behavioral plasticity: Some implications. In L. Wheeler & P. Shaver (Eds.), *Review of personality and social psychology* (Vol. 4, pp. 237–271). Beverly Hills, CA: Sage.

Brockner, J., & Wiesenfeld, B. M. (1996). An integrative frame-work for explaining reactions to decisions: Interactive effects of outcomes and procedures. *Psychological Bulletin, 120,* 189–208.

Brodish, A. B., & Devine, P. G. (2009). The role of performance-avoidance goals and worry in mediating the relationship between stereotype threat and performance. *Journal of Experimental Social Psychology, 45,* 180–185.

Brodish, A. B., Brazy, P. C., & Devine, P. G. (2008). More eyes on the prize: Variability in White Americans' perceptions of progress toward racial equality. *Personality and Social Psychology Bulletin, 34,* 513–527.

Bronfenbrenner, U. (1961). The mirror-image in Soviet-American relations. *Journal of Social Issues, 17,* 45–56.

Brooks, R., & Meltzoff, A. N. (2002). The importance of eyes: How infants interpret adult looking behavior. *Developmental Psychology, 38,* 958–966.

Brown, E., Deffenbacher, K., & Sturgill, W. (1977). Memory for faces and the circumstances of encounter. *Journal of Applied Psychology, 62,* 311–318.

Brown, J. D. (2003). The self-enhancement motive in collectivistic cultures: The rumors of my death have been greatly exaggerated. *Journal of Cross-Cultural Psychology, 34,* 603–605.

Brown, J. D., & Dutton, K. A. (1995). The thrill of victory, the complexity of defeat: Self-esteem and people's emotional reactions to success and failure. *Journal of Personality and Social Psychology, 68,* 712–722.

Brown, J. M. (2003). Eyewitness memory for arousing events: Putting things into context. *Applied Cognitive Psychology, 17,* 93–106.

Brown, R. (1986). *Social psychology* (2nd ed.). New York: Free Press.

Brown, R., & Kulik, J. (1977). Flashbulb memories. *Cognition, 5,* 73–99.

Brown, W. A. (1998, January). The placebo effect. *Scientific American,* pp. 90–95.

Brownstein, A., Read, S. J., & Simon, D. (2004). Bias at the racetrack: Effects of individual expertise and task importance on predecision reevaluation of alternatives. *Personality and Social Psychology Bulletin, 30,* 891–904.

Bruch, M. A., Gorsky, J. M., Collins, T. M., & Berger, P. A. (1989). Shyness and sociability examined: A multicomponent analysis. *Journal of Personality and Social Psychology, 57,* 904–915.

Bruck, M., & Ceci, S. J. (1999). The suggestibility of children's memory. *Annual Review of Psychology, 50,* 419–439.

Bruner, J. S., & Potter, M. C. (1964). Interference in visual recognition. *Science, 144,* 424–425.

Bruner, J. S., & Tagiuri, R. (1954). Person perception. In G. Lindzey (Ed.), *Handbook of social psychology* (Vol. 2, pp. 634–654). Reading, MA: Addison-Wesley.

Bryan, J. H., & Test, M. A. (1967). Models and helping: Naturalistic studies in aiding behavior. *Journal of Personality and Social Psychology, 6,* 400–407.

Buckholtz, J. W., Meyer-Lindenberg, A. (2008). MAOA and the neuroge-netic architecture of human aggression. *Trends in Neurosciences, 31,* 120–129.

Buckhout, R. (1974, December). Eyewitness testimony. *Scientific American,* pp. 23–31.

Buhs, E. S., Ladd, G. W., & Herald, S. L. (2006). Peer exclusion and victimization: Processes that mediate the relation between peer group rejection and children's classroom engagement and achievement. *Journal of Educational Psychology, 98,* 1–13.

Burger, J. M. (1986). Increasing compliance by improving the deal: The that's-not-all technique. *Journal of Personality and Social Psychology, 51,* 277–283.

Burger, J. M. (1999). The foot-in-the-door compliance procedure: A multiple-process analysis and review. *Personality and Social Psychology Review, 3,* 303–325.

Burger, J. M. (2009). Replicating Milgram: Would people still obey today? *American Psychologist, 64,* 1–11.

Burger, J. M., & Caldwell, D. F. (2003). The effects of monetary incentives and labeling on the foot-in-the-door effect: Evidence for a self-perception process. *Basic and Applied Social Psychology, 25,* 235–241.

Burger, J. M., & Cornelius, T. (2003). Raising the price of agreement: Public commitment and the low-ball compliance procedure. *Journal of Applied Social Psychology, 33,* 923–934.

Burger, J. M., Horita, M., Kinoshita, L., Roberts, K., & Vera, C. (1997). Effects of time on the norm of reciprocity. *Basic and Applied Social Psychology, 19,* 91–100.

Burger, J. M., Messian, N., Patel, S., del Prado, A., & Anderson, C. (2004). What a coincidence! The effects of incidental similarity on compliance. *Personality and Social Psychology Bulletin, 30,* 35–43.

Burger, J. M., & Petty, R. E. (1981). The low-ball compliance technique: Task or person commitment? *Journal of Personality and Social Psychology, 40,* 492–500.

Burger, J. M., Sanchez, J., Imberi, J. E., & Grande, L. R. (2009). The norm of reciprocity as an internalized social norm: Returning favors even when no one finds out. *Social Influence, 4,* 11–17.

Burns, J. M. (1978). *Leadership.* New York: Harper & Row.

Burns, J. M. (2003). *Transformational leadership.* New York: Atlantic Monthly Press.

Burnstein, E., & Schul, Y. (1982). The informational basis of social judgments: The operations in forming an impression of another person. *Journal of Experimental Social Psychology, 18,* 217–234.

Burnstein, E., Crandall, C., & Kitayama, S. (1994). Some neo-Darwinian decision rules for altruism: Weighing cues for inclusive fitness as a function of the biological importance of the decision. *Journal of Personality and Social Psychology, 67,* 773–789.

Burt, M. C. (1980). Cultural myths and supports for rape. *Journal of Personality and Social Psychology, 38,* 217–230.

Bushman, B. J. (1988). The effects of apparel on compliance: A field experiment with a female authority figure. *Personality and Social Psychology Bulletin, 14,* 459–467.

Bushman, B. J. (1996). Individual differences in the extent and development of aggressive cognitive-associative networks. *Personality and Social Psychology Bulletin, 22,* 811–819.

Bushman, B. J. (1998). Priming effects of violent media on the accessibility of aggressive constructs in memory. *Personality and Social Psychology Bulletin, 24,* 537–545.

Bushman, B. J. (2002). Does venting anger feed or extinguish the flame? Catharsis, rumination, distraction, anger, and aggressive responding. *Personality and Social Psychology Bulletin, 28,* 724–731.

Bushman, B. J., & Anderson, C. A. (2009). Comfortably numb: Desensitizing effects of violent media on helping others. *Psychological Science, 20,* 273–277.

Bushman, B. J., Baumeister, R. F., Thomaes, S., Ryu, E., Begeer, S., & West, S. G. (2009). Looking again, and harder, for a link between low self-esteem and aggression. *Journal of Personality, 77,* 427–446.

Bushman, B. J., & Cooper, H. M. (1990). Effects of alcohol on human aggression: An integrative research review. *Psychological Bulletin, 107,* 341–354.

Bushman, B. J., & Huesmann, L. R. (2001). Effects of televised violence on aggression. In D. G. Singer & J. L. Singer (Eds.), *Handbook of children and the media* (pp. 223–254). Thousand Oaks, CA: Sage.

Buss, A. H. (1980). *Self-consciousness and social anxiety.* San Francisco: Freeman.

Buss, D. M. (1989). Sex differences in human mate preferences: Evolutionary hypotheses tested in 37 cultures. *Behavioral and Brain Sciences, 12,* 1–14.

Buss, D. M. (2000). *The dangerous passion: Why jealousy is as necessary as love and sex.* New York: Free Press.

Buss, D. M. (2003). *The evolution of desire: Strategies of human mating* (rev. ed.). New York: Basic Books.

Buss, D. M. (2004). *Evolutionary psychology: The new science of the mind* (2nd ed.). Boston: Allyn & Bacon.

Buss, D. M. (2007). The evolution of human mating strategies: Consequences for conflict and cooperation. In S. W. Gangestad & J. A. Simpson (Eds.), *The evolution of mind: Fundamental questions and controversies.* New York: Guilford.

Buss, D. M., & Duntley, J. D. (2005). The evolution of gender differences in aggression. In S. Fein, G. R. Goethals, & M. J. Sandstrom (Eds.), *Gender and aggression: Interdisciplinary perspectives.* Mahwah, NJ: Erlbaum.

Buss, D. M., & Schmitt, D. P. (1993). Sexual strategies theory: An evolutionary perspective on human mating. *Psychological Review, 100,* 204–232.

Buss, D. M., & Shackelford, T. K. (1997). From vigilance to violence: Mate retention tactics in married couples. *Journal of Personality and Social Psychology, 72,* 346–361.

Buss, D. M., Larsen, R. J., Westen, D., & Semmelroth, J. (1992). Sex differences in jealousy: Evolution, physiology, and psychology. *Psychological Science, 3,* 251–255.

Butler, B., & Moran, G. (2007). The impact of death qualification, belief in a just world, legal authoritarianism, and locus of control on venirepersons' evaluations of aggravating and mitigating circumstances in capital trials. *Behavioral Sciences and the Law, 25,* 57–68.

Bylsma, W. H., Major, B., & Cozzarelli, C. (1995). The influence of legitimacy appraisals on the determinants of entitlement beliefs. *Basic and Applied Social Psychology, 17,* 223–237.

Byrne, D. (1971). *The attraction paradigm.* New York: Academic Press.

Byrne, D. (1997). An overview (and underview) of research and theory within the attraction paradigm. *Journal of Social and Personal Relationships, 14,* 417–431.

Byrne, D., & Clore, G. L. (1970). A reinforcement model of evaluative processes. *Personality: An International Journal, 1,* 103–128.

Byrne, D., Clore, G. L., & Smeaton, G. (1986). The attraction hypothesis: Do similar attitudes affect anything? *Journal of Personality and Social Psychology, 51,* 1167–1170.

Byrne, R. M. J., & McEleney, A. (2000). Counterfactual thinking about actions and failures to act. *Journal of Experimental Psychology: Learning, Memory, and Cognition, 26,* 1318–1331.

Byrne, S. (2009). Media literacy interventions: What makes them boom or boomerang? *Communication Education, 58,* 1–14.

Cacioppo, J. T., Crites, S. L., Berntson, G. G., & Coles, M. G. H. (1993). If attitudes affect how stimuli are processed, should they not affect the event-related brain potential? *Psychological Science, 4,* 108–112.

Cacioppo, J. T., Gardner, W. L., & Bernston, G. G. (1997). Beyond bipolar conceptualizations and measures: The case of attitudes and evaluative space. *Personality and Social Psychology Review, 1,* 3–25.

Cacioppo, J. T., & Patrick, W. (2008). *Loneliness: Human nature and the need for social connection.* New York: Norton.

Cacioppo, J. T., Hawkley, L. C., Berntson, G. G., Ernst, J. M., Gibbs, A. C., Stickgold, R., & Hobson, J. A. (2002). Lonely days invade the nights: Social modulation of sleep efficiency. *Psychological Science, 13,* 385–388.

Cacioppo, J. T., Hughes, M. E., Waite, L. J., Hawkley, L. C., & Thisted, R. A. (2006). Loneliness as a specific risk factor for depressive symptoms: Cross-sectional and longitudinal analyses. *Psychology and Aging, 21,* 140–151.

Cacioppo, J. T., & Petty, R. E. (1981). Electromyograms as measures of extent and affectivity of information processing. *American Psychologist, 36,* 441–456.

Cacioppo, J. T., & Petty, R. E. (1982). The need for cognition. *Journal of Personality and Social Psychology, 42,* 116–131.

Cacioppo, J. T., Petty, R. E., & Morris, K. (1983). Effects of need for cognition on message evaluation, recall, and persuasion. *Journal of Personality and Social Psychology, 45,* 805–818.

Cacioppo, J. T., Petty, R. E., Feinstein, J. A., & Jarvis, W. B. G. (1996). Dispositional differences in cognitive motivation: The life and times of individuals varying in need for cognition. *Psychological Bulletin, 119,* 197–253.

Cacioppo, J. T., Petty, R. E., Losch, M. E., & Kim, H. S. (1986). Electromyographic activity over facial muscle regions can differentiate the valence and intensity of affective reactions. *Journal of Personality and Social Psychology, 50,* 260–268.

Camara, W. J., & Schneider, D. L. (1994). Integrity tests: Facts and unresolved issues. *American Psychologist, 49,* 112–119.

Cameron, J., & Pierce, W. D. (1994). Reinforcement, reward, and intrinsic motivation: A meta-analysis. *Review of Educational Research, 64,* 363–423.

Cameron, J., Pierce, W. D., Banko, K. M., & Gear, A. (2005). Achievement-based rewards and intrinsic motivation: A test of cognitive mediators. *Journal of Educational Psychology, 97,* 641–655.

Campbell, A. (1999). Staying alive: Evolution, culture, and women's intrasexual aggression. *Behavioral and Brain Sciences, 22,* 203–252.

Campbell, D. J., & Lee, C. (1988). Self-appraisal in performance evaluation: Development versus evaluation. *Academy Management Review, 13,* 302–313.

Campion, M. A., Pursell, E. D., & Brown, B. K. (1988). Structured interviewing: Raising the psychometric properties of the employment interview. *Personnel Psychology, 41,* 25–42.

Cannon, W. B. (1932). *The wisdom of the body.* New York: Norton.

Capozza, D., & Brown, R. (2000). *Social identity processes: Trends in theory and research.* London: Sage.

Capozza, D., Voci, A., & Licciardello, O. (2000). Individualism, collectivism, and social identity theory. In D. Capozza & R. Brown (Eds.), *Social identity processes: Trends in theory and research.* London: Sage.

Caprariello, P. A., Cuddy, A. J. C., & Fiske, S. T. (2009). Social structure shapes cultural stereotypes and emotions: A causal test of the stereotype content model. *Group Processes & Intergroup Relations, 12,* 147–155.

Card, N. A., Stucky, B. D., Sawalani, G. M., & Little, T. D. (2008). Direct and indirect aggression during childhood and adolescence: A meta-analytic review of gender differences, intercorrelations, and relations to maladjustment. *Child Development, 79,* 1185–1229.

Carey, B. (1997, April). Don't face stress alone. *Health,* pp. 74–76, 78.

Carlo, G., Koller, S. H., Eisenberg, N., Da Silva, M. S., & Frohlich, C. B. (1996). A cross-national study on the relations among prosocial moral reasoning, gender role orientations, and pro-social behaviors. *Developmental Psychology, 32,* 231–240.

Carlo, G., Okun, M. A., Knight, G. P., & de Guzman, M. R. T. (2005). The interplay of traits and motives on volunteering: Agreeableness, extraversion and prosocial value motivation. *Personality and Individual Differences, 38,* 1293–1305.

Carlsmith, K. M. (2006). The roles of retribution and utility in determining punishment. *Journal of Experimental Social Psychology, 42,* 437–451.

Carlsmith, K. M., Darley, J. M., & Robinson, P. H. (2002). Why do we punish? Deterrence and just deserts as motives for punishment. *Journal of Personality and Social Psychology, 83,* 284–299.

Carlsmith, K. M., Wilson, T. D., & Gilbert, D. T. (2008). The paradoxical consequences of revenge. *Journal of Personality and Social Psychology, 95,* 1316–1324.

Carlson, M. (2008). I'd rather go along and be considered a man: Masculinity and bystander intervention. *Journal of Men's Studies, 16,* 3–17.

Carlson, M., & Miller, N. (1987). Explanation of the relation between negative mood and helping. *Psychological Bulletin, 102,* 91–108.

Carnagey, N. L., Bushman, B. J., & Anderson, C. A. (2007). The effect of video game violence on physiological desensitization and helping behavior. *Journal of Experimental Social Psychology, 43*(3): 489–496.

Carnaghi, A., & Yzerbyt, V. Y. (2007). Subtyping and social consensus: The role of the audience in the maintenance of stereotypic beliefs. *European Journal of Social Psychology, 37,* 902–922.

Carnahan, T., & McFarland, S. (2007). Revisiting the Stanford Prison Experiment: Could participant self-selection have led to the cruelty? *Personality and Social Psychology Bulletin, 33,* 603–614.

Carnevale, P. J. (2002). Mediating from strength. In J. Bercovitch (Ed.), *Studies in international mediation: Essays in honor of Jeffrey Z. Rubin* (pp. 25–40). London: Palgrave-MacMillan.

Carpenter, S. (2005). The rich science of economic choice. *APS Observer, 18,* No. 4, 21–27.

Carr, J. L., & VanDeusen, K. M. (2004). Risk factors for male sexual aggression on college campuses. *Journal of Family Violence, 19,* 279–289.

Carrillo, M., Ricci, L. A., Coppersmith, G. A., & Melloni, R. H., Jr. (2009). The effect of increased serotonergic neurotransmission on aggression: A critical meta-analytic review of preclinical studies. *Psychopharmacology, 205,* 349–368.

Carroll, J. (2006, September 1). Americans prefer male boss to a female boss. Gallup News Service (http://www.gallup.com/poll/24346/americans-prefer-male-boss-female-boss.aspx#).

Carron, A. V., Colman, M. M., Wheeler, J., & Stevens, D. (2002). Cohesion and performance in sport: A meta analysis. *Journal of Sport and Exercise Psychology, 24,* 168–188.

Cartwright, D. (1971). Risk taking by individuals and groups: An assessment of research employing choice dilemmas. *Journal of Personality and Social Psychology, 20,* 245–261.

Cartwright, D., & Zander, A. (1960). Group cohesiveness: Introduction. In D. Cartwright & A. Zander (Eds.), *Group dynamics: Research and theory* (2nd ed., pp. 69–94). Evanston, IL: Row, Peterson.

Carver, C. S., & Scheier, M. F. (1981). *Attention and self-regulation: A control-theory approach to human behavior.* New York: Springer-Verlag.

Carver, C. S., & Scheier, M. F. (1990). Origins and functions of positive and negative affect: A control-process view. *Psychological Review, 97,* 19–35.

Carver, C. S., & Scheier, M. F. (1998). *On the self-regulation of behavior.* New York: Cambridge University Press.

Carver, C. S., Harris, S. D., Lehman, J. M., Durel, L. A., Antoni, M. H., Spencer, S. M., & Pozo-Kaderman, C. (2000). How important is the perception of personal control? Studies of early stage breast cancer patients. *Personality and Social Psychology Bulletin, 26,* 139–149.

Carver, C. S., Scheier, M. F., & Weintraub, J. K. (1989). Assessing coping strategies: A theoretically based approach. *Journal of Personality and Social Psychology, 56,* 267–283.

Case, R. B., Moss, A. J., Case, N., McDermott, M., & Eberly, S. (1992). Living alone after myocardial infarction: Impact on prognosis. *Journal of the American Medical Association, 267,* 515–519.

Cashdan, E. (2003). Hormones and competitive aggression in women. *Aggressive Behavior, 29,* 107–115.

Caspi, A. (2000). The child is the father of man: Personality continuities from childhood to adulthood. *Journal of Personality and Social Psychology, 78,* 158–172.

Cassidy, J., & Shaver, P. R. (Eds.). (1999). *Handbook of attachment: Theory, research, and clinical applications.* New York: Guilford Press.

Cassidy, J., Kirsh, S. J., Scolton, K. L., & Parke, R. D. (1996). Attachment and representations of peer relationships. *Developmental Psychology, 32,* 892–904.

Cassidy, T. (2009). Bullying and victimisation in school children: The role of social identity, problem-solving style, and family and school context. *Social Psychology of Education, 12,* 63–76.

Castano, E., Yzerbyt, V. Y., Bourguignon, D., & Seron, E. (2002). Who may enter? The impact of in-group identification on in-group/out-group categorization. *Journal of Experimental Social Psychology, 38,* 315–322.

Castelli, L., De Dea, C., & Nesdale, D. (2008). Learning social attitudes: Children's sensitivity to the nonverbal behaviors of adult models during interracial interactions. *Personality and Social Psychology Bulletin, 34,* 1504–1513.

Castelli, L., Macrae, N., Zogmaister, C., Arcuri, L. (2004). A tale of two primes: Contextual limits on stereotype activation. *Social Cognition, 22,* 233–247.

Castelli, L., Zogmaister, C., & Tomelleri, S. (2009). The transmission of racial attitudes within the family. *Developmental Psychology, 45,* 586–591.

Cate, R. M., & Lloyd, S. A. (1992). *Courtship.* Newbury Park, CA: Sage.

Ceci, S. J., Ross, D. F., & Toglia, M. P. (1987). Suggestibility of children's memory: Psycholegal implications. *Journal of Experimental Psychology, 116,* 38–49.

Ceci, S. J., Williams, W. M., & Barnett, S. M. (2009). Women's underrepresentation in science: Sociocultural and biological considerations. *Psychological Bulletin, 135,* 218–261.

Cesarani, D. (2004). *Eichmann: His life and crimes.* London: Heinemann.

Cesario, J., & Higgins, E. T. (2008). Making message recipients "feel right": How nonverbal cues can increase persuasion. *Psychological Science, 19,* 415–420.

Cesario, J., Grant, H., & Higgins, E. T. (2004). Regulatory fit and persuasion: Transfer from "feeling right." *Journal of Personality and Social Psychology, 86,* 388–404.

Cesario, J., Plaks, J. E., & Higgins, E. T. (2006). Automatic social behavior as motivated preparation to interact. *Journal of Personality and Social Psychology, 90,* 893–910.

Cha, A. E. (2005, March 27). Employers relying on personality tests to screen applicants. *Washington Post,* p. A01.

Chaiken, S. (1979). Communicator physical attractiveness and persuasion. *Journal of Personality and Social Psychology, 37,* 1387–1397.

Chaiken, S. (1980). Heuristic versus systematic information processing and the use of source versus message cues in persuasion. *Journal of Personality and Social Psychology, 39,* 752–766.

Chaiken, S. (1987). The heuristic model of persuasion. In M. P. Zanna, J. M. Olson, & C. P. Herman (Eds.), *Social influence: The Ontario symposium* (Vol. 5, pp. 3–39). Hillsdale, NJ: Erlbaum.

Chaiken, S., & Baldwin, M. W. (1981). Affective-cognitive consistency and the effect of salient behavioral information on the self-perception of attitudes. *Journal of Personality and Social Psychology, 41,* 1–12.

Chaiken, S., & Maheswaran, D. (1994). Heuristic processing can bias systematic processing: Effects of source credibility, argument ambiguity, and task importance on attitude judgment. *Journal of Personality and Social Psychology, 66,* 460–473.

Chan, D. K., & Fishbein, M. (1993). Determinants of college women's intentions to tell their partners to use condoms. *Journal of Applied Social Psychology, 23,* 1455–1470.

Chandrashekaran, M., Walker, B. A., Ward, J. C., & Reingen, P. H. (1996). Modeling individual preference evolution and choice in a dynamic group setting. *Journal of Marketing Research, 33,* 211–223.

Chang, A., Duck, J., & Bordia, P. (2006). Understanding the multidimensionality of group development. *Small Group Research, 37,* 327–350.

Chang, H. (2007). Psychological distress and help-seeking among Taiwanese college students: Role of gender and student status. *British Journal of Guidance & Counselling, 35,* 347–355.

Chao, G. T., & Moon, H. (2005). The cultural mosaic: A metatheory for understanding the complexity of culture. *Journal of Applied Psychology, 90,* 1128–1140.

Chapdelaine, A., Kenny, D. A., & LaFontana, K. M. (1994). Matchmaker, matchmaker, can you make me a match? Predicting liking between two unacquainted persons. *Journal of Personality and Social Psychology, 67,* 83–91.

Chapleau, K., Oswald, D., & Russell, B. (2007). How ambivalent sexism toward women and men supports rape myth acceptance. *Sex Roles, 57,* 131–136.

Chapman, D. S., Uggerslev, K. L., & Webster, J. (2003). Applicant reactions to face-to-face and technology-mediated interviews: A field investigation. *Journal of Applied Psychology, 88,* 944–953.

Chartrand, T. L., & Bargh, J. A. (1999). The chameleon effect: The perception-behavior link and social interaction. *Journal of Personality and Social Psychology, 76,* 893–910.

Chasteen, A. L., Bhattacharyya, S., Horhota, M., Tam, R., & Hasher, L. (2005). How feelings of stereotype threat influence older adults' memory performance. *Experimental Aging Research, 31,* 235–260.

Cheek, J. M., & Melchior, L. A. (1990). Shyness, self-esteem, and self-consciousness. In H. Leitenberg (Ed.), *Handbook of social and evaluation anxiety.* New York: Plenum.

Chemers, M. M., Hays, R. B., Rhodewalt, F., & Wysocki, J. (1985). A person-environment analysis of job stress: A contingency model explanation. *Journal of Personality and Social Psychology, 49,* 628–635.

Chen, F. F., & Kenrick, D. T. (2002). Repulsion or attraction: Group membership and assumed attitude similarity. *Journal of Personality and Social Psychology, 83,* 111–125.

Chen, S., & Chaiken, S. (1999). The heuristic-systematic model in its broader context. In S. Chaiken & Y. Trope (Eds.), *Dual-process theories in social psychology* (pp. 73–96). New York: Guilford.

Chen, S., Langner, C. A., & Mendoza-Denton, R. (2009). When dispositional and role power fit: Implications for self-expression and self–other congruence. *Journal of Personality and Social Psychology, 96,* 710–727.

Chen, Y.-R., Brockner, J., & Chen, X.-P. (2002). Individual-collective primacy and ingroup favoritism: Enhancement and protection effects. *Journal of Experimental Social Psychology, 38,* 482–491.

Cheng, C. M., & Chartrand, T. L. (2003). Self-monitoring without awareness: Using mimicry as a nonconscious affiliation strategy. *Journal of Personality and Social Psychology, 85,* 1170–1179.

Cheng, P. W., & Novick, L. R. (1990). A probabilistic contrast model of causal induction. *Journal of Personality and Social Psychology, 58,* 545–567.

Cheng, P.-Y., & Chiou, W.-B. (2008). Framing effects in group investment decision making: Role of group polarization. *Psychological Reports, 102,* 283–292.

Cherry, E. C. (1953). Some experiments on the recognition of speech, with one and with two ears. *Journal of the Acoustical Society of America, 25,* 975–979.

Cheryan, S., & Bodenhausen, G. V. (2000). When positive stereotypes threaten intellectual performance: The psychological hazards of "model minority" status. *Psychological Science, 11,* 399–402.

Chesler, P., & Goodman, E. J. (1976). *Women, money, and power.* New York: Morrow.

Chia, S. C., & Lee, W. (2008). Pluralistic ignorance about sex: The direct and the indirect effects of media consumption on college students' misperception of sex-related peer norms. *International Journal of Public Opinion Research, 20,* 52–73.

Chiesa, M., & Hobbs, S. (2008). Making sense of social research: How useful is the Hawthorne Effect? *European Journal of Social Psychology, 38,* 67–74.

Chiroro, P. M., Tredoux, C. G., Radaelli, S., & Meissner, C. A. (2008). Recognizing faces across continents: The effect of within-race variations on the own-race bias in face recognition. *Psychonomic Bulletin & Review, 15,* 1089–1092.

Choi, J. N., & Kim, M. U. (1999). The organizational application of groupthink and its limitations in organizations. *Journal of Applied Psychology, 84,* 297–306.

Choi, S. M., Lee, W.-N., & Kim, H.-J. (2005). Lessons from the rich and famous: A cross-cultural comparison of celebrity endorsement in advertising. *Journal of Advertising, 34,* 85–98.

Christensen, A. J., Turner, C. W., Smith, T. W., Holman, J. M., Jr., & Gregory, M. C. (1991). Health locus of control and depression in end-stage renal disease. *Journal of Counseling and Clinical Psychology, 59,* 419–424.

Christensen, A., & Heavey, C. L. (1993). Gender differences in marital conflict: The demand/withdraw interaction pattern. In S. Oskamp & M. Costanzo (Eds.), *Gender issues in contemporary society* (pp. 113–141). Newbury Park, CA: Sage.

Christensen, L. (1988). Deception in psychological research: When is its use justified? *Personality and Social Psychology Bulletin, 14,* 664–675.

Christianson, S. (1992). Emotional stress and eyewitness memory: A critical review. *Psychological Bulletin, 112,* 284–309.

Chung, C. K., & Pennebaker, J. W. (2008). Revealing dimensions of thinking in open-ended self-descriptions: An automated meaning extraction method for natural language. *Journal of Research in Personality, 42,* 96–132.

Cialdini, R. B. (2003). Crafting normative messages to protect the environment. *Current Directions in Psychological Science, 12,* 105–109.

Cialdini, R. B. (2007). *Influence: The psychology of persuasion.* New York: HarperCollins.

Cialdini, R. B., & Ascani, K. (1976). Test of a concession procedure for inducing verbal, behavioral, and further compliance with a request to give blood. *Journal of Applied Psychology, 61,* 295–300.

Cialdini, R. B., & De Nicholas, M. E. (1989). Self-presentation by association. *Journal of Personality and Social Psychology, 57,* 626–631.

Cialdini, R. B., & Goldstein, N. J. (2004). Social influence: Compliance and conformity. *Annual Review of Psychology, 55,* 591–621.

Cialdini, R. B., Baumann, D. J., & Kenrick, D. T. (1981). Insights from sadness: A three-step model of the development of altruism as hedonism. *Developmental Review, 1,* 207–223.

Cialdini, R. B., Borden, R. J., Thorne, A., Walker, M. R., Freeman, S., & Sloan, L. R. (1976). Basking in reflected glory: Three (football) field studies. *Journal of Personality and Social Psychology, 34,* 366–375.

Cialdini, R. B., Cacioppo, J. T., Bassett, R., & Miller, J. A. (1978). Lowball procedure for producing compliance: Commitment then cost. *Journal of Personality and Social Psychology, 36,* 463–476.

Cialdini, R. B., Kallgren, C. A., & Reno, R. R. (1991). A focus theory of normative conduct: A theoretical refinement and reevaluation of the role of norms in human behavior. *Advances in Experimental Social Psychology, 24,* 201–234.

Cialdini, R. B., Reno, R. R., & Kallgren, C. A. (1990). A focus theory of normative conduct: Recycling the concept of norms to reduce littering in public places. *Journal of Personality and Social Psychology, 58,* 1015–1026.

Cialdini, R. B., Schaller, M., Houlihan, D., Arps, K., Fultz, J., & Beaman, A. L. (1987). Empathy-based helping: Is it selflessly or selfishly motivated? *Journal of Personality and Social Psychology, 52,* 749–758.

Cialdini, R. B., Trost, M. R., & Newsom, J. T. (1995). Preference for consistency: The development of a valid measure and the discovery of surprising behavioral implications. *Journal of Personality and Social Psychology, 69,* 318–328.

Cialdini, R. B., Vincent, J. E., Lewis, S. K., Catalan, J., Wheeler, D., & Darby, B. L. (1975). Reciprocal concessions procedure for inducing compliance: The door-in-the-face technique. *Journal of Personality and Social Psychology, 31,* 206–215.

Cioffi, D., & Holloway, J. (1993). Delayed costs of suppressed pain. *Journal of Personality and Social Psychology, 64,* 274–282.

Clark, M. S. (1984). Record keeping in two types of relationships. *Journal of Personality and Social Psychology, 47,* 549–557.

Clark, M. S., & Mills, J. (1979). Interpersonal attraction in exchange and communal relationships. *Journal of Personality and Social Psychology, 37,* 12–24.

Clark, M. S., & Mills, J. (1993). The difference between communal and exchange relationships: What it is and is not. *Personality and Social Psychology Bulletin, 19,* 684–691.

Clark, R. D., III. (2001). Effects of majority defection and multiple minority sources on minority influence. *Group Dynamics, 5,* 57–62.

Clark, R. D., III, & Maass, A. (1990). The effects of majority size on minority influence. *European Journal of Psychology, 20,* 99–117.

Clark, R. D., III, & Word, L. E. (1972). Why don't bystanders help? Because of ambiguity? *Journal of Personality and Social Psychology, 24,* 392–400.

Clifford, M. M., & Walster, E. H. (1973). The effect of physical attractiveness on teacher expectations. *Sociology of Education, 46,* 248–258.

Cochran, S. D., Mays, V. M., Ciarletta, J., Caruso, C., & Mallon, D. (1992). Efficacy of the theory of reasoned action in predicting AIDS-related sexual risk reduction among gay men. *Journal of Applied Social Psychology, 22,* 1481–1501.

Coe, C. L. (1993). Psychosocial factors and immunity in nonhuman primates: A review. *Psychosomatic Medicine, 55,* 298–308.

Coenders, M., Lubbers, M., Scheepers, P., & Verkuyten, M. (2008). More than two decades of changing ethnic attitudes in the Netherlands. *Journal of Social Issues, 64,* 269–285.

Cohen, D., & Nisbett, R. E. (1997). Field experiments examining the culture of honor: The role of institutions in perpetuating norms about violence. *Personality and Social Psychology Bulletin, 23,* 1188–1199.

Cohen, D., Nisbett, R. E., Bowdle, B. F., & Schwarz, N. (1996). Insult, aggression, and the southern culture of honor: An "experimental ethnography." *Journal of Personality and Social Psychology, 70,* 945–960.

Cohen, D., Vandello, J., & Rantilla, A. K. (1998). The sacred and the social: Cultures of honor and violence. In P. Gilbert & B. Andrews (Eds.), *Shame: Interpersonal behavior, psychopathology, and culture* (pp. 261–282). Cambridge: Oxford University Press.

Cohen, G. L. (2003). Party over policy: The dominating impact of group influence on political beliefs. *Journal of Personality and Social Psychology, 85,* 808–822.

Cohen, G. L., Garcia, J., Apfel, N., & Master, A. (2006). Reducing the racial achievement gap: A social-psychological intervention. *Science, 313,* 1307–1310.

Cohen, G. L., Steele, C. M., & Ross, L. D. (1999). The mentor's dilemma: Providing critical feedback across the racial divide. *Personality and Social Psychology Bulletin, 25,* 1302–1318.

Cohen, J. B., & De La Torre, V. (2009, May 16). A year later, would bystanders lend hand? *Hartford Courant,* p. A1.

Cohen, S. (2004). Social relationships and health. *American Psychologist, 59,* 676–684.

Cohen, S., Alper, C. M., Doyle, W. J., Adler, N. E., Treanor, J. J., & Turner, R. B. (2008). Objective and subjective socioeconomic status and susceptibility to the common cold. *Health Psychology, 27,* 268–274.

Cohen, S., Doyle, W. J., Turner, R., Alper, C. M., & Skoner, D. P. (2006). Sociability and susceptibility to the common cold. *Psychological Science, 14,* 389–395.

Cohen, S., Frank, E., Doyle, W. J., Skoner, D. P., Rabin, B. S., & Gwaltney, J. M. (1998). Types of stressors that increase susceptibility to the common cold in healthy adults. *Health Psychology, 17,* 214–223.

Cohen, S., & Herbert, T. (1996). Health psychology: Psychological factors and physical disease from the perspective of human psychoneuroimmunology. *Annual Review of Psychology, 47,* 113–142.

Cohen, S., & Janicki-Deverts, D. (2009). Can we improve our physical health by altering our social networks? *Perspectives on Psychological Science, 4,* 375–378.

Cohen, S., Janicki-Deverts, D., & Miller, G. E. (2007). Psychological stress and disease.

Cohen, S., Kessler, R. C., & Gordon, L. U. (1995). *Measuring stress: A guide for health and social scientists.* New York: Oxford University Press.

Cohen, S., Tyrrell, D. A. J., & Smith, A. P. (1993). Negative life events, perceived stress, negative affect, and susceptibility to the common cold. *Journal of Personality and Social Psychology, 64,* 131–140.

Cohen, S., Underwood, L. G., & Gottlieb, B. H. (Eds.). (2000). *Social support measurement and intervention: A guide for health and social scientists.* New York: Oxford University Press.

Cohen, S., & Williamson, G. (1991). Stress and infectious disease in humans. *Psychological Bulletin, 109,* 5–24.

Cohen-Ketteinis, P. T., & Van Goozen, S. H. M. (1997). Sex reassignment of adolescent transsexuals: A follow-up study. *Journal of the American Academy of Child and Adolescent psychiatry, 36,* 263–271.

Cole, S. W., Kemeny, M. E., Taylor, S. E., Visscher, B. R., & Fahey, J. L. (1996). Accelerated course of human immunodeficiency virus infection in gay men who conceal their homosexual identity. *Psychosomatic Medicine, 58,* 219–231.

Cole, T. B. (2006). Rape at U.S. colleges often fueled by alcohol. *Journal of the American Medical Association, 296,* 504–505.

Collins, N. L., & Feeney, B. C. (2000). A safe haven: An attachment theory perspective on support seeking and caregiving in intimate relationships. *Journal of Personality and Social Psychology, 78,* 1053–1073.

Collins, N. L., & Miller, L. C. (1994). Self-disclosure and liking: a meta-analytic review. *Psychological Bulletin, 116,* 457–475.

Colvin, C. R., Block, J., & Funder, D. C. (1995). Overly positive self-evaluations and personality: Negative implications for mental health. *Journal of Personality and Social Psychology, 68,* 1152–1162.

Conger, R. D., Reuter, M. A., & Elder, G. H., Jr. (1999). Couple resilience to economic pressure. *Journal of Personality and Social Psychology, 76,* 54–71.

Conger, R. D., Wallace, L. E., Sun, Y., Simons, R. L., McLoyd, V. C., & Brody, G. H. (2002). Economic pressure in African American families: A replication and extension of the family stress model. *Developmental Psychology, 38,* 179–193.

Conklin, L. R., Strunk, D. R., & Fazio, R. H. (2009). Attitude formation in depression: Evidence for deficits in forming positive attitudes. *Journal of Behavior Therapy and Experimental Psychiatry, 40,* 120–126.

Conner, M., Norman, P., & Bell, R. (2002). The theory of planned behavior and healthy eating. *Health Psychology, 21,* 194–201.

Connors, E., Lundregan, T., Miller, N., & McEwen, T. (1996). *Convicted by juries, exonerated by science: Case studies in the use of DNA evidence to establish innocence after trial.* Washington, DC: U.S. Department of Justice.

Conroy, S. (2007, August 25). Iraq whistleblowers vilified, demoted. CBS News. Retrieved July 26, 2008, from cbsnews.com.

Conway, J. M., & Huffcutt, A. I. (1997). Psychometric properties of multisource performance ratings: A meta-analysis of subordinate, supervisor, peer, and self-ratings. *Human Performance, 10,* 331–360.

Conway, L. G., III, & Schaller, M. (2005). When authorities' commands backfire: Attributions about consensus and effects on deviant decision making. *Journal of Personality and Social Psychology, 89,* 311–326.

Conway, M. A. (1995). *Flashbulb memories.* Mahwah, NJ: Erlbaum.

Conway, M. A., & Pleydell-Pearce, C. W. (2000). The construction of autobiographical memories in the self-memory system. *Psychological Review, 107,* 261–288.

Conway, M. A., Wang, Q., Hanyu, K., & Haque, S. (2005). A cross-cultural investigation of autobiographical memory: On the universality and cultural variation of the "Reminiscence Bump." *Journal of Cross-Cultural Psychology, 36,* 739–749.

Cook, K. S., & Yamagishi, T. A. (2008). Defense of deception on scientific grounds. *Social Psychology Quarterly, 71,* 215–221.

Cook, T. D., & Campbell, D. T. (1979). *Quasi-experimentation: Design and analysis issues for field settings.* Chicago: Rand McNally.

Cooke, C. A. (2004). Young people's attitudes towards guns in America, Great Britain, and Western Australia. *Aggressive Behavior, 30,* 93–104.

Cooley, C. H. (1902). *Human nature and the social order.* New York: Schocken Books.

Cooper, J. (2007). *Cognitive dissonance: Fifty years of classic theory.* London: Sage.

Cooper, J., & Fazio, R. H. (1984). A new look at dissonance theory. In L. Berkowitz (Ed.), *Advances in experimental social psychology* (Vol. 17, pp. 229–267). New York: Academic Press.

Cooper, J., & Hogg, M. (2007). Feeling the anguish of others: A theory of vicarious dissonance. *Advances in Experimental Social Psychology, 39,* 359–403.

Cooper, J., & Neuhaus, I. M. (2000). The "hired gun" effect: Assessing the effect of pay, frequency of testifying, and credentials on the perception of expert testimony. *Law and Human Behavior, 24,* 149–171.

Cooper, J., Zanna, M. P., & Goethals, G. R. (1974). Mistreatment of an esteemed other as a consequence affecting dissonance reduction. *Journal of Experimental Social Psychology, 10,* 224–233.

Cooper, M. L., Frone, M. R., Russell, M., & Mudar, P. (1995). Drinking to regulate positive and negative emotions: A motivational model of alcohol use. *Journal of Personality and Social Psychology, 69,* 990–1005.

Cooper, W. H. (1981). Ubiquitous halo. *Psychological Bulletin, 90,* 218–224.

Coopersmith, S. (1967). *The antecedents of self-esteem.* San Francisco: Freeman.

Copeland, J. T. (1994). Prophecies of power: Motivational implications of social power for behavioral confirmation. *Journal of Personality and Social Psychology, 67,* 264–277.

Cordery, J. L., & Soo, C. (2008). Overcoming impediments to virtual team effectiveness. *Human Factors and Ergonomics in Manufacturing, 18,* 487–500.

Correll, J., Park, B., Judd, C. M., & Wittenbrink, B. (2002). The police officer's dilemma: Using ethnicity to disambiguate potentially threatening individuals. *Journal of Personality and Social Psychology, 83,* 1314–1329.

Correll, J., Park, B., Judd, C. M., & Wittenbrink, B. (2007a). The influence of stereotypes on decisions to shoot. *European Journal of Social Psychology, 37,* 1102–1117.

Correll, J., Park, B., Judd, C. M., Wittenbrink, B., Sadler, M. S., & Keesee, T. (2007b). Across the Thin Blue Line: Police officers and racial bias in the decision to shoot. *Journal of Personality and Social Psychology, 92,* 1006–1023.

Correll, J., Urland, G. R., & Ito, T. A. (2006). Event-related potentials and the decision to shoot: The role of threat perception and cognitive control. *Journal of Experimental Social Psychology, 42,* 120–128.

Cose, E. (1997). *Color-blind: Seeing beyond race in a race-obsessed world.* New York: HarperCollins.

Costa, R. M. (1982, March 6). Latin and Greek are good for you. *New York Times,* p. 23.

Costanzo, M. (1997). *Just revenge: Costs and consequences of the death penalty.* New York: St. Martin's Press.

Cottrell, N. B., Wack, D. L., Sekerak, G. J., & Rittle, R. H. (1968). Social facilitation of dominant responses by the presence of an audience and the mere presence of others. *Journal of Personality and Social Psychology, 9,* 245–250.

Cousins, A. J., Fugére, M. A., & Franklin, M. (2009). Digit ratio (2D:4D), mate guarding, and physical aggression in dating couples. *Personality and Individual Differences, 46,* 709–713.

Cousins, N. (1989). *Head first: The biology of hope.* New York: Dutton.

Cowan, C. L., Thompson, W. C., & Ellsworth, P. C. (1984). The effects of death qualification on jurors' predisposition to convict and on the quality of deliberation. *Law and Human Behavior, 8,* 53–80.

Cowley, G. (1996, June 3). The biology of beauty. *Newsweek,* pp. 61–69.

Cox, M., & Tanford, S. (1989). An alternative method of capital jury selection. *Law and Human Behavior, 13,* 167–183.

Coyne, S. M., & Archer, J. (2004). Indirect aggression in the media: A content analysis of British television programs. *Aggressive Behavior, 30,* 254–271.

Coyne, S. M., Archer, J., & Eslea, M. (2004). Cruel intentions on television and in real life: Can viewing indirect aggression increase viewers' subsequent indirect aggression? *Journal of Experimental Child Psychology, 88,* 234–253.

Coyne, S. M., Manning, J. T., Ringer, L., & Bailey, L. (2007). Directional asymmetry (right-left differences) in digit ratio (2D:4D) predict indirect aggression in women. *Personality and Individual Differences, 43*, 865–872.

Coyne, S. M., Nelson, D. A., Lawton, F., Haslam, S., Rooney, L., Titterington, L., et al. (2008). The effects of viewing physical and relational aggression in the media: Evidence for a cross-over effect. *Journal of Experimental Social Psychology, 44*, 1551–1554.

Craig, S. B., & Hannum, K. (2006). Research update: 360-degree performance assessment. *Consulting Psychology Journal: Practice and Research, 58*, 117–124.

Craig, W. M., Pepler, D., & Atlas, R. (2000). Observations of bullying in the playground and in the classroom. *School Psychology International, 21*, 22–36.

Cramer, R. E., McMaster, M. R., Bartell, P. A., & Dragna, M. (1988). Subject competence and the minimization of the bystander effect. *Journal of Applied Social Psychology, 18*, 1133–1148.

Crandall, C. S., & Eshleman, A. (2003). A justification-suppression model of the expression and experience of prejudice. *Psychological Bulletin, 129*, 414–446.

Crano, W. D. (2000). Milestones in the psychological analysis of social influence. *Group Dynamics: Theory, Research, and Practice, 4*, 68–80.

Crano, W. D., & Prislin, R. (Eds.). (2008). *Attitudes and attitude change.* New York: Psychology Press.

Crescioni, A. W., & Baumeister, R. F. (2009). Alone and aggressive: Social exclusion impairs self-control and empathy and increases hostile cognition and aggression. In M. J. Harris (Ed.), *Bullying, rejection, and peer victimization: A social cognitive neuroscience perspective* (pp. 251–277). New York: Springer.

Crick, N. R., & Dodge, K. A. (1994). A review and reformulation of social information-processing mechanisms in children's social adjustment. *Psychological Bulletin, 115*, 74–101.

Crick, N. R., & Rose, A. J. (2000). Toward a gender-balanced approach to the study of social-emotional development: A look at relational aggression. In R. G. Geen & E. Donnerstein (Eds.), *Human aggression: Theories, research, and implications for social policy* (pp. 153–168). San Diego: Academic Press.

Crocker, J., & Park, L. E. (2004). The costly pursuit of self-esteem. *Psychological Bulletin, 130*, 392–414.

Crocker, J., Voelkl, K., Testa, M., & Major, B. (1991). Social stigma: The affective consequences of attributional ambiguity. *Journal of Personality and Social Psychology, 60*, 218–228.

Crockett, M. J., Clark, L., Tabibnia, G., Lieberman, M. D., & Robbins, T. W. (2008). Serotonin modulates behavioral reactions to unfairness. *Science, 320*, 1739.

Croizet, J. C., & Claire, T. (1998). Extending the concept of stereotype and threat to social class: The intellectual underperformance of students from low socioeconomic backgrounds. *Personality and Social Psychology Bulletin, 24*, 588–594.

Croizet, J. C., Després, G., Gauzins, M. E., Huguet, P., Leyens, J.-P., & Meot, A. (2004). Stereotype threat undermines intellectual performance by triggering a disruptive mental load. *Personality and Social Psychology Bulletin, 30*, 721–731.

Cronbach, L. J. (1955). Processes affecting scores on "understanding of others" and "assumed similarity." *Psychological Bulletin, 52*, 177–193.

Cronin, P., & Reicher, S. (2009). Accountability processes and group dynamics: A SIDE perspective on the policing of an anti-capitalist riot. *European Journal of Social Psychology, 39*, 237–254.

Cropanzano, R. (Ed.). (1993). *Justice in the workplace: Approaching fairness in human resource management.* Hillsdale, NJ: Erlbaum.

Crosby, F. (1982). *Relative deprivation and working women.* New York: Oxford University Press.

Crosby, F. J., Iyer, A., & Sincharoen, S. (2006). Understanding affirmative action. *Annual Review of Psychology, 57*, 585–611.

Crosby, J. R., Monin, B., & Richardson, D. (2008). Where do we look during potentially offensive behavior? *Psychological Science, 19*, 226–228.

Croyle, R., & Cooper, J. (1983). Dissonance arousal: Physiological evidence. *Journal of Personality and Social Psychology, 45*, 782–791.

Crozier, W. R. (Ed.). (2001). *Shyness: Development, consolidation, and change.* London: Routledge.

Crozier, W. R., & Alden, L. E. (Eds.). (2005). *The essential handbook of social anxiety for clinicians.* New York: John Wiley & Sons.

Crutchfield, R. S. (1955). Conformity and character. *American Psychologist, 10*, 195–198.

Csikszentmihalyi, M. (1999). If we are so rich, why aren't we happy? *American Psychologist, 54*, 821–827.

Csikszentmihalyi, M., & Figurski, T. J. (1982). Self-awareness and aversive experience in everyday life. *Journal of Personality, 50*, 15–28.

Cuddy, A. J. C., Fiske, S. T., & Glick, P. (2008). Warmth and competence as universal dimensions of social perception: The Stereotype Content Model and the BIAS Map. In M. P. Zanna (Ed.), *Advances in Experimental Social Psychology* (Vol. 40, pp. 61–149). New York: Academic Press.

Cuddy, A. J. C., Norton, M. I., & Fiske, S. T. (2004). This old stereotype: The pervasiveness and persistence of the elderly stereotype. *Journal of Social Issues, 61*, 267–285.

Cuddy, A. J. C., Rock, M. S., & Norton, M. I. (2007). Aid in the aftermath of Hurricane Katrina: Inferences of secondary emotions and intergroup helping. *Group Processes & Intergroup Relations, 10*, 107–118.

Cuddy, A. J., Fiske, S. T., Kwan, V., S. Y. Glick, P., Demoulin, S., Leyens, J. P., et al. (2009). Stereotype content model across cultures: Towards universal similarities and some differences. *British Journal of Social Psychology, 48*, 1–33.

Culbertson, F. M. (1997). Depression and gender: An international review. *American Psychologist, 52*, 25–31.

Cunningham, J. H. (2009, May 11). Doctor shares 3 steps to save lives; Shows workers Heimlich moves. *The Record* (Bergen County, NJ), p. L6.

Cunningham, M. R. (1979). Weather, mood, and helping behavior: Quasi experiments with the sunshine Samaritan. *Journal of Personality and Social Psychology, 37*, 1947–1956.

Cunningham, M. R., Roberts, A. R., Wu, C., Barbee, A. P., & Druen, P. B. (1995). "Their ideas of beauty are, on the whole, the same as ours": Consistency and variability in the cross-cultural perception of female physical attractiveness. *Journal of Personality and Social Psychology, 68*, 261–279.

Cunningham, M. R., Steinberg, J., & Grev, R. (1980). Wanting to and having to help: Separate motivations for positive mood and guilt-induced helping. *Journal of Personality and Social Psychology, 38*, 181–192.

Cunningham, M. R., Wong, D. T., & Barbee, A. P. (1994). Self-presentation dynamics on overt integrity tests: Experimental studies of the Reid Report. *Journal of Applied Psychology, 79*, 643–658.

Cunningham, W. A., Johnson, M. K., Gatenby, J. C., Gore, J. C., & Banaji, M. R. (2003). Neural components of social evaluation. *Journal of Personality and Social Psychology, 85*, 639–649.

Cunningham, W. A., Johnson, W. A., Raye, C. L., Gatenby, J. C., Gore, J. C., & Banaji, M. R. (2004). Separable neural components in the processing of black and white faces. *Psychological Science, 15*, 806–813.

Curtis, R. C., & Miller, K. (1986). Believing another likes or dislikes you: Behaviors making the beliefs come true. *Journal of Personality and Social Psychology, 51*, 284–290.

Curtis, N. M., Ronan, K. R., Heiblum, N., & Crellin, K. (2009). Dissemination and effectiveness of multisystemic treatment in New Zealand: A benchmarking study. *Journal of Family Psychology, 23*, 119–129.

Cutler, B. L. (Ed.). (2009). *Expert testimony on the psychology of eyewitness identification.* New York: Oxford University Press.

Cutler, B. L., & Penrod, S. D. (1995). *Mistaken identification: The eyewitness, psychology, and the law.* New York: Cambridge University Press.

Cutler, B. L., Penrod, S. D., & Stuve, T. E. (1988). Juror decision making in eyewitness identification cases. *Law and Human Behavior, 12*, 41–55.

Dabbs, J. M., & Dabbs, M. G. (2000). *Heroes, rogues, and lovers: Testosterone and behavior.* New York: McGraw-Hill.

Dabbs, J. M., Jr., Hargrove, M. F., & Heusel, C. (1996). Testosterone differences among college fraternities: Well-behaved vs. rambunctious. *Personality and Individual Differences, 20,* 157–161.

Daly, M., & Wilson, M. (1988). *Homicide.* New York: Aldine de Gruyter.

Daly, M., & Wilson, M. (1989). Homicide and cultural evolution. *Ethology and Sociobiology, 10,* 99–110.

Daly, M., & Wilson, M. (1996). Violence against stepchildren. *Current Directions in Psychological Science, 5,* 77–81.

Daly, M., & Wilson, M. (2005). The 'Cinderella effect' is no fairy tale: Comment. *Trends in Cognitive Sciences, 9,* 507–508.

Darke, P. R., & Chaiken, S. (2005). The pursuit of self-interest: Self-interest bias in attitude judgment and persuasion. *Journal of Personality and Social Psychology, 89,* 864–883.

Darley, J. M., & Batson, C. D. (1973). From Jerusalem to Jericho: A study of situational and dispositional variables in helping behavior. *Journal of Personality and Social Psychology, 27,* 100–108.

Darley, J. M., & Fazio, R. (1980). Expectancy confirmation processes arising in the social interaction sequence. *American Psychologist, 35,* 867–881.

Darley, J. M., & Gross, P. H. (1983). A hypothesis-confirming bias in labeling effects. *Journal of Personality and Social Psychology, 44,* 20–33.

Darley, J. M., & Latané, B. (1968). Bystander intervention in emergencies: Diffusion of responsibility. *Journal of Personality and Social Psychology, 8,* 377–383.

Darley, J. M., & Latané, B. (1970). Norms and normative behavior: Field studies of social interdependence. In J. Macauley & L. Berkowitz (Eds.), *Altruism and helping behavior* (pp. 83–101). New York: Academic Press.

Darley, J. M., & Pittman, T. S. (2003). The psychology of compensatory and retributive justice. *Personality and Social Psychology Review, 7,* 324–336.

Darley, J. M., Carlsmith, K. M., & Robinson, P. H. (2000). Incapacitation and just deserts as motives for punishment. *Law and Human Behavior, 24,* 659–684.

Darwin, C. (1872). *The expression of the emotions in man and animals.* London: John Murray.

Das, E. H. H. J., de Wit, J. B. F., & Stroebe, W. (2003). Fear appeals motivate acceptance of action recommendations: Evidence for a positive bias in the processing of persuasive messages. *Personality and Social Psychology Bulletin, 29,* 650–664.

Dasgupta, N. (2009). Mechanisms underlying the malleability of implicit prejudice and stereotypes: The role of automaticity and cognitive control. In T. D. Nelson (Ed.), *Handbook of prejudice, stereotyping, and discrimination* (pp. 267–284). New York: Psychology Press.

David, N., Bewernick, B. H., Cohen, M. X., Newen, A., Lux, S., Fink, G. R., Shah, N. J., & Vogeley, K. (2006). Neural representations of self versus other: Visual-spatial perspective taking and agency in a virtual ball-tossing game. *Journal of Cognitive Neuroscience, 18,* 898–910.

Davidson, A. R., & Jaccard, J. J. (1979). Variables that moderate the attitude-behavior relation: Results of a longitudinal survey. *Journal of Personality and Social Psychology, 37,* 1364–1376.

Davidson, A. R., Yantis, S., Norwood, M., & Montano, D. E. (1985). Amount of information about the attitude object and attitude-behavior consistency. *Journal of Personality and Social Psychology, 49,* 1184–1198.

Davies, P. G., Spencer, S. J., Quinn, D. M., & Gerhardstein, R. (2002). Consuming images: How television commercials that elicit stereotype threat can restrain women academically and professionally. *Personality and Social Psychology Bulletin, 28,* 1615–1628.

Davies, P. T., & Cummings, E. M. (1994). Marital conflict and child adjustment: An emotional security hypothesis. *Psychological Bulletin, 116,* 387–411.

Davis, B. P., & Knowles, E. S. (1999). A Disrupt-Then-Reframe technique of social influence. *Journal of Personality and Social Psychology, 76,* 192–199.

Davis, J. H., Au, W. T., Hulbert, L., Chen, X., & Zarnoth, P. (1997). Effects of group size and procedural influence on consensual judgments of quantity: The example of damage awards and mock civil juries. *Journal of Personality and Social Psychology, 73,* 703–718.

Davis, J. H., Kameda, T., Parks, C., Stasson, M., & Zimmerman, S. (1989). Some social mechanics of group decision-making: The distribution of opinion, polling sequence, and implications for consensus. *Journal of Personality and Social Psychology, 57,* 1000–1012.

Davis, J. L., & Rusbult, C. E. (2001). Attitude alignment in close relationships. *Journal of Personality and Social Psychology, 81,* 65–84.

Davis, J. P., & Hall, J. W. (2003). A software-supported process for assembling evidence and handling uncertainty in decisionmaking. *Decision Support Systems, 35,* 415–433.

Davis, M. C., Matthews, K. A., & McGrath, C. (2000). Hostile attitudes predict elevated vascular resistance during interpersonal stress in men and women. *Psychosomatic Medicine, 62,* 17–25.

Davis, M. H., Soderlund, T., Cole, J., Gadol, E., Kute, M., Myers, M., & Wiehing, J. (2004). Cognitions associated with attempts to empathize: How do we imagine the perspective of another? *Personality and Social Psychology Bulletin, 30,* 1625–1635.

Davis, S. (1990). Men as success objects and women as sex objects: A study of personal advertisements. *Sex Roles, 23,* 43–50.

Davison, K. P., Pennebaker, J. W., & Dickerson, S. S. (2000). Who talks? The social psychology of illness support groups. *American Psychologist, 55,* 205–217.

Dawes, R. M. (1980). Social dilemmas. *Annual Review of Psychology, 31,* 169–193.

Dawkins, R. (1989). *The selfish gene* (2nd ed.). Oxford: Oxford University Press.

Day, D. D., & Sulsky, L. M. (1995). Effects of frame-of-reference training and information configuration on memory organization and rating accuracy. *Journal of Applied Psychology, 80,* 158–167.

Day, D. V., Shleicher, D. J., Unckless, A. L., & Hiller, N. J. (2002). Self-monitoring personality at work: A meta-analytic investigation of construct validity. *Journal of Applied Psychology, 87,* 390–401.

DeAngelis, T. (1993, August). It's baaack: TV violence, concern for kid viewers. *APA Monitor,* p. 16.

"Dear Abby." (2003, December 17). *The Berkshire Eagle,* p. C7.

Deater-Deckard, K., Dodge, K. A., Bates, J. E., & Pettit, G. S. (1998). Multiple-risk factors in the development of externalizing behavior problems: Group and individual differences. *Development and Psychopathology, 10,* 469–493.

Deaux, K., & Emswiller, T. (1974). Explanations for successful performance on sex-linked tasks: What is skill for the male is luck for the female. *Journal of Personality and Social Psychology, 29,* 80–85.

DeBono, K. G., Leavitt, A., & Backus, J. (2003). Product packaging and product evaluation: An individual difference approach. *Journal of Applied Social Psychology, 33,* 513–521.

Decety, J., Michalska, K. J., Akitsuki, Y., & Lahey, B. B. (2009). Atypical empathic responses in adolescents with aggressive conduct disorder: A functional MRI investigation. *Biological Psychology, 80*(2), 203–211.

Deci, E. L. (1971). Effects of externally mediated rewards on intrinsic motivation. *Journal of Personality and Social Psychology, 18,* 105–115.

Deci, E. L., & Ryan, R. M. (1985). *Intrinsic motivation and self-determination in human behavior.* New York: Plenum.

De Cremer, D. (2004). The influence of accuracy as a function of leader's bias: The role of trustworthiness in the psychology of procedural justice. *Personality and Social Psychology Bulletin, 30,* 293–304.

De Cremer, D., Van Knippenberg, D., Van Dijk, E., & Van Leeuwen, E. (2008). Cooperating if one's goals are collective-based: Social identification effects in social dilemmas as a function of goal transformation. *Journal of Applied Social Psychology, 38,* 1562–1579.

De Dreu, C. K. W. (2010). Social conflict: The emergence and consequences of struggle and negotiation. In S. T. Fiske, D. T. Gilbert,

& G. Lindzey (Eds.), *Handbook of social psychology* (5th ed.). New York: Wiley.

De Dreu, C. K. W., Beersma, B., Steinel, W., Van Kleef, G. A. (2007). The psychology of negotiation: Principles and basic processes (pp. 608–629). In A. W. Kruglanski & E. T. Higgins (Eds.), *Social psychology: Handbook of basic principles* (2nd ed.). New York: Guilford.

De Dreu, C. K. W., Beersma, B., Stroebe, K., & Euwema, M. C. (2006). Motivated information processing, strategic choice, and the quality of negotiated agreement. *Journal of Personality and Social Psychology, 90,* 927–943.

De Dreu, C., & De Vries, N. (Eds.). (2001). *Group consensus and minority influence: Implications for innovation.* London: Blackwell.

Deffenbacher, K. A., Bornstein, B. H., & Penrod, S. D. (2006). Mugshot exposure effects: Retroactive interference, mugshot commitment, source confusion, and unconscious transference. *Law and Human Behavior, 30,* 287–307.

de Hoog, N., Stroebe, W., & de Wit, J. B. F. (2005). The impact of fear appeals on processing and acceptance of action recommendations. *Personality and Social Psychology Bulletin, 31,* 24–33.

de Hoog, N., Stroebe, W., & de Wit, J. B. F. (2007). The impact of vulnerability to and severity of a health risk on processing and acceptance of fear-arousing communications: A meta-analysis. *Review of General Psychology, 11,* 258–285.

De Houwer, J., Thomas, S., & Baeyens, F. (2001) Associative learning of likes and dislikes: A review of 25 years of research on human evaluative conditioning. *Psychological Bulletin, 127,* 853–869.

DeKeseredy, W. S., Schwartz, M. D., & Tait, K. (1993). Sexual assault and stranger aggression on a Canadian university campus. *Sex Roles, 28,* 263–277.

Demaré, D., Lips, H. M., & Briere, J. (1993). Sexually violent pornography, anti-women attitudes, and sexual aggression: A structural equation model. *Journal of Research in Personality, 27,* 285–300.

DeMarree, K. G., Wheeler, S. C., & Petty, R. E. (2005). Priming a new identity: Self-monitoring moderates the effects of nonself primes on self-judgments and behavior. *Journal of Personality and Social Psychology, 89,* 657–671.

Demoulin, S., Pozo, B. C., & Leyens, J.-P. (2009). Infrahumanization: The differential interpretation of primary and secondary emotions. In S. L. Demoulin, J.-P. Leyens, & J. F. Dovidio (Eds.), *Intergroup misunderstandings: Impact of divergent social realities* (pp. 153–171). New York: Psychology Press.

DeNeve, K. M., & Cooper, H. (1998). The happy personality: A meta-analysis of 137 personality traits and subjective well-being. *Psychological Bulletin, 124,* 197–229.

Denissen, J. A., Penke, L., & Schmitt, D. P. (2008). Self-esteem reactions to social interactions: Evidence for sociometer mechanisms across days, people, and nations. *Journal of Personality and Social Psychology, 95,* 181–196.

DePaulo, B. M., Lindsay, J. J., Malone, B. E., Muhlenbruck, L., Charlton, K., & Cooper, H. (2003). Cues to deception. *Psychological Bulletin, 129,* 74–112.

Deppe, R. K., & Harackiewicz, J. M. (1996). Self-handicapping and intrinsic motivation: Buffering intrinsic motivation from the threat of failure. *Journal of Personality and Social Psychology, 70,* 868–876.

De Raad, B. (2000). *The big five personality factors: Theory and applications.* Germany: Hogrefe & Huber.

Derlega, V. J., Metts, S., Petronio, S., & Margulis, S. T. (1993). *Self-disclosure.* Newbury Park, CA: Sage.

Derlega, V. J., Wilson, M., & Chaikin, A. L. (1976). Friendship and disclosure reciprocity. *Journal of Personality and Social Psychology, 34,* 578–587.

DeRosa, D. M., Smith, C. L., & Hantula, D. A. (2007). The medium matters: Mining the long-promised merit of group interaction in creative idea generation tasks in a meta-analysis of the electronic group brainstorming literature. *Computers in Human Behavior, 23,* 1549–1581.

Dershowitz, A. M. (1982). *The best defense.* New York: Vintage Books.

DeSteno, D. A., & Salovey, P. (1996). Evolutionary origins of sex differences in jealousy? Questioning the "fitness" model. *Psychological Science, 7,* 367–372.

De Steno, D. M., Valdesolo, P., & Bartlett, M. Y. (2006). Jealousy and the threatened self: Getting to the heart of the green-eyed monster. *Journal of Personality and Social Psychology, 91,* 626–641.

Deutsch, F. M. (1989). The false consensus effect: Is the self-justification hypothesis justified? *Basic and Applied Social Psychology, 10,* 83–99.

Deutsch, M., & Gerard, H. B. (1955). A study of normative and informational social influences upon individual judgment. *Journal of Abnormal and Social Psychology, 51,* 629–636.

Deutsch, M., & Krauss, R. M. (1960). The effect of threat upon interpersonal bargaining. *Journal of Abnormal and Social Psychology, 61,* 181–189.

De Veer, M. W., Gallup, G. G., Theall, L. A., van den Bos, R., & Povinelli, D. J. (2003). An 8-year longitudinal study of mirror self-recognition in chimpanzees *(Pan troglodytes). Neuropsychologia, 41,* 229–234.

Devenport, J. L., Penrod, S. D., & Cutler, B. L. (1997). Eyewitness identification evidence: Evaluating commonsense evaluations. *Psychology, Public Policy, and Law, 3,* 338–361.

Devine, P. G. (1989). Stereotypes and prejudice: Their automatic and controlled components. *Journal of Personality and Social Psychology, 56,* 5–18.

Devine, P. G., Brodish, A. B., & Vance, S. L. (2005). Self-regulatory processes in interracial interactions: The role of internal and external motivation to respond without prejudice. In J. P. Forgas, K. D. Williams, & W. von Hippel (Eds.), *Social motivation: Conscious and unconscious processes* (pp. 249–273). New York: Psychology Press.

de Waal, F. B., & Berger, M. L. (2000). Payment for labor in monkeys. *Nature, 404,* 563.

de Waal, F. B. M. (1996). *Good natured: The origins of right and wrong in humans and other animals.* Cambridge, MA: Harvard University Press.

de Waal, F. B. M. (2003). The chimpanzee's service economy: Evidence for cognition-based reciprocal exchange. In E. Ostrom & J. Walker (Eds.), *Trust and reciprocity: Interdisciplinary lessons from experimental research* (pp. 128–143). New York: Russell Sage.

de Waal, F. B. M. (2006a). Joint ventures require joint pay-offs: Fairness among primates. *Social Research, 73,* 349–364.

de Waal, F. B. M. (2006b). *Primates and philosophers: How morality evolved.* Princeton, NJ: Princeton University Press.

de Waal, F. B. M. (2008). Putting the altruism back into altruism: The evolution of empathy. *Annual Review of Psychology, 59,* 279–300.

de Waal, F. B. M. (2009). *The age of empathy: Nature's lesson for a kinder society.* New York: Harmony.

DeWall, C. N., & Bushman, B. J. (2009). Hot under the collar in a lukewarm environment: Words associated with hot temperature increase aggressive thoughts and hostile perceptions. *Journal of Experimental Social Psychology, 45,* 1045–1047.

DeWall, C. N., Maner, J. K., & Rouby, D. A. (2009). Social exclusion and early-stage interpersonal perception: Selective attention to signs of acceptance. *Journal of Personality and Social Psychology, 96,* 729–741.

Diamond, L. M. (2003). Was it a phase? Young women's relinquishment of lesbian/bisexual identities over a 5-year period. *Journal of Personality and Social Psychology, 84,* 352–364.

Diamond, L. M. (2007). A dynamical systems approach to female same-sex sexuality. *Perspectives on Psychological Science, 2,* 142–161.

Diamond, M. (1993). Homosexuality and bisexuality in different populations. *Archives of Sexual Behavior, 22,* 291–310.

Diamond, S. S., Rose, M. R., & Murphy, B. (2006). Revisiting the unanimity requirement: The behavior of the non-unanimous civil jury. *Northwestern Law Review, 100,* 201–230.

Diehl, M., & Stroebe, W. (1987). Productivity loss in brainstorming groups: Toward the solution of a riddle. *Journal of Personality and Social Psychology, 53,* 497–509.

Diekmann, K. A., Tenbrunsel, A. E., & Galinsky, A. D. (2003). From self-prediction to self-defeat: Behavioral forecasting, self-fulfilling prophecies, and the effect of competitive expectations. *Journal of Personality and Social Psychology, 85,* 672–683.

Diener, E. (1979). Deindividuation, self-awareness, and disinhibition. *Journal of Personality and Social Psychology, 37,* 1160–1171.

Diener, E. (1980). Deindividuation: The absence of self-awareness and self-regulation in group members. In P. B. Paulus (Ed.), *Psychology of group influence* (pp. 209–242). Hillsdale, NJ: Erlbaum.

Diener, E. (2000). Subjective well-being: The science of happiness, and a proposal for a national index. *American Psychologist, 55,* 34–43.

Diener, E., & Seligman, M. E. P. (2004). Beyond money: Toward an economy of well-being. *Psychological Science in the Public Interest, 5,* whole No. 1.

Diener, E., & Suh, E. M. (Eds.). (2000). Culture and subjective well-being. Cambridge, MA: MIT Press.

Diener, E., & Biswas-Diener, R. (2008). *Happiness: Unlocking the mysteries of psychological wealth.* Malden, MA: Blackwell.

Diener, E., Emmons, R. A., Larsen, R. J., & Griffin, S. (1984). The Satisfaction with Life Scale. *Journal of Personality Assessment, 49,* 71–75.

Diener, E., Fraser, S. C., Beaman, A. L., & Kelem, R. T. (1976). Effects of deindividuation variables on stealing among Halloween trick-or-treaters. *Journal of Personality and Social Psychology, 33,* 178–183.

Diener, E., Suh, E. M., Lucas, R. E., & Smith, H. L. (1999). Subjective well-being: Three decades of progress. *Psychological Bulletin, 125,* 276–302.

Diener, E., Wolsic, B., & Fujita, F. (1995). Physical attractiveness and subjective well-being. *Journal of Personality and Social Psychology, 69,* 120–129.

Dietz, T. L. (1998). An examination of violence and gender role portrayals in video games: Implications for gender socialization and aggressive behavior. *Sex Roles, 38,* 425–442.

Dietz-Uhler, B. (1996). The escalation of commitment in political decision-making groups: A social identity approach. *European Journal of Social Psychology, 26,* 611–629.

DiFonzo, N., & Bordia, P. (1997). Rumor and prediction: Making sense (but losing dollars) in the stock market. *Organizational Behavior and Human Decision Processes, 71,* 329–353.

Dijksterhuis, A., & Aarts, H. (2003). Of wildebeests and humans: The preferential detection of negative stimuli. *Psychological Science, 14,* 14–18.

Dijksterhuis, A., & Bargh, J. A. (2001). The perception-behavior expressway: Automatic effects of social perception on social behavior. *Advances in Experimental Social Psychology, 33,* 1–40.

Dijkstra, P., & Buunk, B. P. (1998). Jealousy as a function of rival characteristics: An evolutionary perspective. *Personality and Social Psychology Bulletin, 24,* 1158–1166.

Dill, K. E., Anderson, C. A., Anderson, K. B., & Deuser, W. E. (1997). Effects of aggressive personality on social expectations and social perceptions. *Journal of Research in Personality, 31,* 272–292.

Dillard, A. J., Schiavone, A., & Brown, S. L. (2008). Helping behavior and positive emotions: Implications for health and well-being. In S. J. Lopez (Ed.), *Positive psychology: Exploring the best in people: Vol. 2. Capitalizing on emotional experiences* (pp. 101–114). Westport, CT: Praeger.

Dimberg, U., Thunberg, M., & Elmehed, K. (2000). Unconscious facial reactions to emotional facial expressions. *Psychological Science, 11,* 86–89.

Dimberg, U., & Ohman, A. (1996). Behold the wrath: Psychophysiological responses to facial stimuli. *Motivation and Emotion, 20,* 149–181.

Dindia, K., & Allen, M. (1992). Sex differences in self-disclosure: A meta-analysis. *Psychological Bulletin, 112,* 106–124.

Dion, K. K., & Dion, K. L. (1996). Cultural perspectives on romantic love. *Personal Relationships, 3,* 5–17.

Dion, K. K., Berscheid, E., & Walster, E. (1972). What is beautiful is good. *Journal of Personality and Social Psychology, 24,* 285–290.

Dion, K. L. (2000). Group cohesion: From "field of forces" to multidimensional construct. *Group Dynamics, 4,* 7–26.

Dion, K. L., & Dion, K. K. (1976). Love, liking and trust in heterosexual relationships. *Personality and Social Psychology Bulletin, 2,* 187–190.

Dionisio, D. P., Granholm, E., Hillix, W. A., & Perrine, W. F. (2001). Differentiation of deception using pupillary responses as an index of cognitive processing. *Psychophysiology 38,* 205–211.

Dittmann, M. (2005). After the wave. *APA Monitor on Psychology, 36,* No. 3, p. 36.

Dolinski, D. (2000). On inferring one's beliefs from one's attempt and consequences for subsequent compliance. *Journal of Personality and Social Psychology, 78,* 260–272.

Dollard, J., Doob, L. W., Miller, N. E., Mowrer, O. H., & Sears, R. R. (1939). *Frustration and aggression.* New Haven, CT: Yale University Press.

Donnellan, M. B., Trzesniewski, K. H., Robins, R. W., Moffitt, T. E., & Caspi, A. (2005). Low self-esteem is related to aggression, antisocial behavior, and delinquency. *Psychological Science, 16,* 328–335.

Donnelly, M., & Straus, M. A. (Eds.). (2005). *Corporal punishment of children in theoretical perspective.* New Haven, CT: Yale University Press.

Donnerstein, E., & Berkowitz, L. (1981). Victim reactions in aggressive erotic films as a factor in violence against women. *Journal of Personality and Social Psychology, 41,* 710–724.

Donnerstein, E., & Donnerstein, M. (1976). Research in the control of interracial aggression. In R. G. Geen and E. C. O'Neal (Eds.), *Perspectives on aggression* (pp. 133–168). New York: Academic Press.

Donnerstein, E., & Malamuth, N. (1997). Pornography: Its consequences on the observer. In L. B. Schlesinger & E. Revitch (Eds.), *Sexual dynamics of anti-social behavior* (2nd ed., pp. 30–49). Springfield, IL: Charles C Thomas.

Donnerstein, E., Linz, D., & Penrod, S. (1987). *The question of pornography.* New York: Free Press.

Dooley, P. A. (1995). Perceptions of the onset controllability of AIDS and helping judgments: An attributional analysis. *Journal of Applied Social Psychology, 25,* 858–869.

Dornbusch, S. M., Hastorf, A. H., Richardson, S. A., Muzzy, R. E., & Vreeland, R. S. (1965). The perceiver and the perceived: Their relative influence on categories of interpersonal perception. *Journal of Personality and Social Psychology, 1,* 434–440.

Dougherty, T. W., Turban, D. B., & Callender, J. C. (1994). Confirming first impressions in the employment interview: A field study of interviewer behavior. *Journal of Applied Psychology, 79,* 659–665.

Douglas, E. M., & Straus, M. A. (2006). Assault and injury of dating partners by university students in 19 countries and its relation to corporal punishment experienced as a child. *European Journal of Criminology, 7,* 293–318.

Douglas, E., & Straus, M. A. (2007). Discipline by parents and child psychopathology. In A. Felthous & H. Sass (Eds.), *International handbook of psychopathology and the law.* New York: Wiley.

Douglass, A. B., & Steblay, N. (2006). Memory distortion in eyewitnesses: A meta-analysis of the post-identification feed-back effect. *Applied Cognitive Psychology, 20,* 859–869.

Dovidio, J. F. (1984). Helping behavior and altruism: An empirical and conceptual overview. In L. Berkowitz (Ed.), *Advances in experimental social psychology* (Vol. 17, pp. 361-427). New York: Academic Press.

Dovidio, J. F., Brigham, J. C., Johnson, B. T., & Gaertner, S. L. (1996). Stereotyping, prejudice, and discrimination: Another look. In C. N. Macrae, C. Stangor, & M. Hewstone (Eds.), *Stereotypes and stereotyping* (pp. 276–319). New York: Guilford.

Dovidio, J. F., & Gaertner, S. L. (2004). Aversive racism. In M. P. Zanna (Ed.), *Advances in experimental social psychology* (Vol. 36, pp. 1–52). San Diego, CA: Elsevier.

Dovidio, J. F., & Gaertner, S. L. (2010). Intergroup bias. In S. T. Fiske, D. T. Gilbert, & G. Lindzey (Eds.), *Handbook of social psychology* (5th ed.). New York: Wiley.

Dovidio, J. F., Gaertner, S. E., Kawakami, K., & Hodson, G. (2002). Why can't we just get along? Interpersonal biases and interracial distrust. *Cultural Diversity and Ethnic Minority Psychology, 8,* 88–102.

Dovidio, J. F., Gaertner, S., & Saguy, T. (2009). Commonality and the complexity of 'we': Social attitudes and social change. *Personality and Social Psychology Review, 13,* 3–20.

Dovidio, J. F., Kawakami, K., Johnson, C., Johnson, B., & Howard, A. (1997). On the nature of prejudice: Automatic and controlled processes. *Journal of Experimental Social Psychology, 33,* 510–540.

Downie, M., Mageau, G. A., & Koestner, R. (2008). What makes for a pleasant social interaction? Motivational dynamics of interpersonal relationships. *Journal of Social Psychology, 148,* 523–534.

Downs, A. C., & Lyons, P. M. (1991). Natural observations of the links between attractiveness and initial legal judgments. *Personality and Social Psychology Bulletin, 17,* 541–547.

Doyle, J. M. (2005). *True witness: Cops, courts, science, and the battle against misidentification.* New York: Palgrave MacMillan.

Dreher, G. F., & Cox, T. H., Jr. (1996). Race, gender, and opportunity: A study of compensation attainment and the establishment of mentoring relationships. *Journal of Applied Psychology, 81,* 297–308.

Drigotas, S. M., & Rusbult, C. E. (1992). Shall I stay or should I go? A dependence model of breakups. *Journal of Personality and Social Psychology, 62,* 62–87.

Drigotas, S. M., Rusbult, C. E., & Verette, J. (1999). Level of commitment, mutuality of commitment, and couple well-being. *Personal Relationships, 6,* 389–409.

Druckman, D. (1994). Determinants of compromising behavior in negotiation: A meta-analysis. *Journal of Conflict Resolution, 38,* 507–556.

Duck, S., & Wright, P. H. (1993). Reexamining gender differences in same-gender friendships: A close look at two kinds of data. *Sex Roles, 28,* 709–727.

Duckitt, J., & Mphuthing, T. (1998). Group identification and intergroup attitudes: A longitudinal analysis in South Africa. *Journal of Personality and Social Psychology, 74,* 80–85.

Duckitt, J., & Sibley, C. G. (2009). A dual process motivational model of ideological attitudes and system justification. In J. T. Jost & A. C. Kay (Eds.), *Social and psychological bases of ideology and system justification* (pp. 292–313). New York: Oxford University Press.

Duckworth, K. L., Bargh, J. A., Garcia, M., & Chaiken, S. (2002). The automatic evaluation of novel stimuli. *Psychological Science, 13,* 513–519.

Duclos, S. E., Laird, J. D., Schneider, E., Sexter, M., Stern, L., & Van Lighten, O. (1989). Emotion-specific effects of facial expressions and postures on emotional experience. *Journal of Personality and Social Psychology, 57,* 100–108.

Dudley, N. M., Orvis, K. A., Lebiecki, J. E., & Cortina, J. M. (2006). A meta-analytic investigation of conscientiousness in the prediction of job performance: Examining the intercorrelations and the incremental validity of narrow traits. *Journal of Applied Psychology, 91,* 40–57.

Due, P., & Holstein, B. (2008). Bullying victimization among 13 to 15 year old school children: Results from two comparative studies in 66 countries and regions. *International Journal of Adolescent Medicine and Health, 20,* 209–221.

Dueck, L. (2006, November 3). There's a lot we can learn from the Amish. *The Globe and Mail* (Canada), p. A25.

Dunbar, R. I. M. (2008). Cognitive constraints on the structure and dynamics of social networks. *Group Dynamics: Theory, Research, and Practice, 12,* 7–16.

Dunham, Y., Baron, A. S., & Banaji, M. R. (2008). The development of implicit intergroup cognition. *Trends in Cognitive Sciences, 12,* 248–253.

Dunning, D. (2005). *Self-insight: Roadblocks and detours on the path to knowing thyself.* New York: Psychology Press.

Dunning, D., & Hayes, A. F. (1996). Evidence for egocentric comparison in social judgment. *Journal of Personality and Social Psychology, 71,* 213–229.

Dunning, D., & Sherman, D. A. (1997). Stereotypes and tacit inference. *Journal of Personality and Social Psychology, 73,* 459–471.

Dunning, D., Griffin, D. W., Milojkovic, J. D., & Ross, L. (1990). The overconfidence effect in social prediction. *Journal of Personality and Social Psychology, 58,* 568–581.

Dunning, D., Heath, C., & Suls, J. M. (2004). Flawed self-assessment: Implications for health, education, and the workplace. *Psychological Science in the Public Interest, 5,* 69–106.

Duntley, J., & Buss, D. (2008). The origins of homicide. In J. D. Duntley & T. K. Shackelford (Eds.), *Evolutionary forensic psychology: Darwinian foundations of crime and law* (pp. 41–63). New York: Oxford University Press.

Dunton, B. C., & Fazio, R. H. (1997). An individual difference measure of motivation to control prejudiced reactions. *Personality and Social Psychology Bulletin, 23,* 316–326.

Durantini, M. R., Albarracín, D., Mitchell, A. L., Earl, A. N., & Gillette, J. C. (2006). Conceptualizing the influence of social agents of behavior change: A meta-analysis of the effectiveness of HIV-prevention interventionists for different groups. *Psychological Bulletin, 132,* 212–248.

Durik, A. M., & Harackiewicz, J. M. (2007). Different strokes for different folks: Individual interest as a moderator of the effects of situational factors on task interest. *Journal of Educational Psychology, 99,* 597–610.

Dutton, D. G., & Aron, A. P. (1974). Some evidence for heightened sexual attraction under conditions of high anxiety. *Journal of Personality and Social Psychology, 30,* 510–517.

Duval, S., & Wicklund, R. A. (1972). *A theory of objective self-awareness.* New York: Academic Press.

Duval, S., Duval, V. H., & Mulilis, J. P. (1992). Effects of self-focus, discrepancy between self and standard, and outcome expectancy favorability on the tendency to match self to standard or to withdraw. *Journal of Personality and Social Psychology, 62,* 340–348.

Dweck, C. S., Chiu, C., & Hong, Y. (1995). Implicit theories and their role in judgments and reactions: A world from two perspectives. *Psychological Inquiry, 6,* 267–285.

Dysart, J. E., Lindsay, R. C. L., MacDonald, T. K., & Wicke, C. (2002). The intoxicated witness: Effects of alcohol on identification accuracy from showups. *Journal of Applied Psychology, 87,* 170–175.

Eagly, A. H. (1987). *Sex differences in social behavior: A social-role interpretation.* Hillsdale, NJ: Erlbaum.

Eagly, A. H. (2004). Few women at the top: How role incongruity produces prejudice and the glass ceiling. In D. van Knippenberg & M. A. Hogg (Eds.), *Leadership and power: Identity processes in groups and organizations* (pp. 79–93). London: Sage Publications.

Eagly, A. H., & Carli, L. L. (1981). Sex of researchers and sex-typed communications as determinants of sex differences in influenceability: A meta-analysis of social influence studies. *Psychological Bulletin, 90,* 1–20.

Eagly, A. H., & Carli, L. L. (2007). *Through the labyrinth: The truth about how women become leaders.* Boston: Harvard Business School Publishing.

Eagly, A. H., & Crowley, M. (1986). Gender and helping behavior: A meta-analytic review of the social psychological literature. *Psychological Bulletin, 100,* 283–308.

Eagly, A. H., & Fischer, A. (2009). Gender inequalities in power in organizations. In B. van Knippenberg & D. Tjosvold (Eds.), *Power and interdependence in organizations.* New York: Cambridge University Press.

Eagly, A. H., & Karau, S. J. (2002). Role congruity theory of prejudice toward female leaders. *Psychological Review, 109,* 573–598.

Eagly, A. H., Ashmore, R. D., Makhijani, M. G., & Longo, L. C. (1991). What is beautiful is good, but . . . : A meta-analytic review of research on the physical attractiveness stereotype. *Psychology Bulletin, 110,* 107–128.

Eagly, A. H., Johannesen-Schmidt, M. C., & van Engen, M. L. (2003). Transformational, transactional, and laissez-faire leadership styles: A meta-analysis comparing women and men. *Psychological Bulletin, 129,* 569–591.

Eagly, A. H., Mladinic, A., & Otto, S. (1994). Are women evaluated more favorably than men? An analysis of attitudes, beliefs, and emotions. *Psychology of Women Quarterly, 15,* 203–216.

Eagly, A. H., Wood, W., & Chaiken, S. (1978). Causal inferences about communicators and their effect on opinion change. *Journal of Personality and Social Psychology, 36,* 424–435.

Eagly, A. H., Wood, W., & Johannesen-Schmidt, M. C. (2004). Social role theory of sex differences and similarities: Implications for the partner preferences of women and men. In A. H. Eagly, A. Beall, & R. J. Sternberg (Eds.), *The psychology of gender* (2nd ed.). New York: Guilford.

Easton, J., Schipper, L., & Shackelford, T. (2007). Morbid jealousy from an evolutionary psychological perspective. *Evolution and Human Behavior, 28,* 399–402.

Earl, A., Albarracín, D., Durantini, M., Gunnoe, J., Leeper, J., & Levitt, J. (2009). Participation in counseling programs: High-risk participants are reluctant to accept HIV-prevention counseling. *Journal of Consulting and Clinical Psychology, 77,* 668–679.

Easton, J. A., & Shackelford, T. K. (2009). Morbid jealousy and sex differences in partner-directed violence. *Human Nature, 20,* 342–350.

Eastwick, P. W., & Finkel, E. J. (2008). Sex differences in mate preferences revisited: Do people know what they initially desire in a romantic partner? *Journal of Personality and Social Psychology, 94,* 245–264.

Eberhardt, J. L., Davies, P. G., Purdie-Vaughns, V. J., & Johnson, S. L. (2006). Looking deathworthy: Perceived stereotypicality of black defendants predicts capital-sentencing outcomes. *Psychological Science, 17,* 383–386.

Eberhardt, J. L., & Goff, P. A. (2004). Seeing race. In C. S. Crandall & M. Schaller (Eds.), *The social psychology of prejudice: Historical perspectives.* Seattle, WA: Lewinian.

Eberle, M., & Kappeler, P. M. (2008). Mutualism, reciprocity, or kin selection? Cooperative rescue of a conspecific from a boa in a nocturnal solitary forager the gray mouse lemur. *American Journal of Primatology, 70,* 410–414.

Eden, D. (1990). Pygmalion without interpersonal contrast effects: Whole groups gain from raising manager expectations. *Journal of Applied Psychology, 75,* 394–398.

Eder, R. W., & Harris, M. M. (Eds.). (1999). *The employment interview handbook* (2nd ed.). Thousand Oaks, CA: Sage.

Edlund, J. E., & Sagarin, B. J. (2009). Sex differences in jealousy: Misinterpretation of nonsignificant results as refuting the theory. *Personal Relationships, 16,* 67–78.

Edwards, K., & Smith, E. E. (1996). A disconfirmation bias in the evaluation of arguments. *Journal of Personality and Social Psychology, 71,* 5–24.

Ehrlichman, H., & Eichenstein, R. (1992). Private wishes: Gender similarities and differences. *Sex Roles, 26,* 399–422.

Ehrlinger, J., Gilovich, T., & Ross, L. (2005). Peering into the bias blind spot: People's assessments of bias in themselves and others. *Personality and Social Psychology Bulletin, 31,* 680–692.

Eibach, R. P., & Ehrlinger, J. (2006). "Keep your eyes on the prize": Reference points and racial differences in assessing progress toward equality. *Personality and Social Psychology Bulletin, 32,* 66–77.

Eichstaedt, J., & Silvia, P. J. (2003). Noticing the self: Implicit assessment of self-focused attention using word recognition latencies. *Social Cognition, 21,* 349–361.

Eisenberg, N., & Eggum, N. D. (2008). Empathy-related and prosocial responding: Conceptions and correlates during development. In B. A. Sullivan, M. Snyder, & J. L. Sullivan (Eds.), *Cooperation: The political psychology of effective human interaction* (pp. 53–74). Oxford: Blackwell.

Eisenberg, N., Guthrie, I. K., Cumberland, A., Murphy, B. C., Shepard, S. A., Zhou, Q., & Carlo, G. (2002). Prosocial development in early adulthood: A longitudinal study. *Journal of Personality and Social Psychology, 82,* 993–1006.

Eisenberg, N., Spinrad, T. L., & Sadovsky, A. (2006). Empathy-related responding in children. In M. Killen & J. G. Smetana (Eds.), *Handbook of moral development* (pp. 517–549). Mahwah, NJ: Erlbaum.

Eisenberger, N. I., Gable, S. L., & Lieberman, M. D. (2007). fMRI responses relate to differences in real world social experiences. *Emotion, 7,* 745–754.

Eisenberger, N. I., Lieberman, M. I., & Williams, K. D. (2003). Does rejection hurt? An fMRI study of social exclusion. *Science, 302,* 290–292.

Eisenberger, N. I., Way, B. M., Taylor, S. E., Welch, W. T., & Lieberman, M. D. (2007). Understanding genetic risk for aggression: Clues from the brain's response to social exclusion. *Biological Psychiatry, 61,* 1100–1108.

Eisenberger, R., & Cameron, J. (1996). Detrimental effects of reward: Reality or myth? *American Psychologist, 51,* 1153–1166.

Eisenberger, R., & Rhoades, L. (2001). Incremental effects of reward on creativity. *Journal of Personality and Social Psychology, 81,* 728–741.

Eisenberger, R., Cotterell, N., & Marvel, J. (1987). Reciprocation ideology. *Journal of Personality and Social Psychology, 53,* 743–750.

Ekman, P., & Friesen, W. V. (1974). Detecting deception from the body or face. *Journal of Personality and Social Psychology, 29,* 288–298.

Ekman, P., & O'Sullivan, M. (1991). Who can catch a liar? *American Psychologist, 46,* 913–920.

Ekman, P., Friesen, W. V., O'Sullivan, M., Chan, A., Diacoyanni-Tarlatzis, I., Heider, K., Krause, R., LeCompte, W. A., Pitcairn, T., Ricci-Bitti, P., Scherer, K., Tomita, M., & Tzavaras, A. (1987). Universals and cultural differences in the judgments of facial expressions of emotion. *Journal of Personality and Social Psychology, 53,* 712–717.

Elfenbein, H. A., & Ambady N. (2002). On the universality and cultural specificity of emotion recognition: A meta-analysis. *Psychological Bulletin, 128,* 203–235.

Elfenbein, H. A., & Ambady, N. (2003). When familiarity breeds accuracy: Cultural exposure and facial emotion recognition. *Journal of Personality and Social Psychology, 85,* 276–290.

Elkin, R. A., & Leippe, M. R. (1986). Physiological arousal, dissonance, and attitude change: Evidence for a dissonance-arousal link and a "don't remind me" effect. *Journal of Personality and Social Psychology, 51,* 55–65.

El Leithy, S., Brown, G. P., & Robbins, I. (2006). Counterfactual thinking and posttraumatic stress reactions. *Journal of Abnormal Psychology, 115,* 629–635.

Ellemers, N., Haslam, S. A., Platow, M. J., & van Knippenberg, D. (2003). Social identity at work: Developments, debates, directions. In S. A. Haslam, D. van Knippenberg, M. J. Platow, & N. Ellemers (Eds.), *Social identity at work: Developing theory for organizational practice* (pp. 3–26). New York: Psychology Press.

Elliot, A. J., & Devine, P. G. (1994). On the motivational nature of cognitive dissonance: Dissonance as psychological discomfort. *Journal of Personality and Social Psychology, 67,* 382–394.

Elliot, A. J., & Niesta, D. (2008). Romantic red: Red enhances men's attraction to women. *Journal of Personality and Social Psychology, 95,* 1150–1164.

Elliott, M. A., Armitage, C. J., & Baughan, C. J. (2003). Drivers' compliance with speed limits: An application of the theory of planned behavior. *Journal of Applied Psychology, 88,* 964–972.

Elliott, R. (1991). Social science data and the APA: The Lockhart brief as a case in point. *Law and Human Behavior, 15,* 59–76.

Ellsworth, P. C. (1991). To tell what we know or wait for Godot? *Law and Human Behavior, 15,* 77–90.

Elms, A. C. (2009). Obedience lite. *American Psychologist, 64,* 32–36.

Elms, A., & Milgram, S. (1966). Personality characteristics associated with obedience and defiance toward authoritative command. *Journal of Experimental Research in Personality, 1,* 282–289.

Elwork, A., Sales, B. D., & Alfini, J. J. (1982). *Making jury instructions understandable.* Charlottesville, VA: Miche.

Englich, B., Mussweiler, T., & Strack, F. (2006). Playing dice with criminal sentences: The influence of irrelevant anchors on experts' judicial decision making. *Personality and Social Psychology Bulletin, 32,* 188–200.

English, P. W., & Sales, B. D. (1997). A ceiling or consistency effect for the comprehension of jury instructions. *Psychology, Public Policy, and Law, 3,* 381–401.

English, T., & Chen, S. (2007). Culture and self-concept stability: Consistency across and within contexts among Asian Americans and European Americans. *Journal of Personality and Social Psychology, 93,* 478–490.

Epley, N., & Huff, C. (1998). Suspicion, affective response, and educational benefit as a result of deception in psychology research. *Personality and Social Psychology Bulletin, 24,* 759–768.

Erber, R., & Tesser, A. (1992). Task effort and the regulation of mood: The absorption hypothesis. *Journal of Experimental Social Psychology, 28,* 339–359.

Erber, R., & Tesser, A. (1994). Self-evaluation maintenance: A social psychological approach to interpersonal relationships. In R. Erber & R. Gilmour (Eds.), *Theoretical frameworks for personal relationships* (pp. 211–233). Hillsdale, NJ: Erlbaum.

Ericksen, J. A., & Steffen, S. A. (1999). *Kiss and tell: Surveying sex in the twentieth century.* Cambridge, MA: Harvard University Press.

Eslea, M., Menesini, E., Morita, Y., O'Moore, M., Mora-Merchán, J. A., Pereira, B., & Smith, P. K. (2003). Friendship and loneliness among bullies and victims: Data from seven countries. *Aggressive Behavior, 30,* 71–83.

Esser, J. K. (1998). Alive and well after 25 years: A review of groupthink research. *Organizational Behavior and Human Decision Processes, 73,* 116–141.

Esses, V. M., Veenvliet, S., Hodson, G., & Mihic, L. (2008). Justice, morality, and the dehumanization of refugees. *Social Justice Research, 21,* 4–25.

Estrada-Hollenbeck, M., & Heatherton, T. F. (1998). Avoiding and alleviating guilt through prosocial behavior. In J. Bybee (Ed.), *Guilt and children* (pp. 215–231). San Diego: Academic Press.

Evans, G. W., & Lepore, S. J. (1993). Household crowding and social support: A quasiexperimental analysis. *Journal of Personality and Social Psychology, 65,* 308–316.

Evans, G. W., & Wener, R. E. (2006). Rail commuting duration and passenger stress. *Health Psychology, 25,* 408–412.

Evans, R. I., Smith, C. K., & Raines, B. E. (1984). Deterring cigarette smoking in adolescents: A psychosocial-behavioral analysis of an intervention strategy. In A. Baum, S. E. Taylor, & J. E. Singer (Eds.), *Handbook of psychology and health: Vol. 4. Social psychological aspects of health* (pp. 301–318). Hillsdale, NJ: Erlbaum.

Everson, S. A., Goldberg, D. E., Kaplan, G. A., Cohen, R. D., Pukkala, E., Tuomiletho, P., & Salonen, J. T.. (1996). Hopelessness and risk of mortality and incidence of myocardial infarction and cancer. *Psychosomatic Medicine, 58,* 113–121.

Everson, S. A., Goldberg, D. E., Kaplan, G. A., Julkunen, J., & Salonen, J. T. (1998). Anger expression and incident hypertension. *Psychosomatic Medicine, 60,* 730–735.

Everson-Rose, S. A., & Lewis, T. T. (2005). Psychosocial factors in cardiovascular diseases. *Annual Review of Public Health, 26,* 469–500.

Exum, M. L. (2006). Alcohol and aggression: An integration of findings from experimental studies. *Journal of Criminal Justice, 34,* 131–145.

Fagan, A. A. (2005). The relationship between adolescent physical abuse and criminal offending: Support for an enduring and generalized cycle of violence. *Journal of Family Violence, 20,* 279–290.

Fagin-Jones, S., & Midlarsky, E. (2007). Courageous altruism: Personal and situational correlates of rescue during the Holocaust. *Journal of Positive Psychology, 2,* 136–147.

Fairburn, C. G., & Brownell, K. D. (Eds.). (2002). *Eating disorders and obesity: A comprehensive handbook.* New York: Guilford Press.

Falk, C. F., Heine, S. J., Yuki, M., & Takemura, K. (2009). Why do Westerners self-enhance more than East Asians? *European Journal of Personality, 23*(3), 183–203.

Fanti, K., Vanman, E., Henrich, C. C., & Avraamides, M. N. (2009). Desensitization to media violence over a short period of time. *Aggressive Behavior, 35,* 179–187.

Farrelly, D., Lazarus, J., & Roberts, G. (2007). Altruists attract. *Evolutionary Psychology, 5,* 313–329.

Farris, C., Treat, T. A., Viken, R. J., & McFall, R. M. (2008). Sexual coercion and the misperception of sexual intent. *Clinical Psychology Review, 28,* 48–66.

Fay, R. E., Turner, C. F., Klassen, A. D., & Gagnon, J. H. (1989). Prevalence and patterns of same-gender sexual contact among men. *Science, 243,* 343–348.

Fazio, R. H. (1990). Multiple processes by which attitudes guide behavior: The MODE model as an integrative framework. In M. P. Zanna (Ed.), *Advances in experimental social psychology* (Vol. 23, pp. 75–109). New York: Academic Press.

Fazio, R. H., & Olson, M. A. (2003). Implicit measures in social cognition research: Their meaning and use. *Annual Review of Psychology, 54,* 297–327.

Fazio, R. H., & Petty, R. E. (Eds.). (2008). *Attitudes: Their structure, function, and consequences.* New York: Psychology Press.

Fazio, R. H., & Towles-Schwen, T. (1999). The MODE model of attitude-behavior processes. In S. Chaiken & Y Trope (Eds.), *Dual-process theories in social psychology* (pp. 97–116). New York: Guilford.

Fazio, R. H., & Zanna, M. P. (1981). Direct experience and attitude-behavior consistency. In L. Berkowitz (Ed.), *Advances in experimental social psychology* (Vol. 14, pp. 162–202). New York: Academic Press.

Fazio, R. H., Ledbetter, J. E., & Towles-Schwen, T. (2000). On the costs of accessible attitudes: Detecting that the attitude object has changed. *Journal of Personality and Social Psychology, 78,* 197–210.

Fazio, R. H., Zanna, M. P., & Cooper, J. (1977). Dissonance and self perception: An integrative view of each theory's proper domain of application. *Journal of Experimental Social Psychology, 13,* 464–479.

Feeney, J. A., & Noller, P. (1990). Attachment style as a predictor of adult romantic relationships. *Journal of Personality and Social Psychology, 58,* 281–291.

Fehr, B., & Russell, J. A. (1991). The concept of love viewed from a prototype perspective. *Journal of Personality and Social Psychology, 60,* 425–438.

Fein, S., & Eustis, E. F. (2001). *Effects of violent and sexist content in video games on men's sexist attitudes and judgments.* Paper presented at the second annual meeting of the Society of Personality and Social Psychology, San Antonio, TX.

Fein, S., Goethals, G. R., & Kugler, M. B. (2007). Social influence on political judgments: The case of presidential debates. *Political Psychology, 28,* 165–192.

Fein, S., Hoshino-Browne, E., Davies, P. G., & Spencer, S. J. (2003). Self-image maintenance goals and sociocultural norms in motivated social perception. In S. J. Spencer, S. Fein, M. P. Zanna, & J. M. Olson (Eds.), *Motivated social perception: The Ontario symposium* (Vol. 9, pp. 21–44). Mahwah, NJ: Erlbaum.

Fein, S., Morgan, S. J., Norton, M. I., & Sommers, S. R. (1997). Hype and suspicion: The effects of pretrial publicity, race, and suspicion on jurors' verdicts. *Journal of Social Issues, 53,* 487–502.

Fein, E., & Schneider, S. (1996). *The rules: Time-tested secrets for capturing the heart of Mr. Right.* New York: Warner Books.

Feinberg, T. E., & Keenan, J. P. (Eds.). (2005). *The lost self: Pathologies of the brain and identity.* New York: Oxford University Press.

Feingold, A. (1988). Matching for attractiveness in romantic partners and same-sex friends: A meta-analysis and theoretical critique. *Psychological Bulletin, 104,* 226–235.

Feingold, A. (1992a). Gender differences in mate selection preferences: A test of the parental investment model. *Psychological Bulletin, 112,* 125–139.

Feingold, A. (1992b). Good-looking people are not what we think. *Psychological Bulletin, 111,* 304–341.

Fejfar, M. C., & Hoyle, R. H. (2000). Effect of private self-awareness on negative affect and self-referent attribution: A quantitative review. *Personality and Social Psychology Review, 4,* 132–142.

Fenigstein, A., & Abrams, D. (1993). Self-attention and the egocentric assumption of shared perspectives. *Journal of Experimental Social Psychology, 29,* 287–303.

Fenigstein, A., Scheier, M. F., & Buss, A. H. (1975). Public and private self-consciousness: Assessment and theory. *Journal of Consulting and Clinical Psychology, 43,* 522–527.

Fennelly, G. (2009, February 12). Amazon selling rape simulation game. *Belfast Telegraph.*

Ferguson, E., Farrell, K., & Lawrence, C. (2008). Blood donation is an act of benevolence rather than altruism. *Health Psychology, 27,* 327–336.

Ferguson, M. (2007). On the automatic evaluation of end-states. *Journal of Personality and Social Psychology, 92,* 596–611.

Ferrari, J. R. (1998). Procrastination. In H. S. Friedman (Ed.), *Encyclopedia of mental health* (pp. 5.1–5.7). San Diego: Academic Press.

Ferrari, J. R., Johnson, J. A., & McCowan, W. G. (1995). *Procrastination and task avoidance: Theory, research, and treatment.* New York: Plenum.

Ferreira, A., Picazo, O., Uriarte, N., Pereira, M., & Fernandez-Guasti, A. (2000). Inhibitory effect of buspirone and diazepam, but not of 8-OH-DPAT, on maternal behavior and aggression. *Pharmacology, Biochemistry and Behavior, 66,* 389–396.

Festinger, L. (1950). Informal social communication. *Psychological Review, 57,* 271–282.

Festinger, L. (1954). A theory of social comparison processes. *Human Relations, 7,* 117–140.

Festinger, L. (1957). *A theory of cognitive dissonance.* Stanford, CA: Stanford University Press.

Festinger, L., & Carlsmith, J. M. (1959). Cognitive consequences of forced compliance. *Journal of Abnormal and Social Psychology, 58,* 203–210.

Festinger, L., Pepitone, A., & Newcomb, T. (1952). Some consequences of de-individuation in a group. *Journal of Abnormal and Social Psychology, 47,* 382–389.

Fiedler, F. E. (1967). *A theory of leadership effectiveness.* New York: McGraw-Hill.

Fiedler, F. E., & Chemers, M. M. (1984). *Improving leadership effectiveness: The leader match concept* (2nd ed.). New York: Wiley.

Fiedler, F. E., & Garcia, J. E. (1987). *Leadership: Cognitive resources and performance.* New York: Wiley.

Fiedler, F. E., Murphy, S. E., & Gibson, F. W. (1992). Inaccurate reporting and inappropriate variables: A reply to Vecchio's (1990) examination of cognitive resource theory. *Journal of Applied Psychology, 77,* 372–374.

Fincham, F. D. (2003). Marital conflict, correlates, structure, and context. *Current Directions in Psychological Science, 12,* 23–27.

Fincham, F., Beach, S., & Davila, J. (2007). Longitudinal relations between forgiveness and conflict resolution in marriage. *Journal of Family Psychology, 21,* 542–545.

Fincham, F. D., Harold, G. T., & Gano-Phillips, S. (2000). The longitudinal association between attributions and marital satisfaction: Direction of effects and role of efficacy expectations. *Journal of Family Psychology, 14,* 267–285.

Fine, M. A., & Harvey, J. H. (Eds.). (2006). *Handbook of divorce and relationship dissolution.* Hillsdale, NJ: Erlbaum.

Fine, M. A., & Sacher, J. A. (1997). Predictors of distress following relationship termination among dating couples. *Journal of Social and Clinical Psychology, 16,* 381–388.

Finkel, E. J., & Eastwick, P. W. (2008). Speed-dating. *Current Directions in Psychological Science, 17,* 193–197.

Finkel, E. J., Rusbult, C. E., Kumashiro, M., & Hannon, P. A. (2002). Dealing with betrayal in close relationships: Does commitment promote forgiveness? *Journal of Personality and Social Psychology, 82,* 956–974.

Finkel, N. J. (1995). *Commonsense justice: Jurors' notions of the law.* Cambridge, MA: Harvard University Press.

Finkelstein, M. A. (2009). Intrinsic vs. extrinsic motivational orientations and the volunteer process. *Personality and Individual Differences, 46,* 653–658.

Fischer, C. S. (1976). *The urban experience.* New York: Harcourt Brace Jovanovich.

Fischer, P., & Greitemeyer, T. (2006). Music and aggression: The impact of sexual-aggressive song lyrics on aggression-related thoughts, emotions, and behavior toward the same and the opposite sex. *Personality and Social Psychology Bulletin, 32,* 1165–1176.

Fishbein, M. (1980). A theory of reasoned action: Some applications and implications. In H. E. Howe & M. M. Page (Eds.), *Nebraska Symposium on Motivation* (Vol. 27, pp. 65–116). Lincoln: University of Nebraska Press.

Fishbein, M., & Ajzen, I. (1972). Attitudes and opinions. In P. H. Mussen & M. R. Rosenzweig (Eds.), *Annual Review of Psychology, 23,* 487–544.

Fisher, H. E. (2004). *Why we love: The nature and chemistry of romantic love.* New York: Henry Holt.

Fisher, J. D., & Fisher, W. A. (1992). Changing AIDS-risk behavior. *Psychological Bulletin, 111,* 455–474.

Fisher, J. D., Fisher, W. A., Bryan, A. D., & Misovich, S. J. (2002). Information-motivation-behavioral skills model-based HIV risk behavior change intervention for inner-city high school youth. *Health Psychology, 21,* 177–186.

Fisher, J. D., Fisher, W. A., Williams, S. S., & Malloy, T. E. (1994). Empirical tests of an information-motivation-behavioral skills model of AIDS-preventive behavior with gay men and heterosexual university students. *Health Psychology, 13,* 238–250.

Fisher, J. D., Nadler, A., & Whitcher-Alagna, S. (1982). Recipient reactions to aid. *Psychological Bulletin, 91,* 27–54.

Fisher, R. J., Vandenboosh, M., & Kersi, A. (2008). An empathy-helping perspective on consumers' responses to fund-raising appeals. *Journal of Consumer Research, 35,* 519–531.

Fiske, A. P. (1992). The four elementary forms of sociality: Framework for a unified theory of social relations. *Psychological Review, 99,* 689–723.

Fiske, A. P. (2002). Using individualism and collectivism to compare cultures—A critique of the validity and measurement of the constructs: Comment on Oyserman et al. (2002). *Psychological Bulletin, 128,* 78–88.

Fiske, S. T., & Neuberg, S. L. (1990). A continuum model of impression formation: From category-based to individuating processes: Influence of information and motivation on attention and interpretation. In M. P. Zanna (Ed.), *Advances in experimental social psychology* (Vol. 23, pp. 1–74). San Diego, CA: Academic Press.

Fiske, S. T., Bersoff, D. N., Borgida, E., Deaux, K., & Heilman, M. E. (1991). Social science research on trial: Use of sex stereotyping research in *Price Waterhouse v. Hopkins. American Psychologist, 46,* 1049–1060.

Fiske, S. T., Cuddy, A., & Glick, P. (2007). Universal dimensions of social cognition: Warmth and competence. *Trends in Cognitive Sciences, 11,* 77–83.

Fiske, S. T., Harris, L. T., Russell, A. M., & Shelton, J. N. (2009). Divergent social realities, depending on where you sit: Perspectives from the stereotype content model. In S. Demoulin, J. P. Leyens, & J. F. Dovidio (Eds.), *Intergroup misunderstandings: Impact of divergent social realities* (pp. 173–189). New York: Psychology Press.

Fiske, S. T., Lin, M., & Neuberg, S. L. (1999). The continuum model: Ten years later. In S. Chaiken & Y. Trope (Eds.), *Dual-process theories in social psychology* (pp. 231–254). New York: Guilford.

Fiske, S. T., & Taylor, S. E. (2008). *Social cognition: From brains to culture.* New York: McGraw-Hill.

Fitzgerald, C. J. (2009). Altruism and reproductive limitations. *Evolutionary Psychology, 7,* 234–252.

Fitzgerald, J. M. (1988). Vivid memories and the reminiscence phenomenon: The role of self-narrative. *Human Development, 31,* 261–273.

Fitzgerald, R., & Ellsworth, P. C. (1984). Due process vs. crime control: Death qualification and jury attitudes. *Law and Human Behavior, 8,* 31–52.

Fivush, R., Haden, C. A., & Dimmick, J. W. (Eds.). (2003). *Autobiographical memory and the construction of a narrative self: Developmental and cultural perspectives.* Mahwah, NJ: Erlbaum.

Flack, W. F., Jr., Laird, J. D., & Cavallaro, L. A. (1999). Separate and combined effects of facial expressions and bodily postures on emotional feelings. *European Journal of Social Psychology, 29,* 203–217.

Fleming, M. A., Wegener, D. T., & Petty, R. E. (1999). Procedural and legal motivations to correct for perceived judicial biases. *Journal of Experimental Social Psychology, 35,* 186–203.

Fletcher, G. J. O., Danilovics, P., Fernandez, G., Peterson, D., & Reeder, G. D. (1986). Attributional complexity: An individual differences measure. *Journal of Personality and Social Psychology, 51,* 875–884.

Florian, V., Mikulincer, M., & Taubman, O. (1995). Does hardiness contribute to mental health during a stressful real-life situation? The roles of appraisal and coping. *Journal of Personality and Social Psychology, 68,* 687–695.

Flory, J. D., Raikkonen, K., Matthews, K. A., & Owens, J. F. (2000). Self-focused attention and mood during everyday social interactions. *Personality and Social Psychology Bulletin, 26,* 875–883.

Folger, R. (1986). Rethinking equity theory: A referent cognitions model. In H. W. Bierhoff, R. L. Cohen, & J. Greenberg (Eds.), *Justice in social relations* (pp. 145–162). New York: Plenum.

Folger, R., & Cropanzano, R. (1998). *Organizational justice and human resource management.* Thousand Oaks, CA: Sage.

Folger, R., & Greenberg, J. (1985). Procedural justice: An interpretive analysis of personnel systems. In K. Rowland & G. Ferris (Eds.), *Research in personnel and human resource management* (Vol. 3, pp. 141–183). Greenwich, CT: JAI Press.

Folger, R., Konovsky, M. A., & Cropanzano, R. (1992). A due process metaphor for performance appraisal. *Research in Organizational Behavior, 14,* 129–177.

Folkman, S., & Moskowitz, J. T. (2000). Positive affect and the other side of coping. *American Psychologist, 55,* 647–654.

Follett, M. P. (1942). Constructive conflict. In H. C. Metcalf & L. Urwick (Eds.), *Dynamic administration: The collected papers of Mary Parker Follett* (pp. 30–49). New York: Harper.

Forbes, G. B., Adams-Curtis, L. E., Pakalka, A. H., & White, K. B. (2006). Dating aggression, sexual coercion, and aggression-supporting attitudes among college men as a function of participation in aggressive high school sports. *Violence Against Women, 12,* 441–455.

Ford, T. E., & Tonander, G. R. (1998). The role of differentiation between groups and social identity in stereotype formation. *Social Psychology Quarterly, 61,* 372–384.

Ford, T. E., Ferguson, M. A., Brooks, J. L., & Hagadone, K. M. (2004). Coping sense of humor reduces effects of stereotype threat on women's math performance. *Personality and Social Psychology Bulletin, 30,* 643–653.

Forgas, J. P. (Ed.). (2000). *Feeling and thinking: Affective influences on social cognition.* New York: Cambridge University Press.

Forgas, J. P., Baumeister, R. F., & Tice, D. M. (Eds.). (2009). *Psychology of self-regulation: Cognitive, affective, and motivational processes.* New York: Psychology Press.

Forgas, J. P., & Bower, G. H. (1987). Mood effects on person perception judgments. *Journal of Personality and Social Psychology, 53,* 53–60.

Forgas, J. P., Dunn, E., & Granland, S. (2008). Are you being served . . . ? An unobtrusive experiment of affective influences on helping in a department store. *European Journal of Social Psychology, 38,* 333–342.

Forgas, J. P., & East, R. (2008). How real is that smile? Mood effects on accepting or rejecting the veracity of emotional facial expressions. *Journal of Nonverbal Behavior, 32,* 157–170.

Forgas, J. P., & Fitness, J. (Eds.). (2008). *Social relationships: Cognitive, affective, and motivational processes.* New York: Psychology Press.

Forgas, J. P., & Locke, J. (2005). Affective influences on causal inferences: The effects of mood on attributions for positive and negative interpersonal episodes. *Cognition and Emotion, 19,* 1071–1081.

Foster, C. A., & Campbell, W. K. (2005). The adversity of secret relationships. *Personal Relationships, 12,* 125–143.

Foster, C. A., Witcher, B. S., Campbell, W. K., & Green, J. D. (1998). Arousal and attraction: Evidence for automatic and controlled processes. *Journal of Personality and Social Psychology, 74,* 86–101.

Fosterling, F. (1992). The Kelley model as an analysis of variance analogy: How far can it be taken? *Journal of Experimental Social Psychology, 28,* 475–490.

Fox, E., Russo, R., & Dutton, K. (2002). Attentional bias for threat: Evidence for delayed disengagement from emotional faces. *Cognition and Emotion, 16,* 355–379.

Franck, K. A. (1980). Friends and strangers: The social experience of living in urban and non-urban settings. *Journal of Social Issues, 36*(3), 52–71.

Frank, J. (1949). *Courts on trial.* Princeton, NJ: Princeton University Press.

Frantz, C. M., Cuddy, A. J. C., Burnett, M., Ray, H., & Hart, A. (2004). A threat in the computer: The race Implicit Association Test as a stereotype threat experience. *Personality and Social Psychology Bulletin, 30,* 1611–1624.

Frattaroli, J. (2006). Experimental disclosure and its moderators: A meta-analysis. *Psychological Bulletin, 132,* 823–865.

Frazier, P. A. (2003). Perceived control and distress following sexual assault: A longitudinal test of a new model. *Journal of Personality and Social Psychology, 84,* 1257–1269.

Frazier, P., & Schauben, L. (1994). Causal attributions and recovery from rape and other stressful events. *Journal of Social and Clinical Psychology, 13,* 1–14.

Frazier, P., Steward, J., & Mortensen, H. (2004). Perceived control and adjustment to trauma: A comparison across events. *Journal of Social and Clinical Psychology, 23,* 303–324.

Fredrickson, B. L. (2009). *Positivity: Groundbreaking research reveals how to embrace the hidden strength of positive emotions, overcome negativity, and thrive.* New York: Crown Books.

Frederickson, B. L., Maynard, K. E., Helms, M. J., Haney, T. L., Siegler, I. C., & Barefoot, J. C. (2000). Hostility predicts magnitude and duration of blood pressure response to anger. *Journal of Behavioral Medicine, 23,* 229–243.

Fredrickson, B. L., Tugade, M. M., Waugh, C. E., & Larkin, G. R. (2003). What good are positive emotions in crisis? A prospective study of resilience and emotions following the terrorist attacks on the United States on September 11th, 2001. *Journal of Personality and Social Psychology, 84,* 365–376.

Freedman, J. L., & Fraser, S. C. (1966). Compliance without pressure: The foot-in-the-door technique. *Journal of Personality and Social Psychology, 4,* 195–202.

Freedman, J. L., & Sears, D. O. (1965). Warning, distraction, and resistance to influence. *Journal of Personality and Social Psychology, 1,* 262–266.

Freud, S. (1905). Fragments of an analysis of a case of hysteria. *Collected papers* (Vol. 3). New York: Basic Books. (Reprinted in 1959).

Frey, K. S., Hirschstein, M. K., Edstrom, L. V., & Snell, J. L. (2009). Observed reductions in school bullying, nonbullying aggression, and destructive bystander behavior: A longitudinal evaluation. *Journal of Educational Psychology, 101,* 466–481.

Frey, A., Ruchkin, V., Martin, A., & Schwab-Stone, M. (2009). Adolescents in transition: School and family characteristics in the development of violent behaviors entering high school. *Child Psychiatry and Human Development, 40,* 1–13.

Friedland, N., Keinan, G., & Regev, Y. (1992). Controlling the uncontrollable: Effects of stress on illusory perceptions of controllability. *Journal of Personality and Social Psychology, 63,* 923–931.

Friedman, H. S. (1991). *The self-healing personality.* New York: Henry Holt.

Friedman, H. S., & Booth-Kewley, S. (1987). The "disease-prone personality": A meta-analytic view of the construct. *American Psychologist, 42,* 539–555.

Friedman, H. S., & Silver, R. C. (Eds.). (2007). *Foundations of health psychology.* New York: Oxford University Press.

Friedman, M. J., Keane, T. M., & Resick, P. A. (Eds.). (2007). *Handbook of PTSD: Science and Practice.* New York: Guilford.

Friedrich, J., Fethersonhaugh, D., Casey, S., & Gallagher, D. (1996). Argument integration and attitude change: Suppression effects in the integration of one-sided arguments that vary in persuasiveness. *Personality and Social Psychology Bulletin, 22,* 179–191.

Friend, R., Rafferty, Y., & Bramel, D. (1990). A puzzling misinterpretation of the Asch "conformity" study. *European Journal of Social Psychology, 20,* 29–44.

Fritzsche, B. A., Finkelstein, M. A., & Penner, L. A. (2000). To help or not to help: Capturing individuals' decision policies. *Social Behavior and Personality, 28,* 561–578.

Frye, N. E., & Karney, B. R. (2006). The context of aggressive behavior in marriage: A longitudinal study of newlyweds. *Journal of Family Psychology, 20,* 12–20.

Fujino, N., & Okamura, H. (2009, April). Factors affecting the sense of burden felt by family members caring for patients with mental illness. *Archives of Psychiatric Nursing, 23*(2), 128–137.

Fujita, F., & Diener, E. (2005). Life satisfaction set point: Stability and change. *Journal of Personality and Social Psychology, 88,* 158–164.

Funk, S. C. (1992). Hardiness: A review of theory and research. *Health Psychology, 11,* 335–345.

Furche, A., & Johnstone, D. (2006). Evidence of the endowment effect in stock market order placement. *Journal of Behavioral Finance, 7,* 145–154.

Furnham, A. (2003). Belief in a just world: Research progress over the past decade. *Personality and Individual Differences, 34,* 795–817.

Furnham, A., Simmons, K., & McClelland, A. (2000). Decisions concerning the allocation of scarce medical resources. *Journal of Social Behavior and Personality, 15,* 185–200.

Gabbert, F., Memon, A., & Allan, K. (2003). Memory conformity: Can eyewitnesses influence each other's memories for an event? *Applied Cognitive Psychology, 17,* 533–543.

Gabel, M., & Brunner, H. (2003). *Global Inc.: An atlas of the multinational corporation.* New York: New Press.

Gaertner, S. L., & Dovidio, J. F. (1986). The aversive form of racism. In J. F. Dovidio & S. L. Gaernter (Eds.), *Prejudice, discrimination, and racism* (pp. 61–89). San Diego, CA: Academic Press.

Gaertner, S. L., & Dovidio, J. F. (2009). A common intergroup identity: A categorization-based approach for reducing intergroup bias. In T. D. Nelson (Ed.), *Handbook of prejudice, stereotyping, and discrimination* (pp. 489–505). New York: Psychology Press.

Gaertner, S. L., Dovidio, J. F., & Houlette, M. A. (2010). Social categorization. In J. F. Dovidio, M. Hewstone, P. Glick, & V. M. Esses (Eds.), *Handbook of prejudice, stereotyping, and discrimination.* London: Sage.

Gaertner, L., Iuzzini, J., & O'Mara, E. M. (2008). When rejection by one fosters aggression against many: Multiple-victim aggression as a consequence of social rejection and perceived groupness. *Journal of Experimental Social Psychology, 44,* 958–970.

Gagne, F. M., & Lydon, J. E. (2001). Mindset and relationship illusions: The moderating effects of domain specificity and relationship commitment. *Personality and Social Psychology Bulletin, 27,* 1144–1155.

Gagnon, A., & Bourhis, R. Y. (1996). Discrimination in the minimal group paradigm: Social identity or self-interest? *Personality and Social Psychology Bulletin, 22,* 1289–1301.

Gailliot, M., Baumeister, R., DeWall, C., Maner, J., Plant, E., Tice, D., Brewer, L., & Schmeichel, B. (2007). Self-control relies on glucose as a limited energy source: Willpower is more than just a metaphor. *Journal of Personality and Social Psychology, 92,* 325–336.

Gailliot, M. T., Peruche, B. M., Plant, E. A., & Baumeister, R. F. (2009). Stereotypes and prejudice in the blood: Sucrose drinks reduce prejudice and stereotyping. *Journal of Experimental Social Psychology, 45,* 288–290.

Galanter, M. (1999). *Cults: Faith, healing, and coercion* (2nd ed.). New York: Oxford University Press.

Galea, S., Ahern, J., Resnick, H., Kilpatrick, D., Bucuvalas, M., Gold, J., & Vlahov, D. (2002). Psychological sequelae of the September 11 terrorist attacks in New York City. *New England Journal of Medicine, 346,* 982–987.

Galen, B. R., & Underwood, M. K. (1997). A developmental investigation of social aggression among children. *Developmental Psychology, 33,* 589–600.

Galinsky, A. D., & Kray, L. J. (2004). From thinking about what might have been to sharing what we know: The role of counterfactual mind-sets in information sharing in groups. *Journal of Experimental Social Psychology, 40,* 606–618.

Galinsky, A. D., Stone, J., & Cooper, J. (2000). The reinstatement of dissonance and psychological discomfort following failed affirmations. *European Journal of Social Psychology, 30,* 123–147.

Galinsky, A. D., Wang, C. S., & Ku, G. (2008). Perspective-takers behave more stereotypically. *Journal of Personality and Social Psychology, 95,* 404–419.

Gallo, L. C., & Matthews, K. A. (2003). Understanding the association between socioeconomic status and physical health: Do negative emotions play a role? *Psychological Bulletin, 129,* 10–51.

Gallup Poll Editors (2002). *Gallup poll of the Islamic world: Subscriber report.* Princeton, NJ: Gallup Press.

Gallup, G. G., Jr. (1977). Self-recognition in primates: A comparative approach to the bidirectional properties of consciousness. *American Psychologist, 32,* 329–337.

Game, F., Carchon, I., & Vital-Durand, F. (2003). The effect of stimulus attractiveness on visual tracking in 2- to 6-month-old infants. *Infant Behavior & Development, 26,* 135–150.

Gammie, S. C., Olaghere-da-Silva, U. B., & Nelson, R. J. (2000). 3-Bromo–7-nitroindazole, a neuronal nitric oxide synthase inhibitor, impairs maternal aggression and citrulline immunoreactivity in prairie voles. *Brain Research, 870,* 80–86.

Gamson, W. A., Fireman, B., & Rytina, S. (1982). *Encounters with unjust authority.* Homewood, IL: Dorsey.

Gangestad, S. W. (1993). Sexual selection and physical attractiveness: Implications for mating dynamics. *Human Nature, 4,* 205–235.

Gangestad, S. W., & Simpson, J. A. (2000). The evolution of human mating: Trade-offs and strategic pluralism. *Behavioral and Brain Sciences, 23,* 573–587.

Gangestad, S. W., & Snyder, M. (1991). Taxonomic analysis redux: Some statistical considerations for testing a latent class model. *Journal of Personality and Social Psychology, 61,* 141–146.

Gannon, T. A., Keown, K., & Polaschek, D. L. L. (2007). Increasing honest responding on cognitive distortions in child molesters: The bogus pipeline revisited. *Journal of Research and Treatment, 19,* 5–22.

Garcia, S. M., Tor, A., Bazerman, M. H., & Miller, D. T. (2005). Profit maximization versus disadvantageous inequality: The impact of self-categorization. *Journal of Behavioral Decision Making, 18,* 187–198.

Garcia, S. M., Weaver, K., Moskowitz, G. B., & Darley, J. M. (2002). Crowded minds: The implicit bystander effect. *Journal of Personality and Social Psychology, 83,* 843–853.

Gardner, W. L., & Knowles, M. L. (2008). Love makes you real: Favorite television characters are perceived as "real" in a social facilitation paradigm. *Social Cognition, 26,* 156–168.

Gardner, W. L., Gabriel, S., & Hochschild, L. (2002). When you and I are "we," you are not threatening: The role of self-expansion in social comparison. *Journal of Personality and Social Psychology, 82,* 239–251.

Garland, H., & Conlon, D. E. (1998). Too close to quit: The role of project completion in maintaining commitment. *Journal of Applied Social Psychology, 28*, 2025–2048.

Garrett, B. (2008). Judging innocence. *Columbia Law Review, 108*, 55–142.

Gawronski, B., & Bodenhausen, G. V. (2006). Associative and propositional processes in evaluation: An integrative review of implicit and explicit attitude change. *Psychological Bulletin, 132*, 692–731.

Gawronski, B., Peters, K. R., Brochu, P. M., & Strack, F. (2008). Understanding the relations between different forms of racial prejudice: A cognitive consistency perspective. *Personality and Social Psychology Bulletin, 34*, 648–665.

Geary, D. C. (2000). Evolution and proximate expression of human paternal investment. *Psychological Bulletin, 126*, 55–77.

Geary, D. C. (2005). Evolution of life-history trade-offs in mate attractiveness and health: Comment on Weeden and Sabini. *Psychological Bulletin, 131*, 654–657.

Gee, C. J., & Leith, L. M. (2007). Aggressive behavior in professional ice hockey: A cross-cultural comparison of North American and European born NHL players. *Psychology of Sport and Exercise, 8*, 567–583.

Geen, R. G. (1981). Behavioral and physiological reactions to observed violence: Effects of prior exposure to aggressive stimuli. *Journal of Personality and Social Psychology, 40*, 868–875.

Geen, R. G. (1991). Social motivation. *Annual Review of Psychology, 42*, 377–399.

Geen, R. G., & Quanty, M. B. (1977). The catharsis of aggression: An evaluation of a hypothesis. In L. Berkowitz (Ed.), *Advances in experimental social psychology* (Vol. 10, pp. 1–37). New York: Academic Press.

Geis, F. L., Brown, V., Jennings (Walstedt), J., & Porter, N. (1984). TV commercials as achievement scripts for women. *Sex Roles, 10*, 513–525.

Geiselman, R. E., Haight, N. A., & Kimata, L. G. (1984). Context effects in the perceived physical attractiveness of faces. *Journal of Experimental Social Psychology, 20*, 409–424.

Gelfand, M. J., Erez, M., & Aycan, Z. (2007). Cross-cultural organizational behavior. *Annual Review of Psychology, 58*, 479–514.

Gendar, A., Burke, K., & McShane, L. (2009, July 16). "Fight Club" bomber: Teen nabbed in Memorial Day blast at East Side Starbucks. *New York Daily News*, p. 7.

Gentile, D. A., Anderson, C. A., Yukawa, S., Ihori, N., Saleem, M., Ming, L. M., et al. (2009). The effects of prosocial video games on prosocial behaviors: International evidence from correlational, longitudinal, and experimental studies. *Personality and Social Psychology Bulletin, 35*, 752–763.

George, D. M., Carroll, P., Kersnick, R., & Calderon, K. (1998). Gender-related patterns of helping among friends. *Psychology of Women Quarterly, 22*, 685–704.

Georgesen, J. C., & Harris, M. J. (1998). Why's my boss always holding me down? A meta-analysis of power effects on performance evaluations. *Personality and Social Psychology Review, 2*, 184–195.

Gerard, H. B., Whilhelmy, R. A., & Connolley, R. S. (1968). Conformity and group size. *Journal of Personality and Social Psychology, 8*, 79–82.

Gerbner, G., Gross, L., Morgan, M., & Signorielli, N. (1986). Living with television: The dynamics of the cultivation process. In J. Bryant & D. Zillmann (Eds.), *Perspectives on media effects* (pp. 17–40). Hillsdale, NJ: Erlbaum.

Gergen, K. J. (1973). Social psychology as history. *Journal of Personality and Social Psychology, 26*, 309–320.

Gerhart, B., & Rynes, S. (1991). Determinants and consequences of salary negotiations by male and female MBA graduates. *Journal of Applied Psychology, 76*, 256–262.

Gerrard, M., Gibbons, F. X., & Bushman, B. J. (1996). Relation between perceived vulnerability in HIV and precautionary sexual behavior. *Psychological Bulletin, 119*, 390–409.

Gershoff, E. T. (2002). Corporal punishment by parents and associated child behaviors and experiences: A meta-analytic and theoretical review. *Psychological Bulletin, 128*, 539–579.

Gersick, C. J. G. (1988). Time and transition in work teams: Toward a new model of group development. *Academy of Management Journal, 21*, 9–41.

Gersick, C. J. G. (1994). Pacing strategic change: The case of a new venture. *Academy of Management Journal, 37*, 9–45.

Gerson, J. (2006, September 21). Montreal shootings disturb Columbine game creator. *Toronto Star*, p. A12.

Giancola, P. R., Roth, R. M., & Parrott, D. J. (2006). The mediating role of executive functioning in the relation between difficult temperament and physical aggression. *Journal of Psychopathology and Behavioral Assessment, 28*, 211–221.

Gibbons, F. X. (1990). Self-attention and behavior: A review and theoretical update. In M. P. Zanna (Ed.), *Advances in experimental social psychology* (Vol. 23, pp. 249–303). New York: Academic Press.

Gibbons, F. X., & McCoy, S. B. (1991). Self-esteem, similarity, and reactions to active versus passive downward comparison. *Journal of Personality and Social Psychology, 60*, 414–424.

Gibbons, F. X., Gerrard, M., Cleveland, M. J., Wills, T. A., & Brody, G. (2004). Perceived discrimination and substance use in African American parents and their children: A panel study. *Journal of Personality and Social Psychology, 86*, 517–529.

Gibbons, F. X., Lane, D. J., Gerrard, M., Reis-Bergan, M., Lautrup, C., Pexa, N., & Blanton, H. (2002). Comparison level preferences after performance: Is downward comparison theory still useful? *Journal of Personality and Social Psychology, 83*, 865–880.

Gibbons, S. L., & Ebbeck, V. (1997). The effect of different teaching strategies on the moral development of physical education students. *Journal of Teaching in Physical Education, 17*, 85–98.

Gibson, B., & Sachau, D. (2000). Sandbagging as a self-presentational strategy: Claiming to be less than you are. *Personality and Social Psychology Bulletin, 26*, 56–70.

Giebels, E., & Taylor, P. J. (2009). Interaction patterns in crisis negotiations: Persuasive arguments and cultural differences. *Journal of Applied Psychology, 94*, 5–19.

Giesler, R. B., Josephs, R. A., & Swann, W. B., Jr. (1996). Self-verification in clinical depression: The desire for negative evaluation. *Journal of Abnormal Psychology, 105*, 358–368.

Gigerenzer, G., Todd, P. M., & the ABC Research Group. (1999). *Simple heuristics that make us smart.* New York: Oxford University Press.

Gilbert, D. (2006). *Stumbling on happiness.* New York: Alfred A. Knopf.

Gilbert, D. T., & Hixon, J. G. (1991). The trouble of thinking: Activation and application of stereotypic beliefs. *Journal of Personality and Social Psychology, 60*, 509–517.

Gilbert, D. T., & Jones, E. E. (1986). Perceiver-induced constraint: Interpretations of self-generated reality. *Journal of Personality and Social Psychology, 50*, 269–280.

Gilbert, D. T., & Malone, P. S. (1995). The correspondence bias. *Psychological Bulletin, 117*, 21–38.

Gilbert, D. T., Giesler, R. B., & Morris, K. A. (1995). When comparisons arise. *Journal of Personality and Social Psychology, 69*, 227–236.

Gilbert, D. T., McNulty, S. E., Giuliano, T. A., & Benson, J. E. (1992). Blurry words and fuzzy deeds: The attribution of obscure behavior. *Journal of Personality and Social Psychology, 62*, 18–25.

Gilbert, D. T., Morewedge, C. K., Risen, J. L., & Wilson, T. D. (2004). Looking forward to looking backward: The misprediction of regret. *Psychological Science, 15*, 346–350.

Gilbert, D. T., Pelham, B. W., & Krull, D. S. (1988). On cognitive busyness: When person perceivers meet persons perceived. *Journal of Personality and Social Psychology, 54*, 733–740.

Gilbert, D. T., Pinel, E. C., Wilson, T. D., Blumberg, S. J., & Wheatley, T. (1998). Immune neglect: A source of durability bias in affective forecasting. *Journal of Personality and Social Psychology, 75*, 617–638.

Gilbert, S. J. (1981). Another look at the Milgram obedience studies: The role of the gradated series of shocks. *Personality and Social Psychology Bulletin, 7*, 690–695.

Gillig, P. M., & Greenwald, A. G. (1974). Is it time to lay the sleeper effect to rest? *Journal of Personality and Social Psychology, 29*, 132–139.

Gilovich, T. (1991). *How we know what isn't so: The fallibility of human reason in everyday life*. New York: Free Press.

Gilovich, T., Griffin, D., & Kahneman, D. (Eds.). (2002). *Heuristics and biases: The psychology of intuitive judgment*. New York: Cambridge University Press.

Gilovich, T., Medvec, V. H., & Savitsky, K. (2000). The spotlight effect in social judgment: An egocentric bias in estimates of the salience of one's own actions and appearance. *Journal of Personality and Social Psychology, 78,* 211–222.

Giner-Sorolla, R., & Chaiken, S. (1997). Selective use of heuristic and systematic processing under defensive motivation. *Personality and Social Psychology Bulletin, 23,* 84–97.

Gioia, D. A., & Longnecker, C. O. (1994). Delving into the dark side: The politics of executive appraisal. *Organizational Dynamics, 22,* 47–58.

Gladstone, G. L., Parker, G. B., & Malhi, G. S. (2006). Do bullied children become anxious and depressed adults? A cross-sectional investigation of the correlates of bullying and anxious depression. *Journal of Nervous and Mental Disease, 19,* 201–208.

Gladue, B. A., Boechler, M., & McCaul, K. D. (1989). Hormonal response to competition in human males. *Aggressive Behavior, 15,* 409–422.

Gladwell, M. (2005). *Blink: The power of thinking without thinking*. New York: Little, Brown, and Company.

Glanz, J., & Schwartz, J. (September 26, 2003). Dogged engineer's effort to assess shuttle damage. *New York Times,* p. A1.

Glasø, L., Nielsen, M. B., & Einarsen, S. (2009). Interpersonal problems among perpetrators and targets of workplace bullying. *Journal of Applied Social Psychology, 39,* 1316–1333.

Glass, D. C., & Singer, J. E. (1972). *Urban stress*. New York: Academic Press.

Gleicher, F., & Petty, R. E. (1992). Expectations of reassurance influence the nature of fear-stimulated attitude change. *Journal of Experimental Social Psychology, 28,* 86–100.

Glick, P. (2008). Restating the case: The benefits of diverse samples for theory development. *Psychological Inquiry, 19,* 78–83.

Glick, P., & Fiske, S. T. (2001). Ambivalent sexism. In M. P. Zanna (Ed.), *Advances in experimental social psychology* (Vol. 33, pp. 115–188). San Diego, CA: Academic Press.

Glick, P., Fiske, S. T., et al. (2000). Beyond prejudice as simple antipathy: Hostile and benevolent sexism across cultures. *Journal of Personality and Social Psychology, 79,* 763–775.

Godfrey, D. K., Jones, E. E., & Lord, C. G. (1986). Self-promotion is not ingratiating. *Journal of Personality and Social Psychology, 50,* 106–115.

Goethals, G. R. (2005). Presidential leadership. *Annual Review of Psychology, 56,* 545–570.

Goethals, G. R., & Darley, J. (1977). Social comparison theory: An attributional approach. In J. M. Suls & R. L. Miller (Eds.), *Social comparison processes: Theoretical and empirical perspectives* (pp. 259–278). Washington, DC: Hemisphere.

Goethals, G. R., & Reckman, R. (1973). The perception of consistency in attitudes. *Journal of Experimental Social Psychology, 9,* 491–501.

Goethals, G. R., Sorensen, G., & Burns, J. M. (Eds.). (2004). *Encyclopedia of leadership*. Thousand Oaks, CA: Sage.

Goetz, A. T., Shackelford, T. K., Romero, G. A., Kaighobadi, F., & Miner, E. J. (2008). Punishment, proprietariness, and paternity: Men's violence against women from an evolutionary perspective. *Aggression and Violent Behavior, 13,* 481–489.

Goff, P. A., Eberhardt, J. L., Williams, M. J., & Jackson, M. C. (2008). Not yet human: Implicit knowledge, historical dehumanization, and contemporary consequences. *Journal of Personality and Social Psychology, 94,* 292–306.

Goff, P. A., Steele, C. M., & Davies, P. G. (2008). The space between us: Stereotype threat and distance in interracial contexts. *Journal of Personality and Social Psychology, 94,* 91–107.

Goffman, E. (1955). On face-work: An analysis of ritual elements in social interaction. *Psychiatry, 18,* 213–231.

Goffman, E. (1959). *The presentation of self in everyday life*. Garden City: Doubleday.

Goldberg, L. R., Grenier, J. R., Guion, R., Sechrest, L. B., & Wing, H. (1991). *Questionnaires used in the prediction of trustworthiness in pre-employment selection decisions: An A.P.A. task force report*. Washington, DC: American Psychological Association.

Goldberg, P. (1968). Are women prejudiced against women? *Transaction, 5,* 28–30.

Goldfarb, Z. A. (2009, July 2). Staffer at SEC had warned of Madoff; Lawyer raised alarm, then was pointed elsewhere. *Washington Post,* p. A1.

Goldhagen, D. J. (1996). *Hitler's willing executioners: Ordinary Germans and the Holocaust*. New York: Knopf.

Goldin, C. (1990). *Understanding the gender gap: An economic history of American women*. New York: Oxford University Press.

Goldstein, N. J., & Cialdini, R. B. (2007). The spyglass self: A model of vicarious self-perception. *Journal of Personality and Social Psychology, 92,* 402–417.

Gollwitzer, P. M., & Schaal, B. (2001). How goals and plans affect action. In J. M. Collis & S. Messick (Eds.), *Intelligence and personality: Bridging the gap in theory and measurement* (pp. 139–161). Mahwah, NJ: Erlbaum.

Gonzaga, G., Campos, B., & Bradbury, T. (2007). Similarity, convergence, and relationship satisfaction in dating and married couples. *Journal of Personality and Social Psychology, 93,* 34–48.

Gonzales, P. M., Blanton, H., & Williams, K. J. (2002). The effects of stereotype threat and double-minority status on the test performance of Latino women. *Personality and Social Psychology Bulletin, 28,* 659–670.

Goodwin, S. A., Fiske, S. T., Rosen, L. D., & Rosenthal, A. M. (2002). The eye of the beholder: Romantic goals and impression biases. *Journal of Experimental Social Psychology, 38,* 232–241.

Gopnik, A., Meltzoff, A. N., & Kuhl, P. K. (1999). *The scientist in the crib: Minds, brains, and how children learn*. New York: Morrow.

Gorchoff, S., John, O., & Helson, R. (2008). Contextualizing change in marital satisfaction during middle age: An 18-year longitudinal study. *Psychological Science, 19,* 1194–1200.

Gordijn, E. H., Hindriks, I., Koomen, W., Dijksterhuis, A., & van Knippenberg, A. (2004). Consequences of stereotype suppression and internal suppression motivation: A self-regulation approach. *Personality and Social Psychology Bulletin, 30,* 212–224.

Gorman, C. (1994, September 19). Let's not be too hasty. *Time,* p. 71.

Gorman, E. H., & Kmec, J. A. (2009). Hierarchical rank and women's organizational mobility: Glass ceilings in corporate law firms. *American Journal of Sociology, 114,* 1428–1474.

Gosling, P., Denizeau, M., & Oberlé, D. (2006). Denial of responsibility: A new mode of dissonance reduction. *Journal of Personality and Social Psychology, 90,* 722–733.

Gosling, S. (2008). *Snoop: What your stuff says about you*. New York: Basic Books.

Gossett, J. L., & Byrne, S. (2002). "CLICK HERE": A content analysis of Internet rape sites. *Gender and Society, 16,* 689–709.

Gotlib, I. H., & Hammen, C. L. (Eds.). (2009). *Handbook of depression* (2nd ed.). New York: Guilford.

Gottfredson, L. S. (2002). Where and why *g* matters: Not a mystery. *Human Performance, 15,* 25–46.

Gottfried, M. (2007, August 23). A rape witnessed, a rape ignored. *St. Paul Pioneer Press*.

Gottfried, M. (2008, July 18). Man gets 12 years for hallway rape captured on video. *St. Paul Pioneer Press*.

Gottman, J. M. (1994). *What predicts divorce?* Hillsdale, NJ: Erlbaum.

Gottman, J. M. (1998). Psychology and the study of marital processes. *Annual Review of Psychology, 49,* 169–197.

Gottman, J. M., & Levenson, R. W. (1992). Marital processes predictive of later dissolution: Behavior, physiology, and health. *Journal of Personality and Social Psychology, 63,* 221–233.

Gouin, J., Kiecolt-Glaser, J., Malarkey, W., & Glaser, R. (2008). The influence of anger expression on wound healing. *Brain, Behavior, and Immunity, 22,* 699–708.

Gouldner, A. W. (1960). The norm of reciprocity: A preliminary statement. *American Sociological Review, 25,* 161–178.

Govorun, O., & Payne, B. K. (2006). Ego-depletion and prejudice: Separating automatic and controlled components. *Social Cognition, 24,* 111–136.

Graham, K., Osgood, D. W., Wells, S., & Stockwell, T. (2006). To what extent is intoxication associated with aggression in bars? A multilevel analysis. *Journal of Studies on Alcohol, 67,* 382–390.

Grammer, K., Fink, B., Moller, A. P., & Manning, J. T. (2005). Physical attractiveness and health: Comment on Weeden and Sabini. *Psychological Bulletin, 131,* 658–661.

Graña, J. L., Cruzado, J. A., Andreu, J. M., Muñoz-Rivas, M. J., Peña, M. E., & Brain, P. F. (2004). Effects of viewing videos of bullfights on Spanish children. *Aggressive Behavior, 30,* 16–28.

Granberg, D., & Bartels, B. (2005). On being a lone dissenter. *Journal of Applied Social Psychology, 35,* 1849–1858.

Granhag, P. A., & Strömwall. L. A. (Eds.). (2004). *Deception detection in forensic contexts.* Cambridge, England: Cambridge University Press.

Gray, H. M., Gray, K., & Wegner, D. M. (2007, February 2). Dimensions of mind perception. *Science, 315,* 619.

Gray, J. (1997). *Men are from Mars, women are from Venus.* New York: HarperCollins.

Gray, J. J., & Ginsberg, R. L. (2007). Muscle dissatisfaction: An overview of psychological and cultural research and theory. In J. K. Thompson & G. Cafri (Eds.), *The muscular ideal: Psychological, social, and medical perspectives* (pp. 15–39). Washington, DC: American Psychological Association.

Gray, R. (2004). Attending to the execution of a complex sensorimotor skill: Expertise differences, choking, and slumps. *Journal of Experimental Psychology: Applied, 10,* 42–54.

Gray-Little, B., & Hafdahl, A. R. (2000). Factors influencing racial comparisons of self-esteem: A quantitative review. *Psychological Bulletin, 126,* 26–54.

Greathouse, S. M., & Kovera, M. B. (2009). Instruction bias and lineup presentation moderate the effects of administrator knowledge on eyewitness identification. *Law and Human Behavior, 33,* 70–82.

Green, D. P., Glaser, J., & Rich, A. (1998). From lynching to gay bashing: The elusive connection between economic conditions and hate crime. *Journal of Personality and Social Psychology, 75,* 82–92.

Green, J. D., Sedikides, C., & Gregg, A. P. (2008). Forgotten but not gone: The recall and recognition of self-threatening memories. *Journal of Experimental Social Psychology, 44,* 547–561.

Greenberg, D. L. (2004). President Bush's false "flashbulb" memory of 9/11/01. *Applied Cognitive Psychology, 18,* 363–370.

Greenberg, J. (1988). Equity and workplace status: A field experiment. *Journal of Applied Psychology, 73,* 606–613.

Greenberg, J. (1990). Employee theft as a reaction to underpayment inequity: The hidden costs of pay cuts. *Journal of Applied Psychology, 75,* 561–568.

Greenberg, J. (2006). Losing sleep over organizational injustice: Attenuating insomniac reactions to underpayment inequity with supervisory training in interactional justice. *Journal of Applied Psychology, 91,* 58–69.

Greenberg, J., Landau, M., Kosloff, S., & Solomon, S. (2009). How our dreams of death transcendence breed prejudice, stereotyping, and conflict: Terror Management Theory. In T. D. Nelson (Ed.), *Handbook of prejudice, stereotyping, and discrimination* (pp. 309–332). New York: Psychology Press.

Greenberg, J., Solomon, S., & Pyszczynski, T. (1997). Terror management theory of self-esteem and cultural worldviews: Empirical assessments and conceptual refinements. *Advances in Experimental Social Psychology, 29,* 61–139.

Greenberg, M. S., & Westcott, D. R. (1983). Indebtedness as a mediator of reactions to aid. In J. D. Fisher, A. Nadler, & B. M. DePaulo (Eds.), *New directions in helping: Vol. 1. Recipient reactions to aid* (pp. 85–112). New York: Academic Press.

Greene, E., & Bornstein, B. (2003). *Determining damages: The psychology of jury awards.* Washington, DC: American Psychological Association.

Greene, E., Heilbrun, K., Fortune, W. H., & Nietzel, M. T. (2007). *Wrightsman's psychology and the legal system* (6th ed.). Belmont, CA: Wadsworth.

Greenhause, S. (2001, September 1). Report shows Americans have more "Labor Days." *New York Times,* p. A6.

Greenwald, A. G. (1980). The totalitarian ego: Fabrication and revision of personal history. *American Psychologist, 35,* 603–618.

Greenwald, A. G. (1992). New look 3: Unconscious cognition reclaimed. *American Psychologist, 47,* 766–779.

Greenwald, A. G., & Farnham, S. D. (2000). Using the Implicit Association Test to measure self-esteem and self-concept. *Journal of Personality and Social Psychology, 79,* 1022–1038.

Greenwald, A. G., McGhee, D. E., & Schwartz, J. L. K. (1998). Measuring individual differences in implicit cognition: The implicit association test. *Journal of Personality and Social Psychology, 74,* 1464–1480.

Greenwald, A. G., Nosek, B. A., & Banaji, M. R. (2003). Understanding and using the Implicit Association Test: I. An improved scoring algorithm. *Journal of Personality and Social Psychology, 85,* 197–216.

Greenwald, A. G., Oakes, M. A., & Hoffman, H. G. (2003). Targets of discrimination: Effects of race on responses to weapons holders. *Journal of Experimental Social Psychology, 39,* 399–405.

Greenwald, A. G., Poehlman, T. A., Uhlmann, E. L., & Banaji, M. R. (2009). Understanding and using the Implicit Association Test: III. Meta-analysis of predictive validity. *Journal of Personality and Social Psychology, 97,* 17–41.

Greenwald, A. G., Pratkanis, A. R., Leippe, M. R., & Baumgardner, M. H. (1986). Under what conditions does theory obstruct research progress? *Psychological Review, 93,* 216–229.

Greenwald, A. G., Spangenberg, E. R., Pratkanis, A. R., & Eskenazi, J. (1991). Double-blind tests of subliminal self-help audiotapes. *Psychological Science, 2,* 119–122.

Gregory, A. M., Light-Häusermann, J. H., Rijsdijk, F., & Eley, T. C. (2009). Behavioral genetic analyses of prosocial behavior in adolescents. *Developmental Science, 12,* 165–174.

Greitemeyer, T. (2009). Effects of songs with prosocial lyrics on prosocial thoughts, affect, and behavior. *Journal of Experimental Social Psychology, 45,* 186–190.

Greitemeyer, T., Schulz-Hardt, S., Brodbeck, F. C., & Frey, D. (2006). Information sampling and group decision making: The effects of an advocacy decision procedure and task experience. *Journal of Experimental Psychology: Applied, 12,* 31–42.

Griskevicius, V., Goldstein, N. J., Mortensen, C. R., Cialdini, R. B., & Kenrick, D. T. (2006). Going along versus going alone: When fundamental motives facilitate strategic nonconformity. *Journal of Personality and Social Psychology, 91,* 281–294.

Griskevicius, V., Tybur, J. M., Gangestad, S. W., Perea, E. F., Shapiro, J. R., & Kenrick, D. T. (2009). Aggress to impress: Hostility as an evolved context-dependent strategy. *Journal of Personality and Social Psychology, 96,* 980–994.

Gross, J. J., & Levenson, R. W. (1997). Hiding feelings: The acute effects of inhibiting negative and positive emotion. *Journal of Abnormal Psychology, 106,* 95–103.

Grossman, M., & Wood, W. (1993). Sex differences in intensity of emotional experience: A social role interpretation. *Journal of Personality and Social Psychology, 65,* 1010–1020.

Grote, N. K., & Clark, M. S. (2001). Perceiving unfairness in the family: Cause or consequence of marital distress? *Journal of Personality and Social Psychology, 80,* 281–293.

Gudjonsson, G. H. (2003). *The psychology of interrogations and confessions.* London: Wiley.

Gudykunst, W., & Bond, M. H. (1997). Intergroup relations across cultures. In J. W. Berry, M. H. Segall, & C. Kagitçibasi (Eds.), *Handbook of cross-cultural psychology: Social behavior and applications* (2nd ed., Vol. 3, pp. 119–161). Needham Heights, MA: Allyn & Bacon.

Guéguen, N. (2007). Bust size and hitchhiking: A field study. *Perceptual and Motor Skills, 105,* 1294–1298.

Guéguen, N., & Fischer-Lokou, J. (2004). Hitchhikers' smiles and receipt of help. *Psychological Reports, 94,* 756–760.

Guéguen, N., & Martin, A. (2009). Incidental similarity facilitates behavioral mimicry. *Social Psychology, 40,* 88–92.

Guerin, B. (2003). Social behaviors as determined by different arrangements of social consequences: Diffusion of responsibility effects with competition. *Journal of Social Psychology, 143,* 313–329.

Guerra, N. G., Huesmann, L. R., Hanish, L., Font, E., & Henry, D. (1993). *Normative beliefs about aggression as a function of acculturation status among Hispanic children.* Toronto: American Psychological Association.

Guerrero, L. K., La Valley, A. G., & Farinelli, L. (2008). The experience and expression of anger, guilt, and sadness in marriage: An equity theory explanation. *Journal of Social and Personal Relationships, 25,* 699–724.

Gully, S. M., Devine, D. J., & Whitney, D. J. (1995). A meta-analysis of cohesion and performance: Effects of level of analysis and task interdependence. *Small Group Research, 26,* 497–520.

Gump, B. B., & Kulik, J. A. (1997). Stress, affiliation, and emotional contagion. *Journal of Personality and Social Psychology, 72,* 305–319.

Gurtner, A.,Tschan, F., Semmer, N. K., & Nägele, C. (2007). Getting groups to develop good strategies: Effects of reflexivity interventions on team process, team performance, and shared mental models. *Organizational Behavior and Human Decision Processes, 102,* 127–142.

Gurung, R. A. R. (2010). *Health psychology: A cultural approach* (2nd ed.). Belmont, CA: Wadsworth.

Haberstroh, S., Oyserman, D., Schwarz, N., Kuehnen, U., & Ji, L. J. (2002). Is the interdependent self more sensitive to question context than the independent self? Self-construal and the observation of conversational norms. *Journal of Experimental Social Psychology, 38,* 323–329.

Hackman, J. R., & Katz, N. (2010). Group behavior and performance. In S. T. Fiske, D. T. Gilbert, & G. Lindzey (Eds.), *Handbook of social psychology* (5th ed.). New York: McGraw-Hill.

Haddock, G., Maio, G., Arnold, K., & Huskinson, T. (2008). Should persuasion be affective or cognitive? The moderating effects of need for affect and need for cognition. *Personality and Social Psychology Bulletin, 34,* 769–778.

Hafer, C. L. (2000). Do innocent victims threaten the belief in a just world? Evidence from a modified Stroop task. *Journal of Personality and Social Psychology, 79,* 165–173.

Haidt, J. (2006). *The happiness hypothesis: Finding modern truth in ancient wisdom.* New York: Basic Books.

Hakmiller, K. L. (1966). Threat as a determinant of downward comparison. *Journal of Experimental Social Psychology* (Suppl. 1), 32–39.

Halberstadt, J., & Rhodes, G. (2000). The attractiveness of non-face averages: Implications for an evolutionary explanation of the attractiveness of average faces. *Psychological Science, 11,* 285–289.

Halberstadt, J., & Rhodes, G. (2003). It's not just average faces that are attractive: Computer-manipulated averageness makes birds, fish, and automobiles attractive. *Psychonomic Bulletin and Review, 10,* 149–156.

Halberstam, D. (1972). *The best and the brightest.* New York: Random House.

Halbesleben, J. R. B., Wheeler, A. R., & Buckley, M. R. (2007). Understanding pluralistic ignorance in organizations: Application and theory. *Journal of Managerial Psychology, 22,* 65–83.

Hall, A. (2009, March 13). I'm fed-up with this life; Riddle over last message from teenager in gun massacre. *Daily Mail* (London), p. 31.

Hall, J. A., Coats, E. J., & LeBeau, L. S. (2005). Nonverbal behavior and the vertical dimension of social relations: A metaanalysis. *Psychological Bulletin, 131,* 898–924.

Hall, S., French, D. P., & Marteau, T. M. (2003). Causal attributions following serious unexpected negative events: A systematic review. *Journal of Social and Clinical Psychology, 22,* 515–536.

Halpern, D. F., & Cheung, F. M. (2008). *Women at the top: Powerful leaders tell us how to combine work and family.* New York: Wiley-Blackwell.

Hamer, D. H., Rice, G., Risch, N., & Ebers, G. (1999). Genetics and male sexual orientation. *Science, 285,* 803.

Hamermesh, D. S., & Biddle, J. E. (1994). Beauty and the labor market. *American Economic Review, 84,* 1174–1195.

Hamilton, D. L., & Rose, T. L. (1980). Illusory correlation and the maintenance of stereotypic beliefs. *Journal of Personality and Social Psychology, 39,* 832–845.

Hamilton, W. D. (1964). The genetical evolution of social behavior: I and II. *Journal of Theoretical Biology, 7,* 1–52.

Hammel, P. (2008, November 29). Psychologist had dual role in confessions of Beatrice 6. *Omaha World-Herald.*

Hammersla, J. F., & Frease-McMahan, L. (1990). University students' priorities: Life goals vs. relationships. *Sex Roles, 23,* 1–14.

Hampson, R. B. (1984). Adolescent prosocial behavior: Peer-group and situational factors associated with helping. *Journal of Personality and Social Psychology, 46,* 153–162.

Hamrick, N., Cohen, S., & Rodriguez, M. S. (2002). Being popular can be healthy or unhealthy: Stress, social network diversity, and incidence of upper respiratory infection. *Health Psychology, 21,* 294–298.

Han, S., & Shavitt, S. (1994). Persuasion and culture: Advertising appeals in individualistic and collectivistic societies. *Journal of Experimental Social Psychology, 30,* 326–350.

Hanc, J. (2006, September 12). Muscle men: Today's culture has produced fitness buffs obsessed with becoming muscular. But how much is too much? *Newsday* (New York), p. B12.

Haney, C. (1984). On the selection of capital juries: The biasing effects of the death-qualification process. *Law and Human Behavior, 8,* 121–132.

Haney, C., Banks, C., & Zimbardo, P. (1973). Interpersonal dynamics in a simulated prison. *International Journal of Criminology and Penology, 1,* 69–97.

Haney, C., Hurtado, A., & Vega, L. (1994). "Modern" death qualification: New data on its biasing effects. *Law and Human Behavior, 18,* 619–633.

Haney, C., & Zimbardo, P. G. (1998). The past and future of U.S. prison policy: Twenty-five years after the Stanford Prison Experiment. *American Psychologist, 53,* 709–727.

Haney, C., & Zimbardo, P. G. (2009). Persistent dispositionalism in interactionist clothing: Fundamental attribution error in explaining prison abuse. *Personality and Social Psychology Bulletin, 35,* 807–814.

Hans, V. P. (2000). *Business on trial: The civil jury and corporate responsibility.* New Haven, CT: Yale University Press.

Hansen, C. H., & Hansen, R. D. (1988). Finding the face in the crowd: An anger superiority effect. *Journal of Personality and Social Psychology, 54,* 917–924.

Harackiewicz, J. M., & Elliot, A. J. (1993). Achievement goals and intrinsic motivation. *Journal of Personality and Social Psychology, 65,* 904–915.

Hardin, C., & Banaji, M. R. (1993). The influence of language on thought. *Social Cognition, 11,* 277–308.

Hardin, G. (1968). The tragedy of the commons. *Science, 162,* 1243–1248.

Hargreaves, D. A., & Tiggemann, M. (2009). Muscular ideal media images and men's body image: Social comparison processing and individual vulnerability. *Psychology of Men and Masculinity, 10,* 109–119.

Harinck, F., & De Dreu, C. K. W. (2008). Take a break! Or not? The impact of mindsets during breaks on negotiation processes and outcomes. *Journal of Experimental Social Psychology, 44,* 397–404.

Haritos-Fatouros, M. (2002). *Psychological origins of institutionalized torture.* London: Routledge.

Harkins, S. G., & Petty, R. E. (1981). Effects of source magnification of cognitive effort on attitudes: An information processing view. *Journal of Personality and Social Psychology, 40,* 401–413.

Harkins, S. G., & Petty, R. E. (1987). Information utility and the multiple source effect. *Journal of Personality and Social Psychology, 52,* 260–268.

Harmon-Jones, E., & Mills, J. (Eds.). (1999). *Cognitive dissonance: Progress on a pivotal theory in social psychology.* Washington, DC: American Psychological Association.

Harmon-Jones, E., Brehm, J. W., Greenberg, J., Simon, L., & Nelson, D. E. (1996). Evidence that the production of aversive consequences is not necessary to create cognitive dissonance. *Journal of Personality and Social Psychology, 70,* 5–16.

Harris, C. R. (2002). Sexual and romantic jealousy in heterosexual and homosexual adults. *Psychological Science, 13,* 7–12.

Harris, C. R. (2003). A review of sex differences in sexual jealousy, including self-report data, psychophysiological responses, interpersonal violence, and morbid jealousy. *Personality and Social Psychology Review, 7,* 102–128.

Harris, C. R. (2005). Male and female jealousy: Still more similar than different: Reply to Sagarin. *Personality and Social Psychology Review, 9,* 76–86.

Harris, C. R., & Christenfeld, N. (1996). Gender, jealousy, and reason. *Psychological Science, 7,* 364–366.

Harris, L. T., & Fiske, S. T. (2006). Dehumanizing the lowest of the low: Neuroimaging responses to extreme out-groups. *Psychological Science, 17,* 847–853.

Harris, M. B. (1995). Ethnicity, gender, and evaluations of aggression. *Aggressive Behavior, 21,* 343–357.

Harris, M. J., & Perkins, R. (1995). Effects of distraction on interpersonal expectancy effects: A social interaction test of the cognitive busyness hypothesis. *Social Cognition, 13,* 163–182.

Harris, M. J., & Rosenthal, R. (1985). Mediation of interpersonal expectancy effects. *Psychological Bulletin, 97,* 363–386.

Harrison, D. A., & Shaffer, M. A. (1994). Comparative examinations of self-reports and perceived absenteeism norms: Wading through Lake Wobegon. *Journal of Applied Psychology, 79,* 240–251.

Harrison, D. A., Kravitz, D. A., Mayer, D. M., Leslie, L. M., & Lev-Arey, D. (2006). Understanding attitudes toward affirmative action programs in employment: Summary and meta-analysis of 35 years of research. *Journal of Applied Psychology, 91,* 1013–1036.

Hart, A. J. (1995). Naturally occurring expectation effects. *Journal of Personality and Social Psychology, 68,* 109–115.

Hart, A. J., Whalen, P. J., Shin, L. M., McInerney, S. C., Fischer, H., & Rauch, S. L. (2000). Differential response in the human amygdala to racial outgroup vs ingroup face stimuli. *Neuro-Report, 11,* 2351–2355.

Hart, J. W., Karau, S. J., Stasson, M. F., & Kerr, N. A. (2004). Achievement motivation, expected coworker performance, and collective task motivation: Working hard or hardly working? *Journal of Applied Social Psychology, 34,* 984–1000.

Hartwig, M., Granhag, P. A., Strömwall, L. A., & Vrij, A. (2005). Detecting deception via strategic disclosure of evidence. *Law and Human Behavior, 29,* 469–484.

Hasel, L. E., & Kassin, S. M. (2009). On the presumption of evidentiary independence: Can confessions corrupt eyewitness identifications? *Psychological Science, 20,* 122–126.

Hasel, L. E., & Wells, G. L. (2007). Catching the bad guy: Morphing composite faces helps. *Law and Human Behavior, 31,* 193–207.

Haslam, N., Loughnan, S., Kashima, Y., & Bain, P. (2008). Attributing and denying humanness to others. *European Review of Social Psychology, 19,* 55–85.

Haslam, S. A., & Reicher, S. (2007). Beyond the banality of evil: Three dynamics of an interactionist social psychology of tyranny. *Personality and Social Psychology Bulletin, 33,* 615–622.

Haslam, S. A., Jetten, J., Postmes, T., Haslam, C. (2009). Social identity, health and well-being: An emerging agenda for applied psychology. *Applied Psychology: An International Review, 58,* 1–23.

Haslam, S. A., Ryan, M. K., Postmes, T., Spears, R., Jetten, J., & Webley, P. (2006). Sticking to our guns: Social identity as a basis for the maintenance of commitment to faltering organizational projects. *Journal of Organizational Behavior, 27,* 607–628.

Hass, R. G. (1981). Effects of source characteristics on the cognitive processing of persuasive messages and attitude change. In R. Petty, T. Ostrom, & T. Brock (Eds.), *Cognitive responses in persuasion* (pp. 141–172). Hillsdale, NJ: Erlbaum.

Hass, R. G. (1984). Perspective taking and self-awareness: Drawing an E on your forehead. *Journal of Personality and Social Psychology, 46,* 788–798.

Hass, R. G., & Eisenstadt, D. (1990). The effects of self-focused attention on perspective-taking and anxiety. *Anxiety Research, 2,* 165–176.

Hass, R. G., & Grady, K. (1975). Temporal delay, type of forewarning, and resistance to influence. *Journal of Experimental Social Psychology, 11,* 459–469.

Hass, R. G., Katz, I., Rizzo, N., Bailey, J., & Moore, L. (1992). When racial ambivalence evokes negative affect, using a disguised measure of mood. *Personality and Social Psychology Bulletin, 18,* 786–797.

Hassin, R. R., Bargh, J. A., & Zimerman, S. (2009). Automatic and flexible: The case of nonconscious goal pursuit. *Social Cognition, 27*(1), 27–36.

Hassin, R., & Trope, Y. (2000). Facing faces: Studies on the cognitive aspects of physiognomy. *Journal of Personality and Social Psychology, 78,* 837–852.

Hastie, R., & Kameda, T. (2005). The robust beauty of majority rules in group decisions. *Psychological Review, 112,* 494–508.

Hastie, R., Penrod, S. D., & Pennington, N. (1983). *Inside the jury.* Cambridge, MA: Harvard University Press.

Hater, J. J., & Bass, B. M. (1988). Superiors' evaluations and subordinates' perceptions of transformational and transactional leadership. *Journal of Applied Psychology, 73,* 695–702.

Hatfield, E. (1988). Passionate and companionate love. In R. J. Sternberg & M. L. Barnes (Eds.), *The psychology of love* (pp. 191–217). New Haven, CT: Yale University Press.

Hatfield, E., & Rapson, R. L. (1993). *Love, sex, and intimacy: Their psychology, biology, and history.* New York: HarperCollins.

Hatfield, E., Greenberger, E., Traupmann, J., & Lambert, P. (1982). Equity and sexual satisfaction in recently married couples. *Journal of Sex Research, 18,* 18–32.

Hatfield, E., Rapson, R. L., & Aumer-Ryan, K. (2008). Social justice in love relationships: Recent developments. *Social Justice Research, 21,* 413–431.

Hatfield, E., Rapson, R. L., & Martel, L. D. (2007). Passionate love. In S. Kitayama & D. Cohen (Eds.), *Handbook of cultural psychology.* New York: Guilford.

Hawkins, D. L., Pepler, D. J., & Craig, W. M. (2001). Naturalistic observations of peer interventions in bullying. *Social Development, 10,* 512–527.

Hawkley, L. C., Burleson, M. H., Berntson, G. G., & Cacioppo, J. T. (2003). Loneliness in everyday life: Cardiovascular activity, psychosocial context, and health behaviors. *Journal of Personality and Social Psychology, 85,* 105–120.

Hawkley, L. C., Thisted, R. A., & Cacioppo, J. T. (2009). Loneliness predicts reduced physical activity: Cross-sectional & longitudinal analyses. *Health Psychology, 28,* 354–363.

Hay, D. F., & Cook, K. V. (2007). The transformation of prosocial behavior from infancy to childhood. In C. A. Brownell & C. B. Kopp (Eds.), *Socioemotional development in the toddler years: Transitions and transformations* (pp. 100–131). New York: Guilford.

Hayes, T. C., & Lee, M. R. (2005). The southern culture of honor and violent attitudes. *Sociological Spectrum, 25,* 593–617.

Hays, R. B. (1985). A longitudinal study of friendship development. *Journal of Personality and Social Psychology, 48,* 909–924.

Hays, G. (2008). Central Washington offers the ultimate act of sportsmanship. Retrieved July 5, 2009, from http://sports.espn.go.com/ncaa/columns/story?columnist=hays_graham&id=3372631.

Hazan, C., & Diamond, L. M. (2000). The place of attachment in human mating. *Review of General Psychology, 4,* 186–204.

Hazan, C., & Shaver, P. (1987). Romantic love conceptualized as an attachment process. *Journal of Personality and Social Psychology, 52,* 511–524.

Hearold, S. (1986). A synthesis of 1043 effects of television on social behavior. In G. Comstock (Ed.), *Public communication and behavior* (Vol. 1, pp. 65–133). Orlando, FL: Academic Press.

Hearst, P. C. (1982). *Every secret thing.* New York: Doubleday.

Heatherton, T. F., & Polivy, J. (1991). Development and validation of a scale for measuring state self-esteem. *Journal of Personality and Social Psychology, 60,* 895–910.

Heatherton, T. F., & Vohs, K. D. (2000). Interpersonal evaluations following threats to self: Role of self-esteem. *Journal of Personality and Social Psychology, 78,* 725–736.

Heatherton, T. F., & Wyland, C. L. (2003). Assessing self-esteem. In S. J. Lopez & C. R. Snyder (Eds.), *Positive psychological assessment: A handbook of models and measures* (pp. 219–233). Washington, DC: American Psychological Association.

Hebl, M., Dovidio, J. F., Richeson, J. A., Shelton, J. N., Gaertner, S. L., & Kawakami, K. (2009). Interpretation of interaction: Responsiveness to verbal and nonverbal cues. In S. Demoulin, J. P. Leyens, & J. F. Dovidio (Eds.), *Intergroup misunderstandings: Impact of divergent social realities* (pp. 101–116). New York: Psychology Press.

Hebl, M. R., & Heatherton, T. F. (1998). The stigma of obesity in women: The difference is black and white. *Personality and Social Psychology Bulletin, 24,* 417–426.

Hebl, M. R., & Turchin, J. M. (2005). The stigma of obesity: What about men? *Basic and Applied Social Psychology, 27,* 267–275.

Hedge, A., & Yousif, Y. H. (1992). Effects of urban size, urgency, and cost on helpfulness: A cross-cultural comparison between the United Kingdom and the Sudan. *Journal of Cross Cultural Psychology, 23,* 107–115.

Hedge, J. W., & Kavanagh, M. J. (1988). Improving the accuracy of performance evaluations: Comparison of three methods of performance appraiser training. *Journal of Applied Psychology, 73,* 68–73.

Hedges, C. (2008, December 8). The best and the brightest led America off a cliff. Retrieved July 26, 2008, from Truthdig.com.

Heider, F. (1958). *The psychology of interpersonal relations.* New York: Wiley.

Heilman, M. E., & Alcott, V. B. (2001). What I think you think of me: Women's reactions to being viewed as beneficiaries of preferential selection. *Journal of Applied Psychology, 86,* 574–582.

Heilman, M. E., Battle, W. S., Keller, C. E., & Lee, R. A. (1998). Type of affirmative action policy: A determinant of reactions to sex-based preferential selection? *Journal of Applied Psychology, 83,* 190–205.

Heilman, M. E., Block, C. J., & Lucas, J. A. (1992). Presumed incompetent? Stigmatization and affirmative action efforts. *Journal of Applied Psychology, 77,* 536–544.

Heilman, M. E., McCullough, W. F., & Gilbert, D. (1996). The other side of affirmative action: Reactions of nonbeneficiaries to sex-based preferential selection. *Journal of Applied Psychology, 81,* 346–357.

Heilman, M. E., & Okimoto, T. G. (2008). Motherhood: A potential source of bias in employment decisions. *Journal of Applied Psychology, 93,* 189–198.

Heilman, M. E., Simon, M. C., & Repper, D. P. (1987). Intentionally favored, unintentionally harmed? Impact of sex-based preferential selection on self-perceptions and self-evaluations. *Journal of Applied Psychology, 72,* 62–68.

Heine, S. J. (2005). Where is the evidence for pancultural self-enhancement? A reply to Sedikides, Gaertner, & Toguchi (2003). *Journal of Personality and Social Psychology, 89,* 531–538.

Heine, S. J. (2007). Culture and motivation. In S. Kitayama & D. Cohen (Eds.), *Handbook of cultural psychology.* New York: Guilford.

Heine, S. J., & Hamamura, T. (2007). In search of East Asian self-enhancement. *Personality and Social Psychology Review, 11,* 1–24.

Heine, S. J., Kitayama, S., Lehman, D. R., Takata, T., Ide, E., Lueng, C., & Matsumoto, H. (2001). Divergent consequences of success and failure in Japan and North America: An investigation of self-improving motivations and malleable selves. *Journal of Personality and Social Psychology, 81,* 599–615.

Heine, S. J., Lehman, D. R., Markus, H. R., & Kitayama, S. (1999). Is there a universal need for positive self-regard? *Psychological Review, 106,* 756–794.

Heine, S. J., Takata, T., & Lehman, D. R. (2000). Beyond self-presentation: Evidence for self-criticism among Japanese. *Personality and Social Psychology Bulletin, 26,* 71–78.

Heine, S. J., Takemoto, T., Moskalenko, S., Lasaleta, J., & Henrich, J. (2008). Mirrors in the head: Cultural variation in objective self-awareness. *Personality and Social Psychology Bulletin, 34,* 879–887.

Helgesen, S. (1995). *Web of inclusion: A new architecture for building great organizations.* New York: Doubleday.

Helgeson, V. S. (1992). Moderators of the relation between perceived control and adjustment to chronic illness. *Journal of Personality and Social Psychology, 63,* 652–666.

Helgeson, V. S., Cohen, S., Schulz, R., & Yasko, J. (2000). Group support interventions for women with breast cancer: Who benefits from what? *Health Psychology, 19,* 107–114.

Helgeson, V. S., Reynolds, K. A., & Tomich, P. L. (2006). A meta-analytic review of benefit finding and growth. *Journal of Consulting and Clinical Psychology, 74,* 797–816.

Heller, J. F., Pallak, M. S., & Picek, J. M. (1973). The interactive effects of intent and threat on boomerang attitude change. *Journal of Personality and Social Psychology, 26,* 273–279.

Henchy, T., & Glass, D. C. (1968). Evaluation apprehension and the social facilitation of dominant and subordinate responses. *Journal of Personality and Social Psychology, 10,* 446–454.

Henderlong, J., & Lepper, M. R. (2002). The effects of praise on children's intrinsic motivation: A review and synthesis. *Psychological Bulletin, 128,* 774–795.

Henderson, L., & Zimbardo, P. (1998). Shyness. In H. S. Friedman (Ed.), *Encyclopedia of mental health.* San Diego: Academic Press.

Henderson-King, D., Henderson-King, E., & Hoffman, L. (2001). Media images and women's self-evaluations: Social context and importance of attractiveness as moderators. *Personality and Social Psychology Bulletin, 27,* 1407–1416.

Henderson-King, E., & Henderson-King, D. (1997). Media effects on women's body esteem: Social and individual differences factors. *Journal of Applied Social Psychology, 27,* 399–417.

Hendrick, C., & Hendrick, S. S. (Eds.). (2000). *Close relationships: A sourcebook.* Thousand Oaks, CA: Sage.

Hendrick, S. S., & Hendrick, C. (1995). Gender differences and similarities in sex and love. *Personal Relationships, 2,* 55–65.

Heneman, H. G., & Schwab, D. P. (1985). Pay satisfaction: Its multidimensional nature and measurement. *International Journal of Psychology, 20,* 129–141.

Henggeler, S. W., Letourneau, E. J., Chapman, J. E., Borduin, C. M., Schewe, P. A., & McCart, M. R. (2009). Mediators of change for multisystemic therapy with juvenile sexual offenders. *Journal of Consulting and Clinical Psychology, 77,* 451–462.

Henig, R. M. (2006, February 5). Looking for the lie. *The New York Times.*

Henle, C. A., Kohut, G., & Booth, R. (2009). Designing electronic use policies to enhance employee perceptions of fairness and to reduce cyberloafing: An empirical test of justice theory. *Computers in Human Behavior, 25,* 902–910.

Henley, N. M. (1977). *Body politics: Power, sex, and nonverbal communication.* Englewood Cliffs, NJ: Prentice-Hall.

Henningsen, D. D., Henningsen, M. L. M., Eden, J., & Cruz, M. G. (2006). Examining the symptoms of groupthink and retrospective sensemaking. *Small Group Research, 37,* 36–64.

Henry, J. D., von Hippel, W., & Baynes, K. (2009). Social inappropriateness, executive control, and aging. *Psychology and Aging, 24,* 239–244.

Henry, P. J. (2008). College sophomores in the laboratory redux: Influences of a narrow data base on social psychology's view of the nature of prejudice. *Psychological Inquiry, 19,* 49–71.

Heppner, P. P., Heppner, M. J., Lee, D., Wang, Y., Park, H., & Wang, L. (2006). Development and validation of a collectivist coping styles inventory. *Journal of Counseling Psychology, 53,* 107–125.

Herdt, G. (1998). *Same sex, different cultures: Exploring gay and lesbian lives.* Boulder, CO: Westview Press.

Herek, G. M. (2006). Legal recognition of same-sex relationships in the United States: A social science perspective. *American Psychologist, 61,* 607–621.

Herring, C. (2009). Does diversity pay? Race, gender, and the business case for diversity. *American Sociological Review, 74,* 208–224.

Hertwig, R., & Ortmann, A. (2008). Deception in experiments: Revisiting the arguments in its defense. *Ethics & Behavior, 18,* 59–92.

Herzberger, S. D. (1996). *Violence within the family: Social psychological perspectives.* Madison, WI: Brown & Benchmark.

Hewitt, P. L., Flett, G. L., Sherry, S. B., Habke, M., Parkin, M., Lam, R., McMurtry, B., Ediger, E., Fairlie, P., & Stein, M. B. (2003). The interpersonal expression of perfection: Perfectionistic self-presentation and psychological distress. *Journal of Personality and Social Psychology, 84,* 1303–1325.

Hewstone, M., & Lord, C. G. (1998). Changing intergroup cognitions and intergroup behavior: The role of typicality. In C. Sedikides, J. Schopler, & C. A. Insko (Eds.), *Intergroup cognition and intergroup behavior* (pp. 367–392). Mahwah, NJ: Erlbaum.

Heyes, C. M., & Galef, B. G., Jr. (1996). *Social learning in animals: The roots of culture.* New York: Academic Press.

Higgins, C. A., & Judge, T. A. (2004). The effect of applicant influence tactics on recruiter perceptions of fit and hiring recommendations: A field study. *Journal of Applied Psychology, 89,* 622–632.

Higgins, E. T. (1999). Self-discrepancy: A theory relating self and affect. In R. F. Baumeister (Ed.), *The self in social psychology* (pp. 150–181). Philadelphia, PA: Psychology Press/Taylor & Francis.

Higgins, E. T., & Rholes, W. S. (1978). "Saying is believing": Effects of message modification on memory and liking for the person described. *Journal of Experimental Social Psychology, 14,* 363–378.

Higgins, E. T., King, G. A., & Mavin, G. H. (1982). Individual construct accessibility and subjective impressions and recall. *Journal of Personality and Social Psychology, 43,* 35–47.

Higgins, E. T., Rholes, C. R., & Jones, C. R. (1977). Category accessibility and impression formation. *Journal of Experimental Social Psychology, 13,* 141–154.

Higgins, L. T., Zheng, M., Liu, Y., & Sun, C. H. (2002). Attitudes to marriage and sexual behaviors: A survey of gender and culture differences in China and the United Kingdom. *Sex Roles, 46,* 75–89.

Higgins, R. L., & Harris, R. N. (1988). Strategic "alcohol" use: Drinking to self-handicap. *Journal of Social and Clinical Psychology, 6,* 191–202.

Hill, C. A. (1987). Affiliation motivation: People who need people . . . but in different ways. *Journal of Personality and Social Psychology, 52,* 1008–1018.

Hill, C., Memon, A., & McGeorge, P. (2008). The role of confirmation bias in suspect interviews: A systematic evaluation. *Legal and Criminological Psychology, 13,* 357–371.

Hill, J., & Nathan, R. (2008). Childhood antecedents of serious violence in adult male offenders. *Aggressive Behavior, 34,* 329–338.

Hilmert, C. J., Kulik, J. A., & Christenfeld, N. J. S. (2006). Positive and negative outcome modeling: The influence of another's similarity and dissimilarity. *Journal of Personality and Social Psychology, 90,* 440–452.

Hilton, J. L., & Darley, J. M. (1985). Constructing other persons: A limit on the effect. *Journal of Experimental Social Psychology, 21,* 1–18.

Hilton, J. L., & Darley, J. M. (1991). The effects of interaction goals on person perception. *Advances in Experimental Social Psychology, 24,* 235–267.

Hilton, J. L., & Fein, S. (1989). The role of typical diagnosticity in stereotype-based judgments. *Journal of Personality and Social Psychology, 57,* 201–211.

Hines, D. A., & Saudino, K. J. (2002). Intergenerational transmission of intimate partner violence: A behavioral genetic perspective. *Trauma Violence and Abuse, 3,* 210–225.

Hinsz, V. B., Tindale, R. S., & Vollrath, D. A. (1997). The emerging conceptualization of groups as information processors. *Psychological Bulletin, 121,* 43–64.

Hinsz, V. B., Tindale, R. S., Nagao, D. H., Davis, J. H., & Robertson, B. A. (1988). The influence of the accuracy of individuating information on the use of base rate information in probability judgment. *Journal of Experimental Social Psychology, 24,* 127–145.

Hirt, E. R., Deppe, R. K., & Gordon, L. J. (1991). Self-reported versus behavioral self-handicapping: Empirical evidence for a theoretical distinction. *Journal of Personality and Social Psychology, 61,* 981–991.

Hirt, E. R., Zillman, D., Erickson, G. A., & Kennedy, C. (1992). Costs and benefits of allegiance: Changes in fans' self-ascribed competencies after team victory versus defeat. *Journal of Personality and Social Psychology, 63,* 724–738.

Hitler, A. (1933). *Mein Kampf* (E. T. S. Dugdale, Trans.). Cambridge, MA: Riverside.

Hittner, J. B., & Kennington, L. E. (2008). Normative perceptions, substance use, age of substance use initiation, and gender as predictors of HIV-risky sexual behavior in a college student sample. *Journal of Applied Biobehavioral Research, 13,* 86–101.

Hixon, J. G., & Swann, W. B., Jr. (1993). When does introspection bear fruit? Self-reflection, self-insight, and interpersonal choices. *Journal of Personality and Social Psychology, 64,* 35–43.

Hoaken, P. N. S., Allaby, D. B., & Earle, J. (2007). Executive cognitive functioning and the recognition of facial expressions of emotion in incarcerated violent offenders, non-violent offenders, and controls. *Aggressive Behavior, 33,* 412–421.

Hobfoll, S. E., Canetti-Nisim, D., & Johnson, R. J. (2006). Exposure to terrorism, stress-related mental health symptoms, and defensive coping among Jews and Arabs in Israel. *Journal of Consulting and Clinical Psychology, 74,* 207–218.

Hobfoll, S. E., Palmieri, P. A., Johnson, R. J., Canetti-Nisim, D., Hall, B. J., & Galea, S. (2009). Trajectories of resilience, resistance, and distress during ongoing terrorism: The case of Jews and Arabs in Israel. *Journal of Consulting and Clinical Psychology, 77,* 138–148.

Hobza, C. L., & Rochlen, A. B. (2009). Gender role conflict, drive for muscularity, and the impact of ideal media portrayals on men. *Psychology of Men and Masculinity, 10,* 120–130.

Hodson, G., Hooper, H., Dovidio, J. F., & Gaertner, S. L. (2005). Aversive racism in Britain: The use of inadmissible evidence in legal decisions. *European Journal of Social Psychology, 35,* 437–448.

Hoffman, M. L. (2000). *Empathy and moral development: Implications for caring and justice.* New York: Cambridge University Press.

Hofling, C. K., Brotzman, E., Dalrymple, S., Graves, N., & Pierce, C. (1966). An experimental study of nurse-physician relations. *Journal of Nervous and Mental Disease, 143,* 171–180.

Hofstede, G. (1980). *Culture's consequences.* Beverly Hills, CA: Sage.

Hogan, R., Curphy, G. J., & Hogan, J. (1994). What we know about leadership: Effectiveness and personality. *American Psychologist, 49,* 493–504.

Hoigaard, R., & Ommundsen, Y. (2007). Perceived social loafing and anticipated effort reduction among young football (soccer) players: An achievement goal perspective. *Psychological Reports, 100,* 857–875.

Hollander, E. P. (1958). Conformity, status, and idiosyncrasy credit. *Psychological Review, 65,* 117–127.

Hollander, E. P. (1985). Leadership and power. In G. Lindzey & E. Aronson (Eds.), *Handbook of social psychology* (3rd ed., Vol. 2, pp. 485–537). New York: Random House.

Holloway, R., & Johnston, L. (2006). Evaluating the evaluators: Perceptions of interviewers by rejected job applicants as a function of interviewer and applicant sex. *Journal of Applied Social Psychology, 36*, 2635–2648.

Holloway, R. A., Waldrip, A. M., & Ickes, W. (2009). Evidence that a simpático self-schema accounts for differences in the self-concepts and social behavior of Latinos versus Whites (and Blacks). *Journal of Personality and Social Psychology, 96*, 1012–1028.

Holmes, T. H., & Rahe, R. H. (1967). The Social Readjustment Rating Scale. *Journal of Psychosomatic Research, 11*, 213–218.

Homans, G. C. (1961). *Social behavior.* New York: Harcourt, Brace & World.

Hönekopp, J. (2006). Once more: Is beauty in the eye of the beholder? Relative contributions of private and shared taste to judgments of facial attractiveness. *Journal of Experimental Psychology: Human Perception and Performance, 32*, 199–209.

Honeycutt, J. M., Woods, B. L., & Fontenot, K. (1993). The endorsement of communication conflict rules as a function of engagement, marriage and marital ideology. *Journal of Social and Personal Relationships, 10*, 285–304.

Hong, L. (2000). Toward a transformed approach to prevention: Breaking the link between masculinity and violence. *Journal of American College Health, 48*, 269–279.

Hong, Y., Morris, M. W., Chiu, C., & Benet-Martinez, V. (2000). Multicultural minds: A dynamic constructivist approach to culture and cognition. *American Psychologist, 55*, 709–720.

Hong, Y.-y., Wyer, R. S., Jr., & Fong, C. P. S. (2008). Chinese working in groups: Effort dispensability versus normative influence. *Asian Journal of Social Psychology, 11*, 187–195.

Honts, C. R. (1996). Criterion development and validity of the CQT in field application. *Journal of General Psychology, 123*, 309–324.

Honts, C. R., Raskin, D. C., & Kircher, J. C. (1994). Mental and physical countermeasures reduce the accuracy of polygraph tests. *Journal of Applied Psychology, 79*, 252–259.

Honts, C. R., Raskin, D. C., & Kircher, J. C. (2002). The scientific status of research on polygraph techniques: The case for polygraph tests (pp. 446–483). In D. L. Faigman, D. Kaye, M. J. Saks, & J. Sanders (Eds.), *Modern scientific evidence: The law and science of expert testimony.* St. Paul, MN: West.

Hoobler, J. M., & Brass, D. J. (2006). Abusive supervision and family undermining as displaced aggression. *Journal of Applied Psychology, 91*, 1125–1133.

Hoorens, V., & Nuttin, J. M. (1993). Overvaluation of own attributes: Mere ownership or subjective frequency? *Social Cognition, 11*, 177–200.

Hope, L., Memon, A., & McGeorge, P. (2004). Understanding pretrial publicity: Predecisional distortion of evidence by mock jurors. *Journal of Experimental Psychology: Applied, 10*, 111–119.

Hope, L., & Wright, D. (2007). Beyond unusual? Examining the role of attention in the weapon focus effect. *Applied Cognitive Psychology, 21*, 951–962.

Hornsey, M. J., & Jetten, J. (2004). The individual within the group: Balancing the need to belong with the need to be different. *Personality and Social Psychology Review, 8*, 248–264.

Horowitz, I. A., & Willging, T. E. (1991). Changing views of jury power: The nullification debate, 1787–1988. *Law and Human Behavior, 15*, 165–182.

Horstmann, G., & Bauland, A. (2006). Search asymmetries with real faces: Testing the anger-superiority effect. *Emotion, 6*, 193–207.

Horvath, A. O., & Luborsky, L. (1993). The role of the therapeutic alliance in psychotherapy. *Journal of Consulting and Clinical Psychology, 61*, 561–573.

Hoshino-Browne, E., Zanna, A. S., Spencer, S. J.; Zanna, M. P., Kitayama, S., & Lackenbauer, S. (2005). On the cultural guises of cognitive dissonance: The case of Easterners and Westerners. *Journal of Personality and Social Psychology, 89*, 294–310.

Hosoda, M., Stone-Romero, E. F., & Coats, G. (2003). The effects of physical attractiveness on job-related outcomes: A metaanalysis of experimental studies. *Personnel Psychology, 56*, 431–462.

Houghton, D. P. (2008). Invading and occupying Iraq: Some insights from political psychology. *Peace and Conflict: Journal of Peace Psychology, 14*, 169–192.

Houldsworth, C., & Mathews, B. P. (2000). Group composition, performance and educational attainment. *Education and Training, 42*, 40–53.

House, J. S., Landis, K. R., & Umberson, D. (1988). Social relationships and health. *Science, 241*, 540–545.

Hovland, C. I., & Sears, R. R. (1940). Minor studies in aggression: VI. Correlation of lynchings with economic indices. *Journal of Psychology, 9*, 301–310.

Hovland, C. I., & Weiss, W. (1951). The influence of source credibility on communication effectiveness. *Public Opinion Quarterly, 15*, 635–650.

Hovland, C. I., Janis, I. L., & Kelley, H. H. (1953). *Communication and persuasion: Psychological studies of opinion change.* New Haven, CT: Yale University Press.

Hovland, C. I., Lumsdaine, A. A., & Sheffield, F. D. (1949). *Experiments on mass communication.* Princeton, NJ: Princeton University Press.

Howard, D. E., Griffin, M. A., & Boekeloo, B. O. (2008). Prevalence and psychosocial correlates of alcohol-related sexual assault among university students. *Adolescence, 43*, 733–750.

Howard, D. J. (1990). The influence of verbal responses to common greetings on compliance behavior: The foot-in-the-mouth effect. *Journal of Applied Social Psychology, 20*, 1185–1196.

Huesmann, L. R. (1998). The role of social information processing and cognitive schema in the acquisition and maintenance of habitual aggressive behavior. In R. G. Geen & E. Donnerstein (Eds.), *Human aggression: Theories, research, and implications for social policy* (pp. 73–109). San Diego: Academic Press.

Huesmann, L. R., Dubow, E. F., & Boxer, P. (2009). Continuity of aggression from childhood to early adulthood as a predictor of life outcomes: Implications for the adolescent-limited and life-course-persistent models. *Aggressive Behavior, 35*, 136–149.

Huesmann, L. R., & Guerra, N. G. (1997). Children's normative beliefs about aggression and aggressive behavior. *Journal of Personality and Social Psychology, 72*, 408–419.

Huesmann, L. R., Moise-Titus, J., Podolski, C. P., & Eron, L. D. (2003). Longitudinal relations between children's exposure to TV violence and their aggressive and violent behavior in young adulthood: 1977–1992. *Developmental Psychology, 39*, 201–229.

Huffcutt, A. I., & Roth, P. L. (1998). Racial group differences in employment interview evaluations. *Journal of Applied Psychology, 83*, 179–189.

Hugenberg, K., & Bodenhausen, G. V. (2003). Facing prejudice: Implicit prejudice and the perception of facial threat. *Psychological Science, 14*, 640–643.

Hugenberg, K., & Bodenhausen, G. V. (2004). Ambiguity in social categorization: The role of prejudice and facial affect in race categorization. *Psychological Science, 15*, 342–345.

Hugenberg, K., & Corneille, O. (2009). Holistic processing is tuned for in-group faces. *Cognitive Science, 33*, 1173–1181.

Hull, J. G., & Young, R. D. (1983). Self-consciousness, self-esteem, and success-failure as determinants of alcohol consumption in male social drinkers. *Journal of Personality and Social Psychology, 44*, 1097–1109.

Huntsinger, J. R., Lun, J., Sinclair, S., & Clore, G. L. (2009). Contagion without contact: Anticipatory mood matching in response to affiliative motivation. *Personality and Social Psychology Bulletin, 35*, 909–922.

Hur, M. H. (2006). Exploring the motivation factors of charitable giving and their value structure: A case study of Seoul, Korea. *Social Behavior and Personality, 34*, 661–680.

Hurtz, G. M., & Donovan, J. J. (2000). Personality and job performance: The Big Five revisited. *Journal of Applied Psychology, 85*, 869–879.

Huston, T. L., & Vangelisti, A. L. (1991). Socioemotional behavior and satisfaction in marital relationships: A longitudinal study. *Journal of Personality and Social Psychology, 61,* 721–733.

Hutchings, P. B., & Haddock, G. (2008). Look black in anger: The role of implicit prejudice in the categorization and perceived emotional intensity of racially ambiguous faces. *Journal of Experimental Social Psychology, 44,* 1418–1420.

Hyde, M. K., & White, K. M. (2009). To be a donor or not to be? Applying an extended theory of planned behavior to predict posthumous organ donation intentions. *Journal of Applied Social Psychology, 39,* 880–900.

Iacono, W. G., & Lykken, D. T. (1997). The validity of the lie-detector test: Two surveys of scientific opinion. *Journal of Applied Psychology, 82,* 426–433.

Igou, E. R. (2008). "How long will I suffer?" versus "How long will you suffer?" A self-other effect in affective forecasting. *Journal of Personality and Social Psychology, 95,* 899–917.

Imai, Y. (1991). Effects of influence strategies, perceived social power and cost on compliance with requests. *Japanese Psychological Research, 33,* 134–144.

Inbau, F. E., Reid, J. E., Buckley, J. P., & Jayne, B. C. (2001). *Criminal interrogation and confessions* (4th ed.). Gaithersburg, MD: Aspen.

Ingham, A. G., Levinger, G., Graves, J., & Peckham, V. (1974). The Ringelmann effect: Studies of group size and group performance. *Journal of Experimental Social Psychology, 10,* 371–384.

Inglehart, R., Foa, R., Peterson, C., & Welzel, C. (2008). Development, freedom, and rising happiness: A global perspective (1981–2007). *Current Perspectives on Psychological Science, 3,* 264–285.

Ingoldsby, B. B. (1991). The Latin American family: Familism vs. machismo. *Journal of Comparative Family Studies, 23,* 47–62.

Ingram, R. E. (1990). Self-focused attention in clinical disorders: Review and a conceptual model. *Psychological Bulletin, 107,* 156–176.

Innocence Project. (2009). Know the causes. Retrieved September 6, 2009, from http://www.innocenceproject.org/understand/.

Insko, C. A., Sedlak, A. J., & Lipsitz, A. (1982). A two-valued logic or two-valued balance resolution of the challenge of agreement and attraction effects in p-o-x triads, and a theoretical perspective on conformity and hedonism. *European Journal of Social Psychology, 12,* 143–167.

International Labour Office. (2008). LABORSTA Internet. Retrieved October 1, 2009, from http://laborsta.ilo.org/.

Internet World Stats. (2009). Internet usage statistics: The big picture. Retrieved October 9, 2009, from http://www.internetworldstats.com/stats.htm.

Inzlicht, M., Kaiser, C. R., & Major, B. (2008). The face of chauvinism: How prejudice expectations shape perceptions of facial affect. *Journal of Experimental Social Psychology, 44,* 758–766.

Ireland, T. O., & Smith, C. A. (2009). Living in partner-violent families: Developmental links to antisocial behavior and relationship violence. *Journal of Youth and Adolescence, 38,* 323–339.

Irons, E. D., & Moore, G. W. (1985). *Black managers: The case of the banking industry.* New York: Praeger.

Irwin, M., Mascovich, S., Gillin, J. C., Willoughby, R., Pike, J., & Smith, T. L. (1994). Partial sleep deprivation reduces natural killer cell activity in humans. *Psychosomatic Medicine, 56,* 493–498.

Isen, A. M. (1984). Toward understanding the role of affect in cognition. In R. S. Wyer & T. K. Srull (Eds.), *Handbook of social cognition* (Vol. 3, pp. 179–236). Hillsdale, NJ: Erlbaum.

Isen, A. M. (2008). Positive affect and decision processes: Some recent theoretical developments with practical implications. In C. P. Haugtvedt, P. M. Herr, & F. R. Kardes (Eds), *Handbook of consumer psychology* (pp. 273–296). NY: Taylor & Francis.

Isen, A. M., & Levin, P. A. (1972). Effect of feeling good on helping: Cookies and kindness. *Journal of Personality and Social Psychology, 21,* 384–388.

Ishii, K., & Kurzban, R. (2008). Public goods games in Japan: Cultural and individual differences in reciprocity. *Human Nature, 19,* 138–156.

Ishii, K., Reyes, J., & Kitayama, S. (2003). Spontaneous attention to word content versus emotional tone: Differences among three cultures. *Psychological Science, 14,* 39–46.

Ito, T. A., Chiao, K. W., Devine, P. G., Lorig, T. S., & Cacioppo, J. T. (2006). The influence of facial feedback on race bias. *Psychological Science, 17,* 256–261.

Ito, T. A., Larsen, J. T., Smith, N. K., & Cacioppo, J. T. (1998). Negative information weighs more heavily on the brain: The negativity bias in evaluative categorizations. *Journal of Personality and Social Psychology, 75,* 887–900.

Ito, T. A., Miller, N., & Pollock, V. E. (1996). Alcohol and aggression: A meta-analysis on the moderating effects of inhibitory cues, triggering events, and self-focused attention. *Psychological Bulletin, 120,* 60–82.

Ito, T. A., & Urland, G. R. (2003). Race and gender on the brain: Electrocortical measures of attention to the race and gender of multiply categorizable individuals. *Journal of Personality and Social Psychology, 85,* 616–626.

Izard, C. E. (1990). Facial expressions and the regulation of emotions. *Journal of Personality and Social Psychology, 58,* 487–498.

Jacks, J. Z., & Cameron, K. A. (2003). Strategies for resisting persuasion. *Basic and Applied Social Psychology, 25,* 145–161.

Jackson, J. M. (1986). In defense of social impact theory: Comment on Mullin. *Journal of Personality and Social Psychology, 50,* 511–513.

Jackson, L. M., Esses, V. M., & Burris, C. T. (2001). Contemporary sexism and discrimination: The importance of respect for men and women. *Personality and Social Psychology Bulletin, 27,* 48–61.

Jackson, T., Chen, H., Guo, C., & Gao, X. (2006). Stories we love by: Conceptions of love among couples from People's Republic of China and the United States. *Journal of Cross-Cultural Psychology, 4,* 446–464.

Jackson, T., Fritch, A., Nagasaka, T., & Gunderson, J. (2002). Towards explaining the association between shyness and loneliness: A path analysis with American college students. *Social Behavior and Personality, 30,* 263–270.

James, W. (1890). *Principles of psychology* (Vols. 1–2). New York: Holt.

James, W. H. (2005). Biological and psychosocial determinants of male and female human sexual orientation. *Journal of Biosocial Science, 37,* 555–567.

Jamjoom, M. (2009, May 10). Saudi judge: It's OK to slap spendthrift wives. *CNN.com.*

Janis, I. L. (1968). Attitude change via role playing. In R. Abelson, E. Aronson, W. McGuire, T. Newcomb, M. Rosenberg, & P. Tennenbaum (Eds.), *Theories of cognitive consistency: A sourcebook* (pp. 810–818). Chicago: Rand McNally.

Janis, I. L. (1982). *Groupthink* (2nd ed.). Boston: Houghton Mifflin.

Janis, I. L., & Feshbach, S. (1953). Effects of fear arousing communications. *Journal of Abnormal and Social Psychology, 48,* 78–92.

Janis, I. L., & King, B. T. (1954). The influence of role playing on opinion change. *Journal of Abnormal and Social Psychology, 49,* 211–218.

Janis, I. L., Kaye, D., & Kirschner, P. (1965). Facilitating effects of "eating while reading" on responsiveness to persuasive communications. *Journal of Personality and Social Psychology, 1,* 181–186.

Jankowiak, W. R., & Fischer, E. F. (1992). A cross-cultural perspective on romantic love. *Ethnology, 31,* 149–155.

Janoff-Bulman, R. (1979). Characterological versus behavioral self-blame: Inquiries into depression and rape. *Journal of Personality and Social Psychology, 37,* 1798–1809.

Janoff-Bulman, R. (1992). *Shattered assumptions: Towards a new psychology of trauma.* New York: Free Press.

Jansari, A., & Parkin, A. J. (1996). Things that go bump in your life: Explaining the reminiscence bump in autobiographical memory. *Psychology and Aging, 11,* 85–91.

Jarvis, W. B. G., & Petty, R. E. (1996). The need to evaluate. *Journal of Personality and Social Psychology, 70,* 172–194.

Jawahar, I. M., & Mattsson, J. (2005). Sexism and beautyism effects in selection as a function of self-monitoring level of decision maker. *Journal of Applied Psychology, 90,* 563–573.

Jenkins, G. D., Jr., Mitra, A., Gupta, N., & Shaw, J. D. (1998). Are financial incentives related to performance? A meta-analytic review of empirical research. *Journal of Applied Psychology, 83,* 777–787.

Jennings (Walstedt), J., Geis, F. L., & Brown, V. (1980). Influence of television commercials on women's self-confidence and independent judgment. *Journal of Personality and Social Psychology, 38,* 203–210.

Jepson, C., & Chaiken, S. (1990). Chronic issue-specific fear inhibits systematic processing of persuasive communications. *Journal of Social Behavior and Personality, 5,* 61–84.

Jetten, J., Hornsey, M. J., & Adarves-Yorno, I. (2006). When group members admit to being conformist: The role of relative intragroup status in conformity self-reports. *Personality and Social Psychology Bulletin, 32,* 162–173.

Johansson, G., von Hofsten, C., & Jansson, G. (1980). Event perception. *Annual Review of Psychology, 31,* 27–53.

Johns, G. (1994). Absenteeism estimates by employees and managers: Divergent perspectives and self-serving perceptions. *Journal of Applied Psychology, 79,* 229–239.

Johns, M., Schmader, T., & Martens, A., (2005). Knowing is half the battle: Teaching stereotype threat as a means of improving women's math performance. *Psychological Science, 16,* 175–179.

Johnson v. Louisiana, 406 U.S. 356 (1972).

Johnson, D. J., & Rusbult, C. E. (1989). Resisting temptation: Devaluation of alternative partners as a means of maintaining commitment in close relationships. *Journal of Personality and Social Psychology, 57,* 967–980.

Johnson, H. M., & Seifert, C. M. (1998). Updating accounts following a correction of misinformation. *Journal of Experimental Psychology: Learning, Memory, and Cognition, 24,* 1483–1494.

Johnson, R. D., & Downing, L. L. (1979). Deindividuation and valance of cues: Effects on prosocial and antisocial behavior. *Journal of Personality and Social Psychology, 37,* 1532–1538.

Johnson, R. W., Kelly, R. J., & LeBlane, B. A. (1995). Motivational basis of dissonance: Aversive consequences or inconsistency. *Personality and Social Psychology Bulletin, 21,* 850–855.

Johnson, W., & Krueger, R. F. (2006). How money buys happiness: Genetic and environmental processes linking finances and life satisfaction. *Journal of Personality and Social Psychology, 90,* 680–691.

Johnston, K. E., & Jacobs, J. E. (2003). Children's illusory correlations: The role of attentional bias in group impression formation. *Journal of Cognition and Development, 4,* 129–160.

Jones, B. C., DeBruine, L. M., & Little, A. C. (2007). The role of symmetry in attraction to average faces. *Perception & Psychophysics, 69,* 1273–1277.

Jones, E. E. (1964). *Ingratiation: A social psychological analysis.* New York: Appleton-Century-Crofts.

Jones, E. E. (1990). *Interpersonal perception.* New York: Freeman.

Jones, E. E., & Davis, K. E. (1965). From acts to dispositions: The attribution process in person perception. *Advances in Experimental Psychology, 2,* 219–266.

Jones, E. E., & Harris, V. A. (1967). The attribution of attitudes. *Journal of Experimental Social Psychology, 3,* 1–24.

Jones, E. E., & Pittman, T. S. (1982). Toward a general theory of strategic self presentation. In J. Suls (Ed.), *Psychological perspectives on the self.* Hillsdale, NJ: Erlbaum.

Jones, E. E., & Sigall, H. (1971). The bogus pipeline: A new paradigm for measuring affect and attitude. *Psychological Bulletin, 76,* 349–364.

Jones, E. E., Davis, K. E., & Gergen, K. (1961). Role playing variations and their informational value for person perception. *Journal of Abnormal and Social Psychology, 63,* 302–310.

Jones, E. E., Rhodewalt, F., Berglas, S., & Skelton, J. A. (1981). Effects of strategic self-presentation on subsequent self-esteem. *Journal of Personality and Social Psychology, 41,* 407–421.

Jones, E. E., Rock, L., Shaver, K. G., Goethals, G. R., & Ward, L. M. (1968). Pattern of performance and ability attribution: An unexpected primary effect. *Journal of Personality and Social Psychology, 10,* 317–340.

Jones, J. H. (1997a). *Alfred C. Kinsey: A public/private life.* New York: Norton.

Jones, J. M. (1997b). *Prejudice and racism* (2nd ed.). New York: McGraw-Hill.

Jones, J. T., Pelham, B. W., Carvallo, M., & Mirenberg, M. C. (2004). How do I love thee? Let me count the Js: Implicit egotism and interpersonal attraction. *Journal of Personality and Social Psychology, 87,* 665–683.

Jones, S. S. (2007). Imitation in infancy: The development of mimicry. *Psychological Science, 18,* 593–599.

Jones, T. F., Craig, A. S., Hoy, D., Gunter, E. W., Ashley, D. L., Barr, D. B., Brock, J. W., & Schaffner, W. (2000). Mass psychogenic illness attributed to toxic exposure at a high school. *New England Journal of Medicine, 342,* 96–100.

Jordan, J., Bardé, B., & Zeiher, A. M. (Eds.). (2007). *Contributions toward evidence-based psychocardiology: A systematic review of the literature.* Washington, DC: American Psychological Association.

Josephs, R. A., Bosson, J. K., & Jacobs, C. G. (2003). Self-esteem maintenance processes: When low self-esteem may be resistant to change. *Personality and Social Psychology Bulletin, 29,* 920–933.

Jost, J. T., Federico, C. M., & Napier, J. L. (2009a). Political ideology: Its structure, functions, and elective affinities. *Annual Review of Psychology, 60,* 307–337.

Jost, J. T., Kay, A. C., & Thorisdottir, H. (Eds.). (2009b). *Social and psychological bases of ideology and system justification.* New York: Oxford University Press.

Joyce, C. (2005, May 16). Japanese women escape subway gropers: Transit officials tackle problems with women-only cars. *Ottawa Citizen,* p. A6.

Judge, T. A., Bono, J. E., & Locke, E. A. (2000). Personality and job satisfaction: The mediating role of job characteristics. *Journal of Applied Psychology, 85,* 237–249.

Judge, T. A., Hurst, C., & Simon, L. S. (2009). Does it pay to be smart, attractive, or confident (or all three)? Relationships among general mental ability, physical attractiveness, core self-evaluations, and income. *Journal of Applied Psychology, 94,* 742–755.

Judge, T. A., & Welbourne, T. M. (1994). A confirmatory investigation of the dimensionality of the Pay Satisfaction Questionnaire. *Journal of Applied Psychology, 79,* 461–466.

Jung, J., & Lee, S. H. (2006). Cross-cultural comparisons of appearance self-schema, body image, self-esteem, and dieting behavior between Korean and U.S. women. *Family and Consumer Sciences Research Journal, 34,* 350–365.

Jussim, L., Cain, T. R., Crawford, J. T., Harber, K., & Cohen, F. (2009). The unbearable accuracy of stereotypes. In T. D. Nelson (Ed.), *Handbook of prejudice, stereotyping, and discrimination* (pp. 199–227). New York: Psychology Press.

Jussim, L., & Harber, K. D. (2005). Teacher expectations and self-fulfilling prophecies: Knowns and unknowns, resolved and unresolved controversies. *Personality and Social Psychology Review, 9,* 131–155.

Jussim, L., Eccles, J., & Madon, S. (1996). Social perception, social stereotypes, and teacher expectations: Accuracy and the quest for the powerful self-fulfilling prophecy. In M. P. Zanna (Ed.), *Advances in experimental social psychology* (Vol. 28, pp. 281–388). San Diego, CA: Academic Press.

Juvonen, J., Nishina, A., & Graham, S. (2006). Ethnic diversity and perceptions of safety in urban middle schools. *Psychological Science, 17,* 393–400.

Kagan, J. (1994). *Galen's prophecy: Temperament in human nature.* New York: Basic Books.

Kahneman, D., & Miller, D. T. (1986). Norm theory: Comparing reality to its alternatives. *Psychological Review, 93,* 136–153.

Kahneman, D., Knetsch, J. L., & Thaler, R. H. (1990). Experimental tests of the endowment effect and the coase theorem. *Journal of Political Economy, 98,* 1325–1348.

Kahneman, D., Slovic, P., & Tversky, A. (Eds.). (1982). *Judgment under uncertainty: Heuristics and biases.* New York: Cambridge University Press.

Kahneman, D., & Tversky A. (1979). Prospect theory: An analysis of decisions under risk. *Econometrika, 47,* 263–291.

Kaiser, C. R., Drury, B. J., Spalding, K. E., Cheryan, S., & O'Brien, L. T. (2009). The ironic consequences of Obama's election: Decreased support for social justice. *Journal of Experimental Social Psychology, 45,* 556–559.

Kalichman, S. C. (Ed.). (2006). *Positive prevention: Reducing HIV transmission among people living with HIV/AIDS.* New York: Springer.

Kallgren, C. A., & Wood, W. (1986). Access to attitude-relevant information in memory as a determinant of attitude-behavior consistency. *Journal of Experimental Social Psychology, 22,* 328–338.

Kalven, H., & Zeisel, H. (1966). *The American jury.* Boston: Little, Brown.

Kamen-Siegel, L., Rodin, J., Seligman, M. E. P., & Dwyer, J. (1991). Explanatory style and cell-mediated immunity in elderly men and women. *Health Psychology, 10,* 229–235.

Kampis, J. (2005, February 15). Lawsuit claims video violence precipitated Fayetteville shootings. *Tuscaloosa News* (Alabama).

Kanetsuna, T., Smith, P. K., & Morita, Y. (2006). Coping with bullying at school: Children's recommended strategies and attitudes to school-based interventions in England and Japan. *Aggressive Behavior, 32,* 570–580.

Kaplan, M. F., & Schersching, C. (1981). Juror deliberation: An information integration analysis. In B. Sales (Ed.), *The trial process* (pp. 235–262). New York: Plenum.

Karau, S. J., & Williams, K. D. (1993). Social loafing: A meta-analytic review and theoretical integration. *Journal of Personality and Social Psychology, 65,* 681–706.

Karau, S. J., & Williams, K. D. (2001). Understanding individual motivation in groups: The collective effort model. In M. E. Turner (Ed.), *Groups at work: Theory and research. Applied social research* (pp. 113–141). Mahwah, NJ: Erlbaum.

Kark, R., Shamir, B., & Chen, G. (2003). The two faces of transformational leadership: Empowerment and dependency. *Journal of Applied Psychology, 88,* 246–255.

Karney, B. R., & Bradbury, T. N. (1995). The longitudinal course of marital quality and stability: A review of theory, method, and research. *Psychological Bulletin, 118,* 3–34.

Karney, B. R., & Bradbury, T. N. (2000). Attributions in marriage: State or trait? A growth curve analysis. *Journal of Personality and Social Psychology, 78,* 295–309.

Karniol, R. (2003). Egocentrism versus protocentrism: The status of self in social prediction. *Psychological Review, 110,* 564–580.

Karpinski, A., & Hilton, J. L. (2001). Attitudes and the Implicit Association Test. *Journal of Personality and Social Psychology, 81,* 774–788.

Karpinski, A. T., & von Hippel, W. (1996). The role of the linguistic intergroup bias in expectancy maintenance. *Social Cognition, 14,* 141–163.

Karremans, J. C., Stroebe, W., & Claus, J. (2006). Beyond Vicary's fantasies: The impact of subliminal priming and brand choice. *Journal of Experimental Social Psychology, 42,* 792–798.

Kashima, Y., & Kerekes, A. R. Z. (1994). A distributed memory model of averaging phenomena in person impression formation. *Journal of Experimental Social Psychology, 30,* 407–455.

Kassin, S. M. (2002, November 1). False confessions and the jogger case. *New York Times,* p. A31.

Kassin, S. M. (2005). On the psychology of confessions: Does innocence put innocents at risk? *American Psychologist, 60,* 215–228.

Kassin, S. M. (2008). The psychology of confessions. *Annual Review of Law and Social Science, 4,* 193–217.

Kassin, S. M., Drizin, S. A., Grisso, T., Gudjonsson, G. H., Leo, R. A., & Redlich, A. D. (2010). Police-induced confessions: Risk factors and recommendations. *Law and Human Behavior.*

Kassin, S. M., Goldstein, C. J., & Savitsky, K. (2003). Behavioral confirmation in the interrogation room: On the dangers of presuming guilt. *Law and Human Behavior, 27,* 187–203.

Kassin, S. M., & Gudjonsson, G. H. (2004). The psychology of confession evidence: A review of the literature and issues. *Psychological Science in the Public Interest, 5,* 35–69.

Kassin, S. M., & Kiechel, K. L. (1996). The social psychology of false confessions: Compliance, internalization, and confabulation. *Psychological Science, 7,* 125–128.

Kassin, S. M., Leo, R. A., Meissner, C. A., Richman, K. D., Colwell, L. H., Leach, A.-M., & LaFon, D. (2007). Police interviewing and interrogation: A self-report survey of police practices and beliefs. *Law and Human Behavior, 31,* 381–400.

Kassin, S. M., Meissner, C. A., & Norwick, R. J. (2005). "I'd know a false confession if I saw one": A comparative study of college students and police investigators. *Law and Human Behavior, 29,* 211–227.

Kassin, S. M., & Sommers, S. R. (1997). Inadmissible testimony, instructions to disregard, and the jury: Substantive versus procedural considerations. *Personality and Social Psychology Bulletin, 23,* 1046–1054.

Kassin, S. M., Tubb, V. A., Hosch, H. M., & Memon, A. (2001). On the "general acceptance" of eyewitness testimony research: A new survey of the experts. *American Psychologist, 56,* 405–416.

Katz, R., Amichai-Hamburger, Y., Manisterski, E., & Kraus, S. (2008). Different orientations of males and females in computer-mediated negotiations. *Computers in Human Behavior, 24,* 516–534.

Kaufman, D. Q., Stasson, M. F., & Hart, J. W. (1999). Are the tabloids always wrong or is that just what we think? Need for cognition and perceptions of articles in print media. *Journal of Applied Social Psychology, 29,* 1984–1997.

Kawakami, K., Dion, K. L., & Dovidio, J. F. (1998). Racial prejudice and stereotype activation. *Personality and Social Psychology Bulletin, 24,* 407–416.

Kawakami, K., Dovidio, J. F., & van Kamp, S. (2007). The impact of naïve theories related to strategies to reduce biases and correction processes on the application of stereotypes. *Group Processes and Intergroup Relations, 10,* 139–156.

Kawakami, K., Dovidio, J. F., Moll, J., Hermsen, S., & Russin, A. (2000). Just say no (to stereotyping): Effects of training in the negation of stereotypic association on stereotype activation. *Journal of Personality and Social Psychology, 78,* 871–888.

Kay, A. C., & Jost, J. T. (2003). Complementary justice: Effects of "poor but happy" and "poor but honest" stereotype exemplars on system justification and implicit activation of the justice motive. *Journal of Personality and Social Psychology, 85,* 823–837.

Kay, A. C., Jost, J. T., & Young, S. (2005). Victim derogation and victim enhancement as alternate routes to system justification. *Personality and Social Psychology Bulletin, 16,* 240–246.

Keelan, J. P. R., Dion, K. L., & Dion, K. K. (1994). Attachment style and heterosexual relationships among young adults: A short-term panel study. *Journal of Social and Personal Relationships, 11,* 201–214.

Keil, M., Depledge, G., & Rai, A. (2007). Escalation: The role of problem recognition and cognitive bias. *Decision Sciences, 38,* 391–421.

Keillor, J. M., Barrett, A. M., Crucian, G. P., Kortenkamp, S., & Heilman, K. M. (2003). Emotional experience and perception in the absence of facial feedback. *Journal of the International Neurological Society, 8,* 130–135.

Keller, J., & Dauenheimer, D. (2003). Stereotype threat in the classroom: Dejection mediates the disrupting threat effect on women's math performance. *Personality and Social Psychology Bulletin, 29,* 371–381.

Keller, P. A. (1999). Converting the unconverted: The effect of inclination and opportunity to discount health-related fear appeals. *Journal of Applied Psychology, 84,* 403–415.

Kelley, H. H. (1950). The warm-cold variable in first impressions of persons. *Journal of Personality, 18,* 431–439.

Kelley, H. H. (1967). Attribution in social psychology. *Nebraska Symposium on Motivation, 15,* 192–238.

Kelley, M. W., Macrae, C. N., Wyland, C. L., Caglar, S., Inati, S., & Heatherton, T. F. (2002). Finding the self? An event-related fMRI study. *Journal of Cognitive Neuroscience, 14,* 785–794.

Kelly, A. E., & McKillop, K. J. (1996). Consequences of revealing personal secrets. *Psychological Bulletin, 120,* 450–465.

Kelly, A. E., & Rodriguez, R. R. (2006). Publicly committing oneself to an identity. *Basic and Applied Social Psychology, 28,* 185–191.

Kelly, J. A., St. Lawrence, J. S., Diaz, Y. E., Stevenson, L. Y., Hauth, A. C., Brasfield, T. L., Kalichman, S. C., Smith, J. E., & Andrew, M. E. (1991). HIV risk behavior reduction following intervention with key opinion leaders of a population: An experimental community-level analysis. *American Journal of Public Health, 81,* 168–171.

Kelly, M. M., Tyrka, A. R., Anderson, G. M., Price, L. H., Carpenter, L. L. (2008). Sex differences in emotional and physiological responses to the Trier Social Stress Test. *Journal of Behavior Therapy and Experimental Psychiatry, 39,* 87–98.

Kelman, H. C. (1961). Processes of opinion change. *Public Opinion Quarterly, 25,* 57–78.

Kelman, H. C. (1967). Human use of human subjects: The problem of deception in social psychology experiments. *Psychological Bulletin, 67,* 1–11.

Kelman, H. C., & Hamilton, V. L. (1989). *Crimes of obedience: Toward a social psychology of authority and responsibility.* New Haven, CT: Yale University Press.

Kelman, H. C., & Hovland, C. I. (1953). "Reinstatement" of the communicator in delayed measurement of opinion change. *Journal of Abnormal and Social Psychology, 48,* 327–335.

Kemmelmeier, M., Jambor, E. E., & Letner, J. (2006). Individualism and good works: Cultural variation in giving and volunteering across the United States. *Journal of Cross-Cultural Psychology, 37,* 327–344.

Kennedy, H. (2003, February 2). He takes fatal OD as internet pals watch: Chatroom vultures egged him to pop more Rx pills. *New York Daily News,* p. 5.

Kennedy, H. (2009, June 15). GOP activist DePass apologizes after joking on Facebook that gorilla is related to Michelle Obama. *NewYorkDailyNews.com.*

Kenny, D. A. (1994). *Interpersonal perception: A social relations analysis.* New York: Guilford.

Kenny, D. A., & Acitelli, L. K. (2001). Accuracy and bias of perceptions of the partner in close relationships. *Journal of Personality and Social Psychology, 80,* 439–448.

Kenny, D. A., & DePaulo, B. M. (1993). Do people know how others view them? An empirical and theoretical account. *Psychological Bulletin, 114,* 145–161.

Kenny, D. A., & Zaccaro, S. J. (1983). An estimate of variance due to traits in leadership. *Journal of Applied Psychology, 68,* 678–685.

Kenny, D. A., Albright, L., Malloy, T. E., & Kashy, D. A. (1994). Consensus in interpersonal perception: Acquaintance and the Big Five. *Psychological Bulletin, 116,* 245–258.

Kenrick, D. T., & Keefe, R. C. (1992). Age preferences in mates reflect sex differences in human reproductive strategies. *Behavioral and Brain Sciences, 15,* 75–133.

Kenrick, D. T., & MacFarlane, S. W. (1986). Ambient temperature and horn honking: A field study of the heat/aggression relationship. *Environment and Behavior, 18,* 179–191.

Kenrick, D. T., Gabrielidis, C., Keefe, R. C., & Cornelius, J. S. (1996). Adolescents' age preferences for dating partners: Support for an evolutionary model of life-history strategies. *Child Development, 67,* 1499–1511.

Kenrick, D. T., Neuberg, S. L., Griskevicius, V., Becker, D. V., & Schaller, M. (2009). Goal-driven cognition and functional behavior: The fundamental motives framework. *Current Directions in Psychological Science.*

Kernis, M. H., & Waschull, S. B. (1995). The interactive roles of stability and level of self-esteem: Research and theory. *Advances in Experimental Social Psychology, 27,* 93–141.

Kerr, N. L. (1981). Social transition schemes: Charting the group's road to agreement. *Journal of Personality and Social Psychology, 41,* 684–702.

Kerr, N. L. (1983). Motivation losses in small groups: A social dilemma analysis. *Journal of Personality and Social Psychology, 45,* 819–828.

Kerr, N. L., & Levine, J. M. (2008). The detection of social exclusion: Evolution and beyond. *Group Dynamics: Theory, Research, and Practice, 12,* 39–52.

Kerr, N. L., Hymes, R. W., Anderson, A. B., & Weathers, J. E. (1995). Defendant-juror similarity in mock juror judgments. *Law and Human Behavior, 19,* 545–567.

Kerr, N. L., Kramer, G. P., Carroll, J. S., & Alfini, J. J. (1991). On the effectiveness of voir dire in criminal cases with prejudicial pretrial publicity: An empirical study. *American University Law Review, 40,* 665–701.

Kerr, N. L., Niedermeier, K. E., & Kaplan, M. F. (1999). Bias in jurors vs. bias in juries: New evidence from the SDS perspective. *Organizational Behavior and Human Decision Processes, 80,* 70–86.

Kersten, G. E., & Lai, H. (2007). Negotiation support and E-negotiation systems: An overview. *Group Decision and Negotiation, 16,* 553–586.

Kessler, R. C., et al. (1994). Lifetime and 12-month prevalence of DSM-III-R psychiatric disorders in the United States. *Archives of General Psychiatry, 51,* 8–19.

Kessler, R. C., Sonnega, A., Bromet, E., Hughes, M., & Nelson, C. B. (1995). Posttraumatic stress disorder in the National Comorbidity Survey. *Archives of General Psychiatry, 52,* 1048–1060.

Kestilä, L., Rahkonen, O., Martelin, T., Lahti-Koski, M., & Koskinen, S. (2009). Do childhood social circumstances affect overweight and obesity in early adulthood? *Scandinavian Journal of Public Health, 37,* 206–219.

Key, W. B. (1973). *Subliminal seduction.* Englewood Cliffs, NJ: Signet.

Key, W. B. (1989). *The age of manipulation.* New York: Holt.

Keysar, B., & Henly, A. S. (2002). Speakers' overestimation of their effectiveness. *Psychological Science, 13,* 207–212.

Kiecolt-Glaser, J. K. (2009). Psychoneuroimmunology: Psychology's gateway to the biomedical future. *Perspectives on Psychological Science, 4,* 367–369.

Kiecolt-Glaser, J. K., & Newton, T. L. (2001). Marriage and health: His and hers. *Psychological Bulletin, 127,* 472–503.

Kiecolt-Glaser, J. K., McGuire, L., Robles, T., & Glaser, R. (2002). Psychoneuroimmunology: Psychological influences on immune function and health. *Journal of Consulting and Clinical Psychology, 70,* 537–547.

Kierein, N. M., & Gold, M. A. (2000). Pygmalion in work organizations: A meta-analysis. *Journal of Organizational Behavior, 21,* 913–928.

Kiesler, C. A. (1971). *The psychology of commitment.* New York: Academic Press.

Kiesler, C. A., & Kiesler, S. B. (1969). *Conformity.* Reading, MA: Addison-Wesley.

Kilham, W., & Mann, L. (1974). Level of destructive obedience as a function of transmitter and executant roles in the Milgram obedience paradigm. *Journal of Personality and Social Psychology, 29,* 696–702.

Kilianski, S. E., & Rudman, L. A. (1998). Wanting it both ways: Do women approve of benevolent sexism? *Sex Roles, 39,* 333–352.

Kim, H., & Markus, H. R. (1999). Deviance or uniqueness, harmony or conformity? A cultural analysis. *Journal of Personality and Social Psychology, 77,* 785–800.

Kim, H. S., Sherman, D. K., Taylor, S. (2008). Culture and social support. *American Psychologist, 63,* 518–526.

Kimmel, P. R. (1994). Cultural perspectives on international negotiations. *Journal of Social Issues, 50,* 179–196.

Kimmel, P. R. (2000). Culture and conflict. In M. Deutsch & P. T. Coleman (Eds.), *The handbook of conflict resolution: Theory and practice* (pp. 453–474). San Francisco, CA: Jossey-Bass.

Kingston, D. A., Malamuth, N. M., Fedoroff, P., & Marshall, W. L. (2009). The importance of individual differences in pornography use: Theoretical perspectives and implications for treating sexual offenders. *Journal of Sex Research, 46,* 216–232.

Kinsey, A. C., Pomeroy, W. B., & Martin, C. E. (1948). *Sexual behavior in the human male.* Philadelphia: Saunders.

Kinsey, A. C., Pomeroy, W. B., Martin, C. E., & Gebhard, P. H. (1953). *Sexual behavior in the human female.* Philadelphia: Saunders.

Kinzer, S. (1999, September 13). A sudden friendship blossoms between Greece and Turkey. *New York Times.*

Kirkman, B. L., Rosen, B., Gibson, C. B., Tesluk, P., & McPherson, S. O. (2002). Five challenges to virtual team success: Lessons from Sabre, Inc. *Academy of Management Executive, 16,* 67–79.

Kirkpatrick, L. A., & Hazan, C. (1994). Attachment styles and close relationships: A four-year prospective study. *Personal Relationships, 1,* 123–142.

Kirkpatrick, S. A., & Locke, E. A. (1991). Leadership: Do traits matter? *Academy of Management Executive, 5,* 48–60.

Kitayama, S., & Uchida, Y. (2003). Explicit self-criticism and implicit self-regard: Evaluating self and friend in two cultures. *Journal of Experimental Social Psychology, 39,* 476–482.

Kitayama, S., Duffy, S., Kawamura, T., & Larsen, J. T. (2003). Perceiving an object and its context in different cultures: A cultural look at New Look. *Psychological Science, 14,* 201–206.

Kitayama, S., Snibbe, A. C., Markus, H. R., & Suzuki, T. (2004). Is there any "free" choice? Self and dissonance in two cultures. *Psychological Science, 15,* 527–533.

Kite, M. E. (1992). Age and the spontaneous self-concept. *Journal of Applied Social Psychology, 22,* 1828–1837.

Kivimäki, M., Vahtera, J., Elovainio, M., Helenius, H., Singh-Manoux, A., & Pentti, J. (2005). Optimism and pessimism as predictors of change in health after death or onset of severe illness in family. *Health Psychology, 24,* 413–421.

Klapwijk, A., & Van Lange, P. A. M. (2009). Promoting cooperation and trust in 'noisy' situations: The power of generosity. *Journal of Personality and Social Psychology, 96,* 83–103.

Klassen, R. M., & Krawchuk, L. L. (2009). Collective motivation beliefs of early adolescents working in small groups. *Journal of School Psychology, 47,* 101–120.

Klauer, K. C., & Voss, A. (2008). Effects of race on responses and response latencies in the weapon identification task: A test of six models. *Personality and Social Psychology Bulletin, 34,* 1124–1140.

Klein, H., & Shiffman, K. (2009). Underrepresentation and symbolic annihilation of socially disenfranchised groups ('out groups') in animated cartoons. *Howard Journal of Communications, 20,* 55–72.

Klein, J. G. (1991). Negativity effects in impression formation: A test in the political arena. *Personality and Social Psychology Bulletin, 17,* 412–418.

Klein, O., Spears, R., & Reicher, S. (2007). Social identity performance: Extending the strategic side of SIDE. *Personality and Social Psychology Review, 11,* 1–18.

Klein, W. M. (1997). Objective standards are not enough: Affective, self-evaluative, and behavioral responses to social comparison information. *Journal of Personality and Social Psychology, 72,* 763–774.

Kleinke, C. L. (1986). Gaze and eye contact: A research review. *Psychological Bulletin, 100,* 78–100.

Kleinke, C. L., Paterson, T. R., & Rutledge, T. R. (1998). Effects of self-generated facial expressions of mood. *Journal of Personality and Social Psychology, 74,* 272–279.

Klinesmith, J., Kasser, T., & McAndrew, F. T. (2006). Guns, testosterone, and aggression: An experimental test of a mediational hypothesis. *Psychological Science, 17,* 568–571.

Kling, K. C., Hyde, J. S., Showers, C. J., & Buswell, B. N. (1999). Gender differences in self-esteem: A meta-analysis. *Psychological Bulletin, 125,* 470–500.

Kmec, J. A. (2005). Setting occupational sex segregation in motion: Sex traditional employment. *Work and Occupations, 32,* 322–354.

Knafo, A., & Plomin, R. (2006). Prosocial behavior from early to middle childhood: Genetic and environmental influences on stability and change. *Developmental Psychology, 42,* 771–786.

Knafo, A., Zahn-Waxler, C., Van Hulle, C., Rhee, S., & Robinson, J. L. (2008). The developmental origins of a disposition toward empathy: Genetic and environmental contributions. *Emotion, 8,* 737–752.

Knee, C. R., Canevello, A., Bush, A. L., Cook, A. (2008). Relationship-contingent self-esteem and the ups and downs of romantic relationships. *Journal of Personality and Social Psychology, 95,* 608–627.

Kniffin, K., & Wilson, D. S. (2004). The effect of nonphysical traits on the perception of physical attractiveness: Three naturalistic studies. *Evolution and Human Behavior, 25,* 88–101.

Knobloch, S., Callison, C., Chen, L., Fritzsche, A., & Zillmann, D. (2005). Children's sex-stereotyped self-socialization through selective exposure to entertainment: Cross-cultural experiments in Germany, China, and the United States. *Journal of Communication, 55,* 122–138.

Knoll, C., Blankstein, A., & Winton, R. (2009, June 16). Lakers melee tests new LAPD policies. *Los Angeles Times,* p. A3.

Knowles, E. S. (1983). Social physics and the effects of others: Tests of the effects of audience size and distance on social judgments and behavior. *Journal of Personality and Social Psychology, 45,* 1263–1279.

Knox, N. (2000, September 15). Wall Street battles sexual bias: Even as brokerage industry fights discrimination, women regularly make accusations. *USA Today,* p. 1B.

Knox, R. E., & Inskter, J. A. (1968). Postdecision dissonance at posttime. *Journal of Personality and Social Psychology, 8,* 319–323.

Knox, R. E., & Safford, R. K. (1976). Group caution at the race track. *Journal of Experimental Social Psychology, 12,* 317–324.

Ko, S. J., Judd, C. M., & Blair, I. V. (2006). What the voice reveals: Within- and between-category stereotyping on the basis of voice. *Personality and Social Psychology Bulletin, 32,* 806–819.

Kobasa, S. C., Maddi, S. R., & Kahn, S. (1982). Hardiness and health: A prospective study. *Journal of Personality and Social Psychology, 42,* 168–177.

Kogut, T., & Ritov, I. (2007). 'One of us': Outstanding willingness to help save a single identified compatriot. *Organizational Behavior and Human Decision Processes, 104,* 150–157.

Kohn, A. (1993). *Punished by rewards.* Boston: Houghton Mifflin.

Kohn, P. M., Lafreniere, K., & Gurevich, M. (1991). Hassles, health, and personality. *Journal of Personality and Social Psychology, 61,* 478–482.

Kohut, A., & Wike, R. (2008, October 30). Xenophobia on the Continent. Retrieved June 16, 2009, from http://nationalinterest.org/Article.aspx?id=20124.

Kokko, K., Pulkkinen, L., Huesmann, L. R., Dubow, E. F., & Boxer, P. (2009). Intensity of aggression in childhood as a predictor of different forms of adult aggression: A two-country (Finland and the United States) analysis. *Journal of Research on Adolescence, 19,* 9–34.

Kolditz, T. A., & Arkin, R. M. (1982). An impression management interpretation of the self-handicapping strategy. *Journal of Personality and Social Psychology, 43,* 492–502.

Konijn, E. A., Nije Bijvank, M., & Bushman, B. J. (2007). I wish I were a warrior: The role of wishful identification in the effects of violent video games on aggression in adolescent boys. *Developmental Psychology, 43,* 1038–1044.

Kopelman, S. (2009). The effect of culture and power on cooperation in commons dilemmas: Implications for global resource management. *Organizational Behavior and Human Decision Processes, 108,* 153–163.

Kopelman, S., & Rosette, A. S. (2008). Cultural variation in response to strategic emotions in negotiations. *Group Decision and Negotiation, 17,* 65–77.

Korchmaros, J. D., Kenny, D. A., & Flory, K. (2006). An evolutionary and close-relationship model of helping. *Journal of Social and Personal Relationships, 23,* 21–43.

Korte, C. (1980). Urban-nonurban differences in social behavior and social psychological models of urban impact. *Journal of Social Issues, 36*(3), 29–51.

Korte, C., Ypma, I., & Toppen, A. (1975). Helpfulness in Dutch society as a function of urbanization and environmental input level. *Journal of Personality and Social Psychology, 32,* 996–1003.

Koslowski, S. W., Kirsch, M. P., & Chao, G. T. (1986). Job knowledge, ratee familiarity, conceptual similarity, and halo error: An exploration. *Journal of Applied Psychology, 71,* 45–49.

Koslowsky, M., Kluger, A., & Reich, M. (1995). *Commuting stress: Causes, effects, and methods of coping.* New York: Plenum Press.

Kosonen, P., & Winne, P. (1995). Effects of teaching statistical laws of reasoning about everyday problems. *Journal of Educational Psychology, 87,* 33–46.

Kovacs, L. (1983). A conceptualization of marital development. *Family Therapy, 3,* 183–210.

Kovera, M. B. (2002). The effects of general pretrial publicity on juror decisions: An examination of moderators and mediating mechanisms. *Law and Human Behavior, 26,* 43–72.

Kovera, M. B., Penrod, S. D., Pappas, C., & Thill, D. L. (1997). Identification of computer-generated facial composites. *Journal of Applied Psychology, 82,* 235–246.

Kowalski, R. M. (1993). Inferring sexual interest from behavioral cues: Effects of gender and sexually relevant attitudes. *Sex Roles, 29,* 13–36.

Kowalski, R. M. (1996). Complaints and complaining: Functions, antecedents, and consequences. *Psychological Bulletin, 119,* 179–196.

Kozak, M. N., Marsh, A. A., & Wegner, D. M. (2006). What do I think you're doing? Action identification and mind attribution. *Journal of Personality and Social Psychology, 90,* 543–555.

Kozel, F., Johnson, K., Mu, Q., Grenesko, E., Laken, S., & George, M. (2005). Detecting deception using functional magnetic resonance imaging. *Biological Psychiatry, 58,* 605–613.

Kramer, G. P., Kerr, N. L., & Carroll, J. S. (1990). Pretrial publicity, judicial remedies, and jury bias. *Law and Human Behavior, 14,* 409–438.

Kramer, R. M. (1998). Revisiting the Bay of Pigs and Vietnam decisions 25 years later: How well has the groupthink hypothesis stood the test of time? *Organizational Behavior and Human Decision Processes, 73,* 236–271.

Krams, I., Krama, T., Igaune, K., & Mänd, R. (2008). Experimental evidence of reciprocal altruism in the pied flycatcher. *Behavioral Ecology and Sociobiology, 62,* 599–605.

Krantz, D. S., & McCeney, M. K. (2002). Effects of psychological and social factors on organic disease: A critical assessment of research on coronary heart disease. *Annual Review of Psychology, 53,* 341–369.

Kraus, S. J. (1995). Attitudes and the prediction of behavior: A meta-analysis of the empirical literature. *Personality and Social Psychology Bulletin, 21,* 58–75.

Kravitz, D. A., & Martin, B. (1986). Ringelmann rediscovered: The original article. *Journal of Personality and Social Psychology, 50,* 936–941.

Kravitz, D. A., & Platania, J. (1993). Attitudes and beliefs about affirmative action: Effects of target and of respondent sex and ethnicity. *Journal of Applied Psychology, 78,* 928–938.

Kray, L. J., Galinsky, A. D., & Thompson, L. (2002). Reversing the gender gap in negotiations: An exploration of stereotype regeneration. *Organizational Behavior and Human Decision Processes, 87,* 386–409.

Krebs, D. (1987). The challenge of altruism in biology and psychology. In C. Crawford, M. Smith, & D. Krebs (Eds.), *Sociobiology and psychology: Ideas, issues, and applications* (pp. 81–118). Hillsdale, NJ: Erlbaum.

Krebs, D., & Rosenwald, A. (1994). Moral reasoning and moral behavior in conventional adults. In B. Puka (Ed.), *Fundamental research in moral development* (pp. 111–121). New York: Garland.

Kressel, N. J., & Kressel, D. F. (2002). *Stack and sway: The new science of jury consulting.* Boulder, CO: Westview Press.

Kringelbach, M. L., et al. (2008). A specific and rapid neural signature for parental instinct. *PLoS ONE, 3*(2): 1–7.

Krizan, Z., & Windschitl, P. D. (2007). The influence of outcome desirability on optimism. *Psychological Bulletin, 133,* 95–121.

Kroon, M. B. R., t'Hart, P., & van Kreveld, D. (1991). Managing group decision making processes: Individual versus collective accountability and groupthink. *International Journal of Conflict Management, 2,* 91–115.

Krueger, J. (1998). On the perception of social consensus. *Advances in Experimental Social Psychology, 30,* 163–240.

Krueger, J. (2000). The projective perception of the social world: A building block of social comparison processes. In J. Suls & L. Wheeler (Eds.), *Handbook of social comparison: Theory and research* (pp. 323–351). New York: Plenum/Kluwer.

Krueger, J., Rothbart, M., & Sriram, N. (1989). Category learning and change: Differences in sensitivity to information that enhances or reduces intercategory distinctions. *Journal of Personality and Social Psychology, 56,* 866–875.

Krug, E. G., Kresnow, M., Peddicord, J. P., Dahlberg, L. L., Powell, K. E., Crosby, A. E., & Annest, J. L. (1998). Suicide after natural disasters. *New England Journal of Medicine, 338,* 373–378.

Kruger, J., & Dunning, D. (1999). Unskilled and unaware of it: How difficulties in recognizing one's own incompetence lead to inflated self-assessments. *Journal of Personality and Social Psychology, 77,* 1121–1134.

Kruger, J., Wirtz, D., & Miller, D. T. (2005). Counterfactual thinking and the first instinct fallacy. *Journal of Personality and Social Psychology, 88,* 725–735.

Kruglanski, A. W. (2001). That "vision thing": The state of theory in social and personality psychology at the edge of the new millennium. *Journal of Personality and Social Psychology, 80,* 871–875.

Kruglanski, A. W., & Freund, T. (1983). The freezing and unfreezing of lay-inferences: Effects of impressional primacy, ethnic stereotyping, and numerical anchoring. *Journal of Experimental Social Psychology, 19,* 448–468.

Kruglanski, A. W., & Mayseless, O. (1988). Contextual effects in hypothesis testing: The role of competing alternatives and epistemic motivations. *Social Cognition, 6,* 1–20.

Kruglanski, A. W., & Webster, D. M. (1996). Motivated closing of the mind: "Seizing" and "freezing." *Psychological Review, 103,* 263–283.

Kubany, E. S., Leisen, M. B., Kaplan, A. S., Watson, S. B., Haynes, S. N., Owens, J. A., & Burns, K. (2000). Development and preliminary validation of a brief broad-spectrum measure of trauma exposure: The Traumatic Life Events Questionnaire. *Psychological Assessment, 12,* 210–224.

Kubzansky, L. D., Sparrow, D., Vokonas, P., & Kawachi, I. (2001). Is the glass half empty or half full? A prospective study of optimism and coronary heart disease in the Normative Aging Study. *Psychosomatic Medicine, 63,* 910–916.

Kugihara, N. (1999). Gender and social loafing in Japan. *Journal of Social Psychology, 139,* 516–526.

Kulik, J. A., & Mahler, H. I. M. (1989). Stress and affiliation in a hospital setting: Preoperative roommate preferences. *Personality and Social Psychology Bulletin, 15,* 183–193.

Kulik, J. A., Mahler, H. I. M., & Earnest, A. (1994). Social comparison and affiliation under threat: Going beyond the affiliate-choice paradigm. *Journal of Personality and Social Psychology, 66,* 301–309.

Kulik, J. A., Mahler, H. I. M., & Moore, P. J. (1996). Social comparison and affiliation under threat: Effects of recovery from major surgery. *Journal of Personality and Social Psychology, 71,* 967–979.

Kumkale, G. T., & Albarracín, D. (2004). The sleeper effect in persuasion: A meta-analytic review. *Psychological Bulletin, 130,* 143–172.

Kunda, Z., & Spencer, S. J. (2003). When do stereotypes come to mind and when do they color judgment? A goal-based theoretical framework for stereotype activation and application. *Psychological Bulletin, 129,* 522–544.

Kunda, Z., Adams, B., Davies, P. G., Hoshino-Browne, E., & Jordan, C. (2003). The impact of comprehension goals on the ebb and flow of stereotype activation during interaction. In Spencer, S. J., Fein, S., Zanna, M. P., & Olson, J. M. (Eds.), *Motivated social perception: The Ontario symposium* (Vol. 9, pp. 1–20). Mahwah, NJ: Erlbaum.

Kunda, Z., Sinclair, L., & Griffin, D. (1997). Equal ratings but separate meanings: Stereotypes and the construal of traits. *Journal of Personality and Social Psychology, 72,* 720–734.

Kuntz-Wilson, W., & Zajonc, R. B. (1980). Affective discrimination of stimuli that cannot be recognized. *Science, 207,* 557–558.

Kupers, T. A. (1999). *Prison madness: The mental health crisis behind bars and what we must do about it.* New York: Jossey-Bass.

Kurbat, M. A., Shevell, S. K., & Rips, L. J. (1998). A year's memories: The calendar effect in autobiographical recall. *Memory and Cognition, 26,* 532–552.

Kurdek, L. (2008). Change in relationship quality for partners from lesbian, gay male, and heterosexual couples. *Journal of Family Psychology, 22,* 701–711.

Kurdek, L. A. (1991a). Correlates of relationship satisfaction in cohabiting gay and lesbian couples: Interpretation of contextual, investment, and problem-solving models. *Journal of Personality and Social Psychology, 61,* 910–922.

Kurdek, L. A. (1991b). The dissolution of gay and lesbian couples. *Journal of Social and Personal Relationships, 8,* 265–278.

Kurdek, L. A. (1999). The nature and predictors of the trajectory of change in marital quality for husbands and wives over the first 10 years of marriage. *Developmental Psychology, 35,* 1283–1296.

Kurdek, L. A. (2005). What do we know about gay and lesbian couples? *Current Directions in Psychological Science, 14,* 251–254.

Kuwabara, K. (2005). Nothing to fear but fear itself: Fear of fear, fear of greed and gender effects in two-person asymmetric social dilemmas. *Social Forces, 84,* 1257–1272.

Kwan, V. S. Y., & Fiske, S. T. (2008). Missing links in social cognition: The continuum from nonhuman agents to dehumanized humans. *Social Cognition, 26,* 125–128.

Ladd, G., Herald-Brown, S., & Reiser, M. (2008). Does chronic classroom peer rejection predict the development of children's classroom participation during the grade school years? *Child Development, 79,* 1001–1015.

Laird, J. D. (1974). Self-attribution of emotion: The effects of expressive behavior on the quality of emotional experience. *Journal of Personality and Social Psychology, 29,* 475–486.

Lakey, B., & Cassady, P. B. (1990). Cognitive processes in perceived social support. *Journal of Personality and Social Psychology, 59,* 337–343.

Lakin, J. L., Chartrand, T. L., & Arkin, R. M. (2008). I am too just like you: Nonconscious mimicry as an automatic behavioral response to social exclusion. *Psychological Science, 19,* 816–822.

Lalwani, A. K., Shavitt, S., & Johnson, T. (2006). What is the relation between cultural orientation and socially desirable responding? *Journal of Personality and Social Psychology, 90,* 165–178.

Lamb, M. E., Hershkowitz, I., Orbach, Y., & Esplin, P. W. (2008). *Tell me what happened: Structured investigative interviews of child victims and witnesses.* West Sussex, England: Wiley.

Lambert, A. J., Payne, B. K., Jacoby, L. L., Shaffer, L. M., Chasteen, A. L., & Khan, S. R. (2003). Stereotypes as dominant responses: On the "social facilitation" of prejudice in anticipated public contexts. *Journal of Personality and Social Psychology, 84*(2), 277–295.

Lamm, H., & Myers, D. G. (1978). Group-induced polarization of attitudes and behavior. In L. Berkowitz (Ed.), *Advances in experimental social psychology* (Vol. 11, pp. 145–195). New York: Academic Press.

Landau, M. J., Solomon, S., Greenberg, J., Cohen, F., Pyszczynski, T., Arndt, J., Miller, C. H., Ogilvie, D. M., & Cook, A. (2004). Deliver us from evil: The effects of mortality salience and reminders of 9/11 on support for President George W. Bush. *Personality and Social Psychology Bulletin, 30,* 1136–1150.

Landau, T. (1989). *About faces: The evolution of the human face.* New York: Anchor Books.

Landy, F. J., & Farr, J. L. (1983). *The measurement of work performance: Methods, theory, and applications.* New York: Academic Press.

Lane, C. (2007). *Shyness: How normal behavior became a sickness.* New Haven, CT: Yale University Press.

Lane, K. A., Kang, J., & Banaji, M. R. (2007). Implicit social cognition and law. *Annual Review of Law and Social Science, 3,* 427–451.

Lane, L. W., Groisman, M., & Ferreira, V. S. (2006). Don't talk about pink elephants! Speakers' control over leaking private information during language production. *Psychological Science, 17,* 273–277.

Langer, E. J. (1975). The illusion of control. *Journal of Personality and Social Psychology, 32,* 311–328.

Langer, E. J. (1989). *Mindfulness.* Reading, MA: Addison-Wesley.

Langer, E. J., & Rodin, J. (1976). The effects of choice and enhanced personal responsibility for the aged: A field experiment in an institutional setting. *Journal of Personality and Social Psychology, 34,* 191–198.

Langer, E. J., Blank, A., & Chanowitz, B. (1978). The mindlessness of ostensibly thoughtful action. *Journal of Personality and Social Psychology, 36,* 635–642.

Langlois, J. H., & Roggman, L. A. (1990). Attractive faces are only average. *Psychological Science, 1,* 115–121.

Langlois, J. H., Kalakanis, L., Rubenstein, A. J., Larson, A., Hallam, M., & Smoot, M. (2000). Maxims or myths of beauty? A meta-analytic and theoretical review. *Psychological Bulletin, 126,* 390–423.

Langlois, J. H., Ritter, J. M., Roggman, L. A., & Vaughn, L. S. (1991). Facial diversity and infant preferences for attractive faces. *Developmental Psychology, 27,* 79–84.

Langlois, J. H., Roggman, L. A., & Musselman, L. (1994). What is average and what is not average about attractive faces? *Psychological Science, 5,* 214–220.

Langton, S. R. H., Watt, R. J., & Bruce, V. (2000). Do the eyes have it? Cues to the direction of social attention. *Trends in Cognitive Sciences, 4,* 50–59.

LaPiere, R. T. (1934). Attitudes vs. action. *Social Forces, 13,* 230–237.

Larrick, R. P., Morgan, J. N., & Nisbett, R. E. (1990). Teaching the use of cost-benefit reasoning in everyday life. *Psychological Science, 1,* 362–370.

Larsen, J. T., Noms, C. J., & Cacioppo, J. T. (2003). Effects of positive and negative affect on electromyographic activity over zygomaticus major and corrugator supercilii. *Psychophysiology, 40,* 776–785.

Larsen, K. S. (1990). The Asch conformity experiment: Replication and transhistorical comparisons. *Journal of Social Behavior and Personality, 5,* 163–168.

Larsen, R. J., & Kasimatis, M. (1990). Individual differences in entrainment of mood to the weekly calendar. *Journal of Personality and Social Psychology, 58,* 164–171.

Larson, J. R., Jr., Foster-Fishman, P. G., & Franz, T. M. (1998). Leadership style and the discussion of shared and unshared information in decision-making groups. *Personality and Social Psychology Bulletin, 24,* 482–495.

Lassiter, G. D., Diamond, S. S., Schmidt, H. C., & Elek, J. K. (2007). Evaluating videotaped confessions: Expertise provides no defense against the camera-perspective effect. *Psychological Science, 18,* 224–226.

Lassiter, G. D., Geers, A. L., Munhall, P. J., Handley, I. M., & Beers, M. J. (2001). Videotaped confessions: Is guilt in the eye of the camera? *Advances in Experimental Social Psychology, 33,* 189–254.

Lassiter, G. D., Stone, J. I., & Rogers, S. L. (1988). Memorial consequences of variation in behavior perception. *Journal of Experimental Social Psychology, 24,* 222–239.

Latané, B. (1981). The psychology of social impact. *American Psychologist, 36,* 343–356.

Latané, B., & Darley, J. M. (1968). Group inhibition of bystander intervention. *Journal of Personality and Social Psychology, 10,* 215–221.

Latané, B., & Darley, J. M. (1970). *The unresponsive bystander: Why doesn't he help?* New York: Appleton-Century-Crofts.

Latané, B., & L'Herrou, T. (1996). Spatial clustering in the conformity game: Dynamic social impact in electronic groups. *Journal of Personality and Social Psychology, 70,* 1218–1230.

Latané, B., & Nida, S. (1981). Ten years of research on group size and helping. *Psychological Bulletin, 89,* 308–324.

Latané, B., & Werner, C. (1978). Regulation of social contact in laboratory rats: Time, not distance. *Journal of Personality and Social Psychology, 36,* 1128–1137.

Latané, B., & Wolf, S. (1981). The social impact of majorities and minorities. *Psychological Review, 88,* 438–453.

Latané, B., Liu, J. H., Nowak, A., Bonevento, M., & Zheng, L. (1995). Distance matters: Physical space and social impact. *Personality and Social Psychology Bulletin, 21,* 795–805.

Latané, B., Williams, K., & Harkins, S. (1979). Many hands make light the work: The causes and consequences of social loafing. *Journal of Personality and Social Psychology, 37,* 822–832.

Latham, G. P., & Locke, E. A. (2007). New developments in and directions for goal-setting research. *European Psychologist, 12,* 290–300.

Lau, R. R. (1985). Two explanations for negativity effects in political behavior. *American Journal of Political Science, 29,* 119–138.

Laughlin, P. R., Carey, H. R., & Kerr, N. L. (2008). Group-to-individual problem-solving transfer. *Group Processes and Intergroup Relations, 11,* 319–330.

Laughlin, P. R., Hatch, E. C., Silver, J. S., & Boh, L. (2006). Groups perform better than the best individuals on letters-to-numbers problems: Effects of group size. *Journal of Personality and Social Psychology, 90,* 644–651.

Lawrence, E., Rothman, A., Cobb, R., Bradbury, T., & Rothman, M. (2008). Marital satisfaction across the transition to parenthood. *Journal of Family Psychology, 22,* 41–50.

Lazarus, R. S., & Folkman, S. (1984). *Stress, appraisal, and coping.* New York: Springer.

Le, B., & Agnew, C. R. (2003). Commitment and its theorized determinants: A meta-analysis of the investment model. *Personal Relationships, 10,* 37–57.

Leary, M. R. (Ed.). (2001). *Interpersonal rejection.* New York: Oxford University Press.

Leary, M. R., & Baumeister, R. F. (2000). The nature and function of self-esteem: Sociometer theory. *Advances in Experimental Social Psychology, 32,* 1–62.

Leary, M. R., & Kowalski, R. M. (1995). *Social anxiety.* New York: Guilford Press.

Leary, M. R., & Tangney, J. P. (Eds.). (2003). *Handbook of self and identity.* New York: Guilford.

Leary, M. R., Kowalski, R. M., Smith, L., & Phillips, S. (2003). Teasing, rejection, and violence: Case studies of the school shootings. *Aggressive Behavior, 29,* 202–214.

Leary, M. R., Tchividjian, L. R., & Kraxberger, B. E. (1994). Self-presentation can be hazardous to your health: Impression management and health risk. *Health Psychology, 13,* 461–470.

Leary, M. R., Twenge, J. M., & Quinlivan, E. (2006). Interpersonal rejection as a determinant of anger and aggression. *Personality and Social Psychology Review, 10,* 111–132.

Le Bon, G. (1895). *Psychologie des foules.* Paris: Félix Alcan.

LeDoux, J. (2002). *The synaptic self: How our brains become who we are.* New York: Penguin Books.

LeDoux, J. E. (1996). *The emotional brain: The mysterious underpinnings of emotional life.* New York: Simon & Schuster.

Lee, E.-J. (2008). When are strong arguments stronger than weak arguments? Deindividuation effects on message elaboration in computer-mediated communication. *Communication Research, 35,* 646–665.

Lee, J. A. (1988). Love-styles. In R. J. Sternberg & M. L. Barnes (Eds.), *The psychology of love* (pp. 38–67). New Haven, CT: Yale University Press.

Lee, L., Loewenstein, G., Ariely, D., Hong, J., & Young, J. (2008). If I'm not hot, are you hot or not? Physical-attractiveness evaluations and dating preferences as a function of one's own attractiveness. *Psychological Science, 19,* 669–677.

Lee, R. T., & Ashforth, B. E. (1996). A meta-analytic examination of the correlates of the three dimensions of job burnout. *Journal of Applied Psychology, 81,* 123–133.

Lehman, D. R., Chiu, C.-Y., & Schaller, M. (2004). Psychology and culture. *Annual Review of Psychology, 55,* 689–714.

Lehman, D. R., Lempert, R. O., & Nisbett, R. E. (1988). The effects of graduate training on reasoning: Formal discipline and thinking about everyday-life events. *American Psychologist, 43,* 431–442.

Leicht, K. T. (2008). Broken down by race and gender? Sociological explanations of new sources of earnings inequality. *Annual Review of Sociology, 34,* 237–255.

Leichtman, M. D., & Ceci, S. J. (1995). The effects of stereotypes and suggestions on preschoolers' reports. *Developmental Psychology, 31,* 568–578.

Leigh, B. C., & Stacy, A. W. (1993). Alcohol outcome expectancies: Scale construction and predictive utility in higher-order confirmatory models. *Psychological Assessment, 5,* 216–229.

Leiker, M., & Hailey, B. J. (1988). A link between hostility and disease: Poor health habits? *Behavioral Medicine, 14,* 129–133.

Leinbach, M. D., & Fagot, B. I. (1993). Categorical habituation to male and female faces: Gender schematic processing in infancy. *Infant Behavior and Development, 16,* 317–332.

Leippe, M. R., & Eisenstadt, D. (1994). Generalization of dissonance reduction: Decreasing prejudice through induced compliance. *Journal of Personality and Social Psychology, 67,* 395–413.

Leland, J. (1995, December 11). "Copycat" crimes in New York's subways reignite the debate: Do TV and movies cause actual mayhem? *Newsweek,* p. 46.

Lench, H. C. (2009). Automatic optimism: The affective basis of judgments about the likelihood of future events. *Journal of Experimental Psychology: General, 138,* 187–200.

Lenhart, A., Kahne, J., Middaugh, E., Macgill, A. R., Evans, C., & Vitak, J. (2008, September 16). *Teens, video games, and civics.* Washington, DC: Pew Internet and American Life Project.

Leo, R. A. (1996). Inside the interrogation room. *Journal of Criminal Law and Criminology, 86,* 266–303.

Leo, R.A. (2008). *Police interrogation and American justice.* Cambridge, MA: Harvard University Press.

Leonard, K. E. (1989). The impact of explicit aggressive and implicit nonaggressive cues on aggression in intoxicated and sober roles. *Personality and Social Psychology Bulletin, 15,* 390–400.

Leonard, K. E., Collins, R. L., & Quigley, B. M. (2003). Alcohol consumption and the occurrence and severity of aggression: An event-based analysis of male-to-male barroom violence. *Aggressive Behavior, 29,* 346–365.

Lepore, L., & Brown, R. (1997). Category and stereotype activation: Is prejudice inevitable? *Journal of Personality and Social Psychology, 72,* 275–287.

Lepore, L., & Brown, R. (2002). The role of awareness: Divergent automatic stereotype activation and implicit judgment correction. *Social Cognition, 20,* 321–351.

Lepore, S. J., & Smyth, J. M. (2002). *The writing cure: How expressive writing promotes health and emotional well-being.* Washington, DC: American Psychological Association.

Lepore, S. J., Ragan, J. D., & Jones, S. (2000). Talking facilitates cognitive-emotional processes of adaptation to an acute stressor. *Journal of Personality and Social Psychology, 78,* 499–508.

Lepper, M. R., & Greene, D. (Eds.). (1978). *The hidden costs of reward.* Hillsdale, NJ: Erlbaum.

Lepper, M. R., Greene, D., & Nisbett, R. E. (1973). Undermining children's intrinsic interest with extrinsic reward: A test of the "overjustification" hypothesis. *Journal of Personality and Social Psychology, 28,* 129–137.

Lepsinger, R., & Lucia, A. D. (2009). *The art and science of 360–degree feedback* (2nd ed.). New York: Wiley.

Lerner, M. J. (1980). *The belief in a just world: A fundamental delusion.* New York: Plenum.

Lerner, M. J. (1998). The two forms of belief in a just world: Some thoughts on why and how people care about justice. In L. Montada, & M. J. Lerner (Eds.), *Responses to victimization and belief in a just world: Critical issues in social justice* (pp. 247–269). New York: Plenum.

Lerner, M. J., & Simmons, C. H. (1966). Observers' reaction to the "innocent victim": Compassion or rejection? *Journal of Personality and Social Psychology, 4,* 203–210.

Letourneau, E. J., Henggeler, S. W., Borduin, C. M., Schewe, P. A., McCart, M. R., Chapman, J. E., & Saldana, L. (2009). Multisystemic therapy for juvenile sexual offenders: 1-year results from a randomized effectiveness trial. *Journal of Family Psychology, 23,* 89–102.

Levashina, J., & Campion, M. A. (2007). Measuring faking in the employment interview: Development and validation of an interview faking behavior scale. *Journal of Applied Psychology, 92,* 1638–1656.

LeVay, S. (1991). A difference in hypothalamic structure between heterosexual and homosexual men. *Science, 253,* 1034–1037.

Leventhal, H. (1970). Findings and theory in the study of fear communications. In L. Berkowitz (Ed.), *Advances in experimental social psychology* (Vol. 5, pp. 119–186). New York: Academic Press.

Leventhal, H., Watts, J. C., & Pagano, F. (1967). Effects of fear and instructions on how to cope with danger. *Journal of Personality and Social Psychology, 6,* 313–321.

Leventhal, H., Weinman, J., Leventhal, E. A., & Phillips, L. A. (2008). Health psychology: The search for pathways between behavior and health. *Annual Review of Psychology, 59,* 477–505.

Levesque, M. J. (1997). Meta-accuracy among acquainted individuals: A social relations analysis of interpersonal perception and metaperception. *Journal of Personality and Social Psychology, 72,* 66–74.

Levesque, M. J., Nave, C. S., & Lowe, C. A. (2006). Toward an understanding of gender differences in inferring sexual interest. *Psychology of Women Quarterly, 30,* 150–158.

Levett, L. M., & Kovera, M. B. (2008). The effectiveness of opposing expert witnesses for educating jurors about unreliable expert evidence. *Law and Human Behavior, 32,* 363–374.

Levi, A. S., & Fried, Y. (2008). Differences between African Americans and Whites in reactions to affirmative action programs in hiring, promotion, training, and layoffs. *Journal of Applied Psychology, 93,* 1118–1129.

Levin, S., Henry, P. J., Pratto, F., & Sidanius, J. (2009). Social dominance and social identity in Lebanon: Implications for support of violence against the West. In J. Victoroff & A. W. Kruglanski (Eds.), *Psychology of terrorism: Classic and contemporary insights* (pp. 253–267). New York: Psychology Press.

Levin, S., Taylor, P. L., & Caudle, E. (2007). Interethnic and interracial dating in college: A longitudinal study of social psychological predictors and outcomes. *Journal of Social and Personal Relationships, 24,* 323–341.

Levine, J. M. (1989). Reaction to opinion deviance in small groups. In P. B. Paulus (Ed.), *Psychology of group influence* (2nd ed., pp. 187–231). Hillsdale, NJ: Erlbaum.

Levine, J. M., & Choi, H.-S. (2010). Newcomers as change agents: Minority influence in task groups. In R. Martin & M. Hewstone (Eds.), *Minority influence and innovation: Antecedents, processes, and consequences.* New York: Psychology Press.

Levine, J. M., & Moreland, R. L. (1998). Small groups. In D. T. Gilbert, S. T. Fiske, & G. Lindzey (Eds.), *The handbook of social psychology* (4th ed., Vol. 2, pp. 415–469). New York: McGraw-Hill.

Levine, M., & Crowther, S. (2008). The responsive bystander: How social group membership and group size can encourage as well as inhibit bystander intervention. *Journal of Personality and Social Psychology, 95,* 1429–1439.

Levine, M., Prosser, A., Evans, D., & Reicher, S. (2005, April). Identity and emergency intervention: How social group membership and inclusiveness of group boundaries shape helping behavior. *Personality and Social Psychology Bulletin, 31,* 443–453.

Levine, R., Sato, S., Hashimoto, T., & Verma, J. (1995). Love and marriage in eleven cultures. *Journal of Cross-Cultural Psychology, 26,* 554–571.

Levine, R. A., & Campbell, D. T. (1972). *Ethnocentrism: Theories of conflict, ethnic attitudes, and group behavior.* New York: Wiley.

Levine, R. V., Norenzayan, A., & Philbrick, K. (2001). Cross-cultural differences in helping strangers. *Journal of Cross-Cultural Psychology, 32,* 543–560.

Levine, R. V., Reysen, S., & Ganz, E. (2008). The kindness of strangers revisited: A comparison of 24 US cities. *Social Indicators Research, 85,* 461–481.

Levy, D. A., & Nail, P. R. (1993). Contagion: A theoretical and empirical review and reconceptualization. *Genetic, Social, and General Psychology Monographs, 119,* 233–284.

Levy, S. R., Chiu, C.-Y., & Hong, Y.-Y. (2006). Lay theories and intergroup relations. *Group Processes and Intergroup Relations, 9,* 5–24.

Levy, S. R., & Hughes, J. M. (2009). Development of racial and ethnic prejudice among children. In T. D. Nelson (Ed.), *Handbook of prejudice, stereotyping, and discrimination* (pp. 23–42). New York: Psychology Press.

Lewin, K. (1935). *A dynamic theory of personality.* New York: McGraw-Hill.

Lewin, K. (1947). Group decision and social change. In T. M. Newcomb & E. L. Hartley (Eds.), *Readings in social psychology* (pp. 330–344). New York: Holt.

Lewin, K. (1951). Problems of research in social psychology. In D. Cartwright (Ed.), *Field theory in social science* (pp. 155–169). New York: Harper & Row.

Lewis, B. P., & Linder, D. E. (1997). Thinking about choking? Attentional processes and paradoxical performance. *Personality and Social Psychology Bulletin, 23,* 937–944.

Lewis, M. A., & Neighbors, C. (2004). Gender-specific misperceptions of college student drinking norms. *Psychology of Addictive Behaviors, 18,* 334–339.

Lewis, M., & Brooks-Gunn, J. (1979). *Social cognition and the acquisition of self.* New York: Plenum.

Leye, E., Powell, R. A., Nienhuis, G., Claeys, P., & Temmerman, M. (2006). Health care in Europe for women with genital mutilation. *Health Care for Women International, 27,* 362–378.

Li, N. P., & Kenrick, D. T. (2006). Sex similarities and differences in preferences for short-term mates: What, whether, and why. *Journal of Personality and Social Psychology, 90,* 468–489.

Li, N. P., Bailey, J. M., Kenrick, D. T., & Linsenmeier, J. A. W. (2002). The necessities and luxuries of mate preferences: Testing the tradeoffs. *Journal of Personality and Social Psychology, 82,* 947–955.

Liden, R. C., Wayne, S. J., Jaworski, R. A., & Bennett, N. (2004). Social loafing: A field investigation. *Journal of Management, 30,* 285–304.

Lieberman, J. D., & Arndt, J. (2000). Understanding the limits of limiting instructions. *Psychology, Public Policy, and Law, 6,* 677–711.

Lieberman, M. D. (2010). Social cognitive neuroscience. In S. T. Fiske, D. T. Gilbert, & G. Lindzey (Eds.), *Handbook of social psychology* (5th ed.). NY: McGraw-Hill.

Lieberman, M. D., Gaunt, R., Gilbert, D. T., & Trope, Y. (2004). Reflection and reflexion: A social cognitive neuroscience approach to attributional inference. In M. P. Zanna (Ed.), *Advances in experimental social psychology* (Vol. 34, pp. 199–249). San Diego, CA: Academic Press.

Lieberman, J., & Sales, B. (2007). *Scientific jury selection.* Washington, DC: American Psychological Association.

Lierbman, M. D., & Eisenberger, N. I. (2009). Pains and pleasures of social life. *Science, 323,* 890–891.

Lifton, R. J. (1986). *The Nazi doctors: Medical killing and the psychology of genocide.* New York: Basic Books.

Light, K. C., & Obrist, P. A. (1980). Cardiovascular response to stress: Effects of opportunity to avoid shock experience, and performance feedback. *Psychophysiology, 17,* 243–252.

Likert, R. (1932). A technique for the measurement of attitudes. *Archives of Psychology, 140,* 1–55.

Lim, J., & Guo, X. (2008). A study of group support systems and the intergroup setting. *Decision Support Systems, 45,* 452–460.

Lind, E. A., Erickson, B. E., Friedland, N., & Dickenberger, M. (1978). Reactions to procedural models for adjudicative conflict resolution: A cross national study. *Journal of Conflict Resolution, 22,* 318–341.

Lind, E. A., Kanfer, R., & Farley, P. C. (1990). Voice, control, and procedural justice: Instrumental and noninstrumental concerns in fairness judgments. *Journal of Personality and Social Psychology, 59,* 952–959.

Linde, J. A., Rothman, A. J., Baldwin, A. S., & Jeffery, R. W. (2006). The impact of self-efficacy on behavior change and weight change among overweight participants in a weight loss trial. *Health Psychology, 25,* 282–291.

Linder, D. E., Cooper, J., & Jones, E. E. (1967). Decision freedom as a determinant of the role of incentive magnitude in attitude change. *Journal of Personality and Social Psychology, 6,* 245–254.

Lindsay, R. C. L., & Bellinger, K. (1999). Alternatives to the sequential lineup: The importance of controlling the pictures. *Journal of Applied Psychology, 84,* 315–321.

Lindsay, R. C. L., Lea, J. A., & Fulford, J. A. (1991). Sequential lineup presentation: Technique matters. *Journal of Applied Psychology, 76,* 741–745.

Lindsay, R. C. L., Ross, D. F., Read, J. D., & Toglia, M. P. (Eds.). (2007). *The handbook of eyewitness psychology: Vol. 2, Memory for people.* Mahwah, NJ: Erlbaum.

Lindsay, R. C. L., & Wells, G. L. (1985). Improving eyewitness identifications from lineups: Simultaneous versus sequential lineup presentations. *Journal of Applied Psychology, 70,* 556–564.

Lindsay, R. C. L., Wells, G. L., & Rumpel, C. M. (1981). Can people detect eyewitness-identification accuracy within and across situations? *Journal of Applied Psychology, 66,* 79–89.

Lindskold, S., & Han, G. (1988). GRIT as a foundation for integrative bargaining. *Personality and Social Psychology Bulletin, 14,* 335–345.

Linville, P. (1998). The heterogeneity of homogeneity. In J. Cooper & J. Darley (Eds.), *Attribution processes, person perception, and social interaction: The legacy of Ned Jones.* Washington, DC: American Psychological Association.

Linville, P. W., & Jones, E. E. (1980). Polarized appraisals of out-group members. *Journal of Personality and Social Psychology, 38,* 689–703.

Linville, P. W., Fischer, G. W., & Fischoff, B. (1992). Perceived risk and decision making involving AIDS. In J. B. Pryor & G. D. Reeder (Eds.), *The social psychology of HIV infection.* Hillsdale, NJ: Erlbaum.

Linville, P. W., Fischer, G. W., & Salovey, P. (1989). Perceived distributions of the characteristics of in-group and out-group members: Empirical evidence and a computer simulation. *Journal of Personality and Social Psychology, 57,* 165–188.

Linz, D., Donnerstein, E., & Penrod, S. (1987). The findings and recommendations of the Attorney General's Commission on Pornography: Do the psychological "facts" fit the political fury? *American Psychologist, 42,* 946–953.

Linz, D., Wilson, B. J., & Donnerstein, E. (1992). Sexual violence in the mass media: Legal solutions, warnings, and mitigation through education. *Journal of Social Issues, 48,* 145–171.

Lippa, R. A. (2006). Is high sex drive associated with increased sexual attraction to both sexes? *Psychological Science, 17,* 46–52.

Littlepage, G. E., Hollingshead, A. B., Drake, L. R., & Littlepage, A. M. (2008). Transactive memory and performance in work groups: Specificity, communication, ability differences, and work allocation. *Group Dynamics: Theory, Research, and Practice, 12,* 223–241.

Livers, A. B., & Caver, K. A. (2003). *Leading in black and white: Working across the racial divide in corporate America.* San Francisco: Jossey-Bass.

Lobchuk, M. M., McClement, S. E., McPherson, C., & Cheang, M. (2008). Does blaming the patient with lung cancer affect the helping behavior of primary caregivers? *Oncology Nursing Forum, 35,* 681–689.

Locke, E. A. (2000). *The prime movers: Traits of the great wealth creators.* New York: Amacomb.

Locke, E. A., & Latham, G. P. (1990). *A theory of goal setting and task performance.* Englewood Cliffs, NJ: Prentice Hall.

Locke, E. A., & Latham, G. P. (2002). Building a practically useful theory of goal setting and task motivation: A 35-year odyssey. *American Psychologist, 57,* 705–717.

Locke, K. (2009). Aggression, narcissism, self-esteem, and the attribution of desirable and humanizing traits to self versus others. *Journal of Research in Personality, 43,* 99–102.

Lockhart v. McCree, 54 U.S.L.W. 4449 (1986).

Loewenstein, G. F., Weber, E. U., Hsee, C. K., & Welch, N. (2001). Risk as feelings. *Psychological Bulletin, 127,* 267–286.

Loftus, E. F. (1996). *Eyewitness testimony* (reprint ed.). Cambridge, MA: Harvard University Press.

Loftus, E. F., & Ketcham, K. (1991). *Witness for the defense: The accused, the eyewitness, and the expert who puts memory on trial.* New York: St. Martin's Press.

Loftus, E. F., & Palmer, J. C. (1974). Reconstruction of automobile destruction: An example of the interaction between language and memory. *Journal of Verbal Learning and Verbal Behavior, 13,* 585–589.

Loftus, E. F., Loftus, G. R., & Messo, J. (1987). Some facts about "weapon focus." *Law and Human Behavior, 11,* 55–62.

Logel, C., Iserman, E. C., Davies, P. G, Quinn, D. M, & Spencer, S. J. (2009). The perils of double consciousness: The role of thought suppression in stereotype threat. *Journal of Experimental Social Psychology, 45,* 299–312.

Loiselle, M., & Fuqua, W. R. (2007). Alcohol's effects on women's risk detection in a date-rape vignette. *Journal of American College Health, 55,* 261–266.

Loken, B. (2006). Consumer psychology: Categorization, inferences, affect, and persuasion. *Annual Review of Psychology, 57,* 453–485.

London, K., & Nunez, N. (2000). The effect of jury deliberations on jurors' propensity to disregard inadmissible evidence. *Journal of Applied Psychology, 85,* 932–939.

Long, E. C. J., & Andrews, D. W. (1990). Perspective taking as a predictor of marital adjustment. *Journal of Personality and Social Psychology, 59,* 126–131.

Lopez, J. A. (1992, March 3). Study says women face glass walls as well as ceilings. *Wall Street Journal,* pp. B1, B8.

Lortie-Lussier, M. (1987). Minority influence and idiosyncrasy credit: A new comparison of the Moscovici and Hollander theories of innovation. *European Journal of Social Psychology, 17,* 431–446.

Losch, M. E., & Cacioppo, J. T. (1990). Cognitive dissonance may enhance sympathetic tonus, but attitudes are changed to reduce negative affect rather than arousal. *Journal of Experimental Social Psychology, 26,* 289–304.

Lott, A. J., & Lott, B. E. (1974). The role of reward in the formation of positive interpersonal attitudes. In T. L. Huston (Ed.), *Foundations of interpersonal attraction* (pp. 171–189). New York: Academic Press.

Lott, B. (1985). The devaluation of women's competence. *Journal of Social Issues, 41,* 43–60.

Loula, F., Prasad, S., Harber, K., & Shiffrar, M. (2005). Recognizing people from their movement. *Journal of Experimental Psychology: Human Perception & Performance, 31,* 210–220.

Lowe, K., Kroeck, K., & Sivasubramaniam, N. (1996). Effectiveness correlates of transformational and transactional leadership: A meta-analytic review of the MLQ literature. *Leadership Quarterly, 7,* 385–425.

Lu, H., While, A. E., & Barriball, K. L. (2008). Role perceptions and reported actual role content of hospital nurses in Mainland China. *Journal of Clinical Nursing, 17,* 1011–1022.

Lucas, R. E. (2005). Time does not heal all wounds: A longitudinal study of reaction and adaptation to divorce. *Psychological Science, 16,* 945–950.

Lund, R., Nielsen, K. K., Hansen, D. H., Kriegbaum, M., Molbo, D., Due, P., et al. (2009). Exposure to bullying at school and depression in adulthood: A study of Danish men born in 1953. *European Journal of Public Health, 19,* 111–116.

Luus, C. A. E., & Wells, G. L. (1994). The malleability of eyewitness confidence: Co-witness and perseverance effects. *Journal of Applied Psychology, 79,* 714–723.

Luo, S., & Klohnen, E. C. (2005). Assortative mating and marital quality in newlyweds: A couple-centered approach. *Journal of Personality and Social Psychology, 88,* 304–326.

Lutz, A., Slagter, H. A., Dunne, J. D., & Davidson, R. J. (2008). Attention regulation and monitoring in meditation. *Trends in the Cognitive Sciences, 12,* 163–169.

Lykken, D. T. (1998). *A tremor in the blood: Uses and abuses of the lie detector* (2nd ed.). Cambridge, MA: Perseus.

Lykken, D. T. (2000). *Happiness: The nature and nurture of joy and contentment.* New York: St. Martin's Press.

Lykken, D. T., & Tellegen, A. (1993). Is human mating adventitious or the result of lawful choice? A twin study of mate selection. *Journal of Personality and Social Psychology, 65,* 56–68.

Lyness, K. S., & Thompson, D. E. (2000). Climbing the corporate ladder: Do female and male executives follow the same route? *Journal of Applied Psychology, 85,* 86–101.

Lyons, A., & Kashima, Y. (2001). The representation of culture: Communication processes tend to maintain cultural stereotypes. *Social Cognition, 19,* 372–394.

Lyubomirsky, S. (2007). *The how of happiness: A scientific approach to getting the life you want.* New York: Penguin.

Lyubomirsky, S., Sheldon, K. M., & Schkade, D. (2005). Pursuing happiness: The architecture of sustainable change. *Review of General Psychology, 9,* 111–131.

Maass, A., & Clark, R. D., III. (1984). Hidden impact of minorities: Fifteen years of minority influence research. *Psychological Bulletin, 95,* 428–450.

Maass, A., D'Ettole, C., & Cadinu, M. (2008). Checkmate? The role of gender stereotypes in the ultimate intellectual sport. *European Journal of Social Psychology, 38,* 231–245.

Maass, A., & Kohnken, G. (1989). Eyewitness identification: Simulating the "weapon effect." *Law and Human Behavior, 13,* 397–408.

Maass, A., Volpato, C., & Mucchi-Faina, A. (1996). Social influence and the verifiability of the issue under discussion: Attitudinal versus objective items. *British Journal of Social Psychology, 35,* 15–26.

MacCoun, R. J., & Kerr, N. L. (1988). Asymmetric influence in mock jury deliberation: Jurors' bias for leniency. *Journal of Personality and Social Psychology, 54,* 21–33.

MacDonald, G., & Leary, M. R. (2005). Why does social exclusion hurt? The relationship between social and physical pain. *Psychological Bulletin, 131,* 202–223.

MacDonald, T. K., Fong, G. T., Zanna, M. P., & Martineau, A. M. (2000). Alcohol myopia and condom use: Can alcohol intoxication be associated with more prudent behavior? *Journal of Personality and Social Psychology, 78,* 605–619.

Macionis, J. J. (2003). *Sociology* (9th ed.). Upper Saddle River, NJ: Prentice-Hall.

Mackay, N., & Barrowclough, C. (2005). Accident and emergency staff's perceptions of deliberate self-harm: Attributions, emotions, and willingness to help. *British Journal of Clinical Psychology, 44,* 255–267.

Mackenzie, C. S., Gekoski, W. L., & Knox, V. J. (2006). Age, gender, and the underutilization of mental health services: The influence of help-seeking attitudes. *Aging & Mental Health, 10,* 574–582.

Mackie, D. M., & Worth, L. T. (1989). Processing deficits and the mediation of positive affect in persuasion. *Journal of Personality and Social Psychology, 57,* 27–40.

Mackie, D. M., Asuncion, A. G., & Rosselli, F. (1992). Impact of positive affect on persuasion processes. *Review of Personality and Social Psychology, 14,* 247–270.

Mackie, D. M., Worth, L. T., & Asuncion, A. G. (1990). Processing of persuasive in-group messages. *Journal of Personality and Social Psychology, 58,* 812–822.

MacLeod, C., & Campbell, L. (1992). Memory accessibility and probability judgments: An experimental evaluation of the availability heuristic. *Journal of Personality and Social Psychology, 63,* 890–902.

MacNeil, S., & Byers, E. S. (2009). Role of sexual self-disclosure in the sexual satisfaction of long-term heterosexual couples. *Journal of Sex Research, 46,* 3–14.

Macrae, C. N., Bodenhausen, G. V., Milne, A. B., & Jetten, J. (1994). Out of mind but back in sight: Stereotypes on the rebound. *Journal of Personality and Social Psychology, 67,* 808–817.

Madden, T. J., Ellen, P. S., & Ajzen, I. (1992). A comparison of the theory of planned behavior and the theory of reasoned action. *Personality and Social Psychology Bulletin, 18,* 3–9.

Madon, S., Guyll, M., Aboufadel, K., Montiel, E., Smith, A., Palumbo, P., & Jussim, L. (2001). Ethnic and national stereotypes: The Princeton trilogy revisited and revised. *Personality and Social Psychology Bulletin, 27,* 996–1010.

Maddux, J. E. (1995). *Self-efficacy, adaptation, and adjustment: Theory, research, and application.* New York: Perseus.

Maddux, J. E., & Rogers, R. W. (1980). Effects of source expertness, physical attractiveness, and supporting arguments on persuasion: A case of brains over beauty. *Journal of Personality and Social Psychology, 39,* 235–244.

Madey, S. F., Simo, M., Dillworth, D., Kemper, D., Toczynski, A., & Perella, A. (1996). They do get more attractive at closing time, but only when you are not in a relationship. *Basic and Applied Social Psychology, 18,* 387–393.

Madon, S., Guyll, M., Spoth, R., Cross, S. E., & Hilbert, S. J. (2003). The self-fulfilling influence of mother expectations on children's underage drinking. *Journal of Personality and Social Psychology, 84,* 1188–1205.

Madon, S., Jussim, L., Keiper, S., Eccles, J., Smith, A., & Palumbo, P. (1998). The accuracy and power of sex, social class, and ethnic stereotypes: A naturalistic study in person perception. *Personality and Social Psychology Bulletin, 24,* 1304–1318.

Madon, S., Willard, J., Guyll, M., Trudeau, L., & Spoth, R. (2006). Self-fulfilling prophecy effects of mothers' beliefs on children's alcohol use: Accumulation, dissipation, and stability over time. *Journal of Personality and Social Psychology, 90,* 911–926.

Madsen, E. A., Tunney, R. J., Fieldman, G., Plotkin, H. C., Dunbar, R. I. M., Richardson, J. M., & McFarland, D. (2007). Kinship and altruism: A cross-cultural experimental study. *British Journal of Psychology, 98,* 339–359.

Magnussen, S., Wise, R. A., Raja, A. Q., Safer, M. A., Pawlenko, N., & Stridbeck, U. (2008). What judges know about eyewitness testimony: A comparison of Norwegian and US judges. *Psychology, Crime & Law, 14,* 177–188.

Maio, G., & Olson, J. M. (Eds.). (2000). *Why we evaluate: Functions of attitudes.* Mahwah, NJ: Erlbaum.

Major, B., & Crocker, J. (1993). Social stigma: The affective consequences of attributional ambiguity. In D. M. Mackie & D. L. Hamilton (Eds.), *Affect, cognition, and stereotyping: Interactive processes in intergroup perception* (pp. 345–370). New York: Academic Press.

Major, B., & Deaux, K. (1982). Individual differences in justice behavior. In J. Greenberg & R. L. Cohen (Eds.), *Equity and justice in social behavior* (pp. 13–76). New York: Academic Press.

Major, B., & Gramzow, R. H. (1999). Abortion as stigma: Cognitive and emotional implications of concealment. *Journal of Personality and Social Psychology, 77,* 735–745.

Major, B., & Konar, E. (1984). An investigation of sex differences in pay expectations and their possible causes. *Academy of Management Journal, 27,* 777–792.

Major, B., Carrington, P. I., & Carnevale, P. J. D. (1984). Physical attractiveness and self-esteem: Attributions for praise from an other-sex evaluator. *Personality and Social Psychology Bulletin, 10,* 43–50.

Major, B., Feinstein, J., & Crocker, J. (1994). Attributional ambiguity of affirmative action. *Basic and Applied Social Psychology, 15,* 113–142.

Major, B., Kaiser, C. R., O'Brien, L. T., & McCoy, S. K. (2007). Perceived discrimination as worldview threat or worldview confirmation: Implications for self-esteem. *Journal of Personality and Social Psychology, 92,* 1068–1086.

Major, B., McFarlin, D. B., & Gagnon, D. (1984). Overworked and underpaid: On the nature of gender differences in personal entitlement. *Journal of Personality and Social Psychology, 47,* 1399–1412.

Major, B., Quinton, W. J., & Schmader, T. (2003). Attributions to discrimination and self-esteem: Impact of group identification and situational ambiguity. *Journal of Experimental Social Psychology, 39,* 220–231.

Malamuth, N. M. (1983). Factors associated with rape as predictors of laboratory aggression against women. *Journal of Personality and Social Psychology, 45,* 432–442.

Malamuth, N. M. (1986). Predictors of naturalistic sexual aggression. *Journal of Personality and Social Psychology, 50,* 953–962.

Malamuth, N. M. (1996). The confluence model of sexual aggression: Feminist and evolutionary perspectives. In D. M. Buss & N. M. Malamuth (Eds.), *Sex, power, conflict: Evolutionary and feminist perspectives* (pp. 269–295). New York: Oxford University Press.

Malamuth, N. M., & Donnerstein, E. I. (1982). The effects of aggressive-pornographic mass media stimuli. In L. Berkowitz (Ed.), *Advances in experimental social psychology* (Vol. 15, pp. 103–136). New York: Academic Press.

Malhotra, D., & Bazerman, M. H. (2008). Psychological influence in negotiation: An introduction long overdue. *Journal of Management, 34*(3), 509–531.

Malkiel, B. G. (2007). *A random walk down Wall Street: The time-tested strategy for successful investing* (9th ed.). New York: Norton.

Malle, B. F., & Knobe, J. (1997). Which behaviors do people explain? A basic actor-observer asymmetry. *Journal of Personality and Social Psychology, 72,* 288–304.

Malle, B. F., Knobe, J. M., & Nelson, S. E. (2007). Actor-observer asymmetries in explanations of behavior: New answers to an old question. *Journal of Personality and Social Psychology, 93,* 491–514.

Malloy, T. E., & Albright, L. (1990). Interpersonal perception in a social context. *Journal of Personality and Social Psychology, 58,* 419–428.

Malpass, R. S., & Devine, P. G. (1981). Eyewitness identification: Lineup instructions and the absence of the offender. *Journal of Applied Psychology, 66,* 482–489.

Malpass, R. S., & Kravitz, J. (1969). Recognition for faces of own and other race. *Journal of Personality and Social Psychology, 13,* 330–334.

Malti, T., Gasser, L., & Buchmann, M. (2009). Aggressive and prosocial children's emotion attributions and moral reasoning. *Aggressive Behavior, 35,* 90–102.

Man, D. C., & Lam, S. K. (2003). The effects of job complexity and autonomy on cohesiveness in collectivistic and individualistic work groups: A cross-cultural analysis. *Journal of Organizational Behavior, 24,* 979–1001.

Maner, J., Gailliot, M., Rouby, D., & Miller, S. (2007). Can't take my eyes off you: Attentional adhesion to mates and rivals. *Journal of Personality and Social Psychology, 93,* 389–401.

Maner, J. K., Kenrick, D. T., Becker, D. V., Robertson, T. E., Hofer, B., Neuberg, S. L., et al. (2005). Functional projection: How fundamental social motives can bias interpersonal perception. *Journal of Personality and Social Psychology, 88,* 63–78.

Mann, J. M. (1992). AIDS—The second decade: A global perspective. *Journal of Infectious Diseases, 165,* 245–250.

Manning, R., Levine, M., & Collins, A. (2008). The legacy of the 38 witnesses and the importance of getting history right. *American Psychologist, 63,* 562–563.

Mannix, E., & Neale, M. A (2005). What differences make a difference? The promise and reality of diverse teams in organizations. *Psychological Science in the Public Interest, 6,* 31–55.

Maoz, I., & McCauley, C. (2008). Threat, dehumanization, and support for retaliatory aggressive policies in asymmetric conflict. *Journal of Conflict Resolution, 52,* 93–116.

Marcus-Newhall, A., Pedersen, W. C., Carlson, M., & Miller, N. (2000). Displaced aggression is alive and well: A meta-analytic review. *Journal of Personality and Social Psychology, 78,* 670–689.

Mares, M.-L., & Woodard, E. (2005). Positive effects of television on children's social interactions: A meta-analysis. *Media Psychology, 7,* 301–322.

Margolin, G., & Wampold, B. E. (1981). A sequential analysis of conflict and accord in distressed and nondistressed marital partners. *Journal of Consulting and Clinical Psychology, 49,* 554–567.

Markey, P. M. (2000). Bystander intervention in computer-mediated communication. *Computers in Human Behavior, 16,* 183–188.

Marks, J. (1995). *Human biodiversity: Genes, race, and history.* New York: Aldine de Gruyter.

Markus, H. (1977). Self-schemata and processing information about the self. *Journal of Personality and Social Psychology, 35,* 63–78.

Markus, H. R. (2008). Pride, prejudice, and ambivalence: Toward a unified theory of race and ethnicity. *American Psychologist, 63,* 651–670.

Markus, H. R., & Kitayama, S. (1991). Culture and the self: Implications for cognition, emotion, and motivation. *Psychological Review, 98,* 224–253.

Markus, H. R., & Lin, L. R. (1999). Conflictways: Cultural diversity in the meanings and practices of conflict. In D. A. Prentice & D. T. Miller (Eds.), *Cultural divides: Understanding and overcoming group conflict* (pp. 302–333). New York: Russell Sage.

Markus, H. R., Uchida, Y., Omoregie, H., Townsend, S. M., & Kitayama, S. (2006). Going for the gold: Models of agency in Japanese and American contexts. *Psychological Science, 17,* 103–112.

Markus, H., Hamill, R., & Sentis, K. P. (1987). Thinking fat: Self-schemas for body weight and the processing of weight-relevant information. *Journal of Applied Social Psychology, 17,* 50–71.

Marlowe, C. M., Schneider, S. L., & Nelson, C. E. (1996). Gender and attractiveness biases in hiring decisions: Are more experienced managers less biased? *Journal of Applied Psychology, 81,* 11–21.

Martey, R. M., & Stromer-Galley, J. (2007). The digital dollhouse: Context and social norms in The Sims online. *Games and Culture: A Journal of Interactive Media, 2,* 314–334.

Martin, C. L., Eisenbud, L., & Rose, H. (1995). Children's gender-based reasoning about toys. *Child Development, 66,* 1453–1471.

Martin-Albo, J., Nuñez, J. L., Navrro, J. G., Grijalvo, F., & Navascues, V. (2007). The Rosenberg Self-Esteem Scale: Translation and validation in university students. *The Spanish Journal of Psychology, 10,* 458–467.

Marx, B. P., Gross, A. M., & Adams, H. E. (1999). The effect of alcohol on the responses of sexually coercive and noncoercive men to an experimental rape analogue. *Sexual Abuse: Journal of Research and Treatment, 11,* 131–145.

Maslach, C. (1979). Negative emotional biasing of unexplained arousal. *Journal of Personality and Social Psychology, 37,* 953–969.

Maslach, C. (1982). *Burnout: The cost of caring.* Englewood Cliffs, NJ: Prentice-Hall.

Maslach, C., Schaufeli, W. B., & Leiter, M. P. (2001). Job burnout. *Annual Review of Psychology, 52,* 397–422.

Mason, M. F., Tatkow, E. P., & Macrae, C. N. (2005). The look of love: Gaze shifts and person perception. *Psychological Science, 16,* 236–239.

Masten, A. S. (2001). Ordinary magic: Resilience processes in development. *American Psychologist, 56,* 227–238.

Masuda, T., & Kitayama, S. (2004). Perceiver-induced constraint and attitude attribution in Japan and the US: A case for the cultural dependence of the correspondence bias. *Journal of Experimental Social Psychology, 40,* 409–416.

Masuda, T., & Nisbett, R. E. (2001). Attending holistically vs. analytically: Comparing the context sensitivity of Japanese and Americans. *Journal of Personality and Social Psychology, 81,* 922–934.

Mathieu, J., Maynard, M. T., Rapp, T., & Gilson, L. (2008). Team effectiveness 1997–2007: A review of recent advancements and a glimpse into the future. *Journal of Management, 34,* 410–476.

Mathur, M., & Chattopadhyay, A. (1991). The impact of moods generated by TV programs on responses to advertising. *Psychology and Marketing, 8,* 59–77.

Matthews, K. A. (1988). Coronary heart disease and Type A behaviors: Update on and alternative to the Booth-Kewley and Friedman (1987) quantitative review. *Psychological Bulletin, 104,* 373–380.

Matthews, K. A. (2005). Psychological perspectives on the development of coronary heart disease. *American Psychologist, 60,* 783–796.

Matz, D. C., & Wood, W. (2005). Cognitive dissonance in groups: The consequences of disagreement. *Journal of Personality and Social Psychology, 88,* 22–37.

Mayer, J. (2007, August 13). The black sites: A rare look into the CIA's secret interrogation program. *The New Yorker,* pp. 1–24.

Maznevski, M. L. (1994). Understanding our differences: Performance in decision-making groups with diverse members. *Human Relations, 47,* 531–552.

Mazur, A., Booth, A., & Dabbs, J. M. (1992). Testosterone and chess competition. *Social Psychology Quarterly, 55,* 70–77.

McAdams, D. P. (1989). *Intimacy: The need to be close.* New York: Doubleday.

McArthur, L. A. (1972). The how and what of why: Some determinants and consequences of causal attribution. *Journal of Personality and Social Psychology, 22,* 171–193.

McAuliffe, B. J., Jetten, J., Hornsey, M. J., & Hogg, M. A. (2003). Individualist and collectivist norms: When it's ok to go your own way. *European Journal of Social Psychology, 33,* 57–70.

McCall, C., Blascovich, J., Young, A., & Persky, S. (2009). Proxemic behaviors as predictors of aggression towards Black (but not White) males in an immersive virtual environment. *Social Influence, 4,* 1–17.

McCarthy, E. (2009, April 24). On dating: Shared qualities for a successful relationship. *The Washington Post.*

McCarty-Gould, C. (2000). *Crisis and chaos: Life with the combat veteran.* New York: Nova Kroshka Books.

McCauley, J. L., & Calhoun, K. S. (2008). Faulty perceptions? The impact of binge drinking history on college women's perceived rape resistance efficacy. *Addictive Behaviors, 33,* 1540–1545.

McClam, E. (2009, January 17). Pilot's life had prepared him for "miracle" flight. *Associated Press.*

McCowan, B., & Hooper, S. L. (2002). Individual acoustic variation in Belding's ground squirrel alarm chirps in the High Sierra Nevada. *Journal of the Acoustical Society of America, 111,* 1157–1160.

McCrae, R. R., & Costa, P. T., Jr. (2003). *Personality in adulthood: A five-factor theory perspective* (2nd ed.). New York: Guilford Press.

McCullough, M. E., Hoyt, W. T., Larson, D. B., Koenig, H. G., & Thoresen, C. (2000). Religious involvement and mortality: A meta-analytic review. *Health Psychology, 19,* 211–222.

McCullough, M. E., Kimeldorf, M. B., & Cohen, A. D. (2008). An adaptation for altruism? The social causes, social effects, and social evolution of gratitude. *Current Directions in Psychological Science, 17,* 281–285.

McDougall, W. (1908). *An introduction to social psychology.* London: Methuen.

McElwee, R. O., Dunning, D., Tan, P. L., & Hollmann, S. (2001). Evaluating others: The role of who we are versus what we think traits mean. *Basic and Applied Social Psychology, 23,* 123–136.

McGarty, C., Turner, J. C., Hogg, M. A., David, B., et al. (1992). Group polarization as conformity to the prototypical group member. *British Journal of Social Psychology, 31,* 1–19.

McGlynn, R. P., Harding, D. J., & Cottle, J. L. (2009). Individual-group discontinuity in group-individual interactions: Does size matter? *Group Processes & Intergroup Relations, 12,* 129–143.

McGuire, A. M. (1994). Helping behaviors in the natural environment: Dimensions and correlates of helping. *Personality and Social Psychology Bulletin, 20,* 45–56.

McGuire, W. J. (1964). Inducing resistance to persuasion. In L. Berkowitz (Ed.), *Advances in experimental social psychology* (Vol. 1, pp. 192–229). New York: Academic Press.

McGuire, W. J. (1967). Some impending reorientations in social psychology: Some thoughts provoked by Kenneth Ring. *Journal of Experimental Social Psychology, 3,* 124–139.

McGuire, W. J. (1968). Personality and susceptibility to social influence. In E. F. Borgatta & W. W. Lambert (Eds.), *Handbook of personality theory and research* (pp. 1130–1187). Chicago: Rand McNally.

McGuire, W. J. (1969). The nature of attitudes and attitude change. In G. Lindzey & E. Aronson (Eds.), *Handbook of social psychology* (2nd ed., Vol. 3, pp. 136–314). Reading, MA: Addison-Wesley.

McGuire, W. J., & McGuire, C. V. (1988). Content and process in the experience of self. In L. Berkowitz (Ed.), *Advances in experimental social psychology* (Vol. 20, pp. 97–144). New York: Academic Press.

McIntyre, R. B., Paulson, R. M., & Lord, C. G. (2003). Alleviating women's mathematics stereotype threat through salience of group achievements. *Journal of Experimental Social Psychology, 39,* 83–90.

McKelvey, T. (2007). *Monstering: Inside America's policy of secret interrogations and torture in the terror war.* New York: Basic Books.

McKenna, K. Y. A., & Bargh, J. A. (1998). Coming out in the age of the Internet: "Demarginalization" through virtual group participation. *Journal of Personality and Social Psychology, 75,* 681–694.

McKimmie, B. M., Terry, D. J., Hogg, M. A., Manstead, A. S. R., Spears, R., & Doosje, B. (2003). I'm a hypocrite, but so is everyone else: Group support and the reduction of cognitive dissonance. *Group Dynamics: Theory, Research, and Practice, 7,* 214–224.

McNatt, D. B. (2000). Ancient Pygmalion joins contemporary management: A meta-analysis of the result. *Journal of Applied Psychology, 85,* 314–322.

McPherson, M., Smith-Lovin, L., & Cook, J. M. (2001). Birds of a feather: Homophily in social networks. *Annual Review of Sociology, 27,* 415–444.

McQuiston-Surrett, D., Malpass, R. S., & Tredoux, C. G. (2006). Sequential vs. simultaneous lineups: A review of methods, data, and theory. *Psychology, Public Policy, and Law, 12,* 137–169.

Mead, G. H. (1934). *Mind, self, and society.* Chicago: University of Chicago Press.

Mealey, L., Bridgstock, R., & Townsend, G. C. (1999). Symmetry and perceived facial attractiveness: A monozygotic co-twin comparison. *Journal of Personality and Social Psychology, 76,* 151–158.

Medvec, V. H., & Savitsky, K. (1997). When doing better means feeling worse: The effects of categorical cutoff points on counterfactual thinking and satisfaction. *Journal of Personality and Social Psychology, 72,* 1284–1296.

Medvec, V. H., Madey, S. F., & Gilovich, T. (1995). When less is more: Counterfactual thinking and satisfaction among Olympic medalists. *Journal of Personality and Social Psychology, 69,* 603–610.

Meek, J. G. (2009, August 13). Extremist militias see resurgence under President Obama's tenure. *NYDailyNews.com.*

Meeus, W. H. J., & Raaijmakers, Q. A. W. (1995). Obedience in modern society: The Utrecht studies. *Journal of Social Issues, 51,* 155–175.

Meiser, T., & Hewstone, M. (2006). Illusory and spurious correlations: Distinct phenomena or joint outcomes of exemplar-based category learning? *European Journal of Social Psychology, 36,* 315–336.

Meissner, C. A., & Brigham, J. C. (2001). 30 years of investigating the own-race bias in memory for faces: A meta-analytic review. *Psychology, Public Policy, and Law, 7,* 3–35.

Meissner, C. A., & Kassin, S. M. (2002). "He's guilty!" Investigator bias in judgments of truth and deception. *Law and Human Behavior, 26,* 469–480.

Meissner, C. A., Brigham, J. C., & Butz, D. A. (2005). Memory for own- and other-race faces: A dual-process approach. *Applied Cognitive Psychology, 19,* 545–567.

Meissner, C. A., Brigham, J. C., & Pfeifer, J. E. (2003). Jury nullification: The influence of judicial instruction on the relationship between attitudes and juridic decision-making. *Basic and Applied Social Psychology, 25,* 243–254.

Melamed, S., Shirom, A., Toker, S., Berliner, S., & Shapira, I. (2006). Burnout and risk of cardiovascular disease: Evidence, possible causal paths, and promising research directions. *Psychological Bulletin, 132,* 327–353.

Mendonca, P. J., & Brehm, S. S. (1983). Effects of choice on behavioral treatment of overweight children. *Journal of Social and Clinical Psychology, 1,* 343–358.

Meneses, R., Ortega, R., Navarro, J., & de Quijano, S. D. (2008). Criteria for assessing the level of group development (LGD) of work groups: Groupness, entitativity, and groupality as theoretical perspectives. *Small Group Research, 39,* 492–514.

Méras, P. (2009, August 25). Egypt bans barbarity of female mutilation. *Providence Journal-Bulletin,* p. 7.

Meriac, J. P., Hoffman, B. J., Woehr, D. J., & Fleisher, M. S. (2008). Further evidence for the validity of assessment center dimensions: A meta-analysis of the incremental criterion-related validity of dimension ratings. *Journal of Applied Psychology, 93,* 1042–1052.

Merikle, P., & Skanes, H. E. (1992). Subliminal self-help audiotapes: A search for placebo effects. *Journal of Applied Psychology, 77,* 772–776.

Mesmer-Magnus, J., & DeChurch, L. (2009). Information sharing and team performance: A meta-analysis. *Journal of Applied Psychology, 94,* 535–546.

Messick, D. M., & Cook, K. S. (Eds.). (1983). *Equity theory: Psychological and sociological perspectives.* New York: Praeger.

Messineo, M. J. (2008). Does advertising on Black Entertainment Television portray more positive gender representations compared to broadcast networks? *Sex Roles, 59,* 752–764.

Meston, C. M., & Frohlich, P. F. (2003). Love at first sight: Partner salience moderates roller-coaster-induced excitation transfer. *Archives of Sexual Behavior, 32,* 537–544.

Metalsky, G. I., Joiner, T. E., Hardin, T. S., & Abramson, L. Y. (1993). Depressive reactions to failure in a naturalistic setting: A test of the hopelessness and self-esteem theories of depression. *Journal of Abnormal Psychology, 102,* 101–109.

Metropolitan Area Child Study Research Group (2007). Changing the way children 'think' about aggression: Social-cognitive effects of a preventive intervention. *Journal of Consulting and Clinical Psychology, 75,* 160–167.

Mezulis, A. H., Abramson, L. Y., Hyde, J. S., & Hankin, B. L. (2004). Is there a universal positivity bias in attributions? A meta-analytic review of individual, developmental, and cultural differences in the self-serving attributional bias. *Psychological Bulletin, 130,* 711–747.

Mezzacappa, E. S., Katkin, E. S., & Palmer, S. N. (1999). Epinephrine, arousal, and emotion: A new look at two-factor theory. *Cognition and Emotion, 13,* 181–199.

Meyer, J. (2009, June 12). Shooting investigators ask why; Suspect James von Brunn is charged with murdering a Holocaust museum guard. *Los Angeles Times,* p. 22.

Mickelson, K. D., Kessler, R. C., & Shaver, P. R. (1997). Adult attachment in a nationally representative sample. *Journal of Personality and Social Psychology, 73,* 1092–1106.

Miczek, K. A., de Almeida, R. M. M, Kravitz, E. A., Rissman, E. F., de Boer, S. F., & Raine, A. (2007). Neurobiology of escalated aggression and violence. *Journal of Neuroscience, 27,* 11803–11806.

Midlarsky, E., Fagan Jones, S., & Corley, R. P. (2005). Personality correlates of heroic rescue during the Holocaust. *Journal of Personality, 73,* 907–934.

Midlarsky, E., Kahana, E., Corley, R., Nemeroff, R., & Schonbar, R. A. (1999). Altruistic moral judgment among older adults. *International Journal of Aging and Human Development, 49,* 27–41.

Mikulincer, M., & Shaver, P. R. (2007). *Attachment patterns in adulthood: Structure, dynamics, and change.* New York: Guilford.

Miles, D. R., & Carey, G. (1997). Genetic and environmental architecture on human aggression. *Journal of Personality and Social Psychology, 72,* 207–217.

Miles, J. A., & Greenberg, J. (1993). Using punishment threats to attenuate social loafing effects among swimmers. *Organizational Behavior and Human Decision Processes, 56,* 246–265.

Milgram, S. (1963). Behavioral study of obedience. *Journal of Abnormal and Social Psychology, 67,* 371–378.

Milgram, S. (1970). The experience of living in cities. *Science, 167,* 1461–1468.

Milgram, S. (1974). *Obedience to authority: An experimental view.* New York: Harper & Row.

Milgram, S., & Toch, H. (1969). Collective behavior: Crowds and social movements. In G. Lindzey & E. Aronson (Eds.), *The handbook of social psychology* (2nd ed., Vol. 4, pp. 507–610). Reading, MA: Addison-Wesley.

Milgram, S., Bickman, L., & Berkowitz, L. (1969). Note on the drawing power of crowds of different size. *Journal of Personality and Social Psychology, 13,* 79–82.

Miller, A. G. (1986). *The obedience experiments: A case study of controversy in social science.* New York: Praeger.

Miller, A. G. (2009). Reflections on "Replicating Milgram" (Burger, 2009). *American Psychologist, 64,* 20–27.

Miller, A. G., Gordon, A. K., & Buddie, A. M. (1999). Accounting for evil and cruelty: Is to explain to condone? *Personality and Social Psychology Review, 3,* 254–268.

Miller, A. G., Jones, E. E., & Hinkle, S. (1981). A robust attribution error in the personality domain. *Journal of Experimental Social Psychology, 17,* 587–600.

Miller-El v. Dretke, 545 U.S. 231 (2005).

Miller, G., Chen, E., & Cole, S. W. (2009). Health psychology: Developing biologically plausible models linking the social world and physical health. *Annual Review of Psychology, 60,* 501–524.

Miller, J. G. (1984). Culture and the development of everyday social explanation. *Journal of Personality and Social Psychology, 46,* 961–978.

Miller, J. G., Bersoff, D. M., & Harwood, R. L. (1990). Perceptions of social responsibility in India and in the United States: Moral imperatives or personal decisions? *Journal of Personality and Social Psychology, 58,* 33–47.

Miller, M. K., & Hayward, R. D. (2008). Religious characteristics and the death penalty. *Law and Human Behavior, 32,* 113–123.

Miller, N. E. (1941). The frustration-aggression hypothesis. *Psychological Review, 48,* 337–342.

Miller, N., & Campbell, D. T. (1959). Recency and primacy in persuasion as a function of the timing of speeches and measurements. *Journal of Abnormal and Social Psychology, 59,* 1–9.

Miller, P. A., & Eisenberg, N. (1988). The relation of empathy to aggressive and externalizing/antisocial behavior. *Psychological Bulletin, 103,* 324–344.

Miller, P. A., Eisenberg, N., Fabes, R. A., & Shell, R. (1996). Relations of moral reasoning and vicarious emotion to young children's prosocial behavior toward peers and adults. *Developmental Psychology, 32,* 210–219.

Miller, R., & Perlman, D. (2009). *Intimate relationships* (5th ed.). New York: McGraw-Hill.

Miller, T. Q., Smith, T. W., Turner, C. W., Guijarro, M. L., & Hallet, A. J. (1996). A meta-analytic review of research on hostility and physical health. *Psychological Bulletin, 119,* 322–348.

Miller, T. Q., Turner, C. W., Tindale, R. S., Posavac, E. J., & Dugon, B. L. (1991). Reasons for the trend toward null findings in research on Type A behavior. *Psychological Bulletin, 110,* 469–485.

Miller, W. R. (1985). Motivation for treatment: A review with special emphasis on alcoholism. *Psychological Bulletin, 98,* 84–107.

Miller, W. R., & Thoresen, C. E. (2003). Spirituality, religion, and health: An emerging research field. *American Psychologist, 58,* 24–35.

Milliken, C. S., Auchterlonie, J. L., & Hoge, C. W. (2007). Longitudinal assessment of mental health problems among active and reserve component soldiers returning from the Iraq war. *JAMA: Journal of the American Medical Association, 298,* 2141–2148.

Mioshi, E., Bristow, M., Cook, R., & Hodges, J. R. (2009). Factors underlying caregiver stress in frontotemporal dementia and Alzheimer's disease. *Dementia and Geriatric Cognitive Disorders, 27,* 76–81.

Miranda, S. M. (1994). Avoidance of groupthink: Meeting management using group support systems. *Small Group Research, 25,* 105–136.

Mita, T. H., Dermer, M., & Knight, J. (1977). Reversed facial images and the mere exposure hypothesis. *Journal of Personality and Social Psychology, 35,* 597–601.

Mitchell, J. P., Ames, D. L., Jenkins, A. C., Banaji, M. R. (2009). Neural correlates of stereotype application. *Journal of Cognitive Neuroscience, 21,* 594–604.

Mitchell, T. R. (1974). Expectancy models of job satisfaction, occupational preference, and effort: A theoretical, methodological, and empirical appraisal. *Psychological Bulletin, 81,* 1096–1112.

Miura, H. (2009). Differences in frontal lobe function between violent and nonviolent conduct disorder in male adolescents. *Psychiatry and Clinical Neurosciences, 63,* 161–166.

Miyamoto, Y., & Kitayama, S. (2002). Cultural variation in correspondence bias: The critical role of attitude diagnosticity of socially constrained behavior. *Journal of Personality and Social Psychology, 83,* 1239–1248.

Mobius, M. M., & Rosenblat, T. S. (2006). Why beauty matters. *American Economic Review, 96,* 222–235.

Möller, I., & Krahé, B. (2009, January). Exposure to violent video games and aggression in German adolescents: A longitudinal analysis. *Aggressive Behavior, 35,* 75–89.

Monat, A., Lazarus, R. S., & Reevy, G. (Eds.). (2007). *The Praeger handbook on stress and coping.* New York: Praeger.

Mondschein, E. R., Adolph, K. E., & Tamis-LeMonda, C. S. (2000). Gender bias in mothers' expectations about infant crawling. *Journal of Experimental Child Psychology, 77,* 304–316.

Monin, B., Sawyer, P. J., & Marquez, M. J. (2008). The rejection of moral rebels: Resenting those who do the right thing. *Journal of Personality and Social Psychology, 95,* 76–93.

Monteith, M. J., & Mark, A.Y. (2005). Changing one's prejudice ways: Awareness, affect, and self-regulation. *European Review of Social Psychology, 16,* 113–154.

Monteith, M. J., & Mark, A. Y. (2009). The self-regulation of prejudice. In T. D. Nelson (Ed.), *Handbook of prejudice, stereotyping, and discrimination* (pp. 507–523). New York: Psychology Press.

Monteith, M. J., Ashburn-Nardo, L., Voils, C. I., & Czopp, A. M. (2002). Putting the brakes on prejudice: On the development and operation of cues for control. *Journal of Personality and Social Psychology, 83,* 1029–1050.

Monteith, M. J., Sherman, J. W., & Devine, P. G. (1998). Suppression as a stereotype control strategy. *Personality and Social Psychology Review, 2,* 63–82.

Montoya, R. M., Horton, R. S., & Kirchner, J. (2008). Is actual similarity necessary for attraction? A meta-analysis of actual and perceived similarity. *Journal of Social and Personal Relationships, 25,* 889–922.

Moon, H. (2001). Looking forward and looking back: Integrating completion and sunk-cost effects within an escalation-of-commitment progress decision. *Journal of Applied Psychology, 86,* 104–113.

Moons, W. G., Mackie, D. M., Garcia-Marques, T. (2009). The impact of repetition-induced familiarity on agreement with weak and strong arguments. *Journal of Personality and Social Psychology, 96,* 32–44.

Moore, D. A. (2005). Myopic biases in strategic social prediction: Why deadlines put everyone under more pressure than everyone else. *Personality and Social Psychology Bulletin, 31,* 668–679.

Moore, T. E. (1982). Subliminal advertising: What you see is what you get. *Journal of Marketing, 46,* 38–47.

Mor, N., & Winquist, J. (2002). Self-focused attention and negative affect: A meta-analysis. *Psychological Bulletin, 128,* 638–662.

Moradi, B., Dirks, D., & Matteson, A. V. (2005). Roles of sexual objectification experiences and internalization of standards of beauty in eating disorder symptomatology: A test and extension of objectification theory. *Journal of Counseling Psychology, 52,* 420–428.

Moran, G., & Comfort, C. (1986). Neither "tentative" nor "fragmentary": Verdict preference of impaneled felony jurors as a function of attitude toward capital punishment. *Journal of Applied Psychology, 71,* 146–155.

Moran, G., & Cutler, B. L. (1991). The prejudicial impact of pretrial publicity. *Journal of Applied Social Psychology, 21,* 345–367.

Moreland, R. L., & Beach, S. R. (1992). Exposure effects in the classroom: The development of affinity among students. *Journal of Experimental Social Psychology, 28,* 255–276.

Moreland, R. L., & Levine, J. M. (2002). Socialization and trust in work groups. *Group Processes and Intergroup Relations, 5,* 185–201.

Morewedge, C. K., Preston, J., & Wegner, D. M. (2007). Timescale bias in the attribution of mind. *Journal of Personality and Social Psychology, 93,* 1–11.

Morgan, C. A., Hazlett, G., Doran, A., Garrett, S., Hoyt, G., Thomas, P., et al. (2004). Accuracy of eyewitness memory for persons encountered during exposure to highly intense stress. *International Journal of Law and Psychiatry, 27,* 265–279.

Morgeson, F. P., Campion, M. A., Dipboye, R. L., Hollenbeck, J. R., Murphy, K., & Schmitt, N. (2007). Reconsidering the use of personality tests in personnel contexts. *Personnel Psychology, 60,* 683–729.

Morgeson, F. P., Mumford, T. V., & Campion, M. A. (2005). Coming full circle: Using research and practice to address 27 questions about 360-degree feedback programs. *Consulting Psychology Journal: Practice and Research, 57,* 196–209.

Moriarty, D., & McCabe, A. E. (1977). Studies of television and youth sport. In *Ontario Royal Commission on Violence in the Communications Industry report* (Vol. 5). Toronto: Queen's Printer for Ontario.

Moriarty, T. (1975). Crime, commitment, and the responsive bystander: Two field experiments. *Journal of Personality and Social Psychology, 31,* 370–376.

Morr Serewicz, M. C., & Gale, E. (2008). First-date scripts: Gender roles, context, and relationship. *Sex Roles, 58,* 149–164.

Morrison, A. M., & Von Glinow, M. A. (1990). Women and minorities in management. *American Psychologist, 45,* 200–208.

Morrongiello, B. A., & Dawber, T. (2000). Mothers' responses to sons and daughters engaging in injury-risk behaviors on a playground: Implications for sex differences in injury rates. *Journal of Experimental Child Psychology, 76,* 89–103.

Morrongiello, B. A., Midgett, C., & Stanton, K. L. (2000). Gender biases in children's appraisals of injury risk and other children's risk-taking behaviors. *Journal of Experimental Child Psychology, 77,* 317–336.

Morse, B. J. (1995). Beyond the Conflict Tactics Scale: Assessing gender differences in partner violence. *Violence and Victims, 10,* 251–272.

Moscovici, S. (1980). Toward a theory of conversion behavior. In L. Berkowitz (Ed.), *Advances in Experimental Social Psychology, 6,* 149–202.

Moscovici, S., & Personnaz, B. (1991). Studies in social influence VI: Is Lenin orange or red? Imagery and social influence. *European Journal of Social Psychology, 21,* 101–118.

Moscovici, S., Lage, E., & Naffrechoux, M. (1969). Influence of a consistent minority on the responses of a majority in a color perception task. *Sociometry, 32,* 365–380.

Moscovici, S., Mugny, G., & Van Avermaet, E. (Eds.). (1985). *Perspectives on minority influence.* New York: Cambridge University Press.

Moskalenko, S., & Heine, S. J. (2003). Watching your troubles away: Television viewing as a stimulus for subjective self-awareness. *Personality and Social Psychology Bulletin, 29,* 76–85.

Moskowitz, G. B., & Grant, H. (Eds.). (2009). *The psychology of goals.* New York: Guilford Press.

Moskowitz, G. B., Li, P., & Kirk, E. R. (2004). The implicit volition model: On the preconscious regulation of temporarily adopted goals. In M. P. Zanna (Ed.), *Advances in experimental social psychology* (pp. 317–413). San Diego, CA: Academic Press.

Mouton, J., Blake, R., & Olmstead, J. (1956). The relationship between frequency of yielding and the disclosure of personal identity. *Journal of Personality, 24,* 339–347.

Moynihan, J. A., & Ader, R. (1996). Psychoneuroimmunology: Animal models of disease. *Psychosomatic Medicine, 58,* 546–558.

Mueller, J. H. (1982). Self-awareness and access to material rated as self-descriptive and nondescriptive. *Bulletin of the Psychonomic Society, 19,* 323–326.

Mugny, G. (1982). *The power of minorities.* London: Academic Press.

Mugny, G., & Perez, J. A. (1991). *Social psychology of minority influence.* Cambridge: Cambridge University Press.

Mulder, L. B. (2008). Undermining trust and cooperation: The paradox of sanctioning systems in social dilemmas. *Journal of Experimental Social Psychology, 42,* 147–162.

Mullen, B. (1983). Operationalizing the effect of the group on the individual: A self-attention perspective. *Journal of Experimental Social Psychology, 19,* 295–322.

Mullen, B. (1985). Strength and immediacy of sources: A meta-analytic evaluation of the forgotten elements of social impact theory. *Journal of Personality and Social Psychology, 48,* 1458–1466.

Mullen, B., & Copper, C. (1994). The relation between group cohesiveness and performance: An integration. *Psychological Bulletin, 115,* 210–227.

Mullen, B., Anthony, T., Salas, E., & Driskell, J. E. (1994). Group cohesiveness and quality of decision making: An integration of tests of the groupthink hypothesis. *Small Group Research, 25,* 189–204.

Mullen, B., Dovidio, J. F., Johnson, C., & Copper, C. (1992). In-group and out-group differences in social projection. *Journal of Experimental Social Psychology, 28,* 422–440.

Mullen, B., Johnson, C., & Salas, E. (1991). Productivity loss in brainstorming groups: A meta-analytic integration. *Basic and Applied Social Psychology, 12,* 3–23.

Mullen, E., & Skitka, L. J. (2009). Comparing Americans' and Ukrainians' allocations of public assistance: The role of affective reactions in helping behavior. *Journal of Cross-Cultural Psychology, 40,* 301–318.

Muraven, M., & Baumeister, R. F. (1998). Self-control as a limited resource: Regulatory depletion patterns. *Journal of Personality and Social Psychology, 74,* 774–789.

Muraven, M., & Baumeister, R. F. (2000). Self-regulation and depletion of limited resources: Does self-control resemble a muscle? *Psychological Bulletin, 126,* 247–259.

Murphy, K. R., & Balzer, W. K. (1986). Systematic distortions in memory-based behavior ratings and performance evaluation: Consequences for rating accuracy. *Journal of Applied Psychology, 71,* 39–44.

Murphy, K. R., Balzer, W. K., Lockhart, M. C., & Eisenman, E. J. (1985). Effects of previous performance on evaluations of present performance. *Journal of Applied Psychology, 70,* 72–84.

Murphy, K. R., Cronin, B. E., & Tam, A. P. (2003). Controversy and consensus regarding the use of cognitive ability testing in organizations. *Journal of Applied Psychology, 88,* 660–671.

Murphy, S. P. (2008, July 17). Big Dig's red ink engulfs state; Cost spirals to $22b. *Boston Globe,* p. A1.

Murray, C. B., Kaiser, R., & Taylor, S. (1997). The O. J. Simpson verdict: Predictors of beliefs about innocence or guilt. *Journal of Social Issues, 53,* 455–475.

Murray, G., Judd, F., Jackson, H., Komiti, A., Wearing, A., Robins, G., et al. (2008). Big boys don't cry: An investigation of stoicism and its mental health outcomes. *Personality and Individual Differences, 44,* 1369–1381.

Murray, S. L., Aloni, M., Holmes, J. G., Derrick, J. L., Stinson, D. A., & Leder, S. (2009). Fostering partner dependence as trust insurance: The implicit contingencies of the exchange script in close relationships. *Journal of Personality and Social Psychology, 96,* 324–348.

Murray, S. L., & Holmes, J. G. (1999). The (mental) ties that bind: Cognitive structures that predict relationship resilience. *Journal of Personality and Social Psychology, 77,* 1228–1244.

Murray, S. L., & Holmes, J. G. (2008). The commitment insurance system: Self-esteem and the regulation of connection in close relationships. *Advances in Experimental Social Psychology, 40,* 1–60.

Murray, S. L., Holmes, J. G., & Collins, N. L. (2006). Optimizing assurance: The risk regulation system in relationships. *Psychological Bulletin, 132,* 641–666.

Murray, S. L., Holmes, J. G., & Griffin, D. W. (1996). The benefits of positive illusions: Idealization and the construction of satisfaction in close relationships. *Journal of Personality and Social Psychology, 70,* 79–98.

Murstein, B. I. (1986). *Paths to marriage.* Beverly Hills, CA: Sage.

Mussweiler, T., & Damisch, L. (2008). Going back to Donald: How comparisons shape judgmental priming effects. *Journal of Personality and Social Psychology, 95,* 1295–1315.

Mussweiler, T., & Ruter, K. (2003). What friends are for! The use of routine standards in social comparison. *Journal of Personality and Social Psychology, 85,* 467–481.

Mussweiler, T., & Strack, F. (2000). The "relative self": Informational and judgmental consequences of comparative self-evaluation. *Journal of Personality and Social Psychology, 79,* 23–38.

Mussweiler, T., Rüter, K., & Epstude, K. (2004). The man who wasn't there: Subliminal social comparison standards influence self-evaluation. *Journal of Experimental Social Psychology, 40,* 689–696.

Myers, D. G., & Diener, E. (1995). Who is happy? *Psychological Science, 6,* 10–19.

Myers, D. G., & Lamm, H. (1976). The group polarization phenomenon. *Psychological Bulletin, 83,* 602–627.

Nabi, R. L., & Sullivan, J. L. (2001). Does television viewing relate to engagement in protective action against crime? A cultivation analysis from a theory of reasoned action perspective. *Communication Research, 28,* 802–825.

Nacoste, R. W. (1996). Social psychology and the affirmative action debate. *Journal of Social and Clinical Psychology, 15,* 261–282.

Nadler, A., & Fisher, J. D. (1986). The role of threat to self-esteem and perceived control in recipient reactions to help: Theory development and empirical validation. In L. Berkowitz (Ed.), *Advances in experimental social psychology* (Vol. 19, pp. 81–122). New York: Academic Press.

Nadler, A., Halabi, S., & Harpaz-Gorodeisky, G. (2009). Intergroup helping as status-organizing processes: Implications for intergroup misunderstandings. In S. Demoulin, J. P. Leyens, & J. F. Dovidio (Eds.), *Intergroup misunderstandings: Impact of divergent social realities* (pp. 311–330). New York: Psychology Press.

Nakao, H., & Itakura, S. (2009). An integrated view of empathy: Psychology, philosophy, and neuroscience. *Integrative Psychological & Behavioral Science, 43,* 42–52.

Nakashima, K., Isobe, C., & Ura, M. (2008). Effect of self-construal and threat to self-esteem on ingroup favouritism: Moderating effect of independent/interdependent self-construal on use of ingroup favouritism for maintaining and enhancing self-evaluation. *Asian Journal of Social Psychology, 11,* 286–292.

Naquin, C. E., & Kurtzberg, T. R. (2009). Team negotiation and perceptions of trustworthiness: The whole versus the sum of the parts. *Group Dynamics: Theory, Research, and Practice, 13,* 133–150.

Narvaez, D., & Lapsley, D. K. (2009). Moral identity, moral functioning, and the development of moral character. In D. M. Bartels, C. W. Bauman, L. J. Sktika, & D. L. Medin (Eds.), *Moral judgment and decision making* (pp. 237–274). San Diego, CA: Elsevier Academic Press.

Nash, R. A., & Wade, K. A. (2009). Innocent but proven guilty: Using false video evidence to elicit false confessions and create false beliefs. *Applied Cognitive Psychology, 23,* 624–637.

Nassif, A., & Gunter, B. (2008). Gender representation in television advertisements in Britain and Saudi Arabia. *Sex Roles, 58,* 752–760.

National Law Journal. (1990, September 10). Rock group not liable for deaths. p. 33.

National Research Council, Committee to Review the Scientific Evidence on the Polygraph, Division of Behavioral and Social Sciences and Education. (2003). *The polygraph and lie detection.* Washington, DC: National Academies Press.

National Television Violence Study, Vol. 2 (1998). Thousand Oaks, CA: Sage.

Nattinger, A. B., et al. (1998). Celebrity medical care decisions can influence others. *Journal of the American Medical Association, 279,* 788–789.

Neff, L. A., & Karney, B. R. (2005). To know you is to love you: The implications of global adoration and specific accuracy for marital relationships. *Journal of Personality and Social Psychology, 88,* 480–497.

Neisser, U. (1981). John Dean's memory: A case study. *Cognition, 9,* 1–22.

Nelissen, R. M. A. (2008). The price you pay: Cost-dependent reputation effects of altruistic punishment. *Evolution and Human Behavior, 29,* 242–248.

Nemeth, C. (1986). Differential contributions of majority and minority influence. *Psychological Review, 93,* 23–32.

Nemeth, C. J., Connell, J. B., Rogers, J. D., & Brown, K. S. (2001). Improving decision making by means of dissent. *Journal of Applied Social Psychology, 31,* 48–58.

Nemeth, C., & Kwan, J. (1987). Minority influence, divergent thinking, and detection of correct solutions. *Journal of Applied Social Psychology, 17,* 788–799.

Nes, L. S., & Segerstrom, S. C. (2006). Dispositional optimism and coping: A meta-analytic review. *Personality and Social Psychology Review, 10,* 235–251.

Nesdale, D., & Naito, M. (2005). Individualism-collectivism and the attitudes to school bullying of Japanese and Australian students. *Journal of Cross-Cultural Psychology, 36,* 537–556.

Neuberg, S. L., Kenrick, D. T., & Schaller, M. (2010). Evolutionary social psychology. In S. T. Fiske, D. T. Gilbert, & G. Lindzey (Eds.), *The handbook of social psychology* (5th ed.). New York: McGraw-Hill.

Neuman, W. R., Marcus, G. E., Crigler, A. N., & MacKuen, M. (Eds.). (2007). *The affect effect: Dynamics of emotion in political thinking and behavior.* Chicago: University of Chicago Press.

Neumann, R., & Strack, F. (2000). "Mood contagion": The automatic transfer of mood between persons. *Journal of Personality and Social Psychology, 79,* 211–223.

Neuschatz, J., Lawson, D. S., Swanner, J. K., Meissner, C. A., & Neuschatz, J. S. (2008). The effects of accomplice witnesses and jailhouse informants on jury decision making. *Law and Human Behavior, 32,* 137–149.

Newby-Clark, I. R., McGregor, I., & Zanna, M. P. (2002). Thinking and caring about cognitive inconsistency: When and from whom does attitudinal ambivalence feel uncomfortable? *Journal of Personality and Social Psychology, 82,* 157–166.

Newcomb, T. M. (1943). *Personality and social change: Attitude formation in a student community.* Ft. Worth, TX: Dryden Press.

Newcomb, T. M. (1961). *The acquaintance process.* New York: Holt, Rinehart and Winston.

Newman, C. (2000, January). The enigma of beauty. *National Geographic,* pp. 94–121.

Newman, L. S., & Uleman, J. S. (1989). Spontaneous trait inference. In J. S. Uleman & J. A. Bargh (Eds.), *Unintended thought* (pp. 155–188). New York: Guilford.

Newman, R. S. (2005). The cocktail party effect in infants revisited: Listening to one's name in noise. *Developmental Psychology, 41,* 352–362.

Newtson, D. (1974). Dispositional inference from effects of actions: Effects chosen and effects foregone. *Journal of Experimental Social Psychology, 10,* 487–496.

Newtson, D., Hairfield, J., Bloomingdale, J., & Cutino, S. (1987). The structure of action and interaction. *Social Cognition, 5,* 191–237.

Nezlek, J. B., Kafetsios, K., & Smith, C. V. (2008). Emotions in everyday social encounters: Correspondence between culture and self-construal. *Journal of Cross-Cultural Psychology, 39,* 366–372.

Ng, K. Y., & Van Dyne, L. (2005). Antecedents and performance consequences of helping behavior in work groups: A multilevel analysis. *Group and Organization Management, 30,* 514–540.

Nguyen, H. H. D., & Ryan, A. M. (2008). Does stereotype threat affect test performance of minorities and women? A meta-analysis of experimental evidence. *Journal of Applied Psychology, 93,* 1314–1334.

Nibler, R., & Harris, K. L. (2003). The effects of culture and cohesiveness in collectivistic and individualistic work groups: A cross-cultural analysis. *Journal of Organizational Behavior, 24,* 979–1001.

Nickerson, C., Schwarz, N., Diener, E., & Kahneman, D. (2003). Zeroing in on the dark side of the American dream: A closer look at the negative consequences of the goal for financial success. *Psychological Science, 14,* 531–536.

Niedermeier, K. E., Horowitz, I. A., & Kerr, N. L. (1999). Informing jurors of their nullification power: A route to a just verdict or judicial chaos? *Law and Human Behavior, 23,* 331–351.

Nieva, V. F., & Gutek, B. A. (1981). *Women and work: A psychological perspective.* New York: Praeger.

Nije Bijvank, M., Konijn, E. A., Bushman, B. J., & Roelofsma, P. H. M. P. (2009). Age and content labels make video games forbidden fruit for youth. *Pediatrics, 123,* 870–876.

Nijstad, B. A., & Stroebe, W. (2006). How the group affects the mind: A cognitive model of idea generation in groups. *Personality and Social Psychology Review, 10,* 186–213.

Nisbett, R. E., & Cohen, D. (1996). *Culture of honor: The psychology of violence in the South.* Boulder, CO: Westview.

Nisbett, R. E., & Ross, L. (1980). *Human inference: Strategies and shortcomings of social judgment.* Englewood Cliffs, NJ: Prentice-Hall.

Nisbett, R. E., & Wilson, T. D. (1977). Telling more than we can know: Verbal reports on mental processes. *Psychological Review, 84,* 231–259.

Nisbett, R. E., Fong, G. T., Lehman, D. R., & Cheng, P. W. (1987). Teaching reasoning. *Science, 238,* 625–631.

Nolen-Hoeksema, S. (1991). Responses to depression and their effects on the duration of depressive episodes. *Journal of Abnormal Psychology, 100,* 569–582.

Nolen-Hoeksema, S., & Girgus, J. S. (1994). The emergence of gender differences in depression during adolescence. *Psychological Bulletin, 115,* 424–443.

Nolen-Hoeksema, S., & Morrow, J. (1991). A prospective study of depression and posttraumatic stress symptoms after a natural disaster: The 1989 Loma Prieta earthquake. *Journal of Personality and Social Psychology, 61,* 115–121.

Nolen-Hoeksema, S., Wisco, B. E., & Lyubomirsky, S. (2008). Rethinking rumination. *Perspectives on Psychological Science, 3,* 400–424.

Norenzayan, A., & Nisbett, R. E. (2000). Culture and causal cognition. *Current Directions in Psychological Science, 9,* 132–135.

North, A. C., Hargreaves, D. J., & McKendrick, J. (1999). The influence of in-store music on wine selections. *Journal of Applied Psychology, 84,* 271–276.

North, A. C., Tarrant, M., & Hargreaves, D. J. (2004). The effects of music on helping behavior: A field study. *Environment and Behavior, 36,* 266–275.

Northoff, G., & Panksepp, J. (2008). The trans-species concept of self and the subcortical-cortical midline system. *Trends in Cognitive Sciences, 12,* 259–264.

Northoff, G., Heinzel, A., de Greck, M., Bermpohl, F., Dobrowolny, H., & Panksepp, J. (2006). Self-referential processing in our brain—a meta-analysis of imaging studies on the self. *NeuroImage, 31,* 440–457.

Norton, K. I., Olds, T. S., Olive, S., & Dank, S. (1996). Ken and Barbie at life size. *Sex Roles, 34,* 287–294.

Nosek, B. A., Banaji, M. R., & Greenwald, A. G. (2002). Harvesting implicit attitudes and stereotype data from the Implicit Association Test website. *Group Dynamics, 6,* 101–115.

Nowak, M. A., & Sigmund, K. (2005). Evolution of indirect reciprocity. *Nature, 437,* 1291–1298.

O'Brien, L. T., & Crandall, C. S. (2003). Stereotype threat and arousal: Effects on women's math performance. *Personality and Social Psychology Bulletin, 29,* 782–789.

O'Connor, S. C., & Rosenblood, L. K. (1996). Affiliation motivation in everyday experience: A theoretical comparison. *Journal of Personality and Social Psychology, 70,* 513–522.

Oddone-Paolucci, E., Genuis, M., & Violato, C. (2000). A metaanalysis of the published research on the effects of pornography. In C. Violato & E. Oddone-Paolucci (Eds.), *The changing family and child development* (pp. 48–59). Aldershot, England: Ashgate.

Oetzel, J., Garcia, A. J., & Ting-Toomey, S. (2008). An analysis of the relationships among face concerns and facework behaviors in perceived conflict situations: A four-culture investigation. *International Journal of Conflict Management, 19*, 382–403.

Ogilvy, D. (1985). *Ogilvy on advertising.* New York: Vintage Books.

Ogloff, J. R. P., & Vidmar, N. (1994). The impact of pretrial publicity on jurors: A study to compare the relative effects of television and print media in a child sex abuse case. *Law and Human Behavior, 18*, 507–525.

O'Gorman, R., Sheldon, K. M., & Wilson, D. S. (2008). For the good of the group? Exploring group-level evolutionary adaptations using multilevel selection theory. *Group Dynamics: Theory, Research, and Practice, 12*, 17–26.

Olczak, P. V., Kaplan, M. F., & Penrod, S. (1991). Attorneys' lay psychology and its effectiveness in selecting jurors: Three empirical studies. *Journal of Social Behavior and Personality, 6*, 431–452.

O'Leary, A., & Wolitski, R. J. (2009). Moral agency and the sexual transmission of HIV. *Psychological Bulletin, 135*(3): 478–494.

O'Leary, K. D., Barling, J., Arias, I., Rosenbaum, A., Malone, J., & Tyree, A. (1989). Prevalence and stability of physical aggression between spouses: A longitudinal analysis. *Journal of Consulting and Clinical Psychology, 57*, 263–268.

O'Leary, K. D., & Smith, D. A. (1991). Marital interaction. *Annual Review of Psychology, 42*, 191–212.

O'Leary-Kelly, A. M., Bowes-Sperry, L., Bates, C. A., & Lean, E. R. (2009). Sexual harassment at work: A decade (plus) of progress. *Journal of Management, 35*, 503–536.

Oleson, E., (2009, July 9). A defibrillator in every building; Pappases want devices for public. *Telegram & Gazette* (Worcester, MA), p. 3.

Oliver, M. G., & Hyde, J. S. (1993). Gender differences in sexuality: A meta-analysis. *Psychological Bulletin, 114*, 29–51.

Olson, J. M., Vernon, P. A., Harris, J. A., & Jang, K. L. (2001). The heritability of attitudes: A study of twins. *Journal of Personality and Social Psychology, 80*, 845–860.

Olson, M. A., & Fazio, R. H. (2001). Implicit attitude formation through classical conditioning. *Psychological Science, 12*, 413–417.

Olson, M. A., & Fazio, R. H. (2004). Reducing the influence of extrapersonal associations on the Implicit Association Test: Personalizing the IAT. *Journal of Personality and Social Psychology, 86*, 653–667.

Olson, M. A., & Fazio, R. H. (2006). Reducing automatically activated racial prejudice through implicit evaluative conditioning. *Personality and Social Psychology Bulletin, 32*, 421–433.

Olweus, D. (2004). The Olweus Bullying Prevention Programme: Design and implementation issues and a new national initiative in Norway. In P. K. Smith, D. Pepler, & K. Rigby (Eds.), *Bullying in schools: How successful can interventions be?* (pp. 13–36). New York: Cambridge University Press.

Omarzu, J. (2000). A disclosure decision model: Determining how and when individuals will self-disclose. *Personality and Social Psychology Review, 4*, 174–185.

Omoto, A. M., Malsch, A. M., & Barraza, J. A. (2009). Compassionate acts: Motivations for and correlates of volunteerism among older adults. In B. Fehr, S. Sprecher, & L. G. Underwood (Eds.), *The science of compassionate love: Theory, research, and applications.* Malden, MA: Wiley-Blackwell.

Omoto, A. M., & Snyder, M. (1995). Sustained helping without obligation: Motivation, longevity of service, and perceived attitude change among AIDS volunteers. *Journal of Personality and Social Psychology, 68*, 671–686.

O'Neil, K. M., Patry, M. W., & Penrod, S. D. (2004). Exploring the effects of attitudes toward the death penalty on capital sentencing verdicts. *Psychology, Public Policy, and Law, 10*, 443–470.

O'Neill, A. M., Green, M., & Cuadros, P. (1996, September 2). *People*, 72.

Ones, D. S., Viswesvaran, C., & Schmidt, F. L. (1993). Comprehensive meta-analysis of integrity test validities: Findings and implications for personnel selection and theories of job performance. *Journal of Applied Psychology, 78*, 679–703.

Ore, T. E. (2000). *The social construction of difference and inequality: Race, gender, and sexuality.* Mountain View, CA: Mayfield.

Orenstein, P. (1994). *Schoolgirls: Young women, self-esteem, and the confidence gap.* New York: Anchor Books.

Orobio de Castro, B., Veerman, J. W., Koops, W., Bosch, J. D., & Monshouwer, H. J. (2002). Hostile attribution of intent and aggressive behavior: A meta-analysis. *Child Development, 73*, 916–934.

Orwell, G. (1942). Looking back on the Spanish War. In S. Orwell & I. Angus (Eds.), *The collected essays, journalism and letters of George Orwell: Vol. 2. My country right or left, 1940–1943* (pp. 249–267). New York: Harcourt, Brace & World.

Osborn, A. F. (1953). *Applied imagination.* New York: Scribner.

Osgood, C. E. (1962). *An alternative to war or surrender.* Urbana: University of Illinois Press.

Oshri, I., van Fenema, P., & Kotlarsky, J. (2008). Knowledge transfer in globally distributed teams: The role of transactive memory. *Information Systems Journal, 18*, 593–616.

Oxley, D. R., Smith, K., Alford, J., Hibbing, M., Miller, J., Scalora, M., Hatemi, P., & Hibbing, J. (2008). Political attitudes vary with physiological traits. *Science, 321*, 667–1670.

Oxley, N. L., Dzindolet, M. T., & Paulus, P. B. (1996). The effects of facilitators on the performance of brainstorming groups. *Journal of Social Behavior and Personality, 11*, 633–646.

Oyserman, D., & Lee, S. W. (2008). Does culture influence what and how we think? Effects of priming individualism and collectivism. *Psychological Bulletin, 134*, 311–342.

Oyserman, D., Coon, H. M., & Kemmelmeier, M. (2002). Rethinking individualism and collectivism: Evaluation of theoretical assumptions and meta-analyses. *Psychological Bulletin, 128*, 3–72.

Ozer, E. J., Best, S. R., Lipsey, T. L., & Weiss, D. S. (2003). Predictors of posttraumatic stress disorder and symptoms in adults: A meta-analysis. *Psychological Bulletin, 129*, 52–71.

Özgen, E. (2004). Language, learning, and color perception. *Current Directions in Psychological Science, 13*, 95–98.

Packer, D. J. (2008). Identifying systematic disobedience in Milgram's obedience experiments. *Perspectives on Psychological Science, 3*, 301–304.

Pagani, L., Tremblay, R. E., Nagin, D., Zoccolillo, M., Vitaro, F., & McDuff, P. (2009). Risk factor models for adolescent verbal and physical aggression toward fathers. *Journal of Family Violence, 24*, 173–182.

Page-Gould, E., Mendoza-Denton, R., & Tropp, L. R. (2008). With a little help from my cross-group friend: Reducing anxiety in intergroup contexts through cross-group friendship. *Journal of Personality and Social Psychology, 95*, 1080–1094.

Pager, D., & Shepherd, H. (2008). The sociology of discrimination: Racial discrimination in employment, housing, credit, and consumer markets. *Annual Review of Sociology, 34*, 181–209.

Paik, H., & Comstock, G. (1994). The effects of television violence on antisocial behavior: A meta-analysis. *Communication Research, 21*, 516–546.

Palazzolo, E. T., Serb, D. A., & She, Y. (2006). Coevolution of communication and knowledge networks in transactive memory systems: Using computational models for theoretical development. *Communication Theory, 16*, 223–250.

Paluck, E. L. (2009). Reducing intergroup prejudice and conflict using the media: A field experiment in Rwanda. *Journal of Personality and Social Psychology, 96*, 574–587.

Panee, C. D., & Ballard, M. E. (2002). High versus low aggressive priming during video-game training: Effects on violent action during game play, hostility, heart rate, and blood pressure. *Journal of Applied Social Psychology, 32*, 2458–2474.

Parducci, A. (1995). *Happiness, pleasure, and judgment: The contextual theory and its applications.* Mahwah, NJ: Erlbaum.

Park, B. (1986). A method for studying the development of impressions of real people. *Journal of Personality and Social Psychology, 51,* 907–917.

Park, L. E., & Maner, J. K. (2009). Does self-threat promote social connection? The role of self-esteem and contingencies of self-worth. *Journal of Personality and Social Psychology, 96,* 203–217.

Park, S., & Catrambone, R. (2007). Social facilitation effects of virtual humans. *Human Factors, 49,* 1054–1060.

Park, S. Y., Yun, G. W., McSweeney, J. H., & Gunther, A. C. (2007). Do third-person perceptions of media influence contribute to pluralistic ignorance on the norm of ideal female thinness? *Sex Roles, 57,* 569–578.

Parker, C. P., Baltes, B. B., & Christiansen, N. D. (1997). Support for affirmative action, justice perceptions, and work attitudes: A study of gender and racial-ethnic group differences. *Journal of Applied Psychology, 82,* 376–389.

Parkinson, S. (1994). Scientific or ethical quality? *Psychological Science, 5,* 137–138.

Parsons, H. M. (1974). What happened at Hawthorne? *Science, 183,* 922–932.

Parsons, C. A., Sulaeman, J., Yates, M. C., & Hamermesh, D. S. (2009). *Strike three: Discrimination, incentives, and evaluation.* University of North Carolina.

Partridge, A., & Eldridge, W. B. (1974). *The second circuit sentencing study: A report to the judges of the second circuit.* Washington, DC: Federal Judicial Center.

Pascoe, E. A., & Smart Richman, L. (2009). Perceived discrimination and health: A meta-analytic review. *Psychological Bulletin, 135,* 531–554.

Patzer, G. L. (2006). *The power and paradox of physical attractiveness.* Boca Raton, FL: Brown Walker Press.

Pauker, K., Weisbuch, M., Ambady, N., Sommers, S. R., Adams, R. B., Jr., & Ivcevic, Z. (2009). Not so black and white: Memory for ambiguous group members. *Journal of Personality and Social Psychology, 96,* 795–810.

Paulhus, D. L. (1998). Interpersonal and intrapsychic adaptiveness of trait self-enhancement: A mixed blessing? *Journal of Personality and Social Psychology, 74,* 1197–1208.

Paulhus, D., Graf, P., & Van Selst, M. (1989). Attentional load increases the positivity of self-presentation. *Social Cognition, 7,* 389–400.

Paulus, P. B. (1988). *Prison crowding: A psychological perspective.* New York: Springer-Verlag.

Paulus, P. B., & Brown, V. R. (2007). Toward more creative and innovative group idea generation: A cognitive-social-motivational perspective of brainstorming. *Social and Personality Psychology Compass, 1,* 248–265.

Paulus, P. B., Nakui, T., Putman, V. L., & Brown, V. (2006). Effects of task instructions and brief breaks on brainstorming. *Group Dynamics: Theory, Research, and Practice, 10,* 206–219.

Pavitt, C. (1994). Another view of group polarizing: The "reasons for" one-sided oral argumentation. *Communication Research, 21,* 625–642.

Pavot, W., & Diener, E. (1993). Review of the Satisfaction with Life Scale. *Psychological Assessment, 5,* 164–172.

Pawlowski, B., Dunbar, R. I. M., & Lipowicz, A. (2000). Evolutionary fitness: Tall men have more reproductive success. *Nature, 403,* 156.

Payne, B. K. (2006). Weapon bias: Split-second decisions and unintended stereotyping. *Current Directions in Psychological Science, 15,* 287–291.

Payne, B. K., Cheng, C. M., Govorun, O., & Stewart, B. D. (2005). An inkblot for attitudes: Affect misattribution as implicit measurement. *Journal of Personality and Social Psychology, 89,* 277–293.

Pedersen, W. C., Bushman, B. J., Vasquez, E. A., & Miller, N. (2008). Kicking the (barking) dog effect: The moderating role of target attributes on triggered displaced aggression. *Personality and Social Psychology Bulletin, 34,* 1382–1395.

Pedersen, W. C., Miller, L. C., Putch-Bhagavatula, A. D., & Yang, Y. (2002). Evolved sex differences in the number of partners desired? The long and the short of it. *Psychological Science, 13,* 157–161.

Pelham, B. W. (1995). Self-investment and self-esteem: Evidence for a Jamesian model of self-worth. *Journal of Personality and Social Psychology, 69,* 1141–1150.

Pelham, B. W., & Swann, W. B., Jr. (1989). From self-conceptions to self-worth: The sources and structure of self-esteem. *Journal of Personality and Social Psychology, 57,* 672–680.

Pelham, B. W., Carvallo, M., & Jones, J. T. (2005). Implicit egotism. *Current Directions in Psychological Science, 14,* 106–110.

Pelham, B. W., Mirenberg, M. C., & Jones, J. T. (2002). Why Susie sells seashells by the seashore: Implicit egotism and major life decisions. *Journal of Personality and Social Psychology, 82,* 469–487.

Peltokorpi, V. (2008). Transactive memory systems. *Review of General Psychology, 12,* 378–394.

Peng, K., & Nisbett, R. E. (1999). Culture, dialectics, and reasoning about contradiction. *American Psychologist, 54,* 741–754.

Pennebaker, J. W. (1997). Writing about emotional experiences as a therapeutic process. *Psychological Science, 8,* 162–166.

Pennebaker, J. W., Dyer, M. A., Caulkins, R. J., Litowitz, D. L., Ackreman, P. L., Anderson, D. B., & McGraw, K. M. (1979). Don't the girls get prettier at closing time: A country and western application to psychology. *Personality and Social Psychology Bulletin, 5,* 122–125.

Penner, L. A. (2004). Volunteerism and social problems: Making things better or worse? *Journal of Social Issues, 60,* 645–666.

Penner, L. A., Dovidio, J. F., Piliavin, J. A., & Schroeder, D. A. (2005). Prosocial behavior: Multiple perspectives. *Annual Review of Psychology, 56,* 365–392.

Pennington, N., & Hastie, R. (1992). Explaining the evidence: Tests of the story model for juror decision making. *Journal of Personality and Social Psychology, 62,* 189–206.

Penrod, S. D., & Cutler, B. (1995). Witness confidence and witness accuracy: Assessing their forensic relation. *Psychology, Public Policy, and Law, 1,* 817–845.

People. (1996, December 30). She gave a helping hand to a distant— very distant—relation. p. 66.

Peplau, L. A. (2003). Human sexuality: How do men and women differ? *Current Directions in Psychological Science, 12,* 37–40.

Peplau, L. A., & Fingerhut, A. W. (2007). The close relationships of lesbians and gay men. *Annual Review of Psychology, 58,* 405–424.

Peplau, L. A., & Perlman, D. (Eds.). (1982). *Loneliness: A sourcebook of current theory, research, and therapy.* New York: Wiley.

Peplau, L. A., Garnets, L. D., Spalding, L. R., Conley, T. D., & Veniegas, R. C. (1998). A critique of Bem's "Exotic becomes erotic" theory of sexual orientation. *Psychological Review, 105,* 387–394.

Pepler, D. J., Craig, W. M., Connolly, J. A., Yuile, A., McMaster, L., & Jiang, D. (2006). A developmental perspective on bullying. *Aggressive Behavior, 32,* 376–384.

Pepler, D., Craig, W., Yuile, A., & Connolly, J. (2004). Girls who bully: A developmental and relational perspective. In M. Putallaz & K. L. Bierman (Eds.), *Aggression, antisocial behavior, and violence among girls: A developmental perspective* (pp. 90–109). New York: Guilford.

Persky, V. W., Kempthorne-Rawson, J., & Shekelle, R. B. (1987). Personality and risk of cancer: 20-year follow-up of the Western Electric Study. *Psychosomatic Medicine, 49,* 435–449.

Peruche, B. M., & Plant, E. A. (2006). The correlates of law enforcement officers' automatic and controlled race-based responses to criminal suspects. *Basic and Applied Social Psychology, 28,* 193–199.

Peters, T. J., & Waterman, R. H. (1982). *In search of excellence: Lessons from America's best-run companies.* New York: Warner.

Peterson, C. (2000). The future of optimism. *American Psychologist, 55,* 44–55.

Peterson, K. S. (1997, November 3). For today's teens, race "not an issue anymore." *USA Today,* p. 1A.

Peterson, R. S., Owens, P. D., Tetlock, P. E., Fan, E. T., & Martorana, P. (1998). Group dynamics in top management teams: Groupthink, vigilance, and alternative models of organizational failure and success. *Organizational Behavior and Human Decision Processes, 73,* 272–305.

Petrie, K. J., Booth, R. J., & Pennebaker, J. W. (1998). The immunological effects of thought suppression. *Journal of Personality and Social Psychology, 75,* 1264–1272.

Pettigrew, T. F., & Tropp, L. R. (2000). Does intergroup contact reduce prejudice: Recent meta-analytic findings. In S. Oskamp (Ed.), *Reducing prejudice and discrimination: The Claremont Symposium on Applied Social Psychology* (pp. 93–114). Mahwah, NJ: Erlbaum.

Pettigrew, T. F., & Tropp, L. R. (2006). A meta-analytic test of intergroup contact theory. *Journal of Personality and Social Psychology, 90,* 751–783.

Pettigrew, T. F., & Tropp, L. R. (2008). How does intergroup contact reduce prejudice? Meta-analytic tests of three mediators. *European Journal of Social Psychology, 38,* 922–934.

Pettigrew, T. F., Christ, O., Wagner, U., van Dick, R., Zick, A., & Meertens, R. W. (2008). Relative deprivation and intergroup prejudice. *Journal of Social Issues, 64,* 385–401.

Petty, R. E., & Cacioppo, J. T. (1983). The role of bodily responses in attitude measurement and change. In J. Cacioppo & R. Petty (Eds.), *Social psychophysiology: A sourcebook* (pp. 51–101). New York: Guilford.

Petty, R. E., & Cacioppo, J. T. (1984). The effects of involvement on response to argument quantity and quality: Central and peripheral routes to persuasion. *Journal of Personality and Social Psychology, 46,* 69–81.

Petty, R. E., & Cacioppo, J. T. (1986). *Communication and persuasion: Central and peripheral routes to attitude change.* New York: Springer-Verlag.

Petty, R. E., & Fazio, R. H., & Brinol, P. (Eds.). (2009). *Attitudes: Insights from the new implicit measures.* New York: Psychology Press.

Petty, R. E., & Krosnick, J. A. (Eds.). (1995). *Attitude strength: Antecedents and consequences.* Mahwah, NJ: Erlbaum.

Petty, R. E., & Wegener, D. T. (1998). Attitude change: Multiple roles for persuasion variables. In D. Gilbert, S. Fiske, & G. Lindzey (Eds.), *The handbook of social psychology* (4th ed., pp. 323–390). New York: McGraw-Hill.

Petty, R. E., Cacioppo, J. T., & Goldman, R. (1981). Personal involvement as a determinant of argument-based persuasion. *Journal of Personality and Social Psychology, 41,* 847–855.

Petty, R. E., Schumann, D. W., Richman, S. A., & Strathman, A. J. (1993). Positive mood and persuasion: Different roles for affect under high- and low-elaboration conditions. *Journal of Personality and Social Psychology, 64,* 5–20.

Petty, R. E., Wegener, D. T., & Fabrigar, L. R. (1997). Attitudes and attitude change. *Annual Review of Psychology, 48,* 609–647.

Petty, R. E., Wegener, D. T., & White, P. (1998). Flexible correction processes in persuasion. *Social Cognition, 16,* 93–113.

Pew Research Center for People & the Press. (2009). Trends in political values and core attitudes: 1987–2009. Retrieved on June 16, 2009, from http://people-press.org/report/?reportid=312.

Pfau, M., Kenski, H. C., Nitz, M., & Sorenson, J. (1990). Efficacy of inoculation strategies in promoting resistance to political attack messages: Application to direct mail. *Communication Monographs, 57,* 25–43.

Phelan, J. E., Moss-Racusin, C. A., & Rudman, L. A. (2008). Competent yet out in the cold: Shifting criteria for hiring reflect backlash toward agentic women. *Psychology of Women Quarterly, 32,* 406–413.

Phelps, E. A., O'Connor, K. J., Cunningham, W. A., Funayama, E. S., Gatenby, J. C., Gore, J. C., & Banaji, M. R. (2000). Performance on indirect measures of race evaluation predicts amygdala activation. *Journal of Cognitive Neuroscience, 12,* 729–738.

Philippot, P. (2005). Stereotyping and action tendencies attribution as a function of available emotional information. *European Journal of Social Psychology, 35,* 517–536.

Phillips, A. G., & Silvia, P. J. (2005). Self-awareness and the emotional consequences of self-discrepancies. *Personality and Social Psychology Bulletin, 31,* 703–713.

Phillips, A. P., & Dipboye, R. L. (1989). Correlational tests of predictions from a process model of the interview. *Journal of Applied Psychology, 74,* 41–52.

Pickel, K. L. (1999). The influence of context on the "weapon focus" effect. *Law and Human Behavior, 23,* 299–311.

Piferi, R. L., Jobe, R. L., Jones, W. H., & Gaines, S. O., Jr. (2006). Giving to others during national tragedy: The effects of altruistic and egoistic motivations on long-term giving. *Journal of Social and Personal Relationships, 23,* 171–184.

Pihl, R. O., Lau, M. L., & Assaad, J. M. (1997). Aggressive disposition, alcohol, and aggression. *Aggressive Behavior, 23,* 11–18.

Piliavin, J. A. (2003). Doing well by doing good: Benefits for the benefactor. In C. L. M. Keyes & J. Haidt (Eds.), *Flourishing: Positive psychology and the life well-lived* (pp. 227–247). Washington, DC: American Psychological Association.

Piliavin, J. A., & Callero, P. L. (1991). *Giving blood: The development of an altruistic identity.* Baltimore: Johns Hopkins.

Piliavin, J. A., Dovidio, J. F., Gaertner, S. L., & Clark, R. D., III. (1981). *Emergency intervention.* New York: Academic Press.

Piliavin, J. A., Grube, J. A., & Callero, P. L. (2002). Role as a resource for action in public service. *Journal of Social Issues, 58,* 469–485.

Piliavin, J. A., & Siegl, E. (2008). Health benefits of volunteering in the Wisconsin Longitudinal Study. *Journal of Health and Social Behavior, 48,* 450–464.

Pillemer, D. B., Picariello, M. L., Law, A. B., & Reichman, J. S. (1996). Memories of college: The importance of educational episodes. In D. C. Rubin (Ed.), *Remembering our past: Studies in autobiographical memory* (pp. 318–337). New York: Cambridge University Press.

Pinderhughes, E. E., Dodge, K. A., Bates, J. E., Pettit, G. S., & Zelli, A. (2000). Discipline responses: Influences of parents' socioeconomic status, ethnicity, beliefs about parenting, stress, and cognitive-emotional processes. *Journal of Family Psychology, 14,* 380–400.

Pinel, E. C., Long, A. E., Landau, M. J., Alexander, K., & Pyszczynski, T. (2006). Seeing I to I: A pathway to interpersonal connectedness. *Journal of Personality and Social Psychology, 90,* 243–257.

Pittman, T. S. (1975). Attribution of arousal as a mediator of dissonance reduction. *Journal of Experimental Social Psychology, 11,* 53–63.

Pittman, T. S., & Heller, J. F. (1987). Social motivation. *Annual Review of Psychology, 38,* 461–489.

Plaks, J. E., & Higgins, E. T. (2000). Pragmatic use of stereotyping in teamwork: Social loafing and compensation as a function of inferred partner-situation fit. *Journal of Personality and Social Psychology, 79,* 962–974.

Plant, E. A., & Butz, D. A. (2006). The causes and consequences of an avoidance-focus for interracial interactions. *Personality and Social Psychology Bulletin, 32,* 833–846.

Plant, E. A., & Devine, P. G. (1998). Internal and external motivation to respond without prejudice. *Journal of Personality and Social Psychology, 75,* 811–832.

Plant, E. A., & Devine, P. G. (2009). The active control of prejudice: Unpacking the intentions guiding control efforts. *Journal of Personality and Social Psychology, 96,* 640–652.

Plant, E. A., Peruche, B. M., & Butz, D. A. (2005). Eliminating automatic racial bias: Making race non-diagnostic for responses to criminal suspects. *Journal of Experimental Social Psychology, 41,* 141–156.

Plante, T. G., & Thoresen, C. E. (Eds.). (2007). *Spirit, science, and health: How the spiritual mind fuels physical wellness.* Westport, CT: Praeger.

Platek, S. M., Wathne, K., Tierney, N. G., & Thomson, J. W. (2008). Neural correlates of self-face recognition: An effect-location meta-analysis. *Brain Research, 1232,* 173–184.

Platow, M. J., Byrne, L., & Ryan, M. K. (2005). Experimentally manipulated high in-group status can buffer personal self-esteem against discrimination. *European Journal of Social Psychology, 35,* 599–608.

Platz, S. J., & Hosch, H. M. (1988). Cross-racial/ethnic eyewitness identification: A field study. *Journal of Applied Social Psychology, 18,* 972–984.

Plaut, V. C., Thomas, K. M., & Goren, M. J. (2009). Is multiculturalism or color blindness better for minorities? *Psychological Science, 20,* 444–446.

Plotnik, J. M., de Waal, F. B. M., & Reiss, D. (2006). Self-recognition in an Asian elephant. *Proceedings of the National Academy of Sciences, 103,* 17053–17057.

Polivy, J., Garner, D. M., & Garfinkel, P. E. (1986). Causes and consequences of the current preference for thin female physiques. In C. P. Herman, M. P. Zanna, & E. T. Higgins (Eds.), *The Ontario symposium: Vol. 3. Physical appearance, stigma, and social behavior* (pp. 89–112). Hillsdale, NJ: Erlbaum.

Polman, H., de Castro, B. O., & van Aken, M. A. G. (2008). Experimental study of the differential effects of playing versus watching violent video games on children's aggressive behavior. *Aggressive Behavior, 34,* 256–264.

Pontari, B. A., & Schlenker, B. R. (2000). The influence of cognitive load on self-presentation: Can cognitive busyness help as well as harm social performance? *Journal of Personality and Social Psychology, 78,* 1092–1108.

Poole, D. A., & White, L. T. (1991). Effects of question repetition on the eyewitness testimony of children and adults. *Developmental Psychology, 27,* 975–986.

Poole, D., & Lindsay, D. S. (2001). Children's eyewitness reports after exposure to misinformation from parents. *Journal of Experimental Psychology: Applied, 7,* 27–50.

Poppen, P. J., & Segal, N. J. (1988). The influence of sex and sex role orientation on sexual coercion. *Sex Roles, 19,* 689–701.

Pornpitakpan, C. (2004). The persuasiveness of source credibility: A critical review of five decades' evidence. *Journal of Applied Social Psychology, 34,* 243–281.

Porter, D. P., & Smith, V. L. (2003). Stock market bubbles in the laboratory. *Journal of Behavioral Finance, 4,* 7–20.

Posavac, H. D., Posavac, S. S., & Posavac, E. J. (1998). Exposure to media images of female attractiveness and concern with body weight among young women. *Sex Roles, 38,* 187–201.

Post, S. G. (2005). Altruism, happiness, and health: It's good to be good. *International Journal of Behavioral Medicine, 12,* 66–77.

Postmes, T., & Jetten, J. (Eds.). (2006). *Individuality and the group: Advances in social identity.* London: Sage.

Postmes, T., Spears, R., & Cihangir, S. (2001). Quality of decision making and group norms. *Journal of Personality and Social Psychology, 80,* 918–930.

Povinelli, D. J., Gallup, G. G., Jr., Eddy, T. J., Bierschwale, D. T., Engstrom, M. C., Perilloux, H. K., & Toxopeus, I. B. (1997). Chimpanzees recognize themselves in mirrors. *Animal Behaviour, 53,* 1083–1088.

Powell, L. H., Shahabi, L., & Thoresen, C. E. (2003). Religion and spirituality: Linkages to physical health. *American Psychologist, 58,* 36–52.

Powers, S. I., Pietromonaco, P. R., Gunlicks, M., & Sayer, A. (2006). Dating couples' attachment styles and patterns of cortisol reactivity and recovery in response to a relationship conflict. *Journal of Personality and Social Psychology, 90,* 613–628.

Pratkanis, A. R. (1992). The cargo-cult science of subliminal persuasion. *Skeptical Inquirer, 16,* 260–272.

Pratkanis, A. R., & Turner, M. E. (1994). Nine principles of successful affirmative action: Mr. Branch Rickey, Mr. Jackie Robinson, and the integration of baseball. *Nine: A Journal of Baseball History and Social Policy Perspectives, 3,* 36–65.

Pratkanis, A. R., & Turner, M. E. (1996). The proactive removal of discriminatory barriers: Affirmative action as effective help. *Journal of Social Issues, 52,* 111–132.

Pratkanis, A. R., Greenwald, A. G., Leippe, M. R., & Baumgardner, M. H. (1988). In search of reliable persuasion effects: III. The sleeper effect is dead. Long live the sleeper effect. *Journal of Personality and Social Psychology, 54,* 203–218.

Pratto, F., & John, O. P. (1991). Automatic vigilance: The attention-grabbing power of negative social information. *Journal of Personality and Social Psychology, 61,* 380–391.

Pratto, F., Stallworth, L. M., Sidanius, J., & Sieres, B. (1997). The gender gap in occupational attainment: A social dominance approach. *Journal of Personality and Social Psychology, 72,* 37–53.

Prentice, D. A., & Carranza, E. (2002). What women should be, shouldn't be, are allowed to be, and don't have to be: The contents of prescriptive gender stereotypes. *Psychology of Women Quarterly, 26,* 269–281.

Prentice, D. A., & Miller, D. T. (1996). Pluralistic ignorance and the perpetuation of social norms by unwitting actors. *Advances in Experimental Social Psychology, 28,* 161–209.

Prentice, D., A. & Miller, D. T. (2003). Pluralistic ignorance and alcohol use on campus: Some consequences of misperceiving the social norm. In P. Salovey & A. J. Rothman (Eds.), *Social psychology of health* (pp. 183–198). NY: Psychology Press.

Prentice-Dunn, S., & Rogers, R. W. (1982). Effects of public and private self-awareness on deindividuation and aggression. *Journal of Personality and Social Psychology, 43,* 503–513.

Prentice-Dunn, S., & Rogers, R. W. (1983). Deindividuation in aggression. In R. G. Geen & E. I. Donnerstein (Eds.), *Aggression: Theoretical and empirical reviews: Vol. 2. Issues in research* (pp. 155–171). New York: Academic Press.

Presidential Commission on the Space Shuttle Challenger Accident. (1986). *Report of the Presidential Commission on the Space Shuttle Challenger Accident.* Washington, DC: U.S. Government Printing Office.

Pressman, S. D., Cohen, S., Miller, G. E., Barkin, A., Rabin, B. S., & Treanor, J. J. (2005). Loneliness, social network size, and immune response to influenza vaccination in college freshmen. *Health Psychology, 24,* 297–306.

Price, M. E. (2008). The resurrection of group selection as a theory of human cooperation. *Social Justice Research, 21,* 228–240.

Prichard, J. S., & Ashleigh, M. J. (2007). The effects of team-skills training on transactive memory and performance. *Small Group Research, 38,* 696–726.

Priester, J. R., & Petty, R. E. (1995). Source attributions and persuasion: Perceived honesty as a determinant of message scrutiny. *Personality and Social Psychology Bulletin, 21,* 637–654.

Priester, J. R., Cacioppo, J. T., & Petty, R. E. (1996). The influence of motor processes on attitudes toward novel versus familiar semantic stimuli. *Personality and Social Psychology Bulletin, 22,* 442–447.

Principe, G. F., & Ceci, S. J. (2002). "I saw it with my own ears": The effects of peer conversations on preschoolers' reports of nonexperienced events. *Journal of Experimental Child Psychology, 83,* 1–25.

Principe, G. F., Ornstein, P. A., Baker-Ward, L., & Gordon, B. N. (2000). The effects of intervening experiences on children's memory for a physical examination. *Applied Cognitive Psychology 14,* 59–80.

Prioleau, L., Murdock, M., & Brody, N. (1983). An analysis of psychotherapy versus placebo studies. *Behavioral and Brain Sciences, 6,* 275–310.

Prokosch, M., Coss, R., Scheib, J., & Blozis, S. (2009). Intelligence and mate choice: Intelligent men are always appealing. *Evolution and Human Behavior, 30,* 11–20.

Pronin, E., Berger, J., & Molouki, S. (2007). Alone in a crowd of sheep: Asymmetric perceptions of conformity and their roots in an introspection illusion. *Journal of Personality and Social Psychology, 92,* 585–595.

Pronin, E., Gilovich, T., & Ross, L. (2004). Objectivity in the eye of the beholder: Divergent perceptions of bias in self versus others. *Psychological Review, 111,* 781–799.

Pronin, E., Wegner, D. M., McCarthy, K., & Rodriguez, S. (2006). Everyday magical powers: The role of apparent mental causation in the overestimation of personal influence. *Journal of Personality and Social Psychology, 91,* 218–231.

Proto-Campise, L., Belknap, J., & Wooldredge, J. (1998). High school students' adherence to rape myths and the effectiveness of high school rape-awareness programs. *Violence Against Women, 4,* 308–328.

Pruitt, D. G. (1998). Social conflict. In D. T. Gilbert, S. T. Fiske, & G. Lindzey (Eds.), *The handbook of social psychology* (4th ed., Vol. 2, pp. 410–503). New York: McGraw-Hill.

Pryor, J. B., & Merluzzi, T. V. (1985). The role of expertise in processing social interaction scripts. *Journal of Experimental Social Psychology, 21,* 362–379.

Pumphrey-Gordon, J. E., & Gross, A. M. (2007). Alcohol consumption and females' recognition in response to date rape risk: The role of sex-related alcohol expectancies. *Journal of Family Violence, 22,* 475–485.

Purdie-Vaughns, V., Steele, C. M., Davies, P. G., Ditlmann, R., & Crosby, J. R. (2008). Social identity contingencies: How diversity cues signal threat or safety for African Americans in mainstream institutions. *Journal of Personality and Social Psychology, 94,* 615–630.

Putnam, R. D. (2001). *Bowling alone: The collapse and revival of American community.* New York: Simon & Schuster.

Putnam, R. D. (2006, July 3). You gotta have friends. *Time,* 36.

Pyszczynski, T. A., Solomon, S., & Greenberg, J. (2002). *In the wake of 9/11: The psychology of terror.* Washington, DC: American Psychological Association.

Pyszczynski, T., & Greenberg, J. (1987). Self-regulatory preservation and the depressive self-focusing style: A self-awareness theory of reactive depression. *Psychological Bulletin, 201,* 122–138.

Pyszczynski, T., & Greenberg, J. (1992). *Hanging on and letting go.* New York: Springer-Verlag.

Pyszczynski, T., Greenberg, J., Solomon, S., Arndt, J., & Schimel, J. (2004). Why do people need self-esteem? A theoretical and empirical review. *Psychological Bulletin, 130,* 435–468.

Qualter, T. H. (1962). *Propaganda and psychological warfare.* New York: Random House.

Quattrone, G. A. (1986). On the perception of a group's variability. In S. Worchel & W. G. Austin (Eds.), *Psychology of intergroup relations* (2nd ed., pp. 25–48). Chicago: Nelson Hall.

Quigley, B. M., & Leonard, K. E. (2006). Alcohol expectancies and intoxicated aggression. *Aggression and Violent Behavior, 11,* 484–496.

Quinn, D. M., Kahng, S. K., & Crocker, J. (2004). Discreditable: Stigma effects of revealing a mental illness history on test performance. *Personality and Social Psychology Bulletin, 30,* 803–815.

Raaijmakers, M. A. J., Smidts, D. P., Sergeant, J. A., Maassen, G. H., Posthumus, J. A., van Engeland, H., et al. (2008). Executive functions in preschool children with aggressive behavior: Impairments in inhibitory control. *Journal of Abnormal Child Psychology, 36,* 1097–1107.

Rabinowitz, J. L., Sears, D. O., Sidanius, J., & Krosnik, J. A. (2009). Why do white Americans oppose race-targeted policies? Clarifying the impact of symbolic racism. *Political Psychology, 30,* 805–828.

Ragins, B. R., & Sundstrom, E. (1989). Gender and power in organizations: A longitudinal perspective. *Psychological Bulletin, 105,* 51–88.

Raine, A. (2008). From genes to brain to antisocial behavior. *Current Directions in Psychological Science, 17,* 323–328.

Rains, S. A. (2005). Leveling the organizational playing field—virtually: A meta-analysis of experimental research assessing the impact of group support system use on member influence behaviors. *Communication Research, 32,* 193–234.

Rajecki, D. W., Bledsoe, S. B., & Rasmussen, J. L. (1991). Successful personal ads: Gender differences and similarities in offers, stipulations, and outcomes. *Basic and Applied Social Psychology, 12,* 457–469.

Ramírez-Esparza, N., Gosling, S. D., & Pennebaker, J. W. (2008). Paradox lost: Unraveling the puzzle of Simpatía. *Journal of Cross-Cultural Psychology, 39,* 703–715.

Ramírez-Esparza, N., Mehl, M., Álvarez-Bermúdez, J., & Pennebaker, J. W. (2009). Are Mexicans more or less sociable than Americans? Insights from a naturalistic observation study. *Journal of Research in Personality, 43,* 1–7.

Raskin, D. C. (1986). The polygraph in 1986: Scientific, professional, and legal issues surrounding application and acceptance of polygraph evidence. *Utah Law Review, 1,* 29–74.

Ray, D. G., Mackie, D. M., Rydell, R. J., & Smith, E. R. (2008). Changing categorization of self can change emotions about outgroups. *Journal of Experimental Social Psychology, 44,* 1210–1213.

Ray, O. (2004). How the mind hurts and heals the body. *American Psychologist, 59,* 29–40.

Read, S. J. (1987). Constructing causal scenarios: A knowledge structure approach to causal reasoning. *Journal of Personality and Social Psychology, 52,* 288–302.

Read, S. J., & Urada, D. I. (2003). A neural network simulation of the outgroup homogeneity effect. *Personality and Social Psychology Review, 7,* 146–159.

Reeder, G. D. (1993). Trait-behavior relations and dispositional inference. *Personality and Social Psychology Bulletin, 19,* 586–593.

Reeder, G. D., & Brewer, M. B. (1979). A schematic model of dispositional attribution in interpersonal perception. *Psychological Review, 86,* 61–79.

Reeder, G. D., Davison, D. M., Gipson, K. L., & Hesson-McInnis, M. S. (2001). Identifying the motivations of African American volunteers working to prevent HIV/AIDS. *AIDS Education and Prevention, 13,* 343–354.

Regan, D. T. (1971). Effects of a favor and liking on compliance. *Journal of Experimental Social Psychology, 7,* 627–639.

Regan, D. T., & Kilduff, M. (1988). Optimism about elections: Dissonance reduction at the ballot box. *Political Psychology, 9,* 101–107.

Regan, P. C. (2008). *The mating game: A primer on love, sex, and marriage.* Thousand Oaks, CA: Sage Publications.

Regan, P. C., & Berscheid, E. (1997). Gender differences in characteristics desired in a potential sexual and marriage partner. *Journal of Psychology and Human Sexuality, 9,* 25–37.

Regan, P. C., & Berscheid, E. (1999). *Lust: What we know about human sexual desire.* Thousand Oaks, CA: Sage.

Regan, P. C., Kocan, E. R., & Whitlock, T. (1998). Ain't love grand! A prototype analysis of the concept of romantic love. *Journal of Social and Personal Relationships, 15,* 411–420.

Reicher, S. D., & Haslam, S. A. (2006). Rethinking the psychology of tyranny: The BBC prison study. *British Journal of Social Psychology, 45,* 1–40.

Reifman, A. S., Larrick, R. P., & Fein, S. (1991). Temper and temperature on the diamond: The heat-aggression relationship in major-league baseball. *Personality and Social Psychology Bulletin, 17,* 580–585.

Reifman, A., Klein, J. G., & Murphy, S. T. (1989). Self-monitoring and age. *Psychology and Aging, 4,* 245–246.

Reinhard, M.-A., Messner, M., & Sporer, S. L. (2006). Explicit persuasive intent and its impact on success at persuasion: The determining roles of attractiveness and likeableness. *Journal of Consumer Psychology, 16,* 249–259.

Reisenzein, R. (1983). The Schachter theory of emotion: Two decades later. *Psychological Bulletin, 94,* 239–264.

Reiss, D., & Marino, L. (2001). Mirror self-recognition in the bottlenose dolphin: A case of cognitive convergence. *Proceedings of the National Academy of the Sciences, 98,* 5937–5942.

Remley, A. (1988, October). The great parental value shift: From obedience to independence. *Psychology Today,* 56–59.

Rendell, L., & Whitehead, H. (2001). Culture in whales and dolphins. *Behavioral and Brain Sciences, 24,* 309–382.

Renfrew, J. W. (1997). *Aggression and its causes: A biopsychosocial approach.* New York: Oxford University Press.

Renteln, A. D. (2004). *The cultural defense.* New York: Oxford University Press.

Responsible citizenship. (2002, December 31). *Ottawa Citizen*, p. A14.

Reysen, S., & Ganz, E. (2006). Gender differences in helping in six U.S. cities. *North American Journal of Psychology, 8*, 63–67.

Rhatigan, D. L., & Axsom, D. K. (2006). Using the investment model to understand battered women's commitment to abusive relationships. *Journal of Family Violence, 21*, 153–162.

Rhee, E., Uleman, J. S., Lee, H. K., & Roman, R. J. (1995). Spontaneous self-descriptions and ethnic identities in individualistic and collectivistic cultures. *Journal of Personality and Social Psychology, 69*, 142–152.

Rhodes, G. (2006). The evolutionary psychology of facial beauty. *Annual Review of Psychology, 57*, 199–226.

Rhodes, G., Simmons, L. W., & Peters, M. (2005). Attractiveness and sexual behavior: Does attractiveness enhance mating success? *Evolution and Human Behavior, 26*, 186–201.

Rhodes, G., Sumich, A., & Byatt, G. (1999). Are average facial configurations attractive only because of their symmetry? *Psychological Science, 10*, 52–58.

Rhodes, G., Zebrowitz, L. A., Clark, A., Kalick, S. M., Hightower, A., & McKay, R. (2001). Do facial averageness and symmetry signal health? *Evolution and Human Behavior, 22*, 31–46.

Rhodes, N., & Wood, W. (1992). Self-esteem and intelligence affect influenceability: The mediating role of message reception. *Psychological Bulletin, 111*, 156–171.

Rhodewalt, F. (1990). Self-handicappers: Individual differences in the preference for anticipatory, self-protective acts. In R. L. Higgins, C. R. Synder, & S. Berglas (Eds.), *Self-handicapping: The paradox that isn't* (pp. 69–106). New York: Plenum.

Rhodewalt, F., & Agustsdottir, S. (1986). Effects of self-presentation on the phenomenal self. *Journal of Personality and Social Psychology, 50*, 47–55.

Rhodewalt, F., Sandonmatsu, D. M., Tschanz, B., Feick, D. L., & Waller, A. (1995). Self-handicapping and interpersonal tradeoffs: The effects of claimed self-handicaps on observers' performance evaluations and feedback. *Personality and Social Psychology Bulletin, 21*, 1042–1050.

Rholes, W. S., & Simpson, J. A. (Eds.). (2004). *Adult attachment: Theory, research, and clinical implications*. New York: Guilford.

Ricciardelli, L. A., McCabe, M. P., & Banfield, S. (2000). Sociocultural influences on body image and body change methods. *Journal of Adolescent Health, 26*, 3–4.

Richardson, M. J., Marsh, K. L., & Schmidt, R. C. (2005). Effects of visual and verbal interaction on unintentional interpersonal coordination. *Journal of Experimental Psychology: Human Perception and Performance, 31*, 62–79.

Richeson, J. A., & Shelton, J. N. (2010). Prejudice and bias in intergroup interactions. In J. F. Dovidio, M. Hewstone, P. Glick, & V. M. Esses (Eds.), *Handbook of prejudice, stereotyping, and discrimination*. London: Sage.

Richeson, J. A., & Trawalter, S. (2005). Why do interracial interactions impair executive function? A resource depletion account. *Journal of Personality and Social Psychology, 88*, 934–947.

Richeson, J. A., & Trawalter, S. (2008). The threat of appearing prejudiced and race-based attentional biases. *Psychological Science, 19*, 98–102.

Richeson, J. A., Todd, A. R., Trawalter, S., & Baird, A. A. (2008). Eye-gaze direction modulates race-related amygdala activity. *Group Processes & Intergroup Relations, 11*, 233–246.

Rieger, G., Chivers, M. L., & Bailey, J. M. (2005). Sexual arousal patterns of bisexual men. *Psychological Science, 16*, 579–584.

Rieger, G., Linsenmeier, J. A. W., Gygax, L., & Bailey, J. M. (2008). Sexual orientation and childhood gender nonconformity: Evidence from home videos. *Developmental Psychology, 44*, 46–58.

Rilling, J. K., Goldsmith, D. R., Glenn, A. L., Jairam, M. R., Elfenbein, H. A., Dagenais, J. E., Murdock, C. D., & Pagnoni, G. (2008). The neural correlates of the affective response to unreciprocated cooperation. *Neuropsychologia, 46*, 1256–1266.

Rilling, J. K., Gutman, D. A., Zeh, T. R., Pagnoni, G., Berns, G. S., & Kilts, C. D. (2002). A neural basis for social cooperation. *Neuron, 35*, 395–405.

Rimal, R. N., & Real, K. (2005). Assessing the perceived importance of skin cancer: How question-order effects are influenced by issue involvement. *Health Education & Behavior, 32*, 398–412.

Rind, B., & Strohmetz, D. B. (2001). Effect on restaurant tipping of a helpful message written on the back of customers' checks. *Journal of Applied Social Psychology, 31*, 1379–1384.

Ringelmann, M. (1913). Recherches sur les moteurs animés: Travail de l'homme. *Annales de l'Institut National Agronomique*, 2e série, tom XII, 1–40.

Riniolo, T. C., Johnson, K. C., Sherman, T. R., & Misso, J. A. (2006). Hot or not: Do professors perceived as physically attractive receive higher student evaluations? *Journal of General Psychology, 133*, 19–35.

Risen, J. L., Gilovich, T., & Dunning, D. (2007). One-shot illusory correlations and stereotype formation. *Personality and Social Psychology Bulletin, 33*, 1492–1502.

Roach, M. (2008). *Bonk: The curious coupling of science and sex*. New York: Norton.

Roane, K. R. (2000, February 28). Boston's big-bucks highway to hell. *U.S. News and World Report*, p. 34.

Robins, R. W., Mendelsohn, G. A., Connell, J. B., & Kwan, V. S. Y. (2004). Do people agree about the causes of behavior? A social relations analysis of behavior ratings and causal attributions. *Journal of Personality and Social Psychology, 86*, 334–344.

Robinson, J. P., Shaver, P. R., & Wrightsman, L. S. (Eds.). (1991). *Measures of personality and social psychological attitudes*. New York: Academic Press.

Robinson, J. P., Shaver, P. R., & Wrightsman, L. S. (Eds.). (1998). *Measures of political attitudes*. New York: Academic Press.

Rockloff, M. J., & Dyer, V. (2007). An experiment on the social facilitation of gambling behavior. *Journal of Gambling Studies, 23*, 1–12.

Rodin, J. (1986). Aging and health: Effects of the sense of control. *Science, 233*, 1271–1276.

Rodkin, P. C., Farmer, T. W., Pearl, R., & van Acker, R. (2000). Heterogeneity of popular boys: Antisocial and prosocial configurations. *Developmental Psychology, 36*, 14–24.

Rodrigues, A., Assmar, E. M. L., & Jablonski, B. (2005). Social-psychology and the invasion of Iraq. *Revista de Psicologia Social, 20*, 387–398.

Rodriguez Mosquera, P. M., Fischer, A. H., & Manstead, A. S. R. (2004). Inside the heart of emotion. On culture and relational concerns. In L. Z. Tiedens & C. W. Leach (Eds.), *The social life of emotions* (pp. 187–202). Cambridge, UK: Cambridge University Press.

Rodriguez Mosquera, P. M.., Fischer, A. H., Manstead, A. S. R., & Zaalberg, R. (2008). Attack, disapproval, or withdrawal? The role of honour in anger and shame responses to being insulted. *Cognition & Emotion, 22*, 1471–1498.

Roese, N. J. (1997). Counterfactual thinking. *Psychological Bulletin, 121*, 133–148.

Roese, N. J., & Jamieson, D. W. (1993). Twenty years of bogus pipeline research: A critical review and meta-analysis. *Psychological Bulletin, 114*, 363–375.

Roese, N. J., & Olson, J. M. (Eds.). (1995). *What might have been: The social psychology of counterfactual thinking*. Hillsdale, NJ: Erlbaum.

Roese, N. J., & Summerville, A. (2005). What we regret most . . . and why. *Personality and Social Psychology Bulletin, 31*, 1273–1285.

Roethlisberger, F. J., & Dickson, W. J. (1939). *Management and the worker*. Cambridge, MA: Harvard University Press.

Rofé, Y. (1984). Stress and affiliation: A utility theory. *Psychological Review, 91*, 235–250.

Rogers, M., Miller, N., Mayer, F. S., & Duval, S. (1982). Personal responsibility and salience of the request for help: Determinants of the relation between negative affect and helping behavior. *Journal of Personality and Social Psychology, 43*, 956–970.

Rogers, R. W. (1983). Cognitive and psychological processes in fear appeals and attitude change: A revised theory of protection motivation. In J. Cacioppo & R. Petty (Eds.), *Social psychophysiology: A sourcebook* (pp. 153–176). New York: Guilford.

Rogers, R. W., & Mewborn, R. C. (1976). Fear appeals and attitude change: Effects of a threat's noxiousness, probability of occurrence, and the efficacy of coping responses. *Journal of Personality and Social Psychology, 34*, 54–61.

Rohrer, J. H., Baron, S. H., Hoffman, E. L., & Swander, D. V. (1954). The stability of autokinetic judgments. *Journal of Abnormal and Social Psychology, 49*, 595–597.

Roig-Franzia, M. (2009, May 26). Credit crisis Cassandra; Brooksley Born's unheeded warning is a rueful echo 10 years on. *Washington Post*, p. C01.

Ronquillo, J., Denson, T., Lickel, B., Nandy, A., Maddox, K., & Lu, Z. (2007). The effects of skin tone on race-related amygdala activity: An fMRI investigation. *Social Cognitive and Affective Neuroscience, 2*, 39–44.

Ronzone, R. (2009, April 2). Video games not just children's play. *The Villanovan*.

Rook, K. S. (1984). The negative side of social interaction: Impact on psychological well-being. *Journal of Personality and Social Psychology, 46*, 1097–1108.

Rook, K. S. (1987). Reciprocity of social exchange and social satisfaction among older women. *Journal of Personality and Social Psychology, 52*, 145–154.

Rook, K. S., & Peplau, L. A. (1982). Perspectives on helping the lonely. In L. A. Peplau & D. Perlman (Eds.), *Loneliness: A sourcebook of current theory, research and therapy* (pp. 351–378). New York: Wiley.

Rose, V. G., & Ogloff, J. R. P. (2001). Evaluating the comprehensibility of jury instructions: A method and an example. *Law and Human Behavior, 25*, 409–431.

Rosenbaum, M. E. (1986). The repulsion hypothesis: On the nondevelopment of relationships. *Journal of Personality and Social Psychology, 51*, 1156–1166.

Rosenberg, S., Nelson, C., & Vivekananthan, P. S. (1968). A multidimensional approach to the structure of personality impressions. *Journal of Personality and Social Psychology, 9*, 283–294.

Rosenbloom, T., Shahr, A., Perlman, A., Estreich, D., & Kirzner, E. (2007). Success on a practical driver's license test with and without the presence of another testee. *Accident Analysis and Prevention, 39*, 1296–1301.

Rosenkoetter, L. I., Rosenkoetter, S. E., & Acock, A. C. (2009). Television violence: An intervention to reduce its impact on children. *Journal of Applied Developmental Psychology, 30*, 381–397.

Rosener, J. B. (1995). *America's competitive secret: Utilizing women as a management strategy.* New York: Oxford University Press.

Rosenman, R. H., Brand, R. J., Jenkins, C. D., Friedman, M., Strau, R., & Wurm, M. (1975). Coronary heart disease in the Western Collaborative Group Study: Final follow-up experience of 8 1/2 years. *Journal of the American Medical Association, 233*, 872–877.

Rosenthal, E. (2006, June 2). Genital cutting raises by 50% likelihood mothers or their newborns will die, study finds. *New York Times*, p. A10.

Rosenthal, H. E. S., & Crisp, R. J. (2006). Reducing stereotype threat by blurring intergroup boundaries. *Personality and Social Psychology Bulletin, 32*, 501–511.

Rosenthal, R. (1976). *Experimenter effects in behavioral research.* New York: Irvington.

Rosenthal, R. (1985). From unconscious experimenter bias to teacher expectancy effects. In J. B. Dusek, V. C. Hall, & W. J. Meyer (Eds.), *Teacher expectancies* (pp. 37–65). Hillsdale, NJ: Erlbaum.

Rosenthal, R. (2002). Covert communication in classrooms, clinics, courtrooms, and cubicles. *American Psychologist, 57*, 839–849.

Rosenthal, R., & Jacobson, L. (1968). *Pygmalion in the classroom: Teacher expectation and pupils' intellectual development.* New York: Holt, Rinehart and Winston.

Rosnow, R. L., & Rosenthal, R. (1993). *Beginning behavioral research: A conceptual primer.* New York: Macmillan.

Ross, A. J., Davies, J. B., & Clarke, P. (2004). Attributing to positive and negative sporting outcomes: A structural analysis. *Athletic Insight: The Online Journal of Sport Psychology, 6*, 19–37.

Ross, E. A. (1908). *Social psychology: An outline and source book.* New York: Macmillan.

Ross, J., & Staw, B. M. (1986). Expo 86: An escalation prototype. *Administrative Science Quarterly, 31*, 274–297.

Ross, L., Bierbrauer, G., & Hoffman, S. (1976). The role of attribution processes in conformity and dissent. *American Psychologist, 31*, 148–157.

Ross, L., Greene, D., & House, P. (1977). The false consensus phenomenon: An attributional bias in self-perception and social-perception processes. *Journal of Experimental Social Psychology, 13*, 279–301.

Ross, M., & Sicoly, F. (1979). Egocentric biases in availability and attribution. *Journal of Personality and Social Psychology, 37*, 322–336.

Rosse, J. G., Miller, J. L., & Stecher, M. D. (1994). A field study of job applicants' reactions to personality and cognitive ability testing. *Journal of Applied Psychology, 79*, 987–992.

Roth, P. L., Huffcutt, A. I., & Bobko, P. (2003). Ethnic group differences in measures of job performance: A new metaanalysis. *Journal of Applied Psychology, 88*, 694–706.

Rothbaum, F., & Tsang, B. Y. (1998). Lovesongs in the United States and China: On the nature of romantic love. *Journal of Cross-Cultural Psychology, 29*, 306–319.

Rothman, D. J., & Rothman, S. M. (2006). *Trust is not enough: Bringing human rights to medicine.* New York: New York Review Books.

Rowatt, W. C., Cunningham, M. R., & Druen, P. B. (1999). Lying to get a date: The effect of facial physical attractiveness on the willingness to deceive prospective dating partners. *Journal of Social and Personal Relationships, 16*, 209–223.

Rowe, R., Rijsdijk, F. V., Maughan, B., Hosang, G. M., & Eley, T. C. (2008). Heterogeneity in antisocial behaviours and comorbidity with depressed mood: A behavioural genetic approach. *Journal of Child Psychology and Psychiatry, 49*, 526–534.

Roxborough, S. (2009, March 19). German retailer pulls violent DVDs, games. *Reuters*. Retrieved August 30, 2009, from http://www.reuters.com/article/filmNews/idUSTRE52I7WC20090319.

Rozin, P., & Fallon, A. E. (1987). A perspective on disgust. *Psychological Review, 94*, 23–41.

Rozin, P., & Royzman, E. B. (2001). Negativity bias, negativity dominance, and contagion. *Personality and Social Psychology Review, 5*, 296–320.

Ruback, R. B., & Wroblewski, J. (2001). The federal sentencing guidelines: Psychological and policy reasons for simplification. *Psychology, Public Policy, and Law, 7*, 739–775.

Rubenowitz, S., Norrgren, F., & Tannenbaum, A. S. (1983). Some social psychological effects of direct and indirect participation in ten Swedish companies. *Organization Studies, 4*, 243–259.

Rubin, D. C. (Ed.). (1996). *Remembering our past: Studies in autobiographical memory.* New York: Cambridge University Press.

Rubin, J. Z., Provenzano, F. J., & Luria, Z. (1974). The eye of the beholder: Parents' views on sex of newborns. *American Journal of Orthopsychiatry, 44*, 512–519.

Rubin, J. Z., Pruitt, D. G., & Kim, S. H. (1994). *Social conflict: Escalation, stalemate, and settlement.* New York: McGraw-Hill.

Rubin, Z. (1973). *Liking and loving.* New York: Holt, Rinehart and Winston.

Ruble, D. N., & Martin, C. L. (1998). Gender development. In W. Damon & N. Eisenberg (Eds.), *Handbook of child psychology, 5th edition: Volume 3: Social, emotional, and personality development* (pp. 933–1016). Hoboken, NJ: Wiley.

Rubonis, A. V., & Bickman, L. (1991). Psychological impairment in the wake of disaster: The disaster-psychopathology relationship. *Psychological Bulletin, 109*, 384–399.

Rudman, L. A., & Borgida, E. (1995). The afterglow of construct accessibility: The behavioral consequences of priming men to view women as sexual objects. *Journal of Experimental Social Psychology, 31*, 493–517.

Rudman, L. A., & Glick, P. (2001). Prescriptive gender stereotypes and backlash toward agentic women. *Journal of Social Issues, 57*, 743–762.

Ruffle, B. J., & Sosis, R. (2006). Cooperation and the in-group-out-group bias: A field test on Israeli kibbutz members and city residents. *Journal of Economic Behavior and Organization, 60,* 147–163.

Rule, B. G., Taylor, B. R., & Dobbs, A. R. (1987). Priming effects of heat on aggressive thoughts. *Social Cognition, 5,* 131–143.

Rule, N. O., & Ambady, N. (2008). The face of success: Inferences from chief executive officers' appearance predict company profits. *Psychological Science, 19,* 109–111.

Rusbult, C. E., & Buunk, B. P. (1993). Commitment processes in close relationships: An interdependence analysis. *Journal of Social and Personal Relationships, 10,* 175–204.

Rusbult, C. E., Martz, J. M., & Agnew, C. R. (1998). The investment model scale: Measuring commitment level, satisfaction level, quality of alternatives, and investment size. *Personal Relationships, 5,* 357–391.

Rushton, J. P. (1981a). Television as a socializer. In J. P. Rushton & R. M. Sorrentino (Eds.), *Altruism and helping behavior: Social, personality, and developmental perspectives* (pp. 91–108). Hillsdale, NJ: Erlbaum.

Rushton, J. P. (1981b). The altruistic personality. In J. P. Rushton & R. M. Sorrentino (Eds.), *Altruism and helping behavior: Social, personality, and developmental perspectives* (pp. 251–266). Hillsdale, NJ: Erlbaum.

Russano, M. B., Meissner, C. A., Narchet, F. M., & Kassin, S. M. (2005). Investigating true and false confessions within a novel experimental paradigm. *Psychological Science, 16,* 481–486.

Russell, G. W., Arms, R. L., & Bibby, R. W. (1995). Canadians' belief in catharsis. *Social Behavior and Personality, 23,* 223–228.

Russell, J. A. (1994). Is there universal recognition of emotion from facial expression? A review of cross-cultural studies. *Psychological Bulletin, 115,* 102–141.

Rutchick, A. M., Hamilton, D. L., & Sack, J. D. (2008). Antecedents of entitativity in categorically and dynamically construed groups. *Journal of Social Psychology, 38,* 905–921.

Rutkowski, G. K., Gruder, C. L., & Romer, D. (1983). Group cohesiveness, social norms, and bystander intervention. *Journal of Personality and Social Psychology, 44,* 545–552.

Ryan, C. S., & Bogart, L. M. (1997). Development of new group members' ingroup and outgroup stereotypes: Changes in perceived group variability and ethnocentrism. *Journal of Personality and Social Psychology, 73,* 719–732.

Rydell, R. J., McConnell, A. R., & Beilock, S. L. (2009). Multiple social identities and stereotype threat: Imbalance, accessibility, and working memory. *Journal of Personality and Social Psychology, 96,* 949–966.

Rynes, S. L., & Connerly, M. L. (1993). Applicant reactions to alternative selection procedures. *Journal of Business and Psychology, 4,* 261–277.

Sackett, P. R., Borneman, M. J., & Connelly, B. S. (2008). High-stakes testing in higher education and employment: Appraising the evidence for validity and fairness. *American Psychologist, 63,* 215–227.

Sackett, P. R., & DuBois, C. L. Z. (1991). Rater-ratee race effects on performance evaluation: Challenging meta-analytic conclusions. *Journal of Applied Psychology, 76,* 873–877.

Sackett, P. R., & Leivens, F. (2008). Personnel selection. *Annual Review of Psychology, 59,* 419–450.

Sackett, P. R., Burris, L. R., & Callahan, C. (1989). Integrity testing for personnel selection: An update. *Personnel Psychology, 42,* 491–525.

Sacks, O. (1985). *The man who mistook his wife for a hat.* New York: Summit.

Sagar, H. A., & Schofield, J. W. (1980). Racial and behavioral cues in black and white children's perceptions of ambiguously aggressive acts. *Journal of Personality and Social Psychology, 39,* 590–598.

Sagarin, B. J. (2005). Reconsidering evolved sex differences in jealousy: Comment on Harris (2003). *Personality and Social Psychology Review, 9,* 62–75.

Saks, M. J. (1974). Ignorance of science is no excuse. *Trial, 10,* 18–20.

Saks, M. J., & Marti, M. W. (1997). A meta-analysis of the effects of jury size. *Law and Human Behavior, 21,* 451–468.

Salas, E., Nichols, D. R., & Driskell, J. E. (2007). Testing three team training strategies in intact teams: A meta-analysis. *Small Group Research, 38,* 471–488.

Saleton, W. (2009, April 15). Sex reversal. *Slate Magazine.*

Salgado, J. F. (1997). The five factor model of personality and job performance in the European community. *Journal of Applied Psychology, 82,* 30–43.

Salomon, K. & Jagusztyn, N. E. (2008). Cardiovascular reactivity to an interpersonal conflict is moderated by reports of ethnic discrimination. *Health Psychology, 27,* 473–481.

Salovey, P. (1992). Mood-induced focus of attention. *Journal of Personality and Social Psychology, 62,* 699–707.

Salovey, P., Mayer, J. D., & Rosenhan, D. L. (1991). Mood and helping: Mood as a motivator of helping and helping as a regulator of mood. In M. S. Clark (Ed.), *Prosocial behavior* (Vol. 12, pp. 215–237). Newbury Park, CA: Sage.

Salvemini, N. J., Reilly, R. R., & Smither, J. W. (1993). The influence of rater motivation on assimilation effects and accuracy in performance ratings. *Organizational Behavior and Human Decision Processes, 55,* 41–60.

Sampson, E. E. (2000). Reinterpreting individualism and collectivism: Their religious roots and monologic versus dialogic person-other relationship. *American Psychologist, 55,* 1425–1432.

Samuels, T., & Goldsmith, S. (2009, March 1). He saves drunk from train death; Heroic PATH guard grabs man with seconds to spare. *New York Daily News,* p. 6.

Sanchez, J. I., & De La Torre, P. (1996). A second look at the relationship between rating and behavioral accuracy in performance appraisal. *Journal of Applied Psychology, 81,* 3–10.

Sanchez-Burks, J., Nisbett, R. E., & Ybarra, O. (2000). Relational schemas, cultural styles, and prejudice against outgroups. *Journal of Personality and Social Psychology, 79,* 174–189.

Sanders, G. S. (1981). Driven by distraction: An integrative review of social facilitation theory and research. *Journal of Experimental Social Psychology, 17,* 227–251.

Sanders, S. A., & Reinisch, J. M. (1999). Would you say you "had sex" if . . . ? *Journal of the American Medical Association, 281,* 275–277.

Sanderson, C. A., & Evans, S. M. (2001). Seeing one's partner through intimacy-colored glasses: An examination of the processes underlying the intimacy goals-relationship satisfaction link. *Personality and Social Psychology Bulletin, 27,* 463–473.

Sands, D. R. (2009, February 5). SEC "overmatched"; Madoff whistleblower blasts regulators as inept. *Washington Times,* p. A14.

Santalahti, P., Sourander, A., Aromaa, M., Helenius, H., Ikäheimo, K., & Piha, J. (2008). Victimization and bullying among 8-year-old Finnish children: A 10-year comparison of rates. *European Child and Adolescent Psychiatry, 17,* 463–472.

Santos, M. D., Leve, C., & Pratkanis, A. R. (1994). Hey buddy, can you spare seventeen cents? Mindful persuasion and the pique technique. *Journal of Applied Social Psychology, 24,* 755–764.

Sapolsky, R. M. (1994). *Why zebras don't get ulcers: A guide to stress, diseases, and coping.* New York: Freeman.

Sapolsky, R. M. (2004). *Why zebras don't get ulcers* (3rd ed.). New York: Owl Books.

Sarason, I. G., Sarason, B. R., Pierce, G. R., Shearin, E. N., & Sayers, M. H. (1991). A social learning approach to increasing blood donations. *Journal of Applied Social Psychology, 21,* 896–918.

Sarat, A. (Ed.). (2005). *Dissent in dangerous times.* Ann Arbor: University of Michigan Press.

Sargent, M. J., & Bradfield, A. L. (2004). Race and information processing in criminal trials: Does the defendant's race affect how the facts are evaluated? *Personality and Social Psychology Bulletin, 30,* 995–1008.

Sarkar, U., Ali, S., & Whooley, M. A. (2009). Self-efficacy as a marker of cardiac function and predictor of heart failure hospitalization and mortality in patients with stable coronary heart disease: Findings from the Heart and Soul Study. *Health Psychology, 28,* 166–173.

Sarnoff, I., & Zimbardo, P. (1961). Anxiety, fear, and social affiliation. *Journal of Abnormal and Social Psychology, 62,* 356–363.

Saucier, D. A., Miller, C. T., & Doucet, N. (2005). Differences in helping whites and blacks: A meta-analysis. *Personality and Social Psychology Review, 9,* 2–16.

Saulny, S. (2002, December 8). Why confess to what you didn't do? *New York Times,* Section 4.

Savin, H. B. (1973). Professors and psychological researchers: Conflicting values in conflicting roles. *Cognition, 2,* 147–149.

Savitsky, K., Epley, N., & Gilovich, T. (2001). Do others judge us as harshly as we think? Overestimating the impact of our failures, shortcomings, and mishaps. *Journal of Personality and Social Psychology, 81,* 44–56.

Savitsky, K., Gilovich, T., Berger, G., & Medvec, V. H. (2003). Is our absence as conspicuous as we think? Overestimating the salience and impact of one's absence from a group. *Journal of Experimental Social Psychology, 39,* 386–392.

Sbarra, D. A., & Nietert, P. J. (2009). Divorce and death: Forty years of the Charleston Heart Study. *Psychological Science, 20,* 107–113.

Schachter, S. (1951). Deviation, rejection, and communication. *Journal of Abnormal and Social Psychology, 46,* 190–207.

Schachter, S. (1959). *The psychology of affiliation: Experimental studies of the sources of gregariousness.* Stanford, CA: Stanford University Press.

Schachter, S. (1964). The interaction of cognitive and physiological determinants of emotional state. In L. Berkowitz (Ed.), *Advances in experimental social psychology* (Vol. 1, pp. 49–80). New York: Academic Press.

Schachter, S., & Singer, J. (1962). Cognitive, social, and physiological determinants of the emotional state. *Psychological Review, 69,* 379–399.

Schachter, S., & Singer, J. (1979). Comments on the Maslach and Marshall-Zimbardo experiments. *Journal of Personality and Social Psychology, 37,* 989–995.

Schachter, S., Hood, D., Gerin, W., Andreasson, P. B., & Rennert, M. (1985). Some causes and consequences of dependence and independence in the stock market. *Journal of Economic Behavior and Organization, 6,* 339–357.

Schachter, S., Ouellette, R., Whittle, B., & Gerin, W. (1987). Effects of trends and of profit or loss on the tendency to sell stock. *Basic and Applied Social Psychology, 8,* 259–271.

Schafer, R. B., & Keith, P. M. (1981). Equity and marital roles across the family life cycle. *Journal of Marriage and the Family, 43,* 359–367.

Schaller, M., Park, J. H., & Faulkner, J. (2003). Prehistoric dangers and contemporary prejudices. *European Review of Social Psychology, 14,* 105–137.

Schaller, M., Simpson, J. A., & Kenrick, D. T. (Eds.). (2006). *Evolution and social psychology.* New York: Taylor & Francis.

Scharfe, E., & Bartholomew, K. (1994). Reliability and stability of adult attachment patterns. *Personal Relationships, 1,* 23–43.

Schechner, S. (2008, October 10). When your political opinion isn't yours alone: Broadcasts of political debates that include live audience feedback can influence what you're thinking—hecklers can too. *Wall Street Journal,* A14.

Scheck, B., Neufeld, P., & Dwyer, J. (2000). *Actual innocence: Five days to execution and other dispatches from the wrongly convicted.* New York: Doubleday.

Scheepers, D. (2009). Turning social identity threat into challenge: Status stability and cardiovascular reactivity during inter-group competition. *Journal of Experimental Social Psychology, 45,* 228–233.

Scheepers, D., & Ellemers, N. (2005). When the pressure is up: The assessment of social identity threat in low and high status groups. *Journal of Experimental Social Psychology, 41,* 192–200.

Scheepers, D., Spears, R., Doosje, B., & Manstead, A. S. R. (2006). The social functions of ingroup bias: Creating, confirming, or changing social reality. *European Review of Social Psychology, 17,* 359–396.

Scheier, M. F., & Carver, C. S. (1983). Two sides of the self: One for you and one for me. In J. Suls and A. G. Greenwald (Eds.), *Psychological perspectives on the self* (Vol. 2, pp. 123–157). Hillsdale, NJ: Erlbaum.

Scheier, M. F., & Carver, C. S. (1985). Optimism, coping, and health: Assessment and implications of generalized outcome expectancies. *Health Psychology, 4,* 219–247.

Scheier, M. F., & Carver, C. S. (1992). Effects of optimism on psychological and physical well-being: Theoretical overview and empirical update. *Cognitive Therapy and Research, 16,* 201–228.

Schel, A. M., Tranquilli, S., & Zuberbühler, K. (2009). The alarm call system of two species of black-and-white colobus monkeys (Colobus polykomos and Colobus guereza). *Journal of Comparative Psychology, 123,* 136–150.

Scher, S. J., & Cooper, J. (1989). Motivational basis of dissonance: The singular role of behavioral consequences. *Journal of Personality and Social Psychology, 56,* 899–906.

Schimel, J., Arndt, J., Pyszczynski, T., & Greenberg, J. (2001). Being accepted for who we are: Evidence that social validation of the intrinsic self reduces general defensiveness. *Journal of Personality and Social Psychology, 80,* 35–52.

Schimmack, U., Oishi, S., & Diener, E. (2005). Individualism: A valid and important dimension of cultural differences between nations. *Personality and Social Psychology Review, 9,* 17–31.

Schino, G. (2007). Grooming and agonistic support: A meta-analysis of primate reciprocal altruism. *Behavioral Ecology, 18,* 115–120.

Schlagman, S., Schulz, J., & Kvavilashvili, L. (2006). A content analysis of involuntary autobiographical memories: Examining the positivity effect in old age. *Memory, 14,* 161–175.

Schlauch, R. C., Lang, A. R., Plant, E. A., Christensen, R., & Donohue, K. F. (2009). Effect of alcohol on race-biased responding: The moderating role of internal and external motivations to respond without prejudice. *Journal of Studies on Alcohol and Drugs, 70,* 328–336.

Schlenger, W. E., et al. (2002). Psychological reactions to terrorist attacks: Findings from the National Study of Americans' Reactions to September 11. *Journal of the American Medical Association, 288,* 581–588.

Schlenker, B. R. (1982). Translating actions into attitudes: An identity-analytic approach to the explanation of social conduct. In L. Berkowitz (Ed.), *Advances in experimental social psychology* (Vol. 15, pp. 193–247). New York: Academic Press.

Schlenker, B. R. (2003). Self-presentation. In M. R. Leary & J. P. Tangney (Eds.), *Handbook of self and identity* (pp. 492–518). New York: Guilford.

Schlenker, B. R., & Trudeau, J. V. (1990). The impact of self-presentations on private self-beliefs: Effects of prior self-beliefs and misattribution. *Journal of Personality and Social Psychology, 58,* 22–32.

Schlenker, B. R., Weigold, M. F., & Hallam, J. R. (1990). Self-serving attributions in social context: Effects of self-esteem and social pressure. *Journal of Personality and Social Psychology, 58,* 855–863.

Schmader, T., & Johns, M. (2003). Converging evidence that stereotype threat reduces working memory capacity. *Journal of Personality and Social Psychology, 85,* 440–452.

Schmader, T., Johns, M., & Forbes, C. (2008). An integrated process model of stereotype threat effects on performance. *Psychological Review, 115,* 336–356.

Schmeichel, B. J., & Vohs, K. (2009). Self-affirmation and self-control: Affirming core values counteracts ego depletion. *Journal of Personality and Social Psychology, 96,* 770–782.

Schmeichel, B. J., Gailliot, M. T., Filardo, E.-A., McGregor, I., Gitter, S., & Baumeister, R. F. (2009). Terror management theory and self-esteem revisited: The roles of implicit and explicit self-esteem in mortality salience effects. *Journal of Personality and Social Psychology, 96,* 1077–1087.

Schmidt, F. L. (2002). The role of general cognitive ability and job performance: Why there cannot be a debate. *Human Performance, 15,* 187–210.

Schmidt, F. L., & Rader, M. (1999). Exploring the boundary conditions for interview validity: Meta-analytic validity findings for a new interview type. *Personnel Psychology, 52,* 445–464.

Schmitt, D. P. (2003). Universal sex differences in the desire for sexual variety: Tests from 52 nations, 6 continents, and 13 islands. *Journal of Personality and Social Psychology, 85,* 85–104.

Schmitt, M. T., & Maes, J. (2002). Stereotypic ingroup bias as self-defense against relative deprivation: Evidence from a longitudinal study of the German unification process. *European Journal of Social Psychology, 32,* 309–326.

Schmitt, M. T., Branscombe, N. R., Silvia, P. J., Garcia, D. M., & Spears, R. (2006). Categorizing at the group-level in response to intragroup social comparisons: A self-categorization theory integration of self-evaluation and social identity motives. *European Journal of Social Psychology, 36,* 297–314.

Schmitt, M. T., Branscrombe, N. R., Kobrynowicz, D., & Owen, S. (2002). Perceiving discrimination against one's gender group has different implications for well-being in women and men. *Personality and Social Psychology Bulletin, 28,* 197–210.

Schmitt, N., & Oswald, F. L. (2006). The impact of corrections for faking on the validity of noncognitive measures in selection settings. *Journal of Applied Psychology, 91,* 613–621.

Schneider, D. J. (1973). Implicit personality theory: A review. *Psychological Bulletin, 79,* 294–309.

Schneider, D. M., & Watkins, M. J. (1996). Response conformity in recognition testing. *Psychonomic Bulletin and Review, 3,* 481–485.

Schneider, M. E., Major, B., Luhtanen, R., & Crocker, J. (1996). Social stigma and the potential costs of assumptive help. *Personality and Social Psychology Bulletin, 22,* 201–209.

Schneider, S. G., Taylor, S. E., Hammen, C., Kemeny, M. E., & Dudley, J. (1991). Factors influencing suicide intent in gay and bisexual suicide ideators: Differing models for men with and without human immunodeficiency virus. *Journal of Personality and Social Psychology, 61,* 776–778.

Schneiderman, R. M. (2008, October 30). Do Americans still hate welfare? *New York Times.*

Schonert-Reichl, K. A. (1999). Relations of peer acceptance, friendship adjustment, and social behavior to moral reasoning during early adolescence. *Journal of Early Adolescence, 19,* 249–279.

Schooler, D. (2008). Real women have curves: A longitudinal investigation of TV and the body image development of Latina adolescents. *Journal of Adolescent Research, 23,* 132–153.

Schoorman, F. D. (1988). Escalation bias in performance appraisals: An unintended consequence of supervisor participation in hiring decisions. *Journal of Applied Psychology, 73,* 58–62.

Schulman, J., Shaver, P., Colman, R., Emrick, B., & Christie, R. (1973, May). Recipe for a jury. *Psychology Today,* pp. 37–44, 77, 79–84.

Schultz, B., Ketrow, S. M., & Urban, D. M. (1995). Improving decision quality in the small group: The role of the reminder. *Small Group Research, 26,* 521–541.

Schulz, R. (1976). Effects of control and predictability on the physical and psychological well-being of the institutionalized aged. *Journal of Personality and Social Psychology, 33,* 563–573.

Schuster, M. A., Stein, B. D., Jaycox, L. H., Collins, R. L., Marshall, G. N., Elliott, M. N., Zhou, A. J., Kanouse, D. E., Morrison, J. L., & Berry, S. H. (2001). A national survey of stress reactions after the September 11, 2001, terrorist attacks. *New England Journal of Medicine, 345,* 1507–1512.

Schützwohl, A. (2004). Which infidelity type makes you more jealous? Decision strategies in a forced-choice between sexual and emotional infidelity. *Evolutionary Psychology, 2,* 121–128.

Schwartz, S. H. (1990). Individualism-collectivism: Critique and proposed refinements. *Journal of Cross-Cultural Psychology, 21,* 139–157.

Schwartz, S. H., & Gottlieb, A. (1980). Bystander anonymity and reaction to emergencies. *Journal of Personality and Social Psychology, 39,* 418–430.

Schwartz, C. E., Wright, C. I., Shin, L. M., Kagan, J., & Rauch, S. L. (2003). Inhibited and uninhibited infants "grow up": Adult amygdalar response to novelty. *Science, 300,* 1952–1953.

Schwarz, N. (1990). Feelings as information: Information and motivational functions as affective states. In E. T. Higgins et al. (Eds.), *Handbook of motivation and cognition: Foundations of social behavior* (Vol. 2, pp. 527–561). New York: Guilford.

Schwarz, N. (1999). Self-reports: How the questions shape the answers. *American Psychologist, 54,* 93–105.

Schwarz, N. (2007). Cognitive aspects of survey methodology. *Applied Cognitive Psychology, 21,* 277–287.

Schwarz, N., & Oyserman, D. (2010). Asking questions about behavior: Self-reports in evaluation research. In M. Mark, S. Donaldson, & B. Campbell (Eds.), *Social psychology and program/policy evaluation.* New York: Guilford.

Schwarz, N., Bless, H., & Bohner, G. (1991). Mood and persuasion: Affective states influence the processing of persuasive communications. In M. P. Zanna (Ed.), *Advances in experimental social psychology* (Vol. 24, pp. 161–199). New York: Academic Press.

Schwarz, N., Oyserman, D., & Peytcheva, E. (2010). Cognition, communication, and culture: Implications for the survey response process. In J. Harkness et al. (Eds.), *Survey methods in multinational, multiregional and multicultural contexts.* New York: Wiley.

Schwarzwald, J., Raz, M., & Zvibel, M. (1979). The applicability of the door-in-the-face technique when established behavioral customs exist. *Journal of Applied Social Psychology, 9,* 576–586.

Scullen, S. E., Mount, M., & Goff, M. (2000). Understanding the latent structure of job performance ratings. *Journal of Applied Psychology, 85,* 956–970.

Seacat, J. D., & Mickelson, K. D. (2009). Stereotype threat and the exercise/dietary health intentions of overweight women. *Journal of Health Psychology, 14,* 556–567.

Sears, D. O., & Henry, P. J. (2005). Over thirty years later: A contemporary look at symbolic racism. In M. P. Zanna (Ed.), *Advances in experimental social psychology* (Vol. 37, pp. 95–150). San Diego: Elsevier.

Sedikides, C. (1992). Attentional effects on mood are moderated by chronic self-conception valence. *Personality and Social Psychology Bulletin, 18,* 580–584.

Sedikides, C. (1993). Assessment, enhancement, and verification determinants of the self-evaluation process. *Journal of Personality and Social Psychology, 65,* 317–338.

Sedikides, C., & Anderson, C. A. (1994). Causal perceptions of intertrait relations: The glue that holds person types together. *Personality and Social Psychology Bulletin, 20,* 294–302.

Sedikides, C., & Gregg, A. P. (2008). Self-enhancement: Food for thought. *Perspectives on Psychological Science, 3,* 102–116.

Sedikides, C., & Jackson, J. M. (1990). Social impact theory: A field test of source strength, source immediacy and number of targets. *Basic and Applied Social Psychology, 11,* 273–281.

Sedikides, C., & Spencer, S. J. (Eds.). (2007). *The self.* New York: Psychology Press.

Sedikides, C., Gaertner, L., & Toguchi, Y. (2003). Pancultural self-enhancement. *Journal of Personality and Social Psychology, 84,* 60–79.

Sedikides, C., Gaertner, L., & Vevea, J. L. (2005). Pancultural self-enhancement reloaded: A meta-analytic reply to Heine (2005). *Journal of Personality and Social Psychology, 89,* 539–551.

Seeman, T. E., Dubin, L. F., & Seeman, M. (2003). Religiosity/spirituality and health: A critical review of the evidence for biological pathways. *American Psychologist, 58,* 53–63.

Segerstrom, S. C. (2006a). *Breaking Murphy's law: How optimists get what they want from life and pessimists can too.* New York: Guilford Press.

Segerstrom, S. C. (2006b). How does optimism suppress immunity? Evaluation of three affective pathways. *Health Psychology, 25,* 653–657.

Segerstrom, S. C., & Miller, G. E. (2004). Psychological stress and the human immune system: A meta-analytic study of 30 years of inquiry. *Psychological Bulletin, 130,* 601–630.

Segerstrom, S. C., Taylor, S. E., Kemeny, M. E., & Fahey, J. L. (1998). Optimism is associated with mood, coping, and immune change in response to stress. *Journal of Personality and Social Psychology, 74,* 1646–1655.

Seguin, J. R., & Zelazo, P. D. (2005). Executive function in early physical aggression. In R. E. Tremblay, W. W. Hartup, & J. Archer (Eds.), *Developmental origins of aggression* (pp. 307–329). New York: Guilford.

Seib, C. (2009, March 16). Storm gathers as propped-up AIG plans to pay 'outrageous' bonuses. *London Times,* p. 38.

Seibert, S. E., & Goltz, S. M. (2001). Comparison of allocations by individuals and interacting groups in an escalation of commitment situation. *Journal of Applied Social Psychology, 31,* 134–156.

Seijts, G. H., & Latham, G. P. (2000). The effects of goal setting and group size on performance in a social dilemma. *Canadian Journal of Behavioural Science, 32,* 104–116.

Sekaquaptewa, D., & Thompson, M. (2003). Solo status, stereotype threat, and performance expectancies: Their effects on women's performance. *Journal of Experimental Social Psychology, 39,* 68–74.

Sekaquaptewa, D., Espinoza, P., Thompson, M., Vargas, P., & von Hippel, W. (2003). Stereotypic explanatory bias: Implicit stereotyping as a predictor of discrimination. *Journal of Experimental Social Psychology, 39,* 75–82.

Seligman, M. E. P. (1975). *On depression, development, and death.* San Francisco: Freeman.

Seligman, M. E. P. (1991). *Learned optimism.* New York: Knopf.

Sellers, R. M., & Shelton, J. N. (2003). The role of racial identity in perceived racial discrimination. *Journal of Personality and Social Psychology, 84,* 1079–1092.

Seltzer, R. (2006). Scientific jury selection: Does it work? *Journal of Applied Social Psychology, 36,* 2417–2435.

Selye, H. (1936). A syndrome produced by diverse nocuous agents. *Nature, 138,* 32.

Senju, A., & Johnson, M. (2009). The eye contact effect: Mechanisms and development. *Trends in Cognitive Sciences, 13,* 127–134.

Serbin, L. A., Poulin-Dubois, D., & Eichstedt, J. A. (2002). Infants' response to gender-inconsistent events. *Infancy, 3,* 531–542.

Sergeant, M. J. T., Dickins, T. E., Davies, M. N. O., & Griffiths, M. D. (2006). Aggression, empathy and sexual orientation in males. *Personality and Individual Differences, 40,* 475–486.

Seta, J. J., Seta, C. E., & McElroy, T. (2003). Attributional biases in the service of stereotype maintenance: A schema-maintenance through compensation analysis. *Personality and Social Psychology Bulletin, 29,* 151–163.

Seto, M. C., Marc, A., & Barbaree, H. E. (2001). The role of pornography in the etiology of sexual aggression. *Aggression and Violent Behavior, 6,* 35–53.

Seyfarth, R. M., & Cheney, D. L. (1984). Grooming, alliances and reciprocal altruism in vervet monkeys. *Nature, 308,* 541–543.

Seyle, D. C., & Newman, M. L. (2006). A house divided? The psychology of red and blue America. *American Psychologist, 61,* 571–580.

Shackelford, T. K. (2001). Cohabitation, marriage, and murder: Woman-killing by male romantic partners. *Aggressive Behavior, 27,* 284–291.

Shackelford, T. K., & Goetz, A. T. (2005). When we hurt the ones we love: Predicting violence against women from men's mate retention tactics. In S. M. Platek & T. K. Shackelford (Eds.), *Human paternal uncertainty and anti-cuckoldry tactics: How males deal with female infidelity.* Cambridge: Cambridge University Press.

Shackelford, T. K., & Larsen, R. J. (1999). Facial attractiveness and physical health. *Evolution and Human Behavior, 20,* 71–76.

Shackelford, T. K., Voracek, M., Schmitt, D. P., Buss, D. M., Weekes-Shackelford, V. A., & Michalski, R. L. (2004). Romantic jealousy in early adulthood and later life. *Human Nature, 15,* 283–300.

Shackelford, T. K., Weekes-Shackelford, V. A., & Schmitt, D. P. (2005). An evolutionary perspective on why some men refuse or reduce their child support payments. *Basic and Applied Social Psychology, 27,* 297–306.

Shanab, M. E., & Yahya, K. A. (1977). A behavioral study of obedience in children. *Journal of Personality and Social Psychology, 35,* 530–536.

Shanab, M. E., & Yahya, K. A. (1978). A cross cultural study of obedience. *Bulletin of the Psychonomic Society, 11,* 267–269.

Shapiro, P. N., & Penrod, S. (1986). Meta-analysis of facial identification studies. *Psychological Bulletin, 100,* 139–156.

Shaver, K. G. (1970). Defensive attribution: Effects of severity and relevance on the responsibility assigned for an accident. *Journal of Personality and Social Psychology, 14,* 101–113.

Shaw, J. S., III. (1996). Increases in eyewitness confidence resulting from postevent questioning. *Journal of Experimental Psychology: Applied, 2,* 126–146.

Shea, C. (1996, January 12). New students uncertain about racial preferences. *Chronicle of Higher Education,* p. A33.

Shefrin, H. (2006). *Greed and fear: Understanding behavioral finance and the psychology of investing.* New York: Oxford University Press.

Shefrin, H. M., & Statman, M. (1985). The disposition to sell winners too early and ride losers too long: theory and evidence. *Journal of Finance, 40,* 777–790.

Shefrin, H. M., & Statman, M. (1986, February). How not to make money in the stock market. *Psychology Today,* pp. 52–57.

Shelton, J. N., Dovidio, J. F., Hebl, M., & Richeson, J. A. (2009). Prejudice and intergroup interaction. In S. Demoulin, J. P. Leyens, & J. F. Dovidio (Eds.), *Intergroup misunderstandings: Impact of divergent social realities* (pp. 21–38). New York: Psychology Press.

Shelton, J. N., & Richeson, J. A. (2005). Intergroup contact and pluralistic ignorance. *Journal of Personality and Social Psychology, 88,* 91–107.

Shelton, J. N., & Richeson, J. A. (2007). Interracial interactions: A relational approach. In M. P. Zanna (Ed.), *Advances in experimental social psychology.* San Diego: Elsevier.

Shepela, S. T., Cook, J., Horlitz, E., Leal, R., Luciano, S., Lutfy, E., Miller, C., Mitchell, G., & Worden, E. (1999). Courageous resistance: A special case of altruism. *Theory and Psychology, 9,* 787–805.

Sheppard, B. H. (1985). Justice is no simple matter: Case for elaborating our model of procedural fairness. *Journal of Personality and Social Psychology, 49,* 953–962.

Shepperd, J. A. (1993a). Productivity loss in performance groups: A motivation analysis. *Psychological Bulletin, 113,* 67–81.

Shepperd, J. A. (1993b). Student derogation of the Scholastic Aptitude Test: Biases in perceptions and presentations of college board scores. *Basic and Applied Social Psychology, 14,* 455–473.

Shepperd, J. A., & Taylor, K. M. (1999). Social loafing and expectancy-value theory. *Personality and Social Psychology Bulletin, 25,* 1147–1158.

Sherer, M. (2007). Advice and help-seeking intentions among youth in Israel: Ethnic and gender differences. *Journal of Sociology & Social Welfare, 34,* 53–76.

Sherer, M. (2009). The nature and correlates of dating violence among Jewish and Arab youths in Israel. *Journal of Family Violence, 24,* 11–26.

Sherif, M. (1936). The psychology of social norms. New York: Harper.

Sherif, M. (1966). *In common predicament: Social psychology of intergroup conflict and cooperation.* Boston: Houghton Mifflin.

Sherif, M., Harvey, L. J., White, B. J., Hood, W. R., & Sherif, C. W. (1961). *The Robbers Cave experiment: Intergroup conflict and cooperation.* Middletown, CT: Wesleyan University Press.

Sherman, D. K., Bunyan, D. P., Creswell, J. D., & Jaremka, L. M. (2009). Psychological vulnerability and stress: The effects of self-affirmation on sympathetic nervous system responses to naturalistic stressors. *Health Psychology, 28,* 554–562.

Sherman, J. W., Kruschke, J. K., Sherman, S. J., Percy, E. J., Petrocelli, J. V., & Conrey, F. R. (2009). Attentional processes in stereotype formation: A common model for category accentuation and illusory correlation. *Journal of Personality and Social Psychology, 96,* 305–323.

Shih, M., Pittinsky, T. L., & Ambady, N. (1999). Stereotype susceptibility: Identity salience and shifts in quantitative performance. *Psychological Science, 10,* 80–83.

Shore, T. H., Shore, L. M., & Thornton, G. C., III. (1992). Construct validity of self- and peer evaluations of performance dimensions in an assessment center. *Journal of Applied Psychology, 77,* 42–54.

Shotland, R. L., & Heinold, W. D. (1985). Bystander response to arterial bleeding: Helping skills, the decision-making process, and differentiating the helping response. *Journal of Personality and Social Psychology, 49,* 347–356.

Shotland, R. L., & Stebbins, C. A. (1980). Bystander response to rape: Can a victim attract help? *Journal of Applied Social Psychology, 10,* 510–527.

Shotland, R. L., & Straw, M. K. (1976). Bystander response to an assault: When a man attacks a woman. *Journal of Personality and Social Psychology, 34,* 990–999.

Shrauger, J. S., & Schoeneman, T. (1979). Symbolic interactionist view of the self-concept: Through the looking-glass darkly. *Psychological Bulletin, 86,* 549–573.

Shteynberg, G., Gelfand, M. J., & Kim, K. (2009). Peering into the "magnum mysterium" of culture: The explanatory power of descriptive norms. *Journal of Cross-Cultural Psychology, 40,* 46–69.

Sidanius, J., Haley, H., Molina, L., & Pratto, F. (2007). Vladimir's choice and the distribution of social resources: A group dominance perspective. *Group Processes and Intergroup Relations, 10,* 259–268.

Siegler, I. C. (1994). Hostility and risk: Demographic and lifestyle variables. In A. W. Siegman & T. W. Smith (Eds.), *Anger, hostility, and the heart* (pp. 199–214). Hillsdale, NJ: Erlbaum.

Siegman, A. W., & Smith, T. W. (1994). *Anger, hostility, and the heart.* Hillsdale, NJ: Erlbaum.

Siever, L. (2008). Neurobiology of aggression and violence. *American Journal of Psychiatry, 165,* 429–442.

Silverstein, B., Perdue, L., Peterson, B., & Kelly, E. (1986). The role of the mass media in promoting a thin standard of bodily attractiveness for women. *Sex Roles, 14,* 519–532.

Silvia, P. (2006). Reactance and the dynamics of disagreement: Multiple paths from threatened freedom to resistance to persuasion. *European Journal of Social Psychology, 36,* 673–685.

Silvia, P. J., & Duval, T. S. (2001). Objective self-awareness theory: Recent progress and enduring problems. *Personality and Social Psychology Review, 5,* 230–241.

Simon, H. A. (1956). Rational choice and the structure of the environment. *Psychological Review, 63,* 129–138.

Simonson, I., & Staw, B. W. (1992). Deescalation strategies: A comparison of techniques for reducing commitment to losing courses of action. *Journal of Applied Psychology, 77,* 419–426.

Simpson, B. (2003). Sex, fear, and greed: A social dilemma analysis of gender and cooperation. *Social Forces, 82,* 35–52.

Simpson, B., & Willer, R. (2008). Altruism and indirect reciprocity: The interaction of person and situation in prosocial behavior. *Social Psychology Quarterly, 71,* 37–52.

Simpson, J. A. (1987). The dissolution of romantic relationships: Factors involved in relationship stability and emotional distress. *Journal of Personality and Social Psychology, 53,* 683–692.

Simpson, J. A., & Kenrick, D. T. (Eds.). (1997). *Evolutionary social psychology.* Mahwah, NJ: Erlbaum.

Simpson, J. A., Campbell, B., & Berscheid, E. (1986). The association between romantic love and marriage: Kephart (1967) twice revisited. *Personality and Social Psychology Bulletin, 12,* 363–372.

Simpson, J. A., Gangestad, S. W., & Lerma, M. (1990). Perception of physical attractiveness: Mechanisms involved in the maintenance of romantic relationships. *Journal of Personality and Social Psychology, 59,* 1192–1201.

Simpson, J. A., Rholes, W. S., & Phillips, D. (1996). Conflicts in close relationships: An attachment perspective. *Journal of Personality and Social Psychology, 71,* 899–914.

Sinclair, L., & Kunda, Z. (1999). Reactions to a black professional: Motivated inhibition and activation of conflicting stereotypes. *Journal of Personality and Social Psychology, 77,* 885–904.

Sinclair, L., & Kunda, Z. (2000). Motivated stereotyping of women: She's fine if she praised me but incompetent if she criticized me. *Personality and Social Psychology Bulletin, 26,* 1329–1342.

Sinclair, R. C., Hoffman, C., Mark, M. M., Martin, L. M., & Pickering, T. L. (1994). Construct accessibility and the misattribution of arousal: Schachter and Singer revisited. *Psychological Science, 5,* 15–19.

Sinervo, B., Chaine, A., Clobert, J., Calsbeek, R., Hazard, L., Lancaster, L., McAdam, A. G., Alonzo, S., Corrigan, G., & Hochberg, M. E. (2006). Self-recognition, color signals, and cycles of greenbeard mutualism and altruism. *Proceedings of the National Academy of Sciences, 103,* 7372–7377.

Singelis, T. M. (1994). The measurement of independent and interdependent self-construals. *Personality and Social Psychology Bulletin, 20,* 580–591.

Singer, T., Seymour, B., O'Doherty, J. P., Stephan, K. E., Dolan, R. J., & Frith, C. D. (2006). Empathic neural responses are modulated by the perceived fairness of others. *Nature, 439,* 466–469.

Singh, D. (1993). Adaptive significance of female physical attractiveness: Role of waist-to-hip ratio. *Journal of Personality and Social Psychology, 65,* 293–307.

Singh, D. (1995). Female judgment of male attractiveness and desirability for relationships: Role of waist-to-hip ratio and financial status. *Journal of Personality and Social Psychology, 69,* 1089–1101.

Singh, D., & Randall, P. K. (2007). Beauty is in the eye of the plastic surgeon: Waist-hip ratio (WHR) and women's attractiveness. *Personality and Individual Differences, 43,* 329–340.

Singh, E. (2009). *Caste system in India: A historical perspective.* New Delhi: Kalpaz Publications.

Sinnott-Armstrong, W. (Ed.). (2008). *Moral psychology: Vol. 1. The evolution of morality.* Cambridge, MA: MIT Press.

Siris, P. (2009, January 19). Survivors of the storm. *New York Daily News,* p. 2.

Sisk, R. (2007, July 29). Bittersweet honor for retired general. *New York Daily News,* p. 27.

Sistrunk, F., & McDavid, J. W. (1971). Sex variable in conforming behavior. *Journal of Personality and Social Psychology, 17,* 200–207.

Siu, A. M. H., Cheng, H. C. H., & Leung, M. C. M. (2006). Pro-social norms as a positive youth development construct: Conceptual bases and implications for curriculum development. *International Journal of Adolescent Medicine and Health, 18,* 451–457.

Skarlicki, D. P., & Folger, R. (1997). Retaliation in the workplace: The roles of distributive, procedural, and interactional justice. *Journal of Applied Psychology, 82,* 434–443.

Skinner, E. A. (1996). A guide to constructs of control. *Journal of Personality and Social Psychology, 71,* 549–570.

Skinner, E. A., Edge, K., Altman, J., & Sherwood, H. (2003). Searching for the structure of coping: A review and critique of category systems for classifying ways of coping. *Psychological Bulletin, 129,* 216–269.

Skitka, L. J., Mullen, E., Griffin, T., Hutchinson, S., & Chamberlin, B. (2002). Dispositions, scripts, or motivated correction? Understanding ideological differences in explanations for social problems. *Journal of Personality and Social Psychology, 83,* 470–487.

Sklar, L. S., & Anisman, H. (1981). Stress and cancer. *Psychological Bulletin, 89,* 369–406.

Skov, R. B., & Sherman, S. J. (1986). Information-gathering processes: Diagnosticity hypothesis confirmatory strategies, and perceived hypothesis confirmation. *Journal of Experimental Social Psychology, 22,* 93–121.

Skowronski, J. J., & Carlston, D. E. (1989). Negativity and extremity biases in impression formation: A review of explanations. *Psychology Bulletin, 105,* 131–142.

Slamecka, N. J., & Graff, P. (1978). The generation effect: Delineation of a phenomenon. *Journal of Experimental Psychology: Human Learning and Memory, 4,* 592–604.

Sloan, R., Bagiella, E., & Powell, T. (1999). Religion, spirituality, and medicine. *Lancet, 353,* 664–667.

Slovic, P. (2000). *The perception of risk*. London: Earthscan.

Smart Richman, L., & Leary, M. R. (2009). Reactions to discrimination, stigmatization, ostracism, and other forms of interpersonal rejection: A multimotive model. *Psychological Review, 116*, 365–383.

Smeaton, G., Byrne, D., & Murnen, S. K. (1989). The repulsion hypothesis revisited: Similarity irrelevance or dissimilarity bias? *Journal of Personality and Social Psychology, 56*, 54–59.

Smith, A., & Williams, K. D. (2004). RU there? Ostracism by cell phone text messages. *Group Dynamics: Theory, Research, and Practice, 8*, 291–301.

Smith, A., Jussim, L., & Eccles, J. (1999). Do self-fulfilling prophecies accumulate, dissipate, or remain stable over time? *Journal of Personality and Social Psychology, 77*, 548–565.

Smith, C. T., & Nosek, B. A. (2010). Implicit Association Test. In I. B. Weiner & W. E. Craighead (Eds.), *Corsini Encyclopedia of Psychology*. Hoboken, NJ: Wiley.

Smith, D. L. (2007). *The most dangerous animal: Human nature and the origins of war*. New York: St. Martin's.

Smith, E. R., & Collins, E. C. (2009). Contextualizing person perception: Distributed social cognition. *Psychological Review, 116*, 343–364.

Smith, H. J., Spears, R., & Hamstra, I. J. (1999). Social identity and the context of relative deprivation. In N. Ellemers, R. Spears, & I. J. Hamstra (Eds.), *Social identity: Context, commitment, content* (pp. 205–229). Oxford, UK: Blackwell.

Smith, M. L., Glass, G. V., & Miller, T. I. (1980). *The benefits of psychotherapy*. Baltimore: Johns Hopkins University Press.

Smith, N. K., Cacioppo, J. T., Larsen, J. T., & Chartrand, T. L. (2003). May I have your attention, please: Electrocortical responses to positive and negative stimuli. *Neuropsychologia, 41*, 171–183.

Smith, P. B., & Bond, M. H. (1993). *Social psychology across cultures: Analysis and perspective*. New York: Harvester/Wheatsheaf.

Smith, S. S., & Richardson, D. (1983). Amelioration of deception and harm in psychological research: The important role of debriefing. *Journal of Personality and Social Psychology, 44*, 1075–1082.

Smith, T. W., Snyder, C. R., & Perkins, S. C. (1983). The self-serving function of hypochondriacal complaints: Physical symptoms as self-handicapping strategies. *Journal of Personality and Social Psychology, 44*, 787–797.

Smither, J. W., Reilly, R. R., & Buda, R. (1988). Effect of prior performance information on ratings of present performance: Contrast versus assimilation revisited. *Journal of Applied Psychology, 73*, 487–496.

Smitherman, H. O. (1992). Helping: The importance of cost/reward considerations on likelihood to help. *Psychological Reports, 71*, 305–306.

Smolak, L., & Thompson, J. K. (Eds.). (2009). *Body image, eating disorders, and obesity in youth: Assessment, prevention, and treatment* (2nd ed.). Washington, DC: American Psychological Association.

Smurda, J. D., Wittig, M. A., & Gokalp, G. (2006). Effects of threat to a valued social identity on implicit self-esteem and discrimination. *Group Processes and Intergroup Relations, 9*, 181–197.

Snibbe, A. C., Kitayama, S., Markus, H. R., & Suzuki, T. (2003). They saw a game: A Japanese and American (football) field study. *Journal of Cross-Cultural Psychology, 34*, 581–595.

Snyder, C. R., & Higgins, R. L. (1988). Excuses: Their effective role in the negotiation of reality. *Psychological Bulletin, 104*, 23–35.

Snyder, C. R., Lassegard, M. A., & Ford, C. E. (1986). Distancing after group success and failure: Basking in reflected glory and cutting off reflected failure. *Journal of Personality and Social Psychology, 51*, 382–388.

Snyder, M. (1974). The self-monitoring of expressive behavior. *Journal of Personality and Social Psychology, 30*, 526–537.

Snyder, M. (1987). *Public appearances/private realities: The psychology of self-monitoring*. New York: Freeman.

Snyder, M. (1993). Basic research and practical problems: The promise of a "functional" personality and social psychology. *Personality and Social Psychology Bulletin, 19*, 251–264.

Snyder, M., & DeBono, K. (1985). Appeals to image and claims about quality: Understanding the psychology of advertising. *Journal of Personality and Social Psychology, 49*, 586–597.

Snyder, M., & Gangestad, S. (1986). On the nature of self-monitoring: Matters of assessment, matters of validity. *Journal of Personality and Social Psychology, 51*, 125–139.

Snyder, M., & Monson, T. C. (1975). Persons, situations, and the control of social behavior. *Journal of Personality and Social Psychology, 32*, 637–644.

Snyder, M., & Omoto, A. (2008). Volunteerism: Social issues perspectives and social policy implications. *Social Issues and Policy Review, 2*, 1–36.

Snyder, M., & Stukas, A. A. (1999). Interpersonal processes: The interplay of cognitive, motivational, and behavioral activities in social interaction. *Annual Review of Psychology, 50*, 273–303.

Snyder, M., & Swann, W. B., Jr. (1978). Behavioral confirmation in social interaction: From social perception to social reality. *Journal of Personality and Social Psychology, 36*, 1202–1212.

Snyder, M., Tanke, E. D., & Berscheid, E. (1977). Social perception and interpersonal behavior: On the self-fulfilling nature of social stereotypes. *Journal of Personality and Social Psychology, 35*, 656–666.

Soll, J. B., & Larrick, R. P. (2009). Strategies for revising judgment: How (and how well) people use others' opinions. *Journal of Experimental Psychology: Learning, Memory, and Cognition, 35*, 780–805.

Sommers, S. (2006). On racial diversity and group decision making: Identifying multiple effects of racial composition on jury deliberations. *Journal of Personality and Social Psychology, 90*, 597–612.

Sommers, S. R., & Ellsworth, P. C. (2001). White juror bias: An investigation of racial prejudice against Black defendants in the American courtroom. *Psychology, Public Policy, and Law, 7*, 201–229.

Sommers, S. R., & Norton, M. I. (2007). Race-based judgments, race-neutral justifications: Experimental examination of peremptory use and the Batson challenge procedure. *Law and Human Behavior, 31*, 261–273.

Sommers, S. R., & Norton, M. I. (2008). Race and jury selection: Psychological perspectives on the peremptory challenge debate. *American Psychologist, 63*, 527–539.

Sommers, S. R., Warp, L. S., & Mahoney, C. C. (2008). Cognitive effects of racial diversity: White individuals' information processing in heterogeneous groups. *Journal of Experimental Social Psychology, 44*, 1129–1136.

Son Hing, L. S., Bobocel, D. R., & Zanna, M. P. (2002). Meritocracy and opposition to affirmative action: Making concessions in the face of discrimination. *Journal of Personality and Social Psychology, 83*, 493–509.

Son Hing, L. S., Chung-Yan, G. A., Hamilton, L. K., & Zanna, M. P. (2008). A two-dimensional model that employs explicit and implicit attitudes to characterize prejudice. *Journal of Personality and Social Psychology, 94*, 971–987.

Song, H., & Schwarz, N. (2009). If it's difficult to pronounce, it must be risky: Fluency, familiarity, and risk perception. *Psychological Science, 20*, 135–138.

Souweidane, V., & Huesmann, L. R. (1999). The influence of American urban culture on the development of normative beliefs about aggression in Middle-Eastern immigrants. *American Journal of Community Psychology, 27*, 239–254.

Spears, R. (2002). Four degrees of stereotype formation: Differentiation by any means necessary. In C. McGarty, V. Y. Yzerbyt, & R. Spears (Eds.), *Stereotypes as explanations: The formation of meaningful beliefs about social groups* (pp. 127–156). Cambridge, UK: Cambridge University Press.

Spencer, B., & Castano, E. (2007). Social class is dead. Long live social class! Stereotype threat among low socioeconomic status individuals. *Social Justice Research, 20*, 418–432.

Spencer, S. J., Fein, S., Wolfe, C. T., Fong, C., & Dunn, M. A. (1998). Automatic activation of stereotypes: The role of self-image threat. *Personality and Social Psychology Bulletin, 24*, 1139–1152.

Spencer, S. J., Fein, S., Zanna, M., & Olson, J. M. (Eds.). (2003). *Motivated social perception: The Ontario symposium* (Vol. 9). Mahwah, NJ: Erlbaum.

Spencer, S. J., Steele, C. M., & Quinn, D. M. (1999). Stereotype threat and women's math performance. *Journal of Experimental Social Psychology, 35,* 4–28.

Spencer-Rodgers, J., Boucher, H. C., Mori, S. C., Wang, L., & Peng, K. (2009). The dialectical self-concept: Contradiction, change, and holism in East Asian cultures. *Personality and Social Psychology Bulletin, 35,* 29–44.

Spiegel, D. (1993). Social support: How friends, family, and groups can help. In D. Goleman & J. Gurin (Eds.), *Mind body medicine: How to use your mind for better health* (pp. 331–350). Yonkers, NY: Consumer Reports Books.

Spivey, C. B., & Prentice-Dunn, S. (1990). Assessing the directionality of deindividuated behavior: Effects of deindividuation, modeling, and private self-consciousness on aggressive and prosocial responses. *Basic and Applied Social Psychology, 11,* 387–403.

Sporer, S. L., Penrod, S. D., Read, J. D., & Cutler, B. L. (1995). Choosing, confidence, and accuracy: A meta-analysis of the confidence-accuracy relation in eyewitness identification studies. *Psychological Bulletin, 118,* 315–327.

Spradley, J., & McCurdy, D. W. (2009). *Conformity and conflict: Readings in cultural anthropology* (13th ed.). Boston: Allyn & Bacon.

Sprafkin, J. N., Liebert, R. M., & Poulos, R. W. (1975). Effects of a prosocial televised example on children's helping. *Journal of Experimental Child Psychology, 20,* 119–126.

Sprecher, S. (1994). Two sides to the breakup of dating relationships. *Personal Relationships, 1,* 199–222.

Sprecher, S. (1999). "I love you more today than yesterday": Romantic partners' perceptions of changes in love and related affect over time. *Journal of Personality and Social Psychology, 76,* 46–53.

Sprecher, S. (2001). Equity and social exchange in dating couples: Associations with satisfaction, commitment, and stability. *Journal of Marriage and the Family, 63,* 599–613.

Sprecher, S., & Hendrick, S. S. (2004). Self-disclosure in intimate relationships: Associations with individual and relationship characteristics over time. *Journal of Social and Clinical Psychology, 23,* 857–877.

Sprecher, S., & Regan, P. C. (1998). Passionate and companionate love in courting and young married couples. *Sociological Inquiry, 68,* 163–185.

Sprecher, S., Sullivan, Q., & Hatfield, E. (1994). Mate selection preferences: Gender differences examined in a national sample. *Journal of Personality and Social Psychology, 66,* 1074–1080.

Sprecher, S., Wenzel, A., & Harvey, J. (Eds.). (2008). *Handbook of relationship initiation.* New York: Psychology Press.

Sriram, N., & Greenwald, A. G. (2009). The Brief Implicit Association Test. *Experimental Psychology, 56,* 283–294.

Staats, A. W., & Staats, C. K. (1958). Attitudes established by classical conditioning. *Journal of Abnormal and Social Psychology, 57,* 37–40.

Stahl, J., Wiese, H., & Schweinberger, S. R. (2008). Expertise and own-race bias in face processing: An event-related potential study. *Neuroreport: For Rapid Communication of Neuroscience Research, 19,* 583–587.

Stalans, L. J., & Diamond, S. S. (1990). Formation and change in lay evaluations of criminal sentencing: Misperception and discontent. *Law and Human Behavior, 14,* 199–214.

Stalder, D. R. (2008). Revisiting the issue of safety in numbers: The likelihood of receiving help from a group. *Social Influence, 3,* 24–33.

Stanca, L. (2009). Measuring indirect reciprocity: Whose back do we scratch? *Journal of Economic Psychology, 30,* 190–202.

Stangor, C. (2009). The study of stereotyping, prejudice, and discrimination within social psychology: A quick history of theory and research. In T. D. Nelson (Ed.), *Handbook of prejudice, stereotyping, and discrimination* (pp. 1–22). New York: Psychology Press.

Stangor, C., & Lange, J. E. (1994). Mental representations of social groups: Advances in understanding stereotypes and stereotyping. In M. P. Zanna (Ed.), *Advances in experimental social psychology* (Vol. 26, pp. 357–416). San Diego, CA: Academic Press.

Stangor, C., Sechrist, G. B., & Jost, J. T. (2001). Changing racial beliefs by providing consensus information. *Personality and Social Psychology Bulletin, 27,* 486–496.

Stanton, A. L., Kirk, S. B., Cameron, C. L., & Danoff-Berg, S. (2000). Coping through emotional approach: Scale construction and validation. *Journal of Personality and Social Psychology, 78,* 1150–1169.

Stapel, D. A., & Blanton, H. (Eds.). (2006). *Social comparison theories.* New York: Psychology Press.

Stapel, D. A., & Koomen, W. (2000). How far do we go beyond the information given? The impact of knowledge activation on interpretation and inference. *Journal of Personality and Social Psychology, 78,* 19–37.

Stark, E. M., Shaw, J. D., & Duffy, M. K. (2007). Preference for group work, winning orientation, and social loafing behavior in groups. *Group & Organization Management, 32,* 699–723.

Starzyk, K., Fabrigar, L., Soryal, A., & Fanning, J. (2009). A painful reminder: The role of level and salience of attitude importance in cognitive dissonance. *Personality and Social Psychology Bulletin, 35,* 126–137.

Stasser, G. (1992). Pooling of unshared information during group discussions. In S. Worchel, W. Wood, & J. A. Simpson (Eds.), *Group process and productivity* (pp. 48–67). Newbury Park, CA: Sage.

Stasser, G., & Davis, J. H. (1981). Group decision making and social influence: A social interaction sequence model. *Psychological Review, 88,* 523–551.

Stasser, G., & Titus, W. (2003). Hidden profiles: A brief history. *Psychological Inquiry, 14,* 304–313.

Stasser, G., Kerr, N. L., & Bray, R. M. (1982). The social psychology of jury deliberations: Structure, process, and product. In N. Kerr & R. Bray (Eds.), *The psychology of the courtroom* (pp. 221–256). New York: Academic Press.

Stasser, G., Stewart, D. D., & Wittenbaum, G. M. (1995). Expert roles and information exchange during discussion: The importance of knowing who knows what. *Journal of Experimental Social Psychology, 31,* 244–265.

Staub, E. (1996). Cultural-societal roots of violence: The examples of genocidal violence and of contemporary youth violence in the United States. *American Psychologist, 51,* 117–132.

Staub, E. (2004). Understanding and responding to group violence: Genocide, mass killing, and terrorism. In F. M. Moghaddam & A. J. Marsella (Eds.), *Understanding terrorism: Psychosocial roots, consequences, and interventions* (pp. 151–168). Washington, DC: American Psychological Association.

Staub, E., & Vollhardt, J. (2008). Altruism born of suffering: The roots of caring and helping after victimization and other trauma. *American Journal of Orthopsychiatry, 78,* 267–280.

Stauffer, J. M., & Buckley, M. R. (2005). The existence and nature of racial bias in supervisory ratings. *Journal of Applied Psychology, 90,* 586–591.

Staw, B. M. (1997). The escalation of commitment: An update and appraisal. In Z. Shapira (Ed.), *Organizational decision making. Cambridge series on judgement and decision making* (pp. 191–215). New York: Cambridge University Press.

Staw, B. M., & Hoang, H. (1995). Sunk costs in the NBA: Why draft order affects playing time and survival in professional basketball. *Administrative Science Quarterly, 40,* 474–493.

Staw, B. M., Barsade, S. G., & Koput, K. W. (1997). Escalation at the credit window: A longitudinal study of bank executives' recognition and write-off of problem loans. *Journal of Applied Psychology, 82,* 130–142.

Steblay, N. M. (1987). Helping behavior in rural and urban environments: A meta-analysis. *Psychological Bulletin, 102,* 346–356.

Steblay, N. M. (1992). A meta-analytic review of the weapon-focus effect. *Law and Human Behavior, 16,* 413–424.

Steblay, N. M. (1997). Social influence in eyewitness recall: A meta-analytic review of lineup instruction effects. *Law and Human Behavior, 21,* 283–297.

Steblay, N., Besirevic, J., Fulero, S., & Jiminez-Lorente, B. (1999). The effects of pretrial publicity on juror verdicts: A meta-analytic review. *Law and Human Behavior, 23,* 219–235.

Steblay, N., Hosch, H. M., Culhane, S. E., & McWethy, A. (2006). The impact on juror verdicts of judicial instruction to disregard inadmissible evidence: A meta-analysis. *Law and Human Behavior, 30,* 469–492.

Steele, C. M. (1988). The psychology of self-affirmation: Sustaining the integrity of the self. In L. Berkowitz (Ed.), *Advances in experimental social psychology* (Vol. 21, pp. 261–302). New York: Academic Press.

Steele, C. M. (1997). A threat in the air: How stereotypes shape intellectual identity and performance. *American Psychologist, 52,* 613–629.

Steele, C. M. (1999). Thin ice: "Stereotype threat" and black college students. *Atlantic Monthly, 284,* 44–47, 50–54.

Steele, C. M., & Aronson, J. (1995). Stereotype vulnerability and the intellectual test performance of African Americans. *Journal of Personality and Social Psychology, 69,* 797–811.

Steele, C. M., & Josephs, R. A. (1990). Alcohol myopia: Its prized and dangerous effects. *American Psychologist, 45,* 921–933.

Steele, C. M., Spencer, S. J., & Aronson, J. (2002). Contending with group image: The psychology of stereotype and social identity threat. In M. P. Zanna (Ed.), *Advances in experimental social psychology* (Vol. 34, pp. 379–440). San Diego, CA: Academic Press.

Steele, C. M., Spencer, S. J., & Lynch, M. (1993). Self-image resilience and dissonance: The role of affirmational resources. *Journal of Personality and Social Psychology, 64,* 885–896.

Stein, M. B., Walker, J. R., & Forde, D. R. (1996). Public-speaking fears in a community sample. *Archives of General Psychiatry, 53,* 169–174.

Steiner, I. D. (1972). *Group process and productivity.* New York: Academic Press.

Stephan, W. G. (1986). The effects of school desegregation: An evaluation 30 years after Brown. In M. J. Saks & L. Saxe (Eds.), *Advances in applied social psychology* (Vol. 3, pp. 181–206). Hillsdale, NJ: Erlbaum.

Stephan, W. G., Renfro, C. L., Esses, V. M., Stephan, C. W., & Martin, T. (2005). The effects of feeling threatened on attitudes toward immigrants. *International Journal of Intercultural Relations, 29,* 1–19.

Stepper, S., & Strack, F. (1993). Proprioceptive determinants of emotional and nonemotional feelings. *Journal of Personality and Social Psychology, 64,* 211–220.

Sternberg, R. J. (1986). A triangular theory of love. *Psychological Review, 93,* 119–135.

Sternberg, R. J. (1997). *Successful intelligence: How practical and creative intelligence determine success in life.* New York: Plume.

Sternberg, R. J. (1999). *Cupid's arrow: The course of love through time.* New York: Cambridge University Press.

Sternberg, R. J., & Hedlund, J. (2002). Practical intelligence, *g,* and work psychology. *Human Performance, 15,* 143–160.

Sternberg, R. J., & Weis, K. (Eds.). (2006). *The new psychology of love.* New Haven, CT: Yale University Press.

Stevens, C. K., & Kristof, A. L. (1995). Making the right impression: A field study of applicant impression management during job interviews. *Journal of Applied Psychology, 80,* 587–606.

Stewart, A. J., Sokol, M., Healy, J. M., Jr., & Chester, N. L. (1986). Longitudinal studies of psychological consequences of life changes in children and adults. *Journal of Personality and Social Psychology, 50,* 143–151.

Stewart, B. D., & Payne, B. K. (2008). Bringing automatic stereotyping under control: Implementation intentions as efficient means of thought control. *Personality and Social Psychology Bulletin, 34,* 1332–1345.

Stewart, B. D., von Hippel, W., & Radvansky, G. A. (2009). Age, race, and implicit prejudice: Using process dissociation to separate the underlying components. *Psychological Science, 20,* 164–168.

Stewart, G. L., Dustin, S. L., Barrick, M. R., & Darnold, T. C. (2008). Exploring the handshake in employment interviews. *Journal of Applied Psychology, 93,* 1139–1146.

Stewart-Williams, S. (2007). Altruism among kin vs. nonkin: Effects of cost of help and reciprocal exchange. *Evolution and Human Behavior, 28,* 193–198.

Stewart-Williams, S. (2008). Human beings as evolved nepotists: Exceptions to the rule and effects of cost of help. *Human Nature, 19,* 414–425.

Stine, G. J. (2007). *AIDS Update 2007.* New York: McGraw-Hill Science.

Stinson, V., Devenport, J. L., Cutler, B. L., & Kravitz, D. A. (1996). How effective is the presence-of-counsel safeguard? Attorney perceptions of suggestiveness, fairness, and correctability of biased lineup procedures. *Journal of Applied Psychology, 81,* 64–75.

Stinson, V., Devenport, J. L., Cutler, B. L., & Kravitz, D. A. (1997). How effective is the motion-to-suppress safeguard? Judges perceptions of the suggestiveness and fairness of biased lineup procedures. *Journal of Applied Psychology, 82,* 26–43.

Stoltzfus, N. (1996). *Resistance of the heart: Intermarriage and the Rosenstrasse protest in Nazi Germany.* New York: Norton.

Stone, A. A., Neale, J. M., Cox, D. S., Napoli, A., Valdimarsdottir, H., & Kennedy-Moore, E. (1994). Daily events are associated with a secretory immune response to an oral antigen in men. *Health Psychology, 13,* 440–446.

Stone, J. (2003). Self-consistency for low self-esteem in dissonance processes: The role of self-standards. *Personality and Social Psychology Bulletin, 29,* 846–858.

Stone, J., Lynch, C. I., Sjomeling, M., & Darley, J. M. (1999). Stereotype threat effects on black and white athletic performance. *Journal of Personality and Social Psychology, 77,* 1213–1227.

Stone, J., Perry, Z. W., & Darley, J. M. (1997). "White men can't jump": Evidence for the perceptual confirmation of racial stereotypes following a basketball game. *Basic and Applied Social Psychology, 19,* 291–306.

Stone, J., Wiegand, A. W., Cooper, J., & Aronson, E. (1997). When exemplification fails: Hypocrisy and the motive for self-integrity. *Journal of Personality and Social Psychology, 72,* 54–65.

Stone, W. F., Lederer, G., & Christie, R. (Eds.). (1993). *Strength and weakness: The authoritarian personality today.* New York: Springer-Verlag.

Strahan, E. J., Spencer, S. J., & Zanna, M. P. (2002). Subliminal priming and persuasion: Striking while the iron is hot. *Journal of Experimental Social Psychology, 38,* 556–568.

Straub, R. O. (2007). *Health psychology: A biopsychosocial approach* (2nd ed.). New York: Worth.

Strauman, T. J. (1992). Self-guides, autobiographical memory, and anxiety and dysphoria: Toward a cognitive model of vulnerability to emotional distress. *Journal of Abnormal Psychology, 101,* 87–95.

Strauman, T. J., Lemieux, A. M., & Coe, C. L. (1993). Self-discrepancy and natural killer cell activity: Immunological consequences of negative self-evaluation. *Journal of Personality and Social Psychology, 64,* 1042–1052.

Strauman, T. J., Woods, T. E., Schneider, K. L., Kwapil, L., & Coe, C. L. (2004). Self-regulatory cognition and immune reactivity: Idiographic success and failure feedback effects on the natural killer cell. *Brain, Behavior and Immunity, 18,* 544–554.

Straus, M. A. (1999). The controversy over domestic violence by women: A methodical, theoretical, and sociology of science analysis. In X. B. Arriaga & S. Oskamp (Eds.), *Violence in intimate relationships* (pp. 17–44). Thousand Oaks, CA: Sage.

Straus, M. A. (2000). *Beating the devil out of them: Corporal punishment in American families and its effects on children* (2nd ed.). New Brunswick, NJ: Transaction Publishers.

Straus, M. A. (2006). Future research on gender symmetry in physical assaults on partners. *Violence Against Women, 12,* 1086–1097.

Straus, M. A., & Douglas, E. M. (2008). Research on spanking by parents: Implications for public policy. *The Family Psychologist: Bulletin of the Division of Family Psychology, 43,* 18–20.

Straus, M. A., & Ramirez, I. L. (2005). Gender symmetry in prevalence, severity, and chronicity of physical aggression against dating partners by university students in Mexico and the USA. In S. Fein, G. R. Goethals, & M. J. Sandstrom (Eds.), *Gender and aggression: Interdisciplinary perspectives.* Mahwah, NJ: Erlbaum.

Straus, S. G., Parker, A. M., Bruce, J. B., & Dembosky, J. W. (2009). *The group matters: A review of the effects of group interaction on processes and outcomes in analytic teams.* Report WR-580-USG. Arlington, VA: Rand Corporation.

Strawbridge, W. J., Shema, S. J., Cohen, R. D., & Kaplan, G. A. (2001). Religious attendance increases survival by improving and maintaining good health behaviors, mental health, and social relationships. *Annals of Behavioral Medicine, 23,* 68–74.

Strentz, T., & Auerbach, S. M. (1988). Adjustment to the stress of simulated captivity: Effects of emotion-focused versus problem-focused preparation on hostages differing in locus of control. *Journal of Personality and Social Psychology, 55,* 652–660.

Strier, F. (1999). Wither trial consulting: Issues and projections. *Law and Human Behavior, 23,* 93–115.

Strodtbeck, F. L., & Hook, L. (1961). The social dimensions of a twelve-man jury table. *Sociometry, 24,* 397–415.

Strodtbeck, F. L., James, R., & Hawkins, C. (1957). Social status in jury deliberations. *American Sociological Review, 22,* 713–719.

Stroessner, S. J., & Plaks, J. E. (2001). Illusory correlation and stereotype formation: Tracing the arc of research over a quarter century. In G. B. Moskowitz (Ed.), *Cognitive social psychology: The Princeton symposium on the legacy and future of social cognition* (pp. 247–259). Mahwah, NJ: Erlbaum.

Strohmetz, D. B., Rind, B., Fisher, R., & Lynn, M. (2002). Sweetening the till: The use of candy to increase restaurant tipping. *Journal of Applied Social Psychology, 32,* 300–309.

Strube, M. J. (2005). What did Triplett really find? A contemporary analysis of the first experiment in social psychology. *American Journal of Psychology, 118,* 271–286.

Struck, D. (2006, September 15). Gunman's writings presaged rampage; blog described fascination with death, laid out events that would unfold in Montreal. *Washington Post,* p. A12.

Struckman-Johnson, C., & Struckman-Johnson, D. (1994). Men pressured and forced into sexual experience. *Archives of Sexual Behavior, 23,* 93–114.

Strupp, H. H. (1996). The tripartite model and the Consumer Reports study. *American Psychologist, 51,* 1017–1024.

Studebaker, C. A., & Penrod, S. D. (1997). Pretrial publicity: The media, the law, and common sense. *Psychology, Public Policy, and Law, 3,* 428–460.

Stürmer, S., Snyder, M., & Omoto, A. M. (2005). Prosocial emotions and helping: The moderating role of group membership. *Journal of Personality and Social Psychology, 88,* 532–546.

Stürmer, S., Snyder, M., Kropp, A., & Siem, B. (2006). Empathy-motivated helping: The moderating role of group membership. *Personality and Social Psychology Bulletin, 32,* 943–956.

Stuhlmacher, A. F., Citera, M., & Willis, T. (2007). Gender differences in virtual negotiation: Theory and research. *Sex Roles, 57,* 329–339.

Stuhlmacher, A. F., & Walters, A. E. (1999). Gender differences in negotiation outcome: A meta-analysis. *Personnel Psychology, 52,* 653–677.

Stutzer, A. (2004). The role of income aspirations in individual happiness. *Journal of Economic Behavior and Organization, 54,* 89–109.

Suarez, E. C., & Krishnan, K. R. R. (2006). The relation of free plasma tryptophan to anger, hostility, and aggression in a nonpatient sample of adult men and women. *Annals of Behavioral Medicine, 31,* 254–260.

Sue, S., Smith, R. E., & Caldwell, C. (1973). Effects of inadmissible evidence on the decisions of simulated jurors: A moral dilemma. *Journal of Applied Social Psychology, 3,* 345–353.

Suh, E., Diener, E., & Fujita, F. (1996). Events and subjective well-being: Only recent events matter. *Journal of Personality and Social Psychology, 70,* 1091–1102.

Suls, J. M., & Wheeler, L. (Eds.). (2000). *Handbook of social comparison: Theory and research.* New York: Plenum.

Sundstrom, E. (1986). *Work places.* New York: Cambridge University Press.

Surowiecki, J. (2005). *The wisdom of crowds.* New York: Anchor Books.

Susskind, J. (2003). Children's perception of gender-based illusory correlations: Enhancing preexisting relationships between gender and behavior. *Sex Roles, 48,* 483–494.

Swaab, R. I., & Swaab. D. F. (2009). Sex differences in the effects of visual contact and eye contact in negotiations. *Journal of Experimental Social Psychology, 45,* 129–136.

Swami, V., & Furnham, A. (2008). *The psychology of physical attraction.* New York: Routledge/Taylor & Francis.

Swann, W. B., Jr. (1984). Quest for accuracy in person perception: A matter of pragmatics. *Psychological Review, 91,* 457–477.

Swann, W. B., Jr. (1987). Identity negotiation: Where two roads meet. *Journal of Personality and Social Psychology, 53,* 1038–1051.

Swann, W. B., Jr., & Bosson, J. K. (2010). Self and identity. In S. T. Fiske, D. T. Gilbert, & G. Lindzey (Eds.), *Handbook of social psychology* (5th ed.). New York: McGraw-Hill.

Swann, W. B., Jr., & Ely, R. J. (1984). A battle of wills: Self-verification versus behavioral confirmation. *Journal of Personality and Social Psychology, 46,* 1287–1302.

Swann, W. B., Jr., & Hill, C. A. (1982). When our identities are mistaken: Reaffirming self-conceptions through social interaction. *Journal of Personality and Social Psychology, 43,* 59–66.

Swann, W. B., Jr., Chang-Schneider, C. S., & McClarty, K. L. (2007). Do our self-views matter? Self-concept and self-esteem in everyday life. *American Psychologist, 62,* 84–94.

Swann, W. B., Jr., Hixon, J. G., & De La Ronde, C. (1992). Embracing the bitter "truth": Negative self-concepts and marital commitment. *Psychological Science, 3,* 118–121.

Swim, J. K., & Hyers, L. L. (2009). Sexism. In T. D. Nelson (Ed.), *Handbook of prejudice, stereotyping, and discrimination* (pp. 407–430). New York: Psychology Press.

Swim, J. K., & Sanna, L. J. (1996). He's skilled, she's lucky: A meta-analysis of observers' attributions for women's and men's successes and failures. *Personality and Social Psychology Bulletin, 22,* 507–519.

Swim, J. K., Mallett, R., Russo-Devosa, Y., & Stangor, C. (2005). Judgments of sexism: A comparison of sexism measures and sources of variability in judgments of sexism. *Psychology of Women Quarterly, 29,* 406–411.

Syeed, N. (2009, June 19). FBI: Child porn on accused museum shooter computer. *Associated Press.*

Sypeck, M. F., Gray, J. J., Etu, S. F., Ahrens, A. H., Mosimann, J. E., & Wiseman, C. V. (2006). Cultural representations of thinness in women, redux: Playboy magazine's depiction of beauty from 1979 to 1999. *Body Image, 3,* 229–235.

Tajfel, H. (1982). Social psychology of intergroup relations. *Annual Review of Psychology, 33,* 1–39.

Tajfel, H., Billig, M. G., Bundy, R. P., & Flament, C. (1971). Social categorization and intergroup behavior. *European Journal of Social Psychology, 1,* 149–178.

Takahasi, H., Kato, M., Matsuura, M., Mobbs, D., Suhara, T., & Okubo, Y. (2009). When your gain is my pain and your pain is my gain: Neural correlates of envy and schadenfreude. *Science, 323,* 937–939.

Takemura, K., & Yuki, M. (2007). Are Japanese groups more competitive than Japanese individuals? A cross-cultural validation of the interindividual-intergroup discontinuity effect. *International Journal of Psychology, 42,* 27–35.

Talarico, J. M., & Rubin, D. C. (2007). Flashbulb memories are special after all; in phenomenology, not accuracy. *Applied Cognitive Psychology, 21,* 557–578.

Tan, H. H., & Tan, M.-L. (2008). Organizational citizenship behavior and social loafing: The role of personality, motives, and contextual factors. *Journal of Psychology: Interdisciplinary and Applied, 142,* 89–108.

Tanford, S., & Penrod, S. (1984). Social influence model: A formal integration of research on majority and minority influence processes. *Psychological Bulletin, 95,* 189–225.

Tang, S., & Hall, V. C. (1995). The overjustification effect: A meta-analysis. *Applied Cognitive Psychology, 9,* 365–404.

Tangney, J. P., Wagner, P. E., Hill-Barlow, D., Marschall, D. E., & Gramzow, R. (1996). Relation of shame and guilt to constructive versus destructive responses to anger across the lifespan. *Journal of Personality and Social Psychology, 70,* 797–809.

Tannen, D. (1990). *You just don't understand: Women and men in conversation.* New York: Morrow.

Tarde, G. (1890). *Les lois de l'imitation. Étude sociologique.* Paris: Félix Alcan.

Tassinary, L. G., & Cacioppo, J. T. (1992). Unobservable facial actions and emotion. *Psychological Science, 3,* 28–33.

Tay, C., Ang, S., & Linn, V. (2006). Personality, biographical characteristics, and job interview success: A longitudinal study of the mediating effects of interviewing self-efficacy and the moderating effects of internal locus of causality. *Journal of Applied Psychology, 91,* 446–454.

Taylor, D. (2006, September 13). Get fit now, pay later: More and more men want a body like David Beckham's—even if they have to take dangerous short cuts to get them. *The Guardian* (London), p. 16.

Taylor, K. A., Mesmer-Magnus, J., & Burns, T. M. (2008). Teaching the art of negotiation: Improving students' negotiating confidence and perceptions of effectiveness. *Journal of Education for Business, 83,* 135–140.

Taylor, R. B. (2000). *Breaking away from broken windows: Baltimore neighborhoods and the nationwide fight against crime, grime, fear, and decline.* Boulder, CO: Westview Press.

Taylor, S. E. (1989). *Positive illusions: Creative self-deceptions and the healthy mind.* New York: Basic Books.

Taylor, S. E. (1990). Health psychology: The science and the field. *American Psychologist, 45,* 40–50.

Taylor, S. E. (1991). Asymmetrical effects of positive and negative events: The mobilization-minimization hypothesis. *Psychological Bulletin, 110,* 67–85.

Taylor, S. E. (2002). *The tending instinct: Women, men, and the biology of nurturing.* New York: Times Books.

Taylor, S. E. (2006). Tend and befriend: Biobehavioral bases of affiliation under stress. *Current Directions in Psychological Science, 15,* 273–277.

Taylor, S. E. (2009). *Health psychology* (7th ed.). New York: McGraw-Hill.

Taylor, S. E., & Brown, J. D. (1988). Illusion and well-being: A social psychological perspective on mental health. *Psychological Bulletin, 103,* 193–210.

Taylor, S. E., & Fiske, S. T. (1975). Point of view and perceptions of causality. *Journal of Personality and Social Psychology, 32,* 439–445.

Taylor, S. E., & Lobel, M. (1989). Social comparison activity under threat: Downward evaluation and upward contacts. *Psychological Review, 96,* 569–575.

Taylor, S. E., Lerner, J. S., Sherman, D. K., Sage, R. M., & McDowell, N. K. (2003). Portrait of the self-enhancer: Well adjusted and well liked or maladjusted and friendless? *Journal of Personality and Social Psychology, 84,* 165–176.

Taylor, S. E., Sherman, D. K., Kim, H. S., Jarcho, J., Takgi, K., & Dunagan, M. S. (2004). Culture and social support: Who seeks it and why? *Journal of Personality and Social Psychology, 87,* 354–362.

Taylor, S. E., Welch, W. T., Kim, H. S., & Sherman, D. K. (2007). Cultural differences in the impact of social support on psychological and biological stress responses. *Psychological Science, 18,* 831–837.

Tedeschi, J. T., & Bond, M. H. (2001). Aversive behavior and aggression in cultural perspective. In R. M. Kowalski (Ed.), *Behaving badly:*

Aversive behaviors in interpersonal relationships (pp. 257–293). Washington, DC: American Psychological Association.

Tedeschi, J. T., Schlenker, B. R., & Bonoma, T. V. (1971). Cognitive dissonance: Private ratiocination or public spectacle? *American Psychologist, 26,* 685–695.

Teger, A. (1980). *Too much invested to quit.* New York: Pergamon Press.

Tekleab, A. G., Quigley, N. R., & Tesluk, P. E. (2009). A longitudinal study of team conflict, conflict management, cohesion, and team effectiveness. *Group & Organization Management, 34,* 170–205.

Tenenbaum, H. R., & Leaper, C. (2002). Are parents' gender schemas related to their children's gender-related cognitions? A meta-analysis. *Developmental Psychology, 38,* 615–630.

Tepper, B. J. (2001). Health consequences of organizational injustice: Tests of main and interactive effects. *Organizational Behavior and Human Decision Processes, 86,* 197–215.

Tesser, A. (1978). Self-generated attitude change. In L. Berkowitz (Ed.), *Advances in experimental social psychology* (Vol. 11, pp. 288–338). New York: Academic Press.

Tesser, A. (1988). Toward a self-evaluation maintenance model of social behavior. In L. Berkowitz (Ed.), *Advances in experimental social psychology* (Vol. 21, pp. 181–227). New York: Academic Press.

Tesser, A. (1993). The importance of heritability in psychological research: The case of attitudes. *Psychological Review, 100,* 129–142.

Tesser, A., & Collins, J. E. (1988). Emotion in social reflection and comparison situations: Intuitive, systematic, and exploratory approaches. *Journal of Personality and Social Psychology, 55,* 695–709.

Tesser, A., Pilkington, C. J., & McIntosh, W. D. (1989). Self-evaluation maintenance and the mediational role of emotion: The perception of friends and strangers. *Journal of Personality and Social Psychology, 57,* 442–456.

Testa, M., VanZile-Tamsen, C., Livingston, J. A., & Buddie, A. M. (2006). The role of women's alcohol consumption in managing sexual intimacy and sexual safety motives. *Journal of Studies on Alcohol, 67,* 665–674.

Tetlock, P. E. (1998). Social psychology and world politics. In D. T. Gilbert, S. T. Fiske, & G. Lindzey (Eds.), *The handbook of social psychology* (4th ed., Vol. 2, pp. 868–912). New York: McGraw-Hill.

Thaler, R. (1980). Toward a positive theory of consumer choice. *Journal of Economic Behavior and Organization, 1,* 39–60.

t'Hart, P. (1998). Preventing groupthink revisited: Evaluating and reforming groups in government. *Organizational Behavior and Human Decision Processes, 73,* 306–326.

t'Hart, P., Stern, E., & Sundelius, B. (1995). *Beyond groupthink.* Stockholm: Stockholm Center for Organizational Research.

The Detroit News (1997, November 25). Belle Isle bridge murder verdict upheld. p. C3.

Thibaut, J. W., & Kelley, H. H. (1959). *The social psychology of groups.* New York: Wiley.

Thibaut, J., & Walker, L. (1975). *Procedural justice: A psychological analysis.* Hillsdale, NJ: Erlbaum.

Thibaut, J., & Walker, L. (1978). A theory of procedure. *California Law Review, 66,* 541–566.

Thomaes, S., Bushman, B. J., Stegge, H., & Olthof, T. (2008). Trumping shame by blasts of noise: Narcissism, self-esteem, shame, and aggression in young adolescents. *Child Development, 79,* 1792–1801.

Thomaes, S., Reijntjes, A., Orobio de Castro, B., & Bushman, B. J. (In press). Do inflated self-views buffer or fuel the negative impact of threatening events? *Psychological Science.*

Thomas, A. K., & Loftus, E. F. (2002). Creating bizarre false memories through imagination. *Memory and Cognition, 30,* 423–431.

Thomas, D. A., & Gabarro, J. J. (1999). *Breaking through: The making of minority executives in corporate America.* Cambridge, MA: Harvard Business School Press.

Thompson, J. K. (Ed.). (2003). *Handbook of eating disorders and obesity.* New York: Wiley.

Thompson, L. (1990). Negotiation behavior and outcomes: Empirical evidence and theoretical issues. *Psychological Bulletin, 108,* 515–532.

Thompson, L. (1991). Information exchange in negotiation. *Journal of Experimental Social Psychology, 27,* 161–179.

Thompson, L., & Hrebec, D. (1996). Lose-lose agreements in interdependent decision making. *Psychological Bulletin, 120,* 396–409.

Thompson, L., Wang, J., & Gunia, B. (2010, January). Negotiation. In S. Fiske (Ed.), *Annual Review of Psychology, 61,* 491–515.

Thompson, S. C. (1999). Illusions of control: How we overestimate our personal influence. *Current Directions in Psychological Science, 8,* 187–190.

Thompson, S. C., Sobolew-Shubin, A., Galbraith, M. E., Schwankovsky, L., & Cruzen, D. (1993). Maintaining perceptions of control: Finding perceived control in low-control circumstances. *Journal of Personality and Social Psychology, 64,* 293–304.

Thompson, W. M., Dabbs, J. M., Jr., & Frady, R. L. (1990). Changes in saliva testosterone levels during a 90-day shock incarceration program. *Criminal Justice and Behavior, 17,* 246–252.

Thornhill, R., & Gangestad, S. W. (1993). Human facial beauty: Averageness, symmetry, and parasite resistance. *Human Nature, 4,* 237–269.

Thornton, B. (1992). Repression and its mediating influence on the defensive attribution of responsibility. *Journal of Research in Personality, 26,* 44–57.

Thornton, G. C., & Rupp, D. E. (2006). *Assessment centers in human resource management: Strategies for prediction, diagnosis, and development.* Mahwah, NJ: Erlbaum.

Thorsteinsson, E. B., James, J. E., & Gregg, M. E. (1998). Effects of video-relayed social support on hemodynamic reactivity and salivary cortisol during laboratory-based behavioral challenge. *Health Psychology, 17,* 436–444.

Thurstone, L. L. (1928). Attitudes can be measured. *American Journal of Sociology, 33,* 529–544.

Tice, D. M. (1991). Esteem protection or enhancement? Self-handicapping motives and attributions differ by trait self-esteem. *Journal of Personality and Social Psychology, 60,* 711–725.

Tice, D. M., & Baumeister, R. F. (1997). Longitudinal study of procrastination, performance, stress, and health: The costs and benefits of dawdling. *Psychological Science, 8,* 454–458.

Tice, D. M., & Wallace, H. M. (2003). The reflected self: Creating yourself as (you think) others see you. In M. R. Leary & J. P. Tangney (Eds.), *Handbook of self and identity* (pp. 91–105). New York: Guilford.

Tilker, H. A. (1970). Socially responsible behavior as a function of observer responsibility and victim feedback. *Journal of Personality and Social Psychology, 14,* 95–100.

Time (1994, June 27). p. 26.

Timmons-Mitchell, J., Bender, M. B., Kishna, M. A., & Mitchell, C. C. (2006). An independent effectiveness trial of multisystemic therapy with juvenile justice youth. *Journal of Clinical Child and Adolescent Psychology, 35,* 227–236.

Tjaden, P., & Thoennes, N. (2000). *Extent, nature, and consequences of intimate partner violence.* Washington, DC: U.S. Department of Justice.

Tjosvold, D., Hui, C., & Sun, H. (2004). Can Chinese discuss conflicts openly? Field and experimental studies of face dynamics in China. *Group Decision and Negotiation, 13,* 351–373.

Tobin, A. M. (2006, October 3). "Copycat effect" may explain cluster. *Toronto Star,* p. A7.

Todorov, A., & Uleman, J. S. (2004). The person reference process in spontaneous trait inferences. *Journal of Personality and Social Psychology, 87,* 482–493.

Todorov, A., Said, C. P., Engell, A. D., & Oosterhof, N. A. (2008). Understanding evaluation of faces on social dimensions. *Trends in Cognitive Sciences, 12,* 455–460.

Tolin, D. F., & Foa, E. B. (2006). Sex differences in trauma and post-traumatic stress disorder: A quantitative review of 25 years of research. *Psychological Bulletin, 132,* 959–992.

Tolstedt, B. E., & Stokes, J. P. (1984). Self-disclosure, intimacy, and the depenetration process. *Journal of Personality and Social Psychology, 46,* 84–90.

Toma, C. L., Hancock, J. T., Ellison, N. B. (2008). Separating fact from fiction: An examination of deceptive self-presentation in online dating profiles. *Personality and Social Psychology Bulletin, 34,* 1023–1036.

Tomada, G., & Schneider, B. H. (1997). Relational aggression, gender, and peer acceptance: Invariance across culture, stability over time, and concordance among informants. *Developmental Psychology, 33,* 601–609.

Toobin, J. (1996, September 9). The Marcia Clark verdict. *New Yorker,* pp. 58–71.

Top, T. J. (1991). Sex bias in the evaluation of performance in the scientific, artistic, and literary professions: A review. *Sex Roles, 24,* 73–106.

Tormala, Z. L., & Petty, R. E. (2002). What doesn't kill me makes me stronger: The effects of resisting persuasion on attitude certainty. *Journal of Personality and Social Psychology, 83,* 1298–1313.

Tormala, Z. L., Brinol, P., & Petty, R. E. (2006). When credibility attacks: The reverse impact of source credibility on persuasion. *Journal of Experimental Social Psychology, 42,* 684–691.

Törngren, G., & Montgomery, H. (2004). Worse than chance? Performance and confidence among professionals and lay-people in the stock market. *Journal of Behavioral Finance, 5,* 148–153.

Tourangeau, R., Rips, L. J., & Rasinksi, K. (2000). *The psychology of survey response.* New York: Cambridge University Press.

Tourangeau, R., Smith, T. W., & Rasinski, K. A. (1997). Motivation to report sensitive behaviors on surveys: Evidence from a bogus pipeline experiment. *Journal of Applied Social Psychology, 27,* 209–222.

Trafimow, D., Silverman, E. S., Fan, R. M. T., & Law, J. S. F. (1997). The effects of language and priming on the relative accessibility of the private self and collective self. *Journal of Cross-Cultural Psychology, 28,* 107–123.

Trafimow, D., Triandis, H. C., & Goto, S. G. (1991). Some tests of the distinction between the private and collective self. *Journal of Personality and Social Psychology, 60,* 649–655.

Trawalter, S., Todd, A. R., Baird, A. A., & Richeson, J. A. (2008). Attending to threat: Race-based patterns of selective attention. *Journal of Experimental Social Psychology, 44,* 1322–1327.

Triandis, H. C. (1994). *Culture and social behavior.* New York: McGraw-Hill.

Triandis, H. C. (1995). *Individualism and collectivism.* Boulder, CO: Westview.

Triandis, H., Chen, X. P., & Chan, D. K. (1998). Scenarios for the measurement of collectivism and individualism. *Journal of Cross-Cultural Psychology, 29,* 275–289.

Triplett, N. (1897–1898). The dynamogenic factors in pacemaking and competition. *American Journal of Psychology, 9,* 507–533.

Tripp, C., Jensen, T. D., & Carlson, L. (1994). The effects of multiple product endorsements by celebrities on consumers' attitudes and intentions. *Journal of Consumer Research, 20,* 535–547.

Trivers, R. L. (1971). The evolution of reciprocal altruism. *Quarterly Review of Biology, 46,* 35–57.

Trivers, R. L. (1972). Parental investment and sexual selection. In B. Campbell (Ed.), *Sexual selection and the descent of man* (pp. 136–179). Chicago: Aldine-Atherton.

Trivers, R. L. (1985). *Social evolution.* Menlo Park, CA: Benjamin/Cummings.

Troll, L. E., & Skaff, M. M. (1997). Perceived continuity of self in very old age. *Psychology and Aging, 12,* 162–169.

Trope, Y. (1986). Identification and inferential processes in dispositional attribution. *Psychological Review, 93,* 239–257.

Trope, Y., & Alfieri, T. (1997). Effortfulness and flexibility of dispositional judgment processes. *Journal of Personality and Social Psychology, 73,* 662–674.

Trope, Y., Bassock, M., & Alon, E. (1984). The questions lay interviewers ask. *Journal of Personality, 52,* 90–106.

Trzesniewski, K. H., Donnellan, M. B., & Robins, R. W. (2003). Stability of self-esteem across the life span. *Journal of Personality and Social Psychology, 84,* 205–220.

Tsai, W. C., Chen, C. C., & Liu, H. L. (2007). Test of a model linking employee positive moods and task performance. *Journal of Applied Psychology, 92,* 1570–1583.

Tsapelas, I., Aron, A., & Orbuch, T. (2009). Marital boredom now predicts less satisfaction 9 years later. *Psychological Science, 20,* 543–545.

Tubre, T. C., & Collins, J. M. (2000). Jackson and Schuler (1985) revisited: A meta-analysis of the relationships between role ambiguity, role conflict, and job performance. *Journal of Management, 26,* 155–169.

Tuckman, B. W. (1965). Developmental sequence in small groups. *Psychological Bulletin, 63,* 384–399.

Tuckman, B. W., & Jensen, M. A. (1977). Stages of small-group development revisited. *Group and Organization Studies, 2,* 419–427.

Turner, J. C. (1987). *Rediscovering the social group: A self-categorization theory.* Oxford, UK: Basil Blackwell.

Turner, J. C. (1991). *Social influence.* Pacific Grove, CA: Brooks/ Cole.

Tversky, A., & Kahneman, D. (1973). Availability: A heuristic for judging frequency and probability. *Cognitive Psychology, 5,* 207–232.

Tversky, A., & Kahneman, D. (1974). Judgment under uncertainty: Heuristics and biases. *Science, 185,* 1124–1131.

Twenge, J. M. (2006). *Generation me: Why today's young Americans are more confident, assertive, entitled—and more miserable than ever before.* New York: Free Press.

Twenge, J. M. (2009). Change over time in obedience: The jury's still out, but it might be decreasing. *American Psychologist, 64,* 28–31.

Twenge, J. M., & Crocker, J. (2002). Race and self-esteem: Metaanalyses comparing Whites, Blacks, Hispanics, Asians, and American Indians. *Psychological Bulletin, 128,* 371–408.

Tyler, T. R. (2006a). Viewing *CSI* and the threshold of guilt: Managing truth and justice in reality and fiction. *Yale Law Journal, 115,* 1050–1085.

Tyler, T. R. (2006b). *Why people obey the law.* Princeton, NJ: Princeton University Press.

Uchino, B. N. (2006). Social support and health: A review of physiological processes potentially underlying links to disease outcomes. *Journal of Behavioral Medicine, 29,* 377–387.

Uchino, B. N. (2009). Understanding the links between social support and physical health: A life-span perspective with emphasis on the separability of perceived and received support. *Perspectives on Psychological Science, 4,* 236–255.

Uchino, B. N., Cacioppo, J. T., & Kiecolt-Glaser, J. K. (1996). The relationship between social support and physiological processes: A review with emphasis on underlying mechanisms and implications for health. *Psychological Bulletin, 119,* 488–531.

Underwood, J., & Pezdek, K. (1998). Memory suggestibility as an example of the sleeper effect. *Psychonomic Bulletin and Review, 5,* 449–453.

Underwood, M. K., Beron, K. J., Gentsch, J. K., Galperin, M. B., & Risser, S. D. (2008). Family correlates of children's social and physical aggression with peers: Negative interparental conflict strategies and parenting styles. *International Journal of Behavioral Development, 32,* 549–562.

United States v. Scheffer, 523 U.S. 303 (1998).

Unkelbach, C., Forgas, J. P., & Denson, T. F. (2008). The turban effect: The influence of Muslim headgear and induced affect on aggressive responses in the shooter bias paradigm. *Journal of Experimental Social Psychology, 44,* 1409–1413.

USA Today. (2003, June 23). Gallup Poll results. Retrieved August 25, 2003, from http://www.usatoday.com/news/polls/tables/live/0623.htm.

U.S. Bureau of Labor Statistics. (2008).

U.S. Bureau of Labor Statistics. (2009).

U.S. Department of Justice. (1998). *Prevalence, incidence, and consequences of violence against women: Findings from the national violence against women survey, U.S.* Washington, DC: U.S. Government Printing Office.

Uziel, L. (2007). Individual differences in the social facilitation effect: A review and meta-analysis. *Journal of Research in Personality, 41,* 579–601.

Vaillancourt, T. (2005). Indirect aggression among humans: Social construct or evolutionary adaptation? In R. E. Tremblay, W. W. Hartup, & J. Archer (Eds.), *Developmental origins of aggression* (pp.158–177). New York: Guilford.

Vaillancourt, T., & Hymel, S. (2006). Aggression and social status: The moderating roles of sex and peer-valued characteristics. *Aggressive Behavior, 32,* 396–408.

Vaish, A., Carpenter, M., & Tomasello, M. (2009). Sympathy through affective perspective taking and its relation to prosocial behavior in toddlers. *Developmental Psychology, 45,* 534–543.

Vaish, A., Grossmann, T., & Woodward, A. (2008). Not all emotions are created equal: The negativity bias in social-emotional development. *Psychological Bulletin, 134,* 383–403.

Vallacher, R. R., Read, S. J., & Nowak, A. (2002). The dynamical perspective in personality and social psychology. *Personality and Social Psychology Review, 6,* 264–273.

Van Bavel, J. J., & Cunningham, W. A. (2009). Self-categorization with a novel mixed-race group moderates automatic social and racial biases. *Personality and Social Psychology Bulletin, 35,* 321–335.

Van Bavel, J. J., Packer, D. J., & Cunningham, W. A. (2008). The neural substrates of in-group bias: A functional magnetic resonance imaging investigation. *Psychological Science, 19,* 1131–1139.

van Bokhoven, I., van Goozen, S. H. M., van Engeland, H., Schaal, B., Arseneault, L., Séguin, J. R., Assaad, J.-M., Nagin, D. S., Vitaro, F., & Tremblay, R. E. (2006). Salivary testosterone and aggression, delinquency, and social dominance in a population-based longitudinal study of adolescent males. *Hormones and Behavior, 50,* 118–125.

Vandello, J. A., Cohen, D., Grandon, R., & Franiuk, R. (2009). Stand by your man: Indirect prescriptions for honorable violence and feminine loyalty in Canada, Chile, and the United States. *Journal of Cross-Cultural Psychology, 40,* 81–104.

Vandello, J. A., Cohen, D., & Ransom, S. (2008). U.S. Southern and Northern differences in perceptions of norms about aggression: Mechanisms for the perpetuation of a culture of honor. *Journal of Cross-Cultural Psychology, 39,* 162–177.

Van Dijk, E., De Kwaadsteniet, E. W., & De Cremer, D. (2009). Tacit coordination in social dilemmas: The importance of having a common understanding. *Journal of Personality and Social Psychology, 96,* 665–678.

Van Dyne, L., & Saavedra, R. (1996). A naturalistic minority influence experiment: Effects on divergent thinking, conflict, and originality in work-groups. *British Journal of Social Psychology, 35,* 151–167.

Van Eerde, W., & Thierry, H. (1996). Vroom's expectancy models and work-related criteria: A meta-analysis. *Journal of Applied Psychology, 81,* 575–586.

Van Goozen, S. H. M., Cohen-Kettenis, P. T., Gooren, L. J. G., & Frijda, N. H., et al. (1995). Gender differences in behaviour: Activating effects of cross-sex hormones. *Psychoneuroendocrinology 20,* 343–363.

Van Iddekinge, C. H., Raymark, P. H., & Roth, P. L. (2005). Assessing personality with a structured employment interview: Construct-related validity and susceptibility to response inflation. *Journal of Applied Psychology, 90,* 536–552.

van Knippenberg, D., & Schippers, M. C. (2007). Work group diversity. *Annual Review of Psychology, 58,* 515–541.

van Koppen, P. J., & Penrod, S. D. (Eds.). (2003). *Adversarial versus inquisitorial justice: Psychological perspectives on criminal justice systems.* New York: Kluwer Academic/Plenum.

Van Prooijen, J.-W., Van den Bos, K., Lind, E. A., & Wilke, H. (2006). How do people react to negative procedures? On the moderating role of authority's biased attitudes. *Journal of Experimental Social Psychology, 42*, 632–645.

van Straaten, I., Engels, R., Finkenauer, C., & Holland, R. W. (2009). Meeting your match: Attractiveness similarity affects approach behavior in mixed-sex dyads. *Personality and Social Psychology Bulletin, 35*, 685–697.

Vandello, J. A., & Cohen, D. (1999). Patterns of individualism and collectivism across the United States. *Journal of Personality and Social Psychology, 77*, 279–292.

Vandello, J. A., & Cohen, D. (2003). Male honor and female fidelity: Implicit cultural scripts that perpetuate domestic violence. *Journal of Personality and Social Psychology, 84*, 997–1010.

Vandello, J. A., & Cohen, D. (2004). When believing is seeing: Sustaining norms of violence in cultures of honor. In M. Schaller & C. S. Crandall (Eds.), *The psychological foundations of culture* (pp. 281–304). Mahwah, NJ: Erlbaum.

VanderStoep, S. W., & Shaughnessy, J. J. (1997). Taking a course in research methods improves reasoning about real-life events. *Teaching of Psychology, 24*, 122–124.

Van Vugt, M., & Schaller, M. (2008). Evolutionary approaches to group dynamics: An introduction. *Group Dynamics: Theory, Research, and Practice, 12*, 1–6.

Vathanophas, V., & Liang, S. Y. (2007). Enhancing information sharing in group support systems (GSS). *Computers in Human Behavior, 23*, 1675–1691.

Vecchio, R. P. (2002). Leadership and the gender advantage. *Leadership Quarterly, 13*, 643–671.

Veenhoven, R. (1993). *Happiness in nations.* Rotterdam, The Netherlands: Risbo.

Vega, V., & Malamuth, N. M. (2007). Predicting sexual aggression: The role of pornography in the context of general and specific risk factors. *Aggressive Behavior, 33*, 104–117.

Vermillion, M., & Dodder, R. A. (2007). An examination of the Rosenberg Self-esteem Scale using collegiate wheelchair basketball student athletes. *Perceptual and Motor Skills, 104*, 416–418.

Verona, E., Patrick, C. J., & Lang, A. R. (2002). A direct assessment of the role of state and trait negative emotion in aggressive behavior. *Journal of Abnormal Psychology, 111*, 249–258.

Vetlesen, A. J. (2005). *Evil and human agency.* Cambridge, UK: Cambridge University Press.

Vidmar, N., & Hans, V. P. (2007). *American juries: The verdict.* Amherst, NY: Prometheus.

Vierikko, E., Pulkkinen, L., Kaprio, J., & Rose, R. J. (2006). Genetic and environmental sources of continuity and change in teacher-rated aggression during early adolescence. *Aggressive Behavior, 32*, 308–320.

Viki, G. T., Abrams, D., & Masser, B. (2004). Evaluating stranger and acquaintance rape: The role of benevolent sexism in perpetrator blame and recommended sentence length. *Law and Human Behavior, 28*, 295–303.

Vinokur, A., & Burnstein, E. (1974). Effects of partially shared persuasive arguments on group-induced shifts: A group-problem-solving approach. *Journal of Personality and Social Psychology, 29*, 305–315.

Visintainer, M., Volpicelli, J., & Seligman, M. (1982). Tumor rejection in rats after inescapable or escapable shock. *Science, 216*, 437–439.

Visser, P. S., & Mirabile, R. R. (2004). Attitudes in the social context: The impact of social network composition on individual-level attitude strength. *Journal of Personality and Social Psychology, 87*, 779–795.

Viswesvaran, C., Sanchez, J. I., & Fisher, J. (1999). The role of social support in the process of work stress: A meta-analysis. *Journal of Vocational Behavior, 54*, 314–334.

Vittengl, J. R., & Holt, C. S. (2000). Getting acquainted: The relationship of self-disclosure and social attraction to positive affect. *Journal of Social and Personal Relationships, 17*, 53–66.

Vogel, D. L., Wester, S. R., & Heesacker, M. (1999). Dating relationships and the demand/withdraw pattern of communication. *Sex Roles, 41*, 297–306.

Vohs, K. D., & Finkel, E. J. (Eds.). (2006). *Self and relationships: Connecting intrapersonal and interpersonal processes.* New York: Guilford.

Vohs, K. D., & Heatherton, T. F. (2000). Self-regulatory failure: A resource-depletion approach. *Psychological Science, 11*, 249–252.

Vohs, K. D., Baumeister, R. F., & Ciarocco, N. J. (2005). Self-regulation and self-presentation: Regulatory resource depletion impairs impression management and effortful self-presentation depletes regulatory resources. *Journal of Personality and Social Psychology, 88*, 632–657.

Vohs, K. D., Mead, N. L., & Goode, M. R. (2006). The psychological consequences of money. *Science, 314*, 1154–1156.

Vollhardt, J. R. (2009). Altruism born of suffering and prosocial behavior following adverse life events: A review and conceptualization. *Social Justice Research, 22*, 53–97.

von der Pahlen, B., Lindman, R., Sarkola, T., Maekisalo, H., & Eriksson, C. J. P. (2002). An exploratory study on self-evaluated aggression and androgens in women. *Aggressive Behavior, 28*, 273–280.

von Hippel, W., & Ronay, R. (2009). Executive functions and self-control. In J. P. Forgas, R. Baumeister, & D. Tice (Eds.), *Self regulation: Cognitive, affective, and motivational processes.* New York: Psychology Press.

von Hippel, W., Sekaquaptewa, D., & Vargas, P. T. (2009). Linguistic markers of implicit attitudes. In R. E. Petty, R. H. Fazio, & P. Brinol (Eds.), *Attitudes: Insights from the new wave of implicit measures.* New York: Psychology Press.

Von Lang, J., & Sibyll, C. (Eds.). (1983). *Eichmann interrogated* (R. Manheim, Trans.). New York: Farrar, Straus & Giroux.

Vonk, R. (1998). The slime effect: Suspicion and dislike of likeable behavior toward superiors. *Journal of Personality and Social Psychology, 74*, 849–864.

Voracek, M., & Fisher, M. L. (2002). Shapely centrefolds? Temporal change in body measures: Trend analysis. *British Medical Journal, 325*, 1447–1448.

Vorauer, J. D. (2003). Dominant group members in intergroup interaction: Safety or vulnerability in numbers? *Personality and Social Psychology Bulletin, 29*, 498–511.

Vorauer, J. D., & Claude, S. D. (1998). Perceived versus actual transparency of goals in negotiation. *Personality and Social Psychology Bulletin, 24*, 371–385.

Vorauer, J. D., & Turpie, C. (2004). Disruptive effects of vigilance on dominant group members' treatment of outgroup members: Choking versus shining under pressure. *Journal of Personality and Social Psychology, 87*, 384–399.

Vorauer, J. D., Cameron, J. J., Holmes, J. G., & Pearce, D. G. (2003). Invisible overtures: Fears of rejection and the signal amplification bias. *Journal of Personality and Social Psychology, 84*, 793–812.

Vorauer, J. D., Martens, V., & Sasaki, S. (2009). When trying to understand detracts from trying to behave: Effects of perspective taking in intergroup interaction. *Journal of Personality and Social Psychology, 96*, 811–827.

Vorauer, J. D., & Sasaki, S. J. (2009). Helpful only in the abstract? Ironic effects of empathy in intergroup interaction. *Psychological Science, 20*, 191–197.

Vrij, A. (2008). *Detecting lies and deceit: Pitfalls and opportunities.* Chichester, UK: Wiley.

Vrij, A., Mann, S., Fisher, R., Leal, S., Milne, R., & Bull, R. (2008). Increasing cognitive load to facilitate lie detection: The benefit of recalling an event in reverse order. *Law and Human Behavior, 32*, 253–265.

Vroom, V. H., & Jago, A. G. (1988). *Managing participation in organizations.* Englewood Cliffs, NJ: Prentice-Hall.

Vroom, V. H., & Jago, A. G. (2007). The role of the situation in leadership. *American Psychologist, 62*, 17–24.

Vroom, V. H., & Yetton, P. W. (1973). *Leadership and decisionmaking.* Pittsburgh: University of Pittsburgh Press.

Wageman, R., Fisher, C. M., & Hackman, J. R. (2009). Leading teams when the time is right: Finding the best moments to act. *Organizational Dynamics, 38*, 192–203.

Wagstaff, G. F., Wheatcroft, J., Cole, J. C., Brunas-Wagstaff, J., Blackmore, V., & Pilkington, A. (2008). Some cognitive and neuropsychological aspects of social inhibition and facilitation. *European Journal of Cognitive Psychology, 20*, 828–846.

Waldman, D. A., & Avolio, B. J. (1991). Race effects in performance evaluations: Controlling for ability, education, and experience. *Journal of Applied Psychology, 76*, 897–901.

Walker, L., LaTour, S., Lind, E. A., & Thibaut, J. (1974). Reactions of participants and observers to modes of adjudication. *Journal of Applied Social Psychology, 4*, 295–310.

Walker, I., & Smith, H. J. (2002). *Relative deprivation: Specification, development, and integration.* Cambridge, UK: Cambridge University Press.

Walster, E. (1966). Assignment of responsibility for important events. *Journal of Personality and Social Psychology, 3*, 73–79.

Walster, E., & Festinger, L. (1962). The effectiveness of "overheard" persuasive communications. *Journal of Abnormal and Social Psychology, 65*, 395–402.

Walster, E., Aronson, V., Abrahams, D., & Rottman, L. (1966). The importance of physical attractiveness in dating behavior. *Journal of Personality and Social Psychology, 4*, 508–516.

Walster, E., Walster, G. W., & Berscheid, E. (1978). *Equity: Theory and research.* Boston: Allyn & Bacon.

Walster, E., Walster, G. W., Piliavin, J., & Schmidt, L. (1973). "Playing hard-to-get": Understanding an elusive phenomenon. *Journal of Personality and Social Psychology, 26*, 113–121.

Walther, E., Nagengast, B., & Trasselli, C. (2005). Evaluative conditioning in social psychology: Facts and speculations. *Cognition and Emotion, 19*, 175–196.

Walton, G., & Cohen, G. (2003). Stereotype lift. *Journal of Experimental Social Psychology, 39*, 456–467.

Wampold, B. E., Mondin, G. W., Moody, M., Stich, F., Benson, K., & Ahn, H. (1997). A meta-analysis of outcome studies comparing bona fide psychotherapies: Empirically, "all must have prizes." *Psychological Bulletin, 122*, 203–215.

Wang, S. (2006). Contagious behavior. *APS Observer, 19*, 2.

Wann, D. L., & Grieve, F. G. (2005). Biased evaluation of in-group and out-group spectator behavior at sporting events: The importance of team identification and threats to social identity. *Journal of Social Psychology, 145*, 531–545.

Warburton, W. A., Williams, K. D., & Cairns, D. R. (2006). When ostracism leads to aggression: The moderating effects of control deprivation. *Journal of Experimental Social Psychology, 42*, 213–220.

Ward, L. M., & Friedman, K. (2006). Using TV as a guide: Associations between television viewing and adolescents' sexual attitudes and behavior. *Journal of Research on Adolescence, 16*, 133–156.

Ward, M. L., Hansbrough, E., & Walker, E. (2005). Contributions of music video exposure to black adolescents' gender and sexual schemas. *Journal of Adolescent Research, 20*, 143–166.

Warneken, F., & Tomasello, M. (2006). Altruistic helping in human infants and young chimpanzees. *Science, 311*, 1301–1303.

Warren, B. L. (1966). A multiple variable approach to the assortive mating phenomenon. *Eugenics Quarterly, 13*, 285–298.

Watkins, E. R. (2008). Constructive and unconstructive repetitive thought. *Psychological Bulletin, 134*, 163–206.

Watson, D., Wiese, D., Vaidya, J., & Tellegen, A. (1999). The two general activation systems of affect: Structural findings, evolutionary considerations, and psychobiological evidence. *Journal of Personality and Social Psychology, 76*, 820–838.

Wax, E. (2008, November 22). Can love conquer caste? *Washington Post.*

Wayment, H. A. (2004). It could have been me: Vicarious victims and disaster-focused distress. *Personality and Social Psychology Bulletin, 30*, 515–528.

Weary, G., & Edwards, J. A. (1994). Individual differences in causal uncertainty. *Journal of Personality and Social Psychology, 67*, 308–318.

Webster, D. M., Richter, L., & Kruglanski, A. W. (1996). On leaping to conclusions when feeling tired: Mental fatigue effects on impressional primacy. *Journal of Experimental Social Psychology, 32*, 181–195.

Weeden, J., & Sabini, J. (2005). Physical attractiveness and health in Western societies: A review. *Psychological Bulletin, 131*, 635–653.

Wegener, D. T., & Petty, R. E. (1994). Mood management across affective states: The hedonic contingency hypothesis. *Journal of Personality and Social Psychology, 66*, 1034–1048.

Wegener, D. T., Petty, R. E., & Smith, S. M. (1995). Positive mood can increase or decrease message scrutiny: The hedonic contingency view of mood and message processing. *Journal of Personality and Social Psychology, 69*, 5–15.

Wegge, J., Bipp, T., & Kleinbeck, U. (2007). Goal setting via videoconferencing. *European Journal of Work and Organizational Psychology, 16*, 169–194.

Wegner, D. M. (1994). Ironic processes of mental control. *Psychological Review, 101*, 34–52.

Wegner, D. M. (1997). When the antidote is the poison: Ironic mental control processes. *Psychological Science, 8*, 148–153.

Wegner, D. M., Ansfield, M., & Pilloff, D. (1998). The putt and the pendulum: Ironic effects of the mental control of action. *Psychological Science, 9*, 196–199.

Wegner, D. M., Erber, R., & Raymond, P. (1991). Transactive memory in close relationships. *Journal of Personality and Social Psychology, 61*, 923–929.

Wegner, D. M., Lane, J. D., & Dimitri, S. (1994). The allure of secret relationships. *Journal of Personality and Social Psychology, 66*, 287–300.

Weiner, B. (1985). "Spontaneous" causal thinking. *Psychological Bulletin, 97*, 74–84.

Weiner, B. (2008). Reflections on the history of attribution theory and research. *Social Psychology, 39*, 151–156.

Weinstein, N. D. (1980). Unrealistic optimism about future life events. *Journal of Personality and Social Psychology, 39*, 806–820.

Weinstein, N. D. (1989). Effects of personal experience on self-protective behavior. *Psychological Bulletin, 105*, 31–50.

Weisbuch, M., Ivcevic, Z., & Ambady, N. (2009). On being liked on the web and in the "real world": Consistency in first impressions across personal webpages and spontaneous behavior. *Journal of Experimental Social Psychology, 45*, 573–576.

Weiss, E., & Marksteiner, J. (2007). Alcohol-related cognitive disorders with a focus on neuropsychology. *International Journal on Disability and Human Development, 6*, 337–342.

Weldon, M. S., Blair, C., & Huebsch, D. (2000). Group remembering: Does social loafing underlie collaborative inhibition? *Journal of Experimental Psychology: Learning, Memory, and Cognition, 26*, 1568–1577.

Wells, G. L., & Bradfield, A. L. (1998). "Good, you identified the suspect": Feedback to eyewitnesses distorts their reports of the witnessing experience. *Journal of Applied Psychology, 83*, 360–376.

Wells, G. L., Charman, S. D., & Olson, E. A. (2005). Building face composites can harm lineup identification performance. *Journal of Experimental Psychology: Applied, 11*, 147–156.

Wells, G. L., Lindsay, R. C. L., & Ferguson, T. J. (1979). Accuracy, confidence, and juror perceptions in eyewitness identification. *Journal of Applied Psychology, 64*, 440–448.

Wells, G. L., Memon, A., & Penrod, S. (2007). Eyewitness evidence: Improving its probative value. *Psychological Science in the Public Interest, 7*, 45–75.

Wells, G. L., & Murray, D. M. (1984). Eyewitness confidence. In G. Wells & E. Loftus (Eds.), *Eyewitness testimony: Psychological perspectives* (pp. 155–170). New York: Cambridge University Press.

Wells, G. L., & Petty, R. E. (1980). The effects of overt head-movements on persuasion: Compatibility and incompatibility of responses. *Basic and Applied Social Psychology, 1*, 219–230.

Wells, G. L., & Quinlivan, D. S. (2009). Suggestive eyewitness identification procedures and the Supreme Court's reliability test in light of eyewitness science: 30 years later. *Law and Human Behavior, 33,* 1–24.

Wells, G. L., Small, M., Penrod, S., Malpass, R. S., Fulero, S. M., & Brimacombe, C. A. E. (1998). Eyewitness identification procedures: Recommendations for lineups and photospreads, *Law and Human Behavior, 22,* 603–648.

Wenzlaff, R. M., & Wegner, D. M. (2000). Thought suppression. *Annual Review of Psychology, 51,* 59–91.

Werner, N. E., & Grant, S. (2009). Mothers' cognitions about relational aggression: Associations with discipline responses, children's normative beliefs, and peer competence. *Social Development, 18,* 77–98.

West, S. G., & Brown, T. J. (1975). Physical attractiveness, the severity of the emergency and helping: A field experiment and interpersonal simulation. *Journal of Experimental Social Psychology, 11,* 531–538.

West, T. V., Shelton, J. N., & Trail, T. E. (2009). Relational anxiety in interracial interactions. *Psychological Science, 20,* 289–292.

Westen, D. (2007). *The political brain: The role of emotion in deciding the fate of the nation.* New York: Public Affairs.

Westen, D., Kilts, C., Blagov, P., Harenski, K., & Hamann, S. (2006). The neural basis of motivated reasoning: An fMRI study of emotional constraints on political judgment during the U.S. presidential election of 2004. *Journal of Cognitive Neuroscience, 18,* 1947–1958.

Wheelan, S. A. (2009). Group size, group development, and group productivity. *Small Group Research, 40,* 247–262.

Wheeler, B. C. (2008). Selfish or altruistic? An analysis of alarm call function in wild capuchin monkeys, Cebus apella nigritus. *Animal Behaviour, 76,*1465–1475.

Wheeler, L., & Kim, Y. (1997). What is beautiful is culturally good: The physical attractiveness stereotype has different content in collectivist cultures. *Personality and Social Psychology Bulletin, 23,* 795–800.

Wheeler, L., Koestner, R., & Driver, R. E. (1982). Related attributes in the choice of comparison others. *Journal of Experimental Social Psychology, 18,* 489–500.

Wheeler, M. E., & Fiske, S. T. (2005). Controlling racial prejudice: Social-cognitive goals affect amygdala and stereotype activation. *Psychological Science, 16,* 56–63.

Whitbeck, L. B., & Hoyt, D. R. (1994). Social prestige and assortive mating: A comparison of students from 1956 and 1988. *Journal of Social and Personal Relationships, 11,* 137–145.

White, G. L., Fishbein, S., & Rutstein, J. (1981). Passionate love: The misattribution of arousal. *Journal of Personality and Social Psychology, 41,* 56–62.

Whiteside, K. (2006, June 2). Pockets of intolerance raise Cup concerns: Players feel the reality of racism in soccer as tensions continue to boil in Europe. *USA Today.*

Whittaker, J. O., & Meade, R. D. (1967). Social pressure in the modification and distortion of judgment: A cross-cultural study. *International Journal of Psychology, 2,* 109–113.

Whorf, B. L. (1956). Science and linguistics. In J. B. Carroll (Ed.), *Language, thought, and reality: Selected writings of Benjamin Lee Whorf* (pp. 207–219). Canbridge, MA: MIT Press.

Wilson, D. S., Van Vugt, M., & O'Gorman, R. (2008). Multilevel selection theory and major evolutionary transitions: Implications for psychological science. *Current Directions in Psychological Science, 17,* 6–9.

Wilson, D. W. (1978). Helping behavior and physical attractiveness. *Journal of Social Psychology, 104,* 313–314.

Whyte, G. (1998). Recasting Janis's groupthink model: The key role of collective efficacy in decision fiascoes. *Organizational Behavior and Human Decision Processes, 73,* 185–209.

Wicker, B., Keysers, C., Plailly, J., Royet, J. P., Gallese, V., & Rizzolatti, G. (2003). Both of us disgusted in *my* insula: The common neural basis of seeing and feeling disgust. *Neuron, 40,* 655–664.

Wicklund, R. A. (1975). Objective self-awareness. In L. Berkowitz (Ed.), *Advances in experimental social psychology* (Vol. 8, pp. 233–275). New York: Academic Press.

Widmeyer, W. N., & Loy, J. W. (1988). When you're hot, you're hot! Warm-cold effects in first impressions of persons and teaching effectiveness. *Journal of Educational Psychology, 80,* 118–121.

Wiener, R. L., Hackney, A., Kadela, K., Rauch, S., Seib, H., Warren, L., & Hurt, L. E. (2002). The fit and implementation of sexual harassment law to workplace evaluations. *Journal of Applied Psychology, 87,* 747–764.

Wiener, R. L., Prichard, C. C., & Weston, M. (1995). Comprehesibility of approved jury instructions in capital murder cases. *Journal of Applied Psychology, 80,* 455–467.

Wiesner, W. H., & Cronshaw, S. F. (1988). A meta-analytic investigation of the impact of interview format and degree of structure on the validity of the employment interview. *Journal of Occupational Psychology, 61,* 275–290.

Wiggins, J. S. (Ed.). (1996). *The five-factor model of personality: Theoretical perspectives.* New York: Guilford.

Wilder, D. A. (1977). Perception of groups, size of opposition, and social influence. *Journal of Experimental Social Psychology, 13,* 253–268.

Wilder, D. A., Simon, A. F., & Myles, F. (1996). Enhancing the impact of counterstereotypic information: Dispositional attributions for deviance. *Journal of Personality and Social Psychology, 71,* 276–287.

Wilkinson, D. L., & Carr, P. J. (2008). Violent youths' response to high levels of exposure to community violence: What violent events reveal about youth violence. *Journal of Community Psychology, 36,* 1026–1051.

Willer, R. (2004). The effects of government-issued terror warnings on presidential approval ratings. *Current Research in Social Psychology, 10,* 1–12.

Williams v. Florida, 399 U.S. 78 (1970).

Williams, D. R., Neighbors, H. W., & Jackson, J. S. (2003). Racial/ethnic discrimination and health: Findings from community studies. *American Journal of Public Health, 93,* 200–208.

Williams, J. E., & Best, D. L. (1982). *Measuring sex stereotypes: A thirty nation study.* Beverly Hills, CA: Sage.

Williams, K. D. (2007a). Ostracism. *Annual Review of Psychology, 58,* 425–452.

Williams, K. D. (2007b, November). Ostracism: The kiss of social death. *Social and Personality Psychology Compass, 1,* 236–247.

Williams, K. D. (2009). Ostracism: A temporal need-threat model. In M. P. Zanna (Ed.), *Advances in experimental social psychology* (Vol. 41), pp. 275–314. Burlington: Academic Press.

Williams, K. D., Cheung, C., & Choi, W. (2000). Cyberostracism: Effects of being ignored over the internet. *Journal of Personality and Social Psychology, 79,* 748–762.

Williams, K. D., Govan, C. L., Croker, V., Tynan, D., Cruickshank, M., & Lam, A. (2002). Investigations into differences between social- and cyberostracism. *Group Dynamics: Theory, Research, and Practice, 6,* 65–77.

Williams, K. Y., & O'Reilly, C. A. (1998). Demography and diversity in organizations: A review of 40 years of research. *Research in Organizational Behavior, 20,* 77–140.

Williams, M. J., & Eberhardt, J. L. (2008). Biological conceptions of race and the motivation to cross racial boundaries. *Journal of Personality and Social Psychology, 94,* 1033–1047.

Williams, M. J., & Mendelsohn, G. A. (2008). Gender clues and cues: Online interactions as windows into lay theories about men and women. *Basic and Applied Social Psychology, 30,* 278–294.

Williams, R. (1993). *Anger kills.* New York: Times Books.

Williamson, G. M., Clark, M. S., Pegalis, L. J., & Behan, A. (1996). Affective consequences of refusing to help in communal and exchange relationships. *Personality and Social Psychology Bulletin, 22,* 34–47.

Willis, J., & Todorov, A. (2006). First impressions: Making up your mind after a 100-ms exposure to a face. *Psychological Science, 17,* 592–598.

Wills, T. A. (1981). Downward comparison principles in social psychology. *Psychological Bulletin, 90,* 245–271.

Wills, T. A., & DePaulo, B. M. (1991). Interpersonal analysis of the help-seeking process. In C. R. Snyder & D. R. Forsyth (Eds.), *Handbook of social and clinical psychology: The health perspective* (pp. 350–375). New York: Pergamon Press.

Wilson, A. E., & Ross, M. (2000). The frequency of temporal and social comparisons in people's personal appraisals. *Journal of Personality and Social Psychology, 78,* 928–942.

Wilson, T. D. (2002). *Strangers to ourselves: Discovering the adaptive unconscious.* Cambridge, MA: Belknap Press.

Wilson, T. D., & Gilbert, D. T. (2003). Affective forecasting. *Advances in Experimental Social Psychology, 35,* 345–411.

Wilson, T. D., & Gilbert, D. T. (2005). Affective forecasting: Knowing what to want. *Current Directions in Psychological Science, 14,* 131–134.

Wilson, T. D., Lindsey, S., & Schooler, T. Y. (2000). A model of dual attitudes. *Psychological Review, 107,* 101–126.

Wilson, T. D., Wheatley, T., Meyers, J. M., Gilbert, D. T., & Axsom, D. (2000). Focalism: A source of durability bias in affective forecasting. *Journal of Personality and Social Psychology, 78,* 821–836.

Winch, R. F., Ktsanes, T., & Ktsanes, V. (1954). The theory of complementary needs in mate selection: An analytic and descriptive study. *American Sociological Review, 19,* 241–249.

Winter, D. G. (1987). Leader appeal, leader performance, and the motive profiles of leaders and followers: A study of American presidents and elections. *Journal of Personality and Social Psychology, 52,* 41–46.

Wise, R. A., & Safer, M. A. (2004). What U.S. judges know and believe about eyewitness testimony. *Applied Cognitive Psychology, 18,* 427–443.

Wishman, S. (1986). *Anatomy of a jury: The system on trial.* New York: Times Books.

Wissler, R. L., & Saks, M. J. (1985). On the inefficacy of limiting instructions: When jurors use prior conviction evidence to decide on guilt. *Law and Human Behavior, 9,* 37–48.

Wittenbrink, B., & Schwarz, N. (Eds.). (2007). *Implicit measures of attitudes.* New York: Guilford.

Wittenbrink, B., Judd, C. M., & Park, B. (1997). Evidence for racial prejudice at the implicit level and its relationship with questionnaire measures. *Journal of Personality and Social Psychology, 72,* 262–274.

Wolf, S., & Montgomery, D. A. (1977). Effects of inadmissible evidence and level of judicial admonishment to disregard on the judgments of mock jurors. *Journal of Applied Social Psychology, 7,* 205–219.

Wolgemuth, L. (2009, June 17). Why a psychologist might be at your next interview. *U.S. News & World Report.*

Wong, R. Y.-m., & Hong, Y.-y. (2005). Dynamic influences of culture on cooperation in the prisoner's dilemma. *Psychological Science, 16,* 429–434.

Wood, J. V. (1989). Theory and research concerning social comparisons of personal attributes. *Psychological Bulletin, 106,* 231–248.

Wood, N., & Cowan, N. (1995). The cocktail party phenomenon revisited: How frequent are attention shifts to one's name in an irrelevant auditory channel? *Journal of Experimental Psychology: Learning, Memory, and Cognition, 21,* 255–260.

Wood, W., & Quinn, J. M. (2003). Forewarned and forearmed? Two meta-analysis syntheses of forewarnings of influence appeals. *Psychological Bulletin, 129,* 119–138.

Wood, W., Kallgren, C. A., & Preisler, R. M. (1985). Access to attitude-relevant information in memory as a determinant of persuasion: The role of message attributes. *Journal of Experimental Social Psychology, 21,* 73–85.

Wood, W., Lundgren, S., Ouellette, J. A., Busceme, S., & Blackstone, T. (1994). Minority influence: A meta-analytic review of social influence processes. *Psychological Bulletin, 115,* 323–345.

Wood, W., Pool, G. J., Leck, K., & Purvis, D. (1996). Self-definition, defensive processing, and influence: The normative impact of majority and minority groups. *Journal of Personality and Social Psychology, 71,* 1181–1193.

Woodward, B. (2006). *State of denial: Bush at war, part III.* New York: Simon & Schuster.

Woolley, A. W., Gerbasi, M. E., Chabris, C. F., Kosslyn, S. M., & Hackman, J. R. (2008). Bringing in the experts: How team composition and collaborative planning jointly shape analytic effectiveness. *Small Group Research, 39,* 352–371.

Woolley, A. W., Hackman, J. R., Jerde, T. E., Chabris, C. F., Bennett, S. L., & Kosslyn, S. M. (2007). Using brain-based measures to compose teams: How individual capabilities and team collaboration strategies jointly shape performance. *Social Neuroscience, 2,* 96–105.

Word, C. O., Zanna, M. P., & Cooper, J. (1974). The nonverbal mediation of self-fulfilling prophecies in interracial interaction. *Journal of Experimental Social Psychology, 10,* 109–120.

Worth, L. T., & Mackie, D. M. (1987). Cognitive mediation of positive affect in persuasion. *Social Cognition, 5,* 76–94.

Worthy, D. A., Markman, A. B., & Maddox, W. T. (2009). Choking and excelling at the free throw line. *The International Journal of Creativity and Problem Solving, 19,* 53–58.

Wright, L., von Bussman, K., Friedman, A., Khoury, M., & Owens, F. (1990). Exaggerated social control and its relationship to the Type A behavior pattern. *Journal of Research in Personality, 24,* 258–269.

Wright, N. S., & Drewery, G. P. (2006). Forming cohesion in culturally heterogeneous teams differences in Japanese, Pacific Islander and Anglo experiences. *Cross Cultural Management, 13,* 43–53.

Wright, P. H. (1982). Men's friendships, women's friendships and the alleged inferiority of the latter. *Sex Roles, 8,* 1–20.

Wright, R. A., & Contrada, R. J. (1986). Dating selectivity and interpersonal attraction: Toward a better understanding of the "elusive phenomenon." *Journal of Social and Personal Relationships, 3,* 131–148.

Wright, R. A., Wadley, V. G., Danner, M., & Phillips, P. N. (1992). Persuasion, reactance, and judgments of interpersonal appeal. *European Journal of Social Psychology, 22,* 85–91.

Wrightsman, L. S. (2006). *The psychology of the Supreme Court.* New York: Oxford University Press.

Wrightsman, L. S. (2008). *Oral arguments before the Supreme Court: An empirical approach.* NY: Oxford University Press.

Wrightsman, L. S., & Fulero, S. M. (2008). *Forensic psychology* (3rd ed.). Belmont, CA: Wadsworth.

Wyer, N. A. (2004). Not all stereotypic biases are created equal: Evidence for a stereotype disconfirmation bias. *Personality and Social Psychology Bulletin, 30,* 706–720.

Wyer, N. A. (2007). Motivational influences on compliance with and consequences of instructions to suppress stereotypes. *Journal of Experimental Social Psychology, 43,* 417–424.

Wyer, N. A., Sadler, M. S., & Judd, C. M. (2002). Contrast effects in stereotype formation and change: The role of comparative context. *Journal of Experimental Social Psychology, 38,* 443–458.

Xu, X., Zuo, X., Wang, X., & Han, S. (2009). Do you feel my pain? Racial group membership modulates empathic neural responses. *Journal of Neuroscience, 29,* 8525–8529.

Yablo, P. D., & Field, N. P. (2007). The role of culture in altruism: Thailand and the United States. *Psychologia: An International Journal of Psychology in the Orient, 50,* 236–251.

Yamagishi, T., Makimura, Y., Foddy, M., Matsuda, M., Kiyonari, T., & Platow, M. J. (2005). Comparisons of Australians and Japanese on group-based cooperation. *Asian Journal of Social Psychology, 8,* 173–190.

Yamagishi, T., Mifune, N., Liu, J. H., & Pauling, J. (2008). Exchanges of group-based favours: Ingroup bias in the prisoner's dilemma game with minimal groups in Japan and New Zealand. *Asian Journal of Social Psychology, 11,* 196–207.

Yamawaki, N. (2007). Rape perception and the function of ambivalent sexism and gender-role traditionality. *Journal of Interpersonal Violence, 22,* 406–423.

Yantz, C. L., & McCaffrey, R. J. (2007). Social facilitation effect of examiner attention or inattention to computer-administered neuropsychological testing: First sign that the examiner may affect result. *Clinical Neuropsychologist, 21,* 663–671.

Yeung, N. C. J., & von Hippel, C. (2008). Stereotype threat increases the likelihood that female drivers in a simulator run over jaywalkers. *Accident Analysis and Prevention, 40,* 667–674.

Yopyk, D. J. A., & Prentice, D. A. (2005). Am I an athlete or a student? Identity salience and stereotype threat in student-athletes. *Basic and Applied Social Psychology, 27,* 329–336.

Young, R. K., Kennedy, A. H., Newhouse, A., Browne, P., & Thiessen, D. (1993). The effects of names on perceptions of intelligence, popularity, and competence. *Journal of Applied Social Psychology, 23,* 1770–1788.

Yu, D. W., & Shepard, G. H. (1998). Is beauty in the eye of the beholder? *Nature, 296,* 321–322.

Yuille, J. C., & Tollestrup, P. A. (1990). Some effects of alcohol on eyewitness memory. *Journal of Applied Psychology, 75,* 268–273.

Yuki, M. (2003). Intergroup comparison versus intragroup relationships: A cross-cultural examination of social identity theory in North American and East Asian cultural contexts. *Social Psychology Quarterly, 66,* 166–183.

Yzerbyt, V., & Demoulin, S. (2010). Intergroup relations. In S. T. Fiske, D. T. Gilbert, & G. Lindzey (Eds.), *The handbook of social psychology* (5th ed.). New York: McGraw-Hill.

Yzerbyt, V. Y., Dardenne, B., & Leyens, J.-Ph. (1998). Social judgeability concerns in impression formation. In V. Y. Yzerbyt, G. Lories, & B. Dardenne (Eds.), *Metacognition: Cognitive and social dimensions* (pp. 126–156). London: Sage.

Zaccaro, S. J. (2007). Trait-based perspectives of leadership. *American Psychologist, 62,* 6–16.

Zajonc, R. B. (1965). Social facilitation. *Science, 149,* 269–274.

Zajonc, R. B. (1968). Attitudinal effects of mere exposure. *Journal of Personality and Social Psychology Monograph Supplement, 9*(2), 1–27.

Zajonc, R. B. (1980). Compresence. In P. B. Paulus (Ed.), *Psychology of group influence* (pp. 35–60). Hillsdale, NJ: Erlbaum.

Zajonc, R. B. (1993). Brain temperature and subjective emotional experience. In M. Lewis & J. M. Haviland (Eds.), *Handbook of emotions* (pp. 209–220). New York: Guilford.

Zajonc, R. B. (2001). Mere exposure: A gateway to the subliminal. *Current Directions in Psychological Science, 10,* 224–228.

Zajonc, R. B., Heingartner, A., & Herman, E. M. (1969). Social enhancement and impairment of performance in the cockroach. *Journal of Personality and Social Psychology, 13,* 82–92.

Zajonc, R. B., Murphy, S. T., & Inglehart, M. (1989). Feeling and facial efference: Implications of the vascular theory of emotion. *Psychological Review, 96,* 395–416.

Zanna, M. P., & Cooper, J. (1974). Dissonance and the pill: An attribution approach to studying the arousal properties of dissonance. *Journal of Personality and Social Psychology, 29,* 703–709.

Zárate, M. A., Garcia, B., Garza, A. A., & Hitlan, R. T. (2004). Cultural threat and perceived realistic group conflict as dual predictors of prejudice. *Journal of Experimental Social Psychology, 40,* 99–105.

Zebrowitz, L. A., & Montepare, J. M. (2005). Appearance DOES Matter. *Science, 308,* 1565–1566.

Zebrowitz, L. A., Luevano, V. X., Bronstad, P. M., & Aharon, I. (2009). Neural activation to babyfaced men matches activation to babies. *Social Neuroscience, 4,* 1–10.

Zeisel, H., & Diamond, S. (1978). The effect of peremptory challenges on jury and verdict: An experiment in a federal district court. *Stanford Law Review, 30,* 491–531.

Zell, E., & Alicke, M. D. (2009). Self-evaluative effects of temporal and social comparison. *Journal of Experimental Social Psychology, 45,* 223–227.

Zemack-Rugar, Y., Bettman, J. R., & Fitzsimons, G. J. (2007). The effects of nonconsciously priming emotion concepts on behavior. *Journal of Personality and Social Psychology, 93,* 927–939.

Zentall, T. R. (2003). Imitation by animals: How do they do it? *Current Directions in Psychological Science, 12,* 91–95.

Zhang, L., & Baumeister, R. F. (2006). Your money or your self-esteem: Threatened egotism promotes costly entrapment in losing endeavors. *Personality and Social Psychology Bulletin, 32,* 881–893.

Zhang, S., & Kline, S. L. (2009). Can I make my own decision? A cross-cultural study of perceived social network influence in mate selection. *Journal of Cross-Cultural Psychology, 40,* 3–23.

Zhang, J., & Shavitt, S. (2003). Cultural values in advertisements to the Chinese X-generation. *Journal of Advertising, 32,* 23–33.

Zhou, X., Vohs, K. D., & Baumeister, R. F. (2009). The symbolic power of money: Reminders after money alter social distress and physical pain. *Psychological Science, 20,* 700–706.

Zhu, Y., McKenna, B., & Sun, Z. (2007). Negotiating with Chinese: Success of initial meetings is key. *Cross Cultural Management: An International Journal, 14,* 354–364.

Zick, A., Pettigrew, T. E., & Wagner, U. (2008). Ethnic prejudice and discrimination in Europe. *Journal of Social Issues, 64,* 233–251.

Zillmann, D. (1979). *Hostility and aggression.* Hillsdale, NJ: Erlbaum.

Zillmann, D. (1983). Arousal and aggression. In R. G. Geen & E. I. Donnerstein (Eds.), *Aggression: Theoretical and empirical reviews: Vol. l. Theoretical and methodological issues* (pp. 75–101). New York: Academic Press.

Zillmann, D. (1984). *Connections between sex and aggression.* Hillsdale, NJ: Erlbaum.

Zillmann, D. (2003). Theory of affective dynamics: Emotions and moods. In J. Bryant, D. Roskos-Ewoldsen, & J. Cantor (Eds.), *Communication and emotion: Essays in honor of Dolf Zillmann* (pp. 533–567). Mahwah, NJ: Erlbaum.

Zillmann, D., Bryant, J., Cantor, J. R., & Day, K. D. (1975). Irrelevance of mitigating circumstances in retaliatory behavior at high levels of excitation. *Journal of Research in Personality, 9,* 282–293.

Zimbardo, P. G. (1967, June). The psychology of police confessions. *Psychology Today, 1,* 17–27.

Zimbardo, P. G. (1969). The human choice: Individuation, reason, and order versus deindividuation, impulse, and chaos. *Nebraska Symposium on Motivation, 17,* 237–307.

Zimbardo, P. G. (1985, June). Laugh where we must, be candid where we can. *Psychology Today,* pp. 43–47.

Zimbardo, P. G. (2007). *The Lucifer effect: How good people turn evil.* New York: Random House.

Zimbardo, P. G., Banks, W. C., Haney, C., & Jaffe, D. (1973, April 8). The mind is a formidable jailer: A Pirandellian prison. *New York Times Magazine,* pp. 38–60.

Zimbardo, P. G., LaBerge, S., & Butler, L. D. (1993). Psychophysiological consequences of unexplained arousal: A posthypnotic suggestion paradigm. *Journal of Abnormal Psychology, 102,* 466–473.

Zitek, E. M., & Hebl, M. R. (2007). The role of social norm clarity in the influenced expression of prejudice over time. *Journal of Experimental Social Psychology, 43,* 867–876.

Zongker, B., & Nuckols, B. (2009, June 12). For accused museum shooter, a downward spiral. *Associated Press.*

Zuckerman, M., DePaulo, B. M., & Rosenthal, R. (1981). Verbal and nonverbal communication of deception. In L. Berkowitz (Ed.), *Advances in experimental social psychology* (Vol. 14, pp. 1–59). New York: Academic Press.

Zuckerman, M., Knee, C. R., Hodgins, H. S., & Miyake, K. (1995). Hypothesis confirmation: The joint effect of positive test strategy and acquiescence response set. *Journal of Personality and Social Psychology, 68,* 52–60.

Zuwerink, J. R., & Devine, P. G. (1996). Attitude importance and resistance to persuasion: It's not just the thought that counts. *Journal of Personality and Social Psychology, 70,* 931–944.

Credits

Chapter 3

Figure 3.1, p. 63: From M. R. Lepper, D. Greene, and K. E. Nisbett, "Undermining children's intrinsic interest with extrinsic reward: A test of the 'overjustification' hypothesis," *Journal of Personality and Social Psychology,* 28, (1973): 129–137. Copyright © 1973 by the American Psychological Association. Reprinted by permission. **Figure 3.3, p. 69:** From Bahrick et al., *Psychological Science,* 1996, Vol. 7, p. 266–271. Copyright © 1996. Reprinted by permission of Blackwell Publishing. **Figure 3.4, p. 70:** From H. R. Markus and S. Kitayama, "Culture and the self: Implications for cognition, emotion, and motivation," *Psychological Review,* 98 (1991): 226. Copyright © 1991 by the American Psychological Association. Reprinted by permission. **Figure 3.5, p. 71:** From H. Kim and H. R. Markus, "Deviance or Uniqueness, Harmony or Conformity? A Cultural Analysis," *Journal of Personality and Social Psychology,* 77, (1999): 785–800. Copyright © 1999 by the American Psychological Association. Reprinted by permission. **Figure 3.6, p. 75:** From Twenge, J. M. and Crocker, J. (2002). Race and Self-Esteem: Meta-Analysis Comparison Whites, Blacks, Hispanics, Asians, and American Indians. *Psychological Bulletin,* 128, 371–408. Copyright © 2002 by the American Psychological Association. Reprinted by permission. **Table 3.1, p. 78:** From A. Fenigstein, M. F. Scheier, and A. H. Buss, "Public and Private Self-Consciousness: Assessment and Theory," *Journal of Consulting and Clinical Psychology,* 43, 522–527, 1975. Copyright © 1975 by the American Psychological Association. Reprinted by permission. **Table 3.3, p. 94:** From M. Snyder and S. Gangestad, "On the Nature of Self-Monitoring: Matters of Assessment, Matters of Validity," *Journal of Personality and Social Psychology,* 51, 125–139, 1986. Copyright © 1986 by the American Psychological Association. Reprinted by permission.

Chapter 4

Figure 4.1, p. 108: From Elfenbein, H. A. and Ambady, N. (2002). How Good are People at Identifying Emotions in the Face? *Psychological Bulletin,* 128, 203–235. Copyright © 2002 by the American Psychological Association. Reprinted by permission. **Figure 4.2, p. 109:** Reprinted with permission from "Smileys" © 1996 O'Reilly & Associates, Inc. All rights reserved. Orders and Information: 800-998-9938, www.oreilly.com. **Table 4.2, p. 111:** From P. Ekman and M. O'Sullivan, "Who Can Catch a Liar?" *American Psychologist,* Vol. 46, 913–920, 1991. Copyright © 1991 by the American Psychological Association. Reprinted by permission. **Figure 4.3, p. 114:** From E. G. Jones and K. E. Harris, "The Attribution of Attitudes," *Journal of Experimental Social Psychology,* Vol. 3, p. 1–24. Copyright © 1967, with permission from Elsevier. **Figure 4.5, p. 119:** From L. Ross, T. M. Amabile, and J. L. Steinmetz, "Social Roles, Social Control, and Biases in Social Perception Process," *Journal of Personality and Social Psychology,* Vol. 35, 485–494, 1977. Copyright © 1977 by the American Psychological Association. Reprinted by permission. **Figure 4.7, p. 122:** From J. G. Miller, "Culture and the Development of Everyday Social Explanation," *Journal of Personality and Social Psychology,* Vol. 46, 961–978, 1984. Copyright © 1984 by the American Psychological Association. Reprinted by permission. **Figure 4.8, p. 123:** From Y. Hong, M. W. Morris, C. Chiu and V. Benet-Martinez, "Multicultural Minds: A Dynamic Constructivist Approach to Culture and Cognition," *American Psychologist,* Vol. 55, 709–720, 2000. Copyright © 2000 by the American Psychological Association. Reprinted by permission. **Figure 4.9, p. 124:** Balcetis, E., & Dunning, D. (2006). See what you want to see: motivational influences on visual perception. *Journal of Personality and Social Psychology,* 91, 612–625, Figure 1, p. 615. Copyright © 2006 by the American Psychological Association. Reprinted by permission. **Figure 4.10, p. 128:** From J. A. Bargh, M. Chen and L. Burrows, "Automaticity of Social Behavior: Direct Effects of Trait Construct and Stereotype Activation on Action," *Journal of Personality and Social Psychology,* Vol. 71, 23–244, 1996. Copyright © 1996 by the American Psychological Association. Reprinted by permission. **Figure 4.11, p. 131:** Rosenberg, S., Nelson, C., & Vivekananthan, P. S. (1968). A multidimensional approach to the structure of personality impressions. *Journal of Personality and Social Psychology,* 9, 283–294, Figure 3, p. 290. Copyright © 1968 by the American Psychological Association. Reprinted by permission.

Chapter 5

Figure 5.1, p. 147: Kohut, A., & Wike, R. "Xenophobia on the Continent." *National Interest,* Oct. 30, 2008. www.nationalinterest.org. Reprinted by permission. **Figure 5.5, p. 153:** Hutchings, P. B., & Haddock, G. (2008). Look black in anger: The role of implicit prejudice in the categorization and perceived emotional intensity of racially ambiguous faces. *Journal of Experimental Social Psychology,* 44, 1418–1420. Reprinted by permission of Elsevier. **Figure 5.13, p. 180:** From L. Sinclair and Z. Kunda, "Reactions to a Black Professional: Motivated Inhibition and Activation of Conflicting Stereotypes," *Journal of Personality and Social Psychology,* Vol. 77, 885–904. Copyright © the American Psychological Association. Reprinted by permission. **Figure 5.14, p. 181:** Gaertner, S. L., Dovidio, J. F., & Houlette, M. A. (2010). Social categorization. In J. F. Dovidio, M. Hewstone, P. Glick, & V. M. Esses (Eds.), *Handbook of prejudice, stereotyping, and discrimination.* London: Sage. Copyright © 2010. Reprinted by permission of Sage Publications, Inc. **Figure 5.16, p. 188:** From Claude Steele, *Journal of Personality and Social Psychology,* 69, 797–811, 1995. Copyright © 1995 by the American Psychological Association. Reprinted by permission.

Name Index

Subject Index

Evolutionary psychology
    aggression, 444–46
    attraction, 344
    definition of, 18
    helping others, 391–97
    mate selection, 358–60
    punishment, 325
The Evolution of Desire (Buss), 358
Exchange relationships, 367, 426
Excitation transfer, 371, 458–59
Executive functioning, 448, 461
Exercise, 371, 458–59
Exhaustion stage, 575
Expectancy theory, 553
Expectations
    of experimenters, 15, 44
    and first impressions, 133
    positive and helping behavior, 418*t*
    and self-fulfilling prophecy, 135–38
    social exchange theory, 364–65
    and stress treatment success, 602
The Experiment, 520
Experimental realism, 45–46
Experimenter expectancy effects, 44
Experiments
    vs. correlations, 40*t*
    deception in, 46
    definition and characteristics of, 39–40
    ethical issues, 15, 48–49
    example of, 7–9
    field, 41
    independent vs. dependent variables, 42
    internal vs. external validity, 43–46
    laboratory, 40–41
    random assignment, 39–40
    replication, 43
    statistical significance, 43
    subject variables, 42–43
Experts, persuasive communication of, 218–19
Expert witnesses, 219, 508–9
The Expression of the Emotions in Man and Animals (Darwin), 107
External validity, 44–46
Extreme positions, 225–26
Extrinsic motivation, 63–64, 554
Extroversion, 128, 134, 138
Eye contact, 109
Eye-tracking technology, 33
Eyewitness testimony, 257, 499–509

Facebook, 90, 295*c*
Facial electromyograph (EMG), 206–7
Facial features and expressions
    as attitude measure, 206–7
    beauty associated with, 347
    and death penalty, 151*f*
    and emotion identification, 61–62, 107–8
    and fertility, 362
    first impressions from, 102–3, 104
    interracial perceptions, 152–53, 168
Facial feedback hypothesis, 61–62
Failure
    downward social comparisons, 86–88
    and self-handicapping, 84–85
Fairness, 420, 545
Fairy tales, 350
Faking behavior, 532–33, 535
False confessions, 495–98
False-consensus effect, 116–17, 123
Familiarity, 344–45
Familiarity-induced bias, 506
Family violence, 445, 475, 478. *See also* Domestic violence

Fathers, 361–62
Fear appeals, 226–27
Federal Bureau of Investigation (FBI), 438*t*
Female genital mutilation, 440
Fertility, 362
Field experiments, 41
Fields, W. C., 558
50 Cent, 468*c*
Fight Club, 464*c*
"Fight or flight," 576–77
File sharing, 394
Financial crisis (2008–2009), 293, 294*c,* 299, 314
Financial pressure, personal, 575
Finger-length ratios, 446–47
Finland, school shooting in, 28*c*
First dates, 105
First impressions. *See* Impression formation
Fish test, 121–22, 123*f*
Fixed-pie syndrome, 329, 330
Flashbulb memories, 68
Flash mobs, 251
FMRI (functional magnetic resonance imaging), 20, 153, 258–59, 342, 349, 499
Focused relaxation, 596
Foot-in-the-door technique, 270–71
Forepersons, 514
Forewarning, 232–33
Forgiveness, 283
Forming stage, of groups, 270*t*
Fortune 500 companies, 551
Frank, Barney, 318
Fraternity members, 446
Freedom of choice, 240
Free riding, 312*t*
Friendship
    health benefits, 4, 598
    helping behavior in, 426
    proximity effect, 344
    Sternberg's triangular theory of love, 370
Frontal lobe, 448
Frustration-aggression hypothesis, 454–57
F-Scale, 279
Fundamental attribution error, 118–20, 497
Funt, Allen, 275–76

Gallup surveys, 36, 134, 219, 529
Gambling, 84, 302
Gates, Bill, 422, 549
Gaze, 109
Gender differences
    aggression, 442–43, 445–47, 451–52
    conflict in intimate relationships, 382
    in conformity, 263
    depression, 583
    helping others, 426–27
    jurors, 488
    leadership, 551–52
    mate selection, 357–63
    negotiation, 330
    research issues, 19–20
    salary negotiation, 557
    self-concept, 65
    self-disclosure in intimate relationships, 374
    self-esteem, 74
    sexual attitudes and behavior, 377
    sexual orientation, 379
    social loafing, 306
    social value orientation, 326
    sports team cohesiveness, 299
    stress response, 576–77, 596
Gender identity, 174
Gender roles, 175, 451–52
Gender stereotypes, 155, 173–78, 189, 190, 551–52

Gender wage gap, 557–58
General adaptation syndrome, 575–77
Generation Me (Twenge), 283
Genetic factors
    aggression, 446
    attitude formation, 210
    helping behaviors, 391–93, 421
    homosexuality, 379
    race, 166
Genetics, behavior, 18, 446
Genovese, Kitty, 405, 411
Germany, 164
GHB (Gamma Hydroxy Butyrate), 474
Gill, Kimveer, 463
Giuliani, Rudolph, 547
Glass ceiling, 157–58, 551
Globalization, 540
Glucose, 80
Glwi culture, 441*t*
Goals
    group, 320
    work, 553–54
Good mood effect, 417
Good Samaritan laws, 399
Good Samaritan parable, 413
Google, 553*c*
Gorillas, 395
Gossiping, 162
Government employees, 299
Grade inflation, 68, 69*f*
Grades, 83
Gradual escalation, 281
Graduated and reciprocated initiatives in tension-reduction (GRIT), 329
Great Person Theory, 546
Greece, 161
GRIT (graduated and reciprocated initiatives in tension-reduction), 329
Group cohesiveness, 299–300
Group development stages, 296–97
Group-level altruism, 394–95
Group performance, 310–22
    brainstorming, 311–12
    and diversity, 322
    escalation effect, 317–18
    and group cohesiveness, 300
    and group polarization, 312–14
    and groupthink, 314–17
    improvement strategies, 319–21
    information and skill utilization, 318–19
    process loss, 310–11
    and social facilitation, 300–304
    and social loafing, 304–7
    virtual teams, 321–22
Group polarization, 312–14
Groups
    cohesiveness, 299–300
    conflicts and conflict resolution, 160–61, 323–33
    definition of, 148, 294–95
    deindividuation, 307–9
    development stages, 296–97
    fundamental motives between, 159–60
    goals, 320
    ingroups vs. outgroups, 148
    intergroup contact, 192–95
    minimal, 162
    norms, 255, 298–99, 319–20
    presence of others, 300–309
    reasons for joining, 295–96
    roles, 297–98
    size of and conformity levels, 261
    social dominance orientation, 165
    social facilitation effects, 300–304

Teachers, 135–36, 346
Technology, 20–21, 33–34. *See also* Computers; Internet
Teenagers. *See* Adolescents
Television
 and aggression in children, 450
 commercials, 176
 helping others impact, 419
 quiz show study, 119
 reality, 4c, 48
 and self-discrepancies, 77
 social facilitation effects, 303
 violence, 463–70, 476–77
Temperature, and aggression, 457–58
Temporal comparisons, 86–87
Terror alerts, 227c
Terror Management Theory, 73, 160
Testimony
 eyewitness, 499–509
 inadmissible, 510–11
Testosterone, 446–47, 460
Tests, academic, 188–89, 190
Thai students, altruistic behavior study, 421
That's-not-all technique, 273–74
Theories, 29
Theory of planned behavior, 212
Theory of reasoned action, 212, 604
Thompson, Jennifer, 499
Threat capacity, 327–28
Threat-to-self-esteem model, 427–28
360-degree assessment, 544–45
Tiller, George, 435, 455
Time pressure, and helping others, 412–13
Timing, 225
Titus, Steve, 505
TMS (transcranial magnetic stimulation), 20
Torres, Angel Arce, 390–91
Touch, 109–10
Tragedy of the commons, 324–25
Training, of groups, 320
Traits. *See* Personality traits
Transactional leadership, 548–49, 550
Transactive memory, 319
Transcranial magnetic stimulation (TMS), 20
Transformational leadership, 549–51
Transitional periods, 67
Translations, 47
Transsexuals, 447
Trebek, Alex, 120c
Treeing, 28
Trials
 context of, 486
 cultural differences, 523
 inadmissible testimony, 510–11
 judge's instructions, 511–13
 jury deliberation, 513–17
 jury selection, 487–93
 pretrial publicity, 509–10
 sentencing process, 517–19
 See also Evidence
Triangular theory of love, 369–70
True acceptance (private conformity), 259–60, 265
Truman, Harry, 36c
Trust, 325
Trust-insurance system, 366–67
Trustworthiness, 104, 219
Truth, 110–12
Tucholosky, Sara, 400–401

Turkey, 161
Turner, Ted, 422
TV. *See* Television
Twelve Angry Men, 264, 513
Twin studies, 210, 378, 421, 446, 608–9
Two-factor theory of emotion, 66–67, 370
Type A personality, 443, 577–78
Tyson, Mike, 437c

Ukrainians, organ donation study, 428–29
Unemployment, 529
Urban areas, helpfulness in, 413–14
U.S. Department of Justice, 442, 499–500
U.S. News & World Report, 534
U.S. Supreme Court. *See* Supreme Court

Validity
 construct, 31
 internal vs. external, 43–46
Values, and scientific research, 49–50
Vandalism, 476
Variables
 conceptual, 30–31
 in correlational research, 37
 definitions, 30–31
 dependent, 42
 independent, 42
 measurement, 31–34
 subject, 42–43
Vedas, Brandon, 410
Verdicts, 513–17
Vicarious self-perception, 61
Victims, 124–25, 280, 405–12, 441–42
Video games, 11, 39f, 463–70, 472
Videotaping, 206, 498
Vietnam veterans, 86c
Violence
 child abuse, 445, 475, 478
 in cultures of honor, 442, 452–54
 cycle of, 475
 definition of, 437
 and deindividuation, 307–9
 desensitization to, 468–69
 in media, 462–70, 476–77
 in schools, 28c, 435–36, 455, 464, 479
 See also Domestic violence
Violent crime
 age of perpetuators, 441
 alcohol-related, 461
 archival measures, 35
 cultural differences, 438
 gun-related, 459
 and heat, 442, 457
 social learning theory, 451
 statistics, 438t, 439f, 441–42, 473, 474
 in U.S., 438t
 See also Rape
Violent pornography, 471–72
Virginia Tech shooting, 5c
Virtual teams, 321–22
Virtual world, 303
Viruses, 581–82, 598
Visual perception experiments, 124f, 255
Voice, 104
Voir dire, 488, 490, 493
Volunteering, 402–4, 415–16
Von Brunn, James, 435, 455
Voting, 239

Wage gap, 557–58
Waist-to-hip ratio (WHR), 346
Wallace, Liz, 400c
War and warfare, 444–45, 572–73
Warmth, 130
Watergate hearings, 68
Wealth, 267, 606–9
Weapon-focus effect, 500–501
Weapons effect, 459–60
Weather, 6, 416, 457–58
What-is-beautiful-is-good stereotype, 350
Whistleblowers, 298–99
Who Wants to Be a Millionaire?, 258
WHR (waist-to-hip ratio), 346
Williams v. Florida, 515–16
Winfrey, Oprah, 6c
Witnesses
 bystander effect, 406, 410–12
 eyewitness testimony, 257, 499–509
Women
 affirmative action, 537–40
 body image, 176–77
 leadership, 551–53
 obedience, 279
 stereotypes, 155, 173–78, 552
 stereotype threat, 189, 190, 191
 wage gap, 557–58
 See also Gender differences
Women at Ground Zero (Hagen and Carouba), 427
Woods, Tiger, 218, 220
Word, Deletha, 411
Word search study, 127
Work hours, 530c
Workplace
 burnout, 574
 commuting stressors, 575
 discrimination, 157–59, 531–35
 diversity, 540–42
 Hawthorne effect, 530
 injuries, 531
 leadership, 545–53
 motivation, 553–58
 performance appraisals, 542–45
 stress, 574
 See also Personnel selection
World Cup soccer (2006), 101, 102c, 113, 149, 341c
World Health Organization, 570
World views, 73
World War I, 573–74
World War II, 14–15, 48, 276, 280, 283, 314, 328, 523, 573
Wrestling, professional, 472

Yale Communication and Attitude Change Program, 215
You Just Don't Understand (Tannen), 382

Zapotec culture, 441t
Zelmanowitz, Abraham, 399
Zidane, Zinedine, 101, 102c

Study Guide

Social Psychology

EIGHTH EDITION

Saul Kassin
Williams College

Steven Fein
Williams College

Hazel Rose Markus
Stanford University

Prepared by

Billa Reiss
St. John's University

WADSWORTH
CENGAGE Learning™

Australia • Brazil • Japan • Korea • Mexico • Singapore • Spain • United Kingdom • United States

Contents

To the Student

Students often ask us for ideas or tips about how best to study for their social psychology quizzes or exams. Some worry that because there are so many important concepts and findings reported in the textbook, and because the field of social psychology covers such a diverse set of topics, there is no way they can learn them all. They worry that they will confuse concepts that seem similar but have subtle, yet important, differences. They want to know not only on *what* they should focus, but also *how* they should study. We emphasize to these students the importance of doing three things: (1) try to organize the material so that you understand "the big picture" and can see which details are most important toward this end; (2) take an active approach to learning in which you test yourself, put concepts into your own words, etc.; and (3) always ask yourself *why* – *why* this theory predicts what it does, *why* this study found what it did and not something else, *why* this principle is thought to tie together the theory and research so well, and so on.

We have designed this *Study Guide* with these three goals in mind. The material in this guide is designed to help you organize the material and identify the details that are most important in shaping "the big picture," to give you opportunities to take an active approach in your studying by providing various exercises, and to offer explanations for the practice questions that emphasize *why* the answers are correct – and why others are *not* correct.

This *Study Guide* is designed to accompany *Social Psychology*, Eighth Edition, by Saul Kassin, Steven Fein, and Hazel Rose Markus. If followed properly, the materials and exercises found in this guide will not only increase your mastery of the concepts, ideas, and facts found in the textbook, but also enhance your ability to "show what you know" on exams covering material from the textbook.

For every chapter in your textbook, there is a corresponding chapter in the *Study Guide*. Each of these chapters is divided into four major sections: Learning Objectives, Major Concepts: The Big Picture, Key Term Exercise, and a Practice Quiz which itself is divided into Multiple-Choice Questions (along with answers to these questions and explanations for why the correct answers are correct and why the alternative answers are not) and Essay Questions (along with sample essays). These sections are designed to enhance your comprehension of the material in the textbook – each in a different way.

LEARNING OBJECTIVES: GUIDELINES FOR STUDY

The Learning Objectives section that begins each *Study Guide* chapter provides you with an explicit and thorough list of the most important ideas and points of each textbook chapter. A student who masters a chapter's Learning Objectives can be confident that he or she has a thorough understanding of the most important material in the textbook chapter. These Learning Objectives provide you with a detailed road map that points toward command of the material. Keep them in mind as you study the chapters.

Note that page numbers locating the relevant material in the textbook are included next to each objective. Ideally, these objectives should be read *after* you have read the corresponding textbook chapter once, but *before* you read the chapter a second time. The use of these Learning Objectives as a guide for studying will help you organize your studying and make the most of your time.

MAJOR CONCEPTS: THE BIG PICTURE

The learning of complex material is best enhanced not by focusing on details but by understanding how those details fit into the general principles. So, where the Learning Objectives provide you with the important details of the corresponding textbook chapter, the Major Concepts section of each *Study Guide* chapter is provided to help you see where these details fit in "the big picture" of the textbook chapter. For each chapter, therefore, we have provided a summary of the basic issues and principles that organize the chapter. You should know these issues and principles well as they will help you put the more specific details in context, thus improving both your overall understanding of these details and your chances of recalling them successfully when tested later.

KEY TERM EXERCISE: THE CONCEPTS YOU SHOULD KNOW

The Learning Objectives and the Major Concepts sections of each *Study Guide* chapter are designed to help you learn and study the material. The Key Term Exercise and the Practice Quiz are designed to show you, in part, how well you know your stuff. By actually doing these exercises, rather than reading and rereading the material, you will not only improve your comprehension and ability to recall the material but also receive feedback that indicates what you need to spend more time studying. In short, you will use your time more efficiently and wisely.

A clear understanding of the key terms from each chapter is essential. If the authors of the textbook think that these terms are important enough to be highlighted in **bold** and defined in the margins of the textbook and in the glossary, then it's a good bet that your instructor will expect you to know them. The Key Term Exercise in each *Study Guide* chapter is designed to help you study these terms and concepts, and to provide you with a way to test your understanding of them. All of the key terms highlighted in bold in the corresponding textbook chapter are included in the Key Term Exercise.

The Key Term Exercise can be done in one of several different ways, depending on your ambition and the kinds of tests your instructor gives. The simplest way is to treat it like a matching test. That is, try to match each term from the exercise to its textbook definition. But a more complete way of doing the exercise – the method that should promote the deepest understanding – is to take each of the key terms and concepts listed first in the exercise and define them *in your own words*. Challenging yourself to explain these terms in your own words is an excellent way to study, allowing you to find out how well you *really* know them. Once you have defined these terms in your own words, try to match each one to the textbook definitions that are provided. Note how your own definitions compare to the textbook definitions. Are they very similar? Or do these comparisons reveal that you were a bit confused about the meaning of some of these terms? Yet another way to do this exercise is a compromise between the other two ways. That is, define as many terms as you can, and simply try to match the rest of the terms with the corresponding textbook definitions.

PRACTICE QUIZ

The best test of your knowledge of the chapter is to take the Practice Quiz. The Practice Quiz is designed to give you experience with the kinds of questions that are likely to appear on an exam. Thus, we have included multiple-choice questions as well as essay questions in each Practice Quiz. Some of the multiple-choice questions concern factual or conceptual information stated in the textbook; others ask you to *apply* the theories, concepts, and research findings to some practical problem or situation. The multiple-choice questions and the essay questions pose a diverse set of challenges, sometimes asking you to differentiate one concept from another, sometimes asking you to distinguish the predictions of one theory from another, and sometimes asking you to apply your knowledge of social psychological research to predict how people would respond in particular situations. Thus, these questions require a fine-tuned understanding of ideas, terms, and facts in social psychology.

This *Study Guide* is rather unusual in that it not only gives the correct answers to the multiple-choice questions contained in the Practice Quiz, but it also *explains* these answers. That is, in the answer section, we repeat the question (so you won't have to flip pages back and forth constantly), identify the correct answer, and explain *why* that response is the best way to answer the question. In addition, we also explain why the other choices are incorrect, with special attention to alternative responses that *seem* to be appropriate answers but in actuality are not. Because we knew these explanations would be included, we did not hesitate to make many of these questions rather challenging; that is, we often included several possible answers to a question that appear to be plausible. By reading our explanations as to why one response is correct and the others are incorrect, you will have a much more comprehensive understanding of the material.

This *Study Guide* is also somewhat unusual in that it provides brief sample essays to illustrate how to answer the essay questions. We do not want you to consider these sample essays as the *only* way to answer the essay questions; rather, they are included to provide you with examples of good answers. For even more practice writing short essays concerning the material in the chapter, you may wish to return to the Learning Objectives at the start of each *Study Guide* chapter and treat them as essay questions.

If you achieve all of the Learning Objectives, understand the Major Concepts, and perform well in the Key Term Exercises and Practice Quizzes, you can be confident that you have a solid command of the material in the textbook. Remember, however, that learning the material in this guide is not a substitute for a careful reading of the textbook or thorough preparation for an exam. The *Study Guide* cannot begin to cover the breadth of concepts, theories, and research findings discussed in the textbook. But it will prepare you well for the kinds of questions you're likely to encounter on a test. That, in turn, should help you master this course in social psychology.

I would like to thank Steven Fein, Steven Spencer, and Fred Whitford for their substantial contributions to earlier editions of this *Study Guide*.

Billa Reiss

St. John's University

CHAPTER 1

What is Social Psychology?

OUTLINE

LEARNING OBJECTIVES: GUIDELINES FOR STUDY

You should be able to do each of the following by the conclusion of Chapter 1.

1.   Define social psychology. Identify the kinds of questions that social psychologists try to answer. (*pp. 5-9*)

2.   Explain how social psychology differs from sociology and other fields of psychology. Assess the limitations of the following statement: *all social psychological findings are simply common sense.* (*pp. 9-12*)

3.   Describe the early origins of social psychology and the state of the field up until 1950. Identify when the field of social psychology became a distinct field of study, the various founders of the field, and the historical event that inspired interest in and shaped the field of social psychology. Explain the contributions made by Allport, Sherif, and Lewin. (*pp. 12-15*)

4.   Describe the state of social psychology from the 1960s to the mid-1970s, and from the mid-70s to the 1990s. Explain the various ways in which contemporary social psychology can be referred to as "pluralistic." (*pp. 15-16*)

5. Distinguish between different perspectives social psychologists use to understand human behavior. Define social cognition. Summarize the increasing effort in social psychology to develop an international and multicultural perspective. (*pp. 17-18*)

6. Explain how social psychology incorporates biological, evolutionary, and sociocultural perspectives of human behavior. Describe the role of new technologies such as PET and fMRI in the investigation of social behavior. (*pp. 18-21*)

MAJOR CONCEPTS: THE BIG PICTURE

Below are three basic issues or principles that organize Chapter 1. You should know these issues and principles well.

1. Social psychology is the scientific study of the way individuals think, feel, and behave in a social context. Social psychology often emphasizes the power of the situation in affecting people. Social psychology can be distinguished from other disciplines, including sociology, clinical psychology, personality psychology, and cognitive psychology; however, social psychology overlaps with each of these disciplines as well. Social psychology may at first appear to be common sense, but common sense often makes contradictory claims, and many of the findings in social psychology would not be predicted by common sense.

2. Social psychology has a relatively brief history. Early social psychology began in the late 1800s with research by Triplett on how the presence of others affects performance, and the field took root as several textbooks were written on social psychology in the early 1900s. From the 1930s to 1950s the field grew quickly as it tried to understand the horrors of World War II and Nazi Germany. Kurt Lewin was a particularly important figure who fled Nazi Germany for the United States during this period. The 1960s and early 1970s saw a rise in confidence and expansion of the field, but was also a time of questioning and debate. The late 1970s to the 1990s saw the birth of a new subfield, social cognition, and greater international and cultural perspectives in social psychology.

3. In the 21st century it appears that there will be several important new emphases in social psychology. The integration of emotion, motivation, and cognition, biological and evolutionary perspectives, sociocultural perspectives, and new technologies are all likely to shape the field in the near future.

KEY TERM EXERCISE: THE CONCEPTS YOU SHOULD KNOW

Below are all of the key terms that appear in **boldface** in Chapter 1. To help you better understand these concepts, rather than just memorize them, write a definition for each term in your own words. After doing so, look at the next section where you'll find a list of definitions from the textbook for each of the key terms presented in random order. For each of your definitions, find the corresponding textbook definition. Note how your definitions compare with those from the textbook.

Key Terms

1. social psychology
2. cross-cultural research
3. interactionist perspective
4. behavioral genetics
5. evolutionary psychology
6. social cognition
7. multicultural research
8. social neuroscience
9. culture

Textbook Definitions

a. The study of how people perceive, remember, and interpret information about themselves and others.

b. A subfield of psychology that uses the principles of evolution to understand human social behavior.

c. The scientific study of how individuals think, feel, and behave in a social context.

d. Research designed to compare and contrast people of different cultures.

e. A subfield of psychology that examines the role of genetic factors on behavior.

f. A system of enduring meanings, beliefs, values, assumptions, institutions and practices shared by a large group of people and transmitted from one generation to the next.

g. Research designed to examine racial and ethnic groups within cultures.

h. An emphasis on how both an individual's personality and environmental characteristics influence behavior.

i. The study of the relationship between neural and social processes.

ANSWERS FOR KEY TERM EXERCISE

Answers for the key terms exercise are listed below.

1. **c**
2. **d**
3. **h**
4. **e**
5. **b**
6. **a**
7. **g**
8. **i**
9. **f**

PRACTICE QUIZ: TEST YOUR KNOWLEDGE OF THE CHAPTER

Multiple-Choice Questions

1. Kattie and Ernest both study human behavior. Kattie is a social psychologist, and Ernest is a journalist. Based on the definition of social psychology, one can assume that an important difference between Kattie and Ernest is likely to be that Kattie
    a. uses statistics, whereas Ernest does not.
    b. uses the scientific method to study people, whereas Ernest does not.
    c. studies various groups of people, whereas Ernest studies various individuals.
    d. is interested in how people behave toward each other, whereas Ernest is interested in people's attitudes toward each other.

2. Jeannette is a psychologist who specializes in neuroscience. Jeannette studies the effects that drinking alcohol has on the brain. Carmen is a social psychologist, and also is interested in the effects of alcohol. Compared to Jeannette, Carmen is *more* likely to
    a. apply the principles of the scientific method in her research on alcohol.
    b. examine the effects of alcohol from an applied research perspective.
    c. conduct experiments on the effects of alcohol.
    d. focus on the effects of alcohol on social behavior.

3. A major difference between social psychologists and sociologists is that social psychologists tend to focus on _____ while sociologists tend to focus on _____.
    a. prejudice; culture
    b. aggression; violence
    c. the individual level; the group level
    d. social cognition; political attitudes

4. Social psychology started to become established as a distinct field of study in the
    a. late seventeenth century.
    b. late eighteenth century and early nineteenth century.
    c. late nineteenth century and early twentieth century.
    d. mid-1950s.

5. Which of the following is *least* consistent with the ideas of Kurt Lewin?
   a. Behavior is a function of the person and the environment.
   b. Social psychologists should concentrate on basic research rather than on applied research, which represents the "selling out" of social psychology.
   c. Social psychologists should integrate research from personality psychology into their own theories and research.
   d. The behavior of different people may vary even if they are placed in the exact same social situation.

6. Personality psychologists are generally *more* interested than social psychologists in
   a. how people think, feel, and behave.
   b. understanding the underlying causes of behavior.
   c. the scientific approach to psychology.
   d. differences between individuals that are stable across situations.

7. Constantine and Chad are interested in social cognition. Therefore, they should be most inclined to conduct a study in which
   a. personality factors are combined with social factors.
   b. people's interpretations of information about other people are examined.
   c. the level of analysis is the social group, rather than the individual.
   d. an applied, rather than a basic, approach is taken.

8. The German immigrant who made a major contribution to the development of social psychology by helping to establish principles like "behavior is a function of the interaction between the person and the environment" was
   a. Allport.
   b. Festinger.
   c. Ringelmann.
   d. Lewin.

9. In the 1960s and early 1970s, social psychology experienced a period of
   a. expansion and debate.
   b. introspection and stagnation.
   c. pluralism and development.
   d. foundation and reform.

10. The most famous research in the history of social psychology concerns which of the following topics?
    a. How people's attitudes can change by observing their own behavior
    b. The extent to which individuals are vulnerable to the destructive commands of authority
    c. How willing people are to conform to an obviously wrong majority
    d. The effect of the presence of others on the performance of individuals

11. Leroy is a social psychologist and Barney is a clinical psychologist. If they both study aggression, Leroy is *more* likely than Barney to
    a. examine the situational determinants of aggression in an experiment.
    b. develop therapeutic techniques to control people's aggression.
    c. develop theories about what leads people to be aggressive.
    d. develop a questionnaire to measure which people are most likely to be aggressive.

12. Many of the strong disagreements that occurred during the period of "Confidence and Crisis" were a reaction to the predominant use of
    a.   archival methods.
    b.   unobtrusive measures.
    c.   the interactionist perspective.
    d.   laboratory experiments.

13. Of the following individuals, the one who is credited as being one of the founders of social psychology is
    a.   Norman Triplett.
    b.   Kenneth Gergen.
    c.   James Blascovich.
    d.   Harry Triandis.

14. Martha is a cognitive psychologist and Valerie is a social psychologist. Martha is *less* likely than Valerie to be interested in
    a.   reasoning about risky decisions.
    b.   how quickly people can learn new tasks.
    c.   the thinking required to solve a problem.
    d.   how social interactions affect memory for people.

15. Which one of the following is *not* a characteristic of social psychology?
    a.   A broad perspective
    b.   A focus on the individual
    c.   The frequent use of experiment methodology
    d.   A focus on observation of behaviors

16. Unlike common sense, social psychological theories are
    a.   always accurate.
    b.   put to the test.
    c.   based on educated guesses.
    d.   always hard to anticipate.

17. Each of the following is true about the current period of pluralism in social psychology *except* that
    a.   laboratory experiments have been discontinued and replaced by unobtrusive studies that take advantage of archival or correlational techniques.
    b.   there are important variations in the aspects of human behavior being emphasized.
    c.   the "socialness" of social psychology has increased owing to the influence of European social psychologists.
    d.   cross-cultural research is being conducted more extensively than in previous periods.

18. In the 21st century, all of the following are likely to be emphasized in social psychology *except*
    a.   biological and evolutionary perspectives.
    b.   new technologies.
    c.   the separation of emotion, motivation, and cognition.
    d.   sociocultural perspectives.

19. Who was credited with the creation of social psychology as a distinct field of study?
    a.   McDougall
    b.   Ross
    c.   Allport
    d.   All of the above are correct

20. The 1950s saw a major contribution to the field of social psychology by which of the following individuals?
    a. Gordon Allport for publishing *The Nature of Prejudice*
    b. Solomon Asch for studies in conformity
    c. Leon Festinger for two theories on how people learn about themselves and about how attitudes can be changed
    d. All of the above are correct

21. _____ is the scientific study of how individuals think, feel, and behave in a social context.
    a. Social psychology
    b. Cognitive psychology
    c. Clinical psychology
    d. Behavioral psychology

22. An emphasis on how both an individual's personality and environmental characteristics influence the social environment best describes the
    a. evolutionary perspective.
    b. behavioral perspective.
    c. psychoanalytic perspective.
    d. interactionist perspective.

23. The study of the relationship between neural and social processes is best represented by the
    a. social neuroscience perspective.
    b. behavioral perspective.
    c. evolutionary perspective.
    d. cross-cultural perspective.

Essay Questions

24. Provide a definition of social psychology and note how it is different from other similar fields.

25. Describe three periods in the history of social psychology and note two major characteristics of each period.

26. Explain two major differences between common sense understandings and social psychological theories.

27. Discuss the recent findings by Fein et al., 2007, on the effects of social context.

ANSWERS TO THE PRACTICE QUIZ

Multiple-Choice Questions: Correct Answers and Explanations

1. b.   **uses the scientific method to study people, whereas Ernest does not.** Social psychology is the *scientific* study of the way individuals think, feel, desire, and act in social situations. Social psychologists, therefore, apply the scientific method of systematic observation, description, and measurement in their research; journalists, in contrast, can and do use other methods. Journalists, like social psychologists, often use statistics in their work. The level of analysis for social psychologists typically is the individual, not the group. Social psychologists are interested in people's attitudes as well as their behaviors.

2. d.   **focus on the effects of alcohol on social behavior.** An important distinction between social psychology and other sub disciplines within psychology is social psychology's focus on social behavior and social situations. But someone specializing in neuroscience should be no less likely than a social psychologist to apply the scientific method of systematic observation, description, and measurement in her research; to take an applied research perspective by attempting to increase the understanding of naturally occurring events and to find solutions to practical problems; and to conduct experiments.

3. c.   **the individual level; the group level.** This distinction is one important way that social psychologists and sociologists tend to differ. Both social psychologists and sociologists are likely to study prejudice, culture, aggression, violence, and political attitudes. They will tend to focus on different aspects of these topics, but both groups of social scientists study them. Social cognition is a subfield of social psychology which studies how people perceive, remember, and interpret information about themselves and others.

4. c.   **in the late nineteenth century and early twentieth century.** The first research article in social psychology (by Triplett) was published at the end of the nineteenth century, and the field began to be a distinct discipline with the publication of the first three textbooks in social psychology, from 1908 to 1924.

5. b.   **Social psychologists should concentrate on basic research rather than on applied research, which represents the "selling out" of social psychology.** Lewin showed a persistent interest in the application of social psychology, such as in his research on how to promote more economical and nutritious eating habits, so Lewin would not have warned against applied research. Lewin proposed that behavior is a function of the person and the environment. By emphasizing both the person and the environment, Lewin advocated what today is known as the *interactionist perspective*, which combines personality psychology and social psychology. Lewin proposed that even if people are placed in the exact same social situation, their behavior will vary to the extent that they perceive and interpret the situation differently.

6. d.   **differences between individuals that are stable across situations.** Personality psychologists are usually quite interested in studying differences between individuals that are stable across situations. Although some social psychologists might be interested in some individual differences, they are usually less interested in this problem than personality psychologists. Both personality and social psychologists are interested in how people think, feel, and behave; understanding the underlying causes of behavior; and the scientific approach to psychology.

7. b.   **people's interpretations of information about other people are examined.** Social cognition is the study of how people perceive, remember, and interpret information about themselves and others. Social cognition research is no more likely than other forms of research within social psychology to combine personality factors with social factors, or to take an applied (research whose goal is to increase the understanding of naturally occurring events or to find solutions to practical problems), rather than a basic (research whose goal is to increase the understanding of human behavior, often by testing hypotheses based on a theory), approach. The level of analysis of most research within social psychology, including social cognition, is the individual rather than the group.

8. d.   **Lewin.** Kurt Lewin was the psychologist who made this classic statement. He was a very important figure in social psychology who fled Nazi Germany and came to the United States in the 1930s. Allport was another important psychologist from the early 1900s whose works included a seminal book on *The Nature of Prejudice*. Festinger introduced theories in the areas of attitude change and self-perception. Ringelmann, one of the earliest social psychology researchers, was a French engineer who conducted research in the 1880s. He studied the effect of the presence of others on the performance of individuals.

9. a.   **expansion and debate.** This is the period that the book called "Confidence and Crisis." During this time there was a lot of new research and an expansion of research into new topic areas. However, this was also a time of intense discussion and debate about the use of experiments in the field. Although there was some introspection during this period it was not a period of stagnation. Pluralism emerged on a larger scale after this period, so although it was a period of development, pluralism and development does not seem to be the best answer. Finally, this period is probably best characterized as a period of building on the foundation rather than the foundational period, so although there were some reform movements during this period, foundation and reform is probably not the best answer either.

10. b.   **The extent to which individuals are vulnerable to the destructive commands of authority.** Stanley Milgram's experiments on obedience, which were inspired by the behavior of Nazi officers and citizens in Hitler's Germany, are considered the most famous research in the history of social psychology.

11. a.   **examine the situational determinants of aggression in an experiment.** Social psychologists are often interested in the situational determinants of behavior. They are more likely to be interested in this aspect of a topic than clinical psychologists. Clinical psychologists are more likely to develop therapeutic techniques to control people's aggression than social psychologists. Both groups of psychologists might be interested in developing theories about what leads people to be aggressive, and developing a questionnaire to measure which people are most likely to be aggressive.

12. d.   **laboratory experiments.** The dominant research method in social psychology up to the period of "Confidence and Crisis" was the laboratory experiment. Many people questioned the ethics and validity of this research strategy. Archival research, which involves the use of existing records of human behavior, has never been a predominant research strategy in social psychology. Unobtrusive measures, involving assessments of behavior that do not interfere with a subject's spontaneous and natural reactions, were not used predominantly during this period; their use can help researchers avoid some of the criticisms raised at the time about laboratory experiments. Finally, the interactionist perspective, which combines personality and social psychology, was neither predominant at the time nor seen as a controversial practice.

13. a. **Norman Triplett.** Triplett published the first research article in social psychology at the end of the nineteenth century. The work of the other three social psychologists has been much more recent, extending from the 1970s through the present. Gergen played an important role in the 1961–1975 period of "Confidence and Crisis" by arguing that the theories being tested in the social psychology laboratory were historically and culturally limited. James Blascovich is a contemporary researcher who has been exploring conformity, group dynamics, aggression, altruism, and eyewitness testimony. And in Chapter 1, Triandis's work is cited as an example of the increase in work on multiculturalism.

14. d. **how social interactions affect memory for people.** The investigation of reasoning about risky decisions, how quickly people can learn new tasks, and the thinking required to solve a problem are all topics that a cognitive psychologist might be interested in. How social interactions affect memory for people, however, is a topic that social psychologists are more likely to investigate. In particular, this topic is more likely to be studied by a psychologist interested in social cognition—the study of how people perceive, remember, and interpret information about themselves and others.

15. d. **A focus on observation of behaviors.** Social psychologists sometimes study topics by observing behaviors, but this is not a focus or a characteristic of social psychology per se. Conversely, a broad perspective, a focus on the individual, and the frequent use of experiment methodology are all characteristics of social psychology.

16. b. **put to the test.** Because social psychology is a scientific study, its theories are tested. Common sense ideas on the other hand are often contradictory and taken at face value without being tested. Social psychological theories are not always correct, sometimes they are proven wrong. And although social psychological findings are often hard to anticipate, they are not always so. Finally, social psychological theories are often based on educated guesses, but common sense ideas often are as well.

17. a. **laboratory experiments have been discontinued and replaced by unobtrusive studies that take advantage of archival or correlational techniques.** Laboratory experiments continue to be used in social psychology; other approaches, however, are used as well. Each of the other statements is true.

18. c. **the separation of emotion, motivation, and cognition.** It seems that in the 21st century, the integration rather than the separation of emotion, motivation, and cognition is likely to be emphasized. Biological and evolutionary perspectives, new technologies, and sociocultural perspectives are all topics that are likely to see extensive research scrutiny in the next century as well.

19. d. **all of the above are correct.** Credit for this creation goes to the writers of the first three textbooks in social psychology: the English psychologist William McDougall (1908) and two Americans, Edward Ross (1908) and Floyd Allport (1924). Allport's book in particular, with its focus on the interaction of individuals and their social context and its emphasis on the use of experimentation and the scientific method, helped establish social psychology as the discipline it is today. These authors announced the arrival of a new approach to the social aspects of human behavior.

20. d.   **all of the above are correct.** Gordon Allport (1954) published *The Nature of Prejudice*, a book that continues to inspire research on stereotyping and prejudice more than a half century later. Solomon Asch (1951) demonstrated how willing people are to conform to an obviously wrong majority. Leon Festinger (1954, 1957) introduced two important theories—one concerning how people try to learn about themselves by comparing themselves to other people, and one about how people's attitudes can be changed by their own behavior. These individuals are just a sample of a long list of landmark contributions made during the 1950s.

21. a.   **Social psychology.** There are many approaches to understanding how people think, feel, and behave. We can learn about human behavior from novels, films, history, and philosophy to name just a few possibilities. What makes social psychology different from these artistic and humanistic endeavors is that social psychology is a science. It applies the scientific method of systematic observation, description, and measurement to the study of the human condition

22. d.   **interactionist perspective.** Lewin's conviction that both internal and external factors affect behavior helped create a unified view that was distinct from the other major psychological paradigms during his lifetime: psychoanalysis, with its emphasis on internal motives and fantasies, and behaviorism, with its focus on external rewards and punishments. Lewin's position was an early version of what today is known as the interactionist perspective. This approach combines personality psychology (stressing internal, psychological differences among individuals) with social psychology (stressing differences among external situations).

23. a.   **social neuroscience perspective.** Social psychologists have been concerned with physiological influences and responses for many years. A particularly exciting recent development is the emergence of the subfield of social neuroscience, the study of the relationship between neural and social processes. Social neuroscience is part of a flourishing set of research that explores how the social world affects the brain and biology, and vice versa. Recent research has investigated such issues as how individuals' likelihood of acting aggressively may be influenced by their neurological responses to social rejection, and gender differences in neuroendocrine reactivity in response to stress.

Answers to Essay Questions: Sample Essays

24. Social psychology can be defined as the scientific study of how individuals think, feel, and behave in regard to other people and how individuals' thoughts, feelings, and behaviors are affected by other people. Social psychology is different from sociology in that it focuses on the individual level rather than the group level of analysis. Social psychology is different from clinical psychology in that it is primarily concerned with the typical ways that people think, feel, and behave and is less concerned with people who have psychological difficulties and disorders. Social psychology is different from personality psychology in that it is less concerned with individual differences between people that are consistent across situations. Finally, social psychology is different from cognitive psychology in that it is more concerned with how thinking, learning, remembering, and reasoning are relevant to social behavior.

25.   Early social psychology began in the late 1800s. This period had two defining characteristics – the beginning of research, with a study by Triplett on how the presence of others affects performance, and the defining of the field, as several textbooks were written on social psychology in the early 1900s. From the 1930s to 1950s, the field grew quickly as it tried to understand the horrors of World War II and Nazi Germany. Kurt Lewin was a particularly important figure who fled Nazi Germany for the United States during this time. He proposed what later became known as the interactionist perspective and also lobbied for the application of social psychology principles to real-life problems. Generally, this period can be characterized as a period with foundational theories and groundbreaking experiments. The 1960s and early 1970s saw a rise in confidence and expansion of the field, but was also a time of questioning and debate. This period can thus best be characterized as a time of expansion and debate. The late 1970s to the 1990s saw the birth of a new subfield, social cognition, and greater international and cultural perspectives in social psychology. This period can be seen as a time of pluralism and redefinition.

26.   Many people think the findings of social psychology are just common sense, but social psychology differs from common sense in two important ways. First, social psychology, unlike common sense, puts its ideas to the test. This scientific approach is the chief difference between social psychology and common sense. Second, common sense is often contradictory and thus can appear to explain everything. For example, common sense suggests that birds of a feather flock together and that opposites attract. So, if people are attracted to similar others, common sense appears to be true and if people are attracted to dissimilar others, common sense also appears to be true. It is no wonder that sometimes social psychological findings appear to be predicted by common sense after the fact. Common sense also tends to oversimplify complex issues, overlooking the fact that there may be many factors responsible for a single effect. Social psychology's research explores all the components that affect an issue.

27.   The main point of these results from a social psychological standpoint is that the students' judgments were influenced more by other people's reactions to what Reagan said (that is, whether or not the audience appeared to laugh) than by the content of what he said (that is, whether or not the one-liners were edited out of the tape). Additionally, it is important to note that these "other people" were not in the room with the students; they were simply sounds on a videotape recorded many years before. These findings demonstrate that the "social context" can be very subtle, and yet can have very powerful effects on our thoughts, feelings, and behaviors.

CHAPTER 2

Doing Social Psychology Research

OUTLINE

LEARNING OBJECTIVES: GUIDELINES FOR STUDY

You should be able to do each of the following by the conclusion of Chapter 2.

1.   Describe the process of generating research ideas in social psychology, searching the relevant literature, and developing hypotheses. Understand the differences between applied and basic research. (*pp. 27-30*)

2.   Distinguish between hypotheses and theories, and between conceptual variables and operational definitions. (*pp. 30-31*)

3.   Explain self-report and observational research practices, including the advantages and disadvantages of each. (*pp. 31-34*)

4.   Understand the usefulness of traditional research methodologies, such as archival studies and surveys, as well as explain the potential contributions of new technologies to contemporary social psychology research. (*pp. 34-36*)

5.   Contrast correlational research with descriptive research. Define the correlation coefficient, and explain what it means to say that two variables are negatively correlated, positively correlated, or uncorrelated. Summarize the advantages and one major disadvantage of correlational research designs. (*pp. 36-39*)

6.   Explain the importance of control and random assignment in experimental research. Differentiate random sampling from random assignment, as well as an independent variable from a dependent variable. (*pp. 39-43*)

7.   Explain the importance of the following terms with regard to experimental research design: statistical significance, internal validity, and external validity. Explain what is meant by a meta-analysis. (*pp. 43-46*)

8.   Discuss the advantages of cross-cultural research and the challenges that doing such studies present to researchers. (*pp. 46-48*)

9.   Discuss the function of ethics in social psychological research, including the use of deception and confederates. Describe the roles of institutional review boards, informed consent, and debriefing in protecting the welfare of human participants. Summarize the competing points of view about the role of values in science. (*pp. 48-50*)

MAJOR CONCEPTS: THE BIG PICTURE

Following are five basic issues or principles that organize Chapter 2. You should know these issues and principles well.

1.   Learning about social psychology research methods should enable you to better understand the material presented in the textbook, as well as to improve your reasoning about real-life events.

2.   The research process in social psychology begins with coming up with ideas, asking questions about one's social world, and searching the relevant literature to determine what research has already been done on these issues. Social psychologists develop testable hypotheses and theories. An important aspect of social psychological hypotheses and theories is that they can be put to the test and eventually improved upon. Social psychologists test their hypotheses and theories both in basic and applied settings.

3.   A challenging part of the research process is developing specific definitions and measurements of social psychological variables. Researchers typically begin with rather vague, abstract conceptualizations of the variables of interest and eventually make them more concrete and specific. Researchers may measure variables using self-report or observational techniques; each of these approaches has its strengths and potential weaknesses.

4.   Social psychological researchers use descriptive, correlational, experimental, and meta-analytic methods to test their ideas. The goal of descriptive research is to describe people and their behavior. Correlational research examines the association between variables. Experimental research examines the cause-and-effect relationship between variables. Researchers analyze the results of their research and evaluate the research in terms of internal and external validity. Meta-analysis involves using statistical techniques to combine the results of a number of other studies that have already been conducted. Exciting new methods in cultural research can now analyze social data.

5.   Ethical issues must always be considered when research is conducted. In social psychology, the use of deception can be of particular ethical concern. Through institutional review boards, informed consent, and debriefing, social psychologists try to ensure the welfare of their research participants. The issue of values is also important in social psychological research. There are differences of opinion about whether social psychological research – like other research – can or even should be value free.

KEY TERM EXERCISE: THE CONCEPTS YOU SHOULD KNOW

Below are all of the key terms that appear in **boldface** in Chapter 2. To help you better understand these concepts, rather than just memorize them, write a definition for each term in your own words. After doing so, look at the next section where you'll find a list of definitions from the textbook for each of the key terms presented in random order. For each of your definitions, find the corresponding textbook definition. Note how your definitions compare with those from the textbook.

Key Terms

1. internal validity

2. theory

3. debriefing

4. experimental realism

5. correlational research

6. dependent variables

7. mundane realism

8. interrater reliability

9. meta-analysis

10. hypothesis

11. experiment

12. random sampling

13. basic research

14. experimenter expectancy effects

15. random assignment

16. subject variables

17. deception

18. external validity

19. correlation coefficient

20. informed consent

21. independent variables

22. construct validity

23. applied research

24. confederates

25. operational definition

26. interaction

27. bogus pipeline technique

Textbook Definitions

a.   Variables that characterize pre-existing differences among the participants in a study.

b.   The extent to which the measures used in a study measure the variables they were designed to measure and the manipulations in an experiment manipulate the variables they were designed to manipulate.

c.   A set of statistical procedures used to review a body of evidence by combining the results of individual studies to measure the overall reliability and strength of particular effects.

d.   A testable prediction about the conditions under which an event will occur.

e.   An organized set of principles used to explain observed phenomena.

f.   Research whose goal is to increase the understanding of human behavior, often by testing hypotheses based on a theory.

g.   Research whose goal is to enlarge the understanding of naturally occurring events and to find solutions to practical problems.

h.   A statistical measure of the strength and direction of the association between two variables. The correlation coefficient can range from -1.0 to +1.0.

i.   A form of research that can demonstrate causal relationships because (1) the experimenter has control over the events that occur and (2) the participants are randomly assigned to conditions.

j.   In an experiment, the factors experimenters manipulate to see if they affect the dependent variables.

k.   In an experiment, the factors experimenters measure to see if they are affected by the independent variables.

l.   The degree to which there can be reasonable certainty that the independent variables in an experiment caused the effects obtained on the dependent variables.

m.   The effects produced when an experimenter's expectations about the results of an experiment affect his or her behavior toward a participant and thereby influence the participant's responses.

n.   A procedure in which participants are falsely led to believe that their responses will be verified by an infallible lie detector.

o.   Accomplices of an experimenter who, in dealing with the real participants in an experiment, act as if they also are participants.

p.   A method of selecting participants for a study so that everyone in a population has an equal chance of being in the study.

q.   A method of assigning participants to the various conditions of an experiment so that each participant in the experiment has an equal chance of being in any of the conditions.

r. The degree to which the experimental situation resembles places and events that exist in the real world.

s. The degree to which experimental procedures are involving to participants and lead them to behave naturally and spontaneously.

t. Research methods that provide false information to participants.

u. The degree to which different observers agree on their observations.

v. An individual's deliberate, voluntary decision to participate in research, based on the researcher's description of what will be required during such participation.

w. A disclosure made to participants after research procedures are completed in which the researcher explains the purpose of the research, attempts to resolve any negative feelings, and emphasizes the scientific contribution made by participants' participation.

x. Research designed to measure the association between variables that are not manipulated by the researcher.

y. The degree to which one can be reasonably confident that the same results would be obtained for other people and in other situations.

z. The specific procedures for manipulating or measuring a conceptual variable.

aa. A statistical term indicating that the effect that an independent variable has on the dependent variable is different as a function of another independent variable.

ANSWERS FOR KEY TERM EXERCISE

Answers for the key terms exercise are listed below.

1. l
2. e
3. w
4. s
5. x
6. k
7. r
8. u
9. c
10. d
11. i
12. p
13. f
14. m
15. q
16. a
17. t
18. y
19. h
20. v
21. j
22. b
23. g
24. o
25. z
26. aa
27. n

PRACTICE QUIZ: TEST YOUR KNOWLEDGE OF THE CHAPTER

Multiple-Choice Questions

1. Hannah developed an explicit, testable prediction about what kind of advertising campaign would be most effective in selling a particular product. Specifically, she predicted that a campaign that makes an emotional appeal would be more effective than one that focuses more on appeals to logic. She tested her prediction in an experiment that compared both types of appeals. Hannah's prediction is an example of

    a. archival research.
    b. a hypothesis.
    c. a meta-analysis.
    d. survey research.

2. Which of the following studies is probably *highest* in experimental realism?

    a. Participants sit in a waiting room and are observed secretly using hidden video cameras while they wait for the experimenter to call them in to begin the study.
    b. Participants try to memorize a long list of words either alone or in the presence of other participants.
    c. Participants try to make judgments about each other's personalities based on small clues about each other, with the incentive that the participants whose judgments are most accurate will win $50.
    d. Participants from several different countries are selected through random sampling to participate in this study, in which they receive a questionnaire asking them their opinions about a variety of global economic and health issues.

3. Drew conducted an experiment to examine the effects of uncomfortably loud noise on the likelihood that people will aggress against each other. He manipulated the amount of noise in the room, and he measured the number of times that the participants looked at each other in threatening, aggressive ways. After reporting the results of his experiment, some researchers criticized Drew's measure of aggression as having poor construct validity. This criticism suggests that

    a. the operational definition of aggression that Drew used was flawed.
    b. the results of the study are not statistically significant.
    c. the independent variable was poorly designed.
    d. Drew did not use random assignment in his measure of aggression.

4. Some researchers conducted an experiment to examine the effects of noise and test difficulty on students' test performance. The researchers manipulated how much noise was present in a room (either a little or a lot) and how difficult the test was (either easy or very difficult). The researchers analyzed the results of their experiment and found that the manipulation of noise had little effect on test performance when the test was easy, but that it had a strong effect when the test was difficult—students did much worse on the difficult test if the room was noisy than if it was quiet. This pattern of results suggests that

    a. there was an interaction between the two independent variables.
    b. the correlation between noise and test difficulty was negative.
    c. the correlation between noise and test difficulty was positive.
    d. the manipulation of noise was strong in external validity.

5.   Alan wanted to test his hypothesis that people are more likely to vote in presidential elections when the economy of the country is bad rather than good. He decided to conduct archival studies to test this. Which of the following is the kind of archival study that Alan would be *most* likely to do?

   a.   Randomly assign some participants to conditions so that some read information indicating that the economy of the country is strong, and others read information indicating that the economy is weak and vulnerable. Next, give participants a chance to register to vote for an election.

   b.   Look at existing records to determine the strength of the country's economy at different points in time and at other records to record the percentage of the eligible population who voted in presidential elections.

   c.   Collect a number of published studies on the topic and calculate statistically how strong the effects are.

   d.   Randomly sample the population of registered voters and distribute a survey that asks them to describe their feelings about the economy, and then ask them if they voted in the last election.

6.   Angelia recruits participants for an experiment on crowding. She randomly assigns some participants to a small room and other participants to a large room. Through random assignment, Angelia hopes to ensure that

   a.   differences that appear between conditions cannot be attributed to differences in the personal characteristics of the participants in the two conditions.

   b.   the study is high in external validity.

   c.   she will have a representative sample and not have to resort to using a convenience sample.

   d.   the welfare of the participants will be protected.

7.   Some researchers investigated the relationship between smoking and the likelihood of dying of cancer. The researchers found that as the amount one smoked increased, the likelihood of dying of cancer increased as well. Similarly, as the amount of smoking decreased, the likelihood of dying of cancer decreased as well. Which of the following correlation coefficients is *most* likely to reflect this relationship between amount of smoking and the likelihood of dying of cancer?

   a.   A correlation coefficient of −.30

   b.   A correlation coefficient of +.30

   c.   A correlation coefficient of −10.00

   d.   A correlation coefficient of +100.00

8.   Some researchers measured the amount of television a number of boys watched when they were five years old, and then measured how creative they were when they were fifteen years old. They found that the boys who were relatively high in amount of television watching at age five tended to be relatively low in creativity at age fifteen, and that those who had watched the least amount of television at age five were the most creative at age fifteen. This is an example of

   a.   descriptive research.

   b.   an experiment.

   c.   an archival study.

   d.   correlational research.

9. Some researchers found a negative correlation between the number of fans attending hockey games and the number of fights that occurred during the games. Several other groups of researchers found the same negative correlation between these variables. This suggests that

   a. there is a very weak relationship between the number of fans attending hockey games and the number of fights that occur during the games.
   b. the presence of relatively large crowds causes hockey teams to play in a way that produces fewer fights.
   c. there is a greater chance that fights will occur during a hockey game at which relatively few fans are present than during a game at which many fans are present.
   d. fans are turned off by violence in hockey games and will stay away from games between teams that tend to fight a lot.

10. Surveys are much more likely to produce accurate results if

    a. the participants were randomly assigned to conditions.
    b. they are high in experimental realism.
    c. the participants were chosen using a random sample of the population.
    d. their design has strong internal validity.

11. Imagine two alien species: the Romulans and the Klingons. The Romulans were interested in developing a technique for use in extracting secrets from Klingon prisoners. The Romulans wanted to test Klingons' tolerance for pain under different conditions, so they gave some Klingons electric shocks after depriving them of sleep and gave other Klingons the same magnitude of shocks after letting them sleep as much as they wanted. They then measured the decibel level of the Klingons' screams. The independent variable in this experiment is

    a. the amount of pain the Klingons could tolerate.
    b. the intensity of shock voltage.
    c. whether or not the Klingons were deprived of sleep.
    d. the loudness of screams of the Klingons.

12. Min wants to assess people's attitudes about sex education in grade school. To do so, she mails a questionnaire to a large sample of individuals and asks the individuals to answer questions about their attitudes and then to mail the questionnaire back to her. Min's method of measurement is a(n)

    a. event-contingent method.
    b. archival record.
    c. self-report measure.
    d. behavioral observation.

13. Researchers found that the results of their study were statistically significant. Thus they concluded that

    a. the research is relatively high in internal validity.
    b. there is only a very small probability that the results occurred by chance.
    c. the results should generalize to different populations in different settings.
    d. the correlation found between the variables was positive and strong.

14. To study aggression, Neil randomly assigns participants to one of two movies. He makes the specially prepared movies equal in every way except aggressive content. The experimenters are kept uninformed about the hypotheses of the study. This study appears to have

    a. statistical significance.
    b. experimental realism.
    c. a representative sample.
    d. internal validity.

15. Margot hires some research assistants to help her conduct a laboratory experiment. She trains them so that they know exactly what to say or do with participants. However, she does not tell them what the hypotheses or predictions of the research are. By omitting this information, Margot hopes to protect the experiment from
    a. unethical practices.
    b. convenience sampling.
    c. experimenter expectancy effects.
    d. mundane realism.

16. One way to increase the chances that a study will be high in external validity is to use
    a. random assignment.
    b. random sampling.
    c. behavioral observations.
    d. self-report measures.

17. Elissa was given a government grant to investigate what kinds of leaders have the most positive impact on the efficiency of groups of soldiers. She designs a series of experiments to examine this issue. She expects to share her results with military commanders. Elissa is most likely to be interested in
    a. laboratory research.
    b. archival research.
    c. basic research.
    d. applied research.

18. Greta wants to know whether racially diverse work groups typically perform better or worse as a function of how task-oriented the group leader is. She searches the literature on this topic and finds a number of previously conducted studies that have investigated this issue. She determines that, rather than focusing on any single study, a more reliable and valid conclusion could be reached by examining these studies together and combining their results statistically. To reach such a conclusion, Greta should conduct a(n)
    a. correlational study.
    b. analysis of the interrater reliability of the studies.
    c. narrative study.
    d. meta-analysis.

19. The use of deception in some studies highlights the need for researchers to
    a. conduct a thorough debriefing at the conclusion of each study.
    b. conduct research that is not influenced by their own values.
    c. use self-reports as well as behavioral observations whenever possible.
    d. create operational definitions of their variables that are high in external validity.

20. At the start of his experiment, Conrad made sure to ask all participants whether they wanted to take part in the research. He also provided them with a great deal of information about what they could expect if they participated in the study. Conrad took these steps in order to
    a. obtain informed consent.
    b. increase the external validity of the experiment.
    c. debrief the participants..
    d. create mundane realism.

21. An advantage of cross-cultural or multicultural research methods is that they allow better tests of
    a. external validity.
    b. mundane realism.
    c. internal validity.
    d. deception in social research.

22. Dr. Jones has been hired to investigate sexist bias in men employed in a certain government agency. She intends to make use of fMRI (functional magnetic resonance imaging) in her study. When the men view pictures of women, the use of this technology will allow Dr. Jones to do which of the following:
    a. Discern what sexist views the men harbor about women
    b. Measure exactly at which part and for how long the men look at the pictures.
    c. Take note of the men's physiological responses, such as changes in heartbeat
    c. Tell which parts of the men's brains are activated

23. Basic research can best be described as
    a. an attempt to increase understanding of human behavior.
    b. an attempt to decrease understanding of human behavior.
    c. an attempt to understand naturally occurring events.
    d. using the correlational method to understand human behavior.

24. Applied research can best be described as
    a. an attempt to increase understanding of human behavior.
    b. an attempt to decrease understanding of human behavior.
    c. an attempt to understand naturally occurring events.
    d. using the correlational method to understand human behavior.

Essay Questions

25. Craig conducted a study in which he put some participants in very hot rooms and others in comfortably cool rooms, and then measured their levels of aggressiveness by observing their behavior. Craig found that those in the hot rooms were more aggressive than those in the cooler rooms. What further information would you need to determine whether this study was an experiment rather than a correlational study? What further information would you need to evaluate the external validity of this study?

26. Describe the primary disadvantages in using self-report measures in social psychology research. Then discuss the role of interrater reliability in another type of measure used by social psychologists.

27. Summarize three different positions that have been taken concerning the influence of values on science.

28. Describe how new technologies are being used in research by social psychologists.

ANSWERS TO THE PRACTICE QUIZ

Multiple-Choice Questions: Correct Answers and Explanations

1. b.   **a hypothesis.** A hypothesis is a testable prediction about the conditions under which an event will occur; Hannah developed such a prediction for her research. The other three answers are specific types of research, rather than a type of prediction, and there is nothing indicated in the question to suggest that Hannah conducted any one of these types of studies. Archival research involves examining existing records of past events and behaviors. A meta-analysis is a set of statistical procedures used to review a number of previously conducted studies. Survey research involves asking people to indicate their attitudes, beliefs, or behaviors.

2. c.   **Participants try to make judgments about each other's personalities based on small clues about each other, with the incentive that the participants whose judgments are most accurate will win $50.** Experimental realism is the degree to which experimental procedures are involving to participants and lead them to behave naturally and spontaneously. Trying to judge each other's personalities and winning money should be relatively involving to the participants and motivate them to take the tasks in the study seriously. In contrast, the study set in the waiting room should be very low in experimental realism, although it may be high in mundane realism (the degree to which the experimental situation resembles places and events that exist in the real world), since sitting in a waiting room might be a familiar, ordinary situation for the participants. Trying to memorize a long list of words is likely to be a rather dull task, neither very engaging nor interesting to the participants; therefore, the experimental realism is not likely to be very high. Surveys like the kind described in the final option do not have experimental realism.

3. a.   **the operational definition of aggression that Drew used was flawed.** In an experiment, a measure that is said to have poor construct validity does not correctly measure the conceptual variable it was designed to measure. In this case, the conceptual variable was "aggression," and the specific way that Drew measured aggression was his operational definition of aggression. Drew operationally defined aggression in his study as the number of times participants looked at each other in threatening or aggressive ways; this definition is likely to be flawed, as such looks are likely to be ambiguous and may have little to do with aggression. Thus, the measure has poor construct validity. Statistical significance refers to the likelihood that the results of a study could have occurred by chance; this question indicates nothing about whether the results were analyzed statistically to determine whether or not they were statistically significant. The independent variable is the variable that the experimenter manipulated. Drew manipulated the amount of noise in the laboratory room; the validity of this manipulation was not questioned. In an experiment, participants are assigned randomly to the different conditions of the independent variable(s); there is no random assignment of the dependent variable, which in this case was the measure of aggression.

4. a.   **there was an interaction between the two independent variables.** There is said to be an interaction between two independent variables if the effect that one of the independent variables has on the dependent variable depends on the other independent variable. In this study, the effect that the manipulation of noise had on the students' test performance depended on the manipulation of test difficulty (the effect of noise was strong only if the test difficulty was high). A correlation is a measure of the association between two variables; the independent variables in this study were manipulated, not measured, and therefore there is no association to be measured, positive or negative. External validity refers to the degree to which one can be reasonably confident that the same results would be obtained for other people and in other situations. There is nothing indicated in this question that is relevant to the issue of external validity.

5.   b.   **Look at existing records to determine the strength of the country's economy at different points in time and at other records to record the percentage of the eligible population who voted in presidential elections.** Archival research involves examining existing records of past events and behaviors. Using existing records of economic indicators and voting patterns, Alan could test his hypothesis. The other three potential answers to this question describe kinds of research other than archival. Answer "a" describes an experiment, including random assignment to different conditions. Answer "c" describes a meta-analysis—statistical procedures used to review a number of previously conducted studies. The final option describes a survey rather than an archival study.

6.   a.   **differences that appear between conditions cannot be attributed to differences in the personal characteristics of the participants in the two conditions.** Random assignment is an essential characteristic of an experiment. By randomly assigning participants to the different conditions, the participants assigned to one condition should not initially be different from those assigned to any other condition. External validity is the degree to which one can be reasonably confident that the same results would be obtained for other people and in other situations. The setting of the experiment and the type of sample used to obtain participants affect the external validity; random assignment cannot ensure high external validity. Random assignment also does not affect whether or not there is a representative sample, which is a sample of participants that reflects the characteristics of the population of interest; random sampling, in contrast, does affect whether a representative sample is likely to be obtained. The welfare of the participants is protected by following codes of ethics, including the use of informed consent and institutional review boards; random assignment by itself does not protect the welfare of human participants.

7.   b.   **a correlation coefficient of +.30.** Correlation coefficients range from +1.0 to −1.0. A positive correlation indicates that as one variable increases, so does the other, or that as one variable decreases, so does the other. This is the kind of relationship that the researchers found between amount of smoking and likelihood of dying of cancer. A negative correlation indicates that as one variable increases, the other decreases. This is the opposite of what the researchers found. Because correlation coefficients range from +1.0 to −1.0, correlation coefficients of −10.00 and +100.00 are not possible.

8.   d.   **correlational research.** Correlational research measures the relationship between different variables. In this case, the variables are hours of television viewing at age 5 and creativity at age 15. Descriptive research describes people or psychological phenomena through the use of observation. It does not examine associations or correlations between variables. This study does not seem to have been an experiment; there was no random assignment to conditions, and the researchers did not control and manipulate any independent variables. Archival studies involve the examination of existing records of past events. This study involves the measurement of behaviors at two different points of time, not a mere examination of past records.

9.   c.   **there is a greater chance that fights will occur during a hockey game at which relatively few fans are present than during a game at which many fans are present.** A negative correlation indicates that as one variable (such as the number of fans attending a game) increases, the other variable (such as the number of fights in the game) decreases. Correlations can be used to make accurate predictions about the relationship between two variables. A negative correlation does not imply that the relationship is weak. Instead, the magnitude of the correlation coefficient, not the direction of the correlation (whether it is positive or negative), indicates the strength of the correlation—but the magnitude of the correlation coefficient is not indicated in this question. The other possible answers suggest that there is a causal relationship between the two variables, but one should never infer causality from a correlation.

10.   c.   **the participants were chosen using a random sample of the population.** Random sampling ensures that everyone in a population has an equal chance of being in a study. Surveys that use random sampling have a much better chance of truly representing the population and, therefore, of producing accurate results. Randomly assigning participants to conditions is important for experiments, rather than surveys; in addition, surveys typically do not have different conditions to which participants are assigned. Experimental realism, the degree to which experimental procedures are involving to participants and lead them to behave naturally and spontaneously, is relevant for experiments, not surveys. Internal validity, which concerns how well an experiment establishes a causal relationship between the independent and dependent variables, is also relevant for experiments rather than surveys.

11.   c.   **whether or not the Klingons were deprived of sleep.** Independent variables are the factors manipulated in an experiment to see if they affect the dependent variable. The Romulans manipulated whether or not the Klingons were sleep deprived to see the effect of this manipulation on tolerance for pain. The amount of pain the Klingons could tolerate was the conceptual dependent variable, and the loudness of their screams was the operational definition of this conceptual dependent variable. The intensity of shock voltage was not varied in the study, so it was not an independent variable.

12.   c.   **self-report measure.** A self-report measure is one in which people are asked to tell about their own thoughts, feelings, and actions. Despite some limitations, questionnaires and other self-report measures are widely used. An event-contingent method is a specific method of using self-report measures. With event-contingent self-reports, respondents report on a designated set of events as soon as possible after such an event has occurred. Because Min did not ask the respondents to report on specific events as soon as the events occurred, Min's study did not use an event-contingent method. Archival records are existing records of human behavior. This question does not suggest that Min consulted any such records. Behavioral observation involves the direct measurement of actions, in contrast to self-reports. Min did not observe her participants' behaviors or measure their actions.

13.   b.   **there is only a very small probability that the results occurred by chance.** Statistical significance means that the odds that the results were obtained by chance alone are quite low (less than 5 out of 100). Internal validity refers to the degree to which there can be reasonable certainty that the independent variable in an experiment caused the effects obtained on the dependent variable. Although statistical significance indicates that the effects probably did not occur by chance, it does not indicate that the effects were necessarily caused by the independent variable itself; if, for example, the experiment did not contain the proper controls, there could be alternative explanations to account for the differences between conditions. Whether the results should generalize to different populations in different settings—in other words, whether the study is high in external validity—depends on the setting of the experiment and the sampling used; statistically significant results may not generalize to other settings or people if the study is low in external validity. There is no mention of whether the results of this study included any correlations; moreover, a negative correlation is just as likely as a positive correlation to be statistically significant.

14. d. **internal validity.** Internal validity is the degree to which there can be reasonable certainty that the independent variables in an experiment caused the effects obtained on the dependent variables. Neil's use of random assignment and the control he used to ensure that the only difference between the conditions was the manipulated independent variable gives this study a high degree of internal validity. Statistical significance means that the odds that the results were obtained by chance alone are quite low (less than 5 out of 100); but there is no mention made of the results in this example. Experimental realism is the degree to which experimental procedures are involving to participants and lead them to behave naturally and spontaneously; but in this example, there is no information given about how involving and real the procedures were for the participants. This question similarly offers no information about the sampling used, so there is no way to know whether a representative sample, which is a sample of participants that reflects the characteristics of the population of interest, was used.

15. c. **experimenter expectancy effects.** Experimenter expectancy effects refer to the influence of experimenters' expectations on participants' behavior. Margot tried to minimize the chances of these effects by keeping the research assistants unaware of the hypotheses and predictions so that they would be unlikely to have strong expectations that might influence their behavior toward the participants. Keeping the research assistants unaware of the hypotheses and predictions would not help protect the experiment from unethical practices; rather, the use of institutional review boards, informed consent, and debriefing are relevant to ethical considerations. Keeping the research assistants unaware of the hypotheses and predictions is irrelevant to the sampling procedure used (a convenience sample is a sample selected because the participants are readily available), and it is irrelevant to the mundane realism of the experiment (mundane realism is the degree to which the experimental situation resembles places and events that exist in the real world).

16. b. **random sampling.** External validity is the degree to which one can be reasonably confident that the same results would be obtained for other people and in other situations. One way to increase this confidence is to have a sample of participants that is representative of the broader population. How can you get such a sample? One way is to use random sampling, in which every individual in a population has an equal chance of being in the study. Random assignment, in which all participants in an experiment have an equal chance of being assigned to any of the conditions, is essential for establishing cause-and-effect relationships in experiments but does not by itself increase external validity. Behavioral observations, which involve the direct measurement of actions, and self-reports, in which participants disclose their own thoughts, feelings, desires, and behavior, are two methods of measuring variables; neither method necessarily increases external validity.

17. d. **applied research.** The goal of applied research is to increase the understanding of naturally occurring events or to find solutions to practical problems; Elissa's interest in factors affecting the efficiency of groups of soldiers is consistent with this approach. Elissa may or may not be interested in laboratory research—experiments conducted in a controlled setting such as in a university lab; it is very possible (and rather likely) that she would instead conduct field research—real-world settings outside of the laboratory. In archival research, records of previous behavior rather than on-going actions are studied. There is no evidence that Elissa is interested in using such methods; she clearly is interested, however, in doing experiments. Basic research involves the testing of theories in order to increase scientific knowledge. Elissa is more concerned with the practical application of knowledge.

18.   d.   **a meta-analysis.** A meta-analysis is a set of statistical procedures used to review a body of evidence by combining the results of individual studies to measure the overall reliability and strength of particular effects. This is exactly what Greta is interested in doing. A correlational study could examine the relationship between the variables that Greta is interested in investigating, however, it would not involve combining the results of previously conducted studies. Interrater reliability refers to the degree to which different observers agree on their observations of the same behavior. Although interrater reliability may be relevant to some of the specific studies that Greta has discovered, it is not relevant to her general interest in combining the results of these studies. A narrative study is a method of self-report that involves a lengthy response on a general topic. Such studies are not designed for the examination of relationships among variables.

19.   a.   **conduct a thorough debriefing at the conclusion of each study.** A debriefing is the disclosure made to participants after research procedures are completed in which the researcher explains the purpose of the research, attempts to resolve any negative feelings, and emphasizes the scientific contribution made by their participation. Deceptions are revealed during the debriefing, and the researchers explain the purpose of using deception. Failure to "correct" these deceptions during debriefing would be unethical. Although some people believe that it is unethical or poor science to conduct research that is influenced by the researchers' own values, others believe that it is impossible to conduct value-free research, and still others believe that researchers should be encouraged to design their research according to their own values. While all are valid positions, there is no clear connection between the use of deception in studies and the role of values in research. Self-reports and behavioral observations are two ways of measuring variables; deception does not raise any issues concerning how best to measure variables. Operational definitions are the specific ways in which researchers manipulate or measure the variables they are studying, and external validity is the degree to which one can be reasonably confident that the same results would be obtained for other people and in other situations; the use of deception in studies is not relevant to these issues.

20.   a.   **obtain informed consent.** Informed consent is an individual's deliberate, voluntary decision to participate in research, based on the researcher's description of what will be required during such participation; Conrad's actions were taken in order to inform the participants and to obtain their informed consent. These actions would not increase the experiment's external validity, which is the degree to which one can be reasonably confident that the same results would be obtained for other people and in other situations. Debriefing refers to a process that takes place after an experiment is done, whereby researchers explain the procedures, reveal any deceptions, and discuss the purpose of the research with the participants. Finally, Conrad's actions would not create mundane realism, which is the degree to which the experimental situation resembles places and events that exist in the real world.

21.   a.   **external validity.** One of the advantages of the cultural approach is that it provides better tests of the external validity of the research that has been conducted in any one setting. By examining whether the results of an experiment generalize to a very different culture, social psychologists can begin to answer questions about the universality or cultural specificity of their research. It is important to keep in mind that when a finding in one culture does not generalize well to another culture, this should be seen not simply as a failure to replicate but also as an opportunity—an opportunity to learn about potentially interesting and important cultural differences, and how and why these differences affect the issue being studied.

22. d.   **Tell which parts of the brain are activated.** An fMRI (functional magnetic resonance imaging) scan can provide researchers with visual images of activity in parts of the brain while a research subject is thinking, making decisions, or responding to perceptual stimuli, such as photos. Although, the technique will not enable the researcher to discern exactly what sexist views the subject harbors, it will show the level of activity in specific brain areas, such as those associated with feelings of threat or strong emotions. Eye-tracking technology, not fMRI, is used to record exactly where and for how long subjects stare at a photo. fMRI technology is not used to measure physiological responses, such as heartbeat.

23. a.   **an attempt to increase understanding of human behavior.** Basic research seeks to increase our understanding of human behavior and is often designed to test a specific hypothesis from a specific theory. Applied research has a different purpose: to make use of social psychology's theories or methods to enlarge our understanding of naturally occurring events and to contribute to the solution of social problems.

24. c.   **an attempt to understand naturally occurring events.** Applied research is an attempt to make use of social psychology's theories or methods to enlarge our understanding of naturally occurring events and to contribute to the solution of social problems. On the other hand, basic research seeks to increase our understanding of human behavior and is often designed to test a specific hypothesis from a specific theory.

Answers to Essay Questions: Sample Essays

25. In order to determine whether the study was an experiment, one would need to know how much control the researcher had over the procedures and how the participants were assigned to the two conditions (i.e., to the hot versus comfortably cool rooms). This study would be an experiment if the researcher had control over the experimental procedures (i.e., if all those who participated in the study were treated in exactly the same manner except for the specific differences the experimenter wanted to create) and if the participants were assigned randomly to the two conditions. External validity is the degree to which one can be reasonably confident that the same results would be obtained for other people and in other situations. Both the participants in the study and the setting of the study have an impact on external validity, so one would need to know information about these two factors. To the extent that the sample of participants used in the study resembles a representative sample, which is a sample that reflects the characteristics of the population of interest, external validity should be higher than if the sample is a convenience sample, which is a sample selected because the participants are readily available. External validity may also be affected by the mundane realism and/or experimental realism of the study. There is a difference of opinion concerning the relative importance of these two types of realism. Mundane realism is the degree to which the experimental situation resembles places and events that exist in the real world, and experimental realism is the degree to which experimental procedures are involving to participants and lead them to behave naturally and spontaneously. To assess either form of realism in this study, one must know more both about the details of the procedure and about how the participants perceived the procedure. If the participants felt that the situation in which they found themselves resembled situations from their everyday lives, the study would be high in mundane realism; if the procedures were very involving to the participants and led them to behave spontaneously, the study would be high in experimental realism. If the study is high in both types of realism, external validity would be increased. If it is low in both, external validity would be decreased.

26. Self-reports are the most widely used measurement technique. In self-reports, participants disclose their own thoughts, feelings, desires, and behavior. Self-reports can give researchers direct access to an individual's beliefs and perceptions. But self-reports are not always accurate and can be misleading. Participants' concerns with looking good – both to themselves and to others – can bias their responses on self-report measures. The wording or ordering of questions can also affect their responses. For example, the way a question is structured, the "political correctness" of the terms used, and the available response alternatives can all affect participants' responses. In addition, participants may be unaware of some of their own desires or behaviors, or of the causes of their own actions, and thus give inaccurate responses. Interrater reliability is an important concern with observational measures. In contrast to self-reports, observational measures involve researchers observing people's actions. Interrater reliability refers to the level of agreement among multiple observers of the same behavior. The data collected using observational measures can be trusted to the extent that interrater reliability is high.

27. One position is that science should be value free. Adherents of this position argue that science should be totally objective and unbiased. A second position is that science cannot be value free and, thus, political advocacy is appropriate. That is, given that values always influence science, it would be irresponsible of researchers to try to ignore these influences. Instead, scientists should acknowledge the role of values in their work and use their research to help advocate for these values. A third position also acknowledges that science cannot be value free, but this position differs from the second position by advocating methods that try to reduce the biasing influence of these values. By adhering rigorously to the scientific method, scientists can attempt to free themselves of their preconceptions and weaken the influence of their values on their research as much as possible.

28. Social psychologists use more than merely their eyes and ears to observe their subjects. Advances in technology offer researchers exciting new tools that enable them to make extremely precise, subtle, and complex observations that were beyond the methods of social psychologists just a generation ago. Various kinds of apparatus are used to measure physiological responses such as changes in heart rate, levels of hormones, and sexual arousal. Computers are used to record the speed with which participants respond to stimuli, for example how quickly they can identify the race of people in photographs, or the presence of a weapon in the hands of a white or black man. Eye-tracking technology can be used to measure exactly where and for how long participants look at particular parts of a stimulus, such as the face, an advertisement, or a video.

CHAPTER 3

The Social Self

OUTLINE

LEARNING OBJECTIVES: GUIDELINES FOR STUDY

You should be able to do each of the following by the conclusion of Chapter 3.

1. Explain the idea of the self-concept and how it relates to the ways in which we attend to, interpret, and remember the world around us. Understand the ways in which studying the brain can shed light on the nature of the self-concept. *(pp. 56-57)*

2. Explain what is meant by describing the self as "relational." Discuss the social factors that contribute to the self-concept. *(p. 58)*

3. Discuss the limitations of introspection when it comes to achieving self-insight. Explain the relevance of affective forecasting to this issue. *(pp. 58-60)*

4. Describe self-perception theory, and explain how it can be applied to human emotion, behavior, and motivation. Define the overjustification effect and discuss the relationship between intrinsic and extrinsic motivation. (*pp. 60-64*)

5. Explain social comparison theory, identifying when people tend to engage in social comparison and with whom they tend to compare themselves. Explain the two-factor theory of emotion and its relevance to social comparison theory. (*pp. 65-67*)

6. Discuss autobiographical memories and explain how they are influenced by our self-concept. (*pp. 67-69)*

7. Describe the influences of gender, race, and culture on our understanding of self. Define dialecticism and discuss how the dialectical style of thought influences the self-concept. (*pp. 69-72)*

8. Define self-esteem. Explain the basis for the claim that people have a "need for self-esteem." Discuss the potential costs associated with the pursuit of self-esteem. (*pp. 72-75*)

9. Explain how self-discrepancy theory accounts for the general level of and changes in people's self-esteem, and impacts emotional states such as shame, guilt, and anxiety. (*pp. 75-76*)

10. Identify different types of self-focusing situations and personality types. Explain the self-awareness "trap." (*pp. 76-79*)

11. Explain the limitations of self-regulation. Explain what is meant by "ironic processes of self-control" and how this concept relates to self-regulation. (*pp. 79-82*)

12. Identify four ways that people strive for self-enhancement (i.e., positive illusions) and discuss the implications of self-enhancement for mental health and the perception of reality. Discuss the debate regarding whether or not such self-enhancement is adaptive. (*pp. 82-91*)

13. Compare and contrast strategic self-presentation and self-verification. (*pp. 91-93*)

14. Describe the differences between people who are high and low in self-monitoring. Explain how both of these strategies can be useful. (*pp. 93-95*)

MAJOR CONCEPTS: THE BIG PICTURE

Below are three basic issues or principles that organize Chapter 3. You should know these issues and principles well.

1. We have detailed and elaborate knowledge of ourselves – a self-concept. Gaining information about the self is more difficult than it might first appear, so although our self-impressions are not always reliable, we gain information about the self from thinking about ourselves, watching ourselves, comparing ourselves to others, and assimilating to our culture. Once we gain information about the self, we organize our memories around these beliefs.

2. We evaluate ourselves; that is, we have a sense of self-esteem. We evaluate ourselves in comparison to how we think we ought to be and how we think we could ideally be. In addition, we vary in when and how much we evaluate ourselves. Some situations lead to self-evaluation more than others, and some people experience more self-evaluation than others. Yet, in general, we maintain a positive image of ourselves. We are able to think about most situations in ways that enhance our self-image. Cultural influences play an important role in self esteem.

3. We present an image of ourselves to others. We usually try to present ourselves so that others will perceive us in a favorable way, but we also want people to view us accurately.

KEY TERM EXERCISE: THE CONCEPTS YOU SHOULD KNOW

Below are all of the key terms that appear in **boldface** in Chapter 3. To help you better understand these concepts, rather than just memorize them, write a definition for each term in your own words. After doing so, look at the next section where you'll find a list of definitions from the textbook for each of the key terms presented in random order. For each of your definitions, find the corresponding textbook definition. Note how your definitions compare with those from the textbook.

Key Terms

1. overjustification effect

2. self-monitoring

3. downward social comparison

4. self-presentation

5. facial feedback hypothesis

6. bask in reflected glory (BIRG)

7. private self-consciousness

8. self-esteem

9. self-concept

10. self-perception theory

11. social comparison theory

12. public self-consciousness

13. two-factor theory of emotion

14. self-awareness theory

15. self-handicapping

16. affective forecasting

17. implicit egotism

18. terror management theory

19. self-schemas

20. dialecticism

Textbook Definitions

a. Increasing self-esteem by associating with others who are successful.

b. Defensive tendency to compare ourselves to others who are worse off than we are.

c. The hypothesis that changes in facial expression can lead to corresponding changes in emotion.

d. The theory that people evaluate their own abilities and opinions by comparing themselves to others.

e. Behaviors designed to sabotage one's performance in order to provide a subsequent excuse for failure.

f. The tendency for intrinsic motivation to diminish for activities that have become associated with reward or other extrinsic factors.

g. The theory that the experience of emotion is based on two factors: physiological arousal and a cognitive interpretation of that arousal.

h. The theory that when internal cues are difficult to interpret, people gain self-insight by observing their own behavior.

i. The tendency to change behavior in response to the self-presentation concerns of the situation.

j. A personality characteristic of individuals who are introspective, often attending to their own inner states.

k. The theory that self-focused attention leads people to notice self-discrepancies, thereby motivating either an escape from self-awareness or a change in behavior.

l. An affective component of the self, consisting of a person's positive and negative self-evaluations.

m. Strategies people use to shape what others think of them.

n. A personality characteristic of individuals who focus on themselves as social objects, as seen by others.

o. The sum total of an individual's beliefs about his or her own personal attributes.

p. People's difficulty projecting forward and predicting how they would feel in response to future emotional events.

q. A nonconscious and subtle form of self-enhancement.

r. A system of thought characterized by acceptance of contradictions through compromise.

s. Explains our relentless need for self-esteem.

t. A belief people hold about themselves that guides the processing of self-relevant information.

ANSWERS FOR KEY TERM EXERCISE

Answers for the key terms exercise are listed below.

1.   f
2.   i
3.   b
4.   m
5.   c
6.   a
7.   j
8.   l
9.   o
10. h
11. d
12. n
13. g
14. k
15. e
16. p
17. q
18. s
19. t
20. r

PRACTICE QUIZ: TEST YOUR KNOWLEDGE OF THE CHAPTER

Multiple-Choice Questions

1. According to the two-factor theory of emotion, the experience of particular emotions requires both physiological arousal and
    a.   public self-consciousness.
    b.   downward comparison.
    c.   a cognitive interpretation.
    d.   autobiographical memory.

2. Introspection can impair self-knowledge for behaviors that
    a.   consist of flashbulb memories.
    b.   result from facial feedback.
    c.   depend on social comparison.
    d.   are caused by affective factors.

3. Herbert has a crush on Beth, but after thinking it over and weighing the pros and cons, he decides to date Joan instead. Research by Wilson (2002) on the utility of introspection suggests that Herbert probably would enjoy dating
    a.   Beth more than Joan.
    b.   Joan more than Beth.
    c.   Beth in the short run but Joan in the long run.
    d.   Joan in the short run but Beth in the long run.

4. As a child, Pete played baseball because it was fun. Now that he is a professional, he receives $1.9 million a year. Given his salary, he will probably experience
    a.   social comparison jealousy.
    b.   choking under pressure.
    c.   an overjustification effect.
    d.   self-handicapping.

5. Researchers found that when asked "Who are you?" people spontaneously rely on
    a.   the hindsight bias.
    b.   self-verification.
    c.   distinguishing features.
    d.   rewards for competence.

6. Elena spends a lot of time in introspection. She is very much "in touch" with her attitudes, values, and opinions. Elena is someone who is high in
    a.   self-monitoring.
    b.   self-handicapping.
    c.   private self-consciousness.
    d.   public self-consciousness.

7. Jennifer is preparing for an important interview. In order to appear upbeat but also to feel upbeat, she sits alone before the interview and smiles for a while. Jennifer is making use of the
    a.   two-factor theory of emotion.
    b.   self-reference effect.
    c.   egocentric bias.
    d.   facial feedback hypothesis.

8. Which of the following is a finding of the research on self-regulation?
    a. Acts requiring self-control reduce blood glucose levels.
    b. Human beings have an infinite reservoir of self-control.
    c. Self-regulation fatigue cannot be counteracted by psychological intervention.
    d. When people exert self-control in one task, their capacity for self-regulation in the next task increases.

9. People from Western cultures tend to be more _____ than people from Eastern cultures.
    a. interdependent
    b. compassionate
    c. shy
    d. individualistic

10. The fact that Paula, an Asian-American, regards herself as both introverted and extraverted at the same time can be explained by which of the following?
    a. Dialecticism
    b. Implicit egotism
    c. Private self-consciousness
    d. The two-factor theory of emotion

11. Monica thinks that she ought to spend more time with her family, but try as she may, she just can't seem to do it and also get her work done. Based on research concerning the self-concept and self-guides, one can predict that Monica is likely to feel
    a. disappointment.
    b. agitation.
    c. envy.
    d. shame.

12. The desire to have others perceive us as we perceive ourselves is called
    a. self-presentation.
    b. self-verification.
    c. self-consciousness.
    d. self-monitoring.

13. In their research on optimism and mental health Taylor and Brown (1988) argue that positive illusions about ourselves can
    a. be serious signs of mental disturbance.
    b. lead others to reject us.
    c. cause people to react violently in response to negative feedback.
    d. be adaptive in that they promote mental health.

14. People who drink alcohol often avoid the negative aspects of focusing on themselves and downplay the discrepancy between their real and ideal self-concepts. This process is called
    a. drunken self-inflation.
    b. self-monitoring.
    c. private self-awareness.
    d. self-handicapping.

15. Jim is a big fan of his college's football team. After the team wins the league championship, Jim wears his baseball cap with the college's logo for a week straight. Jim is probably

    a. high in self-esteem.
    b. a high self-monitor.
    c. making downward social comparisons.
    d. basking in reflected glory.

16. Jerry is a high school senior with slightly above-average grades. In order to feel good about his intellectual abilities, he selects a college with average-ability students. In doing so, Jerry makes it possible to engage in

    a. BIRGing.
    b. overjustification.
    c. downward social comparisons.
    d. drunken self-inflation.

17. During her job interview, Rachel goes out of her way to congratulate her prospective employers on their successful year and to agree with their strategies for the next fiscal year. Rachel's behavior is an example of

    a. the cocktail party effect.
    b. affective forecasting.
    c. ingratiation.
    d. basking in reflected glory.

18. Preoccupied with their self-image, people who are high in self-monitoring go out of their way to learn about

    a. their autobiographical memory.
    b. self-verification strategies.
    c. their self-discrepancies.
    d. others with whom they'll interact.

19. The _____ theory helps explain our relentless need for self-esteem.

    a. terror management
    b. self-handicapping
    c. social comparison
    d. two-factor

20. People who score on the high-end range on a self-esteem test are most likely

    a. Canadian.
    b. Japanese.
    c. Korean.
    d. Vietnamese.

21. The desire to have others perceive us as we truly perceive ourselves is a good example of

    a. self-schema.
    b. self-esteem.
    c. self-monitoring.
    d. self-verification.

Essay Questions

22. Describe how the self-concept develops from the perception of one's own behavior and from comparisons with other people.

23. Explain how the self-concept shapes our personal memories.

24. Describe two ways in which people can enhance their self-image and cope with their faults and inadequacies. Explain how these self-enhancing biases can promote positive mental health.

25. Describe Terror Management Theory and discuss how it explains modern-day life.

ANSWERS TO THE PRACTICE QUIZ

Multiple-Choice Questions: Correct Answers and Explanations

1. c.   **a cognitive interpretation.** The two factors that the two-factor theory suggests are necessary and sufficient for an emotional response are physiological arousal and a cognitive label or a cognitive interpretation of the situation. Schachter emphasized in this model that we are particularly likely to look to others and their responses in the situation when forming a cognitive interpretation. Public self-consciousness, downward comparison, and autobiographical memory are not included in the two-factor theory.

2. d.   **are caused by affective factors.** Common sense tells us that introspection should lead to accurate self-knowledge, but Wilson's (2002) research suggests that introspection often leads to inaccurate self-knowledge. False feedback and social comparisons have not been shown to have an affect on introspection, and flashbulb memories are unrelated to the issue of introspection.

3. a.   **enjoy dating Beth more than Joan.** Wilson's research suggests that introspection often leads to inaccurate self-knowledge. This research implies that Herbert should probably go with his gut instinct and go out with Beth rather than Joan. This is true for both the short run and the long run.

4. c.   **an overjustification effect.** Pete used to play baseball for the fun of it (he was intrinsically motivated). Now he gets paid big money to play. Self-perception theory suggests that, when he interprets his own behavior, he will now begin to believe that he plays baseball at least partly for the money. This will undermine his intrinsic motivation—an effect known as overjustification. There is no reason to expect that he will choke under pressure or that he will engage in social comparison jealousy or self-handicapping. These processes are unaffected by the salary that he is earning.

5. c.   **distinguishing features.** The research (McGuire & McGuire, 1988) shows that, when spontaneously describing themselves, people tend to point out how they differ from others in their social environment. For example, a girl in a group of all boys is more likely to describe herself in terms of her sex than if she were in a group of all girls or in a group with a more equal mix of boys and girls. Answers to the question "Who are you?" reveal little evidence of the hindsight bias or of self-verification, and they do not appear to be affected by rewards for competence.

6.   c.   **private self-consciousness.** People high in private self-consciousness know their attitudes well and spend a lot of time introspecting about them. Elena seems to be such a person. She certainly is not someone high in public self-consciousness, concerned with her effects upon others, and there is no evidence that she is high in self-monitoring or self-handicapping.

7.   d.   **facial feedback hypothesis.** Research on the facial feedback hypothesis suggests that people's facial expressions can often influence their moods. Therefore, smiling might make Jennifer not only look more upbeat, but also feel more upbeat. The two-factor theory of emotion suggests that physiological arousal that is labeled cognitively gives rise to emotion. However, since there was no mention of physiological arousal or a cognitive label, the two-factor theory would be incorrect. The self-reference effect and the egocentric bias are unrelated to emotion.

8.   a.   **acts requiring self-control reduce blood glucose levels.** Research by Gailliot and others (2007) found that acts of self-control, such as suppressing a word, thought, or emotion, led to reduced blood glucose levels. Self-control does not appear to be an infinite capacity. Rather, it appears to be a limited inner resource that can temporarily be depleted by usage. Schmeichel and Vohs (2009) found that the psychological intervention of self-affirmation did enable people to sustain pain tolerance levels even after they exercised self-control. Muraven and Baumeister (1998) found that those who exercised self-control while watching a film subsequently exerted less self-control when squeezing a handgrip.

9.   d.   **individualistic.** Research cited in the textbook suggests that people from Western cultures are more individualistic than people from Eastern cultures. People in Eastern cultures tend to be more interdependent than Westerners. There have been no differences noted in shyness or compassion between Easterners or Westerners.

10.   a.   **dialecticism**. Dialecticism is the Eastern system of thought characterized by an acceptance of contradictions within one's self. Implicit egotism is a subtle, unconscious bias that people demonstrate when they favor the letters in their own names. Private self-consciousness is the tendency to introspect about private thoughts and feelings. It is not about accepting contradictions within one's self. The two-factor theory of emotion posits that experiencing of emotion takes place in two stages: physical arousal followed by cognitive interpretation.

11.   a.   **disappointment.** Monica is likely to feel a discrepancy between her ideal self (which wants to be with her family) and her actual self (which is not spending time with them). Research on the self-concept and self-guides (Boldero & Francis, 2000; Higgins, 1999; Strauman, 1992) suggests that such ideal/actual self-discrepancies should lead to disappointment. The model does not predict other emotional reactions such as agitation, envy, or shame.

12.   b.   **self-verification.** Self-verification is the desire to have others perceive us as we truly perceive ourselves. Self-presentation encompasses the various strategies people use to shape what others think of them. Self-consciousness occurs when people focus on themselves. This self-consciousness can be public, where people focus on how others see them, or private, where people focus on how they see themselves. Self-monitoring is the tendency to change behavior in response to the self-presentation concerns of the situation.

13.   d.   **be adaptive in that they promote mental health.** Taylor and Brown (1988) argue that positive illusions are adaptive in that they promote happiness, caring for others, and productive work—in short, mental health. This view is at odds with what many psychologists previously claimed: That accurate perceptions of reality are crucial for mental health. More recently, some have noted the shortcomings to Taylor and Brown's argument. Colvin and colleagues (1995) have noted that positive illusions can lead to negative evaluations by others. In a similar vein, a study by Heatherton and Vohs (2000) found that students who were deemed to have high self-esteem were also regarded as rude, unfriendly, and arrogant.

14. a. **drunken self-inflation.** Drunken self-inflation is the tendency to discount real and ideal self-discrepancies when drinking. Drinking is sometimes used as a self-handicapping strategy, but self-handicapping has little to do with focus of attention. Private self-awareness occurs when people focus on their self-concepts and is decreased when people drink alcohol, but may or may not be related to discrepancies between real and ideal self-concepts. As self-monitoring is the tendency to focus on the immediate social situation and adjust one's behavior accordingly, it has little to do with drinking alcohol.

15. d. **basking in reflected glory.** Cialdini's research on basking in reflected glory demonstrates that people like to identify with groups that they are a part of when those groups succeed. Jim is probably basking in reflected glory by identifying himself with the team as it wins. There is little reason to expect that Jim is high in self-esteem, and his self-esteem could not explain why he wore his cap more after the team won. Jim is not engaging in downward social comparisons either; such comparisons involve interactions with others who are doing worse than oneself. Finally, there is no evidence that Jim is a high self-monitor.

16. c. **downward social comparisons.** Attending a less selective school should give Jerry plenty of opportunity for contact with others who are not as smart as he is. It should also allow him to engage in downward social comparisons—comparisons with others that would put him in a positive light. Such comparisons can be self-enhancing. There is no evidence that Jerry is basking in reflected glory or engaging in overjustification or drunken self-inflation. These processes have little or nothing to do with comparisons that allow people to feel good about themselves.

17. c. **ingratiation.** Ingratiation is a tactic of strategic self-presentation. It includes such behaviors as flattery, agreement, and putting one's best foot forward. If successful, ingratiation results in liking by others. There is no evidence that Rachel's behavior exemplifies the cocktail party effect, affective forecasting, or basking in reflected glory. These processes have little to do with flattery and congratulation.

18. d. **others with whom they'll interact.** Since high self-monitors tailor their behavior to fit the situation they are in, they are very sensitive to the people with whom they interact. They recognize that other people are an important part of the situation. However, there is little reason to expect that self-monitors will try to learn about their autobiographical memories, self-discrepancies, or self-verifications. These concepts are probably unrelated to self-monitoring.

19. a. **terror management.** Terror management helps to explain our relentless need for self-esteem. According to this theory, we humans are biologically programmed for life and self-preservation. Yet we are conscious of—and terrified by—the inevitability of our own death. To cope with this paralyzing, deeply rooted fear, we construct and accept cultural worldviews about how, why, and by whom the earth was created; religious explanations of the purpose of our existence; and a sense of history filled with heroes, villains, and momentous events. These worldviews provide meaning and purpose and a buffer against anxiety.

20. a. **Canadian.** Cultures have differing effects on the pursuit of self-esteem. Comparing the distribution of self-esteem test scores in Canada and Japan, researchers have found that whereas most Canadians' scores clustered in the high-end range, the majority of Japanese respondents scored in the center of that same range.

21. d. **self-verification.** People are highly motivated in their social encounters to confirm or verify their existing self-concept in the eyes of others. Researchers have gathered a great deal of evidence for this hypothesis and have found that people selectively elicit, recall, and accept personality feedback that confirms their self-conceptions. In fact, people sometimes bend over backward to correct others whose impressions are positive but mistaken.

Answers to Essay Questions: Sample Essays

22. Self-perception theory describes how people often infer their beliefs and attitudes from their actions. This theory suggests that people make inferences about their own behavior in the same way that they make inferences about other people's behavior. They assume that if someone engages in a behavior, then he or she probably has attitudes and beliefs consistent with this behavior unless there is a good reason to believe otherwise. For example, if someone spends a lot of time playing basketball, then he or she would probably infer that basketball is an important part of his or her self-concept. Social comparison theory describes how people develop their attitudes and behaviors by comparing themselves with others. In particular, it suggests that people make comparisons with others who are similar, especially those who are doing just slightly better. By making these comparisons, we gain a sense of what our beliefs and abilities are.

23. Autobiographical memories concerning childhood, family members, and successes and failures in and out of school help to shape the core of a person's identity or self-concept. That the self-concept, in turn, shapes memories was shown in several studies. For example, in one study, when prompted to recall personal experiences, older adults tended to remember events from their formative teen and early adult years. In another study, people of all ages were more likely to remember "firsts" (such as the first day in college). In these studies, the things that were remembered were those that had the most impact on the self-concept. Other studies showed how the self-concept influences the reconstruction of memory, motivating people to remember the past in ways that flatter their self-concept. For example, when college students were asked to recall grades, errors tended to be inflationary, reflecting the use of memory to boost self-esteem. Another example of this self-serving bias was evident when John Dean's Watergate testimony was compared with tapes of his meetings with president Nixon. Discrepancies between the two showed that Dean had exaggerated his role and importance. Researchers concluded that the past is remembered as a drama in which one's self has the starring role.

24. The text discusses three ways in which people can enhance their self-image: basking in reflected glory, downward social comparison, and self-handicapping. Basking in reflected glory occurs when people come to identify with a group that is succeeding. For example, when a student at a prestigious university points to the accomplishments of the professors and identifies with them, he or she is able to share in their success. Downward social comparison entails making contact with others who are doing worse than oneself. This type of comparison allows one to feel relatively better off. For example, the cancer patient who meets other patients in worse shape can derive some comfort in the thought that at least he or she is doing better than they are. But, downward social comparison is not always an option, as when the successful person is a close friend or relative. In that case, Abraham Tesser suggests that there are two possibilities: one can take pride and bask in the reflected glory or feel jealousy and anger at the other's success. The deciding factor is the importance of the domain in which the success was achieved to one's self. Self-handicapping is a strategy that some people use in order to provide an excuse for poor performance on an upcoming threatening event. For example, the student who gets drunk the night before an exam will have a ready explanation for why he or she fails the exam the next day. Note that while this behavior may soften the negative impact of a poor performance, it may also cause the poor performance. Taylor and Brown present evidence that such self-enhancing biases may be beneficial to our mental health. They suggest that we may need such biases to cope with the difficult problems we face in daily life. Their evidence suggests that people who do not show these biases tend to be depressed.

25. According to Terror Management Theory, we humans are biologically programmed for life and self-preservation. Yet we are conscious of—and terrified by—the inevitability of our own death. To cope with this paralyzing, deeply rooted fear, we construct and accept cultural worldviews about how, why, and by whom the earth was created; religious explanations of the purpose of our existence; and a sense of history filled with heroes, villains, and momentous events. These worldviews provide meaning and purpose and a buffer against anxiety. In a series of experiments, investigators found that people react to graphic scenes of death, or to the thought of their own death, with intense defensiveness and anxiety. When given positive feedback on a test, however, which boosts their self-esteem, that reaction is muted. This theory has been used to explain how Americans coped with the trauma of 9/11 and the terror that it triggered by resorting to worldviews that preserved their self-esteem. Self-esteem thus becomes the protective shield against the anxiety-provoking possibility that our existence on earth is fragile and meaningless.

CHAPTER 4

Perceiving Persons

OUTLINE

LEARNING OBJECTIVES: GUIDELINES FOR STUDY

You should be able to do each of the following by the conclusion of Chapter 4.

1. Explain the importance of first impressions in social perception. Consider the cues (facial features, name, style of dress) that contribute to these snap judgments. (*pp. 102-104*)

2. Explain the function of scripts in social perception. Define mind perception. Discuss the two dimensions that people consider when deciding how much "mind" to attribute to objects and explain the consequences of such decisions. (*pp. 105-107*)

3. Explain the role of nonverbal cues in social perception. Summarize the research concerning perception of angry faces. Explain what is meant by "thin slicing." Discuss the roles of other nonverbal cues, including body language, eye contact, and touch. Discuss the role of cultural norms in evaluating nonverbal behavior. (*pp. 107-110*)

4. Describe people's ability to detect deception. Contrast the channels of communication that are most likely to reveal that someone is lying with the channels that perceivers typically try to use to detect deception. (*pp. 110-112*)

5. Define what is meant by attribution. Distinguish between personal and situational attributions. Summarize Jones's correspondent inference theory and Kelley's covariation theory. (*pp. 112-116*)

6. Describe cognitive heuristics in general and the availability heuristic in particular. Explain the relationship between the availability heuristic, the false-consensus effect, and the base-rate fallacy. (*pp. 116-118*)

7. Define counterfactual thinking and identify when it is likely to occur. (*pp. 118-119*)

8. Define the fundamental attribution error and describe the factors that make this error more or less likely to occur. Compare the fundamental attribution error with the actor-observer effect, and discuss the two explanations for the actor-observer effect. Understand the role of culture in the attribution process. (*pp. 119-123*)

9. Explain how attribution biases may stem from motivational factors, such as the desire to take more credit for success than for failure. Define what is meant by the "belief in a just world," and identify the factors that lead to defensive attributions. (*pp. 123-126*)

10. Explain the summation and averaging models of impression formation. Explain the role of perceiver characteristics (including the effects of individual differences, priming, and mood) and of target characteristics (including the trait negativity bias) on impression formation. (*pp. 126-129*)

11. Explain how people's implicit personality theories affect their impressions of other people. Describe the effects of central traits and the primacy effect on these impressions. Identify two explanations for the primacy effect. (*pp. 130-132*)

12. Define confirmation bias. Describe how belief perseverance, confirmatory hypothesis testing, and the self-fulfilling prophecy can each contribute to this bias. Discuss the relationship between confirmation bias and belief perseverance. (*pp. 132-138*)

13. Describe generally how people fare as social perceivers, listing reasons for being both optimistic and pessimistic regarding people's competence as social perceivers. (*pp. 138-141*)

MAJOR CONCEPTS: THE BIG PICTURE

Below are four basic issues or principles that organize Chapter 4. You should know these issues and principles well.

1. To understand other people's emotions, motives, and personal dispositions, social perceivers rely on indirect clues. These indirect clues—the elements of social perception—include information about persons, situations, and behavior. People's perceptions of others are influenced by others' physical appearance, by preconceptions about various types of situations, and by nonverbal communication.

2. People try to understand each other by attributing the causes of their behavior to personal factors or situational factors. Although these attributions often are consistent with the logic represented in theories of the attribution process, there are several ways in which people's attributions often depart from the logic of these theories, resulting in attribution biases.

3. Perceivers combine different pieces of information about a person to form a coherent overall impression. The integration of this information depends in part on characteristics of the perceiver, such as the perceiver's sensitivity to particular information, and in part on characteristics of the target, such as the presence or absence of particular types of traits.

4. Once an impression is formed, people become less likely to change their minds when confronted with nonsupportive evidence. Rather, they tend to interpret, seek, and even create information in ways that confirm their existing beliefs.

KEY TERM EXERCISE: THE CONCEPTS YOU SHOULD KNOW

Below are all of the key terms that appear in **boldface** in Chapter 4. To help you better understand these concepts, rather than just memorize them, write a definition for each term in your own words. After doing so, look at the next section where you'll find a list of definitions from the textbook for each of the key terms presented in random order. For each of your definitions, find the corresponding textbook definition. Note how your definitions compare with those from the textbook.

Key Terms

1. base-rate fallacy

2. central traits

3. situational attribution

4. belief in a just world

5. primacy effect

6. false-consensus effect

7. social perception

8. correspondent inference theory

9. information integration theory

10. availability heuristic

11. personal attribution

12. implicit personality theory

13. covariation principle

14. fundamental attribution error

15. confirmation bias

16. impression formation

17. actor-observer effect

18. nonverbal behavior

19. counterfactual thinking

20. priming

21. self-fulfilling prophecy

22. attribution theory

23. belief perseverance

24. need for closure

25. mind perception

Textbook Definitions

a.   A general term for the processes by which people come to understand one another.

b.   A tendency to estimate the likelihood that an event will occur by how easily instances of it come to mind.

c.   Behavior that reveals a person's feelings through facial expressions, body language, and vocal cues.

d.   A group of theories that describe how people explain the causes of behavior.

e.   Attribution to internal characteristics of an actor, such as ability, personality, mood, or effort.

f.   Attribution to factors external to an actor, such as the task, other people, luck.

g.   A theory holding that we make inferences about a person when his or her actions are freely chosen, are unexpected, and result in a small number of desirable effects.

h.   A principle of attribution theory holding that people attribute behavior to factors that are present when a behavior occurs and absent when it does not.

i.   The tendency to focus on the role of personal causes and underestimate the impact of situations on other people's behavior.

j.   The tendency to attribute our own behavior to situational causes and the behavior of others to personal factors.

k.   A tendency to imagine alternative events or outcomes that might have occurred but did not.

l.   The tendency for people to overestimate the extent to which others share their opinions, attributes, and behavior.

m.   The finding that people are relatively insensitive to consensus information presented in the form of numerical base rates.

n.   The belief that individuals get what they deserve in life, an orientation that leads people to disparage victims.

o.   The process of integrating information about a person to form a coherent impression.

p.   The theory that impressions are based on (1) perceiver dispositions and (2) a weighted average of a target person's traits.

q.   The tendency for recently used words or ideas to come to mind easily and influence the interpretation of new information.

r.   A network of assumptions people make about the relationships among traits and behaviors.

s.   Traits that exert a powerful influence on overall impressions.

t.   The tendency for information presented early in a sequence to have more impact on impressions than information presented later.

u.   A desire to reduce cognitive uncertainty, which heightens the importance of first impressions.

v.   The process by which people attribute humanlike mental states to various animate and inanimate objects.

w.   The tendency to seek, interpret, and create information that verifies existing beliefs.

x.   The tendency to maintain beliefs even after they have been discredited.

y.   The process by which one's expectations about a person eventually lead that person to behave in ways that confirm those expectations.

ANSWERS FOR KEY TERM EXERCISE

Answers for the key terms exercise are listed below.

1.   m
2.   s
3.   f
4.   n
5.   t
6.   l
7.   a
8.   g
9.   p
10.   b
11.   e
12.   r
13.   h
14.   i
15.   w
16.   o
17.   j
18.   c
19.   k
20.   q
21.   y
22.   d
23.   x
24.   u
25.   v

PRACTICE QUIZ: TEST YOUR KNOWLEDGE OF THE CHAPTER

Multiple-Choice Questions

1. Charlene finishes second in a swim meet and wins the silver medal, but she is depressed because she can't stop thinking about the fact that she was so close to winning the gold medal. Liv finishes third and wins the bronze medal, and she feels great relief and satisfaction because she realizes how close she came to finishing fourth and therefore not winning a medal. Charlene's and Liv's reactions reflect
    a.   belief in a just world.
    b.   counterfactual thinking.
    c.   the fundamental attribution error.
    d.   the covariation principle.

2. Diane sees Carla make a strong speech *against* legalized gambling. She learns that Carla had free choice to make a speech on any issue she chose, and Diane knows that most of the students in Carla's class are in *favor* of legalized gambling. Diane infers that Carla truly is opposed to legalized gambling. This is most consistent with the
    a.   self-fulfilling prophecy.
    b.   correspondent inference theory.
    c.   fundamental attribution error.
    d.   false-consensus effect.

3. Yvonne has small eyes, low eyebrows, a small forehead, and an angular chin. Vickie has large round eyes, high eyebrows, round cheeks, a large forehead, smooth skin, and a rounded chin. According to research concerning social perception, Yvonne would be more likely than Vickie to
    a.   be hired as a day-care teacher.
    b.   get an acting job playing the part of someone who is seen as submissive.
    c.   be accused of negligence as an adult.
    d.   be hired as a banker.

4. Joyce expected that her new roommate, Chrissie, would be somewhat cold and unfriendly. Because of this expectation, Joyce did not welcome Chrissie into her room very warmly. In turn, Chrissie did not act very warmly toward Joyce, and even began to be unfriendly toward Joyce and her friends. This best illustrates the
    a.   negative effects of counterfactual thinking.
    b.   self-fulfilling prophecy.
    c.   false-consensus effect.
    d.   correspondent inference theory.

5. Facial expressions, body language, eye contact, and touch are all forms of
    a.   the actor-observer effect..
    b.   the priming process.
    c.   nonverbal behavior.
    d.   situational attribution.

6. The principal looked at the four boys and said, "I know one of you is not telling the truth." Then, because he had read the latest research concerning the channels of communication that are used to detect deception, he was able to accurately guess that the liar was
   a. Joey, who looked very stressed when he professed his innocence
   b. Kenneth, who avoided making eye contact when he claimed to be telling the truth
   c. Larry, who squirmed, fidgeted, and stuttered when he said he wasn't lying
   d. Mark, who hesitated, sped up, and raised the pitch of his voice when he said he wasn't guilty

7. Jose hires someone from an escort service to be his date for the evening at a company party and to act very warmly toward him. During the party, Jose comes to believe that his date's behavior suggests that she really is warm and friendly. Jose's inference is most likely an example of
   a. the primacy effect.
   b. the fundamental attribution error.
   c. trait negativity bias.
   d. a situational attribution.

8. According to research conducted across different cultures concerning people's attributions, which of the following pairs of people should show the biggest discrepancy in terms of whether they attribute someone's negative behavior to the person or to the situation?
   a. A child in India and a child in the United States
   b. An adult in India and an adult in the United States
   c. An adult in India and a child in the United States
   d. A child in India and an adult in India

9. Persons, situations, and behavior are the three major elements in
   a. central traits.
   b. cognitive heuristics.
   c. self-fulfilling prophecies.
   d. social perception.

10. Ed observes Mary Ann behaving in a particular way and considers whether or not he has learned anything about her personal characteristics on the basis of this behavior. Based on the correspondent inference theory, Ed would be most likely to infer that her behavior does correspond to an enduring personal characteristic if
    a. Mary Ann was behaving in front of other people rather than alone.
    b. Mary Ann's behavior was likely to earn her both a lot of money and a great deal of respect.
    c. Mary Ann's behavior was consistent with a social norm.
    d. Mary Ann had a high degree of choice concerning whether or not to behave in that way.

11. While busy doing something else, and without fully realizing it, Sophia heard the lyrics to a song, which included words such as "punch," "fight," "threaten," and "hurt." Jennifer did not hear the song. Later, Sophia and Jennifer watched a video of a man pushing another man. Sophia interpreted the push as more hostile and threatening than did Jennifer. This outcome is an example of the effects of
    a. priming.
    b. the base-rate fallacy.
    c. the actor-observer difference.
    d. the trait negativity bias.

12. If we know that Juan's perception was influenced by a script, we can reasonably conclude that Juan
    a. was unable to detect deception accurately.
    b. was affected by his expectations.
    c. ignored cognitive heuristics.
    d. made attributions that were biased to make himself look good.

13. Research concerning the base-rate fallacy shows that, when asked to make predictions about the future actions of others, people tend to rely on
    a. graphic, dramatic events.
    b. numerical base rates.
    c. abstract laws of probability.
    d. hard statistical facts.

14. The day before Brenda's roommate Rhoda is supposed to turn in a term paper, Rhoda experiences a very painful headache and blurred vision and goes to the infirmary. Brenda has noticed that Rhoda gets these symptoms whenever she has to turn in a term paper. Brenda also has noticed that Rhoda gets similar symptoms whenever she is excited, stressed, or required to do a lot of work. None of the other students whom Brenda knows well experiences these symptoms. According to Kelley's covariation theory, Brenda should make a personal attribution for Rhoda's experiences because her experiences are
    a. low in consensus, low in consistency, and low in distinctiveness.
    b. high in consensus, high in consistency, and low in distinctiveness.
    c. low in consensus, high in consistency, and low in distinctiveness.
    d. high in consensus, high in consistency, and high in distinctiveness.

15. Of the following, the person most likely to make the fundamental attribution error when observing someone's behavior is
    a. Reed, who is distracted while observing the behavior
    b. Pamela, who is focusing on the situation
    c. Angie, who is not cognitively busy
    d. Sirajul, who is an adult in India

16. Lance suspects that Marcia has low self-esteem. Lance asks Marcia, "Do you sometimes feel that you can't do anything right?" When Marcia answers "yes," Lance concludes that he was right about Marcia having low self-esteem. This conclusion is an example of
    a. confirmatory hypothesis testing.
    b. the summation model of impression formation.
    c. the primacy effect.
    d. priming.

17. Michael often physically touches the people with whom he works, patting them on the back or elbowing them in the ribs. Research suggests that Michael's behavior may be a sign of
    a. dominance.
    b. priming.
    c. suspicion.
    d. personal attributions.

18. According to research concerning the belief in a just world, which of the following people should be *least* likely to be critical of or derogate the plight of a victim?
    a. Mick, who sees the victim as similar to himself in many respects
    b. Charlie, who is prompted to take the victim's perspective
    c. Ron, who is emotionally aroused by observing the victim
    d. Keith, who sees the consequences to the victim as being severe and negative

19. Stacey, a high school student, came home past her curfew. She claimed the fog was so bad that she couldn't drive. Her parents argued that she was just being thoughtless. This difference in views is consistent with the
    a. confirmation bias.
    b. false-consensus effect.
    c. self-fulfilling prophecy.
    d. actor-observer effect.

20. Researchers have found that when participants are asked whether there are more English words that start with the letter *r* or that have the letter *r* as the third letter, most participants guess that there are more words that start with the letter *r*. This phenomenon most clearly reflects the
    a. covariation theory.
    b. primacy effect.
    c. availability heuristic.
    d. confirmation bias.

21. For the first time since he began college, Brad goes to his professor for help. His professor shows him some new study techniques. Brad thinks his instructor is a genuinely dedicated teacher. Brad's opinion is an example of a
    a. situational attribution.
    b. primacy effect.
    c. personal attribution.
    d. central trait.

22. When asked whether a variety of human and nonhuman characters, such as a fetus, a man in a vegetative state, and a sociable robot, had minds, participants appeared to make the decision with regard to two dimensions:
    a. agency and experience.
    b. reliability and validity.
    c. familiarity and utility.
    d. language and motion.

23. The tendency for people to overestimate the extent to which others share their opinions, attributes, and behaviors is a good description of
    a. the covariation principle.
    b. the base-rate fallacy.
    c. counterfactual thinking.
    d. the false-consensus effect.

Essay Questions

24. While observing someone's behavior, why are people more likely to commit the fundamental attribution error when they are cognitively busy or distracted?

25. What is the primacy effect? Describe two major reasons for this effect.

26. Imagine the following study. Participants read about a number of experiments, each of which supports the idea that introverted people make better psychiatrists than extroverted people. The participants are given time to think about this information. Later, they are informed that the experiments they had read were fictitious – they were fabricated by the experimenter for purposes of the experiment. Despite the fact that the information was discredited, however, the participants continue to believe that introverted people probably would make better psychiatrists than extroverted people. What social psychological concept best describes the results of this study? Why does this phenomenon occur?

27. What kind of nonverbal cues do people use to judge how someone else is feeling?

ANSWERS TO THE PRACTICE QUIZ

Multiple-Choice Questions: Correct Answers and Explanations

1. b. **counterfactual thinking.** Counterfactual thinking involves imagining alternative events or outcomes that might have occurred but did not, which is what the two swimmers were reacting to. Belief in a just world is the belief that individuals get what they deserve in life, but there is no evidence that the two swimmers are reacting to such a belief. The fundamental attribution error and the covariation principle both concern attribution theory, but the swimmers' reactions are not due to how they explained the causes of their performances in the meet, but rather are influenced by their thoughts of "what might have been."

2. b. **the correspondent inference theory.** This theory proposes that when perceivers learn that an actor's behavior was performed under free choice, and that it departed from social norms, they are likely to infer that the behavior reflects the actor's true disposition. Because Carla had free choice, and because her speech against gambling departed from her class's norm of supporting gambling, Diane inferred that Carla's speech did indeed reflect her attitudes. Because Diane's attribution was consistent with this theory, there is no evidence of an attribution bias; options "c" and "d" therefore are incorrect as they each concern an attribution bias. The other option, the self-fulfilling prophecy, refers to the process by which one's expectations about a person eventually lead that person to behave in ways that confirm those expectations; there is nothing stated in the question about Diane's expectations or any effects on Carla's behavior.

3. d. **be hired as a banker.** Yvonne's facial features are considered to be mature features, whereas Vickie's are considered baby-faced features. Research has shown that adults with baby-faced features are more likely to be perceived in ways consistent with negligence. Conversely, these same adults are more likely to be seen as appropriate for a day-care teacher, as submissive, and as less likely to engage in intentional wrongdoing. People with mature features tend to be seen as stronger, competent, and more dominant, thus why they might get hired as bankers faster than people with baby-faced features.

4.   b.   **self-fulfilling prophecy.** The self-fulfilling prophecy occurs when one's expectations about a person eventually lead that person to behave in ways that confirm those expectations; this is what apparently happened here, as Joyce's expectations about Chrissie caused Chrissie to behave in ways that confirmed Joyce's expectations. Counterfactual thinking involves imagining alternative events or outcomes that might have occurred but did not; there is no evidence of that in this question. The false-consensus effect is the tendency for people to overestimate the extent to which others share their opinions, attributes, and behavior; again, there is no evidence of this indicated. The correspondent inference theory maintains that we make inferences about a person when his or her actions are freely chosen, are unexpected, and result in a small number of desirable effects; although this theory might be relevant to predicting how Joyce and Chrissie explain each other's behaviors, it is less clearly relevant to what happened between them than is the self-fulfilling prophecy.

5.   c.   **nonverbal behavior.** Nonverbal behavior communicates a person's feelings without words, such as through facial expressions, body language, eye contact, and touch. The other options are not comprised of these particular behaviors.

6.   d.   **Mark, who hesitated, sped up, and raised the pitch of his voice when he said he wasn't guilty.** Research on the four channels of communication that people use to detect deception, found that of the spoken word, the face, the body, and the voice, the only reliable signal was the voice. Liars, typically, hesitate, speed up, and raise the pitch of their voice. In important life situations, such as being called up to the principal's office, truth tellers are as likely to show signs of stress as are liars. Research also shows that liars do not avoid direct eye contact, nor are they more likely to squirm, stutter, or fidget.

7.   b.   **the fundamental attribution error.** The fundamental attribution error is the tendency to underestimate the impact of situations on other people's behavior and to focus on the role of personal causes. José ignores the fact that his date was required to act friendly as part of the job (a situational cause) and instead attributes her behavior to her being a warm and friendly person (a personal cause). José does not, therefore, make a situational attribution. The primacy effect and trait negativity bias are concepts concerning the integration of a number of traits in the impression formation process, rather than attributions of a specific type of behavior.

8.   b.   **an adult in India and an adult in the United States.** According to cross-cultural research, adults in India tend to avoid the fundamental attribution error, whereas adults in the United States tend to make this error. All of the individuals in the other three choices for this question are relatively unlikely to commit the fundamental attribution error.

9.   d.   **social perception.** Social perception is the general term for the processes by which people come to understand each other, and the information used in these processes concerns persons, situations, and behaviors. This set of three elements is not of central importance in any of the three other choices, which are concerned with more specific concepts.

10.   d.   **Mary Ann had a high degree of choice concerning whether or not to behave in that way.** Correspondent inference theory proposes that when perceivers learn that an actor's behavior was performed under free choice, departs from social norms, and results in a small number of desirable effects, they are more likely to infer that the actor's behavior reflects their true disposition. Thus, Ed should make this inference if Mary Ann had a high degree of choice, but not if her behavior was likely to earn money and respect (which are multiple desirable effects) or if it was consistent with social norms. Whether she behaved in front of other people is information, which, by itself, is not relevant to this theory.

11.   a.   **priming.** Priming refers to the tendency for recently used words or ideas to influence the interpretation of new information. Sophia's recent exposure to aggressive words influenced her interpretation of the behavior depicted on the video. The base-rate fallacy and the actor-observer difference are not relevant to this question. Because Sophia and Jennifer were not presented with multiple traits about the man in the video, the trait negativity bias is not relevant either.

12.   b.   **was affected by his expectations.** Scripts are preconceived notions about a sequence of events likely to occur in a particular situation. Perceivers' expectations about the likely occurrence of a sequence of events can influence their perceptions. Detection of deception, cognitive heuristics, and biased attributions are not as likely to depend on perceivers' preconceived notions about a sequence of events.

13.   a.   **graphic, dramatic events.** The base-rate fallacy is the tendency to rely on graphic, dramatic events when making predictions, and to be relatively insensitive to numerical base rates, abstract laws of probability, and hard statistical facts.

14.   c.   **low in consensus, high in consistency, and low in distinctiveness.** The fact that no other students get these symptoms indicates low consensus. The fact that Rhoda always gets these symptoms whenever she faces a deadline indicates high consistency. And the fact that Rhoda experiences similar symptoms in a number of different situations indicates low distinctiveness.

15.   a.   **Reed, who is distracted while observing the behavior.** Distraction inhibits a perceiver's ability to adjust personal attributions to take into account situational causes, thus making the fundamental attribution error more likely to occur. The other three individuals are all more likely to take into account situational factors, and thus less likely to commit the fundamental attribution error.

16.   a.   **confirmatory hypothesis testing.** Because Lance hypothesized that Marcia has low self-esteem, he asked Marcia a question that was likely to elicit confirmation of his hypothesis. The summation model and the primacy effect are not correct because this question does not concern Lance's integration of multiple traits about Marcia. Priming is not relevant because there is no mention of any recently used words or ideas influencing Lance's interpretation of new information.

17.   a.   **dominance.** Research has shown that touch can be a sign of friendship, intimacy, and related feelings, or a sign of dominance and control. There is no evidence that touch is related to priming, which concerns the effects of recently used words on perceivers' perceptions, or to suspicion or personal attributions, both of which are concepts relevant to attribution theory.

18.   b.   **Charlie, who is prompted to take the victim's perspective.** Taking the victim's perspective is one way to reduce the tendency to be critical of a victim. The individuals described in the other choices for this question have an *increased* likelihood of derogating victims, due to people's tendency to want to believe in a just world – the belief that individuals get what they deserve in life, an orientation that leads people to disparage victims.

19.   d.   **actor-observer effect.** The actor-observer effect is the tendency to attribute one's own behavior to situational causes and others' behavior to personal causes. Stacey attributed her own behavior to a situational cause (the fog), whereas her parents attributed her behavior to a personal cause (her thoughtlessness). The confirmation bias concerns the impact of expectations, which is irrelevant to this question. The false-consensus effect concerns overestimating the consensus for one's opinions, attributes, and behaviors; there is no mention of estimates concerning consensus in this question. The self-fulfilling prophecy refers to the process by which one's expectations about a person eventually lead that person to behave in ways that confirm those expectations; there is no mention in this question about the effect of someone's expectations on another's behavior.

20. c. **the availability heuristic.** The availability heuristic is the tendency to estimate the likelihood of an event on the basis of how easily instances of it come to mind. Although the English language contains many more words with r as the third letter rather than the first, it is easier for most people to bring to mind words that start with r, and thus they judge these words to be more common. The covariation theory is an attribution model, so it cannot account for this phenomenon. The primacy effect and the confirmation bias are relevant to impression formation, not to these types of judgment.

21. c. **personal attribution.** A personal attribution focuses on the internal characteristics of an actor. Brad's explanation of the teacher's behavior indeed focuses on internal qualities of the teacher. This is in contrast to a situational attribution, which focuses on factors external to the actor. The primacy effect concerns the strong impact that information learned early in a sequence has on impressions; because there is no mention in this question of a sequence of events that began with his going to the teacher for help, there is no reason to believe the primacy effect is relevant. Central traits exert powerful influence on overall impressions, causing people to assume the presence of other traits as well. In this example, no specific traits (such as warm or cold) were specified and no other traits assumed.

22. a. **agency and experience.** When Heather Gray and colleagues (2007) asked online participants to rate the extent to which an array of human and nonhuman characters possessed various mental capacities, they found that people perceive minds along two dimensions: agency, the ability to plan and execute behavior and experience, the ability to feel pain, pleasure, and other sensations and emotions.

23. d. **false-consensus effect.** A type of availability heuristic, the false-consensus effect is a tendency for people to overestimate the extent to which others share their opinions, attributes, and behaviors. This bias is pervasive. Regardless of whether people are asked to predict how others feel about military spending, abortion, gun control, Campbell's soup, certain types of music, or norms for appropriate behavior, they exaggerate the percentage of others who behave similarly or share their views. The covariation principle was proposed by Harold Kelley to explain how people consider the three dimensions of consensus, distinctiveness, and consistency when making sense of others' behavior. The base-rate fallacy refers to people's lack of sensitivity to probabilities when making decisions. Counterfactual thinking is the tendency to imagine alternative outcomes that might have occurred but did not.

Answers to Essay Questions: Sample Essays

24. According to the two-step model of the attribution process, people first identify a behavior and make a quick personal attribution, and then correct or adjust this initial inference to account for situational influences. The first step then is simple and automatic and being cognitively busy should not interfere with the simple and automatic step of making a personal attribution. The second step, correcting the inference to take into account situational influences, however, requires attention, thought, and effort. Being cognitively busy reduces a perceiver's ability to give the second step the attention, thought, and effort needed to correct the initial inference to account for situational influences; therefore, the result is a personal attribution that does not take into sufficient account the situational influences that may have affected the behavior. In other words, the result is the fundamental attribution error. If, in contrast, perceivers are not cognitively busy (that is, if they are not distracted by other demands on their attention), then they will have a better chance of dedicating the attention, thought, and effort needed for the second step of the process. Thus, these perceivers would be more likely to take situational influences into account, thereby avoiding the fundamental attribution error.

25. The primacy effect refers to the tendency for information presented early in a sequence to have more impact on impressions than information presented later. One reason for this effect is that once perceivers think they have formed an accurate impression, they become less attentive to subsequent information. Thus, this later information has less impact on the overall impression. A second reason for the primacy effect is known as the change-of-meaning hypothesis. According to this hypothesis, once people form an initial impression, they interpret subsequent information in light of that impression. Thus, initial information influences the interpretation of later information, resulting in the initial information having a particularly strong influence on the overall judgment.

26. This study illustrates the concept of belief perseverance. Individuals exhibit belief perseverance when they stick to an initial belief even after it has been discredited. The reason this phenomenon occurs is that once people come up with explanations to account for some theory or belief, those explanations take on a life of their own. The more they think about this belief, the more explanations or support they come up with to increase their confidence in the belief. Thus, even when the information on which the belief or theory was initially based is discredited, people may have generated enough alternative explanations or recalled enough other evidence consistent with the belief that they continue to believe it.

27. In *The Expression of the Emotions in Man and Animals*, Charles Darwin (1872) proposed that the face expresses emotion in ways that are innate and understood by people all over the world. Contemporary research supports this notion. Numerous studies have shown that when presented with photographs, people can reliably identify at least six "primary" emotions: happiness, fear, sadness, anger, surprise, and disgust. In one study, participants from ten different countries exhibited high levels of agreement in their recognition of these emotions. From one end of the world to the other, it is clear that a smile is a smile and a frown is a frown, and that just about everyone knows what they mean—even when these expressions are "put on" by actors and not genuinely felt.

CHAPTER 5

Stereotypes, Prejudice, and Discrimination

OUTLINE

LEARNING OBJECTIVES: GUIDELINES FOR STUDY

You should be able to do each of the following by the conclusion of Chapter 5.

1. Define and distinguish the concepts of racism, sexism, stereotypes, prejudice, and discrimination. Define <u>group</u> and differentiate between ingroups and outgroups. (*pp. 147-148*)

2. Discuss the evidence that racial prejudice has been lessening over the past several decades in the United States. (*pp. 148-149*)

3.   Define modern racism and discuss how it differs from old-fashioned racism. Define implicit racism and discuss the challenges involved in measuring it. Describe how the IAT measures implicit racism. Discuss some of the findings of the IAT and explain why these findings are controversial. (*pp. 149-152*)

4.   Discuss the recent research on interracial perception. Describe the factors that complicate interracial interaction and the psychological impact of such interactions on the individuals involved. (*pp. 152-155*)

5.   Explain how gender stereotypes differ from all other stereotypes and how sexism differs from racism. Explain what is meant by the concept of ambivalent sexism. Discuss how sex discrimination continues to negatively impact working women. (*pp. 155-159*)

6.   Explain how the motive of self-protection leads to negative stereotyping of outgroup members. Describe the Robbers Cave study. Explain how prejudice between groups develops in terms of realistic conflict theory. (*pp. 159-162*)

7.   Explain social identity theory and how it accounts for ingroup favoritism. Discuss cultural differences in social identity processes. (*pp. 162-165*)

8.   Discuss how social dominance and system justification beliefs promote ingroup/outgroup conflict. (*p. 165*)

9.   Describe the human tendencies towards social categorization and the formation of ingroup/outgroup distinctions, and discuss the repercussions of these tendencies. Explain the reasons for the outgroup homogeneity effect and discuss how it can lead to dehumanization. (*pp. 166-169*)

10.   Describe the ways in which stereotypes are perpetuated, including illusory correlation, attributional processes, subtyping, confirmation bias, and self-fulfilling prophecies. (*pp. 169-172*)

11.   Explain how socialization by parents and other role models might perpetuate stereotypes. Discuss the gender stereotypes and sexist ideas that continue to exist at the present time. (*pp. 172-175*)

12.   Define social role theory and discuss the relationship between sex stereotypes and social roles. Discuss the role of the media in shaping men and women's gender-based attitudes. (*pp. 175-177*)

13.   Define the stereotype content model. Explain how the two dimensions of relative group status and perceived intergroup competition help to create stereotypes of women. (*pp. 177-178*)

14.   Discuss the factors that increase the likelihood of automatic stereotype activation. Describe how successful internally or externally driven motivation is in inhibiting automatic stereotype activation. Discuss the factors that affect quantity of cognitive resources available to suppress stereotypes and the techniques used to give people better control over stereotypes. (*pp. 178-182*)

15.   Discuss the research on the impact of racial stereotyping on social judgment that followed the police shooting of Amadou Diallo. Discuss the effectiveness of training in eliminating racial biases. Discuss the relationship between the racial bias seen in "shoot/don't shoot" simulations and racial prejudice. (*pp. 182-186*)

16.   Describe the factors that determine the perception of discrimination. Describe the effects of discrimination from the target's perspective. Explain the concept of stereotype threat, including the reasons it happens and its range of consequences. Consider the different situations likely to elicit stereotype threat, and the different populations susceptible to stereotype threat effects. Discuss ways to protect individuals from stereotype threat. (*pp. 186-192*)

17. Explain the contact hypothesis and the conditions that enable intergroup contact to reduce prejudice. Describe the jigsaw classroom and how it can reduce prejudice. Discuss the role of culture in reducing prejudice and discrimination. (*pp. 192-196*)

MAJOR CONCEPTS: THE BIG PICTURE

Below are six basic issues or principles that organize Chapter 5. You should know these issues and principles well.

1. Stereotypes are beliefs about others based on their group membership. People share the tendency to put individuals into social categories. This social categorization leads people to see outgroup members as all the same and to generalize from characterizations of individual members to characterizations of the group and vice versa. Stereotypes lead to the distortion of people's perception of others and can be self-perpetuating. Further they are often activated without people's awareness and can affect people's perceptions without their awareness. With effort, people can sometimes overcome the use of stereotypes, but suppression of their use is difficult on a long-term basis.

2. Prejudice consists of negative feelings about others based on their group membership. Such feelings of prejudice can arise from conflicts with others, as demonstrated in the Robbers Cave experiment. They can also arise from an effort to maintain a positive sense of self-esteem and a positive group identity.

3. Sexism is discrimination based on a person's gender. Gender stereotypes are prevalent the world over and are often activated in our personal interactions. Although differences do exist between men and women on some traits, gender stereotypes typically exaggerate these differences. The media and social roles help perpetuate gender stereotypes. The impact of sexism is clearly seen in the context of occupational access: Both men and women are judged more favorably when they apply for jobs that are consistent with gender stereotypes.

4. Racism is discrimination based on a person's skin color or ethnic origin. Although most research has focused on Blacks and Whites, the growing number of multiracial people in North America is bound to change this. While overt endorsement of racist statements on surveys has declined over the years, subtle forms of prejudice are still pervasive and can take the form of ambivalence or even unconscious discrimination. Recently a number of researchers have made important advances in detecting such forms of modern racism by using computer tasks.

5. The targets of discrimination often cope with negative feedback by attributing it to prejudice. While this strategy appears to have positive consequences for self-esteem, targets may feel a lack of control over their lives. The targets of stereotyping are affected by the threat that the stereotype implies about their ability. Research on stereotype threat shows that when people believe others may view them stereotypically, it can undermine their academic performance; however, when this stereotype threat is removed, the stereotyped perform just as well as the unstereotyped.

6. Intergroup contact can lead to better intergroup relations, but only when the groups have equal status and are characterized by personal interactions, the need to achieve common goals, and supportive social norms. The jigsaw classroom is one technique that has consistently improved race relations. Changes in the kinds of information perpetuated in one's culture can alter how an individual perceives social groups.

KEY TERM EXERCISE: THE CONCEPTS YOU SHOULD KNOW

Below are all of the key terms that appear in **boldface** in Chapter 5. To help you better understand these concepts, rather than just memorize them, write a definition for each term in your own words. After doing so, look at the next section where you'll find a list of definitions from the textbook for each of the key terms presented in random order. For each of your definitions, find the corresponding textbook definition. Note how your definitions compare with those from the textbook.

Key Terms

1. contact hypothesis
2. relative deprivation
3. modern racism
4. superordinate goals
5. contrast effect
6. illusory correlation
7. social identity theory
8. outgroup homogeneity effect
9. realistic conflict theory
10. stereotype
11. ingroup favoritism
12. prejudice
13. sexism
14. social role theory
15. social categorization
16. discrimination
17. jigsaw classroom
18. racism
19. group
20. subliminal presentation
21. ambivalent sexism
22. ingroups
23. outgroups
24 social dominance orientation

Textbook Definitions

a. The tendency to discriminate in favor of ingroups over outgroups.

b. A method of presenting stimuli so faintly or rapidly that people do not have any conscious awareness of having been exposed to them.

c. Feelings of discontent aroused by the belief that one fares poorly compared to others.

d. The classification of persons into groups on the basis of common attributes.

e. Any behavior directed against persons because of their identification with a particular group.

f. Prejudice and discrimination based on a person's racial background.

g. The theory that hostility between groups is caused by direct competition for limited resources.

h. Shared goals that can be achieved only through cooperation among individuals or groups.

i. A form of prejudice that surfaces in subtle ways when it is safe, socially acceptable, and easy to rationalize.

j. Two or more persons perceived as related because of their interaction with each other over time, membership in the same social category, or common fate.

k. A belief that associates a group of people with certain traits.

l. Negative feelings toward persons based solely on their membership in certain groups.

m. A cooperative learning method used to reduce racial prejudice through interaction in group efforts.

n. Discrimination based on a person's gender.

o. The theory that small gender differences are magnified in perception by the contrasting social roles occupied by men and women.

p. The theory that people favor ingroups over outgroups in order to enhance their self-esteem.

q. The tendency to perceive stimuli that differ from expectations as being even more different than they really are.

r. The tendency to assume that there is a greater similarity among members of outgroups than of ingroups.

s. The theory that direct contact between hostile groups will reduce prejudice under certain conditions.

t. An overestimate of the association between variables that are only slightly correlated or not correlated at all.

u. Comprised of two elements: *hostile* sexism, which concerns negative, resentful feelings about women's abilities, value, and challenging of men's power, and *benevolent* sexism, which concerns affectionate, chivalrous, but potentially patronizing feelings of women needing and deserving protection.

v. Groups to which we belong.

w. Different from groups to which we do not belong.

x. A desire to see one's ingroups as dominant over other groups, and a willingness to adopt cultural values that facilitate oppression over other groups.

ANSWERS FOR KEY TERM EXERCISE

Answers for the key terms exercise are listed below.

1. s
2. c
3. i
4. h
5. q
6. t
7. p
8. r
9. g
10. k
11. a
12. l
13. n
14. o
15. d
16. e
17. m
18. f
19. j
20. b
21. u
22. v
23. w
24. x

PRACTICE QUIZ: TEST YOUR KNOWLEDGE OF THE CHAPTER

Multiple-Choice Questions

1. Social categorization and ingroup favoritism are two processes that lead to
   a. stereotypes.
   b. superordinate goals.
   c. contrast effects.
   d. contact hypotheses.

2. The blue gang and the red gang are having a dispute about who controls the turf around the vacant lot next to the high school. During this dispute, fighting between the two groups escalates. This result could be most easily predicted from
   a. social categorization theory.
   b. modern racism.
   c. confirmation biases.
   d. realistic conflict theory.

3. Lisa thinks that women are more critical than men. At parties, she is more likely to notice a sarcastic remark from a woman than from a man. Lisa's perceptions illustrate
   a. ingroup favoritism.
   b. the confirmation bias.
   c. contrast effects.
   d. ambivalent sexism.

4. Frank thinks that all his instructors are windbags, but he also thinks there are two kinds of instructors: those who are knowledgeable but unable to teach and those who don't know very much. Frank's classification of his instructors is an example of
   a. a contrast effect.
   b. subtyping.
   c. ingroup bias.
   d. the confirmation bias.

5. Illusory correlations, attributions about men's and women's behavior, subtyping men and women who are not representative, and seeking information that supports one's views are four ways in which
   a. gender roles develop.
   b. gender stereotypes endure.
   c. all stereotypes are overcome.
   d. prejudice is minimized.

6. In the Robbers Cave experiment, young boys came to dislike each other intensely after a period of
   a. striving to attain superordinate goals.
   b. forming friendships with one another.
   c. competing with one another.
   d. fighting a common enemy.

7. At the car dealership, Michele encountered ambivalent sexism when her new boss
   a. exhorted the women workers to use their "feminine charms" to increase sales while urging the men to finalize more deals by displaying "manly fortitude."
   b. exhibited favoritism for males over females when it came to promotions, even though she, herself, was female.
   c. acted protectively towards the women under his charge but devalued their work.
   d. told sexual jokes and made derogatory comments about her and the other female workers when they were not around.

8. For Joel, being a part of the basketball team is very important. When asked to compare the basketball team to the football team, he states, "We're a lot better than they are." According to social identity theory, this ingroup favoritism should make Joel
   a. feel better about himself and the basketball team.
   b. pay less attention to football.
   c. feel guilty that he judged the football team so arbitrarily.
   d. concerned about the status of the football team.

9. Karen divides her class into small, racially mixed groups. Each student learns part of the assigned work and then teaches it to others in the group. This procedure is an example of
   a. a jigsaw classroom.
   b. a minimal group.
   c. ingroup favoritism.
   d. realistic conflict.

10. According to cross-cultural research, men are widely seen as more _____ than women.
    a. emotional
    b. sensitive
    c. aggressive
    d. people-oriented

11. Which of the following was a reported result of the research that followed the Amadou Diallo shooting:
    a. Trained police officers were more likely to "shoot" an unarmed black person than an unarmed white person.
    b. The magnitude of the racial bias in the "shoot" or "don't shoot" simulations was directly related to the levels of racial prejudice exhibited by the participants.
    c. Trained police officers were quicker to "shoot" an armed black person than an armed white person.
    d. Training of participants was ineffective in reducing racial bias in "shoot" or "don't shoot" scenarios.

12. The cognitive capacity to process information carefully and the motivation to be accurate are two factors that enable people to
    a. engage in modern racism.
    b. avoid using stereotypes.
    c. feel relative deprivation.
    d. form illusory correlations.

13. Stereotypes about men and women present
    a. a totally biased picture of men and women.
    b. a kernel of the truth that is oversimplified and exaggerated.
    c. an accurate description of the differences between men and women.
    d. unrealistic expectations for men and women.

14. Gender stereotypes result from expectations created by a sex-based division of the labor market, according to which theory?
    a. Realistic conflict
    b. Social identity
    c. Social role
    d. Outgroup homogeneity

15. Recent research on the measurement of modern racism shows that it
    a. is easily measured with a questionnaire.
    b. is impossible to measure.
    c. can be measured with computer tasks without the respondent's awareness.
    d. is difficult to measure with a questionnaire, but possible if anonymity is assured.

16. According to theories of modern racism, discrimination against Blacks is most likely to occur when it is
    a. explicit and obvious.
    b. socially unacceptable.
    c. easy to rationalize.
    d. confrontational in form.

17. Tom is prejudiced against Blacks but doesn't admit it. He sees a Black store owner being robbed. Although he would ordinarily try to help in such emergencies, he does nothing. Tom's lack of action is an example of
    a. old-fashioned racism.
    b. reaction time.
    c. outgroup homogeneity.
    d. modern racism.

18. Melanie describes herself as a "morning person." Her younger sister Nicole describes herself as a "night person." When it comes to unconsciously using stereotypes, which of the following is probably true?
    a. Melanie is more likely to do so in the evening, whereas Nicole is more likely to do so in the morning.
    b. Both girls are more likely to do so in the morning than in the evening.
    c. Both girls are more likely to do so in the evening than in the morning.
    d. Melanie is more likely to do so in the morning, whereas Nicole is more likely to do so in the evening.

19. In one high school, students from the country have always fought with students from the city. In order to reduce this intergroup hostility, the principal decides that the people in the two groups need to have personal contact on an equal-status basis. What else might he do to try to achieve more harmonious relations between the groups?
    a. Have them work together on a school wide project.
    b. Have them identify the strengths of their own group.
    c. Have them take classes designed to teach the value of getting along with others.
    d. Have teachers identify students based on their group affiliation.

20. Research on stereotype threat shows that stereotypes can
    a. motivate people to try harder in order to improve their performance.
    b. undermine the academic performance of women and minorities.
    c. only affect members of groups who do not have power in society.
    d. lower the self-esteem of members of stereotyped groups.

Essay Questions

21. Describe how social categorization can lead people to see all members of an outgroup in the same way. Discuss the implications of this process for intergroup perceptions and interactions.

22. Explain how social identity theory accounts for favoritism of the ingroup over the outgroup.

23. Characterize modern racism. Describe when it is most, and least, likely to be evident.

ANSWERS TO THE PRACTICE QUIZ

Multiple-Choice Questions: Correct Answers and Explanations

1. a. **stereotypes.** Social categorization and ingroup favoritism are two mechanisms that produce stereotyping. Social categorization is the dividing of people into groups based on salient differences between those individuals. Research has demonstrated that once people are categorized into groups, their differences are exaggerated. Ingroup favoritism takes social categorization one step further. When people make social categorizations, they not only exaggerate group differences but they do so in a way that favors their own group. Social categorization and ingroup bias are less likely to produce contrast effects. These emerge when people face disconfirming information. Superordinate goals are goals that can only be achieved through mutual cooperation by groups. Contact hypotheses suggest that intergroup contact can diminish stereotypes and prejudice.

2. d. **realistic conflict theory.** The two gangs appear to be fighting over a scarce resource – the vacant lot. Realistic conflict theory tries to account for such situations, predicting that, when such a conflict occurs, animosity between the groups will increase. Social categorization could also predict animosity between the groups, but not the escalation of conflict during the dispute. Confirmation biases and modern racism would not make clear predictions about this situation because there is insufficient information about the gangs' racial compositions or their expectations about one another.

3. a. **the confirmation bias.** The confirmation bias, or the tendency to pay particular attention to information that confirms one's beliefs, is evident in the fact that Lisa finds it easy to notice sarcastic remarks made by women at parties. This phenomenon is unlikely to result from ingroup favoritism, because Lisa is a woman herself, and there is no evidence that it is related to contrast effects. Ambivalent sexism refers to feelings of hostility and benevolence toward women rooted in men's fear that women will challenge their power and at the same time perceive women as weak and in need of protection.

4. b. **subtyping.** Frank seems to have a negative stereotype about instructors, but he has also differentiated them into two subcategories. Frank's classification of the instructors does not show evidence of contrast effects, ingroup bias, or confirmation bias. If his views depicted contrast effect, one would expect him to have an overly positive view of instructors if they gave a good lecture. If his views depicted ingroup bias, one would expect him to state how people in his group (i.e., students) are so much better than instructors. Finally, if his views depicted the confirmation bias, he would be searching for evidence that the instructors are windbags.

5. b. **gender stereotypes endure.** Illusory correlations work to exaggerate any gender differences that do exist. Research suggests that people make different attributions for men's and women's behaviors and these attributions bolster stereotypes. By subtyping people as "exceptions to the rule," people can maintain their stereotypes even when they are faced with people who do not fit the stereotypes. Finally, people tend to seek out information that supports their stereotypes about men and women. This confirmation bias causes stereotypes to endure. Gender roles may be reinforced by attributions and people's seeking of information, but it is unclear how illusory correlations or subtyping would lead to gender role development. These processes help stereotypes to endure, rather than allowing stereotypes to be overcome or allowing prejudice to be minimized.

6. c. **competing with one another.** In this classic experiment, the researchers devised a situation whereby two groups of boys competed with one another. After this period of competition, the two groups began to show intense animosity and dislike for one another. In this early part of the experiment, there was no evidence of striving to attain superordinate goals, forming friendships with one another, or fighting a common enemy.

7. c. **acted protectively towards the women in his department but devalued their work.** Ambivalent sexism consists of two elements: hostile sexism, characterized by negative, resentful feelings about women's abilities to compete with men and benevolent sexism characterized by chivalrous and protective feelings toward women in general. Asking women to use "feminine wiles" and men to display "manly fortitude" is an example of stereotypical thinking and gender-discriminatory behavior, but does not demonstrate ambivalent sexism. Similarly, promoting males ahead of females simply because of gender is an example of sexism, whether practiced by men or women, but is not ambivalent sexism. Making sexual jokes or derogatory comments about one sex constitutes sexual harassment.

8. a. **feel better about himself and the basketball team.** Social identity theory suggests that ingroup favoritism makes people feel better about their group, which in turn makes them feel better about themselves. Social identity theory has little to say about where people focus their attention. It would suggest, however, that Joel would not feel guilty about his evaluation of the football team and that he would be unconcerned about their status.

9. a. **a jigsaw classroom.** In a jigsaw classroom the instructor arranges for students of different racial groups to interact together on joint tasks in an equal-status environment. Karen's class is an excellent example. None of her actions are related to minimal groups, ingroup favoritism, or realistic conflict. Instead, she seems to have developed an environment with real groups that undermines ingroup favoritism and realistic conflict.

10. c. **aggressive.** Cross-cultural research suggests that, in almost all countries that have been studied, men are seen as more aggressive than women. In most of these countries, women are seen as more emotional, sensitive, and people-oriented.

11. c. **Trained police officers were quicker to "shoot" an armed black person than an armed white person.** Joshua Correll (2007b) found that trained police officers were quicker to decide to "shoot" a black person than a white person. However, when it came to "shooting" unarmed targets, the trained police officers were less likely than civilians to show racial bias and "shoot" at blacks more than whites. The magnitude of racial bias shown in "shoot" or "don't shoot" simulations is not related to the participants' racial prejudice. Training of participants did result in a reduction in the racial bias seen in the "shoot" or "don't shoot" simulations.

12. b.   **avoid using stereotypes.** Some research suggests that when people have the cognitive capacity to process information (they are not distracted) and try hard to be accurate they can also avoid using stereotypes. By making this effort, they are also less likely to display modern racism, to feel relative deprivation, and form illusory correlations.

13. b.   **a kernel of the truth that is oversimplified and exaggerated.** There are some differences between men and women (e.g., men tend to be more aggressive than women), but gender stereotypes exaggerate these differences and fail to take into account that there are more similarities between men and women than there are differences. Thus gender stereotypes are not totally biased, and they do not portray an accurate description of the differences between men and women. Gender roles sometimes present demanding and unrealistic expectations of men and women, but this feature is less characteristic of gender stereotypes.

14. c.   **Social role.** Social role theory suggests that the sex-based division of labor provides a justification for gender stereotypes. From this perspective, gender roles, which contain a stereotypical component, create a sex-based division of labor. This division of labor is then used as a justification for the original stereotype. Realistic conflict theory, social identity theory, and outgroup homogeneity all have little to say about sex-based division of labor.

15. c.   **can be measured with computer tasks without the respondent's awareness.** Recent research has shown that bias in the measurement of modern racism occurs when it is measured with a questionnaire, even if anonymity is assured. Several researchers, however, have developed computer tasks that measure modern racism without the respondent being aware that the measurement is occurring. These tasks appear to have avoided the problems associated with questionnaire measures.

16. c.   **easy to rationalize.** Theories of modern racism suggest that many people are torn between egalitarian values and lingering beliefs in the inferiority of Blacks. For these people, overt endorsement of stereotypes is difficult because it conflicts with their egalitarian values, but when stereotyping and prejudice can be easily rationalized, the lingering belief in the inferiority of Blacks is expressed. Modern racists are unlikely to discriminate against Blacks when the discrimination is explicit and obvious, socially unacceptable, or confrontational in form because these kinds of discrimination may challenge their egalitarian values.

17. d.   **modern racism.** Tom's actions illustrate modern racism because he failed to help the store owner in a situation that offered a good rationalization not to help. In this sort of situation, Tom would be unlikely to feel that he was not being egalitarian. Tom's behavior is less an example of old-fashioned racism because, if he were an old-fashioned racist, he would be more likely to admit his prejudice. Reaction time and outgroup homogeneity have no clear relationship to Tom's behavior.

18. a.   **Melanie is more likely to do so in the evening, whereas Nicole is more likely to do so in the morning.** A study by Galen Bodenhausen (1990) found that "morning persons" were more likely to use stereotypes when tested at 8:00PM, whereas "night persons" were more likely to use stereotypes when tested at 9:00AM. The justification for the finding is that cognitive resources are required to exert the effort necessary to control stereotypical thinking. "Morning persons" are less likely to have such control in the evening and "Night persons" are less likely to have sufficient control in the morning.

19. a. **have them work together on a school wide project.** The principal has met most of the necessary conditions for establishing intergroup contacts that promote racial harmony, personal contacts, equal status, and norms that support positive relations. One condition he has not met is the establishment of superordinate goals. By having the students work together on a school wide project, he could meet this condition as well. Having students identify their group's strengths, giving students lessons about the values of getting along with each other, and having teachers identify students based on their group affiliation have not been shown to promote racial harmony.

20. b. **undermine the academic performance of women and minorities.** Research on stereotype threat shows that when members of a stereotype group are in a situation where others may stereotype them, they perform below their potential; but, when this stereotype threat is lifted, their performance improves. Although most of the research on stereotype threat has been on groups that have less power in society (women and minorities), there is some evidence that stereotype threat can affect dominant groups as well. There is no evidence that stereotype threat lowers self-esteem; in fact, the theory behind stereotype threat predicts that when people face stereotype threat they will protect their self-esteem rather than have their self-esteem lowered. Finally, although it is an interesting idea, there is no evidence that stereotype threat motivates people to try harder in order to improve their performance.

Answers to Essay Questions: Sample Essays

21. Social categorization can lead people to see all members of an outgroup in the same way through the outgroup homogeneity effect. When people categorize others as belonging to social groups, they exaggerate the differences between these groups. They also tend to see their own group as being comprised of many different types of people, whereas they see the outgroup as being composed of people who are all basically the same. One reason for this outgroup homogeneity effect is that people usually have a lot more contact with people in their own group than they have with people in another group. Therefore, they get to know more types of people in their own group. A second reason for this effect is that even if people have contact with members of the outgroup, this contact might reflect a biased sample. They might only have contact with a certain type of member of the outgroup. The outgroup homogeneity effect has important implications. If people perceive all outgroup members as being the same, then they will evaluate the whole group based on the actions of one individual, and they will evaluate the individual based on their perceptions of the group.

22. Social identity theory suggests that people favor their own group over other groups because they want to maintain a positive social identity; they want to see their group as being a good group and as having status. This positive social identity, in turn, makes people feel better about themselves and raises their self-esteem. Thus people favor their own group over other groups in order to feel better not only about the group they belong to but also about themselves.

23. Modern racism is a recent form of racism characterized by a tension between two values: an egalitarian value which maintains that all people are created equal and deserve equal treatment, and traditional racial prejudice which maintains that certain racial groups are inferior to other groups. The latter value, often expressed in old-fashioned racism, is not as often expressed in modern racism. Modern racists rarely endorse overt prejudice and discrimination because it contradicts their egalitarian values. Yet the influence of racist values can be seen in situations where prejudice and discrimination can be justified. Under such conditions, modern racists will engage in discriminatory actions. However, when the discrimination calls into question their egalitarian values, they are less likely to discriminate.

CHAPTER 6

Attitudes

OUTLINE

LEARNING OBJECTIVES: GUIDELINES FOR STUDY

You should be able to do each of the following by the conclusion of Chapter 6.

1. Define what is meant by "attitudes." Discuss how attitudes are measured, including both self-report and covert techniques, as well as measurement of implicit attitudes. (*pp. 203-209*)

2. Discuss how attitudes are formed. Discuss the relationship between attitudes and behaviors. Explain what types of attitudes are most likely to predict behavior, and under what circumstances. (*pp. 209-214*)

3. Define and distinguish the peripheral and central routes to persuasion. Identify factors that dictate which route of processing is taken. (*pp. 215-218*)

4. Explain how and under what circumstances message source affects whether people are likely to be persuaded. Discuss the reasons behind the sleeper effect. (*pp. 218-224*)

5. Explain how the content of a message affects whether people are likely to be persuaded. Describe how the cognitive and emotional content affects message persuasiveness. Discuss the effect of message order. Consider evidence regarding the effectiveness of subliminal persuasive messages. (*pp. 224-230*)

6. Explain how characteristics of the audience, including need for cognition, self-monitoring, and regulatory fit, can moderate the extent to which it is persuaded by a message. Describe strategies for enabling an audience to resist efforts at persuasion. Discuss cultural considerations in persuasion. (*pp. 230-234*)

7. Discuss how role-playing can lead to a change in attitude. Explain the elements of the classic version of cognitive dissonance theory, and the relevance of this theory to understanding attitude change. (*pp. 235-239*)

8. Explain the "new look" of cognitive dissonance and how it expands upon the original theory. (*pp. 239-242*)

9. Consider alternate routes to self-persuasion such as those described by self-perception theory, impression-management theory, and theories of self-esteem. Explain how the processes postulated by these theories differ from those described by cognitive dissonance theory. Discuss cultural influences on cognitive dissonance. (*pp. 242-246*)

MAJOR CONCEPTS: THE BIG PICTURE

Below are three basic issues or principles that organize Chapter 6. You should know these issues and principles well.

1. The study of attitudes has been one of the foundations of social psychology. Researchers measure attitudes by asking people direct questions about their attitudes or by assessing people's behavior or physiological responses. In general, our attitudes are not as strong a predictor of our behaviors as one might think. However, attitudes do a better job of predicting behavior when the attitude is specific to a behavior or particularly important.

2. One of the earliest fields of study in social psychology focused on persuasion, the changing of people's attitudes through communication. Research in this field has found that there are two basic routes to persuasion: a central route that emphasizes the content of a message and systematic deliberate processing of information, and a peripheral route that emphasizes more rules of thumb or heuristic processing of information. The source of a message, its content, and the audience that hears the message all affect whether the message will be persuasive.

3. People are also persuaded by their own actions and the roles that they play. Cognitive dissonance theory maintains that when people engage in an action that conflicts with their attitudes they will feel tension, and that the easiest way to reduce this tension is to change their attitude. In this way, the theory predicts that people will change their attitudes to match their behavior. Recent revisions to cognitive dissonance theory suggest that this attitude change occurs mostly when people take responsibility for their actions. Other approaches emphasize that people rationalize their behaviors by changing them to manage a positive impression with others, to maintain a positive view of themselves, or to be consistent with the way in which they perceive their own behavior.

KEY TERM EXERCISE: THE CONCEPTS YOU SHOULD KNOW

Below are all of the key terms that appear in **boldface** in Chapter 6. To help you better understand these concepts, rather than just memorize them, write a definition for each term in your own words. After doing so, look at the next section where you'll find a list of definitions from the textbook for each of the key terms presented in random order. For each of your definitions, find the corresponding textbook definition. Note how your definitions compare with those from the textbook.

Key Terms

1. theory of planned behavior

2. cognitive dissonance theory

3. persuasion

4. inoculation hypothesis

5. central route to persuasion

6. insufficient deterrence

7. peripheral route to persuasion

8. attitude

9. elaboration

10. sleeper effect

11. need for cognition (NC)

12. insufficient justification

13. psychological reactance

14. attitude scale

15. implicit attitudes

16. facial electromyograph (EMG)

17. bogus pipeline

18. Implicit Association Test (IAT)

Textbook Definitions

a.　A condition in which people freely perform an attitude-discrepant behavior without receiving a large reward.

b.　The process by which a person does not think carefully about a communication and is influenced instead by superficial cues.

c.　A personality variable that distinguishes people on the basis of how much they enjoy effortful cognitive activities.

d.　The theory that attitudes toward a specific behavior combine with subjective norms and perceived control to influence a person's actions.

e.　The process by which a person thinks carefully about a communication and is influenced by the strength of its arguments.

f.　An electronic instrument that records facial muscle activity associated with emotions and attitudes.

g.　A phony lie-detector device that is sometimes used to get respondents to give truthful answers to sensitive attitude questions.

h.　The process by which attitudes are changed.

i.　The theory that holding inconsistent cognitions arouses psychological tension that people become motivated to reduce.

j.　A delayed increase in the persuasive impact of a noncredible source.

k.　A multiple-item questionnaire designed to measure a person's attitude toward some object.

l.　Attitudes that we cannot report in questionnaires because we're not aware of having them

m.　A condition in which people refrain from engaging in a desirable activity, even when only mild punishment is threatened.

n.　The idea that exposure to weak versions of a persuasive argument increases later resistance to that argument.

o.　A positive or negative reaction to a person, object, or idea.

p.　The theory that people react against threats to their freedom by asserting themselves and perceiving the threatened freedom as more attractive.

q.　The process of thinking about and scrutinizing the arguments contained in a persuasive communication.

r.　A covert measure of unconscious attitudes, it is derived from the speed at which people respond to pairings of concepts—such as *black* or *white* with *good* or *bad*.

ANSWERS FOR KEY TERM EXERCISE

Answers for the key terms exercise are listed below.

1. **d**
2. **i**
3. **h**
4. **n**
5. **e**
6. **m**
7. **b**
8. **o**
9. **q**
10. **j**
11. **c**
12. **a**
13. **p**
14. **k**
15. **l**
16. **f**
17. **g**
18. **r**

PRACTICE QUIZ: TEST YOUR KNOWLEDGE OF THE CHAPTER

Multiple-Choice Questions

1. Attitudes are often measured by means of self-reports, questionnaires on which respondents endorse their attitudes. Another technique often used is to collect covert measures. Covert measures are
   a. collected from the respondent's friends, who describe what his or her attitudes are.
   b. more easily controlled by the respondent than are self-measures.
   c. collected by use of a bogus pipeline.
   d. measures collected indirectly.

2. The theory of planned behavior suggests that one reason attitudes might not always predict behaviors is that
   a. people may not have strong enough attitudes.
   b. people's attitudes may be outside their awareness.
   c. people may have only false attitudes.
   d. people's intentions to act may be different from their attitudes.

3. In a television commercial for dental floss, the spokesperson (a well-known TV celebrity) says that eight out of ten dentists recommend the product. The reference to dentists is an attempt to establish
   a. communicator credibility.
   b. cognitive dissonance.
   c. psychological reactance.
   d. fear arousal.

4. Central and peripheral routes to persuasion are proposed by
   a. the dual-process.model.
   b. cognitive dissonance theory.
   c. self-perception theory.
   d. the theory of planned behavior.

5. In their campaigns, John Smith and Jane Doe both present arguments stressing the logic of their positions and detailing the many reasons for their views. These candidates are trying to persuade voters through
   a. attitude-discrepant behavior.
   b. heuristics.
   c. the peripheral route.
   d. the central route.

6. If we must make a choice between two equally desirable options, the positive attributes of the alternative we ultimately do *not* choose will cause
   a. a sleeper effect.
   b. a primacy effect.
   c. cognitive dissonance.
   d. attitude inoculation.

7. Harry is listening to a debate. Harry assumes that the person with the most arguments is the best-qualified candidate. Harry's reasoning is an example of
   a. cognitive dissonance.
   b. elaboration.
   c. a heuristic.
   d. impression management.

8. Jeanne has a negative attitude toward bikes but a positive attitude toward skateboards. If she has spent a lot of time biking and very little time skateboarding, which of the following is likely true about the stability of these attitudes?
   a. Her attitude toward biking is likely to be more stable.
   b. Her attitude toward skateboarding is likely to be more stable.
   c. Both attitudes are likely to be highly stable.
   d. Both attitudes are likely to be unstable.

9. Yvonne is buying a new car. The salesman sees a school sticker on her old car and says he went to the same university. The reference to a common alma mater is an attempt to create
   a. self-monitoring.
   b. communicator likeability.
   c. a need for cognition.
   d. psychological reactance.

10. Mindy chose to write an essay for her English class that argued for a tuition hike even though she didn't want one. Her instructor sent the essay to the president of the university, who decided that if students could write so well then there should *not* be a tuition hike. Recent research on cognitive dissonance theory would suggest that Mindy will
    a. experience physiological arousal.
    b. feel responsible for her essay.
    c. experience no cognitive dissonance.
    d. change her attitude about tuition hikes.

11. Personal involvement and the sleeper effect are two limitations on the persuasive impact of
    a. fear-arousing communications.
    b. communicator credibility.
    c. attitude-discrepant behavior.
    d. self-perception processes.

12. The mayor and her challenger set up a debate three weeks before the election. They both agree that this will be the one and only debate. The challenger gets the opportunity to decide whether to go first or last in the debate. What advice would you give her?
    a. She should go first.
    b. She should go last.
    c. It doesn't matter whether she goes first or last.
    d. Whether she should go first or last depends on what she is going to say.

13. In theory, people who are high in the need for cognition should receive persuasive communications that rely on
    a. strong arguments.
    b. rules-of-thumb or heuristics.
    c. celebrity endorsements.
    d. emotional appeals.

14. Helen has always been upset by doctors who are late for appointments and believes that people should criticize them for this behavior. Yet she has taken a job as a sales representative for a drug company and must try to schmooze with the doctors on her route. In time, Helen is likely to
    a.   learn to dislike doctors even more.
    b.   dislike her job.
    c.   be less concerned with doctors' tardiness.
    d.   feel stress in most of her interactions.

15. Which ad is most likely to appeal to an individual who takes the central route to persuasion?
    a.   An ad featuring a top football player extolling the virtues of a particular SUV
    b.   An ad for an SUV that stresses the fact that it's the number one selling SUV in the world
    c.   An ad for an SUV featuring a well-known car magazine article detailing why the editors chose to recommend this particular model over all others
    d.   An ad for an SUV that makes much of the fact that it is available in many designer colors guaranteed to garner attention wherever it is driven

16. Carly decides to write a paper for her English class that argues for capital punishment even though she is against it. Cognitive dissonance theory would predict that Carly is
    a.   likely to favor capital punishment more.
    b.   likely to favor capital punishment less.
    c.   unlikely to change her views on capital punishment.
    d.   likely to find the experience enjoyable.

17. People are most likely to be in a state of cognitive dissonance if they
    a.   experience no physiological arousal.
    b.   engage in attitude-inconsistent behavior.
    c.   engage in attitude-consistent behavior.
    d.   experience negative unforeseeable consequences.

18. Advertisers and others often use the "overheard communicator" technique to enhance a speaker's
    a.   likeability.
    b.   perceived competence.
    c.   reactance.
    d.   trustworthiness.

19. Gabriella decides to buy a portable tape player rather than a portable CD player. She wonders if she made the right decision. After discussing her purchase with a friend, she is reminded that she is a good student and a good friend. Research on self-affirmation theory would predict that Gabriella will
    a.   experience physiological arousal.
    b.   feel bad about her decision.
    c.   experience no cognitive dissonance.
    d.   come to a stronger conviction that she made the right decision.

20. During assembly, Jane and Rick were listening to candidates for student council president. Jane found herself most comfortable listening to the laid-back candidate who spoke methodically about how he would prop up existing programs so that their school will retain its high reputation. Rick, on the other hand, was most receptive to the animated candidate who spoke enthusiastically about the programs he would inaugurate that would enhance the school's high reputation. Rick and Jane's contrasting listening preferences reflect differences in
    a. psychological reactance.
    b. self-monitoring.
    c. need for cognition.
    d. regulatory fit.

21. Self-perception theory suggests that people change their attitudes to match their behaviors because they
    a. feel a psychological tension.
    b. want to maintain a positive self-image.
    c. infer their attitudes from their behaviors.
    d. want to impress other people.

22. The phenomenon whereby people tend to forget the source but not the message, so the effects of source credibility dissipate over time is called the
    a. insufficient justification effect
    b. elaboration effect
    c. bogus pipeline effect
    d. sleeper effect

23. The theory that says people are motivated only to appear consistent to others is
    a. impression-management theory.
    b. the elaboration model.
    c. self-perception theory.
    d. cognitive dissonance theory.

Essay Questions

24. Discuss whether attitudes lead to behaviors that are consistent with those attitudes. Describe aspects of attitudes that can strengthen their relationship to behavior.

25. Compare and contrast the central and peripheral routes to persuasion.

26. Explain how cognitive dissonance theory accounts for changes in people's attitudes based on changes in their behavior.

27. Discuss the effects of fear arousal in politics.

ANSWERS TO THE PRACTICE QUIZ

Multiple-Choice Questions: Correct Answers and Explanations

1.   d.   **measures collected indirectly.** Covert measures, like facial movements, physiological recordings, and brain-wave patterns, are collected indirectly without the respondents being able to control their responses. The bogus pipeline is not a covert measure as respondents are aware their attitudes are being measured and can control their responses. This procedure attempts to get respondents to give accurate responses. Finally, asking a respondent's friends about the respondent's attitudes is usually viewed as assessing the friend's attitudes about the respondent's attitude via self-report.

2.   d.   **people's intentions to act may be different from their attitudes.** The theory of planned behavior stresses that in order for an attitude to predict behavior, that attitude must lead to an intention to act in a specific situation. But such intentions to act do not always follow from people's attitudes, which prevents their attitudes from predicting their behavior. The theory of planned behavior does not encompass the strength of attitudes, the awareness of attitudes, or the falseness of attitudes.

3.   a.   **communicator credibility.** In referring to the expert's opinion, the spokesperson is drawing upon the credibility of the expert in an attempt to influence the audience. It does not appear that the spokesperson is arousing fear, creating cognitive dissonance, which occurs when a behavior causes a person to change an attitude, or establishing psychological reactance, which occurs when a communicator comes on so strong that the person reacts with a negative attitude change, opposite to the one that is desired.

4.   a.   **the dual-process model.** The dual-process model of persuasion suggests that people process information through one of two channels: a central channel in which the quality of the arguments affects people's response to a persuasive message, and a peripheral channel in which heuristics or simplistic rules affect people's response to a persuasive message. Cognitive dissonance theory, self-perception theory, and the theory of planned behavior do not propose central and peripheral routes to persuasion.

5.   d.   **the central route.** The central route to persuasion, as elaborated by the dual-process model, leads to persuasion through the quality of the arguments that are presented for or against a position. John Smith and Jane Doe appear to be trying to use this route to persuasion. The peripheral route to persuasion, also elaborated by the dual-process model, leads to persuasion through the use of heuristics or simplistic rules that people may use without even being aware of it. There is no evidence that John Smith and Jane Doe are trying to use heuristics or a peripheral route to persuasion. Finally, it does not appear that the campaigners are trying to use attitude-discrepant behavior to influence voters. This strategy would require the voters to engage in actions that would later lead to a change in their attitudes.

6.   c.   **cognitive dissonance.** When people make a choice, the positive features of the option they did not choose are inconsistent with their choice. This inconsistency creates cognitive dissonance. For example, if I choose between a chocolate chip cookie and a molasses cookie, and pick the molasses cookie, the fact that I love chocolate would be inconsistent with my choice and would create cognitive dissonance. There is no evidence that the positive attributes of the alternative not chosen (chocolate chips in my example) create a sleeper effect, a primacy effect, or attitude inoculation.

7. c. **a heuristic.** Here Harry is using a simplistic rule, or heuristic – whoever makes the most arguments is the best-qualified candidate. He is not elaborating on what the candidate is saying, and there is no evidence that Harry is experiencing cognitive dissonance or that he is concerned with impression management.

8. a. **Her attitude toward biking is likely to be more stable.** Jeanne has spent more time biking and thus has more personal contact with biking. Research shows that attitudes about objects with which people have more direct personal experience tend to be more stable and predictive of behavior. Jeanne's attitude toward skateboarding is less likely to be as stable because she has had much less contact with skateboarding.

9. b. **communicator likeability.** The salesman is establishing that in at least one respect (attending the same school) he is similar to Yvonne. This similarity may increase Yvonne's liking for the salesman, which in turn may increase his likeability. It does not appear that the salesman is arousing fear, and need for cognition is a personality construct that distinguishes people on how much they enjoy effortful cognition, so neither of these answers is correct. The salesman would also not be trying to establish psychological reactance because that would mean that Yvonne would be so turned off by his tactics that she'll become determined not to buy the car.

10. c. **experience no cognitive dissonance.** Even though Mindy chose to write a counter-attitudinal essay, she is unlikely to experience cognitive dissonance because her actions had no negative consequences. In fact, her actions produced a result that was consistent with her attitude; her essay actually prevented the tuition hike she opposed. Because Mindy is unlikely to feel cognitive dissonance, she is also unlikely to experience physiological arousal, take responsibility for her essay, or change her attitude about tuition hikes.

11. b. **communicator credibility.** When people are personally involved with a topic, they are more likely to process information about that topic through the central route to persuasion. Processing information in this way should lead them to be less concerned with communicator credibility and more concerned with the content of the message. The sleeper effect is the tendency for people to lose track of which message was associated with which communicator such that, over time, the effect of communicator credibility becomes increasingly less and people evaluate the message more on its own merit. Fear-arousing messages may have less affect for people who are personally involved with a topic, but there is no evidence that the sleeper effect influences fear-arousing communications. Finally, attitude-discrepant behavior and self-perception processes are more likely to occur when people are personally involved with a topic and thus probably not affected by the sleeper effect.

12. a. **She should go first.** Because the election is just a few weeks away, the challenger would probably be better off going first, so she could take advantage of the primacy effect. Research shows that when two messages are presented together and there is a time separation before people make a decision about the quality of the messages, as is the case in this example, people tend to prefer the first message – a primacy effect. Recency effects tend to occur when people make a decision about the quality of the messages immediately after the messages are presented. Primacy and recency effects are general effects and seem to be the result of the way people's memories work; as such, they do not seem to be affected by the content of messages.

13. a. **arguments.** The dual-process model suggests that people who are high in the need for cognition are more likely to process information through the central route to persuasion and, therefore, are more likely to rely on the quality or strength of arguments for or against a position. By the same token, they are less likely to rely on rules-of-thumb or heuristics, celebrity endorsements, or emotional appeals, as all of those are associated with the peripheral route to persuasion.

14.   c.   **be less concerned with doctors' tardiness.** On her route, Helen will probably meet a lot of doctors who are late for their appointments with her, but Helen will probably have to say things like, "That's OK. I don't mind that you are late for your appointment." This action that is discrepant with her attitude will likely set the wheels of justification in motion, and Helen will likely change her attitude to match her behavior. As she makes this transition, it is unlikely that she will dislike doctors more, dislike her job, or be stressed in most of her interactions.

15.   c.   **An ad for an SUV featuring a well-known car magazine article detailing why the editors chose to recommend this particular model over all others.** Taking the central route to persuasion means being influenced by the strength and quality of arguments. An article in a car magazine detailing why the editors chose this particular model over all others is likely to present a strong argument. A celebrity endorsement, the popularity of the car, and the colors it comes in are likely to appeal to someone taking the peripheral route.

16.   a.   **likely to favor capital punishment more.** Early research testing cognitive dissonance theory found that when people write essays that are contrary to their attitudes, they often change their attitudes so that they are closer to their essays. Cognitive dissonance explained this finding by noting that the act of writing the essay is inconsistent with the writer's attitudes, which should produce cognitive dissonance. The easiest way to reduce this dissonance is for the people to change their attitudes; after all, they cannot take back their essays. Therefore, in this example, cognitive dissonance theory would predict that Carly will change her attitude about capital punishment and become more in favor of it; and because she has experienced cognitive dissonance, she probably has not found the experience enjoyable.

17.   b.   **engage in attitude-inconsistent behavior.** An inconsistency between people's attitudes and their behavior is likely to produce cognitive dissonance. Cognitive dissonance is associated with physiological arousal, so if people experience no physiological arousal they probably have no cognitive dissonance. Attitude-consistent behavior does not produce cognitive dissonance because the attitudes and behavior in this case are consonant, not dissonant. Finally, research has shown that unforeseeable consequences often prevent cognitive dissonance in situations when it might otherwise be present.

18.   d.   **trustworthiness.** People will often discount a persuasive communication if they know that the person is trying to persuade them. The "overheard communicator" technique tries to nullify this discounting by presenting the persuasive appeal as if it were not directed at the audience. This technique gives the impression that the communicator is quite sincere and trustworthy. The "overheard communicator" technique has not been shown to have an affect on likeability or the perceived competence of the communicator, nor has it been shown to create reactance.

19.   c.   **experience no cognitive dissonance.** Self-affirmation theory proposes that people experience cognitive dissonance because their actions have threatened their self-image and that if their self-image is repaired after it has been threatened then they will no longer experience cognitive dissonance. In this case, making a difficult decision may have threatened Gabriella's confidence that she is a competent decision maker, thus perhaps initially creating cognitive dissonance; but when she was reminded she is a good student and a good friend, this information should have repaired her self-image and removed any cognitive dissonance she may have felt. Because Gabriella is unlikely to experience cognitive dissonance, she is unlikely to experience physiological arousal, feel bad about her decision, or come to a stronger conviction that she made the right decision.

20. d.   **regulatory fit.** Regulatory fit means that in an effort to regulate their emotions, some individuals are promotion-oriented, being drawn to the pursuit of success and achievement, and so more likely to respond to arguments framed in promotional terms; whereas others are more prevention-oriented, protective of what they have and wary of losing it and so more likely to respond to arguments framed in defensive terms. Rick appears to be more promotion-oriented, whereas Jane appears to be more prevention-oriented. Psychological reactance does not apply because it means doing the opposite of what the persuader wants. Individuals who differ in self-monitoring are likely to differ in preference for imagery-based versus information-based appeals. Neither of the candidates' appeals appears to be image-based. Jane and Rick also appear to have the same need for cognition, as both are paying attention to the argument in the message.

21. c.   **infer their attitudes from their behaviors.** Self-perception theory proposes that people infer their own attitudes in the same way that they infer other people's attitudes: on the basis of behaviors. Therefore, self-perception theory suggests that people make inferences about their own attitudes from their behaviors. Self-perception theory does not propose that people change their attitudes because they feel a psychological tension, want to maintain a positive self-image, or want to manage the impressions of others.

22. d.   **The Sleeper Effect**. Time may heal the effects of a bad reputation. Hovland and Weiss (1951) varied communicator credibility (for example, the physicist versus the Soviet-controlled newspaper) and found that the change had a large and immediate effect on persuasion. But when they re-measured attitudes four weeks later, the effect had vanished. Over time, the attitude change produced by the high-credibility source decreased, and the change caused by the low-credibility source increased. This latter finding of a delayed persuasive impact of a low-credibility communicator is called the sleeper effect.

23. a.   **Impression-management theory.** An alternative to a dissonance view of self-persuasion is impression-management theory, which says that what matters is not a motive to be consistent but a motive to appear consistent. Nobody wants to be called fickle or be seen by others as a hypocrite. So we calibrate our attitudes and behaviors publicly just to present ourselves to others in a particular light (Baumeister, 1982; Tedeschi et al., 1971). Or perhaps we are motivated not by a desire to appear consistent but by a desire to avoid being held responsible for the unpleasant consequences of our actions (Schlenker, 1982). Either way, this theory places the emphasis on our concern for self-presentation

Answers to Essay Questions: Sample Essays

24. In general, attitudes show a weak relationship to behavior; they predict behaviors, but not very well. For one thing, people are not always thinking about their attitudes. Indeed, attitudes are better predictors of behavior when the attitudes are accessible – that is, when people are thinking about their attitudes. In addition, not all attitudes are well thought out and clear in the minds of the people who hold them. Some attitudes are closer to a weak impression than to a strong feeling that people have toward an object. Attitudes generally are better predictors if they are strong.

25.   The dual-process model proposes that there are two basic routes by which persuasive communication leads to changes in attitudes: the central route and the peripheral route. The central route to persuasion leads to attitude change that occurs when the audience pays attention to the quality of the arguments and elaborates or thinks about the content of the message. When people are persuaded via the central route to persuasion, they systematically process the information with which they are presented. The peripheral route to persuasion leads to attitude change that occurs when the audience pays attention to heuristics that suggest what attitude change should take place. When people are persuaded via the peripheral route, they spend little time analyzing the information that is being presented, and they may not even be aware that they are being persuaded.

26.   Cognitive dissonance theory proposes that when people have two thoughts that are psychologically inconsistent, they will experience physiological arousal and cognitive dissonance. In addition, the theory suggests that people will be motivated to reduce this cognitive dissonance by changing whatever thought is easiest to change. When people engage in a behavior that is inconsistent with their attitudes, they are likely to have conflicting thoughts such as "I just did that" and "I don't think people should do that." These two thoughts are psychologically inconsistent and, as such, lead to physiological arousal and cognitive dissonance. To reduce this dissonance, people are more likely to change their attitudes – that is, to think "Maybe it is OK if people do that." This thought is much easier to change than the thought that they had engaged in the action.

27.   Guided by Terror Management Theory and the prediction that a deeply rooted fear of death motivates people to rally around their leaders as a way to ward off anxiety, Mark Landau and his colleagues (2004) found that college students expressed more support for President George W. Bush and his policies if they were reminded of their own mortality or were subliminally exposed to images of 9/11 than if they were not. This result is not limited to the laboratory. Analyzing patterns of government issued terror warnings and Gallup polls, Robb Willer (2004) found that increased terror alerts were predictably followed by increases in Presidential approval ratings.

CHAPTER 7

Conformity

OUTLINE

LEARNING OBJECTIVES: GUIDELINES FOR STUDY

You should be able to do each of the following by the conclusion of Chapter 7.

1. Explain the process and purposes of mimicry. Discuss the implications of mimicry for questions concerning the automaticity of social influence. (*pp. 252-254*)

2. Define conformity. Describe Sherif's and Asch's classic studies on conformity. (*pp. 254-257*)

3. Compare normative and informational influence. Explain each in the context of Sherif's and Asch's studies, and in relation to public and private conformity. Discuss the relationship between research on ostracism and the concept of conformity. (*pp. 257-260*)

4. Explain how group size, awareness of norms, having an ally, and gender are related to and predict levels of conformity. (*pp. 260-263*)

5. Differentiate between majority and minority influence. Explain how to account for the effects of minority influence, and how majorities and minorities exert pressure to affect people's behavior. (*pp. 263-266*)

6.   Discuss the relationship between culture and conformity. (*pp. 266-268*)

7.   Define compliance. Describe the ways in which the discourse of making requests affects compliance with reference to mindlessness. Explain the role of the norm of reciprocity in such efforts to elicit compliance. (*pp. 268-270*)

8.   Define and explain the sequential request strategies known as the foot-in-the-door technique, low-balling, the door-in-the-face technique, and the that's-not-all technique. Explain why each works. Address strategies for resisting these strategies. (*pp. 270-275*)

9.   Define obedience. Discuss blind obedience as a possible explanation for the Nazis' actions during the Holocaust. (*pp. 275-276*)

10. Describe the procedures used in Milgram's research on obedience to authority. Compare the predictions made about how participants would behave to what actually happened. Summarize how each of the following predicted levels of obedience in the study: participant characteristics (e.g., gender, personality), authority figure characteristics (e.g., prestige, presence), proximity of victim, and the procedure (e.g., relieving the participant of responsibility, gradual escalation). (*pp. 276-281*)

11. Compare the findings of Milgram to the more recent studies of obedience by Meeus and Raaijmakers (1995) and Burger (2009). Explain the similarities and differences in the procedures and findings of these studies compared to those of the Milgram study. Describe the Gamson et al. (1982) study and discuss why its participants displayed defiance as opposed to obedience. (*pp. 281-284*)

12. Summarize social impact theory. Identify the factors that influence a source's strength, immediacy, and number, and the aspects of the target that facilitate resistance. Explain the relevance of this theory to conformity, compliance, and obedience. (*pp. 285-288*)

MAJOR CONCEPTS: THE BIG PICTURE

Below are four basic issues or principles that organize Chapter 7. You should know these issues and principles well.

1.   Conformity is the tendency for people to change their behavior to be consistent with group norms. Sherif and Asch conducted two classic studies that illustrate different types of influence and conformity, including informational influence, normative influence, private conformity, and public conformity. A number of situational factors affect majority influence, and a number of other factors affect minority influence. Majorities and minorities may exert different kinds of pressure and elicit different types of conformity. Resistance to conformity is enhanced by having allies in dissent. Cultural influences are important factors in the understanding of both conformity and independence.

2.   In conformity situations, people follow implicit group norms; but in compliance situations, people are influenced by direct *explicit* requests. The style of a request may affect the likelihood that someone will comply with the request even if its content is not very reasonable. People are more likely to comply when they feel indebted to a requester. A number of sequential request strategies can effectively trap people into compliance. Compliance techniques are more likely to work if they are subtle and if people are not vigilant.

3. In contrast to situations eliciting compliance, if the request is a command and the requester is (or seems to be) a figure of authority, the resulting social influence is obedience. Milgram's research on the forces of destructive obedience demonstrated dramatically how susceptible people are to obedience to authority, and how a number of situational factors can increase or decrease the chances that people will obey an authority's command to harm another human being. Milgram's original research continues to hold in the twenty-first century. Just as processes of social influence breed obedience, they can also support acts of defiance against authority.

4. Social influence situations vary in their impact on people. Social Impact Theory maintains that three factors—strength, immediacy, and number—affect the impact of a social influence situation. Strength refers to the power that the influence source has over those being influenced. Immediacy refers to the proximity in time and space between the influence source and the target of influence; the closer the source, the greater its impact. And finally, number refers to the number of influence sources; the larger the number of sources, the greater their impact—at least up to a point.

KEY TERM EXERCISE: THE CONCEPTS YOU SHOULD KNOW

Below are all of the key terms that appear in **boldface** in Chapter 7. To help you better understand these concepts, rather than just memorize them, write a definition for each term in your own words. After doing so, look at the next section where you'll find a list of definitions from the textbook for each of the key terms presented in random order. For each of your definitions, find the corresponding textbook definition. Note how your definitions compare with those from the textbook.

Key Terms

1. individualism
2. that's-not-all technique
3. conformity
4. foot-in-the-door technique
5. idiosyncrasy credits
6. private conformity
7. collectivism
8. compliance
9. normative influence
10. low-balling
11. public conformity
12. social impact theory
13. door-in-the-face technique
14. obedience
15. informational influence
16. minority influence

Textbook Definitions

a. Tendency to change perceptions, opinions, or behavior in ways that are consistent with group norms.

b. Influence that produces conformity because a person believes others are correct in their judgments.

c. Influence that produces conformity because a person fears the negative social consequences of appearing deviant.

d. Change of mind that occurs when a person privately accepts the position taken by others.

e. A superficial change in observable behavior, without a corresponding change of opinion, produced by real or imagined group pressure.

f. A cultural orientation in which independence, autonomy, and self-reliance take priority over group allegiances.

g. A cultural orientation in which interdependence, cooperation, and social harmony take priority over purely personal goals.

h. Interpersonal "credits" a person earns by following group norms.

i. Changes in behavior that are elicited by direct requests.

j. A two-step compliance technique in which an influencer sets the stage for the real request by first getting a person to comply with a much smaller one.

k. A two-step compliance technique in which the influencer secures agreement with a request but then increases the size of that request by revealing hidden costs.

l. A two-step compliance technique in which an influencer prefaces the real request with one so large that it is sure to be rejected.

m. A two-step compliance technique in which the influencer begins with an inflated request, then immediately decreases its apparent size by offering a discount or bonus.

n. The process by which dissenters produce change within a group.

o. Behavior change produced by the commands of authority.

p. Theory that social influence depends on the strength, immediacy, and number of source persons relative to target persons.

ANSWERS FOR KEY TERM EXERCISE

Answers for the key terms exercise are listed below.

1. **f**
2. **m**
3. **a**
4. **j**
5. **h**
6. **d**
7. **g**
8. **i**
9. **c**
10. **k**
11. **e**
12. **p**
13. **l**
14. **o**
15. **b**
16. **n**

PRACTICE QUIZ: TEST YOUR KNOWLEDGE OF THE CHAPTER

Multiple-Choice Questions

1. Jane conducts a new experiment based on Milgram's study of destructive obedience. She manipulates the number of authorities and participants present in the room. She finds that when there are three people in authority present all giving similar commands to one participant, obedience rates are extremely high. However, when there are several participants and only one person in authority giving orders, obedience rates are quite low. These findings are most consistent with

    a.   research findings on informational influence.
    b.   social impact theory.
    c.   dual-process theory.
    d.   reciprocation ideology.

2. Which of the following people is *least* likely to conform to group pressure?

    a.   An adolescent in eighth grade
    b.   A person from an individualistic culture
    c.   A person from a collectivistic culture
    d.   A person whose attention has been drawn to the group norm

3. Before registering for class, Susan asks her friends about a professor. They all say the professor is a great teacher. Not knowing the professor, Susan therefore comes to believe that he is a great teacher and looks forward to taking his class. This illustrates

    a.   reciprocal concessions.
    b.   perceptual contrast.
    c.   informational influence.
    d.   public conformity.

4. Although they are distinct techniques, the foot-in-the-door, door-in-the-face, low-balling, and that's-not-all techniques are similar in that they all involve

    a.   starting with a small request and subsequently raising the costs.
    b.   normative influence.
    c.   two steps.
    d.   the norm of reciprocity.

5. Joanie asked an acquaintance named Chachi if he would do a small favor for her. After he agreed and did the small favor, Joanie then asked him to do an even larger favor for her. This scenario describes

    a.   the foot-in-the-door technique.
    b.   reciprocal concessions.
    c.   low-balling.
    d.   minority influence.

6. Hector's friends all say a recent test was difficult. Hector thinks the test was easy. When asked what he thought, Hector agrees with his friends. This outcome illustrates

    a.   normative influence.
    b.   private conformity.
    c.   reciprocity norms.
    d.   obedience.

7. A dozen participants were gathered into a group. An authority figure approached the group and ordered the group to do something most of the participants thought was morally wrong. The group defied the authority, refusing to obey. According to social impact theory, a factor likely to have helped the group defy the authority is that the
   a. social impact of the authority was divided among the dozen targets.
   b. source of the social influence was not immediate.
   c. situation created normative influence rather than informational influence.
   d. situation was ambiguous.

8. Which of the following people should be *least* likely to conform to a unanimous majority in a situation similar to that faced by the participants in Asch's study concerning line judgments?
   a. Jeff, who is not confident about his eyesight
   b. Shari-Beth, who made her responses in public
   c. Jacob, who comes from a collectivistic culture
   d. Benjamin, who saw someone else dissent

9. When Milgram exposed participants to an authority who demanded that they harm another person by administering electric shocks of up to 450 volts to him, he initially found that the percentage of participants who obeyed the authority's orders to administer all of these shocks was
   a. 0.1 percent.
   b. 10 percent among the male participants and 50 percent among the female participants.
   c. 65 percent.
   d. more than 97 percent.

10. Karen needs to type a term paper. To persuade her roommate, Nancy, to let her use her computer, Karen first lends Nancy some notes that Nancy needs and then asks if she can use her computer. Karen is using the
    a. social impact theory.
    b. that's-not-all technique.
    c. low-balling technique.
    d. norm of reciprocity.

11. Although neither group makes any explicit requests or demands of her, Sheetal expresses pro-conservative opinions when she is with her conservative friends and she expresses anti-conservative opinions when she is with her liberal friends. Sheetal's actions best illustrate
    a. compliance.
    b. individualism.
    c. conformity.
    d. obedience.

12. A majority is more likely to be persuaded to change its views if the dissenting minority
    a. has accumulated idiosyncrasy credits.
    b. seems very obstinate and unusual.
    c. keeps changing back and forth from conforming to dissenting.
    d. is perceived as an outgroup.

13. Which of the following is most accurate concerning gender differences in levels of conformity?
    a. Across situations, men are reliably more likely than women to conform to a group norm.
    b. Across situations, women are reliably more likely than men to conform to a group norm.
    c. When they think they are being observed, women conform more and men conform less than they do in more private situations.
    d. There is no evidence of gender differences in levels of conformity.

14. Sherif conducted a study in which participants in totally darkened rooms estimated how far a dot of light appeared to move. Asch conducted a study in which participants were asked to report which of three lines was identical in length to a standard line. Compared to the participants in Sherif's study, those in Asch's study exhibited more

   a.   vulnerability to informational influence.
   b.   private conformity.
   c.   obedience.
   d.   public conformity.

15. Though in the minority and new to the Senate, a group of senators argued consistently, persuasively, and successfully against a particular bill. Most of the other senators eventually agreed with them that the bill should not be approved. In this example, the first group of senators derived their power to influence from their

   a.   idiosyncrasy credits.
   b.   style of behavior.
   c.   sheer number.
   d.   reciprocation ideology.

16. Keana hopes that Naomi will pledge $5 and sign a petition in support of a community center. Keana first asks Naomi if she'd be willing to pledge $50 in support of a proposed community center. Naomi politely declines. Keana then asks Naomi if she'd be willing to pledge $5 and sign a petition in support of the community center. Naomi complies. Keana's ability to get Naomi to pledge $5 and sign the petition is likely to have been enhanced by Keana's use of the

   a.   foot-in-the-door technique.
   b.   low-balling technique.
   c.   door-in-the-face technique.
   d.   that's-not-all technique.

17. Oscar was walking in a relatively clean parking lot. Walking a few feet in front of him was a man named Felix. Oscar observed Felix stop to pick up some litter that someone had thrown on the ground and throw it into a garbage can. Having seen Felix do this, Oscar, who was just about to throw his gum wrapper on the ground, stopped himself from doing so and instead threw the wrapper into the garbage can. Oscar was influenced by Felix's behavior because it

   a.   made Oscar more aware of injunctive norms.
   b.   elicited obedience in Oscar.
   c.   made Oscar exhibit reciprocal concessions.
   d.   was a sequential strategy.

18. Bickman and his colleagues had a stranger (actually a confederate) approach people on the street and order them to do something. People were most willing to comply with these orders when the

   a.   stranger was a female.
   b.   stranger was dressed in a uniform.
   c.   the initial command was extreme and a subsequent one was smaller.
   d.   participants were not authoritarian.

19. In which of the following situations is Matthew most likely to exhibit private conformity?
    a. Matthew is sure of the proper way to behave, but he is faced with a very large group that is behaving in a very different way.
    b. Matthew is not at all sure of the proper way to behave, and he is in the presence of three other people who are confident that their behavior is correct.
    c. Matthew is sure of the proper way to behave, but he is faced with a small but unanimous group that is behaving in a very different way.
    d. Matthew is commanded by an authority to behave in a particular way.

20. By their willingness to maintain independence from the majority, people in the minority force other group members to
    a. publicly, but not privately, conform.
    b. respond with informational influence.
    c. issue idiosyncrasy credits to them.
    d. think carefully about a problem.

21. A cultural orientation in which independence, autonomy, and self-reliance take priority over group allegiances best describes
    a. individualism.
    b. collectivism.
    c. public conformity .
    d. private conformity.

22. The tendency to change our perception, opinions, or behavior in ways that are consistent with group norms best describes
    a. conformity.
    b. minority influence.
    c. compliance.
    d. idiosyncrasy credit.

Essay Questions

23. Sherif conducted a study in which participants in totally darkened rooms estimated how far a dot of light appeared to move. Asch conducted a study in which participants were asked to report which of three lines was identical in length to a standard line. Was the conformity found in Sherif's study private conformity, public conformity, or both? Was the conformity found in Asch's study private conformity, public conformity, or both? How can one tell the difference? Explain your answers.

24. Summarize the door-in-the-face technique. Give two reasons why this is such an effective strategy for eliciting compliance.

25. Summarize the ways in which Milgram varied the authority in different conditions of his research on destructive obedience. How did these variations affect the levels of obedience observed?

26. What determines whether a culture becomes individualistic or collectivistic?

ANSWERS TO THE PRACTICE QUIZ

Multiple-Choice Questions: Correct Answers and Explanations

1. b.   **social impact theory.** Social impact theory holds that social influence depends on the strength, immediacy, and number of source persons relative to target persons. In Jane's study, the levels of obedience are affected by the number of source persons relative to target persons. Informational influence produces conformity because a person believes others are correct in their judgments. There is no evidence that the participants would have this belief; in addition, Jane's study is about obedience to commands rather than conformity to a group norm. The dual-process theory concerns the belief that, when it comes to conformity, majorities and minorities exert influence in different ways and for different reasons. Since this example is about obedience, not conformity, this theory does not apply. A person's reciprocation ideology refers to his or her individual motives in using the norm of reciprocity; this is not relevant here.

2. b.   **A person from an individualistic culture.** An individualistic culture is one that values independence, autonomy, and self-reliance over group allegiances. People from such a culture are more likely to exert their independence and autonomy over group allegiances and hence to resist conformity than are people from a collectivistic culture, which is one that values interdependence, cooperation, and social harmony over purely personal goals. Adolescents are particularly vulnerable to peer pressure, so an adolescent in eighth grade is relatively likely to conform to group pressure. And making people aware of a group norm increases the likelihood that they will conform to the group norm.

3. c.   **informational influence.** Informational influence is influence that produces conformity because a person believes others are correct in their judgments. Faced with a clear consensus among her friends, and not having had any opportunity to form her own opinion about the professor, Susan reasonably assumes that her friends' judgments are valid; hence, she adopts their opinion. The notion of reciprocal concessions refers to the pressure to respond to changes in a bargaining position; there is no bargaining going on in this example. In the context of social influence, perceptual contrast refers to the tendency to perceive a request as smaller if it was preceded by a larger request than if it was not; this is not relevant in this example. Public conformity is a superficial change in observable behavior, without a corresponding change of opinion, produced by real or imagined group pressure; but there is no evidence that Susan was responding to real or imagined group pressure, and in any case Susan's opinion *did* change.

4. c.   **two steps.** All of these techniques involve a two-step, sequential trap. In the foot-in-the-door technique, the influencer first gets a person to comply with a relatively small request, and next makes a much larger request. The door-in-the-face technique involves the opposite sequence: first a large request (one so large that it is likely to be rejected), followed by a much smaller request. In low-balling, the influencer first secures an agreement, and next changes the agreement by revealing hidden costs. In the that's-not-all technique, the influencer first begins with an inflated request, then immediately decreases the apparent size of that request by offering a discount or bonus. Thus, each of these techniques involves two steps. As is particularly evident in the door-in-the-face technique, they do not all start with a small request and subsequently raise the costs. Normative influence, which is influence that produces conformity because a person fears the negative social consequences of appearing deviant, is not relevant here because these techniques do not involve groups (against which one could appear deviant) or conformity. And finally, the norm of reciprocity dictates that we should treat others as they treat us; but this is not relevant in the foot-in-the-door technique, in which the influencer does not do anything that would make the person feel the need to reciprocate.

5. a. **the foot-in-the-door technique.** The foot-in-the-door technique is a two-step compliance technique in which an influencer prefaces the real request by first getting a person to comply with a much smaller one; this is what is described in this example. Reciprocal concessions refer to changes one makes in a bargaining position to reciprocate the opposing side's changes in their bargaining position; there is no bargaining going on in this example. Low-balling is a two-step compliance technique in which the influencer secures agreement with a request but then increases the size of that request by revealing hidden costs. In this example, Joanie did not change an already secured agreement by revealing extra costs; rather, she secured an agreement, and then made a *separate* request that did not change the original agreement. Finally, minority influence is the process by which dissenters produce change within a group. There is no issue between a group and some dissenter(s) in this question.

6. a. **normative influence.** Normative influence is influence that produces conformity because a person fears the negative social consequences of appearing deviant. Hector's behavior is consistent with this influence; rather than stand out from his friends, Hector decides to agree with them even though he had a different opinion. Because Hector's personal opinion was that the test was easy, there is no evidence of private conformity, which refers to a change of mind that occurs when a person privately accepts the position taken by others. The reciprocity norm dictates that we should treat others as they treat us; but there is no evidence that Hector was reciprocating for a previous favor or for previous conformity on the part of his friends. Finally, obedience is behavior change produced by the commands of authority; but Hector was not commanded by an authority.

7. a. **social impact of the authority was divided among the dozen targets.** Social impact theory maintains that social influence depends on the strength, immediacy, and number of source persons relative to target persons. According to this theory, resistance to the social influence is more likely to occur to the extent that the social impact of the source (in this case, the authority figure) is divided among many targets (in this case, the dozen participants). In this example, the source of the social influence was immediate; the authority was described as having *approached* the group to give the order. Normative influence is influence that produces conformity because a person fears the negative social consequences of appearing deviant; but there is no evidence that this was a factor in this example. Indeed, the fear of appearing deviant might have prevented anyone from starting the resistance against the authority in the first place. The situation did not seem to have been ambiguous—most of the participants thought that the order they had received was morally wrong. Moreover, they probably would have been more likely to obey if the situation were ambiguous because they'd have had little reason to defy the command.

8. d. **Benjamin, who saw someone else dissent.** The research of Asch and of others has shown that having an ally in dissent can break the spell cast by a unanimous majority and reduce the normative pressure to conform. Jeff, who is not confident in his eyesight, is vulnerable not only to normative influence in this study but also to informational influence because he would not be sure what the correct answers are. Thus, Jeff would be especially likely to conform. Because the conformity typically elicited in the situation faced by Asch's participants is public conformity, Shari-Beth would be likely to publicly conform. Finally, since collectivistic cultures value interdependence, cooperation, and social harmony over purely personal goals, Jacob, who is from such a culture, would be more likely to conform in order to cooperate and preserve social harmony with the group.

9.   c.   **65 percent.** Although psychiatrists who were told about Milgram's experimental procedure *predicted* that only about 0.1 percent of participants would obey through the maximum level of shock, 65 percent of the participants did so all the way to 450 volts. This was true of both male and female participants.

10. d.   **norm of reciprocity.** The norm of reciprocity dictates that we should treat others as they treat us. Karen apparently assumes that if she does her roommate a favor, then her roommate will feel obligated to return the favor later. Social impact theory maintains that social influence depends on the strength, immediacy, and number of source persons relative to target persons; but Karen has not manipulated any of these factors, so this theory is not relevant here. The that's-not-all technique is a two-step compliance technique in which the influencer begins with an inflated request, then immediately decreases the apparent size of that request by offering a discount or bonus; but Karen has not offered a discount or bonus. The low-balling technique is a two-step compliance technique in which the influencer secures agreement with a request but then increases the size of that request by revealing hidden costs; but Karen has not increased the size of her request in any way.

11. c.   **conformity.** Conformity is the tendency to change perceptions, opinions, or behavior in ways that are consistent with group norms. In this example, the norm (pro- versus anti-conservative) varies among Sheetal's friends, and she changes her opinions to be consistent with the norm of each friendship group. Compliance refers to changes in behavior that are elicited by direct requests; but in this example, Sheetal was not requested to act in a particular way. Individualism is a cultural orientation in which independence, autonomy, and self-reliance take priority over group allegiances, but this is not relevant in this example. And obedience is behavior change produced by the commands of authority, but Sheetal was not commanded by an authority to change her opinions.

12. a.   **has accumulated idiosyncrasy credits.** Idiosyncrasy credits are interpersonal "credits" a person earns by following group norms. Research has shown that by first conforming and then dissenting, minorities may be effective in influencing the majority. Minorities are *less* effective if they seem very obstinate or unusual, do not appear to be sure of themselves because they keep changing back and forth from conforming to dissenting, or are perceived as an outgroup.

13. c.   **When they think they are being observed, women conform more and men conform less than they do in more private situations.** This is one of the few reliable sex differences reported in the literature.

14. d.   **public conformity.** Public conformity is a superficial change in observable behavior, without a corresponding change of opinion, produced by real or imagined group pressure. Because the correct answers in Asch's study were so obvious, the participants' conformity reflected the desire to *seem* to agree with the majority; privately, they knew the correct answers. Because the correct answers were obvious to them, the participants in Asch's study were protected from informational influence, which is influence that produces conformity because a person believes others are correct in their judgments. In contrast, Sherif's participants were not at all sure what the correct answers were, so they looked to the other participants to provide them with information about these answers. Thus vulnerable to informational influence, the participants in Sherif's study exhibited private conformity, which is a change of mind that occurs when a person privately accepts the position taken by others, but Asch's participants did not *privately* accept the position taken by the others. Obedience is a behavior change produced by the commands of authority, but there were no commands given by an authority in either of these two studies.

15. b. **style of behavior.** According to Moscovici, people in the *majority* derive social influence power by virtue of their sheer number and inherent power, but people in the *minority* derive social influence power from the style of their behavior. These senators, who were in the minority, argued in a consistent and persuasive style. Idiosyncrasy credits are interpersonal "credits" a person earns by following group norms, but there is no evidence that these senators had any such credits or that they had followed group norms; indeed, because they were new to the Senate, they probably hadn't had time to earn any idiosyncrasy credits, and they certainly were not earning any by arguing consistently against the majority in this example. A person's reciprocation ideology refers to his or her individual motives in the use of the norm of reciprocity; but this is not relevant here because no mention is made either of the senators' motives or attitudes about this norm or of any behaviors that the senators might want to reciprocate.

16. c. **door-in-the-face technique.** All of the possible answers to this question are two-step compliance techniques. It is important to recognize the differences among them. In the door-in-the-face technique, an influencer prefaces the real request with one so large that it is sure to be rejected. This is the technique described here—by prefacing the request to pledge $5 and sign a petition with a request for a much larger pledge, Keana increased the chances that Naomi would comply with the smaller, second request. In contrast, in the foot-in-the-door technique an influencer prefaces the real request by first getting a person to comply with a much smaller one; this is the *opposite* of what transpired in this example. In the technique of low-balling, the influencer secures agreement with a request but then increases the size of that request by revealing hidden costs; Keana did not secure an agreement first and then reveal hidden costs. And finally in the that's-not-all technique, the influencer begins with an inflated request, then immediately decreases the apparent size of that request by offering a discount or bonus. Keana did not immediately decrease the apparent size of her request by offering a discount or bonus; rather, she first made one request, which was rejected, and then made a different, smaller request.

17. a. **made Oscar more aware of injunctive norms.** Injunctive norms specify how people in general *should* behave; for example, they should clean up litter. Research by Cialdini and others has shown that making people aware of group or situational norms increases the likelihood that they will be influenced by these norms. Because no authority commanded anyone in this example, there was no evidence of obedience, which is a behavior change produced by the commands of authority. The notion of reciprocal concessions refers to the pressure to respond to changes in a bargaining position; but there was no bargaining going on in this example. And finally, although several compliance techniques involve a sequential strategy, in which two or more related requests are made in a sequence, no such requests were made in this example.

18. b. **stranger was dressed in a uniform.** The presence of a uniform suggests authority. Even when those authorities are not very powerful, they can elicit obedience. The confederate used in this study was always a male. In this study, the stranger did not make an initial extreme command followed by a subsequent, smaller command, nor did this study measure how authoritarian (a personality dimension characterized by attitudes and behaviors concerning authority, rigidity, dissent, ethnocentrism, etc.) the participants were.

19.   b.   **Matthew is not at all sure of the proper way to behave, and he is in the presence of three other people who are confident that their behavior is correct.** Private conformity is most likely to occur when there is no obviously correct or incorrect opinion. Because it is not clear to Matthew what the correct or incorrect opinion is, he is vulnerable to private conformity, particularly because the confidence of the other people should make their opinion a source of informational influence for him. If Matthew were sure of the proper way to behave, he would have been less likely to exhibit private conformity. The presence of a large group, or of a small but unanimous group, that was behaving in a very different way would increase the chances of *public* conformity, but Matthew's confidence would leave him less vulnerable to private conformity. If Matthew were commanded by an authority, he might exhibit obedience, which is a behavior change produced by the commands of authority, but he would not exhibit private conformity.

20.   d.   **think carefully about a problem.** When faced with a persistent minority, majorities often think about a problem more carefully than they would otherwise. As a result, the overall quality or creativity of group decisions is enhanced. Minority influence is more likely to lead to private, rather than public, conformity. Minorities are not particularly likely to cause other group members to respond with informational influence, which is influence that produces conformity because a person believes others are correct in their judgments; instead, the group members are likely to apply their sheer number and power and use normative influence. Idiosyncrasy credits are interpersonal "credits" a person earns by following group norms, but minorities are not in a position of power to "issue" credits to the rest of the group. Indeed, by going against the majority, the minorities are acting in a way that should *cost* them idiosyncrasy credits.

21.   a.   **individualism.** There are different cultural orientations toward persons and their relationships to groups. Some cultures primarily value individualism and the virtues of independence, autonomy, and self-reliance, while others value collectivism and the virtues of interdependence, cooperation, and social harmony. Under the banner of individualism, personal goals take priority over group allegiances. Yet in collectivistic cultures, the person is first and foremost a loyal member of a family, team, company, church, and state.

22.   a.   **conformity.** When social psychologists talk of conformity, they specifically refer to the tendency of people to change their perceptions, opinions, and behavior in ways that are consistent with group norms.

Answers to Essay Questions: Sample Essays

23.   Private conformity is a change of mind that occurs when a person privately accepts the position taken by others. Public conformity is a superficial change in observable behavior, without a corresponding change of opinion, produced by real or imagined group pressure. The conformity found in Sherif's study was primarily private conformity, whereas that found in Asch's study was primarily public conformity. The situation was very ambiguous for the participants in Sherif's study; they could not be sure how far the dot of light really moved. Hence, these participants looked to the other participants to provide them with information about what the correct answers were. Thus vulnerable to the informational influence that the participants provided for each other, the participants in Sherif's study exhibited private conformity to the group norm. One can tell that this was private and not merely public conformity because, when participants in Sherif's study were later asked to make the same judgments alone (in a situation where there would be little pressure against deviating from a group norm), they continued to make judgments consistent with the group norm. By contrast, the situation in Asch's study was not ambiguous; the correct answers were obvious to the participants. When these participants conformed to the judgments given by the majority, they were publicly, but not privately, conforming. That is, they continued to believe their original judgments, but they responded by giving a different judgment so as not to deviate from the rest of the group. One can tell that the conformity was more public than private here because, when participants were asked to write down their answers privately (in a situation where there was much less pressure against deviating from a group norm), levels of conformity dropped sharply.

24.   The door-in-the-face technique is a two-step compliance technique in which an influencer prefaces the real request with one so large that it is sure to be rejected. One reason this technique works may have to do with the principle of perceptual contrast. The contrast effect is the tendency to perceive stimuli that differ from expectations or other stimuli as even more different than they really are. In this case, after exposure to the very large request, the second request may seem even smaller than it would otherwise. Cialdini and his colleagues concluded that perceptual contrast is only partly responsible for the effectiveness of the door-in-the-face technique. A second, and possibly more compelling, reason for the effectiveness of this technique concerns reciprocal concessions – namely, the pressure to respond to changes in a bargaining position. When the influencer backs down from the original large request and makes a subsequent smaller request, the person who rejected the original request may perceive the influencer's second request as a concession or gesture of compromise and thus feel pressure to respond in kind by complying with this second request.

25.   Milgram varied the apparent status of the experimenter (the authority) by moving his lab from the prestigious Yale University to a rundown urban office building with no university affiliation. The rate of total obedience dropped from 65 percent at Yale to 48 percent at the office building – still a surprisingly high level of obedience. When the authority of the experimenter was diminished even more by replacing him with what appeared to be another participant, there was a dramatic drop in total obedience to 20 percent. In another condition, the experimenter issued his commands to the participants by telephone. This condition also showed a dramatic drop in obedience from the original condition – only 21 percent of the participants obeyed all the way.

26.   There are three key factors. The first is the complexity of a society. As people come to live in more complex industrialized societies, there are more groups to identify with, which means less loyalty to any one group and a greater focus on personal rather than collective goals. Second is the affluence of a society. As people prosper, they gain financial independence from each other, a condition that promotes social independence as well as mobility and a focus on personal rather than collective goals. The third factor is heterogeneity. Societies that are homogeneous, sharing the same language, religion, and social customs, tend to be rigid and intolerant of those who deviate from the norm. Societies that are culturally diverse, where two or more cultures coexist, tend to be more permissive of dissent, allowing for more individual expression. Cultural orientations may also be rooted in religious ideologies; for example, the link between Christianity and individualism.

CHAPTER 8

Group Processes

OUTLINE

LEARNING OBJECTIVES: GUIDELINES FOR STUDY

You should be able to do each of the following by the conclusion of Chapter 8.

1. Define group. Describe the reasons that people join a group and discuss the process of adjustment to a new group. Explain the processes of group development. (*pp. 294-297*)

2. Describe roles, norms, and cohesiveness, and explain their influence on group behavior and performance. Describe the effect that the type of work group members' culture, collectivistic or individualistic, has on issues related to group cohesiveness. (*pp. 297-300*)

3. Explain how the presence of others affects task performance and how Zajonc's social facilitation model accounts for these effects. Describe three alternative explanations for these effects. (*pp. 300-304*)

4. Describe how working with others on a task affects productivity. Explain the concept of social loafing, identify factors that can reduce the likelihood of loafing, and distinguish between situations likely to lead to social facilitation versus social loafing. Discuss group and cultural differences in social loafing. (*pp. 304-307*)

5. Define deindividuation. Describe how environmental cues and a sense of identity can affect this process. (*pp. 307-309*)

6. Define process loss. Discuss the types of tasks that lead to process loss and those that lead to process gain. Define brainstorming and list its ground rules. Discuss the effectiveness of group brainstorming in comparison to individual brainstorming. Discuss the effectiveness of electronic brainstorming. (*pp. 310-312*)

7. Describe group polarization and distinguish between the informational and normative processes through which it occurs. (*pp. 312-314*)

8. Define groupthink and its antecedents, behavioral symptoms, and consequences. Address how groupthink can be prevented. (*pp. 314-317*)

9. Define escalation effect. Define biased sampling and discuss its impact on group discussion and decision-making. Discuss the causes of biased sampling and what can be done to prevent it. Define transactive memory and discuss how it relates to utilizing expertise. (*pp. 317-319*)

10. Describe some of the factors that promote better group dynamics, including group norms and goals, training and intervention, computer technology and group support systems, and virtual teams. (*pp. 319-322*)

11. Describe the role diversity plays in group communication and performance. (*p. 322*)

12. Define social dilemma. Describe the prisoner's dilemma and resource dilemmas. Discuss mixed motives in the context of these dilemmas, and delineate psychological and cultural factors that influence behavior in social dilemmas. (*pp. 323-327*)

13. Discuss how threat capacity and perceptions of others can lead to the escalation of group conflict. Explain how GRIT and negotiation can reduce group conflict. Discuss gender and culture differences in negotiation. Discuss the role of superordinate goals and superordinate identity in helping conflicted groups find common ground. (*pp. 327-333*)

MAJOR CONCEPTS: THE BIG PICTURE

Below are four basic issues or principles that organize Chapter 8. You should know these issues and principles well.

1. Human beings appear to be naturally predisposed to join groups, both for safety and for identity needs. People tend to interact most with others in their group. This group interaction is facilitated by the existence of roles for various members, shared norms for group activity, and group cohesiveness.

2. The presence of others can have a major impact on people's behavior. It improves our performance on simple tasks, but impairs our performance on difficult tasks. If people work with others on a joint project, they tend to slack off and do less work than if they worked individually. And, when people form together in an unorganized crowd, they often lose their sense of identity and can be spurred to violent and destructive acts.

3. Group discussion tends to intensify the original position of the group and make it more extreme in a process called group polarization. Interacting with others with shared convictions can strengthen convictions and lead people to lose perspective on problems and engage in an excessive tendency to seek concurrence, called groupthink. Research on the performance of groups shows that they often do not perform as well as most people think; however, diversity in an integrated group can enhance the group's performance.

4. People bring different motives to their group interactions. These motives can lead to cooperation, competition, or conflict. Research on social dilemmas suggests that people often respond in kind to others, and that they can be cooperative but will also take unfair rewards if they can get away with it. Conflict between groups can escalate, even if one or both groups have the capacity to harm the other and have little to gain from the conflict. This escalation is often fueled by distorted views of the other group. Fortunately, conflict can also be reduced. Strategies such as negotiating, finding common ground, and using graduated and reciprocated initiatives in tension-reduction (GRIT) are effective in resolving conflict.

KEY TERM EXERCISE: THE CONCEPTS YOU SHOULD KNOW

Below are all of the key terms that appear in **boldface** in Chapter 8. To help you better understand these concepts, rather than just memorize them, write a definition for each term in your own words. After doing so, look at the next section where you'll find a list of definitions from the textbook for each of the key terms presented in random order. For each of your definitions, find the corresponding textbook definition. Note how your definitions compare with those from the textbook.

Key Terms

1. social dilemma

2. evaluation apprehension theory

3. mere presence theory

4. social loafing

5. graduated and reciprocated initiatives in tension-reduction (GRIT)

6. deindividuation

7.   group support systems

8.   resource dilemma

9.   group polarization

10. groupthink

11. group cohesiveness

12. brainstorming

13. distraction-conflict theory

14. escalation effect

15. integrative agreement

16. collective effort model

17. prisoner's dilemma

18. process loss

19. transactive memory

20. social identity model of deindividuation (SIDE)

21. social facilitation

22. biased sampling

Textbook Definitions

a.   A group-produced reduction in individual output on easy tasks where contributions are pooled.

b.   When commitments to a failing course of action are increased to justify investments already made.

c.   Which concern how two or more people share a limited resource.

d.   A technique that attempts to increase the production of creative ideas by encouraging group members to speak freely without criticizing their own or others' contributions.

e.   A situation in which a self-interested choice by everyone creates the worst outcome for everyone.

f.   A process whereby the presence of others enhances performance on easy tasks but impairs performance on difficult tasks.

g.   Interactive computer-mediated programs that help remove communication barriers and provide structure and incentives for group discussions and decisions.

h.   The theory that individuals will exert effort on a collective task to the degree that they think their individual efforts will be important, relevant, and meaningful for achieving outcomes that they value.

i.   A theory holding that the presence of others will produce social facilitation effects only when those others are seen as potential evaluators.

j.   A group decision-making style characterized by an excessive tendency among group members to seek concurrence.

k.   A negotiated resolution to a conflict in which all parties obtain outcomes that are superior to what they would have obtained from an equal division of the contested resources.

l.   A theory holding that the mere presence of others is sufficient to produce social facilitation effects.

m.   The loss of a person's sense of individuality and the reduction of normal constraints against deviant behavior.

n.   A strategy for unilateral, persistent efforts to establish trust and cooperation between opposing parties.

o.   The exaggeration through group discussion of initial tendencies in the thinking of group members.

p.   A theory holding that the presence of others will produce social facilitation effects only when those others distract from the task and create attentional conflict.

q.   In the prisoner's dilemma, participants are given a series of choices in which they have the option of cooperating or competing.

r.   A group may perform worse than it would if every individual performed up to his or her potential.

s.   A shared system for remembering information that enables multiple people to remember information together more efficiently than they could alone.

t.   When group discussion is dominated by information everyone in the group already knows, while the unshared information never makes it to the table.

u.   The forces exerted on a group that push its members closer together.

v.   The idea that whether deindividuation affects people for better or for worse reflects the characteristics and norms of the group immediately surrounding the individual, as well as the group's power to act according to these norms.

ANSWERS FOR KEY TERM EXERCISE

Answers for the key terms exercise are listed below.

1. e
2. i
3. l
4. a
5. n
6. m
7. g
8. c
9. o
10. j
11. u.
12. d
13. p
14. b
15. k
16. h
17. q
18. r
19. s
20. v
21. f
22. t

PRACTICE QUIZ: TEST YOUR KNOWLEDGE OF THE CHAPTER

Multiple-Choice Questions

1. Dave is a novice tennis player. He is more anxious when being watched by a group of instructors than by a group of novice players. This difference in anxiety illustrates the process of
   a. social comparison.
   b. evaluation apprehension.
   c. social loafing.
   d. mere presence.

2. Groups vary in specific characteristics, but all groups can be defined by three essential components:
   a. attitudes, values, and norms.
   b. roles, values, and ideologies.
   c. roles, norms, and cohesiveness.
   d. values, goals, and cohesiveness.

3. Ben manages an automobile assembly plant. Since he started requiring workers to inscribe their names on the cars they assemble, quality control has found fewer defective cars. Ben reduced social loafing by making
   a. integrative agreements.
   b. superordinate goals.
   c. contributions identifiable.
   d. cohesive work teams.

4. When people work with others on a task, they
   a. work harder than when they work alone.
   b. work just as hard as when they work alone.
   c. don't work as hard as when they work alone.
   d. tend to slack off at the start and then work harder as time progresses.

5. The marketing staff reports to the marketing director, who in turn reports to the president. This system is an example of
   a. a communication network.
   b. production blocking.
   c. performance matching.
   d. an integrative agreement.

6. One consequence of deindividuation is that people experience a decrease in
   a. social comparison.
   b. anonymity.
   c. self-awareness.
   d. goal striving.

7. Mr. Allen's homeroom class of high school seniors is washing cars, in small groups, in order to raise money for a class trip. Of the following students, who is most likely, according to research, to be *least* susceptible to the phenomenon of social loafing?

    a. Maxine, a recent immigrant from Thailand, who is washing cars with a couple of girls who are fooling around
    b. Josh, who was raised in Canada and is in a group with four girls
    c. Valerie, who grew up in New Jersey, and is part of a mixed-gender group
    d. Roberto, an Italian-American, who is a year and a half younger than the other five boys in his group

8. The kind of exchange that usually reduces cooperation and escalates conflict between parties involves the use of

    a. perceived competence.
    b. threat capacity.
    c. public goods.
    d. persuasive arguments.

9. The mere presence account of social facilitation suggests that people do better on easy tasks and worse on hard tasks when performing in front of others than when performing alone because

    a. they are concerned about the impression they are making.
    b. they are distracted by the other people.
    c. the presence of other people produces arousal, which in turn affects performance.
    d. they don't like to exert too much effort in the presence of others.

10. When people discuss a topic with others in their own social group who agree with them, they are likely to

    a. shift their position away from the initial leanings of the group.
    b. reverse their position altogether.
    c. exhibit no change in their position.
    d. enhance or exaggerate the initial leanings of the group.

11. Which of the following is true about the relationship between cohesiveness and performance?

    a. Cohesiveness is more positively related to performance in large groups than in small groups.
    b. The relationship between cohesiveness and performance is stronger for female groups than for male groups.
    c. The relationship between cohesiveness and performance is correlational as opposed to causal.
    d. Cohesiveness affects performance more than performance affects cohesiveness.

12. According to Janis, groupthink is likely to result when groups are

    a. heterogeneous.
    b. led by a weak leader.
    c. highly cohesive.
    d. indecisive.

13. Jane's company is developing a new product. There are indications that the product may be defective and could result in substantial liability for the company. Jane argues that the company's strong record of developing and marketing products suggests that they will pull through this time as well. The board members quickly decide to go ahead with the product despite its dangers. Their reasoning is an example of

    a. group roles.
    b. mutual cooperation.
    c. social loafing.
    d. groupthink.

14. The people in Everytown are celebrating the victory of their town's soccer team in a championship tournament. A large number of people crowd together in the town center to celebrate the victory and soon those in the crowd begin to feel anonymous. Because people are part of this crowd they are more likely to

    a. engage in destructive behaviors.
    b. act reserved.
    c. celebrate the victory through group cooperation.
    d. be concerned with the evaluations of others.

15. Which of the following is a conjunctive group task?

    a. A three-men swim-team is competing in a relay race.
    b. The women's gymnastics team is entered in the individual balance beam competition.
    c. Three runners from the same country are running in the marathon.
    d. In an international bicycle race, the members of the team include the world champion and two cyclists who ride in support positions.

16. The 15 members of the student council of the local high school are meeting in the cafeteria and brainstorming ideas for their senior prom. They can increase the productivity of the session by

    a. evaluating ideas as good or bad as soon as they are uttered.
    b. limiting the number of ideas that can be mentioned and sticking to that number.
    c. only expressing out loud ideas that sound feasible.
    d. having an individual brainstorming session before or after the group session.

17. When two people are faced with a situation in which mutual cooperation by both is beneficial to both, competition by both is harmful to both, but competition by only one is beneficial to the competitor and harmful to the cooperator, the situation can be described as

    a. the prisoner's dilemma.
    b. the tragedy of the commons.
    c. a public goods dilemma.
    d. a free-rider problem.

18. Which of the following is a commons dilemma?

    a. The poor people in the village are unable to afford nutritious food.
    b. The governments of two neighboring countries focus on developing weapons instead of on using their resources to improve the lives of their citizens.
    c. Everyone in the world is eating more fish while the supply in the oceans is being depleted.
    d. Because no one volunteered to help clean the vacant lot, it remained as an eyesore in the community.

19. Specific behaviors, either formal or informal, that are expected for different positions within a group are called

   a.   norms.
   b.   social roles.
   c.   disjunctive tasks.
   d.   superordinate goals.

20. Stating one's intentions to reduce tension and taking unilateral cooperative actions to reduce tension are steps in

   a.   GRIT.
   b.   SIDE.
   c.   integrative agreements.
   d.   social dilemmas.

21. Stephanie and Keith both want to use their jointly owned wagon at the same time. Their mother tells them that dessert depends on their taking turns with the wagon. Her use of dessert to foster turn-taking illustrates the application of

   a.   integrative agreements.
   b.   superordinate goals.
   c.   group polarization.
   d.   social dilemmas.

22. People from different cultures may have very different assumptions and styles concerning negotiations. Which of the following is from the Western perspective?

   a.   The first step in negotiating is to develop a trusting relationship between the individual negotiators.
   b.   Arguments may be more holistic, and emotionality and contradiction tolerated.
   c.   Some of the most important communications are nonverbal or indirect.
   d.   Written contracts are binding; oral commitments are not.

23. Nine-year-old Rhonda and her 11-year-old sister Ellen often argue over who can choose what to watch on their one television. One day, they reached an integrative agreement when they agreed

   a.   to put away the remote and not watch TV for 24 hours and then renegotiate the terms.
   b.   to share equitably by taking turns, each being in control of the remote on alternate days.
   c.   that because Ellen was older, she would get to choose what they would watch four days a week, whereas Rhonda would get to choose three days a week.
   d.   to find TV shows that both wanted to watch instead of dividing up their total TV time.

Essay Questions

24. Describe three ways in which the presence of others can have an impact on people's behavior.

25. Explain how interacting with others who have shared convictions can lead to the strengthening of those convictions.

26. Discuss two techniques that can lead to the reduction of conflict between groups.

27. Discuss the collectivistic perspective versus the individualistic perspective in avoiding direct conflict.

ANSWERS TO THE PRACTICE QUIZ

Multiple-Choice Questions: Correct Answers and Explanations

1.   b.   **evaluation apprehension.** Because Dave is more nervous in front of experts, he is probably concerned about others evaluating him. After all, the experts can be harsher and more detailed critics than the novices. There is no evidence to show that he is comparing himself with others or engaging in social comparison. Social loafing is unlikely to occur in this situation because Dave is not working on a joint task where individual productivity is unobservable. Finally, the mere presence explanation of the social facilitation phenomenon does not distinguish between types of people, so Dave's differential reaction to experts and novices is inconsistent with mere presence.

2.   c.   **roles, norms, and cohesiveness.** The main text argues that all groups can be characterized by the three components: roles, norms, and cohesiveness. Values, ideologies, and goals are all likely to be important to groups but they are not one of the three essential components.

3.   c.   **contributions identifiable.** Social loafing is the tendency for people to work less productively when they work with others on a joint product. Research shows that social loafing is reduced when people's contributions are identifiable. When Ben required workers to put their names on the cars they assemble, he made their contributions identifiable and thereby reduced social loafing. There is no evidence that Ben used integrative agreements, superordinate goals, or cohesive work teams.

4.   c.   **don't work as hard as when they work alone.** When people work with others on a joint task, they tend to work less productively than when they work alone. This phenomenon is called social loafing. People do not tend to work harder as time progresses when working with others.

5.   a.   **communication network.** A communication network is the chain of transmission of messages within an organization. This example clearly shows who communicates with whom, but it contains no evidence of production blocking, performance matching, or an integrative agreement.

6.   c.   **self-awareness.** When people experience deindividuation, they become less self-aware. This decrease in self-awareness is probably responsible for many of the effects of deindividuation: increased aggression, increased helpfulness, etc. There is no evidence that deindividuation leads to a decrease in social comparison or goal striving, and it increases anonymity.

7.   c.   **Valerie, who grew up in New Jersey and is part of a mixed-gender group.** Social loafing is less likely to occur among females than among males. So, Valerie is less likely to loaf than Josh. Social loafing is also less likely to occur among people from Eastern, collectivist cultures, such as Thailand, than among those from Western, individualist cultures, such as the United States, However, research has shown that there are times when people from collectivist cultures are especially likely to social loaf: when they are grouped with others who are social loafing, because they are liable to be concerned about deviating from the norm. So Maxine, who comes from a collectivist culture, is likely to do as the other girls in her group and social loaf. As for Roberto, he comes from an individualist, Western culture and being a male is more likely to social loaf than a female. Moreover, his age is not a factor, as research has documented social loafing in children as young as five years of age.

8. b. **threat capacity.** When two groups emphasize threat capacity (i.e., how much they could hurt each other), they are likely to escalate conflict between themselves. This form of exchange often leads to a cycle of deepening tension between the groups. An arms race is a clear example of the way threat capacity can lead to increased tension and conflict. Perceived competence and persuasive arguments have little to do with reciprocity or reducing cooperation. And public goods, what people fail to share in the public goods dilemma, have some connection to reciprocity but have little to do with the escalation of conflict between parties.

9. c. **the presence of other people produces arousal, which in turn affects performance.** This explanation of social facilitation suggests that the mere presence of other people causes one to become aroused and that this arousal improves performance on easy tasks and impairs performance on difficult tasks. It does not, however, propose that people's performance is affected by the impression they are making, by the distraction they face, or by how hard they are working.

10. d. **enhance or exaggerate the initial leanings of the group.** Group polarization is exaggeration through group discussion of initial tendencies in the thinking of group members. Because of group polarization, it is very unlikely that people would shift or reverse their position, or even have no change in their position, when discussing their views with like-minded others.

11. b. **The relationship between cohesiveness and performance is stronger for female groups than for male groups.** In a meta-analysis of the research on cohesiveness in sports teams, Carron, et al., (2002) found that the relationship between team performance and cohesiveness was especially strong for female teams, possibly because women tend to be more interdependent. The relationship between cohesiveness and performance tends to be stronger for small, rather than large, groups. The relationship between cohesiveness and group performance appears to be causal; cohesiveness makes a group perform better and a good performance makes a group more cohesive. There is stronger evidence that performance affects cohesiveness than that cohesiveness affects performance.

12. c. **highly cohesive.** According to Janis, groupthink develops when groups are highly cohesive, close-minded, under stress, homogeneous, isolated, led by a strong leader, more interested in agreement than in being correct, and lacking in procedures for making and reviewing decisions.

13. d. **groupthink.** The board members appear to be overestimating the ability of the group to carry off the project. They also seem to be using a closed-minded approach that rationalizes the correctness of their decision. Finally, because the group makes the decision so quickly, there appears to be some pressure toward uniformity in the group. These are all behavioral symptoms of groupthink. Although people in this situation might be enacting slightly different roles, their reasoning has little to do with their respective roles. In addition, the actions of the group seem to have little to do with either social loafing or mutual cooperation.

14. a. **engage in destructive behaviors.** When people gather together into a crowd, their behavior often becomes violent and destructive. This phenomenon, known as deindividuation, may be responsible for the wanton and disturbing acts committed during riots. When people experience deindividuation, they seem to lose awareness of their own inner standards; this loss of awareness may be responsible for the increase in destructive behaviors. Deindividuation does not, however, cause people to become reserved, to engage in group cooperation, or to be concerned with evaluations by others.

15.   a.   **A three-men swim-team is competing in a relay race.** In a conjunctive task, the group product is determined by the weakest performance. If three good swimmers compete in a relay race against another team of three good swimmers and one person in the first team gets a cramp and swims very slowly, his team's performance is likely to suffer. The women's gymnastics team is engaging in an individual task, where each is competing on her own. If looked on as a team effort to win as many gold medals as possible for the team, the task becomes an additive one, where the best performer can help by winning a large number of the medals, but a weak performer will not prevent the others on the team from doing so. The marathon runners are also engaging in an individual, not group, task. As for the bicyclists, they are engaging in a disjunctive task where only the performance of the top player will count.

16.   d.   **having an individual brainstorming session before or after the group session.** The ground rules of brainstorming require the expression of all ideas, the more the better, even those that sound crazy, without evaluation. And although group brainstorming is not as effective as individual brainstorming, alternating group sessions with individual sessions of brainstorming can increase the effectiveness of group brainstorming.

17.   a.   **the prisoner's dilemma.** The prisoner's dilemma is a classic paradigm in which two people have the option of cooperating or competing. If one player cooperates and the other player competes, the player who competes gets a big payoff. If both players cooperate, then they both receive a moderate payoff. But if they both compete, they both lose a substantial amount. People usually respond to others in kind in this paradigm. The tragedy of the commons, the public goods dilemma, and the free-rider problem are all dilemmas faced by large social groups, so they are easily represented by two people.

18.   c.   **Everyone in the world is eating more fish while the supply in the oceans is being depleted.** A commons dilemma is a situation in which, if people take as much as they want of a limited resource that does not replenish itself, nothing will be left. Overfishing is such a situation. The inability of poor people to get adequately nutritious food is not a commons dilemma because it does not involve the depletion of a limited resource. When two poor countries are locked in an arms race, the situation is analogous to the prisoner's dilemma. When a vacant lot remains an eyesore because no one volunteers to clean it up, that is a public goods dilemma.

19.   b.   **social roles.** Social roles are the specific behaviors carried out by individuals in a group that are expected by most of the group members. Norms are shared expectations for the group that help define the social roles, but they are not the behaviors themselves. Superordinate goals are also shared by the group, but they are not associated with positions within the group. Finally, disjunctive tasks are not related to expectations in a group.

20.   a.   **GRIT.** GRIT is the acronym for the strategy known as graduated and reciprocated initiatives in tension-reduction. This strategy allows one party, without the cooperation of the other party, to attempt to reduce conflict. It involves clear statements of one's desire to reduce tension, followed by unilateral cooperative actions. If any of these actions elicits cooperation from the other party, then a higher-level cooperative action is initiated in response. GRIT has been shown to be effective in reducing tension between parties. SIDE (social identity model of deindividuation effects) and social dilemmas have little to do with reducing tension, and integrative agreements may be enacted to reduce tension but are not a unilateral solution.

21. b.   **superordinate goals.** Superordinate goals are common goals that people share and must
     work together to obtain. It seems likely that Stephanie and Keith both want dessert, and their turn-
     taking is definitely an activity on which they will have to work together. There is little evidence of
     group polarization or social dilemmas in this example; and although the mother's solution may be
     innovative, it does not constitute an integrative agreement because no bargaining is involved.

22. d.   **Written contracts are binding, oral commitments are not.** As the world becomes
     smaller due to advances in technology and the globalization of business and the economy, as well
     as due to global threats concerning the environment and terrorism, the ability to negotiate
     effectively across cultures becomes increasingly important. Table 8.7 lists some common
     assumptions made by negotiators from western, individualistic cultures that are not always shared
     by representatives from other cultures.

23. d.   **to find TV shows that both wanted to watch instead of dividing up their total TV time.**
     An integrative agreement is reached when both parties obtain outcomes that are superior to a 50-
     50 split. By agreeing to find TV shows that both like to watch, the girls will end up watching more
     TV than if they equitably split up their allotted TV time. Agreeing not to watch anything for 24
     hours does not qualify as an integrative agreement because neither girl benefits. Controlling the
     TV on alternate days amounts to a 50-50 split, which does not qualify as an integrative agreement.
     Letting Ellen have more time than Rhonda because she's older does not qualify as an integrative
     agreement because Rhonda ends up with even less than a 50 percent chunk of the time.

Answers to Essay Questions: Sample Essays

24.   The presence of others can affect people's performance, productivity, and inclination to engage in destructive acts. When people are in the presence of others, they tend to do better on easy tasks and worse on hard tasks than when they do these tasks alone. This phenomenon, known as social facilitation, may be the result of arousal, distraction, or evaluation apprehension that develops in the presence of others. When people work together on a joint task with others and individual contributions are not identifiable, people tend to be less productive. This phenomenon, known as social loafing, may be the result of a decreased sense of personal responsibility for the outcome of the group's work. Finally, when people are grouped together with others they do not know, as in a crowd, they tend to engage in destructive actions. This phenomenon, known as deindividuation, seems to result from the reduced focus on internal standards of conduct when a person's attention is redirected away from the self by the presence of others.

25.   Group polarization is the exaggeration through group discussion of initial tendencies in the thinking of group members. This exaggeration or enhancement of convictions appears to result from three processes. First, people hear more persuasive arguments that are consistent with their views when they discuss these views with people who share them. Second, their views may be strengthened when people draw on the support of others as evidence that the views are valid and should be held. Third, an ingroup (consisting of people who share their views) and an outgroup (consisting of people who do not share their views) may be formed. As this social categorization process occurs, the differences between the two groups may become accentuated, thus strengthening the convictions of the individual members.

26.   Two techniques that can lead to the reduction of conflict between groups are graduated and reciprocated initiatives in tension-reduction (GRIT) and negotiation. GRIT is a peacemaking strategy that can be used even if the other side is hostile toward the party using it. GRIT involves four basic components. First, a general statement is issued about the group's intention to reduce conflict. Second, the group carries out an announced tension-reducing initiative even if there is no immediate reciprocation. Third, if the other group initiates cooperation, the group using GRIT responds with at least as much cooperation. But fourth, the group using GRIT must retain enough retaliatory capability to prevent the other group from exploiting the cooperative overtures. Alternatively, negotiation attempts to reduce conflict without actually engaging in destructive activity. Negotiation works best when the negotiators use flexible behavior at the negotiation table to arrive at integrative agreements, resolutions in which all parties obtain outcomes that are superior to what they would have obtained from an equal distribution of the contested resources.

27. Good communication is a key ingredient in successful negotiation. Communication across
     cultures can present special challenges. Whereas an individualistic perspective emphasizes direct
     communication and confrontation, a collectivistic perspective emphasizes more indirect
     information sharing and a desire to avoid direct conflict. Individualistic negotiators may
     emphasize rationality and a lack of emotion in negotiation, whereas a greater tolerance of
     contradiction and emotionality is characteristic of a collectivistic style—although emotionality
     should not be confrontational. Individualists tend to prefer to make compromises and concessions
     toward the end of a negotiation, whereas collectivists may prefer to begin with generous
     concessions and gradually reduce their concessions later. Even something that may seem as basic
     as time is perceived and valued differently as a function of culture.

CHAPTER 9

Attraction and Close Relationships

OUTLINE

LEARNING OBJECTIVES: GUIDELINES FOR STUDY

You should be able to do each of the following by the conclusion of Chapter 9.

1.   Describe social anxiety and the need for affiliation. Address the relationship between affiliation and stress. (*pp. 340-342*)

2.   Summarize the social difficulties associated with shyness and loneliness. Discuss factors that predict loneliness (e.g., age, transitions) and coping strategies that can be employed to deal with loneliness. (*pp. 342-343*)

3.   Describe the role of familiarity in attraction, including issues of proximity and mere exposure effects. (*pp. 343-345*)

4.   Distinguish between objective and subjective perspectives on physical attractiveness, drawing on data and observations that support both ideas. Discuss the link between the color red and physical and sexual attraction. (*pp. 345-349*)

5.   Describe the what-is-beautiful-is-good stereotype and why it endures. Explain the benefits and costs of being someone who is perceived to be beautiful. (*pp. 349-352*)

6.   Explain the influence of similarity on attractiveness, including the matching and complementarity hypotheses. Discuss the role of reciprocity in liking. Discuss the research on the hard-to-get effect. (*pp. 352-357*)

7.   Explain the differences between evolutionary and sociocultural perspectives on mate preference. (*pp. 357-363*)

8.   List the basic components of an intimate relationship. Explain social exchange theory. Define the concepts of comparison level, comparison level for alternatives, and investment. Explain how equity theory differs from social exchange theory. Describe how people repair imbalances in their relationships according to Murray and Holmes' trust-insurance system. (*pp. 363-367*)

9.   Distinguish between exchange and communal relationships and consider the role of attachment style in studying intimate relationships. (*pp. 367-369*)

10. Summarize different approaches to classifying love such as Lee's love styles, Sternberg's triangular theory of love, and Hatfield's distinction between passionate and companionate love. (*pp. 369-370*)

11. Explain the relationship between arousal and attraction, as well as the role that both play in passionate love. (*pp. 370-372*)

12. Define self-disclosure, and describe typical patterns of disclosure in relationships. (*pp. 372-374*)

13. Discuss cultural and gender differences with regard to issues of attraction, intimate relationships, and sexuality. (*pp. 374-375*)

14. Describe Kinsey's studies of sexual behavior and discuss the limitations of such surveys. Summarize gender differences evident in surveys of sexual attitudes and behavior. (*pp. 375-377*)

15. Define sexual orientation. Discuss the biological and psychological influences that are theorized to affect sexual orientation. Discuss how same-sex couples differ from straight couples when it comes to forming intimate relationships. (*pp. 377-380*)

16. Describe the marital trajectory. Discuss communication and attribution patterns that can lead to conflict in relationships. Describe patterns of marital satisfaction and issues regarding the end of intimate relationships. (*pp. 380-384*)

MAJOR CONCEPTS: THE BIG PICTURE

Below are three basic issues or principles that organize Chapter 9. You should know these issues and principles well.

1.   Being with others appears to be a fundamental human motive. We are drawn to affiliate with others and are quite good at regulating the level of interactions with others that we desire. We are especially likely to seek affiliation when we experience stress and can affiliate with people who share our fate. But not everyone is able to gain the intimacy that they desire. Loneliness is a persistent problem for some.

2.   There are many factors that lead us to be attracted to others. We are attracted to people who we live near and encounter frequently. We are also attracted to people we find physically attractive. Certain features tend to be seen as more attractive by most people – even babies appear to find these features more attractive. However, there also appear to be significant variations due to culture, time, and circumstances in what people find attractive. When getting acquainted with others, we tend to like those who are similar rather than those who are different or opposite. We also like people who like us; and this is especially true if they are somewhat selective in whom they like. Finally, evolutionary perspectives suggest that men and women have important differences in what they find attractive. Men focus more on physical attractiveness as a sign of fertility and become jealous when they believe their partner has become unfaithful. Women focus on a man's ability to care for children and on his financial resources and become jealous when their partner forms an intimate relationship with someone else.

3. Social psychologists have devised several models to explain the development of intimate relationships. One model, social exchange theory, tries to explain relationship formation in terms of a marketplace. People develop intimate relationships if they provide more rewards and fewer costs than not being in the relationship or being in another relationship. Other researchers argue that in some relationships we are only initially concerned with exchange, while in other relationships we take a more communal approach and are concerned with meeting the needs of our partner. Still others note that our relationship styles may mirror the attachments that we had with our caregivers in early childhood. There are many different ways to classify love in relationships, but a common classification recognizes passionate love, an emotionally intense state of absorption in the other person that is characteristic of early relationships, and companionate love, a secure, trusting, and stable partnership that is characteristic of later relationships. Cultural influences play an important role in the understanding of attraction and close relationships.

KEY TERM EXERCISE: THE CONCEPTS YOU SHOULD KNOW

Below are all of the key terms that appear in **boldface** in Chapter 9. To help you better understand these concepts, rather than just memorize them, write a definition for each term in your own words. After doing so, look at the next section where you'll find a list of definitions from the textbook for each of the key terms presented in random order. For each of your definitions, find the corresponding textbook definition. Note how your definitions compare with those from the textbook.

Key Terms

1. intimate relationship
2. hard-to-get effect
3. passionate love
4. loneliness
5. matching hypothesis
6. mere exposure effect
7. equity theory
8. self-disclosure
9. need for affiliation
10. reciprocity
11. communal relationship
12. companionate love
13. social exchange theory
14. attachment style
15. excitation transfer
16. triangular theory of love
17. exchange relationship
18. what-is-beautiful-is-good stereotype
19. sexual orientation

Textbook Definitions

a.   A relationship in which the participants expect and desire strict reciprocity in their interactions.

b.   The theory that people are most satisfied with a relationship when the ratio between benefits and contributions is similar for both partners.

c.   The belief that physically attractive individuals also possess desirable personality characteristics.

d.   A quid-pro-quo mutual exchange – for example, liking those who like us.

e.   The tendency to prefer people who are highly selective in their social choices over those who are more readily available.

f.   The process whereby arousal caused by one stimulus is added to arousal from a second stimulus and the combined arousal is attributed to the second stimulus.

g.   The proposition that people are attracted to and form relationships with those who are similar to them in particular characteristics, such as physical attractiveness.

h.   A secure, trusting, stable partnership.

i.   The desire to establish and maintain many rewarding interpersonal relationships.

j.   A feeling of deprivation about existing social relations.

k.   A theory proposing that love has three basic components – intimacy, passion, and commitment – which can be combined to produce eight subtypes.

l.   Revelations about the self that a person makes to other people.

m.   A perspective that views people as motivated to maximize benefits and minimize costs in their relationships with others.

n.   The way a person typically interacts with significant others.

o.   The phenomenon whereby the more often people are exposed to a stimulus, the more positively they evaluate that stimulus.

p.   Romantic love characterized by high arousal, intense attraction, and fear of rejection.

q.   A close relationship between two adults involving at least one of the following: emotional attachment, fulfillment of psychological needs, and interdependence.

r.   A relationship in which the participants expect and desire mutual responsiveness to each other's needs.

s.   A person's preference for members of the same sex (homosexuality), opposite sex (heterosexuality), or both sexes (bisexuality).

ANSWERS FOR KEY TERM EXERCISE

Answers for the key terms exercise are listed below.

1. **q**
2. **e**
3. **p**
4. **j**
5. **g**
6. **o**
7. **b**
8. **l**
9. **i**
10. **d**
11. **r**
12. **h**
13. **m**
14. **n**
15. **f**
16. **k**
17. **a**
18. **c**
19. **s**

PRACTICE QUIZ: TEST YOUR KNOWLEDGE OF THE CHAPTER

Multiple-Choice Questions

1. Muhammad does not like Joe. Howard does not like Joe. Muhammad and Howard like each other. Joe does not like either Muhammad or Howard. This pattern is consistent with

    a.   balance theory.
    b.   internal attributions.
    c.   contrast effects.
    d.   psychological reactance.

2. The kind of attachment in which people report that they desire attachment but are afraid of being hurt is called

    a.   secure.
    b.   avoidant.
    c.   anxious/ambivalent.
    d.   fearful.

3. When people like her, Jenny likes them. When people dislike her, Jenny dislikes them. Jenny's likes and dislikes exemplify

    a.   the matching hypothesis.
    b.   reciprocity.
    c.   resource exchange.
    d.   complementarity.

4. All but one of the following have been suggested as explanations for the bias for beauty. Which is the *exception*?

    a.   The aesthetic appeal of an individual affects others' responses to him or her.
    b.   Men are interested in physical appearance, whereas women are interested in interpersonal warmth.
    c.   People believe in the what-is-beautiful-is-good stereotype.
    d.   Interactions with physically attractive people are likely to be more rewarding because physically attractive people tend to have higher levels of social skills than do physically unattractive people.

5. Exchange relationships are characterized by

    a.   deep affection and commitment.
    b.   a high degree of self-disclosure.
    c.   strict payment and repayment of benefits by one partner to the other.
    d.   insecurity due to the nature of the interaction.

6. When Gene meets an attractive member of the other sex, his only thoughts concern how he can have a good time without making a commitment. Gene's approach illustrates

    a.   companionate love.
    b.   social exchange theory.
    c.   self-disclosure reciprocity.
    d.   jealousy.

7. Jamal and Veronica have been married for ten years. While their marriage was exciting and wild in its early days, they have since settled into a routine of care, nurturance, and friendship with one another. The changes in Jamal and Veronica's relationship illustrate the difference between

    a. passionate and companionate love.
    b. secure and insecure attachments.
    c. self-disclosure and social penetration.
    d. exchange and communal relationships.

8. Luis and Shelia consoled each other when their parents passed away, supported each other's careers, and provided comfort for each other in times of loneliness. Research on _____ shows that these rewarding interactions are strongly associated with the couple's satisfaction and commitment.

    a. self-disclosure reciprocity
    b. the triangular theory of love
    c. the social exchange framework
    d. the two-factor theory of emotion

9. Ruth thinks that people find her physically unattractive. Tina thinks that people find her physically attractive. Both Ruth and Tina received very favorable evaluations of their work on some task. How would the two women feel about the feedback when they find out that the evaluator saw their photos?

    a. Both will feel good about the favorable evaluation.
    b. Both will feel undeserving of the favorable evaluation.
    c. Ruth will feel better about the favorable evaluation than Tina.
    d. Tina will feel better about the favorable evaluation than Ruth.

10. Bobby and Joan have been going out for some time. They began dating very casually, but then Bobby revealed that he was having trouble with his roommates and Joan revealed that she was still broken up by her father's death two years ago. As they shared these experiences, Bobby and Joan became closer. Their actions illustrate

    a. self-disclosure reciprocity.
    b. the triangular theory of love.
    c. social rewards in their relationship.
    d. the two-factor theory of emotion.

11. Graciella tends to play "hard to get" and appears not to like most people. Social psychological research suggests that

    a. people will be attracted to Graciella because she shows no interest in them.
    b. Graciella will be seen as *more* attractive by people who think that she is committed to someone else.
    c. Graciella will be viewed as *more* attractive if she seems moderately selective rather than extremely selective in her social choices.
    d. Graciella will be viewed as *less* attractive if others think that her reasons for playing hard-to-get are external.

12. David is a heterosexual 45-year-old man who is very outgoing. Research suggests that he is most likely to be attracted to a

    a. woman whose needs are opposite his; for example, if David needs to control others, he should be most attracted to someone who likes to be controlled.
    b. shy woman.
    c. financially successful 45-year-old woman.
    d. woman who he thinks has the same attitudes as he does.

13. Brenda and Chris have been having difficulty in their relationship. Brenda thinks that Chris puts less than his share of time into the relationship and doesn't try to please her. Chris gets quiet and sulks when Brenda makes these accusations. Brenda and Chris's relationship seems to display

   a.   negative reciprocity.
   b.   the demand/withdraw interaction pattern.
   c.   lack of social support.
   d.   anxious/ambivalent attachment.

14. In order to manage conflict in a relationship, each partner should try to

   a.   engage in negative affect reciprocity.
   b.   recognize the other's behavioral problems as inherent and permanent personality traits.
   c.   understand the other partner's point of view.
   d.   make his or her demands for the relationship known to the other partner.

15. Intimacy, passion, and commitment are three components of

   a.   John Alan Lee's theory of three primary love styles.
   b.   companionate love.
   c.   the triangular theory of love.
   d.   fatuous love.

16. Jim often forgets to finish the chores he has agreed to do around the house and sometimes is insensitive toward Molly. Molly usually brushes off such instances, saying that it isn't Jim's fault he's often too stressed out. Such attributions for Jim's behavior are

   a.   distress-maintaining attributions.
   b.   characteristic of happy couples.
   c.   likely to create communication difficulties.
   d.   likely to cause trouble for Molly but not for Jim.

17. People who have an interdependent self-concept – that is, those who include others in their definition of themselves – are likely to

   a.   make self-serving attributions.
   b.   have enduring relationships.
   c.   have low self-esteem.
   d.   have high self-esteem.

18. Stanley, a fourth-grader, is anxious because he's about to receive his first flu vaccine from the school nurse. Under what circumstance, would Stanley *most* prefer to wait in the company of other children to waiting alone?

   a.   If he expected to embarrass himself by crying when given the shot
   b.   If the other children were not getting vaccinated
   c.   If the other children were about to receive the shot, as well
   d.   If the other children already had the shot

19. José and Lucinda have a happy marriage. They spend a lot of time together and see themselves as being interdependent. If José were to pass away, Lucinda is likely to

   a.   be able to handle it well.
   b.   be more broken up than the typical spouse.
   c.   never recover.
   d.   form other relationships quickly.

20. In this country, which of the following people is likely to be the loneliest?
    a. A ten-year-old child
    b. A twenty-two-year-old young adult
    c. A forty-five year-old adult
    d. A seventy-year-old grandparent

21. In a recent study of Internet ratings of professors' teaching ability, high ratings were associated with being
    a. "hot."
    b. "cool."
    c. smart.
    d. funny.

22. When it comes to self-reports on the subject of sex, one gender difference that emerges is that men are
    a. less likely than women to think about sex every day.
    b. less likely than women to fantasize about sex with multiple partners.
    c. more likely than women to enjoy sex only if they are emotionally involved.
    d. more likely than women to desire sexual variety.

Essay Questions

23. Compare and contrast companionate and passionate love.

24. Describe two communication patterns that may lead to conflict in relationships.

25. Discuss the positive and negative consequences of having an interdependent relationship.

26. Discuss how people's attachment styles influence their physiological reactions to relationship conflict.

ANSWERS TO THE PRACTICE QUIZ

Multiple-Choice Questions: Correct Answers and Explanations

1.   a.   **balance theory.** Fritz Heider (1958) theorized that people desire balance, or consistency, in their social relationships. A balanced pattern of attraction requires that we like someone whose relationships with others parallel our own. Usually, we like those who are friends of our friends and enemies of our enemies. Consistent with this, Muhammad and Howard see each other as enemies of their enemy, Joe, and therefore like each other. Joe's dislike of the other two men reciprocates their dislike of him, and so this pattern, too, is balanced. Internal attributions locate the cause of a condition or event in the person rather than in external circumstances, but attributions are not described in this question. Contrast effects concern the tendency to perceive stimuli that differ from expectations or other stimuli as even more different than they really are, but, again, there is no evidence of this phenomenon in this question. Psychological reactance refers to the theory that people react against threats to specific behavioral freedoms by perceiving a threatened freedom as more attractive and trying to re-establish it; in this question, however, no freedom was threatened.

2.   c.   **anxious/ambivalent.** Anxious/ambivalent attachments are characterized by a strong desire for a relationship, together with a fear that the relationship will not work out properly. Secure attachments are characterized by warmth and affection, together with a sense of independence and self-worth. And avoidant attachments are characterized by a reluctance to develop relationships. Although people may be fearful in a relationship, this trait is not usually called an attachment style.

3.   b.   **reciprocity.** Reciprocity is a quid-pro-quo mutual exchange between what we give and what we receive – for example, liking those who like us. Consistent with this idea, Jenny likes those who like her and dislikes those who dislike her. The matching hypothesis is the idea that people tend to become romantically involved with people who are their equal in physical attractiveness. Resource exchange involves the resources that people possess, but this question does not give any information about the resources Jenny possesses or is seeking. Complementarity refers to a fit between opposites; it is consistent with the idea that "opposites attract." However, this question gives no indication that Jenny is attracted to people who have needs or personality traits opposite, or complementary, to hers.

4.   b.   **Men are interested in physical appearance, whereas women are interested in interpersonal warmth.** Both men and women are attracted to and react more favorably toward people who are physically attractive. Therefore, the difference between men and women alleged in this question could not explain the general bias for beauty. The other three alternatives have been offered as explanations for this bias. (A fourth explanation is that people desire to increase their own perceived attractiveness through association with attractive others.)

5.   c.   **strict payment and repayment of benefits by one partner to the other.** Exchange relationships are defined by the strict equity in exchanges between partners. They are usually casual or business-type relationships and, as such, they are not characterized by deep affection and commitment or a high degree of self-disclosure. These relationships can be quite stable and are not typically characterized by insecurity.

6.　b.　**social exchange theory.** Social exchange theory suggests that people try to maximize their rewards and minimize their costs in a relationship. Therefore, when Gene tries to maximize his fun while minimizing his commitment, his approach illustrates social exchange theory. Companionate love emphasizes a concern for the other person that has developed into a deep friendship, so this characteristic does not fit Gene. Likewise, self-disclosure reciprocity and jealousy do not emphasize maximizing rewards and minimizing costs in a relationship.

7.　a.　**passionate and companionate love.** Passionate love often characterizes the early days of a relationship and contains a strong emotional component, much like the exciting and wild days of Jamal and Veronica. Companionate love is usually seen later in a relationship and is characterized by a deep loving friendship, much like the routine of care, nurturance, and friendship in Jamal and Veronica's relationship. There is no evidence that Jamal and Veronica have insecure attachments; and while their strong relationship might indicate a secure attachment, there is no illustration of the difference between these kinds of attachments. Likewise, Jamal and Veronica's description can tell us little about self-disclosure and social penetration or about exchange and communal relationships.

8.　c.　**the social exchange framework.** Luis and Shelia have given each other comfort, support, and companionship – clear rewards that they receive from their relationship. Rewards, along with costs and comparison level, are one of the building blocks of social exchange. It seems likely that Luis and Shelia have self-disclosed to each other, but this is not stated in the question. Similarly, there is no evidence of the triangular theory of love or the two-factor theory of emotion.

9.　c.　**Ruth will feel better about the favorable evaluation than Tina.** People, like Tina, who think that they are judged as physically attractive, often discount the praise they receive for their work because they suspect that the evaluation they received was influenced by their physical appearance. People, like Ruth, who think of themselves as physically unattractive, in contrast, often feel better about the quality of their work after getting a favorable evaluation from someone who they think was aware, rather than unaware, of their physical appearance. Therefore, Ruth will feel better about the positive evaluation than will Tina.

10.　a.　**self-disclosure reciprocity.** When Bobby revealed something important about himself (that he was having fights with his roommates), Joan responded by revealing something even more personal about herself (her feelings about the loss of her father). This back-and-forth exchange of personal, meaningful information, which gradually gets more personal and more meaningful, is self-disclosure reciprocity. The triangular theory of love and the two-factor theory of emotion do not entail information exchange in a relationship. One of the social rewards in a relationship is having someone who listens, but this concept also does not explain the exchange of information between Bobby and Joan.

11.　c.　**Graciella will be viewed as more attractive if she seems moderately selective rather than extremely selective in her social choices.** As the text indicates, the hard-to-get effect – the tendency to prefer people who are highly selective in their social choices over those who are more readily available – has been very hard to substantiate in social psychological research. People are especially unlikely to be attracted to someone who plays hard to get if the person has shown no interest in them or if the person is fully committed to someone else. In contrast, someone who appears to be moderately selective tends to be viewed as more attractive than someone who appears to be extremely selective. On the other hand, if the person playing "hard to get" appears to have an external reason for doing so, such as religion or parental constraint, he or she will be viewed as more, not less, attractive because of psychological reactance.

12. d.   **woman who he thinks has the same attitudes as he does.** Perceived (though not necessarily actual) similarity in attitudes is associated with attraction. Because complementarity, which is a fit between opposites, does not tend to affect attraction, there is no reason to assume that David will like someone whose needs or personality are opposite his, such as a shy woman. Cross-cultural research has found that men prefer mates who are younger than they are, and that they rate the financial status or potential of a mate as less important than women do. Thus, there is little reason to assume that David will be especially attracted to a woman who is 45 years old and is financially successful.

13. b.   **the demand/withdraw interaction pattern.** Brenda seems to be making demands in this relationship that Chris feels he cannot meet. In turn, Chris seems to be withdrawing. This demand/withdraw pattern of interaction has been associated with conflict in relationships. There is no evidence of negative reciprocity, or the escalation of the perception of negative affect in the partner, in Brenda and Chris's relationship. Likewise, we might guess that Chris and Brenda offer each other little social support or have an anxious/ambivalent attachment, but there is no clear evidence for either of these conclusions in the question.

14. c.   **understand the other partner's point of view.** When partners make an effort to understand each other's point of view, conflict in a relationship can be diminished. Engaging in negative affect reciprocity, or a tit-for-tat exchange of negative feelings, can only increase conflict. Attributing the other's behavioral problems to inherent, permanent personality traits will maintain the distress in the relationship. Making demands known to the partner might lead to the demand/withdraw pattern of behavior, which characterizes unhappy relationships.

15. c.   **the triangular theory of love.** The three components of love according to Sternberg's triangular theory of love are intimacy, passion, and commitment. John Alan Lee's proposed three primary love styles are erotic, game-playing, and friendship. In Sternberg's theory, companionate love does not include passion and fatuous love does not include intimacy.

16. b.   **characteristic of happy couples.** Happy couples usually make relationship-enhancing attributions for each other's actions. That's what Molly is doing. She is attributing Jim's problem behaviors to factors that are situational, temporary, and limited in scope. In this way, she is minimizing the bad and maximizing what's good about Jim, something couples in successful relationships routinely do.

17. b.   **have enduring relationships.** People who are interdependent and include others in their definition of themselves have particularly strong attachments to others. These attachments make it more likely that these people will have enduring relationships. There is no evidence that people who include others in their definition of themselves have higher or lower self-esteem, or are more likely to engage in self-serving biases.

18. d.   **If the other children already had the shot.** Stress increases people's desire to affiliate with others. This is particularly true when the stress is not linked to embarrassment. People facing an imminent threat seek the company of others in order to gain information about the threat. Consequently, research has shown that people prefer the company of those who had already faced the threat. So, although Stanley would probably opt to be with either those expecting the shot or those who have already received it, as opposed to those who will not be receiving the shot at all, he would much prefer the latter because they could ease his anxiety by telling him what to expect.

19. b. **be more broken up than the typical spouse.** Interdependent relationships are more likely to endure, but when such relationships end, either in death or in a breakup, the partners are more likely to have difficulty coping with the loss. These people do seem to recover eventually, even though they are unlikely to form other relationships quickly.

20. b **A twenty-two-year-old young adult.** The loneliest people in our society are adolescents and young adults, ages eighteen to thirty years old.

21. a. **being "hot."** An analysis of ratings of student evaluations posted on www.ratemyprofessor.com, a popular web site, reveals that both male and female professors who were rated highly for their teaching were also more likely to be described as "hot" (Riniolo et al., 2006).

22. d. **more likely than women to desire sexual variety.** In a large-scale study of 16,000 respondents from 52 countries, David Schmitt (2003) found that most men desire more sexual partners and more sexual variety than most women do. In another survey, Longer et al., (2004) found that men are more likely than women to think about sex every day. And Oliver and Hyde (1993) found that men are more likely to fantasize about sex with multiple partners and to enjoy casual sex without emotional commitment.

Answers to Essay Questions: Sample Essays

23. Passionate love is more typical of the early stages of a relationship. It is characterized by high states of arousal and strong emotions. Being passionately loved is joyous; being rejected is heartbreaking. Companionate love, on the other hand, is more typical of the later stages of a relationship. It is comfortable and warm, characterized by stability, security, trust, and deep friendship. Most people admire both kinds of love. They enjoy the intense emotion of passionate love and the stable trust of companionate love.

24. One communication pattern that may lead to conflict is negative affect reciprocity. In this pattern, one partner notices a small negative reaction in the other partner and follows it with a negative reaction of his or her own. This back-and-forth exchange continues and escalates. After a while, expressions of positive affect are ignored, whereas expressions of negative affect become the focus of the relationship. A second communication pattern that can lead to conflict is the demand/withdraw interaction pattern. In this interaction pattern, one partner initiates and demands discussion, while the other partner seeks to avoid discussion. The demanding partner nags and criticizes; the withdrawing partner remains silent and defensive. This pattern can lead to a regular pattern of conflict with little or no resolution.

25. When two people are involved in an interdependent relationship, such that they include their partner in their definition of themselves, their commitment is likely to be stronger and more enduring. They are more likely to spend time together, to engage in shared activities, and to influence each other. However, when such a relationship ends, either in a breakup or at death, they tend to have more difficulty coping with the loss of the relationship. Perhaps it is because these individuals have lost a more significant part of themselves – relative to others not involved in an interdependent relationship – that they have greater difficulty dealing with this outcome.

26.   There is reason to believe that people's attachment styles influence their physiological reactions to relationship conflict. In one study, Powers (2006) brought 124 college-aged dating couples into the laboratory to discuss a heated conflict they'd been having. Before and after this "conflict negotiation task," the researchers took saliva samples from all participants to measure levels of cortisol, a stress hormone. The results showed that boyfriends and girlfriends who were insecurely attached exhibited more physiological stress in response to the conflict task than did those who were securely attached.

CHAPTER 10

Helping Others

OUTLINE

LEARNING OBJECTIVES: GUIDELINES FOR STUDY

You should be able to do each of the following by the conclusion of Chapter 10.

1.   Discuss how evolutionary theory accounts for helping behavior. Explain kin selection, reciprocal altruism, and indirect reciprocity. Discuss evidence that morality and empathy evolved due to the social nature of primates, in general, and are not exclusively human constructs. (*pp. 391-397*)

2.   Discuss the arousal: cost-reward model of helping. Identify some of the rewards of helping. Discuss how the negative-relief model accounts for helping behavior. Identify some of the costs of helping and discuss how "Good Samaritan" laws both lower the costs of helping and increase the costs of not helping. (*pp. 397-399*)

3. Compare and contrast egoistic and altruistic motives for helping. Explain the empathy-altruism hypothesis and identify why a distinction between these two types of motives is important. (*pp. 399-404*)

4. Explain the bystander effect. Identify and explain the five steps in the helping process, discussing obstacles to each step. Consider how each of these obstacles contributes to the bystander effect. (*pp. 404-412*)

3. Describe the influence of other situational factors on helping behavior, such as time pressure, location, culture, mood, role models, and social norms. (*pp. 412-421*)

4. Explain how individual differences such as personality, moral reasoning, and family background may affect a person's likelihood of helping others. (*pp. 421-423*)

5. Describe how characteristics of people in need (e.g., attractiveness, perceived responsibility, gender) influence the likelihood that others will help them. Consider the relationship between the characteristics of the help giver and receiver (i.e., similarity, ingroup status, and closeness). (*pp. 423-426*)

6. Discuss the relationship between gender and helping behavior. (*pp. 426-427*)

8. Identify the factors that influence people's different reactions to receiving help. Discuss how cultural factors impact on who will receive help. (*pp. 427-429*)

MAJOR CONCEPTS: THE BIG PICTURE

Below are five basic issues or principles that organize Chapter 10. You should know these issues and principles well.

1. There are several motivational factors that affect why people help. Evolutionary factors may lead us to help those who are close relatives, those with whom we have reciprocal relationships, and those who are part of our group. Egoistic factors might also lead to helping because helping makes most people feel good. On the other hand, it seems that at times we help for altruistic motives. This is especially true when we have empathy for those we help, or when we do so because it seems the "right thing to do.". The debate between whether we help for altruistic or egoistic motives continues and is not resolved at the present time. Distinguishing among the motivations to help is important because different motives are likely to affect behavioral and emotional responses to helping, attribution for helping, and the role of rewards in helping.

2. The situation can also influence helping. For instance, research shows that the presence of others actually inhibits helping by making it harder to recognize the need for help, causing situations to be more ambiguous, and diffusing individual responsibility for helping. Other situations that inhibit helping include time pressure, living in a city, and belonging to a "non-simpatico" culture. Situations can also influence helping by affecting our emotions. Positive moods, and, in some situations, negative moods can all lead to helping. Finally, role models and social norms can be powerful situational factors that lead individuals to help others.

3. Despite the strong situational influences on helping, some people are simply more likely to help than others. Indeed, there is some evidence that helping may have a genetic component. In addition, other personality characteristics, such as empathy and moral reasoning, appear to work together in promoting helping.

4.   Some people are more likely to receive help than others. Attractive individuals, as well as those seen as innocent victims, are more likely to receive help. People are also more likely to help those who are similar to themselves. Men are more likely to help in situations that are somewhat dangerous, whereas women are more likely to provide long-term social support to friends and relatives.

5.   People exhibit varied reactions to receiving help. Sometimes they see help as supportive; at other times they see it as threatening. For instance, help received from a similar other on an important task is often seen as threatening rather than supportive. There are gender differences in seeking help, with men being more reluctant to seek others' help.

KEY TERM EXERCISE: THE CONCEPTS YOU SHOULD KNOW

Following are all of the key terms that appear in **boldface** in Chapter 10. To help you better understand these concepts, rather than just memorize them, write a definition for each term in your own words. After doing so, look at the next section where you'll find a list of definitions from the textbook for each of the key terms presented in random order. For each of your definitions, find the corresponding textbook definition. Note how your definitions compare with those from the textbook.

Key Terms

1.   prosocial behaviors

2.   audience inhibition

3.   norm of social responsibility

4.   threat-to-self-esteem model

5.   altruistic

6.   empathy-altruism hypothesis

7.   social norm

8.   good mood effect

9.   bystander effect

10. negative state relief model

11. pluralistic ignorance

12. diffusion of responsibility

13. kin selection

14. arousal: cost-reward model

15. egoistic

16. empathy

Textbook Definitions

a.   The proposition that people react to emergency situations by acting in the most cost-effective way to reduce the arousal of shock and alarm.

b.   The proposition that people help others in order to counteract their own feelings of sadness.

c.   The theory that reactions to receiving assistance depend on whether help is perceived as supportive or threatening.

d.   The effect whereby the presence of others inhibits helping.

e.   Actions intended to benefit others

f.   The belief that others will or should take the responsibility for providing assistance to a person in need.

g.   Motivated by the desire to increase another's welfare.

h.   A moral standard emphasizing that people should help those who need assistance.

i.   The proposition that empathic concern for a person in need produces an altruistic motive for helping.

j.   Reluctance to help for fear of making a bad impression on observers.

k.   A general rule of conduct reflecting standards of social approval and disapproval.

l.   Motivated by the desire to increase one's own welfare.

m.   Understanding or vicariously experiencing another individual's perspective and feeling sympathy and compassion for that individual.

n.   The effect whereby a good mood increases helping behavior.

o.   The state in which people mistakenly believe that their own thoughts and feelings are different from those of others, even though everyone's behavior is the same.

p.   Preferential helping of genetic relatives so that genes held in common survive.

ANSWERS FOR KEY TERM EXERCISE

Answers for the key terms exercise are listed below.

1. **e**
2. **j**
3. **h**
4. **c**
5. **g**
6. **i**
7. **k**
8. **n**
9. **d**
10. **b**
11. **o**
12. **f**
13. **p**
14. **a**
15. **l**
16. **m**

PRACTICE QUIZ: TEST YOUR KNOWLEDGE OF THE CHAPTER

Multiple-Choice Questions

1. Reciprocal helping and kin selection are two main kinds of helping, according to the
    a. arousal: cost-reward model.
    b. empathy-altruism hypothesis.
    c. negative state relief model.
    d. evolutionary perspective.

2. Beth wants to borrow notes for the class she skipped on Friday. If she tells a classmate that she needs the notes because she skipped class rather than offering a good excuse (e.g., she was home sick), the classmate will probably be
    a. less likely to help because Beth doesn't deserve help.
    b. more likely to help because Beth was honest.
    c. more likely to help because she'll admire Beth for doing as she pleases.
    d. no more or less likely to help.

3. Norm is in a bad mood because he accidentally broke his roommate's stereo. He sees an elderly woman who needs help crossing the street. Because Norm is in a bad mood, he is
    a. less likely to help.
    b. more likely to help.
    c. no more or less likely to help.
    d. more likely to help but only if he is very self-focused.

4. Bob has to drive his beat-up old car across the country. He knows that the car is likely to break down and that he may need help. According to research on bystander intervention, Bob would be best advised to
    a. take the rural route and avoid cities.
    b. make sure others know it was his decision to drive the car.
    c. drive through as many cities as possible.
    d. "dress down" so that if he does need help, others won't find him intimidating.

5. Michelle feels sorry for homeless people. To ease their suffering, she organizes a campaign to find clothing, food, and shelter for them. Michelle's actions illustrate
    a. reciprocity norms.
    b. good mood effects.
    c. empathic concern.
    d. kin selection.

6. When people are in a good mood, they are
    a. less likely to help.
    b. more likely to help.
    c. no more or less likely to help.
    d. more likely to help but less likely to notice that others need help.

7. David and Lisa are both good friends of Ron, who has been in an accident. According to research concerning gender differences in helping, which of the two is more likely to stop by and help Ron with his daily chores when he comes home from the hospital?

    a. David is more likely to do so.
    b. Lisa is more likely to do so.
    c. David and Lisa are equally likely to stop by.
    d. It depends on the severity of Ron's accident.

8. Bobby helps his classmates with their homework because he wants them to like him. Bobby's behavior is

    a. cost-free.
    b. heroic.
    c. altruistic.
    d. egoistic.

9. Alexandra, who is an excellent diver and swimmer, is one of many people walking on a bridge one sunny day when she witnesses a person slip and fall in the water. Alexandra becomes very distressed and thinks, "If I jump in to save the guy, my hair will be ruined and so will my clothes. On the other hand, I will feel so good knowing that I helped save a person's life and everyone will call me a hero." Consequently, she jumps in and saves the man. Alexandra's bystander calculus is associated with which theory?

    a. Arousal: cost-reward model
    b. Bystander effect theory
    c. Empathy-altruism hypothesis
    d. Threat-to-self-esteem model

10. Collectivist and individualist participants were asked to pick which of 16 fictitious patients should receive a donated organ. The decision was to be based on two factors: how responsible the patients were for their illness and how much the patients contributed to society. What were the results of that study?

    a. Only individualist participants were more likely to favor those who contributed to society over those who didn't.
    b. Only collectivist participants were more likely to favor those who were not responsible for their illness over those who were.
    c. The individualist participants were more affected by the issue of personal responsibility, whereas the collectivist participants were more affected by the issue of contribution to society.
    d. Both issues affected individualist and collectivist participants to the same degree.

11. Although tennis is not important to Randy, he would still like to play better. His brother spends three weekends coaching Randy. Randy is likely to interpret his brother's actions as a form of

    a. empathic concern.
    b. self-threatening help.
    c. supportive help.
    d. negative state relief.

12. Perspective taking is the major cognitive component of

    a. docility.
    b. empathy.
    c. pluralistic ignorance.
    d. audience inhibition.

13. Noticing incidents, interpreting situations, and taking responsibility for action are three steps specified by the

    a.   just-world belief.
    b.   self-evaluation maintenance model.
    c.   empathy-altruism hypothesis.
    d.   bystander intervention model.

14. A crowd of people has gathered at a bar. Suddenly smoke fills the whole room. The people are most likely to interpret the situation as an emergency if

    a.   the crowd is very large.
    b.   they are enjoying themselves.
    c.   they know each other.
    d.   they are mingling rather than staying in one place.

15. When a large group of people fails to help an innocent victim of a crime, the most likely cause is

    a.   callousness of the people in the group.
    b.   the tendency to blame the victim of the crime.
    c.   diffusion of responsibility for helping.
    d.   lack of empathy for the victim.

16. Isaac and Tina are making supper and run out of flour. Who is most likely to ask the neighbor for help?

    a.   Isaac is most likely to do so.
    b.   Tina is most likely to do so.
    c.   Isaac and Tina are equally likely to ask for help.
    d.   Whether Isaac or Tina asks for help depends on the gender of their neighbor.

17. Tasha has received threatening help in the past. How does this experience affect her desire to seek help?

    a.   She is more likely to seek help later.
    b.   She is less likely to seek help later.
    c.   She is no more or less likely to seek help later.
    d.   Whether she seeks help depends on her perceived control of the situation.

18. Molly thinks she's a first-rate parent. A friend points out that Molly should teach her children self-control by setting standards for them. Molly is likely to see this advice as

    a.   empathic concern.
    b.   self-threatening help.
    c.   supportive help.
    d.   negative state relief.

19. The social norm that motivates us out of a sense of duty and obligation to help those who are dependent on us is the norm of

    a.   reciprocity.
    b.   equity.
    c.   social responsibility.
    d.   justice.

20. Feeling a sense of connection to other people should

    a.   increase helping.
    b.   decrease helping.
    c.   neither increase nor decrease helping.
    d.   sometimes increase helping and sometimes decrease helping.

21. I help you and somebody else helps me is an example of
    a.   indirect reciprocity.
    b.   altruistic behavior.
    c.   bystander effect.
    d.   cost-reward model.

22. In the "Good Samaritan" study, the deciding factor as to whether or not the students would help a needy victim was
    a.   mood.
    b.   the topic of the students' upcoming talk.
    c.   time pressure.
    d.   location.

23. Empathic concern is to other-directed feelings as _____ is to self-directed feelings.
    a.   sympathy
    b.   personal distress
    c.   compassion
    d.   tenderness

Essay Questions

24. Describe how a person's mood can affect the likelihood that he or she will help others. Analyze the effect of both positive and negative moods.

25. Discuss three ways in which the presence of others can affect the likelihood that people will help someone in need.

26. Discuss gender differences in giving and receiving help.

27. Discuss charitable giving and volunteerism in the United States in terms of individualism.

ANSWERS TO THE PRACTICE QUIZ

Multiple-Choice Questions: Correct Answers and Explanations

1.   d.   **evolutionary perspective.** According to the evolutionary perspective, people help others because doing so enhances the possibility that they will be able to pass on their genes. Kin selection is the helping of relatives, and, since relatives share genes, helping a relative increases the chance that one's genes will be passed on. Reciprocal helping is helping someone who will help you in the future and thus can also increase the chances of passing on one's genes. The arousal: cost-reward model, the empathy-altruism hypothesis, and the negative state relief model do not try to explain kin selection or reciprocal helping.

2.   a.   **less likely to help because Beth doesn't deserve help.** Research shows that when people are blamed or judged to be responsible for their bad outcomes others are less likely to help them. If the classmate assumes Beth is to blame for skipping class, or that she stayed home because she wanted to, as appears to be the case, then the classmate will probably be less likely to help her.

3.   b.   **more likely to help.** Research shows that when adults are in a bad mood they are more likely to help others, perhaps as a way to improve their mood. However, if people in a bad mood are very self-focused, they are not likely to help.

4.   a.   **take the rural route and avoid cities.** Research shows that people are more likely to help in rural areas than in cities, so Bob should take the rural routes because he is more likely to receive help there. If people knew it was his decision to drive this particular car, they might be less likely to help because they might infer that the breakdown was his responsibility. Finally, there is no clear evidence that "dressing down" will increase Bob's chances of being helped.

5.   c.   **empathic concern.** Empathic concern involves other-oriented feelings, which Michelle demonstrates. Research shows that such feelings often lead to helping. It is unlikely that Michelle's actions result from a reciprocity norm, as it seems unlikely that she was previously helped by these homeless people. It is also unlikely that her actions are the result of good mood effects, because her empathic concern for the homeless is really more likely to put her in a bad mood. Finally, it is unlikely that her actions result from kin selection, as the homeless people she is trying to help do not appear to be her relatives.

6.   b.   **more likely to help.** Research shows that when people are in a good mood they are more likely to help others, perhaps as a way to maintain their good mood. There is no documentation regarding the effect of mood on noticing that others need help.

7.   b.   **Lisa is more likely to do so.** Research shows that women are more likely than men to provide supportive and caring help, especially to friends and family members. The seriousness of the accident is unlikely to affect the gender difference in helping, although when helping could be dangerous or embarrassing, men are more likely to help than women.

8.   d.   **egoistic.** Bobby seems to be helping because of what he can get out of doing so. This kind of helping is called egoistic helping. There is no indication that the helping is cost-free; he does have to expend some time and energy helping his classmates. And his helping surely isn't altruistic or heroic if he is helping solely for his own sake.

9.   a.   **Arousal: cost-reward model.** According to arousal: cost-reward model, both emotional and cognitive factors determine whether bystanders to an emergency will intervene. Emotionally, bystanders experience the shock and alarm of personal distress; this unpleasant state of arousal motivates them to do something to reduce it. What they do, however, depends on the "bystander calculus," their computation of the costs and rewards associated with helping. When potential rewards (to self and victim) outweigh potential costs (to self and victim), bystanders will help. The bystander effect states that the presence of others inhibits helping. Alexandra is not inhibited from jumping in and saving the man by the fact that there others around. According to the empathy-altruism hypothesis, taking the perspective of a person in need leads to empathic feelings, which in turn lead to altruistic action. There is no evidence that Alexandra is empathizing with the man in the water. As for the threat-to-self-esteem model, that has to do with the reactions of those receiving help, not with the helpers.

10.   c.   **The individualist participants were more affected by the issue of personal responsibility, whereas the collectivist participants were more affected by the issue of contribution to society.** Mullen and Skitka (2009) found that although both groups of participants were less likely to award organs to those who were responsible for their illness or those who did not contribute to society, collectivist participants from the Ukraine placed more weight on the patients' contributions to society when making their decisions, whereas the American participants considered the issue of personal responsibility to be more important when making their decisions.

11.   c.   **supportive help.** Because tennis is not important to Randy, it is unlikely that his brother's help will be perceived as self-threatening. Self-threatening help occurs when the help challenges an important area of one's self-concept. Empathic concern and negative state relief help have not been documented as ways in which people perceive help that they are receiving; therefore, it is difficult to say whether Randy would interpret his brother's help as empathic concern or negative state relief help.

12.   b.   **empathy.** When people feel empathy, they take the other person's perspective. Docility is a sense of withdrawal and thus has little to do with perspective taking. Pluralistic ignorance is the mistaken belief that one's thoughts and feelings are different from others', and audience inhibition is the reluctance to help stemming from fear of making a bad impression. Both of these concepts are unrelated to perspective taking.

13.   d.   **bystander intervention model.** The bystander intervention model proposes that people help when they notice an incident, interpret the situation as one in which help is needed, and take responsibility for helping. Just-world beliefs do not involve noticing incidents or interpreting situations, and the self-evaluation maintenance model and empathy-altruism hypothesis do not involve noticing incidents.

14.   c.   **they know each other.** The people are most likely to interpret the situation as an emergency if they know each other because they will have an easier time reading each other's reactions; these reactions will be less ambiguous. A large crowd would tend to be more distracting, making it harder for people to recognize the situation as an emergency. And there is no clear evidence that people who are mingling or enjoying themselves would have an easier or harder time recognizing an emergency.

15. c. **diffusion of responsibility for helping.** The bystander intervention model was developed to help explain why large groups of people do not help in such instances. One of the important factors in this model is diffusion of responsibility, which describes the tendency for groups of people to be less likely to help than individuals would be. In a group, people tend to believe that other people will help and thus everyone is less likely to help. There is no clear evidence that groups who do not help are especially callous, are especially likely to blame the victim of a crime, or lack empathy for the victim.

16. b. **Tina is most likely to do so.** Research has shown that women are more likely than men to ask for help, especially in cases of simple requests. There is no clear evidence that the gender of the helper affects this basic finding.

17. d. **Whether she seeks help depends on her perceived control of the situation.** Research shows that people who receive threatening help will seek help only if they think they have little control of the situation. Therefore, they are likely to seek help in some situations but not in others.

18. b. **self-threatening help.** Self-threatening help is help that challenges an important aspect of one's self-concept. For Molly, being a good parent seems to be an important part of her self-concept, and her friend's advice seems to be challenging her belief that she is a first-rate parent; so the help her friend is giving is likely to be perceived as self-threatening. For the same reason, it is unlikely that Molly will see the help as supportive. In addition, there is no evidence that the help is based on empathic concern or negative state relief.

19. c. **social responsibility.** The norm of social responsibility is a moral standard emphasizing that we should help those in need, thus motivating us to help out of a sense of duty or obligation. The norm of reciprocity is the sense that we should help others who have helped us, and the norm of equity prescribes that those who have the most should help those who have the least. These two norms have less to do with helping people out of a sense of duty because they are dependent. Finally all of these norms describe different notions of justice, but there is no specific norm of justice.

20. a. **increase helping.** Feelings of interdependence and connection with other people usually lead to greater helping of those people. At present, there is no indication that feelings of connection to other people lead to decreased helping.

21. a. **indirect reciprocity.** Indirect reciprocity can be described as: "I help you and somebody else helps me." This more complex system of altruism may play a role in group selection. The idea behind group selection is that groups with altruistic members are more likely to thrive and avoid extinction than groups with only selfish individuals. Cooperation and helpfulness among members of a social group appears to be an evolved tendency, especially when the group faces external threats.

22. c. **time pressure.** In Darley and Batson's (1973) study, seminary students were asked to prepare a talk about one of two topics: the parable of the Good Samaritan or the favorite jobs of seminary students. They were then instructed to walk over to another building. At this point, they were also either told that they were ahead of schedule, right on time, or late. On their way to the building where they were to present their talk, the students passed a confederate who was slumped in a doorway, groaning and coughing and obviously in need of help. Those who were told they were early were much more likely to stop and offer help than those who were told they were on time or late. The topic of the talk had little effect. Location and mood were not variables in this study.

23.   b.   **personal distress**. Empathic concern is a key emotional component of empathy, which involves other-oriented feelings such as compassion, tenderness, and sympathy. In contrast, personal distress involves self-oriented reactions to a person in need, such as feeling alarmed, troubled, or upset.

Answers to Essay Questions: Sample Essays

24.   Both a good mood and a bad mood can increase the likelihood that people will help others. When people are in a good mood, positive thoughts are primed, thus leading to helping behavior. Alternatively, people may help others when they are in a good mood because they want to stay in a good mood. Adults in a bad mood are also more likely to help others, partly in order to dispel their bad mood. Children are less likely to help when they are in a bad mood; only at a later developmental stage will helping others lead to a more positive mood. However, negative moods don't always lead to more helping among adults. Negative moods are less likely to promote helping if one blames an individual for his or her bad mood. Also, negative moods are less likely to increase helping if they cause one to become very self-focused.

25.   When a group of people that do not know each other are faced with an emergency, each individual in the group is less likely to help than if they faced the emergency alone. The presence of others can lead to a decrease in helping in three ways. First, when other people are around, everyone is likely to be distracted and thus less likely to notice the emergency. Second, when other people are around, the ambiguous actions of others are often taken as cues that the situation may not be an emergency. Each person may believe that he or she is the only one who thinks it is an emergency, even though everyone thinks it is an emergency – a state called pluralistic ignorance. This state can make it difficult for people to interpret the situation as an emergency. Third, when other people are around, individuals are less likely to take responsibility for helping in an emergency – a phenomenon called diffusion of responsibility. In this situation, everyone seems to say, "Someone else will do it." However, despite the fact that crowds inhibit individuals from helping, the individual in need is more likely to receive help from a large group of witnesses than from a lone witness, simply because as the crowd gets larger, the odds are that somebody will decide to help, even if the probability that any particular witness would help is reduced by the bystander effect.

26.   When it comes to providing help, men are more likely to do so for strangers, in a one-time emergency situation, under dangerous circumstances that require some bravery and in front of others. They are also more likely to provide help to females in need than to males. Women, on the other hand, are more likely to provide social support, over a long time period, to a friend or family member. They are likely to do so without anyone else being present and they are just as likely to help a male as a female. There are no marked gender differences in help that do not fit into these two categories. For example, males and females are equally likely to help someone who dropped a bag of groceries on the sidewalk. As for receiving help, the stereotype is true worldwide; women seek help more often than men do. Apparently, men find asking for help threatening to their self-esteem.

27. Using data from random samples drawn from 40 of the 50 states in the U.S., Markus
      Kemmelmeier and others (2006) examined the relationship between the degree of individualism
      associated with each state and the amount of helping the individuals from within those states
      offered to strangers in the form of donations and volunteering. The states' degree of individualism
      was determined in a previous study by Vandello and Cohen (1999) using a number of variables,
      such as the percentage of people living alone, the percentage of people with no religious
      affiliation, and the percentage of people self-employed. In general, states in the Mountain West
      and Great Plains were the most individualistic, followed by the Northeast and Midwest. The least
      individualistic states tended to be in the South and Southwest. Kemmelmeier and colleagues
      found that people from the more individualistic states tended to exhibit greater charitable giving
      and volunteering than people from the more collectivistic states, particularly for donations and
      volunteering that were not specific to one's ingroup affiliations. The authors propose that when
      helping involves this more abstract kind of giving—as opposed to, for example, helping someone
      from within one's ingroup—individualism may be associated with greater helping.

CHAPTER 11

Aggression

OUTLINE

LEARNING OBJECTIVES: GUIDELINES FOR STUDY

You should be able to do each of the following by the conclusion of Chapter 11.

1. Define aggression as well as related concepts, such as anger, hostility, and violence. Distinguish between instrumental aggression and emotional aggression. (*pp. 436-437*)

2. Discuss the role of culture in aggression and attitudes towards aggression. Consider various explanations for differences in aggression across cultures and across groups within cultures. (*pp. 437-442*)

3. Discuss gender differences in physical aggression. Differentiate between overt and relational, or indirect, aggression. Discuss rates of indirect aggression as a function of gender and sexual orientation. (*pp. 442-443*)

4. Elaborate on individual differences in aggression, with reference to stability, correlated personality characteristics, and tendency to aggress only upon provocation. (pp. *443-444*)

5. Consider whether aggression is innate by reviewing instinct theories, the evolutionary perspective, and the role of biological factors. Discuss how these different explanations account for gender differences in aggression. (*pp. 444-448*)

4. Consider whether aggression is learned by reviewing the concepts of reinforcement, punishment, and the social learning theory of aggression. Discuss how socialization accounts for gender and cultural variations in aggression. (*pp. 448-454*)

5. Explain the original version of the frustration-aggression hypothesis, including discussion of the concepts of displacement and catharsis. Identify problems with this hypothesis and summarize its subsequent reformulation. (*pp. 454-457*)

6. Discuss the role of affect, arousal, and cognition when it comes to aggression as captured by the negative affect escape model and the process of excitation transfer. Consider situational factors that influence these processes. (*pp. 457-462*)

7. Summarize the immediate as well as long-term effects on aggression of exposure to violent forms of media. Explain the concepts of desensitization and cultivation. (*pp. 462-470*)

8. Discuss the influence of nonviolent and violent forms of pornography on nonsexual and sexual aggression, and consider the factors and psychological processes responsible for these effects. Consider types of interventions or education that might reduce these effects. (*pp. 470-472*)

9. Discuss the antecedents, prevalence, and consequences of different forms of violence among intimates. Discuss the role played by alcohol and rape myth attitudes in sexual aggression among college students and other populations. Discuss effective ways of reducing these forms of violence. (*pp. 473-478*)

MAJOR CONCEPTS: THE BIG PICTURE

Below are six basic issues or principles that organize Chapter 11. You should know these issues and principles well.

1. Pinning down what is meant exactly by "aggression" can be rather difficult. This chapter emphasizes the role of one's intention to harm another person in its definition of aggression. Other concepts defined and discussed include violence, anger, and hostility. Two types of aggression are distinguished – aggression that is a means to some other end, and aggression that is impulsive and not intended to achieve some other end.

2. There are a number of ways in which patterns of aggression are similar and different across cultures and gender. Rates of violent crimes vary widely across countries, and across different regions within a particular culture – as in subcultures within a society that emphasize the use of violence to protect or establish one's honor. There are also significant variations in rates of aggression as a function of age, economic class, and race. In virtually every culture ever studied, men are much more likely than women to commit, and to be victims of, violent crime. Males tend to be more physically aggressive than females, but this difference is weakened under a variety of conditions. For more indirect, relational forms of aggression, females are often more aggressive than males.

3. Various theories and research findings concerning the origins of aggression differ in their perspectives. These perspectives vary in terms of the degree to which they emphasize the "nature" or "nurture" origins of aggression. Perspectives emphasizing the former include those that regard aggression as an innate instinct, as a characteristic favored by natural selection and other processes of evolution, as produced by genetic heritability, and as influenced by biological factors such as hormones and neurotransmitters. Perspectives emphasizing the latter include social learning theory, which focuses on the influence of models of aggression. These perspectives are not necessarily mutually exclusive, and they can be seen together as illustrating the interaction between nature and nurture, or biological and social factors.

4. There are numerous situational influences on aggression. Among these influences are frustration, negative and positive affect, and arousal. Thought – both automatic and deliberate – can also play an important role in influencing aggression.

5. The media have many important effects on aggression. Depictions of nonsexual violence can increase aggressive behavior among adults and children, and it can lead to changes in people's sensitivity to and attitudes about violence. Exposure to pornographic materials can also influence aggressive behavior and attitudes. The nature of the relationship between exposure to such materials and aggressive behavior depends in part on the arousal elicited by the materials, whether the pornography is nonviolent or violent, and whether the people depicted in the pornography are portrayed as enjoying or suffering through their experience.

6. Violence is not limited to strangers or competing groups. A great deal of violence occurs within familiar contexts and intimate relationships, as is evident in research concerning sexual aggression among college students, physical aggression between spouses or partners, and child abuse.

KEY TERM EXERCISE: THE CONCEPTS YOU SHOULD KNOW

Below are all of the key terms that appear in **boldface** in Chapter 11. To help you better understand these concepts, rather than just memorize them, write a definition for each term in your own words. After doing so, look at the next section where you'll find a list of definitions from the textbook for each of the key terms presented in random order. For each of your definitions, find the corresponding textbook definition. Note how your definitions compare with those from the textbook.

Key Terms

1. displacement

2. instrumental aggression

3. pornography

4. hostile attribution bias

5. frustration-aggression hypothesis

6.   emotional aggression

7.   cultivation

8.   cycle of violence

9.   aggression

10. catharsis

11. desensitization

12. social learning theory

13. weapons effect

Textbook Definitions

a.   Behavior intended to injure another person who does not want to be injured.

b.   Inflicting harm in order to obtain something of value.

c.   Inflicting harm for its own sake.

d.   The proposition that behavior is learned through the observation of others as well as through the direct experience of rewards and punishments.

e.   The idea that (1) frustration always elicits the motive to aggress and (2) all aggression is caused by frustration.

f.   Aggressing against a substitute target because aggressive acts against the source of the frustration are inhibited by fear or lack of access.

g.   A reduction of the motive to aggress that is said to result from any imagined, observed, or actual act of aggression.

h.   The tendency of weapons to increase the likelihood of aggression by their mere presence.

i.   Reduction in emotion-related physiological reactivity in response to a stimulus

j.   The process by which the mass media (particularly television) construct a version of social reality for the public.

k.   Explicit sexual material.

l.   The transmission of aggressive behavior across generations.

m.   Individuals who tend to perceive hostile intent in others.

ANSWERS FOR KEY TERM EXERCISE

Answers for the key terms exercise are listed below.

1. **f**
2. **b**
3. **k**
4. **m**
5. **e**
6. **c**
7. **j**
8. **l**
9. **a**
10. **g**
11. **i**
12. **d**
13. **h**

PRACTICE QUIZ: TEST YOUR KNOWLEDGE OF THE CHAPTER

Multiple-Choice Questions

1. The region of the United States that typically has the highest rates of violence is the

    a.   Northeast.
    b.   South.
    c.   Midwest.
    d.   West.

2. The idea that arousal produced by one stimulus can increase a person's emotional reaction to another stimulus is called

    a.   excitation transfer.
    b.   cultivation.
    c.   emotional aggression.
    d.   displacement.

3. Males are to _____ aggression, as females are to _____ aggression.

    a.   instrumental; emotional
    b.   overt; indirect
    c.   emotional; instrumental
    d.   indirect; overt

4. Research on the effects of pornography on aggression has found that

    a.   the effects of violent pornography tend to be strong only among men who fit the rapist's profile.
    b.   catharsis is much stronger in response to violent pornography than in response to nonviolent pornography.
    c.   nonviolent pornography tends to increase aggression primarily when arousal is low.
    d.   violent pornography tends to have greater immediate effects on male-to-female aggression than on male-to-male aggression.

5. In some samples of preschool children studied, children living with a stepparent or foster parent were much more likely to be fatally abused than were children living with both biological parents. This finding is most consistent with

    a.   negative affect theory.
    b.   a cycle of violence.
    c.   the concept of catharsis.
    d.   evolutionary psychology.

6. Which of the following four teens is most likely to respond aggressively when another teen makes disparaging remarks about his looks:

    a.   Kevin, who has low self-esteem
    b.   Scott, who has a Type B personality
    c.   Tom, who is very narcissistic
    d.   Craig, who is the least impulsive of the four

7. According to social learning theory, an effective way to strengthen existing restraints against aggression is to
   a. discourage displaced aggression.
   b. encourage catharsis through socially acceptable means of displacing aggression.
   c. punish acts of aggression quickly, consistently, and with obvious hostility.
   d. demonstrate nonaggressive responses to a provoking situation.

8. The idea that repeated exposure to violent crimes on the local and national television news leads individuals to become overly fearful, distrustful, and more likely to feel threatened is most consistent with the concept of
   a. cultivation.
   b. habituation.
   c. social learning.
   d. displacement.

9. John read a magazine containing several pictures of very attractive nude models. John found this to be a very pleasant but not particularly arousing experience. Immediately afterward, John was put in a situation in which he had the opportunity to aggress against another man who had acted toward John in a way that might be considered insulting. Compared to someone who had *not* just seen the pictures, the degree of John's retaliatory aggression against this individual would likely have been
   a. increased.
   b. reduced.
   c. increased, unless the material that John read elicited feelings of empathy.
   d. reduced if John had already had a great deal of experience with pornography, but increased if he had not.

10. When Carl thinks of any of the *Lethal Weapon* movies, he imagines violence and mayhem. His thoughts are so strong that he's ready to start a fight at the drop of a hat. For Carl, these movies are most clearly a(n)
    a. source of frustration.
    b. aggression-enhancing situational cue.
    c. trigger for death instincts.
    d. outlet for catharsis.

11. Jerry angered Tom, and now Tom has an opportunity to retaliate by aggressing against Jerry. Assume that Jerry could do each of the following just before Tom has the chance to aggress against him. Of these actions, which, according to the research, should be most successful in reducing the degree of aggression that Tom would use against Jerry in retaliation?
    a. Jerry tricks Tom into drinking a great deal of alcohol, and then tells Tom that he hadn't meant to anger Tom.
    b. Jerry shows Tom a series of violent cartoons in which both characters depicted in the cartoon are killed.
    c. Jerry shows Tom a picture of a kitten who has lost its mother, causing Tom to feel sympathy and empathy for the kitten.
    d. Jerry gives Tom a punching bag and has Tom punch it a few minutes.

12. When a witness went to the police and told them that she saw Jim leaving the scene of the crime, Jim did not get very upset but instead hired someone to kill her before she could testify in court. Jim's actions illustrate

    a.   emotional aggression.
    b.   instrumental aggression.
    c.   a cycle of violence.
    d.   excitation transfer.

13. According to research by Malamuth, men who fit the rapist's profile report more sexually coercive behavior in the past and more sexually aggressive intentions for the future than do men who do not fit this profile. Men who fit the rapist's profile are also more likely than other men to

    a.   express attitudes toward women that are very positive, whereas their behaviors are more negative.
    b.   be habituated to violent pornography, such that they are no longer aroused by exposure to it.
    c.   be vulnerable to the weapons effect.
    d.   have high levels of arousal in response to violent pornography.

14. Whenever people stop Lynda from getting what she wants, she verbally attacks them. But she attacks people only when they stand in her way. Lynda's behavior is an example of

    a.   the frustration-aggression hypothesis.
    b.   the hostile attribution bias.
    c.   the cycle of violence.
    d.   social learning theory.

15. On the hottest day of the summer, Spike, who is usually not very aggressive, is walking down a noisy street in Brooklyn. He passes an appliance store and stops to watch a weatherman on television who is talking about poor air quality and issuing a high-ozone alert. As he continues walking, an acquaintance named Tony sees Spike and comes over to ask him a question. Spike is verbally aggressive to Tony. Spike's aggression is most likely a reaction to

    a.   habituation.
    b.   desensitization.
    c.   noxious stimuli.
    d.   machismo.

16. After the home team loses the championship game, many fans of the home team run into the streets and vandalize the neighborhood while yelling, drinking, and fighting. This behavior is *least* likely to reflect

    a.   emotional aggression.
    b.   excitation transfer.
    c.   instrumental aggression.
    d.   the relationship between frustration and aggression.

17. Paolo, who comes from Brazil, a culture of honor, is presented with two court cases: In the first, a husband hit his wife after she lost a substantial amount of money gambling. In the second, a husband hit his wife because he saw her flirt with their neighbor. How is Paolo likely to regard the husbands' behaviors in these cases?

    a.   He is likely to find the husbands' behaviors to be unacceptable in both cases.
    b.   He is likely to find the husbands' behaviors to be justifiable in both cases.
    c.   He is likely to say that the behavior of the first husband (with the gambling wife) was justified, but the behavior of the second husband (with the flirting wife) was unacceptable.
    d.   He is likely to say that the behavior of the first husband (with the gambling wife) was unacceptable, but that the behavior of the second husband (with the flirting wife) was justified

18. In a bar, Mick aggressed successfully against a man named Walt. A few minutes later, Mick encountered some other men in the bar whom he found to be annoying. According to social learning theory, Mick's motivation to aggress against these other men may have been relatively high because his previous act of aggressing against Walt was likely to

    a. reduce Mick's levels of arousal and negative affect.
    b. reinforce aggressive actions for Mick.
    c. strengthen Mick's positive affect.
    d. produce catharsis for Mick.

19. Warren had a very bad day in school. Not only did he get an "F" on his paper, the teacher also humiliated him by reading aloud from his paper as an example to the other students of how not to write. He was so mad at his teacher, he wanted to punch him, but of course he wouldn't do that. So, when he came home, he picked up his kid brother's favorite toy robot and smashed it against the wall. The research on catharsis predicts that now Warren will

    a. continue to feel hostile and angry, possibly even more than before.
    b. experience lower arousal levels and be less likely to aggress further.
    c. no longer be angry at his teacher but be very angry toward his brother.
    d. experience higher arousal levels but be less likely to aggress further.

20. Which of the following would the social psychological research on aggression suggest is most likely to reduce aggression in society?

    a. Reducing the prevalence of displays of weapons
    b. Exposing people to movies in which the use of violence by "the bad guys" is met with even stronger, successful violence by "the good guys"
    c. Encouraging parents to respond to their children's aggression by punishing them quickly with spanking and other kinds of non-abusive but very strong physical punishments
    d. Teaching people to be true to themselves by responding directly to their emotional states

21. Based on data from INTERPOL reports, the rates of violent crimes are higher in _____ than in many other regions in the world.

    a. the Americas
    b. Western Europe
    c. Asia
    d. Australia

22. There is considerable variation in how acceptable students found different actions, such as a husband slapping a wife or vice versa. In which country did students find these types of behaviors *least* acceptable?

    a. United States
    b. India
    c. Australia
    d. New Zealand

23. What is true about the 25 nonviolent societies reported on by Bonta?

    a. All but two espouse rugged individualism.
    b. All but two are situated quite far from violent societies.
    c. All but two are located in Asia.
    d. All but two are opposed to competition.

Essay Questions

24. How are men and women similar or different in terms of aggression?

25. Explain what is meant by the weapons effect. Describe an experiment, discussed in the main text, that illustrates the weapons effect.

26. Discuss whether users of violent pornography differ from users of nonviolent pornography in male-to-male and male-to-female aggression.

27. Discuss how testosterone and serotonin influence aggression.

ANSWERS TO THE PRACTICE QUIZ

Multiple-Choice Questions: Correct Answers and Explanations

1. b.   **South.** Over the years, the highest rates of recorded violence in the United States have been reported in the South, followed by the West. This is consistent with the idea that there exists a strong "culture of violence" among White men in the South, as well as in the West. Alternatively, some scholars cite the South's hot weather as a factor.

2. a.   **excitation transfer.** Excitation transfer occurs when arousal experienced in one setting carries over to another setting. This residual arousal can enhance aggressive responding. Cultivation is the process by which television constructs a social reality for the viewer. Emotional aggression means inflicting harm for its own sake. Displacement has to do with aggressing against a substitute because aggression against the real target is blocked.

3. b.   **overt; indirect.** Although males tend to be more overtly aggressive than females, females tend to engage to a greater degree in indirect aggression, especially relational aggression, which targets a person's relationships or social status. Instrumental aggression is the infliction of harm to gain something of value. Emotional aggression is the infliction of harm for its own sake. Neither is gender-specific.

4. d.   **violent pornography tends to have greater immediate effects on male-to-female aggression than on male-to-male aggression.** Male-to-male aggression is no greater after exposure to violent pornography than after exposure to highly arousing but nonviolent pornography; male-to-female aggression, however, is markedly increased. The effects of violent pornography are not limited to those men who fit the rapist's profile. There is no evidence that catharsis is stronger in response to violent pornography than in response to nonviolent pornography. Nonviolent pornography does not tend to increase aggression primarily when arousal is low; indeed, it tends to *decrease* aggression when arousal is low and the emotional response to the pornography is positive.

5. d.   **evolutionary psychology.** According to evolutionary psychology, behaviors can be interpreted as attempts to increase the odds of one's genes being passed on to future generations. Research on child abuse shows that parents are more likely to fatally abuse children if they do not share their genes. Although it is possible that stepparents or foster parents experience more negative affect or have more violence in their family background, there is no clear evidence that either would be the case; thus, there is no compelling reason to suspect a strong role of negative affect or of a cycle of violence. Catharsis is the reduction of the motive to aggress that is said to result from any imagined, observed, or actual act of aggression, but there is no reason to infer any role of catharsis in this research finding.

6. c. **Tom, who is very narcissistic.** Narcissism, the tendency to possess an inflated sense of self-worth and self-love without a strong set of beliefs to support these feelings, is positively and consistently correlated with aggression in response to provocation. Low self-esteem is not a great predictor of aggression. In fact, some researchers have found that those with high self-esteem and a narcissistic personality are more likely to aggress in response to provocation that involves threats to their egos, as are those with low self-esteem. Having a Type B personality is not a predictor of aggression, having a Type A personality is. Impulsive individuals, those unable to control thoughts and actions, are more likely to aggress than individuals who are low in impulsivity.

7. d. **demonstrate nonaggressive responses to a provoking situation.** This method teaches a peaceful alternative. But there is nothing in social learning theory that suggests that discouraging displacement would be effective, and encouraging catharsis or modeling punishment should, according to this theory, both increase aggression.

8. a. **cultivation.** Cultivation is the process by which the mass media (particularly television) construct a version of social reality for the viewing public. The version constructed by television news shows is very violent and threatening. Habituation would be evident to the extent that the individuals adapt to such exposure on the news and no longer become aroused by it. Social learning is not implicated because there is no evidence that the individuals learned acts of aggression. And displacement refers to aggressive acts directed at someone other than the source of provocation, so it is not relevant here.

9. b. **reduced.** Experiences that produce pleasant affect and low levels of arousal tend to reduce aggression.

10. b. **aggression-enhancing situational cue.** Any object or external characteristic that is associated with successful aggression or with the negative affect of pain or unpleasantness can serve as an aggression-enhancing situational cue. For Carl, these movies have some of these associations and make him more likely to be aggressive.

11. c. **Jerry shows Tom a picture of a kitten who has lost its mother, causing Tom to feel sympathy and empathy for the kitten.** By causing Tom to feel sympathy and empathy, Jerry has created a response in Tom that is incompatible with aggression; by this means, the aggression should be reduced. In contrast, exposure to alcohol or to violent cartoons tends to increase aggression, and giving Tom a punching bag could have any of a number of different effects.

12. b. **instrumental aggression.** Instrumental aggression is inflicting harm in order to obtain something of value. Jim's action is intended to eliminate the witness in order to obtain his freedom. Because the aggression is a means to some end, rather than aggression for its own sake, Jim's actions do not reflect emotional aggression. No information is given about Jim's family background or levels of arousal, so there is no evidence suggesting a cycle of violence or excitation transfer.

13. d. **have high levels of arousal in response to violent pornography.** In addition to having relatively high levels of arousal in response to violent pornography, men who fit this profile express attitudes and opinions indicating acceptance of violence toward women. Finally, men who fit this profile are as vulnerable to the weapons effect – in which the mere presence of weapons increases the likelihood of aggression – as anyone else.

14. a.   **the frustration-aggression hypothesis.** The frustration-aggression hypothesis proposes that frustration causes the drive to aggress, and that aggression is the result of frustration. Consistent with this hypothesis, whenever Lynda is frustrated she aggresses, and she aggresses only when frustrated. The hostile attribution bias is the tendency to perceive hostile intent in others. Lynda appears to aggress against those who stand in her way regardless of their intent. The cycle of violence refers to the transmission of domestic violence across generations. There is no mention here of Lydia's family. Social learning theory emphasizes the role of models in learning. Lynda is not copying the behavior of a model.

15. c.   **noxious stimuli.** A noxious stimulus is an unpleasant event (such as heat, pollution, or noise). Exposure to noxious stimuli tends to increase people's likelihood of aggressing. Habituation is the adaptation to something familiar so that psychological and physiological responses are reduced; Spike's reactions indicate that he had not habituated to the noxious stimuli around him. Similarly, desensitization, which is a form of habituation, refers to a reduction in reactivity in someone witnessing real violence, as a result of having been exposed to violence in the media. Machismo, a code of behavior seen in cultures of honor, prescribes that challenges, abuse, and even differences of opinion must be met with fists or other weapons. Brooklyn is not considered a culture of honor. Moreover, there is no indication that Tony presented a challenge to Spike's social status or reputation.

16. c.   **instrumental aggression.** Instrumental aggression is inflicting harm in order to obtain something of value. The fans' behavior in this example is not intended to get them anything of value. Rather, their behavior can be seen as aggressive behavior for its own sake, which is consistent with emotional aggression. It is likely that the fans were aroused by the game, and that this arousal may have enhanced their negative feelings after their team lost, leading to an excitation transfer. In short, the fans were probably frustrated by the loss, and their frustration may have caused their desire to aggress.

17. d.   **He is likely to say that the behavior of the first husband (with the gambling wife) was unacceptable, but that the behavior of the second husband (with the flirting wife) was justified.** In cultures of honor, aggressive responses to honor-based threats are the norm. Vandello, Cohen, and others (2009) found that participants, from a culture of honor (Chile), rated a husband positively when he behaved violently toward his wife because she flirted with another man. But they rated such violent behavior as unacceptable when a husband behaved violently toward his wife in a matter that did not threaten his honor.

18. b.   **reinforce aggressive actions for Mick.** Because Mick's aggression was successful, aggression was positively reinforced for him. Social learning theory does not propose that aggression reduces arousal, strengthens positive affect, or produces catharsis.

19. a.   **continue to feel hostile and angry, possibly even more than before.** Dollard and his colleagues believed that catharsis involved a two-step process: first, aggression reduces the level of arousal, and second, with reduced arousal, people are less likely to aggress. However, research has shown that not to be true. Instead, researchers found that feelings of hostility and anger persist after displaced aggression is expressed and sometimes even increase. Although catharsis does reduce arousal, that does not necessarily result in reduction of aggressive feelings, especially if reduced arousal feels good or if aggressive intent remains. Moreover, it's unlikely that Warren will now only be angry with his brother and not with his teacher, as there's no reason to think that he'll forget the source of his frustration.

20. a. **Reducing the prevalence of displays of weapons.** By this means, people's exposure to aggression-enhancing cues would be lessened, thereby reducing the likelihood that they would aggress. Exposing people to violent movies, even those in which the violence is met with stronger violence, is likely to increase, rather than decrease, real-world violence; the successful, justifiable violence used by "the good guys" is likely to reinforce the use of violence as a way to solve problems and succeed. Research suggests that parents who punish their children may serve as models of aggression, and that the children are likely to imitate such models eventually. Finally, responding directly to one's emotional states is likely to cause more, rather than less, aggression; for example, people so responding would be less likely to be sensitive to norms against aggression.

21. a. **the Americas**. Based on data from INTERPOL, the world's largest police organization, Nigel Barber (2006) reports that rates of violent crimes are higher in the Americas than many other regions in the world. According to these data, the rates of murder, rape, and assault among 11 countries in the Americas (including Argentina, Bahamas, Chile, Costa Rica, and the U.S.) were about double the world averages. Barber proposes that a key factor that may explain this difference is the relatively high rate of single parenthood in the Americas, which correlates with violent crime.

22. a. **United States**. Cultures also differ in their attitudes about aggression. In a study involving students at 36 universities in 19 different countries around the world, there was considerable variation in how acceptable the students found different actions, such as a husband slapping a wife or vice versa (Douglas & Straus, 2006). For example, almost 80 percent of the respondents from a university in India did not strongly disapprove of a husband slapping a wife, compared to only about 24 percent at a university in the United States. In general, samples from Europe were more approving of a husband slapping a wife than were samples from Australia and New Zealand, which in turn tended to be somewhat more approving than samples from North America.

23. d. **All but two are opposed to competition.** All but two of the 25 nonviolent societies identified by Bonta endorse cooperation in every aspect of their lives and oppose competition. Consequently, as cooperative societies, they are not likely to promote rugged individualism. At least four of the societies, the Amish, the Mennonites, the Hutterites, and the Zapotec are located within or near violent societies. Of the 10 societies mentioned in the text, only 3 are located in Asia.

Answers to Essay Questions: Sample Essays

23. In virtually all cultures studied in virtually any time period, men are more violent than women. Men, for example, are much more likely to commit, and be the victims of, murder. Males in general (both young boys and adult men) are more likely to engage in overt, physical acts of aggression than females (both young girls and adult women). Even in the toddler years, gender differences can be seen – two-year-old boys are more likely to be interested in violent, scary books than are two-year-old girls. But the gender differences in aggression become less clear when considering measures of non-physical aggression. Although they are less physically aggressive than boys, girls are often more indirectly, or relationally, aggressive than boys, especially from around age eleven until they become young adults. An example of indirect or relational aggression is spreading mean-spirited, false stories about someone in order to get others to dislike the person. In addition, with regard to overt aggression, the gender difference may be more complicated than had been realized previously. When the aggression can be hidden – from others or from themselves – the tendency for males to be more overtly aggressive than females may be reduced or even eliminated. For example, in one study, male participants behaved more aggressively than female participants under ordinary conditions. However, when experimental conditions made participants feel anonymous and deindividuated, female participants were just as aggressive as the males.

24. The weapons effect refers to the tendency for the presence of guns and other weapons associated with aggression to increase aggression. The presence of a gun can serve as an aggression-enhancing situational cue for an angered individual, making the individual more likely to resort to aggression or to engage in greater degrees of aggression. As Berkowitz said, "The finger pulls the trigger, but the trigger may also be pulling the finger." An experiment that illustrates the weapons effect was conducted by Berkowitz and LePage (1967). In this study, male participants were provoked by a confederate, and subsequently were given the opportunity to deliver shocks to the confederate. The participants delivered more shocks to the confederate if a revolver and rifle were present in the room with them than if badminton racquets and shuttlecocks were present. The weapons – the revolver and the rifle – apparently served as aggression-enhancing cues.

25. Several studies have shown that violent pornography has a gender-specific effect. That is, male-to-male aggression is no greater after exposure to violent pornography than after exposure to highly arousing but nonviolent pornography; male-to-female aggression, however, is markedly increased after exposure to violent pornography. Violent pornography increases aggression even without provocation, especially if the women portrayed appear to enjoy their own victimization. Violent pornography is most likely to have an effect on men who have relatively high levels of sexual arousal in response to violent pornography and who express attitudes and opinions indicating acceptance of violence against women.

26. There is a positive correlation between levels of the "male sex hormone", testosterone, and physical aggression or violence for both men and women. The correlation, however, does not necessarily mean that higher levels of testosterone cause people to aggress. There might be a third variable, such as stress that causes an increase in both or aggressive actions might stimulate the production of higher levels of testosterone. In order to determine causation, researchers administered tests of aggression to transsexuals, just before they were about to undergo hormone treatment and three months after treatment began. They found that those undergoing female-to-male transformation (with an increase in testosterone) exhibited an increase in aggression-proneness. Conversely, those undergoing a male-to-female sex change (with a reduction in testosterone), showed a decline in aggression-proneness. The study does not, however, point to testosterone as a definite cause of aggression. The researchers noted that the results might simply be due to expectations. As for the neurotransmitter serotonin, it has the opposite effect from testosterone. It puts the brakes on impulsive acts of aggression. When serotonin levels in the nervous system are low, aggression levels rise. Conversely, high levels of serotonin are associated with lower levels of aggression. Therefore, drugs that boost serotonin's activity act to dampen aggressiveness. One example in the use of such drugs has been for the treatment of individuals who are prone to acts of "road rage."

CHAPTER 12

Law

OUTLINE

LEARNING OBJECTIVES: GUIDELINES FOR STUDY

You should be able to do each of the following by the conclusion of Chapter 12.

1. Identify the three stages of jury selection. Consider the role of intuition and scientific data in the process of jury selection. (*pp. 487-491*)

2. Consider the role of race in legal decision-making. Discuss how and under what circumstances the race of a defendant and the racial composition of a jury can affect verdicts. (*pp. 491-492*)

3. Describe the purpose of death qualification and the controversy surrounding the effects of this process on trial verdicts. (*pp. 492-493*)

4. Describe the approaches used by police to extract confessions from suspects. Differentiate false confessions that result from compliance from those that result from internalization, and identify the conditions under which people are most likely to internalize false confessions. Discuss the difficulties that juries face when they try to evaluate a confession introduced into evidence at trial. (*pp. 494-498*)

5. Describe a polygraph, and identify the assumptions and potential problems underlying its use. (*p. 498-499*)

6. Summarize the acquisition, storage, and retrieval stages of eyewitness testimony. Describe how these stages are susceptible to errors caused by factors such as arousal, the weapon-focus effect, the cross-race identification bias, misinformation, the suggestibility of young children, and lineup procedures. (*pp. 499-508*)

7. Explain why jurors often cannot distinguish credible from noncredible eyewitnesses. Summarize how experts may help jurors become more competent judges of eyewitnesses. (*pp. 508-509*)

8. Summarize the general effects of pretrial publicity and inadmissible evidence on jurors' perceptions of defendants. Identify the factors that contribute to the finding that judges' instructions often have little impact on jurors. (*pp. 509-513*)

9. Describe the jury deliberation process. Discuss the importance of a jury's first vote and explain the concept of the leniency bias produces. Describe factors that affect jury deliberation, including informational and normative influences, jury size, and the unanimous decision rule. (*pp. 513-517*)

10. Discuss how defendants are treated after being found guilty in a court of law. Define the sentencing disparity and why it occurs. Describe the Stanford prison study. Discuss the implications of the study and cite the conclusions of replication studies. (*pp. 517-521*)

11. Differentiate between decision and process control and their effects on perceptions of justice. Contrast the adversarial and inquisitorial models of justice. (*pp. 521-522*)

12. Discuss how cultural influences affect what is considered lawful behavior, the procedures used to enforce laws, and the consequences of breaking the law. (*pp. 522-524*)

MAJOR CONCEPTS: THE BIG PICTURE

Below are five basic issues or principles that organize Chapter 12. You should know these issues and principles well.

1. The selection of jurors is an often controversial process. Through the voir dire and peremptory challenges, potential jurors are excluded from serving on the jury. Lawyers often rely on intuition – including implicit personality theories and stereotypes – in trying to select jurors who they believe will be most favorable to their side. Lawyers sometimes hire consultants to help them conduct scientific jury selection. These consultants may determine correlations between demographics and attitudes relevant to a specific trial, and these correlations can be used to guide a lawyer's selection of jurors. The issue of race in jury matters is complex and depends on several factors. Jurors with positive attitudes toward the death penalty are more likely to find a defendant guilty than jurors who are against the death penalty.

2. Once the jury is selected, evidence is presented in court. Underlying the courtroom drama are problems concerning the accuracy of the evidence, the biasing effects of factors extraneous to the evidence, and the ineffectiveness of judges' instructions. Confessions and eyewitness testimony have strong effects on verdicts, but judges and juries often do not reject coerced confessions and are often unable to distinguish credible from noncredible eyewitnesses. Pretrial publicity and inadmissible testimony that leaks into court – both of which juries are instructed to ignore – can bias the jury.

3. Jury deliberations pass through multiple stages. Informational and normative influences may pressure jurors toward conforming to the majority opinion. Despite the deliberation process, the initial majority opinion typically wins, although deliberation produces a bias toward leniency. Deliberation and verdicts are affected both by the size of the jury and whether or not verdicts must be unanimous.

4. Sentencing decisions are usually made by judges, and these are often controversial. A common complaint is that punishments are inconsistent from one judge to the next. A source of this sentencing disparity is that judges receive sentencing recommendations from people who have different views of the goals of sentencing. Once sentenced to prison, convicts – and their guards – may find themselves becoming dehumanized by their institutional roles in this setting.

5. Satisfaction with justice depends not only on winning and losing but also on the procedures used to achieve the outcome. In general, people are more satisfied with the adversarial model of justice than with the inquisitorial model. More generally, any method that offers participants a voice in the proceedings is more likely to be seen as fair and just than is a method that does not offer this opportunity.

KEY TERM EXERCISE: THE CONCEPTS YOU SHOULD KNOW

Below are all of the key terms that appear in **boldface** in Chapter 12. To help you better understand these concepts, rather than just memorize them, write a definition for each term in your own words. After doing so, look at the next section where you'll find a list of definitions from the textbook for each of the key terms presented in random order. For each of your definitions, find the corresponding textbook definition. Note how your definitions compare with those from the textbook.

Key Terms

1. weapon-focus effect

2. inquisitorial model

3. sentencing disparity

4. peremptory challenge

5. leniency bias

6. scientific jury selection

7. polygraph

8. misinformation effect

9. adversarial model

10.   voir dire

11.   death qualification

12.   jury nullification

13.   cross-race identification bias

Textbook Definitions

a.   The pretrial examination of prospective jurors by the judge or opposing lawyers to uncover signs of bias.

b.   A means by which lawyers can exclude a limited number of prospective jurors without the judge's approval.

c.   A method of selecting juries through surveys that yield correlations between demographics and trial-relevant attitudes.

d.   Inconsistency of sentences for the same offense from one judge to another.

e.   A jury-selection procedure used in capital cases that permits judges to exclude prospective jurors who say they would not vote for the death penalty.

f.   A mechanical instrument that records physiological arousal from multiple channels; it is often used as a lie-detector test.

g.   The tendency for the presence of a weapon to draw attention and impair a witness's ability to identify the culprit.

h.   The tendency for people to have difficulty identifying members of a race other than their own.

i.   The tendency for false postevent information to become integrated into people's memory of an event.

j.   The jury's power to disregard, or "nullify," the law when it conflicts with personal conceptions of justice.

k.   The tendency for jury deliberation to produce a tilt toward acquittal.

l.   A dispute-resolution system in which the prosecution and the defense present opposing sides of the story.

m.   A dispute-resolution system in which a neutral investigator gathers evidence from both sides and presents the findings in court.

ANSWERS FOR KEY TERM EXERCISE

Answers for the key terms exercise are listed below.

1. **g**
2. **m**
3. **d**
4. **b**
5. **k**
6. **c**
7. **f**
8. **i**
9. **l**
10. **a**
11. **e**
12. **j**
13. **h**

PRACTICE QUIZ: TEST YOUR KNOWLEDGE OF THE CHAPTER

Multiple-Choice Questions

1. Marie is accused of stealing money from the store where she works. Marie claims she did not steal. The director of security at the store hires a trained examiner to administer a polygraph on her. The examiner would determine that Marie is lying if

    a. Marie's level of arousal is higher than other people's when asked about stealing from the store.
    b. the measures of Marie's conscience indicate that she is trying to suppress some thoughts or memories.
    c. Marie's level of arousal is higher in response to questions about stealing from the store than it is in response to other arousing questions that are not about stealing from the store.
    d. the measures of Marie's eye movements indicate that Marie's eyes keep shifting and not focusing on her examiner.

2. The police arrest Fred for a crime. Earlier that night, during the time that the crime occurred, Fred had been drinking. The police tell him that people often do unusual things when they've been drinking, things they can't always remember doing. The police act very friendly toward Fred, and they advise him to plea-bargain for a lesser charge. This scenario exemplifies

    a. the misinformation effect.
    b. the leniency bias.
    c. the kind of misleading questions that bias the acquisition process.
    d. tactics used to extract confessions.

3. Research on eyewitness testimony suggests that

    a. there is no reliable method to distinguish accurate from inaccurate eyewitness identifications.
    b. jurors underestimate eyewitness accuracy.
    c. eyewitness confidence does not reliably predict their accuracy.
    d. eyewitnesses are more likely to remember the face of an armed criminal than an unarmed one.

4. After a woman was mugged on the subway, four witnesses came forward to the police at different times. Each witness, in turn, was shown a lineup of suspect photos. Which of the witnesses was most likely to make an unbiased identification?

    a. Ray, who was shown sequential photos by a policeman who did not know who the suspect was
    b. Harlan, who was shown simultaneous photos by a policeman who did not know who the suspect was
    c. Kelly, who was shown sequential photos by a policeman who knew which one of the photos was of the suspect
    d. Emma, who was shown simultaneous photos by a policeman who knew which one of the photos was of the suspect

5. The voir dire is one stage of the

    a. jury selection process.
    b. jury deliberation process.
    c. inquisitorial model.
    d. jury nullification process.

6. Jury nullification is one reason why jurors might

    a. exhibit familiarity-induced biases.
    b. exhibit misinformation effects.
    c. disregard judges' instructions.
    d. favor sentencing disparity.

7. Orientation, open conflict, and reconciliation best describe the three stages in

    a. jury nullification.
    b. eyewitness memory.
    c. jury deliberation.
    d. peremptory challenges.

8. In court, a lawyer calls witnesses and introduces evidence suggesting that Anne is guilty of drunk driving. Anne's lawyer then cross-examines witnesses and discredits evidence to suggest that Anne is innocent. This process illustrates

    a. the adversarial model.
    b. the open-conflict stage of deliberations.
    c. peremptory challenges.
    d. the inquisitorial model.

9. What did Philip Zimbardo mean when he attributed the results of his Stanford Prison study to the *Lucifer Effect*?

    a. That the study attracted individuals who were prone to antisocial behavior
    b. That the study attracted people who were overly aggressive
    c. That the study attracted people who had an authoritarian personality
    d. That the study attracted good people who behaved badly because of the situation

10. The defense attorney in a trial thought that jurors living in a particular neighborhood would be prejudiced against her client. During the jury selection process, the attorney noted that one of the prospective jurors was from that particular neighborhood. The attorney didn't think that the judge would agree with her that this prospective juror would be biased, but the attorney wanted to exclude this juror anyway. To exclude this person from serving on the jury, the attorney most probably would use

    a. jury nullification.
    b. the adversarial model.
    c. peremptory challenge.
    d. an appeal based on normative influence.

11. According to research, prospective jurors who favor the death penalty are

    a. highly suspicious of police.
    b. cynical about defense lawyers.
    c. tolerant of protecting the accused.
    d. less likely to find a defendant guilty.

12. The fact that people divulge information that isn't allowed into trial records is one of the potential dangers of

    a. peremptory challenges.
    b. pretrial publicity.
    c. expert witnesses.
    d. the leniency bias.

13. Research on jury deliberation suggests that verdicts tend to be

   a. determined by whatever the majority of jurors initially believe even before the deliberation, although deliberation tends to produce a bias toward acquittal.
   b. mostly random, and therefore it is virtually impossible to make any generalizations about how most jurors reach their verdicts.
   c. determined largely by the initial opinion of the foreperson.
   d. influenced more by the judge's instructions than by the initial opinions of the jurors, although deliberation tends to produce a bias toward conviction.

14. Research on confessions has found that

   a. under some conditions suspects will confess to a crime they did not commit, and they will believe their confessions.
   b. suspects may be coerced or tricked into confessing when they had not planned to, but they will confess only if they actually committed the crime.
   c. confessions have less effect on jurors if they see a videotape that focuses on the defendant confessing than if they learn about the confession through testimony.
   d. suspects may be coerced into confessing to a crime they did not commit, but they will not be led to believe that they may have actually committed the crime.

15. Wayne was waiting in line at the bank. Suddenly, he saw three people in the bank pull out guns, go to a few cashiers, demand and receive money, and run out the door. Research suggests that because Wayne saw the guns, he will

   a. be especially able to accurately identify the bank robbers.
   b. be less able to accurately identify the bank robbers.
   c. have very accurate acquisition but less accurate retrieval.
   d. be too traumatized to be able to describe the weapons to the police.

16. Jenny is a lawyer very familiar with social psychological research. Jenny asks an eyewitness to a car accident to "please estimate the speed of the green car when it contacted the red car." Based on this wording, one can infer that because she said

   a. "speed" rather than "miles per hour," Jenny is hoping to raise the witness's estimate of how fast the green car was going.
   b. "car" rather than a specific make and model of car, Jenny is trying to make the eyewitness look less competent.
   c. "please estimate," Jenny is trying to make the witness feel less pressure to be specific, which should cause the witness to exaggerate the speed of the car.
   d. "contacted" rather than "collided" or "smashed," Jenny is trying to lower the witness's estimate of how fast the green car was going.

17. The following people all witnessed a crime. All other things being equal, which one is most likely to *falsely* identify a suspect as the criminal?

   a. A witness who sees five people in a line-up who resemble each other
   b. A witness who is told before observing a line-up that the real criminal might or might not be present
   c. A witness who is brought to a show-up in which the police bring the suspect in alone
   d. A witness who sees the mug shot of the suspect and then sees the suspect and four other people in a line-up

18. Critics of scientific jury selection oppose this process because they claim that it
    a. tends to result in hung juries.
    b. tips the scales of justice in favor of wealthy clients.
    c. biases jurors against the defendant.
    d. produces the leniency bias.

19. During police questioning, Gary confessed to a crime. All other things being equal, in which of the following cases are jurors in Gary's trial most likely to find Gary guilty?
    a. The jurors learn that the police had extracted the confession by threatening Gary with harm if he didn't confess.
    b. The jurors see a videotape that focuses on the coercive interrogation that the police used to extract the confession from Gary.
    c. The jurors learn that the police had extracted the confession by offering Gary favorable treatment.
    d. Gary's confession is ruled inadmissible in a pretrial hearing and it is not introduced in the trial.

20. While witnessing a crime, Rose was highly aroused, saw a weapon, and observed that the criminal was of a different race than hers. The defense lawyer argues that these are all factors that may make her testimony less reliable because each can affect
    a. acquisition.
    b. storage.
    c. retrieval.
    d. informational influence.

21. Research shows that reconstructing a culprit's face by selecting a set of eyes, a nose, a mouth, and a hairstyle _____ produces a face that resembles the actual culprit.
    a. seldom
    b. usually
    c. always
    d. never

22. The "CSI effect" is purported to lead jurors to hold unrealistically high expectations that cause them to cautiously vote
    a. for conviction.
    b. for acquittal.
    c. not guilty by reason of insanity.
    d. for jury nullification.

Essay Questions

23. Explain scientific jury selection. What are the arguments supporting and opposing the use of this technique?

24. Briefly describe the three stages of eyewitness memory. Describe a bias that might influence the third stage of an eyewitness memory.

25. What are two situational factors that affect which juror is selected as foreperson? Describe the impact that the foreperson typically has on the jury's deliberations.

26. To what extent does a juror's race affect his or her decision-making on a jury?

ANSWERS TO THE PRACTICE QUIZ

Multiple-Choice Questions: Correct Answers and Explanations

1.   c.   **Marie's level of arousal is higher in response to questions about stealing from the store than it is in response to other arousing questions that are not about stealing from the store.** The polygraph is a mechanical instrument that records physiological arousal from multiple channels; it is often used as a lie-detector test. In theory, the polygraph should reveal that guilty suspects who deny that they are guilty show more arousal when asked crime-relevant questions than when asked other questions that are arousing but not relevant to the crime. The suspect's levels of arousal are not compared with other people's levels because people's baseline levels of arousal are likely to vary dramatically from one person to another. Rather, the suspect's levels of arousal in response to crime-relevant questions are compared to his or her own levels of arousal in response to questions that are arousing but not relevant to the crime. The polygraph is designed to measure levels of arousal; it cannot measure people's conscience to determine whether they are trying to suppress thoughts or memories, and it cannot measure eye movements.

2.   d.   **the tactics used to extract confessions.** Police use a wide variety of tactics to get confessions from suspects. Minimizing the offense by offering excuses (i.e., by telling Fred that people do unusual things when drinking) and pretending to befriend the suspect and offer advice are among these tactics. The misinformation effect has to do with postevent information compromising eyewitnesses.. The leniency bias is the tendency for jury deliberation to produce a tilt toward acquittal. Neither term is relevant in this example. The acquisition process is the first stage of human memory, followed by storage and retrieval. Acquisition refers to one's perceptions at the time of the event to be remembered. In this example, the event had already happened, so acquisition is not an issue. In addition, there is no mention of the police asking misleading questions.

3.   c.   **eyewitnesses' confidence does not reliably predict their accuracy.** Surprisingly, a witness's confidence is not a good predictor of the accuracy of his or her testimony. Eyewitnesses can become more or less confident as a result of social factors that are unrelated to eyewitness accuracy. Research suggests that it *is* possible to distinguish between accurate and inaccurate eyewitness identifications by asking witnesses to describe how they came to their judgments; they are more likely to be accurate to the extent that they describe their judgments as quick, effortless, and automatic. Jurors tend to overestimate, not underestimate, eyewitness accuracy. The weapons effect refers to the fact that eyewitnesses are less able to accurately identify a criminal with a weapon than one without because, during the crime, they tend to focus on the weapon instead of on the face.

4.   a.   **Ray, who was shown sequential photos by a policeman who did not know who the suspect was.** In their recent study, Greathouse and Kovera (2009) found that witnesses made the least suspect identifications when shown a sequential photo lineup under "double-blind" conditions, where neither the eyewitness or the administrator of the lineup was aware of the suspect's identity.

5.   a.   **jury selection process.** The voir dire is the pretrial examination of prospective jurors by the judge or opposing lawyers to uncover signs of bias. This is the third stage of the jury selection process. The first two stages involve identifying potential jurors and selecting a representative sample. The jury deliberation process is the decision-making process juries go through after the testimony has been presented in court. The inquisitorial model is a system of resolving disputes in which a neutral investigator gathers evidence from both sides and then presents the findings in court. Jury nullification refers to the jury's power to disregard, or "nullify," the law when it conflicts with the jurors' personal conceptions of justice.

6.   c.   **disregard judges' instructions.** Jury nullification refers to the jury's power to disregard, or "nullify," the law when it conflicts with the jurors' personal conceptions of justice. Because juries deliberate in private, they can choose to disregard their judge's instructions. Jury nullification does not explain familiarity-induced biases, misinformation effects, or sentence disparity. Familiarity-induced biases refer to the tendency for witnesses to be more likely to identify someone in a line-up if they had previously seen that person before, such as in a mugshot, but this tendency has nothing to do with juries. Misinformation effects are also not relevant here; rather, they refer to the finding that eyewitness memory can be altered by exposure to postevent information. Finally, sentencing disparity refers to judges' assignment of different sentences to criminals who have committed similar offenses. As such, it is not a reaction on the part of jurors. Moreover, few jurors would favor such disparity.

7.   c.   **jury deliberation.** After the evidence is presented and the judge gives the jurors instructions and tells them to return with a verdict, the jury deliberates and tries to reach a verdict. The jury deliberation process typically moves through three stages. First, juries begin in a relaxed, orientation period during which they set an agenda, raise questions, and explore the facts. Second, as soon as differences of opinion are revealed, a period of open conflict develops during which jurors debate evidence and dispute interpretations. Third, the jury smoothes over the conflicts and affirms its satisfaction with the outcome during the period of reconciliation. Jury nullification refers to the jury's power to disregard, or "nullify," the law when it conflicts with the jurors' personal conceptions of justice, but it does not necessarily proceed through any stages. Orientation, open conflict, and reconciliation are not relevant to eyewitness memory, which involves acquisition, storage, and retrieval. Peremptory challenges are the means by which lawyers can exclude a limited number of prospective jurors without having to state reasons or get the judge's approval, but these challenges do not progress through the stages of orientation, open conflict, and reconciliation.

8.   a.   **the adversarial model.** The adversarial model is a dispute-resolution system in which the prosecution and the defense present opposing sides of the same story; this model is illustrated in Anne's case. The open-conflict stage of deliberations is the second of three stages of jury deliberation, during which jurors debate evidence and dispute interpretations; but the example does not mention the role or behaviors of a jury. Peremptory challenges are the means by which lawyers can exclude a limited number of prospective jurors without having to state reasons or get the judge's approval; this example does not mention anything about the jury selection process. Finally, the inquisitorial model differs from the adversarial model in that it is a system of resolving disputes in which a neutral investigator gathers evidence from both sides and then presents the findings in court.

9.   d.   **That the study attracted good people who behaved badly because of the situation.** In the Stanford Prison study, participants were assigned to play the role of either prisoners or guards. As the study progressed, the "guards" became more and more abusive and cruel. The "prisoners" were so shaken by the experience, that by the sixth day, the study had to be called off. Some researchers (Carnahan & McFarland, 2007) suggested that the study attracted individuals who were prone to antisocial behavior. Philip Zimbardo disagreed. He said there were no personality differences between the participants and the general population or between those randomly assigned to play guards and those assigned to play prisoners. In his opinion, the behavior of the guards was due to the situation. He termed this transformation, of good people into people who behave in evil ways, the *Lucifer Effect*, after God's favorite angel, Lucifer, who fell from grace and became Satan.

10. c.   **peremptory challenge.** A peremptory challenge is a means by which lawyers can exclude a limited number of prospective jurors without the judge's approval; this is what the attorney could use to exclude the prospective juror she feared would be biased, without having to get the judge's approval. Jury nullification refers to the jury's power to disregard, or "nullify," the law when it conflicts with the jurors' personal conceptions of justice, but this is not relevant here. The adversarial model is not a technique used by an attorney to exclude certain people from serving on the jury, but rather is a dispute-resolution system in which the prosecution and the defense present opposing sides of the story. Normative influence produces conformity because a person fears the negative social consequences of appearing deviant, but this influence is not relevant in this question.

11. b.   **cynical about defense lawyers.** Prospective jurors who favor the death penalty are more prosecution-minded on a host of issues. For example, they are more concerned about crime, more trustful of the police, more cynical about defense lawyers, and less tolerant of procedures that protect the accused. Consequently, they are also more likely to find a defendant guilty.

12. b.   **pretrial publicity.** Pretrial publicity often includes information (such as prior convictions of the defendant) that may not be admissible in court. Hence, to the extent that jurors are exposed to this publicity, it could jeopardize a fair trial. A peremptory challenge is a means by which lawyers can exclude a limited number of prospective jurors without the judge's approval, but there is no danger in this process that is related to the issue raised in the question. There is no reason to assume that expert witnesses are particularly likely to divulge information that isn't allowed into trial records, nor is the leniency bias (the tendency for jury deliberation to produce a tilt toward acquittal) relevant in this example.

13. a.   **determined by whatever the majority of jurors initially believe even before the deliberation, although deliberation tends to produce a bias toward acquittal.** The initial majority opinion is the best predictor of eventual verdicts, although a bias toward leniency does often emerge from deliberation. These research findings suggest that verdicts are not simply random. Forepersons do not exert more than their fair share of influence on the verdict. Judge's instructions often are too complex, come too late, and may rely on details of laws that jurors disagree with – each of these problems contributes to the fact that judge's instructions often do not have that much impact; in addition, the second part of this answer – that deliberation produces a bias toward conviction -- is the opposite of the real bias toward leniency.

14. a.   **under some conditions, suspects will confess to a crime they did not commit, and they will believe their confessions.** Although rare, suspects may be led to believe that they committed a crime they had not committed under a particular set of conditions. Research has suggested that when people are uncertain about their own actions and are presented with false evidence that points strongly to their guilt, people may come to believe that they are guilty even if they are not guilty. The issue of false confessions is particularly important because confessions often have a very strong effect on verdicts. Showing the jury a videotape that focuses on the defendant confessing *increases* the effect of the confession on the jury's interpretations.

15. b.   **be less able to accurately identify the bank robbers.** There is a tendency for weapons to draw witnesses' attention and impair their ability to identify the culprit – this phenomenon is known as the weapon-focus effect. When a criminal pulls out a weapon, witnesses are less able to identify the culprit than if no weapon were present. This is probably because the witnesses either are agitated by the sight of the weapon or tend to focus on the weapon and have their attention drawn away from the face(s) of the culprit(s). By interfering with their observation of the event as it occurred, the weapon-focus effect interferes with the acquisition stage of eyewitness memory, which refers to one's perceptions at the time of the event to be remembered. Because the eyewitness is so focused on the weapon(s), it is probable that he or she would be able to describe it to the police.

16. d.   **"contacted" rather than "collided" or "smashed," Jenny is trying to lower the witness's estimate of how fast the green car was going.** Research has shown that the wording of a question such as this can affect a witness's response, and may even influence the witness's memory for the event in question. For example, research has found that participants give lower estimates of the speed of a car involved in an accident that they had witnessed if the verb "contacted" is used in the question than if the verb "collided" or "smashed" is used. There is no research evidence to support any of the alternative answers for this example.

17. d.   **a witness who sees the mug shot of the suspect and then sees the suspect and four other people in a line-up.** When witnesses view a line-up after having looked at mug shots, they are inclined to identify anyone whose photograph they have previously seen. This tendency, known as a familiarity-induced bias, can result in false identifications. The three alternative answers to this question all concern factors that *reduce* the chances of inducing a witness to falsely identify someone as the criminal.

18. b.   **tips the scales of justice in favor of wealthy clients.** Scientific jury selection is a method of selecting juries through surveys that yield correlations between demographics and trial-relevant attitudes. Because hiring experts to conduct scientific jury selection is expensive, this method favors wealthy clients who can afford the service. Clients without the resources to pay for these services cannot afford to use this selection procedure even though it might benefit them. Scientific jury selection is not typically criticized for the reasons stated in the alternative answers to this question. There is no evidence that scientific jury selection tends to result in hung juries, that it biases jurors against the defendant, or that it produces the leniency bias, which is the tendency for jury deliberation to produce a tilt toward acquittal.

19. c.   **The jurors learn that the police had extracted the confession by offering Gary favorable treatment.** Research suggests that when a defendant is said to have confessed in response to an offer of favorable treatment, jurors may not completely disregard the confession. They may recognize that the confession was involuntary, but they vote guilty anyway. In contrast, if jurors learn that the confession came in response to a threat of harm or punishment, they are much more likely to completely discount the confession and are thus less likely to vote guilty. Seeing a videotape that focuses on the coercive interrogation that the police used on the defendant to extract the confession makes jurors more likely to discount the confession as involuntary, making them less likely to vote guilty. If the defendant's confession is ruled inadmissible in a pretrial hearing and is not introduced in the trial, the confession should have absolutely no impact on the jurors (unless they were exposed to it in pretrial publicity – but this is not suggested in this example), and thus they should be less likely to vote guilty than if they learned of the confession.

20.   a.   **acquisition.** Acquisition is the first stage of human memory, followed by the stages of storage and retrieval. Acquisition refers to one's perceptions at the time of the event to be remembered. During this stage, information about a crime is gathered. Arousal, the weapon-focus effect (which is the tendency for weapons to draw witness's attention and impair their ability to identify the culprit), and the cross-race identification bias (which refers to the finding that people are better able to identify members of their own race than members of other races) are all factors that can interfere with the acquisition stage. Because these factors have their effects as the witness observes the event, they are most relevant to acquisition rather than to the later stages of storage and retrieval. Informational influence is influence that produces conformity because a person believes others are correct in their judgment; this is relevant to the jury deliberation process, but not to the situation outlined in this example.

21.   a.   **seldom.** Imagine trying to reconstruct a culprit's face by selecting a set of eyes, a nose, a mouth, a hairstyle, and so on, from vast collections of features, and then combining them into a composite of the face. Research shows that this process seldom produces a face that resembles the actual culprit (Kovera et al., 1997). To further complicate matters, the face construction process itself may confuse witnesses, making it more difficult for them later to identify the culprit. In one study, for example, participants were asked to select from six pictures a person's face they had seen two days earlier. Sixty percent accurately identified the target. When they first tried to reconstruct the face using a computerized facial composite program, however, their identification accuracy dropped to 18 percent (Wells et al., 2005).

22.   b.   **for acquittal.** Perhaps you have watched the popular television drama CSI, which stands for Crime Scene Investigation and focuses on the process by which police investigators collect and analyze fingerprints, bodily fluids, and other types of forensic evidence. Many legal commentators are speculating that the public's exposure to this show is influencing jury verdicts. Legal commentators speculate that the "CSI effect" leads jurors to hold unrealistically high expectations that cause them to vote cautiously for acquittal because they find the actual evidence insufficient to support a guilty verdict. If true, then the CSI effect would represent a special type of pretrial publicity, potentially influencing an entire population of juries. Tom Tyler (2006) is quick to note, however, that although the hypothesis is plausible, there is at present no hard evidence to support it.

Answers to Essay Questions: Sample Essays

23.   Scientific jury selection is a method of selecting juries through surveys that yield correlations between demographics and trial-relevant attitudes. During the voir dire, lawyers ask prospective jurors about their backgrounds and then use peremptory challenges to exclude those whose profiles are associated with unfavorable attitudes. Proponents of scientific jury selection argue that picking juries according to survey results is simply a more refined version of what lawyers are permitted to do by intuition. They argue that as long as it is legal for lawyers to use peremptory challenges, there is nothing unethical about using a scientific technique to accomplish what other lawyers try to do using their own intuition, implicit theories, and stereotypes. However, because hiring experts to conduct scientific jury selection is expensive, critics of the use of this technique argue that it favors wealthy clients who can afford it. Clients without the resources to pay for this service are thus essentially discriminated against.

24.   Eyewitness memory is divided into three stages. The first stage is the acquisition stage. Acquisition involves the perceptions of an event at the time of occurrence. The second stage is the storage stage. Storage involves the placing and keeping in memory of those perceptions to avoid forgetting. The third stage is the retrieval stage. Retrieval involves the recall from memory of those perceptions. One kind of bias that can create errors in the retrieval stage is a familiarity-induced bias. When witnesses view a line-up after having looked at mug shots, for example, they are more likely to identify someone in the line-up as the culprit of the crime they had witnessed if they saw this person's photograph among the mug shots than if they did not. When witnesses see someone in a line-up whose face looks familiar, they may confuse the familiarity resulting from exposure to the person's mug shot with that of having witnessed this person at the crime. Thus they are impaired in their ability to accurately retrieve the face of the culprit from memory.

25.   Several factors are related to the selection of a foreperson. People of higher occupational status or with prior experience on a jury are frequently chosen. More subtle, situational factors include who speaks first and where people sit. The person who speaks first as the jury is about to begin deliberations is often chosen as foreperson. If the seating arrangements are such that there are particularly salient seats, such as at the head of the table, the people who sit in these seats are more likely to be chosen than are those who sit at other, less salient seats. During the deliberation process, the foreperson calls for votes, acts as a liaison between the judge and jury, and, at the conclusion of the deliberations, announces the verdict in court. The foreperson spends more time than other jurors talking about procedural matters, but less time than the other jurors expressing opinions on the verdict. Forepersons do not exert a disproportionate amount of influence over the jury.

26. Research suggests that there is no simple answer. In one study, Norbert Kerr and others (1995) tested the most intuitive hypothesis of all, that jurors favor defendants who are similar to themselves. They presented mixed-race groups with a strong or weak case involving a black or white defendant. They found that when the evidence was weak, the participants were more lenient in their verdicts toward the defendant of the same race. Yet when the evidence was strong, they were harsher against that similar defendant—as if distancing themselves from his wrongdoing. In a second study, Samuel Sommers and Phoebe Ellsworth (2001) tested the popular notion that jurors would show preference for others of their racial group when a crime involves race—as when it is a motivated hate crime or when attorneys "play the race card" in arguments to the jury. Yet they found the opposite pattern. When race was not an "on the radar" issue, white jurors predictably treated the defendant more favorably when he was white than when he was black. Yet when race was made a prominent issue at trial, the white jurors bent over backward not to appear prejudiced; hence, they did not discriminate. Other research as well has shown that jurors may, at times, be motivated to serve as watchdogs against racist tendencies, leading them to process trial information even more carefully when a defendant is black than when he or she is white (Sargent & Bradfield, 2004).

CHAPTER 13

Business

OUTLINE

LEARNING OBJECTIVES: GUIDELINES FOR STUDY

You should be able to do each of the following by the conclusion of Chapter 13.

1.   Define industrial/organizational psychology. Explain the Hawthorne effect and its role in triggering interest in industrial/organizational psychology. (*pp. 529-530*)

2.   Describe the effectiveness of the traditional employment interview when it comes to personnel selection. Consider the role of expectations in job interviews. Discuss the effectiveness of the various alternatives to the traditional job interview. (*pp. 531-537*)

3.   Discuss social psychological perspectives on the debate concerning affirmative action in hiring and promotion. Discuss the effects of diversity on organizational morale and performance. (*pp. 537-542*)

4.   Differentiate objective from subjective criteria for performance appraisals. Identify the potential problems associated with supervisors' evaluations of their subordinates as well as self-evaluations. Identify factors that improve the accuracy of performance appraisals and explain the due process model of performance appraisal. (*pp. 542-545*)

5.   Compare and contrast views of leadership that emphasize a trait approach with those that emphasize interactions between the person and situation. Explain the concepts of transactional and transformational leaderships. Discuss some of the problems faced by women and ethnic minorities when it comes to advancement in the workplace, and consider gender differences in leadership styles and preferences. (*pp. 545-553*)

6.   Summarize the economic factors that affect employee satisfaction. Discuss expectancy theory, equity theory, and the differences between intrinsic and extrinsic motivation. (*pp. 553-558*)

7.   Consider psychological perspectives on economic decision-making. In particular, identify the influence of money on social judgment, social influences on investor behavior, and the significance of concepts such as commitment, entrapment, and escalation. (*pp. 558-563*)

MAJOR CONCEPTS: THE BIG PICTURE

Below are five basic issues or principles that organize Chapter 13. You should know these issues and principles well.

1.   In business, behavior is influenced not only by economic factors but by social psychology as well. This is evident in all aspects of business, including one of the first steps in the development of a successful business or organization: personnel selection. Most employers use traditional employment interviews in their hiring decisions. Such interviews have mixed effects on these decisions; they reduce the effects of some biases but increase the effects of others. Standardized tests, structured interviews, and assessment centers have been developed as alternatives to the traditional employment interviews. Affirmative action in hiring and promotion can lead to either positive or negative reactions depending on the way it is structured and implemented. Affirmative action and the globalization of business have combined to increase diversity in the workplace.

2.   The processes by which employees' performances are evaluated and the means by which these evaluations are communicated to the employees can have profound effects on organizations. Performance appraisals are often based on ratings of employees given by their supervisors. Although such ratings have their benefits, they are also vulnerable to several biases. Self-evaluations are sometimes used, but they tend to be self-serving and inflated and may be biased by power and gender differences. New and improved methods of appraisal have been, and continue to be, developed. These new approaches have been designed to improve not only the accuracy of performance appraisals but also their fairness.

3. The work experience in an organization often depends in large part on the quality of leadership in the organization. There are two general approaches to understanding the determinants of good leadership: the trait approach and interactional models. The trait approach to understanding good leadership emphasizes the role of personal traits that characterize people who are good leaders. Interactional models emphasize the interaction of personal and situational factors. Despite recent gains, women and minorities are still underrepresented in positions of leadership and face various obstacles, such as stereotypes and exclusion from social networks.

4. Both economic and social factors influence worker motivation. Various economic incentive programs are used to motivate by reward. The ways in which these rewards are perceived influence whether the rewards enhance or decrease workers' intrinsic motivation. Concerns about equity have significant effects on motivation and performance.

5. Social psychological factors, such as social comparison, conformity, and attribution, have important effects on economic decision making. For example, investors are influenced by the kinds of attributions they and others make for rising and falling stock prices, and these attributions can in turn affect the stock prices. Individuals and organizations often get psychologically entrapped by initial commitments, leading them to continue with failing courses of action.

KEY TERM EXERCISE: THE CONCEPTS YOU SHOULD KNOW

Below are all of the key terms that appear in **boldface** in Chapter 13. To help you better understand these concepts, rather than just memorize them, write a definition for each term in your own words. After doing so, look at the next section where you'll find a list of definitions from the textbook for each of the key terms presented in random order. For each of your definitions, find the corresponding textbook definition. Note how your definitions compare with those from the textbook.

Key Terms

1. performance appraisal

2. integrity test

3. contingency model of leadership

4. industrial/organizational (I/O) psychology

5. structured interview

6. Hawthorne effect

7. transformational leader

8. assessment center

9. transactional leader

10. escalation effect

11. expectancy theory

12. sunk cost principle

13. normative model of leadership

14. endowment effect

Textbook Definitions

a.   The study of human behavior in business and other organizational settings.

b.   The finding that workers who were observed increased their productivity regardless of what actual changes were made in the work setting.

c.   Paper-and-pencil questionnaire designed to test a job applicant's honesty and character.

d.   Interview in which each job applicant is asked a standard set of questions and evaluated on the same criteria.

e.   Structured setting in which job applicants are exhaustively tested and judged by multiple evaluators.

f.   The process of evaluating an employee's work within the organization.

g.   The theory that leadership effectiveness is determined both by the personal characteristics of leaders and by the control afforded by the situation.

h.   The theory that leadership effectiveness is determined by the amount of feedback and participation that leaders invite from workers.

i.   Leader who gains compliance and support from followers primarily through goal setting and the use of rewards.

j.   Leader who inspires followers to transcend their own needs in the interest of a common cause.

k.   The theory that workers become motivated when they believe that their efforts will produce valued outcomes.

l.   The tendency for investors to remain committed to a losing course of action.

m.   The economic rule of thumb that only future costs and benefits, not past commitments, should be considered in making a decision.

n.   A tendency to inflate the value of objects they already own.

ANSWERS FOR KEY TERM EXERCISE

Answers for the key terms exercise are listed below.

1. **f**
2. **c**
3. **g**
4. **a**
5. **d**
6. **b**
7. **j**
8. **e**
9. **i**
10. **l**
11. **k**
12. **m**
13. **h**
14. **n**

PRACTICE QUIZ: TEST YOUR KNOWLEDGE OF THE CHAPTER

Multiple-Choice Questions

1. The owner of a baseball team has lost more than $15 million of his own money trying to build a team that would win a championship. Not only has the team never won, but the players whose contracts he had purchased are now past their prime. The owner receives an offer from someone who is interested in buying the team at a reduced price. Rather than sell, the owner decides that since he already spent so much on the team, he will continue to put money into it until he can win a championship and justify his expenditures. This reasoning illustrates

    a.   expectancy theory.
    b.   a failure to apply the contingency model of leadership.
    c.   the halo effect.
    d.   a violation of the sunk cost principle.

2. Most evaluations of employee performance are made using

    a.   subjective measures.
    b.   self-evaluations.
    c.   peer-rating processes.
    d.   objective criteria.

3. Research suggests that when it comes to promoting sound, unbiased hiring, traditional live interviews have

    a.   positive effects.
    b.   negative effects.
    c.   mixed effects.
    d.   effects no different from those of other techniques.

4. The idea that a leader is effective if he or she listens to followers and fulfills their needs in exchange for expected levels of job performance is most consistent with the

    a.   normative model.
    b.   contingency model.
    c.   trait approach.
    d.   transactional model.

5. A major problem with using employees' self-evaluations for performance appraisals is that

    a.   employees tend to overestimate their performance and worth in an organization.
    b.   self-evaluations are more affected by contrast effects than are supervisors' evaluations.
    c.   men tend to be more negative on self-evaluations compared to women.
    d.   people who lack power in the organization tend to be more positive on self-evaluations compared to people with significant power.

6. A team of researchers varied the pay schedules of some of the employees in a company to see which schedule would lead to the greatest amount of productivity. If the results of this research were consistent with the Hawthorne effect, it would mean that the researchers found that the

    a.   workers who were paid most frequently had the highest levels of satisfaction but the lowest levels of productivity.
    b.   workers who were paid most frequently had the highest levels of productivity.
    c.   extra attention paid to these workers led to an increase in their productivity regardless of changes in their pay schedule.
    d.   extra attention paid to these workers angered them, leading to a drop in their productivity regardless of changes in their pay schedule.

7. An employer wants to hire salespeople who are extroverted rather than introverted. She has all candidates complete a questionnaire that has been designed by personality psychologists to measure a person's degree of extroversion, and she hires the candidates who score highest on this scale. This employer's method of personnel selection illustrates the use of

    a. standardized tests.
    b. integrity tests.
    c. an assessment center.
    d. performance appraisals.

8. As factory supervisor, Harry annually scrutinizes each employee's productivity rate and quality control record. He then gives each employee feedback on his or her job. Harry's behavior is an example of

    a. contingency leadership.
    b. high situational control.
    c. performance appraisal.
    d. an interactional model of leadership.

9. Which of the following statements is an accurate characterization of assessment centers?

    a. They are relatively ineffective.
    b. They involve groups of activities and evaluators.
    c. They provide employees a chance to give feedback to their supervisors.
    d. They are used primarily by transformational leaders.

10. A company is actively trying to recruit more women for entry-level executive positions. After standardized testing, a dozen new people are hired and four them are women: Glenda, who is told that she was hired because of her gender; Mindy, who is told that she was hired because of her gender and because she got the minimum acceptable score; Eva, who is told that she was hired because of her gender and the fact that she received a score equivalent to that of Ned, the man who had the top score among those not hired; and Topanga, who is told that she was hired because she received one of the top scores. Subsequently, which two women are likely to rate their ability and performance favorably and view the selection process as fair?

    a. Glenda and Mindy
    b. Mindy and Eva
    c. Eva and Topanga
    d. Topanga and Glenda

11. Xavier, who owns a small chocolate factory, is concerned about hiring workers who might steal from the company. Research suggests that Xavier would have the best chance of hiring only honest people if he makes all the job candidates

    a. take a lie-detector test.
    b. submit to live, unstructured interviews.
    c. turn in self-evaluations.
    d. take integrity tests.

12. Adequate notice, fair hearing, and a focus on evidence are all components of the

    a. expectancy theory of worker motivation.
    b. sunk cost principle of decision making.
    c. contingency model of leadership.
    d. due-process model of performance appraisal.

13. Patrick was elected leader of a group. He seemed identical to the other candidates for the leadership role except that he was the tallest. This outcome is most consistent with

    a.   the trait approach to leadership.
    b.   interactional models of leadership.
    c.   the inherently random processes involved in selections of leaders.
    d.   expectancy theory.

14. Jerry and Dean have shared an office for several years. They do the same work, and Jerry feels that they are equally effective in the organization. One day their boss tells them that they will be getting their own offices. Jerry is initially glad but becomes very upset when he sees that Dean has been given an office that is bigger and in a more desirable location than his. Jerry's performance in his job worsens. This outcome is most consistent with

    a.   intrinsic motivation.
    b.   equity theory.
    c.   the sunk cost principle.
    d.   the Hawthorne effect.

15. A particular business uses a structured setting for personnel selection in which several job applicants take part in a series of activities – including written tests, activities in which they play the role of workers in various situations, and so on – that are monitored by a group of evaluators. This is an example of

    a.   equity considerations.
    b.   an assessment center.
    c.   an affirmative action policy.
    d.   a structured interview.

16. While screening candidates for a job, Erica uses a traditional employment interview for Isabella, a self-report personality test for Melanie, a structured interview for Franco, and a polygraph for Ouida. Erica is most likely to be accurate in her assessment of

    a.   Isabella.
    b.   Melanie.
    c.   Franco.
    d.   Ouida.

17. Tara is intelligent, self-assured, and task-oriented. Her boss, nevertheless, does not recommend Tara for the company's management training program because he thinks she's unsuited to be a manager. This outcome is most consistent with

    a.   expectancy theory.
    b.   the notion of the glass ceiling.
    c.   the restriction of range problem.
    d.   the problems of having a transactional leader.

18. Brooke is a department store manager. Her employees are part-time students. To increase sales, Brooke starts a program in which the ten workers with the highest summer sales earn a stipend for college tuition. After she starts this program, Brooke observes that sales increase by 25 percent. This outcome is most consistent with

    a.   the endowment effect.
    b.   the escalation effect.
    c.   expectancy theory.
    d.   the halo effect.

19. Ron runs a six-person real estate office. In order to increase the intrinsic motivation of his sales staff, Ron might consider which of the following?

    a. Deducting ten percent off the paycheck of the salesperson who brings in the least money each month
    b. Raising salaries across the board
    c. Offering a bonus to the employee who brings in the most money in sales each month
    d. Setting up a monthly competition to see who could sell the house that has been on the market longest

20. Stephanie instills a sense of purpose in her employees. Lydia is single-mindedly focused on the job. Wanda insists that all of the members of the organization have a say in all decisions. Beverly likes to "rally the troops" and ensure positive relations and energy. In a situation in which leaders have high situational control, the contingency model would predict that the most effective leader would be

    a. Stephanie.
    b. Lydia.
    c. Wanda.
    d. Beverly.

21. Levi and Fried (2008) found that business school students favor an affirmative action policy that is _____ and that impacted _____

    a. hard; promotions and layoffs of existing employees
    b. hard; the hiring and training of new employees
    c. soft; promotions and layoffs of existing employees
    d. soft; the hiring and training of new employees

22. Which of the following describes the essence of a 360-degree performance appraisal:

    a. The employee is rated on the full spectrum of social and work-related skills required for the job.
    b. The employee is rated, in turn, by every supervisor who works in the same division.
    c. The employee is rated at the end of each workday by a supervisor for a period of one year.
    d. The employee is rated by superiors, peers, subordinates, the employee, and outside stakeholders.

23. In a pair of studies exploring the relationship between money and social rejection, Chinese researchers found that students who had experienced rejection drew _____ coins than did students who experienced acceptance, and were also more distressed following rejection if they had counted _____ beforehand.

    a. larger; money, rather than paper,
    b. larger; paper, rather than money,
    c. smaller; money, rather than paper,
    d. smaller; paper, rather than money,

Essay Questions

24. Describe an alternative to the traditional interview that research suggests may be more effective.

25. Discuss two factors that can boost the accuracy of performance evaluations.

26. Describe what is meant by transformational leaders. Are such leaders more consistent with the trait approach or with interactional models? Why?

27. In terms of cultural influences on organizational diversity, discuss the effects of affirmative action programs and globalization.

ANSWERS TO THE PRACTICE QUIZ

Multiple-Choice Questions: Correct Answers and Explanations

1. d.   **a violation of the sunk cost principle.** The sunk cost principle is a principle of economics stating that only future benefits and costs, not past commitments, should be considered in making a decision. In this example, the owner of the baseball team is considering his past commitments as he makes his decision, and he decides not to sell the team even though the future costs of owning the team look like they will be higher than the benefits. He is thus in violation of the principle. Expectancy theory proposes that people analyze the benefits and costs of possible courses of action and exert effort when they believe it will produce a desired outcome (monetary or symbolic), but this example is not concerned with the amount of effort that the owner exerts or that he expects his employees to exert. The contingency model of leadership proposes that leadership effectiveness is determined both by the personal characteristics of leaders and by the control afforded by the situation; but this example is not about leadership, and it does not indicate the personal characteristics of the owner or the control afforded by the situation. Finally, the halo effect is a failure to discriminate among distinct aspects of a worker's performance; but it is not relevant in this example.

2. a.   **subjective measures.** Objective, quantifiable criteria of workers' performances are often unavailable and frequently do not take into account the quality, as opposed to the quantity, of work. Therefore, performance appraisals are usually based on subjective measures – perceptions of employees by their supervisors, coworkers, customers, and so on. Although employees or their peers are sometimes asked for their subjective evaluations, it is supervisors who are most often asked to appraise employee performance.

3. c.   **mixed effects.** Research suggests that, on the positive side, live interviews may actually diminish the tendency to make stereotyped judgments. On the negative side, they often lack predictive validity and can be distorted by employers' preconceptions. Such distortions may be less likely to emerge when interviewers use structured questions or when assessment centers rather than traditional interviews are used.

4. d.   **transactional model.** According to the transactional model of leadership, leadership is a two-way street in which there is a mutual influence between a leader and follower. An effective leader sets clear goals for the followers, provides tangible rewards, listens to followers, and fulfills their needs in exchange for an expected level of job performance. The other potential answers to this question all may be considered "top-down" approaches in which the followers are portrayed as passive creatures to be soothed or aroused at management's discretion. The normative model judges the effectiveness of a leader according to how much participation and feedback he or she invites from the workers. Too much participation is deemed inefficient, whereas too little lowers worker morale. The contingency model is the theory that leadership effectiveness is determined both by the personal characteristics of leaders and by the control afforded by the situation; this model would predict that the kind of leader described in this example would be effective only in certain situations (probably those that afford the leader a moderate degree of situational control). The trait approach to understanding leadership is to identify traits that characterize leaders. The idea described in this question emphasizes that effective leadership is determined not only by the personal characteristics of the leader but by the interaction of the leader and the followers; thus, as would not be considered by the trait approach, the kinds of traits that might be found in a good leader in one situation might make for a poor leader in another situation.

5.   a.   **employees tend to overestimate their performance and worth in an organization.**
People's tendency to overestimate their performance and worth is a principal reason why self-evaluations often are flawed. The three other potential answers to this question are all opposite to the truth. Contrast effects are more likely to affect supervisors' ratings than self-evaluations; for example, supervisors who first observe a very positive performance by one worker are more likely to judge an average subsequent performance by another worker as less positive, and supervisors who first observe a very negative performance by one worker are more likely to judge an average subsequent performance by another worker as more positive. Men tend to be more boastful on their self-evaluations than women, and people with relatively low power tend to make more modest self-evaluations than people high in power.

6.   c.   **extra attention paid to these workers led to an increase in their productivity, regardless of changes in their pay schedule.** The Hawthorne effect refers to the finding that workers who were observed increased their productivity regardless of what actual changes were made in the work setting. This effect is consistent with the outcome illustrated in this selection but inconsistent with the three alternative answers provided.

7.   a.   **standardized tests.** Many companies today use standardized written tests in their personnel selection process. These tests may be designed to measure (1) various cognitive abilities such as intelligence, (2) personality traits such as extroversion, which was the focus in this question, or (3) a candidate's honesty and character. An integrity test is an example of the third kind of standardized test, but it is not what the employer in this question was trying to measure. An assessment center is a structured setting in which job applicants are exhaustively tested and judged by multiple evaluators, but this employer simply gave the candidates one test. Performance appraisals concern the evaluation of an employee's work within the organization, but this is not relevant here.

8.   c.   **performance appraisal.** Performance appraisal is the process of evaluating an employee's work within the organization and communicating the results to that person; this is what Harry is described as doing in this example. The contingency model of leadership emphasizes that leadership effectiveness is determined both by the personal characteristics of leaders and by the control afforded by the situation. There is no evidence of such leadership in this example. According to the contingency model of leadership, leaders enjoy high situational control when they have good relations with their staff, a position of power, and a clearly structured task. Although Harry *may* be in such a situation, it is impossible to determine from this question. Interactional models of leadership emphasize the interaction between personal and situational factors. There is no mention of Harry's personal characteristics or of the situational factors in the factory.

9.   b.   **They involve groups of activities and evaluators.** In an assessment center, a group of applicants takes part in a set of activities (such as written tests and role-playing exercises) that are monitored by a group of evaluators. Assessment centers are said to be more effective than traditional interviews at finding applicants who will succeed in a particular position. They are not designed to provide employees a chance to give feedback to their supervisors. Transformational leaders are leaders who inspire followers to transcend their own needs in the interest of a common cause; there is no evidence that assessment centers are primarily used by these leaders.

10.   c.   **Eva and Topanga.** Heilman and her colleagues (1998) found that female leaders, who had been told that their appointment was based on merit (as Topanga was), rated their own performance and leadership abilities most favorably and saw the selection process as fair. The same was true for female leaders (such as Eva), who were told that their test score matched that of the top rejected male.

11.   d.   **take integrity tests.** Integrity tests are paper-and-pencil questionnaires designed to test a job applicant's honesty and character. Research has found that these tests are predictive of job performance and counterproductive behaviors such as theft. Using integrity tests would be an improvement over live, unstructured interviews, which fail to identify people prone to dishonesty. The use of lie detectors, or polygraphs, is prohibited in the workplace, except in matters involving large sums of money, public safety, and national security. None of those exceptions appears to apply here. Self-evaluations are sometimes used in performance appraisals, but because people often present themselves quite favorably in these self-evaluations, it is unlikely that they could be used to exclude dishonest people.

12.   d.   **due-process model of performance appraisal.** The due-process model is designed to enhance fairness in performance appraisals. According to this model, fairness can be enhanced by such factors as adequate notice, fair hearing, and a focus on evidence of job performance. However, these factors are not components of expectancy theory of worker motivation, the sunk cost principle of decision making, or the contingency model of leadership. Expectancy theory proposes that people analyze the benefits and costs of possible courses of action and exert effort when they believe it will produce a desired outcome (monetary or symbolic). The sunk cost principle is a principle of economics stating that only future benefits and costs, not past commitments, should be considered in making a decision. The contingency model of leadership emphasizes that leadership effectiveness is determined both by the personal characteristics of leaders and by the control afforded by the situation.

13.   a.   **the trait approach to leadership.** The trait approach to understanding leadership emphasizes identification of traits that characterize leaders. One characteristic associated with leadership is height. For example, between the years 1900 and 2000, the tallest candidate for U.S. president won an astonishing twenty-three out of twenty-five elections. Research suggests that this finding is not a random coincidence. Interactional models of leadership, in contrast, emphasize the interaction between personal and situational factors. But this example makes no mention of situational factors. Expectancy theory maintains that people analyze the benefits and costs of possible courses of action and exert effort when they believe it will produce a desired outcome (monetary or symbolic). But the example does not concern worker motivation or performance.

14.   b.   **equity theory.** According to equity theory, people want rewards to be equitable, such that the ratio between inputs and outcomes is the same for the self as for others. In this example, which resembles the situation faced by some of the subjects in Greenberg's (1988) study of employees in a large insurance firm, Jerry perceives the distribution of offices to be inequitable. Because Jerry believes that he works as hard and is as valuable as Dean, Jerry is not happy when Dean is rewarded more than he is. When people feel undercompensated for their work, as Jerry does, they become more likely to lower their job performance. People are intrinsically motivated when they engage in an activity for the sake of interest, challenge, or sheer enjoyment. If Jerry were very intrinsically motivated, he would not care about his compensation relative to Dean's, and he would continue to work hard and perform well. The sunk cost principle is a principle of economics stating that only future benefits and costs, not past commitments, should be considered in making a decision, but this principle is not relevant in this example. The Hawthorne effect refers to the finding that workers who were observed increased their productivity, regardless of what actual changes were made in the work setting. In contrast to the Hawthorne effect, but consistent with equity theory, Jerry's productivity *decreased* after the change.

15.   b.   **an assessment center.** Assessment centers are used to evaluate candidates for hiring and promotion. In an assessment center, a group of applicants takes part in a series of activities that are monitored by a group of evaluators. Equity considerations concern the perception that the benefits one receives for working are fair. Although considerations of fairness are important for personnel selection as well, there is no direct evidence that such considerations were relevant in the business or setting described in this question. Affirmative action policies give preference in hiring, admissions, and promotion to women and underrepresented minority groups; there is no evidence that such policies are used in the setting described here. Finally, a structured interview is one in which each job applicant is asked a standard set of questions and evaluated on the same criteria. Although structured interviews may be included among the activities evaluated at an assessment center, they are not the only activity.

16.   c.   **Franco.** Structured interviews are interviews in which each job applicant is asked a standard set of questions and evaluated on the same criteria. This standardization prevents interviewers from unwittingly conducting biased interviews that merely confirm their preconceptions. Some research suggests that structured interviews are better than traditional interviews in the selection of qualified workers. Although certain personality traits are associated with productivity on the job, self-report personality measures are easily faked and are therefore not highly predictive. The polygraph is a mechanical instrument that records physiological arousal from multiple channels; it is often used as a lie-detector test. However, there are ethical and legal problems associated with the use of the polygraph in personnel selection, such as suggesting that people are lying when they are not.

17.   b.   **the notion of the glass ceiling.** The glass ceiling refers to a barrier that women and minorities come up against – a barrier so subtle that it's transparent, yet so strong that it keeps them from reaching the top of the hierarchy. Despite the progress that women and minorities have made in entry-level and middle-level positions, they still seem to be blocked by this glass ceiling when seeking positions of leadership. This example is not relevant to expectancy theory, which is the theory that people analyze the benefits and costs of possible courses of action and exert effort when they believe it will produce a desired outcome (monetary or symbolic). The restriction of range problem refers to the failure of people to make adequate distinctions in evaluating workers (e.g., some people may give everyone positive evaluations). But there is no evidence that Tara's boss thinks everyone is unsuited for the job, so this example is not consistent with this problem. Tara's situation is also not the kind of problem that would more likely result from having a transactional leader. The transactional model of leadership emphasizes that an effective leader provides tangible rewards, listens to followers, and fulfills their needs in exchange for an expected level of job performance, but Tara's boss is *not* providing Tara with tangible rewards and is *not* fulfilling her needs, despite Tara's effective job performance.

18.   c.   **expectancy theory.** Expectancy theory maintains that people analyze the benefits and costs of possible courses of action and exert effort when they believe it will produce a desired outcome (monetary or symbolic). In this example, the part-time students believe that exerting effort might produce a desired outcome, so they have exerted the effort. The endowment effect is the tendency to inflate the value of things already in one's possession. It does not apply here. The escalation effect is the tendency for investors to remain committed to a losing course of action, but this is not relevant here. A halo effect is a failure to discriminate among distinct aspects of a worker's performance, but there is no evidence of such an effect here.

19. c.   **Offering a bonus to the employee who brings in the most money in sales each month.** People are intrinsically motivated when they engage in an activity for the sake of interest, challenge, or sheer enjoyment. Rewards that have informational value by offering positive feedback about the quality of one's performance can enhance intrinsic motivation. Performance bonuses are an example of such rewards. In contrast to rewards perceived as serving an informational function, those perceived as serving a controlling function (e.g., a raise in salary) are likely to undermine intrinsic motivation. Similarly, punishment and competition would make employees feel as if they're being controlled by external forces and thus would decrease their intrinsic motivation.

20. b.   **Lydia.** According to Fiedler's contingency model of leadership, task-oriented leaders (who are single-mindedly focused on the job, as Lydia is) are more effective than relations-oriented leaders (who are more concerned about the feelings of the employees, as Stephanie, Wanda, and Beverly seem to be) in situations in which leaders have high situational control (that is, when leaders have good relations with staff, a position of power, and a clearly structured task). This model also states that task-oriented leaders such as Lydia are more effective than relations-oriented leaders when the leader has low situational control. Relations-oriented leaders are said to perform better in situations that afford a moderate degree of control.

21. d.   **soft; the hiring and training of new employees.** When Levi and Fried (2008) described various affirmative action plans to business school students, they found that the students favored a "soft" policy, such as having an outreach program to identify, recruit, and train minority group members, rather than a "hard" policy that involved preferential hiring practices to members of outgroups. They also found that the students favored a policy that influenced the hiring and training of new employees as opposed to a policy that affected promotions and layoffs for existing employees.

22. d.   **The employee is rated by superiors, peers, subordinates, the employee, and outside stakeholders.** The 360-degree performance appraisal utilizes a multiple-rater system in which a final evaluation represents the average of ratings made by independent sources with different perspectives. In a typical 360-degree assessment, an employee's performance is rated by superiors, peers, subordinates, the employees themselves, and even outside stakeholders such as customers, clients, students, and patients. In this way, whatever idiosyncratic bias a single individual brings to his or her ratings can be offset by others. Although there is debate over how to combine, compare, and contrast different sources, research shows that this approach in general is an improvement over single-rater methods (Craig & Hannum, 2006; Morgeson et al., 2005).

23. b.   **larger; paper, rather than money.** Chinese researchers (Xinyue Zhou and others, 2009) explored the relationship between money and social rejection in two studies. In the first study, university students were made to feel either rejected or accepted by their peers. Later they were asked to draw Chinese coins from memory. The ones who thought they had been rejected drew larger coins. In the second study, students were asked to count either 80 pieces of paper or 80 $100 bills. Next they played a computerized ball toss game. Again, some were rejected and others were accepted. The rejected ones felt more distress if they had been in the group that counted plain paper. The members of the group that counted money were not as distressed in the face of social rejection. Why did money provide a buffer against social rejection? The researchers theorized that money makes people feel less interconnected and more self-sufficient.

Answers to Essay Questions: Sample Essays

24. One approach to improving personnel selection involves the use of structured interviews. In such interviews, each job applicant is asked a standard set of questions and evaluated on the same criteria as those applied to every other job applicant. This standardization prevents interviewers from unwittingly conducting biased interviews that merely confirm their preconceptions. Some research suggests that structured interviews are more effective than traditional interviews in the selection of qualified workers.

25. One factor concerns the timing of evaluations in relation to the observation of performance. Evaluations are less prone to error when they are made immediately after performance than after a delay. Once memory for the details of the performance begins to fade over time, evaluators are more likely to be affected by stereotypes, halo effects, and other biases. A second factor that can boost the accuracy of performance evaluations is the number of evaluators used. A system that utilizes multiple raters is better than a system that utilizes just one. Because the individual biases or tendencies of multiple raters largely cancel each other out, the average across raters tends to be more accurate than the ratings of any single evaluator. Assessment centers use multiple raters when evaluating candidates for hiring or promotion.

26. Transformational leaders inspire followers to transcend their own needs in the interest of a common cause, articulate a vision for the future, and are able to mobilize others to share that vision. They are likely to be charismatic, inspirational, intellectually stimulating, and considerate of others. This characterization of good leaders is more consistent with the trait approach than with interactional models. The trait approach to the understanding of effective leadership identifies traits that characterize great leaders – and, indeed, transformational leaders are identified by the traits and characteristics they possess, such as charisma. Interactional models, in contrast, view leadership as an interaction between personal and situational factors. The idea of the transformational leader is not consistent with the interactional approach because this approach would expect similar leaders to rise to the top and lead and inspire others in any situation.

27. For many years, the study of organizational behavior was "culture blind and culture bound" (Triandis, 1994; Gelfand et al., 2007). In light of two dramatic historical changes, researchers now look at the workplace through a broader lens. The first change has resulted from affirmative action programs, which forced an increase in the number of women and minorities who populate most organizations. The second is the worldwide trend toward globalization, which has brought more and more people from disparate cultures into daily contact with each other, often as coworkers. Georgia Chao and Henry Moon (2005) note that every individual worker has a multidimensional identity that can be characterized within a cultural mosaic consisting of the various "tiles" of his or her demographic characteristics (such as age, gender, race, and ethnic heritage), geographical background (such as country of origin, region, climate, and population density), and personal associations (such as with religion, profession, and political affiliation). In some ways, everyone is similar; in other ways, no two people are alike. For researchers who study organizational behavior, the challenge is to represent the full complexity that comes with a diverse workplace.

CHAPTER 14

Health

OUTLINE

LEARNING OBJECTIVES: GUIDELINES FOR STUDY

You should be able to do each of the following by the conclusion of Chapter 14.

1. Define health psychology. Define stress and identify its causes, including major crises, positive and negative life events, and microstressors of everyday life. (*pp. 569-575*)

2. Consider how the body responds to stress. Describe the three stages of the general adaptation syndrome. Explain how the experience of stressful events affects the heart, the immune system, and the likelihood of experiencing other short-term and chronic disease. (*pp. 575-583*)

3. Discuss the physical and mental health implications of attributional and explanatory tendencies. Discuss the negative effects engendered by learned helplessness and a depressive explanatory style. (*pp. 583-584*)

4. Consider the psychological tendencies that contribute to the human capacity for resilience, including self-efficacy and optimism. (*pp. 584-588*)

5. Define the two principal types of coping with stress, problem- and emotion-focused coping. Identify the strengths and limitations of each coping style, as well as the types of stress towards which each is best suited. (*pp. 588-596*)

6. Explain what is meant by "proactive coping." Discuss the role of self-complexity, social support, religion, and culture on the manner in which people cope with stress. (*pp. 596-601*)

7. Identify the social psychological components of a successful approach to treatment, and explain why they are effective. Outline factors that promote prevention of risky behaviors. (*pp. 601-605*)

8. Consider the wide range factors that affect the pursuit of happiness and subjective well-being. Describe when people are most likely to be happy and when they are least likely to be happy. (*pp. 605-609*)

MAJOR CONCEPTS: THE BIG PICTURE

Below are five basic issues or principles that organize Chapter 14. You should know these issues and principles well.

1. Theorists have proposed that all change ends up being stressful, but negative events tend to be more stressful than positive events. Simple daily hassles can be an especially important source of stress in our lives, as can major crises like a catastrophe or a war.

2. Stress can have strong negative effects on the body. Selye proposed a three-stage model called the general adaptation syndrome to describe how the body responds to stress. According to this model, people have an initial alarm reaction to stress, followed by a resistance stage, which eventually leads to an exhaustion stage where the body breaks down. Stress, particularly when it is associated with the Type A behavior pattern, has been shown to have strong negative effects on the heart. Stress also affects the immune system by reducing the body's natural defense system. This probably is part of the reason that people under stress are more susceptible to a number of different illnesses.

3. People may view the same stressful event quite differently. Some may view it as an indication of their incompetence and their general weaknesses, which they believe they cannot overcome. This sort of appraisal, characteristic of learned helplessness, is associated with depression. Others may view the same event as a challenge and as an opportunity for them to take charge of their lives. Such optimism and appraisals of agency are associated with positive health outcomes.

4. When coping with a negative event, some people will focus on how to overcome the problem whereas others will focus on how to deal with their emotions. People can deal with their emotions by distracting themselves from them or by opening up and expressing them. They can also cope proactively before a stressful event occurs. Self-complexity and social support are two important resources that people can use when they confront stress. There is an influence of culture on methods of coping.

5. Social psychologists have also examined ways to promote health and have found that social ingredients in a medical intervention can be crucial to its effectiveness. Research on persuasion has also provided important lessons in how to encourage people to engage in behaviors that prevent illness.

KEY TERM EXERCISE: THE CONCEPTS YOU SHOULD KNOW

Following are all of the key terms that appear in **boldface** in Chapter 14. To help you better understand these concepts, rather than just memorize them, write a definition for each term in your own words. After doing so, look at the next section where you'll find a list of definitions from the textbook for each of the key terms presented in random order. For each of your definitions, find the corresponding textbook definition. Note how your definitions compare with those from the textbook.

Key Terms

1. health psychology

2. Type A behavior pattern

3. stress

4. general adaptation syndrome

5. immune system

6. posttraumatic stress disorder (PTSD)

7. emotion-focused coping

8. learned helplessness

9. depressive explanatory style

10. placebo effect

11. self-efficacy

12. proactive coping

13. psychoneuroimmunology (PNI)

14. coping

15. problem-focused coping

16. appraisal

17. stressor

18. social support

19. subjective well-being

Textbook Definitions

a. A phenomenon in which experience with an uncontrollable event creates passive behavior toward a subsequent threat to well-being.

b. A condition in which a person experiences enduring physical and psychological symptoms after an extremely stressful event.

c. Cognitive and behavioral efforts to alter a stressful situation.

d. A person's belief that he or she is capable of the specific behavior required to produce a desired outcome in a given situation.

e. The helpful coping resources provided by friends and other people.

f. Anything that causes stress.

g. Up-front efforts to ward off or modify the onset of a stressful event.

h. An unpleasant state of arousal in which people perceive the demands of an event as taxing or exceeding their ability to satisfy or alter those demands.

i. The study of physical health and illness by psychologists from various areas of specialization.

j. A habitual tendency to attribute negative events to causes that are stable, global, and internal.

k. A subfield of psychology that examines the links among psychological factors, brain and nervous system, and the immune system.

l. Efforts to reduce stress.

m. A biological surveillance system that detects and destroys "nonself" substances that invade the body.

n. The tendency for an ineffectual drug or treatment to improve a patient's condition because he or she believes in its effectiveness.

o. The process by which people make judgments about the demands of potentially stressful events and their ability to meet those demands.

p. A three-stage process (alarm, resistance, and exhaustion) by which the body responds to stress.

q. Cognitive and behavioral efforts to reduce the distress produced by a stressful situation.

r. A pattern of behavior characterized by extremes of competitive striving for achievement, a sense of time urgency, hostility, and aggression.

s. A term used by social psychologists to describe the pursuit of happiness.

ANSWERS FOR KEY TERM EXERCISE

Answers for the key terms exercise are listed below.

1. **i**
2. **r**
3. **h**
4. **p**
5. **m**
6. **b**
7. **q**
8. **a**
9. **j**
10. **n**
11. **d**
12. **g**
13. **k**
14. **l**
15. **c**
16. **o**
17. **f**
18. **e**
19. **s**

PRACTICE QUIZ: TEST YOUR KNOWLEDGE OF THE CHAPTER

Multiple-Choice Questions

1. Gretchen recently lost her job, became engaged to be married, started classes at a junior college, and moved into a new apartment. Which change in Gretchen's life is most likely to produce harmful stress?

    a. Losing her job
    b. Becoming engaged to be married
    c. Starting classes at a junior college
    d. Moving into her own apartment

2. Research suggests that the component of Type A behavior pattern that is most likely to lead to heart disease is

    a. time-consciousness.
    b. hostility.
    c. competitiveness.
    d. a hard-driving attitude.

3. Paul and Ann were recently married. They have since experienced several disagreements over childrearing and money matters. These conflicts that Paul and Ann are having could be categorized as

    a. major life changes.
    b. microstressors.
    c. a form of burnout.
    d. catastrophes.

4. Julio was living near Los Angeles when an earthquake occurred in the area. He is particularly likely to feel stress from the earthquake if he

    a. was distressed before the earthquake.
    b. exhibits a Type A behavior pattern.
    c. has never been in an earthquake before.
    d. is suffering from depression.

5. Steve has a depressive explanatory style. Consequently, when asked why he thought he did not make the cut for the football team, he might have said:

    a. "I didn't get enough sleep last night."
    b. "I can't seem to do anything right, ever."
    c. "That coach doesn't know anything about football."
    d. "I guess I just wasn't good enough, but there's always basketball."

6. At the present time, Americans are most likely to die from

    a. AIDS.
    b. accidents.
    c. heart disease.
    d. pneumonia.

7. Stress hormones such as adrenaline

    a. "charge up" the immune system to fight off disease.
    b. have little effect on the immune system.
    c. suppress the immune system, thereby lowering the body's resistance to disease.
    d. cause people to engage in dangerous behaviors that compromise the immune system.

8. Which of the following is most likely to be causing considerable stress for the average person in the US today:

   a. Our military's involvement in foreign conflicts
   b. Social relationships
   c. Money
   d. Work

9. After becoming a victim of date rape, Eleanor has been feeling extremely anxious, has trouble falling asleep, is unable to pay attention in class, and is constantly thinking about the night of the rape. When her best friend calls and suggests that they go out, Eleanor always finds an excuse to say "No." Eleanor appears to be suffering from

   a. burnout.
   b. learned helplessness.
   c. posttraumatic stress disorder.
   d. Type A behavior pattern.

10. Anna is facing a serious bout with cancer. She remains steadfastly optimistic in the face of her diagnosis. Her positive attitude is likely to

    a. help cure her cancer.
    b. have a small effect on her immune system.
    c. make her less likely to follow her doctor's advice.
    d. cause her cancer to progress more quickly.

11. Allison's car broke down on the way to work. She checks to see whether there is a bus on this route and whether a coworker who lives nearby can give her a ride. Allison's actions illustrate

    a. emotion-focused coping.
    b. problem-focused coping.
    c. proactive coping.
    d. avoidance coping.

12. Allowing patients to decide on the type of treatment they receive for conditions like alcoholism and obesity is likely to

    a. increase the effectiveness of the treatment.
    b. decrease the effectiveness of the treatment.
    c. neither increase nor decrease the effectiveness of the treatment.
    d. increase the effectiveness of treatment for obesity, but decrease the effectiveness of treatment for alcoholism.

13. After being at home all week with his children, Charlie feels extremely stressed. To relax, he tries meditating for thirty minutes every night. Charlie's use of meditation illustrates

    a. social support.
    b. emotion-focused coping.
    c. social-clinical interfaces.
    d. negative affectivity.

14. Pete has taken up golf as a hobby. After weeks of practice, he is now confident that he can drive the ball off the tee and keep it in the fairway. Pete's belief is an example of

    a. self-efficacy.
    b. vulnerability factors.
    c. help-seeking.
    d. role enhancement.

15. Wayne just came face-to-face with a black bear while hiking on a trail. His sympathetic nervous system is activated. Therefore, which of the following is happening:

    a.   His liver is pouring extra sugar into his bloodstream.
    b.   His blood clots slower.
    c.   His saliva flow increases.
    d.   His pupils contract.

16. The finding that women are less likely to become depressed when they are involved with a spouse or boyfriend is consistent with the _____ model of social support.

    a.   number of social contacts
    b.   number of helpers
    c.   intimacy
    d.   perceived availability

17. Research on psychotherapy has shown that one factor that may lead to its effectiveness is the

    a.   theoretical orientation of the therapist.
    b.   experience of the therapist.
    c.   amount of schooling the therapist has had.
    d.   hope and positive expectations offered by the therapy.

18. Efforts to fend off stressful situations before they occur are termed

    a.   emotion-focused coping.
    b.   problem-focused coping.
    c.   avoidance coping.
    d.   proactive coping.

19. Women who are upset tend to _____, whereas men who are upset tend to _____.

    a.   brood; act out
    b.   engage in antisocial behavior; seek treatment
    c.   distract themselves with physical activity; ruminate
    d.   use drugs or alcohol; confront negative feelings

20. Sometimes people want to change their health behaviors but feel they cannot do so. In such cases persuasion should be used in an effort to

    a.   arouse fear.
    b.   impart credible information.
    c.   increase self-efficacy.
    d.   stress the rewards of the health behavior.

21. Social psychologists are most likely to use which of the following to measure the subjective well-being of individuals:

    a.   Self-reports
    b.   Polygraph data
    c.   The opinions of friends
    d.   The opinions of family members

22. Asians are more likely than European Americans to cope with stress by

    a.   turning to others for support.
    b.   seeking explicit social support.
    c.   joining a self-help group.
    d.   utilizing implicit social support.

23. Highlighting a dark side to the "American dream," research shows that the
_____ materialistic people are, the _____ satisfied they seem to be.
   a. more; less
   b. less; more
   c. less; less
   d. more; more

Essay Questions

24. Explain how change can lead to stress in one's life. Give examples of minor and major events that can cause stress.

25. Compare and contrast problem-focused and emotion-focused coping.

26. Describe how a sense of control over one's life and one's medical treatment can promote health.

27. Discuss how stress can have both positive and negative effects on the immune system.

28. Discuss the general point that resilience, or hardiness, serves as a buffer against stress.

29. Discuss differences in coping styles between collectivist and individualist cultures.

ANSWERS TO THE PRACTICE QUIZ

Multiple-Choice Questions: Correct Answers and Explanations

1.   a.   **losing her job.** Although it was originally proposed that all life changes lead to stress, it is now generally believed that *negative* life changes produce harmful stress. For Gretchen, losing her job is the negative event that she faced that is most likely to produce harmful stress. Becoming engaged, starting classes, and moving into a new apartment are unlikely to produce harmful stress.

2.   b.   **hostility.** Research on Type A behavior pattern has shown that of the various components of this behavior pattern hostility seems to be the most closely linked to heart disease. Time-consciousness, competitiveness, and a hard-driving attitude are components of the Type A behavior pattern, but they have not shown the strong link to heart disease that hostility has.

3.   b.   **microstressors.** Paul and Ann seem to have many daily hassles or microstressors in their marriage. These minor daily stressors can accumulate and affect people's health. While Paul and Ann's marriage certainly was a life change for them, their current stressors (arguing over finances and childrearing) are not a cause of major change in an aspect of their lives. Burnout is a prolonged response to job stress, not marriage. Catastrophes are traumatic events such as war, car accidents, plane crashes, violent crime, sexual or physical abuse, death of a loved one, or natural disasters, such as hurricanes, fires, floods, or earthquakes.

4.   a.   **was distressed before the earthquake.** As reported in the main text, a study that examined stress levels both before and after an earthquake found that people who were distressed before the earthquake were among those most likely to suffer additional stress from the earthquake. This research emphasizes the effect of major stressors on people's lives. There is no evidence that people with Type A behavior pattern, people who have never experienced an earthquake, or people who are suffering from depression are more likely to feel stress from an earthquake.

5.   b.   **"I can't seem to do anything right, ever."** The depressive explanatory style refers to a tendency to attribute bad events to factors that are internal rather than external ("It's my fault"), stable rather than unstable ("It will not change"), and global rather than specific ("It spreads to all parts of my life"). The answer "I can't seem to do anything right, ever" is internal, stable, and global. In contrast, the answer "I didn't get enough sleep last night" is unstable, "That coach doesn't know anything about football" is external, and "I guess I just wasn't good enough, but there's always basketball" is specific.

6.   c.   **heart disease.** Heart disease is now the leading cause of death in the US. AIDS is the twentieth on the list of leading causes. Accidents are the fifth leading cause, topped by heart disease, cancer, strokes, and respiratory illnesses. Pneumonia used to be a leading cause of death in the past, along with other infectious diseases, but that is no longer the case.

7.   c.   **suppress the immune system, thereby lowering the body's resistance to disease.** Research in psychoneuroimmunology demonstrates that adrenaline and other stress hormones weaken the immune system. They do not "charge it up" and they do have a negative effect. And there is no evidence that adrenaline leads to negative behaviors that weaken the immune system.

8.   c.   **Money.** According to an APA (2008) survey, 4 out of 5 Americans report being stressed about money and the economy. Our military's involvement in foreign conflicts was not reported as one of the top stressors. Neither was the topic of social relationships. Work was one of the top stressors, but did not rank as high as money.

9. c. **posttraumatic stress disorder.** Eleanor is manifesting many of the symptoms typical of those suffering from posttraumatic stress disorder (PTSD): recurring anxiety, sleeplessness, nightmares, intrusive bad thoughts, attention problems, and social withdrawal. Burnout is a prolonged response to job stress and does not, therefore, apply here. Learned helplessness is the acquired expectation that one cannot control important outcomes. There is no indication that Eleanor has feelings of hopelessness. Type A behavior pattern is characterized by extreme competitiveness, time urgency and hostility or aggression. Clearly that does not apply here.

10. b. **have a small effect on her immune system.** Optimism usually provides a small boost to the immune system, but this effect is unlikely to be the sole reason for the impact of optimism on health. Other ways in which optimism promotes health have yet to be discovered. There is no clear evidence that optimism helps cure cancer, makes people less likely to follow a doctor's advice, or makes people's cancer progress more quickly.

11. b. **problem-focused coping.** Allison has taken several steps to remedy the problem that is causing her stress. If she is able to catch the bus or hitch a ride, her current situation will be remedied, which should lower her stress. Allison does not seem to be engaging in emotion-focused coping, which has to do with managing stressful emotions rather than taking action against the stressor. There is also no evidence that she used proactive coping, which involves up-front efforts to modify or suppress an upcoming stressful event. Or that she used avoidance coping, which involves shutting down and not acknowledging stressful thoughts.

12. a. **increase the effectiveness of the treatment.** Generally, when alcoholics or obese people are given the opportunity to choose their own treatment, the treatment is more effective.

13. b. **emotion-focused coping.** Charlie is using a strategy, meditation, that removes the harmful emotional effects of stress he is experiencing without eliminating the cause of the stress, staying home with the kids. This type of coping is called emotion-focused coping. Charlie does not seem to be seeking social support from others, and his actions bear little resemblance to social-clinical interfaces or negative affectivity.

14. a. **self-efficacy.** Pete's belief that he can hit a good drive is an example of self-efficacy, the belief that one is capable of doing what needs to be done in a specific situation. Vulnerability factors, help-seeking, and role enhancement are concepts that do not address the belief that one can succeed at such a task.

15. a. **His liver is pouring extra sugar into his bloodstream.** When a person is confronted with danger, the sympathetic nervous system activates and adrenaline is secreted. That increases the heart rate and heightens arousal. Consequently, the liver pours extra sugar into the bloodstream to provide needed energy for fight or flight. At the same time, blood clots faster to heal wounds, saliva flow is inhibited as digestion slows down to divert blood to the brain and skeletal muscles, the pupils dilate to allow in more light, and breathing speeds up to allow for more oxygen,

16. a.   **number of social contacts** According to the number of social contacts model of social support, the more contact that people have with others, the more social support they will receive and the better their health outcomes will be. There is a considerable amount of evidence that supports this model. For example, women who are involved in a relationship and have regular contact with their spouse or boyfriend tend to have better health outcomes than women not involved in a relationship. The number of helpers model of social support proposes that it is not the number of social contacts that leads to better health outcomes, but rather the number of contacts with people who can help. The intimacy model of social support suggests that only those contacts with someone whom one can share his or her innermost thoughts are likely to lead to better health outcomes. Finally, the perceived availability model of social support suggests that only those contacts that one believes are available lead to positive health outcomes. These models maintain that only some relationships (i.e., better-quality relationships) lead to better health outcomes (e.g., less depression), and thus all of them are inconsistent with the basic finding that relationships tend to make women less depressed. Nevertheless, these other models represent useful developments in the concept of social support.

17. d.   **the hope and positive expectations offered by the therapy.** Research suggests that a therapist's theoretical orientation, experience, and amount of schooling all bear little relationship to how effective the psychotherapy is. One factor that may make psychotherapy effective, however, is the sense of hope and positive expectations offered by the therapy.

18. d.   **proactive coping.** Proactive coping involves up-front efforts to ward off or modify the onset of stressful situations. Problem-focused coping is an effort to alter a stressful situation, whereas emotion-focused coping is an effort to reduce the distress caused by a stressful situation. Both of these are enacted after the situation occurs. Similarly, avoidance coping involves blocking stressful thoughts from awareness after the stressful event.

19. a.   **brood; act out.** Women who are upset tend to brood, ruminate, confront negative feelings, and seek treatment for depression. Men who are upset tend to act out, resort to drug and alcohol, engage in antisocial behavior, and distract themselves with physical activity.

20. c.   **increase self-efficacy.** People may want to change their health behavior, have developed a positive attitude toward health outcomes, and have even developed an intention to engage in healthy behavior. However, they think that they cannot follow through on these behaviors. What these people need to develop is a sense of self-efficacy, a sense that they can carry out the positive health behaviors. Arousing their fear and giving them credible information might help to change their attitudes, and stressing the rewards of health behaviors may increase their intentions to engage in these behaviors, but the people described in the question already have positive attitudes and intentions to act, so these modes of persuasion are likely to be insufficient for them.

21. a.   **Self-reports.** To study subjective well-being one must be able to measure it. How do researchers know if someone is happy? Simple: They ask. Better yet, they use questionnaires such as the *Satisfaction with Life Scale*, in which people respond to statements such as "If I could live my life over, I would change almost nothing."

22. d   **utilizing implicit social support.** Kim (2008) distinguished between two types of social support: explicit (disclosing one's problems to others and seeking their comfort) and implicit (merely thinking about being close to others without asking for their help). People from Asian cultures are less likely than European Americans to seek social support in times of stress. That's because people in collectivist societies are reluctant to strain their relations with others. So, while they are less likely to tell their troubles to others, they are more likely to cope by thinking about the others in their lives. Self-help groups are a form of explicit social support, and so, are likely to be less popular with Asians than with European Americans.

23. a.   **more, less.** Highlighting a dark side to the "American dream," research shows that the more materialistic people are, the less satisfied they seem to be (Nickerson et al., 2003). Economists are thus coming to appreciate the point that to some extent, our sense of well being stems from the gap between income and material aspirations (Stutzer, 2004).

Answers to Essay Questions: Sample Essays

24. Stress occurs when people perceive that the demands of a situation exceed their ability to meet those demands. Change in people's lives can place a number of demands on them. These demands may result from microstressors or hassles of everyday life, such as child-care duties, work pressure, traffic, inadequate living space, and many other small events that place demands on people's time and energy. Demands may also result from major crises such as divorce, the death of a spouse, or war. Under these conditions people face many new obstacles and tasks to which they are likely to be unaccustomed, thus becoming especially vulnerable to stress.

25. When people face a stressful situation, they can cope with it either by trying to change the situation or by dealing with the emotions it gives rise to. Problem-focused coping is an attempt to change the situation that is provoking stress. The advantage of this coping strategy is that if it is effective, the person using it will no longer experience stress. Alternatively, emotion-focused coping is an attempt to relieve the negative emotions that accompany stress without changing the situation that is provoking the stress. The advantage of this strategy is that it may be used to cope with a number of different stressful situations.

26. In general, when people have a sense of control over their lives, especially over the stressful situations they encounter, they experience better health outcomes. This may be true even when the sense of control over the situation and one's ability to handle the situation are illusions. Optimism seems to promote health. Similarly, when people are accurately informed about their medical treatment and choose their own course of treatment, they seem to recover from illnesses more quickly and are better able to end destructive behavior patterns.

27. Hundreds of studies now show that the effects of stress on the immune system are complex. Brief stressors (such as a shark attack or difficult exam) can enhance the immune response in ways that are adaptive in the short term, but chronic life stressors (such as a high-pressure job or distressed marriage) can suppress the immune response over time, putting the organism at risk (Segerstrom & Miller, 2004).

28. Research supports the general point that resilience, or hardiness, serves as a buffer against stress (Funk, 1992). As you might expect, most people are exposed to at least one highly traumatic event during the course of a lifetime. Yet while many react with PTSD, others maintain their equilibrium and mental health: "Roughly 50% to 60% of the U.S. population is exposed to traumatic stress but only 5% to 10% develop PTSD" (Ozer et al., 2003, p. 54). Thus, Ann Masten (2001) and George Bonanno (2004) both argue that most human beings are highly resilient, exhibiting a remarkable capacity to thrive in the wake of highly aversive events. In fact, Vicki Helgeson and her colleagues (2006) note that many people who confront heart attacks, cancer, divorce, war, family illness, and other traumas find ways to accept, benefit, and grow from the experience.

29. Most of the research on coping is conducted with people from Western cultures, in which individualism and independence are highly valued. In view of the differences between Eastern and Western cultures, it seems that Asians might be more likely than Americans to cope with stress by turning to others for support. Yet Taylor and her colleagues (2004) found that when they asked college students to describe what they do to relieve stress, 57% of Americans—but only 39% of South Koreans—cited social support seeking. A possible reason is that in collectivist cultures, where social groups take precedence over the self, people are more reluctant to strain their relationships by calling on others for support. Instead, Asians tend to rely more on implicit social support, merely thinking about their close relations with others in times of stress, but not explicitly asking for help (Kim and colleagues, 2008). As for their most preferred method of coping, when college students in Taiwan were asked how they coped with the traumatic events in their lives, they reported the following strategies in order of how often they are used: (1) Acceptance, reframing, and striving, (2) avoidance and detachment, (3) family support, (4) religion and spirituality, and (5) private emotional outlets. Of these, participants rated acceptance as the most helpful (Heppner and others, 2006).